Connect Government is an application-based assignment platform containing engaging, user-friendly tools that help students better understand and connect with the concepts and language used in the American Government course. Political Scientists have reported deeper critical thinking, improved student performance, and increased classroom efficiency as a result of using Connect Government, which includes innovative tools that are often auto-gradable, such as:

SmartBook®

Described as a "textbook for the 21st century" by a political scientist, SmartBook gives students a road map to success through an adaptive reading experience that changes the way students read. It creates a personalized, interactive reading environment by highlighting important concepts, while helping students identify their strengths and weaknesses. This ensures that he or she is focused on the content needed to close specific knowledge gaps, while it simultaneously promotes long-term learning.

NewsFlash

Responding to the need for currency in the American Government course, this new Connect assignment pairs fresh content on a rolling basis with auto-grade questions that allow instructors to assess student understanding of the important news of the day.

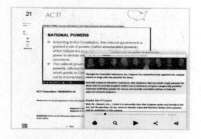

Applied Critical Thinking

Nicknamed ACT!, these new activities encourage students to apply critical thinking skills to core course content through political research and reflection. First, students assess their understanding of content, then gather applicable political research, and lastly, critically reflect on the results.

Practice Government Missions

Practice Government, McGraw-Hill's educational game focused on the American political system, can now be played inside of Connect American Government! Two introductory missions have now been paired with auto-grade and critical thinking questions that harness the power of "learning by doing" right within Connect. Additional missions are available through mhpractice.com.

Concept Clips

Expanded to now include audio, Concept Clips are engaging videos that walk students through the more difficult concepts in the American government course (such as the Electoral College, Supreme Court procedures, or how to evaluate a public opinion poll).

Podcasts

Deepen understanding of how politics happens in the real world by leveraging the most popular podcasts available with our new **Podcast Assignments**. These assignments allow you to bring greater context and nuance to your courses while engaging students through the storytelling power of podcasts.

87%
of college students report that access to learning analytics can positively impact their learning experience.

75%
of students using adaptive technology report that it is "very helpful" or "extremely helpful" in aiding their ability to retain new concepts.

"I can honestly say that the first time I used SmartBook after reading a chapter I understood what I had just read better than I ever had in the past."
– Nathan Herrmann, Oklahoma State University

"I really enjoy how it has gotten me engaged in the course and it is a great study tool without having to carry around a heavy textbook."
– Madeline Uretsky, Simmons College

Professors spend:

Less time on administrative tasks
75%

90%
More time on active learning

"Connect keeps my students engaged and motivated. Requiring Connect assignments has improved student exam grades."
– Sophia Garcia, Tarrant County College

Mc Graw Hill Education

Because learning changes everything.™

To learn more about American Government visit the McGraw-Hill Education American Government page: bit.ly/MHEAmGov

AMERICAN DEMOCRACY NOW

SIXTH EDITION

AMERICAN DEMOCRACY NOW

SIXTH EDITION

BRIGID CALLAHAN HARRISON

Montclair State University

JEAN WAHL HARRIS

University of Scranton

MICHELLE D. DEARDORFF

University of Tennessee at Chattanooga

Mc
Graw
Hill
Education

AMERICAN DEMOCRACY NOW: SIXTH EDITION

Published by McGraw-Hill Education, 2 Penn Plaza, New York, NY 10121. Copyright © 2019 by McGraw-Hill Education. All rights reserved. Printed in the United States of America. Previous editions © 2017, 2015, and 2013. No part of this publication may be reproduced or distributed in any form or by any means, or stored in a database or retrieval system, without the prior written consent of McGraw-Hill Education, including, but not limited to, in any network or other electronic storage or transmission, or broadcast for distance learning.

Some ancillaries, including electronic and print components, may not be available to customers outside the United States.

This book is printed on acid-free paper.

1 2 3 4 5 6 7 8 9 LWI 21 20 19 18

ISBN 978-1-259-91239-9 (bound edition)
MHID 1-259-91239-6 (bound edition)
ISBN 978-1-260-16458-9 (loose-leaf edition)
MHID 1-260-16458-6 (loose-leaf edition)

Senior Portfolio Manager: *Jason Seitz*
Product Development Manager: *Dawn Groundwater*
Senior Digital Product Developer: *Sarah Colwell*
Marketing Manager: *Will Walter*
Lead Core Content Project Manager: *Rick Hecker*
Assessment Content Project Manager: *George Theofanopoulos*
Media Content Project Manager: *Sandra Schnee*
Senior Buyer: *Susan K. Culbertson*
Design: *Egzon Shaqiri*
Lead Content Licensing Specialist: *Carrie Burger*
Cover Image: *©Trevor Carpenter/Getty Images*
Compositor: *Aptara®, Inc.*

All credits appearing on page or at the end of the book are considered to be an extension of the copyright page.

Library of Congress Cataloging-in-Publication Data

Names: Harrison, Brigid C., author. | Harris, Jean (Jean Wahl), 1960- author.
 | Deardorff, Michelle D., author.
Title: American democracy now / Brigid Callahan Harrison, Montclair State
 University, Jean Wahl Harris, University of Scranton, Michelle D.
 Deardorff, University of Tennessee at Chattanooga.
Description: Sixth Edition. | New York : McGraw-Hill Education, [2019]
Identifiers: LCCN 2018046757 | ISBN 9781259912399 (acid-free paper)
Subjects: LCSH: Political participation–United States–Textbooks. | United
 States–Politics and government–Textbooks.
Classification: LCC JK276 .H36 2019 | DDC 320.473–dc23 LC record available at https://lccn.loc.gov/2018046757

The Internet addresses listed in the text were accurate at the time of publication. The inclusion of a website does not indicate an endorsement by the authors or McGraw-Hill Education, and McGraw-Hill Education does not guarantee the accuracy of the information presented at these sites.

mheducation.com/highered

Brief Contents

Contents

Part II Fundamental Principles

Part III

Linkages Between the People and Government

6 POLITICAL SOCIALIZATION AND PUBLIC OPINION 196

7 INTEREST GROUPS 226

8   POLITICAL PARTIES   258

9   CAMPAIGNS, ELECTIONS, AND VOTING   298

Part IV Institutions of Government

12 CONGRESS 390

13 THE PRESIDENCY 426

Part V

Public Policy

17 DOMESTIC POLICY   564

18 FOREIGN POLICY AND NATIONAL SECURITY   596

Part VI State and Local Government

Currency, Compelling Content,

American Democracy Now **engages** students in American politics through **relevant** content and supportive digital tools that **enrich and reinforce learning**. **Accessible** to students at all levels, the narrative is brought to life through **compelling features**, such as **rich visuals and graphics** and the ***Then, Now, Next*** framework, helping students gain a **comprehensive** understanding of American government yesterday, today, and through development of **critical thinking skills**, tomorrow.

Better Data, Smarter Revision, Improved Results

Students helped inform the revision strategy:

STEP 1. Over the course of three years, data points showing concepts that caused students the most difficulty were anonymously collected from McGraw-Hill Education's Connect® American Government's SmartBook for *American Democracy Now*.

STEP 2. The data from SmartBook were provided to the authors in the form of a ***Heat Map***, which graphically illustrated "hot spots" in the text that affected student learning (see image to left).

STEP 3. The authors used the ***Heat Map*** data to refine the content and reinforce student comprehension in the new edition. Additional quiz questions and assignable activities were created for use in Connect American Government to further support student success.

RESULT: Because the ***Heat Map*** gave the authors empirically based feedback at the paragraph and even sentence level, they were able to develop the new edition using precise student data that pinpointed concepts that caused students the most difficulty.

Heat Map data also inform the activities and assessments in Connect American Government, McGraw-Hill Education's assignable and assessable learning platform. Where the ***Heat Map*** data show students struggle with specific learning objectives or concepts, we created new Connect assets—Concept Clips, Applied Critical Thinking (ACT), and NewsFlash current event activities—to provide another avenue for students to learn and master the content.

Make It Effective. SmartBook creates a personalized reading experience by highlighting the most impactful concepts a student needs to learn at that moment in time. This ensures that every minute spent with SmartBook is returned to the student as the most value added minute possible.

Make It Informed. The reading experience continuously adapts by highlighting content based on what the student knows and doesn't know. Real-time reports quickly identify the concepts that require more attention from individual students—or the entire class. SmartBook detects the content a student is most likely to forget and brings it back to improve long-term knowledge retention.

SMARTBOOK™

New to this edition, SmartBook is now optimized for mobile and tablet and is accessible for students with disabilities. And as part of any American government course, SmartBook now focuses on the broader context for and building blocks of the political system. Specifically, it has been enhanced with improved learning objectives to ensure that students gain foundational knowledge while they also learn to make connections for broader understanding of government institutions, events, and behavior. SmartBook personalizes learning to individual student needs, continually adapting to pinpoint knowledge gaps and focus learning on topics that need the most attention. Study time is more productive, and as a result, students are better prepared for class and coursework. For instructors, SmartBook tracks student progress and provides insights that can help guide teaching strategies.

Informing and Engaging Students on American Government Concepts

Using Connect American Government, students can learn the course material more deeply and study more effectively than ever before.

©Image Credit

At the *remember* and *understand* levels of Bloom's taxonomy, **Concept Clips** help students break down key concepts in American Government. Using easy-to-understand audio narration, visual cues, and colorful animations, Concept Clips provide a step-by-step presentation that aids in student retention. New Concept Clips for this edition include the following:

■ What are the Types of Government?
■ Federalists and Antifederalists
■ What is Devolution?
■ Regulation of the Media

- Who Participates?
- Presidency: Going Public
- U.S. Foreign Policy

In addition to the concept-based clips, the new edition also offers several skills-based clips that equip students for work within and outside the classroom. These skills-based clips include the following:

- Evaluating the News
- Critical Thinking
- How to Read a Court Case
- How to Understand Charts and Graphs
- Political Cartoons
- How to Avoid Plagiarism

Also at the remember and understand levels of Bloom's taxonomy **NewsFlash** exercises tie current news stories to key American government concepts and learning objectives. After interacting with a contemporary news story, students are assessed on their ability to make the connections between real-life events and course content. Examples include the 2018 midterm election results, 2017 tax reform legislation, and trade tariffs.

Deepen understanding of how politics happens in the real world by leveraging the most popular podcasts available with our new **Podcast Assignments.** These assignments allow you to bring greater context and nuance to your courses while engaging students through the storytelling power of podcasts.

At the *apply, analyze,* and *evaluate* levels of Bloom's taxonomy, **critical thinking activities** allow students to engage with the political process and learn by doing. Examples are:

- Quiz: What Is Your Political Ideology?
- Poll: Americans' Confidence in the Police
- Research: Find Your Senator
- Infographic: Compare the Courts

Practice Government, McGraw-Hill's educational game focused on the American political system, is fully integrated inside of Connect American Government! A set of focused introductory missions are paired with auto-grade and critical thinking.

At the heart of *American Democracy Now* is a rich set of instructional tools that move students along the path to critical thinking.

A "**Then, Now, Next**" framework encourages students to understand historical contexts and precedents so that they can weigh them against current political events and actions, begin to formulate an informed judgment about politics, and consider how the past and present might shape the future. For example, in Chapter 9 on interest groups, the feature highlights how group participation has changed in the United States since the 1960s and asks students to consider how media technology might affect interest-group mobilization, for better or worse, in the future.

THEN NOW NEXT

How Group Participation Has Changed in the United States

Then (1960s)	Now
Individuals joined bowling leagues, civic associations, and community service organizations.	People join virtual communities and use social networking sites to keep in touch with others who share their personal and public interests.
Many people entertained and socialized a great deal at home.	People are more likely to visit with friends and relatives in restaurants, cafés, and other public settings, as well as online through "virtual visits," like Facetiming and Snapchatting.
Groups used traditional activities to communicate their interests to policy-makers, including letter writing and lobbying.	Groups rely on traditional activities but also increasingly use social media, including Twitter, to communicate with members, to fund-raise, and to lobby policymakers.

WHAT'S NEXT?

> What new media technologies and strategies might shape how interest groups organize and mobilize members in the future?

> Are there *negative* consequences to relying on the Internet as an organizing tool? What obstacles will some Internet-based organizations face in mobilizing their supporters around a given issue?

> In what ways will technology change how policymakers are influenced in the future?

"**Analyzing the Sources**" guides students in interpreting data, images, maps, and primary sources and poses questions that prompt analytical thinking. For example, in Chapter 11 on politics and technology, the feature asks students to evaluate whether Facebook ads generated by Russian operatives were effective.

Analyzing the Sources

TROLLING FOR VOTES

In the 18 months leading up to the 2016 presidential election, about 126 million Americans saw Facebook content that included ads and posts generated by Russian operatives. Using bots, the Russians sought to influence the outcome of the election and foment divisions and dissent among the American people. Using Facebook's advertiser tools, the Russians targeted Americans based on their self-professed "likes"—algorithms that indicate users' political preferences—and demographic characteristics including age, sex, and geography.

Practice Analytical Thinking

1. Why would Russian operatives seek to create divisions within the American electorate?

2. What are the obstacles to preventing such covert disinformation attacks?

3. How can social media users protect themselves from being the target of disinformation campaigns?

Source: Being Patriotic (Facebook event)

Source: BM (Facebook event)

"Thinking Critically" is a debate feature that gives students a comprehensive appreciation of multiple sides of a political issue and an opportunity to formulate their own positions by evaluating the data, information, or sources provided. For example, in Chapter 4 on civil liberties, the feature explores the current debate regarding whether college campuses should be allowed to limit speech.

Thinking Critically

Should College Campuses Be Allowed to Limit Speech?

The Issue: The faculty and administrators of public universities are struggling with the meaning of the First Amendment's free speech protections on college campuses. As student bodies become more diverse, students expect to have their identities and beliefs treated with respect, and current student bodies often do not want to hear perspectives that are directly different from their own. Speech in the United States has become more polarized and extreme, and speakers who gain fame from social media often are not temperate or reasoned in their analysis, but focus on being provocative.

All Speech Should Be Allowed: Without exposure to sometimes offensive and difficult views, future Americans will not be capable of engaging in a public debate that forces one to confront contrary perspectives. In light of our great polarization as a nation, the onus is on universities to educate our students to be capable citizens in our democracy. And at the heart of our democracy is the First Amendment, with its guarantee that all citizens can participate in the debates that will direct our governance.

Free speech has historically been essential to advancing equal rights and political equality. Students do not know the history of free speech or the ways in which contrary views have been shut down and dissenters persecuted by the government. The First Amendment and the value of academic freedom are clear. The Supreme Court clearly states that public institutions cannot punish speech or exclude speakers based on the content of their speech.

found in a 2015 survey that 40 percent of college students believe that the government should prevent people from making statements offensive to minority groups. They want to make campuses inclusive for all, and they know that hate speech is harmful, especially to those who have been traditionally excluded from higher education. The university is a special place. It exists to educate and create knowledge, both of which require the evaluation of the quality of ideas. We teach students to do this and grade them on the merit of their own arguments and understandings. Faculty teach content discrimination, and their ideas are evaluated based on their judgments regarding content. A classroom and the university are not an open forum. They promote freedom of ideas, but this does not mean that all ideas have equal value; universities must teach students the skill of facing and evaluating threatening and dangerous ideas. This does not mean that students should be exposed to abuse and threatening language. For a university to do its job, it must encourage and tolerate offensive ideas while rejecting and refusing personal incivility.

What do you think?

1. Is there a difference between speakers sponsored by professors and departments versus those sponsored by student organizations? Explain your answer.

2. What role should a university play in distinguishing between the quality of ideas and the manner in which they are

"Evaluating the Facts" seeks to create students who are wise consumers of information by developing critical thinking skills that will assist them in evaluating information they encounter daily and determining both the legitimacy of the source and the motivation or agenda of the source. For example, Chapter 6 on political socialization focuses on the gender gap in party identification, asking students to identify trends over time and consider reasons for these trends.

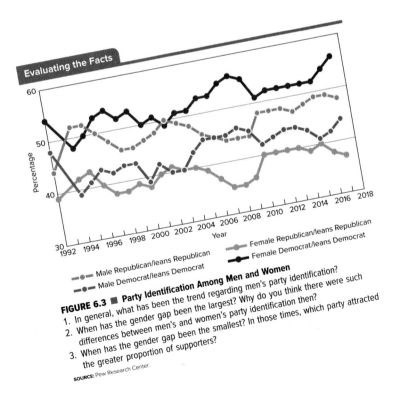

FIGURE 6.3 ■ **Party Identification Among Men and Women**
1. In general, what has been the trend regarding men's party identification?
2. When has the gender gap been the largest? Why do you think there were such differences between men's and women's party identification then?
3. When has the gender gap been the smallest? In those times, which party attracted the greater proportion of supporters?

SOURCE: Pew Research Center.

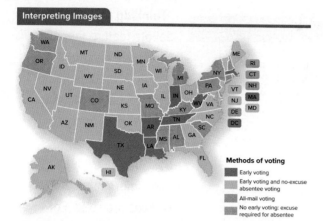

FIGURE 9.2 ■ Methods of Voting in the States What is the most prevalent available form of voting in the states? Where do we find the strictest voting laws? What effect would the available method of voting have on voter turnout?

SOURCE: National Conference of State Legislatures, "Absentee and Early Voting," 2017.

Students continue to build skills through additional tools, such as "**Interpreting Images**," which encourages the development of analytic skills to interpret original-source visual elements, including photographs, documents, maps, tables, and graphs. For example, in Chapter 9 on campaigns, elections, and voting, the feature presents data on the varied methods of voting across the country and asks students to consider patterns and possible impacts.

Staying Current

This edition reflects the November 2018 election results. Also, as mentioned, the authors revised in response to student Heat Map data that pinpointed the topics and concepts with which students struggled the most. This Heat Map-directed revision is reflected primarily in Chapters 1, 2, 6, 8, 9, 11, 12, 13, and 18. Other content changes include the following:

CHAPTER 1 PEOPLE, POLITICS, AND PARTICIPATION

- Added new discussion on the importance of tolerant, civic discourse in our nation.
- Updated discussion of the current political context, including Russian intervention in the 2016 presidential election and U.S. engagement with North Korea.
- Updated voter turnout data.
- Added new discussion of the politics of Generation Z.
- Added new Analyzing the Sources that frames the issues of increased ideological polarization in the United States by generation.
- Updated data about the U.S. population.

CHAPTER 2 THE CONSTITUTION

- Revised section "British Policies Incite Revolution in the Colonies."
- Revised Then, Now, Next feature.
- Added new Thinking Critically feature on Census 2020.
- Revised Analyzing the Sources feature on convening a Constitutional Convention.
- Revised the section on "The Constitution as a Living, Evolving Document."
- Updated inquiry questions in the annotated Constitution.

CHAPTER 3 FEDERALISM

- Reorganized chapter sections to foster understanding of foundational structures and concepts of our federal system.
- Added new section on "Partisan Federalism."
- Revised Thinking Critically feature, "Can State Governments Nullify National Marijuana Law?"
- Revised section on "Tools of Intergovernmental Relations," including new sections on "Nullification" and "Intergovernmental Tensions."
- Revised Then, Now, Next feature, "Americans' Trust in Their Governments."
- Updated Recommended Readings.

CHAPTER 4 CIVIL LIBERTIES

- Updated statistics, data, and Supreme Court rulings from the previous edition.
- Provided a greater emphasis on selective incorporation and its significance.
- Introduced decisions and policies of the Trump administration, as opposed to prior focus on the Obama administration.
- Updated campus policies on concealed weapons.
- Moved focus from Millennials to Generation Z.
- Introduced a new section on free speech on campus.

CHAPTER 5 CIVIL RIGHTS

- Updated statistics, data, and Supreme Court rulings from the previous edition.
- Included coverage of current issues, such as the #MeToo movement and diversity within the Asian American community.
- Added new Thinking Critically on the impact of illegal immigration.
- Updated all references and citations.

CHAPTER 6 POLITICAL SOCIALIZATION AND PUBLIC OPINION

- Added new Thinking Critically feature that asks whether the United States should have stricter gun safety laws.
- Explored new data concerning the gender gap in political party identification between men and women.
- Evaluated new data about the policy priorities of men and women in the 2016 presidential election.
- Evaluated the gender gap in presidential vote choice in 2016.
- Updated information about the opinions of Millennials.
- Added new information on the politics of Generation Z.
- Included new discussion of the new "most important problem."
- Included new data concerning trust in government.

CHAPTER 7 INTEREST GROUPS

- Included a new discussion of the Women's March protests.
- Included additional explanation of the role of group competition in determining interest group success.
- Included a discussion of the effect of *Janus v. United States* on interest groups.
- Updated information on the top lobbying interests in the United States.

CHAPTER-BY-CHAPTER CHANGES

- Included more detailed discussion of *Citizens United v. Federal Election Commission.*
- Added a new Analyzing the Sources feature demonstrating the importance of considering interest groups' perspective when evaluating interest group ratings.

CHAPTER 8 POLITICAL PARTIES
- Included a new discussion titled "A Democratic Party Struggling to Define Itself."
- Included a new discussion titled "The Republican Party in the Era of President Trump."
- Updated data concerning Americans' opinions of the two political parties.
- Added new information about the role of the parties in the 2018 midterm congressional elections.
- Updated the discussion of the responsible party model.
- Provided new data concerning post-2018 election party control of state legislatures.
- Added a new Analyzing the Sources feature that asks students to evaluate the characteristics of voters who have switched political party preference since 2011.
- Updated data on Americans' support for a third party.

CHAPTER 9 CAMPAIGNS, ELECTIONS, AND VOTING
- Explained the U.S. Intelligence Community's conclusions about Russian interference in the 2016 presidential election.
- Enhanced the discussion of the importance of fair, independent elections.
- Explained why election meddling matters.
- Highlighted the idea of political participation as an expression of the will of the people.
- Discussed 2018 ballot initiatives in the states.
- Explained campaign finance regulations for the 2018 elections.
- Updated data concerning age and presidential election turnout.
- Revised an Analyzing the Sources feature examining race and presidential elections.
- Included new research concerning reasons for low voter turnout.

CHAPTER 10 THE MEDIA
- Contextualized the current debate about media accuracy.
- Revised the Analyzing the Sources feature examining new data on confidence in the media.
- Added new data on the increasing diversity in newsrooms.
- Included new research on the demographics of increasing online news consumption.
- Reexamined the question of media bias.

CHAPTER 11 POLITICS AND TECHNOLOGY
- Discussed social media hacking and data breaches.
- Updated data on Internet usage.
- Updated research on the use of technology in the 2018 elections.
- Added information on the use of social media as a tool of macro-protests, including facilitating the #MeToo movement.
- Added a new Analyzing the Sources feature that asks students to evaluate whether Facebook ads generated by Russian operatives were effective.
- Added new information and research on election infiltration.
- Described the effects of FCC Chairman Ajit Pai's rollback of the net neutrality order.

CHAPTER 12 CONGRESS
- Added a new Thinking Critically feature that asks whether congressional elections are "rigged" through gerrymandering.
- Described new trends regarding the use of congressional earmarks.
- Added a new discussion of the filibuster.
- Updated the congressional leadership section.
- Discussed the role of Congress in supporting special counsel Robert Mueller.
- Added updates on the 2018 elections and the party composition of Congress.
- Described congressional action on President Trump's policy agenda, including the overhaul of the federal tax plan.
- Included new discussion on the diversity in Congress after the 2018 elections.

CHAPTER 13 THE PRESIDENCY
- Examined the revolutionizing effect on the presidency of President Trump's use of social media.
- Added new discussion of the Electoral College.
- Examined President Trump's role in managing the economy, looking at the issue of tariffs and the overhaul of the federal tax structure.

- Updated information on Trump administration officials, including the cabinet.
- Included new comparative data on women and minorities appointed to presidential cabinets.
- Updated discussion of the use of executive privilege.
- Included new comparative data on presidential public approval.
- Examined the geographical variation of President Trump's popularity.
- Added information on First Lady Melania Trump's priorities for her role.

CHAPTER 14   THE BUREAUCRACY

- Added new Then, Now, Next feature, "Federal Civil Service Hiring Process."
- Added new discussion of President Trump's budget proposals and their potential impact on federal civil service hiring.
- Updated data on pay scale for white-collar (GS) federal civil servants.
- Revised section on "State, Local, and Shadow Bureaucrats."
- Revised (to make more clear and concise) sections on bureaucratic accountability.
- Updated data and analysis in section "Can Bureaucratic Performance Be Improved?"
- Added new Analyzing the Sources feature, "Is it Government Performance or Partisanship?"
- Updated discussion and analysis in section "Does Contracting-Out Improve Performance?"
- Updated Recommended Readings.

CHAPTER 15   THE JUDICIARY

- Reorganized sections to foster understanding of foundational structures and concepts of the federal judiciary.
- Added new Analyzing the Sources features on judicial independence.
- Revised Then, Now, Next feature, "Supreme Court Diversity."
- Updated data on demographics of federal judges to include those confirmed during first years of the Trump administration.
- Revised discussion on judicial policy making, including comparisons of judicial activism, judicial restraint, and originalism and the Constitution as a living document
- Added discussion of the most recent personnel changes to the Roberts Court and their potential ramifications.

CHAPTER 16   ECONOMIC POLICY

- Integrated discussion of the Trump administration's economic policy initiatives supporting supply-side economics, including the Tax Cuts & Jobs Act (2017) and deregulation.
- Updated survey data on Americans' views about the American dream.
- Reorganized sections to foster understanding of foundational concepts and theories.

- Added new Then, Now, Next feature on tax law.
- Updated data on the health of the U.S. economy.
- Updated federal budget data.
- Reviewed the use of continuing resolutions in the FY 2018 budget process.
- Revised (and streamlined) discussion of trade policy.
- Revised section on "The American Dream and the American Economy," which integrates Trump administration policies and Americans' policy preferences.

CHAPTER 17   DOMESTIC POLICY

- Added new Analyzing the Sources feature, "Partisan Differences on Top Priorities for President Trump and Congress."
- Added new Critically Thinking feature, "Should the National Government Mandate Flood Insurance?"
- Added new Then, Now, Next feature, "Federal Websites and Climate Change."
- Integrated the Trump administration's environmental, energy, health care, and immigration policy initiatives.
- Updated data on safety net programs (income security, housing security, health insurance programs).
- Updated data on immigrants.
- Eliminated section on Homeland Security policy.

CHAPTER 18   FOREIGN POLICY AND NATIONAL SECURITY

- Described the context for current foreign policy.
- Updated the "The Military Option" section to include U.S. air strikes in Syria.
- Updated coverage of the use of new technologies in foreign policy.
- Added new Analyzing the Sources feature that asks students to evaluate recent U.S. troop deployment.
- Examined President Trump's America First foreign policy in the context of Huntington's clash of civilizations thesis.
- Described future challenges in foreign policy, including trade policy, the renewed threat of terrorism, and Russian expansion and efforts to increase influence.

CHAPTER 19   STATE AND LOCAL GOVERNMENT   ▣ connect

- Added new Thinking Critically feature, "Is Direct Democracy the Fix for Misrepresentation in a Representative Democracy?"
- Relocated the direct democracy section to earlier in chapter.
- Added new section on "Intergovernmental Relations."
- Added new data on citizens' trust in state and local governments.
- Updated data on state and local government revenues and expenditures.
- Revised Analyzing the Sources feature comparing state voting laws.
- Updated data on diversity in state governments.

Acknowledgments

We owe a debt of thanks to all of the people who contributed their thoughts and suggestions to the development of *American Democracy Now.*

Manuscript Reviewers

Stephen Anthony, *Georgia State University*
Stephen Baker, *Jacksonville University*
Michael Baranowski, *Northern Kentucky University*
Kyle Barbieri, *Georgia Perimeter College*
Donna Bennett, *Trinity Valley Community College*
Amy Brandon, *El Paso Community College–Valle Verde*
Wendell Broadwell, *Georgia Perimeter College*
Monique Bruner, *Rose State College*
Joseph Campbell, *Rose State College*
Kathleen Collihan, *American River College*
Joe Corrado, *Clayton State University*
Vida Davoudi, *Lone Star College–Kingwood*
Julia Decker, *Texas State University–San Marcos*
William Delehanty, *Missouri Southern State University*
Jacqueline DeMerritt, *University of North Texas*
Kevin Dockerty, *Kalamazoo Valley Community College*
Cecil Dorsey, *San Jacinto College*
Walle Engedayehu, *Prairie View A&M University*
Matthew Eshbaugh-Soha, *University of North Texas*
Heather Evans, *Sam Houston State University*
Glen Findley, *Odessa College*
David Fistein, *Gulf Coast Community College*
John Forshee, *San Jacinto College*
Myrtle Freeman, *Tarrant County College–South*
Crystal Garrett, *Georgia Perimeter College*
Sandra Gieseler, *Palo Alto College*
Dana Glencross, *Oklahoma City Community College*
James Michael Greig, *University of North Texas*
Alexander Hogan, *Lone Star College–CyFair*
Richard Kiefer, *Waubonsee Community College*
Robert King, *Georgia Perimeter College–Dunwoody*
Melinda Kovacs, *Sam Houston State University*
Nancy Kral, *Lone Star College–Tomball*
Fred Lokken, *Truckee Meadows*
Becky Lubbers, *Saint Clair County Community College*
Joseph Mancos, *Lenoir-Rhyne University*
Roger Marietta, *Darton College*
Vinette Meikle-Harris, *Houston Community College–Central*

Brooke Miller, *Middle Georgia State College*
Shea Mize, *Georgia Highlands College*
Fran Moran, *New Jersey City University*
Joseph Moskowitz, *New Jersey City University*
Yamini Munipalli, *Florida State College*
Kathleen Murnan, *Ozarks Technical Community College*
Martha Musgrove, *Tarrant County College–South*
Glynn Newman, *Eastfield College*
John Osterman, *San Jacinto College–Pasadena*
Cecil Larry Pool, *El Centro College*
Robert K. Postic, *University of Findlay*
Sean Reed, *Wharton County Junior College*
Shauna Reilly, *Northern Kentucky University*
Elizabeth Rexford, *Wharton County Junior College*
Sonja M. Siler, *Cuyahoga Community College*
Shyam Sriram, *Georgia Perimeter College*
Adam Stone, *Georgia Perimeter College*
Steve Tran, *Houston Community College*
Dennis Toombs, *San Jacinto College–North*
David Uranga, *Pasadena City College*
Ronald Vardy, *University of Houston–Houston*
Sarah Velasquez, *Fresno Community College*
Peter Wielhouwer, *Western Michigan University–Kalamazoo*
Robert Wilkes, *Atlanta Metropolitan State College*

American Government Symposia

Since 2006, McGraw-Hill has conducted several symposia in American Government for instructors from across the country. These events offered a forum for instructors to exchange ideas and experiences with colleagues they might not have met otherwise. They also provided an opportunity for editors from McGraw-Hill to gather information about what instructors of American Government need and the challenges they face. The feedback we have received has been invaluable and has contributed—directly and indirectly—to the development of *American Democracy Now.* We would like to thank the participants for their insights:

Melvin Aaron, *Los Angeles City College*

Yan Bai, *Grand Rapids Community College*

Leslie Baker, *Mississippi State University*

Evelyn Ballard, *Houston Community College*

Robert Ballinger, *South Texas College*

Nancy Bednar, *Antelope Valley College*

Jeffrey Birdsong, *Northeastern Oklahoma A&M College*

Madelyn Bowman, *Tarrant County College–South*

Amy Brandon, *San Jacinto College–North*

Jane Bryant, *John A. Logan College*

Dan R. Brown, *Southwestern Oklahoma State University*

Monique Bruner, *Rose State College*

Anita Chadha, *University of Houston–Downtown*

John Clark, *Western Michigan University–Kalamazoo*

Kathleen Collihan, *American River College*

Steven Collins, *Oklahoma State University–Oklahoma City*

Daphne Cooper, *Indian River State College, Central*

John Davis, *Howard University*

Kevin Davis, *North Central Texas College*

Paul Davis, *Truckee Meadows Community College*

Vida Davoudi, *Lone Star College–Kingwood*

Robert De Luna, *Saint Philips College*

Jeff DeWitt, *Kennesaw State University*

Hien Do, *San Jose State University*

Kevin Dockerty, *Kalamazoo Valley Community College*

Cecil Dorsey, *San Jacinto College–South*

Jay Dow, *University of Missouri–Columbia*

Manar Elkhaldi, *University of Central Florida*

Emily Erdmann, *Blinn College, Bryan*

Henry Esparza, *University of Texas at San Antonio*

Karry Evans, *Austin Community College*

Kahlib Fischer, *Helms School of Government, Liberty University*

Marie Flint, *San Antonio College*

Reynaldo Flores, *Richland College*

Pearl Ford, *University of Arkansas–Fayetteville*

John Forshee, *San Jacinto College–Central*

Ben Riesner Fraser, *San Jacinto College*

Daniel Fuerstman, *Dutchess Community College*

Marilyn Gaar, *Johnson County Community College*

Jarvis T. Gamble, *Owens Community College*

Crystal Garrett, *Perimeter College at Georgia State University–Dunwoody*

Michael Gattis, *Gulf Coast Community College*

Patrick Gilbert, *Lone Star College–Tomball*

William Gillespie, *Kennesaw State University*

Dana K. Glencross, *Oklahoma City Community College*

Larry Gonzalez, *Houston Community College–Southwest*

Nirmal Goswami, *Texas A&M University–Kingsville*

Daniel Gutierrez, *El Paso Community College*

Richard Gutierrez, *University of Texas, El Paso*

Precious Hall, *Truckee Meadows Community College*

Michelle Kukoleca Hammes, *St. Cloud State University*

Cathy Hanks, *University of Nevada, Las Vegas*

Wanda Hill, *Tarrant County Community College*

Joseph Hinchliffe, *University of Illinois at Urbana–Champaign*

John Hitt, *North Lake College*

Mark Jendrysik, *University of North Dakota*

Brenda Jones, *Houston Community College–Central*

Franklin Jones, *Texas Southern University*

Lynn Jones, *Collin County Community College*

James Joseph, *Fresno City College*

Jason Kassel, *Valdosta State University*

Manoucher Khosrowshahi, *Tyler Junior College*

Rich Kiefer, *Waubonsee Community College*

Robert J. King, *Georgia Perimeter College*

Orin Kirshner, *Florida Atlantic University*

Melinda Kovacs, *Sam Houston State University*

Chien-Pin Li, *Kennesaw State University*

Fred Lokken, *Truckee Meadows Community College*

Mary Louis, *Houston Community College*

Kenneth Mariano, *Rowan College at Burlington County*

Jan McCauley, *Tyler Junior College*

John Mercurio, *San Diego State University*

Janna Merrick, *University of South Florida*

Joe Meyer, *Los Angeles City College*

Eric Miller, *Blinn College*

Kent Miller, *Weatherford College*

Charles Moore, *Georgia State University*

Patrick Moore, *Richland College*

Eduardo Munoz, *El Camino College*

Kay Murnan, *Ozarks Technical Community College*

Carolyn Myers, *Southwestern Illinois College*

Sharon Navarro, *University of Texas at San Antonio*

Blaine Nelson, *El Paso Community College*

Theresa Nevarez, *El Paso Community College*

James A. Norris, *Texas A&M International University*

Kent Park, *U.S. Military Academy at West Point*

Sylvia Peregrino, *El Paso Community College*

Amy Perry, *Texas State University*

Eric Rader, *Henry Ford Community College*

Elizabeth Rexford, *Wharton County Junior College*

Tara Ross, *Keiser University*

Carlos Rovelo, *Tarrant Community College–South*

Ryan Rynbrandt, *Collin County Community College*

Ray Sandoval, *Richland College*

Craig Scarpelli, *California State University–Chico*

Louis Schubert, *City College of San Francisco*

Edward Senu-Oke, *Joliet Junior College*
Mark Shomaker, *Blinn College*
Thomas Simpson, *Missouri Southern University*
Henry Sirgo, *McNeese State University*
Amy Smith, *North Lake College*
Daniel Smith, *Northwest Missouri State University*
John Speer, *Houston Community College–Southwest*
Jim Startin, *University of Texas at San Antonio*
Matt Stellges, *Blinn College, Bryan*
Sharon Sykora, *Slippery Rock University*
Tressa Tabares, *American River College*
Beatrice Talpos, *Wayne County Community College*
Alec Thomson, *Schoolcraft College*
Judy Tobler, *Northwest Arkansas Community College*
Steve Tran, *Houston Community College*
Beth Traxler, *Greenville Technical College*
William Turk, *University of Texas–Pan American*
Ron Vardy, *University of Houston*
Sarah Velasquez, *Fresno City College*
Ron VonBehren, *Valencia Community College–Osceola*
Albert C. Waite, *Central Texas College*
Van Allen Wigginton, *San Jacinto College–Central*
Geoffrey Willbanks, *Tyler Junior College*
Charlotte Williams, *Pasadena City College*
Theodore Williams, *Kennedy-King College, City Colleges of Chicago*
Ike Wilson, *U.S. Military Academy*
Paul Wilson, *San Antonio College*
John Wood, *University of Central Oklahoma*
Robert Wood, *University of North Dakota*
Larry Wright, *Florida A&M University*
Ann Wyman, *Missouri Southern State University*
Kathryn Yates, *Richland College*

Personal Acknowledgments

We must thank our team at McGraw-Hill: Katie Stevens, managing director; Jason Seitz, portfolio manager; Dawn Groundwater, product development manager; Will Walter, marketing manager; Susan Messer, product developer; and David Tietz, photo researcher. We are extraordinarily grateful to all of you.

For their patience, understanding, and support, the authors also wish to thank: Paul Meilak; Caroline, Alexandra, and John Harrison; Rosemary Fitzgerald; Patricia Jillard; Kathleen Cain; John Callahan; Teresa Biebel; Thomas Callahan; Michael Harris; Audrey Wahl and the Wahl "girls"—Eileen Choynowski, Laura McAlpine, Audrey Messina, and Jaimee Conner; David Deardorff; Amy Donaldson; and Michael, Kelly, Logan, and Lauren Donaldson.

John and Rosemary Callahan, Jim and Audrey Wahl, and Earl and Fonda Donaldson first began the conversation of democracy with us, and we thank them and all of the students and colleagues, friends, and family members who continue that conversation now.

BRIGID CALLAHAN HARRISON
JEAN WAHL HARRIS
MICHELLE D. DEARDORFF

©Mike Peters   ©Eileen Notarianni   ©Jaimie Davis

From the Authors

Welcome to the sixth edition of *American Democracy Now!* In this program, we share our passion for politics while providing students with the foundation they need to become informed citizens in a rapidly changing democracy.

In creating the first edition of *American Democracy Now,* we merged our years of experience as classroom instructors and our desire to captivate students with the compelling story of their democracy into a student-centered program. We refined those goals with an integrated learning program for American government to maximize student performance in the second edition. The third edition revolutionized how we think about American democracy by incorporating for the first time a chapter on Politics and Technology, demonstrating the extent to which technology has become integral to how citizens participate in their democracy and how governments serve their citizenry. The fifth edition continued this tradition, tackling new ways in which technology is changing how politics happens—for both the good and the bad. The goals of the sixth edition stem from the necessities of our times: We seek to help students navigate the vast array of information that technology provides by strengthening their ability to evaluate information for accuracy. We also hope to encourage civil discourse by providing students with critical thinking skills that will enable them to develop an empathy with understanding of the positions held by those whose views differ from their own.

More than any previous edition, the sixth edition of *American Democracy Now* relies on technological advances to improve how we deliver information to students in a way that they can best understand, enjoy, and share our passion for political life. Informed by data garnered from thousands of students who have used our Connect and SmartBook platforms, we have revised our program to ensure greater clarity in areas that have proven complex for past student readers. We have continued to integrate an examination of the increasing role technology is playing in politics. And we have continued our quest to create a student-centered program that increases students' sense of political efficacy by exciting them about the political conversations of the day and by integrating a critical thinking framework that not only explains the past and present of politics, but also asks them to think critically about the future: What's next for their democracy? In *American Democracy Now,* sixth edition, students learn how the fundamental principles of American democracy inform their understanding of the politics and policies of today so that they can think about the policies they would like to see take shape tomorrow. In short, they learn to inquire: How do *then* and *now* shape what's going to happen *next?* This "Then, Now, Next" approach to critical thinking serves as the basis for student participation.

American Democracy Now, sixth edition, takes a broader, more contemporary view of participation than other programs. To us, participation encompasses a variety of activities from the modest, creative, local, or even personal actions students can take to the larger career choices they can make. And choosing how to participate makes American government matter.

Today's hyper-partisan politics and ever-changing technology provide challenges for those seeking to ensure that the rights guaranteed by the Constitution are protected, and they present opportunities for those striving to fulfill the responsibilities that come with living in a constitutional democracy. *American Democracy Now,* sixth edition, enables students to garner a solid understanding of the essential elements, institutions, and dynamics of national government and politics, while fostering critical thinking skills that are essential to meeting these novel challenges and realizing these new opportunities.

Facilitating success—as students, but also as citizens and participants—means honing their critical thinking skills, harnessing their energy, and creating tools that foster success in the American government course and in our polity. We know we have succeeded when students apply their knowledge and sharpened skills to consider the outcomes they—as students, citizens, and participants—would like to see.

Creating this success means joining increasingly diverse students where they are so that they can see the relevance of politics in their everyday lives. Instagram, YouTube, Snapchat, and Twitter are not only powerful social networking tools, but also powerful political and educational tools. New technologies help politicians to communicate with citizens, citizens to communicate with each other, and you to communicate with your students. The sixth edition of *American Democracy Now* further integrates technology into our students' study of politics so that their engagement with content is seamless.

We are excited to present you with the sixth edition of *American Democracy Now,* and we wish you and your students success.

BRIGID CALLAHAN HARRISON
JEAN WAHL HARRIS
MICHELLE D. DEARDORFF

BRIGID CALLAHAN HARRISON specializes in the civic engagement and political participation of Americans, especially the Millennial generation and Generation Z, the U.S. Congress, and the presidency. Brigid has taught American government for 24 years at Montclair State University in New Jersey. She takes particular pride in creating a learning experience in the classroom that shapes students' lifelong understanding of American politics, sharpens their critical thinking about American government, and encourages their participation in civic life. She enjoys supervising student internships in political campaigns and government and is a frequent commentator in print and electronic media on national and New Jersey politics. She is past president of the New Jersey Political Science Association and of the National Women's Caucus for Political Science. She received her B.A. from Stockton University; her M.A. from Rutgers, The State University of New Jersey; and her Ph.D. from Temple University. Harrison lives in Longport, New Jersey, with her husband, Paul Meilak, a retired New York City police detective. She has three children: Caroline (24), Alexandra (18), and John (16). Born and raised in New Jersey, Harrison is a fan of Bruce Springsteen and in her spare time, she enjoys reading on the beach, traveling, cycling, and binge-watching political thrillers on Netflix. Like her on Facebook at Brigid Callahan Harrison, and follow her on Twitter @BriCalHar.

JEAN WAHL HARRIS'S research interests include political socialization and engagement, federalism, and the gendered nature and effects of U.S. politics. She teaches introductory courses in local, state, and national government and upper-level courses in public administration, public policy, and judicial politics. As a faculty member in the Political Science Department and the director of the Women's & Gender Studies Program at the University of Scranton, Jean seeks to cultivate students' sense of political efficacy, empowering and inspiring them to engage in local, state, national, and/or international politics. She earned her B.A., M.A., and Ph.D. from the State University of New York at Binghamton. In 1994, the University of Scranton named her its CASE (Council for Advancement and Support of Education) professor of the year. She was an American Council on Education (ACE) Fellow during the 2007–2008 academic year. Jean lives in Nicholson, Pennsylvania, with her husband, Michael. She enjoys reading on her deck overlooking the Endless Mountains of Northeast Pennsylvania.

MICHELLE D. DEARDORFF'S teaching and research focus on the constitutional and statutory protections surrounding gender, race, and religion. She particularly enjoys developing classes that allow students to apply their understandings of law, politics, and political theory to current events; she seeks to foster critical citizens prepared to participate in governing our communities and nation. Deardorff is currently head of Political Science and Public Service at the University of Tennessee at Chattanooga. Before coming to UTC, she spent 10 years teaching at Jackson State, a historically black university in Mississippi, and another decade at Millikin University, a small private college in Illinois. She recently served on the Council of the American Political Science Association and is a founding faculty member of the Fannie Lou Hamer National Institute on Citizenship and Democracy, a coalition of academics who promote civic engagement and popular sovereignty through the study of the struggle for civil rights in the United States. She lives in Chattanooga with her husband, David, where they enjoy kayaking, hiking, live music, and reading in beautiful places.

The Sixth Edition of *American Democracy Now* is dedicated to the memory of Jim Wahl and Sue Tolchin, both of whom taught us a lot about politics.

CHAPTER 1

People, Politics, and Participation

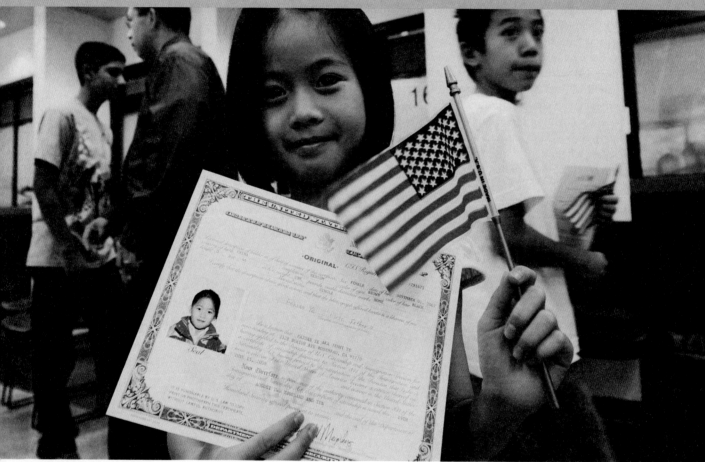

©Kevork Djansezian/Getty Images

THEN

Cynicism, distrust, and apathy characterized Americans' relationship with their government for the past generation.

NOW

Anger and divisiveness characterize segments of the American electorate, but new information technologies, generational politics, and a diversifying population give some cause for optimism as the nation responds to today's challenges, including terrorism, inequality, and violence.

NEXT

Will the present generation break the cycle of cynicism and increasingly, anger, that has pervaded the politics of the recent past?

Will new information technologies continue to facilitate and energize political participation?

Will our nation's increasing diversity continue to tear our nation apart or eventually serve to create compassion, respect, and unity?

The United States was

founded by individuals who believed in the power of democracy to respond to the will of citizens. Historically, citizen activists have come from all walks of life, but they have shared one common attribute: the belief that, in the ongoing conversation of democracy, their government listens to *people like them*. This idea is vital if individuals are to have an impact on their government; people who don't believe they can have any influence rarely try. The story of the United States is the story of people who are involved with their government, who know what they want their government to do, and who have confidence in their ability to influence its policies.[1] *American Democracy Now* tells the story of how today's citizen activists are participating in the conversation of democracy in a tumultuous and transformational time in which an increasingly diverse population faces sweeping technological changes and unprecedented global change. This story is the next chapter in America's larger story.

The history of democracy in the United States is rife with examples of ordinary people who have made and are making a difference.[2] Throughout this book, we describe the effects that individuals and groups have had, and continue to have, in creating and changing the country's institutions of government. We also explore how individuals have influenced the ways in which our governments—national, state, and local—create policy.[3] These stories are important not only in and of themselves but also as motivators for all of us who want to live in a democracy that responds to all its citizens.

A fundamental principle underlying this book is that your beliefs and your voice—and ultimately how you use those beliefs and that voice—matter. Whatever your beliefs, it is important that you come to them thoughtfully, by employing introspection and critical thinking, and it is our hope that you leave this course with the tools to discuss and advocate and act for your views civilly, in a manner that contributes to the tolerant, civic discourse of our nation. This book seeks both to inform and to inspire your participation. A sentiment voiced by American anthropologist Margaret Mead expresses a powerful truth: "Never doubt that a small group of thoughtful, committed citizens can change the world. Indeed, it's the only thing that ever has."

Learning Objectives

After reading this chapter, students should be able to:

- Define *politics*.
- Describe the functions of government.
- Explain the types of government.
- Explain the origins of American democracy.
- Identify and describe the key components of American political culture.
- Understand the concept of political ideology.
- Explain how the demographic characteristics of the U.S. population are changing.

y shd u stdy am dem now? Or, Why Should You Study American Democracy Now?

politics
The process of deciding who gets benefits in society and who does not.

Politics as practiced today is not your parents' brand of politics. **Politics**—the process of deciding who benefits in society and who does not—is a much different process today than it was even a decade ago. Advances in technology have altered the political landscape in many ways. In some countries, these advances have facilitated the overthrow of governments. In other countries, they are changing how voters and candidates communicate with each other, how governments provide information to individuals, how people get their news about events, and how governments administer laws. The political landscape has also changed because of world events.

How Technology Has Changed Politics

It would be difficult to overstate the influence of the technological revolution on politics as it is practiced today. President Donald Trump regularly relies on Twitter to voice his views and to make major policy statements. But he is not alone. In electoral politics, faster computers, the Internet, microtargeting, and social media have revolutionized a process that, until the advent of the personal computer, the Internet, and cellular technology, was not very different in 1990 from the way it was carried out in 1890. Today, many voters get much of their information from Facebook, Twitter, and Internet-based news sites and blogs. Campaigns rely on e-mail and text messaging, and they use websites and social networking sites such as Instagram, Facebook, and Twitter to communicate with and organize supporters. State governments rely on computers to conduct elections, and cities use computers to provide services to their residents.

Because of these unprecedented shifts in the ways politics happens and how government is administered, Americans today face both new opportunities and new challenges. Evidence demonstrating Russia's efforts to influence the 2016 election using social media have led many citizens to ask how we might use technology to ensure that elections are conducted fairly.

THEN NOW NEXT

Technology and Political Participation

Then (1970s)	Now
47 percent of 18- to 20-year-olds voted in the 1976 presidential election.	About 50 percent of 18- to 20-year-olds voted in the 2016 presidential election.
People got their national news from one-half-hour-long nightly news broadcasts.	People get their news from an array of sources, including Twitter feeds, Internet news services, and 24-hour news networks available on demand via computers and cell phones.
Many people participated in civic life primarily through demonstrations, protests, and voting.	Internet activism is now mainstream: Online protests and petitions are commonplace, and Facebook groups designed to express viewpoints and mobilize activists have replaced many in-real-life (IRL) groups.

WHAT'S NEXT?

> Will the upswing of voter participation by 18- to 20-year-olds continue?

> How might advancing media technologies further transform the ways that people "consume" their news?

> What new forms of civic participation will emerge?

How might the abundance and reach of media technology be directed toward informing and enriching us rather than overwhelming us or perpetuating the citizen cynicism of recent years? What privacy rights can we be sure of in the present digital age? Whatever your age, as a student, you are a member of one of the most tech-savvy groups in the country, and your input, expertise, and participation are vital to sorting out the opportunities and obstacles of this next stage of American democracy. Throughout this text, we examine the many ways in which people are using technology to link with each other and with the branches of government in an effort to influence those branches.

The Political Context Now

The political context today centers on a debate taking place in Washington, D.C., and throughout the nation about the appropriate size and role of government. Should economic development be fostered through tax cuts to corporations, in the hope that they will increase wages and create jobs, or should the federal government spend more money on services that benefit people directly, such as schools? Should the federal government repeal all aspects of the health care plan passed during the Obama administration? What is the obligation of the federal government in guaranteeing that law enforcement and the criminal justice system treat all Americans fairly and impartially? These issues have sparked great passion among many Americans on both sides of these and many other issues. Government officials today seek to walk a fine line between placating those demanding action by the government and those who fear that increased government action will result in too strong a government with too much power over its people.

Also part of the U.S. political context is a global environment characterized by uncertainty and instability on many fronts: uncertainty is still the guiding principle concerning North Korea and its nascent nuclear program; Russia seems bent on increasing its sphere of influence, both formally and subversively. In the meantime, China stands by, awaiting a coherent and consistent policy from the Trump administration, as a multitude of mixed signals emanate from Washington, D.C.[4] And the United States and the rest of the world continue to cope with multiple issues in the Middle East, where the retaliatory wars fought in Afghanistan and Iraq by the United States after the September 11, 2001, attacks, increased violence and instability. In recent years, ISIS—the insurgent group also known as Islamic State in Iraq and Syria, spawned in part by the power vacuum left when the United States pulled out of Iraq in 2011—perpetrated terror attacks by beheading Western journalists and aid workers. In response to those attacks, and the ongoing civil wars in those nations, the United States initiated air strikes first in Iraq and then in Syria, targeting areas where ISIS had taken control.

Americans' Efficacy

Since the early 1970s—a decade blemished by the intense unpopularity of the Vietnam War and by scandals that ushered in the resignation of President Richard Nixon in 1974—Americans' attitudes about government have been dismal.[5] Numerous surveys of the American public, including an ongoing Gallup poll, have demonstrated low levels of trust in government and of confidence in government's ability to solve problems, and today those levels have reached historically

efficacy

Citizens' belief that they have the ability to achieve something desirable and that the government listens to people like them.

low numbers, with only 20 percent of Americans saying they trust the government to do what's right always or most of the time.[6] Young people's views have mirrored those of the nation as a whole.[7] Distrust; lack of **efficacy,** which is a person's belief that he or she has the ability to achieve something desirable and that the government genuinely listens to individuals; and apathy are prevalent among young people.

These attitudes are expressed through one of the most easily measured contexts: voter turnout. Figure 1.1 shows the trend of participation by young voters in presidential elections. From Figure 1.1, we see that about 43 percent of young Americans (aged 18–29) voted in 2016, a slight increase from the 2012 presidential election. Since the drastic uptick in youth voter participation in 2004, majorities of young American typically have supported Democratic candidates for president, especially Barack Obama, whose 2008 candidacy generated record turnout and support among young Americans. But early research shows that the youngest of the young voters—members of Generation Z—may be somewhat more likely to support Republican candidates than were Millennials.

Despite the complexity of the youth vote issue, there remain lingering media characterizations of a cynical, nonparticipatory youth electorate. But evidence indicates that many young people are enthusiastic participants in civic and political life.[8] Others are taking part in ways that have not traditionally been thought of, and measured as, participation, including Internet activism and using one's power as a consumer to send political messages. For many students, that foundation of political participation, volunteerism, or community action has already provided them with a rationale for increasing their knowledge of, and participation in, their communities.

Individuals who engage in politics and civic life experience many benefits. Engaged citizens are knowledgeable about public issues; actively communicate with policymakers and others; press government officials to carry out the people's will; advocate for their own self-interest and the interests of others; and hold public officials accountable for their decisions and actions. You will find that advocating for your own interests or working with others in similar situations sometimes (perhaps to your surprise) leads to desired outcomes. This is efficacy in action. And you will discover that with experience you will become more effective at advocacy—the more you do, the better you get. Furthermore, you will derive social and psychological benefits from being civically engaged.

In addition, and equally important, local communities, states, and the nation benefit from an engaged populace. Governments are more effective when people voice their views. As we will see as we explore *American Democracy Now,* today's citizens and others have more opportunities to influence

Evaluating the Facts

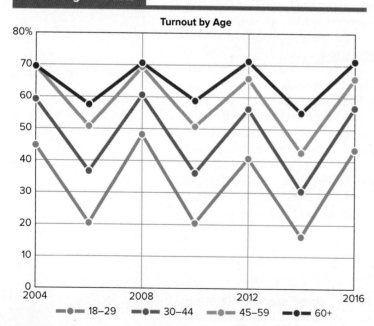

FIGURE 1.1 ■ Voter Turnout in Presidential Elections (2004–2016) by Voter Age. How has the turnout rate changed over time for voters aged 18–29? For other age groups?

SOURCE: United States Elections Project.

Facts Matter

In 1971, a whistleblower employee of the Department of Defense, Daniel Ellsberg, leaked a document that would come to be known as the Pentagon Papers, which was a history of the United States' political-military involvement in Vietnam from 1945 to 1967. Published by *The New York Times,* the Papers demonstrated that successive presidents had "systematically lied, not only to the public but also to Congress." The Pentagon Papers caused a huge controversy at the time and undermined the confidence of the American people in their government, generally, and in the presidency, specifically.

Since then, it seems that Americans have more to worry about than their government lying to them. Thanks to the Internet, information is abundant but often unreliable. And increasingly, those who disseminate misinformation appear to be doing so as a political tactic, a strategy made particularly effective with the advent of social media.

Consider: During the presidential campaign, a physician "diagnosed" Democratic candidate Hillary Clinton with Parkinson's disease, despite the fact that he had never examined her, and he posted a YouTube video of his diagnosis. Today, more than 800,000 websites repeat this claim in some form, even though Clinton's physician has rejected the diagnosis.

A website announced that "Pope Francis Shocks World, Endorses Donald Trump for President." The story gained enough traction that Pope Francis noted in a press conference that he does not endorse political candidates.

After President Donald Trump was inaugurated, and during a tour of the Oval Office, a *Time* magazine reporter tweeted that the incoming president had removed a bust of iconic Civil Rights leader Dr. Martin Luther King Jr. Twenty-three minutes later, the reporter tweeted that he was mistaken, claiming someone was standing in front of the bust so he couldn't see it, but by then the claim had gone viral.

How can a student think critically about the facts and determine whether information being presented is accurate? In each chapter that follows, "Thinking Critically" will coach students in evaluating facts and data and in considering perspective and biases in their analyses. This kind of careful evaluation occurs on three tiers:

- *Tier One—Gut Check:* Using common sense, ask yourself: Is the information consistent with what I already know about the subject? Is the claim outlandish or implausible? Does the source appear legitimate? Red flags for fake news include a multitude of exclamation marks, misspelled words, all caps headlines, or claims of "Not a Hoax!"

- *Tier Two—Credibility Check:* Is the information current (i.e., the timing of information can matter)? Is the material copyrighted (typically indicated after the headline or at the bottom of a news story)? Is the website a legitimate one (beware of slight adaptations of traditional news outlets, and consult Snopes' list of fake news sites [www.snopes.com/2016/01/14/fake-news-sites/])? Is the source known to be a reliable one, and if so, how does he or she have access to the information being described? Is the information from a satirical site, meant to be funny, like the *Onion* or the *Borowitz Report*? Does the source seem to have an agenda? Is the author or source of information a recognized expert?

- *Tier Three—Accuracy Check:* Can the information be independently verified or corroborated? Just because information appears on multiple sites does not mean that it is corroborated. Rather, look to see if multiple sources are independently reporting similar versions of events. Do sources contain links to verifiable data sources, independent accounts of events, or other verifying statements? Multiple resources are available for you to double-check accuracy, particularly before you pass information on. These include websites like Snopes, factcheck.org, and PolitiFact's Truth-O-Meter.

What do you think?

Each chapter's *Thinking Critically* will ask students to evaluate how a source of data, the perspective of a reporter or viewer, and/or the timing of information can affect the interpretation of "facts." For example:

1. In evaluating Hillary Clinton health, Dr. Ted Noel characterized Clinton as "a politician who lies about everything." In addition, he is an anesthesiologist and would likely have little experience in diagnosing Parkinson's disease. A quick gut check reveals the flaws with this claim.

2. A credibility check of the original Pope Francis post, on the WTOE 5 News website, reveals that the site lacks credibility. In its "About" page, it says, "WTOE 5 News is a fantasy news website."

3. An accuracy check shows that *Time*'s Zeke Miller was the only reporter to note the removal of the Martin Luther King Jr. bust, and then White House Spokesman Sean Spicer tweeted a rebuttal photo, showing the bust in place, indicating the claim was inaccurate.

> One way individuals articulate their political views is through the products they purchase. In 2017, Proctor & Gamble created a stir with an ad called The Talk, in which African American mothers talk to their children about racial bias. The company paired the ads with a social media campaign encouraging everyone to #talkaboutbias. The ads were met with widespread support among many African Americans who identified with the theme of the ads, but critics, including the conservative-leaning *National Review,* characterized the ad as "identity-politics pandering." Have you ever boycotted or buycotted a manufacturer because of your political views?
Source: BBDO NY for Proctor and Gamble

civic engagement
Individual and collective actions designed to identify and address issues of public concern.

political engagement
Citizen actions that are intended to solve public problems through political means.

government
The institution that creates and implements policy and laws that guide the conduct of the nation and its citizens.

citizens
Members of the polity who, through birth or naturalization, enjoy the rights, privileges, and responsibilities attached to membership in a given nation.

governmental action than at any other time in history. If you have the knowledge and tools, you should be able to make the most of these opportunities.

Civic Engagement: Acting on Your Views

One vitally important goal of this book is to encourage you to engage in a respectful, continuing conversation about your views and to make the connection between having ideas and opinions and acting on them. Political scientist Michael Delli Carpini has defined **civic engagement** as

individual and collective actions designed to identify and address issues of public concern. Civic engagement can take many forms, from individual voluntarism to organizational involvement to electoral participation. It can include efforts to directly address an issue, work with others in a community to solve a problem or interact with the institutions of representative democracy.[9]

The possibilities for citizen involvement are so broad and numerous that the idea of civic engagement encompasses a range of activities. Civic engagement might include everything from tutoring an underprivileged child to volunteering at a conservative think tank. In this book, we focus in particular on civic engagement that takes the form of **political engagement**—that is, citizen actions that are intended to solve public problems through political means. As you read this book, you will find that a variety of political actions are possible, from boycotting and *buycotting* (buying goods produced by companies whose policies you agree with) to running for office.

We hope that this book not only empowers you by teaching you about the institutions, policies, and processes of government but also inspires you to become civically and politically engaged. Today, many students choose to stick their toes into the waters of political activism by using the Internet—by following an elected official on Twitter, for example. You can take part in your democracy by joining a Facebook group advocating for an issue you care about, organizing a fundraising event, signing an e-petition, joining a volunteer group, volunteering for a campaign, or even participating in a protest march, to name just a few of the many options available to you. Consider which potential volunteer activities pique your interest. Think about what might best suit your schedule, lifestyle, and personal and professional goals. By taking part, you will ensure that your voice is heard, and you will derive the satisfaction of knowing that your community and the nation benefit from your actions as well.

What Government Does

In this section, we look at the nature of government and the functions a government performs. **Government** is an institution that creates and implements the policy and laws that guide the conduct of a nation and its citizens. **Citizens** are those members of a political community—town, city, state, or country—who, through birth or naturalization, enjoy the rights, privileges, and responsibilities attached to membership in a given nation. **Naturalization** is the process of becoming a citizen by means other than birth, as in the case of immigrants. Although governments vary widely in how well they perform, most national governments share some common functions.

To get a clear sense of the business of government, consider the following key functions performed by government in the United States and many other national governments:

- **To protect their sovereign territory and their citizenry and to provide national defense.** Governments protect their *sovereign territory* (that is, the territory over which they have the ultimate governing authority) and their citizens at home and abroad. Usually they carry out this responsibility by maintaining one or more types of armed services, but governments also provide for the national defense through counterterrorism efforts.

  In the United States, the armed services include the Army, Navy, Marines, Air Force, and Coast Guard. Governments also preserve order domestically. In the United States, domestic order is preserved through the National Guard and federal, state, and local law enforcement agencies.

- **To preserve order and stability.** Governments also preserve order by providing emergency services and security in the wake of disasters. Governments also maintain stability by providing a political structure that has **legitimacy:** a quality conferred on government by citizens who believe that its exercise of power is right and proper.[10]

- **To establish and maintain a legal system.** Governments create legal structures by enacting and enforcing laws that restrict or ban certain behaviors. In the United States, the foundation of this legal structure is the federal Constitution.[11] Governments also provide the means to implement laws through the actions of local police and other state and national law enforcement agencies. By means of the court system, governments administer justice and impose penalties.

- **To provide services.** Governments distribute a wide variety of services to their citizens. In the United States, government agencies provide services ranging from inspecting the meat we consume to ensuring the safety of our workplaces. Federal, state, and local governments provide roads, bridges, transportation, education, and health services. They facilitate communication, commerce, air travel, and entertainment.

  Many of the services governments provide are called **public goods** because their benefits, by their nature, cannot be limited to specific groups or individuals. For example, everyone enjoys national defense, equal access to clean air and clean water, airport security, highways, and other similar services. Because the value and the benefits of these goods are extended to everyone, government makes them available through revenue collected by taxes.

- **To raise and spend money.** All the services that governments provide, from national protection and defense to health care, cost money.[12] Governments at all levels spend money collected through taxes. Depending on personal income, between 25 and 35 cents of every dollar earned by those working in the United States and earning above a certain level goes toward federal, state, and local income taxes. Governments also tax *commodities* (commercially exchanged goods and services) in various ways—through sales taxes, property taxes, "sin" taxes, and luxury taxes.

naturalization
The process of becoming a citizen by means other than birth, as in the case of immigrants.

legitimacy
A quality conferred on government by citizens who believe that its exercise of power is right and proper.

public goods
Goods whose benefits cannot be limited and that are available to all.

> Children are socialized to the dominant political culture from a very early age. When children emulate police officers, for example, they begin the process of learning about the functions governments perform.
©Huntstock/AGE Fotostock

monarchy
Government in which a member of a royal family, usually a king or queen, has absolute authority over a territory and its government.

oligarchy
Government in which an elite few hold power.

democracy
Government in which supreme power of governance lies in the hands of its citizens.

totalitarianism
System of government in which the government essentially controls every aspect of people's lives.

authoritarianism
System of government in which the government holds strong powers but is checked by some forces.

- **To socialize new generations.** Governments play a role in *socialization,* the process by which individuals develop their political values and opinions. Governments perform this function, for example, by providing funding for schools, by establishing standards for curriculum, by introducing young people to the various "faces" of government (perhaps through a police officer's visiting a school or a mayor's bestowing an honor on a student), and by facilitating participation in civic life through institutions such as libraries, museums, and public parks. In these ways, governments transmit cultural norms and values such as patriotism and build commitment to fundamental values such as those we explore later in this chapter. For a detailed discussion of political socialization, see Chapter 6.

Types of Government

When social scientists categorize the different systems of government operating in the world today, two factors influence their classifications. The first factor is *who participates in governing or in selecting those who govern.* These participants vary as follows, depending on whether the government is a monarchy, an oligarchy, or a democracy:

- In a **monarchy,** a member of a royal family, usually a king or a queen, has absolute authority over a territory and its government. Monarchies typically are inherited—they pass down from generation to generation. Most modern monarchies, such as those in Great Britain and Spain, are *constitutional monarchies,* in which the monarch plays a ceremonial role but has little say in governance, which is carried out by elected leaders. In contrast, in traditional monarchies, such as the Kingdom of Saudi Arabia, the monarch is both the ceremonial and the governmental head of state.
- In an **oligarchy,** an elite few hold power. Some oligarchies are *dictatorships,* in which a small group, such as a political party or a military junta, supports a dictator. North Korea is a present-day example of an oligarchy.
- In a **democracy,** the supreme power of governance lies in the hands of citizens. The United States and most other modern democracies are *republics,* sometimes called *representative democracies,* in which citizens elect leaders to represent their views. We discuss the republic form of government in Chapter 2.

When classifying governments, social scientists also consider *how governments function* and *how they are structured:*

- Governments that rule according to the principles of **totalitarianism** essentially control every aspect of their citizens' lives. In these tyrannical governments, citizens enjoy neither rights nor freedoms, and the state is the tool of the dictator. Totalitarian regimes tend to center on a particular ideology, religion, or personality. North Korea is a contemporary example of a totalitarian regime.
- When a government rules by the principles of **authoritarianism,** it holds strong powers, but they are checked by other forces within the society. China and Cuba are examples of authoritarian states, because their leaders are restrained in their exercise of power by political parties, constitutions, and the military. Individuals living under an authoritarian regime may enjoy some rights, but often those rights are not protected by the government.

- **Constitutionalism,** a form of government structured by law, provides for **limited government**—a government that is restricted in what it can do so that the rights of the people are protected. Constitutional governments can be democracies or monarchies. In the United States, the federal Constitution created the governmental structure, and this system of government reflects both the historical experiences and the norms and values of the founders.

The Constitution's framers (authors) structured American government as a *constitutional democracy*. In this type of government, a constitution creates a representative democracy in which the rights of the people are protected. We can trace the roots of this modern constitutional democracy back to ancient times.

constitutionalism
Government that is structured by law, and in which the power of government is limited.

limited government
Government that is restricted in what it can do so that the rights of the people are protected.

The Origins of American Democracy

The ancient Greeks first developed the concept of a democracy. The Greeks used the term *demokratia* (literally, "people power") to describe some of the 1,500 *poleis* ("city-states"; also the root of *politics*) on the Black and the Mediterranean Seas. These city-states were not democracies in the modern sense of the term, but the way they were governed provided the philosophical origins of American democracy. For example, citizens decided public issues using majority rule in many of the city-states. However, in contrast to modern democracies, the Greek city-states did not count women as citizens. The Greeks also did not count slaves as citizens. American democracy also traces some of its roots to the Judeo-Christian tradition and the English common law, particularly the ideas that thrived during the Protestant Reformation.[13]

Democracy's Origins in Popular Protest: The Influence of the Reformation and the Enlightenment

We can trace the seeds of the idea of modern democracy almost as far back as the concept of monarchy—back to several centuries ago, when the kings and emperors who ruled in Europe claimed that they reigned by divine sanction, or God's will. The monarchs' claims reflected the political theory of the **divine right of kings,** articulated by Jacques-Benigne Bossuet (1627–1704), who argued that monarchies, as a manifestation of God's will, could rule absolutely without regard to the will or well-being of their subjects. Challenging the right of a monarch to govern or questioning one of his or her decisions thus represented a challenge to the will of God.

divine right of kings
The assertion that monarchies, as a manifestation of God's will, could rule absolutely without regard to the will or well-being of their subjects.

At odds with the theory of the divine right of kings was the idea that people could challenge the Crown and the church—institutions that seemed all-powerful. This idea took hold during the Protestant Reformation, a movement to reform the Catholic Church. In October 1517, Martin Luther, a German monk who would later found the Lutheran Church, affixed his *95 Theses,* criticizing the harmful practices of the Catholic Church, to the church at Wittenberg Castle. The Reformation continued throughout the sixteenth century, during which time reform-minded Protestants (whose name is derived from *protest*) challenged basic tenets of Catholicism and sought to *purify* the church.

In England, some extreme Protestants, known as Puritans, thought that the Reformation had not gone far enough in reforming the church. Puritans asserted their right to communicate directly with God through prayer rather than through an intermediary such as a priest. This idea that an individual could speak directly with God lent support to the notion that the people could govern themselves. Faced with persecution in England, congregations of Puritans, known to us today

> In his scientific work, Sir Isaac Newton demonstrated the power of science to explain phenomena in the natural world and discredited prevalent ideas based on magic and superstition. Newton's ideas laid the foundation for the political philosophers of the Enlightenment.
©Pixtal/AGE Fotostock

social contract
An agreement between people and their leaders in which the people agree to give up some liberties so that their other liberties are protected.

natural law
The assertion that standards that govern human behavior are derived from the nature of humans themselves and can be applied universally.

popular sovereignty
The theory that government is created by the people and depends on the people for the authority to rule.

as the Pilgrims, fled to America, where they established self-governing colonies, a radical notion at the time. Before the Pilgrims reached shore in 1620, they drew up the Mayflower Compact, an example of a **social contract**—an agreement between people and their leaders, whereby the people give up some liberties so that their other liberties will be protected. In the Mayflower Compact, the Pilgrims agreed to be governed by the structure of government they formed, thereby establishing the idea of consent of the governed.

In the late seventeenth century came the early beginnings of the Enlightenment, a philosophical movement that stressed the importance of individuality, reason, and scientific endeavor. Enlightenment scientists such as Sir Isaac Newton (1642–1727) drastically changed how people thought about the universe and the world around them, including government. Newton's work in physics, astronomy, math, and mechanics demonstrated the power of science and repudiated prevalent ideas based on magic and superstition. Newton's ideas about **natural law,** the assertion that the laws that govern human behavior are derived from the nature of humans themselves and can be applied universally, laid the foundation for the ideas of the political philosophers of the Enlightenment.

The Modern Political Philosophy of Hobbes and Locke

The difficulty of individual survival under the rule of an absolute monarch is portrayed in British philosopher Thomas Hobbes's book *Leviathan* (1651). Hobbes (1588–1679), who believed in the righteousness of absolute monarchies, argued that the strong naturally prey on the weak and that through a social contract, individuals who relinquish their rights can enjoy the protection offered by a sovereign. Without such a social contract and without an absolute monarch, Hobbes asserted, anarchy prevails, describing this state as one lived in "continuall feare, and danger of violent death; And the life of man, solitary, poore, nasty, brutish, and short."[14]

John Locke (1632–1704) took Hobbes's reasoning concerning a social contract one step further. In the first of his *Two Treatises on Civil Government* (1689), Locke systematically rejected the notion that the rationale for the divine right of kings is based on scripture. By providing a theoretical basis for discarding the idea of a monarch's divine right to rule, Locke paved the way for more radical notions about the rights of individuals and the role of government. In the second *Treatise,* Locke argued that individuals possess certain unalienable (or natural) rights, which he identified as the rights to life, liberty, and property, ideas that would prove pivotal in shaping Thomas Jefferson's articulation of the role of government and the rights of individuals found in the Declaration of Independence. Locke, and later Jefferson, stressed that these rights are inherent in people as individuals; that is, government can neither bestow them nor take them away. When people enter into a social contract, Locke said, they do so with the understanding that the government will protect their natural rights. At the same time, according to Locke, they agree to accept the government's authority; but if the government fails to protect the inherent rights of individuals, the people have the right to rebel.

The French philosopher Jean-Jacques Rousseau (1712–1778) took Locke's notion further, stating that governments formed by social contract rely on **popular sovereignty,** the theory that government is created by the people and depends on the people for the authority to rule. **Social contract theory,** which assumes that individuals possess free will and that every individual possesses the God-given right of self-determination and the ability to consent to be governed, would eventually form the theoretical framework of the Declaration of Independence.

The Creation of the United States as an Experiment in Representative Democracy

The American colonists who eventually rebelled against Great Britain and who became the citizens of the first 13 states were shaped by their experiences of living under European monarchies. Many rejected the ideas of absolute rule and the divine right of kings, which had been central to rationalizing the monarchs' authority. The logic behind the rejection of the divine right of kings—the idea that monarchs were not chosen by God—was that people could govern themselves.

In New England, where many colonists settled after fleeing England to escape religious persecution, a form of **direct democracy,** a structure of government in which citizens discuss and decide policy through majority rule, emerged in *town meetings* (which still take place today). In every colony, the colonists themselves decided who was eligible to participate in government, and so in some localities, women and people of color who owned property participated in government well before they were granted formal voting rights under amendments to the federal Constitution.

Beyond the forms of direct democracy prevalent in the New England colonies, nearly all the American colonies had councils structured according to the principle of representative democracy, sometimes called **indirect democracy,** in which citizens elect representatives who decide policies on their behalf. These representative democracies foreshadow important political values that founders such as Thomas Jefferson and James Madison would incorporate into key founding documents, including the Declaration of Independence and the Constitution.

Political Culture and American Values

American democracy rests on a set of ideals rooted in the founding of our republic—concepts of liberty, freedom, and equality that were born of the Enlightenment. These and other core values—capitalism; consent of the governed; and the importance of the individual, family, and community—shape our beliefs about government and inform our views as we react and reconsider our values and beliefs in our dynamic, rapidly changing society. While the importance we place on certain ideals may ebb and flow—for example, in an age of terrorism, some might weigh security more important than liberty—nonetheless, their underpinnings remain constant. These ideals are part of American

social contract theory
The idea that individuals possess free will, and every individual is equally endowed with the God-given right of self-determination and the ability to consent to be governed.

direct democracy
A structure of government in which citizens discuss and decide policy through majority rule.

indirect democracy
Sometimes called a *representative democracy,* a system in which citizens elect representatives who decide policies on behalf of their constituents.

>Thomas Jefferson's ideas about the role of government shaped the United States for generations to come. In 2008, descendants of Thomas Jefferson, including those he fathered with his slave, Sally Hemings, who was also his wife's half-sister, posed for a group photo at his plantation, Monticello, in Charlottesville, Virginia.
©Paul J. Richards/AFP/Getty Images

political culture
The people's collective beliefs and attitudes about government and political processes.

political culture—the people's collective beliefs and attitudes about government and the political process. Individuals' differing perception of these core values—and how they weight the importance of each—affects not only the relationship citizens have with their federal government, but also the relationship they have with each other. Indeed, much of the political division seen in recent times in the United States lies in individuals' differing concepts of our core values and the relative importance of these values.

Liberty

liberty
The most essential quality of American democracy; it is both the freedom from governmental interference in citizens' lives and the freedom to pursue happiness.

The most essential quality of American democracy, **liberty** is both freedom from government interference in our lives (limited government) and freedom to pursue happiness. Many of the colonies that eventually became the United States were founded by people who were interested in one notion of liberty: religious freedom. Those who fought in the War of Independence were intent on obtaining economic and political freedom. The framers of the Constitution added to the structure of the U.S. government many other liberties,[15] including freedom of speech, freedom of the press, and freedom of association.[16]

Throughout history and to the present day, liberties have often conflicted with efforts by the government to ensure a secure and stable society by exerting restraints on liberties. When government officials infringe on personal liberties, they often do so in the name of security, arguing that such measures are necessary to protect the rights of other individuals, institutions (including the government itself), or society as a whole. Such was the case when it was revealed that the National Security Agency had recorded information about 125 million cell phone communications in a 30-day period in 2013, including 3 million communications originating in the United States.

The meaning of liberty—how we define our freedoms—is constantly evolving. Today, technological innovation prompts new questions about individual privacy, including what information the government should be privy to. Should the government be permitted to collect metadata—data about communications data (the length of calls, for example)—of members of suspected terror cells? Should government officials be able to monitor phone calls and text messages to individuals in these cells? What if that person is suspected of plotting a terrorist attack—should officers be required to obtain a warrant first in that situation? Should law enforcement officers be allowed to track a person's movements using GPS (Global Positioning System) if that person is suspected of a crime? Or should they be required to get a warrant first? What if one of the suspected plotters is not a U.S. citizen?

Equality

The Declaration of Independence states that "all men are created equal...." But the founders' notions of equality were vastly different from those that prevail today. Their ideas of equality evolved from the emphasis the ancient Greeks placed on equality of opportunity. The Greeks envisioned a merit-based system in which educated freemen could participate in democratic government rather than inheriting their positions as a birthright. The Judeo-Christian religions also emphasize the idea of equality. All three major world religions—Christianity, Judaism, and Islam—stress that all people are equal in the eyes of God. These notions of equality informed both Jefferson's assertion about equality in the Declaration of Independence and, later, the framers' structuring of the U.S. government in the Constitution.[17]

The idea of equality evolved during the 19th and 20th centuries. In the early American republic, all women, as well as all men of color, were denied fundamental rights, including the right to vote. Through long, painful struggles—including the abolition movement to free enslaved people; the suffrage movement to gain women the right to vote; various immigrants' rights movements; and later the civil rights, Native American rights, and women's rights movements of the 1960s and 1970s (Chapter 5)—members of these disenfranchised groups won the rights previously denied to them. Several groups are still engaged in the struggle for legal equality today, notably those that advocate for equality in the criminal justice and legal systems, including groups that fight for the rights of transgender, bisexual, gay, and lesbian individuals, and of immigrants.

Beyond these questions of legal equality, today many arguments focus on issues of economic equality, a concept about which there is substantial disagreement. Many people in the United States believe that the government should do more to eliminate disparities in wealth—by taxing wealthy people more heavily than others, for example, or by providing more subsidies and services to the poor. Others disagree, however, and argue that although people should have equal opportunities for economic achievement, their attainment of that success should depend on factors such as education and hard work, and that success should be determined in the marketplace rather than through government intervention.

Capitalism

Although the founders valued the notion of equality, capitalism was enormously important to them. **Capitalism** is an economic system in which the means of producing wealth are privately owned and operated to produce profits. In a pure capitalist economy, the marketplace determines the regulation of production, the distribution of goods and services, wages, and prices. In this type of economy, for example, businesses pay employees the wage that they are willing to work for, without the government's setting a minimum wage by law. Although capitalism is an important value in American democracy, the U.S. government imposes certain regulations on the economy. For example, it mandates a minimum wage, regulates and inspects goods and services, and imposes tariffs on imports and taxes on domestically produced goods that have an impact on pricing.

capitalism
An economic system in which the means of producing wealth are privately owned and operated to produce profits.

One key component of capitalism is **property**—anything that can be owned. There are various kinds of property: businesses, homes, farms, the material items we use every day, and even ideas are considered property. Property holds such a prominent position in American culture that it is considered a natural right, and the Constitution protects some aspects of property ownership.

property
anything that can be owned

Consent of the Governed

The idea that, in a democracy, the government's power derives from the consent of the people is called the **consent of the governed.** As we have seen, this concept, a focal point of the rebellious American colonists and eloquently expressed in Jefferson's Declaration of Independence, is based on John Locke's idea of a social contract. Implicit in Locke's social contract is the principle that the people agree to the government's authority, and if the government no longer has the consent of the governed, the people have the right to revolt.

consent of the governed
The idea that, in a democracy, the government's power derives from the consent of the people.

The concept of consent of the governed also implies **majority rule**—the principle that, in a democracy, only policies with 50 percent plus one vote are enacted. Governments based on majority rule include the idea that the majority has the right of self-governance and typically also protect the rights of people in the minority. A particular question about this ideal of governing by the consent of

majority rule
The idea that in a democracy, only policies with 50 percent plus one vote are enacted, and only candidates that win 50 percent plus one vote are elected.

the governed has important implications for the United States in the early 21st century: Can a democracy remain stable and legitimate if less than a majority of its citizens participate in elections?

Individual, Family, and Community

Emphasis on the individual is a preeminent feature of American democratic thought. In the Constitution, rights are bestowed on, and exercised by, the individual. The importance of the individual—an independent, hearty entity exercising self-determination—has powerfully shaped the development of the United States, both geographically and politically.

Family and community have also played central roles in the U.S. political culture, both historically and in the present day. A child first learns political behavior from his or her family, and in this way the family serves to perpetuate the political culture. From the earliest colonial settlements to Snapchat today, communities have channeled individuals' political participation. Indeed, the intimate relationship between individualism and community life is reflected in the First Amendment of the Constitution, which ensures individuals' freedom of assembly—one component of which is their right to form or join any type of organization, political party, or club without penalty.

Ideology: A Prism for Viewing American Democracy

political ideology
An integrated system of ideas or beliefs about political values in general and the role of government in particular.

Besides focusing on the demographic characteristics of the U.S. population, we can also analyze political events and trends by looking at them through the prism of ideology. **Political ideology** is an integrated system of ideas or beliefs about political values in general and the role of government in particular (see "Analyzing the Sources"). Political ideology provides a framework for thinking about politics, about policy issues, and about the role of government in society. In the United States, one key component of various ideologies is the *extent* to which adherents believe that the government should have a role in people's everyday lives. Table 1.1 summarizes the key ideologies we consider in this section.

TABLE 1.1 The Traditional Ideological Spectrum

	SOCIALISM	LIBERALISM	MIDDLE OF ROAD (MODERATE)	CONSERVATISM	LIBERTARIANISM
GOAL OF GOVERNMENT	Equality	Equality of opportunity; protection of fundamental liberties	Nondiscrimination in opportunity; protection of some economic freedoms; security; stability	Traditional values; order; stability; economic freedom	Absolute economic and social freedom
ROLE OF GOVERNMENT	Strong government control of economy	Government action to promote opportunity	Government action to balance the wants of workers and businesses; government fosters stability	Government action to protect and bolster capitalist system; few limitations on fundamental rights	No governmental regulations of economy; no limitations on fundamental rights

A NATION DIVIDED?

The figure below shows the ideological affiliation of generations of Americans.

Percentage of each generation who are . . .

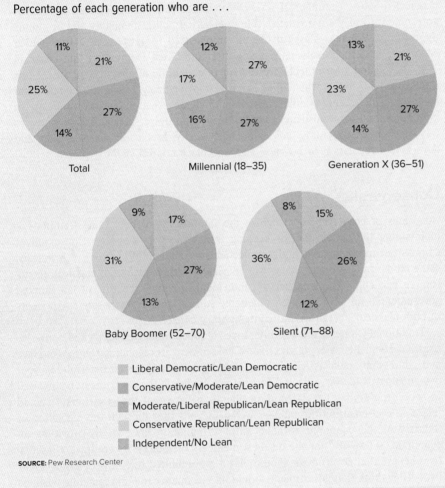

Total

Millennial (18–35)

Generation X (36–51)

Baby Boomer (52–70)

Silent (71–88)

■ Liberal Democratic/Lean Democratic
■ Conservative/Moderate/Lean Democratic
■ Moderate/Liberal Republican/Lean Republican
■ Conservative Republican/Lean Republican
■ Independent/No Lean

SOURCE: Pew Research Center

Practice Analytical Thinking

1. Contrast the ideological affiliations of Millennials and Gen Xers compared with Boomers and the Silent Generation. What is the major difference between these two groups?

2. Historically, Baby Boomers were known to be a liberal generation, but like previous generations, they became more conservative as they have grown older. In addition, initial data indicate that the generation following Millennials—Generation Z—is more conservative than Millennials. Given these trends, analyze what you believe this distribution will look like in 10 years.

3. In the United States, most large cities tend to vote Democratic (liberal), while rural areas are more Republican (conservative). With these facts in mind, can you make any deductions about specific areas where Millennials are most likely to live? What about members of the Silent Generation?

Liberalism

Modern **liberalism** in the United States is associated with the ideas of liberty and political equality; its advocates favor change in the social, political, and economic realms to better protect the well-being of individuals and to produce equality within society. They emphasize the importance of civil liberties, including freedom of speech, assembly, and the press, as outlined in the Bill of Rights. Modern liberals also advocate the separation of church and state, often opposing measures that bring religion into the public realm, such as prayer in the public schools. In addition, they support political equality, advocating contemporary movements that

liberalism

An ideology that advocates change in the social, political, and economic realms to better protect the well-being of individuals and to produce equality within society.

promote the political rights of gay and lesbian couples and voting rights for the disenfranchised.

The historical roots of modern liberalism reach back to the ideals of classical liberalism: freedom of thought and the free exchange of ideas, limited governmental authority, the consent of the governed, the rule of law in society, the importance of an unfettered market economy, individual initiative as a determinant of success, and access to free public education. These also were some of the founding ideals that shaped American democracy as articulated in the Declaration of Independence and the Constitution.

Modern liberalism, which emerged in the early 20th century, diverged from its classical roots in a number of ways. Most important, modern liberals expect the government to play a more active role in ensuring political equality and economic opportunity. Whereas classical liberals emphasized the virtues of a free market economy, modern liberals, particularly after the Great Depression that began in 1929, advocated government involvement in economic affairs. Today, we see this expectation in action when liberals call for prioritizing economic policies that benefit the poor and middle class, including job creation and tax policies. In modern times, liberals also are likely to advocate for universal health care; increases in social welfare programs such as Social Security, Medicare, and Medicaid; and government regulation of business and workplace conditions.

Conservatism

Advocates of **conservatism** recognize the importance of preserving tradition—of maintaining the status quo, or keeping things the way they are. Conservatives emphasize community and family as mechanisms of continuity in society. Ironically, some modern conservative ideals are consistent with the views of classical liberalism. In particular, the emphasis on individual initiative, the rule of law, limited governmental authority, and an unfettered market economy are key components of both classical liberalism and contemporary conservatism.

Traditionally, one of the key differences between modern liberals and conservatives has been their view of the role of government in regulating the marketplace and addressing social issues. In fact, one of the best ways of determining your own ideology is to ask yourself, "To what extent should the government be involved in people's everyday lives?" Modern liberals believe that the government should play a role in ensuring the public's well-being, whether through the regulation of industry or the economy, through antidiscrimination laws, or by providing an economic "safety net" for the neediest members of society. By contrast, conservatives believe that government should play a more limited role in people's everyday lives. They think that government should have a smaller role in regulating business and industry and that market forces, rather than the government, should largely determine economic policy. Conservatives believe that families, faith-based groups, and private charities should be more responsible for protecting the neediest and the government less so. When governments must act, conservatives prefer decentralized action by state governments rather than a nationwide federal policy.

Other Ideologies on a Traditional Spectrum: Socialism and Libertarianism

Although liberals and conservatives dominate the U.S. political landscape, other ideologies reflect the views of some Americans. In general, those ideologies tend to be more extreme than liberalism or conservatism. Advocates of certain of these ideologies call for *more* governmental intervention than modern liberalism does, and supporters of other views favor even *less* governmental interference than conservatism does.

For example, **socialism**—an ideology that stresses economic equality, theoretically achieved by having the government or workers own the means of production (businesses and industry)—lies to the left of liberalism on the political spectrum.[18] Socialists play a very limited role in modern American politics, though 2016 Democratic presidential candidate Bernie Sanders, who identifies himself as a "democratic socialist," brought new focus to this ideology's ideals, which were once more prominent in American politics.[19] In the early part of the 20th century, socialists had a good deal of electoral success, electing two members of Congress, more than 70 mayors of cities of various sizes, and numerous state legislators.

According to **libertarianism,** in contrast, government should take a "hands-off" approach in most matters. This ideology can be found to the right of conservatism on a traditional ideological spectrum. Libertarians believe that the less government intervention, the better. They chafe at attempts by the government to foster economic equality or to promote a social agenda, whether that agenda is the equality espoused by liberals or the traditional values espoused by conservatives. Libertarians strongly support the rights of property owners and a *laissez-faire* (French for "let it be") capitalist economy.

socialism
An ideology that advocates economic equality, theoretically achieved by having the government or workers own the means of production (businesses and industry).

libertarianism
An ideology whose advocates believe that government should take a "hands off" approach in most matters.

A Multidimensional Political Model

A one-dimensional ideological continuum is limited, however, because it sometimes fails to reflect the complexity of many individuals' views. For example, although an individual may believe that government should play a strong role in regulating the economy, he or she may also believe that the government should allow citizens a high degree of personal freedom of speech or religion. Even the traditional ideologies do not always fit easily into a single continuum that measures the extent to which the government should play a role in citizens' lives. Liberals supposedly advocate a larger role for the government. But although this may be the case in matters related to economic equality, liberals generally take a more laissez-faire approach when it comes to personal liberties, advocating strongly for privacy and free speech. And although conservatives support less governmental intervention in the economy, they sometimes advocate government action to promote traditional values, such as constitutional amendments to ban gay marriage, flag burning, and abortion and laws that mandate prayer in public schools.

Scholars have developed various *multidimensional scales* that attempt to represent people's ideologies more accurately.[20] Many of these scales measure people's opinions on the proper role of government in the economy—whether the government should act aggressively to ensure economic equality (fiscal liberalism) or prioritize a hands-off approach to the economy (social conservatism) on one axis and their beliefs about personal freedom on social issues on a second axis. These scales demonstrate that traditional liberals and traditional conservatives believe in social liberty and economic equality, and economic liberty and social conservatism, respectively. But the scale also acknowledges that some people prioritize economic equality and social order, whereas others embrace economic liberty and social order.

Ideology is one of the most important factors influencing people's belief structure about the types of issues they prioritize and the solutions they see to various policy challenges. But ideology alone does not explain priorities and preferred

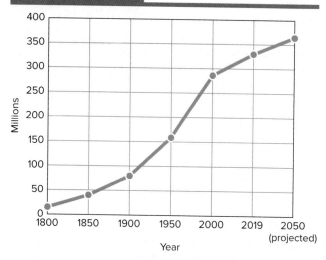

FIGURE 1.2 ■ **Growth of the U.S. Population from 1800 to 2050** The U.S. population increased gradually, and it did not reach 100 million until the second decade of the 20th century. What factors caused the steep rise during the 20th century? How will these forces continue to affect the size of the U.S. population during this century?

SOURCE: U.S. Census Bureau.

solutions. Also important are the characteristics of who we are, as these characteristics often make us more likely to identify certain issues as important, or render us more likely to favor one policy solution over another.

The Changing Face of American Democracy

Figure 1.2 shows how the U.S. population has grown since the first census in 1790. At that point, there were fewer than 4 million Americans. By 2019, the U.S. population had reached more than 330 million.

Immigrants have always been part of the country's population growth, and over the centuries they have made innumerable contributions to American life and culture.[21] Immigrants from lands all around the world have faced the kinds of struggles that today's undocumented immigrants encounter. And efforts to improve the lot of immigrant populations are not new either: Chinese Americans, for example, were instrumental in pioneering the West and completing the construction of the transcontinental railroad in the mid-19th century, but the Chinese Exclusion Act of 1881 prevented them from becoming U.S. citizens. Faced with the kinds of persecution that today would be considered hate crimes, Chinese Americans used civil disobedience to fight against the so-called Dog Tag Laws that required them to carry registration cards. In one incident, in 1885, they fought back against unruly mobs that drove them out of the town of Eureka, California, by suing the city for reparations and compensation.[22]

A Population That Is Growing—and on the Move

Between the 1960 census and the Census Bureau's 2017 Population Estimates, the population of the United States increased by more than 50 percent. As the population increases, measures of who the American people are and what percentage of each demographic group makes up the population have significant implications for the policies, priorities, values, and preferred forms of civic and political participation of the people. All the factors contributing to U.S. population growth—including immigration, the birth rate, falling infant mortality rates, and longer life spans—influence both politics and policy.

Accompanying the increase in population over the years has been a shift in the places where people live. Figure 1.3 shows that much of the population in the United States is concentrated in just a few densely populated areas: the Northeast, the Great Lake states, the Carolinas, Florida, Texas, and California. Between 2000 and 2010, the South and West accounted for 84 percent of the country's increase in population. Though not shown in Figure 1.3, census data indicates that many of the states in the Midwest are facing an out-migration of population, particularly of younger residents who are moving to metropolitan areas seeking employment. Over the past 10 years, all of the 10 most populous metropolitan areas grew, as

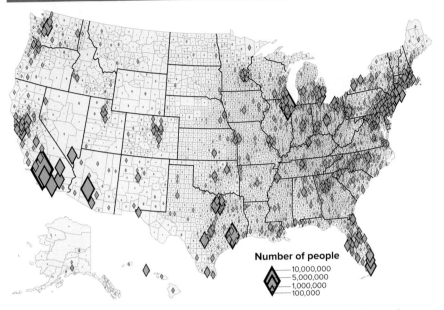

FIGURE 1.3 ■ **Population Distribution by County** The area of each diamond symbol is proportioned by the number of people in a county. The legend presents example symbol sizes from the many symbols shown on the map. Where are the largest population centers in the United States? What areas have comparatively sparse population?

SOURCE: U.S. Census Bureau.

did 9 of the 10 most populous cities. In part of the rural Midwest, though, some of this out-migration is counterbalanced by migration into these areas by families and retirees attracted by the comparatively low cost of living characteristic of such places.

An Aging Population

As the U.S. population increases and favors new places of residence, it is also aging. Figure 1.4 shows the distribution of the population by age and by sex as a series of three pyramids for three different years. The 2000 pyramid shows the "muffin top" of the Baby Boomers, who were 36–55 years old in that year. A quarter century later, the echo boom of the Millennials, who will be between the ages of 30 and 55 in 2025, is clearly visible. The pyramid evens out and thickens by 2050, showing the effects of increased population growth and the impact of extended longevity, with a large number of people (women, in particular) expected to live to the age of 85 and older.

Some areas of the United States are well-known meccas for older Americans. For example, the reputation of Florida and the Southwest as the premier retirement destinations in the United States is well-earned, and many senior citizens also reside in a broad north-south band that runs down the United States' midsection. Older people are concentrated in the Midwest and Plains states because of the high levels of out-migration from these areas by younger Americans, who are leaving their parents behind to look for opportunity elsewhere.

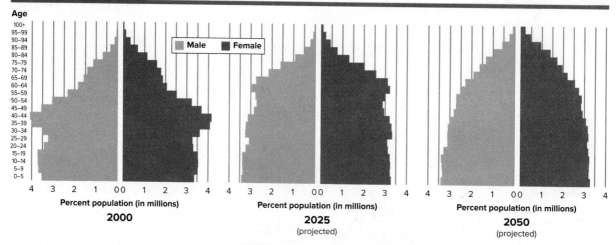

FIGURE 1.4 ■ **The Aging U.S. Population, 2000–2050** What effect will the changing age distribution of the U.S. population have on demand for services in 2025? In 2050? Given what you know about the racial composition of the Millennial generation, what will that mean for the racial composition of the U.S. population as it ages?

SOURCE: U.S. Census Bureau.

A Changing Complexion: Race and Ethnicity in the United States Today

The population of the United States is becoming not only older but also more racially and ethnically diverse. Today, non-Hispanic whites constitute a majority of the population, with 62 percent of Americans identifying themselves as "white alone." But according to the Census Bureau, by 2060, non-Hispanic whites will be only 44 percent of the U.S. population. Figure 1.5 shows the racial and ethnic composition of the U.S. population over time. Notice that Hispanics* now make up a greater proportion of the U.S. population than do blacks. As Figure 1.5 also shows, this trend has been continuous over the past several decades. Figure 1.5 also indicates that the percentage of Asian Americans has more than doubled in recent decades, from just over 2 percent of the U.S. population in 1980 to nearly 6 percent today, and is projected to increase to 12 percent by 2060. The Native American population remains just below 1 percent of the whole population. Figure 1.5 also shows the proportion of people reporting that they belonged to two or more racial groups—2.3 percent of the population today. This category was not an option on the census questionnaire until 2000, and the population proportion of this group has nearly doubled since that time. It will double again to over 6 percent by 2060. The increasing diversity of the U.S. population can be seen too in the Census Bureau's population projections: by 2044, more than half of all Americans will belong to a minority group (any group other than non-Hispanic white alone); and by 2060, nearly one in five of the nation's total population will be foreign born.[23]

* A note about terminology: When discussing data for various races and ethnicities to make comparisons, we use the terms *black* and *Hispanic* because these labels are typically used in measuring demographics by the U.S. Census Bureau and other organizations that collect this type of data. In more descriptive writing that is not comparative, we use the terms *African American* and *Latino* and *Latina*, which are the preferred terms at this time. Although the terms *Latino* and *Latina* exclude Americans who came from Spain (or whose ancestors did), these people compose a very small proportion of this population in the United States.

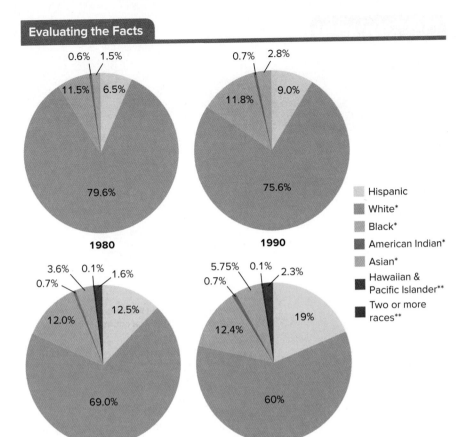

*Non-Hispanic only; in 1980 and 1990 "Asians" included Hawaiians and Pacific Islanders.
**Option available for the first time in 2000 census.

FIGURE 1.5 ■ **Population by Race, 1980–2020** Describe the general trend regarding the racial distribution of the U.S. population. Analyze whether you believe this trend will continue or whether it will change in some way. Why?

SOURCES: Social Science Data Analysis Network, University of Michigan; and U.S. Census Bureau.

As Figures 1.6 and 1.7 show, minority populations tend to be concentrated in different areas of the United States. Figure 1.6 shows the concentration of non-Hispanic African Americans. At over 13 percent of the population, African Americans are the largest racial minority in the United States. (Hispanics are an ethnic minority.) As the map illustrates, the African American population tends to be centered in urban areas and in the South, where, in some counties, African Americans constitute a majority of the population.

Hispanics, in contrast, historically have tended to cluster in Texas, Arizona, and California along the border between the United States and Mexico and in the urban centers of New Mexico (as shown in Figure 1.7), but recent years have seen significant growth in the number of Hispanics living in the South. Since 2000, there have been sizable increases in Hispanic populations in Florida and the Northeast as well. Hispanics are the fastest-growing ethnic group in the United States, with over 17 percent of the U.S. population identifying themselves as Hispanic in 2014, an increase of over 180 percent since 1980. By 2060, the Hispanic population is projected to grow to nearly 120 million, a 115 percent increase from today. Among

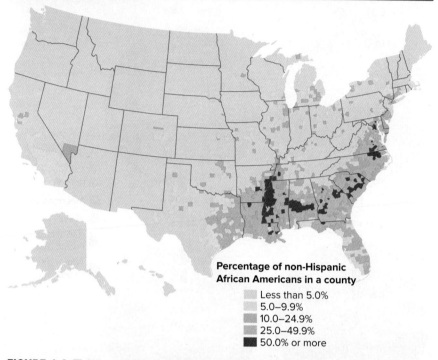

Percentage of non-Hispanic
African Americans in a county

Less than 5.0%
5.0–9.9%
10.0–24.9%
25.0–49.9%
50.0% or more

FIGURE 1.6 ■ **Where African Americans Live** From this figure, we see that the African American population in the United States is centered in the South, along the Eastern Seaboard, and in major cities. Given that African American voters are a core constituency of the Democratic Party, how might the distribution of this group of voters affect electoral politics in these regions? Are there national implications for this trend?

SOURCE: U.S. Census Bureau, Census Data Mapper.

people of Hispanic ethnicity, Mexicans make up the largest number (about 7 percent of the total U.S. population), followed by Puerto Ricans and Cubans.

Changing Households: American Families Today

The types of families that are counted by the U.S. census are also becoming more diverse. The traditional nuclear family, consisting of a stay-at-home mother, a breadwinning father, and their children, was at one time the stereotypical "ideal family" in the United States. Many—though hardly all—American families were able to achieve that cultural ideal during the prosperous 1950s and early 1960s. But since the women's liberation movement of the 1970s, in which women sought equal rights with men, the American family has changed drastically. As a result, the proportion of single-person households has increased significantly (from 13 percent in 1960 to 28 percent in 2017). Explanations for these trends include the tendency of people to marry at an older age and the fact that, as the population ages, increasing numbers of individuals are left widowed. The percentage of female householders without spouses (both with and without children) remained constant between 2000 and 2017 after a significant increase from 1970 through 1990. The proportion of male householders without spouses increased slightly, and men without a spouse are more likely to be raising children than they were

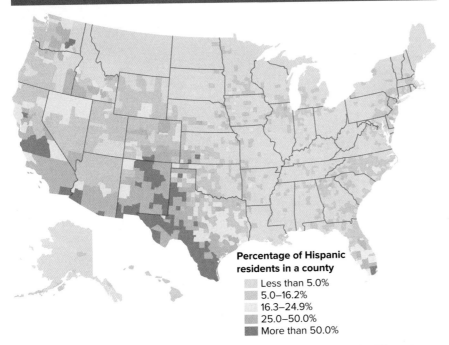

Percentage of Hispanic residents in a county

- Less than 5.0%
- 5.0–16.2%
- 16.3–24.9%
- 25.0–50.0%
- More than 50.0%

FIGURE 1.7 ■ Where Hispanics Live From this figure, we see that the Hispanic population in the United States is centered in the Southwest and the Eastern Seaboard. How might higher populations of Hispanics influence political culture in these regions? Do you think these Hispanic populations are homogeneous in their outlook? What policies might be priorities for majorities of Hispanics?

SOURCE: U.S. Census Bureau, Census Data Mapper.

in 1980. Finally, the proportion of the population living in nonfamily households, both those living alone and those living with others, rose slightly.

Why the Changing Population Matters for Politics and Government

Each of the changes to the U.S. population described here has implications for American democracy. As the nature of the electorate shifts, a majority of the nation's people may have different priorities, and various policies may become more or less important. For example, in recent years, we have seen increased demands for comprehensive immigration reform, often propelled by immigrants or families of immigrants with a vested interest in this reform. In addition, the swift growth in U.S. population means that demand for the services government provides—from schools, to highways, to health care—will continue to increase. The aging population will inevitably increase the burden on the nation's Social Security and government-supported health care system, which will be forced to support the needs of that older, growing population.

Changes in the population's racial and ethnic composition also matter, as does the concentration of racial minorities in specific geographic areas. The racial and ethnic makeup of the population (along with other influences) can significantly affect the nation's political culture and people's political attitudes, as can be seen

THEN

KNOW-NOTHINGISM IN BROOKLYN.
"None but citizens of the United States can be licensed to ngage in any employment in this city."
Brooklyn Board of Aldermen.

NOW

MR. TRUMP BUILD THAT WALL

> The Chinese Exclusion Act of 1881 prevented Chinese from becoming U.S. citizens, and local laws, including one in Brooklyn depicted here, banned them from employment. Faced with the kinds of persecution that today would be considered hate crimes, Chinese Americans used civil disobedience to fight against the so-called Dog Tag Laws that required them to carry registration cards. President Donald Trump supports the building of a wall between the United States and Mexico, in an effort to prevent undocumented immigrants from entering the United States. This controversial proposal has ignited passions on both sides of the immigration issue. What are the circumstances that cause increases in anti-immigrant sentiments in the United States?

Cartoon: Library of Congress, Prints and Photographs Division [LC-USZC2-761]; protest photo: ©Ethan Miller/Getty Images.

both in the viewpoints of young Americans concerning the fairness of the judicial system and in the prioritization of issues associated with immigration by many Hispanics, particularly those who are themselves recent immigrants. It has implications too for who will govern, as more and more representatives of the country's various racial and ethnic groups become candidates for political office and as *all* political candidates must reach out to increasingly diverse groups of voters—or possibly pay the price at the ballot box for failing to do so.

Conclusion

Thinking Critically About What's Next in American Democracy

Now is an exciting time to study American democracy. The fast-paced changes in American society today make participation in government and civic life more vitally important than ever. The effects of participating in the continuing conversation of American democracy through both words and actions are unequivocally positive—for you, for others, and for the government—and can have large ripple effects.

Will the present generation break the cycle of cynicism, anger, and division that has pervaded the politics of the recent past? Today, it is clear that the differing political viewpoints between generations of Americans will have repercussions in our polity. Technology will continue to play a significant role in how we communicate and participate in politics and how government creates and administers policy. Major transformations have come to pass in the political realm, and there is no end to them in sight.

Demographic changes in American society—particularly the growing diversity and the aging of the U.S. population—are giving rise to new public policy demands and creating new challenges. Challenges mean opportunities for those who are ready for them, and citizens who respond to those challenges will have an impact on the future of the nation.

Learning Summary

1. Define *politics*.
   a. Explain the current political context.
   b. Describe the role technology plays in the political arena.
   c. Compare and contrast how different generations participate in politics.
   d. Summarize the importance of being politically and civically engaged, both for the individual and for the polity.

2. Describe the functions of government.
   a. Explain the six functions of government.
   b. Explain the concept of public goods, and provide an example.

3. Explain the types of government.
   a. Describe the various types of government as determined by who participates in governing.
   b. Describe the various types of government as determined by how governments function and how they are structured.

4. Explain the origins of American democracy.
   a. Recall how the republican form of government is rooted in the Reformation and the Enlightenment.
   b. Compare and contrast the philosophies of Hobbes and Locke.

5. Describe the core values of American political culture and how individuals' perception of these values shapes their views of government.

6. Understand the concept of political ideology.
   a. Compare and contrast liberalism and conservatism.
   b. Understand the other ideologies on the spectrum.
   c. Describe the multidimensional political model.

7. Explain the changing face of American democracy.
   a. Summarize how the demographic characteristics of the U.S. population are changing.
   b. Analyze the effects these changes might have on policy priorities, policy making, and representation.

Key Terms

authoritarianism 10

capitalism 15

citizens 8

civic engagement 8

consent of the
governed 15

conservatism 18

constitutionalism 11

democracy 10

direct democracy 13

divine right of kings 11

efficacy 6

government 8

indirect democracy 13

legitimacy 9

liberalism 17

libertarianism 19

liberty 14

limited government 11

majority rule 15

monarchy 10

natural law 12

naturalization 9

oligarchy 10

political culture 14

political engagement 8

political ideology 16

politics 4

popular sovereignty 12

property 15

public goods 9

social contract 12

social contract theory 13

socialism 19

totalitarianism 10

For Review

1. In what ways has technology changed how politics happens and how government works? What impact has terrorism had on how Americans think about government?

2. Explain the functions that governments perform.

3. Describe how social scientists categorize governments.

4. How did the ideas of the Enlightenment shape people's views on the proper role of government?

5. Explain the fundamental values of American democracy.

6. Contrast liberals' and conservatives' views on government.

7. Describe the general trends with regard to population change in the United States.

For Critical Thinking and Discussion

1. In what ways do you use technology in your daily life? Do you use it to get information about politics or to access government services? How do your practices differ from those in your parents' generation?

2. Do you believe there are differences between your political views and those held by members of other generations? Explain. If your answer is yes, why do you believe these differences have emerged?

3. Why do governments perform the functions they do? Can you think of any private entities that provide public goods?

4. Think of the advantages and disadvantages of direct versus indirect democracies. Do you participate in any form of direct decision making? If you do, how well, or poorly, does it work?

5. Examine the demographic maps of the United States in this chapter, and describe what they reveal about the population in your home state.

Resources for Research AND Action

Internet Resources

Association of American Colleges and Universities
www.aacu.org/resources/civicengagement/index.cfm The AACU's website offers a clearinghouse of Internet resources on civic engagement.

American Political Science Association
www.apsanet.org The professional association for political scientists offers many resources on research about civic engagement, education, and participation.

CIRCLE: The Center for Information & Research on Civic Learning & Engagement
www.civicyouth.org Circle is the premier clearinghouse for research and analysis on civic engagement.

Factcheck
www.factcheck.org Factcheck is a project of the Annenberg Center for Public Policy. It provides a mechanism for individuals to debunk "fake news" by flagging inaccurate content.

PolitiFact's
www.polifact.com Polifact's Truth-O-Meter evaluates the claims made by political leaders to test for accuracy.

Snopes
www.snopes.com Snopes is a useful resource in determining the accuracy of information.

The Harvard Public Opinion Project
www.iop.harvard.edu/HPOP The Harvard Public Opinion Project is one of the leading research institutes that examines the opinions of Millennial Americans through its biennial surveys.

The U.S. Census
www.census.gov The U.S. Census Bureau's website is a clearinghouse for information about the census, including information on why the census is important, data, and how you can get involved in the census.

Recommended Readings

Grinspan, Jon. *The Virgin Vote: How Young Americans Made Democracy Social, Politics Personal, and Voting Popular in the Nineteenth Century.* Chapel Hill: University of North Carolina Press, 2016. Grinspan explores the idea of generational politics, examining the specific role that young people play in shaping American democracy.

Henriquez, Cristina. *The Book of Unknown Americans.* New York: Knopf, 2015. This poignant fictional account of immigration is told from various perspectives, including a young woman from Mexico and a first-generation American teenager, whose parents immigrated from Panama.

Howe, Neil, and William Strauss. *Millennials Rising: The Next Great Generation.* New York: Vintage, 2000. A pre–September 11, 2001, examination of the unique characteristics of the Millennial generation.

Levine, Peter. *We Are the Ones We Have Been Waiting For: The Promise of Civic Renewal in America.* New York: Oxford University Press, 2013. Levine offers a theory of active citizenship, in which he argues that the problems the United States faces can be addressed by individuals engaged in civic activism in their communities.

Putnam, Robert D. *Bowling Alone: The Collapse and Revival of American Community.* New York: Touchstone, 2000. A classic volume demonstrating the decline in traditional forms of civic participation.

Rather, Dan, and Elliot Kirschner. *What Unites Us.* New York: Algonquin Books, 2017. Written by iconic veteran newscaster Rather, this book discusses the common core of political values that unite Americans.

Verba, Sidney, Kay Lehman Schlozman, and Henry E. Brady. *Voice and Equality: Civic Voluntarism in American Politics.* Cambridge, MA: Harvard University Press, 1995. An analysis of how people come to be activists in their communities, what issues they raise when they participate, and how activists from various demographic groups differ.

Winograd, Morley, and Michael D. Hais. *Millennial Makeover: MySpace, YouTube, and the Future of American Politics.* New Brunswick, NJ: Rutgers University Press, 2008. A study of the impact of Millennials' use of changing technology on political life.

Zukin, Cliff, Scott Keeter, Molly Andolina, Krista Jenkins, and Michael X. Delli Carpini. *A New Engagement? Political Participation, Civic Life and the Changing American Citizen.* Oxford: Oxford University Press, 2006. A study of participation and political viewpoints across generations.

Movies of Interest

I Learn America (2013)

This documentary film by Jean-Michel Dissard and Gitte Peng tells the story of five immigrant teenagers studying at the International High School as they strive to learn the values and culture of their new country.

The Messenger (2009)

This film, starring Ben Foster and Woody Harrelson, depicts one side of the ravages of war through the experiences of the U.S. Army's Casualty Notification officers. Through their experiences, viewers explore the values of the families of fallen soldiers, as well as those of society at large.

V for Vendetta (2005)

Actress Natalie Portman becomes a revolutionary in this thriller, which depicts an uprising against an authoritarian government.

Blind Shaft (2003)

This Chinese thriller explores the interaction between free market incentives and aspects of political culture, including traditional communal values and human decency, in the context of an increasingly globalized economy.

Blue Collar (1978)

This classic film tracing the experience of three autoworkers in the late 1970s explores racial and economic strife in the United States.

References

1. Rogers Smith, *Civic Ideals: Conflicting Visions of Citizenship in U.S. History* (New Haven, CT: Yale University Press, 1997).
2. Robert A. Dahl, *Who Governs? Democracy and Power in an American City* (New Haven, CT: Yale University Press, 1961).
3. E. E. Schattschneider, *The Semi-Sovereign People* (New York: Holt, Rinehart, and Winston, 1960).
4. Ken Thomas, "White House Sends Mixed Signals on Trade Fight; Markets Dive," *Associated Press.* April 8, 2018.
5. E. J. Dionne Jr., *Why Americans Hate Politics: The Death of the Democratic Process,* 2nd ed. (New York: Touchstone, 1992).
6. Gallup Poll, "Trust in Government."
7. www.people-press.org/2017/05/03/public-trust-in-government-remains-near-historic-lows-as-partisan-attitudes-shift/.
8. Barbara Roswell, "From Service-Learning to Service Politics: A Conversation with Rick Battistoni."
9. Michael Delli Carpini, Director Pew Charitable Trusts.
10. S. E. Finer, *The History of Government,* 3 vols. (London: Oxford University Press, 1997).
11. Martin A. Reddish, *The Constitution as Political Structure* (London: Oxford University Press, 1995).
12. Theodore Sky, *To Provide for the General Welfare: A History of the Federal Spending Power* (Newark: University of Delaware Press, 2003).
13. David Epstein, *The Political Theory of the Federalist* (Chicago: University of Chicago Press, 1984).
14. Thomas Hobbes, *Leviathan* (1651; New York: Oxford University Press, 1996), chap. 14.
15. Oscar Handlin and Mary Handlin, *The Dimensions of Liberty* (Cambridge, MA: Harvard University Press, 1961).
16. Richard Labunski, *James Madison and the Struggle for the Bill of Rights* (London: Oxford University Press, 2006).
17. Jack N. Rakove, *Original Meanings: Politics and Ideas in the Making of the Constitution* (New York: Knopf, 1996).
18. Clyde W. Barrow, *Critical Theories of the State: Marxist, Neo-Marxist, Post-Marxist* (Madison: University of Wisconsin Press, 1993).
19. Seymour Martin Lipset and Gary Marks, *It Didn't Happen Here: Why Socialism Failed in the United States* (New York: W. W. Norton, 2001).
20. Giovanni Sartori and Peter Mair, *Parties and Party Systems: A Framework for Analysis* (Oxford, England: European Consortium for Political Research).
21. Ira Katznelson and Martin Shefter, eds., *Shaped by War and Trade: International Influences on American Political Development* (Princeton, NJ: Princeton University Press, 2002).
22. *Wing Hing v. City of Eureka* (Calif.), 1886.
23. www.census.gov/content/dam/Census/library/publications/2015/demo/p25-1143.pdf.

CHAPTER 2

The Constitution

©Bruce Glikas/FilmMagic/Getty Images

THEN

To establish a representative democracy that protects individual liberties, the Constitution's framers divided governmental power between the federal and the state governments and created checks and balances among the three separate branches of the national government.

NOW

Questions about how to properly interpret constitutionally established governing structures and procedures, rights, and liberties regularly end up at the doorstep of the U.S. Supreme Court as the nation continues to pursue a more perfect union.

NEXT

Will the courts continue to expand limits on U.S. governments?

Will court interpretations alter the balance of power between national and state governments?

Will courts interpret the constitutional separation of powers and checks and balances in ways that will change the balance of power among the three separate branches of the national government?

To secure their rights to

life, liberty, and the pursuit of happiness, colonists in North America declared their independence from Britain in 1776. At the same time, they claimed the right to institute a new government. In 1777, the First Continental Congress approved and sent to the 13 colonies-now-states for ratification a constitution, the Articles of Confederation. This constitution created a confederal system of government: a friendly alliance among the states, with a weak national government.

By 1787, weaknesses in the confederal system sparked a call for each state to send delegates to meet in Philadelphia to revise the Articles in a way that would make the government more effective and preserve the union. Through long debates, tough negotiations, and major compromises, the delegates drafted the Constitution of the United States.

In effect since 1789, this Constitution is the oldest written, national constitution in the world. Scholars attribute its long life to several factors. One is the basic governmental structures it creates: a federal system with two levels of sovereign governments (national and state) and the separation of basic government functions among three branches in the national government. A second factor is the fundamental principles on which the framers built the government: popular sovereignty balanced with protection of life, liberty, and the pursuit of happiness. Finally, scholars attribute the Constitution's longevity to its vague and ambiguous language, which allows each generation to debate, deliberate, and interpret it to meet the needs and demands of an ever-changing nation in an ever-changing world.

Today, it is almost impossible to engage in a conversation about government, politics, or public policy without debating differing understandings of what is and is not constitutional.

What Is a Constitution?

A **constitution** presents the fundamental principles of a government and establishes the basic structures and procedures by which the government operates to fulfill those principles. Constitutions may be written or unwritten. An *unwritten constitution,* such as the constitution of Great Britain, is a collection of written laws approved by a legislative body and unwritten common laws established by judges, based on custom, culture, habit, and previous judicial decisions. A *written constitution,* such as the Constitution of the United States, is one specific document, ratified at one point in time, formally amended (through a deliberate process to change the written document) and informally amended (by judicial interpretations that clarify its meaning) over time.

constitution
The fundamental principles of a government and the basic structures and procedures by which the government operates to fulfill those principles; may be written or unwritten.

>People demonstrating against the U.S. Supreme Court decision in *Citizens United v. Federal Election Commission* (2010) display a banner with the Preamble to the Constitution printed on it. According to the Preamble, what was the mission of "we the people" that led to the drafting and ratification of the U.S. Constitution to replace the Articles of Confederation? After reviewing the constitution and/or by-laws of your institution's student government, can you identify the mission of the student government?

©Chip Somodevilla/Getty Images

If you read a government's written constitution, or even your school's student government constitution, you will find three essential pieces of information about the government. First, you will find a statement of the government's mission or the long-term goals of the government as envisioned by its framers. Second, you will discover a description of how the government is organized into foundational structures, core government bodies that accomplish its mission. Finally, you will uncover details of the government's essential operating procedures.

Typically, constitutions begin with a description of the mission of the government. For example, the first sentence in the Constitution of the United States, known as the Preamble, states:

We the People of the United States, in Order to form a more perfect Union, establish Justice, insure domestic Tranquility, provide for the common defence, promote the general Welfare, and secure the Blessings of Liberty to ourselves and our Posterity, do ordain and establish this Constitution for the United States of America.

After the Preamble, the first three articles (main sections) of the U.S. Constitution describe the structure of the national government. Specifically the articles describe three foundational government bodies—the legislative, executive, and judicial branches—and articulate the responsibilities of each body as well as the relationships among those bodies. The Constitution also details essential operating procedures, including those used to select national government officials, to make laws, and to formally amend the Constitution (by changing language in the document), as well as the process by which the Constitution itself was to be ratified.

In addition to finding the mission statement, descriptions of foundational structures, and details of essential operating procedures in a constitution, you will typically find some vague and ambiguous language. For example, reread the Constitution's Preamble. What do you think "promote the general welfare" means? Does it mean that the government is responsible for ensuring that all people living in the nation have decent health care? Does it mean that everyone needs access to a good education and a job with a living wage so that they can be financially independent? Does it mean that the government needs to ensure that all people have sufficient and nutritious food and safe housing?

Debates over the meaning of constitutional language were taking place in living rooms, bars, government offices, courtrooms, and on the streets even before the states ratified the Constitution. Ultimately, the U.S. Supreme Court has the final word on the meaning of constitutional language. You will learn as you read the chapters in this book that members of the Supreme Court do not always agree on the meaning of constitutional language. Moreover, throughout U.S. history, as the members of the Supreme Court changed and the nation's economy, technology, and culture evolved, societal understanding of constitutional language changed, as did judicial interpretation of the language.

To comprehend today's debates about the meanings of constitutional language, we need to first develop an understanding of what the framers of the Constitution and the citizens who debated it were hoping to achieve. What was their vision of a more perfect union?

The Creation of the United States of America

In the 1600s, waves of Europeans made the dangerous sea voyage to America to start new lives. Some people with connections to the king of England received large grants of land and the authority to govern. Many more voyagers came as *indentured servants,* who would work for a number of years for a master who paid for their passage. Others came to create communities with people of the same religion so that they could practice their faith without government interference. Countless others—Africans brought to the colonies as slaves—came against their will. In short, a diversity of people and a mix of economic classes migrated to the colonies, joining the Native American peoples who already inhabited North America.

By the early 18th century, a two-tier system of governing the British colonies in America had evolved, with governance split between the colonies and Britain. The colonists elected local officials to colonial assemblies that had the authority to rule on day-to-day matters (including criminal law and civil law) and to set and collect taxes to implement laws regarding day-to-day matters. Back in England, Parliament, with no elected representatives from the colonies, enacted laws with which the British government expected the colonists to comply. Governors appointed by the king oversaw the enforcement of British law in the colonies. For the colonists, this combination of colonial assemblies close to home and a faraway Parliament represented by an appointed governor living in the colonies worked well: life went on without much interference from the British Parliament and Crown.

In the latter half of the 18th century, this relationship began to change. Parliament tried to raise additional revenue to pay for its growing debt (due to war expenses in Europe and America) and to confirm its sovereignty over its colonists. To accomplish these goals, Parliament approved legislation that put more and more restrictions on the colonists' freedoms and their pursuit of economic well-being. Colonists began to complain among themselves about the British government's damaging treatment of them. Eventually those conversations coalesced around their preference for a government by the people (popular sovereignty) and for the people (government established to protect the people's liberties). Criticism turned into rebellion, which became a revolution. In the process, a new country was born.

British Policies Incite Revolution in the Colonies

Between 1756 and 1763, Britain was engaged in the Seven Years' War in Europe, a military conflict that involved all the major European powers of the era. At the same time, British and French forces (and France's Native American allies) were battling in North America, in a conflict known as the French and Indian War. To help pay the costs of waging those wars and the postwar costs of maintaining peace in America, the British Parliament turned to the colonies for increased revenues and to provide support and housing for British soldiers. As colonists criticized and then protested the new laws, Parliament continued to enact additional laws that limited the colonists' liberties and pursuit of happiness. Eventually the colonists' protests turned to revolution.

TAXATION WITHOUT REPRESENTATION In 1764, Parliament enacted the Sugar Act, which increased taxes on goods imported into the colonies and directed that all taxes collected be sent directly to Britain instead of to the colonial

>Participation by women, as supported by the Daughters of Liberty, was essential to the success of the boycotts. What explains why women's participation was essential to the success of boycotts?

Library of Congress, Prints and Photographs Division [LC-USZC4-9905]

assemblies, as had been the practice.[1] Then, in 1765, Parliament passed the Stamp Act, which taxed the paper used for all legal documents, advertisements, and newspapers.[2]

Colonists condemned these laws and called for their repeal, claiming they had no obligation to pay the taxes because they had no representation in the parliament that created them. In addition, the colonists boycotted goods imported from Britain. Women, who substituted homegrown or homespun goods for the boycotted items, were key to the success of the boycotts, which, according to historian Glenna Matthews "proved to be the single most valuable tool, short of war, that the patriots possessed."[3]

To support the growing number of troops it was sending to the colonies as protests grew, Parliament enacted the Quartering Act in 1765. This act directed each colonial assembly to provide supplies to meet the basic needs of the British soldiers stationed in the colonies. An expansion of this act in 1766 required the colonial assemblies to ensure housing for the soldiers as well.[4] Many colonists viewed the Quartering Act as an indirect tax forcing them to pay some of the costs of the troops, whose presence the colonists saw as a threat to their liberties.[5]

In response to protests, Parliament repealed the Stamp Act in 1766. However, at the same time, it enacted the Declaratory Act, which confirmed Parliament's power to make laws that the colonists were legally required to follow.[6] The Townshend Act of 1767 confirmed Parliament's power to impose taxes that the colonists were obligated to pay. It also expanded the list of imported goods to be taxed.[7]

A "MASSACRE," A MONOPOLY, AND A TEA PARTY   By 1770, thousands of British soldiers were quartered in the homes of the civilians living in Boston. To make matters worse, the British soldiers, who were financially supported by the colonists due to the Quartering Act, sought additional paid labor, competing with the colonists for jobs. Growing tensions came to a head in Boston on March 5, 1770, when an angry mob of nearly 1,800 struggling colonists clashed with British soldiers. The soldiers shot into the crowd, leaving five dead and six wounded.[8] The Sons of Liberty and Samuel Adams—an expert at "spinning" a news story—condemned the event as "the Boston Massacre." Colonists' calls for resistance and protests grew.

In 1772, Samuel Adams created the Massachusetts Committee of Correspondence, a group dedicated to encouraging and maintaining the free flow of information and the spread of calls for rebellion among the Massachusetts colonists. Angry and disaffected people in other colonies followed suit, creating their own correspondence committees to encourage and organize acts of resistance and protest.[9]

Adding fuel to the fire of rebellion, in 1773 Parliament passed the Tea Act, which gave the East India Tea Company a monopoly on importing tea into the colonies. The Sons of Liberty questioned the act's legitimacy, vowed they would block the Company's ships from docking in ports, and called for renewed boycotts of British goods. The Sons of Liberty successfully swayed public opinion and became the catalyst for the Boston Tea Party. In November 1773, the first post–Tea Act shipment of tea arrived in Boston Harbor on three East India Company ships. On the night of December 16, 1773, more than 100 colonists, dressed as Mohawk Indians, boarded the three ships, broke open hundreds of crates, and dumped thousands of pounds of tea into the harbor.[10] The Boston Tea Party had a cataclysmic effect, not only on the relationship between Britain and the colonies but also on relationships among the colonists themselves.

Parliament responded to the Boston Tea Party with the Coercive Acts (Intolerable Acts) in 1774, which closed the port of Boston with the intent of keeping it closed until the colonists paid for the lost tea. In addition, the act imposed martial law, shut down the colonial assembly, and banned virtually all town meetings, thus curtailing legal opportunities for Massachusetts colonists to engage in politics.[11]

THE DESTRUCTION OF TEA AT BOSTON HARBOR.

> The Boston Tea Party (1773) was a rebellious act of colonists angered by Parliament's string of new tax laws, including a tax on imported tea, and the Tea Act which gave the East India Tea Company a monopoly on importing tea to the American colonies. Without representation in Parliament, the rebellious colonists did not believe they were obligated to comply with the laws. How did Parliament respond to the Boston Tea Party?
Library of Congress, Prints and Photographs Division [LC-USZC4-523]

THE FIRST CONTINENTAL CONGRESS: A DECLARATION OF RIGHTS AND GRIEVANCES Sympathy among the colonies for Massachusetts's plight, along with rising colonists' concerns about how the British government was generally abusing its powers, reinforced the colonists' growing sense of community and their shared consciousness of the need to engage in collective action. The Massachusetts and Virginia colonial assemblies requested a meeting of delegates from all the colonies to develop a joint statement of concern they would send to the king. In September 1774, every colony but Georgia sent delegates to Philadelphia for what became known as the First Continental Congress.

The First Continental Congress adopted and sent to King George III the Declaration of Rights and Grievances. This document listed numerous rights to which the delegates argued the colonists were entitled. Some of the rights included in the list were life, liberty, and property; representation in Parliament; and consideration of their grievances and petitions to the king.[12] The Congress also adopted the Articles of Association, which put forth a plan to create a parliament for the colonies.[13] Finally, the Congress scheduled a second meeting of delegates—the Second Continental Congress—to discuss the anticipated king's response to their declaration of rights and list of grievances.

King George III refused to respond to the First Continental Congress's declarations and grievances. Colonists' talk about pursuing independence grew louder. On April 19, 1775, before the Second Continental Congress met, shots rang out at Lexington and Concord, Massachusetts, as British troops moved to seize the colonists' store of guns and ammunition. The rebellion—sparked by more than a decade's worth of Parliament's policies that threatened the life, liberties, and pursuit of happiness of the colonists—was now a military conflict, a revolutionary war for independence, that would last for eight years (1775–1783).

The Common Sense of Declaring Independence

On May 10, 1775, the Second Continental Congress convened. The assembled delegates authorized the Congress to function as an independent government and to prepare for war with Britain. The Congress also appointed George Washington to command the to-be-created Continental Army.

In July 1775, the Second Continental Congress made one last effort to avert a full-blown war. It petitioned King George III to end hostile actions against the colonists. The king refused and sent even more troops to the colonies to put down the growing rebellion. Yet even as the Congress prepared for war, many colonists remained unsure about cutting their ties with Britain. A pamphlet written by Thomas Paine, a recently arrived radical from Britain, and published in January 1776, transformed many such wavering colonists into revolutionary patriots. Paine's *Common Sense* argued that war with Great Britain was not only necessary but also unavoidable. Only through independence would Americans attain civil and religious liberty.[14]

In May 1776, Richard Henry Lee, a Virginia delegate to the Congress, asserted "that these united Colonies are, and of right ought to be free and independent States, [and] that they are absolved from all allegiance to the British crown."[15] Lee's resolution also called for the drafting of a plan of union for the colonies, each of which would become an independent state. This "declaration of independence," which congressional delegates from other colonies subsequently echoed, led the Second Continental Congress to establish a committee to write down, in formal language, a declaration of independence on behalf of all the colonies. The committee selected Virginia delegate Thomas Jefferson, a wealthy plantation owner, to draft the declaration.

Unanimously endorsed by the Second Continental Congress on July 4, 1776, Jefferson's Declaration of Independence was groundbreaking. It put forth three principles that at the time were radical. First, he held that all men are equal, with **natural rights** (also called *unalienable rights*), which are rights possessed by all humans as a gift from nature, or God; not rights established by government. Jefferson stated that the natural rights that all men have are the rights to life, liberty, and the pursuit of happiness. Second, he proposed that all governments must be based on the consent of the people they serve. Finally, he stated that if a government is not protecting the rights of the people, then the people have the duty to abolish it and to create a new government.

After establishing those three radical principles, the Declaration spelled out a list of grievances against King George III in an attempt to convince the colonists and the European powers that the colonists' break with Great Britain was necessary and justified. The Declaration won the hearts and minds of people in the colonies and abroad. Until this point, the colonists were united in their hatred toward Britain but lacked a rallying point for moving forward. The Declaration provided that rallying point by promising a new government that would be based on the consent of the people, with liberty and equality as its central goals.

The War for Independence (the American Revolutionary War), which began at Lexington and Concord in 1775, would end eight years later with the signing of a peace treaty in Paris (1783). However, the colonists could not wait until the end of the war to establish a new government. Even before the colonial delegates at the Second Continental Congress endorsed the Declaration of Independence, they encouraged the legislative assembly of each colony to write a constitution establishing a state government, independent of Great Britain. In addition, by 1777, the Second Continental Congress drafted and submitted to the states a constitution, the Articles of Confederation, which designed a collaborative governing alliance among the independent, sovereign states.

The State Constitutions

By the end of 1776, eight of the 13 colonies had ratified state constitutions. New York and Georgia followed suit in 1777. After four years of intense deliberation, Massachusetts adopted a state constitution in 1780. Connecticut and Rhode Island continued to operate under revised royal charters (governing documents from the British government with references to the king removed) until they enacted new constitutions in 1818 and 1843, respectively.[16]

The new state constitutions were revolutionary for three primary reasons. First, they were each a single, written document that specified the principles, structures, and operating procedures of the government established by the consent of the people. Second, they were adopted at a specific moment in time, unlike constitutions before them, which were accumulations of disparate laws written over time or created by judges through the years, based on customs and traditions.[17] So, the state constitutions were the first written constitutions in the world. Third, they transformed the legal status of people from that of "subjects" under the rule of a king, who was sovereign, into citizens sharing in popular sovereignty. The state constitutions instituted governments created by and for the people.

BASIC STRUCTURES AND PROCEDURES   The framers of the first state constitutions attempted to implement the principles of popular sovereignty and natural rights presented in the Declaration of Independence through the governing structures and procedures they instituted. Each state constitution established a **republic,** better known today as a representative democracy. Moreover, most state constitutions asserted explicitly that the people held the power—government was instituted by the consent of the people and was to serve the people. State governments included three governing bodies—the legislative, executive, and judicial branches. **Bicameral legislatures,** which are legislatures comprising two parts (or chambers), were the norm in the states. State legislators, who were elected directly by voters in most states, were delegated more governing powers than members of the other two branches, who were not typically elected by voters. The prevailing view of people of the time was that the legislature offered the best prospects for representative government that would ensure popular sovereignty and protection of life, liberty, and the pursuit of happiness.

republic
A government that derives its authority from the people and in which citizens elect government officials to represent them in the processes by which laws are made; a representative democracy.

bicameral legislature
Legislature comprising two parts, called *chambers*.

FUNDAMENTAL PRINCIPLES   The mission of each state government was to ensure natural rights. This is evident in state constitutions' bills of rights. State bills of rights affirmed that all government's power derives from the people; endorsed rights such as trial by jury and religious freedom; and included protections for free speech and press, protection from excessive fines and bail, and protection from unreasonable search and seizure. Authors of the first state constitutions wrote into them limits on government power to prevent state governments from infringing on individuals' liberties and pursuit of happiness, infringements the colonists experienced under British rule. Hence, the inclusion of a written list of citizens' liberties, a *bill of rights,* limited government by ensuring that both the people and the government knew what freedoms the government could not violate.

The states of the newly forming union used their constitutions to guide them in handling day-to-day domestic matters. Meanwhile, members of the Second

Continental Congress turned their attention to developing a system of government that would retain each state's independence and sovereignty while allowing them to engage collectively in international affairs and providing for the common defense of all the states and their people.

The Articles of Confederation (1781–1788)

Because of the colonists' bitter experience under the British Crown, the people and their delegates to the Second Continental Congress distrusted a strong, distant central government; they preferred limited governments, close to home, which they established in their state constitutions. The delegates nevertheless recognized the need for a unified authority to engage in international trade, foreign affairs, and defense.

The Second Continental Congress drafted and submitted to the states for ratification the Articles of Confederation and Perpetual Union in 1777. The Articles established a **confederation:** a union of independent states in which each state retains its sovereignty—that is, its ultimate power to govern—and agrees to work collaboratively on matters the states expressly agree to delegate to a central (national) governing body. Through the Articles of Confederation, the states created an alliance for mutual well-being in the international realm, yet continued to pursue independently their own self-interests within their own borders. In 1781, after the 13 states ratified it, the Articles of Confederation officially went into effect, while the War for Independence continued for another two years.

STRUCTURE AND AUTHORITY OF THE CONFEDERATION   Structurally, the Articles created only one governing body in the national government, a congress. The Congress was a **unicameral legislature,** meaning that it had only one chamber. Every state had from two to seven delegates in Congress, but only one vote on policies, treaties, and constitutional amendments. Each state determined how its congressional delegates would be selected. Approving policies and ratifying treaties required affirmative votes from nine of the state delegations in Congress. The Articles did not create a judicial branch, an executive branch, or a president. Congressional delegates would select one of their members to serve as president, to preside over the meetings of Congress. State courts would resolve legal conflicts, unless the dispute was between states, in which case Congress would resolve it. State governments would implement and pay for (if they agreed to congressional requests for money) policies approved by Congress. Finally, and important to remember, amending the Articles of Confederation required unanimous agreement among all 13 state congressional delegations.

The structure of national government instituted by the Articles was a product of its framers' experiences under the British government; the framers wanted to avoid structures and procedures they feared would lead to tyranny. Congress had very limited authority. Although it could approve policies relevant to foreign affairs, defense, and the coining of money, it was not authorized to raise revenue through taxation. Only state governments could levy and collect taxes. Therefore, to pay the national government's bills, Congress had to request money from each state. State governments, the governments closer to the people, with elected representatives, remained sovereign and more powerful than the national government.

WEAKNESSES OF THE CONFEDERATION   The Articles of Confederation emphasized the sovereignty of individual, independent states at the expense of a powerful national government. Citizens' allegiance was to their states; there was no mass national conscience. Under the Articles of Confederation, the states retained

confederation
A union of independent states in which each state retains its sovereignty, that is, its ultimate power to govern, and agrees to work collaboratively on matters the states expressly agree to delegate to a central governing body.

unicameral legislature
A legislative body with a single chamber.

ultimate authority in matters of day-to-day life, commerce, and currency. There was no centralized economic policy. In addition, each state taxed goods coming into the state from foreign nations and from other states. Moreover, several states issued their own money and required the use of that currency for all business within the state. At the national level, Congress lacked authority to collect taxes and lacked the power to compel states to honor national policies and obligations, including state cooperation in building roads and canals, which were the infrastructure needed for a healthy economy that supports general welfare.

The cumulative effect of each state's having its own economic policies was that interstate and international commerce was hampered, putting the nation's economic health in jeopardy.[18] At the same time, the national government had war debt to pay. Farmers (a substantial component of the economy) were struggling financially and losing their farms, which were sold at public auctions. Veterans of the Revolutionary War were waiting for pay. State governments threw debtors in jail. When petitions to state governments calling for them to address the problems of those suffering financially went unanswered, debt-burdened citizens protested and rebelled, some taking up arms. Rebellions occurred in most states, but the most serious, known as Shays's Rebellion, occurred in Massachusetts between 1786 and 1787.

>This image depicts a fight between a Shays's Rebellion rebel, fighting to protect debtors, and a supporter of the Massachusetts government, which enacted laws that criminalized protests and anti-government speech. How does the First Amendment to the Constitution, adopted in 1788, address speech, protests, and complaints against the government?

©Bettmann/Getty Images

Farmer and war veteran Daniel Shays led hundreds of debt-burdened rebels in protests at Massachusetts courthouses, closing them down and burning debtor records. As such protests spread to other states, Congress voted to establish a national army and requested that each state provide money to pay for it. Only the state of Virginia agreed to provide the requested money. At the same time, the Massachusetts state government enacted laws to criminalize protests against, and speech critical of, the government. In addition, the Massachusetts governor raised money from wealthy merchants to support a private militia to battle Shays's Rebellion. In the winter of 1787, the state militia crushed Shays's Rebellion.[19]

The weaknesses of the confederal system—including its barriers to the development of national economic policies and to defense against domestic uprisings—were becoming apparent to the nation's political and business leaders.

CALLS TO REMEDY DEFECTS OF THE ARTICLES OF CONFEDERATION As Congress faced an inability to pay the costs of governing, and as violent rebellions threatened peace and security in the states, five states sent delegates to Annapolis, Maryland, in 1786, to discuss ways to "remedy defects of the Federal Government," as the national government created by the Articles of Confederation was known at that time. The states charged their Annapolis delegates with considering the trade and commerce problems of the United States. However, in the report of their proceedings, the delegates noted that the "embarrassments which characterize the present State of our national affairs, foreign and domestic" suggested that trade and commerce were not the only problems of the federal government. Therefore, the delegates called for a future convention, to be attended by representatives from all 13 states, to devise amendments to the Articles of Confederation that would fix its weaknesses and to submit its proposals to "the United States in Congress assembled."[20]

Crafting the Constitution of the United States

The convention called to address the defects of the Articles of Confederation was held in Philadelphia from May 25 through September 17, 1787. All states except Rhode Island sent delegates. The delegates to this Constitutional Convention were among the most elite Americans. Some 80 percent had served as members of the Continental Congresses, and most were lawyers, businessmen, or plantation owners. Many were engaged in highly lucrative international trade, and all were wealthy men. These elites contrasted sharply with the majority of the population, who included the country's hard-pressed farmers, struggling local merchants, and those engaged in trade. In fact, historian Charles Beard contended in 1913 that the Constitution's framers succeeded in forging a government that protected their elite status.[21]

Although very early in the convention the delegates agreed on the need for a stronger national government than the Articles had created, there was conflict over how best to structure a stronger national government while incorporating principles of representative democracy and protecting liberties. There was also conflict over the issue of slavery. In working through those conflicts to create compromises they could support, the delegates were pragmatic. They had to balance their preference for a strong central government with the citizens' distrust of a strong central government. Ultimately, the delegates framed a new constitution, instituting new foundational government structures and operating procedures in an effort to fulfill the principles laid out in the Declaration of Independence. Thereafter, proponents of the proposed new constitution would win its ratification only after acknowledging the need to amend it quickly by adding a bill of rights to limit the power of the national government it created.

Areas of Consensus

Early in the convention, consensus developed on the need for dual sovereignty (a federal system of government) to address the Article's weaknesses while at the same time winning the votes needed to support a new constitution. The delegates also reached quick consensus on the need to establish the new constitution as the supreme law of the country, with which the national and state governments must all comply. In addition, the delegates' views coalesced around the principle of distributing the basic governing functions among three branches of the national government, each with capabilities to monitor the other branches, a structure that was evident in the state constitutions.

A FEDERAL SYSTEM: DUAL SOVEREIGNTY   According to the congressional charge to the convention, the convention delegates had to send their final proposal to the existing Congress for action. Remember that Congress, as structured by the Articles of Confederation (the constitution in effect at the time of the Constitutional Convention), was made up of representatives of the state governments. The convention delegates recognized that these representatives, selected by the states, were not likely to ratify a document that created a strong central government at the expense of the existing state governments. Therefore, the framers had to balance a strong central government (national sovereignty) and existing state sovereignty.

That balance would hinge on delegating governing powers to the national government in the policy areas that were problematic under the Articles of Confederation—interstate and international trade, foreign affairs, and defense—and leaving the remaining domestic matters with the states.

The framers created an innovative system of government with **dual sovereignty**—one in which ultimate governing authority is divided between two levels of government—a central government and regional governments—with each level having ultimate authority over different policy matters and different geographic areas. Today, we call this a *federal system* of government. Article I of the Constitution lists the matters over which the national legislature (Congress) has lawmaking authority, such as regulating interstate and foreign commerce, coining money, raising and funding an army, and declaring war. Article I also prohibits state governments from engaging in several specific activities, such as negotiating treaties. (Chapter 3 focuses on dual sovereignty and the constitutional distribution of power between the national and the state governments in the U.S. federal system of government.)

Although the Constitution's first three articles list powers and responsibilities of the national government, nowhere in the document that was drafted at the convention were states' powers and responsibilities listed. Therefore, the distribution of sovereignty in the federal system was not clearly articulated in the proposed Constitution.

CONSTITUTIONAL SUPREMACY   The framers anticipated that this system of dual sovereignty would cause tension between the national government and the state governments. Therefore, they included in Article VI of the Constitution a **supremacy clause,** which states that the Constitution and the treaties and laws created by the national government in compliance with the Constitution are the supreme law of the land.

The framers did not include a list or even a vague outline of the matters over which the states had sovereignty. Citizens apprehensive of a strong central government, recollecting the colonists' experiences under the British government, would argue that this vacuum of information on state sovereignty was a major fault in the Constitution, because it would allow the national government to infringe on state sovereignty. The lack of a list of individual liberties to limit the power of the national government, a bill of rights such as each state constitution had, was also a major concern for citizens afraid of a strong central government.

SEPARATION OF POWERS WITH INTEGRATED CHECKS AND BALANCES   Another area where there was convergence of opinion among the framers was that of the foundational structures of the new government they were creating. Borrowing from the states, the framers separated the primary governing functions among three branches of government—referred to as the **separation of powers**—so that no one group of government officials controlled all the governing functions. Under the terms of the separation of powers, each branch of the government has specific powers and responsibilities that allow it to operate independently of the other branches: the legislative branch has authority to formulate policy; the executive branch has authority to implement policy; and the judicial branch has authority to resolve conflicts over the law.

Once the framers separated the primary functions, they established various mechanisms by which each branch can monitor and limit the functions of the other branches to ensure that no branch acts to the detriment of citizens' natural rights. These mechanisms collectively form a system of **checks and balances.**

dual sovereignty
A system of government in which ultimate governing authority is divided between two levels of government, a central government and regional governments, with each level having ultimate authority over different policy matters.

supremacy clause
A clause in Article VI of the Constitution that states that the Constitution and the treaties and laws created by the national government in compliance with the Constitution are the supreme law of the land.

separation of powers
The Constitution's delegation of authority for the primary governing functions among three branches of government so that no one group of government officials controls all the governing functions.

checks and balances
A system in which each branch of government can monitor and limit the functions of the other branches.

Separation of Powers with Checks and Balances

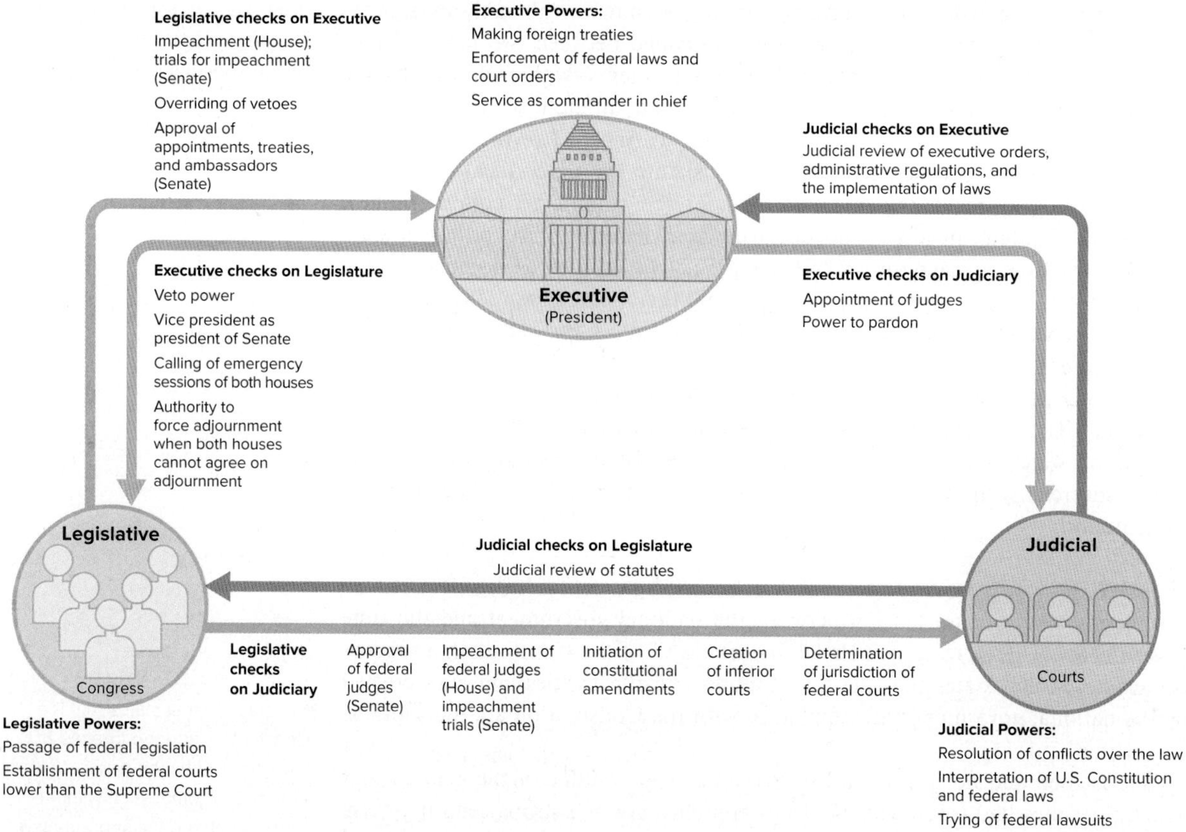

Legislative checks on Executive

Impeachment (House);
trials for impeachment
(Senate)

Overriding of vetoes

Approval of
appointments, treaties,
and ambassadors
(Senate)

Executive Powers:

Making foreign treaties

Enforcement of federal laws and
court orders

Service as commander in chief

Executive
(President)

Judicial checks on Executive

Judicial review of executive orders,
administrative regulations, and
the implementation of laws

Executive checks on Legislature

Veto power

Vice president as
president of Senate

Calling of emergency
sessions of both houses

Authority to
force adjournment
when both houses
cannot agree on
adjournment

Executive checks on Judiciary

Appointment of judges

Power to pardon

Legislative

Congress

Judicial checks on Legislature

Judicial review of statutes

Judicial

Courts

Legislative checks on Judiciary	Approval of federal judges (Senate)	Impeachment of federal judges (House) and impeachment trials (Senate)	Initiation of constitutional amendments	Creation of inferior courts	Determination of jurisdiction of federal courts

Legislative Powers:

Passage of federal legislation

Establishment of federal courts
lower than the Supreme Court

Judicial Powers:

Resolution of conflicts over the law

Interpretation of U.S. Constitution
and federal laws

Trying of federal lawsuits

FIGURE 2.1 ■ **Why Did the Constitution's Framers Separate Powers Among the Three Branches of the National Government?** What specific powers does each branch have? What is the purpose of the Constitution's checks and balances? For each branch of the government—legislative, executive, judicial—name a specific check that it can exert on each of the other two. Which, if any, branch is the most powerful? Explain.

If one branch tries to move beyond its own sphere or to behave tyrannically, this arrangement ensures that the other branches can take action to stop it. For example, Congress formulates and approves legislation; however, before legislation becomes law, the president has the opportunity to approve or reject it (through the veto process). Although the president has authority to nominate top executive branch officials and federal judges, the Senate has the authority to confirm or reject the nominees. Figure 2.1 shows how specific checks and balances contribute to the separation of powers.

The delegates spent most of the first two months of the Constitutional Convention arguing about the national legislature and focused primarily on the question of state representation in Congress. They devoted less than a month to the other issues before them, including the structure of the executive and judicial branches; the relationship between the federal and the state governments; the process for amending the new constitution, should the need arise to do so; the procedures for the Constitution's ratification; and perpetuation of the slave trade.[22]

Conflict and Compromise over Representation

Among the delegates' top points of contention was representation in the national government. There was disagreement about two elements of representation. First, how should the government officials in each of the three branches of this newly formed republican national government be selected? Second, how would the states be represented in the national government?

THE CONNECTICUT COMPROMISE Virginian James Madison arrived at the convention with a plan in hand for restructuring the national government. The **Virginia Plan,** drafted by Madison and proposed by the Virginia delegation, called for a radically restructured national government, consisting of three branches: a bicameral legislature (Congress), an executive elected by the legislature, and a separate national judiciary. Under the Virginia Plan, state representation in both chambers of Congress would be proportional, based on state population. The people would elect members to the lower house, and members elected by the people to the lower house would select the members of the upper house.

Under the Virginia Plan, states with larger populations would have more representatives, each with a vote, and therefore more votes. On behalf of the less populous states, William Paterson of New Jersey presented a series of resolutions known as the **New Jersey Plan,** which essentially reworked the Articles of Confederation. Under the New Jersey Plan, a unicameral national legislature would remain the centerpiece of the government, and all states would have an equal voice (equal representation) in this government. The New Jersey Plan also called for Congress to elect several people to form an executive office, and the executive office had the authority to appoint members to a Supreme Court.

The disagreement and negotiation over the Virginia and the New Jersey Plans resulted in several compromises, most notably the **Connecticut Compromise** (also known as the *Great Compromise*). This compromise created today's bicameral Congress, with state representation in the House of Representatives based on state population and equal state representation in the Senate (two senators per state).

THE CONSTITUTION'S LIMITS ON REPRESENTATIVE DEMOCRACY At the heart of representative democracy is the participation of citizens in electing their government officials. Yet the framers allowed citizens, whose eligibility to vote was determined by state constitutions instead of the Constitution of the United States, to elect directly only the members of the House of Representatives, thereby placing tremendous limits on representative democracy.

The process that the framers devised for the election of the president and the vice president prevents citizens from directly selecting them. The Constitution delegates to states the authority to appoint individuals (*electors*), using a process determined by the state legislature, to elect the president and the vice president. Before ratification of the Twelfth Amendment (1804), each elector would cast two votes for president. The candidate receiving the largest majority of electors' votes would become president and the candidate receiving the second largest number of votes would become vice president. Since ratification of the Twelfth Amendment, each elector casts one vote for president and one vote for vice president. Today, in nearly every state, your presidential vote, combined with the votes of other citizens from your state, determines which political party's slate of representatives (*electors*) will participate on behalf of your state in the **Electoral College,** the name given to the body of electors that actually selects the president and the vice president.

Virginia Plan
The new governmental structure proposed by the Virginia delegation to the Constitutional Convention, which consisted of a bicameral legislature (Congress), an executive elected by the legislature, and a separate national judiciary; state representation in Congress would be proportional, based on state population; the people would elect members to the lower house, and members of the lower house would elect the members of the upper house.

New Jersey Plan
The proposal presented in response to the Virginia Plan by the less populous states at the Constitutional Convention, which called for a unicameral national legislature in which all states would have an equal voice (equal representation), an executive office composed of several people elected by Congress, and a Supreme Court whose members would be appointed by the executive office.

Connecticut Compromise
The compromise between the Virginia Plan and the New Jersey Plan that created a bicameral legislature with one chamber's representation based on population and the other chamber having two members for each state (also known as the *Great Compromise*).

Electoral College
The name given to the body of representatives elected by voters in each state to elect the president and the vice president.

THEN NOW NEXT

Evolution of Representation in the National Government

	Then (1790)	Now
Number of voting members in the House	106 based on 1790 Census**	435**
Number of people represented by each House member	Approximately 34,000**	Approximately 710,000, with a high of 1 million in Montana and a low of 583,000 in Wyoming
Number of U.S. senators	36	100
Number of people represented by each Senator	Varies; highest number was in Virginia and lowest number was in Delaware*	Varies: highest is 38 million in California; lowest is 583,000 in Wyoming*
Who votes for U.S. House members?	Determined by the states; in all states, white men who own property can vote	Citizens 18 years and older (per U.S. Constitution)
Who selects U.S. Senators?	State legislatures (per Constitution of 1789)	Citizens 18 years and older (per 17th Amendment of 1913)
Who votes for president and vice president?	Members of the Electoral College; each elector has two votes. Candidate with the most electoral votes wins the presidency; candidate with the second-most votes wins the vice presidency.	Members of the Electoral College. Electors each have one vote for president and one vote for vice president.

WHAT'S NEXT?

> Will calls to improve quality and fairness of representation in the Senate be heard by Congress, resulting in a proposed constitutional amendment that ameliorates the huge differences in the number of constituents represented by each senator in the U.S. Senate?

> Will calls to improve popular sovereignty by replacing the Electoral College with direct election of the president and vice president by citizen voters be heard by Congress, resulting in a constitutional amendment?

*1790 and 2010 Census data, respectively.
**U.S. Census Bureau, "Apportionment Data."

Until the Seventeenth Amendment was passed in 1913, state legislators (not the voting citizens) selected the state's representatives in the national senate (U.S. senators). The Seventeenth Amendment gave voters in each state the power to elect their representatives in the U.S. Senate.

In addition to limiting the national government officials directly elected by citizens to just their representative in the House of Representatives, the framers effectively limited voting rights to a minority of citizens. The framers left to the states the authority to determine eligibility to vote. Existing state constitutions allowed only property-owning white men to vote. The one exception was New Jersey, where property-owning white women could also vote until 1807, when the state constitution was amended to deny all women the right to vote. Hence, all women (except in New Jersey from 1776 to 1807) and many men, including Native Americans and enslaved African Americans, were denied the right to vote under the new Constitution. Therefore, representative democracy in the national government was very limited under the Constitution as ratified in 1788. Most inhabitants could not vote, and those who could voted to elect representatives to only one chamber of Congress.

Conflict and Compromise over Slavery

Delegates to the Constitutional Convention disagreed on the "peculiar institution" (as Thomas Jefferson called it) of slavery. In 1790, slaves made up 18 percent of the U.S. population, and most were enslaved in the southern states.[23] Delegates from the southern states, whose economy relied on slave labor, feared that a strong central government would abolish slavery. Meanwhile, northern delegates, who were widely concerned that a weak national government would limit the

United States' ability to engage in commerce and international trade, believed that the nation needed a more powerful central government than had existed under the Articles of Confederation. Ultimately, to get the southern states to agree to the strong central government established in the Constitution, the northern states compromised on the slavery issue by agreeing to a delay in debating the issue.

A provision in Article I, Section 9, of the Constitution postponed debate on the legality of slavery—and consequently kept it legal—by prohibiting Congress from addressing the importation of new slaves into the United States until January 1, 1808. Moreover, Article IV, which deals with interstate relations, established the states' obligation to deliver all fugitive slaves back to their owners. This measure aimed to ensure that people in non-slaveholding states would continue to respect the property rights of slaveholders—including the right to own slaves, who were legally defined as property, not people with natural rights guaranteed by government.

Although enslaved African and African American people were legally property, Article I, Section 2, established a formula for "counting" slaves for purposes of representation in the House of Representatives, apportionment of electors for the Electoral College, and the allocation of tax burdens among the states. This **Three-Fifths Compromise** counted each enslaved person as three-fifths of a free man. The southern states benefited from this compromise: they gained greater representation in the House and in the Electoral College than they would have if only nonslaves

Three-Fifths Compromise
The negotiated agreement by the delegates to the Constitutional Convention to count each slave as three-fifths of a free man for the purpose of representation and taxes.

> Before the Fifteenth Amendment was added to the Constitution in 1870, the Constitution did not guarantee anyone the right to vote. Voting rights were established by state governments. Today, due to the Fifteenth, Nineteenth, and Twenty-Sixth amendments, female and male citizens, no matter their race, color, or ancestry, who are 18 years of age or older have the right to vote. However, there are some limits on citizen voting rights. Since the Jones-Shafroth Act (1917), people born in Puerto Rico, a U.S. territory; are U.S. citizens; however, their right to vote is guaranteed only when they reside within one of the 50 states—they do not participate in elections to elect national officials while residing in Puerto Rico. A shrinking number of state governments deny convicted felons the right to vote during their incarceration. Some states permanently take away the right to vote for citizens convicted of felonies. Does your state limit voting rights of felons?

THEN

NOW

>The architects of the Constitution of the United States gathered in Philadelphia beginning on May 25, 1787. On September 17, 1787, 39 of the 42 delegates present signed the proposed constitution. Today, you can walk among bronze statues of the framers in attendance at the signing in Signers Hall at the National Constitution Center, located in Philadelphia. What do the images tell us about diversity among the Constitution's framers?

Painting photo: ©WDC Photos/Alamy Stock Photo; photo: ©Richard Cummins/Corbis Documentary/Getty Images

were counted. The benefit to the northern states was that if the national government imposed a direct tax on the states based on their populations, southern states would pay more than they would if only nonslaves were counted. (The national government has never imposed such a direct tax on the states.)

James Madison, while deploring slavery, argued that the delegates' "compromise" over slavery was "in the spirit of accommodation which governed the Convention." He insisted that without the Three-Fifths Compromise, the Constitution would never have been signed.

So, at the Constitutional Convention, delegates resolved some disagreements through accommodations and compromises, such as the large state–small state conflict over congressional representation. They put on hold other differences, such as their divisions over slavery. In the end, the document that the framers sent to the states for ratification described a government structure that aimed to fulfill the principles of the Declaration of Independence, for a select group of people. Foremost among those principles was the idea that it is up to the people to create a government that protects their natural rights to life, liberty, and the pursuit of happiness.

To ensure those rights, which were initially meant only for white property-owning men, the framers devised two key arrangements: the separation of powers with an integrated system of checks and balances, and a federal system in which the national and state governments had distinct, ultimate authorities. Although there was consensus on the mission of the new government, the conflict and arguments over the appropriate structure of government and government processes resulted in compromises and often vague language that the framers anticipated would be clarified in the future.

What About a Bill of Rights?

While the Declaration of Independence argued that governments were created by the people to protect their natural rights to life, liberty, and the pursuit of happiness, unlike state constitutions, the Constitution as drafted by the framers did not provide protections for these rights in the form of a list of limits on the national government. On September 12, 1787, George Mason, a delegate from Virginia, called for a bill of rights such as those found in state constitutions, which would list fundamental freedoms that the national government could not infringe. Roger Sherman, a delegate from Connecticut, argued that there was no need for one, because state constitutions included bills of rights. With hardly any discussion, the delegates decided not to add a bill of rights to the proposed constitution.[24] The lack of a bill of rights would become a main target for critics of the proposed constitution.

Congress Sends the Constitution to the States for Ratification

On September 17, 1787, thirty-nine convention delegates signed the Constitution. Following the amendment process in the Articles of Confederation, the delegates delivered their proposed constitution to the standing Congress. However, fearful that the document would not garner the approval of all 13 state legislatures as mandated by the Articles of Confederation's amendment process, the framers included in the proposed constitution a new ratification process that required just 9 of the 13 states to approve it for it to replace the Articles.

The framers requested that Congress send the proposed constitution to the states and that the state legislatures each establish a special, popularly elected convention to review and ratify the Constitution. One argument made to support this ratification process, which violated the Articles of Confederation, was that ratification by popularly elected conventions would validate the Constitution as the supreme law of the land, legitimized by the consent of the people. Congress acquiesced to the framers' request, and sent the proposed constitution to the states for ratification votes in special conventions.

The proposed constitution sent to the states was a product of conflict, deliberation, compromise, and pragmatism. In seven articles, the framers established a new national government with structures modeled after the state governments—distributing the basic governing functions among three branches and giving each branch means to check the others—and a radical new system of government, a federal system, with dual sovereignty. Before exploring the states' debate and ratification of the Constitution, we review the blueprint of government embodied in the constitution sent to the states. To explore the entire Constitution, as amended since 1791, turn to the annotated Constitution that follows this chapter.

ARTICLE I: THE LEGISLATIVE BRANCH Article I of the Constitution delegates lawmaking authority to Congress, describes the structure of the legislative branch, and outlines the legislative process. Article I specifies that the legislature is bicameral, comprising the House of Representatives and the Senate. Each state is represented in the House based on its population, with each elected representative having one vote. To ensure representation based on state population, Article 1 also calls for a census every 10 years, as discussed in this chapter's "Thinking Critically" feature. In contrast, state representation in the Senate is equal, with each state having two senators, with one vote each.

According to Article I, a proposed piece of legislation—a *bill*—requires simple majority votes (50 percent plus one vote) in each chamber, the House and the Senate, to become a law. This requirement means that the House and the Senate can check each other in the legislative process, because even if one chamber

A Debate Over One 2020 Census Question

"The Census has to be credible."

—Robert Grove, Director of the U.S. Census Bureau, 2009–2012

Article 1, Section 2 of the U.S. Constitution mandates a count of all people living in the United States every 10 years since the first such count occurred in 1790. For each census, the national government attempts to count everyone living in the United States.

The Importance of the Census: Congress

uses the data collected in the decennial census to redistribute (reapportion) the 435 voting seats of the House of Representatives among the 50 states. Based on changes in population, some states gain seats, some lose seats, and other states see no change in their representation in the House. If a state's number of House seats changes, the number of the state electors participating in the Electoral College will also change.

The Census Bureau also shares data with each state government so it can redraw (redistrict) its U.S. House districts to contain just about the same number of residents in each. This supports the democratic principle of "one person, one vote." That is, with each House member acting on behalf of the same number of people, each U.S. resident has the same vote/influence in House policy making. The states also use the data to redistrict their state House and Senate districts to comply with the one person, one vote principle.

The national government also uses the census data to distribute more than $600 billion of federal support to state and local governments annually. The states use the federal funds for a broad range of public policies—from infrastructure to health care to subsidies for farmers.

Concern About a Threat to the Credibility of the 2020 Census: In a December 2016

letter to the Census Bureau, the Department of Justice (DOJ) requested that a question on citizenship be added to the 2020 census. The DOJ argued that with this question, it could better enforce the section of the national Voting Rights Act that protects voting rights of minority groups during the redistricting process. The DOJ letter claims that "to fully enforce those requirements, the Department needs a reliable calculation of the citizen voting-age population in localities where voting rights violations are alleged or suspected."*

On December 29, 2017, Justin Elliott of ProPublica.org described the DOJ request as "a move that observers say could depress participation by immigrants who fear that the government could use the information against them."* If Elliott's statement is correct, and immigrants, documented and undocumented, fear the government will use their responses to census questions against them, they will be less willing to answer the census questions.

Michael Wines, a *New York Times* journalist, states in a January 2, 2018, article that the DOJ request "is stirring a broad backlash from census experts and others who say the move could wreck chances for an accurate count of the population—and, by extension, a fair redistricting of the House and state legislatures next decade." Wines also reports that voting rights advocates say "adding a citizenship question to the census would not enhance voting rights, but suppress them by reducing the head count of already undercounted minority groups, particularly the fast-growing Hispanic population."**

What do you think?

1. Do you agree or disagree with Grove's statement that the census must be credible? Justify your answer.

2. Do the sources of information presented above influence your belief in the credibility of their claims?

   a. Does the fact that the DOJ is a government agency influence your view about the need to add the citizenship question to the census? Please explain your answer.

   b. Does the reputation of a news source influence your view about the creditability of the concerns raised in its articles? Is ProPublica a reputable news source? Is it known to have a bias (liberal? conservative?)? How can you evaluate the quality of ProPublica as a news source?

   c. Is *The New York Times* a reputable news source? Is it known to have a bias? How does your view of *The New York* Times influence your view of the credibility of the concerns raised by Michael Wines?

*Justin Elliott, "Trump Justice Department Pushes for Citizenship Question on Census, Alarming Experts," December 29, 2017.

**Michael Wines, "Critics Say Questions about Citizenship Could Wreck Chances for an Accurate Census."

garners a majority vote, the other chamber can kill the bill if its majority does not support it. Because all pieces of legislation supported by the majority of the House and the majority of the Senate go to the president for approval or rejection, the president has a check on the legislative authority of Congress.

ARTICLE II: THE EXECUTIVE BRANCH   Article II of the Constitution describes the authority of the president. This article gives the president authority to ensure that the laws are faithfully executed, to appoint people to assist in administering the laws, to negotiate treaties, and to command the military. In addition to those executive functions, Article II allows the president several checks on the power of the other two branches of government.

All pieces of legislation approved by the House and the Senate must be forwarded to the president's desk. The president has 10 days to act on a bill, or it will automatically become law. Within those 10 days, the president can either sign the bill into law or **veto** it—that is, reject it, sending it back to Congress with his objections noted. Because Congress has primary responsibility for the legislative function, it can set aside the president's veto—that is, override the veto—with two-thirds of House members and two-thirds of the senators voting to approve the vetoed bill. Therefore, a bill can become law without the president's approval, once he has had the opportunity to approve it, but a bill cannot become law without the approval of at least a simple majority in each chamber of Congress.

With respect to the legislature's checks on the executive, the Constitution gives the Senate the power of **advice and consent**—the power to approve or reject—for treaties and presidential appointments. The Senate's advice and consent authority extends to the president's judicial nominees, as well.

ARTICLE III: THE JUDICIAL BRANCH   Article III describes the judicial branch. More specifically, Article III establishes the U.S. Supreme Court, and it delegates to Congress the authority to establish other, inferior (lower) courts. The Supreme Court and the other federal courts established by Congress have the authority to resolve lawsuits arising under the Constitution, national laws, and international treaties. In 1803, in the case of *Marbury v. Madison,*[25] the Supreme Court interpreted Article III to mean that the Court has the authority to determine whether an action taken by any government official or governing body violates the supreme law of the land, the Constitution; this is the power of **judicial review.**

ARTICLE IV: STATE-TO-STATE RELATIONS   The Constitution does not include a list of state powers, rights, or responsibilities as it does for the national government. However, in Article IV, the Constitution does describe how the states must respect the rights and liberties of the citizens of all states, as well as the legal proceedings and decisions of the other states. Article IV also establishes the means by which Congress can add new states to the union at the same time it prohibits Congress from changing state borders without consent of the affected states. Article IV also obligates the national government to ensure that all states are representative democracies.

ARTICLE V: THE AMENDMENT PROCESS   The framers recognized that the Constitution was a compromise born of their attempts to resolve existing problems, and therefore future generations would want to, and need to, revise the document in light of their own experiences, circumstances, and problems. Therefore, the framers provided processes to amend the Constitution.

veto
The president's rejection of a bill, which is sent back to Congress with the president's objections noted.

advice and consent
The Senate's authority to approve or reject the president's top appointments and negotiated treaties.

Marbury v. Madison
The 1803 Supreme Court case that established the power of judicial review, which allows the Court to strike down laws passed by the other branches that it views to be in conflict with the Constitution.

judicial review
Court authority to determine that an action taken by any government official or governing body violates the Constitution; established by the Supreme Court in the 1803 *Marbury v. Madison* case.

Amending the Constitution

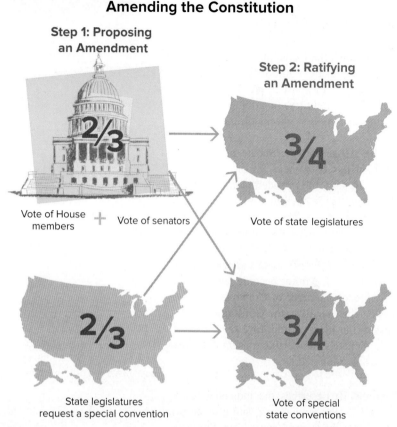

Step 1: Proposing an Amendment

2/3

Vote of House members + Vote of senators

2/3

State legislatures request a special convention

Step 2: Ratifying an Amendment

3/4

Vote of state legislatures

3/4

Vote of special state conventions

FIGURE 2.2 ■ **What Steps Are Involved in Proposing a Constitutional Amendment?** In what two ways can an amendment be ratified? Who has the authority to ratify amendments to the Constitution? Why is the designation of this authority important to the balance of power between the national and state governments? Explain.

The Constitution's framers wanted to ensure that widespread deliberation among the American people would precede any and all changes in the written Constitution. Thus, they made it no easy matter to amend formally the U.S. Constitution—that is, to change its written language. Constitutional amendment is a two-step process, entailing, first, the proposal of the amendment and, second, the ratification of the proposed amendment. Article V describes two different procedures for *proposing* an amendment (see Figure 2.2). The first method requires a two-thirds majority vote in each chamber, the House and the Senate, after which Congress sends the approved proposal to the states for ratification. The second method (which has never been used) requires a special constitutional convention. If two-thirds of the state legislatures petition Congress to consider an amendment, such a convention, where state delegates vote on the possible amendment, takes place; an approved proposal then goes to the states for ratification.

Article V also outlines two avenues by which the second step, ratifying a proposed amendment, may occur. An amendment is ratified by a vote of approval in either three-quarters of the state legislatures or three-quarters of special state conventions. The "Analyzing the Sources" feature explores Article V of the Constitution.

ARTICLE VI: SUPREMACY OF THE CONSTITUTION Article VI proclaims that the new national government will be legally responsible for all debts incurred by the Congress of the United States established by the Articles of Confederation. In addition, the article states that the Constitution, and laws and treaties made in compliance with it by the national government, are the supreme law of the land. Moreover, all national and state government officials must uphold the Constitution of the United States.

ARTICLE VII: THE CONSTITUTIONAL RATIFICATION PROCESS According to Article VII of the Constitution, ratification of the Constitution required the affirmative vote of special conventions in 9 of the 13 original states. After the delegates signed the Constitution, the standing Congress forwarded it to the states, directing them to hold ratification conventions according to Article VII of the Constitution, instead of implementing the constitutional amendment process established in the Articles of Confederation (the constitution in effect at the time).

ARTICLE V: CONVENING A CONSTITUTIONAL CONVENTION

Thomas Jefferson and James Madison both believed that Americans would need to review the Constitution critically and revise it over time to keep up with human development, technological advances, and changes in opinions and values as society evolved. Article V of the Constitution establishes the following processes by which the Constitution can be formally revised (its language changed):

The Congress, whenever two thirds of both Houses shall deem it necessary, shall propose Amendments to this Constitution, or on the Application of the Legislatures of two thirds of the several States, shall call a Convention for proposing Amendments, which in either Case, shall be valid to all Intents and Purposes, as part of this Constitution, when ratified by the Legislatures of three fourths of the several States, or by Conventions in three fourths thereof, as the one or the other Mode of Ratification may be proposed by the Congress: Provided that no Amendment which may be made prior to the Year One thousand eight hundred and eight shall in any Manner affect the first and fourth Clauses of the Ninth Section of the first Article; and that no State, without its Consent, shall be deprived of its equal suffrage in the Senate.

* Robert Gehrke, "Lawmakers Meet in Utah to Draw Blueprint for Constitutional Convention," *The Salt Lake Tribune*, November 11, 2015.

Practice Analytical Thinking

1. In November 2015, 100 legislators from 30 states met in Utah to develop rules and procedures for a constitutional convention.* Do state legislators have the authority to establish rules and procedures for a constitutional convention, or can they only propose rules and procedures to Congress for its approval?

2. Once the required number of states have applied to Congress to call for a convention, is Congress constitutionally bound to call a convention, or is it up to Congress's discretion?

3. For which, if any, of these questions does Article V provide clear, unambiguous answers?

The Ratification Debate: Federalists versus Anti-Federalists

Two days after 39 delegates signed the Constitution, it was published in a special issue of a newspaper called the *Pennsylvania Packet.* Almost immediately, opponents of the proposed Constitution began to write letters, issue pamphlets, and make stirring speeches urging the state legislatures to reject the document. The debate developed as one between the Federalists and the Anti-Federalists. The **Federalists** supported the Constitution as presented by the convention delegates. The **Anti-Federalists** opposed the Constitution because it gave the national government too much power—power that would erode states' authority, which was left undefined in the document, and endanger individual freedoms because it was not limited by a bill of rights.

It was in the Pennsylvania debate between the Federalists and the Anti-Federalists that the public call for the inclusion of a bill of rights to limit the powers of the federal government clearly emerged. Geared toward addressing the main Anti-Federalist complaints about the Constitution, the proposal for a bill of rights became the dominant point of contention in the ratification campaign.

Federalists
Individuals who supported the new Constitution as presented by the Constitutional Convention in 1787.

Anti-Federalists
Individuals who opposed ratification of the Constitution because they were deeply suspicious of the powers it gave to the national government and of the impact those powers would have on states' authority and individual freedoms.

>Mercy Otis Warren was a politically engaged woman of the 18th century who influenced many of the framers of the new nation, including Thomas Jefferson, George Washington, and Alexander Hamilton. Her letters, plays, poems, and pamphlets influenced the debates over declaring independence from Britain, ratification of the Articles of Confederation, ratification of the Constitution, and proposing and ratifying the Bill of Rights. Have you heard of her? One reason you may not know about Mercy Otis Warren is that she was an Anti-Federalist (on the losing side of the ratification debate). Another reason you might not have heard about her is she was a politically engaged woman at a time when society believed women should not be involved in politics. What are some signs that today most U.S. citizens accept women's political participation?

©Art Reserve/Alamy Stock Photo

The Federalist Papers
A series of essays, written by James Madison, Alexander Hamilton, and John Jay, that argued for the ratification of the Constitution.

In the end, the success or failure of the ratification process would hinge on the debate over a bill of rights.

THE ANTI-FEDERALISTS' CONCERNS WITH THE PROPOSED CONSTITUTION
Numerous Anti-Federalists penned countless letters, speeches, and essays warning of the dangers of the proposed new constitution and urging Americans to reject it. Under the pen name "A Columbian Patriot," Mercy Otis Warren wrote several pieces critical of the proposed constitution, including her "Observations on the New Constitution, and on the Federal and State Conventions" (1788), which presented a comprehensive summary of the Anti-Federalist arguments against the proposed Constitution of the United States. The circulation of Mercy Otis Warren's pamphlet was larger than that of *The Federalist Papers* written by James Madison, Alexander Hamilton, and John Jay to win support for ratification of the proposed constitution.[26]

The bottom line for Warren and the Anti-Federalists was that the foundational structures in the proposal threatened protection of citizens' natural rights in several ways. First, the Constitution gave too much power to the national government at the expense of the state governments that were closer to the people and therefore better understood their concerns and problems. Next, it delegated too much power to the executive branch at the expense of the legislative branch, which in a republic should have the most power because it is composed of representatives elected by the people (not by an Electoral College). Finally, the Constitution lacked a bill of rights to limit the vague powers delegated to the national government, including Congress's ambiguous power to make all laws it deems necessary and proper to promote the general welfare. Without a bill of rights, there was no way of truly limiting the actions the national government might take to achieve its goals, actions that might threaten states' rights (sovereignty) and the liberties and rights of the people.

Articulating Anti-Federalist views, Thomas Jefferson, author of the Declaration of Independence, insisted that the inclusion of a bill of rights in the Constitution was essential to protecting citizens' rights. Federalist Alexander Hamilton countered that listing those rights might endanger the very kind of individual freedoms and rights they sought to safeguard. It was possible, Hamilton reasoned, that the list would be incomplete and that at some future time people might legitimately argue that because a given right was not specifically enumerated, it did not exist. Jefferson's response was that "half a loaf is better than no bread" and that "if we cannot secure all our rights, let us secure what we can."[27]

THE FEDERALIST PAPERS: IN SUPPORT OF THE CONSTITUTION   The Federalists made their most famous arguments in support of the proposed constitution in a series of essays known as *The Federalist Papers*. The authors of *The Federalist Papers,* James Madison, Alexander Hamilton, and John Jay, knew that achieving ratification depended on convincing the public and state legislators that the Constitution would empower the new nation to succeed. They also understood that many of the Anti-Federalists' concerns centered on how much power the national government would have under the Constitution and how that authority would affect the states and individual freedoms. Consequently, they approached the ratification debate strategically, penning eloquently reasoned essays (in the form of letters) to consider those specific issues.

With regard to protecting individual rights, in *Federalist* No. 10, Madison reassuringly details how the republican government created by the Constitution would ensure that many views would be heard and that a majority of the population would not be permitted to trample the rights of the numerical minority. Writing in *Federalist* No. 84, Hamilton argues that because "the people surrender nothing, and as they retain every thing" by way of the Constitution, there was no danger that the new government would usurp individual rights and liberties.

In *Federalist* No. 51, Madison explains that there is a "double security" for protecting individual rights and liberties. In the federal system, "the power surrendered by the people is first divided between two distinct governments," the national and the state, and each government will control the other. In addition, both levels of government are "subdivided among distinct and separate departments" (branches of government) that check each other.

With regard to loss of state power, James Madison argues in *Federalist* No. 45 that the states retain "a very extensive portion of active sovereignty" because "the powers delegated by the proposed Constitution to the federal government are few and defined. Those which are to remain in the State governments are numerous and indefinite." Therefore, the listed national powers are limited while the lack of a list of state powers means the states have fewer limits than does the national government.

For the Federalists, the foundational structures of the new government, which included the federal system of government (dual sovereignty), the separation of powers, and the system of checks and balances, would protect individual liberties and states' rights. For the Anti-Federalists, those structures were not sufficient. An enumeration of limits on the national government was also essential to protect individual liberties and states' rights.

Ratification: Constitution (1788) and Bill of Rights (1791)

In the end, the concerns of the Anti-Federalists and the larger public conversation about states' rights and individuals' liberties placed significant pressure on the Federalists to reconsider the need for inclusion of a bill of rights. With the proviso that a bill of rights would be the first order of business for the new Congress, Massachusetts, Maryland, South Carolina, and New Hampshire—the last four states of the nine needed for ratification—ratified the Constitution in 1788. In 1790, Rhode Island was the last of the original 13 states to ratify the Constitution.

In the opening days of the first session of the newly constituted Congress in March 1789, Virginia congressman James Madison introduced a bill of rights. Comprising 12 amendments, this proposed addition to the Constitution powerfully reflected the public concerns voiced during the ratification debates by enumerating limits on the national government's right to infringe on the natural rights of life, liberty, and the pursuit of happiness and by preserving the states' sovereignty. Congress passed all 12 proposed amendments and sent them to the states for ratification. By 1791, the required number of states had quickly ratified 10 of the 12 amendments, which we refer to today as the **Bill of Rights.**

The first eight amendments in the Bill of Rights establish the government's legal obligation to protect several specific liberties to which the Declaration of Independence referred when it stated that men were "endowed by their creator with certain unalienable rights." These natural rights became government-protected liberties, *civil liberties,* through the ratification process. With the Jefferson and Hamilton debate over the pros and cons of listing citizens' rights in mind, the Ninth Amendment indicates that the list of liberties in the first eight amendments is not exhaustive and therefore "shall not be construed to deny or disparage others retained by the people." (Chapter 4 discusses in depth the civil liberties established in the Bill of Rights.) The tenth and last amendment in the Bill of Rights preserves

Bill of Rights
The first 10 amendments to the Constitution, which were ratified in 1791, constituting an enumeration of the individual liberties with which the government is forbidden to interfere.

the states' rights. The Tenth Amendment states that the powers not delegated to the national government by the Constitution "nor prohibited by it to the states, are reserved to the states respectively, or to the people." By listing rights of citizens and the states, the Bill of Rights addressed the core concerns raised by the Anti-Federalists by imposing limits on the national government.

The Constitution as a Living, Evolving Document

The authors of the Constitution were pragmatic men who were willing to compromise to resolve the problems confronting the new nation and to get a new constitution ratified.[28] To win the votes needed to move the document from first draft through ratification, the framers had to negotiate and compromise over constitutional language. As a result of this give-and-take, the Constitution is replete with vague and ambiguous phrases, which the framers expected would be reviewed and revised through both formal amendment of the Constitution and judicial interpretation.

According to James Madison's convention notes on the discussion of Article V, the formal amendment process, delegate "Elbridge Gerry noted that 'the novelty and difficulty of the experiment requires periodical revisions.'"[29] Thomas Jefferson even proposed during the discussion of Article V that a constitutional convention be called at the beginning of each new century.[30] At the time of his retirement, President George Washington (1789–1797) stated that he thought "the People (for it is with them to Judge) can as they will have the advantage of experience on their Side, decide with as much propriety on the alterations and amendments which are necessary [as] ourselves. I do not think we are more inspired, have more wisdom, or posses more virtue, than those who will come after us."[31]

Viewing the Constitution as a living document that should evolve along with the nation, through conventions and formal amendment, the framers also expected judges to interpret the Constitution, and laws made under its provisions, in light of the realities of their own time. Alexander Hamilton wrote in *Federalist* No. 78, "A constitution is in fact, and must be, regarded by judges as a fundamental law. It therefore belongs to them to ascertain its meaning as well as the meaning of any particular act proceeding from the legislative body. . . . The courts must declare the sense of the law. . . ."[32] As Supreme Court justice Charles Evans Hughes (1862–1948) later observed, "The Constitution is what the Judges say it is."[33]

The alteration of this document—through both the passage of formal amendments and judicial (re)interpretation of key clauses—derives from a continuing conversation among citizens about the core beliefs and principles of the framers and the generations that have followed them, including Americans today, and what those beliefs mean for contemporary realities. Hence, the Constitution continues to be a living and evolving document.

Formal Amendment of the Constitution

Every term, members of Congress introduce between 100 and 200 proposals for new constitutional amendments. Members of Congress who oppose a ruling by the U.S. Supreme Court or a law that creates a great deal of public debate may propose a constitutional amendment to supersede the Court ruling or the controversial law. Often, members of Congress introduce constitutional amendments knowing that they will never be ratified but wanting to appease their core constituencies by at least instigating public conversation about how our government should function and what rights and freedoms individuals possess.

Only a tiny fraction of the thousands of proposed amendments have cleared Congress—in fact, only 33 have achieved the two-thirds vote necessary in both the House and the Senate—and, as noted, the states have ratified only 27 of those congressional proposed amendments. The amendments that the states have ratified fit into one of three categories: They have (1) extended civil liberties and civil rights (equal protection of laws for citizens), (2) altered the selection of officials or the operation of the branches of the national government, or (3) dealt with important policy issues. The annotated Constitution that follows this chapter indicates the three categories in which each constitutional amendment fits.

One possible explanation for the relatively low number of constitutional amendments is that the framers established a difficult amendment process, requiring super-majority votes: two-thirds of the members in each chamber in Congress and three-quarters approval among the states. They did so to ensure that nationwide public discourse would take place before the written words in the Constitution, the supreme law of the land, could be changed.

Interpretation by the U.S. Supreme Court

Beyond the addition of formal amendments, the Constitution has changed over time through interpretation by the courts. This interpretation began with the U.S. Supreme Court's landmark *Marbury v. Madison* decision in 1803, in which the Court established the important power of judicial review—the authority of the courts to rule on whether acts of government officials and governing bodies violate the Constitution. Although the U.S. Supreme Court's interpretation is final, if the Supreme Court does not review constitutional interpretations made by lower federal courts, then the interpretations of those lower courts are the final word on the Constitution's meaning.

According to constitutional law scholars Laurence Tribe and Joshua Matz, a wealth of scholarly literature discusses the varied factors influencing judges' decisions that "define the framework of our fundamental law" as established in the Constitution. That literature indicates that when resolving a conflict over the meaning of constitutional language, the judges "look to the Constitution's text, how it was understood when it was ratified, our national history, judicial precedent [previous court opinions and decisions], the Constitution's values, and the practical needs of our time."[34]

Judges have interpreted and reinterpreted (changed previous judicial interpretations of) constitutional clauses regularly. Such interpretations and reinterpretations are discussed throughout this book, particularly in the chapters on civil liberties and civil rights.

Richard Beeman, a widely respected constitutional scholar, identifies three recurring themes evident in Supreme Court rulings: (1) the nature of the Constitution as a document that continues evolving as the courts interpret changing social norms, (2) the tensions created by the foundational structures established in the Constitution (separation of powers, checks and balances, and the dual sovereignty of our federal system), and (3) the clarification of fundamental rights guaranteed by the Bill of Rights.[35] With regard to changing societal norms, Court decisions reflect an expansion of the principle of equality, as well as of the liberties and rights granted by the Bill of Rights and subsequent amendments.

In most cases, the Court's rulings are in step with public opinion. Analysts note that the Court does not often lead public opinion—in fact, it more often follows it.[36] And even if the justices wanted to take some very controversial and unpopular action, the system of checks and balances forces them to consider how the other branches would react. Recall that the Court has the power to interpret the law; it does not have the power to implement or to enforce the law and must be concerned about how the other branches might retaliate against it for highly unpopular decisions. Therefore, for the most part, changes to the Constitution, both formal (constitutional amendment) and informal (court interpretation), are incremental and further the will of the people because they are the product of a government with separation of powers and a system of checks and balances, a written constitution that establishes fundamental law, and widespread public discourse—an ongoing conversation of democracy.

Conclusion

Thinking Critically About What's Next for the Constitution

The governing principles proclaimed in the Declaration of Independence successfully unified American colonists to fight the War for Independence. However, government created by the consent of the people with the mission of protecting the people's natural rights to life, liberty, and the pursuit of happiness has proven difficult. Economic upheaval and domestic uprisings experienced under the Articles of Confederation sparked the call for a convention to amend the constitution. The product of the convention to amend the Articles, a convention in which the "spirit of accommodation" governed, was a proposed new constitution replete with compromises over major issues (such as how to implement representative government and the right to enslave people) and vague language.

The foundational structures established by the Constitution (federal system, separation of powers with integrated system of checks and balances), the core governing procedures, and the values and principles articulated in the Preamble (mission) have been perpetually questioned, debated, clarified, and amended since day one of the new union. Indeed, the Constitution is an ever evolving and living document, just as the framers predicted.

In response to lawsuits, the courts continue to determine what is and is not constitutional through judicial review. In addition, citizens and elected officials continue to debate possible amendments to the Constitution. The framers' mission to create a more perfect union through the Constitution of the United States is still a work in progress.

Learning Summary

1. Define what a constitution is.
   a. Describe the key differences between a written and an unwritten constitution.
   b. Describe the three essential pieces of information about a government contained in a written constitution.

2. Summarize key events that sparked and structured the creation of the United States of America.
  a. Name policies and actions taken by the British government that led the British colonists to declare independence.
  b. Outline actions the colonists took, before they declared their independence, in response to the British government's policies and actions.
  c. Contrast the key structures, procedures, and principles found in the first state constitutions with those in the Articles of Confederation.
  d. Describe at least two major weaknesses in the Articles of Confederation that led to calls to remedy its defects.

3. Summarize the major issues deliberated and resolved in the crafting of the Constitution of the United States.
  a. Describe the people who participated in the Constitutional Convention of 1787.
  b. Recall the issues on which the Constitutional Convention delegates came to quick consensus.
  c. Recall the issues on which the delegates conflicted and eventually compromised.
  d. Describe the structures, procedures, and principles found in the seven articles in the Constitution of the United States.
  e. Summarize the concerns the Anti-Federalists raised in the ratification process.
  f. Summarize the arguments the Federalists made in support of ratifying the Constitution.
  g. Explain how the Bill of Rights addressed concerns raised by the Anti-Federalists.

4. Explain why the Constitution is an evolving document and how it evolves.
  a. Explain why the Constitution is considered a living document.
  b. Outline the process by which the Constitution can be formally amended.
  c. Describe how and why the courts amend the Constitution through interpretation.

Key Terms

advice and consent 51

Anti-Federalists 53

bicameral legislature 39

Bill of Rights 55

checks and balances 43

confederation 40

Connecticut Compromise (Great Compromise) 45

constitution 33

dual sovereignty 43

Electoral College 45

Federalists 53

judicial review 51

Marbury v. Madison 51

natural rights (unalienable rights) 38

New Jersey Plan 45

republic 39

separation of powers 43

supremacy clause 43

The Federalist Papers 54

Three-Fifths Compromise 47

unicameral legislature 40

veto 51

Virginia Plan 45

For Review

1. Describe the three essential pieces of information contained in a written constitution.

2. How did the policies and actions of the British government leading up to the War for Independence shape the core principles of the U.S. Constitution, including representative democracy and protection of life, liberty, and the pursuit of happiness?

3. How did conflict and compromise influence the basic structures and procedures established in the Constitution? What specific issues caused conflict and required compromise for their resolution? On what matters was there early consensus among the framers?

4. Differentiate the formal constitutional amendment process from the informal process by which the Constitution's meaning is changed.

For Critical Thinking and Discussion

1. Think about important debates in American society today. Describe one that you think is linked in some way to the compromises upon which the Constitution is based and its often vague and ambiguous language.

2. What liberties and rights being debated today would you argue are rational extensions of the liberties and rights established in the Constitution (as amended) and properly extended through the Ninth Amendment, which states that "The enumeration in the Constitution, of certain rights, shall not be construed to deny or disparage others retained by the people"?

3. What do you think would have happened had the Anti-Federalists, rather than the Federalists, prevailed in the ratification process of the Constitution? Would the Articles of Confederation still be in effect today? Would its amendment process (requiring all states to approve constitutional amendments) have prevented formal amendment? How would the confederal government have dealt with the difficult issues facing the new republic—slavery, concerns about mob rule, and continuing hostility in the international community?

Resources for Research AND Action

Internet Resources

Constitutional Center's Interactive Constitution
www.constitutioncenter.org/interactive-constitution This site presents constitutional experts who discuss their differing perspectives on the Constitution's history and the (re)interpretations of constitutional language.

FindLaw
www.findlaw.com This site offers links to news regarding current cases before the U.S. Supreme Court as well as access to decisions of all federal and state appellate courts.

Library of Congress Memory Project
www.ourdocuments.gov/content.php?page=milestone This comprehensive website provides links to 100 milestone documents, compiled by the National Archives and Records Administration, that chronicle U.S. history, from Lee's Resolution calling for independence in 1776 through the Voting Rights Act of 1965.

The U.S. Constitution Online
www.USConstitution.net This interesting site helps to place the U.S. Constitution in a contemporary context. Its current events section discusses how the pending issues are affected by constitutional principles.

Recommended Readings

Beeman, Richard. *The Penguin Guide to the United States Constitution.* New York: Penguin Books, 2010. This book has a fully annotated Declaration of Independence, a fully annotated U.S. Constitution, selections from *The Federalist Papers,* chapters presenting the history of the making and the initial enactment of the Constitution, and brief overviews of several landmark Supreme Court decisions.

Hamilton, Alexander, James Madison, and John Jay. *The Federalist Papers.* Cutchogue, NY: Buccaneer Books, 1992. A compilation of the 85 newspaper articles written by the authors to persuade the voters of New York to ratify the proposed Constitution of the United States, featuring a comprehensive introduction that puts the articles in context and outlines their principal themes—and hence, the underlying principles of the Constitution.

Roberts, Cokie. *Founding Mothers: The Women Who Raised Our Nation.* New York: Perennial Press, 2004. An examination of the Revolution and its aftermath, focusing on how women contributed to the war effort and to wider discussions about how the new government should be structured and what goals it should advance.

Sabato, Larry. *A More Perfect Constitution: 23 Proposals to Revitalize Our Constitution and Make America a Fairer Country.* New York: Walker Publishing, 2007. An exploration by political scientist Larry Sabato into why a constitutional convention is needed. The book includes proposals for 23 amendments—many of which citizens support, according to a poll commissioned by the author—that Sabato argues will perfect the Constitution. His real goal in writing the book was to kindle a national conversation on what he perceives as the deficiencies in U.S. representative democracy.

Tribe, Laurence, and Joshua Matz. *Uncertain Justice: The Roberts Court and the Constitution.* New York: Picador, 2014. The authors show how the Supreme Court has (re)interpreted the Constitution, specifically civil liberties and rights, since Chief Justice Roberts joined the Court in 2005.

Wittes, Benjamin, and Pietro S. Nivola. *What Would Madison Do? The Father of the Constitution Meets Modern American Politics.* Washington, DC: Brookings Institution Press, 2015. The collection of papers in this book addresses two questions. First, how well is the system of government constructed by Madison and his colleagues working? Second, would Madison be pleased or dissatisfied with contemporary policy processes and policies?

Movies of Interest

Return to the Land of Wonders (2004)

This documentary follows Adnan Pachachi's return to Iraq in 2003, after 37 years in exile, to head a committee charged with drafting a new constitution and bill of rights. The movie focuses on the torturous process of trying to resolve conflicts created by the demands of the United States and the expectations of Iraqis, as well as the realities of everyday life in Iraq in 2003.

An Empire of Reason (1998)

A thought-provoking answer to an intriguing "what if?" question: What if the ratification debates were held using the media tools of the 21st century, specifically, television?

Amistad (1997)

This film depicts the mutiny and subsequent trial of Africans aboard the ship *Amistad* in 1839–1840. Viewers get a glimpse of the intense civic discourse over slavery in the period leading up to the Civil War.

1776 (1972)

A musical that depicts what occurred during the crafting of the Declaration of Independence.

References

1. "Sugar Act of 1764," www.u-s-history.com/pages/h1211.html.
2. "Great Britain: Parliament-The Stamp Act, March 22, 1765," http://avalon.law.yale.edu/18th_century/stamp_act_1765.asp.
3. Glenna Matthews, *The Rise of Public Woman: Women's Power and Women's Place in the United States 1630-1970* (New York: Oxford University Press, 1992), 56.
4. "Prelude to Revolution," www.history-place.con/unitedstates/revolution/rev-prel.htm.
5. J. Alan Rogers, "Colonial Opposition to the Quartering of Troops During the French and Indian War," *Military Affairs* (1970): 7.
6. "Great Britain: Parliament—The Declaratory Act, March 18, 1766," http://avalon.law.yale.edu/18th_century/declaratory_act_1767.html.
7. America's Homepage, "The Townshend Act," http://ahp.gatech.edu/townshend_act_1767.html.
8. Russell Bourne, *Cradle of Violence: How Boston's Waterfront Mobs Ignited the American Revolution* (Hoboken, NJ: Wiley, 2006).
9. "Committees of Correspondence," www.u-s-history.com/pages/h675.html.
10. Boston Tea Party Ships & Museums, www.bostonteapartyship.com/.
11. "The Intolerable Acts," www.ushistory.org/declaration/related/intolerable.htm.
12. "The Declaration of Rights and Grievances," www.usconstitution.net/intol.html#Rights.
13. "The Articles of Association," www.usconstitution.net/assocart.html.
14. For further discussion of the impact of *Common Sense* on colonial attitudes and beliefs, see Edmund S. Morgan, *The Birth of the Republic: 1763-89* (Chicago: University of Chicago Press, 1992), 71-76.
15. "Lee's Resolutions," http://avalon.law.yale.edu/18th_century/lee.asp.
16. You can find these constitutions at Yale Law School's Avalon Project, http://avalon.law.yale.edu/subject_menus/18th.asp.
17. Jack N. Rakove, "A Tradition Born of Strife," in *American Politics: Classic and Contemporary Readings,* 6th ed., ed. Allan J. Cigler and Burdett A. Loomis (Boston: Houghton Mifflin, 2005), 4-5.
18. For an excellent discussion of how the Articles benefited the states, see Keith L. Dougherty, *Collective Action Under the Articles of Confederation* (New York: Cambridge University Press, 2001), 76-82.
19. "Shays Rebellion," www.government-and-constitution.org/history-us-political-parties/shays-rebellion.htm.
20. "Proceedings of Commissioners to Remedy Defects of the Federal Government: 1786," http://avalon.law.yale.edu/18th_century/annapoli.asp.
21. Charles Beard, *An Economic Interpretation of the Constitution of the United States* (New York: Macmillan, 1913).
22. "The Constitutional Convention," www.usconstitution.net/consttop_ccon.html.
23. Eddie Becker, "Chronology on the History of Slavery and Racism," http://innercity.org/holt/chron_1790_1829.html.
24. Richard Beeman, *The Penguin Guide to the United States Constitution* (New York: Penguin Books, 2010), 161.
25. *Marbury v. Madison,* 5 U.S. 137 (1803).
26. Larry M. Lane and Judith J. Lane, "The Columbian Patriot: Mercy Otis Warren and the Constitution," in *Women, Politics, and the Constitution,* ed. Naomi B. Lunn (New York: Harrington Park Press, 1990), 17-31.
27. Thomas Jefferson, letter to James Madison on the Bill of Rights debate, March 15, 1789. Courtesy of *Eigen's Political & Historical Quotations.*
28. John P. Roche, "The Founding Fathers: A Reform Caucus in Action,"*American Political Science Review,* LV (1961).
29. Larry J. Sabato, *A More Perfect Constitution: Why the Constitution Must Be Revised—Ideas to Inspire a New Generation* (New York: Walker Publishing Company), 315, fn 4.
30. Ibid., 218.
31. Ibid., 221.
32. Alexander Hamilton, "Federalist No. 78," *The Federalist Papers* (Cutchogue, NY: Buccaneer Books, 1992), 395-396.
33. "Charles Evans Hughes," http://c250.columbia.edu/c250_celebrates/remarkable_columbians/charles_hughes.
34. Laurence Tribe and Joshua Matz, *Uncertain Justice: The Roberts Court and the Constitution* (New York: Picador, 2014), 5.
35. Richard Beeman, *The Penguin Guide to the United States Constitution* (New York: Penguin Books, 2010), 190.
36. Thomas Marshall, "Representing Public Opinion: American Courts and the Appeals Process," *Politics and Policy,* 31 (December 2003): 726-739.

The Constitution of the United States of America

Preamble

We the People of the United States, in Order to form a more perfect Union, establish Justice, insure domestic Tranquility, provide for the common defence, promote the general Welfare, and secure the Blessings of Liberty to ourselves and our Posterity, do ordain and establish this Constitution for the United States of America.

> The Preamble states that "the People" are creating a new government, which is described in the Constitution. The Preamble also decrees that it is the mission of this new government to serve the people better than did the government established by the Articles of Confederation, which had been in effect since before the end of the War for Independence.

POLITICAL INQUIRY:

1. *What did the people of the United States in the late 18th century mean by "promote the general Welfare"?*

2. *What are some of the debates among people of the United States today related to the goal of promoting the general welfare?*

ARTICLE I. (Legislative Branch)

Section 1. (Bicameral Legislative Branch)

All legislative Powers herein granted shall be vested in a Congress of the United States, which shall consist of a Senate and House of Representatives.

> Article I presents the organization, procedures, and authority of the lawmaking branch, the Congress, a bicameral (two-chamber) legislature comprising the House of Representatives and the Senate.

POLITICAL INQUIRY:

1. *Why did the framers establish a bicameral legislature instead of a unicameral legislature such as existed under the Articles of Confederation?*

2. *In 1934, as a cost-cutting measure, the state of Nebraska adopted a unicameral legislature (one chamber) to replace its bicameral legislature. What are some advantages and disadvantages of a bicameral legislature compared to a unicameral (one chamber) legislature?*

Section 2. (The House of Representatives)

Clause 1: The House of Representatives shall be composed of Members chosen every second Year by the People of the several States, and the Electors in each State shall have the Qualifications requisite for Electors of the most numerous Branch of the State Legislature.

> House members are elected to serve a two-year term.

> The Constitution specifies only three qualifications to be elected to the House: You must be at least 25 years old; you must be a U.S. citizen for at least seven years (so a foreign-born, naturalized citizen can be a House member); and you must be a resident of the state you will represent. By tradition, House members live in the district that they represent.

> The "three-fifths" clause called on the government to count enslaved people as three-fifths of a person when conducting the decennial (every ten years) census, which measures how many people live in the country and where they live.

> Census data is also used in the distribution of more than $600 billion in federal funds to state and local governments annually.

> The population count is used to distribute the 435 House seats among the states—the goal being that each House member represents about the same number of constituents.

> Governors have the authority to call for a special election to fill any of their states' House seats that become vacant.

> House members select their presiding officer, the Speaker of the House. The Speaker is in line to succeed the president if both the president and the vice president are unable to serve.

> The Constitution gives the House a check on officials of the executive and judicial branches through its power of impeachment: the power to accuse such officials formally of offenses such as treason, bribery, and abuse of power. If the officials are subsequently found guilty in a trial held by the Senate, they are removed from office.

> Before the Seventeenth Amendment was passed (1913), state legislatures selected their state's two U.S. senators, each of whom served a 6-year term.

> Today, every even-numbered year, congressional elections are held in which one-third of the Senate's 100 seats and all 435 House seats are up for election. Thanks to the Seventeenth Amendment (1913), each state's governor is authorized to call for elections to fill a vacancy in a Senate seat; in addition, each state legislature is authorized to determine the process by which a vacant Senate seat will be temporarily filled until the election of a new senator.

Clause 2: No Person shall be a Representative who shall not have attained to the age of twenty five Years, and been seven Years a Citizen of the United States, and who shall not, when elected, be an Inhabitant of that State in which he shall be chosen.

Clause 3: Representatives and direct Taxes shall be apportioned among the several States which may be included within this Union, according to their respective Numbers, which shall be determined by adding to the whole Number of free Persons, including those bound to Service for a Term of Years, and excluding Indians not taxed, three fifths of all other Persons. The actual Enumeration shall be made within three Years after the first Meeting of the Congress of the United States, and within every subsequent Term of ten Years, in such Manner as they shall by Law direct. The Number of Representatives shall not exceed one for every thirty Thousand, but each State shall have at Least one Representative; and until such enumeration shall be made, the State of New Hampshire shall be entitled to chuse three, Massachusetts eight, Rhode-Island and Providence Plantations one, Connecticut five, New-York six, New Jersey four, Pennsylvania eight, Delaware one, Maryland six, Virginia ten, North Carolina five, South Carolina five, and Georgia three.

Clause 4: When vacancies happen in the Representation from any State, the Executive Authority thereof shall issue Writs of Election to fill such Vacancies.

Clause 5: The House of Representatives shall chuse their Speaker and other Officers; and shall have the sole Power of Impeachment.

Section 3. (The Senate)

Clause 1: The Senate of the United States shall be composed of two Senators from each State, chosen by the Legislature thereof, for six Years; and each Senator shall have one Vote.

POLITICAL INQUIRY: *In the 1960s, the U.S. Supreme Court ruled that in state government the proper implementation of representative democracy must follow the principle of one person, one vote. This means that each elected representative in a state House should represent about the same number of constituents, and each elected state senator must represent about the same number of constituents. However, the Great Compromise of the Constitutional Convention established the U.S. Senate such that today Wyoming's 583,000 residents are represented by two U.S. senators, and so are California's 38 million residents.*

1. *Do you support the Great Compromise, or do you think that the principle of one person, one vote should be upheld, which would mean amending the Constitution? Justify your answer.*

2. *What are the chances that states with small populations would support an amendment that would apportion senators based on state population, as is done for the House of Representatives? Explain.*

Clause 2: Immediately after they shall be assembled in Consequence of the first Election, they shall be divided as equally as may be into three Classes. The Seats of the Senators of the first Class shall be vacated at the Expiration of the second Year, of the second Class at the Expiration of the fourth Year, and of the third Class at the Expiration of the sixth Year, so that one third may be chosen every second Year; and if Vacancies happen by Resignation, or otherwise, during the Recess of the Legislature of any State, the Executive thereof may make temporary Appointments until the next Meeting of the Legislature, which shall then fill such Vacancies.

Clause 3: No Person shall be a Senator who shall not have attained to the Age of thirty Years, and been nine Years a Citizen of the United States, and who shall not, when elected, be an Inhabitant of that State for which he shall be chosen.

> Senators must be at least 30 years old, either natural-born citizens or immigrants who have been citizens for at least nine years, and—like members of the House—residents of the state they are elected to represent.

Clause 4: The Vice President of the United States shall be President of the Senate but shall have no Vote, unless they be equally divided.

> The vice president serves as the president of the Senate, with the authority to preside over meetings of the Senate and to vote when there is a tie.

Clause 5: The Senate shall chuse their other Officers, and also a President pro tempore, in the Absence of the Vice President, or when he shall exercise the Office of President of the United States.

> Although the first few vice presidents did preside over daily meetings of the Senate, the vice president rarely does so today.

Clause 6: The Senate shall have the sole Power to try all Impeachments. When sitting for that Purpose, they shall be on Oath or Affirmation. When the President of the United States is tried the Chief Justice shall preside: And no Person shall be convicted without the Concurrence of two thirds of the Members present.

> The Senate exercises a check on officials of the executive and judicial branches of the federal government by trying them once they have been impeached by the House of Representatives.

Clause 7: Judgment in Cases of Impeachment shall not extend further than to removal from Office, and disqualification to hold and enjoy any Office of honor, Trust or Profit under the United States: but the Party convicted shall nevertheless be liable and subject to Indictment, Trial, Judgment and Punishment, according to Law.

> If the Senate convicts an impeached official, he or she is removed from office and may be subject to prosecution in the criminal courts.

Section 4. (Congressional Elections)

Clause 1: The Times, Places and Manner of holding Elections for Senators and Representatives, shall be prescribed in each State by the Legislature thereof; but the Congress may at any time by Law make or alter such Regulations, except as to the Places of chusing Senators.

> Though states have the authority to organize and conduct elections, today they rely heavily on local governments to assist them. Congress has passed numerous laws to ensure constitutionally guaranteed voting rights. The first such law was passed shortly after ratification of the Fifteenth Amendment to criminalize attempts to deny black men their newly won right to vote. Congress has also enacted laws to make voter registration easier. For example, a 1996 federal law requires states to allow citizens to register to vote through the mail.

POLITICAL INQUIRY: *To increase voter turnout (the percentage of eligible voters that vote on Election Day), states have enacted laws allowing voters to vote by mail, to register to vote on Election Day, and even to vote during a two-week window instead of only on Election Day (known as early voting). Within the last few years, several states have repealed early voting or shortened the time period for early voting.*

1. *Would you support or oppose allowing voters to vote by Internet? Explain your response.*

2. *What are some advantages of and some concerns raised by allowing voters to vote during a two-week window?*

Clause 2: The Congress shall assemble at least once in every Year, and such Meeting shall be on the first Monday in December, unless they shall by Law appoint a different Day.

> The Twentieth Amendment (1933) changed the date on which the annual meeting of Congress must begin.

> Each chamber decides whether the election of each of its members is legitimate. A majority of the members of each chamber must be present to conduct business: at least 218 members for the House and 51 senators for the Senate.

> After each congressional election, both the House and the Senate determine how they will conduct their business, and each chamber selects from among its members a presiding officer. Moreover, the members of each chamber establish codes of behavior, which they use to judge and—if necessary—punish members' misconduct.

> The House and the Senate must keep and publish records of their proceedings, including a record of all votes for and against proposals, except those that they decide require secrecy. However, if one-fifth of the members of a chamber demand that a vote be recorded, it must be recorded. Congress publishes a record of its debates, called the Congressional Record.

> To close down business for more than three days during a session, or to conduct business at another location, each chamber needs to get approval from the other one. This ensures that one chamber cannot stop the legislative process by refusing to meet.

> Today, each member of Congress earns at least $174,000 per year, paid by taxes collected by the national government. Members of Congress are protected from civil lawsuits and criminal prosecution for the work they do as legislators. They are also protected from arrest while Congress is in session except for a charge of treason, of committing a felony, or of committing a breach of the peace.

> To ensure the separation of basic governing functions, no member of Congress can hold another federal position while serving in the House or the Senate. Moreover, members of Congress cannot be appointed to a position in the executive or judicial branch that was created during their term of office.

> This section details the legislative process.

> Although all revenue-raising bills, such as tax bills, must originate in the House, the Senate reviews them and has the authority to make modifications; ultimately the House and the Senate must each approve the identical bill for it to become law.

> After the House and the Senate approve the identical bill by a simple majority vote in each chamber, it is sent to the president for approval or rejection. The president has 10 days in which to act, or the bill will automatically become law (unless Congress has adjourned, in which case the bill dies—a pocket veto). If the president signs the bill within 10 days, it becomes law. If the president rejects—vetoes—the bill, he or she sends it back to the chamber of its origin with objections. Congress can then rewrite the vetoed bill and send the revised bill through the legislative process. Or Congress can attempt to override the veto by garnering a super-majority vote of approval (two-thirds majority) in each chamber.

Section 5. (Powers and Responsibilities of the House)

Clause 1: Each House shall be the Judge of the Elections, Returns and Qualifications of its own Members, and a Majority of each shall constitute a Quorum to do Business; but a smaller Number may adjourn from day to day, and may be authorized to compel the Attendance of absent Members, in such Manner, and under such Penalties as each House may provide.

Clause 2: Each House may determine the Rules of its Proceedings, punish its Members for disorderly Behaviour, and, with the Concurrence of two thirds, expel a Member.

Clause 3: Each House shall keep a Journal of its Proceedings, and from time to time publish the same, excepting such Parts as may in their Judgment require Secrecy; and the Yeas and Nays of the Members of either House on any question shall, at the Desire of one fifth of those Present, be entered on the Journal.

Clause 4: Neither House, during the Session of Congress, shall, without the Consent of the other, adjourn for more than three days, nor to any other Place than that in which the two Houses shall be sitting.

Section 6. (Rights of Congressional Members)

Clause 1: The Senators and Representatives shall receive a Compensation for their Services, to be ascertained by Law, and paid out of the Treasury of the United States. They shall in all Cases, except Treason, Felony and Breach of the Peace, be privileged from Arrest during their Attendance at the Session of their respective Houses, and in going to and returning from the same; and for any Speech or Debate in either House, they shall not be questioned in any other Place.

Clause 2: No Senator or Representative shall, during the Time for which he was elected, be appointed to any civil Office under the Authority of the United States, which shall have been created, or the Emoluments whereof shall have been encreased during such time; and no Person holding any Office under the United States, shall be a Member of either House during his Continuance in Office.

Section 7. (The Legislative Process)

Clause 1: All Bills for raising Revenue shall originate in the House of Representatives; but the Senate may propose or concur with amendments as on other Bills.

Clause 2: Every Bill which shall have passed the House of Representatives and the Senate, shall, before it become a law, be presented to the President of the United States: If he approve he shall sign it, but if not he shall return it, with his Objections to that House in which it shall have originated, who shall enter the Objections at large on their Journal, and proceed to reconsider it. If after such Reconsideration two thirds of that House shall agree to pass the Bill, it shall be sent, together with the Objections, to the other House, by which it shall likewise be reconsidered, and if approved by two thirds of that House, it shall become a Law. But in all such Cases the Votes of both Houses shall be determined by Yeas and Nays, and the Names of the Persons voting for and against the Bill shall be entered on the Journal of each House respectively. If any Bill shall not be returned by the President within ten Days (Sundays excepted) after it shall have been presented to him, the Same shall be a Law, in like Manner as if he had signed it, unless the Congress by their Adjournment prevent its Return, in which Case it shall not be a Law.

Clause 3: Every Order, Resolution, or Vote to which the Concurrence of the Senate and House of Representatives may be necessary (except on a question of Adjournment) shall be presented to the President of the United States; and before the Same shall take Effect, shall be approved by him, or being disapproved by him, shall be repassed by two thirds of the Senate and House of Representatives, according to the Rules and Limitations prescribed in the Case of a Bill.

Section 8. (The Lawmaking Authority of Congress)

Clause 1: The Congress shall have Power To lay and collect Taxes, Duties, Imposts and Excises, to pay the Debts and provide for the common Defence and general Welfare of the United States; but all Duties, Imposts and Excises shall be uniform throughout the United States;

Clause 2: To borrow Money on the credit of the United States;

> The president must approve or veto everything that Congress approves, except its vote to adjourn or any resolutions that do not have the force of law.

> This section specifies the constitutionally established congressional powers. These powers are limited to those listed and any other powers that Congress believes are "necessary and proper" for Congress to fulfill its listed powers. Congress has used the "necessary and proper" clause (Clause 18) to justify laws that expand its powers that are listed in Article I of the Constitution. Laws that appear to go beyond the listed powers can be challenged in the courts, with the Supreme Court ultimately deciding their constitutionality.

> The power to raise money and to authorize spending it for common defense and the general welfare is one of the most essential powers of Congress. The Sixteenth Amendment (1913) authorizes a national income tax, which was not previously possible given the "uniformity" requirement in Clause 1.

> Today, after years of borrowing money to pay current bills, the national government has a debt of over $19 trillion.

POLITICAL INQUIRY: *Some economists, politicians, and citizens fear that the national debt harms the United States by limiting the amount of money available to invest in growing the economy. Moreover, citizens worry that their children and grandchildren, saddled with the obligation of paying back this debt, may face limited government services. Therefore, there have been repeated calls for a balanced budget amendment, which would force Congress to spend no more than the money it raises in each budget year.*

1. *What arguments might the members of Congress, elected officials who want to be reelected, put forth against ratification of a balanced budget amendment?*

2. *What national situations might require spending more money than is raised in a budget year?*

Clause 3: To regulate Commerce with foreign Nations, and among the several States, and with the Indian Tribes;

Clause 4: To establish an uniform Rule of Naturalization, and uniform Laws on the subject of Bankruptcies throughout the United States;

Clause 5: To coin Money, regulate the Value thereof, and of foreign Coin, and fix the Standard of Weights and Measures;

Clause 6: To provide for the Punishment of counterfeiting the Securities and current Coin of the United States;

Clause 7: To establish Post Offices and post Roads;

Clause 8: To promote the Progress of Science and useful Arts, by securing for limited Times to Authors and Inventors the exclusive Right to their respective Writings and Discoveries;

Clause 9: To constitute Tribunals inferior to the supreme Court;

Clause 10: To define and punish Piracies and Felonies committed on the high Seas, and Offences against the Law of Nations;

> With the Supreme Court's support, Congress has interpreted Clause 3 in a way that has allowed it to expand its involvement in the economy and the daily lives of U.S. citizens. However, state governments have frequently challenged Congress's expansion of power by way of the commerce clause when they believe that Congress is infringing on their constitutional authority.

> Congress has the authority to establish the process by which foreigners become citizens (Clause 4). Recently, national legislation has made it more difficult for individuals to file for bankruptcy.

> Congressional authority to make and regulate money as well as to standardize weights and measures is essential to the regulation of commerce (Clause 5).

> This is the constitutional basis for copyright laws, which protect people's rights to their intellectual products.

> Congress exercised its authority under Clause 9 to create the federal court system, other than the Supreme Court, which was established under Article III of the Constitution.

> Every nation in the world possesses the authority to establish its own laws regarding crimes outside its borders and violations of international law (Clause 10).

> Clauses 11 through 15 collectively delegate to Congress the authority to raise and support military troops, to enact rules to regulate the troops, to call the troops to action, and to declare war. However, the president as commander in chief (Article II) has the authority to wage war. Presidents have committed armed troops without a declaration of war, leading to disputes over congressional and presidential war powers. Clause 11 also provides Congress with the authority to hire an individual for the purpose of retaliating against another nation for some harm it has caused the United States—that is, to provide a letter of Marque, an outdated practice.

> Clauses 15 and 16 guarantee the states the right to maintain and train a militia (today's National Guard), but state control of the militia is subordinate to national control when the national government needs the support of these militias to ensure that laws are executed, to suppress domestic uprisings, and to repel invasion.

> Congress has the authority to govern Washington, D.C., which is the seat of the national government. Today, citizens living there elect local officials to govern the city with congressional oversight. The national government also governs federal lands throughout the states that are used for federal purposes, such as military installations.

> Clause 18 grants Congress authority to make all laws it deems necessary and proper to fulfill its responsibilities under the Constitution, including those listed in Section 8. This clause also authorizes Congress to pass laws it deems necessary to ensure that the other two branches are able to fulfill their responsibilities. Congress has used this clause to expand its powers.

> Article I, Section 9 limits Congress's lawmaking authority, thereby protecting rights of the people, and mandates that Congress be accountable to the people in how it spends the public's money.

> Without using the word "slave," Clause 1 barred Congress from passing laws to prohibit the slave trade until 1808 at the earliest. The Thirteenth Amendment (1865) made slavery illegal.

Clause 11: To declare War, grant Letters of Marque and Reprisal, and make Rules concerning Captures on Land and Water;

Clause 12: To raise and support Armies, but no Appropriation of Money to that Use shall be for a longer Term than two Years;

Clause 13: To provide and maintain a Navy;

Clause 14: To make Rules for the Government and Regulation of the land and naval Forces;

Clause 15: To provide for calling forth the Militia to execute the Laws of the Union, suppress Insurrections and repel Invasions;

Clause 16: To provide for organizing, arming, and disciplining, the Militia, and for governing such Part of them as may be employed in the Service of the United States, reserving to the States respectively, the Appointment of the Officers, and the Authority of training the Militia according to the discipline prescribed by Congress;

Clause 17: To exercise exclusive Legislation in all Cases whatsoever, over such District (not exceeding ten Miles square) as may, by Cession of Particular States, and the Acceptance of Congress, become the Seat of the Government of the United States, and to exercise like Authority over all Places purchased by the Consent of the Legislature of the State in which the Same shall be, for the Erection of Forts, Magazines, Arsenals, dock-Yards and other needful Buildings;—And

POLITICAL INQUIRY: *Article IV of the Constitution delegates to Congress the authority to admit new states to the union. The citizens of Washington, D.C., the seat of national government over which Congress has legislative power, have petitioned Congress to become a state.*

1. *What would be the benefits to its residents if Washington, D.C., became a state? What would be the benefits for the rest of the nation?*

2. *What problems might arise for the residents of Washington, D.C., if it were to become a state? What problems might arise for the rest of the nation?*

Clause 18: To make all Laws which shall be necessary and proper for carrying into Execution the foregoing Powers and all other Powers vested by this Constitution in the Government of the United States, or in any Department or Officer thereof.

Section 9. (Prohibitions on Congress)

Clause 1: The Migration or Importation of such Persons as any of the States now existing shall think proper to admit, shall not be prohibited by the Congress prior to the Year one thousand eight hundred and eight, but a Tax or duty may be imposed on such Importation, not exceeding ten dollars for each Person.

Clause 2: The Privilege of the Writ of Habeas Corpus shall not be suspended, unless when in Cases of Rebellion or Invasion the public Safety may require it.

Clause 3: No Bill of Attainder or ex post facto Law shall be passed.

Clause 4: No Capitation, or other direct, Tax shall be laid, unless in Proportion to the Census of Enumeration herein before directed to be taken.

Clause 5: No Tax or Duty shall be laid on Articles exported from any State.

Clause 6: No Preference shall be given by any Regulation of Commerce or Revenue to the Ports of one State over those of another: nor shall Vessels bound to, or from, one State, be obliged to enter, clear or pay Duties in another.

Clause 7: No Money shall be drawn from the Treasury, but in Consequence of Appropriations made by Law; and a regular Statement and Account of the Receipts and Expenditures of all public Money shall be published from time to time.

POLITICAL INQUIRY: *Today there exists a secret budget (black budget) for some military operations, intelligence operations, and counter-terrorism operations. The black budget is estimated to be more than $52 billion per year. Some argue that the existence of the black budget violates the Constitution's requirement for "a regular Statement and Account of the Receipts and Expenditures of all public Money."*

1. *What justification does the federal government use for the black budget?*

2. *Are you comfortable with the existence of a black budget? Explain your answer.*

Clause 8: No Title of Nobility shall be granted by the United States: And no Person holding any Office of Profit or Trust under them, shall, without the Consent of the Congress, accept of any present, Emolument, Office, or Title, of any kind whatever, from any King, Prince or foreign State.

POLITICAL INQUIRY: *Several lawsuits were filed in 2017 that accused President Trump of violating the constitutional clause that restricts government officials from receiving gifts or emoluments (money payments for work done) from any King, Prince or foreign government. The lawsuits claimed that Trump was receiving emoluments from foreign governments through his continued ownership of profit-making businesses, including hotels.*

1. *What do you think the framers were trying to prevent by prohibiting government officials from accepting gifts and emoluments from foreign governments?*

2. *Do you think President Trump has violated the Constitution by the fact that his hotels accept payments from foreign officials who use the services of the hotels he owns? Why or why not?*

> Clauses 2 and 3 guarantee protections to those accused of crimes. Clause 2 establishes the right of imprisoned persons to challenge their imprisonment in court (through a writ of habeas corpus). It notes that Congress can deny the right to a writ of habeas corpus during times of a rebellion or invasion if public safety is at risk.

> Clause 3 prohibits Congress from passing laws that declare a person or a group of people guilty of an offense (bills of attainder). Only courts have the authority to determine guilt. Congress is also prohibited from passing laws that punish a person tomorrow for an action he or she took that was legal today (ex post facto laws).

> Clause 4 prohibits Congress from directly taxing individual people, such as imposing an income tax. The Sixteenth Amendment (1913) authorized congressional enactment of a direct income tax on individual people.

> Congress is prohibited from taxing goods that are exported from any state, either those sent to foreign lands or to other states (Clause 5).

> Congress cannot favor any state over another in its regulation of trade (Clause 6).

> The national government can spend money only as authorized by Congress through enacted laws (no more than authorized and only for the purpose authorized) and must present a public accounting of revenues and expenditures.

> Congress cannot grant individuals special rights, privileges, or a position in government based on their heredity (birth into a family designated as nobility), which is how kings, queens, and other officials were granted their positions in the British monarchy. In addition, federal officials cannot accept gifts from foreign nations except those Congress allows (which today are gifts of minimal value).

> Clause 1 specifically prohibits states from engaging in several activities that the Constitution delegates to the national government, including engaging in foreign affairs and creating currency. It also extends prohibitions on the states that are imposed on Congress in Section 9 of this Article, including prohibitions on enacting a law that declares a person or group guilty of an offense (bill of attainder) or a law that punishes a person tomorrow for an action that was legal when the person took the action (ex post facto law).

> Clause 2 prevents states from interfering in foreign trade without congressional approval.

> States cannot, without congressional approval, levy import taxes, build an army, or keep war ships during times of peace; neither can they enter into interstate compacts with other states or agreements with other countries.

> Article II outlines the authority of the president and the vice president and the process of their selection.

> The Constitution delegates to the president the authority to administer the executive branch of the national government. The term of office for the president and his vice president is four years. No term limit was specified; until President Franklin D. Roosevelt (1933–1945), there was a tradition of a two-term limit. President Roosevelt served four terms.

> The Electoral College system was established as a compromise between those who wanted citizens to elect the president directly and others who wanted Congress to elect the president. Each state government has the authority to determine how their state's electors will be selected.

> Electors, who are selected through processes established by the legislatures of each state, have the authority to select the president and the vice president. Citizens' votes determine who their state's electors will be. Electors are individuals selected by officials of the state's political parties to participate in the Electoral College if the party wins the presidential vote in the state. Before passage of the Twelfth Amendment (1804), each elector had two votes. The candidate receiving the majority of votes won the presidency, and the candidate with the second highest number of votes won the vice presidency.

Section 10. (Prohibitions on the States)

Clause 1: No State shall enter into any Treaty, Alliance, or Confederation; grant Letters of Marque and Reprisal; coin Money; emit Bills of Credit; make any Thing but gold and silver Coin a Tender in Payment of Debts; pass any Bill of Attainder, ex post facto Law, or Law impairing the Obligation of Contracts, or grant any Title of Nobility.

Clause 2: No State shall, without the Consent of the Congress, lay any Imposts or Duties on Imports or Exports, except what may be absolutely necessary for executing its inspection Laws: and the net Produce of all Duties and Imposts, laid by any State on Imports or Exports, shall be for the Use of the Treasury of the United States; and all such Laws shall be subject to the Revision and Control of the Congress.

Clause 3: No State shall, without the Consent of Congress, lay any Duty of Tonnage, keep Troops, or Ships of War in time of Peace, enter into any Agreement or Compact with another State, or with a foreign Power, or engage in War, unless actually invaded, or in such imminent Danger as will not admit of delay.

ARTICLE II. (Executive Branch)

Section 1. (Executive Powers of the President)

Clause 1: The executive Power shall be vested in a President of the United States of America. He shall hold his Office during the Term of four Years, and, together with the Vice President, chosen for the same Term, be elected, as follows:

Clause 2: Each State shall appoint, in such Manner as the Legislature thereof may direct, a Number of Electors, equal to the whole Number of Senators and Representatives to which the State may be entitled in the Congress: but no Senator or Representative, or Person holding an Office of Trust or Profit under the United States, shall be appointed an Elector.

Clause 3: The Electors shall meet in their respective States, and vote by Ballot for two Persons, of whom one at least shall not be an Inhabitant of the same State with themselves. And they shall make a List of all the Persons voted for, and of the Number of Votes for each; which List they shall sign and certify, and transmit sealed to the Seat of the Government of the United States, directed to the President of the Senate. The President of the Senate shall, in the Presence of the Senate and House of Representatives, open all the Certificates, and the Votes shall then be counted. The Person having the greatest Number of Votes shall be the President, if such Number be a Majority of the whole Number of Electors appointed; and if there be more than one who have such Majority, and have an equal Number of Votes, then the House of Representatives shall immediately chuse by Ballot one of them for President; and if no Person have a Majority, then from the five highest on the List the said House shall in like Manner chuse the President. But in chusing the President, the Votes shall be taken by States, the Representatives from each State having one Vote; a quorum for this Purpose shall consist of a Member or Members from two thirds of the States, and a Majority of all the States shall be necessary to a Choice. In every Case, after the Choice of the President, the Person having the greatest Number of Votes of the Electors shall be the Vice President. But if there should remain two or more who have equal Votes, the Senate shall chuse from them by Ballot the Vice President.

POLITICAL INQUIRY: *The Electoral College system is criticized for many reasons. Some critics argue that deciding the presidential election by any vote other than that of the citizens is undemocratic and, therefore, the Electoral College system should be eliminated and replaced by direct popular election of the president and vice president.*

1. *What might be the benefits of eliminating the Electoral College?*

2. *What might be the potential harm to the nation of eliminating the Electoral College?*

Clause 4: The Congress may determine the Time of chusing the Electors, and the Day on which they shall give their Votes; which Day shall be the same throughout the United States.

Clause 5: No Person except a natural born Citizen, or a Citizen of the United States, at the time of the Adoption of this Constitution, shall be eligible to the Office of President; neither shall any person be eligible to that Office who shall not have attained to the Age of thirty five Years, and been fourteen Years a Resident within the United States.

Clause 6: In Case of the Removal of the President from Office, or of his Death, Resignation, or Inability to discharge the Powers and Duties of the said Office, the Same shall devolve on the Vice President, and the Congress may by Law provide for the Case of Removal, Death, Resignation or Inability, both of the President and Vice President, declaring what Officer shall then act as President, and such Officer shall act accordingly, until the Disability be removed, or a President shall be elected.

> Today, by law, national elections are held on the Tuesday following the first Monday in November, in even-numbered years. During presidential election years, the electors gather in their state capitals on the Monday after the second Wednesday in December to vote for the president and the vice president. When Congress convenes in January after the presidential election, its members count the electoral ballots and formally announce the newly elected president and vice president.

> The president (and the vice president) must be at least 35 years old and must have lived within the United States for at least 14 years. Unlike the citizenship qualification for members of the House and the Senate, the president and the vice president must be natural-born citizens; they cannot be immigrants who have become citizens after arriving in the United States.

> Clause 6 states that the powers and duties of the presidency are transferred to the vice president when the president is no longer able to fulfill them. It also states that Congress can pass legislation to indicate who shall act as president if both the president and the vice president are unable to fulfill the president's powers and duties. The "acting" president would serve until the disability is removed or a new president is elected. The Twenty-Fifth Amendment (1967) clarifies when the vice president acts as president temporarily—such as when the president undergoes surgery—and when the vice president actually becomes president.

POLITICAL INQUIRY: *The vice president's constitutional responsibilities are to act as president (temporarily or to complete the term, depending on the situation) and to be president of the Senate (see Article 1, Section 3). However, since Vice President Walter Mondale (1977–1981), vice presidents have been important, active members of presidential administrations. Yet, citizens do not get to vote for the vice president. Presidential candidates choose the person who will be their running mate but citizens have one vote with which they select a president. They do not have a second vote to select a vice president.*

1. *What responsibilities do you think are appropriate for the vice president?*

2. *Should the Constitution be amended to include an enumeration of vice-presidential responsibilities and constraints? Why or why not?*

Clause 7: The President shall, at stated Times, receive for his Services, a Compensation, which shall neither be increased nor diminished during the Period for which he shall have been elected, and he shall not receive within that Period any other Emolument from the United States, or any of them.

> Currently the president's salary is $400,000 per year plus numerous benefits, including a nontaxable expense account.

> The president is the commander of the military and of the National Guard (militia of the several states) when it is called to service by the president. When they are not called to service by the president, the state divisions of the National Guard are commanded by their governors. The president is authorized to establish the cabinet, the presidential advisory body comprising the top officials (secretaries) of each department of the executive branch. As the chief executive officer, the president can exercise a check on the judicial branch by decreasing or eliminating sentences and even pardoning (eliminating guilty verdicts of) federal prisoners.

> The Constitution provides a check on the president's authority to negotiate treaties and appoint foreign ambassadors, top officials in the executive branch, and Supreme Court justices by requiring that treaties be ratified or appointments confirmed by the Senate. Congress can create additional executive branch positions and federal courts and can decree how these legislatively created positions will be filled.

> In 2014, the Supreme Court clarified when the president can make "recess appointments"—that is, appointment to fill vacancies that occur when the Senate is not in session and is therefore not available to confirm presidential appointees. In *National Labor Relations Board v. Noel Canning,* the Court found that the president can make recess appointments only during Senate recesses that last no fewer than 10 days. Such recess appointees serve through the end of the congressional session.

> As chief executive officer of the nation, the president is required to ensure that laws are properly implemented by overseeing the executive branch agencies to be sure they are doing the work of government as established in law. The president is also required from time to time to give an assessment of the status of the nation to Congress and to make recommendations for the good of the country. This has evolved into the annual televised State of the Union Address, which is followed within days by the presentation of the president's budget proposal to Congress. The president can also call special sessions of Congress.

> Presidents, vice presidents, and other federal officials can be removed from office if the members of the House of Representatives formally accuse them of treason (giving assistance to the nation's enemies), bribery, or other vaguely defined abuses of power ("high Crimes and Misdemeanors") and two-thirds of the Senate members find them guilty of these charges.

> Article III presents the organization and authority of the U.S. Supreme Court and delegates to Congress the authority to create other courts as its members deem necessary.

> To ensure that judges make neutral and objective decisions, and are protected from political influences, federal judges serve until they retire, die, or are impeached by the House and convicted by the Senate. In addition, Congress cannot decrease a judge's pay.

Clause 8: Before he enter on the Execution of his Office, he shall take the following Oath or Affirmation:—"I do solemnly swear (or affirm) that I will faithfully execute the Office of President of the United States, and will to the best of my Ability, preserve, protect and defend the Constitution of the United States."

Section 2. (Powers of the President)

Clause 1: The President shall be Commander in Chief of the Army and Navy of the United States, and of the Militia of the several States, when called into the actual Service of the United States; he may require the Opinion, in writing, of the principal Officer in each of the executive Departments, upon any Subject relating to the Duties of their respective Offices, and he shall have Power to Grant Reprieves and Pardons for Offences against the United States, except in Cases of Impeachment.

Clause 2: He shall have Power, by and with the Advice and Consent of the Senate, to make Treaties, provided two thirds of the Senators present concur; and he shall nominate, and by and with the Advice and Consent of the Senate, shall appoint Ambassadors, other public Ministers and Consuls, Judges of the supreme Court, and all other Officers of the United States, whose Appointments are not herein otherwise provided for, and which shall be established by Law: but the Congress may by Law vest the Appointment of such inferior Officers, as they think proper, in the President alone, in the Courts of Law, or in the Heads of Departments.

Clause 3: The President shall have Power to fill up all Vacancies that may happen during the Recess of the Senate, by granting Commissions which shall expire at the End of their next Session.

Section 3. (Responsibilities of the President)

He shall from time to time give to the Congress Information on the State of the Union, and recommend to their Consideration such Measures as he shall judge necessary and expedient; he may, on extraordinary Occasions, convene both Houses, or either of them, and in Case of Disagreement between them, with Respect to the Time of Adjournment, he may adjourn them to such Time as he shall think proper; he shall receive Ambassadors and other public Ministers; he shall take Care that the Laws be faithfully executed, and shall Commission all the Officers of the United States.

Section 4. (Impeachment)

The President, Vice President and all Civil Officers of the United States, shall be removed from Office on Impeachment for and Conviction of, Treason, Bribery, or other high Crimes and Misdemeanors.

ARTICLE III. (Judicial Branch)

Section 1. (Federal Courts and Rights of Judges)

The judicial Power of the United States, shall be vested in one supreme Court, and in such inferior Courts as the Congress may from time to time ordain and establish. The Judges, both of the supreme and inferior Courts, shall hold their Offices during good Behaviour, and shall, at stated Times, receive for their Services, a Compensation, which shall not be diminished during their Continuance in Office.

Section 2. (Jurisdiction of Federal Courts)

Clause 1: The judicial Power shall extend to all Cases, in Law and Equity, arising under this Constitution, the Laws of the United States, and Treaties made, or which shall be made, under their Authority;—to all Cases affecting Ambassadors, other public ministers and Consuls;—to all Cases of admiralty and maritime Jurisdiction;—to Controversies to which the United States shall be a Party;—to Controversies between two or more States;—between a State and Citizens of another State;—between Citizens of different States;—between Citizens of the same State claiming Lands under Grants of different States, and between a State, or the Citizens thereof, and foreign States, Citizens or Subjects.

> Federal courts have the authority to hear all lawsuits pertaining to national laws, the Constitution of the United States, and treaties. They also have jurisdiction over cases involving citizens of different states and citizens of foreign nations. Note that the power of judicial review—that is, the power to declare acts of government officials or bodies unconstitutional—is not articulated in the Constitution.

Clause 2: In all Cases affecting Ambassadors, other public Ministers and Consuls, and those in which a State shall be Party, the supreme Court shall have original Jurisdiction. In all the other Cases before mentioned, the supreme Court shall have appellate Jurisdiction, both as to Law and Fact, with such Exceptions, and under such Regulations as the Congress shall make.

> The Supreme Court hears cases involving foreign diplomats and cases in which states are a party. Today, such cases are rare. For the most part, the Supreme Court hears cases on appeal from lower federal courts.

Clause 3: The Trial of all Crimes, except in Cases of Impeachment, shall be by Jury; and such Trial shall be held in the State where the said Crimes shall have been committed; but when not committed within any State, the Trial shall be at such Place or Places as the Congress may by Law have directed.

> Defendants accused of federal crimes have the right to a jury trial in a federal court located in the state in which the crime was committed.

Section 3. (Treason)

Clause 1: Treason against the United States, shall consist only in levying War against them, or in adhering to their Enemies, giving them Aid and Comfort. No Person shall be convicted of Treason unless on the Testimony of two Witnesses to the same overt Act, or on Confession in open Court.

> This clause defines treason as making war against the United States or helping its enemies. At least two witnesses to the crime are required for a conviction.

Clause 2: The Congress shall have Power to declare the Punishment of Treason, but no Attainder of Treason shall work Corruption of Blood, or Forfeiture except during the Life of the Person attainted.

> This clause prevents Congress from redefining treason. Those found guilty of treason can be punished, but their family members cannot be (no "Corruption of Blood").

ARTICLE IV. (State-to-State Relations)

Section 1. (Full Faith and Credit of Legal Proceedings and Decisions)

Full Faith and Credit shall be given in each State to the public Acts, Records, and judicial Proceedings of every other State. And the Congress may by general Laws prescribe the Manner in which such Acts, Records and Proceedings shall be proved, and the Effect thereof.

> Article IV establishes the obligations states have to each other and to the citizens of other states.

> States must respect one another's legal judgments and records, and a contract agreed to in one state is binding in the other states.

> No matter what state they find themselves in, all U.S. citizens are entitled to the same privileges and rights as the citizens of that state.

> If requested by a governor of another state, a state is obligated to return an accused felon to the state from which he or she fled.

> The Thirteenth Amendment (1865) eliminated a state's obligation to return slaves fleeing from their enslavement in another state.

> Congress can admit new states to the union, but it cannot alter established state borders without the approval of the states that would be affected by the change.

> The federal government has authority to administer all federal lands, wherever they are located, including national parks and historic sites as well as military installations. Today, the federal government owns 640 million acres, which is about 28% of all the land in the country.

> The national government must ensure that every state has a representative democracy, protect each state from foreign invasion, and assist states in addressing mass breaches of domestic tranquility. Under this section, Congress has authorized the president to send in federal troops to protect public safety. During the civil rights movement, for example, federal troops ensured the safety of black students attending newly desegregated high schools and colleges.

> Article V details the process by which the Constitution can be amended.

> Amendments can be proposed either by Congress or by a special convention called at the request of the states. States have the authority to ratify amendments to the Constitution; three-fourths of the state legislatures must ratify an amendment for it to become part of the Constitution. Every year dozens of constitutional amendments are proposed in Congress, yet only 27 have been ratified since 1789.

Section 2. (Privileges and Immunities of Citizens)

Clause 1: The Citizens of each State shall be entitled to all Privileges and Immunities of Citizens in the several States.

Clause 2: A Person charged in any State with Treason, Felony, or other Crime, who shall flee from Justice, and be found in another State, shall on Demand of the executive Authority of the State from which he fled, be delivered up, to be removed to the State having Jurisdiction of the Crime.

Clause 3: No Person held to Service or Labour in one State, under the Laws thereof, escaping into another, shall, in Consequence of any Law or Regulation therein, be discharged from such Service or Labour, but shall be delivered up on Claim of the Party to whom such Service or Labour may be due.

Section 3. (Admission of New States)

Clause 1: New States may be admitted by the Congress into this Union; but no new State shall be formed or erected within the Jurisdiction of any other State; nor any State be formed by the Junction of two or more States, or Parts of States, without the Consent of the Legislatures of the States concerned as well as of the Congress.

Clause 2: The Congress shall have Power to dispose of and make all needful Rules and Regulations respecting the Territory or other Property belonging to the United States; and nothing in this Constitution shall be so construed as to Prejudice any Claims of the United States, or of any particular State.

Section 4. (National Government Obligations to the States)

The United States shall guarantee to every State in this Union a Republican Form of Government, and shall protect each of them against Invasion; and on Application of the Legislature, or of the Executive (when the Legislature cannot be convened) against domestic Violence.

ARTICLE V. (Formal Constitutional Amendment Process)

The Congress, whenever two thirds of both Houses shall deem it necessary, shall propose Amendments to this Constitution, or, on the Application of the Legislatures of two thirds of the several States, shall call a Convention for proposing Amendments, which, in either Case, shall be valid to all Intents and Purposes, as Part of this Constitution, when ratified by the Legislatures of three fourths of the several States, or by Conventions in three fourths thereof, as the one or the other Mode of Ratification may be proposed by the Congress; Provided that no Amendment which may be made prior to the Year One thousand eight hundred and eight shall in any Manner affect the first and fourth Clauses in the Ninth Section of the first Article; and that no State, without its Consent, shall be deprived of its equal Suffrage in the Senate.

POLITICAL INQUIRY: *The framers of the Constitution indicated that they believed each generation should make the Constitution its own. Although more than 10,000 amendments have been introduced in Congress, only 33 earned the votes required to be a proposal sent to the* states, with only 27 of those ratified by the states. In addition, Congress has never called for a constitutional convention even though each of the 50 states has applied for a constitutional convention at least once since 1789.

1. What is a potential benefit of calling a constitutional convention at regular intervals, as is done in several states?

2. What is a potential problem of calling a constitutional convention at regular intervals?

ARTICLE VI. (Supremacy of the Constitution)

Clause 1: All Debts contracted and Engagements entered into, before the Adoption of this Constitution, shall be as valid against the United States under this Constitution, as under the Confederation.

Clause 2: This Constitution, and the Laws of the United States which shall be made in Pursuance thereof; and all Treaties made, or which shall be made, under the Authority of the United States, shall be the supreme Law of the Land; and the Judges in every State shall be bound thereby, any Thing in the Constitution or Laws of any state to the Contrary notwithstanding.

Clause 3: The Senators and Representatives before mentioned, and the Members of the several State Legislatures, and all executive and judicial Officers, both of the United States and of the several States, shall be bound by Oath or Affirmation, to support this Constitution; but no religious Test shall ever be required as a Qualification to any Office or public Trust under the United States.

ARTICLE VII. (Constitutional Ratification Process)

Clause 1: The Ratification of the Conventions of nine States, shall be sufficient for the Establishment of this Constitution between the States so ratifying the same.

> Article VI decrees that the Constitution is the supreme law of the land.

> This provision states that the new federal government created by the Constitution was responsible for the financial obligations of the national government created by the Articles of Confederation.

> The Constitution, and all laws made to fulfill its mission that are in compliance with it, are the supreme law of the land; no one is above the supreme law of the land.

> All national and state officials must take an oath promising to uphold the Constitution. This article also prohibits the government from requiring officeholders to submit to a religious test or swear a religious oath, hence supporting a separation of government and religion.

> Article VII outlines the process by which the Constitution will be ratified.

POLITICAL INQUIRY: The framers of the Constitution developed a ratification process that violated the process of constitutional amendment established in the Articles of Confederation. Not only did their process allow for the new constitution to replace the constitution in effect since 1781 with nine votes of approval instead of a unanimous vote of approval, but they also suggested that special state conventions, not the state legislatures, vote to ratify the new constitution.

1. Do you think ratification of the Constitution would have occurred in just two years if ratification required approval by the existing state legislatures instead of special conventions? Explain your answer.

2. With the fact that no delegates from Rhode Island signed the proposed constitution, do you think ratification would have occurred in just two years (or at all) if the vote had to be unanimous (as called for in the Articles of Confederation)? Explain your answer.

Clause 2: Done in Convention by the Unanimous Consent of the States present the Seventeenth Day of September in the Year of our Lord one thousand seven hundred and Eighty seven and of the Independence of the United States of America the Twelfth. In witness whereof We have hereunto subscribed our Names,

G. Washington—Presid't. and deputy from Virginia

Delaware	George Read
	Gunning Bedford, Jr.
	John Dickinson
	Richard Bassett
	Jacob Broom
Maryland	James McHenry
	Daniel of St. Thomas Jenifer
	Daniel Carroll
Virginia	John Blair
	James Madison, Jr.
North Carolina	William Blount
	Richard Dobbs Spaight
	Hugh Williamson
South Carolina	John Rutledge
	Charles Cotesworth Pinckney
	Charles Pinckney
	Pierce Butler
Georgia	William Few
	Abraham Baldwin
New Hampshire	John Langdon
	Nicholas Gilman
Massachusetts	Nathaniel Gorham
	Rufus King
Connecticut	William Samuel Johnson
	Roger Sherman
New York	Alexander Hamilton
New Jersey	William Livingston
	David Brearley
	William Paterson
	Jonathan Dayton
Pennsylvania	Benjamin Franklin
	Thomas Mifflin
	Robert Morris
	George Clymer
	Thomas FitzSimons
	Jared Ingersoll
	James Wilson
	Gouverneur Morris

Amendments to the Constitution of the United States of America

Amendment I (1791)

Congress shall make no law respecting an establishment of religion, or prohibiting the free exercise thereof; or abridging the freedom of speech, or of the press; or the right of the people peaceably to assemble, and to petition the Government for a redress of grievances.

> Government cannot make laws that limit freedom of expression, which includes freedom of religion, speech, and the press, as well as the freedom to assemble and to petition the government to address grievances. None of these individual freedoms is absolute, however; courts balance the protection of individual freedoms (as provided for in this Constitution) with the protection of public safety, including national security.

Amendment II (1791)

A well regulated Militia, being necessary to the security of a free State, the right of the people to keep and bear Arms, shall not be infringed.

> Today, states and the federal government balance the right of the people to own guns with the need to protect the public.

POLITICAL INQUIRY: *Public debates and debates among government officials over Second Amendment rights and gun control are sparked every time people are killed in a mass shooting in the United States.*

1. *Is the right to own a gun absolute, or does the right have to be balanced with public safety and general welfare, as are the other individual rights established in the Constitution? Explain your answer.*

2. *Does your state allow colleges to prohibit weapons on their campuses?*

Amendment III (1791)

No Soldier shall, in time of peace be quartered in any house, without the consent of the Owner, nor in time of war, but in a manner to be prescribed by law.

> Military troops cannot take control of private homes during peacetime.

Amendment IV (1791)

The right of the people to be secure in their persons, houses, papers, and effects, against unreasonable searches and seizures, shall not be violated, and no Warrants shall issue, but upon probable cause, supported by Oath or affirmation, and particularly describing the place to be searched, and the persons or things to be seized.

> Government officials must obtain approval before they search or seize a person's property. The approval must come either from the person whose private property they are searching or seizing or from a judge who determines that the government is justified in taking this action to protect public safety and who therefore signs a search warrant.

POLITICAL INQUIRY: *Since the terrorist attacks on September 11, 2001, the national government has tried to balance the right of people to be secure in their person and property with public safety and national security.*

1. *What reasons have the president and members of Congress offered in defense of allowing intelligence agencies to bypass the requirement that they obtain judicial permission to conduct searches or seizures of phone records?*

2. *How valid are those reasons? In your opinion, can they be reconciled with constitutional protections?*

> The Fifth Amendment provides much more than the familiar protection against self-incrimination that we hear people who are testifying before Congress and the courts claim by "taking the Fifth." For example, before the government can punish a person for a crime (take away a person's life, liberty, or pursuit of happiness), it must follow certain procedures specified in law; it must follow due process of the law. The federal government guarantees those accused of federal crimes a grand jury hearing in which the government presents its evidence to a selected group of citizens who determine whether there is sufficient evidence to go to trial. If a defendant is found not guilty of a specific criminal offense, he or she cannot be brought to trial again by the same government for the same offense. If the government determines it needs private property for a public use, the owner is compelled to sell the land, and the government must pay a fair price based on the market value of the property.

> The Sixth Amendment outlines additional procedures that the government must follow before taking away a person's life, liberty, or pursuit of happiness. People accused of crimes have the right to know what they are accused of doing, to hear from witnesses against them, and to defend themselves in a trial that is open to the public within a reasonable amount of time after the accusations are made. An indigent (very poor) person is guaranteed a government-provided lawyer in serious criminal cases. It is assumed all others can afford to hire a lawyer.

> Either party (the complainant or the person accused of causing harm or violating a contract) in a federal civil lawsuit involving more than $20 can demand a jury trial.

> The Eighth Amendment protects those accused of crimes as well as those found guilty from overly punitive decisions. Bail, a payment to the government that can be required to avoid incarceration before and during trial, cannot be set at an excessively high amount, unless the judge determines that freedom for the accused would jeopardize public safety or that he or she might flee. The punishment imposed on those convicted of crimes is expected to "fit" the crime: It is to be reasonable given the severity of the crime. Punishment cannot be excessive or cruel.

> The Ninth Amendment acknowledges that there are additional rights, not listed in the preceding eight amendments, that the government cannot deny to citizens. The Supreme Court has interpreted the First, Fourth, Fifth, and Ninth Amendments collectively to provide individuals with a right to privacy.

> The Tenth Amendment acknowledges that state governments retain all authority they had before ratification of the Constitution that has not been delegated to the national government by the Constitution. This amendment was demanded by the Anti-Federalists, who opposed ratification of this Constitution. The Anti-Federalists feared that the national government would infringe on people's freedoms and on the authority of the state governments. The vagueness of the rights retained by the states continues to cause tensions and disputes between the state governments and the national government.

Amendment V (1791)

No person shall be held to answer for a capital, or otherwise infamous crime, unless on a presentment or indictment of a Grand Jury, except in cases arising in the land or naval forces, or in the Militia, when in actual service in time of War or public danger; nor shall any person be subject for the same offence to be twice put in jeopardy of life or limb; nor shall be compelled in any criminal case to be a witness against himself, nor be deprived of life, liberty, or property, without due process of law; nor shall private property be taken for public use, without just compensation.

Amendment VI (1791)

In all criminal prosecutions, the accused shall enjoy the right to a speedy and public trial, by an impartial jury of the State and district wherein the crime shall have been committed, which district shall have been previously ascertained by law, and to be informed of the nature and cause of the accusation; to be confronted with the witnesses against him; to have compulsory process for obtaining witnesses in his favor, and to have the Assistance of Counsel for his defence.

Amendment VII (1791)

In Suits at common law, where the value in controversy shall exceed twenty dollars, the right of trial by jury shall be preserved, and no fact tried by a jury, shall be otherwise re-examined in any Court of the United States, than according to the rules of the common law.

Amendment VIII (1791)

Excessive bail shall not be required, nor excessive fines imposed, nor cruel and unusual punishments inflicted.

Amendment IX (1791)

The enumeration in the Constitution, of certain rights, shall not be construed to deny or disparage others retained by the people.

POLITICAL INQUIRY: *Thomas Jefferson and Alexander Hamilton debated the need for a bill of rights. Hamilton argued that a list of rights would be incomplete and therefore, people might argue that because a given right was not listed, it did not exist.*

1. *How well do you think the Ninth Amendment addresses Hamilton's argument against a bill of rights? Explain.*

2. *What rights has the Supreme Court identified that are not enumerated in the Constitution?*

Amendment X (1791)

The powers not delegated to the United States by the Constitution, nor prohibited by it to the States, are reserved to the States respectively, or to the people.

POLITICAL INQUIRY: *Go back and read Article 1, Section 8, Clause 18, of the Constitution and compare its meaning with that of the Tenth Amendment.*

1. *How do these two sections of the Constitution make it difficult to distinguish between national authority to act and state authority to act?*

2. *Ultimately, who resolves the conflict when the national government claims that its action is "necessary and proper" and a state claims that the national action is unconstitutional because it violates its constitutionally reserved powers?*

▬ Amendments to Protect Civil Rights and Liberties
▬ Amendments Related to Selection of Government Officials or Government Operations
▬ Amendments That Address a Specific Public Policy

Amendment XI (1795)

The Judicial power of the United States shall not be construed to extend to any suit in law or equity, commenced or prosecuted against one of the United States by Citizens of another State, or by Citizens or Subjects of any Foreign State.

> The courts have interpreted this amendment to mean that federal courts do not have the authority to hear lawsuits brought by citizens against their own state or against another state, or brought by foreigners against a state.

Amendment XII (1804)

The Electors shall meet in their respective states and vote by ballot for President and Vice-President, one of whom, at least, shall not be an inhabitant of the same state with themselves; they shall name in their ballots the person voted for as President, and in distinct ballots the person voted for as Vice-President, and they shall make distinct lists of all persons voted for as President, and of all persons voted for as Vice-President, and of the number of votes for each, which lists they shall sign and certify, and transmit sealed to the seat of the government of the United States, directed to the President of the Senate;—The President of the Senate shall, in the presence of the Senate and House of Representatives, open all the certificates and the votes shall then be counted;—The person having the greatest Number of votes for President, shall be the President, if such number be a majority of the whole number of Electors appointed; and if no person have such majority, then from the persons having the highest numbers not exceeding three on the list of those voted for as President, the House of Representatives shall choose immediately, by ballot, the President. But in choosing the President, the votes shall be taken by states, the representation from each state having one vote; a quorum for this purpose shall consist of a member or members from two-thirds of the states, and a majority of all the states shall be necessary to a choice. And if the House of Representatives shall not choose a President whenever the right of choice shall devolve upon them, before the fourth day of March next following, then the Vice-President shall act as President, as in the case of the death or other constitutional disability of the President—The person having the greatest number of votes as Vice-President, shall be the Vice-President, if such number be a majority of the whole number of Electors appointed, and if no person have a majority, then from the two highest numbers on the list, the Senate shall choose the Vice-President; a quorum for the purpose shall consist of two-thirds of the whole number of Senators, and a majority of the whole number shall be necessary to a choice. But no person constitutionally ineligible to the office of President shall be eligible to that of Vice-President of the United States.

> The presidential election in 1800 ended with a tie in Electoral College votes between Thomas Jefferson and Aaron Burr. Because the candidate with the most votes was to become president and the candidate with the second highest number of votes was to become vice president, the tie meant that the job of selecting the president was turned over to the House of Representatives. The House selected Jefferson. Calls to change the procedure were answered by the enactment of this amendment.

> Today, each elector has two votes: one for a presidential candidate and one for a vice-presidential candidate. The presidential candidate who wins the majority of electoral votes wins the presidency, and the same is true for the vice-presidential candidate. If no presidential candidate wins a majority of the votes, the House selects the president. If no vice-presidential candidate wins a majority of the votes, the Senate selects the vice president.

POLITICAL INQUIRY: *Electors in the Electoral College have two votes: one vote for a presidential candidate and one vote for a vice-presidential candidate. Citizens have just one vote; citizens vote for a ticket that includes both a presidential candidate and the vice-presidential candidate selected by the presidential candidate.*

1. *What effect might each citizen having two votes as do the electors—one vote for a presidential candidate and one vote for a vice-presidential candidate—have on presidential campaigns?*

2. *What effect might it have on the ability of the president to govern?*

Amendment XIII (1865)

Section 1. Neither slavery nor involuntary servitude, except as a punishment for crime whereof the party shall have been duly convicted, shall exist within the United States, or any place subject to their jurisdiction.

Section 2. Congress shall have power to enforce this article by appropriate legislation.

Amendment XIV (1868)

Section 1. All persons born or naturalized in the United States and subject to the jurisdiction thereof, are citizens of the United States and of the State wherein they reside. No State shall make or enforce any law which shall abridge the privileges or immunities of citizens of the United States; nor shall any State deprive any person of life, liberty, or property, without due process of law; nor deny to any person within its jurisdiction the equal protection of the laws.

POLITICAL INQUIRY: *In January 2017, President Trump issued an executive order known as the "Muslim Ban" that prohibited entrance to the United States to individuals from several Muslim-dominated countries. Immediately, a diverse range of people questioned the order's constitutionality.*

1. *Does the Equal Protection Clause of the Fourteenth Amendment prohibit the government, including the president, from singling out for differential treatment individuals for their religion and nationality?*

2. *The government often must balance individual rights with public safety and welfare. If the answer to question 1 is yes, the next question to be asked is: Is there a compelling public interest that might justify the ban's constitutional violation?*

Section 2. Representatives shall be apportioned among the several States according to their respective numbers, counting the whole number of persons in each State, excluding Indians not taxed. But when the right to vote at any election for the choice of electors for President and Vice President of the United States, Representatives in Congress, the Executive and Judicial officers of a State, or the members of the Legislature thereof, is denied to

> This amendment abolished slavery.

> This amendment extends the rights of citizenship to all those born in the United States and those who have become citizens through naturalization. States are prohibited from denying U.S. citizens their rights and privileges and must provide all people with due process before taking away their life, liberty, or pursuit of happiness. States must also treat all people equally and fairly. The courts have also used this section of the Fourteenth Amendment to require that states ensure citizens their protections under the Bill of Rights.

> This section of the Fourteenth Amendment is the first use of the term *male* in the Constitution. This section requires that if a state denies men over the age of 21 the right to vote, its representation in the House will be diminished accordingly. The Fifteenth Amendment makes this section unnecessary.

any of the male inhabitants of such State, being twenty-one years of age, and citizens of the United States, or in any way abridged, except for participation in rebellion, or other crime, the basis of representation therein shall be reduced in the proportion which the number of such male citizens shall bear to the whole number of male citizens twenty-one years of age in such State.

Section 3. No person shall be a Senator or Representative in Congress, or elector of President and Vice President, or hold any office, civil or military, under the United States, or under any State, who, having previously taken an oath, as a member of Congress, or as an officer of the United States, or as a member of any State legislature, or as an executive or judicial officer of any State, to support the Constitution of the United States, shall have engaged in insurrection or rebellion against the same, or given aid or comfort to the enemies thereof. But Congress may by a vote of two-thirds of each House, remove such disability.

Section 4. The validity of the public debt of the United States, authorized by law, including debts incurred for payment of pensions and bounties for services in suppressing insurrection or rebellion, shall not be questioned. But neither the United States nor any State shall assume or pay any debt or obligation incurred in aid of insurrection or rebellion against the United States, or any claim for the loss or emancipation of any slave; but all such debts, obligations and claims shall be held illegal and void.

Section 5. The Congress shall have power to enforce, by appropriate legislation, the provisions of this article.

Amendment XV (1870)

Section 1. The right of citizens of the United States to vote shall not be denied or abridged by the United States or by any State on account of race, color, or previous condition of servitude.

Section 2. The Congress shall have power to enforce this article by appropriate legislation.

Amendment XVI (1913)

The Congress shall have power to lay and collect taxes on incomes, from whatever source derived, without apportionment among the several States, and without regard to any census or enumeration.

Amendment XVII (1913)

The Senate of the United States shall be composed of two Senators from each State, elected by the people thereof, for six years; and each Senator shall have one vote. The electors in each State shall have the qualifications requisite for electors of the most numerous branch of the State legislatures.

When vacancies happen in the representation of any State in the Senate, the executive authority of such State shall issue writs of election to fill such vacancies: Provided, That the legislature of any State may empower the executive thereof to make temporary appointments until the people fill the vacancies by election as the legislature may direct.

This amendment shall not be so construed as to affect the election or term of any Senator chosen before it becomes valid as part of the Constitution.

■ Amendments to Protect Civil Rights and Liberties
■ Amendments Related to Selection of Government Officials or Government Operations
■ Amendments That Address a Specific Public Policy

> The intent of this section was to prevent government officials who supported the Confederacy during the Civil War from serving in government. Congress voted in 1898 to eliminate this prohibition.

> This section allowed the national and state governments to refuse to pay debts of the Confederate Army as well as claims made by slave owners whose slaves were freed by the Thirteenth Amendment.

> All male citizens meeting their state's minimum age requirement are guaranteed the right to vote.

> This amendment authorizes the national government to establish taxes on personal and corporate income.

> Representative democracy was enhanced by this amendment, which changed the process by which U.S. senators were selected. Senators are now elected by the citizens in each state rather than by state legislatures. The amendment also allows each state legislature to establish the process by which vacancies in the Senate will be filled, either through special election or by gubernatorial appointment.

> The "Prohibition" amendment—making it illegal to manufacture, sell, or transport alcoholic beverages in the United States—was widely disobeyed during the years it was in effect. This is the only amendment that has been repealed.

> All female citizens meeting their state's minimum age requirement are guaranteed the right to vote.

Amendment XVIII (1919)

Section 1. After one year from the ratification of this article the manufacture, sale, or transportation of intoxicating liquors within, the importation thereof into, or the exportation thereof from the United States and all territory subject to the jurisdiction thereof for beverage purposes is hereby prohibited.

Section 2. The Congress and the several States shall have concurrent power to enforce this article by appropriate legislation.

Section 3. This article shall be inoperative unless it shall have been ratified as an amendment to the Constitution by the legislatures of the several States, as provided in the Constitution, within seven years from the date of the submission hereof to the States by the Congress.

Amendment XIX (1920)

The right of citizens of the United States to vote shall not be denied or abridged by the United States or by any State on account of sex. Congress shall have power to enforce this article by appropriate legislation.

POLITICAL INQUIRY: *All male citizens gained the right to vote with the Fifteenth Amendment in 1870, 50 years before all women citizens did. Today, women's voter turnout is typically higher than is men's voter turnout and women voters lean more Democratic than men voters.*

1. *What does the fact that women did not win the vote until 1920 suggest about the status of women in the United States during the 19th and early 20th centuries?*

2. *What effect do you think women's voter turnout patterns have had on campaigns and public policy debates in the 21st century?*

> The first two sections of the Twentieth Amendment establish new starting dates for the president's and vice president's terms of office (January 20) as well as for members of Congress (January 3). Section 2 also decrees that the annual meeting of Congress will begin on January 3 unless Congress specifies a different date.

> Sections 3 and 4 of this amendment establish that if the president elect dies before his or her term of office begins, the vice president elect becomes president. If the president elect has not been selected or is unable to begin the term, the vice president elect serves as acting president until the president is selected or is able to serve.

Amendment XX (1933)

Section 1. The terms of the President and Vice President shall end at noon on the 20th day of January, and the terms of Senators and Representatives at noon on the 3d day of January, of the years in which such terms would have ended if this article had not been ratified; and the terms of their successors shall then begin.

Section 2. The Congress shall assemble at least once in every year, and such meeting shall begin at noon on the 3d day of January, unless they shall by law appoint a different day.

Section 3. If, at the time fixed for the beginning of the term of the President, the President elect shall have died, the Vice President elect shall become President. If a President shall not have been chosen before the time fixed for the beginning of his term, or if the President elect shall have failed to qualify, then the Vice President elect shall act as President until a President shall have qualified; and the Congress may by law provide for the case wherein neither a President elect nor a Vice President elect shall have qualified, declaring who shall then act as President, or the manner in which one who is to act shall be selected, and such person shall act accordingly until a President or Vice President shall have qualified.

Section 4. The Congress may by law provide for the case of the death of any of the persons from whom the House of Representatives may choose a President whenever the right of choice shall have devolved upon them, and for the case of the death of any of the persons from whom the Senate may choose a Vice President whenever the right of choice shall have devolved upon them.

Section 5. Sections 1 and 2 shall take effect on the 15th day of October following the ratification of this article.

Section 6. This article shall be inoperative unless it shall have been ratified as an amendment to the Constitution by the legislatures of three-fourths of the several States within seven years from the date of its submission.

Amendment XXI (1933)

Section 1. The eighteenth article of amendment to the Constitution of the United States is hereby repealed.

Section 2. The transportation or importation into any State, Territory, or possession of the United States for delivery or use therein of intoxicating liquors, in violation of the laws thereof, is hereby prohibited.

Section 3. This article shall be inoperative unless it shall have been ratified as an amendment to the Constitution by conventions in the several States, as provided in the Constitution, within seven years from the date of the submission hereof to the States by the Congress.

Amendment XXII (1951)

Section 1. No person shall be elected to the office of the President more than twice, and no person who has held the office of President, or acted as President, for more than two years of a term to which some other person was elected President shall be elected to the office of the President more than once. But this Article shall not apply to any person holding the office of President, when this Article was proposed by the Congress, and shall not prevent any person who may be holding the office of President, or acting as President, during the term within which this Article becomes operative from holding the office of President or acting as President during the remainder of such term.

Section 2. This article shall be inoperative unless it shall have been ratified as an amendment to the Constitution by the legislatures of three-fourths of the several States within seven years from the date of its submission to the States by the Congress.

■ Amendments to Protect Civil Rights and Liberties
■ Amendments Related to Selection of Government Officials or Government Operations
■ Amendments That Address a Specific Public Policy

> With this amendment, the Eighteenth Amendment's prohibition of the manufacture, sale, and transportation of alcoholic beverages was repealed. This is the only constitutional amendment that was ratified by special state conventions, not by state legislatures.

> This amendment establishes a two-term limit for the presidency, or in the case of a vice president succeeding to the presidency and then running for reelection, a maximum limit of 10 years in office.

POLITICAL INQUIRY: *Critics of term limits in general argue that they are undemocratic because they may force out of office an official whom the voters want to keep in office as their representative.*

1. *What is an additional argument for eliminating the two-term limit for the presidency?*

2. *What is an argument against eliminating the two-term limit for the presidency (other than the argument that it is undemocratic)?*

> Citizens living in Washington, D.C., are given the right to elect three voting members to the Electoral College. Before this amendment, these citizens were not represented in the Electoral College.

Amendment XXIII (1961)

Section 1. The District constituting the seat of Government of the United States shall appoint in such manner as the Congress may direct: A number of electors of President and Vice President equal to the whole number of Senators and Representatives in Congress to which the District would be entitled if it were a State, but in no event more than the least populous State; they shall be in addition to those appointed by the States, but they shall be considered, for the purposes of the election of President and Vice President, to be electors appointed by a State; and they shall meet in the District and perform such duties as provided by the twelfth article of amendment.

Section 2. The Congress shall have power to enforce this article by appropriate legislation.

POLITICAL INQUIRY: *In 1978, Congress approved and sent to the states for ratification an amendment to repeal the Twenty-Third Amendment. Moreover, the proposed amendment provided D.C. residents with full congressional representation (two senators and representation in the House based on population) and the same ability to vote in national elections. The proposed amendment addressed the fact that D.C. residents (who number more than the residents of Wyoming and Vermont, which are each represented in Congress by two senators and one representative) are taxed by laws Congress enacts but have no voting representatives in Congress—taxation without representation.*

1. *Make an argument for this proposed amendment that has yet to be ratified.*

2. *Make an argument against this proposed amendment.*

> Governments are prohibited from requiring a person to pay a tax in order to vote.

Amendment XXIV (1964)

Section 1. The right of citizens of the United States to vote in any primary or other election for President or Vice President, for electors for President or Vice President, or for Senator or Representative in Congress, shall not be denied or abridged by the United States or any State by reason of failure to pay any poll tax or other tax.

Section 2. The Congress shall have power to enforce this article by appropriate legislation.

POLITICAL INQUIRY: *Several states have enacted laws requiring voters to show a government-issued photo ID to vote. However, many elderly, poor, and urban residents do not have a government-issued photo ID and therefore would have to pay for one, or would be prevented from voting.*

1. *Is this a modern poll tax? Why or why not?*

2. *What is the explanation states provide for enacting laws requiring a government-issued photo ID to vote?*

> The vice president becomes president if the president resigns or dies.

Amendment XXV (1967)

Section 1. In case of the removal of the President from office or of his death or resignation, the Vice President shall become President.

Section 2. Whenever there is a vacancy in the office of the Vice President, the President shall nominate a Vice President who shall take office upon confirmation by a majority vote of both Houses of Congress.

Section 3. Whenever the President transmits to the President pro tempore of the Senate and the Speaker of the House of Representatives his written declaration that he is unable to discharge the powers and duties of his office, and until he transmits to them a written declaration to the contrary, such powers and duties shall be discharged by the Vice President as Acting President.

Section 4. Whenever the Vice President and a majority of either the principal officers of the executive departments or of such other body as Congress may by law provide, transmit to the President pro tempore of the Senate and the Speaker of the House of Representatives their written declaration that the President is unable to discharge the powers and duties of his office, the Vice President shall immediately assume the powers and duties of the office as Acting President.

Thereafter, when the President transmits to the President pro tempore of the Senate and the Speaker of the House of Representatives his written declaration that no inability exists, he shall resume the powers and duties of his office unless the Vice President and a majority of either the principal officers of the executive department or of such other body as Congress may by law provide, transmit within four days to the President pro tempore of the Senate and the Speaker of the House of Representatives their written declaration that the President is unable to discharge the powers and duties of his office. Thereupon Congress shall decide the issue, assembling within forty-eight hours for that purpose if not in session. If the Congress, within twenty-one days after receipt of the latter written declaration, or, if Congress is not in session, within twenty-one days after Congress is required to assemble, determines by two-thirds vote of both Houses that the President is unable to discharge the powers and duties of his office, the Vice President shall continue to discharge the same as Acting President; otherwise, the President shall resume the powers and duties of his office.

Amendment XXVI (1971)

Section 1. The right of citizens of the United States, who are eighteen years of age or older, to vote shall not be denied or abridged by the United States or by any State on account of age.

Section 2. The Congress shall have power to enforce this article by appropriate legislation.

Amendment XXVII (1992)

No law varying the compensation for the services of the Senators and Representatives shall take effect, until an election of Representatives shall have intervened.

POLITICAL INQUIRY: Now that you have read the Constitution, do you think three-quarters of state legislatures would ratify this document—even as amended—today? Why or why not?

■ Amendments to Protect Civil Rights and Liberties
■ Amendments Related to Selection of Government Officials or Government Operations
■ Amendments That Address a Specific Public Policy

> The president can nominate a person to fill a vice-presidential vacancy. Congress must approve the nominee. President Richard Nixon appointed and Congress confirmed Gerald Ford to the vice presidency when Vice President Spiro Agnew resigned. When President Nixon resigned, Vice President Ford, who had not been elected, became president. He subsequently appointed and Congress confirmed Nelson Rockefeller to be vice president.

> If the president indicates in writing to Congress that he or she cannot carry out the duties of office, the vice president becomes acting president until the president informs Congress that he or she is again fit to resume the responsibilities of the presidency.

> If the vice president in concert with a majority of cabinet officials (or some other body designated by Congress) declares to Congress in writing that the president is unable to fulfill the duties of office, the vice president becomes acting president until the president claims he or she is again fit for duty. However, if the vice president and a majority of cabinet officials challenge the president's claim, then Congress must decide within three weeks if the president can resume office.

> Citizens 18 years of age and older are guaranteed the right to vote.

> Proposed in 1789, this amendment prevents members of Congress from raising their own salaries. Approved salary increases cannot take effect until after the next congressional election.

CHAPTER 3

Federalism

©Bill Clark/Getty Images

THEN

The newly created national government and the preexisting state governments acted independently as they implemented the innovative federal system of government established in 1789.

NOW

National, state, and local governments challenge one another regularly over the proper interpretation of the Constitution's vague and ambiguous distribution of power in the federal system of U.S. government.

NEXT

Will Supreme Court justices continue to issue conflicting interpretations of the proper balance of power in the federal system of government?

Will state and local governments continue their policy experiments to find more effective means of addressing domestic problems?

Will partisan differences between state governments and the national government perpetuate state legal challenges to national laws?

State governments are

"independent sovereigns in our federal system," and the Obama administration must accept that fact, argued U.S. Supreme Court Justice John Roberts in the 2012 court case that questioned the constitutionality of the national Affordable Care Act (ACA).[1] Although the Supreme Court found the ACA to be constitutional, it found unconstitutional the law's requirement that each state government expand its Medicaid program to provide insurance to more people or lose *all* its federal Medicaid grant money.

As a result of this Supreme Court interpretation of the U.S. Constitution, specifically its distribution of powers between the sovereign state governments and the sovereign national government, individuals throughout the country are required to have health insurance, and some states expanded Medicaid coverage, while others did not. States with Democratic-dominated governments were the first to expand Medicaid coverage. Republican-dominated state governments did not initially expand Medicaid. Moreover, between 2012 and 2017, the Republicans in Congress attempted to repeal the ACA, also called Obamacare, while Democrats in Congress fought to retain it.

The dual sovereignty that defines the U.S. federal system of government distributes ultimate authority (sovereignty) over some governing matters to the national government and sovereignty over different governing matters to the state governments. However, constitutional language that distributes sovereignty is not always clear. Therefore, since 1789, state governments and the national government have battled (in court and in the Civil War) over the proper implementation of the federal system of government.

In the past few decades, partisan battles (conflicts between Democrats and Republicans) over policy matters have fueled state and national conflicts as the parties take advantage of the federal system's dual sovereignty to get their preferred policies approved. At the same time that the state and national governments battle over the constitutional distribution of sovereignty, they also regularly collaborate to fulfill their responsibilities to the people. Intergovernmental relations—or the ways in which the national, state, and state-created local governments deal with each other as they all try to serve the people—can be cooperative, conflictive, and confusing. This is the reality of the U.S. federal system today.

Learning Objectives

After reading this chapter, students should be able to:

- Compare the unitary, confederal, and federal systems of government.
- Explain the constitutional distribution of power and responsibilities between the national and state governments.
- Outline the evolution of the U.S. federal system by discussing the multiple models of federalism and the tools of intergovernmental relations.
- Describe the realities of today's intergovernmental relations.

An Overview of the U.S. Federal System

The U.S. Constitution established an innovative and unique government structure, a federal system. A **federal system** has two constitutionally recognized levels of government, each with *sovereignty*—that is, ultimate governing authority, with no legal superior—over different policy matters and geographic areas. According to the Constitution, the national government has ultimate authority over some matters, and the state governments hold ultimate authority over different matters. In addition, the national government's jurisdiction covers the entire geographic area of the nation, and each state government's jurisdiction covers the geographic area within the state's borders. The existence of two levels of government, each with ultimate authority over different matters and geographic areas—an arrangement called *dual sovereignty*—is what distinguishes the federal system of government from the two other most common systems of government worldwide: the unitary system and the confederal system. The American colonists' experience with a unitary system, and subsequently the early U.S. citizens' life under a confederal system (1781–1788), led to the creation of the innovative federal system.

Unitary System

Today, the majority of countries in the world have unitary governments. In a **unitary system,** the central government is *the* sovereign government. It can create other governments (regional governments) and delegate governing powers and responsibilities to them. In addition, the sovereign central government in a unitary system can unilaterally take away any governing powers and responsibilities it delegated to the regional governments it created. Ultimately, the sovereign central government can even eliminate the regional governments it created.

Indeed, under Britain's unitary system of government during the American colonial period, the British Crown (the sovereign central government) created colonial governments (regional governments) and gave them authority to handle day-to-day matters such as regulating marriages, resolving business conflicts, providing for public safety, and maintaining roads. As the central government in Britain (with no representatives from the colonies) approved tax and trade policies that harmed the colonists' quality of life, growing public discourse and dissension spurred the colonists to protest. The colonists' failed attempts to influence the central government's policies eventually sparked their declaration of independence from Great Britain.

Confederal System

When the colonies declared their independence from Great Britain in 1776, each colony became an independent sovereign state and adopted its own constitution. As a result, no state had a legal superior; each was *the* sovereign government for its geographic area. In 1777, delegates from every state except Rhode Island met in a convention and agreed to a proposed alliance of the 13 sovereign state governments. In 1781, the 13 independent state governments ratified the Articles of Confederation, the first constitution of the United States, which created a confederal system of government.

In a **confederal system,** several independent sovereign governments (such as the first 13 state governments in the case of the United States) agree to cooperate on specified policy matters while each sovereign state retains ultimate authority over

---

federal system
A governmental structure with two levels of government in which each level has sovereignty over different policy matters and geographic areas; a system of government with dual sovereignty.

unitary system
A governmental system in which one central government is *the* sovereign government and it creates other, regional governments to which it delegates some governing powers and responsibilities; however, the central government retains ultimate authority (sovereignty).

confederal system
A government structure in which several independent sovereign states agree to cooperate on specified policy matters by creating a central governing body; each sovereign state retains ultimate authority over other governmental matters within its borders, so the central governing body is not a sovereign government.

all other governmental matters within its borders. The cooperating sovereign state governments delegate some governing responsibilities to a central governing body. However, the sovereign state governments retain ultimate authority and can modify or even eliminate governing responsibilities they agreed to delegate to the central government.

As detailed in Chapter 2, the effectiveness of the confederal system of government created by the Articles of Confederation quickly came into question due to economic problems and domestic rebellions. In 1787, the national Congress (the central governing body created by the sovereign states) called for a constitutional convention "for the sole and express purpose of revising the Articles of Confederation" in order to preserve the union. Clear-eyed about the failures of the unitary system they experienced as British colonies, and the confederal system, the citizens of the United States decided to experiment with a unique government system. The federal system created by the Constitution of the United States has succeeded in strengthening and preserving the union.

Federal System

The state delegates who met in Philadelphia in 1787 drafted a new constitution that created the federal system with dual sovereignty. The Constitution's framers established dual sovereignty by detailing a new, sovereign national government for the United States and modifying the sovereignty of the existing state governments. The sovereign national government thus created has no legal superior on matters over which the Constitution gives it authority, and the sovereign state governments have no legal superior on the matters which the Constitution grants to them.

Such dual sovereignty does not exist in unitary or confederal systems, where sovereignty is held by one level of government (the central government in a unitary system and the regional governments in a confederal system). Figure 3.1 compares the three types of governing systems.

The federal system, as it works in the United States today, can be confusing—not only to citizens, but also to government officials. The confusion is a product of at least three factors. First, vague constitutional language that distributes sovereignty

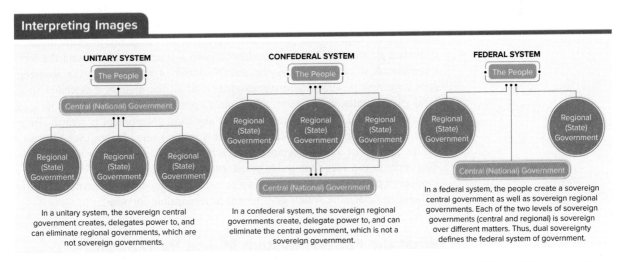

Interpreting Images

UNITARY SYSTEM

In a unitary system, the sovereign central government creates, delegates power to, and can eliminate regional governments, which are not sovereign governments.

CONFEDERAL SYSTEM

In a confederal system, the sovereign regional governments create, delegate power to, and can eliminate the central government, which is not a sovereign government.

FEDERAL SYSTEM

In a federal system, the people create a sovereign central government as well as sovereign regional governments. Each of the two levels of sovereign governments (central and regional) is sovereign over different matters. Thus, dual sovereignty defines the federal system of government.

FIGURE 3.1 ■ Three Governing Systems What does it mean to be a sovereign government? Distinguish between the three systems of government by explaining what level, or levels, of government holds sovereignty in each system.

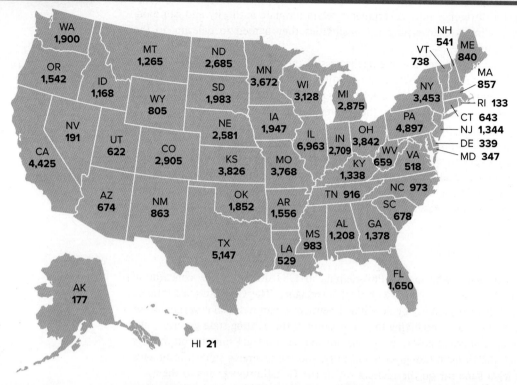

FIGURE 3.2 ■ **Number of Local Governments in Each State** What might explain the range in the number of local governments that exist in the 50 states? Do the states with the largest geographic area have the largest number of local governments? Are there regional patterns? Do states with smaller populations have fewer local governments?

SOURCE: American Fact Finder, "Local Governments by Type and State 2012."

between the national government and the state governments fuels questions about which government is sovereign over specific matters. Second, state governments have established tens of thousands of local governments—a third level of government—delegating some governing powers and responsibilities to them, to assist the state in serving its citizens. The relationship between a state government and the local governments it creates follows the *unitary system* of government; the sovereign state government retains ultimate authority over all the matters it delegates to its local governments, can remove power and responsibilities it delegates to its local governments, and ultimately can eliminate any local government it creates. Today there are more than 89,400 local governments in the United States. (See Figure 3.2 for the number of local governments in each state.) The third factor adding to the confusion is the fact that today, most government services and benefits are a product of collaborative efforts by two or more governments. Therefore, it is often difficult to determine which government is responsible for what.

What the Federal System Means for U.S. Citizens

The majority of U.S. citizens live under the jurisdiction of at least five governments: national, state, county (called *borough* in Alaska and *parish* in Louisiana), municipal or township, and school district. Every one of those governments can enact laws with which the people living in its jurisdiction must comply and from which they may benefit.

Each of these governments can impose responsibilities on the people living in its jurisdiction. The most obvious responsibility is to pay taxes. These taxes can include the national personal income tax; state sales and personal income taxes; and county, municipal/township, and school district property taxes.

Each state and local government can enact laws to regulate behaviors, as long as the law does not violate rights and liberties established in the U.S. Constitution. For example, while some states have tight gun control laws, other states do not, and some local governments even require citizens to have a gun in their home.[2] On January 1, 2016, Hawaii became the first state to raise the legal age for the purchase of tobacco products and electronic smoking devices from 18 years to 21 years. Several cities also have increased the legal age for purchasing tobacco products to 21 years, including New York City and Cleveland, Ohio.[3]

The Constitution lists individual liberties in the Bill of Rights. In addition, every state constitution has its own bill of rights, and some local governments offer further protections to their citizens. For example, some cities and counties prohibit discrimination in employment and public accommodations based on an individual's sexual orientation, yet most states do not, nor does the national government.

Clearly, people's rights and responsibilities vary depending on where they live in the United States (as discussed further in Chapter 4). Thus, the federal system can be confusing for citizens. It can also be confusing for the many governments created to serve the people. Which government is responsible for what services and policies? Because the Constitution of the United States is the supreme law of the land, it is to the Constitution that we must turn to answer that question.

Constitutional Distribution of Authority

By distributing some authority to the national government and different authority to the state governments, the Constitution creates the dual sovereignty that defines the U.S. federal system. The Constitution lists the several matters over which the national government has ultimate authority, and it implies additional national authority. The Constitution spells out just a few matters over which the state governments have authority. The Constitution lacks detail on state authority in part because, at the time of the Constitution's drafting, the states expected to retain their authority, except for matters that, by way of the Constitution, they agreed to turn over to the newly created national government.

To fulfill their responsibilities to their citizens, both the national and the state governments have the authority to engage in basic governing functions inherent to all sovereign governments. The powers that are exercised by both the national and state governments are the first topic in this section.

Concurrent Powers

concurrent powers
Basic governing functions that are exercised by the national and state governments independently, and at the same time, including the power to make policy, raise revenue, implement policies, and establish courts.

To function, sovereign governments need basic governing powers such as the authority to make policy, raise and spend money, implement policies, and establish courts to interpret law when a conflict arises about its meaning. In the U.S. federal system, these basic governing powers are **concurrent powers** because the national

TABLE 3.1 Concurrent Powers of National and State Governments

Make policy

Raise & spend money

Borrow money

Implement policy

Charter banks and corporations

Establish courts

Take private property for public use (eminent domain)

government and all state governments exercise them, independently and at the same time. For example, national and state governments make their own public policies, and raise and spend their own revenues to implement their policies. In addition, the national court system resolves conflicts over the interpretation of national laws and each state has its own court system to resolve conflicts over its state laws. State governments delegate some concurrent powers to the local governments they create so that the local governments can govern. Table 3.1 lists concurrent powers of the national and the state governments.

In addition to the basic governing powers that the national and state governments hold concurrently, in the federal system the national government and the state governments have sovereignty over different matters. We now consider the distinct sovereign powers of the national and state governments.

National Sovereignty

The Constitution distributes powers to the national government's three branches (legislative, executive, and judicial) that are (1) enumerated, or specifically listed, and (2) implied. For example, Article I of the Constitution enumerates the matters over which Congress holds the authority to make laws, including interstate and foreign commerce, the system of money, general welfare, and national defense. These matters are **enumerated powers** of the national government. The Constitution also gives Congress **implied powers**—that is, powers that are not described explicitly but that may be interpreted to be necessary to fulfill the enumerated powers. Congress specifically receives implied powers through the Constitution's **necessary and proper clause,** sometimes called the **elastic clause** because the national government uses this passage to stretch its enumerated authority. The necessary and proper clause in Article I, Section 8, of the Constitution states that Congress has the power to "make all Laws which shall be necessary and proper" for carrying out its enumerated powers.

Articles II and III of the Constitution also enumerate powers of the national government. Article II delegates to the president the responsibility to ensure the proper implementation of national laws and, with the advice and consent of the U.S. Senate, the authority to make treaties with foreign nations and to appoint foreign ambassadors. With respect to the U.S. Supreme Court and the lower federal courts, Article III enumerates jurisdiction over legal cases involving U.S. constitutional issues, national legislation, and treaties. The jurisdiction of the Supreme Court also extends to disagreements between two or more state governments, as well as to conflicts between citizens from different states. Figure 3.3 lists national powers enumerated in Articles I, II, and III of the Constitution.

THE SUPREMACY CLAUSE The country's founders anticipated disagreements over the interpretation of constitutional language and prepared for them by creating the Supreme Court. The Court has mostly supported the national government when states, citizens, or interest groups have challenged Congress's use of the necessary and proper clause to take on new responsibilities beyond its enumerated powers. Unless the Supreme Court finds a national law to be outside of the enumerated or implied powers, that law is constitutional and hence the **supreme law of the land,**

enumerated powers
The powers of the national government that are listed in the Constitution.

implied powers
The powers of the national government that are not enumerated in the Constitution but that Congress claims are necessary and proper for the national government to fulfill its enumerated powers in accordance with the necessary and proper clause of the Constitution.

necessary and proper clause (elastic clause)
A clause in Article I, Section 8, of the Constitution that gives Congress the power to do whatever it deems necessary and constitutional to meet its enumerated obligations; the basis for the implied powers.

supreme law of the land
The U.S. Constitution's description of its own authority, meaning that all laws made by governments within the United States must be in compliance with the Constitution.

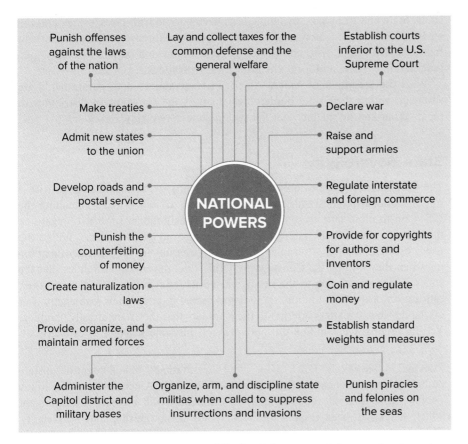

FIGURE 3.3 ■ **Enumerated Powers of National Government** Can you locate each enumerated power in the Constitution that precedes this chapter (by article, section, and clause)?

as defined by the supremacy clause in Article VI of the Constitution: "This Constitution, and the Laws of the United States which shall be made in Pursuance thereof; and all Treaties made, or which shall be made, under the Authority of the United States, shall be the supreme Law of the Land." State and local governments are thereby obligated to comply with national laws that implement national enumerated and implied powers, as well as with treaties—including treaties with Native American nations.

NATIONAL TREATIES WITH INDIAN NATIONS   Throughout U.S. history, the national government has signed treaties with Native American nations, which are legally considered sovereign foreign nations. As with all treaties, treaties with Native American nations are supreme law with which the national, state, and local governments must comply. The core issue in the majority of these treaties is the provision of land (reservations) on which the native peoples would resettle after non-Indians took their lands during the 18th and 19th centuries. Today, the federal government recognizes more than 550 Indian tribes. Although most Native Americans no longer live on reservations, approximately 300 reservations remain, in 34 states.[4]

Even though Indian reservations lie within state borders, national treaties and national laws, not state or local laws, apply to the reservation populations and lands. State and local laws, including laws having to do with taxes, crime, and the environment, are unenforceable on reservations. Moreover, Native American treaty rights to hunt, fish, and gather on reservations and on public lands supersede national, state, and local environmental regulations.[5]

With the exception of Native American reservations, state governments are sovereign within their state borders over matters the Constitution distributes to them. What are the matters that fall within state sovereignty?

State Sovereignty

The Constitution specifies only a few state powers. It provides the states with a role in national politics and gives them the final say on formally amending the U.S. Constitution. One reason for the lack of constitutional specificity regarding the matters over which state governments are sovereign is because, unlike the newly created national government, the state governments were already functioning when they ratified the Constitution. Other than those responsibilities that the states agreed to delegate to the newly created national government through their ratification of the Constitution, the states expected to retain their sovereignty over all the day-to-day matters internal to their borders that they were already handling. Yet the original Constitution did not speak of this state sovereignty explicitly.

POWERS RESERVED TO THE STATES   The Constitution's limited attention to state authority caused concern among citizens of the early American republic. Many people feared that the new national government would meddle in matters for which states had been responsible, in that way compromising state sovereignty. Citizens were also deeply concerned about their own liberties. As described in Chapter 2, within two years of the states' ratification of the Constitution, they ratified the Bill of Rights (1791), the first 10 amendments to the U.S. Constitution, in response to those concerns.

The Tenth Amendment asserts that the "powers not delegated to the United States by the Constitution, nor prohibited by it to the States, are *reserved to the States* respectively, or to the people." This **reserved powers** clause of the Tenth Amendment acknowledged the domestic matters over which the states had exercised authority since the ratification of their own constitutions. These matters included the handling of the daily affairs of the people—laws regarding birth, death, marriage, intrastate business, commerce, crime, health, morals, and safety. The states' reserved powers to protect the health, safety, lives, and property of their citizens are their **police powers.** It was over these domestic matters, internal to each state, that the states retained sovereignty according to the Tenth Amendment.

Figure 3.4 summarizes the constitutionally reserved powers of the states at the time of the Tenth Amendment's ratification, as well as some of the few powers delegated to the states in the Constitution prior to ratification of the Tenth Amendment.

POWERS DELEGATED TO THE STATES   Although the Constitution does not list all the specific powers reserved to the states, it does assign, or delegate, several powers to the states. These powers provide the states with a distinct voice in the composition and priorities of the national government. Members of Congress are elected by voters in their home states (U.S. senators) or their home districts (representatives in the U.S. House). Therefore, members of Congress are accountable to the voters in the state that elected them. State governments also have the authority to redraw the boundaries of the U.S. House districts within the state

reserved powers
The matters referred to in the Tenth Amendment over which states retain sovereignty.

police powers
The states' reserved powers to protect the health, safety, lives, and properties of residents in a state.

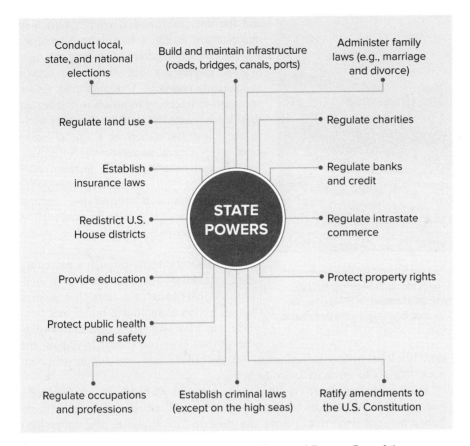

Conduct local, state, and national elections

Build and maintain infrastructure (roads, bridges, canals, ports)

Administer family laws (e.g., marriage and divorce)

Regulate land use

Regulate charities

Establish insurance laws

Regulate banks and credit

Redistrict U.S. House districts

STATE POWERS

Regulate intrastate commerce

Provide education

Protect property rights

Protect public health and safety

Regulate occupations and professions

Establish criminal laws (except on the high seas)

Ratify amendments to the U.S. Constitution

FIGURE 3.4 ■ Constitutionally Delegated and Reserved Powers Few of these powers are specified in the Constitution. Which of these state powers are listed (delegated) in the Constitution? Where do the other powers come from?

after each decennial census. In addition, each state government determines the procedure by which the state's Electoral College electors will be selected to participate in the state's vote for the president and vice president. Overall, state voters expect that the officials whom they elect to the national government will carefully consider their concerns when creating national policy.

In addition to establishing the various electoral procedures that give voice to state interests in the national policy-making process, the Constitution creates a formal means by which the states can ensure that the language in the Constitution is not changed in such a way that their sovereignty is threatened. Specifically, the Constitution stipulates that three-fourths of the states (through votes in either their legislatures or special conventions, as discussed in Chapter 2) must ratify amendments to the Constitution. By having the final say in whether the supreme law of the land will be changed formally through the passage of amendments to the U.S. Constitution, the states can protect their constitutional powers. Indeed, they did just that when they ratified the Tenth Amendment.

State-to-State Relations: Horizontal Federalism

In Article IV, the Constitution sets forth obligations that the states have to one another and to each other's citizens. Collectively, these state-to-state obligations

> The Rio Grande originates in Colorado and flows south into New Mexico and Texas. To resolve disputes over the three states' claims to water rights, Texas, New Mexico, and Colorado signed the Rio Grande Compact in 1938, an agreement that apportions the water of the Rio Grande Basin among the three states.

©William Silver/Shutterstock

horizontal federalism
The state-to-state relationships created by the U.S. Constitution.

interstate compacts
Agreements between states that Congress has the authority to review and reject.

extradition
The return of individuals accused of a crime to the state in which the crime was committed upon the request of that state's governor.

privileges and immunities clause
The Constitution's requirement that a state extend to other states' citizens the privileges and immunities it provides for its citizens.

full faith and credit clause
The constitutional clause that requires states to comply with and uphold the public acts, records, and judicial decisions of other states.

and the intergovernmental relationships they mandate are forms of **horizontal federalism.** For example, state governments have the right to forge agreements with other states, known as **interstate compacts.** Congress must review and approve interstate compacts to ensure that they do not harm the states that are not party to them and the nation as a whole. States enter into cooperative agreements to provide services and benefits for one another, such as monitoring paroled inmates from other states; sharing and conserving natural resources that spill over state borders, such as water; and decreasing pollution that crosses state borders.

States also cooperate through a procedure called **extradition,** the legal process of sending individuals back to a state that accuses them of having committed a crime, and from which they have fled. The Constitution establishes a state governor's right to request the extradition of an accused criminal. Yet the courts have also supported governors' refusals to extradite individuals.

The Constitution asserts, too, that each state must guarantee the same **privileges and immunities** it provides to its citizens to all U.S. citizens, including citizens from other states who visit or move into the state. This guarantee does not prohibit states from imposing reasonable requirements before extending rights to visiting or new state residents. For example, states can and do charge higher tuition costs to out-of-state college students. In addition, in many states, new state residents must wait 30 days before they can register to vote. Yet no state can deny new state residents who are U.S. citizens the right to register to vote once they meet a reasonable state residency requirement.

Because of the ease of traveling between states as well as relocating from state to state, an important component of horizontal federalism stems from the full faith and credit clause of Article IV, Section 1, of the Constitution. The **full faith and credit clause** asserts that each state must recognize as legally binding (that is, valid and enforceable) the public acts, records, and judicial proceedings of every other state. For example, in March 2016, the Supreme Court cited the full faith and credit clause when it ruled that states must honor adoptions by same-sex parents who move across state lines.[6]

Supreme Court Interpretation of the Constitution

Vague language in the U.S. Constitution continues to spark disputes over what are the constitutional powers of the national government versus what are the constitutional powers of the state governments. Some constitutional clauses that the courts have had to interpret repeatedly include the *necessary and proper* powers of Congress and the powers of Congress to provide for the *general welfare* and to regulate *commerce among the several states.* In addition, the courts are continually interpreting and reinterpreting the meaning of the *reserved powers clause* of the Tenth Amendment. The U.S. Supreme Court has the final say over what constitutional language means. In the process of resolving conflicts by distinguishing

WHICH GOVERNMENT HAS SOVEREIGNTY?

First, review Table 3.1, Figure 3.3, and Figure 3.4. Next, reflect on the following list of issue areas for which state legislatures proposed nullification-related proposals from 2010 through 2016. Then answer the questions posed under "Practice Analytical Thinking."

Issue Areas Addressed by Nullification-Related State-Proposed Legislation (2010–2016)

Affordable Care Act

Agenda 21 (United Nations protocols related to environmental and economic regulation)

Common Core [education] Standards

Federal gun regulations

Drones

Hemp farming

Indefinite detention by the national government

License plate tracking

Marijuana use

National Security Administration (NSA) surveillance

Militarization of local police forces (with national military-grade weapons and equipment)

Use by terminally ill patients of drugs not yet FDA approved

SOURCE: Adam Olson, T. Callaghan, and Andrew Karch, "Return of the 'Rightful Remedy'?: Partisan Federalism, Resource Availability, and Nullification Legislation in the American States," *Publius: The Journal of Federalism*, p. 23.

Practice Analytical Thinking

1. Which issues fall under state sovereignty (reserved powers)?

2. Which issues fall under national sovereignty (enumerated or implied powers)?

3. Which issues could be either reserved for the states or implied for the national government? How do your answers compare with those of your classmates?

4. Are your answers facts or opinions?

among national enumerated and implied powers and the powers reserved for the states, the Court has given meaning to the supremacy clause of the Constitution and influenced the relationships among the national and state governments. (See "Analyzing the Sources" to consider the complexity of determining enumerated, reserved, and implied powers.)

THE POWER TO REGULATE COMMERCE The landmark case of *McCulloch v. Maryland* (1819) exemplifies a Supreme Court ruling that established the use of the implied powers to expand the national government's enumerated authority.[7] The case stemmed from Congress's establishment of a national bank, and in particular a branch of that bank located in the state of Maryland, which the Maryland state authorities tried to tax. Maryland's attorneys argued that Congress did not have the constitutional authority to establish a national bank, noting it was not among the enumerated powers. They also argued that if the Court interpreted

McCulloch v. Maryland
The 1819 case that established that the necessary and proper clause justifies broad understandings of enumerated powers.

the Constitution such that the national government did have the implied power to establish a national bank, then Maryland had the concurrent power to tax the bank. Lawyers for the national government in turn argued that the Constitution did indeed imply federal authority to establish a national bank and that Maryland's levying a tax on the bank was unconstitutional, for it impinged on the national government's ability to fulfill its constitutional responsibilities by taking some of its financial resources.

The Supreme Court decided in favor of the national government. The justices based their ruling on their interpretation of the Constitution's necessary and proper clause and the enumerated powers of Congress to "lay and collect taxes, to borrow money . . . and to regulate commerce among the several states." The Court said that, combined, these enumerated powers implied that the national government had the authority to charter a bank and to locate a branch in Maryland. Moreover, the Court found that Maryland did not have the right to tax that bank, because taxation by the state would interfere with the exercise of national authority.

In the *McCulloch* case, the Supreme Court established that the necessary and proper clause allows Congress to broadly interpret the enumerated powers of the national government. Moreover, the Court interpreted the national supremacy clause to mean that in the event of a conflict between national legislation (the law chartering the national bank) and state legislation (Maryland's tax law), the national law is supreme *as long as* it falls under the enumerated and implied powers that the Constitution distributes to the national government.

> In *United States v. Lopez* (1995), the U.S. Supreme Court ruled the national Gun-Free School Zones Act unconstitutional and affirmed that state governments have the right to establish gun-free school zones. What constitutional clauses did the Court have to interpret to resolve the *United States v. Lopez* case?

A few years later, in the case of *Gibbons v. Ogden* (1824), the Supreme Court again justified a particular national action on the basis of the implications of an enumerated power.[8] The *Gibbons* case was the first suit brought to the Supreme Court seeking clarification on the constitutional meaning of *commerce* in the Constitution's clause on the regulation of interstate commerce. The Court established a broad definition of commerce: "all commercial intercourse—meaning all business dealings." The conflict in this case concerned which government, New York State or the national government, had authority to regulate the operation of boats on the waterways between New York and New Jersey. The Court ruled that regulation of commerce implied regulation of navigation and therefore the national government had authority to regulate it, not New York State.

Not until the Great Depression (1930s) did the national government begin to justify new laws by arguing that they were necessary to fulfill its enumerated power to regulate interstate commerce. After some initial conflicts, the Court has more often agreed than disagreed with Congress's broad understanding of what its enumerated powers implied it could do through legislation. In addition to expanding its power through implications of the regulation of interstate commerce clause, Congress has also successfully used the general welfare clause to take on new matters, hence expanding its authority.

THE POWER TO PROVIDE FOR THE GENERAL WELFARE The national government's landmark Social Security Act of 1935 was a response to the Great Depression's devastating impact on the financial security of countless Americans. The congressional vote to establish Social Security was overwhelmingly favorable.

Yet several states challenged the constitutionality of this expansive program shortly after its passage, claiming it infringed on their reserved police powers. In 1937, the Supreme Court had to decide: Was Social Security indeed a matter of general welfare for which Congress is delegated the authority to raise and spend money? Or was Social Security a matter for the state governments to address? The Court found the national policy to be constitutional—a reasonable congressional interpretation, the justices wrote, of the enumerated and implied powers of the national government.[9]

The Supreme Court's decisions in the *McCulloch, Gibbons,* and Social Security cases set the stage for the expansion of national power in domestic policy matters by combining the necessary and proper clause with such enumerated powers as the regulation of commerce and providing for the general welfare. Although throughout U.S. history, particularly since the 1930s, the Court has typically supported Congress's enactment of laws dealing with matters implied by—but not specifically enumerated in—the Constitution, Congress does not always get its way. For example, in 1995 the Supreme Court rejected the national government's claim that its Gun-Free School Zones Act of 1990 was a necessary and proper means to regulate interstate commerce. The Court found the act unconstitutional because it infringed on states' reserved police powers; state governments have authority to create gun-free school zones, and they can extend that authority to their local governments.[10]

In addition to establishing dual sovereignty and creating two independently operating levels of government, the Constitution enumerates some obligations that the national government has to the states. These obligations include guaranteeing a republican form of government, protecting states from foreign invasion and domestic violence, and prohibiting the national government from changing state boundaries without consent of the states concerned.

Judicial Federalism

The Fourteenth Amendment authorizes the national government to ensure that the state governments (1) follow fair procedures (due process) before taking away a person's life, liberties, or pursuit of happiness and (2) guarantee all people the same rights (equal protection of the laws) to life, liberties, and pursuit of happiness without arbitrary discrimination. In addition, the amendment guarantees the privileges and immunities of U.S. citizenship to all citizens in all states.

The rights and privileges guaranteed by the U.S. Constitution are minimums; all governments in the United States must comply with the Constitution. However, state and local governments can guarantee additional rights and privileges to the people in their jurisdictions. Indeed, state and local governments have enacted laws that provide more rights and privileges than found in the Constitution.

For example, the Pennsylvania constitution states that the "people have a right to clean air, pure water, and to the preservation of the natural, scenic, historic and esthetic values of the environment." The U.S. Constitution does not guarantee such a right. The California state constitution protects freedom of speech and expression in privately owned properties, such as shopping centers. The U.S. Constitution's guaranteed freedom of expression does not extend to privately owned properties.[11] In Takoma Park, Maryland, citizens as young as 16 have the right to vote in municipal elections (the voting age for state and federal elections is still 18 in Takoma Park).[12] And in numerous municipalities and counties across the country, laws prohibit discrimination due to a person's sexual orientation, though the U.S. Constitution does not prohibit such discrimination.

Historically, state courts turned to the U.S. Constitution when deciding civil rights and liberties cases. However, beginning in the 1970s, state courts increasingly based these decisions on their own state constitutions, which guaranteed more extensive rights to their citizens than did the U.S. Constitution. For example, after the U.S. Supreme Court's 1973 ruling that the equal protection clause of the Fourteenth Amendment did not require equal funding of schools in Texas,[13] state courts in 15 states ruled that their state constitutions required equal funding of schools.[14] Political scientists refer to the reliance of state courts on their state constitutions as **judicial federalism.**

Evolution of the Federal System

Since 1789, when the U.S. federal system of government was put in place, the roles, responsibilities, and power dynamics among the three levels of U.S. government have evolved. In *Federalist* No. 45, James Madison (1788) stated that the powers delegated to the national government are "few and defined" and primarily focused on "external objects" such as war and peace, foreign relations, and commerce. He also noted that the powers reserved for the states are "numerous and indefinite," extending to matters affecting the daily "lives, liberties and properties of the people; and the internal order, improvement, and prosperity of the state [police powers]."[15]

Gary Gerstle, a respected scholar of American government, agrees with Madison's claims: as written, the Constitution anticipated that the national government would be limited in its roles and responsibilities and the state governments would be expansive. In his book *Liberty and Coercion* (2015), Gerstle argues that the Tenth Amendment's reserved powers grant the state governments "a staggering freedom of action." When balancing the enumerated powers of the federal government and the police powers reserved for the states, Gerstle claims that the federal system as established in the Constitution clearly gave dominant power to the states. However, according to Gerstle, presidents, congresses, and the U.S. Supreme Court have twisted the meaning of the Constitution over the course of U.S. history so that today, the federal government dominates. Therefore, today's federal system is not the system of government envisioned by the framers of the Constitution.[16]

Most government services and benefits today are products of collaborative efforts by two or more governments. To serve its people, a government must have the authority to formulate and approve a plan of action (policy statement), to raise and spend money to finance the plan (policy financing), and to hire workers who put the plan into action (policy implementation). Therefore, all public policies have three elements: the policy statement, the policy financing, and the policy implementation. In the U.S. federal system today, the responsibility for these three elements may rest entirely with one level of government (national, state, or local) or may be shared in a collaborative effort by two or more of these levels. Political scientists label the interactions of two or more governments (national, state, and local) in their collective efforts to provide goods and services to the people they serve **intergovernmental relations (IGR)**. Today, IGR is a dominant characteristic of the U.S. federal system of government.

To understand the intergovernmental relations of today's federal system and the expansion of federal power, we need to first survey several models of federalism, each of which characterizes different roles, responsibilities, and relationships between the national and state governments in the United States.

Dual Federalism

Initially, the dual sovereignty of the U.S. federal system was implemented in such a way that the national and state governments acted independently of each other. The national government raised its own money and spent it on policies it created. Each state government also raised its own money and spent it on policies it created. Political scientists give the name **dual federalism** to this pattern of implementation of the federal system, whereby the national government takes care of its enumerated powers and the states independently take care of their reserved powers. From 1789 through 1932, dual federalism was the dominant pattern of national-state relations. Congresses and presidents did enact some laws that states argued infringed on their powers, and the U.S. Supreme Court typically found in favor of the states in those cases. Yet, as the 1819 *McCulloch* case shows, sometimes the Supreme Court ruled in favor of the national government.

dual federalism
The initial model of national and state relations in which the national government takes care of its enumerated powers while the state governments independently take care of their reserved powers.

Cooperative Federalism

Passage of the Sixteenth Amendment (1913) powerfully enhanced the ability of the national government to raise money. The amendment granted Congress the authority to collect income taxes from workers and corporations without apportioning the taxes among the states on the basis of population (which the Constitution had required before this amendment). With the capacity to raise more revenue, the national government could financially assist states.

To help the state governments deal with the domestic problems spawned by the global economic depression that began in 1929 (the Great Depression), Congress and President Franklin D. Roosevelt (1933-1945) approved numerous policies, collectively called the New Deal. **Grants-in-aid**—transfers of money from one government (the national government) to another government (state and local governments) that need not be paid back—became a main mechanism of President Roosevelt's New Deal programs. State and local governments welcomed the national grants-in-aid, which assisted them in addressing the domestic matters that fell within their sovereignty while allowing them to make most of the specific program decisions to implement the policies. Through grants-in-aid, dual federalism was replaced by **cooperative federalism** in numerous policy matters. Collaborative intergovernmental relations was a product of cooperative federalism, which dominated national and state government relations from the New Deal era to the early 1960s.

grant-in-aid (intergovernmental transfer)
The transfer of money from one government to another government that does not need to be paid back.

cooperative federalism
Intergovernmental relations in which the national government supports state governments' efforts to address the domestic matters reserved to them.

Centralized Federalism

By the time of Lyndon Johnson's presidency (1963-1969), a new kind of federalism was developing. In this new form of federalism, the national government imposed its own policy preferences on state and local governments. Specifically, in **centralized federalism,** directives in national legislation, including grant-in-aid programs with ever-increasing conditions or strings attached to the money, force state and local governments to implement a particular national policy. Therefore, in centralized federalism, the national government dominates intergovernmental relations, imposing its policy preferences on state and local governments.

Presidents since Richard Nixon (1969-1974) have fought against this centralizing tendency by proposing to return policy responsibilities (policy making, policy financing, and policy implementation) to state and local governments. Presidents

centralized federalism
Intergovernmental relations in which the national government imposes its policy preferences on state and local governments.

devolution
The process whereby the national government returns policy responsibilities to state or local governments.

Nixon and Ronald Reagan (1981–1989) gave the name *new federalism* to these efforts, and today we use the term **devolution** to refer to the return of power to state and local governments.

Today, Republicans and Democrats (including presidents, members of Congress, and state and local lawmakers) broadly support devolution, but they debate *which elements of the policy* should be devolved: policy statements, policy financing, and/or policy implementation. They also butt heads over *which policies* to devolve. For example, President George W. Bush signed the No Child Left Behind (2002) education law, which expanded the national government's role in education. His successor, President Obama, signed the Every Student Succeeds Act (2015), which returned elements of education policy to the states.

Conflicted Federalism

conflicted federalism
Intergovernmental relations in which elements of dual federalism, co-operative federalism, and centralized federalism are evident in the domestic policies implemented by state and local governments.

David B. Walker, a preeminent scholar of federalism and intergovernmental relations, argues that the term **conflicted federalism** best describes the intergovernmental relations of the federal system today because conflicting elements of dual federalism, cooperative federalism, and centralized federalism are evident in domestic policies implemented by national, state, and local governments.[17] For some policy matters, the national and state governments operate independently of each other, and hence dual federalism is at work. For most policies, however, intergovernmental efforts are the norm. These efforts may be a means to advance state policy priorities (cooperative federalism), or they may be compelled by national legislation (centralized federalism) to advance national policy priorities.

Partisan Federalism

partisan federalism
The phenomenon of preference for state or national government action (hence, preference for dual federalism, cooperative federalism, or centralized federalism) depending on policy substance and partisan makeup of government at the other levels.

Although conflicts between the states and the national government have been a reality throughout U.S. history, contemporary scholarship on U.S. federalism notes increased "volume and intensity" in intergovernmental tensions.[18] During the 21st century, state governments have filed lawsuits against the national government over national health care policy, immigration policy, education policy, and environmental protection.[19] The national government has filed lawsuits against state and local governments over immigration policy, environmental protection, and voting rights.[20] States have increasingly acted to invalidate (nullify) national laws by enacting state laws that conflict with or modify national laws.[21] During the Obama administration, the governor of Texas even publicly mentioned secession.[22]

Federalism scholars identify increased political polarization and gridlock in Congress as factors that fuel intergovernmental tensions. That is, when there is gridlock in Congress and, therefore, a vacuum in a policy matter salient to states, state governments will step up and enact their preferred policies. With Democrats controlling government in some states and Republicans in others, state-level policies may conflict with each other, and some will conflict with the national government's priorities. In addition, when a state government is dominated by one party and Congress or the presidency is controlled by the opposing one, the state may act on its own, fulfilling its policy preferences. Scholar Jessica Bulman-Pozen argues that the U.S. federal system "provides durable and robust scaffolding for partisan conflict," which allows states and local governments to challenge national policies when the national government is controlled by the opposing party.[23] Bulman-Pozen labels this phenomenon **partisan federalism**—that is, a preference for state or national government action (hence, a preference for dual federalism,

THEN

NOW

>Between 1789 and the Great Depression, the model of federalism implemented in the United States was dual federalism. Dual federalism is often depicted as a slice of layer cake, with three distinct layers—three levels of government with clear distinctions among their responsibilities and powers. Today, conflicted federalism rules the day. In this model of federalism, which is depicted as a slice of marble cake with swirls of colors that flow into each other, the responsibilities and powers of the three levels of government are not clear and distinct. A confusion of conflicting intergovernmental relations dominates most domestic policies.

Layer cake: ©D. Hurst/Alamy Stock Photo; *marble cake:* ©Pawel Horosiewicz/Alamy Stock Photo

cooperative federalism, or centralized federalism) that depends on policy substance and partisan makeup of government at the other levels.[24]

Traditionally, since the New Deal, Democrats have supported federal government expansion in domestic policy matters. Republicans have been viewed as the party that supports states' rights (protects states' reserved powers) over national expansion. However, in today's era of partisan federalism, government officials at all levels of government and from both major political parties will support action by whichever level of government supports their policy preferences; state governments will support national action when it is in line with their preferences or state action when the national government opposes their preferences. The partisans in national government act this way, too. If they cannot obtain what they want through national action, they will support state action. According to a report from the Congressional Research Service, "the historical record suggests that for members of both political parties, regardless of their personal ideological preferences, federalism principles often lose out when in conflict with other policy goals."[25]

Conflicted and partisan federalism are the reality of the U.S. federal system today. What are the tools national and state governments use to foster intergovernmental relations, including intergovernmental cooperation and intergovernmental tensions?

Intergovernmental Relations

Constitutional language establishing our federal system of government, with dual sovereignty, remains essentially as it was in 1791. However, what that looks like on the ground is confusing (look back at that marble cake!). National grants-in-aid, funded and unfunded mandates, and preemption combined with states' rights established in the Tenth Amendment and interstate compacts intermingle to spawn intergovernmental relations that are sometimes cooperative, other times tense, and often downright hostile. Another product of all these elements of today's federalism is wide variation in policy from state to state on numerous domestic issues, from health care to legal use of marijuana to gun control to civil rights and civil liberties. National and state laws also conflict; in some cases states seem to have nullified federal law. We will now look at how intergovernmental tensions are affecting several issues.

Tools of Intergovernmental Relations

Although the national government shared its revenue surplus with the states in the form of grants-in-aid in 1837, it did not make a habit of offering grants-in-aid until the Great Depression of the 1930s. Today, federal grants-in-aid are 17 percent of the national government's annual spending, and they pay for about one-third of total state government funding.[26] Table 3.2 presents data on the state policies receiving the largest federal grants-in-aid. Figure 3.5 presents data on the total dollar value of federal grants-in-aid for select years since 1960.

The pervasiveness of intergovernmental transfers of money has led political scientists to the study of **fiscal federalism**—the intergovernmental relationships between the national government and state and local governments that grow out

fiscal federalism
The relationship between the national government and state and local governments whereby the national government provides grant money to state and local governments.

Evaluating the Facts

TABLE 3.2 Fiscal Federalism: Largest Federal Intergovernmental Transfers (2016)

PROGRAM	COST (IN BILLIONS)
Medicaid	$357
Federal-Aid-Highways	42
Child Nutrition	24
Tenant Based Rental Assistance (Section 8 Vouchers)	20
Accelerating Achievement and Ensuring Equity (Education for the Disadvantaged)	16
Temporary Assistance to Needy Families	15
Children's Health Insurance Fund	14
Special Education	13
State Children and Families Services Programs	11
Urban Mass Transportation Grants	10

Federal grants-in-aid provide approximately one-third of state and local government revenues. What information about each of these grant programs would you need to determine whether the program fits into the cooperative federalism model or the centralized federalism model?

SOURCE: Robert Jay Dilger, *Federal Grants to State and Local Governments: A Historical Perspective on Contemporary Issues* (Washington, D.C.: Congressional Research Service, 2017), 6.

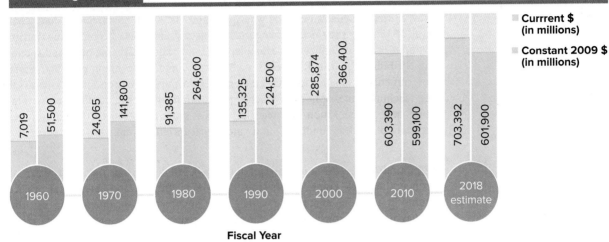

FIGURE 3.5 ■ **Federal Grants to State and Local Governments** State and local governments have come to depend on federal grants-in-aid, which make up about one-third of their budget revenues. The graph presents grant-in-aid data using two measures: the total amount of funds in constant dollars and the total amount of funds in current dollars. *Constant dollars* adjust for inflation (change in the value of the dollar), thereby removing the effect of price changes over time. *Current dollars* represent the dollar value at the time when the money was spent (in this case, transferred from the federal government to the state and local governments). Which measure—constant dollars or current dollars—do you think provides a better understanding of the trend in federal grants-in-aid? Explain your answer.

of the grants of money that the national government provides to state and local governments.

CATEGORICAL GRANTS   Historically, the most common type of grant-in-aid has been the **categorical formula grant**—a grant of money from the federal government to state and local governments for a narrow purpose, as defined by the federal government. The legislation that creates such a grant includes a formula determining how much money is available to each grant recipient. The formula is typically based on factors related to the purpose of the grant, such as the number of people in the state in need of the program's benefits. Categorical grants come with strings attached—that is, rules and regulations with which the recipient government must comply.

categorical formula grant
A grant-in-aid for a narrowly defined purpose, whose dollar value is based on a formula.

One typical string is a **matching funds requirement,** which obligates the government receiving the grant to spend some of its own money to match a specified percentage of the grant money provided. Matching funds requirements allow the national government to influence the budget decisions of state and local governments by forcing them to spend some of their own money on a national priority, which may or may not also be a state priority, in order to receive national funding. Medicaid, a health insurance program the national government created for low-income citizens, is jointly funded by federal and state money due to a matching funds requirement. Put into action primarily by state and local governments, this is one example of a national categorical formula grant program with strings attached.

matching funds requirement
A grant requirement that obligates the government receiving the grant to spend some of its own money to match a specified percentage of the grant money provided.

Since the 1960s, the national government has also offered categorical project grants. Like the categorical formula grant, a **categorical project grant** covers a narrow purpose (program area), but unlike the formula grant, a project grant does

categorical project grant
A grant-in-aid for a narrowly defined purpose for which governments compete with each other by proposing specific projects.

not include a formula specifying how much money a recipient will receive. Instead, state and local governments interested in receiving such a grant must compete for it by writing proposals detailing what programs they wish to implement and what level of funding they need. Categorical project grants have become common in national education policy. For example, in 2014, President Obama proposed spending $5 billion on the RESPECT categorical competitive grant program. State governments competed for this grant money to pursue reforms in all aspects of the teaching profession—from teacher preparation to teacher development, evaluation, and compensation. A categorical project grant has strings attached to it and typically offers less funding than a categorical formula grant.

block grant
A grant-in-aid for a broadly defined policy area, whose funding amount is typically based on a formula.

BLOCK GRANTS   Another type of formula-based intergovernmental transfer of money, the **block grant,** differs from categorical formula and categorical project grants in that the matters for which state and local governments can use the money is not narrowly defined, thus allowing state and local governments more discretion to decide how to spend the money. Whereas a categorical grant might specify that the money is to be used for a child care program, a block grant gives the recipient government more discretion to determine what program it will be used for within a broad policy area such as assistance to economically needy families with children. In 1996, the national government eliminated Aid to Families with Dependent Children (AFDC), its most well-known income assistance program to low-income families, which was a categorical formula grant program for states. It replaced AFDC with a block grant program for the states, Temporary Assistance to Needy Families (TANF).

mandates
Clauses in legislation that direct state and local governments to comply with national legislation and national standards.

When first introduced by the Nixon administration in the 1970s, block grants had fewer strings attached to them than did categorical grants. Today, however, the number and specificity of conditions included in block grants are increasing, which means increasing limits on state and local government discretion in policy making and program implementation.

State and local governments have grown dependent on national financial assistance, and so grants are an essential tool of national power to direct state and local government activity. Although the states welcome federal grant money, they do not welcome the strings attached to the funds, or *mandates.*

>Although in 1987 the Supreme Court found the drinking age mandate to be constitutional because it was attached to a grant, in 2012 the Court found unconstitutional a grant mandate attached to the national Affordable Care Act of 2010. What did the Affordable Care Act mandate require of states? What model of federalism do these two divergent Court decisions support?
©B Christopher/Alamy Stock Photo

MANDATES   National **mandates** are statements in national laws, including the strings attached to grants-in-aid, that require state and local governments to do something specified by the national government. Many national mandates relate to ensuring citizens' constitutional rights. For example, the Equal Employment Opportunity Act of 1972 extended the prohibitions against discrimination in employment established in the Civil Rights Act of 1964 to state and local government employment. In this case, the national government enacted the law to fulfill its constitutional responsibilities and imposes it on state and local governments.

When the national government assumes the entire cost of a mandate it imposes on a state or local government, it is a *funded mandate*. However, more often than not, the national government does not cover the entire cost of its mandates. Often, it does not cover any of the cost, forcing states to pick up the bill. When the state or local government must cover all or some of the cost, it is an *unfunded mandate*. Because grants-in-aid are voluntary—that is, state and local governments can decide to accept a grant-in-aid or to reject it—state and local governments can determine whether or not they can afford to accept the grant and hence its mandate. Although state and local governments have always opposed the strings attached to grants, the attaching of mandates to grant money has come under increasing fire.

In the 1923 case *Massachusetts v. Mellon,*[27] one of the first cases in which state governments questioned the national government's right to attach mandates to grant money, the Supreme Court found the mandates in national grants-in-aid to be constitutional, arguing that grants-in-aid are voluntary cooperative arrangements. By voluntarily accepting the national grant, the justices ruled, the state government agrees to the grant conditions. The Court's decision did not end states' challenges to grant mandates.

In 1987, South Dakota challenged a 1984 national transportation law that penalized states whose legal drinking age was lower than 21 years. The intent of the national law was to decrease driving while intoxicated (DWI) car accidents. States with legal drinking ages lower than 21 years would lose 10 percent of their national grant money for transportation. South Dakota argued that Congress was using grant conditions to put a law into effect that Congress could not achieve through national legislation because the law dealt with a power reserved to the states—determining the legal age for drinking alcoholic beverages.

In its decision in *South Dakota v. Dole,* the Court confirmed that the national government could not impose a national drinking age because setting a drinking age is indeed a reserved power of the states.[28] However, the Court found that the national government could *encourage* states to set a drinking age of 21 years by threatening to decrease their grants-in-aid for transportation. Ultimately, the national policy goal of a drinking age of 21 was indeed accomplished by 1988—not through a national law but through a condition attached to national highway funds offered to state governments, funds on which the states are dependent.

In the summer of 2012, the U.S. Supreme Court ruled on the constitutionality of the Affordable Care Act of 2010 (ACA).[29] In its decision, the Court found unconstitutional the act's mandate requiring states that accepted Medicaid grants to extend Medicaid coverage to additional lower-income citizens. The act mandated that a state that did not expand its coverage to additional citizens would lose all its Medicaid grant money—not just forfeit the new ACA grant money available to them for coverage expansion. Therefore, although state governments "voluntarily" participate in the Medicaid program by accepting Medicaid categorical grants, this ruling appears to limit the "financial penalty" the national government can impose through a grant's mandate. As a result of the Court's ruling, states have a choice to expand Medicaid coverage or not; it is not required. Initially, some states—mostly those with Democratic governors—expanded Medicaid coverage, while states with Republican governors were less apt to do so. However, many Republican-controlled states expanded their coverage after they received from the national government **waivers** that exempted them from some additional conditions attached to the ACA.

waivers
Exemptions from particular conditions normally attached to grants.

Presidents have used waivers to appease those who do not support mandates in a specific law in order to gain their support for it. Waivers often soften partisan opposition to a law with mandates.

preemption
The constitutionally based principle that allows a national law to supersede state or local laws.

PREEMPTION   Another means by which the national government can direct the actions of state and local governments is through preemption. **Preemption** means that a national policy supersedes a state or local policy because it deals with an enumerated or implied national power. Therefore, people must obey, and states must enforce, the national law even if the state or local government has its own law on the matter.

Preemption is common in environmental policy. Although states can enact and enforce laws with greater protections than are established in national environmental law, they cannot do less than what is called for in the national law. In late 2015, the national government's Federal Aviation Administration (FAA) began to warn state and local governments that it had enacted laws regarding the recreational use of drones and public safety, and that it, the FAA, is the top authority in regulating air space. Therefore, its new rules preempt existing state and local laws. State and local governments complained about the FAA's call for them to back off because, they argued, their rules offer better protection of safety and privacy than do the FAA rules.[30]

nullification
A legal theory that state governments have the authority to invalidate national actions they deem unconstitutional.

NULLIFICATION   **Nullification** is a legal theory that state governments have the authority to invalidate national actions they deem unconstitutional. (The Thinking Critically feature focuses on the theory of nullification.) Federalism scholars Adam Olson, Timothy Callaghan, and Andrew Karch investigated more than 2,500 state legislative proposals that fit into three categories of nullification activity from 2010 through 2016.[31] (The issues covered by the legislative proposals are listed in "Analyzing the Sources.")

Olson, Callaghan, and Karch identify three categories of nullification between 2010 and 2016: true nullification, non-acquiescence nullification, and inconsistent legislation. *True nullification* occurs when a state law explicitly declares the national law unconstitutional. This is very rare. More common is *non-acquiescence nullification,* which is when the state law claims the state will not cooperate with a national law without declaring the national law unconstitutional. The most common form of nullification is *inconsistent legislation nullification,* which occurs when the state law conflicts with or attempts to alter the rules or procedures enacted in an existing national law.

According to Olson, Callaghan, and Karch, "contemporary American federalism is characterized by unusually high tensions. These [nullification] bills appeared in every state, and their policy goals spanned the ideological spectrum." They also write that the "new partisan alignment at the national level [that began with Trump's inauguration in January 2017] also represents an opportunity to assess whether state-level Republicans' embrace of nullification during the Obama administration was principled or opportunistic."[32] If principled, then proposing nullification follows the tradition in which Republicans support states' rights. If opportunistic, then proposing nullification indicates that Republicans were opposing the policy preferences of a Democratic president and using nullification to that end, not merely to support states' rights.

The United States' experiment with a federal system of government has lasted more than 225 years. What began as a system of government with dual sovereignty implemented through a model of dual federalism has evolved into a system of government with dual sovereignty implemented through a model of conflicted

Thinking Critically

Can State Governments Nullify National Marijuana Law?

The Issue: Nullification is the theory that states have the authority to invalidate national laws. By 2018, 30 states and the District of Columbia had legalized marijuana in some form. Eight states and D.C. enacted laws legalizing marijuana for recreational use. These states are nullifying national law that criminalizes the growth, sale, possession, and use of marijuana. Do state governments have the constitutional authority to nullify national laws?

Yes: The Tenth Amendment allows a state to nullify a national law that exceeds the enumerated powers of the national government. If the national government enacts a law relevant to a matter that is reserved for the states, the states have the right to declare it void. One benefit of the federal system touted by the framers was that two levels of government exist to doubly protect citizens' rights and liberties. When states believe a national law or court ruling infringes on citizens' rights or liberties, states have an obligation to nullify it. In addition, the Constitution is a compact among the states. The states had to ratify it for it to go into effect. That means the states gave power to the national government and they can reclaim it.

No: In a federal system, neither the state governments nor the national government can nullify laws enacted by other governments because neither is sovereign over the other. Article VI of the Constitution establishes that the Constitution and national laws made in compliance with it are the supreme law of the land. All governments in the United States must comply with the supreme law of the land.

Other Approaches: The power of judicial review allows courts to determine if government actions, including enacted legislation, comply with the Constitution. If states believe that an action of the national government violates their constitutional authority, they can file a lawsuit against the national government. The proper interpretation of the enumerated powers, necessary and proper clause, the supremacy clause, and the Tenth Amendment are vital to the health of the union. If the debate over constitutionality of national or state laws gets too heated, the ultimate means of clarification is through a constitutional convention, which states can call for according to Article V of the Constitution.

What do you think?

1. Do you think a constitutional convention to clarify constitutional language will resolve the perpetual conflicts over state and national authority? Explain.

2. Some people are concerned that recent growth in the number of laws among the states that contradict each other as well as national law will spark domestic upheavals. Do you share this concern? Why or why not?

federalism. Although the national government works independently on some policy matters (such as national defense and foreign policy) and state governments work independently on others (such as land use and the regulation of occupations and professions), most domestic matters are addressed through mutual efforts of at least two, if not three, levels of government, through intergovernmental relations.

Intergovernmental Tensions

The pace of lawsuits filed by state attorneys general against the national government has become extraordinary. According to political scientist Paul Nolette, Republican state attorneys general filed five partisan briefs with the Supreme Court during President Clinton's administration. They filed 97 partisan briefs during the first seven years of Obama's presidency.[33] During the first seven months of Trump's presidency, "State attorneys from Massachusetts to New York to California, often working together, have brought more than 40 legal actions against the Trump administration," which is "an average of one lawsuit or legal motion

>Intergovernmental relations can be cooperative—for example, when national guardsmen assist state and local law enforcement personnel at large events, such as the Super Bowl. This image represents all three levels of government. Can you find the references to each of the three levels?

©Ezra Shaw/Getty Images

every five days since Trump's inauguration, not including many more letters, legal threats and formal comments to federal agencies." The chair of the Republican Attorneys General Association is concerned that the lawsuits are less about the law and more about opposing the president. At the same time, Democratic attorneys general claim their legal actions are based on merit.[34]

For example, on January 1, 2018, the California Values Act went into effect. This state law "restricts state authorities from cooperating with federal immigration agents, and places limits on agents entering schools, churches, hospitals or courthouses to detain undocumented immigrants."[35] Although the law is inconsistent with the national government's efforts to detain and possibly deport undocumented immigrants, other states have also proposed laws to limit the role their local police officers can play in national immigration policy enforcement. In response to such initiatives, Attorney General Jeff Sessions, the head of the national Department of Justice, threatened to withhold federal grant money. At the same time, other states have proposed laws that require local governments to cooperate with Immigration and Customs Enforcement (ICE) officers.[36]

As another example, in 2009, the U.S. attorney general announced that the federal government would not prosecute individuals for dispensing marijuana or using it in compliance with state laws in states that legalized such activity. Then in 2013, as states began to legalize recreational marijuana use, the Department of Justice issued a policy memo that acknowledged marijuana as an illegal drug according to federal law, yet instructed federal prosecutors to deprioritize marijuana-related prosecutions in states that had enacted laws decriminalizing recreational marijuana use (except in cases that were gang related or where marijuana was sold to children).[37] In 2018, however, the Department of Justice rescinded the Obama administration's policy, hence freeing federal prosecutors to enforce national marijuana laws in states whose policies are inconsistent with (nullify) the national laws.[38]

Last, governors, who traditionally steer clear of global issues have become more involved in such issues since the inauguration of President Trump.[39] A dozen governors established a coalition to partially implement the Paris climate agreement after Trump rejected it. Governor Jerry Brown of California even traveled to a meeting on climate with China's president. Foreign trade is another issue on which governors from both major political parties have shown concern with the Trump administration's directions. In one instance, the National Governors Association invited Canadian Prime Minister Justin Trudeau to address the members—the first foreign leader to ever address the group—at its summer 2017 meeting.

The dual sovereignty established in the Constitution has evolved into a complex web of relationships among the national, state, and state-created local governments in the United States. There is both intergovernmental cooperation and intergovernmental tension. And questions continue about the constitutional distribution of sovereignty between the national and state governments; many of these questions end up in front of the courts. After more than 230 years of experience with dual sovereignty, one can identify both advantages and disadvantages in the federal system of government as it functions today.

Advantages and Disadvantages of Today's Federalism

When political scientists discuss the advantages and disadvantages of the federal system, what one person argues is an advantage may look like a disadvantage to another. For example, a frequently stated advantage of the federal system is the numerous access points for citizens to participate in their governments. Citizens can engage with national, state, county, municipal, and school district governments. They elect representatives to multiple governments so that they will be responsive to their needs and protect their rights.

For citizens, however, the availability of so many access points might be confusing and time consuming. Which government is the one with the legal responsibility to solve the problem you want addressed? Which elected official or government has the authority and resources to solve a specific problem? Vague constitutional language does not make these easy questions for either citizens or government officials to answer.

Moreover, each election requires citizens to research candidates running for office. Who has the time? Each year, every state has a primary election day and a general election day. On any given election day, a citizen may be asked to vote for a handful of government officials or dozens. Voters elect more than 500,000 government officials to serve them in the three levels of government. Some political scientists argue that voter turnout would be higher if there were fewer elections.

Another proclaimed advantage of the federal system is that it offers flexibility that makes for more efficient, effective, and responsive government. For example, because of their proximity, local and state governments can respond more quickly, and with a better understanding, to regional problems and needs than can the national government. In addition, what is a problem in one location may not be a problem elsewhere in the nation. Therefore, a national policy may not be appropriate. Moreover, the solution (policy) supported by citizens in one area may not be supported by citizens in a different area. One-size-fits-all national policies are not necessarily effective for all or supported by all.

Yet, some problems and needs cross state borders and affect the entire nation. As a result, we need national policies for some matters, state policies for other

THEN NOW NEXT

Americans' Trust* in Their Governments

	Then (Sep. 7–10, 2001)	Now (Sep. 7–10, 2017)
Your local government handling local affairs	69%	70%
Your state government handling state affairs	65%	63%
The national government handling domestic affairs	60%	45%

*Trust is defined as those responding to the Gallup poll indicating that they have a "great deal" or a "fair amount" of trust and confidence in the government.

SOURCE: Trust in Government, Gallup.

WHAT'S NEXT?

> What will become of the gap between Americans' trust in their state and local governments compared to their national government in its handling of domestic policies? Will that gap be sustained, or even grow larger, as state and local governments' challenges to national policies increase?

> Will Americans' expectations for their state and local governments grow if their trust in the national government's handling of domestic affairs shrinks?

> Will Americans' greater trust in their state and local governments foster increasing support for states' rights over the expansion of national power?

matters, and local policies for still others. A federal system provides for policies at all three levels of government.

However, this flexibility may lead to duplication of effort as multiple governments enact policies to address the same concern of their overlapping citizens. Duplication of effort is costly to taxpayers and inefficient. On the other hand, multiple governments enacting different policies to address the same problem allows for experimentation and innovation in the search for the best solution. Governments observing other governments' efforts to solve a problem can then adopt the policy they deem best for their citizens.

One clear disadvantage to the federal system is that it creates inequalities in services and policies; some state or local governments provide their citizens with better public services or more rights than citizens elsewhere. Today, legal rights and privileges (such as the right to legal use of marijuana or to lower in-state college tuition) depend on the state in which you live. Such inequalities may satisfy those who support state laws on given matters, but they dissatisfy those who do not support the laws and want the same rights as citizens in other states. Vague constitutional language also allows states to enact policies that may infringe on national sovereignty, and it allows the national government to enact policies that may infringe on state sovereignty. Conflicts over sovereignty can disrupt domestic tranquility (via protests and demonstrations) and lead to costly lawsuits. They may also fuel distrust and dissatisfaction with governments.

Today, we see hostility and tension between state governments and the national government over numerous issues, including immigration reform, the right to bear arms and gun control, the right to abortion, the expansion of Medicaid eligibility, and the proper implementation of the Affordable Care Act. Some observers have begun to discuss a new states' rights movement[40] as state governments that do not agree with a national policy enact their own laws that may conflict with national laws.

Polarization in Congress, which leads to gridlock, is fueling the states' rights movement. When Congress cannot agree on policies to solve problems, state governments step into the silence and pass their own policies. The result can be conflicting state policies and state policies that infringe on national sovereignty. Ultimately, the courts may have to resolve these conflicts.

Conclusion Thinking Critically About What's Next for Federalism

Today's federalism (conflicted federalism) is not the framers' federalism (dual federalism). James Madison and other framers argued that the national government's powers were limited by the Constitution and focused on foreign affairs and defense matters, while states' powers were expansive and covered domestic issues. However, the proper distribution of authority and balance of power between the national and state governments has always been controversial. Until recent decades, the Supreme Court's interpretations tended to favor an expansion of the national government's enumerated and implied powers into a growing number of domestic matters. However, the past few decades have witnessed inconsistency in the Court's interpretations. The Court protects and even expands national powers in some cases while protecting states' powers in other cases.

The national government has created a complex web of intergovernmental relations through its application of the Fourteenth Amendment, as well as grants-in-aid, mandates, and preemption. IGR makes it difficult to determine what governments are in charge of making policy, financing policy, and implementing policy; therefore, it can be hard to know which government can solve your particular problem.

Today, we see increasing differences among state policies enacted to address similar needs and concerns of their residents. States are experimenting to find effective policies that their citizens support. Because of years of gridlock in Congress over several policy matters that traditionally were the purview of the national government, we also are witnessing an increase in state and local laws enacted to fill in the national policy silences. Moreover, state governments are enacting laws that often seem to conflict with national laws. IGR, conflicted federalism, and partisan federalism are today's reality.

Learning Summary

1. Compare the unitary, confederal, and federal systems of government.
   a. Describe what living in the U.S. federal system of government means to a citizen's rights, responsibilities, and public services.

2. Explain the constitutional distribution of powers and responsibilities between the national and state governments.
   a. Define concurrent powers and identify them.
   b. Explain the enumerated powers and the implied powers of the national government.
   c. Explain the national supremacy clause.
   d. Describe the rationale for the Tenth Amendment and the reserved powers and police powers that it delegates to state governments.
   e. Explain the constitutional clauses that establish horizontal federalism.
   f. Explain why the Supreme Court must interpret the Constitution.
   g. Explain the main constitutional clauses the Supreme Court has used to expand the responsibilities and power of the national government.
   h. Define and provide examples of judicial federalism.

3. Outline the evolution of the U.S. federal system by discussing the multiple models of federalism and the tools of intergovernmental relations.
   a. Contrast dual federalism, cooperative federalism, centralized federalism, conflicted federalism, and partisan federalism.
   b. Explain the tools of intergovernmental relations: categorical grants, block grants, mandates, preemption, and nullification.

4. Describe the realities of today's intergovernmental relations.
   a. Describe some examples of cooperative intergovernmental relations.
   b. Describe some examples of intergovernmental tensions.
   c. Describe some advantages of the U.S. federal system of government.
   d. Describe some disadvantages of the U.S. federal system of government.

Key Terms

block grant 106

categorical formula grant 105

categorical project grant 105

centralized federalism 101

concurrent powers 91

confederal system 88

conflicted federalism 102

cooperative federalism 101

devolution 102

dual federalism 101

enumerated powers 92

extradition 96

federal system 88

fiscal federalism 104

full faith and credit clause 96

grants-in-aid 101

horizontal federalism 96

implied powers 92

intergovernmental relations (IGR) 100

interstate compacts 96

judicial federalism 100

mandates 106

matching funds requirement 105

McCulloch v. Maryland 97

necessary and proper clause (elastic clause) 92

nullification 108

partisan federalism 102

police powers 94

preemption 108

privileges and immunities clause 96

reserved powers 94

supreme law of the land 92

unitary system 88

waivers 107

For Review

1. In terms of which government is sovereign, differentiate among a unitary system, a confederal system, and a federal system of government.

2. To which level of government does the Constitution distribute the enumerated powers? Implied powers? Concurrent powers? Reserved powers? Provide several examples of each power.

3. What matters fall within the scope of state sovereignty?

4. Differentiate among dual federalism, cooperative federalism, centralized federalism, horizontal federalism, partisan federalism, and conflicted federalism.

5. How does the national government use grants-in-aid, mandates, and preemption to direct the policy of state and local governments?

6. What do we mean by intergovernmental relations? Why is the term a good description of U.S. federalism today?

7. Explain some advantages and some disadvantages for citizens of the U.S. federal system of government.

For Critical Thinking and Discussion

1. Is the federal system of government that provides citizens with the opportunity to elect a large number of officials each year a benefit or a burden for citizens? Explain your answer.

2. Would the amount of money citizens pay for their governments through taxes and fees decrease if there were fewer governments serving them? Defend your answer.

3. Would the quality or quantity of government services decrease if there were fewer governments in the United States? Why or why not?

4. Note at least three societal problems you believe the national government can address best (more effectively and efficiently than state or local governments). Discuss why you believe the national government is best suited to address these problems. Do these problems fit in the category of enumerated national powers? Explain your answer.

5. Note at least three societal problems you believe state or local governments can address best (more effectively and efficiently than the national government). Discuss why you believe state or local governments are best suited to address these problems. Do these problems fit in the category of powers reserved to the states? Explain your answer.

6. Which of your governments (national, state, county, municipal/township, or school district) do you believe has the greatest effect on your daily life? Explain your answer.

Resources for Research AND Action

Internet Resources

Bureau of the Census
www.census.gov Access multiple sources of data about national and state governments at this site.

Catalog of Federal Domestic Assistance
www.cfda.gov On this site you will find a full listing of all federal programs available to state and local governments; federally recognized tribal governments; public and private organizations and institutions; specialized groups; and individuals.

Council of State Governments
www.csg.org At this site, state officials can share information on common problems and possible solutions.

National Conference of State Legislatures
www.ncsl.org This site provides resources to state legislatures to fulfill the NCSL's goals of ensuring positive intergovernmental relations, by fostering a strong cohesive voice for state legislatures in the federal system and promoting policy innovation and communication among the states.

National Governors Association (NGA)
www.nga.org The NGA lobbies the national government on behalf of governors and also provides the governors with opportunities to share information on policies.

Publius
www.publius.oxfordjournals.org This is the website of *Publius,* a scholarly journal for the study of federalism.

Tenth Amendment Center
www.tenthamendcenter.com This Center seeks to educate people about the original meaning of the Constitution, with a focus on states' rights.

Recommended Readings

Gerstle, Gary. *Liberty and Coercion: The Paradox of American Government From the Founding to the Present.* Princeton, NJ: Princeton University Press, 2015. A comprehensive and critical review of the American federal system. Gerstle believes that the federal system is structured to favor state domination; however, presidents, Congresses, and the courts have twisted this vision of state dominance.

Levinson, Sanford (editor). *Nullification and Secession in Modern Constitutional Thought.* Lawrence: University Press of Kansas, 2016. This edited volume offers a survey of nullification and secession that offers new insights and raises questions about federalism and constitutional politics.

O'Toole, Laurence J. *American Intergovernmental Relations: Foundations, Perspectives, and Issues,* 3rd ed. Washington, D.C.: CQ Press, 2000. A collection of readings giving a comprehensive overview of U.S. federalism and intergovernmental relations, covering historical, theoretical, and political perspectives as well as fiscal and administrative views.

Robertson, David Brian. *Federalism and the Making of America.* New York: Routledge, 2012. A comprehensive review of the evolution of federalism in the United States, with a focus on the effect of intergovernmental relations on major policy battles in U.S history.

Walker, David B. *The Rebirth of Federalism: Slouching Toward Washington,* 2nd ed. Washington, D.C.: CQ Press, 2000. Both a history of U.S. federalism and an assessment of the status of U.S. federalism today.

Movies of Interest

Code of the West (2012)
This film documents the human and political story behind the legislative process in Montana's battle over legalized medicinal marijuana. Featuring policy advocates on both sides of the debate—lobbyists, growers, patients, lawmakers—the film provides insights into the challenging legal and moral questions raised in the debate, state political processes, and federalism questions that are evident through the federal crackdown on medical marijuana growers.

When the Levees Broke: A Requiem in Four Acts (2006)
This Spike Lee documentary critically examines the responses of federal, state, and local governments to Hurricane Katrina. Through images of the disaster, interviews with Katrina's victims, and clips of government officials' media interviews, Lee focuses on racial issues and intergovernmental ineptitude—from the poor construction of the levees to the delayed and inadequate federal, state, and local response.

Hoxie: The First Stand (2003)
This documentary presents one of the first integration battles in the South post–*Brown v. Board of Education of Topeka, Kansas.* The opponents are the Hoxie Board of Education, which in the summer of 1955 decided to integrate its schools, and grassroots citizens' organizations that resisted integration through petitions, harassment, and threats of violence against the school board members, their families, and the school superintendent.

Dances With Wolves (1990)
Sent to command the U.S. Army's westernmost outpost in the 1860s, Lieutenant John Dunbar witnesses, as an observer and a participant, the conflicts created in the Dakota Territory as white settlers encroach on territory of the Sioux Indians. Movie critics and historians praised Kevin Costner (the movie's director and lead actor) for correcting the erroneous image of Native Americans presented in classic Hollywood Westerns.

References

1. *National Federation of Independent Business* v. *Sebelius,* 567 U.S. 519 (2012).
2. Anna Fifield, "Kennesaw, Where Everyone Is Armed by Law," *Financial Times,* September 25, 2010.
3. Andrew Blake, "Hawaii Becomes First State to Raise Legal Smoking Age to 21," *The Washington Times,* January 5, 2016.
4. National Conference of State Legislators, "Federal and State Recognized Tribes."
5. Dennis L. Dresang and James J. Gosling, *Politics and Policy in American States and Communities,* 4th ed. (New York: Pearson Longman, 2004).
6. *V.L. v. E.L., et al.* 136 S. Ct. 1017 (2016).
7. *McCulloch v. Maryland,* 17 U.S. 316 (1819).
8. *Gibbons v. Ogden,* 22 U.S. 1 (1824).
9. *Helvering v. Davis,* 301 U.S. 619 (1937).
10. *United States v. Lopez,* 514 U.S. 549 (1995).
11. *Pruneyard Shopping Center & Fred Sahadi v. Michael Robins et al.,* 447 U.S. 74, 100 S. Ct. 2035.
12. "Old Enough to Drive—And Vote?" *Governing* (October 2013): 9.
13. *San Antonio Independent School District v. Rodriguez,* 411 U.S. 1 (1973).
14. G. Alan Tarr, *Judicial Process and Judicial Policymaking,* 6th ed. (Boston, MA: Cengage Learning, 2014), 309.
15. James Madison, "Federalist No. 45," *The Federalist Papers* (Cutchogue, NY: Buccaneer Books, 1992), 236.
16. Gary Gerstle, *Liberty and Coercion: The Paradox of American Government From the Founding to the Present* (Princeton, NJ: Princeton University Press, 2015).
17. David B. Walker, *The Rebirth of Federalism,* 2nd ed. (New York: Chatham House, 2000).
18. Greg Goelzhauser and S. Rose, "The State of American Federalism 2016–2017: Policy Reversals and Partisan Perspectives on Intergovernmental Relations," *Publius: The Journal of Federalism,* 47, no. 3 (2017): 285-313; Adam Olson, T. Callaghan, and A. Karch, "Return of the 'Rightful Remedy': Partisan Federalism, Resource Availability, and Nullification Legislation in the American States," *Publius: The Journal of Federalism,* 48, no. 3 (2018), 1-28.
19. Goelzhauser and Rose, "The State of American Federalism 2016-2017."
20. Daniel C. Vock, "At Odds," *Governing* (June 2016): 24-31.
21. Olson, Callaghan, and Karch. "Return of the 'Rightful Remedy.'"
22. Vock. "At Odds."
23. As quoted in Goelzhauser and Rose, "The State of American Federalism 2016-2017."
24. Jessica Bulman-Pozen, "Partisan Federalism," *Harvard Law Review* 124, no. 4 (2014): 1077-1146.
25. Robert Jay Dilger, *Federal Grants to State and Local Governments: A Historical Perspective on Contemporary Issues* (Washington, DC: Congressional Research Service, 2017), 39.
26. Dilger, *Federal Grants to State and Local Governments.*
27. *Massachusetts v. Mellon,* 262 U.S. 447 (1923).
28. *South Dakota v. Dole,* 483 U.S. 208 (1987).
29. *National Federation of Independent Business v. Sebelius,* 567 U.S. _____, 132 S. Ct. 2566 (2012).
30. Cecilia Kang, "Localities Object as F.A.A. Asserts Drone Authority," *New York Times,* December 28, 2015.
31. Olson, Callaghan, and Karch, "Return of the 'Rightful Remedy.'"
32. Ibid.
33. Alan Greenblatt, "The Pruitt Backlash," *Governing* (February 2017): 9.
34. Steve Peoples, "Dem Attorneys General Escalate Fight vs. Trump," *Times-Tribune,* August 14, 2017: B9.
35. Tim Arango, "In Clash between California and Trump, It's One America versus Another," *New York Times,* January 7, 2018.
36. Jennifer Medina and Jess Bidgood, "California Moves to Add Protections for Immigrants: Other States Follow," *New York Times,* April 11, 2017.
37. "Justice Department Announces Update to Marijuana Enforcement Policy."
38. Charlie Savage and Jack Healy, "Trump Administration to Move to Weaken Marijuana Legalization Movement," *New York Times,* January 4, 2018, https://nyti.ms/2E6rxbE.
39. Alexander Burns, "Going around Trump, Governors Embark on Their Own Diplomatic Missions," *New York Times,* July 15, 2017.
40. Dylan Scott, "The United States of America: In the Absence of Strong Federal Policies, States Have Become More Active—and More Divergent—Than They've Been in Decades," *Governing* (June 2013): 42-47; Peter Harkness, "Shall We Overcome? After 50 Years, a New No-Holds Barred States' Rights Movement Has Emerged," *Governing* (November 2013): 18-19.

CHAPTER 4

Civil Liberties

©Larry Marano/REX/Shutterstock

THEN

The Bill of Rights was designed to protect citizens' rights to speak and act without undue monitoring by or interference from the national government; however, Congress soon legislated exceptions to those protections.

NOW

Ideas about liberty in the context of such areas as religion and privacy often conflict with one another, resulting in tensions that legislatures and courts must resolve.

NEXT

Will the nation find ways to balance the Second Amendment's guarantee of a protected individual right to bear arms with concerns about security and the increased visibility of mass shootings?

How do we protect free speech on public campuses while recognizing a more diverse community?

A strong belief in civil

liberties is deeply embedded in our understanding of what it means to be an American. Civil liberties protect people from government intrusion and allow them to follow their own belief systems. Civil liberties also empower people to speak out against the government, as long as they do not harm others.

Since the nation's founding, political discourse among the people has often focused on the ideals of liberty and freedom. The colonists took up arms against Britain because the king and Parliament refused to recognize their liberties as English citizens: freedom of speech and assembly and the right to be free from unrestrained governmental power, especially in the investigation and prosecution of crimes. Withdrawing their consent to be governed by the king, they created a new government that would tolerate political discourse and disagreement and that could not legally disregard the collective or individual will of citizens.

Ideologies of liberty and freedom inspired the War for Independence and the founding of the new nation.[1] Those rights, though guaranteed, were never absolute. In fact, one of the earliest acts passed by Congress after the Bill of Rights was the Alien and Sedition Acts (1798), which not only limited immigration but also prohibited certain criticisms of the government. From its origins, the Constitution guaranteed basic liberties, but those protections were tempered by other goals and values, perhaps most importantly by the goal of order and the need to protect people and their property. Following the terrorist attacks of September 11, 2001, the national government enacted laws aimed at protecting American citizens and property from further attacks, such as the Parkland shootings in 2018. But those laws, in some cases, overturned decades of legal precedents that protected civil liberties. As technology evolves, the government's ability to engage in surveillance activities that escape public awareness increases, as does the capacity of private individuals and anonymous groups to expose these activities. Is such public exposure a way of holding the government accountable or an act of treason?

Learning Objectives

After reading this chapter, students should be able to:

- Summarize how the Constitution demonstrates a commitment to liberty.
- Define the "right to bear arms."
- Explain how freedoms of speech, press, and assembly are important to democracy.
- Summarize how freedoms of religion, privacy, and criminal due process can be limited.
- Evaluate ways in which liberty and security interests are currently in conflict.

Civil Liberties in the American Legal System

Civil liberties are individual liberties established in the Constitution and safeguarded by state and federal courts. We also refer to civil liberties as *personal freedoms* and often use the concepts of "liberty" and "freedom" interchangeably.

Civil liberties differ from civil rights. **Civil liberties** are constitutionally established guarantees that protect citizens, opinions, and property *against* arbitrary

civil liberties
Constitutionally established guarantees that protect citizens, opinions, and property against arbitrary government interference.

government interference. In contrast, civil rights (the focus of Chapter 5) reflect positive acts of government (in the form of constitutional provisions or statutes) *for* the purpose of protecting individuals against arbitrary or discriminatory actions. For example, the freedom of speech, a liberty established in the First Amendment to the U.S. Constitution, protects citizens against the government's censorship of their words, in particular when those words are politically charged. In contrast, the constitutionally protected right to vote requires the government to step in to ensure that all citizens be allowed to vote, without restriction by individuals, groups, or government officials.

The Freedoms Protected in the American System

The U.S. Constitution, through the Bill of Rights, and state constitutions explicitly recognize and protect civil liberties. As demonstrated in the Constitution in Chapter 2, the first 10 amendments to the Constitution explicitly limited the power of the legislative, executive, and judicial branches of the national government.

The Bill of Rights established freedoms essential to individuals' and groups' free and effective participation in the larger community. Without these protections, citizens could not freely express their opinions through rallies, speeches, protests, letters, pamphlets, tweets, blogs, e-mail, and other forms of civic engagement. The Constitution's framers, who had been denied these liberties under British rule, saw them as indispensable to forming a new democratic republic.

The meanings of these precious freedoms have shifted over the course of U.S. history, as presidents, legislators, judges, and ordinary citizens have changed their minds about how much freedom the people should have. When Americans have not perceived themselves as being under some external threat, they generally have adopted an expansive interpretation of civil liberties. At those times, citizens tend to believe that the government should interfere as little as necessary in individuals' lives, strongly supporting people's right to gather with others and to speak their minds. When the nation has been under some perceived threat, citizens have often allowed the government to limit protected freedoms.[2] (See "Analyzing the Sources.") Limits have also extended to many **due process** protections—legal safeguards that prevent the government from arbitrarily depriving people of life, liberty, or property without adhering to strict legal procedures. In this chapter, we consider not only the historical context of our civil liberties but also recent changes in how Congress, the president, and the courts interpret these liberties.

due process
The legal safeguards that prevent the government from arbitrarily depriving citizens of life, liberty, or property; guaranteed by the Fifth and Fourteenth Amendments.

The Historical Basis for American Civil Liberties: The Bill of Rights

The framers vividly remembered the censorship and suppression of speech that they had suffered under British rule. Colonists had been harshly punished, often by imprisonment and confiscation of their property and even death, if they criticized the British government, through both speech and the publication of pamphlets. The framers understandably viewed liberty as a central principle guiding the creation of a new democratic republic. Federalists such as Alexander Hamilton

Analyzing the Sources

BALANCING THE TENSION BETWEEN LIBERTY AND SECURITY

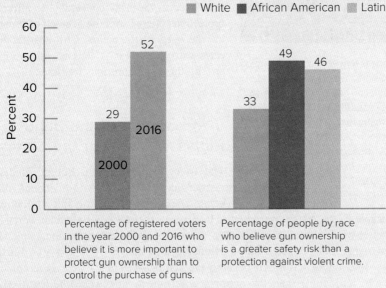

Legend: ■ White ■ African American ■ Latin

Percentage of registered voters in the year 2000 and 2016 who believe it is more important to protect gun ownership than to control the purchase of guns.
- 2000: 29
- 2016: 52

Percentage of people by race who believe gun ownership is a greater safety risk than a protection against violent crime.
- White: 33
- African American: 49
- Latin: 46

SOURCE: Pew Research Center, "Opinions on Gun Policy and the 2016 Campaign," August 26, 2016.

Practice Analytical Thinking

1. In recent years, we have seen an increase in mass shootings in the United States with larger numbers of victims. How might these shootings on U.S. soil affect public opinion on the issue of liberty versus security?

2. What does this public opinion data tell us about perceptions of how tensions between liberty and security can be resolved?

saw the Constitution itself as a bill of rights because it delegated specific powers to the national government and contained specific provisions designed to protect citizens against an abusive government.

Some constitutional protections were designed to protect people from being punished, imprisoned, or executed for expressing political beliefs or opposition. These are noted on the annotated Constitution in Chapter 2. However, the Anti-Federalists still stressed the need for a written bill of rights. As we saw in Chapter 2, the ratification of the Constitution stalled because citizens feared that the government might use its expanded powers to limit individual freedoms, particularly those associated with political speech and engagement. The First Amendment, which ensures freedom of religion, the press, assembly, and speech, was essential to political speech and to discourse in the larger society.

The freedoms embodied in the Bill of Rights are broad principles rather than specific prohibitions against governmental action. From the nation's beginnings, the vagueness of the Bill of Rights led to serious disagreement about how to interpret its amendments. For example, the First Amendment's establishment clause states simply that "Congress shall make no law respecting an establishment of religion." Some commentators, most notably Thomas Jefferson, argued that the clause mandated a "wall of separation between church and state" and barred any

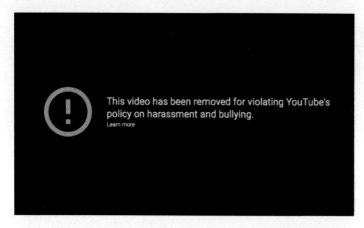

federal support of religion. Others interpreted the clause more narrowly as barring only the establishment of a national religion or the requirement that all public officials swear an oath to some particular religion.

Other freedoms, too, have been subject to differing interpretations, including the First Amendment guarantees of freedom of speech, assembly, and the press. These conflicting interpretations often arise in response to public crises or security concerns. Security concerns also affect the protections offered to those accused of threatening the safety of the nation. Civil liberties advocates worry that fear is causing Americans to give up their most precious freedoms.

>When YouTube began removing posted videos that violated their harassment and bullying policy, some individuals claimed the privately owned company was engaged in viewpoint discrimination and a violation of free speech. While the company is not a government entity limited by the First Amendment, challengers claim that in the twenty-first century, companies like YouTube, Google, and Facebook are the equivalent of the public square. Do you think private companies in cyberspace should give users of these large social media conglomerates the same free speech rights as the government must provide in physical public space?
Source: YouTube

Incorporation of the Bill of Rights to Apply to the States

The framers intended the Bill of Rights to restrict the powers of only the *national government.* They did not see the Bill of Rights as applicable to the state governments. In general, there was little public worry that the states would curtail civil liberties, because most state constitutions included a bill of rights that protected the individual against abuses of state power. Further, it was generally believed that because the state governments were geographically closer to the people than the national government, they would be less likely to encroach upon individual rights and liberties.

Through most of early U.S. history, the Bill of Rights applied to the national government, but not to the states. That assumption is illustrated by the case of *Barron v. Baltimore* (1833), in which a wharf owner named Barron sued the city of Baltimore. Barron claimed that the city had violated the "takings clause" of the Fifth Amendment, which bars the taking of private property for public use without just compensation. *Barron* argued that by paving its streets, the city of Baltimore had changed the natural course of certain streams; the resulting buildup of silt and gravel in the harbor made his wharf unusable. In *Barron,* the Supreme Court determined that the Fifth Amendment applies only to actions taken by the federal government and not to state actions.[3]

In 1868, three years after the Civil War ended, the Fourteenth Amendment was added to the U.S. Constitution. The Fourteenth Amendment reads as if it were meant to extend the protections of the Bill of Rights to citizens' interactions with *state governments:*

> No State shall make or enforce any law which shall abridge the privileges or immunities of citizens of the United States; nor shall any State deprive any person of life, liberty, or property, without due process of law; nor deny to any person within its jurisdiction the equal protection of the laws.

total incorporation
The theory that the Fourteenth Amendment's due process clause requires the states to uphold *all* freedoms in the Bill of Rights; rejected by the Supreme Court in favor of selective incorporation.

Although this language sounds like an effort to protect citizens' rights and liberties from arbitrary interference by state governments, the Supreme Court rejected the doctrine of **total incorporation:** that is, the application of *all* the protections contained in the Bill of Rights to the states. Instead, beginning with a series of cases decided by the Court in the 1880s, the justices formulated a narrower approach, known as **selective incorporation.**[4] This approach considered each protection individually, one case at a time, for possible incorporation into the Fourteenth Amendment and application to the states. The Court determined that due process mandates the incorporation of those rights that serve the fundamental principles of liberty and justice, those that were at the core of the "very idea of free government" and that were unalienable rights of citizenship.

As Table 4.1 shows, it was not until 1925 that the Court gradually began the process of incorporation, starting with the First Amendment protections most central to democratic government and civic engagement. That year, in the case of *Gitlow v. New York,* the Court held that freedom of speech is "among the fundamental personal rights and 'liberties' protected by the due process clause of the

selective incorporation
The process by which, over time, the Supreme Court applied those freedoms that served *some* fundamental principle of liberty or justice to the states, thus rejecting total incorporation.

Evaluating the Facts

TABLE 4.1 Selective Incorporation of the Bill of Rights

The process of selective incorporation has been very slow; while a Supreme Court decision in 1897 was later understood to incorporate a right to the state, the Supreme Court did not deliberately begin the process until 1925, and it continues until today. What trends do you see in the incorporation of the Bill of Rights to the states? What categories of rights were more quickly applied to the states under the Fourteenth Amendment and which ones took longer? Do you think those amendments that have not been currently incorporated might be in the future? Why or why not?

DATE	LIBERTY	AMENDMENT	KEY CASE
1897	Right to just compensation (for property taken by government)	V	*Chicago, B&Q RR Co. v. Chicago*
1925	Freedom of speech	I	*Gitlow v. New York*
1931	Freedom of the press	I	*Near v. Minnesota*
1937	Freedom of assembly and petition	I	*DeJonge v. Oregon*
1940	Freedom to practice religion	I	*Cantwell v. Connecticut*
1947	Freedom from government-established religion	I	*Everson v. Board of Education*
1948	Right to a public trial	VI	*In re Oliver*
1949	No unreasonable searches and seizures	IV	*Wolf v. Colorado*
1961	Exclusionary rule	IV	*Mapp v. Ohio*
1962	No cruel and unusual punishments	VIII	*Robinson v. California*
1963	Right to counsel in criminal cases	VI	*Gideon v. Wainwright*
1964	No compulsory self-incrimination	V	*Malloy v. Hogan*
1965	Right to confront witnesses	VI	*Pointer v. Texas*
1966	Right to an impartial jury	VI	*Parker v. Gladden*
1967	Right to a speedy trial	VI	*Klopfer v. North Carolina*
1968	Right to a jury in criminal trials	VI	*Duncan v. Louisiana*
1969	No double jeopardy	VII	*Benton v. Maryland*
2010	Right to bear arms	II	*McDonald v. City of Chicago*
	No quartering of soldiers	III	Not incorporated
	Right to grand jury indictment	V	Not incorporated
	Right to a jury in civil trials	VII	Not incorporated
	No excessive fines or bail	VIII	Not incorporated

Fourteenth Amendment from impairment by the states."[5] In 1931, in its decision in *Near v. Minnesota,* the Court added freedom of the press, and in 1937 it added freedom of assembly to the list of incorporated protections.[6]

Incorporation progressed further with the landmark case of *Palko v. Connecticut* (1937), in which the Court laid out a formula for defining fundamental rights that later courts have used time and time again in incorporation cases, as well as in due process cases more generally. The justices found that fundamental rights were rooted in the traditions and conscience of the American people. Moreover, if those rights were eliminated, the justices argued, neither liberty nor justice could exist.[7] In case after case, the justices have considered whether such a right is fundamental— that is, rooted in the American tradition and conscience and essential for liberty and justice—and they have been guided by the principle that citizen participation in government and society is necessary for democracy in gauging the importance of each constitutionally protected right.

Freedoms in Practice: Controversy over the Second Amendment and the Right to Bear Arms

The fierce debate today over gun control illustrates much about the conflicts surrounding the civil liberties protected in the United States. Americans disagree about how to interpret the Second Amendment of the Constitution, but they do agree to have their disputes settled through laws and court rulings rather than armed conflict. Private citizens and political interest groups use their First Amendment freedoms of speech and assembly to voice their opinions about the place of guns in society. They also work behind the scenes to influence elected officials through campaign contributions and lobbying (see Chapter 7). At the heart of this debate is the question of the role of guns in creating a safe and free society and negotiating the tension between personal liberty and community security.

Changing Interpretations of the Second Amendment

Over the last decade, the Supreme Court has changed its interpretation of the Second Amendment, which reads

> A well-regulated Militia, being necessary to the security of a free State, the right of the people to keep and bear Arms, shall not be infringed.

The Second Amendment was initially interpreted by the Supreme Court as ensuring that state militias could support the government in maintaining public order; under this interpretation the right to bear arms is a group right subject to regulation by Congress and the states.[8]

In 2008, the Supreme Court ruled in the *District of Columbia v. Heller* that the Second Amendment confers an individual right to possess a firearm for lawful purposes, such as self-defense.[9] In the 2010 case of *McDonald v. Chicago,* the Court incorporated the Second Amendment to the states, requiring states to respect this new individual constitutional right when they regulated citizen access to guns.[10] This forced many states to change their laws to allow individuals to carry concealed weapons, though there remains a great deal of variation in how these laws are implemented (see Figure 4.1).

FIGURE 4.1 ■ **Concealed Carry Laws and College Campuses** All 50 states allow individuals the right to carry a concealed weapon. Only the District of Columbia prohibits it. After a number of campus shootings, some state legislatures have made provisions to allow the carrying of concealed weapons on college campuses. Currently, 23 states allow campuses to make this determination for themselves, and 16 states ban carrying concealed weapons on campuses. What regional variations do you see regarding these laws? How could you use this data to determine whether increased access to weapons on campus could (1) decrease violence on campuses or (2) heighten the potential for additional shootings? What else do you need to know?

SOURCE: National Conference of State Legislatures, "Guns on Campus Overview," May 5, 2017.

Citizens Engaged: Fighting for a Safer Nation

The U.S. gun death rate (homicides and suicides) increased in 2016 and 2017 after 15 years of stability.[11] The increased visibility of mass shootings—such as those in Virginia Tech; Sandy Hook Elementary School; the Aurora movie theater; the church in Charleston; the Orlando Nightclub; Las Vegas; and Parkland—has kept the question of domestic security visible. Some activists, like the interest group The Coalition to Stop Gun Violence, argue that stricter weapons laws are necessary for a safe society.

Other groups, like the National Rifle Association, believe that if more law-abiding citizens can carry weapons, fewer violent crimes will be committed. Both groups have joined vocally in the public debate, exercising their freedom of speech and assembly to influence opinions about guns in the United States and by working to influence policy.

By 2014, every state allowed for some form of concealed-carry protection, permitting citizens to have weapons on them or in close proximity. In addition, the nation has been debating the wisdom of "Stand Your Ground" laws, allowing individuals who feel threatened to fire their weapons in self-defense. The shooting death of Trayvon Martin, a 17-year-old African American high school student, in February 2012 in Stanford, Florida, galvanized many critics of Stand Your Ground laws. George Zimmerman, a 28-year-old neighborhood watch coordinator, claimed that he felt threatened by the unarmed Martin. Later that year, the shooting of Jordan Davis, another unarmed 17-year-old high school student at a Florida convenience store, by Michael David Dunn, sparked protests against liberal gun laws. Dunn objected to the volume of the music playing in the car in which Davis was riding. Unlike Zimmerman, Dunn was convicted of murder and sentenced to life in prison and another 90 years for three counts of attempted murder. Critics argued that the mere perception of a threat does not constitute one, while many civil rights groups contend that Stand Your Ground laws ultimately result in the deaths of innocent, young African American men, like Martin and Davis, who are more likely to be unfairly stereotyped as a threat.

By 2017, numerous states had passed campus carry laws allowing weapons (with an appropriate permit) on public campuses (see Figure 4.1) and others sought to arm trained teachers and security personnel in public schools. Federal legislation allowing soldiers to remain armed on bases has been introduced to Congress, despite dissent from the Pentagon. Advocates of these policies believe that the introduction of personal firearms into these previously gun-free spaces will serve as a deterrent to additional mass shootings. Opponents think it will only increase the likelihood of additional casualties due to the lax regulations of who may legally carry a firearm.

Freedoms of Speech, Assembly, and the Press: Supporting Civic Discourse

Civic discourse and free participation in the political process have certain requirements. As we consider in this section, an individual must be able to express his or her political views through speech, assembly, and petition. Freedom of speech, assembly, petition, and the press is essential to an open society and to democratic rule. These freedoms ensure that individuals can discuss the important issues facing the nation and try to agree about how to address these matters without government censorship. Scholars have referred to this sharing of contrasting opinions as the **marketplace of ideas.** It is through the competition of ideas—some of them radical, some even loathsome—that solutions emerge. Freedom of the press allows for the dissemination and discussion of these varying ideas and encourages consensus building.

marketplace of ideas
A concept at the core of the freedoms of expression and press, based on the belief that true and free political discourse depends on a free and unrestrained discussion of ideas.

The marketplace of ideas enables people to voice their concerns and views freely and allows individuals to reconsider their ideas on important national and local issues. The centrality of the freedom of political expression to the First Amendment reflects the founders' belief that democracy would flourish only through robust discussion and candid debate.

The First Amendment and Political Instability

Over time, the Supreme Court has distinguished between political expression that the First Amendment protects and expression that the government may limit or even prohibit. The government has tried to limit speech, assembly, and the press during times of national emergency, when it has viewed that expression as more threatening than it would be in normal times.

THE TENSION BETWEEN FREEDOM AND ORDER   A fundamental tension exists between the Bill of Rights, with its goal of protecting individual freedoms, and the government's central goal of ensuring order. Not even a decade had gone by after the Constitution's ratification when Congress passed the Alien and Sedition Acts (1798). These laws placed the competing goals of freedom and order directly in conflict. The Sedition Act criminalized all speech and writings judged to be critical of the government, Congress, or the president. This was just the first of many times in U.S. history that lawmakers sacrificed free speech and freedom of the press in an effort to ensure national security and order. For example, President Abraham Lincoln (1861–1865) attempted to silence political dissidents during the Civil War by mandating that they be tried in military courts, without the due process protections afforded in a civilian court. Lincoln also suspended the writ of *habeas corpus* (Latin, meaning "you have the body"), an ancient right and constitutional guarantee that protects an individual in custody from being held without the right to be heard in a court of law.[12] Again, political dissidents were targeted for indefinite detention without trial. Whenever the nation has perceived itself under attack or threat, pressure has been placed on the government by some citizens to limit individual freedom to ensure societal order, and other citizens have pressured the government to maintain freedom while securing order.

habeas corpus
An ancient right that protects an individual in custody from being held without the right to be heard in a court of law.

The struggle for a balance between freedom and order continues today as the United States fights a global war on terrorism. Part of the 1798 Alien and Sedition Acts, known as the Alien Enemies Act, empowered the president to deport aliens suspected of threatening the nation's security or to imprison them indefinitely.[13] Soon after assuming office in January 2017, President Donald J. Trump signed an executive order that identified countries from which the United States would not accept immigrants or visitors and expanded the basis on which immigrants could be deported.[14] A federal district judge determined the order to be biased against Muslims and a constitutional violation of the First Amendment; a revised executive order has been litigated in the federal courts.[15]

THE HISTORICAL CONTEXT FOR FREE SPEECH LAWS   The Supreme Court's willingness to suppress or punish political speech has changed over time in response to perceived internal and external threats to the nation. During World War I, the Court upheld the conviction of socialist and war protester Charles Schenck for distributing a pamphlet to recently drafted men urging them to resist the draft.[16] For the first time, the Court created through its ruling a test to evaluate such government actions, called the **clear and present danger test.** Under this standard, the government may silence speech or expression only when there is an evident and immediate danger that such speech will bring about some harm that the government has the power to prevent. In the *Schenck* case, the Court noted that the circumstances of war permit greater restrictions on the freedom of speech than would be allowable during peacetime. The justices ruled that Schenck's actions could endanger the nation's ability to carry out the draft and prosecute the war.

clear and present danger test
A standard established in the 1919 Supreme Court case *Schenck v. U.S.* whereby the government may silence speech or expression when there is a clear and present danger that this speech will bring about some harm that the government has the power to prevent.

Soon after the *Schenck* case, a majority of the justices adopted a far more restrictive test that made it easier to punish citizens for the content of their speech. This test, known as the **bad tendency test,** was extended in the case of Benjamin

bad tendency test
A standard extended in the 1925 case *Gitlow v. New York* whereby any speech that has the likelihood of inciting crime or disturbing the public peace can be silenced.

>In August 2017, white supremacists and armed militia gathered in Charlottesville, Virginia, under the cry of "Unite the Right." After Virginia and a torch-lit march the first night, counter-demonstrators gathered to challenge the messages of "Blood and Soil" (a Nazi phrase) and "White Lives Matter" as well as the confederate flags and Nazi symbols. In the violent aftermath one protester was killed and two police officers died. What kind of free speech protections should we provide unpopular views that challenge the political rights of others?

©Samuel Corum/Anadolu Agency/Getty Images

Gitlow, who was convicted of violating a New York State criminal anarchy law by publishing pamphlets calling for a revolutionary mass action to create a socialist government.[17] The political context of Gitlow's conviction is revealing: A so-called red scare—fears that the socialist revolution in the Soviet Union would spread to other nations with large populations of workers—was sweeping the nation. Gitlow's lawyer contended that there was no proof that Gitlow's pamphlet created a clear and present danger of a violent uprising. The Court disagreed, however, ruling that any speech that had a likelihood of inciting crime or disturbing the public peace could be silenced.

This highly restrictive test required only that the government demonstrate that some speech may at some time help to bring about harm. The threat did not need to be immediate or even direct. The test sacrificed the freedoms of speech and the press to concerns about public safety and protection of the existing order. The bad tendency test lasted only a short while; by the late 1930s, the Court had reverted to the clear and present danger test, which the justices interpreted more broadly to protect speech and participation. The relative peace and stability of the period between the two world wars is apparent in the Court's handling of speech and press cases, as the justices required government officials to demonstrate that the speech obviously posed a danger to public safety.

Even after the Court returned to the clear and present danger test, however, it still allowed concerns about national security to control its handling of First Amendment cases. In the wake of World War II, a war of conflicting ideologies emerged between the United States and the Soviet Union. Termed the *Cold War* because it did not culminate in a direct military confrontation between the countries, this development nevertheless created a climate of fear and insecurity in both nations. Concerns about the spread of communism in the United States led to prosecutions of individuals deemed to be sympathetic to communism and socialism under the Smith Act of 1940. This federal law barred individuals from advocating or teaching about "the duty, necessity, desirability, or propriety of overthrowing or destroying any government in the United States by force or violence."

In the most important case of this period, the Supreme Court upheld the conviction of several individuals who were using the writings of German philosophers Karl Marx and Friedrich Engels, along with those of Soviet leaders Vladimir Lenin and Josef Stalin, to teach about socialism and communism.[18] In upholding the convictions, the justices found that although the use of these writings did not pose a risk of imminent danger to the government, it created the *probability* that such harm would result. The seriousness of the evil was key to the test that came out of this ruling, known as the **clear and probable danger test.** Because the government was suppressing speech to avoid the gravest danger, an armed takeover of the United States, the Supreme Court majority ruled that it was justified in its actions—even if the risk or probability of this result was relatively remote.

clear and probable danger test
A standard established in the 1951 case *Dennis v. U.S.* whereby the government could suppress speech to avoid grave danger, even if the probability of the dangerous result was relatively remote; replaced by the imminent lawless action (incitement) test in 1969.

As the Cold War subsided and concerns diminished about a potential communist takeover of the United States, the Court shifted to a broader interpretation of the First Amendment speech and press protections. Beginning with *Brandenburg v. Ohio* (1969), the Court signaled that it would give more weight to First Amendment claims and less to government concerns about security and order. In this case, the Court considered the convictions of the leaders of an Ohio Ku Klux Klan group who were arrested after they made a speech at a televised rally, during which they uttered racist and anti-Semitic comments and showed guns and rifles. Local officials charged them with violating a state law that banned speech that disturbed the public peace and threatened armed overthrow. In overturning the convictions, the Court reverted to a strict reading of the clear and present danger test. The justices held that government officials had to demonstrate that the speech they sought to silence went beyond mere advocacy, or words, and that it created the risk of immediate disorder or lawlessness.[19]

THE STANDARD TODAY: THE IMMINENT LAWLESS ACTION TEST The *Brandenburg* test, known as both the **imminent lawless action test** and the **incitement test,** altered the clear and present danger test by making it even more stringent. Specifically, after the *Brandenburg* decision, any government in the United States—national, state, or local—trying to silence speech would need to show that the risk of harm from the speech was highly likely and that the harm was imminent or immediate. The imminent lawless action test is the standard the courts use today to determine whether speech is protected from government interference.

Even though the *Brandenburg* test is well established, the issue of whether speech is protected continues to be debated. For example, public attention has increasingly focused on websites operated by terrorists and terrorist sympathizers, especially members of militant Islamic groups and those of the alt right. Do First Amendment guarantees protect sites on which posters threaten those who disagree with them and equip their followers for violence? What about websites threatening violence against white supremacists or those who are accused of committing sexual assault? Courts examining these questions must determine not only whether the speech intends to bring about a bad result—most would agree that intent exists—but also whether the speech incites lawless action that is imminent.

imminent lawless action test (incitement test)
A standard established in the 1969 *Brandenburg v. Ohio* case, whereby speech is restricted only if it goes beyond mere advocacy, or words, to create a high likelihood of immediate disorder or lawlessness.

Freedom of Speech

The freedom to speak publicly, even critically, about government and politics is central to the democratic process. Citizens cannot participate fully in a political system if they are unable to share information, opinions, advice, and calls to action. Citizens cannot hold government accountable if they cannot criticize government actions or demand change.

PURE SPEECH VERSUS SYMBOLIC SPEECH The Supreme Court has made a distinction between pure speech that is "just words" and advocacy that couples words with actions. With respect to civic discourse, both are important. When speech moves beyond words into the realm of action, it is considered to be **symbolic speech,** nonverbal "speech" in the form of an action such as picketing or wearing an armband to signify a protest.

Unless words threaten imminent lawless action, the First Amendment will likely protect the speaker. But in civic discourse, words are often combined with action. For example, in the 1960s, antiwar protesters were arrested for burning their draft

symbolic speech
Nonverbal "speech" in the form of an action such as picketing, flag burning, or wearing an armband to signify a protest.

>Michael Wolff is a journalist who wrote an insider tell-all book, based on anonymous sources, that is very critical of the Trump White House. Why does the Constitution guarantee that the government cannot prevent such negative portrayals from being published?

©David Levenson/Getty Images

cards to demonstrate their refusal to serve in Vietnam, and public high school students were suspended from school for wearing black armbands to protest the war. When the two groups brought their cases to the Supreme Court, the justices had to determine whether their conduct rose to the level of political expression and merited First Amendment protection. Together, these cases help to define the parameters for symbolic speech.

In the first of these cases, *U.S. v. O'Brien,* the justices considered whether the government could punish several Vietnam War protesters for burning their draft cards in violation of the Selective Service Act, which made it a crime to "destroy or mutilate" those cards. The Court balanced the free expression guarantee against the government's need to prevent the destruction of the cards. Because the cards were critical to the nation's ability to raise an army, the Court ruled that the government had a compelling interest in preventing their destruction. Moreover, because the government had passed the Selective Service Act to facilitate the draft and not to suppress speech, the impact of the law on speech was incidental. When the justices balanced the government's interest in making it easy to raise an army against the incidental impact that this law had on speech, they found that the government's interest overrode that of the political protesters.[20]

In contrast, when the Court considered the other symbolic speech case of this era, *Tinker v. Des Moines,* they found that the First Amendment did protect the speech in question. In this case, the justices ruled that the political expression in the form of the students' wearing black armbands to school to protest the Vietnam War was protected.[21] On what basis did the justices distinguish the armbands in the *Tinker* case from the draft cards in the *O'Brien* case? They cited legitimate reasons for the government to ban the burning of draft cards in a time of war; but there were no comparable reasons to ban the wearing of armbands, apart from the school district's desire to curb or suppress political expression on school grounds. School officials could not show that the armbands had disrupted normal school activities.[22] For that reason, the Court argued, the symbolic speech in *Tinker* warranted more protection than that in *O'Brien.*

The highly controversial case of *Texas v. Johnson* (1989) tested the Court's commitment to protecting symbolic speech of a highly unpopular nature. At issue was a man's conviction under state law for burning the American flag during the Republican National Convention in 1984 to emphasize his disagreement with the policies of the administration of President Ronald Reagan (1981–1989). The Supreme Court overturned the man's conviction, finding that the flag burning was political speech worthy of protection under the First Amendment.[23] After the *Johnson* decision, Congress quickly passed the Flag Protection Act in an attempt to reverse the Court's ruling. Subsequently, however, in the case of *U.S. v. Eichman* (1990), the Court struck down the new law by the same 5–4 majority as in the *Johnson* ruling.[24]

The decisions in these flag-burning cases were very controversial and prompted Congress to pursue the only remaining legal avenue to enact flag protection statutes—a constitutional amendment. Every other year from 1995 to 2006, the proposed amendment has received the two-thirds majority necessary for approval in the U.S.

House of Representatives, but failed to achieve the same constitutionally required supermajority vote in the U.S. Senate. This issue has apparently been resolved in favor of liberty.

NOT ALL SPEECH IS CREATED EQUAL: UNPROTECTED SPEECH The Supreme Court long ago rejected the extreme view that all speech should be free in the United States. Whereas *political speech* tends to be protected against government suppression, other forms of speech can be limited or prohibited.

The courts afford **commercial speech,** that is, advertising statements, limited protection under the First Amendment. According to the Supreme Court, commercial speech may be restricted as long as the restriction "seeks to implement a substantial government interest, directly advances that interest, and goes no further than necessary to accomplish its objective." Restrictions on tobacco advertising, for example, limit free speech in the interest of protecting the health of society. In 2010, the Supreme Court, in the controversial *Citizens United v. Federal Elections Commission* decision, revised its previous rulings and determined that the First Amendment also protected corporate spending during elections as a form of free speech. Legislation that limits such spending was an unconstitutional banning of political speech.[25]

Interpreting Images

>The Slants is an Asian-American band that could not register their name because of a federal law prohibiting disparaging terms from being granted a trademark. In a 2017 decision, the Supreme Court found that law to be a violation of free speech. The Slants said they wanted to reclaim a term that had been used as a racial slur. How might this decision impact other uses of disparaging terms? Should the government forbid groups from naming themselves "Abort the Republicans" or "Democrats Shouldn't Breed" (real groups denied names under this law)?

©Keeton Gale/Shutterstock

Other forms of speech, including libel and slander, receive no protection under the First Amendment. **Libel** (written statements) and **slander** (verbal statements) are false statements that harm the reputation of another person. To qualify as libel or slander, the defamatory statement must be made publicly and with fault, meaning that reporters, for example, must undertake reasonable efforts to verify allegations. The statement must extend beyond mere name-calling or insults that cannot be proven true or false. Those who take a legal action on the grounds that they are victims of libel or slander, such as government officials, celebrities, and people involved with specific public controversies, are required to prove that the defendant acted with malice—with knowledge that the statement was false or that they recklessly disregarded the accuracy of the statement.

Obscenity, indecent or offensive speech or expression, is another form of speech that is not protected under the First Amendment. After many unsuccessful attempts to define obscenity, in 1973 the Supreme Court developed a three-part test in *Miller v. California.*[26] The Court ruled that a book, a film, or another form of expression is legally obscene if

- the average person applying contemporary standards finds that the work taken as a whole appeals to the prurient interest—that is, tends to excite unwholesome sexual desire;
- the work depicts or describes, in an obviously offensive way, a form of sexual conduct specifically prohibited by an anti-obscenity law;
- the work taken as a whole lacks serious literary, artistic, political, or scientific value.

commercial speech
Advertising statements that describe products.

libel
False written statements about others that harm their reputation.

slander
False verbal statements about others that harm their reputation.

obscenity
Indecent or offensive speech or expression.

Of course, these standards do not guarantee that people will agree on what materials are obscene. What is obscene to some may be acceptable to others. For that reason, the Court has been reluctant to limit free speech, even in the most controversial cases.

The Court may also ban speech known as **fighting words**—speech that inflicts injury or results in public disorder. The Court first articulated the fighting-words doctrine in *Chaplinsky v. New Hampshire* (1942). Walter Chaplinsky was convicted of violating a New Hampshire statute that prohibited the use of offensive, insulting language toward persons in public places after he made several inflammatory comments to a city official. The Court, in upholding the statute as constitutional, explained the limits of free speech: "These include the lewd and obscene, the profane, the libelous, and the insulting or fighting words—those which by their very utterance inflict injury or tend to incite an immediate breach of the peace."[27] Thus the Court ruled that, like slander, libel, and obscenity, "fighting words" do not advance the democratic goals of free speech. Cross burning, for example, has been a form of symbolic speech that in the United States has come to represent racial violence and intimidation against African Americans and other vulnerable groups. In 2005, the Supreme Court in *Virginia v. Black* found that a state could ban cross burning when it was used to threaten or attempt to silence other individuals, but that the state law could not assume all cross burnings attempt to communicate that message.[28]

Even the types of "unprotected speech" we have considered enjoy broad protection under the law. Although cigarette ads are banned from television, many products are sold through every media outlet imaginable. Though a tabloid such as the *National Inquirer* sometimes faces lawsuits for the false stories it prints, most celebrities do not pursue legal action because of the high burden of proving that the paper knew the story was false, intended to damage the subject's reputation, and in fact caused real harm. Even though network television is censored for broadcasting objectionable material, the Supreme Court has ruled that the government cannot ban (adult) pornography on the Internet or on paid cable television channels.[29] And despite continued reaffirmation of the fighting-words doctrine, the Supreme Court has declined to uphold any convictions for fighting words since *Chaplinsky*. In short, the Court is reluctant to do anything that might limit the content of adults' free speech and expression, even when that speech is unpopular or offensive.

Freedom of Assembly and Redress of Grievances

The First Amendment says that people have the freedom to assemble peaceably and to seek redress of (compensation for) grievances against the government; yet, there are limits placed on assembly. As the Supreme Court has considered free assembly cases, it has been most concerned about ensuring that individuals and groups can gather to discuss their concerns and that they can take action in the public arena that advances their political goals.

The Court is keenly aware of the need for order in public forums and will clamp down on speech that is intended and likely to incite public unrest and anger. That is one reason the Court has reaffirmed the fighting-words doctrine. Although officials cannot censor speech before it occurs, they can take action to limit speech once it becomes apparent that public disorder is going to erupt. In its rulings, the Court has also allowed content-neutral **time, place, and manner restrictions**—regulations regarding when, where, or how expression may occur. Such restrictions do not target speech based on content, and to stand up in court, they must be applied in a content-neutral manner. For example, people have the right to march in protest, but not while chanting into bullhorns at four o'clock in the morning in a residential neighborhood.

The Court's rulings in these various cases illustrate how the government is balancing the freedom of public assembly against other concerns, notably public safety and the right of an individual to be left alone. The Court is carefully weighing the freedoms of one group of individuals against another and attempting to ensure the protection of free public expression.

Freedom of the Press

Throughout American history, the press has played a crucial role in the larger debate about political expression. Before the War for Independence, when the British monarchy sought to clamp down on political dissent in the colonies, the king and Parliament quickly recognized the urgency of silencing the press. A free press is essential to democratic ideals, and democracy cannot survive when a government controls the press. The First Amendment's guarantees of a free press ensure not only that American government remains accountable to its constituents but also that the people hear competing ideas about how to deal with matters of public concern. Increasingly, ordinary citizens share their views on important political issues on social media.

Ensuring a free press can complicate the work of government. As we have been reminded by the Trump administration, the White House cannot control its press coverage. While this has been a source of frustration of most presidents, President Trump has responded with public expressions of anger and irritation. For instance, in the summer of 2017, President Trump tweeted a video of himself at a wrestling match, throwing a man with the CNN logo over his head to the floor. The president's use of Twitter has been justified by the administration as a way of communicating directly to the public and avoiding a media he perceives to be biased against him. The Committee to Protect Journalists noted its concern that such White House rhetoric "undermines the media in the U.S. and emboldens autocratic leaders around the world."[30]

Certain well-established principles govern freedom of the press in the United States. First and foremost, the courts almost never allow the government to engage in prior restraint. **Prior restraint** means censorship—the attempt to block the publication of material that is considered to be harmful. The Supreme Court established this rule against censorship in 1931 in the landmark case of *Near v. Minnesota*. After editor Jay Near wrote a story in the *Saturday Press* alleging that Jews were responsible for corruption, bribery, and prostitution in Minneapolis, a state judge barred all future sales of the newspaper. The Court overturned the state judge's ruling, finding that the sole purpose of the order was to suppress speech. Because freedom of the press has strong historical foundations, the Court concluded, censorship is clearly prohibited.

In the *Near* ruling, the Court recognized, however, that there might be times when government officials could limit the publication of certain stories. Specifically, such censorship might be justified under extraordinary circumstances related to ensuring public safety or national security or in cases involving obscenity. In reality, though, the Court has disallowed prior restraint in the vast majority of cases. For example, in the most important case examining the national security exception, *New York Times v. U.S.* (1971), the Court rejected the government's attempt to prevent publication of documents that detailed the history of the United States' involvement in Vietnam. In this case, also known as the *Pentagon Papers*

prior restraint
A form of censorship by the government whereby it blocks the publication of news stories viewed as libelous or harmful.

case, the government argued that censorship was necessary to prevent "irreparable injury" to national security. But the Court dismissed that argument, asserting that full disclosure was in the interest of all Americans and that publication of the documents could contribute to the ongoing debate about the U.S. role in the Vietnam War.[31] In their ruling, the justices recognized that some materials are clearly necessary for full and fair discussion of issues facing the nation, whereas others are far less important to political discourse.

Freedoms of Religion, Privacy, and Criminal Due Process: Encouraging Civic Engagement

The Constitution's framers understood that the government they were creating could use its powers to single out certain groups for either favorable or unfavorable treatment. They realized, too, that unequal treatment of that kind could interfere with the creation of community—and with citizens' engagement within that community. The founders' commitment to community building and citizens' engagement lies at the heart of several constitutional amendments in the Bill of Rights. Specifically these are the amendments establishing the freedom of religion, the right to privacy, and the right to due process for individuals in the criminal justice system.

The First Amendment and the Freedom of Religion

The religion clauses of the First Amendment—the establishment clause and the free exercise clause—essentially do two things. First, they bar the government from establishing or supporting any one religious sect over another, and second, they ensure that individuals are not hindered in the exercise of their religion. Whereas the establishment clause requires that the government be neutral toward religious institutions, favoring neither one specific religion over others nor all religious groups over nonreligious groups, the free exercise clause prohibits the government from taking action that is hostile toward individuals' practice of their religion. As we now consider, there is tension between these two clauses.

establishment clause
The First Amendment clause that bars the government from passing any law "respecting an establishment of religion"; often interpreted as a separation of church and state, but this is increasingly challenged.

THE ESTABLISHMENT CLAUSE Stating only that "Congress shall make no law respecting an establishment of religion," the **establishment clause** does little to clarify what the relationship between church and state should be. The Constitution's authors wanted to ensure that Congress could not create a national religion, as a number of European powers (notably France and Spain) had done; the framers sought to avoid that level of government entanglement in religious matters. Further, many colonists had emigrated to America to escape religious persecution in Europe, and although many were deeply religious, uncertainty prevailed about the role that government should play in the practice of religion. That uncertainty, too, is reflected in the brevity of the establishment clause. The question arises, does the clause prohibit the government from simply preferring one sect over another, or is it broader, preventing any kind of government support of religion?

This is a crucial question because religious institutions have always been important forums for community building and engagement in the United States. Americans continue to be a very religious people. In 2016, over 75 percent of Americans surveyed said religion was fairly or very important in their lives.[32] But even given their strong religious affiliations, most Americans believe in some degree of separation between religious organizations and the government. The actual debate has been about how much separation the establishment clause requires.

Over time, scholars and lawyers have considered three possible interpretations of the establishment clause. One interpretation, called separationism, is that the establishment clause requires a *strict separation of church and state* and bars most or all government support for religious sects. Supporters of the strict separationist view invoke the writings of Thomas Jefferson, James Madison, and others that call for a "wall of separation" between church and state.[33] They also point to societies outside the United States in which religious leaders dictate how citizens may dress, act, and pray as examples of what can happen without strict separation.

A second, and more flexible, interpretation allows the government to offer support to religious sects as long as that support is neutral and not biased toward one sect. This interpretation, known as *neutrality* or the *preferential treatment standard,* would permit government support provided that this support extended to all religious groups. The third interpretation is the most flexible and reads the establishment clause as barring only establishment of a state religion. This interpretation, known as *accommodationism,* allows the government to offer support to any or all religious groups provided that this support does not rise to the level of recognizing an official religion.[34]

Which of these three vastly different interpretations of the establishment clause is correct? Over time, the Supreme Court has shifted back and forth in its opinions, usually depending on the kind of government support in question. Overall, the courts have rejected the strictest interpretation of the establishment clause, which would ban virtually any form of aid to religion. Instead, they have allowed government support for religious schools, programs, and institutions if the support advances a secular (nonreligious) goal (such as teaching mathematics) and does not specifically endorse a particular religious belief.

For example, in 1974, the Court upheld a New Jersey program that provided funds to the parents of parochial school students to pay for bus transportation to and from school.[35] The Court reasoned that the program was necessary to help students to get to school safely and concluded that if the state withdrew funding for any of these programs for parochial school students, it would be impossible to operate these schools. The impact would be the hindrance of the free exercise of religion for students and their parents.

In another landmark case, *Lemon v. Kurtzman* (1971), however, the Court struck down a state program that used cigarette taxes to reimburse parochial schools for the costs of teachers' salaries and textbooks. The Court found that subsidizing parochial schools furthered a process of religious teaching and that the "continuing state surveillance" that would be necessary to enforce the specific provisions of the laws would inevitably entangle the state in religious affairs.[36]

In the *Lemon* case ruling, the Court refined the establishment clause standard to include three considerations.

- Does the state program have a secular, as opposed to a religious, purpose?
- Does it have as its principal effect the advancement of religion?
- Does the program create an excessive entanglement between church and state?

This three-part test is known as the **Lemon test.** The programs most likely to withstand scrutiny under the establishment clause are those that have a secular purpose, have only an incidental effect on the advancement of religion, and do not excessively entangle church and state.

Lemon test
A three-part test established by the Supreme Court in the 1971 case *Lemon v. Kurtzman* to determine whether government aid to parochial schools is constitutional; the test is also applied to other cases involving the establishment clause.

THEN

NOW

> Throughout the first decades of the 21st century, the Supreme Court wrestled with protecting student-initiated prayer and study, as demonstrated by this picture of a "Rally Round the Flagpole" prayer. Now the public is wrestling with new issues; in the picture on the right, Milos Yiannopoulos is at an alt-right rally protesting the City University of New York's selection of Muslim-American activist Linda Sarsour as their commencement speaker. Can government entities like public schools provide a platform for speakers who represent a particular religious perspective without unconstitutionally endorsing that religion?

Group prayer: ©Valerie Berta/Journal-Courier/The Image Works; Individual: ©Susan Watts/NY Daily News via Getty Images

More recently, the Court upheld an Ohio program that gave vouchers to parents to offset the cost of parochial schooling.[37] The justices ruled that the purpose of the program was secular, not religious, because it was intended to provide parents with an alternative to the Cleveland public schools. Any aid to religious institutions—in this case, mostly Catholic schools—was indirect, because the primary beneficiaries were the students themselves. Finally, there was little entanglement between the church and state, because the parents received the vouchers based on financial need and then were free to use these vouchers as they pleased. There was no direct relationship between the religious schools and the state.

If a government program offers financial support, the Court has tended to evaluate the program by using either the preferential treatment standard or the accommodationist standard. If a program or policy involves prayer in the schools or issues related to the curriculum, however, the Court has adopted a standard that looks more like strict separatism.

A series of cases beginning with *Engel v. Vitale* (1962) has barred formalized prayer in the schools, finding that such prayer has a purely religious purpose and that prayer is intended to advance religious, as opposed to secular, ideals.[38] For that reason, the Court has barred school-organized prayer in public elementary and secondary schools on the grounds that it constitutes a state endorsement of religion. Student-organized prayer is constitutional because the state is not engaging in any coercion by mandating or encouraging student participation.

free exercise clause

The First Amendment clause prohibiting the government from enacting laws prohibiting an individual's practice of his or her religion; often in contention with the establishment clause.

THE FREE EXERCISE CLAUSE The tension between the establishment and free exercise clauses arises because the establishment clause bars the state from helping religious institutions, whereas the **free exercise clause** makes it illegal for the government to enact laws prohibiting the free practice of religion by individuals. Establishment clause cases often raise free exercise claims, and so courts must frequently consider whether, by banning state aid, they are interfering with the free exercise of religion.

Although free exercise and establishment cases raise many of the same concerns, they are different kinds of cases, whose resolution depends on distinct legal tests. Because establishment clause cases often center on state aid to religious schools, many involve the Roman Catholic Church, which administers the largest number of private elementary and secondary schools in the country. In contrast, free exercise clause cases tend to involve less-mainstream religious groups, among them Mormons, Jehovah's Witnesses, Christian Scientists, and Amish. These groups' practices tend to be less well known—or more controversial. For example, free exercise clause cases have involved the right to practice polygamy, use hallucinogens, refuse conventional medical care for a child, sacrifice animals, and refuse to salute the flag.

The Supreme Court has refused to accept that the government is barred from *ever* interfering with religious exercise. Free exercise claims are difficult to settle because they require that courts balance the individual's right to free practice of religion against the government's need to adopt some policy or program. First and foremost, the Court has always distinguished between religious beliefs, which government may not interfere with, and religious actions, which government is

THEN NOW NEXT

How Does the Changing Religious Affiliation of Americans Affect the First Amendment?

	Then (2000)	Now
Protestant	54%	46.6%
Catholic	24	20.8
Jewish	2	1.9
Islam/Muslim	N/A	.9
Other faith	5	3.5
None	14	22.8

SOURCE: All data derived from the General Social Survey: The Association of Religion Data Archive, Pew Research Center, "Religious Landscape Study."

WHAT'S NEXT?

> As Americans' religious affiliations continue to slowly decline, what might be the implications for the First Amendment? Will the battles around the free exercise clause and the establishment clause become more intense or less relevant?

> The Millennial generation has the highest levels of nonaffiliation of any generation previously. How will Generation Z perceive religion? What might the consequences be for debates surrounding the First Amendment?

permitted to regulate. For example, although adults may refuse lifesaving medical care on the basis of their own religious beliefs, they may not refuse medical procedures required to save the lives of their children.[39] More recently, debates over mandatory vaccination laws for students enrolling in public schools have been challenged as a violation of the free exercise of religion protected in the First Amendment. Lower federal courts have found these regulations to be a lawful exercise of the police power;[40] unless there is conflict among the lower courts over this issue, the Supreme Court most likely will not hear this controversy.

In assessing those laws that interfere with religiously motivated action, the Court has distinguished between laws that are neutral and generally applicable to all religious sects and laws that single out one sect for unfavorable treatment. In *Employment Division, Department of Human Resources v. Smith* (1990), the Court allowed the state of Oregon to deny unemployment benefits to two substance-abuse counselors who were fired from their jobs after using peyote as part of their religious practice. Oregon refused to provide benefits because the two men had been fired for engaging in an illegal activity. The Court concluded that there was no free exercise challenge, because Oregon had good reason for denying benefits to lawbreakers who had been fired from their jobs. The justices concluded that the state was simply applying a neutral and generally applicable law to the men as opposed to singling them out for bad treatment.[41] One consequence of this case was that several states, including Oregon, passed laws excluding members of the Native American Church, who smoke peyote as part of traditional religious rites, from being covered by their controlled-substance laws.

One major change in the free exercise clause has been the extension of the First Amendment constitutional rights to corporations. The 2014 case of *Burwell v. Hobby Lobby* was an appeal of the Affordable Care Act's (Obamacare) requirement that family-owned corporations pay for insurance coverage of birth control for its employees.[42] The two companies, Hobby Lobby and Conestoga Wood Specialties, were owned by families who claimed that they try to run their businesses on Christian principles and that providing contraception coverage burdened their religious liberty. The Court agreed with the companies, but noted the decision applied only to "closely held" for-profit companies run on religious principles. The dissenting justices noted this was the first time the constitutional protection of religious freedom was extended to the commercial world, and more litigation will follow.

In summary, people are free to hold and profess their own beliefs, to build and actively participate in religious communities, and to allow their religious beliefs to inform their participation in politics and civil society. However, individual *actions* based on religious beliefs may be limited if those actions conflict with existing laws that are neutrally applied in a nondiscriminatory fashion. The extension of these rights to some corporations means that our understanding of religious liberty will continue to evolve.

The Right to Privacy

So far in this section, we have explored the relationship between civil liberties and some key themes of this book: civic participation, inclusiveness, community building, and community engagement. We now shift our focus somewhat to consider the **right to privacy,** the right of an individual to be left alone and to make decisions freely, without the interference of others. Privacy is a core principle for most Americans, and the right to make decisions, especially about intimate or personal matters, is at the heart of this right. Yet the right to privacy is also necessary for genuine inclusiveness and community engagement, because it ensures that each individual is able to act autonomously and to make decisions about how he or she will interact with others.

The right to privacy is highly controversial and the subject of much public debate. In large part, the reason is that this right is tied to some of the most divisive issues of our day, including abortion, aid in dying, and sexual orientation. The right to privacy is also controversial because, unlike the freedoms of speech, the press, assembly, and religion, it is not mentioned explicitly anywhere in the Constitution. A further reason for the debate surrounding the right to privacy is that the Supreme Court has only recently recognized it.

right to privacy
The right of an individual to be left alone and to make decisions freely, without the interference of others.

THE EMERGENT RIGHT TO PRIVACY   For more than 100 years, Supreme Court justices and lower-court judges have concluded that the right to privacy is implied in all the other liberties spelled out in the Bill of Rights. Not until the landmark

Supreme Court case *Griswold v. Connecticut* (1965) did the courts firmly establish the right to privacy. The issue in this case may seem strange to us today: whether the state of Connecticut had the power to prohibit married couples from using birth control. In their decision, the justices concluded that the state law violated the privacy right of married couples by preventing them from seeking access to birth control, and the Court struck down the Connecticut prohibition. The Court argued that the right to privacy was inherent within many of the constitutional guarantees, most importantly in the First Amendment freedom of association, the Third Amendment right to be free from the quartering of soldiers, the Fourth Amendment right to be free from unreasonable searches and seizures, the Fifth Amendment protection against self-incrimination, and the Ninth Amendment assurance of rights not explicitly listed in the Bill of Rights. Justice William O. Douglas and his colleagues effectively argued that a zone of privacy surrounded every person in the United States and that government could not pass laws that encroached upon this zone.[43]

In its ruling, the Court asserted that the right to privacy existed quite apart from the law. It was implicit in the Bill of Rights and fundamental to the American system of law and justice. The right to privacy hinged in large part on the right of individuals to associate with one another, and specifically the right of marital partners to engage in intimate association.

In a 1984 case, the Supreme Court ruled that the Constitution protects two kinds of freedom of association: (1) intimate associations and (2) expressive associations.[44] The protection of intimate associations allows Americans to maintain private human relationships as part of their personal liberty. The protection of expressive associations allows people to form associations with others and to practice their First Amendment freedoms of speech, assembly, petition, and religion.

THE RIGHT TO PRIVACY APPLIED TO OTHER ACTIVITIES The challenge for the Court since *Griswold* has been to determine which activities fall within the scope of the privacy right, and that question has placed the justices at the center of some of the most controversial issues of the day. For example, the first attempt to extend the privacy right, which raised the question of whether the right protected abortion, remains at least as controversial today as it was in 1973 when the Court decided the first abortion rights case, *Roe v. Wade*.[45] In *Roe* and the many abortion cases the Court has heard since, the justices have tried to establish whether a woman's right to abortion takes precedence over any interests the state may have in either the woman's health or the fetus's life. Over time, the Court has adopted a compromise position by rejecting the view that the right to abortion is absolute and by attempting to determine when states can regulate, or even prohibit, access to abortion. In 1992, the Court established the "undue burden" test, which asks whether a state abortion law places a "substantial obstacle in the path of a woman seeking an abortion before the fetus attains viability."[46] The Court, in 2016, found that state requirements such as requiring doctors to have admitting rights at local hospitals or that abortions could occur only at surgical centers imposed such an undue burden without significantly protecting women's health.[47] Although the Court used this standard to strike down spousal notification requirements, it has upheld other requirements imposed by some states, including waiting periods, mandatory counseling, and parental consent.

The Court has also stepped gingerly around other privacy rights, such as the right to choose one's sexual partners and the right to terminate medical treatment or engage in physician-assisted suicide. Both of these rights have been presented to the Court as hinging on the much broader right to privacy. With respect to the

>Public debate over abortion was not settled by the Supreme Court's 1973 decision in *Roe v. Wade.* In these photos taken more than four decades later, pro-life and pro-choice activists hold signs supporting their differing viewpoints. Abortion rights advocates frame the issue in terms of a woman's right to privacy and to control her own body without interference from the government. Abortion rights opponents view abortion as murder and frame the issue in terms of the rights of an unborn child. Where do you believe the privacy line should be drawn in the question of abortion?

right to terminate medical treatment, the Court has been fairly clear. Various Court decisions have confirmed that as long as an individual is competent to terminate treatment, the state may not stop him or her from taking this action, even if stopping treatment will lead to the person's death.[48]

The Court has been less clear in its rulings when an incompetent person's right is advanced by another individual, such as a spouse, a parent, or a child. In these circumstances, the Court has accepted the state's argument that before treatment may be terminated, the state may require that the person seeking to end life show that his or her loved one would have wanted that course of action.[49] When a person's wishes are not clear, loved ones may wage legal battles over whether to discontinue life support.

In cases involving the right to engage in consensual sexual activities with a partner of one's choosing, the Supreme Court has also employed a less than absolute approach. For many years, the Court allowed states to criminalize homosexual activity, finding that the right to engage in consensual sexual activity did not extend to same-sex partners.[50] In a 2003 case, *Lawrence v. Texas,* the Court changed course by ruling that the right to engage in intimate sexual activity was protected as a liberty right, especially when the activity occurred inside one's home, and that states could not criminalize this activity.[51] Since that decision, rights activists have worked through the courts and state and federal legislatures to secure for same-sex partners the same rights that heterosexual couples enjoy, including benefits provided by group health insurance and marriage. In the 2015 decision of *Obergefell v. Hodges,* the Supreme Court found that same-sex couples possessed the fundamental right to marry under the Fourteenth Amendment.[52] (See Chapter 5 for further discussion of the ruling.) Despite these rulings, states are still free to prohibit a range of sexual activities, including prostitution, child sexual abuse, and sex in public places.[53] In the Court's view, these activities can be prohibited primarily because they are not consensual or do not take place in the home, a place that accords special protection by the privacy right.

The right to privacy remains very controversial. Cases brought under the right to privacy tend to link this right with some other civil liberty, such as the protection against unreasonable search and seizure, the right to free speech, or the protection against self-incrimination. In other words, the privacy right, which the justices themselves created, seems to need buttressing by other rights that the Bill of Rights *explicitly* establishes. The explanation for this development may be the contentiousness of Americans' civic discourse about abortion, aid in dying, and other privacy issues. In short, continuing civic disagreement may have forced the Court to fall back on rights that are well established and more widely accepted.

GOVERNMENT USE OF SOCIAL MEDIA IN INVESTIGATIONS Public discourse about privacy is constantly evolving as people voluntarily share more and more information about themselves through online networking sites such as Facebook, Pinterest, Twitter, LinkedIn, and Instagram. Users of such sites and bloggers share stories, photos, and videos of themselves—as well as of others, who may be unaware that they are the subject of a posting, a blog, or a video. Civil libertarians worry about the misuse and theft of personal information in a high-tech society where people's financial, employment, consumer, legal, and personal histories are so easily accessible.

In 2013, global media organizations disclosed evidence that the National Security Agency had tracked and reviewed international and domestic phone calls, text messages, and e-mails of an unknown number of Americans without first obtaining a warrant.[54] Social media platforms operated by such entities as Facebook, Apple, Microsoft, LinkedIn, Twitter, and Google are seeking to provide greater transparency as to their cooperation with governmental requests for user information.[55] However, in 2017 Google reported an unprecedented number of governmental requests for personal data from the United States and other nations.[56] Without legislation to determine when and if social media organizations may deny warrantless requests and without legislation that mandates public disclosure of the scope of inquiries, no clear limits exist on the government.

The Fourth, Fifth, Sixth, and Eighth Amendments: Ensuring Criminal Due Process

The last category of civil liberties that bear directly on civic engagement consists of the criminal due process protections established in the Fourth, Fifth, Sixth, and Eighth Amendments. Does it surprise you that so many of the Bill of Rights amendments focus on the rights of individuals accused of crimes? The context for this emphasis is the founders' concern with how the British monarchy had abused its power and used criminal law to impose its will on the American colonists. The British government had used repeated trials, charges of treason, and imprisonment without bail to stifle political dissent. The founders therefore wanted to ensure that there were effective checks on the power of the federal government, especially in the creation and enforcement of criminal law. As we have seen, the Bill of Rights amendments were incorporated to apply to the states and to their criminal codes through the process of selective incorporation. Thus, criminal due process protections are the constitutional limits imposed on law enforcement personnel.

These four amendments together are known as the **criminal due process rights** because they establish the guidelines that the government must follow in investigating, bringing to trial, and punishing individuals who violate criminal law. Each amendment guides the government in administering some facet of law enforcement, and all are intended to ensure justice and fairness in the administration of the law. Criminal due process is essential to guarantee that individuals can participate in the larger society and that no one person is singled out for better or worse treatment under the law. Like the First Amendment, due process protects

criminal due process rights
Safeguards for those accused of crime; these rights constrain government conduct in investigating crimes, trying cases, and punishing offenders.

political speech and freedom. Without these liberties, government officials could selectively target those who disagree with the laws and policies they advocate.

Moreover, without these rights, there would be little to stop the government from using criminal law to punish those who want to take action that is protected by the other amendments we have examined in this chapter. For example, what good would it do to talk about the freedom of speech if the government could isolate or punish someone who spoke out critically against it without having to prove in a public venue that the speech threatened public safety or national security? The criminal due process protections are essential to ensuring meaningful participation and engagement in the larger community and to safeguarding justice and fairness.

THE FOURTH AMENDMENT AND THE PROTECTION AGAINST UNREASONABLE SEARCHES AND SEIZURES The Fourth Amendment requires police to get a warrant before engaging in a search and guides law enforcement personnel in conducting criminal investigations and in searching an individual's body or property. It has its roots in colonial history—specifically, in the British government's abuse of its law enforcement powers to prosecute and punish American colonists suspected of being disloyal to England.

The Fourth Amendment imposes significant limits on law enforcement. In barring police from conducting any unreasonable searches and seizures, it requires that they show probable cause that a crime has been committed before they can obtain a search warrant. The warrant ensures that police officers can gather evidence only when they have probable cause. Further, a judicially created ruling known as the **exclusionary rule** compels law enforcers to carry out searches properly. Established for federal prosecutions in 1914, the exclusionary rule forbids the courts to admit illegally seized evidence during trial.[57] In the Supreme Court decision of *Mapp v. Ohio* (1961), the exclusionary rule was extended to state court proceedings.[58] Here, the Court overturned an Ohio court's conviction of Dollree Mapp for the possession of obscene materials. Police had found pornographic books in Mapp's apartment after searching it without a search warrant and despite the defendant's refusal to let them in. Critics of the exclusionary rule note that securing a warrant is not always necessary or feasible and that guilty people sometimes go free because of procedural technicalities. They argue that reasonable searches should not be defined solely by the presence of a court-ordered search warrant.[59]

What are "reasonable" and "unreasonable" searches under the Fourth Amendment? Over time, the U.S. Supreme Court has established criteria to guide both police officers and judges hearing cases. In the strictest definition of reasonableness, a warrant is always required: where there is no warrant, the search is considered to be unreasonable. However, the Supreme Court has ruled that even without a warrant, some searches would still be reasonable. In 1984, for example, the Court held that illegally obtained evidence could be admitted at trial if law enforcers could prove that they would have obtained the evidence legally anyway.[60] In another case the same year, the Court created a "good faith" exception to the exclusionary rule by upholding the use of evidence obtained with a technically incorrect warrant, because the police officer had acted in good faith.[61]

More broadly, a warrantless search is valid if the person subjected to it has no reasonable expectation of privacy in the place or thing being searched. From colonial times to the present, the assumption has been that individuals have a reasonable expectation of privacy in their homes. Where there is no reasonable expectation of privacy, however, there can be no unreasonable search, and so the police are not required to get a warrant before conducting the search or surveillance. Since the 1990s, the Court has expanded the situations in which there is

exclusionary rule
The criminal procedural rule stating that evidence obtained illegally cannot be used in a trial.

>Jonathan Fleming, who had already served **24 years** in prison for a crime he didn't commit, embraces his mother. Disregarding the constitutional rights of the accused can lead to wrongful convictions, like the **50 cases** currently under review by the Brooklyn district attorney. Is ensuring that innocent people are not wrongfully convicted worth the societal cost of allowing some guilty people to go free?

©Seth Wenig/AP Images

no reasonable expectation of privacy and hence no need for a warrant. For example, there is no reasonable expectation of privacy in one's car, at least in those areas that are in plain view, such as the front and back seats. There is also no expectation of privacy in public places such as parks and stores, because it is reasonable to assume that a person knowingly exposes his or her activities to public view in those places. The same is true of one's trash: because there is no reasonable expectation of privacy in the things that one discards, police may search this material without a warrant.[62]

In instances when there is a reasonable expectation of privacy, individuals or their property may be searched if law enforcement personnel acquire a warrant from a judge. To obtain a warrant, the police must provide the judge with evidence that establishes probable cause that a crime has been committed. Also, the warrant must be specific about the place to be searched and the materials that the agents are seeking. These requirements limit the ability of police simply to go on a "fishing expedition" to find some bit of incriminating evidence.

As society changes, expectations of privacy change as well. For example, technological innovation has given us new technology, such as e-mail and the Internet, and Fourth Amendment law has had to adapt to these inventions. As an example, in 2015, the Supreme Court ruled in *Torrey Dale Grady v. North Carolina* that the placement of a GPS tracking device on a convicted felon in order to monitor his movements is an unlawful search and violation of the Fourth Amendment.[63] Is there a reasonable expectation of privacy in our movements in public spaces? This is an important question, especially in light of citizens' heightened concerns about terrorism and security.

THE FIFTH AND SIXTH AMENDMENTS: THE RIGHT TO A FAIR TRIAL AND THE RIGHT TO COUNSEL The Fifth and Sixth Amendments establish the rules for conducting a trial. These two amendments ensure that criminal defendants are protected at the formal stages of legal proceedings. Although less than 10 percent of all charges result in trials, these protections have significant symbolic and practical importance, because they hold the state to a high standard whenever it attempts to use its significant power to prosecute a case against an individual.

The Fifth Amendment bars **double jeopardy** and compelled self-incrimination. These safeguards mean, respectively, that a person may not be tried twice for the same crime or forced to testify against himself or herself when accused of a crime. These safeguards are meant to protect people from persecution, harassment, and forced confessions. A single criminal action, however, can lead to multiple trials if each trial is based on a separate offense.

The Sixth Amendment establishes the rights to a speedy and public trial, to a trial by a jury of one's peers, to information about the charges against oneself, to the confrontation of witnesses testifying against oneself, and to legal counsel. The protection of these Fifth and Sixth Amendment liberties is promoted by the **Miranda rights,** based on the Supreme Court decision in *Miranda v. Arizona* (1966).[64] In the *Miranda* case, the Court outlined the requirement that "prior to questioning, the person must be warned that he has a right to remain silent, that any statement he does make may be used against him, and that he has a right to the presence of an attorney, either retained or appointed." Later cases have created some exceptions to *Miranda* (see Table 4.2).

Together, the Fourth, Fifth, and Sixth Amendments ensure the protection of individuals against abuses of power by the state, and in so doing they promote a view of justice that the community widely embraces. Because these rights extend to individuals charged with violating the community's standards of right and wrong, they promote a broad sense of inclusiveness—a respect even for persons who allegedly have committed serious offenses, and a desire to ensure that the justice system treats all people fairly.

The Court has considered the community's views in reaching its decisions in cases brought before it. For example, through a series of Supreme Court cases culminating with *Gideon v. Wainwright* (1963), the justices interpreted the right to counsel to mean that the government must provide lawyers to individuals who are too poor to hire their own.[65] The justices adopted this standard because they came to believe that the community's views of fundamental fairness dictated this result. Before this decision, states had to provide attorneys only in cases that could result in capital punishment.

TABLE 4.2 Cases Weakening Protection Against Self-Incrimination

YEAR	CASE	RULING
1986	*Moran v. Burbine*	Confession is not inadmissible because police failed to inform suspect of attorney's attempted contacts.
1991	*Arizona v. Fulminante*	Conviction is not automatically overturned in cases of coerced confession if other evidence is strong enough to justify conviction.
1994	*Davis v. U.S.*	Suspect must unequivocally and assertively state his right to counsel to stop police questioning.
2013	*Salina v. Texas*	Accused must explicitly invoke the Fifth Amendment for it to apply.

THE EIGHTH AMENDMENT: PROTECTION AGAINST CRUEL AND UNUSUAL PUNISHMENT The meaning of *cruel* and *unusual* has changed radically since the Eighth Amendment was ratified, especially with regard to the imposition of capital punishment—the death penalty. Moreover, Americans have always disagreed among themselves about the death penalty itself. Throughout the country's history, citizens and lawmakers have debated the morality of capital punishment as well as the circumstances under which the death penalty should be used. Central to the public debate have been the questions of which crimes should be punished by death and how capital punishment should be carried out.

Generally, the Court has supported the constitutionality of the death penalty. An exception was the landmark case *Furman v. Georgia* (1972), in which, in a 5–4 decision, the Court suspended the use of the death penalty.[66] Justices Brennan and Marshall believed the death penalty to be "incompatible with evolving standards of decency in contemporary society." The dissenting justices argued in turn that capital punishment had always been regarded as appropriate under the Anglo-American legal tradition for serious crimes and that the Constitution implicitly authorized death penalty laws because of the Fourteenth Amendment's reference to the taking of "life." The decision came about as a result of concurring opinions by Justices Stewart, White, and Douglas, who focused on the arbitrary nature with which death sentences had been imposed. The Court's decision forced the states and the national legislature to rethink their statutes for capital offenses to ensure that the death penalty would not be administered in a capricious or discriminatory manner. After states changed their laws regarding the death penalty in order to address legal processes that were unfair or arbitrary, the Court allowed the death penalty to be reinstated in the states (*Gregg v. Georgia,* 1976).[67]

Over time, the courts have also interpreted the Eighth Amendment as requiring that executions be carried out in the most humane and least painful manner. Public discourse and debate have strongly influenced thinking about which methods of execution are appropriate.

Recent studies, however, suggest that states' administration of the sedative sodium pentothal has left individuals conscious and in agony but paralyzed and thus unable to cry out while they are dying. But in 2008, the Supreme Court ruled in a 7–2 decision that lethal injection does not constitute cruel and unusual punishment,[68] paving the way for 10 states, which had halted lethal injections pending the case's outcome, to resume executions. The 2008 decision of *Baze v. Rees* marked the first time the Supreme Court reviewed the constitutionality of a method of execution since 1878, when the Court upheld Utah's use of a firing squad.[69]

After the execution of Clayton Lockett using a three-drug lethal injection resulted in a 40-minute conscious death, Oklahoma created a new death protocol. One remaining option was a drug used in the Lockett execution—midazolam. Twenty-one inmates on death row argued that the use of midazolam violated the Eighth Amendment. The Court found that the Eighth Amendment did not guarantee a pain-free execution and that medical evidence did not demonstrate that midazolam created a risk of severe pain in light of Oklahoma's new safeguards.[70]

Civil Liberties Now

Public discussion about the proper balance of individual freedom with public action extends from First Amendment freedoms to gun laws to the rights of the accused. Debate has intensified as the nation struggles with the threat of terrorism and a growing protest culture at home. Citizens and government leaders are rethinking their beliefs about the proper scope of governmental power.

Over the course of U.S. history, liberty and security have coexisted in a state of tension. This tension has become more acute as the federal, state, and local governments have taken certain actions that directly intrude on individual freedoms. New technologies have increased the government's capacity to invade citizens' privacy, and a heightened fear of internal and external threats has been used to justify such invasions. The government and many citizens argue that these actions are necessary to protect life and property. But civil libertarians shudder at what they see as unprecedented violations of individual freedoms and rights.

Perceived Intrusions on Free Speech and Assembly

Although the tension between liberty and order has been clear since the origins of our republic, this conflict has become more intense in recent years. For instance, the Foreign Intelligence Surveillance Act (FISA) of 1978, which empowers the government to conduct secret searches where necessary to protect national security, significantly broadened the powers of law enforcement agencies to engage in investigation. Agencies must go before a designated court, the Foreign Intelligence Surveillance Act Court, to justify a secret search. Civil libertarians are concerned about the FISA court's concealed location and sealed records, as well as its judicial proceedings, in which the suspect is never told about the investigation and probable cause is not required to approve surveillance or searches of any person suspected of having some link to terrorism.

Following September 11, 2001, a number of government agencies engaged in the surveillance of political groups in the United States. In late 2005, the media exposed a program by the Bush administration and the National Security Agency (NSA) to target U.S. civilians for electronic surveillance without judicial oversight. Members of the Bush administration claimed that they had monitored only communications where one party was suspected of links to terrorism and was currently overseas. Beginning in 2005, however, the American Civil Liberties Union (ACLU) issued a series of reports demonstrating that the Federal Bureau of Investigation (FBI) spied not only on people suspected of taking part in terrorist plots but also on individuals involved in peaceful political activities.[71] The ACLU has released similar reports describing the Pentagon's database of peaceful war protesters.[72]

The ACLU and other critics of the domestic surveillance program have argued that the federal government is targeting political protest, not domestic terrorism plots. Opponents of the policy warn that the FBI and other agencies are infringing upon free speech, assembly, and expression. But employees of the NSA and the Department of Justice have defended the government's expanded investigation and enforcement activities, claiming that the threats to national security are grave and that the government must be given the power it needs to protect against these dangers.[73]

Perceived Intrusions on Criminal Due Process

Attacks in Europe and across the globe, isolated attacks in the U.S. from people claiming sympathies with terrorist organizations and numerous mass shootings, have meant many Americans are willing to accept some infringement on their freedoms if it makes them safer. These citizens assume that criminal activity may be afoot and that the surveillance is not being used to target groups that are politically unpopular or critical of the administration. Much of the debate about the surveillance activities of the FBI and other groups centers on the distinction between criminally active groups and politically unpopular groups. How do we know which groups the federal government is using its powers to investigate?

To what extent must administration officials provide evidence of criminal intent before placing a suspect under surveillance? Since September 11, 2001, the laws that govern domestic spying have been modified in such a way that the government has much more leeway in conducting searches and investigations, even where there is no proof of criminal activity.

One example is the USA PATRIOT Act, which allowed the FBI and other intelligence agencies to access personal information and records without getting permission from, or even informing, targeted individuals.[74] Much of the data come from private sources, which are often ordered to hand over their records.

On July 28, 2007, President George W. Bush (2001–2009) called on Congress to pass legislation to reform the FISA in order to ease restrictions on the surveillance of terrorist suspects in cases where one party or both parties to the communication are located overseas. The Protect America Act of 2007 essentially legalized ongoing NSA practices.[75] Under the act, the U.S. government may wiretap without FISA court supervision any communications that begin or end in a foreign country. The act removes from the definition of "electronic surveillance" in FISA any surveillance directed at a person reasonably believed to be located outside the United States. This means that the government may listen to conversations without a court order as long as the U.S. attorney general approves the surveillance. Supporters stress that flexibility is needed to monitor the communications of suspected terrorists and their networks. Critics, however, worry that the law is too vague and provides the government with the ability to monitor any group or individual it opposes, regardless of whether it has links to terrorism.

In 2009, the Inspectors General of the Department of Defense, the Department of Justice, the CIA, the NSA, and the Office of the Director of National Intelligence revealed that the surveillance program had a much larger scope than previously believed.[76] Edward Snowden, an IT contractor with the NSA, downloaded approximately 200,000 classified documents revealing the NSA's large-scale surveillance of both American citizens and residents of other countries. These metadata collections included most phone calls made in the U.S., e-mail, Facebook, text messages, raw Internet traffic, and an unknown number of phone conversations. In 2013, Snowden fled the U.S. and began slowly sharing this information with *The Guardian* and *The Washington Post.*

The USA Freedom Act was signed into law in 2015, renewing a number of expired elements of the PATRIOT Act until 2019. These controversial aspects included roving wiretaps, the capacity to search business records, and the surveillance of so-called lone wolves, persons who while suspected of terrorist actions do not appear to be formally related to organized terrorist groups. The new law also amended a part of the USA PATRIOT Act to prevent the NSA from collecting telephone data from the masses and then storing the data perpetually. Under the USA Freedom Act, phone companies store the data and the federal government can access data of specified individuals by obtaining a warrant.

Although many Americans are concerned about domestic surveillance, especially in situations where it targets political speech and expression, these laws remain on the books, and this surveillance likely will continue. For the time being, the line between suspected criminal activity and purely political expression remains blurred. Civic discourse about how to balance liberty and national security continues to evolve as Americans consider how much freedom they should sacrifice to protect public safety.

Another place the nation has observed intrusions on criminal due process has been in the response of police forces to public outcry against perceived unjustified killings of civilians. In part because of the visibility of the Black Lives Matter movement (see Chapter 5 for a more detailed discussion) and cell phone videos made public over social media, the public has called for greater police accountability in their use of deadly force. After the police shooting in Ferguson, Missouri, of Michael Brown in 2014, the accompanying protests, additional high-profile shootings, and a Department of Justice investigation of local police practices, the arguments for police accountability have expanded beyond the Black and Latino communities where they originated and become part of a national discussion. As activists recorded similar fatalities from across the country, a disproportionate pattern of officers killing persons of color was evident.

In response to such events, the use of body cameras for police officers has become policy in many communities. The federal government has provided $41 million to fund cameras, and cities are seeking to similarly equip their officers; body cameras are the nation's primary response to claims of systemic racism and police abuse.[77] While these new policies had the stated intention of protecting vulnerable populations, there are no national uniform guidelines of how this equipment can be used. Organizations including the Leadership Conference on Civil and Human Rights are concerned that this taping of civilians (but not of police actions) could simply become a means of government surveillance, absent careful regulations.[78] As this technology becomes integrated into local law enforcement communities, this question becomes increasingly significant: How can we ensure that it improves the quality of policing and relationships with citizens without enabling police to profile and track people of color?

Free Speech on Campus

After a very contentious and polarizing 2016 presidential election season, some of the nation's elite public universities struggled with the meaning and requirements of free speech on campus. Student bodies are more ethnically, racially, and socioeconomically diverse than in previous generations, and these student groups seek to have a voice on campus. Universities are pressured to intellectually welcome traditionally marginalized student voices and value their perspectives on campus, a place from which they had historically been excluded. At the same time, a newly empowered conservative movement, particularly those on the alt-right who are galvanized by white supremacy and threatened by a more diverse and multicultural society, are calling for greater visibility on college campuses. Using the First Amendment to protect their speech, they have challenged public universities to allow their voices to be heard. Students of color and their allies feel they can't be silent because the alt-right is an "existential threat" seeking to destroy their very existence.[79]

For instance, at California State University at Fullerton, Milo Yiannopoulos—an openly gay, former editor at the conservative media outlet Breitbart—who is known for his misogynistic, racist, and homophobic speeches and posts, spoke to an audience of 800 in October 2017. Sponsored by College Republicans, his presence led to fights between protesters and attendees, resulting in seven arrests despite the university's claim that dozens of police officers patrolled the event. The enhanced police presence was considered essential because prior events with polarizing speakers at campuses across the country had resulted in violent responses from protesters, including fires and window smashing. Universities canceled his events, and Yiannopoulos has withdrawn.[80]

Should College Campuses Be Allowed to Limit Speech?

The Issue: The faculty and administrators of public universities are struggling with the meaning of the First Amendment's free speech protections on college campuses. As student bodies become more diverse, students expect to have their identities and beliefs treated with respect, and current student bodies often do not want to hear perspectives that are directly different from their own. Speech in the United States has become more polarized and extreme, and speakers who gain fame from social media often are not temperate or reasoned in their analysis, but focus on being provocative.

All Speech Should Be Allowed: Without exposure to sometimes offensive and difficult views, future Americans will not be capable of engaging in a public debate that forces one to confront contrary perspectives. In light of our great polarization as a nation, the onus is on universities to educate our students to be capable citizens in our democracy. And at the heart of our democracy is the First Amendment, with its guarantee that all citizens can participate in the debates that will direct our governance.

Free speech has historically been essential to advancing equal rights and political equality. Students do not know the history of free speech or the ways in which contrary views have been shut down and dissenters persecuted by the government. The First Amendment and the value of academic freedom are clear. The Supreme Court clearly states that public institutions cannot punish speech or exclude speakers based on the content of their speech. Campuses can regulate where and when the speech occurs to prevent the disruption of learning, and counter-demonstrations are also protected. And just because speakers can express hateful speech, campuses do not have to agree with ideas reflected in the speech and can always denounce the hate behind it.

Some Speech Should Not Be Allowed: Many students want campuses to stop offensive speech and believe that campus officials have the power to do so. Pew Research Institute found in a 2015 survey that 40 percent of college students believe that the government should prevent people from making statements offensive to minority groups. They want to make campuses inclusive for all, and they know that hate speech is harmful, especially to those who have been traditionally excluded from higher education. The university is a special place. It exists to educate and create knowledge, both of which require the evaluation of the quality of ideas. We teach students to do this and grade them on the merit of their own arguments and understandings. Faculty teach content discrimination, and their ideas are evaluated based on their judgments regarding content. A classroom and the university are not an open forum. They promote freedom of ideas, but this does not mean that all ideas have equal value; universities must teach students the skill of facing and evaluating threatening and dangerous ideas. This does not mean that students should be exposed to abuse and threatening language. For a university to do its job, it must encourage and tolerate offensive ideas while rejecting and refusing personal incivility.

What do you think?

1. Is there a difference between speakers sponsored by professors and departments versus those sponsored by student organizations? Explain your answer.

2. What role should a university play in distinguishing between the quality of ideas and the manner in which they are delivered?

3. Does the First Amendment mean something different at a university than it does in a city park?

4. How should universities prepare students to confront ideas they see as "threatening and dangerous"?

SOURCES: Robert C. Post, "There Is No 1st Amendment Right to Speak on a College Campus," *Vox*, December 31, 2017, and Erwin Chemerinsky, "Hate Speech Is Protected Free Speech, Even on College Campuses," *Vox*, December 26, 2017.

These circumstances have raised new questions around the First Amendment and free speech. When speakers—whether liberal or conservative—use abusive and threatening language toward specific groups, does the First Amendment protect them from the government (or state universities) exercising content discrimination? If such controversial speakers as Yiannopoulos and white supremacist Richard Spencer attract counterprotests requiring states to spend much additional money for security, is this considered a legitimate state regulation of the time, place, and manner of speech? When a university allows speakers to appear who offend or threaten students' identities, is it an endorsement of that speech?

Thinking Critically About What's Next for Civil Liberties

At the core of the U.S. political and legal system lies a strong belief in individual liberties and rights. This belief is reflected in the Bill of Rights, the first 10 amendments to the Constitution. The freedoms therein are at the heart of civic engagement and ensure that individuals can freely participate in the political and social life of their communities. But these freedoms are also malleable, and at times the government has starkly limited them, as when officials perceive a threat to national security.

The inevitable tension between freedom and order is heightened as Americans and their government struggle to protect essential liberties while guarding the nation against future terrorist attacks and internal violence. Debates over enhanced Second Amendment rights in a culture of increasing mass shootings remain unresolved and continue to mobilize groups to protest and campaign. Privacy continues to be a concern of citizens as Internet providers create new services that consumers both demand and desire. Tension between national security and personal freedom is reflected in contemporary debates over free speech and hate speech.

Meanwhile, governmental mining of private information through warrantless surveillance of social media sites, as well as the increased reliance on police body cameras, raises new questions regarding the limits of liberty. The issues we confront will continue to evolve as we struggle to maintain the commitment to liberty that defines our nation while preserving the country itself.

Learning Summary

1. Summarize how the Constitution demonstrates a commitment to liberty.
   a. Demonstrate how the Bill of Rights balances liberty and security interests.
   b. Explain the implications of the doctrine of selective incorporation.
2. Define the "Right to Bear Arms."
   a. Explain how the Second Amendment demonstrates a commitment to liberty.
   b. Describe how the Supreme Court interprets individual liberty in the Second Amendment.
   c. Recall how the Supreme Court's interpretation of the Second Amendment has changed over time.

3. Explain how freedoms of speech, press, and assembly are important to democracy.
   a. Identify types of speech protected by the First Amendment.
   b. Describe the principles underlying freedom of the press, including prohibiting prior restraint.
   c. Outline how Supreme Court decisions have balanced liberty and security in the First Amendment in limiting speech.

4. Summarize how freedoms of religion, privacy, and criminal due process can be limited.
   a. Distinguish between the establishment and free exercise clauses of the First Amendment.
   b. Explain how the Supreme Court has interpreted the due process clause to protect the right of privacy.
   c. Recall how the due process clause prevents states from infringing on the individual rights of the criminally accused.

5. Evaluate ways in which liberty and security interests are currently in conflict.
   a. Identify the liberty and security interests in the free speech debates on campus.
   b. Explain how the collection of metadata could either promote or interfere with liberty and security interests.

Key Terms

bad tendency test 127

civil liberties 119

clear and present danger test 127

clear and probable danger test 128

commercial speech 131

criminal due process rights 141

double jeopardy 144

due process 120

establishment clause 134

exclusionary rule 142

fighting words 132

free exercise clause 136

habeas corpus 127

imminent lawless action test (incitement test) 129

Lemon test 135

libel 131

marketplace of ideas 126

Miranda rights 144

obscenity 131

prior restraint 133

right to privacy 138

selective incorporation 123

slander 131

symbolic speech 129

time, place, and manner restrictions 132

total incorporation 122

For Review

1. What are civil liberties? How do civil liberties differ from civil rights? Why do we protect civil liberties?

2. How does the First Amendment support civic discourse?

3. What protections does the Bill of Rights provide to those accused of committing a crime?

4. What are the two sides of the issue of Second Amendment rights? How has the Supreme Court interpreted these rights?

5. How have increased security threats affected civil liberties in the United States?

For Critical Thinking and Discussion

1. Under what circumstances should the government be allowed to regulate or punish speech?

2. How do we protect citizens' Second Amendment rights and still ensure that the public is secured by law enforcement?

3. Under what circumstances should the government be able to punish people for practicing their religious beliefs?

4. Should the government be allowed to search people and property without a warrant based on probable cause that a crime was committed? Explain.

5. Do you believe that the USA Freedom Act and the NSA domestic surveillance program make the nation safer? Why or why not?

6. Will giving up liberty to enhance security protect the nation, or will it destroy the fundamental values on which the nation was founded? Defend your position.

7. Are you concerned that technologies developed to fight wars against terrorism could be used to control the behavior of citizens in the United States? Where do you believe the line should be drawn?

Resources for Research AND Action

Internet Resources

Center for Democracy and Technology
www.cdt.org The effect of new computer and communications technologies on American civil liberties is the subject of this site.

National Rifle Association-Institute for Legislative Action
www.nraila.org The lobbying arm of the National Rifle Association focuses on guaranteeing safe access to guns for law-abiding individuals.

American Civil Liberties Union
www.aclu.org With the tagline "Because Freedom Can't Protect Itself," this national organization with state branches prioritizes liberty over all other priorities.

Recommended Readings

Chemerinsky, Erwin, and Howard Gillman. *Free Speech on Campus*. New Haven: Yale University Press, 2017. A political scientist and law school dean work to balance the needs of students to be welcome on campuses and the demands of free speech.

Denvir, John. *Freeing Speech: The Constitutional War Over National Security*. New York: New York University Press, 2010. Argues that a broad definition of presidential power and a weak interpretation of the First Amendment by Congress and the judiciary have changed American democracy for the worse.

Fisher, Louis. *The Constitution and 9/11: Recurring Threats to America's Freedoms*. Lawrence: University Press of Kansas, 2008. This book, written by one of the nation's foremost experts on separation of powers, surveys the historic responses to threats to national security by the branches of the federal government and then evaluates the current challenges to the constitutional law of national security after 9/11.

Rosen, Jeffrey, and Benjamin Wittes, eds. *Constitution 3.0: Freedom and Technological Change*. Washington, D.C.: Brookings Institution Press, 2011. Considers the way in which future and current technology may affect current constitutional doctrine, evolving into new constitutional challenges and tensions with citizens' right to individual freedom.

Rotenberg, Marc, Julia Horwitz, and Jeramie Scott, eds. *Privacy in the Modern Age: The Search for Solutions*. New York: The New Press, 2015. This collection assumes that privacy is a value worth protecting and that there are solutions to our current and future privacy concerns.

Spitzer, Robert J. *Guns Across America: Reconciling Gun Rules and Rights*. New York: Oxford University Press, 2015. Notes the history of gun regulations in the United States from the founding and its relationship with gun-ownership rights.

Movies of Interest

The Post (2017)
Using the *Pentagon Papers* case litigated in *New York Times v. U.S.* (1971), which protected the press from the prior restraint of publishing, the film examines the *Washington Post* involvement and its first female publisher, Katharine Graham.

The Fifth Estate (2013)
A popular portrayal of the evolution of the WikiLeaks organization and its global impact when it reveals many governments' secrets relative to security, surveillance, and corruption, focusing on WikiLeaks's founder, Julian Assange.

J. Edgar (2011)
A biographic picture of the life and career of J. Edgar Hoover, the head of the FBI from 1924 to his death in 1972. The film explores the ways in which the government, with Hoover's leadership, criminalized and investigated the activities of dissidents in the United States.

Rendition (2007)
When an Egyptian terrorism suspect "disappears" on a flight from Africa to Washington, D.C., his American wife and a CIA analyst struggle to secure his release from a secret detention (and torture) facility somewhere outside the United States.

Good Night and Good Luck (2005)
This film examines the conflict between veteran journalist Edward R. Murrow and Senator Joseph McCarthy as Murrow attempts to investigate and discredit McCarthy's tactics in investigating and destroying communist elements in the federal government and larger society.

The People versus Larry Flynt (1996)
This film documents the economic success, courtroom battles, and personal challenges of *Hustler* magazine publisher Larry Flynt. Flynt is obnoxious and hedonistic in ways that offend and anger "decent people," even as he fights to protect freedom of speech for all.

References

1. For an accessible and lively account of the central role of liberty in the American Revolution, see Thomas Fleming, *Liberty! The American Revolution* (New York: Viking, 1997).
2. For a history of civil liberties in wartime, see Geoffrey R. Stone, *Perilous Times: Free Speech in Wartime From the Sedition Act of 1798 to the War on Terrorism* (New York: W. W. Norton, 2004).
3. *Barron v. Baltimore,* 32 U.S. 243 (1833).
4. See *Hurtado v. California,* 110 U.S. 516 (1884) and *Turning v. New Jersey,* 211 U.S. 78 (1908) for a discussion of the standard the Court uses to determine whether a particular liberty should be incorporated into the Fourteenth Amendment.
5. *Gitlow v. New York,* 268 U.S. 652 (1925).
6. *Near v. Minnesota,* 283 U.S. 697 (1931).
7. *Palko v. Connecticut,* 302 U.S. 319 (1937).
8. For a detailed look at evolution of our constitutional understanding of the Second Amendment, see Michael Waldman, *The Second Amendment: A Biography* (New York: Simon & Schuster, 2014).
9. *District of Columbia v. Heller,* 554 U.S. (2008).
10. *McDonald v. City of Chicago,* 561 U.S. 3025 (2010).
11. F. B. Ahmad and B. Bastian, "Quarterly Provisional Estimates for Selected Indicators of Mortality, 2016–Quarter 4, 2017." National Center for Health Statistics. National Vital Statistics System. 2018.
12. Presidential Proclamation of September 24, 1862, by President Abraham Lincoln, suspending the writ of *habeas corpus.*
13. For two detailed accounts of the acts, see John C. Miller, *Crisis in Freedom: The Alien and Sedition Acts* (Boston: Little, Brown, 1951); and James Morton Smith, *Freedom's Fetters: The Alien and Sedition Laws and American Civil Liberties* (Ithaca, NY: Cornell University Press, 1956).
14. Liz Robbins, Fernando Santos, and Jennifer Medina, "Trump's Immigration Policies Explained," *New York Times,* February 21, 2017 and "President Donald J. Trump Restores Responsibility and the Rule of Law to Immigration," The White House Fact Sheets, September 5, 2017.
15. Garrett Epps, "The Supreme Court's Travel Ban Off-Ramp," *The Atlantic,* December 24, 2017.
16. *Schenck v. United States,* 249 U.S. 47 (1919).
17. *Gitlow v. New York,* 268 U.S. 652 (1925).
18. *Dennis v. U.S.,* 341 U.S. 494 (1951).
19. *Brandenburg v. Ohio,* 395 U.S. 444 (1969).
20. *U.S. v. O'Brien,* 391 U.S. 367 (1968).
21. *Tinker et al. v. Des Moines Independent Community School District et al.,* 393 U.S. 503 (1969).
22. For a discussion of *Tinker* and similar cases, see Jamin B. Baskin, *We the Students: Supreme Court Cases for and About Students,* 3rd ed. (Washington, DC: CQ Press, 2008).
23. *Texas v. Johnson,* 491 U.S. 397 (1989).
24. *U.S. v. Eichman,* 496 U.S. 310 (1990).
25. *Citizens United v. Federal Election Commission,* 558 U.S. 310 (2010).
26. *Miller v. California,* 413 U.S. 15 (1973).
27. *Chaplinsky v. New Hampshire,* 315 U.S. 568 (1942).
28. *Virginia v. Black,* 538 U.S. 343 (2003).
29. *Reno v. ACLU,* 521 U.S. 844 (1997); and *U.S. v. Playboy Entertainment Group,* 529 U.S. 803 (2000).
30. Martin Pengelly and Joanna Walters, "Trump Accused of Encouraging Attacks on Journalists with CNN Body-Slam Tweet," *The Guardian,* July 2, 2017, and Jacey Fortin, "Rough Treatment of Journalists in the Trump Era," *New York Times,* May 25, 2017.
31. *New York Times v. U.S.,* 403 U.S. 713 (1971).
32. Gallup poll, "Religion," www.gallup.com/poll/1690/Religion.aspx.
33. The phrase "wall of separation" first appeared in Thomas Jefferson's 1802 letter to the Danbury Baptist Association. This letter is available at the Library of Congress website: www.loc.gov/loc/lcib/9806/danpre.html.
34. For a discussion of the doctrine of accommodationism, see Kenneth D. Wald, *Religion and Politics in the United States,* 3rd ed. (Washington, DC: CQ Press, 1997). For a discussion of neutrality, see Robert Booth Fowler, Allen D. Hertzke, and Laura R. Olson, *Religion and Politics in America: Faith, Culture, & Strategic Choices,* 2nd ed. (Boulder, CO: Westview Press, 1999).
35. *Everson v. Board of Education,* 330 U.S. 1 (1947).
36. *Lemon v. Kurtzman,* 403 U.S. 602 (1971).
37. *Zelman v. Simmons-Harris,* 539 U.S. 639 (2002).
38. *Engel v. Vitale,* 370 U.S. 421 (1962).
39. *Prince v. Massachusetts,* 321 U.S. 158 (1944).
40. See for instance, *Phillips v. City of New York,* 14-2156-CV, 2015 (2nd Circuit); and *Schenker v. County of Tuscarawas,* 5:12 CV 1020, 2012 (E.D., Ohio).
41. *Employment Division, Department of Human Resources of the State of Oregon et al. v. Smith,* 494 U.S. 872 (1990).
42. *Burwell v. Hobby Lobby,* 573 U.S. 682 (2014).
43. *Griswold v. Connecticut,* 381 U.S. 479 (1965).
44. *Roberts v. U.S. Jaycees,* 468 U.S. 609 (1984).
45. *Roe v. Wade,* 410 U.S. 113 (1973).
46. *Planned Parenthood v. Casey,* 505 U.S. 833 (1992).
47. *Whole Women's Health v. Hellerstedt,* 579 U.S. _____ (2016).
48. *Cruzan v. Director, Missouri Department of Health,* 497 U.S. 261 (1990).
49. Ibid.
50. *Bowers v. Hardwick,* 478 U.S. 186 (1986).
51. *Lawrence v. Texas,* 539 U.S. 558 (2003).
52. *Obergefell v. Hodges,* 576 U.S. _____ (2015).
53. This is a point of agreement among the Court's opinion, the concurring opinion, and the dissenting opinion issued in *Lawrence v. Texas,* 539 U.S. 558 (2003).
54. American Civil Liberties Union, "NSA Documents Released to the Public Since June 2013".
55. Global Government Surveillance Reform, www.reformgovernmentsurveillance.com/.
56. Alfred Ng, "Google Reports All-Time High of Government Data Requests," *C/Net,* September 28, 2017.
57. *Weeks v. U.S.,* 232 U.S. 383 (1914).
58. *Mapp v. Ohio,* 367 U.S. 643 (1961).

59. See Chief Justice Warren E. Burger's dissent in *Coolidge v. New Hampshire,* 403 U.S. 443, 1971.

60. *Segura v. U.S.,* 468 U.S. 796 (1984).

61. *U.S. v. Leon,* 468 U.S. 897 (1984).

62. *California v. Greenwood,* 486 U.S. 35 (1988).

63. *Grady v. North Carolina,* 575 U.S. _____ (2015).

64. *Miranda v. Arizona,* 384 U.S. 436 (1966).

65. *Gideon v. Wainwright,* 312 U.S. 335 (1963).

66. *Furman v. Georgia,* 408 U.S. 238 (1972).

67. *Gregg v. Georgia,* 428 U.S. 153 (1976) was the first of many such cases.

68. *Baze v. Rees,* 553 U.S. 35 (2008).

69. *Wilkerson v. Utah,* 99 U.S. 130 (1878).

70. *Glossip v. Gross,* 576 U.S. _____ (2015).

71. For a recent report, see ACLU, "History Repeated: The Dangers of Domestic Spying by Federal Law Enforcement," May 29, 2007.

72. ACLU, "No Real Threat: The Pentagon's Secret Database on Peaceful Protest," January 17, 2007.

73. Jo Mannies, "Ashcroft Defends Bush on Spying," *St. Louis Post-Dispatch,* February 10, 2008.

74. The full title of the law (H.R. 3162) is the Uniting and Strengthening America by Providing Appropriate Tools Required to Intercept and Obstruct Terrorism (USA PATRIOT) Act of 2001.

75. Protect America Act of 2007 (Pub.L. 110-55, S. 1927) signed into law by George W. Bush on August 5, 2007.

76. Offices of Inspectors General of the Department of Defense, Department of Justice, the Central Intelligence Agency, the National Security Agency, and the Office of the Director of National Intelligence, "Unclassified Report on the President's Surveillance Program," Report No. 2009-0013-AS, July 10, 2009.

77. U.S. Department of Justice, "Body-Worn Camera Program," www.bja.gov/bwc/pdfs/BWCPIP-Factsheet-2016-Update-Final.pdf.

78. National Institute of Justice, "Research on Body-Worn Cameras and Law Enforcement," December 5, 2017.

79. Steve Kolowich, "Hey, Look Over Here!" *The Chronicle of Higher Education,* November 15, 2017.

80. Fernanda Zamudio-Suaréz, "7 Are Arrested outside Milo Yiannopoulos Speech at Cal State-Fullerton," *The Chronicle of Higher Education,* November 1, 2017.

CHAPTER 5
Civil Rights

©Gabriel Olsen/WireImage/Getty Images

THEN

African Americans, women, Native Americans, Latinos, and other groups struggled to achieve equality in the United States.

NOW

Women are challenging current and historic sexual harassment and assault as a violation of civil rights.

Changing understandings of gender identity and sexual orientation are altering our definition of civil rights. Communities of color are protesting abuses from law enforcement through the Black Lives Matter movement.

NEXT

What protections will the nation be willing to extend to undocumented immigrants and their children?

Will access to safe drinking water and water rights become the next front in civil rights battles?

Should quality, affordable housing and child care be considered civil rights?

Although the Declaration of

Independence claims that all men are created equal and are endowed with the natural rights of life, liberty, and the pursuit of happiness, neither the Articles of Confederation nor the Constitution as initially ratified guaranteed that the government would treat or protect all men equally. Indeed, those constitutions did *not* guarantee nonwhite men or women of all races and colors the same legal rights that they guaranteed to white men. For example, African American men and women had no legal rights and were bought and sold as property until 1865, when the Thirteenth Amendment to the Constitution made such enslavement illegal. The Constitution did not guarantee American women the right to sue, nor did it protect married women's right to own property, until well into the 19th century. Many Americans experienced unequal treatment under the law throughout U.S. history.

Fast-forward to today. When asked what principles or ideals they hold most dear, many Americans will mention equality. Yet, even today, not all people in the United States are treated equally under the law. Moreover, people disagree strongly on the meaning of "equal protection of the law," which has been a stated constitutional guarantee since 1868, when the states ratified the Fourteenth Amendment to the U.S. Constitution.

Disagreement about what constitutes "equal treatment" is at the heart of many past and current struggles for equality. Does equal treatment mean that the government must ensure that all people have equal opportunities to pursue their happiness? Does it bar all differential treatment by the government and its officials, or are there certain situations in which it is acceptable for the government to treat people differently to fulfill its mission (establish justice, ensure domestic tranquility, provide for the common defense, promote the general welfare, and secure the blessings of liberty)?

In this chapter, we examine the concept of equality under the law. We focus on how groups of citizens who were originally deprived of equal protection of their liberties and pursuit of happiness have been able to expand their rights in numerous areas, including voting rights and equal access to educational and employment opportunities, marriage, and public accommodations.

The Meaning of Equality Under the Law

Although the issue of protecting civil liberties was in the forefront at the nation's founding, as we discussed in Chapter 4, the issue of guaranteeing civil rights reached the national agenda much later.[1] When we talk about **civil rights** in the

Learning Objectives

After reading this chapter, students should be able to:

- Summarize how the United States defines equality through the law.
- Explain the impact of slavery and its aftermath on the United States.
- Describe how people resisted discrimination in the modern civil rights movement.
- Describe the federal government's response to the civil rights movement.
- Explain the primary concern of the Blacks Lives Matter movement.
- Define the three waves of the movement for women's civil rights.
- Explain how other groups have expanded civil rights.
- Analyze the constitutionality of affirmative action.

civil rights
The rights and privileges guaranteed to all citizens under the equal protection and due process clauses of the Fifth and Fourteenth Amendments; the idea that individuals are protected from discrimination based on characteristics such as race, national origin, religion, and sex.

THEN NOW NEXT

Fighting for Their Rights: How Groups and Issues Change

Then (1960s and 1970s)	Now
African Americans, women, Native Americans, Latinos, and the elderly fought for equal treatment under the law.	Asian citizens, citizens with disabilities, and lesbian, gay, bisexual, and transgender citizens fight for equal treatment under the law.
Key strategies included nonviolent civil disobedience, protests, and seeking remedy through the judicial and legislative processes.	Protests, lobbying, and lawsuits remain important strategies, but today's activists also use social media to organize supporters and political theater to bring attention to their causes.
Important issues included equal access to schools, public accommodations, voting rights, and equal pay.	Important issues include rights for trans persons, ensured access to adequate housing and health care, voting rights, and immigration policy.

WHAT'S NEXT?

> What groups will begin to seek ways of achieving their civil rights?

> How will emerging technologies change the strategies and tactics that civil rights activists use?

> What issues will be at the forefront of the civil rights agenda in the future?

inherent characteristics
Individual attributes such as race, national origin, religion, and sex.

United States, we mean the rights and privileges guaranteed by the government under the equal protection and due process clauses of the Fifth and Fourteenth Amendments and the privileges and immunities clause of the Fourteenth Amendment. These rights are based on the idea that the government should protect individuals from discrimination that results from inherent characteristics. **Inherent characteristics** are individual characteristics that are part of a person's nature, such as race, religion, national origin, and sex. Some of these rights are extended only to citizens (such as the right to vote), but there is a significant debate around what protections are extended to other individuals.[2]

The Constitution imposes constraints (civil liberties) and responsibilities (civil rights) on governments, which includes government officials and employees, but *not* on private individuals or organizations. However, governments can write laws that prohibit private individuals and organizations from infringing on civil liberties and civil rights. For example, the national government enacted the Civil Rights Act of 1964, which prohibited private businesses and organizations from discriminating in hiring decisions based on the inherent characteristics of race, color, religion, national origin, and sex.

Most people agree that no government, private individual, or organization should treat people differently because of these inherent characteristics. The courts have determined that treating citizens differently based on their inherent characteristics is unfair, arbitrary, and in most situations illegal. However, people and even government officials, including judges, disagree about whether the list of inherent characteristics should include such factors as age, physical and mental disabilities, and sexual orientation. For example, should people whose gender identity does not match their birth sex have the right to determine their own gender? Within all of these classifications, there are debates over if and when the government should allow differential treatment in order to encourage greater equality.

As we explored in Chapter 4, no civil liberty is absolute; there are situations in which the government may infringe on an individual's liberty. For example, the government may infringe on an individual's freedom of speech if it views her speech as violating the imminent lawless action test (or incitement test)—that is, if the risk of harm from the speech is highly likely and the harm is imminent or immediate. Civil rights are also not absolute. The national courts have established

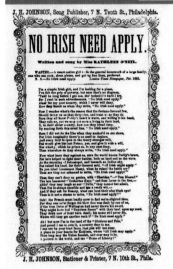

> Historically, people have encountered discrimination because of their ethnicity, race, or gender. In some places, Irish citizens were barred from applying for jobs, African Americans attending theaters were forced to use separate entrances (here with the ironic promise of "good shows in comfort"), and help-wanted ads were segregated based on gender. How do these changing norms demonstrate the way in which civil rights movements have altered our understanding of equality?

poster: ©Everett Collection/SuperStock; *theater:* ©New York Times/Hulton Archive/Getty Images; *newspaper:* ©History Archives/Alamy Stock Photo

"tests" that the government uses to determine when unequal protection under the law (that is, differential or discriminatory treatment) is legal.

Today, the courts use three tests—*strict scrutiny, heightened scrutiny,* and *ordinary scrutiny*—to determine when unequal treatment is legal. Which test the court uses depends on the inherent characteristic that is the basis for differential treatment. For example, courts view race, ethnic origin, and religion to be **suspect classifications,** meaning that judges will assume that the laws treating individuals differently because of these inherent characteristics are unconstitutional and violate the equal protection clauses. When the courts hear a challenge to laws with suspect classifications, they use the **strict scrutiny test,** which requires the government to show that the differential treatment is necessary for it to achieve a compelling public interest for which it is responsible. Using the strict scrutiny test in *Loving v. Virginia* (1967), the Supreme Court determined that laws barring interracial marriage violated the Constitution because there was no compelling public interest for which the government was responsible; hence, the laws were not necessary.[3] Therefore, today it is illegal to deny interracial couples the right to marry.

The courts do not consider the inherent characteristic of sex to be a suspect classification, and therefore laws that allow differential treatment of women and men do not need to pass the strict scrutiny test when challenged. Instead, the courts apply the **heightened scrutiny test** (also known as the **intermediate scrutiny test**) in sex-based discrimination cases, which requires the government to show that the sex-based differential treatment is substantially related to an important public interest for which the government is responsible. The heightened scrutiny test is a weaker test, making it easier for the government to justify sex-based discrimination than discrimination based on race, religion, or ethnic origin. Therefore, today women in the military do not have the same opportunities in combat roles (and hence combat-related benefits) as military men do.

suspect classifications
Distinctions based on race, religion, and national origin, which are assumed to be illegitimate.

strict scrutiny test
Guidelines the courts use to determine the legality of suspect classification based discrimination; on the basis of this test, discrimination is legal if it is a necessary means by which the government can achieve a compelling public interest.

heightened scrutiny test (intermediate scrutiny test)
The guidelines used most frequently by the courts to determine the legality of sex-based discrimination; on the basis of this test, sex-based discrimination is legal if the government can prove that it is substantially related to the achievement of an important public interest.

ordinary scrutiny test (rational basis test)
On the basis of this test, sex-based discrimination is legal if it is a reasonable means by which the government can achieve a legitimate public interest.

The weakest test the courts use when determining if a law allowing discriminatory treatment is legal is the **ordinary scrutiny test** (also called the **rational basis test**). Using the ordinary scrutiny test, courts require governments to show that the differential treatment is a rational means to achieve a legitimate public interest for which the government is responsible. State governments have established minimum ages for numerous legal rights, such as the right to marry, the right to get a driver's license, and the right to purchase alcoholic beverages. Many states have also established a retirement age (a maximum age) for state judges. These are areas of life where the courts, applying the ordinary scrutiny test, have determined age-based discrimination to be legal. Differential treatment based on age is a reasonable way to achieve some legitimate public interests. Can you determine what the public interests are in each of these age-based differential treatment situations?

For most of our nation's history, the law not only allowed unequal treatment for different racial, ethnic, and religious groups as well as for men and women but also *required* this unequal treatment for a majority of the population. Women were not granted the right to vote until 1920, and they faced a wide variety of discriminatory practices. Ethnic and religious groups also faced widespread discrimination, some as a matter of law. For example, more than 120,000 people of Japanese ancestry were forcibly interned in camps during World War II. Mainstream America has most recently become aware of the invidious discrimination that has been exercised against individuals based on their sexual orientation and identity and against women through sexual harassment and violence.

#MeToo: Sexual Violence Promotes Inequality

Unlawful discrimination can be conducted by private individuals, such as in sexual harassment and assault, or by the government or public agencies through unequal policies and laws. While initially, most gender-equity activism focused on equal treatment under the law, by the late-20th century, the focus was on how the law could prevent or punish private behavior that harmed women based on their gender.

Originated by activist Tarana Burke in 2006, #MeToo was intended to remind survivors of sexual violence in communities of color that they were not alone. This movement gained momentum and visibility in the fall of 2017 after a year of women accusing prominent men (including Hollywood producers, directors, and actors; journalists; politicians; photographers; and chefs) of using sexual violence, the threat of violence, or sexual exposure (nakedness or masturbation) to intimidate or coerce women who were politically or economically weaker. Many women claimed that if they did not comply with this coercion, the "gatekeepers" to their professions could harm their careers and opportunities. While many of the allegations made were not criminal, the movement demonstrates the scope of the problem in society and the limited options women have to challenge powerful people who coerce others and abuse their power.[4]

If we expand our definition of gender discrimination and civil rights to include the private exercise of sexual power over women, we must be "clear about what behavior is criminal, what behavior is legal but intolerable in the workplace, and what private intimate behavior is worthy of condemnation."[5] It is not only in the United States where women are protesting this form of private discrimination as harmful to civil rights. This hashtag and the questions it raises have spread globally, and policy analysts are beginning to measure the costs of such gender discrimination on our economy and in our society.[6]

Slavery and Its Aftermath

The most egregious example of civil rights violations in U.S. history is slavery. This practice was protected under the law, and enslaved people were considered to be the property of their owners. When it was first written, the Constitution implicitly endorsed the unequal and discriminatory treatment of African Americans.[7] Some of the most important provisions of the new constitution treated people of African descent as property, allowing states to continue to permit them to be enslaved and to be sold in open markets. Although the movement to abolish slavery was in its early stages in 1787, the year the Constitution was completed, by the early to mid-1800s, it had gained significant momentum in the North, largely because of the activism of various religious and humanitarian groups.[8]

Slavery in the United States

Many African Americans today are the descendants of Africans who were forcibly brought to the New World. In 1619, twenty Africans arrived in Jamestown as *indentured servants,* workers with a fixed term of service. But by the mid-1600s, slavery began to replace indentured servitude.

OPPOSITION TO SLAVERY   Some chafed at the hypocrisy of those who sought freedom and equality but kept slaves. Among the first to challenge slavery were former slaves, who staged both peaceful protests and armed insurrections throughout the late 1700s and early 1800s. These activists successfully rallied support in the North for the gradual abolition of slavery by 1804. They argued forcefully against the injustice of the slave system, moving the opponents of slavery to action by their horrifying firsthand accounts of the treatment of slaves. By 1860, many northern states had abolished slavery.

Despite those arguments, the U.S. Congress, wary of the divisiveness caused by the slavery issue, sought to balance the antislavery position of the abolitionist states with the proslavery sentiments of the slaveholding states. One such attempt was the Missouri Compromise, passed by Congress in 1820. The compromise regulated slavery in the newly acquired western territories: slavery was prohibited north of the 36° 30′ north parallel, except within the state of Missouri.

The abolitionists objected to the efforts of Congress to accommodate the slaveholding states and called for the emancipation of all slaves. Black and white dissenters to slavery were actively engaged in **civil disobedience,** which is nonviolent refusal to comply with laws or government policies that are morally objectionable. Specifically, American Anti-Slavery Society members actively supported the Underground Railroad, a series of safe houses that allowed escaping slaves to flee to the northern states and Canada. But in 1850, the U.S. Congress—in an attempt to stall or prevent the secession, or separation, of southern states from the Union—passed the Fugitive Slave Act. The law required federal marshals to return runaway slaves or risk a $1,000 fine (over $20,000 in today's dollars); private citizens who harbored or abetted runaway slaves could be imprisoned for six months and fined $1,000. Passage of this law meant that "conductors" on the Underground Railroad operated in clear violation of the statute, risking their own livelihoods and property.

civil disobedience
Active, but nonviolent, refusal to comply with laws or government policies that are morally objectionable, while accepting the consequences of violating these laws.

THE CIVIL WAR ERA   Abolitionists were bolstered in their efforts when Harriet Beecher Stowe's popular book *Uncle Tom's Cabin* was published in 1852. Vividly depicting the harsh reality of slavery in the United States, this work inspired many to actively challenge slavery. By the late 1850s, the widespread distribution of *Uncle Tom's Cabin,* as well as the trial and execution of John Brown, a white abolitionist who tried to ignite a slave insurrection in Harpers Ferry, in what was then Virginia and is now West Virginia, had convinced some northerners that slavery was immoral.

Yet the U.S. Supreme Court ruled otherwise. In 1857, Dred Scott, an African American enslaved by a surgeon in the U.S. Army, sued for his freedom, arguing that because he had lived in both a free state (Illinois) and a free territory (the Wisconsin Territory, now Minnesota), he had become a free man and as such he could not be re-enslaved when he moved to Missouri. The Supreme Court rejected Scott's claim and in *Dred Scott v. Sandford* ruled that the Missouri Compromise of 1820 was unconstitutional because the U.S. Congress lacked the authority to ban slavery in the territories.[9] It also ruled that Scott was not a U.S. citizen, asserting that because of their race, African Americans were not citizens with **standing to sue,** or the legal right to bring lawsuits in court. Although the *Dred Scott* decision appeared to be a victory for slaveholding states, it was also pivotal in mobilizing the abolitionist movement and swaying public opinion in favor of a war to prevent secession.

Certain that their way of life was under siege and alarmed by the election of Abraham Lincoln as president in 1860, southern states decided that they should secede from the union. By May 1861, eleven southern states had declared their independence and created the Confederate States of America. A long and bloody civil war followed as the North fought to bring the southern states back into the union.

An important turning point of the Civil War was the Emancipation Proclamation, issued by Abraham Lincoln in April 1862. This order abolished slavery in the states that had seceded from the Union. The Union army and navy were charged with implementing the order. The proclamation had several purposes: It decreed that the abolition of slavery was a goal of the war, and by doing so it effectively prevented Britain and France from intervening in the war on the southern side, because those countries had both renounced the institution of slavery. When the South finally surrendered in April 1865, it did so knowing that its economic way of life, which depended on slave-based plantation farming, was over. At the end of the war, nearly 4 million slaves in the United States were freed. The states then ratified three constitutional amendments to codify the victories won on the battlefield:

- Thirteenth Amendment (1865), which ended slavery throughout the United States and prohibited it in the future.
- Fourteenth Amendment (1868), which defines *citizens* as "all persons born or naturalized in the United States" and mandates the same privileges and immunities for all citizens and due process and equal protection for all people, overturning the *Dred Scott* decision.
- Fifteenth Amendment (1870), which decrees that every man has the right to vote, regardless of color.

Reconstruction and the First Civil Rights Acts

After the North won the war and Lincoln was assassinated in April 1865, members of Congress and others in government disagreed about the best way to proceed in the South. Many Republicans thought that the South should be stabilized and quickly brought back into the political fold. Like Lincoln, these moderates

standing to sue
The legal right to bring lawsuits in court.

endorsed a plan that would enable the southern states to be quickly represented in Congress. Others, however, took a more radical view and argued that all those who had ever supported the Confederacy should be kept out of national and state politics. As the 1860s drew to a close, many of these more radical Republicans had come to power and had strictly limited the people in southern states who could participate in politics. As a result of their activities, during the **Reconstruction era** between 1866 and 1877—when the institutions and the infrastructure of the South were rebuilt—freed slaves, who could easily say they had never supported the Confederacy, made up a sizeable portion of both the electorate and the candidate pool in the southern states. Federal troops provided protection that facilitated their participation. During this decade, African American voters made the most of their position in the South and elected a substantial number of other African Americans to legislative offices in the local, state, and federal governments. In some places, such as South Carolina, African American legislators outnumbered whites, giving them a majority during the Reconstruction years.

Between 1865 and 1875, Congress passed a series of laws designed to solidify the rights and protections outlined in the Thirteenth, Fourteenth, and Fifteenth Amendments. Congress needed to spell out the rights of African Americans because of the pervasiveness of **Black Codes,** laws passed immediately after the Civil War by the confederate states that limited the rights of "freemen," or former slaves. These codes prevented freemen from voting, owning property, or bringing suit. To remedy that situation, Congress passed laws that sought to negate the Black Codes. One law, the Civil Rights Act of 1866, extended the definition of *citizen* to anyone born in the United States (including freemen) and granted all citizens the right to sue, own property, bear witness in a court of law, and enter into legal contracts. The Enforcement Act of 1870 bolstered the Fifteenth Amendment by establishing penalties for interfering with the right to vote. The Civil Rights Act of 1872, also known as the Anti–Ku Klux Klan Act, made it a federal crime to deprive individuals of their rights, privileges, or immunities protected by the Constitution. Although the Reconstruction-era Congress sought to remedy the new forms of inequality that emerged after the Civil War, its efforts would be short-lived.

Backlash: Jim Crow Laws

In 1877, the inauguration of President Rutherford Hayes (1877–1881) brought the Reconstruction era to a decisive end, almost immediately rolling back the gains African Americans had achieved in education and political participation. Under Hayes, the federal troops that had protected African Americans from physical reprisals were withdrawn. State and local governments throughout the South mandated racial segregation by enacting what came to be known as **Jim Crow laws.** These laws required the strict separation of racial groups, with whites and "nonwhites" going to separate schools, being employed in different jobs, and using segregated public accommodations, such as transportation and restaurants. **De jure segregation,** legally mandated separation of the races, became the norm in much of the South. The North, on the other hand, manifested **de facto segregation** in employment and housing, resulting in educational segregation.

The idea behind the Jim Crow laws was that whites and nonwhites should occupy separate societies and have little to do with each other. Many whites feared that racial mixing would result in interracial dating and marriage, which would inevitably lead to the decline of their superior position in society; thus in many southern states, miscegenation laws, which banned interracial marriage, cohabitation, or sex, were passed and severe penalties imposed for those who violated them.

Reconstruction era
The time after the Civil War between 1866 and 1877 when the institutions and infrastructure of the South were rebuilt.

Black Codes
Laws passed immediately after the Civil War by the confederate states that limited the rights of "freemen" (people formerly enslaved).

Jim Crow laws
Laws requiring the strict separation of racial groups, with whites and "nonwhites" required to attend separate schools, work in different jobs, and use segregated public accommodations, such as transportation and restaurants.

de jure segregation
Segregation mandated by law.

de facto segregation
Segregation maintained by practice.

white primary

A primary election in which a party's nominees for general election were chosen but in which only white people were allowed to vote.

literacy test

A test to determine eligibility to vote; designed so that few African Americans would pass.

poll tax

A fee for voting; levied to prevent poor African Americans in the South from voting.

grandfather clause

A clause exempting individuals from voting conditions such as poll taxes or literacy tests if they or their ancestors had voted before 1870, thus sparing most white voters.

State and local governments in the South also found creative ways to prevent African Americans from exercising their right to vote. They relied on several tactics:

- The **white primary** was a primary election in which only white people were allowed to vote. Because Democrats dominated politics so heavily in the post–Civil War South, the only races that really mattered were the primary races that determined the Democratic nominees. But southern states restricted voting in these primaries to whites only.
- The **literacy test** determined eligibility to vote. Literacy tests were designed so that few voters would stand a chance of passing the exam administered to African American voters, whereas the test for white voters was easy to pass. Typically, white voters were exempt from literacy tests because of a grandfather clause.
- A **poll tax,** a fee levied for voting, often presented an insurmountable obstacle to poor African Americans. White voters were often exempt from poll taxes because of a grandfather clause.
- The **grandfather clause** exempted individuals from conditions on voting (such as poll taxes or literacy tests) if they or their ancestors had been eligible to vote before 1870. Because African Americans did not have the right to vote in southern states before the Civil War, the grandfather clause was a mechanism to protect the voting rights of whites.

These laws were enforced not only by government agents, particularly police, but by nongovernmental groups as well. Among the most powerful was the Ku Klux Klan (KKK). During the late 1800s and into the 1900s, the Klan was dreaded and hated throughout the southern states, and it used violence to threaten and intimidate those African Americans and whites who dared to question its core principle: that whites are in every way superior to African Americans. The Klan's brand of intimidation, the burning cross and the lynching noose, was reviled throughout the southern and border states, but few could dispute the power of the Klan there (see Figure 5.1).

Governmental Acceptance of Discrimination

The federal government too had seemingly abandoned African Americans and the quest for equality under the law. In the *Civil Rights Cases* of 1883, the Supreme Court ruled that Congress lacked the authority to prevent discrimination by private individuals and organizations. Rather, Congress's jurisdiction, the Court claimed, was limited to banning discrimination in official acts of state or local governments. The Court also declared that the Civil Rights Act of 1875, which had sought to mandate "full and equal enjoyment" of a wide variety of facilities and accommodations, was unconstitutional.

In 1896, the Court struck what seemed to be the final blow against racial equality. In 1890, Louisiana passed a law that required separate accommodations for blacks and whites on railroad trains. Several citizens of New Orleans sought to test the constitutionality of the law and enlisted Homer Plessy, who was one-eighth African American (but still considered "black" by Louisiana state law) to serve as plaintiff. The choice of Plessy, who could pass for white, was intended to show the arbitrary nature of the statute. On June 7, 1892, Plessy boarded a railroad car designated for whites only. Plessy was asked to leave the whites-only car, and he refused. He was then arrested and jailed, charged with violating the state law. In 1896, the U.S. Supreme Court heard *Plessy v. Ferguson,* in which Plessy's attorneys argued that the Louisiana state law violated the **equal protection clause**

Plessy v. Ferguson

1896 Supreme Court ruling creating the separate but equal doctrine.

equal protection clause

The Fourteenth Amendment clause stating that no state shall "deny to any person within its jurisdiction the equal protection of the laws."

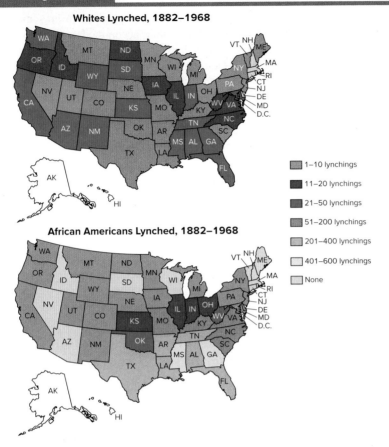

Whites Lynched, 1882–1968

African Americans Lynched, 1882–1968

1–10 lynchings
11–20 lynchings
21–50 lynchings
51–200 lynchings
201–400 lynchings
401–600 lynchings
None

FIGURE 5.1 ■ The Racial Nature of Lynching in the United States The source of these data defines lynching as the ritual murder of one or more people by a group of at least three people, outside of the legal process. Many people associate lynching only with the U.S. South or Far West. However, consider the regional distribution of racialized violence in the United States. What surprises you about these maps? What trends do you observe in terms of the changing demographics? These data come from a single data source; What liabilities might result from relying on them? What might explain the differences between the states that have greater versus those with lesser violence? In considering your answers, you may want to compare these data with some recent recalculations that include other forms of racial violence.

SOURCE: Tuskegee Data, The Racial Nature of Lynching in the United States.

of the Fourteenth Amendment, which states that no state shall "deny to any person within its jurisdiction the equal protection of the laws."

In a 7–1 decision, the Court rejected Plessy's arguments, claiming that segregation based on race was not a violation of the equal protection clause. Rather, the Court made this argument:

> We consider the underlying fallacy of the plaintiff's argument to consist in the assumption that the enforced separation of the two races stamps the colored race with a badge of inferiority. If this be so, it is not by reason of anything found in the act, but solely because the colored race chooses to put that construction upon it.[10]

In its decision, the Court created the **separate but equal doctrine,** declaring that separate but equal facilities do not violate the Fourteenth Amendment's equal protection clause. Under this doctrine, the Court upheld state laws mandating separation of the races in schools and all public accommodations such as businesses, public transportation, restaurants, hotels, swimming pools, and recreational facilities. The only condition the Court placed on these segregated facilities was that the state had to provide public facilities for both whites and nonwhites. The Court paid little attention to whether the school systems or public accommodations were comparable in quality. As long as the state had some kind of facilities in place for both whites and nonwhites, the segregation was permitted. This doctrine would become the legal backbone of segregationist policies for more than five decades to come.

The Modern Civil Rights Movement

In the early decades of the 20th century, African Americans continued their struggle for equal protection of the laws. Though the movement enjoyed some early successes, the century was nearly half over before momentous victories by civil rights activists finally began to change the status of African Americans in revolutionary ways. These victories were the result of strong leadership at the helm of the movement, the effective strategies used by activists, and new national media.

Fighting Back: Early Civil Rights Organizations

In the early years of the 20th century, the political climate was open to reform, with activists in the Progressive and Black Women's Club movements calling for an end to government corruption, reforms to labor laws, and an expansion of rights, including the right of women to vote and the civil rights of African Americans (see Chapter 8 for more on the Progressive movement). In 1909, W. E. B. Du Bois (an influential African American writer and scholar, who is today acknowledged as the father of social science) joined many other prominent African American and white male and female activists to form the National Association for the Advancement of Colored People (NAACP). One of the targets of the NAACP for the next several decades was the separate but equal doctrine, which remained in place.

Citing the lack of graduate and professional schools for African Americans, the NAACP argued that the states had violated the equal protection clause by failing to make such schools available to African Americans. During the 1930s, lawsuits brought by the NAACP in several states ended discriminatory admissions practices in professional schools.[11] Momentum in the movement for equality continued to grow, fueled in part by the growing political activism of African American soldiers returning home after fighting against fascism abroad during World War II. Many of these soldiers began to question why they were denied freedom and equality in their own country, and they mobilized for civil rights in their communities. Although the U.S. Supreme Court had not yet overturned the separate but equal doctrine, by 1950 it had ruled that segregating classrooms, dining rooms, or library facilities in higher education was unconstitutional.

Taking cues from those court decisions, by the 1950s the NAACP and other groups had changed their tactics. Instead of arguing that states had to provide equivalent education for African Americans and whites, these groups began to argue that segregation itself was a violation of the equal protection clause. But it was not until 1954 that the U.S. Supreme Court struck down the separate but equal doctrine, finding it inherently unequal and unconstitutional under the Fourteenth Amendment.

The End of Separate but Equal

In the fall of 1951, Oliver Brown, a welder at the Santa Fe Railroad yard in Topeka, Kansas, sought to have his daughter Linda enrolled in the third grade in an all-white public school seven blocks from their home. The act was not accidental; it was the calculated first step in an NAACP legal strategy that would result in sweeping changes to the nation's public school system, effectively shattering the segregated school system dominant in the South.[12] The Browns lived in an integrated neighborhood in Topeka, and Topeka schools were segregated, as allowed (but not required) under Kansas state law. The Topeka NAACP persuaded them to join a lawsuit against the Topeka Board of Education. Brown agreed and was directed to attempt to register Linda at the all-white public school. Linda was denied admission.

Thurgood Marshall, who later became the first African American to sit on the U.S. Supreme Court, argued the case, and in a unanimous decision in 1954 the Supreme Court ruled in ***Brown v. Board of Education of Topeka*** that segregated schools violate the equal protection clause of the Fourteenth Amendment.[13] In one stroke, the Court concluded that "separate but equal" schools were inherently unequal, because they stamped African American children with a "badge of racial inferiority" that stayed with them throughout their lives.

Brown v. Board of Education of Topeka

This 1954 Supreme Court decision ruled that segregated schools violated the equal protection clause of the Fourteenth Amendment.

The Movement Gains National Visibility

Civil rights activists were buoyed by the *Brown* decision, but white supremacists were mobilized.[14] In 1955, a 14-year-old African American Chicago teen who was visiting his uncle in Mississippi was kidnapped, tortured, and killed because a white female shopkeeper claimed he made offensive comments to her.[15] His mother ensured the nation saw his mutilated corpse by allowing a photograph to run in *Jet* magazine. His white killers, who later confessed in another national magazine, *Life,* were quickly acquitted.

Although African Americans had boycotted segregated public transportation throughout the South since the late 19th century, it would not be until 1955 that this protest would help to spark a national movement. In Montgomery, Alabama, and throughout the South, buses were segregated, with white riders boarding in the front and sitting front to back and African American riders sitting in the rear of the bus.[16] In December, Rosa Parks was on a bus returning home from work. The bus driver asked the 43-year-old African American woman to give

> The 1955 Chicago funeral of Emmett Till, a teenager who was tortured and killed in Mississippi, attracted national attention. His mother insisted on an open casket funeral because she "wanted the whole world to see" what racism had done to her son. Why might the national media attention on this murder have mobilized a generation of young people to push for radical social change in the 1960s?

©Bettmann/Getty

up her seat for a white man; Parks refused and was arrested for violating a local segregation law.

The Montgomery chapter of the NAACP, which Parks helped lead, had sought a test case to challenge the constitutionality of the state's Jim Crow laws. Parks agreed to participate in the case, and her arrest came at a pivotal time in the civil rights movement. Momentum favored the civil rights activists in the South, and their cause was bolstered when civil rights and religious leaders in Montgomery chose a 27-year-old minister, named Martin Luther King, Jr., to lead a bus boycott to protest Parks's arrest and segregated public facilities.[17]

Local Organizing and Civil Disobedience Strategies

The year-long bus boycott garnered national media attention, and King became a national symbol for the civil rights movement. King's leadership skills were put to the test during the battle: He was arrested. His home was bombed. Death threats were made against him. But for 381 days, the buses of Montgomery remained virtually empty, representing a serious loss in revenue to the city and causing the NAACP to be banned in the state of Alabama. Finally, in December 1956, the U.S. Supreme Court ruled that segregated buses were unconstitutional.[18] The bus boycott was a success on many fronts: its justness was confirmed by the Supreme Court, the protests garnered national media attention and evoked public sympathy, and the civil rights movement had gained a powerful leader who was capable of unifying and motivating masses. King advocated protesting government-sanctioned discrimination through civil disobedience, peaceful boycotts, and marches. African American students, as well as white students and national civil rights activists, adopted these tactics to challenge the policies of segregation.

Other groups, including the Student Non-violent Coordinating Committee (SNCC) and the Congress of Racial Equality (CORE), advocated the use of more direct action nonviolent strategies—voter registration drives and sit-ins—in the most violent of the southern states, Mississippi and Georgia. In 1961, SNCC and CORE joined the NAACP and Martin Luther King's Southern Christian Leadership Conference (SCLC) under the umbrella organization of COFO (Coalition of Federated Organizations) to focus on common goals. SNCC, CORE, and the NAACP emphasized building leadership skills of local African American citizens in southern communities based on the groundwork laid by WWII veterans. Emphasizing voter registration and education, one of COFO's most nationally visible endeavors was the 1964 Summer Project in which northern college students came down to work with local communities in Freedom Schools and voter registration drives. One outcome of this work was the establishment of the racially integrated Mississippi Freedom Democratic Party at the 1964 Democratic Convention, which forced presidential candidate Lyndon Johnson and the Democratic Party to refuse to seat future all-white delegations (see "Analyzing the Sources").[19]

Besides political protest, activists from all these groups engaged in mass marches to draw public attention to their challenge to Jim Crow segregation and racial inequality. The violence in such places as Birmingham and Montgomery (Alabama), Jackson (Mississippi), and Albany (Georgia) televised on the evening news kept white America aware of the aims of the protesters. One famous series of marches occurred in early March 1965 from Selma to Montgomery, Alabama. On Sunday, March 7, about 600 civil rights activists began a march out of Selma, protesting the policies of intimidation and violence that prevented African Americans from registering to vote. The demonstrators walked only six blocks to the Edmund Pettus bridge, where law enforcement officials were waiting.[20] When the

Analyzing the Sources

A FAMOUS IMAGE FROM THE CIVIL RIGHTS ERA

In this photograph, Fannie Lou Hamer, a former sharecropper from Mississippi who became an activist with the Student Non-violent Coordinating Committee, testifies before the Democratic National Convention (DNC) held in Atlantic City in 1964. Local Mississippians and civil rights activists joined together in the interracial Mississippi Freedom Democratic Party (MFDP) to challenge the all-white Democratic Party in Mississippi. Mrs. Hamer told the nation of her attempts to register to vote and how, as a result, she and other women were severely beaten in a Winona, Mississippi, jail, and she was thrown off the plantation where she and her husband worked. She asked that the MFDP be seated and that the all-white Mississippi delegation be sent home. President Lyndon Johnson, who was running for reelection, offered to seat two of the MFDP delegates and determined that beginning in 1968 all national convention state delegations had to reflect the demographics of their state, including race, gender, and age. In 1972, the Republican Party made the same ruling.

©AP Images

Practice Analytical Thinking

1. What makes this picture unusual in terms of how we see official governmental actions? Would most Americans have heard stories like Mrs. Hamer's from the people who experienced them? What does this tell us about the power of the media to change democratic society?

2. In 1964, there were only three television networks, so when a national event like the DNC aired, all stations would cover it. Mrs. Hamer spoke during prime evening hours when the viewing audience was the largest. President Johnson attempted to interrupt it with a national address of his own. Why do you think this testimony had such an important impact?

protesters peacefully attempted to cross the bridge, law enforcement officers brutally attacked them, using tear gas, bull whips, and nightsticks. Dubbed Bloody Sunday, the march and the beatings were televised nationally and were instrumental in swaying public opinion in favor of civil rights. The marches sparked a renewed focus on the lack of voting rights for African Americans and ultimately helped to pressure Congress to pass the Voting Rights Act in 1965.[21]

Although the violence used against protesters generated positive opinions of the civil rights movement, another form of violence, urban rebellions, eroded feelings of white goodwill. For five days in 1965, rioting in the Watts neighborhood of Los Angeles resulted in 34 deaths, more than 1,000 injuries, and over

>African American sanitation workers in Memphis, Tennessee, went on strike in 1968 to protest against dangerous working conditions and for better pay. They organized under the slogan "I Am a Man." Martin Luther King, Jr., was in Memphis supporting the strike as part of his Poor People's Campaign when he was assassinated. How does the claim of "I Am a Man" resonate with the promises of our founding documents?
©Bettmann/Getty

4,000 arrests. Although the immediate cause of the violence was an altercation between white police officers and an African American man who had been arrested for drunk driving, the frustration and anger that spilled over had long been brewing in this poor, predominantly African American neighborhood.

On April 4, 1968, Martin Luther King was in Memphis, Tennessee, in support of African American sanitation workers who were striking for equal treatment and pay with white workers. Standing on a balcony at the Lorraine Motel, King was killed by an assassin's bullet. Heartbreak, hopelessness, and despair followed King's assassination—a feeling manifested in part by further rioting in over 100 cities. Many Americans, both black and white, objected to the looting depicted in nightly news broadcasts. But some noted that because of the accumulated injustices against African Americans, the government and the rule of law had lost legitimacy in the eyes of those who were rioting.[22]

The Government's Response to the Civil Rights Movement

The civil rights movement is credited not only with ending segregation in public schools but also with the desegregation of public accommodations such as buses, restaurants, and hotels and with promoting universal suffrage. As a result of the movement, Congress passed the 1965 Voting Rights Act, which aggressively sought to counter nearly 100 years of disenfranchisement, as well as the 1964 Civil Rights Act, which bars racial discrimination in accommodations and private employment, and the 1968 Civil Rights Act, which prohibits racial discrimination in housing.

The Civil Rights Act of 1964

Simultaneously expanding the rights of many Americans and providing them with important protections from discrimination based on race, sex, religion, or ethnicity, the Civil Rights Act of 1964 includes provisions that mandate equality on numerous fronts. The law requires equality in public accommodations, including hotels, restaurants, and theaters, as well as in employment and access to public facilities. It bars government agencies from discriminating and allows the federal government to sue to desegregate public schools. The last part of the act, Title VII, which establishes the equality standard in employment opportunity, provides the legal foundation for a body of law that regulates fair employment practices.

Specifically, Title VII bans discrimination in employment based on inherent characteristics—race, national origin, religion, and sex. Title VII also established the Equal Employment Opportunity Commission (EEOC), a government body that still administers Title VII today.

The Voting Rights Act of 1965

Many civil rights leaders believed that legislation beyond the Civil Rights Act was necessary to protect the voting rights of African Americans in the South because they had been so systematically intimidated and prevented from participating.[23] In some southern counties, less than a third of all eligible African Americans were registered to vote, whereas nearly two-thirds of eligible white voters were registered in the same counties.

During the summer of 1964, thousands of civil rights activists, including many college students, worked to register black voters in southern states where black voter registration was dismal. Within months, a quarter of a million new voters had registered. However, because of violent attacks on civil rights activists and citizens, including the murders of activists in Mississippi in the summer of 1964, Congress determined that it needed to enact a federal law to eliminate discriminatory local and state government registration and voting practices.

The Voting Rights Act of 1965 (VRA) banned voter registration practices such as literacy tests. Moreover, if a county wanted to implement any law that would impact voting procedures—for example, by redrawing districts—and less than 50 percent of that county's eligible voters were registered, the VRA required the county to get approval from the Justice Department. In 2013, the Supreme Court in *Shelby County v. Alabama* found this portion of the law to be unconstitutional. Disagreement on the Court, and in the nation as a whole, centered around whether racial minorities continue to confront barriers to exercising the ballot in states with a history of racial animus.[24]

Impact of the Civil Rights Movement

The culmination of many acts of resistance by individuals and groups, the civil rights movement has had a momentous impact on society by working for the laws and rulings that bar discrimination in employment, public accommodations, education, and housing. The movement has also had a profound impact on voting rights by establishing the principle that the laws governing voter registration and participation should ensure that individuals are permitted to vote regardless of their race. As a result of the Voting Rights Act, in Mississippi, for example, the percentage of African Americans registered to vote jumped from 7 percent in 1965 to 72 percent in 2006, and then to 90 percent in 2012. Today, in some states, including Georgia, Mississippi, and South Carolina, a greater percentage of African Americans are registered than whites. In addition, all states, especially those in the South, have seen an increase in the number of African Americans elected to serve in offices at the state, county, and municipal levels and in school districts. Indeed, more African Americans serve in local elected office in Mississippi than in any other state, and all southern states are among those with the highest numbers of African American local elected officials. However, Mississippi has not elected an African American official to a statewide office since Reconstruction, and 18 states have passed laws limiting voters' access to the ballot, believed by many to harm the election turnout of communities of color.

In addition to having a profound effect on race relations and civil rights law, the civil rights movement soon came to be regarded by other groups as a model of political engagement. Women, ethnic minorities, and persons with disabilities have adopted many tactics of the movement in their own quest to secure their civil rights.

Black Lives Matter

The killing of Michael Brown, an unarmed black 18-year-old, by Darren Wilson, a white police officer in Ferguson, Missouri, initiated the Black Lives Matter movement in Fall 2014. Following reports that Brown was holding his hands over his head when he was shot, "Hands Up, Don't Shoot" became a cry of advocates who gathered in Ferguson to protest the killing of black people, particularly by representatives of the state such as law enforcement.

While subsequent investigations by the Department of Justice (DOJ) found Wilson's shooting of Brown justified, it also found continuous violations of the rights of Black citizens in Ferguson by the local police. The report from the DOJ demonstrated various ways the local government had systematically oppressed its Black citizenry—through excessive and compounding fines, racist attitudes, bias in law enforcement, and the use of targeted excessive force. As the DOJ report noted:

> Our investigation indicates that this disproportionate burden on African Americans cannot be explained by any difference in the rate at which people of different races violate the law. Rather, our investigation has revealed that these disparities occur, at least in part, because of unlawful bias against and stereotypes about African Americans.[25]

>While groups like Black Lives Matter still engage in 1960s-style collective protest, individual protesters have become more visible because of social media. A number of grassroots organizations, advocating for the Muslim community, have challenged popular stereotypes by sharing digital shorts titled "This Is What a Muslim Looks Like." How might generational differences in culture, communication tools such as social media, and the issues faced change the strategies used to advocate for equality?

Protesters: ©AP Images; Woman: ©BijoyVerghese/E+/Getty Images

This report reinforced what many African Americans had assumed about American law enforcement and documented for white America what many communities of color experience. A long and continuous history of state-sanctioned violence against black citizens related earlier in this chapter (see Figure 5.1) reinforces the belief of African Americans that lives of black citizens are of lesser value in white America.

The use of social media to provide a more Afrocentric interpretation of political events and popular culture led to support from other communities of color who share similar fears of law enforcement and concerns that their lives also matter less. Because the movement had no central organizing structure—unlike many civil rights groups of the past—activists challenging perceived injustices from throughout the country simply identified with #BlackLivesMatter.

Future of the Movement

How sustainable are such individualized movements as Black Lives Matter? The attempt to make broad social changes as opposed to changing a specific law or policy means these movements have a less clearly articulated agenda, and the lack of an institutionalized structure means these movements are pulled into competing policy positions. The movement has also sparked counter-protests like "All Lives Matter" and "Blue Lives Matter" (in reference to the police), which seem to perceive the movement as merely a challenge to the authority of law enforcement. However, the movement—when placed in the context of American history—is focusing on the fact that Black Lives *Matter,* just as other lives have been protected in the United States.

As Chapter 4 discusses, the Black Lives Matter movement has resulted in the rethinking of strategies and training for police in their interaction with communities of color and in new policies relative to body cameras and protocol during potential violent scenarios. Further, debates over the militarization of police have led to questions about the purpose and function of local police.

The Movement for Women's Civil Rights

As already noted, the pronouncement in the Declaration of Independence that "all men are created equal" initially applied only to white men, and usually only to those who owned property. Not only did the concept of equal protection of the laws not apply to nonwhite male citizens, until the Civil War amendments to the Constitution and subsequent pieces of national legislation such as the Voting Rights and Civil Rights Acts, it also did not apply to female citizens—white or nonwhite. Like African American men, women had to wait until the Constitution was amended and civil rights legislation was adopted, in response to the women's rights movement, for equal protection of the laws.

Advocates for women's civil rights began their efforts in the mid-1800s, initially focusing on gaining the right to vote for women citizens. That endeavor, the first of three waves of the women's rights movement, won suffrage for women in 1920.

The First Wave of the Women's Rights Movement

The segregation of the women delegates at the 1840 World Anti-Slavery Conference in London was a defining moment for the first wave of the U.S. women's rights movement. Forced to sit in the balcony behind a drawn curtain, Lucretia Mott and Elizabeth Cady Stanton recognized that without improving their own legal and political status, women were not going to be successful in fighting for the legal rights of other groups of people.

In 1848, Mott and Stanton organized a meeting at Seneca Falls, New York, to talk about the lack of legal rights of U.S. citizens who happened to be born female. At the end of the convention, the participants signed the Declaration of Sentiments. This Declaration, modeled after the Declaration of Independence, listed many rights and opportunities that the law did not guarantee women, including the right to vote, educational and employment opportunities equal to those of white men, and married women's rights to own property as well as legal standing to sue. At the end of the convention, the participants signed the Declaration of Sentiments.

Clearly, John Adams and the other architects of the Constitution had ignored Abigail Adams's request to her husband and his colleagues to "remember the ladies" when they created the new system of government. Adams warned her husband that not only would women not feel bound to obey laws in which they had no say but also the ladies would "foment a rebellion" if they were not provided a voice in government.

The signatories of the Declaration of Sentiments began Adams's forecasted rebellion. The document they signed insisted "that [women] have immediate admission to all rights and privileges which belong to them as citizens of these United States." For those women and men who joined this new movement for women's civil rights, the right to vote became the focal point. They recognized that this right was the foundational right that would enable women to win the other rights and privileges of citizenship.

Because the Constitution initially reserved for the states the authority to determine who had the right to vote, as well as to be employed and obtain the best possible education, many of the initial battles for women's rights took place at the state level of government. Eventually, as the national government's responsibilities expanded through court interpretations of the Constitution, especially the Fourteenth Amendment, the federal government's role in guaranteeing civil rights expanded.

STATE-LEVEL RIGHTS   Even after ratification of the Fourteenth Amendment (1868) guaranteeing equal protection of the laws for all people, women's educational and work opportunities were limited by social norms as well as state laws. Education for girls prepared them to be good wives and mothers, not to be economically independent. By the late 1800s, a few colleges began to admit women, and several women's colleges were established. Yet most colleges did not offer women the same educational opportunities as men, and women who graduated and aspired to a career were limited in two ways. First, by choosing a career, these educated women gave up the possibility of marriage. They were not legally banned from marriage, but societal norms prevented them from having both a career and a husband. Second, their career choices were limited: teaching, the developing professions of nursing and social work, or missionary work.

In 1873, Myra Bradwell challenged women's limited career choices when she sued the state of Illinois over its refusal to let her practice law.[26] In this case, the Supreme Court found that women's God-given destiny was to "fulfill the noble and benign offices of wife and mother" and that allowing women to practice law would impinge on that destiny. The *Bradwell* case established the precedent for the Court to justify allowing women to be treated differently than men are (sex-based discrimination) if the different treatment was deemed a *rational* means by which the government could fulfill a *legitimate* public interest. In the *Bradwell* case, the Court applied the *ordinary scrutiny* test, deeming it legitimate for the government to protect the role of women as wives and mothers, and, to accomplish that protection, it was rational to deny them equal employment opportunities.

In 1875, Virginia Minor of Missouri (actually her husband, because she, like all married women, did not have standing to sue) challenged the constitutionality of the Missouri law that guaranteed the right to vote only to male U.S. citizens. In this case, *Minor v. Happersett,* the Supreme Court acknowledged that women were citizens, yet it also decreed that state governments established voting rights, not the U.S. Constitution.[27] Therefore, the justices argued that the Fourteenth Amendment's privileges and immunities clause did not give women rights not established in the Constitution, hence it did not extend to women the right to vote.

> A line of women march for women's suffrage in Chicago in 1916; these are members of the Alpha Suffrage Club, an organization of African American women. How does this image challenge the way we typically conceive of the activists seeking the right to vote for women?

©Afro Newspaper/Gado/Getty Images

Interpreting Images

THE NINETEENTH AMENDMENT TO THE CONSTITUTION The American Women's Suffrage Association (AWSA), directed by Lucy Stone, had been leading the battle to extend the right to vote to women in the states since 1869. Simultaneously, the National Women's Suffrage Association (NWSA), directed by Susan B. Anthony and Elizabeth Cady Stanton, had been fighting to extend to women all rights of citizenship, including but not limited to the right to vote. In 1890, frustrated by their lack of success in the battle to extend suffrage to women, the AWSA and the NWSA joined forces, creating the National American Women's Suffrage Association (NAWSA). The NAWSA focused its efforts on amending the U.S. Constitution.

In 1916, Alice Paul founded the National Women's Party, which adopted more radical tactics than the NAWSA had been willing to use in its fight for suffrage. Noting the lack of support on the part of national officials for suffrage, Paul's organization called on voters in the 1916 election not to vote for candidates who opposed women's suffrage, including President Woodrow Wilson (1913–1921), who was running for reelection. In 1917, after President Wilson was reelected, Paul and other suffragists chained themselves to the White House fence and called on Wilson to support the suffrage amendment. Arrested, jailed, and force-fed when they engaged in a hunger strike, the women gained media attention, which in turn brought national attention to their struggle for suffrage and the president's opposition. After several months and persistent media pressure, President Wilson called on the House and the Senate to approve the women's suffrage amendment.

Congress approved this amendment in June 1919, and by the following year 36 states had ratified it. The Nineteenth Amendment prohibited the national and state governments from abridging or denying citizens the right to vote on account of sex. The right to vote was extended to another group of citizens in 1971 when the states ratified the Twenty-sixth Amendment. This amendment guarantees citizens 18 years of age and older the right to vote.

The Second Wave of the Women's Rights Movement

After the Nineteenth Amendment was added to the Constitution, the push for women's rights ceased to be a mass movement. Women were still organized in groups and lobbied the government for women's civil rights, but the many women's organizations were no longer working collectively toward a single goal, such as the right to vote. Another mass women's movement did not arise until the 1960s. Several factors account for the mobilization of the second wave of the women's movement in the 1960s, which focused this time on the plethora of rights related to the social, economic, and political status of women, many of the same rights originally demanded in the Declaration of Sentiments.

By the 1960s, large numbers of women were working outside the home in the paid labor force. Working women talked with one another about their work and family lives and came to recognize common concerns and problems, including discrimination in educational opportunities, employment opportunities, and pay; lack of child care; domestic violence; the problem of rape, for which *they* were often blamed; and their inability to obtain credit (borrow money) without having a male cosign on the loan. Women recognized that as a class of citizens they did not have equal protection of the laws.

In 1961, at the prodding of Esther Peterson, the director of the Women's Bureau in the Department of Labor, President John F. Kennedy (1961–1963) established a Commission on the Status of Women, chaired by Eleanor Roosevelt. In 1963, the commission reported that women in the United States were discriminated against in many areas of life, including education and employment. In its report, the commission argued that women needed to pursue lawsuits that would allow the Supreme Court to interpret properly the Fourteenth Amendment's equal protection clause, hence prohibiting discrimination against women.

By the mid-1960s, the women's rights movement was rejuvenated with a second wave of mass activity. The goal of this second wave was equal legal rights for women. The means to achieve that goal included public demonstrations, legislation, litigation, and an as yet unsuccessful attempt to enact the Equal Rights Amendment (ERA), which had been written by Alice Paul and first introduced in Congress in 1923.

FEDERAL LEGISLATION AND WOMEN'S RIGHTS In 1955, Edith Green (D-Oreg.) introduced into Congress the first piece of national legislation written specifically to protect women, the Equal Pay Act. Enacted into law in 1963, the Equal Pay Act prohibited employers from paying women less than men were paid for the same job, which was the standard employment practice at the time. There are still concerns that a gender wage gap continues (see Figure 5.2).

The 1964 Civil Rights Act as initially drafted prohibited discrimination in education, employment, and public accommodations based on race, ethnicity, and religion. Yet because of congressional women's efforts, Title VII of the proposed act was rewritten to prohibit discrimination in all personnel decisions based on *sex* as well as the other inherent characteristics. Initially, the EEOC, the federal agency responsible for monitoring Title VII implementation, did not take sex-based discrimination complaints seriously.

To take advantage of Title VII's promise of equal employment opportunities, women needed to pursue educational opportunities on an equal basis with men. Yet Title VI of the 1964 Civil Rights Act does not prohibit sex-based discrimination in institutions that receive federal funds, including educational institutions. By 1972, women's rights advocates won an amendment to the 1964 Civil Rights Act, Title IX, which prohibits sex-based discrimination in educational institutions receiving federal funds.

The Equal Pay Act, Title VII, and Title IX are landmark pieces of national legislation that provide equal protection of the law for women. At the same time that Congress was enacting laws prohibiting sex-based discrimination, the courts were reinterpreting the equal protection clause of the Fourteenth Amendment.

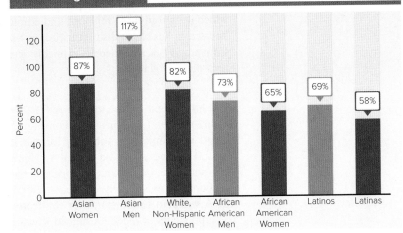

FIGURE 5.2 ■ **The Wage Gap, by Gender and Race** White, non-Hispanic men (not shown on the chart) are at 100 percent, and the bars show the percentage of that amount other demographic groups make. How do these data demonstrate the intersectionality discussed by Third Wave Feminists? What hypotheses can you generate to explain the differences in earnings—across education levels and types of jobs—based on race and gender? Why might civil rights legislation not have remedied this issue? Are these disparities something the government should be concerned about? Why or why not?

SOURCE: Pew Research Center, Eileen Patten, "Racial, Gender Wage Gaps Persist in U.S. Despite Some Progress," July 1, 2016.

WOMEN'S RIGHTS AND THE EQUAL PROTECTION CLAUSE In 1971, in the case of *Reed v. Reed,* the Supreme Court for the first time in history used the equal protection clause of the Fourteenth Amendment to find a law that discriminated against women unconstitutional.[28] In the *Reed* case, the Supreme Court found that an Idaho state law giving automatic preference to men to administer the estate of a deceased person who had not named an administrator was not a rational means to fulfill a legitimate government interest. Hence, using the ordinary scrutiny test established in the 1873 *Bradwell* case, the court ruled this discriminatory treatment of women was unconstitutional.

Then, in 1976, the Supreme Court developed a new test for the legality of sex-based discrimination. Oklahoma law allowed women 18 years of age to buy beer with 3.2% alcohol content. Yet men in Oklahoma had to be 21 years of age to purchase 3.2% beer. Men challenged the law, asking the Court to decide if this sex-based discrimination was constitutional. In this case, *Craig v. Boren,* the Court established the heightened scrutiny test for sex-based discrimination cases: Different treatment is legal if it is substantially related to an important government interest.[29] The Court used this test in the *Craig* case to find the Oklahoma law unconstitutional. The Court also used the heightened scrutiny test in the 1996 *United States v. Virginia* case.[30] In this case, the Court found the male-only admissions policy of the Virginia Military Institute unconstitutional. Justice Ruth Bader Ginsburg noted in her opinion that the state of Virginia had not shown that this discriminatory admissions policy was substantially related to the important government objective of training soldiers.

Today, courts typically use the heightened scrutiny test when deciding sex-based discrimination cases. Proponents of an ERA argue that the strict scrutiny test, which is used in race-, religion-, and ethnic-based discrimination cases, should also be used in sex-based discrimination cases, but that this will not happen until the Constitution is amended to explicitly guarantee equality of rights under the law regardless of gender.

THE PROPOSED EQUAL RIGHTS AMENDMENT During the 1970s, as the Supreme Court was reinterpreting the implications of the Fourteenth Amendment for sex-based discrimination, lobbying for the Equal Rights Amendment increased. In 1972, Congress approved the ERA, which states that "equality of rights under the law shall not be denied or abridged by the United States or by any State on account of sex." Finally, 49 years after it was first introduced in Congress, the ERA was sent to the states for ratification.

Opponents of the ERA argued it was a duplication of the Fourteenth Amendment and therefore was not needed. Opponents also claimed that passage of the amendment would make women subject to the military draft; would lead to the integration of all single-sex institutions, including schools and public bathrooms; and would result in the legalization of and public funding for all abortions. Moreover, they argued that the ERA was not needed because Congress was passing laws that guaranteed women equal protection in employment and education. Whether or not the claims of its opponents were accurate, they were successful in defeating the ERA, which had not been ratified by enough states by the deadline of 1982.

The Third Wave of the Women's Rights Movement

Although the first two waves of the women's movement advocated for formal equality or identical legal treatment with men, by the 1990s, feminists realized that a good deal still needed to be done to realize these goals in practice. Despite legal and constitutional change, women still battle inequities, including unequal pay, sexual harassment, and the glass ceiling (aspiring to higher-level jobs but being unable to win them). Moreover, although the situation for women has greatly improved, not all women have benefited equally from gains in women's rights. Third-wave feminism recognizes that women have unequal access to legal rights owing to differences in race, class, sexual orientation, gender identity, ethnicity, and religion. For example, although *Roe v. Wade* secured a woman's right to an abortion, many women cannot afford one. (Abortions can cost anywhere from a few hundred dollars to many thousands of dollars.) Third-wave organizations, such as the Chicago Abortion Fund, seek to overcome economic barriers to reproductive rights by helping women fund abortions. Another key issue has been the ending of sexual violence, particularly that against women; the #MeToo movement has been an attempt to call attention to the ways sexual violence and harassment limit women's opportunities. Women of color face the intertwined challenges of race and gender, which civil rights laws do not recognize, particularly in the area of employment discrimination. For instance, under the Civil Rights Act of 1964, women of color must challenge employment discrimination as being based on either their gender **or** their race; there is no legal recognition of the ways in which perceptions of their race **and** gender could create difficulties in the workplace. If the white women in the workplace are not similarly mistreated, then it is not gender discrimination, and if the men of color are not similarly mistreated, then it is not considered racial discrimination. Third-wave feminists refer to this as *intersectionality*, the experience of multiple forms of oppression simultaneously. Low-income and working-class women of all ethnicities seek solutions to such problems as affordable child and health care. Lesbian, bisexual, and transgender women are examining the intersection between gender discrimination and oppression based on their sexual identity.

Third-wave feminism has focused on expanding the political and economic gains made for women in the 1970s and 1980s to all women.[31] Third-wave feminism is a broader movement seeking redress on multiple and more individualized fronts—not merely legal and political, but cultural and economic as well.

Expanding Civil Rights

Today, discriminatory treatment is still a reality for many groups of citizens. The civil rights acts notwithstanding, discrimination in employment, education, housing, and due process still occurs. Moreover, battles for civil rights continue. Unfortunately, we cannot discuss all the civil rights movements that have occurred or are ongoing in the United States. Therefore, we will explore the civil rights battles of just a few groups of citizens: Native Americans, Hispanic Americans, Asian Americans, and citizens with disabilities. The hard-fought victories and aspirations of these groups offer an overview of both the history and the breadth of contemporary civil rights movements.

Lesbian, Gay, Bisexual, and Transgender Citizens

Lesbian, gay, bisexual, and **transgender** people, and those questioning their sexual identity or who identify as "queer"—a group often referred to with the abbreviation LGBTQ or GBLTQ—are redefining gender norms as well as actively seeking equal civil rights. Moreover, they are using many of the same strategies other groups have used to obtain legal and social equality. Some of the specific rights LGBTQ persons have organized to fight for focus on employment, housing, and marriage.

transgender
Individuals whose gender identity does not match the sex they were assigned at birth.

RIGHTS FOR TRANS PEOPLE   The number of people who identify as transgender in the U.S. is estimated at .5 percent, or approximately 1.4 million individuals.[32] While transgender citizens and others with fluid gender identities (those who do not identify as either "male" or "female") have been advocating for legal protections for many decades, recently these concerns became more nationally visible, and the public discourse began to more visibly include trans people.

Hate crimes continue to be a problem for members of the LGBTQ community as well as for communities of color, and they have been particularly underreported in the Trans community. The national government enacted its first hate crime law in 1969. Since then, it has expanded the inherent characteristics for which the law guarantees protection. Today, under federal law, a **hate crime** is one in which the offender is motivated in part or entirely by her or his bias against the victim because of the victim's actual or perceived race, color, religion, nationality, ethnicity, gender, sexual orientation, gender identity, or disability. Forty-six states and the District of Columbia also have hate crime laws, but the inherent characteristics covered by those laws vary.

hate crime
A crime committed against a person, property, or society, in which the offender is motivated, in part or in whole, by his or her bias against the victim because of the victim's race, religion, disability, sexual orientation, or ethnicity.

>Delegate Danica Roem, second from left, takes her oath of office at the opening ceremonies of the 2018 session of the Virginia House of Delegates at the Capitol in Richmond, Virginia. She is the first openly transgender elected official to serve in a state legislature in the United States. How important in a representative system of government is it that elected officials reflect the intersectionality of their constituencies?

©Steve Helber/AP Images

intersectionality

The experience of multiple forms of oppression (based on race, gender, class, sexual orientation, or sexual identity) simultaneously.

Violence against transgender people has been a continuous concern. For the first time, in 2014, the FBI released data on violence based on sexual identity of the victim, finding that hate crimes had decreased overall, but had increased based on sexual identity. The National Coalition of Anti-Violence Programs found that 246 trans people were harmed in 2016, with 19 killed.[33] While this type of data is difficult to consistently report, violence and potential violence are clearly concerns for trans people. As with many groups, **intersectionality** complicates this issue. Those who are from communities of color, who are poor, or who identify as female often face greater violence and risk than those who are white or wealthy, or who identify as male.

GROWTH OF THE MOVEMENT Several LGBT civil rights organizations were founded after the Stonewall Rebellion. In June 1969, groups of gay men and lesbians clashed violently with police in New York City, protesting the routine harassment by law enforcement of members of the lesbian and gay community. This influential conflict, which started at the Stonewall bar, marked the first time that members of this community acted collectively and in large numbers to assert their rights. Shortly after this event, in 1970, Lambda Legal, a national organization fighting for full recognition of the civil rights of LGBT citizens, was founded. Within a few years, gays and lesbians began to hold gay pride marches, and many new groups, such as the Human Rights Campaign and the National Gay and Lesbian Task Force, began advocating for LGBT rights.

As a result of organized educational and lobbying efforts by the gay community, during the 1980s a number of state and local governments adopted laws prohibiting discrimination in employment, housing, public accommodations, and employee benefits—that is, guaranteeing equal protection of some laws—for LGBT persons. Yet during the same decade, numerous states had laws on the books prohibiting sex between mutually consenting adults of the same sex, typically in the form of antisodomy laws. In the 1986 case of *Bowers v. Hardwick,* the U.S. Supreme Court upheld Georgia's antisodomy law.[34] In 2003, another lawsuit challenging the constitutionality of a state antisodomy law came before the Supreme Court in the case of *Lawrence v. Texas.*[35] This time, the Court overturned the 1986 *Bowers* decision, finding that the Fourteenth Amendment provides due process and equal protection for sexual privacy, and therefore the Texas law was unconstitutional.

There is still no federal law prohibiting LGBTQ-based discrimination in the private-sector workplace. However, the Equal Employment Opportunity Commission (EEOC) has interpreted the prohibition against sex discrimination in Title VII of the Civil Rights Act of 1964 as including sexual orientation and gender identity within its coverage. These rulings are quite limited, however. Twenty states,

Puerto Rico, and Washington, D.C., prohibit sexual orientation and gender identity discrimination by private and public employers.[36]

Several states passed legislation affirming the religious liberty of business owners to refuse service to lesbians, gay men, and transgender people. These types of religious liberties have been interpreted to preclude individuals, religious organizations, or small businesses from providing services they perceive as contrary to their beliefs. Some examples come from religiously affiliated schools that have fired women who were unmarried and pregnant, pharmacists who refused to fill birth control prescriptions, bakeries and photographers who refused services to same-sex weddings, and graduate students who abstained from counseling gay clients. How do we protect personal religious liberties while simultaneously advancing civil rights?

SAME-SEX MARRIAGE The issue of marriage has been a focal point for LGBTQ rights activists in recent years. With marriage comes a host of advantages, including inheritance rights, rights to governmental benefits, and hospital-visitation rights. Like other struggles for civil rights, the movement for marriage equality has relied on court action, bills in state legislatures, public referenda, and other strategies.

The 2013 Supreme Court case of *United States v. Windsor* paved the way for many states to change their laws when it determined that the federal Defense of Marriage Act (DOMA) defining marriage as inherently heterosexual was unconstitutional under the equal protection clause of the Fifth Amendment.[37]

In 2015, the U.S. Supreme Court decided the landmark case of *Obergefell v. Hodges,* which ruled that the due process clause of the Fourteenth Amendment protects the right to marry as a fundamental liberty—for same-sex couples identically to opposite-sex couples.[38] Denial of this right to marry, according to Justice Kennedy's majority opinion, violates the equal protection clause. The Court made it clear that while the free exercise clause of the First Amendment (Chapter 4) allows religious organizations to refrain from endorsing same-sex unions, it does not allow states to discriminate against their citizens. Although the LGBTQ community is winning many of its civil rights battles, the challenge continues. For example, in the area of family law, issues involving adoption rights and child custody as well as divorce and property rights are now battlegrounds.

Native Americans' Rights

At first, the fledgling nation recognized the native residents of the land that became the United States as members of sovereign and independent nations with inherent rights. The federal government entered into more than 370 treaties with Native American tribes between 1778 and 1870.[39] Most of those treaties promised land to tribes that agreed to move, and almost all those promises were empty, with the government reneging on most of the agreements. In addition, in 1830, Congress passed the Indian Removal Act, which called for the forced relocation of all native peoples to lands west of the Mississippi. In the end, most Native Americans were dispossessed of their lands and wound up living on reservations. The federal government treated Indians as subhumans, relegating them to second-class status, as they had African Americans.

Until Congress passed the Indian Citizenship Act in 1924, Native Americans had virtually no rights to U.S. citizenship, and even the laws that allowed immigrants to become citizens did not apply to Native Americans. The Indian Rights

Association, founded in 1882 and active in lobbying Congress and the state legislatures until the 1930s, was one of the most important of the early groups that actively campaigned for full suffrage for native peoples, in the belief that enfranchisement would help to "civilize" them. The early 1900s also saw the founding of the Society of American Indians and the American Indian Defense Association, both of which fought for citizenship for Native Americans and then for their civil rights. However, for more than 40 years after passage of the Indian Citizenship Act, the basic rights enumerated in the Bill of Rights were not granted to Native Americans. In the 1960s, Indian activists became more radical, occupying government buildings, picketing, and conducting protests. In 1968, the American Indian Movement (AIM) was founded. In the same year, Congress passed the Indian Civil Rights Act, which ensured that Native Americans would have the full protection of the Bill of Rights both on and off their reservations. Although this law had significant symbolic impact, it lacked an enforcement mechanism, and so native peoples continued to be deprived of basic due process protections and equal education and employment opportunities. The National Indian Education Association (NIEA), founded in 1969, continues to confront the lack of quality educational opportunities for Native Americans and the loss of native culture and values.

During the 1970s, Native American organizations began a new effort to force the federal government to honor treaties granting Indians fishing and hunting rights as well as rights to the natural resources buried in their lands. Indians in New York, Maine, and elsewhere sued for land taken from them decades or even a century ago in violation of treaties. Starting with the 1975 Indian Self-Determination and Education Assistance Act, the national government has enacted laws that support greater autonomy for Indian tribes and give them more control of their assets.

The 1988 Indian Gaming Regulatory Act is the best known of the federal laws enacted to support Indian self-determination. This law authorizes Indian tribes to establish gaming operations on their property and requires them to negotiate compacts with the states in which their lands are located. The compacts typically include a profit-sharing understanding that requires the Indian tribe to give a proportion of its profits to the state government and possibly to contiguous local governments. The act mandates that the money made through gaming operations be used for education, economic development, infrastructure (for example, roads and utilities), law enforcement, and courts. By 2016, the National Indian Gaming Commission, the independent agency that regulates Indian gaming, reported that more than 244 of the federally recognized 562 Indian tribes operate more than 450 gaming establishments in 28 states.

Interpreting Images

> Native Americans protest at a burial-ground sacred site that was disturbed by bulldozers building the Dakota Access Pipeline (DAPL). The site was near an encampment where thousands of people had gathered to join the Standing Rock Sioux Tribe's protest of the oil pipeline slated to cross their reservation. Protesters were attacked by dogs, sprayed with irritants, and arrested. While pipeline construction was stopped under the Obama Administration, the Trump Administration reauthorized its construction, and despite global protest the pipeline was completed in April 2017. Why do you think the Standing Rock protests were ultimately ineffective in achieving policy goals despite global attention?

©Robyn Beck/AFP/Getty Images

The gross revenues for these gaming activities totaled $31.2 billion in 2016.[40] Clearly, one goal of the Gaming Act was to generate resources that would increase the educational and employment opportunities on Indian reservations.

Even with gaming profits, however, the prospects for many Native Americans today remain bleak. According to race and ethnic relations scholars Joe R. Feagin and Clairece Booher Feagin, "Native Americans have endured the longest Depression-like economic situation of any U.S. racial or ethnic group."[41] They are among the poorest, least educated U.S. citizens. Native women face some of the highest levels of violence, in part because until 2015 non-Native people were immune from prosecution in tribal courts. Under the Violence Against Women Act reauthorization, tribal sovereignty has now been expanded to cover prosecution of these offenders. Like many other groups of U.S. citizens, Native Americans continue to fight in the halls of government, in the courtrooms, and in the public arena for their constitutionally guaranteed rights and privileges.

Citizens of Latin American Descent

U.S. citizens of Latin American descent (Latinos) include those whose families hail from Central America, South America, or the Caribbean. Latinos are the largest minority group in the United States, making over 17 percent of the total U.S. population. Sixty-five percent of this Latino population is composed of natural-born U.S. citizens, and the majority of growth in the population is from U.S.-born children, not new immigrants.[42]

In the 2016 presidential election, 47.6 percent of eligible Latino voters voted, constituting almost 8 percent of the voters. In contrast, the voter turnout for blacks was 59.6 percent, for Asians was 49.3 percent, and for whites was 65.3 percent.[43] So far, the elections that have occurred in the 21st century have been followed by numerous lawsuits claiming that individual citizens, organized groups, and local governments have prevented eligible Latino voters from voting. Limited English proficiency can create barriers to voting and equal educational and employment opportunities for many U.S. citizens, including Latino citizens. We focus here on U.S. citizens of Mexican origin—the largest Latino population in the United States today.

EARLY STRUGGLES OF MEXICAN AMERICANS In 1846, because of land disputes sparked by white immigrants from the United States encroaching on Mexican territory, the United States declared war on Mexico. By the terms of the 1848 Treaty of Guadalupe Hidalgo, which ended the war, Mexico ceded territory to the United States for $15 million. According to the treaty, Mexicans who stayed on their land would become U.S. citizens, and their civil rights would be protected. Although nearly 77,000 Mexicans chose to do so, their civil rights were *not* protected.[44] Thus began a long and continuing history of discrimination against U.S. citizens of Mexican descent.

At the turn of the 20th century, Mexican Americans organized to protest the various forms of discrimination they were experiencing, which included segregated schools, inequities in employment opportunities and wages, discrimination by law enforcement officers, and barriers to their voting rights such as poll taxes and English-only literacy tests. In 1929, several Mexican American organizations combined to create the League of United Latin American Citizens (LULAC).[45]

In 1945, LULAC successfully challenged the segregated school systems in California, which provided separate schools for Mexican children that were of poorer quality than the schools for white children. In this case, *Mendez v. Westminister,* the federal court set an important precedent by using the Fourteenth Amendment

>Cesar Chavez began his civil rights work as a community organizer in 1952 by encouraging Mexican Americans to vote and use their civil rights. Together with Dolores Huerta, he founded the United Farm Workers. From the early 1960s until his death in 1993, Chavez was the leading voice for and organizer of migrant farmworkers in the United States. Huerta was a prominent Chicana labor leader, developing other leaders and advocating for the rights of immigrant workers, women, and children.
©Arthur Schatz/Getty Images

to guarantee equal educational opportunities.[46] In 1954, the U.S. Supreme Court followed this lower court's precedent when it ended legal race-based segregation in public schools throughout the nation in the *Brown v. Board of Education of Topeka* case. The Supreme Court unanimously agreed in 1954 that Mexican Americans and all nationalities were guaranteed equal protection under the Fourteenth Amendment.[47] Mexican Americans were not explicitly protected under *Brown v. Board of Education* as a minority group until 1971.[48]

THE CHICANO MOVEMENT   In addition to the women's rights movement and the civil rights movement for African American rights, the 1960s witnessed the birth of the Chicano Movement, the mass movement for Mexican American civil rights. The Chicano Movement was composed of numerous Latino organizations focusing on a variety of issues, including rights to equal employment and educational opportunities. One of the most widely recognized leaders in the Chicano Movement was Cesar Chavez.

Cesar Chavez began his civil rights work as a community organizer in 1952, encouraging Mexican Americans to vote and educating them about their civil rights. In the early 1960s, Chavez, along with Jessie Lopez and Dolores Huerta, founded the Agricultural Workers Organizing Committee (AWOC) and the National Farm Workers Association (NFWA). Under Chavez's leadership, the AWOC and the NFWA merged to form the United Farm Workers (UFW) in 1966. The UFW organized successful protests and boycotts to improve working conditions and pay for farmworkers.[49]

IMMIGRATION AND OTHER CIVIL RIGHTS ISSUES   There are approximately 11 million undocumented immigrants in the United States, which is 3.4 percent of the U.S. population. About 66 percent of these adults have lived in the U.S. for at least a decade, and approximately 50 percent of these undocumented aliens are Hispanic.[50] In 2003, as part of the new Department of Homeland Security, U.S. Immigration and Customs Enforcement (ICE) was created to enforce immigration laws by rounding up and deporting individuals and families in the country illegally. Immediately after his inauguration, President Donald J. Trump (2017–) issued an executive order that expanded the grounds of who could be considered "removable aliens" well beyond the previous 2014 focus on convicted felons and those who are safety threats.[51] Beginning in July 2016, ICE deported 226,119 individuals in the following 12 months.[52]

What Is the Impact of Illegal Immigration?

The Issue: Approximately 11 million illegal immigrants live in the United States. These individuals, their impact on the country, and their fate have generated significant political debate in the United States over such issues as legal status, deportation, benefits, criminality, and education. In tandem, governmental and nongovernmental organizations have compiled massive amounts of data on these issues, and these numbers are open to multiple interpretations. How can we best evaluate data we encounter and know which interpretations to trust? Evaluating data and using them to determine policy are particularly difficult when advocates focus on different aspects of the problem. Those who oppose expansion of rights for undocumented citizens focus on their negative impacts on society, while those who support expanding rights focus on their positive societal impacts. How do we determine which arguments are more important?

Criminality of Illegal Aliens

Lott, John R., Undocumented Immigrants, U.S. Citizens, and Convicted Criminals in Arizona (February 10, 2018). Available at SSRN: https://ssrn.com/abstract=3099992.

This author examined the crime rates of illegal versus legal residents of Arizona, using data on prisoners in the state prison system between January 1985 and June 2017. He presents the following numbers: "Undocumented immigrants are at least 142% more likely to be convicted of a crime than other Arizonans. They also tend to commit more serious crimes and serve 10.5% longer sentences, [are] more likely to be classified as dangerous, and [are] 45% more likely to be gang members than U.S. citizens." The author further concluded that these numbers underrepresented the amount of crime committed by undocumented immigrants, noting particularly that undocumented immigrants between 15 and 35 years of age make up 2 percent of the Arizona general population and 8 percent of the Arizona prison population. He also found that the crimes committed by undocumented immigrants tended to be more violent than crimes committed by citizens and documented immigrants. Based on his data, the author concludes that if "undocumented immigrants committed crime nationally as they do in Arizona, in 2016 they would have been responsible for over 1,000 more murders, 5,200 rapes, 8,900 robberies, 25,300 aggravated assaults, and 26,900 burglaries."

Economic Impact of Illegal Aliens

Michael D. Nicholson, "The Facts on Immigration Today: 2017 Edition," *American Progress*, April 20, 2017.

"Immigrants added an estimated $2 trillion to the U.S. GDP in 2016. Immigrants are overrepresented in the labor force and also boost productivity through innovation and entrepreneurship. . . . Over the long run, the net fiscal impact of immigration is positive. From 2011 to 2013, children of immigrants contributed $1,700 per person to state and local budgets, and immigrants' grandchildren contributed another $1,300. Across three generations, immigrants' net contribution, per person, was $900." The author also argues that even undocumented immigrants contribute to Social Security and Medicare. For instance, in 2010 they paid $13 billion into Social Security, while only withdrawing $1 billion in benefits. Similarly, from 2000 to 2011, undocumented immigrants "paid $35.1 billion more into Medicare than they withdrew. Unauthorized immigrants pay an estimated $11.7 billion a year in state and local taxes." As the author concludes, "Granting all unauthorized immigrants legal status would boost their tax contributions an additional $2.2 billion per year. Immigrants—even legal immigrants—pay to support many of the benefits they are statutorily barred from receiving."

What do you think?

Both authors rely on governmental data for their information and have well-documented research, and both authors are arguing for a particular policy outcome.

1. The first author is arguing against expansion of immigration or amnesty for the children of illegal immigrants. What questions does he not answer in his analysis? What else do you want to know?

2. The second group of authors is arguing for the expansion of immigration and the amnesty for children of illegal immigrants. What questions do they not answer in their analysis? What else do you want to know?

3. How do these arguments use evidence about both legal and illegal immigration to make their position stronger?

4. To come up with your own stance on immigration, what information do you want? What is most important to you—crime rates, economic impact, or some other factor?

Over the past several years, four primary approaches have been discussed nationally to address illegal immigration: implementing mass deportations; offering pathways to citizenship for families with children born in the United States; providing temporary reprieves from deportation without a pathway to citizenship; and/or providing refugee status to the increasing numbers of unaccompanied minors fleeing their home countries. Because immigration reform, including building a wall along the U.S./Mexican border, is a key part of President Trump's agenda, this issue will continue to be contentious in U.S. policy.[53]

Citizens of Asian Descent

Asian American citizens come from, or have ancestors from, a number of different countries with diverse cultures, religions, histories, and languages. Today, the largest percentage of Asian Americans have Chinese origins, followed by those of Filipino, Asian Indian, Vietnamese, Korean, and Japanese ancestry. Large numbers of immigrants from Japan came to the United States around the turn of the 20th century, but it was not until the 1940s that the flow of immigrants from other Asian countries began to increase, beginning with the Philippines. In the 1960s, the number of immigrants from Korea and India began to increase significantly, and in the 1970s—as the Vietnam War ended—immigrants from Vietnam began to arrive in large numbers. Today, nearly 6 percent of the U.S. population is of Asian descent. They are the fastest-growing ethnic population in the United States, by 2055 estimated to make up 38% of all immigrants.[54]

Like other U.S. citizens with significant nonwhite ancestry, Asian Americans have had to fight continually for their civil rights, specifically for equal protection under the law and particularly for equal access to educational and employment opportunities as well as citizenship. Asian immigrants and Asian Americans created organizations to fight for citizenship and equal protection of the law. One successful result of those efforts was the 1952 Immigration and Nationality Act, which allowed Asian immigrants to become citizens for the first time. Before passage of this law, only U.S.-born children of Asian immigrants could be citizens.

INTERNMENT OF JAPANESE AMERICANS DURING WORLD WAR II One of the most egregious violations of the civil rights of Asian American citizens occurred during World War II when Americans of Japanese ancestry were forced to move to government-established camps. Under President Franklin Roosevelt's Executive Order 9066, over 120,000 Japanese Americans, two-thirds of whom were native-born U.S. citizens, were relocated from the West Coast of the United States after Japan's attack on Pearl Harbor. During that same period, the federal government also restricted the travel of Americans of German and Italian ancestry who were living on the West Coast (the United States was also fighting against Germany and Italy), but those citizens were not relocated. Many relocated Japanese Americans lost their homes and businesses.

Activists fought for decades to obtain reparations for the citizens who were interned and for the repeal of a section of the 1950 Internal Security Act that allowed the government to imprison citizens deemed enemy collaborators during a crisis. Congress repealed the section of the 1950 law targeted by interest groups, and in 1987 President Ronald Reagan signed a bill providing $1.2 billion in reparations.

CONTEMPORARY ISSUES FOR ASIAN AMERICANS During the 1960s and 1980s, the number of organizations and coalitions pressing for the civil rights of Asian Americans grew as large numbers of new immigrants from Asian countries arrived in the United States in response to changes in U.S. immigration laws. During the 1960s, Asian Americans on college campuses organized and fostered a group consciousness about the need to protect their civil rights. During the 1980s, Asian American organizations began to pay more attention to voting rights as well as to hate crimes and employment discrimination. Then in 1996, numerous organizations, each representing Asian Americans with ancestry from one country, joined to form the National Council of Asian Pacific Americans (NCAPA), which presses for equal protection of the law for all Asians.

Asian Americans have the highest median income compared with the population as a whole, but this varies greatly within Asian origin groups (see Figure 5.3).[55] Asian Americans are also twice as likely as the population as a whole to earn a bachelor's degree or higher but are less likely to own a home.[56] Moreover, Asian Americans are better represented in professional and managerial positions than any other racial or ethnic group, including white Americans. Yet like women, Asian American citizens appear to hit a glass ceiling, for they are not represented in the very top positions in the numbers that their high levels of educational achievement would seem to predict. Therefore, those advocating for Asian American civil rights are increasingly concentrating their efforts on discrimination in employment. Professor Don T. Nakanishi, an expert on Asian Americans, points out that Asian Americans are becoming "more organized, more visible and more effective as participants and leaders in order to advance—as well as to protect—their individual and group interests, and to contribute to our nation's democratic processes and institutions."[57] Today, more than 4,000 Asian Americans serve as elected or appointed officials in all levels of government throughout the nation.[58]

Citizens with Disabilities

The civil rights movements of the 1960s and 1970s made society more aware of the lack of equal protection of the laws for diverse groups of citizens, including people with disabilities. The first law to mandate equal protection for people with physical and mental disabilities was the 1973

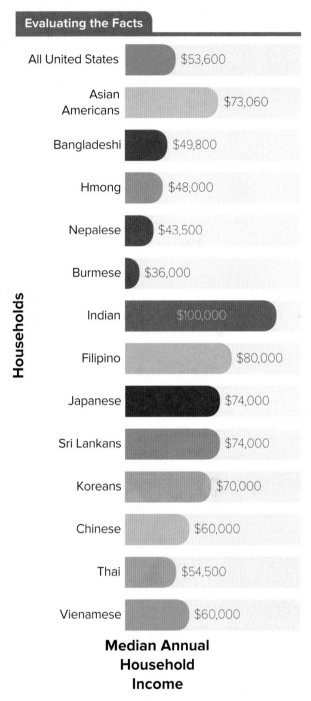

Evaluating the Facts

Households

	Median Annual Household Income
All United States	$53,600
Asian Americans	$73,060
Bangladeshi	$49,800
Hmong	$48,000
Nepalese	$43,500
Burmese	$36,000
Indian	$100,000
Filipino	$80,000
Japanese	$74,000
Sri Lankans	$74,000
Koreans	$70,000
Chinese	$60,000
Thai	$54,500
Vienamese	$60,000

FIGURE 5.3 ■ **Comparative Asian American Household Incomes** This chart shows wide variation in the household incomes of Asian American origin groups. While Asian American groups have the highest median income compared to the population as a whole, how do the numbers in this table clarify this generalization? What might explain the disparities among these origin groups?

SOURCE: Pew Research Center, Asian Americans: A Diverse and Growing Population.

Rehabilitation Act, which prohibited discrimination against people with disabilities in federally funded programs. In 1990, people with disabilities achieved a significant enhancement of this earlier victory in their fight to obtain protection of their civil rights. The Americans with Disabilities Act (ADA), enacted in that year, extends the ban on discrimination against people with disabilities in education, employment, health care, housing, and transportation to all programs and organizations, not just those receiving federal funds. The ADA defines a disability as any "physical or mental impairment that substantially limits one or more of the major life activities of the individual." The ADA does not enumerate every disability that it covers, resulting in much confusion over which conditions it covers and which it excludes.

A series of U.S. Supreme Court rulings in the late 1990s and early 2000s narrowed the interpretation of "disability," decreasing the number of people benefiting from the ADA. For example, the Court determined that if an individual can take an action to mitigate an impairment (such as taking medication to prevent seizures), then the impairment is not a disability protected by the ADA. In response, disability advocates, including the National Coalition of Disability Rights and the ADA Watch, successfully lobbied Congress to propose an act restoring the broader interpretation of the term "disability" and, hence, increasing the number of people benefiting from the ADA. The Americans with Disabilities Act Amendments of 2008 went into effect in January 2009. The act applies to the equal protection guaranteed in the Rehabilitation Act (1973) and the ADA (1990). It does not change the written definition of "disability" that is in the ADA, but broadens what "substantially limits" and "major life activities" mean, and no longer considers actions taken to mitigate impairments as relevant to determining if employers and educational institutions must accommodate a person's mental or physical disability in public facilities and housing.[59]

The ADA has enhanced the civil rights of citizens with disabilities. Before the ADA was enacted, people with disabilities who were fired from their jobs or denied access to schools, office buildings, or other public places had no recourse. Cities were under no obligation to provide even the most reasonable accommodations to people with disabilities who sought employment or the use of public transportation systems. And employers were under no obligation to make even the most minor modifications to their workplaces for employees with disabilities. For example, if a qualified job applicant was wheelchair bound, an employer did not have to consider installing ramps or raising desks to accommodate the wheelchair but could simply refuse to hire the individual. The ADA requires employers and governmental organizations to make it possible for people with disabilities to participate meaningfully in their communities through reasonable accommodations.

Interpreting Images

>Comet is a service dog who attends middle school with a 14-year-old boy who has severe Cerebral Palsy. Federal law requires that schools make the same kinds of accommodations that the ADA requires employers to make, ensuring that when reasonable adjustments to policy or process can allow a student access to education, school boards are obligated to make such changes. What do laws like the ADA tell us about how we pursue equality in the United States?

©Hyoung Chang/The Denver Post via Getty Images

Is Affirmative Action a Constitutional Solution to Discrimination?

Laws reinforcing constitutional guarantees by prohibiting discriminatory treatment are the most common objectives of civil rights battles. Nevertheless, in the 1960s the federal government also began implementing policies aimed at reinforcing equal access to employment by mandating recruitment procedures that actively sought to identify qualified minority men for government positions. This policy of **affirmative action** was extended to women in employment and then to educational opportunities. However, affirmative action policies have been and continue to be very controversial.

affirmative action
In the employment arena, intentional efforts to recruit, hire, train, and promote underutilized categories of workers (women and minority men); in higher education, intentional efforts to diversify the student body.

How Affirmative Action Works

Affirmative action does not require organizations to select unqualified candidates, nor does it require choosing a qualified minority candidate over a qualified nonminority candidate. Affirmative action does require that an organization make intentional efforts to diversify by providing equal opportunity to classes of people that have been historically, and in many cases are currently, subject to discrimination.

In the 1970s, institutions of higher education began to adopt intentional efforts to expand educational opportunities for both men and women from various minority groups. In addition, colleges and universities use affirmative action to ensure a student body that is diverse in race, color, economic status, and other characteristics. These institutions believe that having students on campus from a wide variety of backgrounds enhances all students' educational experience and best prepares them to function successfully in a nation that is increasingly diverse. Critics have argued that admitting minority students over qualified white applicants on the basis of race is unconstitutional discrimination.

Opposition to Affirmative Action

In the important *Bakke* decision in 1978, the U.S. Supreme Court found unconstitutional the University of California at Davis's affirmative action plan for admission to its medical school.[60] The UC Davis plan set aside 16 of the 100 seats in its first-year medical school class for racial minorities (specifically, African Americans, Latinos, Asian Americans, and Native Americans). Justice Powell noted in his opinion that schools can take race into consideration as one of several factors for admission but cannot use it as the sole consideration.

Opponents have challenged affirmative action in the courts as well as through legislative processes and statewide ballot measures. In two cases involving the University of Michigan in 2003, the U.S. Supreme Court upheld the *Bakke* decision that universities can use race as a factor in admissions decisions, but not as the overriding factor. Using the strict scrutiny test, the Court said in the *Grutter v. Bollinger* case that the school's goal of creating a diverse student body serves a *compelling public interest:* a diverse student body enhances "cross-racial understanding . . . breaks down racial stereotypes . . . and helps students better understand persons of different races."[61]

In 2007, however, the Supreme Court found unconstitutional two school districts' policies of assigning students to elementary schools based on race to ensure a diverse student body.[62] The majority of justices argued that those policies violated the equal protection clause of the Fourteenth Amendment. Chief Justice Roberts, writing for the majority, argued that governments should not use laws to remedy racial imbalances caused by economic inequalities, individual choices, and historical biases (de facto imbalances). He stated that such laws put in place discrimination that the Court found unconstitutional in the *Brown* case back in 1954. The justices who dissented from the majority opinion noted that today's policies are trying to ensure inclusion of minorities, not create segregation of, and hence cause harm to, minorities. The dissenters view policies that take race into account to ensure inclusion and balance as necessary means to achieving the compelling public good gained by a diverse student body.

Are affirmative action policies aimed at ensuring equal educational and employment opportunities for all women and minority men constitutional, or do they violate the equal protection clause of the Fourteenth Amendment?

Conclusion

Thinking Critically About What's Next in Civil Rights

For most of U.S. history, the law allowed, and in some cases even required, discrimination against people based on inherent characteristics such as race, ethnicity, and sex. This discriminatory treatment meant that the U.S. government did not guarantee all citizens equal protection of their civil rights. The long and continuing battles for civil rights of African Americans, Native Americans, and women are only part of the story. Latinos, Asian Americans, citizens with disabilities, and LGBT citizens are all currently engaged in political, legal, and civic activities aimed at guaranteeing equal protection of their civil rights. Numerous other groups are working to gain their civil rights as well. These include older Americans, poor Americans, and children born in the United States to parents who are in the country illegally. The Fourteenth Amendment extends citizenship, and hence civil rights, to these children.

Building on the legal gains of previous activists for gender equality, the current movement has expanded its focus to ensure that the concerns of all women, regardless of race, ethnicity, class, religion, or sexual identity, are heard. While legal and political battles are still fought, this movement has expanded to consider cultural and economic challenges to women, and it capitalizes on new techniques provided by social media. Although the goals of the women's movement remain the same, third-wave feminism's aims are more diffuse than in the past and are being pursued through myriad organizations focusing on a wide variety of cultural and policy objectives.

As individuals whose interests were not previously considered in discussions of civil rights intensify their challenges to oppression, the nation will continue to struggle with the scope and meaning of civil rights. Activists are raising access to affordable and safe housing, health care, and drinking water as civil and human rights demands.

Learning Summary

1. Summarize how the United States defines equality through the law.
   a. Compare the protections of civil rights with civil liberties.
   b. Explain the tests courts use to determine when discriminatory treatment is legal.
   c. Outline the difference between allowed and required discriminatory treatment.

2. Explain the impact of slavery and its aftermath on the United States.
   a. Summarize the means private citizens and the government used to restrict the rights of African Americans.
   b. Describe how state violence maintained the system of slavery and limited civil rights.
   c. Explain the governmental acceptance of discrimination.

3. Describe how people resisted discrimination in the modern civil rights movement.
   a. Outline decisions by the government that protected and restricted civil rights.
   b. Define the tools citizens used to challenge oppression.
   c. Recall the reasons citizens decided to challenge governmental policy.

4. Describe the federal government's response to the civil rights movement.
   a. Name the policies the federal government passed in response.
   b. Recall how the Supreme Court used the equal protection clause in challenges to these policies.

5. Explain the primary concern of the Blacks Lives Matter movement.
   a. Compare the arguments of Black Lives Matter advocates with those raised over the history of racial oppression in the United States.

6. Define the three waves of the movement for women's civil rights.
   a. Demonstrate the role of the Fourteenth Amendment in expanding rights.
   b. Describe the tools women used to challenge oppression.
   c. Compare the three waves in terms of strategies and the problems each addresses.

7. Explain how other groups have expanded civil rights.
   a. Contrast how other groups used tools from prior movements to make change.
   b. Outline the difference between private and public discrimination.
   c. Describe some of the current claims for greater civil rights protections.

8. Analyze the constitutionality of affirmative action.
   a. Summarize the arguments of those on both sides of the issue.

Key Terms

affirmative action 189

Black Codes 163

Brown v. Board of Education of Topeka 167

civil disobedience 161

civil rights 157

de facto segregation 163

de jure segregation 163

equal protection clause 164

grandfather clause 164

hate crime 179

heightened scrutiny test (intermediate scrutiny test) 159

inherent characteristics 158

intersectionality 180

Jim Crow laws 163

literacy test 164

ordinary scrutiny test (rational basis test) 160

Plessy v. Ferguson 164

poll tax 164

Reconstruction era 163

separate but equal doctrine 166

standing to sue 162

strict scrutiny test 159

suspect classifications 159

transgender 179

white primary 164

For Review

1. What is meant by *suspect classification*?

2. What tactics did whites in the South use to prevent African Americans from achieving equality before the civil rights era?

3. What strategy did the early civil rights movements employ to end discrimination?

4. What civil rights did the 1964 Civil Rights Act protect for minority, male citizens but not for female citizens?

5. Why did those fighting for women's civil rights begin their work by concentrating their efforts on state governments rather than on the national government?

6. Other than color and sex, what inherent (immutable) characteristics have been used as a basis for discriminatory treatment of citizens?

7. Explain how an approach to improving access to employment and educational opportunity based on affirmative action differs from an approach based on civil rights legislation.

For Critical Thinking and Discussion

1. How do the claims pressed by those seeking legal protections and societal acceptance for trans people differ from those in prior civil rights battles? How are they similar? Explain.

2. Today, more women than men are in college pursuing their bachelor's degrees. Is it legal for schools to give preference to male applicants by accepting men with lower SAT scores and high school grade-point averages than women, to maintain sex balance in the student body? Explain.

3. How has the use of social media and other forms of newer technology changed the way in which civil rights activists promote change? Can you find examples in the Black Lives Matter movement?

4. What would be the effect of using the strict scrutiny test to determine the legality of sex-based discrimination? Would sex-based affirmative action pass the test? Explain.

Resources for
Research AND Action

Internet Resources

Equal Employment Opportunity Commission
www.eeoc.gov/facts/qanda.html This federal government site offers a list of federal laws relevant to equal employment opportunities and includes answers to the most frequently asked questions regarding equal employment laws.

Lambda Legal
www.lambdalegal.org Lambda Legal is a national organization committed to achieving full recognition of the civil rights of lesbians, gay men, transgender people, and people with HIV through litigation, education, and public policy work.

The Southern Poverty Law Center
www.splcenter.org The Southern Poverty Law Center is a nonprofit civil rights organization dedicated to fighting hate and bigotry and is known internationally for tracking and exposing the activities of hate groups.

The United States Department of Justice, Civil Rights Division
www.justice.gov/crt/index.php This site is maintained by the law enforcement arm of the federal government, which researches, investigates, and prosecutes violations of constitutional protections of civil rights.

Recommended Readings

Coates, Ta-Nehisi. *Between the World and Me.* New York: Spiegel and Grau, 2015. A well-published essayist on race writes a series of letters to his son about being Black in America and how his thinking on race has evolved. Along the way he discusses Trayvon Martin, Ferguson, and police shootings as part of a system of oppression.

Davis, Lennard J. *Enabling Acts: The Hidden Story of How the Americans with Disabilities Act Gave the Largest Minority Its Rights.* New York: Beacon Press, 2016. This is the first book that traces the history and development of the ADA, demonstrating how it changed the model of equality in the U.S. and now around the world.

Harrison, Brigid. *Women in American Politics: An Introduction.* Belmont, CA: Wadsworth, 2003. *American Democracy Now* coauthor Brigid Harrison introduces the study of women's participation in American politics, including their historical and contemporary participation in political groups, as voters, and in government.

Klarman, Michael. *From the Closet to the Altar: Courts, Backlash, and the Struggle for Same-Sex Marriage.* New York: Oxford University Press, 2014. A revised version of a book tracing the conflicts among legislatures and courts, state and federal governments, and interest groups over the rapidly changing legal status of same-sex marriage.

Lawson, Steven F., Charles Payne, and James T. Patterson. *Debating the Civil Rights Movement, 1945–1968.* Lanham, MD: Rowman & Littlefield Publishers, 2006. Integrates primary documents with essays comparing visions of the civil rights movement as being "bottom up" with a focus on local people or "top down" with a focus on the national leaders and statutory changes.

Movies of Interest

Selma (2014)
Taking place in the years between the Civil Rights Act of 1964 and the Voting Rights Act of 1965, the movie shows the violence in the South relative to voting. Despite violent opposition, local people and Martin Luther King, Jr., join the nationally visible march from Selma to Montgomery, Alabama.

Milk (2008)
The story of California's first openly gay elected official, San Fransisco Board of Supervisor member Harvey Milk. The movie examines his involvement in local politics, his fight to expand gay rights, and the opposition he faced until his assassination in 1978.

Bury My Heart at Wounded Knee (2007)
Based on Dee Brown's book of the same name, this HBO made-for-television movie chronicles ordeals of Sioux and Lakota tribes as the U.S. government displaces them from their lands.

Iron Jawed Angels (2004)
The little-known story of the tensions between the young, militant women's suffrage advocates, led by Alice Paul, and the older, more conservative advocates, such as Carrie Chapman Catt. The details of the suffrage battle during wartime, with a popular president opposed to women's suffrage, are well presented in this made-for-television movie.

Freedom Song (2000)
Supported by civil rights movement veterans, this movie tells the story of the movement through the eyes of the Student Non-violent Coordinating Committee (SNCC). Danny Glover is a concerned Mississippi father who watches his son become increasingly involved in the civil rights movement and begin agitating for racial equality and social change.

Boys Don't Cry (1999)
A young female-to-male transsexual moves to a new town, falls for a girl, and plans a new life. When his past identity is revealed, members of the community become threatened and violent. Based on a true story.

References

1. David Schultz, John R. Vile, and Michelle D. Deardorff, *Constitutional Law in Contemporary America, Volume II: Civil Rights and Liberties* (Minneapolis: West Academic, 2017).
2. Joseph Landau, "Due Process and the Non-Citizen: A Revolution Reconsidered," *Connecticut Law Review* 47 (2015): 879–936.
3. *Loving v. Virginia,* 388 U.S. 1 (1967).
4. Emily Sugerman, "MeToo: Why Are Women Sharing Stories of Sexual Assault and How Did It Start?" *Independent,* October 17, 2017.
5. Alyssa Rosenberg, "The #MeToo Movement Is at a Dangerous Tipping Point," *Washington Post,* January 17, 2018.
6. Lynn Parramore. "$MeToo: The Economic Cost of Sexual Harassment," *Institute for New Economic Thinking,* January 2018.
7. Timothy S. Huebner, *Liberty and Union* (Lawrence: University Press of Kansas, 2016).
8. John Hope Franklin and Evelyn Higginbotham, *From Slavery to Freedom,* 9th ed. (New York: McGraw-Hill, 2010).
9. *Dred Scott v. Sandford,* 60 U.S. 393 (1857).
10. *Plessy v. Ferguson,* 163 U.S. 537 (1896).
11. Michael Klarman, *From Jim Crow to Civil Rights* (New York: Oxford University Press, 2004).
12. Richard Kluger, *Simple Justice: The History of* Brown v. Board of Education *and Black America's Struggle for Equality* (New York: Knopf, 1976).
13. *Brown v. Board of Education,* 347 U.S. 483 (1954).
14. Klarman, 2004.
15. Timothy B. Dyson, *The Blood of Emmett Till* (New York: Simon & Schuster 2017).
16. Jo Ann Robinson, *The Montgomery Bus Boycott and the Women Who Started It* (Knoxville: University of Tennessee Press, 1987).
17. Taylor Branch, *Parting the Waters: America during the King Years, 1954–1963* (New York: Simon & Schuster, 1988).
18. *Browder v. Gale,* 352 U.S. 903 (1956).
19. John Dittmer, *Local People: The Struggle for Civil Rights in Mississippi* (Champaign: University of Illinois Press, 1995).
20. Robert A. Pratt, *Selma's Bloody Sunday: Protest, Voting Rights, and the Struggle for Racial Equality* (Baltimore: Johns Hopkins University Press, 2016).
21. David J. Garrow, *Protest at Selma: Martin Luther King, Jr., and the Voting Rights Act of 1965* (New Haven, CT: Yale University Press, 2015).
22. Michael Honey, *Going Down Jericho Road: The Memphis Strike, Martin Luther King's Last Campaign* (New York: W. W. Norton, 2008).
23. Charles S. Bullock III and Ronald Keith Gaddie, *The Rise and Fall of the Voting Rights Act* (Norman: University of Oklahoma Press, 2016).
24. *Shelby County, Alabama v. Holder,* 570 U.S. 2 (2013).
25. U.S. Department of Justice, Civil Rights Division, *Investigation of the Ferguson Police Department,* March 4, 2015: 5.
26. *Bradwell v. Illinois,* 83 U.S. 130 (1873).
27. *Minor v. Happersett,* 88 U.S. 162 (1875).
28. *Reed v. Reed,* 404 U.S. 71 (1971).
29. *Craig v. Boren,* 429 U.S. 190 (1976).
30. *U.S. v. Virginia,* 518 U.S. 515 (1996).
31. Jennifer Baumgardner, *F'em: Goo Goo, Gaga, and Some Thoughts on Balls* (New York: Seal Press, 2011).
32. Andrew R. Flores, Jody L. Herman, Gary J. Gates, and Taylor N. T. Brown, *How Many Adults Identify as Trans Gender in the United States?* (Los Angeles: The Williams Institute, 2016).
33. National Coalition of Anti-Violence Programs, *Lesbian, Gay, Bisexual, Trans Gender, Queer, and HIV-Affected Hate Violence in 2016* (New York: Emily Waters, 2017).
34. *Bowers v. Hardwick,* 478 U.S. 186 (1986).
35. *Lawrence and Garner v. Texas,* 539 U.S. 558 (2003).
36. Local Non-Discrimination Ordinances," Movement Advancement Project, 2018,
37. *United States v. Windsor,* 570 U.S. 12, 2013.
38. *Obergefell v. Hodges,* 576 U.S. _____ (2015).
39. Joe R. Feagin and Clairece Booher Feagin, *Racial and Ethnic Relations* (Upper Saddle River, NJ: Prentice Hall, 2003), 135.
40. National Indian Gaming Commission, "2016 Indian Gaming Revenues Increase 4.4 Percent," July 17, 2017.
41. Feagin and Feagin, *Racial and Ethnic Relations,* 135.
42. Antonio Flores, "Facts on U.S. Latinos, 2015," Pew Research Center, September 18, 2017, www.pewhispanic.org/2017/09/18/facts-on-u-s-latinos/.
43. Jens Manuel Krogstad and Mark Hugo Lopez, "Black Voter Turnout Fell in 2016, Even as a Record Number of Americans Cast Ballots," Pew Research Center, May 12, 2017.
44. League of Latin American Citizens, "LULAC History—All for One and One for All," http://lulac.org/about/history/.
45. Ibid.
46. *Mendez v. Westminister,* 64 F. Supp. 544 (1946).
47. *Hernandez v. Texas,* 347 U.S. 475 (1954).
48. *Corpus Christi Independent School District v. Cisneros,* 330 F. Supp 1377 (S.D. Texas, 1977).
49. Feagin and Feagin, *Racial and Ethnic Relations,* 218.
50. Jens Manuel Krogstad, Jeffrey S. Passel, and D'Vera Cohn, "5 Facts About Illegal Immigration the U.S.," Pew Research Center, April 27, 2017.
51. Donald J. Trump, "Executive Order [13,768]: Enhancing Public Safety in the Interior of the United States," January 25, 2017.
52. U.S. Immigration and Customs Enforcement, *FY 2017 ICE Removal Operations Enforcement Report,* December 13, 2017.
53. Donald J. Trump, "Executive Order [13,767]: Border Security and Immigration Enforcement Improvements," January 25, 2017.
54. Gustavo López, Neil G. Ruiz, and Eileen Patten, "Key Facts About Asian Americans, a Diverse and Growing Population," Pew Research Center, September 8, 2017.
55. Ibid.
56. Ibid.

57. Marisa Osorio, "New Edition of National Asian Pacific American Political Almanac Examines Group's Growing Impact," UCLA Newsroom, June 28, 2000.

58. Don T. Nakanishi and James Lai, *National Asian Pacific American Political Almanac, Fifteenth Edition* (Los Angeles: UCLA Asian Pacific American Center Press, 2016).

59. U.S. Equal Employment Opportunity Commission, "The Americans with Disabilities Act Amendments Act of 2008.

60. *Regents of the University of California v. Bakke,* 438 U.S. 265 (1978).

61. *Grutter v. Bollinger,* 539 U.S. 306 (2003).

62. *Parents Involved in Community Schools v. Seattle School District No. 1 et al.,* and *Meredith v. Jefferson County Board of Education,* 551 U.S. 701 (2007).

CHAPTER 6

Political Socialization and Public Opinion

©Chip Somodevilla/Getty Images

THEN

Families and schools were the most important influences on children as they developed their political views.

NOW

Families and schools remain influential, but the media have increased their multiple roles in developing the political views of members of the Millennial generation and Generation Z.

NEXT

How will technology affect the socialization of new generations of Americans?

How will polling organizations find ways to harness the power of the Internet to predict political behavior accurately?

How will government officials reconcile differences in public opinion between generations of Americans?

The process of developing

informed opinions about issues begins with the process of political socialization. Through socialization, we acquire our basic political beliefs and values. Through political socialization, we come to value the attributes of our own political culture. We also develop our ideological outlook and perhaps even begin to identify with a particular political party. Although the process of political socialization begins in early childhood, throughout our lives, institutions, peers, and the media continue to influence our views.

Through the process of socialization, individuals acquire the ideology and the perspective that shape their political opinions. Though seemingly simple, public opinion is a fundamental building block on which American democracy rests. When we discuss public opinion, we often do so in the context of various public opinion polls that ask respondents everything from whether they approve of the president's job performance to how many times they've Instagrammed in the past week. Political scientist V. O. Key, Jr., wrote: "To speak with precision of public opinion is a task not unlike coming to grips with the Holy Ghost."[1] Key was referring to the nebulous nature of public opinion, a particularly apt description of 2016 polls, which failed to show Donald Trump's popularity among voters. The glut in the number of "latest polls" has perhaps made us forget that the act of voting is simply the act of expressing one's opinion. Indeed, the word *poll* means to gauge public opinion as well as the location where one traditionally casts a ballot.

Learning Objectives

After reading this chapter, students should be able to:

- Understand the process of socialization.
- Name the agents of socialization and how they socialize Americans to political life.
- Describe the effects demographic characteristics have on our opinions and attitudes.
- Compare and contrast the behaviors, opinions, and attitudes of Millennial and Generation Z Americans with each other, and with older generations.
- Explain the process of measuring public opinion.
- Analyze what Americans think about politics, including their trust in government in general and various branches of government, and what Americans identify as the "most important problem."

Political Socialization and Civic Participation

How do we acquire our political views? Although an infant would be hard pressed to evaluate the president's job performance, children begin to acquire political opinions at an early age, and this process continues throughout adulthood. As noted earlier, the process by which we develop our political values and opinions is called **political socialization.** As we develop our political values, we form the bedrock of what will become our political ideology, our integrated system of general political values. As this ideology emerges, it shapes how we view most political subjects: what side we take on public issues, how we evaluate candidates for office, and what our opinions on policies will be.

Although many people tend to think that political socialization occurs only as they approach voting age, in reality this process begins at home in very early childhood. Core tenets of our belief system—including our political ideology, our beliefs about people of different races and sexes, even our party identification—are often firmly embedded before we have completed elementary school.

A key aspect of political socialization is whether children are socialized to participate in politics. Simply put, civically engaged parents often have civically

political socialization
The process by which we develop our political values and opinions.

engaged children. Parents who engage in active forms of participation, such as volunteering on a campaign, and passive forms, such as staying informed and discussing important events, watching the news, or reading a newspaper, demonstrate to children what matters to them. Parents who change the channel to a *Modern Family* rerun during an important presidential news conference are also socializing their children to their values. Children absorb the political views of their parents as well: A parent's subtle (or sometimes not so subtle!) comments about the president, a political news story, or a policy debate contribute to a child's political socialization by shaping that child's views.

The Process of Political Socialization

The beliefs and values we learn early in life also help shape how we view new information. Although events may change our views, we often choose to perceive events in a way that is consistent with our earlier beliefs. For example, people's evaluation of which candidate "won" a debate often coincides strongly with their party identification. Thus, the process of political socialization tends to be cumulative.

Historically, most social scientists have agreed that family and school have the strongest influence on political socialization. Our families teach us that it is—or is not—valuable to be an informed citizen and coach us in the ways in which we should participate in the civic life of our communities. For example, if your mother is active in Republican Party politics in your town, you are more likely to be active in that party than someone whose parents are not involved. Is your father active in charitable organizations such as the local food bank? He might ask you to run in a 5K race to raise money to buy food for the upcoming holiday season. Schools also influence our political socialization by teaching us shared cultural values. And in recent times, the omnipresent role that the media play in everyday life warrants their inclusion as one of the prime agents of political socialization.

Participating in Civic Life

Studies indicate that children whose parents are active in politics or in their community are more likely to be active themselves. Schools also play an important role in socializing young people to become active in civic life; college students are more likely to participate than young people of the same age who are not attending school, and the longer people continue their education, the more likely they will be active in their communities.[2]

From our families and schools we also learn the value of becoming informed. Parents and schools, along with the media and the other agents of socialization that are discussed in the next section, provide us with important information that we can use to make decisions about our political actions. People who lack political knowledge, by contrast, tend not to be actively involved in their communities.[3] In fact, research indicates that when young people use any source of information regularly, including newspapers, radio, television, magazines, and the Internet, they are more likely to engage in all forms of civic participation. There is also a strong link between being informed and voting behavior. According to the results of one survey that

>Children are socialized to the views of their parents at a very early age. What opinions were you socialized to as a young child?

©John Gomez/Shutterstock

measured civic engagement among young people, "youth who are registered to vote are more informed than their non-registered peers. Eighty-six percent of young registered voters answered at least one of the knowledge questions (measuring political knowledge) correctly as opposed to 78 percent of youth who are not registered to vote."[4]

Agents of Socialization

Learning, culture, and socialization occur through **agents of socialization,** the individuals, organizations, and institutions that facilitate the acquisition of political views. Among the most important agents of socialization are family, the media, schools, churches, peers, and political and community leaders. Our political views are also shaped by who we are; our race, ethnicity, gender, and age all influence how we become socialized to political and community life.

agents of socialization
The individuals, organizations, and institutions that facilitate the acquisition of political views.

Family Influences on Attitudes, Opinions, and Actions

Family takes one of the most active roles in socializing us to politics and influencing our political views and behaviors. We learn whether our family members value civic activism by observing their actions and listening to their views. The children of political activists are taught to be engaged citizens. They may see their parents attend city council meetings, host Democratic or Republican club meetings in their home, or help local candidates for office by volunteering to campaign door to door on a weekend afternoon. Other parents may teach different forms of political engagement—some young children might attend protests or demonstrations with their parents or boycott a particular product for political reasons. When political activists discuss their own involvement, they often observe that "politics is in my blood." In reality, political activism is passed from one generation to the next *through example.*

In other homes, however, parents are not involved in politics or their communities. They may lack the time to participate in political activities, or they may fail to see the value of doing so. They may have a negative opinion of people who participate in politics, making such comments as "all politicians are corrupt," "they're just in it for themselves," or "it's all about ego." Such opinions convey to children that politics is not valued and may in fact be frowned on. A parent's political apathy need not necessarily sour a son or a daughter on politics or civic engagement permanently, however. Instead, first-generation activists often point to external influences such as school, the media, friends, and public policies, any of which can cause someone to become involved in civic life, regardless of family attitudes.

Our families influence not only whether or not we are civically active participants in the political process but also what we believe. While parents or older siblings may discuss specific issues or policies, their attitudes and outlook

> Saira Blair, a member of the West Virginia House of Delegates, is among the youngest elected officials in the United States. When she was elected in 2014, the then-17-year-old, who defeated a two-term incumbent Republican in the primary and a Democratic opponent in the general election, was not yet eligible to vote. Blair embodies the notion that "politics is in your blood"—that is, the children of many politically oriented people pass on that passion to their children. Saira's father, Craig, is also a member of the West Virginia state legislature. Craig Blair has served intermittently in the House of Delegates since 2003, and was elected to the state Senate in 2013.
©Cliff Owen/AP Images

also shape children's general political attitudes and ideology. Children absorb their parents' beliefs—whether their parents think the government should have a larger or smaller role in people's lives, whether they value equality between the sexes and the races, whether they consider people in government to be trustworthy, and even specific opinions they have about political leaders. In fact, we can see evidence of how strongly parents' views are transmitted to their children in one of the best predictors of the results of presidential elections: Each election year until the publication folded in 2012, the *Weekly Reader,* a current events magazine that many school districts subscribed to, conducted nonrandomized polls of its readers. Since 1956, the first- through twelfth-grade student poll had correctly predicted the outcome of 90 percent of all presidential elections. Children know for whom their parents will vote and mimic that behavior in their responses to the poll.

The Media's Ever-Increasing Role in Socialization

An almost ever-present fixture in the lives of young Americans today, the media contribute to the political socialization of Americans in many ways. Television, radio, social media, the Internet, and various forms of electronic entertainment and print media help shape Americans' political perspectives. First, the media help shape societal norms. In our early lives, the media impart norms and values on children's shows such as *Sesame Street, Barney,* and *Dora the Explorer,* which teach about racial diversity. These shows and others reflect changing societal standards and values. The media also reinforce core democratic values. Television programs such as *Dancing with the Stars, Survivor,* and *The Biggest Loser* incorporate the principle of voting: through telephone, online, or texted votes, viewers decide which contestant stays or goes.

Second, the media also help determine the national agenda. Whether they are covering the civil war in Syria, the latest economic news, or congressional policy debates, the media focus the attention of the American public. This attention may then have spillover effects as people demand action on a policy issue.

Third, the media educate the public about policy issues. Local and national news programs, newsmagazine shows, and even comedies such as *Full Frontal with Samantha Bee* or *Saturday Night Live*'s "Weekend Update" inform viewers about current events, the actions of policymakers, and public policy challenges in communities, states, and the nation.

Schools, Patriotism, and Civic Participation

As early as preschool, children in the United States are socialized to believe in democracy and express patriotism. Schools socialize children to the concept of democracy by making the idea tangible for them. On Election Day, children might vote for their favorite snack and wait for the results at the end of the day. Or they might compare different kinds of apples or grapes, or different books, and then vote for a favorite. Lessons such as these introduce children to processes associated with democracy at its most basic level: They learn about comparing attributes, choosing a favorite, voting, and winning and losing.

Children also are taught patriotism as they recite the Pledge of Allegiance every day, sing patriotic songs, and learn to venerate the "founding fathers," especially George Washington, and other American heroes, including Abraham Lincoln, Dr. Martin Luther King, Jr., and John F. Kennedy. Traditionally, elementary and high schools in the United States emphasized the "great men in great moments" form of history, a history that traditionally concentrated solely on the contributions of men in formal governmental or military settings. Today, however, the curriculum often includes contributions by women and racial and ethnic minorities, including African Americans and Latinos.

Education also plays a pivotal role in determining *who* will participate in the political affairs of the community. Research indicates that higher levels of education are associated with higher levels of political activism, which is passed through generations. In a book on civic voluntarism, Sidney Verba, Kay Schlozman, and Henry Brady wrote: "Well-educated parents are more likely to also be politically active and to discuss politics at home and to produce children who are active in high school. Growing up in a politicized household and being active in high school are associated with political engagement."[5]

Religious Institutions: Faith as an Agent of Socialization

The influence of religious institutions and religion in general on one's political socialization varies a great deal from individual to individual. For some people, faith communities formed at a church, temple, or mosque play a key, defining role in the development of their political beliefs. For some, the body of beliefs their religion conveys are the fundamental building blocks of all other beliefs and actions in their life, including their political views and behaviors. For others, religious institutions and faith are irrelevant.

For many years, political scientists have examined the effect that religious affiliation—whether one is Catholic or Jewish, Protestant or Muslim—has on political preferences. For example, religion is related to how people view various issues, especially the issue of abortion. But more recent analysis shows that a better predictor of the impact of religion on voting is not so much the religion an individual practices but how regularly he or she practices it. In general, it seems that those who regularly attend religious services are more likely to share conservative values—and support Republican candidates in general elections.

Research also shows that this relationship between frequency of church attendance and identification with the Republican Party is particularly strong among white Protestants but less so among Catholics, who are generally more Democratic, and among African Americans. African American voters are even more likely than Catholics to vote for a Democratic candidate but are also likely to have high levels of religiosity, as measured by frequency of attending services.

Figure 6.1 shows the breakdown in party affiliation by religiosity. The results are based on respondents' assessment of the importance of religion in their lives and their frequency of church attendance. Note in this figure that a large proportion—at 49 percent, nearly a majority—of highly religious people (41 percent of Americans, not shown in the figure)

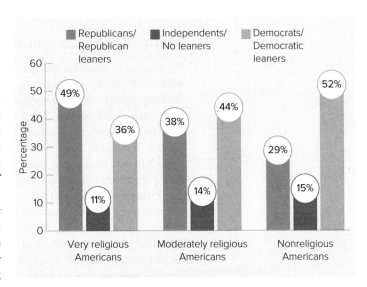

FIGURE 6.1 ■ Political Party Affiliation by Religiosity

SOURCE: Frank Newport, "Religion Remains a Strong Marker of Political Identity in U.S.," July 28, 2014, Gallup.

are Republicans or lean Republican in voting. Among the moderately religious (29 percent of Americans), Democrats held sway with 44 percent leaning Democrat and 38 percent leaning Republican. Among the nonreligious (30 percent of the U.S. population), 52 percent identify themselves as Democratic leaners, while 29 percent of the nonreligious identify as leaning Republican. Although there is a strong link between religiosity and political party, the differences between the proclivities of religious and nonreligious voters are applicable only to white voters—as discussed later in this chapter. African Americans are likely to be Democrats no matter how religious they are—only 10 percent of very religious African Americans identify themselves as Republican. And although religious Latinos and Asian Americans are more likely to be Republican, by and large, majorities of both groups identify as Democrats. Nonetheless, the relationship between religiosity and party identification is an important factor in American politics, particularly to the extent that religiosity shapes political views on social issues—abortion or gay marriage, say—and renders them moral imperatives for voters, rather than mere opinions.

Peers and Group Norms

Friends, neighbors, coworkers, and other peers influence political socialization. Through peers, we learn about community and the political climate and values of the area in which we live. For example, your neighbors might inform you that a particular member of the city council is a strong advocate for your neighborhood on the council, securing funds for recreational facilities or increased police protection in your area. Or a coworker might let you know what your member of Congress is doing to help save jobs in the industry in which you work. Keep in mind, however, that much research indicates that the primary function of peers is to reinforce our already-held beliefs and values. Typically, the people with whom you are acquainted are quite similar to you. Although diversity exists in many settings, the norms and values of the people you know tend to be remarkably similar to your own. Indeed, a 2016 Pew Research Center poll showed that fewer than 25 percent of Americans had close friends who were supporting the opposing candidate in the presidential race.

Political and Community Leaders: Opinion Influencers

Political and community leaders also help to socialize people and influence public opinion. Positions advocated by highly regarded government leaders hold particular sway, and the president plays an especially important role in shaping the views of Americans. Consider, for example, the national debate that occurred when presidential candidate Donald Trump proposed "building a wall" between the United States and Mexico to prevent people from entering the country illegally. Suddenly, what once had been considered a fringe idea was embraced by a sizeable proportion of the population. But political leaders are not the only ones who can influence public opinion. Consider, for example, the influence that student activists from Marjory Stoneman Douglas High School had on public opinion and in compelling action regarding the issue of gun safety after the mass shooting at their high school in 2018. And chances are that in your town, the views of community leaders—elected and not—influence the way the public perceives local policies. Perhaps the fire or police chief endorses a candidate for city council, or the popular football coach for the Police Athletic League makes the funding of a new football field a policy priority in your town. Often we rely on the recommendations and priorities of well-respected leaders who have earned our trust.

Demographic Characteristics: Our Politics Are a Reflection of Us

Who we are often influences our life experiences, which shape our political socialization and therefore what we think. The racial and ethnic groups to which we belong, our gender, our age and the events that have shaped our lives, and where we live all play a role in how we are socialized to political and community life, our values and priorities, and even whom we vote for. Demographic characteristics also shape our levels of civic involvement and may even help determine the ways in which we contribute to the civic life of our communities and our nation.

RACE AND ETHNICITY   In general, whites, African Americans, Latinos, and Asian Americans prefer different candidates, hold different political views, and have different levels of civic involvement. Among the most salient of these differences are candidate preferences, which are reflective of party affiliation and ideology.

When analyzing candidate support by various racial and ethnic groups in the 2016 election, we can see that there are significant differences in the levels of support given to the Democratic and Republican candidates for president among African Americans and non-Hispanic whites, though of course there is variation within these groups. As shown in Figure 6.2, a majority of whites, especially working-class white males, supported Republican Donald Trump, whereas an overwhelming proportion of African Americans (88 percent) supported Democrat Hillary Clinton. Clinton also enjoyed strong support from Hispanics (at 65 percent) and Asian Americans (at 65 percent).

But significant differences exist even within racial and ethnic groups.[6] Table 6.1 shows how the various categories of Latinos differ in terms of party identification. As the table shows, majorities of Latinos who identify themselves as Puerto Ricans, Dominicans, Salvadorans, and Mexican Americans (who constitute the largest nationality of all Hispanic Americans) identify as Democrats; Cubans, however, identify more strongly as Republicans.

Party affiliation among ethnic groups within the Asian American community also varies somewhat. In general, about 60 percent of all Asian Americans are registered Democrats. South Asians are most likely to be Democrats, and majorities

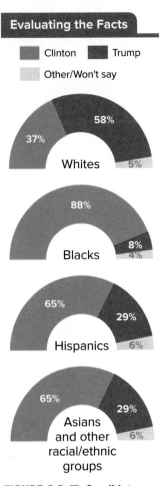

Evaluating the Facts

Clinton   Trump
Other/Won't say

Whites: 58% / 37% / 5%

Blacks: 88% / 8% / 4%

Hispanics: 65% / 29% / 6%

Asians and other racial/ethnic groups: 65% / 29% / 6%

FIGURE 6.2 ■ Candidate Support by Racial and Ethnic Group Which racial group had the highest proportion of Trump supporters? Of Clinton supporters? Which racial or ethnic group was the most unified? Which was the most divided?

SOURCE: Election 2016: Exit Polls, The New York Times.

Evaluating the Facts

TABLE 6.1 Latino Party Identification by National Origin

Which Latino nationality is most likely to identify as Democratic? Which as Republican? Which groups are the least Republican?

NATIONAL ORIGIN	PARTY IDENTIFICATION		
	REPUBLICAN	DEMOCRATIC	INDEPENDENT
Puerto Rican	22%	57%	21%
Mexican	22	55	23
Cuban	33	48	19
Dominican	7	80	13
Salvadoran	12	52	36
Other	15	41	44

SOURCE: Pew Research Center Survey of Hispanic adults, May 24-July 28, 2013, Pew Research Center.

of Chinese and Koreans are Democrats as well. A quarter to a third of all Korean, Southeast Asian, Filipino, and Chinese Americans are unaffiliated with either party.[7]

GENDER   Public opinion polls and voting behavior indicate that men and women have very different views on issues, have different priorities when it comes to public issues, and often favor different candidates, particularly in national elections. This difference in men's and women's views and voting preferences is called the **gender gap,** the measurable difference in the way women and men vote for candidates and in the way they view political issues. Eleanor Smeal, who at the time was president of the National Organization for Women, first noticed the gender gap. In the 1980 presidential election, Democrat incumbent Jimmy Carter lost to Republican challenger Ronald Reagan, but Smeal noticed that in poll after poll, women favored Carter.

Since that watershed 1980 election, the gender gap has been a factor in every subsequent presidential election, and in every presidential election, women are more likely than men to favor Democratic candidates—a fact that is representative of the differing partisan leanings of men and women, as shown in Figure 6.3. The gender gap is particularly pronounced among members of the Millennial generation: while both male and female Millennials are more likely to favor the Democratic Party than other age cohorts, Millennial women overwhelmingly lean Democrat, with 70 percent of Millennial women compared to 49 percent of Millennial men favoring the Democrats. That 21 percent gap is far larger than in other generations: among Gen-Xers, there is an 11-point difference, and among members of the Silent Generation, women are 8 points more favorable to Democrats. Among Boomers, it's 10 points.[8] In the 2016 presidential election, the gender gap was particularly apparent, with Hillary Clinton,

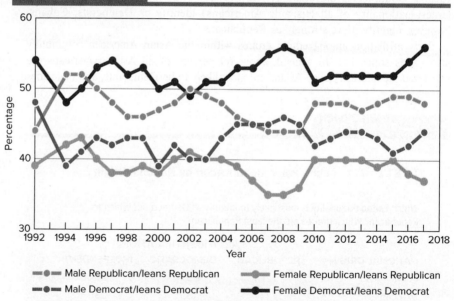

Evaluating the Facts

FIGURE 6.3 ■ **Party Identification Among Men and Women**

1. In general, what has been the trend regarding men's party identification?
2. When has the gender gap been the largest? Why do you think there were such differences between men's and women's party identification then?
3. When has the gender gap been the smallest? In those times, which party attracted the greater proportion of supporters?

SOURCE: Pew Research Center.

the Democratic nominee, garnering a sizeable majority of women's votes. But the pattern of women supporting Democrats in greater proportion than Republicans is not a new phenomenon, or one related exclusively to Clinton's status as the first woman major party nominee for president, as shown in Figure 6.4.

In addition to party affiliation, voting turnout patterns increase the effect of the gender gap. Women in most age groups—except those under age 25—are more likely to vote than their male counterparts. In addition, on average, women also live longer than men, so older women constitute an important voting bloc. The difference in women's candidate preferences and their higher likelihood of voting mean that the gender gap is a political reality that any candidate seeking election cannot ignore.

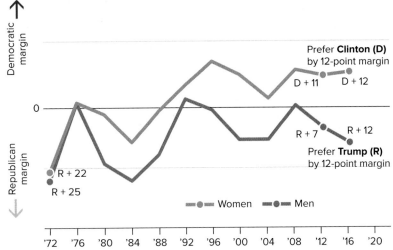

Presidential candidate preference, by gender

FIGURE 6.4 ■ The Gender Gap in Presidential Elections

SOURCE: Pew Research Center.

Women's and men's opinions also differ on public policy issues, although often in unexpected ways. One important way is that men and women differ in the extent to which they *prioritize* various issues. Figure 6.5 shows the top policy issue priorities for men and women during the 2016 presidential election. From this figure, we can see great disparities in the issues men and women identify as "very important." And so while similar percentages of men and women identified the economy, terrorism, immigration, Supreme Court appointments, foreign policy, and Social Security as very important, slightly greater proportions of women identified gun policy, health care, and education as very important issues. Also, women were much more likely than men to identify the treatment of racial and ethnic minorities and gay, lesbian, and transgender people, the environment, and abortion as very important issues. And men were much more likely than women to identify trade policy as a very important issue.

But in addition to sometimes differing priorities, men and women sometimes differ on their viewpoints on issues: women are more likely to believe that a lack of pay equity exists in the United States.[9] Men and women also differ on the issue of the death penalty, as men are about 10 percent more likely than women to favor capital punishment.[10] And men's and women's views on the optimal role of government

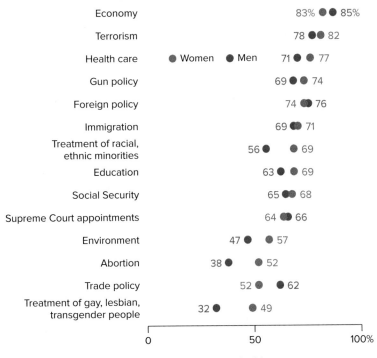

Percent of registered voters saying each is "very important" to their vote in 2016 . . .

FIGURE 6.5 ■ Men's and Women's Policy Priorities

SOURCE: Pew Research Center.

>Eleanor Smeal, president of the Feminist Majority and a former president of the National Organization for Women, coined the term "gender gap" after the 1980 presidential election. Smeal noticed that in poll after poll women favored Democratic incumbent Jimmy Carter over Republican challenger Ronald Reagan. Was there a gender gap in the 2016 presidential election?

©Lawrence Jackson/AP Images

vary greatly: 66 percent of young women believe that government should do more to solve problems (versus 60 percent of young men), whereas only 27 percent of women believe that government does too many things better left to businesses and individuals, as opposed to 35 percent of men.[11]

GEOGRAPHIC REGION Since the nation's founding, Americans have varied in their political attitudes and beliefs and how they are socialized to politics, depending on the region of the United States from which they come. These differences stem in part from historical patterns of immigration: Irish and Italian immigrants generally settled on the northeastern seaboard, influencing the political culture of Boston, New York, Philadelphia, and Baltimore. Chinese immigrants, instrumental in building the transcontinental railroad in the 19th century, settled in California and areas of the Pacific Northwest and have had a major influence on the political life of those areas.

Among the most important regional differences in the United States is the difference in political outlook between those who live in the Northeast and those in the South. The differences between these two regions predate even our nation's founding. During the Constitutional Convention in 1787, northern and southern states disagreed as to the method that should be used to count slaves for the purposes of taxation and representation. The differences between these two regions were intensified in the aftermath of the Civil War—the quintessential manifestation of regional differences in the United States. Since the Republican Party was the party of Lincoln and the North, the South became essentially a one-party region, with all political competition occurring *within* the Democratic Party. The Democratic Party dominated the South until the later part of the 20th century, when many Democrats embraced the civil rights movement (as described in Chapter 5). Differences in regional culture and political viewpoints between North and South remain, as shown in Table 6.2. In most modern national elections, Republicans tend to carry the South, the West, and most of the Midwest, except for large cities in these regions. Democrats are favored in the Northeast, on the West Coast, and in most major cities.

Figure 6.6 illustrates one factor that contributes to these differences in regional political climate: religiosity. As discussed earlier in this chapter, religiosity affects

Evaluating the Facts

TABLE 6.2 Americans' Political Ideology by Region

REGION	CONSERVATIVE	MODERATE	LIBERAL	PERCENTAGE-POINT-DIFFERENCE BETWEEN CONSERVATIVE-LIBERAL
East	29%	35%	32%	−3
Midwest	36	36	24	+12
South	40	35	20	+20
West	32	34	30	+2

1. Which region is the most conservative? The most liberal?

2. Which region is the most evenly divided among the ideologies?

3. Is your ideology and that of your classmates consistent with the dominant views in your region? Why might substantial differences exist within a region?

SOURCE: Lydia Saad, "Conservative Lead in U.S. Ideology Is Down to Single Digits," January 11, 2018, Gallup.

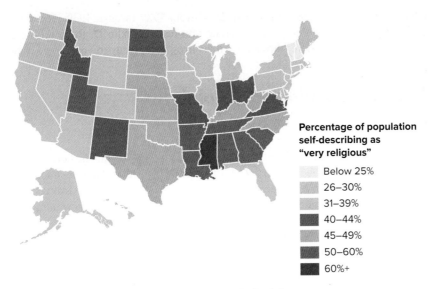

Percentage of population self-describing as "very religious"

Below 25%
26–30%
31–39%
40–44%
45–49%
50–60%
60%+

FIGURE 6.6 ■ **Levels of Religiosity in the United States**

SOURCE: Frank J. Newport, "New Hampshire Now the Least Religious State," February 4, 2016, Gallup.

political viewpoints, and the regional differences in levels of religiosity mean that those differences are manifested as regional differences as well. From Figure 6.6, we can see that the most religious states are found primarily in the South (Mississippi, Alabama, Louisiana, Arkansas, South Carolina, Tennessee, North Carolina, and Georgia), and none of the most religious states are in the Northeast or on the West Coast. Contrast that with where we find the least religious states: Nearly all are found in the Northeast (Vermont, New Hampshire, Maine, Massachusetts, Connecticut, New York, and Rhode Island), and four are in the West (Alaska, Oregon, Nevada, and Washington).

The regional differences in levels of religiosity are compounded by the differences in the dominant religious denominations in each area. The South is much more Protestant than other regions of the United States. Not surprisingly, Republicans dominate in this area, particularly among the most religious Protestants, born-again Christians and Evangelicals. Catholics and Jews tend to dominate in the Northeast along the East Coast; both groups are more frequently supporters of the Democratic Party, which is underscored by their lower levels of religiosity. People without a religious affiliation, who tend to value independence and have negative views of governmental activism, tend to live in the West and vote Republican. We can discern many of the similarities and differences between the political beliefs of members of these various demographic groups because of the increasingly sophisticated and accurate ways in which we can measure public opinion.

AGE AND EVENTS Differences in the candidates voters prefer—including the party, sex, and/or age of the candidates themselves—are one reflection of age and political opinions. People's opinions are also influenced by the events they have lived through and by their political socialization; an epic event may lead to a widespread change in political views. The **generational effect** (sometimes called the *age-cohort effect*) is the influence of a significant external event in shaping the views of a generation. Typically, generational effects are felt most strongly by young people. The major events that occur while we grow up affect our socialization by shaping our viewpoints and our policy priorities. One of the strongest examples of the generational

generational effect
The impact of an important external event in shaping the views of a generation.

effect is the Great Depression, which lasted from 1929 through 1939. Those who came of age during the era of Democratic president Franklin D. Roosevelt's New Deal social programs were, throughout their lives, most likely to vote Democratic.

The Socialization and Opinions of Young Americans

Today, two diverse and different young generations—the Millennials, born between 1980 and 2000, and Generation Z, born after 2000—are making an imprint on the fabric of American political life. The Millennial generation in the United States is an important population politically simply because of their size—now numbering 80 million. Characterized as a "ripple boom"—many are the children of post-World War II Baby Boomers—Millennials are now the largest generation in the United States, comprising about one-third of the population. In addition, research has shown that many Millennials have a strong generational identity.[12] But as the oldest members of Generation Z age, enter college, and begin voting, clear distinctions between this generation and the Millennials who preceded them are becoming apparent.

THEN

NOW

> The 1991 confirmation hearing for Supreme Court Justice Clarence Thomas gave rise to protests after Anita Hill alleged that Thomas had sexually harassed her while they were both employed at the Equal Employment Opportunity Commission (left image). Thomas was confirmed by a 52 to 48 vote margin in the Senate. Twenty-seven years later, protesters again rallied against the nomination of a Supreme Court Justice—Brett Kavanaugh—after Christine Blasey Ford alleged that he had sexually assaulted her when they were teenagers. The Senate confirmed Kavanaugh by a 50 to 48 vote margin.

Rally on steps: ©Luke Frazza/AFP/Getty Images; *Supreme Court protest:* ©Jim Watson/AFP/Getty Images

Several "externalities" have shaped the political development of Millennials. Among the most important is that they are the first generation of Americans born after birth control became widely available. Thus, by and large, they are unique in that a sweeping majority of them were "wanted" by their parents. This reality has informed various spin-off characteristics: the concepts that they have been "helicopter parented" and socialized in a child-centric era during which unique child-rearing patterns—including hyper-scheduled "leisure" activities (play-dates, lessons, sports) and the psychology of "specialness"—prevailed.[13] In addition, American Millennials are the most educated generation in history; 40 percent have graduated with baccalaureate degrees, and their attendance in graduate school also surpasses previous generations.

Finally, Millennials are a very diverse generation of Americans. Many—about 15 percent—are themselves immigrants; others are first-generation Americans whose parents came to the United States as part of a new wave of immigration that followed World War II, and recent waves of Eastern European, Hispanic, and Asian immigration and increasing intermarriage between races. Forty-three percent of Millennials are nonwhite. This trend—both the reality of "being diverse" and the exposure to both racial and cultural diversity—also has a bearing on the formation of attitudes and opinions. One result of this diversity is consistently demonstrated in research: Millennials tend to be the most tolerant of all generations of Americans,[14] embracing what can be considered a "live and let live" philosophy. We can see this ideal of political tolerance manifested in several ways. One example is the overwhelming support of Millennials for gay rights: Millennials supported same-sex marriage earlier than other generations, and greater proportions of Millennials have always supported same-sex marriage.

Another example of Millennials' political tolerance is their support of marijuana legalization. Like same-sex marriage, the issue of marijuana legalization is one in which Millennials appear to be trail-blazing, as their support has been both earlier and more cohesive than among other generations: As shown in Figure 6.7, today, 70 percent of Millennials support legalization, with support more than doubling in less than a decade (Millennials support of legalization stood at 34 percent in 2006). Other generations also are increasingly supporting legalization, but Millennials' support of legalization has foreshadowed other cohorts' changing opinions. Among Gen-Xers, 66 percent agree that marijuana should be legalized (up from 19 points in 2006), and 56 percent of Baby Boomers say it should (up from 18 percent). Members of the Silent Generation (those born between 1928 and 1945) remain largely opposed, with only 35 percent favoring legalization.

A final issue in which we see a "live and let live" philosophy driving opinions among Millennials is immigration

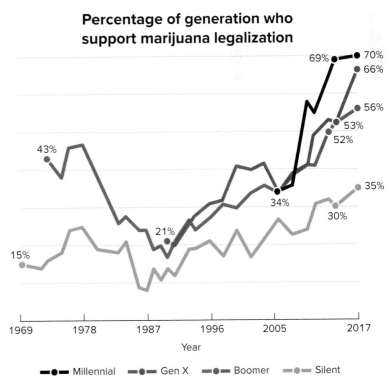

Percentage of generation who support marijuana legalization

FIGURE 6.7 ■ **Support for Marijuana Legalization by Generation**

SOURCE: Pew Research Center.

reform. Millennials are the cohort most likely to support reforms that include a path to citizenship for undocumented immigrants. And 79 percent of Millennials say immigrants strengthen rather than burden the country, compared to 66 percent of Gen Xers, 56 percent of Boomers, and 47 percent of members of the Silent Generation. Millennials' positive views of immigrants carry into specific policies concerning immigration: 72 percent of Millennials oppose expanding the border wall between Mexico and the United States, while 60 percent of Gen Xers oppose it, compared to 48 and 46 percent of Boomers and members of the Silent Generation, respectively.[15] Again, the issue positions of Millennials reflect the worldview to which they have been socialized: a tolerant, global, multicultural environment.

As with other generations, externalities also have played an important role in the political socialization of Millennials. For them, the terrorist attacks of September 11, 2001, and the ripple effects throughout the United States provided an event-centered, cohesive experience, jolting the nation and altering the context that shaped their political socialization. But another, more recent event also appears to be driving many Millennials' opinions and behaviors: the Great Recession. The results of the Great Recession were borne disproportionately by Millennials, who came of age facing higher levels of student loan debt, higher levels of unemployment, higher poverty rates, and lower levels of personal income and accumulated wealth than previous generations.[16] Those economic realities have seemed to affect other attitudes and behaviors: Millennials are more likely to support federal government policies that reduce income inequality, including increasing the minimum hourly wage to $15, and are more likely to support "bigger government providing more services" than other generations, as shown in Table 6.3.

While the oldest members of Generation Z are just coming of age politically, research demonstrates that this generation differs significantly from Millennials. Some evidence indicates that Gen Z will be more conservative than Millennials: for example, one poll indicated that 8 out of 10 members of Generation Z think of themselves as "fiscally conservative."[17] This characteristic may be a generational effect of the Great Recession. Indeed, watching their parents and older siblings struggle with staggering unemployment rates, the mortgage crisis, and record-setting foreclosure rates during their childhoods may have shaped members of Generation Z into a fiscally cautious generation.

Other studies show more conservative personal behaviors: members of Generation Z have lower teen-pregnancy rates, are less likely to engage in substance abuse, and have higher on-time high school graduation rates compared to Millennials,[18] and while only 18 percent of Millennials attend church regularly, 41 percent of members

TABLE 6.3 Preferences for Size of Government by Generation

	PERCENTAGE FAVORING "SMALLER GOVERNMENT, FEWER SERVICES"	PERCENTAGE FAVORING "BIG GOVERNMENT, MORE SERVICES"
Millennials	38%	53%
Gen X	49	43
Baby Boomers	59	32
Silent	64	22

SOURCE: Pew Research Center.

of Generation Z do.[19] And if ink is an indicator of politics, Gen Z may wind up being more conservative than their older siblings: one study found Gen Z participants 10 times more likely than Millennials to dislike tattoos and body piercings.

Generation Z is surpassing Millennials as the most diverse generation, and as we saw with Millennials, diversity tends to breed tolerance. Members of Generation Z are more likely to have positive feelings about diversity, and in general, are opposed to policies or practices that discriminate against immigrants or people of different races, religions, or ethnic groups.[20] Some members of this generation have grown up in same-sex households, and as a whole, they are overwhelmingly supportive of same-sex marriage. They are also more supportive of transgender rights and are more likely to know someone who prefers gender-neutral pronouns such as "they," "them," or "ze," compared to Millennials. And more than 33 percent of Gen Zers strongly agreed that gender does not define a person as much as it used to, compared to 23 percent of Millennials.[21]

Like Millennials, Generation Z is also overwhelmingly supportive of marijuana legalization, and three-quarters of them say they are concerned about the issue of global warming.[22] Having been the generation most likely to witness and be victims of mass shootings, members of Generation Z also are more likely to support gun safety measures than older generations.[23]

And so, while certain elements of Generation Z's character point to an underpinning of conservatism, other components of their beliefs demonstrate a consistency with the more liberal policy positions favored by Millennials. The 2020 presidential election will mark the first opportunity to gauge the political preferences of Generation Z on the national level.

Measuring Public Opinion

Public opinion consists of the public's expressed views about an issue at a specific point in time. Public opinion and ideology are inextricably linked because ideology is the prism through which people view all political issues; hence their ideology informs their opinions on a full range of political issues. Indeed, the growing importance of public opinion has even led some political scientists, such as Elizabeth Noelle-Neumann, to argue that public opinion itself is a socializing agent in that it provides an independent context that affects political behavior.[24] Though we are inundated every day with the latest public opinion polls everywhere and, while 2016 raises questions about their accuracy, public opinion has played an important role historically in American politics.

Public opinion is manifested in various ways: demonstrators protesting on the steps of the state capitol; bloggers posting their opinions; citizens communicating directly with government officials, perhaps by telling their local city council members what they think of the town's plan to increase taxes or by calling their members of Congress to indicate their opinion on a current piece of legislation. One of the most important ways public opinion is measured is through the act of voting, discussed in Chapter 9. But another important tool that policymakers, researchers, and the public rely on as an indicator of public opinion is the **public opinion poll,** a survey of a given population's opinion on an issue at a particular time. Policymakers, particularly elected officials, care about public opinion because they want to develop and implement policies that reflect the public's views.[25] Such policies are more likely to attract support from other government leaders, who are also relying on public opinion as a gauge, but they also help ensure that elected leaders will be reelected, because they are representing their constituent's views.[26]

public opinion
The public's expressed views about an issue at a specific point in time.

public opinion poll
A survey of a given population's opinion on an issue or a candidate at a particular point in time.

How Public Opinion Polls Are Conducted

In politics, public opinion polls are used for many reasons.[27] Political scientist Herbert Asher noted: "Polling plays an integral role in political events at the national, state, and local levels. In any major event or decision, poll results are sure to be a part of the news media's coverage and the decision maker's deliberations."[28] In addition, public opinion polls help determine who those decision makers will be: Candidates for public office use polls to determine their initial name recognition, the effectiveness of their campaign strategy, their opponents' weaknesses, and how potential voters are responding to their message. Once elected to office, policymakers often rely on public opinion polls to gauge their constituents' opinions and to measure how well they are performing on the job.

population

In a poll, the group of people whose opinions are of interest and/or about whom information is desired.

The process of conducting a public opinion poll consists of several steps. Those conducting the poll first need to determine the **population** they are targeting for the survey—the group of people whose opinions are of interest and about whom information is desired. For example, if your neighbor were considering running for the U.S. House of Representatives, she would want to know how many people recognize her name. But she would be interested only in those people who live in your congressional district. Furthermore, she would probably narrow this population by looking only at those people in the district who are registered to vote. She might even want to narrow her target population further by limiting her survey to likely voters, perhaps those who have voted in past congressional elections.

random sampling

A scientific method of selection in which each member of the population has an equal chance of being included in the sample.

SAMPLING Once the target population is determined and the survey measurement instrument, or poll, is designed, pollsters then must select a sample that will represent the views of this population. Because it is nearly impossible to measure all the opinions of any given population, pollsters frequently rely on **random sampling,** a scientific method of selection in which each member of the population has an equal chance of being included in the sample. Relying on random sampling helps to ensure that the sample is not skewed so that one component of the population is overrepresented.

To demonstrate this point, suppose the dean of students asks your class to conduct a public opinion survey that will measure whether students believe that parking facilities are adequate at your school. In this case, the population you need to measure is the entire student body. But clearly, how you conduct the sampling will affect the responses. If you ask only students in your 8:00 a.m. American government class, you might find that they have little trouble parking, because the campus is not crowded at that hour. If you ask students who attend classes only during peak hours, you might get different, yet not necessarily representative, views as well, since these students may have more difficulty parking than average. How then would you obtain a random sample? The best way would be to ask the registrar for a list of all students, determine your sample size, randomly select every *n*th student from the list, contact each *n*th student, and ask for his or her views.

Researchers have noted, however, that one problem with polls is that even those conducted using random samples may not provide the accurate data needed to illuminate political opinions and behaviors. Consider that today, many people use cell phones exclusively. One standard method for conducting telephone surveys is to use random-digit dialing of telephones.[29] Although most major polling organizations now include cell phone users in order to create an accurate sample of Americans, some polling organizations still exclude cellular lines from their population.[30] Today, less than 50 percent of the U.S. population relies exclusively on cell phones and has no landline phone.[31] But even those polling organizations that include cell phone subscribers face a high rate of nonresponse because of the nearly

Analyzing the Sources

EXAMINING AMERICANS' IDEOLOGY

This graph shows the trend over time regarding Americans' self-described ideology. In all the surveys, respondents were asked to describe their political views as very conservative, conservative, moderate, liberal, or very liberal. Very conservative/conservative and very liberal/liberal responses have been consolidated.

Practice Analytical Thinking

1. What does the graph indicate about how most people identify themselves now? What has been the trend in recent years? Why do you think this is the case?

2. Why do the 2009 data stand out? Are the 2009 data consistent with those of previous years?

3. Why was 2017 a watershed year? How would you project the ideological distribution in years to come?

How would you describe your political views?

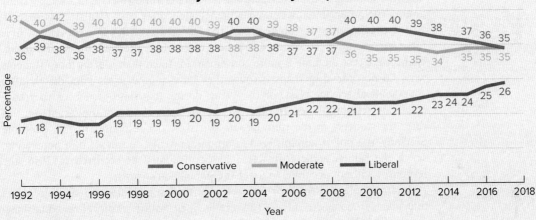

SOURCE: Lydia Saad, "Conservative Lead in U.S. Ideology Is Down to Single Digits," January 11, 2018, Gallup.

universal use of caller ID, and the transportable nature of cell phones that makes their owners less likely to answer calls when involved in other activities.[32] In fact, one study found that those who are willing to respond to pollsters' questions are more politically engaged than those who hit "ignore." (See "Analyzing the Sources" to consider how these and other factors might impact polling results.)

One way pollsters attempt to address these types of concerns is through the use of a **quota sample,** a more scientifically sophisticated method of sampling than random sampling. A pollster using this method structures the sample so that it is representative of the characteristics of the target population. Let's say that your mother is running for mayor of your town, and you would like to conduct a poll that measures opinions of her among various constituencies. From census data, you learn that your town is 40 percent white, 35 percent African American, 20 percent Latino, and 5 percent Asian. Therefore, when conducting a poll you structure your sample so that it reflects the proportions of the population. With a sample of 200 voters, you would seek to include 80 white respondents, 70 African Americans, 40 Latinos, and 10 Asians. Pollsters routinely rely on quota sampling, though often they may not ask participants about their demographic characteristics until the end of the poll.

quota sample

A method by which pollsters structure a sample so that it is representative of the characteristics of the target population.

Another method used to address problems in sampling is **stratified sampling,** in which the national population is divided into fourths and certain areas within these regions are selected as representative of the national population. Although some organizations still rely on quota sampling, larger organizations and media polls now use stratified sampling, the most reliable form of random sampling. Today, nearly every major polling organization relies on U.S. census data as the basis of their four sampling regions. Stratified sampling is the basis for much of the public opinion data used by political scientists and other social scientists, in particular the General Social Survey (GSS) and the American National Election Study.

SAMPLING ERROR   As we have seen, to accurately gauge public opinion, pollsters must obtain an accurate sample from the population they are polling. A sample need not be large to reflect the population's views. In fact, most national polling organizations rarely sample more than 1,500 respondents; most national samples range from 1,000 to 1,500. To poll smaller populations (states or congressional districts, for example), polling organizations routinely use samples of between 300 and 500 respondents.

The key is having a sample that accurately reflects the population. Let's say that your political science instructor offers extra credit if you attend a weekly study group. The group initially convenes immediately after your regular class session. At the conclusion of the study group, the leader asks if this is a convenient time for everyone to meet. Since everyone present has attended the study group, chances are that the time is more convenient for them than it is for those students who did not attend—perhaps because they have another class immediately after your political science class, or they work during that time period, or they have child care responsibilities. In other words, the composition of the sample—in this case, the students in the study group—will skew the responses to this question. Similarly, if a poll is administered to a nonrepresentative sample of a population, say if the sample underestimates a block of voters, as occurred in 2016, the responses will not accurately reflect the population's views.

Internet polls present their own set of obstacles, including the ability of some individuals to complete surveys (or vote for their favorite reality show contestant) repeatedly.[33] Nonetheless, market research firms, public opinion polling organizations, and even political candidates are increasingly relying on the Internet as a survey research tool.[34] Some organizations, such as the Harris Poll Online, offer "memberships": Poll respondents can earn rewards for completing surveys that help the organization create a representative sample of their target population.

To adjust for problems with sampling, every poll that relies on a sample has a **sampling error** (sometimes called a margin of error), which is a statistical calculation of the difference in results between a poll of a randomly drawn sample and a poll of the entire population. Most polls have a sampling error of ±3 percentage points ("plus or minus 3 percentage points"). This means that 3 percentage points should be added and subtracted from the poll results to find the range for the population.

Types of Political Polls

The process of measuring political opinions has evolved drastically over the years.[35] Today, political candidates, parties, and news organizations rely on several types of polls, depending on their goals and objectives. These include tracking polls, push polls, and exit polls.

- **Tracking polls** measure changes in public opinion over the course of days, weeks, or months by repeatedly asking respondents the same questions over time and measuring changes in opinion (see "Thinking Critically"). During

Should the United States Have Stricter Gun Safety Laws?

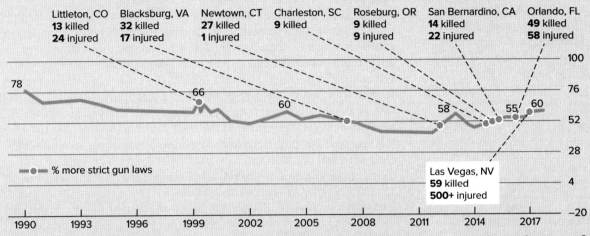

Littleton, CO
13 killed
24 injured

Blacksburg, VA
32 killed
17 injured

Newtown, CT
27 killed
1 injured

Charleston, SC
9 killed

Roseburg, OR
9 killed
9 injured

San Bernardino, CA
14 killed
22 injured

Orlando, FL
49 killed
58 injured

Las Vegas, NV
59 killed
500+ injured

In general, do you feel that the laws covering the sale of firearms should be made more strict, less strict or kept as they are now?

Support for Stricter Gun Laws

SOURCE: Frank Newport and R.J. Reinhard, "Direction From the American Public on Gun Policy," October 30, 2017, Gallup

The Issue: The issue of stricter gun safety laws is contentious, and public opinion surrounding it reflects existing geographic, partisan, and cultural divides. In recent years, numerous polls indicate that a majority of Americans support stricter gun control, but they differ acutely in levels of support for various policies, and while some policies garner overwhelming support, a relatively small proportion of the population ranks gun safety as a salient issue that would determine who they would vote for.

Yes: Support for stricter gun control continues to increase, with more than 60 percent of Americans in favor. Fully 90 percent of Democrats support stricter gun laws. In addition, some policies—including universal background checks—garner almost unanimous support of all Americans (96 percent of Americans support this policy). While other policies may not garner unanimous approval, support is strong for a 30-day waiting period for all gun sales (supported by 75 percent of Americans) and a regulation that would require all guns to be registered with local police (70 percent support).

No: Today, the partisan gap in support of stricter gun laws is greater than ever: only 33 percent of Republicans support increased gun control, creating a 57 percent difference between the proportion of Republicans versus Democrats supporting it. This difference is greater than even the gap between gun owners versus non–gun owners, which tends to hover between a 25- and 38-percentage-point difference. In addition, there is little support for banning specific types of guns: less than a majority of Americans (48 percent) support banning semiautomatic assault weapons, while only 28 percent support a ban on handguns.

Other Approaches: Data appears to support restrictions on the conditions of gun sales rather than bans on specific weapons, which perhaps reflects an effort on the part of Americans to balance the safety of Americans against the Second Amendment. In addition, less than half of Americans believe that new gun safety laws would succeed in reducing the number of mass shootings. Some believe that increased governmental resources should be allocated to address the mental health issues that almost always accompany mass shootings.

What do you think?

1. Do you support increased gun safety laws in general? Do you support specific reforms, including requiring universal background checks, a 30-day waiting period for all gun sales, and the registration of all guns with local police? Do you support banning semiautomatic assault weapons? Handguns?

2. Are your views consistent with your partisan identity? Are they consistent with your status as a gun owner or non-gun owner?

3. Do you believe that stricter gun laws will decrease the number of mass shootings? According to the figure, what effect do mass shootings have on public opinion concerning support of increased gun safety laws? Overall, what is the trend in public opinion on this issue?

SOURCE: Frank Newport and RJ Reinhart, "Direction From the American Public on Gun Policy," http://news.gallup.

Measuring Public Opinion   215

the 2016 Republican presidential primaries, when many candidates faced poll numbers that showed declining support, they withdrew from the race. Tracking polls can indicate the effectiveness of a media strategy in both the long- and short-term, assess the success of a day's worth of campaigning, or measure whether the campaign has gotten its message across during a specific period of time.

- **Push polls** are a special type of poll that both attempts to skew public opinion about a candidate and provides information to campaigns about candidate strengths and weaknesses. Sometimes this is done by presenting survey respondents with a hypothetical situation and then asking them to gauge the importance of the hypothetical issue in determining their vote. For example, a push-pollster might ask: "If you knew that Congresswoman Jackson lives outside the district, how would that affect your vote?" At their best, push polls help gauge voter priorities so that a campaign can better target its message. The campaign can then determine whether to accentuate that message. But push polls have an unsavory reputation, because some campaigns and organizations have used them to smear an opponent, using hypothetical scenarios to make baseless accusations against an opponent without having to substantiate the charges.

- **Exit polls** are conducted at polling places on Election Day to project the winner of an election before the polls close. News organizations frequently sponsor exit polls, which help them predict the outcome of gubernatorial, congressional, and presidential elections. Because of exit polls, news organizations can frequently predict the outcome of a given election shortly after the polls have closed. Exit polls also provide the media, candidates, and political parties with information about why voters voted the way they did.

push polls

A special type of poll that both attempts to skew public opinion about a candidate and provides information to campaigns about candidate strengths and weaknesses.

exit polls

Polls conducted at polling places on Election Day to project the winner of an election before the polls close.

>An important type of poll is the exit poll, conducted on Election Day. From these polls, we learn about why voters voted for their candidates.
©Mario Tama/Getty Images

What Americans Think About Politics

Public opinion research is the means by which individuals can convey their opinions and priorities to policymakers. Consequently, polls connect Americans to their government.[36] Through public opinion polls, whether conducted by campaigns or media organizations, government officials come to know and understand the opinions of the masses.[37] Through polls, leaders learn what issues are important to people, which policy solutions they prefer, and whether they approve of the way government officials are doing their jobs.[38] The role of opinion polls in shaping citizens' involvement with their government is also circular: Polls play a pivotal role in shaping public opinion, and the results of polls, frequently reported by the media, provide an important source of information for the American public.

The Most Important Problem

Several polling organizations routinely ask respondents to identify (either from a list or in their own words) what they view as "the most important problem" facing the country. In 2018, 25 percent of respondents said that dissatisfaction with government/poor leadership was the most important problem, marking the first time in decades that this response was identified as the top concern of Americans. For the past decade, economic issues, including the economy in general, unemployment, and income inequality have dominated, but just 20 percent of Americans identified economic issues as their top concern.

THEN NOW NEXT

Public Opinion Polling

Then (1970s)	Now
Telephone polls replaced mail-in and door-to-door polling, because most American households had landlines.	Internet polls are at the cutting edge of public opinion research, but anonymity and multiple responses from the same person can damage a poll's accuracy.
Early telephone polls overrepresented the views of homemakers and retirees, who were more likely to answer the phone during the day.	Polls in 2016 are distinguished by their inaccuracy in projecting both support of and turnout for Donald Trump among working-class white voters.
Pollsters remedied nonrepresentative sampling through quota sampling.	Pollsters rely on stratified sampling to ensure the most representative sample of the population they are targeting.

WHAT'S NEXT?

> How will technologies such as YouTube and social networking sites shape polling in the future?

> How might pollsters overcome the obstacles associated with Internet polls, in particular, the problem of anonymous respondents giving false answers or responding to the same poll multiple times?

> How will cell phones and text messaging change the way in which public opinion is measured in the future?

Public Opinion About Government

Analysts of public opinion, government officials, and scholars of civic engagement are all concerned with public opinion about the government at all levels, in particular about the institutions of the federal government. For decades, public opinion researchers have measured the public's trust in government by asking survey respondents to rate their level of trust in the federal government's ability to handle domestic and international policy matters and to gauge their amount of trust and confidence in the executive, legislative, and judicial branches of government.

The responses to these questions are important for several reasons. First, although these measures indicate public opinion about institutions rather than individuals, individual officeholders nonetheless can use the data as a measure of how well they are performing their jobs. Lower levels of confidence in the institution of the presidency, for example, tend to parallel lower approval ratings of specific presidents.[39] Second, trust in government is one measure of the public's sense of efficacy, their belief that the government works for people like them, as discussed in Chapter 1. If people trust their government, they are more likely to believe that it is responsive to the needs of citizens. In Chapter 3, we examined the issue of citizens' trust in local, state, and federal governments. Here, we delve further into Americans' trust of the federal government—which branches they view as the most trustworthy, and in which policy areas.

As indicated by the results of a Gallup poll, the public's trust in the ability of the federal government to handle both international affairs and domestic problems had in general declined over the years after rebounding slightly between 2009 and 2016. Many analysts attributed the decline to widespread dissatisfaction with the war in Iraq and the economic downturn during the George W. Bush administration, the temporary rebound caused by optimism during President Obama's first term, and then frustration with many of Obama's policies, particularly concerning the terror group ISIS.

As shown in Figure 6.8, the public's trust in government to handle international problems reached a record high immediately after the September 11, 2001, terror attacks, with 83 percent of those surveyed indicating a great deal or a fair amount of trust. The public's trust in government to handle international problems then declined steadily from 2004 through 2007, reaching 51 percent in 2007, as the war in Iraq dragged on. The effect of President George W. Bush's "surge strategy" in Iraq and then the optimism generated by the election of President Obama accounted for a temporary increase in optimism, but as the war in Afghanistan dragged on, trust declined again, hitting 57 percent in late 2011. Faith in Obama's ability to

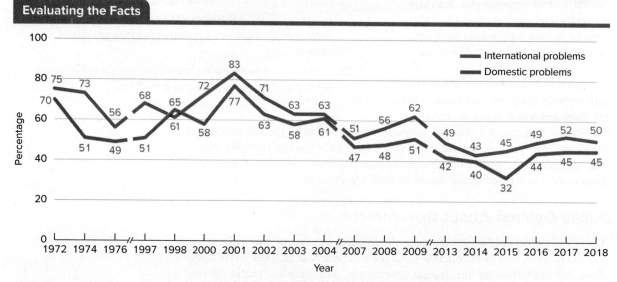

Evaluating the Facts

FIGURE 6.8 ■ **Trust in Government to Handle International and Domestic Problems** Public trust in the government's ability to deal with international problems has decreased since 2012. Why do you think this is the case? What impact does the state of the economy have on the public's trust in government's ability to handle domestic problems? What can you infer about the state of the economy in May 1972? In September 2004? In September 2018?

SOURCE: Jeffrey M. Jones "Trust in Government," Gallup.

handle international problems increased to 66 percent leading up to the 2012 election, but then declined to record lows in 2014 after the administration's early bungled response to the ISIS terror threat. Comparatively low levels of trust concerning the government's ability to handle international problems—pegged at 49 percent in 2016—continued to plague the remainder of Obama's tenure in office. Initial evidence shows that the public trust in government to handle international problems was a mediocre 52 percent in 2017, then dipped slightly to 50 percent in 2018.

The public's trust in the government's ability to handle domestic matters also peaked in 2001. From Figure 6.8, we can see that in 2007, worries about the economy dominated the public's thinking, and trust in government to handle domestic problems dropped to 47 percent, a figure that rivaled the record-low confidence levels of 51 percent to 49 percent seen in the period between 1974 and 1976, following the Watergate scandal. An uptick registered in 2009, coinciding with the start of Barack Obama's presidency. During his years in office, the skepticism and frustration many Americans felt concerning implementation of the Affordable Care Act plagued the public's trust in government to handle domestic matters. But President Trump has not fared much better; he garnered a 45 percent confidence rating in his administration's ability to handle domestic issues. During the beginning of his term, he faced significant opposition from within his own party as well as from outside, where members of Congress and portions of the general public opposed some of his top domestic policy priorities, including tougher immigration laws and the construction of a wall between the United States and Mexico.

The public's trust in specific institutions was also affected by the terror attacks of September 11, 2001, the subsequent weariness with the war in Iraq, the Great Recession, the optimism following Barack Obama's election as president, and the ultimate disappointment in his administration. As Figure 6.9 shows, for example, trust in the executive branch hit a near-record-high mark in 2002, when fully 72 percent of Americans voiced a great deal or a fair amount of trust. But then,

Evaluating the Facts

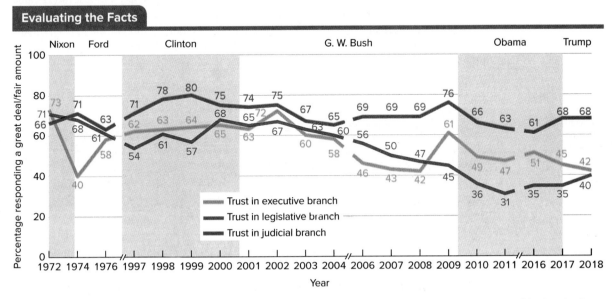

FIGURE 6.9 ■ Trust in the Branches of Government How much trust and confidence do you have at this time in the executive branch headed by the president, the judicial branch headed by the U.S. Supreme Court, and the legislative branch, consisting of the U.S. Senate and House of Representatives—a great deal, a fair amount, not very much, or none at all?

SOURCE: Jeffrey M. Jones, "Trust in Government," Gallup.

in 2007, as this figure shows, public trust in the executive branch dropped to 43 percent, marking a 9-percentage-point decline from 2005. As noted previously, the decline in trust in the institution of the presidency is closely related to public approval of individual presidents: In 2007, only 36 percent of those surveyed approved of the way President Bush was handling his job. Similarly, in 2009, trust in the executive branch spiked up to 61 percent, mirroring Barack Obama's higher approval ratings during that time. By 2014, Obama's popularity had diminished, and correspondingly, trust in the executive branch plummeted to a record low rating of 40 percent in 2014, marking the lowest level of public trust in the executive branch ever measured, including trust in the executive before Richard Nixon resigned the presidency.[40] By 2015, Americans' trust in the executive branch had rebounded to 45 percent, a small improvement that continued throughout Obama's presidency, but dipped slightly during the early portion of President Trump's tenure.

Congress, too, faces ups and downs in terms of its public approval rate, but in general the legislative branch has struggled to maintain approval ratings comparable with the other branches of government. While Congress enjoyed widespread popularity until the early 2000s, since that time the legislative branch has failed to win approval from the majority of Americans, as shown in Figure 6.9. From 2006 through 2010, increasing dissatisfaction with the Democrats in Congress was apparent, and this dissatisfaction culminated in the Republican takeover of the House of Representatives in 2010. But since that time, Republicans have fared no better: often only one-third of Americans approve of the way Congress is handling its job. This is the case today, where we see Congress's approval rating at 35 percent. Nonetheless, this figure is an improvement from its record low of 28 percent in 2014, which reflected the widespread dissatisfaction with partisan bickering within the legislature, and between Congress and the president.

The judicial branch of government consistently scores higher in levels of public trust than do the other two branches. Figure 6.9 shows that confidence in the judiciary typically hovers between 65 percent and 75 percent, sometimes climbing into the high 70s (or even 80 percent in 1999). The judiciary's lowest rating came in 1976, when there was widespread dissatisfaction with government as a whole in the aftermath of the Watergate scandal. But overall, opinion of the judiciary tends to be the most consistent and the most positive of all branches of government.

Conclusion

Thinking Critically About What's Next in Public Opinion

The process of political socialization is quite different from what it was even a generation ago. Although some agents of socialization such as families, peers, and churches remain important, other agents, particularly the media, are more pervasive and influential than ever before. Although television and radio have played their part in socializing the average 40-year-old in 2019, today's younger people are almost constantly bombarded by various other forms of media, which may influence their viewpoints, priorities, behaviors, and opinions.

Technology has also drastically changed the way public opinion is measured. The advent of the computer alone—from powerful mainframes to personal computers—has revolutionized the data-collection process; today, computers facilitate near-instant access to polling data. The problem witnessed in the 2016 campaign was that sometimes this process is flawed and results in inaccurate projections dominating the news.

The catch-22, however, has been the pervasiveness of public opinion polls. People's opinions are solicited by every kind of survey from cheesy Internet polls to reputable polling organizations. As a result, the public has become poll weary, dubious of the value of the pollster's next set of questions. Will increasing weariness with Internet polling result in less representative samples? How might pollsters overcome this challenge? How will the universality of cell phones revolutionize the process of public opinion polling?

Technology has provided—and will continue to provide—ways to solve the problems that technology itself has generated in accurately measuring public opinion. Stratified samples and other increasingly sophisticated microsampling techniques have improved the ability of reputable pollsters to gauge public opinion. And pollsters are incorporating new technologies, including text messaging and cell phone surveys, as they work to develop new ways to accurately measure and convey the public's views to candidates, to policymakers, and, through the media, to the public itself.

Learning Summary

1. Explain the process of political socialization and how family environment influences whether we are socialized to be civically engaged.

2. Explain how agents of socialization influence our political beliefs and behaviors.
   a. Explain how family shapes our political values and ideology from childhood.
   b. Describe how the media have come to rival the family in shaping our views and informing our opinions.
   c. Explain the impact of schools on civic participation and attitudes toward core democratic values, such as the legitimacy of elections and the principle of majority rule.
   d. List the ways in which demographic characteristics—including religiosity, race and ethnicity, gender, geographic region, and age—contribute to how we are socialized to political and community life, shape our values and priorities, and influence the candidates we vote for.

3. Explain the socialization and opinions of young Americans, including the factors that contribute to the unique socialization of Millennials, and how Generation Z appears to differ from Millennials politically.

4. Analyze the obstacles pollsters face in accurately gauging opinions.
   a. Explain the process of polling—including identifying the target population, designing an accurate measure, selecting a sample, and administering the poll.
   b. Describe the types of polls—including tracking polls, push polls, and exit polls—and their differing purposes in political campaigns.

5. Discuss the trends regarding Americans' dissatisfaction with government and levels of trust in the three branches of government.

Key Terms

agents of socialization 199

exit polls 216

gender gap 204

generational effect 207

political socialization 197

population 212

public opinion 211

public opinion poll 211

push polls 216

quota sample 213

random sampling 212

sampling error (margin of error) 214

stratified sampling 214

tracking polls 214

For Review

1. How are political socialization and civic participation linked?
2. Explain in detail the agents of socialization. How does each agent influence an individual's political views over a lifetime?
3. What demographic characteristics contribute to how individuals view politics?
4. How did public opinion polls evolve historically?
5. Explain how public opinion polls are conducted.
6. What factors influence what Americans perceive as the "most important problem"?
7. Describe the most recent trend regarding Americans' trust in government.

For Critical Thinking and Discussion

1. How did your family influence your political views? Does your family believe in the value of political participation? Do you? If not, why do you think that is the case?
2. How have your demographic characteristics—your age, the area of the country in which you were raised, for example—contributed to the formation of your political views? How relevant are the generalities described in the chapter to your own experience and beliefs?
3. What do you think is the "most important problem" facing the United States? Is it a problem discussed in this book? Is it one shared by your classmates?
4. What factors influence how satisfied you feel about the direction of the country?
5. Which branch of government do you trust the most? Why?

Resources for Research AND Action

Internet Resources

American National Election Studies
www.electionstudies.org The American National Election Studies website contains information on American public opinion as well as a valuable user guide that can help acquaint you with using the data.

The Gallup Organization
www.gallup.com You will find both national and international polls and analysis on this site.

Pew Research Center
www.pewresearch.org This nonpartisan fact tank serves to inform the public on national and international issues, conduct public opinion polls, and provide research on a variety of social topics.

Polling Report
www.pollingreport.com This independent, nonpartisan website offers a clearinghouse for a wide range of polls on both elections and public policy issues.

The Roper Center
www.ropercenter.uconn.edu This website features the University of Connecticut's Roper Center polls, the General Social Survey, presidential approval ratings, and poll analysis.

Recommended Readings

Alsop, Ron. *The Trophy Kids Grow Up: How the Millennial Generation Is Shaking Up the Workplace.* New York: John Wiley & Sons, 2008. This book examines how the socialization of Millennials has affected their attitudes and behaviors.

Bishop, George F., and Stephen T. Mockabee. *Taking the Pulse of Public Opinion: Leading and Misleading Indicators of the State of the Nation.* New York: Springer, 2010. This analytical work examines how psychology and the media influence well-established public opinion indicators.

Fiorina, Morris P. *Culture War: The Myth of a Polarized America.* New York: Pearson Longman, 2006. A critical view of the notion that the United States is divided along ideological lines. Fiorina asserts that Americans are generally moderate and tolerant of a wide variety of viewpoints.

Jamieson, Kathleen Hall. *Electing the President, 2008.* Philadelphia: University of Pennsylvania Press, 2008. A fascinating "insider's view" of how public opinion shaped the 2008 presidential campaigns by the director of the Annenberg National Election Studies.

Page, Benjamin I., and Robert Y. Shapiro. *The Rational Public: Fifty Years of Trends in Americans' Policy Preferences.* Chicago: University of Chicago Press, 1992. An analysis of the policy preferences of the American public from the 1930s until 1990. The authors describe opinion on both domestic and foreign policy.

Traugott, Michael W., and Paul J. Lavrakas. *The Voter's Guide to Election Polls,* 4th ed. New York: Chatham House, 2008. A user-friendly approach, written in question-and-answer format, that helps beginners understand the polling process and how to interpret public opinion data.

Welch, Susan, Lee Sigelman, Timothy Bledsoe, and Michael Combs. *Race and Place: Race Relations in an American City* (Cambridge Studies in Public Opinion and Political Psychology). New York: Cambridge University Press, 2001. An analysis of the effect of residential changes on the attitudes and behavior of African Americans and whites.

Movies of Interest

Lions for Lambs (2007)
Directed by Robert Redford and starring Redford, Meryl Streep, and Tom Cruise, this film about a platoon of U.S. soldiers in Afghanistan demonstrates the influence that educational socialization can have on individuals.

Wag the Dog (1997)
A classic Barry Levinson film featuring a spin-doctor (Robert De Niro) and a Hollywood producer (Dustin Hoffman) who team up 11 days before an election to "fabricate" a war to cover up a presidential sex scandal.

References

1. V. O. Key Jr., *Public Opinion and American Democracy* (New York: Knopf, 1961), 8.
2. J. Foster-Bey, *Do Race, Ethnicity, Citizenship and Socio-economic Status Determine Civic-Engagement?* (College Park, MD: CIRCLE: The Center for Information and Research on Civic Learning & Engagement, 2008), 4.
3. Mark Hugo Lopez, Peter Levine, Deborah Both, Abby Kiesa, Emily Kirby, and Karlo Marcelo, *The 2006 Civic and Political Health of the Nation: A Detailed Look at How Youth Participate in Politics and Communities* (College Park, MD: CIRCLE: The Center for Information and Research on Civic Learning and Engagement, 2006), 4.
4. Ibid.
5. Sidney Verba, Kay Lehman Schlozman, and Henry E. Brady, *Voice and Equality: Civic Voluntarism in American Politics* (Cambridge, MA: Harvard University Press, 1995), 439.
6. David L. Leal, Matt A. Barreto, Jongho Lee, and Rodolfo O. de la Garza, "The Latino Vote in the 2004 Election," *PS: Political Science and Politics* (2005): 46.
7. National Asian American Survey, Post Election Survey of Asian Americans and Pacific Island Voters in 2012.
8. Lopez et al., *The 2006 Civic and Political Health of the Nation,* 20–21.
9. www.gallup.com/poll/185213/working-women-lag-men-opinion-workplace-equity.aspx.
10. David W. Moore, "Death Penalty Gets Less Support from Britons, Canadians Than Americans," Gallup News Service, February 20, 2006.
11. Karlo Barrios Marcelo, Mark Hugo Lopez, and Emily Hoban Kirby, *Civic Engagement Among Young Men and Women* (College Park, MD: CIRCLE: The Center for Information and Research on Civic Learning and Engagement, 2007), 12.
12. H.-W. Charng, J. A. Piliavin, and A. P. Callero, "Role Identity and Reasoned Action in the Prediction of Repeated Behavior," *Social Psychology Quarterly,* 1988: 303–317.

13. R. Alsop, *The Trophy Kids Grow Up: How the Millennial Generation Is Shaking Up the Workplace* (New York: John Wiley & Sons, 2008).
14. J. M. Twenge and S. M. Campbell, "Who Are the Millennials? Empirical Evidence for Generational Differences in Work Values, Attitudes and Personality," *Managing the New Workforce: International Perspectives on the Millennial Generation,* 2012, 1-19; B. J. Kowske and J. Wiley, "Millennials' (Lack of) Attitude Problem: An Empirical Examination of Generational Effects on Work Attitudes," *Journal of Business and Psychology,* 2010: 265–279; S. Gonzalez, "Religion and Ethics Newsweekly," *PBS,* November 7, 2014.
15. www.people-press.org/2018/03/01/4-race-immigration-same-sex-marriage-abortion-global-warming-gun-policy-marijuana-legalization/.
16. Don Peck, *Pinched: How the Great Recession Has Narrowed Our Futures and What We Can Do about It* (New York: Broadway Books, 2012).
17. https://public.tableau.com/profile/mycollegeoptions#!/vizhome/PresidentialPolling-Fall2016/PresidentialPolling2016/.
18. www.aecf.org/blog/generation-z-breaks-records-in-education-and-health-despite-growing-economic-instability-of-families/.
19. Joan Hope, "Get Your Campus Ready for Generation Z," *Dean and Provost* 17:8.
20. www.nielsen.com/us/en/insights/news/2017/youth-movement-gen-z-boasts-the-largest-most-diverse-media-users-yet.html.
21. www.jwtintelligence.com/2016/03/gen-z-goes-beyond-gender-binaries-in-new-innovation-group-data/.
22. www.forbes.com/sites/deeppatel/2017/10/04/11-environmental-causes-gen-z-is-passionate-about/#432199501849.
23. www.cnbc.com/2018/03/14/how-gen-z-activists-have-changed-the-conversation-around-guns.html.
24. Elizabeth Noelle-Neumann, *The Spiral of Silence: Public Opinion—Our Social Skin,* 2nd ed. (Chicago: University of Chicago Press, 1993).

25. Susan Herbst, *Numbered Voices: How Opinion Polling Has Shaped American Politics* (Chicago: University of Chicago Press, 1993).
26. Robert S. Erikson, Gerald C. Wright, and John P. McIver, *Statehouse Democracy: Public Opinion and Policy in the American States* (New York: Cambridge University Press, 1994).
27. Herbert Asher, *Polling and the Public: What Every Citizen Should Know* (Washington, DC: CQ Press, 2001).
28. Ibid., 2.
29. Randolph Grossman and Douglas Weiland, "The Use of Telephone Directories as a Sample Frame: Patterns of Bias Revisited, *Journal of Advertising* 7 (1978): 31–36.
30. Stephen J. Blumberg and Julian V. Luke, "Coverage Bias in Traditional Telephone Surveys of Low-Income and Young Adults," *Public Opinion Quarterly* 71 (2007): 734–749.
31. www.statista.com/chart/2072/landline-phones-in-the-united-states/.
32. Clyde Tucker, J. Michael Brick, and Brian Meekins, "Household Telephone Service and Usage Patterns in the United States in 2004: Implications for Telephone Samples," *Public Opinion Quarterly* 71 (2007): 3–22.
33. George Terhanian and John Bremer, "Confronting the Selection-Bias and Learning Effects Problems Associated with Internet Research," Harris Interactive white paper, August 16, 2000.
34. G. Terhanian, R. Smith, J. Bremer, and R. K. Thomas, "Exploiting Analytical Advances: Minimizing the Biases Associated with Internet-Based Surveys of Non-Random Samples," *ARF/ESOMAR: Worldwide Online Measurement* 248 (2001): 247–272.
35. Irving Crespi, *Pre-Election Polling: Sources of Accuracy & Error* (New York: Russell Sage Foundation, 1988).
36. Benjamin I. Page and Robert Y. Shapiro, *The Rational Public: Fifty Years of Trends in Americans' Policy Preferences* (Chicago: University of Chicago Press, 1992).

37. Frank Newport, *Polling Matters: Why Leaders Must Listen to the Wisdom of the People* (New York: Warner Books, 2004).

38. James A. Stimson, *Tides of Consent: How Public Opinion Shapes American Politics* (Cambridge: Cambridge University Press, 2004).

39. Jeffrey M. Jones and Joseph Carroll, "National Satisfaction Level Dips to 25%, One of Lowest Since 1979; Iraq War Remains Top Problem in Americans' Eyes," *The Free Library.* 2007. Gallup Organization.

40. David W. Moore, "Top Ten Gallup Presidential Approval Ratings," Gallup press release, September 24, 2001.

CHAPTER 7

Interest Groups

©J Pat Carter/Getty Images

THEN

Individuals joined voluntary organizations to achieve goals of value to their members and to influence the direction of society and government.

NOW

Interest groups continue to be an important vehicle citizens use to persuade government to act in their interest, but technology has now transformed the tactics these groups rely on.

NEXT

Will digital fund-raising, organizing, and communicating strengthen the clout and efficacy of interest groups?

Will expanding web-based activism change the face of who participates in interest groups?

Will digital group activism have unintended negative consequences?

Organizations that seek to

achieve their goals by influencing government decision making are called interest groups. Also called *special interests,* interest groups differ from political parties in that interest groups do not seek to control the government, as parties do. Interest groups simply want to influence policy making on specific issues, varying from how much the minimum wage is to whether states legalize marijuana. Interest groups are more important in the political process of the United States than anywhere else in the world.[1] Their strong role is due partly to the number of interest groups that attempt to influence U.S. policy.

Interest groups shape the policy process by helping determine which issues policymakers will act on and which options they will consider in addressing a problem.

When we think of interest groups, the typical images that come to mind are of wealthy lobbyists "schmoozing" with easily corrupted politicians. But today, technology has made it possible for organized interests that are not part of the traditional power structure to emerge and exert important influence on policymakers. Increasingly, social media has made it easier to join interest groups, and it has made it easier for interest groups to mobilize supporters, demonstrating that the organized effort of people from all walks of life can influence policy making. Although moneyed interests may dominate politics, interest groups play a crucial role in leveling the political playing field by providing access for organized "average" people.

Learning Objectives

After reading this chapter, students should be able to:

- Explain the value of interest groups as tools of citizen participation, in pluralism, and in elite theory.
- Understand the key functions of interest groups and their downside.
- Understand who joins interest groups and why.
- Discuss the factors that contribute to interest group success.
- Categorize types of interest groups.
- Explain the strategies that interest groups rely on to influence policy making.
- Analyze the role interest group money—particularly in the form of PAC contributions—plays in politics and policy making.

The Value of Interest Groups

The 19th-century French historian and writer Alexis de Tocqueville, author of the influential work *Democracy in America,* dubbed Americans "a nation of joiners" in 1835, and his analysis still rings true today.[2] Indeed, estimates indicate that about 80 percent of all Americans belong to some kind of voluntary group or association, although not every group is an **interest group.**[3] The key role that interest groups would play in politics was foreseen by the founders—James Madison acknowledged the idea that people with similar interests would form and join groups to prompt government action. He believed that the only way to cure "the mischiefs of faction" was by enabling groups to proliferate and compete with one another.[4]

Yet some contemporary scholars argue that Americans today are increasingly staying at home. Political scientist Robert Putnam, author of *Bowling Alone: The Collapse and Revival of American Community,* found a marked decrease in the number of people who belong to interest groups and other types of clubs and organizations. These organizations, Putnam argues, are essential sources of **social capital,** the relationships that improve our lives by giving us social connections with which

interest group
An organization that seeks to achieve goals by influencing government decision making.

social capital
The many ways in which our lives are improved in many ways by social connections.

>Can a conversation over a skim latte create social capital? People may not be joining gardening clubs, but are they really less connected than in the past? Or are their connections just different?

©Mariusz Szczawinski/Alamy Stock Photo

to solve common problems. Putnam demonstrates that social capital improves individual lives in very concrete ways: People with a greater number of social ties live longer, happier, and healthier lives. But social capital also improves communities, and even larger polities, because it stimulates individuals to communicate and interact with their governments. Efficacy increases, because when people are engaged and communicate with government officials, government responds by meeting their needs more effectively. This response in turn creates the feeling among individuals that government listens to people like them. And when government responds, it becomes more likely that those affected will try to influence government decisions again.[5]

One problem with Putnam's work is that it was written almost 20 years ago, while the Internet was blossoming, but while social media had not yet emerged as an important tool for modern social relationships. Thus his work does not analyze the social capital that may be derived from participation in online civic engagement and activism. Critics of Putnam's work have also noted that although the number of people belonging to the kinds of groups he analyzed may be declining, people are engaged in other types of groups and clubs and enjoy various forms of group recreation.[6] For example, it is unlikely that you are a member of a gardening club such as those that Putnam researched. (But if you are, good for you!) Yet it is likely that you belong to an online community such as Instagram or Facebook. Such communities facilitate social relationships and may even provide the opportunity for participants to solve community problems. And although people may be less likely to entertain friends and relatives in their homes today (another activity Putnam measured), they are more likely to socialize with friends and relatives over meals in restaurants. So even if Putnam is correct in his analysis that we are no longer socially engaged the way Americans used to be, we may still be engaged— but through different channels and in different settings.

Political scientist E. E. Schattschneider has written: "Democracy is a competitive political system in which competing leaders and organizations define the alternatives of public policy in such a way that the public can participate in the decision-making process."[7] One of the key types of competitive organizations Schattschneider was describing is interest groups. Schattschneider and other political scientists study and assess the value that interest groups provide in American democracy. This value centrally includes interest groups' usefulness in channeling civic participation—serving as a point of access and a mechanism by which people can connect with their governments. Political scientists also explore interest groups, on the one hand, as valuable avenues by which people can influence the policy process and, on the other hand, as resources for policymakers. In this section, we consider various perspectives on the role of interest groups in a democracy, the diverse value that interest groups confer, and the drawbacks of interest groups.

THEN NOW NEXT

How Group Participation Has Changed in the United States

Then (1960s)	Now
Individuals joined bowling leagues, civic associations, and community service organizations.	People join virtual communities and use social networking sites to keep in touch with others who share their personal and public interests.
Many people entertained and socialized a great deal at home.	People are more likely to visit with friends and relatives in restaurants, cafés, and other public settings, as well as online through "virtual visits," like Facetiming and Snapchatting.
Groups used traditional activities to communicate their interests to policymakers, including letter writing and lobbying.	Groups rely on traditional activities but also increasingly use social media, including Twitter, to communicate with members, to fund-raise, and to lobby policymakers.

WHAT'S NEXT?

> What new media technologies and strategies might shape how interest groups organize and mobilize members in the future?

> Are there *negative* consequences to relying on the Internet as an organizing tool? What obstacles will some Internet-based organizations face in mobilizing their supporters around a given issue?

> In what ways will technology change how policymakers are influenced in the future?

Interest Groups and Civic Participation

Scholars who study civic engagement acknowledge the significant ways in which interest groups channel civic participation. Interest groups afford a way for people to band together to influence government as a *collective force.* Interest groups also seek to involve *individuals* more actively in the political process by encouraging them to vote and to communicate their views one-on-one to their elected officials. In addition, interest groups assist in the engagement of *communities* by providing a forum through which people can come together and form an association. Importantly, too, interest groups offer an alternative means of participation to individuals who are disenchanted with the two-party system, or with the status quo in general. By taking part in interest groups, individuals, acting together, perform important roles in the polity not only by communicating their viewpoints to policymakers but also by providing a medium that other people can use to express their opinions.

Pluralist Theory versus Elite Theory

An interest group can represent a wide variety of interests, as in the case of a community Chamber of Commerce that serves as an umbrella organization for local businesses. Alternatively, an interest group can restrict itself to a narrower focus, as does the Society for the Preservation and Encouragement of Barbershop Quartet Singing. But how one views the role that interest groups play shapes the perception of the representative democracies in which the groups exist. For example, scholars who support **pluralist theory** emphasize how important it is for a democracy to have large numbers of diverse interest groups representing a wide variety of views.[8] Indeed, pluralists view the policy-making process as a crucial competition among diverse groups whose members attempt to influence policy in numerous settings, including agencies in the executive branch of government, Congress, and the courts.[9] Pluralists believe that interest groups are essential players in democracy because they ensure that individual interests are represented in the political arena even if some individuals opt not to participate. Like some of the founders, pluralists argue that individuals' liberties can be protected only through a proliferation of groups representing diverse competing interests, so that no one group dominates.

Pluralists believe, moreover, that interest groups provide a structure for political participation and help ensure that individuals follow the rules in participating in civic society. Following the rules means using positive channels for government action rather than extreme tactics such as assassinations, coups, and other forms of violence. Pluralists also stress that groups' varying assets tend to counterbalance one another. And so although an industry association such as the American Petroleum Institute, an interest group for the oil and natural gas industry, may have a lot of money at its disposal, an environmental group opposing the industry, such as Greenpeace, may have a large membership base from which to launch grass-roots activism.

Proponents of elite theory dispute some claims of pluralist theory. In particular, elite theorists point to the overwhelming presence of elites as political decision makers. According to **elite theory,** a ruling class composed of wealthy, educated individuals wields most of the power in government and also within the top universities, corporations, the military, and media outlets. Elite theorists claim that despite appearances that the political system is accessible to all, elites hold disproportionate power in the United States. They also emphasize that elites commonly use that power to protect their own economic interests, frequently by ensuring the continuation of the status quo. And so, although non-elites represented by interest groups may occasionally win political victories, elites control the direction of major policies. But elite theorists posit that there is mobility into the elite structure; they emphasize that (in contrast to the situation in aristocracies) talented and industrious individuals from non-elite backgrounds can attain elite status in a democracy, often through education. This mobility, they say, gives the political system an even greater façade of accessibility.

Although these theories offer competing explanations for the role and motivation of interest groups in the United States, many political scientists agree that aspects of both theories are true: elites do have disproportionate influence in policy making, but that power is checked by interest groups. Undisputed is that interest groups are an essential feature of American democracy and provide an important medium through which individuals can exercise some control over their government.

pluralist theory
A theory that holds that policy making is a competition among diverse interest groups that ensure the representation of individual interests.

elite theory
A theory that holds that a group of wealthy, educated individuals wields most political power.

Key Functions of Interest Groups

Many Americans join interest groups, and yet interest groups have a generally negative reputation. For example, it has been said of many a politician that he or she is "in the pockets of the special interests." This statement suggests that the politician is not making decisions based on conscience or the public interest but instead has been "bought." This notion is closely linked to the ideas held by elite theorists, who argue that elites' disproportionate share of influence negatively affects the ability of the average person to get the government to do what she or he wants it to. Yet despite the criticisms frequently leveled by politicians, pundits, and the populace about interest groups' efforts to influence government, these groups serve several vital functions in the policy-making process in the United States:

- *Interest groups educate the public about policy issues.* Messages from interest groups abound. For example, thanks to the efforts of organizations such as Mothers Against Drunk Driving (MADD), most people are aware of the dangers of drinking and driving. In educating the public, interest groups often provide a vehicle for civic discourse, so that genuine dialogue about policy problems and potential solutions is part of the national agenda.
- *Interest groups provide average citizens with an avenue of access to activism.* Anyone can join or form an interest group. Although wealthy and well-educated people are most likely to do so, interest groups can speak for all kinds of people on all kinds of issues. Historically in the United States, interest groups have been significant forces for advocates of civil rights for African Americans,[10] as well as for supporters of equal rights for women.[11] Consider, for example, the diverse interests that initially came together as the Women's March in protests targeted at President Trump's 2017 inauguration. These individuals and interest groups have, each year since, continued to march on cities throughout the United States. The organizers seek to "harness the political power of diverse women and their communities to create transformative social change. Women's March is a women-led movement providing intersectional education on a diverse range of issues and creating entry points for new grassroots activists [and] organizers to engage in their local communities through trainings, outreach programs and events."[12]
- *Interest groups mobilize citizens and stimulate them to participate in civic and political affairs.* Some people are "turned off" by politics because they feel that elected officials do not represent their views. In these cases, interest groups, with their typically narrower area of focus, can sometimes fill the void. Interest groups, particularly grassroots organizations that foster community identity among individuals who had previously felt they lacked a voice in government, encourage civic and political participation. Today, groups that advocate for racial equality, immigrant rights, and rights for gays, lesbians, and transgender people all nurture participation among individuals who previously felt excluded from the political process. Moreover, large national interest groups may spawn community involvement by encouraging the formation of local chapters of larger interest groups.
- *Interest groups perform electoral functions.* By endorsing and rating candidates and advertising their positions, interest groups provide voters with cues as to which candidates best represent their views. Interest groups also mobilize campaign volunteers and voters. These activities facilitate informed

civic participation. For example, before the 2018 congressional elections, the Republican-oriented interest group the American Conservative Union rated members of Congress, enabling voters to learn which members are the most conservative; at the same time, Democratically aligned groups, including Democracy for America, used sophisticated get-out-the-vote software to turn Democratic voters out for Democratic candidates.

- *Interest groups provide information and expertise to policymakers.* The private sector often has greater resources than the public sector and can be a source of meaningful data and information for policymakers on pressing social issues. Sometimes, interest group "experts" might include celebrities, who, through their status, not only provide information to legislators but also increase public awareness of their issue. Indeed, some research indicates that when legislators are insulated from the interest group environment, they are less likely to revise policies already on the books.[13]

- *Interest groups can protect the common good.* The federal government is structured so that only one individual (the president) is elected from a national constituency. Interest groups can work to protect the nation's interest as a whole rather than just the needs of a specific constituency. For example, in the months leading up to the Flint, Michigan, water crisis, several interest groups, including the Flint-based Coalition for Clean Water, the American Civil Liberties Union of Michigan, and the Natural Resources Defense Council, petitioned the federal Environmental Protection Agency to investigate Flint's water, as elevated lead levels were found both in the water supply and in blood tests performed on the city's children. They pressured for a declaration of a state of emergency in the city and surrounding county, which allowed the Federal Emergency Management Agency to provide up to $5 million in aid to provide clean water for the city's residents and improve the city's water infrastructure.

- *Interest groups are an integral part of the government's system of checks and balances.* Interest groups often "check" one another's influence with competing interests, and they can similarly check the actions of policymakers. And so, for example, while labor-oriented interest groups advocate for an increase in the federal minimum wage, business groups, including industry associations and the Chamber of Commerce, lobby against such legislation.

The Downside of Interest Groups

Despite the valuable functions of interest groups, certain criticisms of these organizations are valid. Interest groups do contribute to the appearance of (and sometimes the reality of) corruption in the political system. Indeed, there are various criticisms of the "interest group state." Former president Jimmy Carter (1977–1981) bemoaned the influence of special interests, saying that they are "the single greatest threat to the proper functioning of our democratic system," and former president Ronald Reagan charged that interest groups are "placing out of focus our constitutional balance."[14]

political action committee (PAC)

An entity whose specific goal is to raise and spend money to influence the outcome of elections.

Another criticism is that interest groups and their **political action committees (PACs),** entities whose specific goal is to raise and spend money to influence the outcome of elections, have made money a vital force in American politics. (See Chapter 9 for a detailed discussion of PACs.) By contributing large sums of money to political campaigns, interest groups' PACs make campaigns expensive and often lopsided; candidates without well-stuffed campaign war chests have a difficult, if not impossible, task in challenging those who receive large PAC contributions. Money also changes the nature of campaigns, making them less engaging for citizens on a grassroots level and more reliant on the mass media. These concerns have been exacerbated by a 2010 U.S. Supreme Court ruling that enables corporations and labor unions to spend money freely on political ads supporting or targeting candidates for federal office and allows corporations and unions to buy advertisements even in the last days of political campaigns. Critics, say these rule changes are increasing the importance of money in political campaigns and are enabling corporations to exert greater influence over the electoral process.

Interest groups, moreover, are faulted for strengthening the advantages enjoyed by incumbents. Most interest groups want access to policymakers, regardless of these elected officials' party identification. Realizing that the people already in office are likely to be reelected, interest groups use their resources disproportionately to support incumbent candidates. Doing so increases incumbency advantage even further by improving the odds against a challenger.

Finally, although the option to form an interest group is open to any and all activists and would-be activists, elites are more likely to establish and to dominate interest groups than are non-elites. This fact skews the policy process in favor of elites. Interest group activism is much more prominent among the wealthy, the white, the upper middle class, and the educated than among the poor, the non-white, the working class, and the less educated. Although in recent years, Internet-based interest groups have been particularly effective in attracting young people and others not traditionally drawn to such organizations, many of the most effective national interest groups remain dominated by traditional interest group populations.

Who Joins Interest Groups, and Why?

People are not all equally likely to join or form interest groups, and this reality has serious consequences for the ability of interest groups to represent everyone's views. Political scientists agree that income and education tend to be the best predictors of interest group membership. That said, enormous diversity exists in the types of people who choose to join or form interest groups. Even the meaning of "belonging" to these groups varies a great deal. Among both online and traditional interest groups, a small cadre of individuals may be highly active while a large number are passive but counted as members despite their less-active roles. For example, a member of an Internet-based interest group may play a highly active role—communicating with other members regularly, attending rallies and other campus events, and taking concrete actions such as signing an Internet petition and participating in a protest. Others may limit their activity to reading the regular e-mails from the group but may only occasionally participate in events. Or they may be members in name only. And nearly every group has a contingent of "members" who signed up mainly for the free T-shirt, popsocket, or umbrella.

Patterns of Membership

Interest group participation is related to four demographic characteristics: income, social class, education, and race. But these characteristics are increasing related to the types of interest groups individuals participate in. Indeed, while the interest group arena historically had been dominated by white individuals with higher levels of income and education, the increasing prominence of online interest groups (many of which may also rely on off-line strategies) means that, increasingly, young, less-affluent African Americans and Latinos are forming and joining interest groups.

TRADITIONAL INTEREST GROUPS   When we examine patterns of membership of traditional "brick and mortar" interest groups, we see that people with higher incomes are more likely to participate than those with lower incomes. Also, many surveys show that those who identify themselves as upper-middle or middle class are more likely to join these kinds of interest groups than those who self-identify as lower-middle or working class. Similarly, higher education levels are a strong predictor of traditional interest group participation.

Income and Education as Predictors of Membership   Individuals with higher levels of education and income have dominated traditional interest groups for several reasons, and as we shall see, some of these reasons are interconnected. For example, wealthier people have more disposable income to spend on membership dues for organizations. They are also likely to have occupations in which interest group activity is useful (or even required, as in some professional fields such as the law). Doctors and lawyers, for example, are likely to be members of professional associations such as the American Medical Association and the American Bar Association. These organizations give incentives for membership, such as accreditation of qualified professionals, and also attempt to influence government policy on members' behalf. Workers such as teachers and tradespeople are likely to belong to labor unions, while executives in business and industry are likely to be members of industry-specific and general business organizations that advocate on behalf of their members.[15] All these professional associations, labor unions, and business organizations are types of interest groups.

Educational attainment also has a strong influence on whether a person will join an interest group. Individuals with higher education levels are more likely to be informed about issues and more willing to invest the time and energy in joining an interest group that represents their views. They may also be more likely to understand how important interest groups are in shaping public policy.

Interest Group Participation and Social Class   Differentiating the influence of income from that of class can be difficult when examining the impact of social class on the likelihood of joining an interest group. But in general, people who identify themselves as working class are less likely to have been socialized to participate in traditional interest groups, with the important exception of labor unions, which historically have been most likely to organize working-class occupations. As we considered in Chapter 6, an important predictor of political participation (and interest group participation, specifically) is whether a person learns to take part and join from a young age. If your mother participated in your town's historical preservation society, and your father attended meetings of the local Amnesty International chapter, you are likely to view those behaviors as "what people do" and do them yourself. If you come from a working-class family, you are generally less likely to see your parents engage in these participatory behaviors, rendering you similarly less likely to participate. Although scholars trace much of the lack of participation of working-class people to how they are socialized, the overlapping occurrence of working-class status and lower income is also a factor.[16] Working-class people may not be able to afford membership dues or have access to child care that would allow them to attend meetings. Or they may simply lack the leisure time to participate.

MODERN EQUALITY AND RIGHTS MOVEMENTS   Over the past years, several **social movements**—large, often informal groups of individuals or organizations striving for a broad, common goal that is frequently centered on significant change to the social or political order—have emerged in the United States. As discussed in Chapter 5, the women's rights movement and the civil rights movement of the 1960s established a framework for the successful transformation of the social and political order. Today, we see several groups relying on time-tested strategies while also forging new pathways to pressure for change, including the Women's March and the Black Lives Matter movement in recent times. And for decades, activists in the gay rights movement have relied on protest, lobbying, public education, and judicial redress (that is, lawsuits) to win rights for gay and lesbian Americans. The successes seen by the gay rights movement, as well as the increasing prominence of celebrity transgender individuals, has empowered an increasingly active transgender rights movement. In the past several years, immigrant rights groups have also relied on a wide range of tactics to pressure politicians for immigration reform.

These groups, which tend to be loosely organized, have thrived in an era in which the Internet facilitates the organization and mobilization of large numbers of like-minded people. Without a formal membership base and without a hierarchical leadership structure, these groups have resonated particularly with individuals who, typically, are less likely to join traditional interest groups: the young, the poor, African Americans and Latinos, and working-class individuals.

While social movements clearly resonate with many people who agree with the need to change the social and political order in one way or another, in examining online civic participation the evidence suggests that one demographic characteristic remains an important determinant of participation: A recent study surveyed 19- to 23-year-olds and found that those who were college students were more than twice as likely to join a politically motivated interest group as their age-group peers who did not attend college.[17]

social movement
Large, often informal groups of individuals or organizations striving for a broad, common goal, frequently centered on significant change to the social or political order.

Motivations for Joining Interest Groups

Some people may join an interest group for the benefits they can gain. Others may gravitate to a group sponsoring a particular cause. Still others may become members of a group for the simple reason that they want to meet new people. Recognizing that individuals have various motivations for joining, interest groups typically provide a menu of incentives for membership.

SOLIDARY INCENTIVES   Some people join interest groups because they offer **solidary incentives**—the feeling of belonging, companionship, friendship, and the satisfaction derived from socializing with others. Solidary incentives are closely linked to Robert Putnam's idea of social capital: Both solidary incentives and social capital are related to the psychological satisfaction derived from civic participation. For example, your friend might join the Sierra Club because she wants to participate in activities with other people who enjoy hiking or care deeply about wilderness protection. Your uncle might join the National Rifle Association because he likes to compete in shooting contests and wants to get to know others who do the same.

solidary incentive
The motivation to join an interest group based on the companionship and the satisfaction derived from socializing with others that it offers.

PURPOSIVE INCENTIVES   People also join interest groups because of **purposive incentives;** that is, because they believe in the group's cause from an ideological or a moral standpoint. Interest groups pave the way for people to take action with like-minded people. And so you might join People for the Ethical Treatment of Animals (PETA) because you strongly object to animal abuse and want to work with others to prevent cruelty to animals. A friend who is passionately pro-life might join the National Right to Life Committee, whereas your pro-choice cousin might join NARAL Pro-Choice America (formerly the National Abortion Reproductive Rights Action League).

ECONOMIC INCENTIVES   Many people join interest groups because of material or **economic incentives;** that is, they want to support groups that work for policies that will provide them with economic benefits. Sometimes these groups advocate for tangible, concrete items. For example, the National Association of Police Organizations lobbies Congress concerning many appropriations measures that could affect its membership, including bills that would provide or increase funding for Community Oriented Policing Services (COPS) programs, bulletproof vests, and overtime pay for first responders to disasters.

Nearly all corporate and labor interest groups offer economic incentives to their members. They sometimes do so by advocating for policies that support business or labor in general, such as policies focused on the minimum wage, regulations concerning workplace conditions, and laws governing family leave or health coverage.

Other interest groups offer smaller-scale economic benefits to members. Many Americans over age 50 join AARP (formerly the American Association of Retired Persons) because of the discounts members receive on hotels, airfares, and car rentals. Other organizations provide discounts on health insurance, special deals from merchants, or low-interest credit cards. Most people join and remain in interest groups for a combination of reasons, purposive incentive, economic benefits, or even social connections.

How Interest Groups Succeed

Given that interest groups attempt to influence all kinds of policies, why are some interest groups better than others at getting what they want? Political scientists agree on various factors that influence whether an interest group will succeed. These factors include the interest group's *organizational resources,* the tools it has at its disposal to help achieve its goals, and its *organizational environment,* the setting in which it attempts to achieve those goals.

Organizational Resources

The effectiveness of interest groups in influencing government policy often depends on the resources these groups use to sway policymakers.[18] Interest groups rely on two key types of resources: membership, the people who belong to a given group; and financial resources, the money the group can spend to exert influence.

HOW MEMBERSHIP AFFECTS SUCCESS   A large membership enhances an interest group's influence because policymakers are more likely to take note of the group's position. The sheer number of a group's membership is often an important factor in forcing policymakers, the media, and the public to pay attention to an issue. Among the largest U.S. interest groups is the AARP, which boasts a membership of over 38 million people. This vast size gives the organization incredible clout and historically has made policymakers unwilling to take on any issue that would unleash the wrath of AARP's formidable membership. For example, for years many economic analysts have suggested increasing the age at which people become eligible to receive Social Security. They reason that the average life span has risen significantly since the eligibility age was set and that people are working longer because they remain healthier longer. But this potential policy solution has long simmered on the back burner. Indeed, Congress has not tackled the issue of raising the retirement age since 1983, when it phased in a small increase—from 65 to 67—in the age at which an individual could collect full Social Security retirement benefits over 22 years. The reason? Politicians in Congress and the White House have not wanted to incur the disapproval of the AARP's members, who would widely oppose increasing the eligibility age and might respond by voting unsympathetic officials out of office.

But size is not the only important aspect of an interest group's membership. The *cohesion* of a group, or how strongly unified it is, also matters to participants and to policymakers.[19] For example, the Human Rights Campaign (HRC) lobbies for federal legislation to end discrimination on the basis of sexual orientation and provides research to elected officials and policymakers on issues of importance to people who are gay, lesbian, bisexual, transgender, or queer. The HRC has a membership of more than 3 million people, but because the organization limits its advocacy to issues affecting gay, lesbian, bisexual, transgender, and queer people, it is an extremely cohesive association.

Another significant aspect of an interest group's membership is its *intensity*. Intensity is a measure of how strongly members feel about the issues they are targeting. Some organizations may reach an intense crescendo of activism but may find it difficult to sustain that level of intensity. But certain kinds of organizations, including pro-life interest groups such as the National Right to Life Committee, environmental groups such as Greenpeace and the Sierra Club, and animal rights groups such as People for the Ethical Treatment of Animals (PETA), are known for sustaining high levels of intensity. These organizations are more adept at attracting new members and younger members than are older, more entrenched kinds of groups. These newer, youthful members are a significant force behind the persistence and intensity of these groups.

The *demographics* of a group's membership also may increase its success. Members who know policymakers personally and have access to them mean greater influence for the group.[20] Other demographic attributes also matter. Members who are well educated or affluent tend to have more influence. Policymakers perceive these attributes as important because the group's membership is more likely to lobby and to contribute financial resources on behalf of the organization's cause. But today, geographically dispersed members are becoming an increasingly important interest group demographic, as technology enables individuals around the country to have quick input in the policy process.[21] Increasingly, this use of technology in lobbying policymakers means younger citizens are becoming more effective at articulating their concerns to them.

HOW FINANCIAL RESOURCES AFFECT SUCCESS For an interest group, money can buy power.[22] Money fuels the hiring of experienced and effective staff and lobbyists, who communicate directly with policymakers, as well as the undertaking of initiatives that will increase the group's membership. Money also funds the raising of more money.[23] For example, the Business Roundtable represents the

>Intensity is a measure of how strongly members feel about the issues they are targeting. Some organizations, including the National Rifle Association, are known for sustaining high levels of intensity, which helps them pressure policymakers to enact components of their agenda. These organizations are more adept at attracting new members and younger members, including 12-year-old Bailey Chappuis, who attended an NRA Annual Meeting and its exhibits in St. Louis, Missouri.
©Whitney Curtis/Getty Images

interests of 150 chief executive officers of the largest U.S. companies, including American Express, General Electric, IBM, and Verizon. In 2016, it spent over $16 million lobbying the president, Congress, and several cabinet departments for policies that would benefit its member corporations, their shareholders, and their member corporations' 10 million employees.[24] Issues of concern to the Business Roundtable include policies such as Securities and Exchange Commission rules, laws concerning corporate ethics, and immigration reform. Many critics believe that the financial resources of an organization will play an even greater role in determining the group's success in the future because of new campaign finance rules that allow unlimited expenditures by business and labor.

Sometimes interest groups form a political action committee (PAC) to shape the composition of government; that is, they contribute money to the campaigns of favored candidates, particularly incumbents who are likely to be reelected.[25] Interest groups representing the economic concerns of members—business, industry, and union groups—generally tend to have the greatest financial resources for all these activities.[26]

Organizational Environment

The setting in which an interest group attempts to achieve its goals is the *organizational environment*. Key factors in the organizational environment include its leadership and the presence or absence of opposition from other groups.[27]

LEADERSHIP   Strong, charismatic leaders contribute to the influence of an interest group by raising public awareness of the group and its activities, by enhancing its reputation, and by making the organization attractive to new members and

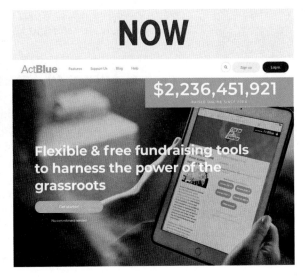

THEN

NOW

ActBlue Features Support Us Blog Help   Sign up Log in

$2,236,451,921
RAISED ONLINE SINCE 2004

Flexible & free fundraising tools to harness the power of the grassroots

Get started

No commitment needed

> In the traditional approach to fundraising, interest groups and candidates met face to face, often with donors attending swanky events, like this one in 1974 at the Helmsley Hotel in New York, attended by former First Lady Jacqueline Kennedy. Today, interest groups, including ActBlue, are more likely to raise money on-line, increasing the role small donors play in politics.

photo: ©Mariette Pathy Allen/Getty Images; ad: Source: actblue.com

contributors. Thomas Donohue became leader of the U.S. Chamber of Commerce in 1997, when he vowed to "build the biggest gorilla in town."[28] Since that time, Donohue, known in D.C. for his straight talk and assertive leadership, has transformed the organization that represents many of the nation's businesses into an enormously powerful force. Today, the U.S. Chamber of Commerce employs more than 170 lobbyists and spends over $100 million annually lobbying policymakers,[29] making it the largest interest group in the nation in terms of its expenditures and financial resources.

OPPOSITION   The presence of opposing interest groups can also have an impact on an interest group's success. When an interest group is "the only game in town" on a particular issue, policymakers are more likely to rely on that group's views. But if groups with opposing views are also attempting to influence policy, getting policymakers to act strongly in any one group's favor is more difficult. Consider this example: Hotel Employees and Restaurant Employees International Union supports increasing the minimum wage, but the National Restaurant Association, which advocates for restaurant owners, opposes a minimum wage hike, arguing that the higher wage would cut into restaurant owners' profits or limit its members' ability to hire as many employees. In the face of such opposing interests, policymakers are often more likely to compromise than to give any one group exactly what it wants.

In addition to opposition, competition influences interest group success.[30] Research indicates that when a group faces an environment in which other groups with similar agendas are forming, competition may damage the older, more established groups, at least initially.[31] One study concluded that if the established groups can withstand the initial challenge, their chances of survival are high.[32]

Although each of these factors—organizational resources and the organizational environment—influences how powerful an interest group will be, no single formula determines an interest group's clout. Sometimes an interest group has powerful advocates in Congress who support its cause. Other times, a single factor can prove essential to an interest group's success.

Types of Interest Groups

A wide variety of political interest groups try to exert influence on virtually every type of policy question, from those concerning birth (such as the minimum hospital stay an insurance company must cover after a woman gives birth) to matters related to death (such as what funeral home practices should be banned by the government). Despite the broad range of issues around which interest groups coalesce, political scientists generally categorize interest groups by what kinds of issues concern them and who benefits from the groups' activities.

Economic Interest Groups

When economic interest groups lobby government, the benefits for their members can be direct or indirect. In some cases, the economic benefits flow directly from the government to the interest group members, as when an agricultural interest group successfully presses for *subsidies,* monies given by the government to the producers of a particular crop or product, often to influence the volume of production of that commodity. In other instances, economic interest groups lobby for or against policies that, though not directly benefiting their members, have an indirect impact on the interest group's membership.

>When President Trump named Alex Michael Azar II to become Secretary of Health and Human Services, the nomination attracted opposition from interest groups, including from the consumer-interest group Public Citizen, which tweeted out its opposition to the former pharmaceutical company executive.
©Tasos Katopodis/Getty Images

CORPORATE AND BUSINESS INTERESTS Large corporate and smaller business interest groups are among the most successful U.S. pressure groups with respect to their influence on government. These groups typically seek policies that benefit a particular company or industry. For example, the Motion Picture Association of America (MPAA) lobbies policymakers (often by hosting prerelease screenings of films and lavish dinner receptions) with the goal of securing the passage of antipiracy laws, which protect the copyrights of their films.

Certain industries' associations are stand-alone organizations, such as the newly formed National Cannabis Industry Association, which encourages marijuana retailers to join the organization this way: "banding together with your fellow business people and entrepreneurs in the only unified, coordinated, and industry-led effort to change federal law increases the power of our new industry."[33] Industry and business groups also commonly advocate for policies using **umbrella organizations,** which are interest groups representing groups of industries or corporations. Examples of umbrella business organizations include the Business Roundtable and the U.S. Chamber of Commerce.

umbrella organizations
Interest groups that represent collective groups of industries or corporations.

Like corporate interest groups, labor interest groups include both national labor unions and umbrella organizations of unions. The AFL-CIO, an umbrella organization made up of more than 50 labor unions, is among the nation's most powerful interest groups, although its influence has waned over the past several decades, as union membership has declined generally. During the 1950s and 1960s, nearly 35 percent of all U.S. workers were union members. By 1983, membership had decreased to about 20 percent, and today about 11 percent of all U.S. workers belong to unions, many of whom are public sector employees, including teachers, police officers, and firefighters. Today, only 7 percent of private sector employees are union members.[34] In part, this decline in private sector union membership stems from changes in the U.S. economy, with many highly unionized manufacturing jobs being replaced by less unionized service sector jobs. Given the drop in union membership, labor interest groups' influence has also waned, although the unions' reduced clout is also due to a lack of cohesion among labor union members.

That lack of cohesion could be seen in the 2018 U.S. Supreme Court case *Janus V. United States,* when Mark Janus, a child support specialist who works for the Illinois Department of Healthcare and Family Services, declined union membership. Under Illinois law, Janus is permitted to decline membership in the American Federation of State, County, and Municipal Employees, which is a **public employee union,** made up of federal, state, and municipal workers. But Janus and others who declined were still required by law to pay an "agency fee," which was to cover expenses associated with negotiating contracts and administering the union, but not for the union's political activities. Janus argued that all public employee spending is linked with the union's political purposes and that he and others who disagree with the union's positions should not have to subsidize its political activities. The Court agreed, saying that as "the compelled subsidization of private speech seriously impinges on First Amendment rights, it cannot be casually allowed," essentially ending compelled union dues for public employees.[35] The impact of the decision will have a widespread effect on the strength of public employee unions, which are among the most unionized workforces, with 35 percent of all governmental employees belonging to a labor union.[36]

public employee unions
Labor organizations comprising federal, state, and municipal workers, including police officers and teachers.

AGRICULTURAL INTERESTS The largest agricultural interest group today is the American Farm Bureau Federation (AFBF), which grew out of the network of county farm bureaus formed in the 1920s. With more than 5 million farming members, the AFBF is one of the most influential interest groups in the United

States, primarily because of its close relations with key agricultural policymakers. It takes stands on a wide variety of issues that have an impact on farmers, including subsidies, budget and tax policies, immigration policies that affect farm workers, energy policies, trade policies, and environmental policies.

In addition to large-scale, general agricultural interest groups such as the AFBF, an industry-specific interest group represents producers for nearly every crop or commodity in the agricultural sector. Think of the growing prevalence of commodities once rare in the American diet. Often, products come into favor through the efforts of interest groups, including those of the American Kale Association and the California Avocado Commission.

TRADE AND PROFESSIONAL INTERESTS   Nearly every professional occupation—doctor, lawyer, engineer, chiropractor, dentist, accountant, and even video game developer—has a trade or professional group that focuses on its interests. These interest groups take stands on a variety of policy matters, many of which indirectly affect their membership.

Public and Ideological Interest Groups

Public interest groups typically are concerned with a broad range of issues that affect the populace at large. These include social issues such as the environmental causes of food safety, clean air and clean water, as well as economic issues such as Social Security reform and revision of the federal tax structure. Examples of public interest groups include National Taxpayers Union, Common Cause, and Sierra Club. Usually, the results of the efforts of a particular public interest group's advocacy cannot be limited to the group's members; rather, these results are **collective goods** (sometimes called *public goods*)—outcomes that are shared by the general public. For example, if an organization like Food and Water Watch succeeds in their goal of getting a law passed that would require food manufacturers to label foods with genetically modified ingredients (GMOs), everyone shares from the benefit of being aware of what ingredients are in the foods they purchase and consume. Specifically, it is impossible to make this information a privilege restricted only to Food and Water Watch members.

The nature of collective goods—the fact that they cannot be limited to those who worked to achieve them—creates a **free rider problem,** the situation whereby someone derives a benefit from the actions of others. You are probably familiar with the free rider problem. Suppose, for example, that you form a study group to prepare for an exam, and four of the five members of the group come to a study session having prepared responses to essay questions. The fifth member shows up but is unprepared. The unprepared group member then copies the others' responses, memorizes them, and does just as well on the exam. The same thing happens to interest groups that advocate for a collective good. The group may work hard to improve the quality of life, but the benefits of its work are enjoyed by many who do not contribute to the effort.

Economist Mancur Olson asserted in his **rational choice theory** that from an economic perspective it is not rational for people to participate in a collective action designed to achieve a collective good when they can secure that good without participating. So, in the study group example, from Olson's perspective, it is not economically rational to spend your time preparing for an exam when you can get the benefits of preparation without the work. Of course, taking this idea to the extreme, one might conclude that if no one advocated for collective

collective goods
Outcomes shared by the general public; also called *public goods.*

free rider problem
The phenomenon of someone deriving benefit from others' actions.

rational choice theory
The idea that from an economic perspective it is not rational for people to participate in collective action when they can secure the collective good without participating.

>Some interest groups rely on confrontational tactics, which serve to attract media attention and sway public opinion. PETA is one interest group known for doing so, like in the protest shown here where PETA members protested the manufacture of high-end outerwear by the company Canada Goose.

©Spencer Platt/Getty Images

goods, they would not exist, and thus free riders could not derive their benefit. In addition, rational choice theory ignores the intangible individuals benefits individuals may receive from collective action, including the solidary incentives discussed earlier in this chapter.

CONSUMER INTERESTS During the 2017 confirmation hearing of Alex Michael Azar II to become President Trump's Secretary of Health and Human Services, the consumer interest group Public Citizen tweeted out its opposition: "Thanks to Big Pharma's stranglehold on Congress, the Senate just installed a former drug company exec with a history of price-spiking lifesaving medicines as the nation's top health official." Public Citizen was founded in 1971 by activist Ralph Nader and other consumer interest groups to promote the rights of consumers. In the 1970s and 1980s, these organizations lobbied primarily—and successfully—for changes in automotive design that would make cars safer. One result was the mandatory installation of harness safety belts in rear seats, which then typically had only lap belts. Today, consumer interest groups advocate for a wide variety of issues, including food safety, fair pricing of pharmaceuticals, commercial airline fliers' rights, an end to predatory lending practices, and more.

ENVIRONMENTAL INTERESTS Many groups that advocate for the protection of the environment and wildlife and for the conservation of natural resources came about as a result of a broader environmental movement in the 1970s. Some environmental groups, such as People for the Ethical Treatment of Animals (PETA) and Greenpeace, use confrontational tactics, such as when PETA members protested the manufacturing tactics of high-end outerwear manufacturer Canada Goose in 2017, trying to compel the company to stop using goose down and coyote fur in its coats (and to dissuade consumers from purchasing the goods). The confrontational protest tactic also has the advantage of attracting media attention, which serves to increase public awareness.[37] Other groups, such as

Environmental Defense Fund, forge partnerships with corporations to research solutions to environmental problems and then persuade the government to provide market incentives for these solutions.

RELIGIOUS INTERESTS   For a long time, organized religions in the United States were essentially uninvolved in politics, partly because they were afraid of losing their tax-exempt status by becoming political entities. But formal religions increasingly have sought to make their voices heard, usually by forming political organizations separate from the actual religious organizations. Today, religious interests are among the most influential interest groups in U.S. politics.

In the early stages of their activism, Christian organizations typically were most politically effective in the Republican presidential nomination process, when the mobilization of their members could alter the outcome in low-turnout primaries. During the 1970s, several conservative Christian organizations, most notably the Moral Majority, became a force in national politics. The Moral Majority helped to elect Ronald Reagan, a Republican, to the presidency in 1980 and was instrumental in shaping the national agenda of the Reagan years, particularly regarding domestic policy. In 1989, another conservative Christian organization, the Christian Coalition, took shape, emphasizing "pro-family" values[38] and becoming a pivotal player in presidential elections. During the 2000 election, the organization was an important supporter of George W. Bush's candidacy for the presidency, and with his election, the group's influence grew considerably. These groups also play a role in Republican primaries.

The Christian Coalition and other religious groups—including Pax Christi USA (the national Catholic peace movement), B'nai B'rith (an interest group dedicated to Jewish interests), and the Council on American-Islamic Relations (CAIR, a Muslim interest group)—also advocate for the faith-based priorities of their members. Many of these organizations have become increasingly active in state and local politics in recent years, by running slates of candidates for local school boards, for example, or by spearheading efforts in state legislatures to pass controversial bills that allow business owners to refuse service to gays and members of other groups.

Foreign Policy Interests

In the United States, interest groups advocate for specific foreign policies and foreign governments, as well as international corporations based abroad, vigorously pressing for U.S. policies beneficial to them. Often a foreign government benefits from the efforts of an interest group made up of U.S. citizens of the foreign nation's heritage. Indeed, one of the more influential interest groups lobbying for foreign concerns is the U.S.-based American Israel Public Affairs Committee (AIPAC), which has 100,000 members. AIPAC lobbies the U.S. government for pro-Israel foreign policies.[39] Sometimes interest groups of expatriates advocate for policies that they feel will improve the conditions in their country of origin. The Cuban American National Foundation, made up largely of Cuban Americans, works to influence Congress to adopt measures that it believes will promote democracy in Cuba, and has been successful in their efforts to convince policymakers to normalize relations with the communist nation.

Although foreign nationals cannot contribute money to political campaigns, foreign entities do lobby the U.S. government—especially for favorable trade policies. One foreign government with increasing political influence on Capitol Hill is China, which has spent millions of dollars trying to influence trade and other U.S. policies to its advantage.[40] It has enjoyed particular success with the 60-member congressional U.S.-China Working Group, which has strengthened diplomatic ties and, in the wake of the imposition of tariffs on China by President Trump, is working to pass the Trade Authority Protection Act, which would allow Congress to review trade actions by presidential administrations. Many members of the working group represent congressional districts that are dependent on China for trade.[41]

Interest Group Strategies

Interest groups use two kinds of strategies to advance their causes. *Direct strategies* involve actual contact between representatives of the interest group and policymakers. *Indirect strategies* use intermediaries to advocate for a cause or generally to attempt to persuade the public, including policymakers, to embrace the group's position.

Direct Strategies to Advance Interests

Groups often opt for direct strategies when they seek to secure passage or defeat of a specific piece of legislation. These strategies include lobbying, entering into litigation to change a law, and providing information or expert testimony to decision makers.

LOBBYING, ISSUE NETWORKS, AND IRON TRIANGLES   Interest groups hire professionals to **lobby,** or to communicate directly with, policymakers on the interest groups' behalf. President Ulysses S. Grant (1869–1877) coined the term *lobbyist* when he walked through the lobby of the Willard Hotel in Washington, D.C., and commented on the presence of "lobbyists" waiting to speak to members of Congress.

lobby
To communicate directly with policymakers on an interest group's behalf.

Today, lobbying is among the most common strategies that interest groups use, and the practice may include scheduled face-to-face meetings, "buttonholing" members of Congress as they walk through the Capitol, telephone calls, and receptions and special events hosted by the interest groups. The professional lobbyists whom interest groups hire are almost always lawyers, and their job is to cultivate ongoing relationships with members of Congress (and their staff) who have influence in a specific policy area. In many situations, lobbyists help navigate access to these policymakers for industry and interest group members.

Interest groups have learned that one of the most effective ways of influencing government is to hire as lobbyists former government officials, including cabinet officials, members of Congress, and congressional staffers. Because these ex-officials often enjoy good relationships with their former colleagues and have an intimate knowledge of the policy-making process, they are particularly effective in influencing government. Frequently, this practice creates an **issue network,** the fluid web of connections among those concerned about a policy and those who create and administer the policy.

issue network
The fluid web of connections among those concerned about a policy and those who create and administer the policy.

Similarly, an interest group's effectiveness often depends on its having close relationships with the policymakers involved in decisions related to the group's causes. During the rough-and-tumble policy-making process, the interaction of mutual interests among a "trio" comprising (1) members of Congress, (2) executive departments and agencies (such as the Department of Agriculture or the Federal Emergency Management Agency), and (3) organized interest groups is

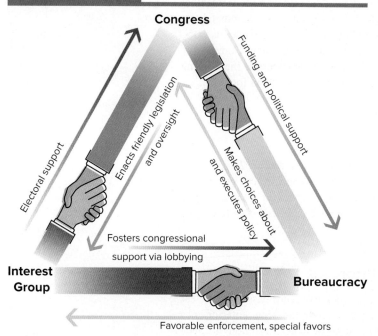

FIGURE 7.1 ■ Iron Triangle Who are the players in an iron triangle? How do interest groups benefit from their iron triangle relationships? Why do you think the triangular relationship has been described as "iron"?

iron triangle
The interaction of mutual interests among members of Congress, executive agencies, and organized interests during policy making.

Citizens United v. Federal Election Commission
Supreme Court ruling that the First Amendment's protection of free speech applies to political advertising and communications of corporations, labor unions, nonprofits, and other organizations.

sometimes referred to as an **iron triangle,** with each of the three players being one side of the triangle (see Figure 7.1).

Although each side in an iron triangle is expected to fight on behalf of its own interests, constituents, or governmental department, the triangle often seeks a policy outcome that benefits all parts of the triangle. Often this outcome occurs because of close personal and professional relationships that develop as a result of the interactions among the sides in an issue-based triangle. (See Chapter 14 for further discussion of the role of iron triangles in policy making.)

LITIGATION BY INTEREST GROUPS   Sometimes interest groups challenge a policy in the courts. For example, the 2010 U.S. Supreme Court case that resulted in a drastically altered political landscape for campaign funding came as the result of a lawsuit filed by an interest group. In ***Citizens United v. Federal Election Commission,*** the interest group Citizens United argued that federal bans on corporate and union expenditures to promote or target candidates for federal office violated the organizations' right to free speech. A 5-4 majority of Supreme Court justices agreed with the interest group and lifted the ban, ruling that the First Amendment's protection of free speech—previously applicable only to individuals—applies to political advertising and the communications of corporations, labor unions, nonprofits, and other organizations.[42]

By litigating, interest groups can ensure that laws passed by legislatures and signed by executives are in keeping with current constitutional interpretation. By bringing their causes before the courts, they also can shape policy and encourage enforcement by executive agencies.

PROVIDING INFORMATION AND EXPERT TESTIMONY   Interest groups are one of the chief sources of information for policymakers. Interest groups have the resources to investigate the impact of policies. They have access to data, technological know-how, and a bevy of experts with extensive knowledge of the issues. Most interest groups provide information to policymakers, and policymakers understand that the information received is slanted toward the group's interest. But if competing interest groups supply information to policymakers, then policymakers can weigh the merits of the various sets of information.

Sometimes interest groups use celebrities as "experts" to testify, knowing that they will attract greater attention than most policy experts—for example, actor George Clooney testified before the U.S. Senate Committee on Foreign Relations concerning findings from his Satellite Sentinel Project, an organization he founded that uses satellites to monitor conflict and human rights abuses in the Sudan.

Indirect Strategies to Advance Interests

Reaching out to persuade the public that their position is right, interest groups rely on citizens as grassroots lobbyists, and they engage in electioneering. These two activities are examples of indirect strategies that interest groups use to pursue their public policy agendas. Indirect tactics are likely to be ongoing rather than targeted at a specific piece of legislation, although that is not always the case.

PUBLIC OUTREACH   Interest groups work hard—and use a variety of strategies—to make the public, government officials, their own members, and potential members aware of issues of concern and to educate people about their positions on the issues. Some interest groups focus solely on educating the public and hope that through their efforts people will be concerned enough to take steps to have a particular policy established or changed. Thus the groups promote civic engagement by informing individuals about important policy concerns, even if the information they provide is skewed toward the group's views. The groups also encourage civic discourse by bringing issues into the public arena. Often they do so by mounting advertising campaigns to alert the public about an issue. Consider, for example, the use of the hashtag #BlackLivesMatter, a phrase that embodied the sentiments of many protesters demanding reforms to the judicial system in the wake of the killing of several African American men by law enforcement officers in various places throughout the nation. On Twitter, Instagram, and social media outlets #BlackLivesMatter became a shorthand rallying cry of a social movement.

Sometimes interest groups and corporations engage in **climate control,** the practice of using public outreach to build favorable public opinion of the organization or company. The logic behind climate control is simple: If a corporation or an organization has the goodwill of the public on its side, enacting its legislative agenda or getting its policy priorities passed will be easier, because government will know of, and may even share, the public's positive opinion of the organization. For example, when Walmart encountered opposition to the construction of its superstores in communities across the country, it relied on public relations techniques, particularly advertising, to convince people that Walmart is a good corporate citizen. As critics complained about Walmart's harmful effects on smaller, local merchants, the firm's ads touted Walmart's positive contributions to its host communities. When opponents publicized the company's low-wage jobs, Walmart countered with ads featuring employees who had started in entry-level positions and risen through the ranks to managerial posts. These ads were viewed both by policymakers (municipal planning board members, for example) and by citizens, whose opinions matter to those policymakers.

Other groups, especially those without a great deal of access to policymakers, may engage in protests and civil disobedience to be heard. Sometimes leaders calculate that media attention to their actions will increase public awareness and spark widespread support for their cause.

ELECTIONEERING   Interest groups often engage in the indirect strategy of **electioneering**—working to influence the election of candidates who support their issues. All the tactics of electioneering are active methods of civic participation. These techniques include endorsing particular candidates or positions and conducting voter-registration and get-out-the-vote drives. Grassroots campaign efforts often put interest groups with large memberships, including labor unions, at an advantage.

Campaign contributions are considered a key element of electioneering. The importance of contributions puts wealthier interest groups, including corporate

climate control
The practice of using public outreach to build favorable public opinion of an organization.

electioneering
Working to influence the election of candidates who support the organization's issues.

EVALUATING INTEREST GROUP STRATEGIES

Interest Group Ratings of Florida Legislators

DISTRICT		PARTY	PLANNED PARENTHOOD ACTION FUND	NATIONAL RIGHT TO LIFE COMMITTEE
Senator	Bill Nelson, Sr.	Democrat	100%	0%
Senator	Marco Rubio	Republican	0	100
Florida - 1	Matt Gaetz	Republican	0	
Florida - 2	Neal Dunn	Republican	0	
Florida - 3	Ted Yoho	Republican	0	100
Florida - 4	John Rutherford	Republican	0	
Florida - 5	Al Lawson, Jr.	Democrat	100	
Florida - 6	Ron DeSantis	Republican	0	100
Florida - 7	Stephanie Murphy	Democrat	100	
Florida - 8	Bill Posey	Republican	0	100
Florida - 9	Darren Soto	Democrat	100	
Florida - 10	Val Demings	Democrat	100	
Florida - 11	Daniel Webster	Republican	0	100
Florida - 12	Gus Bilirakis	Republican	4	100
Florida - 13	Charlie Crist, Jr.	Democrat	100	
Florida - 14	Kathy Castor	Democrat	100	0
Florida - 15	Dennis Ross	Republican	0	100
Florida - 16	Vern Buchanan	Republican	4	100
Florida - 17	Tom Rooney	Republican	0	100
Florida - 18	Brian Mast	Republican	0	
Florida - 19	Francis Rooney	Republican	0	
Florida - 20	Alcee Hastings, Sr.	Democrat	100	0
Florida - 21	Lois Frankel	Democrat	100	0
Florida - 22	Ted Deutch	Democrat	100	0
Florida - 23	Debbie Wasserman Schultz	Democrat	100	0
Florida - 24	Frederica Wilson	Democrat	100	0
Florida - 25	Mario Diaz-Balart	Republican	0	100
Florida - 26	Carlos Curbelo	Republican	16	80
Florida - 27	Ileana Ros-Lehtinen	Republican	3	100

SOURCE: National Rights to Life Committee

Practice Analytical Thinking

1. Why is it important to understand what the interest groups' perspective is when evaluating their ratings? Why does this perspective matter?

2. Describe the relationship between the two groups' ratings of legislators.

3. Explain the relationship between the interest groups' ratings and the legislators' political party affiliation.

The accompanying table shows the ratings of members of Congress from the state of Florida from two interest groups that are concerned with the abortion issue. Interest groups rate legislators and candidates based on their public statements, their voting behavior on key issues (if applicable), and sometimes their responses to interest group surveys about their positions on relevant issues.

According to their ratings sheets, "National Right to Life Committee (NRLC) is the nation's largest pro-life organization, with 50 state affiliates and approximately 3,000 local affiliates nationwide. NRLC works through legislation and education to protect those threatened by abortion, infanticide, euthanasia, and assisted suicide."

"The [Planned Parenthood] Action Fund engages in educational and electoral activity, including legislative advocacy, voter education, and grassroots organizing to promote the Planned Parenthood mission. Planned Parenthood Federation of America, Inc. (PPFA) is the nation's leading provider and advocate of high-quality, affordable health care for women, men, and young people, as well as the nation's largest provider of sex education. With over 650 health centers across the country, Planned Parenthood organizations serve all patients with care and compassion, with respect and without judgment. Through health centers, programs in schools and communities, and online resources, Planned Parenthood is a trusted source of reliable health information that allows people to make informed health decisions."

In general, the National Right to Life Committee is recognized as the nation's leading pro-life interest group, while Planned Parenthood is recognized as a leading pro-choice interest group.

and business groups, at an advantage. Figure 7.2 shows the breakdown of contributions by incumbency status. From this figure, we see that incumbent candidates have a significant edge in raising money from political action committees. The data indicate that most PACs recognize that incumbents—who are most likely to win reelection—are best situated to look after their interests following the election.

The issue of party affiliation also matters to PACs. Business PACs and individuals with business interests make up the largest sources of revenue for political candidates and tend to favor Republicans over Democrats. Labor groups and individuals associated with them give overwhelmingly to Democratic candidates, but they contribute a great deal less money than do business PACs. Ideologically driven PACs and individuals are nearly evenly divided between Democrats and Republicans.

Interest groups also commonly use the tactics of endorsements and ratings to attract support for the candidates whom they favor and to reduce the electoral chances of those whom they do not (see "Analyzing the Sources"). Through endorsements, an interest group formally supports specific candidates and typically notifies its members and the media of that support. An endorsement may also involve financial support from the interest group's PAC. With the technique of rating candidates, the interest group examines candidates' responses to a questionnaire issued by the group. Sometimes a group rates members of Congress on the basis of how they voted on measures important to the group. The ratings of a liberal interest group such as Americans for Democratic Action (ADA) or a conservative interest group such as American Conservative Union (ACU) can serve as an ideological benchmark.

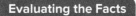

Evaluating the Facts

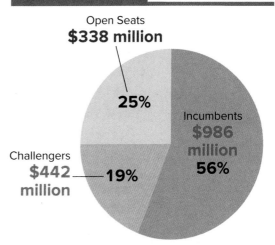

Open Seats
$338 million

25%

Incumbents
$986 million
56%

Challengers
$442 million — **19%**

Contributions to 2018 Congressional Candidates by Political Action Committees

FIGURE 7.2 ■ Incumbents and Challengers 446 incumbents, 1,271 challengers, and 715 candidates for open seats ran for the House or Senate, but incumbents received more than 56 percent of all contributions. What are some of the reasons PACs are more likely to contribute to incumbents? What might be the effect of contributing to challengers?

SOURCE: Center for Responsive Politics, "2016 Election Overview," 2016.

Interest Groups, Politics, and Money: The Influence of Political Action Committees

The influence of money on politics is not a recent phenomenon. Louise Overacker, one of the first political scientists to do research on campaign finance, wrote this in 1932: "Any effective program of control must make it possible to bring into the light the sources and amounts of all funds used in political campaigns, and the way in which those funds are expended."[43] Years later, Congress saw the wisdom of Overacker's analysis and enacted regulations stipulating that a group that contributes to any candidate's campaign must register as a political action committee (PAC). For that reason, most interest groups form PACs as one arm of their organization, although federal law now permits corporations and labor unions to use their financial resources to purchase advertisements for federal campaigns directly.

Whereas an interest group pursues a group's broad goals by engaging in a variety of activities, its PAC raises and spends money to influence the outcome of an election. Typically it will do so by contributing to candidates' campaigns. Funding campaigns helps an interest group in various ways. For one thing, it establishes the interest group as a formal supporter of one or more candidates. And, importantly, campaign contributions are a door opener for an interest group's lobbyists. For a lobbyist, access to policymakers is crucial, and campaign contributions provide a means of contact and help to ensure that a phone call will be returned or an invitation responded to, even if the policymaker does not support the group's position on every issue.

Table 7.1 lists the PACs that contribute the most money to U.S. campaigns and highlights the party their contributions favor. As the table illustrates, labor groups

TABLE 7.1 Top PAC Contributors

PAC NAME	TOTAL AMOUNT	PERCENT TO DEMOCRATS	PERCENT TO REPUBLICANS
National Association of Realtors	$3,973,350	42%	58%
National Beer Wholesalers Association	3,322,700	43	57
AT&T Inc.	2,953,750	38	62
Honeywell International	2,861,364	40	60
National Auto Dealers Association	2,659,250	28	72
Lockheed Martin	2,612,750	38	62
Blue Cross/Blue Shield	2,573,398	36	64
International Brotherhood of Electrical Workers	2,570,650	96	4
American Bankers Association	2,444,007	21	79
Credit Union National Association	2,380,350	47	53

SOURCE: The Center for Responsive Politics, OpenSecrets.org

Thinking Critically

Should Super PACs Enjoy Unlimited Free Speech?

The Issue: Super PACs were enormously important in the 2018 congressional elections, and their presence has been felt in the U.S. political arena since they initially emerged on the political scene in 2012. Super PACs are a special form of political action committee that raise unlimited amounts of money from individuals (or a single individual donor) and then spend unlimited amounts in political races. Unlike traditional PACs, they may not contribute directly to the candidates they are supporting, and they must report their independent expenditures to the Federal Election Commission (FEC). The legal path for the creation of Super PACs was paved in the 2010 D.C. District Court of Appeals decision *SpeechNow.org v. Federal Election Commission*. Some argue that Super PACs represent an important tool of free speech. Others say they constitute merely another avenue for the wealthy to dominate the electoral process. In your view, should Super PACs (and the donors behind them) enjoy unlimited free speech, including unlimited political advertising?

Yes: Some free speech proponents argue that the ruling has increased the amount of information available to voters. Under previous regulations, free speech advocates argue, the contribution limitations to PACs restricted "the individuals' freedom of speech by limiting the amount that an individual can contribute to SpeechNow and thus the amount the organization may spend."* Brad Smith, former chairman of the FEC and founder and chair of the Center for Competitive Politics, argued in favor of the decision: "The rise of independent expenditure groups made possible by the *SpeechNow* ruling has increased the information available to voters and increased the number of competitive races."** Many conservatives also argue that organizations consist of individuals who form associations and that the Constitution protects not only free speech but also freedom of association.

No: Critics of the decision argue that it facilitates unmitigated corporate influence in political campaigns. Giving organizations

protected rights that individuals enjoy, like free speech, detracts from the protection of individual human rights. Some critics argue that enabling these organizations to spend freely to influence campaigns has a detrimental effect on campaigns, which should be a competition of ideas and candidates rather than which candidate has the support of large Super PAC warchests. Others argue against Super PACs because they increase the clout of enormously wealthy individuals who enjoy more than their fair share of influence through their ability to spend unlimited sums.

Other Approaches: In light of the *SpeechNow* ruling, voters need to be increasingly skeptical of claims made by organizations about political candidates. In effect, these Super PACs are only as powerful as average Americans enable them to be, and their influence can be countered through the formation of opposing groups comprising individuals who share a viewpoint. The availability of technology provides a medium for average citizens both to get information and to form groups with like-minded people, thus potentially mitigating the effect of the influence of Super PACs.

*Federal Election Commission, "*SpeechNow.org v. FEC Case Summary*," 2010, www.fec.gov/law/litigation/speechnow.shtml#summary.

**Center for Competitive Politics, "*SpeechNow.org v. FEC*—Protecting Free Speech for the Last 2 Years," 2012.

What do you think?

1. Are you aware of any advertising or information campaigns sponsored by Super PACs in the 2018 election? Do you know who was responsible for funding those ad campaigns?

2. Do you believe that enabling Super PACs to purchase unlimited independent expenditure ads is a protected right?

3. How can average Americans get their opinions about candidates heard? How can they find out whether allegations made by Super PACs are accurate?

tend to support Democrats, whereas many traditional business and corporate PACs favor Republicans. (See "Thinking Critically" for more information on Super PACs.) In addition, PACs, particularly those formed by economic interest groups, overwhelmingly favor incumbents. PACs' powers-that-be know that incumbent candidates are likely to be reelected, and thus the PACs support their reelection bids. As we examine further in Chapter 9, interest groups rely on PACs to channel their support to candidates that espouse their views.

Thinking Critically About What's Next for Interest Groups

Interest groups are powerful vehicles by which individuals can join forces and collectively persuade policymakers to take legislative action on their goals. As such, interest groups play a strong role in the policy-making process. Throughout U.S. history and continuing today, the prevalence of interest groups is testimony to people's desire to influence the pathways of their society and government.

Interest groups have the potential to be one of the great leveling devices in U.S. politics. They are organizations that enable ordinary people to influence policy through collective action and organization. Although not all Americans are equally likely to join and form interest groups, these groups represent an avenue of participation open to all, and with enough variety in tactics and strategies to offer appealing means of civic participation to a broad spectrum of the population. Particularly today, with the Internet providing a highly accessible medium for participation, interest groups give individuals the opportunity to increase their own social capital—to improve their lives and the life of their community by making government more responsive to their needs and concerns and by increasing the effectiveness of the public policy-making process.

Although opinions differ about the role and the value of interest groups in U.S. politics, their influence in policy making is unquestioned. Thus interest groups offer enormous potential for people who wish to become civically engaged. The abundance of groups for virtually every cause (and the ability of anyone to form his or her own group) means that like-minded individuals can work together to ensure that government policy represents their views. How does the number of groups available today differ from decades past? What is the result of that difference in terms of potential members?

Today, through the Internet and other digital technology, interest groups can provide individuals with instantly accessed information and organizational tools. Advances in computing, telephone communications, and television have opened the doors to participation in politics and government in ways that were undreamed of a few decades ago. Thanks to technology, the potential exists for interest groups to reach new and ever-widening audiences. As we have seen, however, the potential audience, at least in the present day, excludes many members of the working class, who may not have been socialized to take part in groups and who may lack the time and means to access computer technology. This lack of access poses a challenge to some interest groups, because they rely ever more heavily on digital recruiting, communicating, organizing, and fund-raising, and likely will continue to depend on these methods in the future.

Learning Summary

1. Explain the value of interest groups.
   a. Explain the value of interest groups as tools of citizen participation, and understand how interest groups are viewed in pluralism and elite theory.
   b. Describe the role interest groups play in a pluralist representative democracy.
   c. Explain elite theory and describe the role of interest groups within that theory.

2. Summarize the key functions of interest groups, and explain their downside.
   a. Describe seven key functions of interest groups, including those related to individuals, the polity, and the policy-making process.
   b. Recall three negative effects of interest groups.

3. Understand who joins interest groups and why.
   a. Explain how income, education, and social class affect interest group participation.
   b. List and explain the categories of incentives that compel people to participate in interest groups.

4. Discuss the various factors that contribute to interest group success. Explain the various components of organizational resources and the organizational environment that contribute to interest group success.

5. Categorize various types of interest groups. Outline the various types of interest groups, and provide examples of each type.

6. Explain the strategies that interest groups rely on to influence policy making.
   a. Recall the types of direct strategies interest groups use to influence policy making.
   b. Define what an "iron triangle" is, and explain who the participants in an iron triangle are.
   c. Summarize the types of indirect strategies that interest groups use to influence policy.

7. Analyze the role that interest group money—particularly in the form of PAC contributions—plays on politics and policy making.
   a. Define what a PAC is, and explain how they influence policy making.
   b. Describe trends of PAC contributions to political candidates.

Key Terms

Citizens United v. Federal Election Commission 246

climate control 247

collective goods 242

economic incentive 236

electioneering 247

elite theory 230

free rider problem 242

interest group 227

iron triangle 246

issue network 245

lobby 245

pluralist theory 230

political action committee (PAC) 232

public employee unions 241

purposive incentive 236

rational choice theory 242

social capital 227

social movement 235

solidary incentive 235

umbrella organizations 241

For Review

1. Explain in detail how the pluralist and elite theories differ in their views of interest groups in U.S. democracy.

2. Why do people join interest groups? Who is most likely to join an interest group? Who is most likely to join a social movement? Why?

3. What kinds of interest groups exist in the United States? Which types are the most influential? Why are they the most influential?

4. What resources help determine how powerful an interest group is?

5. How does electioneering by interest groups help shape policies that these groups favor?

For Critical Thinking and Discussion

1. Were you brought up in a family in which joining groups was important? Do your parents belong to any interest groups? Do you? If not, why do you think that is the case?

2. What interest groups are most prominent today? Are there any social movements that speak on behalf of large swaths of the population?

3. What kinds of interest groups are you and your friends most likely to be involved in (even if you are not)? Why are the issues these groups advocate important to you? How are you most likely to act on the issues that you care about?

4. How has the Internet changed how interest groups operate? What kinds of groups has it made more effective? Has it made any groups less effective?

5. Select a controversial issue such as immigration or gun control, and use the Internet to search for and learn about the interest groups that represent opposing views. What tactics does each group use? Is one strategy more effective than the other?

6. The Supreme Court has ruled that political expenditures constitute a form of free speech. Do you agree? Can you think of any other ways in which "money talks"?

Resources for Research AND Action

Internet Resources

Center for Responsive Politics
www.opensecrets.org This nonpartisan website provides information on the campaign financing of candidates for federal office.

Common Cause
www.commoncause.org This website features a special section on money and politics and provides links to sites related to its endorsed reform measures.

Federal Election Commission
www.fec.org Here you'll find a multitude of information about campaign financing, including regulations, contributions and expenditures, specific candidates, individual donors, political action committees, and political parties.

Recommended Readings

Alexander, Robert M. *Rolling the Dice with State Initiatives: Interest Group Involvement in Ballot Campaigns.* Westport, CT: Praeger, 2001. A probing analysis of the impact of interest groups on gambling initiatives in California and Missouri that, unlike most treatments of interest group activity, focuses on interest group initiatives within states and on lobbying in a nonlegislative arena.

Berry, Jeffrey M., and Clyde M. Wilcox. *The Interest Group Society,* 6th ed. New York: Longman, 2018. Analyzes the proliferation of various types of interest groups in the United States, as well as the strategies interest groups use to sway policymakers.

Cigler, Alan J., and Burnett A. Loomis. *Interest Group Politics,* 9th ed. Washington, DC: CQ Press, 2015. A classic analysis, first published in 1983, detailing the effects of interest groups in modern American politics.

Franz, Michael M. *Choices and Changes: Interest Groups in the Electoral Process.* Philadelphia: Temple University Press, 2008. A comprehensive examination of interest groups' use of electioneering tactics, especially campaign contributions, and how electioneering strategies are shaped by the campaign regulatory environment.

Hays, Richard A. *Who Speaks for the Poor? National Interest Groups and Social Policy.* New York: Routledge, 2001. An examination of how the poor gain political representation in the policy process through the efforts of interest groups.

Herrnson, Paul S., Ronald G. Shaiko, and Clyde J. Wilcox. *The Interest Group Connection: Electioneering, Lobbying, and Policymaking in Washington,* 2nd ed. Washington, DC: CQ Press, 2004. A collection of essays describing the role of interest groups on the federal level. The essays focus on elections, Congress, the president, and the judiciary.

Holyoke, Thomas T. *Interest Groups and Lobbying.* Boulder, CO: Westview Press, 2014. Examines why interest groups form and how they are able to gain influence, as well as why their adversarial nature often makes voters uncomfortable with their role in the political process.

Loomis, Burdett A. (ed.) *Guide to Interest Groups and Lobbying in the United States.* Washington, DC: CQ Press, 2011. Examines how interest groups have grown in scope and size and which tactics they have relied on that have made them an essential part of the U.S. political system.

Miller, Norman. *Environmental Politics: Interest Groups, the Media, and the Making of Policy.* New York: Taylor and Francis, 2017. Miller explores environmental policy making through the prism of interests and interest groups, including the various fronts on which these battles occur: in legislative chambers, in the media, and online.

Wright, John. *Interest Groups and Congress* (Longman Classics Edition). New York: Longman, 2002. A study of the influence of both historical and modern interest groups; it asserts that interest groups' practice of providing specialized information to members of Congress increases their influence there, has an impact on the resultant policy, and shapes opinion.

Movies of Interest

Casino Jack (2010)
Kevin Spacey stars as a K-Street lobbyist (the character was based loosely on Jack Abramoff, a lobbyist who was convicted on multiple federal charges) whose unethical tactics lead to murder.

Thank You for Smoking (2005)
Aaron Eckhart stars as a lobbyist in this satirical comedy about the big tobacco lobby.

Erin Brockovich (2000)
Starring Julia Roberts, this film is based on the true story of Erin Brockovich, an activist fighting for the rights of a community whose water supply has been contaminated.

The Pelican Brief (1993)
Based on the John Grisham novel of the same name, this film, starring Julia Roberts and Denzel Washington, spotlights competition between big business and the environmental movement and illuminates how interested parties can use the courts to make policy.

References

1. Frank R. Baumgartner and Beth L. Leech, *Basic Interests: The Importance of Groups in Politics and in Political Science* (Princeton, NJ: Princeton University Press, 1998).
2. Alexis De Tocqueville, *Democracy in America: The Complete and Unabridged Volumes I and II* (1835–1840; New York: Bantam, 2000), 51.
3. Everett Carll Ladd, *The Ladd Report* (New York: Free Press, 1999).
4. *Federalist no. 10,* Publius (James Madison), 1787.
5. Robert D. Putnam, *Bowling Alone: The Collapse and Revival of American Community* (New York: Touchstone, 2000).
6. Claude S. Fischer, "Bowling Alone: What's the Score?" *Social Networks* 27 (May): 155–167.
7. E. E. Schattschneider, *The Semi-Sovereign People* (New York: Holt, Rinehart, and Winston, 1960), 132.
8. Earl Latham, *The Group Basis of Politics* (Ithaca, NY: Cornell University Press, 1952).
9. David B. Truman, *The Governmental Process* (New York: Knopf, 1951).
10. Hugh Davis Graham, *The Civil Rights Era: Origins and Development of National Policy, 1960–1972* (London: Oxford University Press, 1990).
11. Sidney Verba, Kay Schlozman, and Nancy Burns, *The Private Roots of Public Action: Gender, Equality, and Political Participation* (Cambridge, MA: Harvard University Press, 2001).
12. Silke Adam and Hanspeter Kriesi, "The Network Approach," in Paul A. Sabatier *Theories of the Policy Process* (Boulder, CO: Westview Press, 2007).
13. https://www.womensmarch.com/welcome3/.
14. Quoted in Mark P. Petracca, *The Politics of Interests* (Boulder, CO: Westview, 1992), 347.
15. Julie Greene, *Pure and Simple Politics: The American Federation of Labor and Political Activism, 1881–1917* (New York: Cambridge University Press, 1998).
16. Elizabeth Sanders, *Roots of Reform: Farmers, Workers, and the American State, 1877–1917* (Chicago: University of Chicago Press, 1998).
17. Sharon E. Jarvis, Lisa Montoya, and Emily Mulvoy, *The Civic Participation of Working Youth and College Students: Working Paper 36* (Austin, TX: The Annette Strauss Institute for Civic Participation, and CIRCLE, the Center for Information and Research on Civic Learning and Engagement, 2005).
18. James Q. Wilson, *Political Organizations* (New York: Basic Books, 1973).
19. Jeffrey Berry, *The Interest Group Society,* 3rd ed. (New York: Longman, 1997).
20. Martin J. Smith, *Pressures, Power and Policy: Policy Networks and State Autonomy in Britain and the United States* (Pittsburgh, PA: University of Pittsburgh, 1994).
21. Nina Hall, "Innovations in Activism in the Digital Era," in *The Governance Report 2017,* The Hertie School of Governance (Oxford: Oxford University Press, 2017).
22. Herbert Alexander, *Money in Politics* (Washington, DC: Public Affairs Press, 1972).
23. Frank Sorauf, *Money in American Elections* (New York: Little, Brown, 1988).
24. OpenSecrets.org, www.opensecrets.org/lobby/clientsum.php?id=D000032202.
25. Frank Sorauf, *Inside Campaign Finance: Myths and Realities* (New Haven, CT: Yale University Press, 1992).
26. Gary C. Jacobson, *Money in Congressional Elections* (New Haven, CT: Yale University Press, 1980).
27. Allan J. Cigler and Burdett A. Loomis, *Interest Group Politics* (Washington, DC: CQ Press, 1991).
28. Danny Hakim, "Big Tobacco's Staunch Friend in Washington: U.S. Chamber of Commerce," *The New York Times,* October 9, 2015.
29. Open Secrets, www.opensecrets.org/lobby/clientissues.php?id=D000019798&year=2015.
30. Donald P. Haider-Markel, "Interest Group Survival: Shared Interests versus Competition for Resources," *Journal of Politics* 59 (1997): 903–12.
31. Virginia Gray and David Lowery, "Life in a Niche: Mortality Anxiety Among Organized Interests in the American States, *Political Research Quarterly* 50 (1997): 25–47.
32. Anthony J. Nownes and Daniel Lipinski, "The Population Ecology of Interest Group Death: Gay and Lesbian Rights Interest Groups in the United States, 1945–98," *British Journal of Political Science* 35 (2005): 303–19.
33. https://thecannabisindustry.org/join-now/.
34. U.S. Bureau of Labor Statistics. www.bls.gov/cps/cpslutabs.htm.
35. to come
36. U.S. Bureau of Labor Statistics, "Union Members Summary, January 20, 2016.
37. Lucy G. Barber, *Marching on Washington: The Forging of an American Political Tradition* (Los Angeles: University of California Press, 2002).
38. Christian Coalition of America, "About Us," www.cc.org/about_us.
39. Jeremy M. Sharp, *U.S. Foreign Aid to Israel,* Congressional Research Service, June 10, 2015.
40. John Pomfret, "China's Lobbying Efforts Yield New Influence, Openness on Capitol Hill," *The Washington Post,* January 9, 2010.
41. Ibid.
42. *Citizens United v. Federal Election Commission,* 558 U.S. 310 (2010).
43. Louise Overacker, *Money in Elections* (New York: Macmillan, 1932), 3.

CHAPTER 8
Political Parties

©Jim Watson/AFP/Getty Images

THEN

Political parties relied on patronage and voter loyalty to become powerful entities in American politics.

NOW

The United States seems deeply divided, with rampant partisan rancor.

NEXT

Will the dominance of the Democratic and Republican Parties continue?

Can a viable third party emerge that will satisfy a sizeable bloc of voters?

How will digital technologies further shape parties' strategies and expand their reach—and change the membership of parties?

Political parties have been

essential channels for the realization of American democracy. Political parties serve the American system in many crucial capacities, from recruiting candidates, to conducting elections, to distributing information to voters, to participating in governance. One of their essential functions is to provide an open arena for participation by civic-minded individuals while reaching out to involve those who do not participate.

Because Americans place high value on independent thought and action, some citizens view political parties with suspicion. For such observers, the collective activity of parties brings worries about corruption and control by elite decision makers. In contemporary times, many Americans across the ideological spectrum view the opposing party with hostility, yet both the Democratic and Republican Parties today face serious obstacles in fostering unity within their ranks. Despite these criticisms and challenges, parties remain one of the most accessible forums for citizens' participation in democracy. Indeed, political scientist E. E. Schattschneider, who believed that parties represented the foremost means for citizens to communicate with political decision makers—and in this way to retain control over their government—wrote that "modern democracy is unthinkable save in terms of political parties."[1]

Are Political Parties Today in Crisis?

In the United States today, two major political parties—the Democratic and the Republican Parties—dominate the political landscape. Generally speaking, a **political party** is an organization of ideologically similar people that nominates and elects its members to office in order to run the government and shape public policy. Parties identify potential candidates, nominate them to run for office, campaign for them, organize elections, and govern.

Historically, political parties have performed important functions, discussed later in this chapter. Since the founding of the United States, it has not been uncommon for one political party to dominate the political landscape temporarily, such as when Democrats controlled national politics during the tenure of Franklin D. Roosevelt, or when Republicans did the same during the Reagan years. The popularity of one or the other major political parties ebbs and flows over the decades. However, in recent years, both political parties have struggled to win the approval of the American people, though from Figure 8.1, we can see that Republican party approval has increased dramatically during the Trump presidency. The comparatively low party approval ratings reflect the deep divisions within the United States, where a lack of respect for the other side characterizes many people's views.

A Democratic Party Struggling to Define Itself

The difficulty the Democratic Party faces in terms of defining itself was perhaps best demonstrated in 2016, when Hillary Clinton, the front-runner in her party's

political party
An organization that recruits, nominates, and elects party members to office in order to control the government.

Learning Objectives

After reading this chapter, students should be able to:

- Explain the argument that political parties today are in crisis.
- Describe the functions of political parties today.
- Summarize the three faces of parties—the party in the electorate, the party organization, and the party in government.
- Describe the five party systems identified by political scientists.
- Summarize the arguments advocating that parties are in decline, are resurging, and are in a post-party era.
- Explain why two parties have dominated U.S. politics.
- Outline the nature, electoral record, and influence of third parties in the United States throughout history.
- Describe the effects of new ideologies and new technologies on parties in the contemporary era.

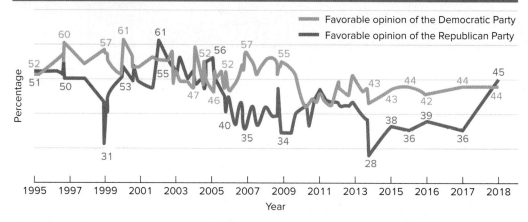

FIGURE 8.1 ■ **The People's Opinion of Democrats and Republicans** The figure shows the percentage of survey respondents who have a favorable view of the Republican and Democratic Parties at selected dates between September 1995 and August 2018. What is the general trend with regard to party favorability ratings? Look at particular high and low points for each political party. What events may have caused people's favorable opinions of the parties to increase or decline?

SOURCE: Gallup, "Party Images," 2018.

presidential primary, faced formidable opposition from the left wing of her party with the candidacy of U.S. Senator Bernie Sanders (I-Vt.), who characterizes himself as a democratic socialist. Clinton was viewed as the moderate standard-bearer, but Sanders managed to attract support within the party, particularly among young Americans, who constituted the core of his constituency. In the 2016 election, dissatisfaction with Clinton—and, as many political observers asserted, with the Democratic Party in general—was apparent when she failed to win the support of many rural white voters without a college degree. Indeed, one study indicated that Clinton managed to win only 78 percent of white voters without a college degree who had voted for President Obama.[2] Other studies indicate that the percentage was even lower in many of the industrial battleground states.[3]

As the 2020 presidential election approaches, Democrats will continue to try to identify ideas, messages, and personalities that will resonate soundly and broadly with party members, including those voters they have lost. Since President Trump has assumed office, they have maintained their approval rating, though it remains below 50 percent, as shown in Figure 8.1.

The Republican Party in the Era of President Trump

As noted from Figure 8.1, we can also see that the Republican Party's favorability ratings have rebounded since President Trump's election. But the Republican Party that President Trump inherited struggled to win the public's approval for more than a decade. After reaching an apex of 61 percent in the immediate aftermath of the September 11, 2001, terrorist attacks, the party's approval rating has hovered between 35 percent and 45 percent. Part of the reason for the trending dissatisfaction with the Republican Party stems from increasing factionalization within party ranks. Republicans struggled with the increasing levels of conservatism espoused by voters, members of Congress, and presidential candidates.

INVESTIGATING PARTY SWITCHERS

In 2017, the Voter Study Group evaluated the behavior of voters who have switched political party preference since 2011. This figure shows the percentage of respondents who have switched parties categorized by their 2011 affiliation (on the left). Their new affiliation is reflected in the bars: red signifies that they switched to become Republicans, blue to Democrats, and green to Independents or "Not Sure."

Practice Analytical Thinking

1. What demographic groups were most likely to have switched affiliation from Democrat to Republican? Which groups were most likely to switch from Republican to Democrat?

2. Who was most likely to become Independents? What does this indicate about how these voters perceive both political parties?

3. Given these data, who do you think each party should target in upcoming elections?

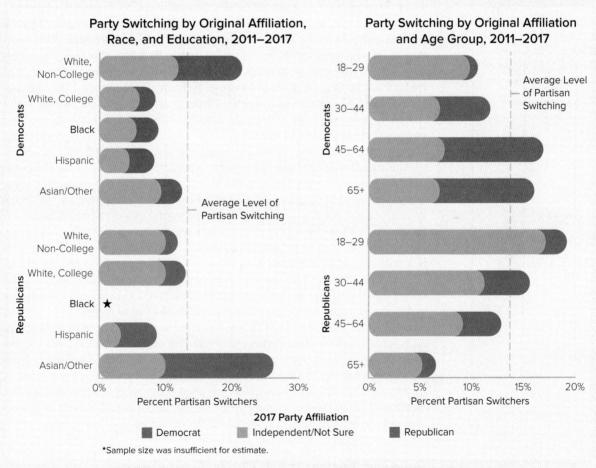

SOURCE: Robert Griffin, "Understanding Voters Who Switched Partisan Affiliation," December, 2017, Voter Study Group.

>**Members of the Democratic National Committee elected Tom Perez as their chairman in 2017. As the leader of the party that does not hold the presidency, his job is to represent the "loyal opposition" to the Republicans.**

©Evan El-Amin/Shutterstock

Tea Party movement

A grassroots, conservative protest movement that opposed recent government actions, including economic stimulus spending and health care reform.

big tent principle

A strategy in which a political party seeks to build a broad coalition among individuals with wide-ranging beliefs, backgrounds, and priorities.

Members of the **Tea Party movement**—a grassroots, conservative protest movement that opposed recent government actions, including economic stimulus spending and health care reform—argue that smaller government should be the main goal of the modern Republican Party. They have flexed considerable muscle to prevent the more moderate members of their political party from compromising.

Before his campaign for the Republican nomination, President Trump had historically backed Democratic candidates and supported liberal causes, but as president, he has successfully worked with members of the Tea Party in Congress. Still, conservatives' increased strength there, particularly in the House of Representatives, prompted the resignation and retirements of several moderate Republicans leading into the 2018 congressional mid-term elections. In some congressional districts held by Republicans, anti-Trump sentiment was enough to spook incumbents and force retirements.[4] In particular, President Trump's use of derogatory rhetoric to disparage various groups—including women, Latinos, and Muslims—was seen as a rejection of the **big tent principle,** a strategy in which a political party seeks to build a broad coalition among individuals with wide-ranging beliefs, backgrounds, and priorities. Iconic Republican campaign strategist Karl Rove supported the concept of the Republican Party as a big tent, and credited this strategy for President George W. Bush's 2004 victory, a win that saw Evangelicals and many deeply religious African American voters supporting Bush's candidacy. Donald Trump's ability in 2016 to forge a new Republican coalition composed of working-class white voters—from union-industrial areas of the Midwest and the rural South—may be the harbinger of a new era in GOP politics.

Although the Republicans have faced significant challenges in satisfying the American people, in general both political parties have witnessed an overall decline in favorabilities over the past two decades. In fact, part of the reason for the overall decline stems from the increasing divide between Democrats and Republicans nationally. This growing schism is particularly evident among members of Congress, who, in general, tend to be more ideologically extreme than in decades past. This is a consequence of the process of congressional elections (discussed in greater detail in Chapter 12), which relies on increasingly sophisticated technology to create congressional districts dominated by one political party. This one-party dominance in districts facilitates the election of more extreme ideological members of Congress, who do not have to appeal to moderate constituents, or those of the opposing party. As political scientists Marc Hetherington and Thomas Rudolph assert, this increasing polarization has meant that in the general population, Democrats and Republicans increasingly do not like each other, and this dislike results in lower levels of trust in government institutions.[5] With increased polarization, disdain, and distrust, members of Congress—and even presidential candidates—have little incentive to moderate their views, behave civilly, work with the other party, or compromise.

Parties Today and Their Functions

Political scientists agree that parties can be distinguished from other political organizations, such as interest groups and political action committees, through four defining characteristics.

First, political parties run candidates under their own label, or affiliation. Most candidates who run for office are identified by their party affiliation. Running a candidate under the party label requires party functions such as recruiting candidates, organizing elections, and campaigning.[6] And political parties typically are the only organizations that regularly run candidates for political office under the party label on a ballot.

Second, unlike interest groups, which hope to have individuals sympathetic to their cause elected but which typically do not want to govern, *political parties seek to govern.* Political parties run candidates hoping that they will win a majority of the seats in a legislature or control the executive branch. Such victories enable the party to enact a broad partisan agenda.

> While historically, political parties excluded various groups, including women, today both political parties actively recruit women voters and candidates. Here, a 2018 session sponsored by EMILY's List trains Democratic women candidates to run for office.
©LM Otero/AP Images

A *third* defining characteristic is that *political parties have broad concerns, focused on many issues.* The major parties in the United States are made up of coalitions of different groups and constituencies who rely on political parties to enact their agendas. That is to say, if we were to look at a party's **platform**—the formal statement of its principles and policy objectives—we would find its stance on all sorts of issues: war, abortion rights, environmental protection, the minimum wage. These positions are one articulation of the interests of that party's coalition constituencies. Typically, interest groups have narrower issue concerns than parties do, and some focus on only a single issue. For example, we know that the National Rifle Association opposes governmental controls on gun ownership, but what is this interest group's position on the minimum wage? On labeling foods with GMOs? Chances are high that the NRA does not have positions on those matters because its concern is with the single issue of gun ownership.

platform
The formal statement of a party's principles and policy objectives.

Finally, political parties are quasi-public organizations that have a special relationship with the government. Some functions of political parties overlap with governmental functions, and some party functions facilitate the creation and perpetuation of government (running elections, for example). The resulting special status subjects political parties to greater scrutiny than private clubs and organizations.

How Parties Engage Individuals

Political scientists who study the nature of Americans' civic engagement recognize that political parties represent one of the main channels through which citizens can make their voices heard. A fixture in the politics of American communities large and small, parties today are accessible to virtually everyone.

Historically, political parties excluded various groups from participating. For example, in many states, women were shut out of party meetings until the mid-20th century.[7] African Americans were formally excluded from voting in

Democratic primaries in the South until the U.S. Supreme Court banned the practice in 1944, though it took decades before the party complied with that decision.[8] But in recent times, political parties have increasingly embraced and championed diversity. Evidence of outreach to diverse constituencies can be seen today. Although President Trump has faced criticism for his rhetoric aimed at diverse constituencies, both the Democrats and Republicans attempt to court women, ethnic and racial minorities, and young voters, providing an important avenue for those traditionally excluded from political life to gain valuable experience as party activists, campaign volunteers, and informed voters. This increasingly diverse participation has also contributed to the parties' health, because it has caused them to recognize that to be successful, candidates must reflect the diverse identities and interests of voters.

What Political Parties Do

grassroots organizing
Tasks that involve direct contact with voters or potential voters.

As we have seen, by promoting political activity, political parties encourage civic engagement and citizen participation and in that way foster democracy. Parties provide a structure for people to participate in **grassroots organizing**—that is, engaging in tasks that involve direct contact with potential voters, including volunteering on and contributing to party-run campaigns, volunteering in party headquarters, and running for office. Today, much of that organizing occurs online, but parties continue to perform this essential function. For example, leading up to the 2018 midterm congressional races, Democratic and Republican activists registered, canvassed, and mobilized voters. Much of their efforts were focused on important competitive elections, particularly in open-seat races, districts where no incumbent was seeking reelection where grassroots organizing efforts were viewed as crucial in determining the outcome of the election in those states.

Political parties also grease the wheels of government and ensure its smooth running. Nearly all legislatures, from town councils to Congress, consist of a majority party, the party to which more than 50 percent of the elected legislators belong, and the minority party, to which fewer than 50 percent of the elected legislators belong. Thus, if five of the nine members of your town council are Republicans and four are Democrats, the Republicans are the majority party and the Democrats are the minority party. The majority party elects the legislature's leaders, makes committee assignments, and holds a majority on those committees.

On the local level, a political party's ability to promote citizen participation varies with its relative influence within the community. Viable political parties—those that effectively contest and win some elections—are more effective at promoting citizen participation than weak political parties. A party that typically is in the minority in a local government—on the town council, in the county legislature—will find it more difficult to attract volunteers, to bring people out to fund-raisers, and to recruit candidates. It follows naturally that parties that are better at attracting public participation are more likely to win elections.

By serving as a training ground for members, political parties also foster effective government. This role of parties is particularly important for groups that traditionally have not been among the power brokers in the government. Historically, African Americans, Latinos, and women have gained valuable knowledge and leadership experience in party organizations—by volunteering on party-run campaigns, assisting with candidate recruitment, or helping with fund-raising endeavors–before running for office.[9] Party credentials established by serving the party in these ways can act as a leveling device that can help make a newcomer's candidacy more viable.

Perhaps most important, political parties promote civic responsibility among elected officials and give voters an important "check" on those elected officials. Undoubtedly, the 2018 congressional midterm elections were partially a mandate on President Trump's tenure, even though his name was not on the ballot. Voters who viewed Trump's tenure favorably were more likely to vote for Republican candidates for Congress, while those who perceived his administration negatively were more likely to support Democratic candidates for the House and Senate. When an elected leader, particularly a chief executive, is the crucial player in enacting an important policy, the existence of political parties enables voters to hold party members responsible even if that particular elected official is not running for reelection. The system thus provides a check on the power of elected officials, because it makes them aware that the policy or position they take may be unpopular, and may have long-lasting repercussions.

Historically, political parties also have fostered cooperation between divided interests and factions, building coalitions even in the most divisive of times, though, as previously discussed, this task is proving increasingly difficult given the growing polarization of political parties. Civic engagement researchers point out that political parties' work in building coalitions and promoting cooperation among diverse groups often occurs away from the bright lights of the media-saturated public arena, where the parties' differences, rather than their common causes, often are in the spotlight.

The Responsible Party Model

Historically, according to one theory, political parties have also made government more effective and have provided important cues for voters. The **responsible party model,** developed by E. E. Schattschneider, posits that a party tries to give voters a clear choice by establishing priorities or policy stances different from those of the rival party or parties. Because a party's elected officials tend to be loyal to their party's stances, voters can readily anticipate how a candidate will vote on a given set of issues if elected and can thus cast their vote according to their preferences on those issues.

The Three Faces of Parties

American political parties perform their various functions through three "faces," or spheres of operation.[10] The three components of the party include the party in the electorate, the party organization, and the party in government (see Figure 8.2).

The Party in the Electorate

All the individuals who identify with or tend to support a particular party make up the **party in the electorate.** Several factors influence which party an individual will identify with, including personal circumstances, demographic characteristics like race and religion, as

responsible party model
Political scientists' view that a function of a party is to offer a clear choice to voters by establishing priorities or policy stances different from those of rival parties.

party in the electorate
Individuals who identify with or tend to support a party.

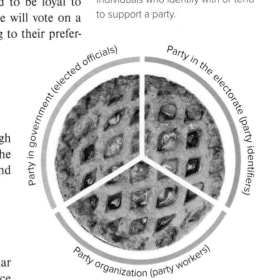

FIGURE 8.2 ■ **The Three Faces of Parties**
©Creativeye99/E+/Getty Images

well as the party's history, ideology, position on issues of importance to the voter, and candidates.[11]

MEASURING THE PARTY IN THE ELECTORATE The term **party identifier** refers to an individual who identifies himself or herself as a member of one party or another; party identifiers typically are measured by party registration. In most states, party registration is a legal process in which a voter formally selects affiliation with one political party. This declaration of affiliation often occurs when a person registers to vote; the prospective voter selects his or her party identification by filling out a voter registration form or party declaration form. Depending on the state, a voter may select the Democratic or the Republican Party, a variety of third parties, or no party. When a voter does not select a party, he or she is technically an unaffiliated voter, but often analysts refer to such a voter as an **independent.**

People's party identification sometimes does not match their actual voting preferences. When we refer to the party in the electorate, we also consider those individuals who express a tendency to vote for one party or a preference for that party.

DETERMINING WHO BELONGS TO EACH POLITICAL PARTY Although we commonly speak in terms of which groups affiliate with and "belong to" each of the political parties, those are just generalizations, with many exceptions. In general, each political party counts specific demographic groups as part of its base of support. A party will often draw party activists and leaders from the ranks of this bloc of individuals who can be counted on for support.

Although whites, men, and people with some college education are naturally found in both parties, they are more likely to be Republicans. For the Democrats, key voting blocs traditionally have included African Americans, women, young people, and people with no college education. In 2016, however, Donald Trump succeeded in attracting the support of many Americans with no college education but struggled to attract the support of more educated voters. Hispanics, a demographic group that is increasing in importance, has traditionally leaned Democratic, though over the years some Hispanics—particularly Cuban Americans and deeply religious Hispanics—were more likely to identify with Republicans, though that was not the case in 2016, when Republican nominee Donald Trump succeeded in alienating many Hispanic voters. Individuals with a college degree or more are divided evenly between the two parties. Social class also plays a role in party preference. The working class is largely Democratic; the upper-middle class is largely Republican; and the middle class, by far the largest class in the United States, is divided between the two parties. But the best predictor of a person's party identification is his or her ideology. People who identify themselves as conservative are much more likely to be Republicans; people who identify themselves as liberal are much more likely to be Democrats. (See the discussion of ideology in Chapter 1.)

DIFFERENCES BETWEEN DEMOCRATS AND REPUBLICANS We can trace to the 1930s some of the differences—in both ideologies and core constituencies—between today's Democrats and Republicans. That was the era of the Great Depression, a time of devastating economic collapse and personal misery for people around the world. President Franklin D. Roosevelt's drive to expand the role of government by providing a safety net for the most vulnerable in society has remained part of

party identifiers
Individuals who identify themselves as a member of one party or the other.

independent
A voter who does not belong to any organized political party; often used as a synonym for an unaffiliated voter.

the Democratic agenda to this day. During the latter half of the 20th century, the Democratic agenda centered on pressing for civil rights for African Americans, equal rights for women, and the expansion of social welfare programs. Evidence of Democrats' continued commitment to a government-provided safety net can be seen in the passage of the Affordable Care Act, which reformed the nation's health care system. Today, key components of the Democratic agenda include immigration reform, particularly passage of a policy that would provide a path to citizenship for so-called dreamers, who are undocumented immigrants who arrived in the United States as children; gay and transgender rights; and freedom of choice with respect to abortion.

Traditionally, Republicans have embraced the idea of smaller government that performs fewer social welfare functions. In modern times, this position is manifested in the Republicans' opposition to the Affordable Care Act. Republicans traditionally have also supported measures that protect business and business owners. For many Republicans today, a key stance is advocacy of a stronger governmental role in regulating traditional moral values. Because of this stance, a solid voting bloc within the Republican Party comprises conservative Christians, sometimes called the Christian Right or the Religious Right, who agree with the Republicans' pro-life position on abortion (which includes support for increased regulation of abortion) and appeals for a constitutional amendment banning gay marriage. Republicans also support measures that protect business and business owners. They generally support a decreased role for the federal government, particularly with respect to the economy and social welfare issues, including staunch opposition to Obamacare, and a corresponding larger role for state governments.

It is not surprising that the base constituencies of the parties are drawn from the groups that each party's platform favors. The base of the Democratic Party prominently includes women, the majority of whom, since 1980, have voted for the Democratic presidential nominee. Since Franklin D. Roosevelt's New Deal social welfare policy during the 1930s, African Americans have been an important voting bloc within the Democratic Party, and this support for the Democratic Party among African Americans was shored up during Obama's presidency. Other ethnic minorities, including Latinos and Asian Americans, also tend to support the Democratic Party (as described in Chapter 6). The base of the Republican Party prominently includes many small-business owners, citizens who identify themselves as being very religious, and upper-middle-class voters, and, under President Trump, increasing numbers of rural voters who have not attended college.[12]

Today, the two political parties have a few similarities. For instance, both parties are perceived as equally adept at keeping the country prosperous. And from Table 8.1, we see that identifiers in both political parties agree on certain policy areas where they want to see the government playing a major role. Among these are managing the immigration system (though we would expect stark differences in how partisans would like to see this done); keeping the country safe from terrorism; and responding to natural disasters.

>Hispanics are an increasingly important demographic group, as both the number of eligible Hispanic voters grows and their participation rates increase. While many Hispanics, including Congresswoman Linda Sanchez (D-CA), are staunchly Democratic, the traditional moral values espoused by the Republican Party often resonate with many religious Latinos.

©Chip Somodevilla/Getty Images

TABLE 8.1 In What Areas Should the Government Play a Major Role? Differences and Similarities Among Democrats and Republicans

	PERCENT WHO SAY GOVERNMENT SHOULD PLAY A MAJOR ROLE		
	REPUBLICAN/LEAN REPUBLICAN	DEMOCRAT/LEAN DEMOCRAT	REPUBLICAN-DEMOCRAT DIFFERENCE
Ensuring access to health care	39%	86%	47
Helping people get out of poverty	44	80	36
Protecting the environment	45	80	35
Ensuring access to quality education	57	89	32
Setting workplace standards	51	75	24
Ensuring basic income for 65+	58	71	13
Strengthening the economy	73	76	3
Maintaining infrastructure	69	76	7
Ensuring safe food and medicine	83	92	9
Responding to natural disasters	86	90	4
Keeping country safe from terrorism	92	98	6
Managing the immigration system	78	86	8

SOURCE: Pew Research Center, "Government Gets Lower Ratings for Handling Health Care, Environment, Disaster Response," Pew Research Center, Washington, DC (November, 2015).

Nonetheless, some differences exist between Democrats and Republicans. Democrats are much more likely to see income inequality as a central problem in the United States, and Republicans are more likely to identify the federal budget deficit as an important issue.[13] And there are sizeable party-based differences in the proportion of Democrats and Republicans who think the government should play a major role in specific policy areas. For example, in Table 8.1 we see that Republicans and Democrats disagree about the issue of ensuring access to health care, with only 39 percent of Republicans and those who lean Republican saying the government should play a major role in ensuring access, while 86 percent of Democrats and Democrat leaners say it should. Another major policy area in which Republicans and Democrats disagree relates to helping people get out of poverty, where 44 percent of Republicans and Republican leaners say the government should play a major role, contrasted with 80 percent of Democrats and Democrat leaners.

The Party Organization

Thomas P. "Tip" O'Neill (D-Mass.), Speaker of the House of Representatives from 1977 until 1987, is often quoted as having said, "All politics is local." In no case is that statement truer than it is for American political parties.

party organization

The formal party apparatus, including committees, party leaders, conventions, and workers.

Party organization refers to the formal party apparatus, including committees, headquarters, conventions, party leaders, staff, and volunteer workers. In the United States, the party organization is most visible at the local level. Yet county and local parties tend to be loosely organized—centered predominantly on elections—and may be dormant after election season passes.[14] Except during presidential elections, state and local political parties typically function quite separately from the national party. Although the number of individuals who actually participate in the party organization is quite small when compared with the party in the electorate, on the local level, political parties offer one of the most accessible means for individuals to participate in politics.

With respect to political power, county and local parties are the most important components of a party organization. Theoretically, political parties' organization resembles a pyramid (see Figure 8.3), with a broad base of support at the bottom and power flowing up to a smaller group at the state level and then to an even smaller, more exclusive group at the national level.[15] In reality, the national committees of both major U.S. political parties exist separately from the committees of the state and local parties (see Figure 8.4), and real political power can usually be found at the local or county party level, as we will see in the following discussion.

NATIONAL PARTIES Every four years, political party activists meet at a national convention to determine their party's nominee for the presidency. At these conventions, the delegates also adopt rules and develop a party platform that describes the party's policy priorities and positions on issues.

The national party committees (the Democratic National Committee, or DNC, and the Republican National Committee, or RNC) are the national party organizations charged with conducting the conventions and overseeing the operation of the national party during the interim between conventions. The national committee elects a national chair, who is often informally selected by the party's presidential nominee. The national chair, along with the paid staff of the national committee, oversees the day-to-day operations of the political party.

The role of the national chair depends to a large extent on whether the party's nominee wins the presidency. If the party's nominee is victorious, the national chair has a less prominent role because the president serves as the most public representative of the party. If the party's nominee loses, however, the national chair may take on a more public persona, serving as the spokesperson for the **loyal opposition**—voicing the out-of-power party's objections to the policies and priorities of the government in power. In recent years, regardless of whether the party's nominee has won or lost, one of the most important roles of the national chair has been to raise funds. Money donated to the national parties is often redirected to the state and local parties, which use it to help contest elections and mobilize voters.

STATE PARTIES Both national parties have committees in each state (the California State Democratic Committee, for example) that effectively *are* the party in that state. State committees act as intermediaries between the national committees and county committees. Typically, state committees are made up of a few members from each county or other geographic subdivision of a given state.

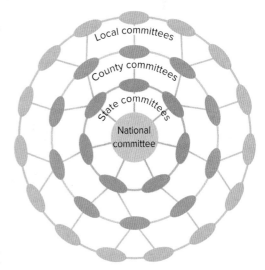

FIGURE 8.3 ■ Theoretical Structure of Political Parties: A Hierarchical Model of Party Organizations

loyal opposition
A role that the party out of power plays, highlighting its objections to policies and priorities of the government in power.

FIGURE 8.4 ■ Modern Structure of Political Parties: Power Diffused Through Many Party Organizations

Historically, state parties were important because of their role in the election of U.S. senators, who until 1913 were elected by their states' legislatures. Since the ratification of the Seventeenth Amendment in that year, the voters of each state have directly elected their senators by popular election.

Later in the 20th century, state political parties began a rebound of power, partly because of the U.S. Supreme Court's decision in *Buckley v. Valeo* (1976). In this case, the Court ruled that political parties are entities with special status because their functions of educating and mobilizing voters and contesting elections help to ensure democracy.[16] This ruling created the so-called **soft money loophole,** through which the political parties could raise unlimited funds for party-building activities such as voter registration drives and get-out-the-vote (GOTV) efforts, although contributions to specific candidates were limited. The Court's decision strengthened the influence of the state parties, which the national parties often relied on to coordinate these efforts. The Bipartisan Campaign Reform Act of 2002 eliminated the soft money loophole, but until that time state parties were strengthened by their ability to channel those contributions to political parties. (See Chapter 9 for further discussion of soft money.)

COUNTY AND LOCAL PARTIES   County committees consist of members of municipal, ward, and precinct party committees. The foot soldiers of the political parties, county committees help recruit candidates for office, raise campaign funds, and mobilize voters. The importance of a given county committee's role depends largely on whether its candidates are elected and whether its party controls the government. Party success tends to promote competition for candidates' slots and for seats on the county committee.

In most major cities, ward committees and precinct committees dominate party politics. Because city council members are often elected to represent a ward, ward committees are a powerful force in city politics, providing the grassroots organization that turns voters out in city elections. Precinct committees (a precinct is usually a subdivision of a ward) also help elect city council members.

Besides fund-raising, county and local political parties still play key roles in shaping both community engagement and individual participation in the political process, as they have done historically. During election season (in most places, from the end of August through the first week in November), county and local parties recruit and rely on volunteers to perform a host of functions, including creating and maintaining electronic databases of supporters' contact information, answering phones in party headquarters, registering voters, coordinating mailings, doing advance work for candidates, compiling lists for GOTV efforts, supervising door-knocking campaigns, and staffing phone banks to remind voters to vote on Election Day.

The Party in Government

When candidates run for local, state, or national office, their party affiliation usually appears next to their names on the ballot. After an elected official takes the oath of office, many people do not think about the official's party affiliation. But in fact, the **party in government**—the partisan identifications of elected leaders in local, county, state, and federal government—significantly influences the organization and running of the government at these various levels.

In most towns, the party identification of the majority of the members of the legislative branch (often called the *city council* or *town council*) determines who

---

soft money loophole
The Supreme Court's interpretation of campaign finance law that enabled political parties to raise unlimited funds for party-building activities such as voter registration drives and get-out-the-vote (GOTV) efforts.

party in government
The partisan identifications of elected leaders in local, county, state, and federal government.

will serve as the head of the legislature (sometimes called the *president of city council*). And in most towns, the president of city council hails from the majority party. In addition, paid professional positions such as city solicitor (the town's lawyer), town planner, and city engineer are often awarded on the basis of the support of the majority of council. Even though the entire council votes on appointments, the minority party members often defer to the majority, since appointments typically are viewed as a privilege of winning a majority. Other appointments might include positions on voluntary boards such as a town planning or zoning board.

On the state level, the party in government plays a similarly prominent role in organizing government work. Typically, state legislatures are organized around political parties, with leadership roles in each legislative chamber being determined by the majority party. Seating assignments and committee assignments are made by the majority party leadership and are based on a legislator's party affiliation. Figure 8.5 illustrates the partisan breakdown of state legislatures. In each state, the party with a majority in the legislature (shown in the figure) also has a majority on the legislature's committees, which decide the outcome of proposed legislation. Parties moreover are important in the executive branch of state government, since state governors typically appoint party loyalists to key positions in their administrations. Depending on the appointment powers of the governor, which vary from state to state, a governor may also appoint party members to plum assignments on state regulatory boards. In states where the governor appoints the judiciary, the governor also frequently selects judicial nominees from his or her own political party.

Parties perform a similar role in the federal government. Presidents draw from party loyalists to fill cabinet and subcabinet appointments and typically appoint federal judges from their own political parties. Congress is organized based on the party affiliation of its members. When representatives or senators refer to a colleague "on the other side of the aisle," they are referring to a member of the other political party, since congressional Democrats and Republicans sit across the aisle from one another. As in state legislatures, the party with the majority in Congress essentially runs the legislative branch. From its ranks comes the congressional leadership, including the Senate majority leader, the Speaker of the House of Representatives, and the House majority leader (see Chapter 11).

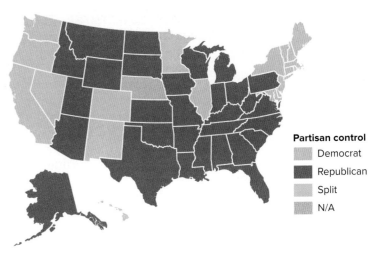

Partisan control
- Democrat
- Republican
- Split
- N/A

FIGURE 8.5 ■ **Partisan Control of State Legislatures, 2018**

SOURCE: https://ballotpedia.org/State_legislative_elections,_2016.

> The party organization includes loyalists on the local, state, and national levels. Here, loyal Texas Republican delegates hold a voice vote on a provision of their state party's platform at a statewide convention.

©LM Otero/AP Images

DIVIDED GOVERNMENT   There are limits to a party's power. Probably the most important check comes from the opposition party, which can openly criticize the party in power and sometimes succeed in obstructing policy initiatives. During some of their years in office, Presidents Barack Obama, Bill Clinton, and George W. Bush faced **divided government,** the situation in which one party controls both houses of Congress and the other party holds the presidency.[17] Because Democrats took control of the House in 2019, President Trump has faced **truncated government,** meaning that one chamber of Congress is controlled by the same party that controls the White House, while the other chamber is controlled by the other party. President Obama faced a similar situation during his tenure. The muscle flexed by Republicans was particularly notable in the fall of 2013, when Republicans shut down the government for 16 days. To strengthen its position, the opposing party has also aggressively investigated alleged misconduct on the part of an elected leader, a common occurrence during the presidencies of both Bill Clinton and George W. Bush.

Political Parties in U.S. History

Modern Americans' divided opinions of political parties would not be surprising to the founders, who viewed political parties with suspicion.[18] Thomas Jefferson said, "If I could not go to heaven but with a party, I would not go there at all." That sentiment was shared by George Washington, who warned of "the baneful effects of the spirit of party."[19] Despite those reservations, political parties began to emerge in the United States during the debate over ratification of the Constitution (with both Washington and Jefferson instrumental in their creation). Those who advocated ratification and a strong central government were called Federalists, and those who opposed ratification and favored states' rights were called Anti-Federalists. Thus began the first party system in the United States. **Party system** refers to the number and competitiveness of political parties in a polity[20]—for example, a government may have a two-party system in which one party is ascending in power. As we will see, the demarcation of party systems typically occurs in hindsight, when social scientists recognize points where there has been **realignment,** a shift in party allegiances or electoral support.[21]

Although these shifting allegiances have played a pivotal role in shaping the context of politics since the country's early days, the founders generally believed that parties threatened the stability of the fledgling democracy.[22] Most thought that political parties enabled individuals and groups to pursue self-serving interests that were often contrary to the common good. Some of the founders argued that parties discouraged independence in thought and action. Some thought that parties exacerbated conflicts and disagreements among the people rather than building consensus. Yet their formation and continued evolution testifies to their important role in achieving political and policy goals for their members.[23]

The First Party System: The Development of Parties, 1789–1828

In 1788, George Washington was elected president, but the consensus surrounding his election proved short-lived. Washington deeply opposed the idea of political parties and ruled during an era without formal parties. But he recognized that despite his popularity, he needed legislators who would push his initiatives through Congress. Washington's secretary of the Treasury and close ally Alexander Hamilton

divided government
The situation that exists when Congress is controlled by one party and the presidency by the other.

truncated government
The situation that exists when one chamber of Congress is controlled by the same party that controls the White House, while the other chamber is controlled by the other party.

party system
The categorization of the number and competitiveness of political parties in a polity.

realignment
A shift in party allegiances or electoral support that propels a political party to majority status.

gathered legislators into a loosely knit party, the Federalists, that favored a strong national government.

Thomas Jefferson, secretary of state during Washington's first term (1789-1793), feared a strong central government, and he and his backers opposed Hamilton's Federalists. But Jefferson's primary concern was that the new government should succeed, and so, despite his opposition, he remained in Washington's cabinet during the president's first term. When Jefferson later resigned his secretarial post, in 1793, many of those who shared his apprehensions about a strong central government remained in Congress.

Although Jefferson lost to Federalist John Adams in the 1796 presidential election, he paved the way for his future electoral success by building a base of support—including partisan groups in the states and newly established political newspapers—that allowed him to get his message out.[24] This direct communication with voters marked a significant step in the civic development of the U.S. electorate. The strategy was effective: Jefferson won election to the presidency in 1800 over Adams, and Adams's defeat marked the end of the Federalist Party. Jefferson was reelected in 1804, and both of his elections demonstrated the important function that political parties would play in elections.[25] His supporters became known as Jeffersonian Republicans; later, Democratic-Republicans. The modern descendants of the Democratic-Republicans today are called Democrats.

The Jeffersonian Republicans' effective campaign tactics of communicating with voters, along with the absence of well-organized opposition, resulted in their continued dominance from 1815 to 1828. Historians call those years the Era of Good Feelings, largely because of the widespread popular support for Democratic-Republican presidents James Madison (1809-1817), James Monroe (1817-1825), and John Quincy Adams (1825-1829).

The Second Party System: The Democrats' Rise to Power, 1828–1860

By 1828, some dissension among the Jeffersonian Republicans was becoming apparent. Members of the party, including the charismatic military general and politician Andrew Jackson (1829-1837) of Tennessee, chafed at the elitism of the party and the era. The Jacksonian Democrats—the name for the new coalition that Jackson formed—emphasized leadership through merit rather than birth.[26] They espoused **populism,** a philosophy supporting the rights and empowerment of the masses, particularly in the area of political participation, and the **spoils system,** in which political supporters were rewarded with jobs (from the phrase "to the victor go the spoils"). The Jacksonian Democrats succeeded in mobilizing the masses, sweeping Jackson to victory in the presidential election of 1828.[27] Political parties had become the medium through which many Americans were politicized, and in 1828, for the first time, more than 1 million Americans cast their ballots in the presidential contest.

Jackson's populism marked a critical step in opening up the civic life of the polity to many new groups of citizens who had not been involved in politics previously.[28] It redefined not only who was eligible to succeed as political leaders but also who should be eligible to participate in the selection of those leaders. Historian Richard P. McCormick noted that the Jacksonian Democrats extended voting rights to all white adult males, changed the mechanism for selecting presidential electors to popular elections by voters instead of by the state legislatures, and increased the importance of the party convention, in effect giving party members

populism
A philosophy supporting the rights and empowerment of the masses as opposed to elites.

spoils system
The practice of rewarding political supporters with jobs.

THEN

NOW

> The American brand of populism espoused by President Andrew Jackson mobilized the masses, and his anti-establishment rhetoric has led to many comparisons with President Trump, who has succeeded in rallying groups of Americans, especially rural, non-college-educated white men, to his side.

Jackson: ©Print Collector/Getty Images; *Trump:* ©Jeff Swensen/Getty Images

more say in candidates' selection. And although women would not gain the right to vote until 1920, the Jacksonian era saw the formal beginnings of the women's suffrage movement with the formation of the two major women's suffrage organizations and the advent of the Seneca Falls Convention (1848) in support of expanded rights for women.[29]

During the 1830s, southern plantation owners and northern industrialists became concerned about the impact the Democrats' populism would have on economic elites.[30] Their mutual interests crystallized in the formation of the Whig Party in 1836, which succeeded in electing William Henry Harrison (1841) as president. Upon Harrison's death, he was succeeded by his vice president and fellow member of the Whig party, John Tyler (1841–1845).[31] But the era of the Second Party System ultimately was defined by the long-standing effects that Jacksonian principles would have on U.S. politics—namely, through the politicization of a previously excluded mass of citizens, many of whom had been initiated into the rites of full citizenship and others of whom had begun the struggle to win recognition of their status as full citizens.[32]

The Third Party System: The Republicans' Rise to Power, 1860–1896

In the 1850s, slavery became the primary concern for both the Whigs and the Democrats.[33] This highly charged issue divided the Whig Party into proslavery and abolitionist factions, and the party consequently faded away.[34] In its place, a new antislavery party, the Republicans (also called the Grand Old Party, or GOP), took shape in 1854 and gained the support of abolitionist Whigs and northern Democrats.[35] The victory of the Republican presidential nominee, Abraham Lincoln, in the election of 1860 marked the beginning of a period of dominance of the antislavery Republicans, which continued even after the Civil War.[36] During this time, the Republican Party enjoyed strong support from newly enfranchised African American voters. Although many African Americans in the South were prevented from exercising their right to vote through threats, intimidation, and tactics such as the white primary (see Chapter 5), African Americans in the North widely voted Republican. They would remain strong supporters of the "party of Lincoln" for decades.

During this time, political parties grew very strong, and political machines came to dominate the political landscape. A **political machine** was both a corrupt and a useful organization that dominated politics around the turn of the 20th century, particularly in cities. Each political machine was headed by a "boss," whose power rested on a system of patronage. A party leader used **patronage** as a device to reward political supporters—rather than individuals who might demonstrate greater merit or particular competence—with jobs or government contracts. In exchange, those receiving patronage would vote for the party and might be expected to volunteer on a campaign or kick back some of their wages to the party.

Although political machines were known for corruption, they did accomplish some good. Richard Croker was political boss of Tammany Hall, New York City's Democratic Party political machine from 1886 until 1902. He explained: "Think of what New York is and what the people of New York are. One half are of foreign birth. . . . They do not speak our language, they do not know our laws. . . . There is no denying the service which Tammany has rendered to the Republic, there is no such organization for taking hold of the untrained, friendless man and converting him into a citizen. Who else would do it if we did not?"[37]

On that score, Croker was right. At the time, political machines provided the vital service of socializing a generation of immigrants to democracy and to the American way of political life. Some machines, including Tammany Hall, generated widespread political participation, and some allowed the participation of women.[38] Political machines helped integrate immigrants into the social, economic, and political fabric of the United States, usually by awarding jobs for loyalty to the party. And in an era when the federal government had not yet become a large-scale provider of social services, urban political machines also provided a safety net for the injured, the elderly, and widows.

> As depicted, after President Abraham Lincoln signed the Emancipation Proclamation in 1863, it meant that for decades after his presidency, African Americans would remain an important Republican party constituency, loyal to "the party of Lincoln."
©Bettmann/Getty Images

political machines
Big-city organizations that exerted control over many aspects of life and lavishly rewarded supporters.

patronage
The system in which a party leader rewarded political supporters with jobs or government contracts in exchange for their support of the party.

The Fourth Party System: Republican Dominance, 1896–1932

The 1896 presidential election between populist Democrat William Jennings Bryan and Republican William McKinley (1897–1901) marked the beginning of a new era in party politics. Bryan appealed widely to Protestants, southerners, midwesterners, and rural dwellers who were suspicious of Catholic, ethnic, working-class immigrants in the urban Northeast. McKinley emphasized economic growth and development and garnered support from industrialists, bankers, and even

THE CURIOUS EFFECT OF CLEAN LINEN UPON THE DEMOCRATIC PARTY

>In this cartoon by the famous 19th-century caricaturist and cartoonist Thomas Nast, what does the tiger represent? What point is the cartoonist making about the "clean linen" the tiger is wearing?

©History Archives/Alamy Stock Photo

working-class factory workers, who saw his backing of business as being good for the economy. McKinley won the election handily, his victory ushering in an era of Republican dominance in presidential politics that would last until the election of 1912.

That year, Theodore Roosevelt (1901–1909), who had succeeded McKinley as president in 1901 after the latter's assassination, and who had been elected president as a Republican in 1904, ran in the presidential election as a Progressive. The Progressive Party advocated widespread governmental reform and sought to limit the power of political bosses. The Republicans' split between William Howard Taft's regular Republicans and Roosevelt's Progressives powered Democrat Woodrow Wilson to the presidency with only 42 percent of the popular vote.

As Wilson's Democratic administration ended up enacting many of the Progressive Party's proposals, the power of the urban political machines declined. For example, recorded voter registration and secret ballot laws were passed, the direct party primary was established, and civil service reform was expanded. The national leaders who spearheaded those measures designed them to take political power out of the bosses' hands and give it to the electorate.

After Wilson's two terms, the Republicans continued to enjoy the support of business elites and the industrial working class. They also benefited from the backing of the many African Americans in the northern cities who continued to support the party of Lincoln, and of women voters, many of whom had been activists in the Progressive movement. With this widespread and diverse support, the Republicans retained control of the presidency throughout the 1920s.

New Deal

Franklin D. Roosevelt's broad social welfare program in which the government would bear the responsibility of providing a safety net to protect the most disadvantaged members of society.

New Deal coalition

The group composed of southern Democrats, northern city dwellers, immigrants, the poor, Catholics, labor union members, blue-collar workers, African Americans, and women who elected Franklin D. Roosevelt to the presidency four times.

The Fifth Party System: Democratic Dominance, 1932–1968

When the stock market crashed in 1929, the economy entered the deep downturn that history remembers as the Great Depression. In the election of 1932, a broad constituency responded to the calls of the Democratic candidate, Franklin D. Roosevelt, for an increased governmental role in promoting the public welfare. Roosevelt pressed tirelessly for a **New Deal** for all Americans, a broad program in which the government would bear the responsibility of providing a safety net to protect the most disadvantaged members of society.

A new alignment among American voters swept "FDR" into presidential office. In fact, the **New Deal coalition**—the name for the voting bloc comprising traditional southern Democrats, northern city dwellers (especially immigrants and the poor), Catholics, unionized and blue-collar workers, African Americans, and women—would elect Roosevelt to the presidency an unprecedented four times.[39]

The era of the Fifth Party System significantly opened up party politics and civic activity to a widening spectrum of Americans. Notably for African Americans and women, Roosevelt's elections marked the first time that they had been actively courted by political parties, and their new political activism—particularly in the form of voting and political party activities—left them feeling they had a voice in their government.

Vice President Harry Truman assumed the presidency on Roosevelt's death in 1945 and was elected in his own right in 1948, but subsequent Democrats were unable to keep Roosevelt's coalition together. Republican Dwight Eisenhower won the White House in 1952 and again in 1956. And although Democrats John F. Kennedy and Lyndon Johnson held the presidency through most of the 1960s, the events of that decade wreaked havoc on the Democratic Party, with deep divisions opening up over the Vietnam War and civil rights for African Americans.[40]

A New Party System?

Donald Trump's election in 2016 raises the question as to whether a new party system is emerging. Until his election, many political scientists expected the trend of Democratic dominance established in the Fifth Party System to continue. But because the recognition of party systems often requires the advantage of hindsight, political scientists are still seeking to determine whether the era that began when Richard Nixon was elected president in 1968 can be considered a separate party system. Republican dominance of the presidency between 1968 and 2008, including the presidencies of presidents Nixon, Ford, Reagan, George H. W. Bush, and George W. Bush, coupled with increasing support of the Republican Party by southern whites and the increasing activism of conservative Christians in the party, gives support to the claim that a new party system has emerged. Also backing this claim is the support President Trump was able to muster from among rural white voters, particularly those who have not attended college and who live in industrial states—including Pennsylvania, Ohio, West Virginia, and southern Michigan, considered to be part of the "Rust Belt."

Additional characteristics of this new party system, according to scholars, include *intense party competition,* in which the two major U.S. political parties have been nearly evenly matched and neither one has dominated; and *divided government,* where a president of one party has to deal with a Congress of the other. This fierce partisan competitiveness is clearly apparent in the outcomes of recent national elections. In particular, the 2000 presidential campaign demonstrated the ferocious rivalry of the two parties, with a presidential election so close that the outcome was in question for weeks after the voting had ended. That year, voters also evenly divided the Senate, electing 50 Democrats and 50 Republicans.

The Party System Today: In Decline, in Resurgence, or a Post-Party Era?

Given the various historical changes to the U.S. political party system that we have examined, many political scientists have inquired into what the impact of those changes will be. Do the changes signify an end to party control in American politics? Or can political parties adapt to the altered environment and find new sources of power?

THEN NOW NEXT

Party Politics in Flux

Then (1889)	Now
Powerful political parties were in their heyday, and party bosses ruled the cities with an iron fist.	The era of party politics in the United States is over, according to some scholars.
The patronage system was in high gear, and political parties derived enormous power and loyalty from the recipients of jobs and lucrative contracts.	A merit-based civil service system has largely replaced patronage, and parties are weakened because of a decline in the number of loyal members.
Elected officials toed the party line, because they depended on the party for their office.	Dissatisfaction with both political parties by most Americans means that elected officials sometimes break with their party and its leaders to attract the public's support.

WHAT'S NEXT?

> How are advancing technologies likely to change political parties and their operations in the future? Will these weaken or strengthen the parties? Explain.

> How do parties today help voters evaluate candidates? Will they still perform this function in the future? Will the nature of this process change? Explain.

> Are there any problems with "independent" elected officials? Will political parties be able to ensure voters that candidates will act consistently with their stated principles in the future?

The Party's Over

Some scholars argue that changes in the political environment have rendered today's political parties essentially impotent to fulfill the functions that parties performed during stronger party systems. In 1982, political scientist Gary Orren wrote: "In a world in which political scientists disagree on almost everything, there is remarkable agreement among the political science profession that the strength of American political parties has declined significantly over the past several decades."[41] Although some political scientists would subsequently challenge Orren's perspective, many still agree with him.

These theorists note several key factors that have contributed to party decline. Some argue that the elimination of political patronage through the requirement of civil service qualifications for government employees has significantly hurt parties' ability to reward loyal followers with government jobs. Patronage jobs still exist, but most government positions are now awarded upon an applicant's successful performance on a civil service exam that is designed to measure qualifications based on objective criteria. Whereas the recipients of patronage jobs were among the most loyal party members in previous decades, party loyalty has decreased as political parties have lost a significant amount of control in the awarding of jobs.

Other political scientists emphasize the government's increased role over time in providing social welfare benefits as a contributor to the decline of political parties. Because of President Franklin D. Roosevelt's New Deal and further expansion of the government's role as the key provider of social services, the parties typically no longer perform that function. Thus, changing times have brought the elimination of another source of party loyalty.

Primary elections—elections in which voters choose the party's candidates who will run in the later general election—also have decreased parties' power by taking the control of nominations from party leaders and handing it to voters. In the past, when a party machine anointed nominees at nominating conventions, those nominees became indebted to the party and typically responded with loyalty if they got elected. But today's candidates are less likely to owe their nomination to the party: Instead, in many cases they have fought for and won the nomination by taking their campaign directly to primary voters. Such was the case in 2016,

primary election
An election in which voters choose the party's candidates who will run in the later general election.

when Donald Trump faced a Republican Party structure that was largely opposed to his nomination. He effectively took his case to primary voters and succeeded in winning the nomination despite efforts to stymie his candidacy by some within the elite of the Republican Party establishment.

Changes in the mass media have also meant a drastically decreased role for political parties. In their heyday, political parties were one of the most important providers of news. Parties published so-called penny papers that reported information to the public. Today, political parties may still provide some information to voters at election time, but most voters rely on other, independent media outlets—including social media, newspapers, television, radio, and Internet news sources—rather than exclusively partisan sources. Take, for example, Donald Trump's bid to win the Republican nomination for president. Trump entered the race with little support from the party establishment, and indeed, many of his supporters were either new to the Republican Party or new to politics in general. Trump used the traditional media wisely, and media outlets, recognizing that the celebrity candidate attracted large ratings, willingly chronicled his every move. But Trump also relied extensively (and infamously) on social media (including the occasional 2 a.m. tweet). Trump's ability to communicate with and mobilize his supporters without relying on the party apparatus demonstrates the ability of candidates to work around the traditional party methods of getting information out to supporters.

The rise in candidate-centered campaigns has also weakened political parties. **Candidate-centered campaigns,** in which an individual seeking election, rather than an entire party slate, is the focus, have come about because of changes in the parties' functions, the advent of direct primaries, trends in the mass media that have shifted the focus to individual office-seekers, and the 2010 U.S. Supreme Court decision *Citizens United v. Federal Election Commission,*[42] which found that the free speech clause of the First Amendment prohibits the government from restricting the amount of money corporations, labor unions, and other organizations can spend on political and election-related communications. This decision paved the way for the explosion of campaign spending by independent groups. Candidate-centered campaigns also must rely more heavily on paid professional campaign workers (instead of party volunteers), making it necessary for contributors to support individual candidates rather than political parties.

These challenges to the ability of political parties to perform their traditional functions, and indeed, the changing nature of the parties themselves, have led some political scientists to conclude that the era of party rule is ending. Other players, they say—including interest groups, candidate-based organizations, and the media—will come to assume the roles traditionally performed by political parties.

candidate-centered campaign
A campaign in which the individual seeking election, rather than an entire party slate, is the focus.

Citizens United v. Federal Election Commission
Landmark 2010 Supreme Court ruling that says the free speech clause of the First Amendment prohibits the government from restricting the amount of money corporations, labor unions, and other organizations can spend on political and election-related communications.

The Party's Just Begun

Pointing to the pervasiveness of political discourse, as well as heightened interest and turnout in several recent presidential primaries and general elections, other political scientists strongly disagree that U.S. parties' prime has passed.[43] While conceding that political parties' functions have changed, these theorists observe that parties have proved themselves remarkably adaptable. When the political environment has changed in the past, political parties have responded by assuming different functions or finding new avenues by which to seed party loyalty. According to this view, the parties' ability to rebound is alive and well.

These scholars also argue that the continued dominance in the United States of two political parties—through decades of threats to their survival—has demonstrated a strength and a resilience that are likely to prevail. Today's Republicans, the party of Lincoln, have endured the assassinations of party leaders, the Great Depression, the four-term presidency of popular Democrat Franklin D. Roosevelt, and the Watergate scandal during the Nixon presidency. Today's Democrats are the same party that opposed suffrage for African Americans in the aftermath of the Civil War, and that survived internal divisions over civil rights through the 1960s, to become strong supporters of African American rights in recent decades. The Democrats too have endured assassinations and scandals and have weathered Republican control of the White House for all but 20 years since 1968. Both political parties have remained remarkably competitive despite the challenges to their success.

Scholars who argue that the two main U.S. political parties are once again rebounding cite the lack of viable alternatives to the two-party system. Yes, third parties garnered increased attention in some recent presidential elections, but the present-day party system has not seen the emergence of a strong, viable third party with a cohesive ideology that has attracted a significant portion of the vote in more than one election. And civic education scholars agree that third parties have served an important function by encouraging the political participation of people who are disenchanted with the current two-party system. They also acknowledge, however, the continued dominance of the two main parties in creating opportunities for civic engagement within communities.

A Post-Party Era?

Whether one views U.S. political parties as in decline or rebounding, the evidence demonstrates that the responsible party model (discussed earlier) is not as strong as it once was. Some scholars argue that, as a nation, we are entering a post-partisan era in which political parties are continually decreasing in their importance in national politics, but retain a role as loose organizing structures in government. These scholars see **dealignment,** the phenomenon in which fewer voters support the two major political parties and instead self-identify as independent, as a notable characteristic of this post-partisan era.[44] Others view the increasing trend toward supporting candidates from both parties (**ticket splitting**) or from other parties as evidence of this phenomenon.

One characteristic that lends credence to the assertion of a post-partisan era is the growing importance of candidate-centered politics. The rise of **candidate committees,** organizations that candidates form to support their individual election as opposed to the party's slate of candidates, is one reflection of how politics has become increasingly candidate centered. Candidate committees compete with political parties in many arenas. They raise and spend money, organize campaigns, and attempt to mobilize voters. One effect of their enhanced influence has been that elected officials, particularly members of Congress, are less indebted to their parties than in previous eras and thus sometimes demonstrate less party loyalty when voting on bills in the legislature.

Whether or not the United States is entering a post-partisan era, we do know that the rise of candidate committees and the increase in ticket splitting mean that parties are less useful to voters as they assess candidates, because the differences between Republican and Democratic candidates may dissipate in the face of constituent opinion. Yet most Americans disagree: A recent Gallup poll indicated that nearly two-thirds of those surveyed believe that there are important differences between the Democratic and the Republican Parties.[45] And the research of some scholars, including David Karol, Hans Noel, John Zaller, and Marty Cohen, indicates that, in most recent election years, party elites, including elected

dealignment

The situation in which fewer voters support the two major political parties, instead identifying themselves as independent, or splitting their ticket between candidates from more than one party.

ticket splitting

The situation in which voters vote for candidates from more than one party.

candidate committees

Organizations that candidates form to support their individual election.

officials and former elected officials, have increased their control in selecting party presidential nominees, suggesting a potential revival of the importance of parties as players in politics today.[46]

Two-Party Domination in U.S. Politics

Since the ratification of the Constitution in 1787, the United States has had a two-party system for all but about 30 years in total. This historical record stands in marked contrast to the experience of the many nations that have third parties.[47] A **third party** is a political party organized as opposition or an alternative to the existing parties in a two-party system. Many countries even have multi-party systems.

The United States' two-party system has had two contradictory influences on people's civic engagement. On the one hand, the dominance of only two strong political parties through most of American history has made it easy for individuals to find avenues for becoming civically engaged. Further, at various historical points, political parties have worked for the outright extension of political rights to groups that were excluded from politics, although often with the foremost aim of bolstering their core supporters. On the other hand—the dominance of just two political parties that tend to be ideologically moderate discourages the political participation of some people, particularly those who hold more extreme ideological positions.

Although the grip of the United States' two-party system is frustrating to people who support a greater diversity of parties, the reasons for the two-party system are numerous and difficult to change.

The Dualist Nature of Most Conflicts

Historically, many issues in the United States have been dualist, or "two-sided." For example, the debate over ratification of the U.S. Constitution found people with two basic opinions. On one side, the Federalists supported ratification of the Constitution, which created a federal government that separated powers among three branches and shared power with state governments. They were opposed by the Anti-Federalists, who campaigned against ratification of the Constitution, supported stronger states' rights, and wanted to see states and individuals enjoy greater protections. This split provided the initial structure for the two-party system, and a multitude of issues followed that format.

Political scientists Seymour Martin Lipset and Stein Rokkan asserted that the dualist nature of voter alignments or cleavages shapes how political parties form. In particular, these alignments or cleavages concern the character of the national fabric (for example, whether religious ideals or secular notions should prevail), and they are determined by function (business versus agrarian interests, for example).[48] These cleavages shaped party formation during the 19th century, when the dualist nature of conflict continued to be in evidence in public affairs. Some states wanted slavery; other states opposed "the peculiar institution" of human bondage. In some states, commercial and industrial interests dominated; in other states, agricultural interests held the reins of power. Immigrants, often Catholics, controlled the politics of some states, whereas native-born Protestants held sway in others.

By the 20th century, the dualist conflict had become more ideological. Some Americans agreed with President Franklin D. Roosevelt's plan to help lift the country out of the Great Depression by significantly increasing the role of government in people's everyday lives. Others opposed this unprecedented expansion of the federal government's power. In later decades, debates over civil rights and women's rights demonstrated the continued dualist nature of conflict in American society and culture, a point underscored in later debate centering on gay rights. During President Obama's tenure, an ideologically centered dualist debate concerned the Patient Protection and Affordable Care Act of 2010, or Obamacare, with many conservatives arguing that the federal government was overstepping its function in mandating and providing mechanisms for health care coverage, while many liberals assert that it is the federal government's responsibility to ensure what they claim is a basic right. Today, the national debate on immigration reform continues to provide evidence of the dualist nature of much of American political discourse, with conservatives taking a hard-line approach to enforcing current immigration laws, while liberals advocate for reform that allows a path to citizenship for undocumented immigrants living in the United States and for allowing more legal immigration.

The Winner-Take-All Electoral System

In almost all U.S. elections, the person with the most votes wins. If a competitor gets just one vote fewer than the victor, he or she wins nothing. If a third party garners a significant proportion of the vote in congressional elections nationwide but does not win the most votes in any given district, the party will not win any seats in Congress.

winner-take-all system
An electoral system in which the candidate who receives the most votes wins that office, even if that total is not a majority.

proportional representation system
An electoral structure in which political parties win the number of parliamentary seats equal to the percentage of the vote the party receives.

Compare the **winner-take-all system** with the proportional representation system found in many nations. In a **proportional representation system,** political parties win the number of parliamentary seats equal to the percentage of the vote each party receives. So, for example, if the Green Party were to capture 9 percent of the vote in a country's election, it would get nine seats in a 100-member parliament. In a proportional representation system, the 19 percent of the vote that Reform Party candidate Ross Perot won in the 1992 U.S. presidential election would have given the Reform Party about 85 seats in the House of Representatives!

In nations with proportional representation, third parties (which we consider in more detail later in the chapter) are encouraged, because such parties can win a few seats in the legislature and use them to further their cause and broaden their support.[49] In addition, in proportional representation systems, third parties sometimes form a *coalition,* or working union, with a larger party so that the two together can control a majority of a legislature. And so, for example, the Green Party that won nine seats in Parliament in the preceding example might form a coalition with another party that had received 42 percent of the vote, together forming a majority government. In this way, a third party can get members appointed to key positions as a reward for forming the coalition. Consequently, societies with proportional representation systems can sometimes be more inclusive of differing points of view, because even those winning a small proportion of the vote achieve representation, and that representation can be pivotal in the formation of coalitions.

Continued Socialization to the Two-Party System

Another reason the two-party system dominates in the United States is that party identification—like ideology, values, and religious beliefs—is an attribute that often passes down from one generation to the next. Hence, many an individual is likely to be a Democrat or a Republican because his or her parents were one or the other. Many people first learn about government and politics at home. Around the dinner table, a child may have heard her parents rail against Donald Trump's incendiary rhetoric or complain about the numerous scandals surrounding Hillary Clinton. Having become socialized to their household's political culture, children are likely to mimic their parents' views.

Even children who do not share their parents' political outlook or who grow apart from it over time (as commonly occurs during the college years) have been socialized to the legitimacy of the two-party system—unless, of course, their parents routinely criticized both Democrats and Republicans or voiced dissatisfaction with the two-party system.

Election Laws That Favor the Two-Party System

At both the federal and the state levels in the United States, election laws benefit the two major parties because they are usually written by members of one of those parties. Although some local governments mandate nonpartisan elections, in most cities and towns, getting on the ballot typically means simply winning the party's nomination and collecting a state-specified number of signatures of registered party members on a nominating petition. Usually, the party organization circulates this petition for a candidate. Third parties have a much steeper climb to get their candidates in office—sometimes, just getting a candidate's name on the ballot is a serious challenge. For example, 2016 Green Party presidential candidate Jill Stein, who succeeded in attracting the support of many of Bernie Sanders's supporters when Sanders dropped out of the race, only succeeded in getting on the ballot in 45 states. Scholars of civic engagement point to the structural impediments to the formation of third parties as key to the low level of civic engagement on the part of individuals who are dissatisfied with the two-party system. Facing seemingly insurmountable structural obstacles to the formation of successful third parties, some Americans shy away from political engagement.

Third Parties in the United States

As we have seen, the absence of viable U.S. political parties beyond the Democrats and the Republicans is a source of frustration for some Americans, and many Americans feel that the Democratic and Republican political parties do not do an adequate job of representing the American people. At different times, the proportions of conservatives, liberals, and moderates vary in their likelihood of agreeing that a third party is needed. According to pollsters, this difference may reflect the respondents' opinions of the effectiveness of their party at representing their views. For example, at high points in Barack Obama's presidency, liberals would have been less likely to say a third party was needed, and the same would hold true for conservatives during the George W. Bush presidency.

One of the most significant obstacles to the formation of a viable third party is that people who are dissatisfied with the two dominant parties fall across the ideological spectrum. In general, about 60 percent of Americans say they think a third party is needed, but these individuals differ as to what that party should stand for. Indeed, the group most likely to support the creation of a third party

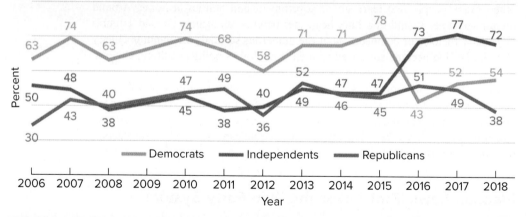

FIGURE 8.6 ■ Support for a Third Party by Party Identification This graph presents responses to the following question: "In your view, do the Republican and Democratic parties do an adequate job of representing the American people, or do they do such a poor job that a third major party is needed?" In general, what has been the recent trend regarding Republican and Democratic support for a third party? Why do you think this is the case? Why would Independents be more likely to support a third party? In your view, given these data, is there ample support to sustain a third party?

SOURCE: Gallup, "Majority in U.S. Need for Third Party," 2018.

is independents. As shown in Figure 8.6, in recent years, nearly four out of five independents see the need for a third party, while fewer than half of individuals who identify as Democrats or Republicans do. Thus, although many Americans are dissatisfied with the current parties, a third party would have difficulty attracting enough support from among these diversely dissatisfied party members.

Because of the differing ideological viewpoints of those who agree a third party is needed, third parties have had little success in contesting elections. Ralph Nader was an influential candidate in 2000, not because he netted a sizeable proportion of votes but because the 3 percent that he did win was enough to change the outcome of that razor-close election. Other third-party candidacies have proved influential because of their role in focusing attention—particularly the attention of the victorious candidate—on an issue that might not otherwise have been addressed.[50] Such was the case in 1912 when Progressive Party candidate Theodore Roosevelt ran against Woodrow Wilson. Although he lost the election, Roosevelt succeeded in shaping public opinion so that Wilson felt compelled to enact part of the Progressives' national agenda, including sweeping changes to the nation's child labor laws.

Nonetheless, third parties have played, and continue to play, an influential role in American electoral politics. Indeed, occasionally even the threat of forming a third party is enough to send tremors through the dominant parties, as was the case in the months leading up to the 2016 presidential election, when Republicans feared that Donald Trump, who was running in the Republican presidential primaries, would run as an Independent in the general election. During early primary campaigning, Republicans believed that an Independent Trump candidacy would mean that he would siphon votes from the Republican nominee, leading to a victory by the Democrat, a scenario that in fact had unfolded in 1992. The chairman of the Republican National Committee, Reince Priebus, convinced Trump to sign a "loyalty pledge" stating that Trump would support whoever the party's nominee

Are Third Parties Bad for the United States?

The Issue: The United States' political culture and electoral structure predispose the country to a two-party system. Historically, two parties have dominated, and when third parties have emerged, they have either been subsumed by the dominant parties or simply disappeared when their primary issue of concern was no longer relevant.

The question of whether third parties are bad or good for American democracy dates back almost as far as the democracy itself. But the question has modern implications. In the 2016 campaign, two third-party candidates, the Libertarian Party's Gary Johnson and the Green Party's Jill Stein attracted the attention and support of many voters who were not satisfied with the major parties' nominees. The fear among many Democrats was that Stein would draw from potential supporters of Hillary Clinton; Republicans were wary that Johnson would siphon off votes from Donald Trump. Many pundits argued that third-party candidates have played the role of spoiler during the 2010, 2012, and 2014 congressional elections, when Tea Party candidates challenged Democrats and Republicans for seats in the U.S. House of Representatives and the U.S. Senate. In some races, critics charged that conservative Tea Party candidates who had won primaries against mainstream candidates were weaker general election candidates, and paved the way for some Democratic victories. In other races, Tea Party candidates who ran as independents may have siphoned votes from Republicans, resulting in a stronger Democratic showing. Similar arguments were made in 1992, when pundits charged Reform Party candidate H. Ross Perot with taking votes away from Republican George H. W. Bush and thus ushering Democrat Bill Clinton into the White House.

Do third-party candidacies hurt American democracy by skewing elections away from the third party's major party rival? Or are they good for democracy because they bring out voters who otherwise would have stayed at home and because they help ensure that issues of crucial concern to the electorate get on the national agenda?

Yes: The presence of third-party candidates on a ballot means that the major political party—Democratic or Republican—that is closest to the third party in ideology and in base of support will be hurt. This effect occurs because if the third-party candidate were not on the ballot, many of his or her supporters would vote for the candidate (Democratic or Republican) who is ideologically closest to the third-party candidate. Thus, that major party candidate is at a disadvantage, because the third-party candidate essentially siphons off or splits the vote for the major party candidate. Democracy is subverted, because often a candidate wins who is least appealing to the majority of voters (that is, those who voted for the losing major party candidate and those who voted for the third-party candidate). As a result, people are highly dissatisfied with both the political process and elected officials.

No: Only through third parties and third-party candidacies can voters get the national agenda they desire. Tea Party candidates have successfully framed the national political agenda, and their prioritization of their key values—including a limited role of government—has attracted many voters who previously had been apathetic to the two-party system. Without third parties to spearhead such conversations of democracy, many more people will be turned off by and disaffected from the political process.

Other Approaches: Third parties are a mixed blessing for the United States. Proponents of third parties are correct in asserting that they provide a safety valve for participation by those dissatisfied with the status quo. Third parties have been effective at getting specific policy concerns on the national agenda, even though frequently that has occurred because one of the major parties co-opts a third party's key issue. But supporters of third parties should realize that the electoral politics in the United States is structured to ensure the perpetuation of the two-party system and that, by supporting a third-party candidate, they run the risk of spoiling the chances of their preferred major party candidate.

What do you think?

1. Do you think third parties help or hurt American democracy? Why?

2. What kind of third party do you think would be successful in winning elections?

3. Are you satisfied with how the Democratic and Republican Parties are performing their jobs? How might an individual's perspective on the current state of political parties affect their evaluation of whether third parties are bad for the United States?

was. Trump created a loophole to the pledge, saying he would abide by it "only if Republicans treated him fairly." In the end, the loyalty pledge was moot, as Trump himself went on to become the Republican Party nominee.

Types of Third Parties

Third parties have existed in the United States since the early 19th century. Over the nation's history, third parties typically have fallen into one of three general categories: issue advocacy parties, ideologically oriented parties, and splinter parties.

ISSUE ADVOCACY PARTIES   Formed to promote a stance on a particular issue, many issue advocacy parties are short-lived. Once the issue is dealt with or fades from popular concern, the mobilizing force behind the party disintegrates. An example is today's United States Marijuana Party, which advocates the legalization of marijuana as well as libertarian views on most issues. The difficulty faced by such parties are exemplified by the struggle of the Green Party, which promotes environmental protection as a primary issue, to become a mainstream party: In the 2000 presidential election, the Green Party sought to win 5 percent of the vote in order to automatically qualify for federal matching funds in the 2004 campaign. It fell short, however, capturing only 3 percent of the vote, and then faded from the national electoral arena.

IDEOLOGICALLY ORIENTED PARTIES   The agenda of an ideologically oriented party is typically broader than that of an issue-oriented party. Ideologically oriented parties are structured around an *ideology*—a highly organized and coherent framework concerning the nature and role of government in society (see Chapter 6). Such parties have broad views about many different aspects of government. For example, the Libertarian Party, which holds the ideological position that government should not interfere with individuals' social, political, and economic rights, advocates a very limited role for government: no guarantees of minimum wages or other forms of governmental regulation of the economy, including environmental regulation; no governmental interference in individuals' privacy; the legalization of prostitution and drugs; and the elimination of major governmental bureaucracies, including the Central Intelligence Agency, the Internal Revenue Service, and the Federal Bureau of Investigation.

Another ideologically oriented party is the Socialist Party, which lies at the other end of the ideological spectrum from the Libertarian Party. The Socialist Party, formed in 1901, is one of the longest-standing ideologically oriented parties in the United States. Socialists believe that government should play a large role in ensuring economic equality for all people.

SPLINTER PARTIES   A splinter party is a political party that breaks off, or "splinters," from one of the two dominant parties. Often a group splinters off because of intraparty (internal, or within the party) disagreement on a particular issue. In 1948, a group of southern Democrats who opposed the Democratic Party's support of civil rights for African Americans splintered from the Democratic Party to form the States' Rights Party, which quickly became known as the Dixiecrat Party. The party called itself the States' Rights Party because it claimed that Congress had no power to interfere with the administration of laws made by the states. It used that claim to retain the policies that created a system of racial segregation in the South. Although the States' Rights Party was a separate, formal organization, many southern Democratic elected officials and party leaders who agreed with the States' Rights Party's platform supported its views from within the Democratic Party.

The Impact of Third Parties

Despite the difficulties associated with sustaining support in American electoral politics, third parties have important effects in the political arena. First, third parties provide a release valve for dissatisfied voters. People who are disgruntled with the two major parties can join or form another political party. This has been the case with the Tea Party, which has channeled the energy of staunch conservatives who view the mainstream Republican Party as too moderate. And while a third party's chances of electoral success are not great, such parties provide a mechanism for like-minded people to come together to try to effect change. At the national level, third parties were a release valve for discontented voters in several elections, as shown in Figure 8.7.

Second, although U.S. third parties usually do not win elections, they can influence electoral outcomes. For example, given the closeness of the 2000 presidential race, many Democrats believe that Green Party candidate Ralph Nader caused Democrat Al Gore to lose the election. They reason that Nader voters would have been more likely to vote for the liberal Gore than for the conservative George W. Bush if Nader had not been a candidate. In a state such as Florida, where the electorate was divided evenly, Nader's candidacy in fact could have changed the outcome of that state's balloting and thus the results of the national election as well. Of course, many third-party advocates claim that supporters of a third-party candidate may not have voted at all if their party had not been on the ballot.

In U.S. history, third-party presidential candidates have won more than 10 percent of the vote seven times, the latest being in 1992, when Independent Party candidate H. Ross Perot captured 19 percent of the vote. As Figure 8.7 illustrates, in five of those seven cases, the incumbent party's presidential nominee lost the presidency. Thus, third parties tend to help the major out-of-power party win election.

Finally, third parties put a variety of issues on the national political agenda. When a third party, especially an issue-oriented third party, draws attention to an issue of concern, sometimes government officials respond to that concern even if the third party fails in its election bid. In some such cases, the issue has not previously been given priority, and the attention the third party draws to it creates a groundswell of political pressure that forces action. In other cases, policymakers might act to address the issue in order to woo the supporters of the third party who have expressed that particular issue concern.

Historically, the two major parties' co-option of issues that were first promoted by third parties has sometimes contributed to the demise of third parties. For example, as we have seen, the Progressives' presidential candidate, Theodore Roosevelt, lost to Democrat Woodrow Wilson in 1912, but Wilson enacted many elements of the Progressive Party's platform, including antitrust regulations, corporate law reforms, and

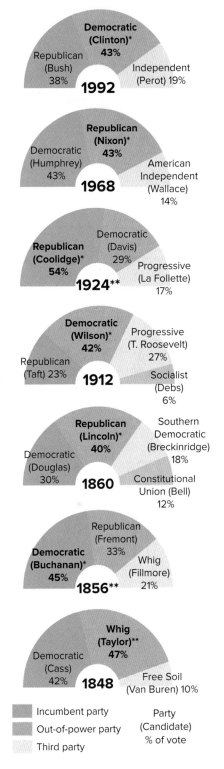

FIGURE 8.7 ■ Third Parties Help the Out-of-Power Party

*Winner.

**Denotes election in which incumbent party retained power in face of a strong third-party challenge.

banking regulations. Lacking a unique platform, and with comparatively little electoral success, the Progressives faded away.

New Ideologies, New Technologies: The Parties in the 21st Century

American political parties have changed dramatically in recent years. Global events such as the end of the Cold War, the rise of international and domestic terrorism and multifront wars, and the impact of the Internet and cellular technologies have partly driven the changes. Within the Republican and Democratic Parties, the changes have reflected an ideological shift from an era when a party's defining position was its position on social welfare policy, to a time when foreign policy issues were central, and back again. Today, issues dominating the national agenda include those related to foreign policy—many centered on trade—as well as a bevy of domestic economic issues, including job creation in the United States' industrial economy. Immigration continues to be a lightning rod issue. There are distinct differences between Democrats' and Republicans' positions on these and other issues. While much emphasis today is placed on the differences between the Democrats and the Republicans, for many citizens there are shades of "purple" between the reds and the blues (see Figure 8.8).

Republicans Today: The Establishment, President Trump, and the Tea Party

The Republican Party today faces a watershed moment. Throughout the country, a battle for the soul of the party is taking place on several fronts. The emergence and success of Donald Trump's candidacy took many Republicans by surprise, but many remained unconvinced that his rhetoric, which often targeted groups that some party members were trying to bring into the GOP fold, is helpful to the future prospects of the Republican Party. For example, Trump's derogatory comments aimed at Mexicans and his mantra of "Build That Wall" (between the United States and Mexico as a mechanism to staunch the flow of undocumented immigrants) is viewed as harmful in the context of attracting Latinos—the fastest-growing voter demographic—into the Republican Party. Others fret over inconsistencies in his policy positions, which sometimes seem to repudiate long-held beliefs within the party.[51] Party leaders fear that these positions might alienate groups that have been core constituents of the Republican Party, including business leaders, members of the military, and veterans, though his appeal to working-class white voters has breathed new life into the Republican Party.

Moderate establishment Republican leaders also seek to fend off attacks and heal wounds caused by devisions between staunchly conservative activists and more moderate members of the party. Conservatism is nothing new to the Republican Party, but the election of Barack Obama in 2008 fueled the flames of a grassroots movement that began growing in communities across the United States. Outraged by what they saw as excessive spending by the administration and the Democrats in Congress, and particularly incensed during the debates concerning health care reform, conservative activists formed the Tea Party movement. The moniker is a reference to the colonial era, when colonists dumped tea into Boston Harbor to protest taxes imposed by the British Crown, an action that contributed to the American Revolution.

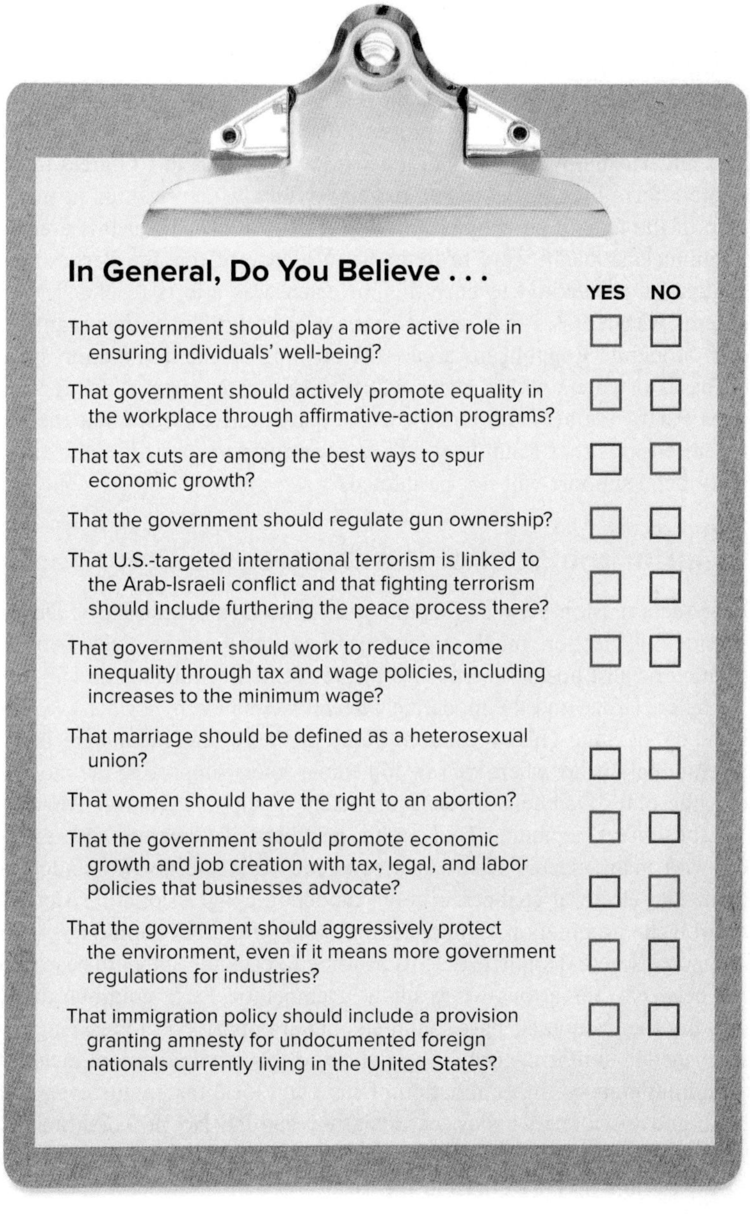

In General, Do You Believe . . .

	YES	NO
That government should play a more active role in ensuring individuals' well-being?	☐	☐
That government should actively promote equality in the workplace through affirmative-action programs?	☐	☐
That tax cuts are among the best ways to spur economic growth?	☐	☐
That the government should regulate gun ownership?	☐	☐
That U.S.-targeted international terrorism is linked to the Arab-Israeli conflict and that fighting terrorism should include furthering the peace process there?	☐	☐
That government should work to reduce income inequality through tax and wage policies, including increases to the minimum wage?	☐	☐
That marriage should be defined as a heterosexual union?	☐	☐
That women should have the right to an abortion?	☐	☐
That the government should promote economic growth and job creation with tax, legal, and labor policies that businesses advocate?	☐	☐
That the government should aggressively protect the environment, even if it means more government regulations for industries?	☐	☐
That immigration policy should include a provision granting amnesty for undocumented foreign nationals currently living in the United States?	☐	☐

FIGURE 8.8 ■ **Are You Red, Blue, or Purple?** News commentators use the terms "red" and "blue" to refer to Republicans and Democrats, respectively. Although the basis for an individual's political ideology is complex (see Chapter 1), party identification in the United States often reflects differences in viewpoint on several key issues. Do you know what each party stands for? Do you know which party best represents your views? Take this brief quiz to find out which party you lean toward. Of course, before voting for candidates of that party or even counting yourself as a party identifier, you should further investigate the positions of the parties and the positions of the candidates. The websites listed at the end of the chapter are a good place to start.

Although plagued with the growing pains characteristic of virtually any large-scale political movement, over the ensuing years since their formation, Tea Partiers have identified six key principles including less government, fiscal responsibility, lower taxes, states' rights, national security, and border security as their priorities. Activism centering on these principles has involved a variety of tactics. Some, such as the formation of a political action committee that contributes donations to endorsed candidates who espouse the Tea Party's views, are standard for such movements. Other strategies have proven more controversial: One example was the effort undertaken by members of the Tea Party Caucus in Congress to defund health care reform by refusing to authorize spending, which resulted in the 16-day shutdown of the federal government in 2013. In the aftermath of this event, moderate Republicans sought ways to limit the influence of the Tea Party and other conservatives. One method to curb this influence was efforts to change nomination systems within states that had caucuses or conventions, rather than primary elections. Moderate Republicans argue that opening up the nomination system to broader bases of voters within states will lead to greater support for their candidates. Tea Party members and more extreme conservatives argue that the convention system ensures that candidates will espouse the party position and that loyal party members' support will not be diluted.

A Battle for the Soul of the Democratic Party Today

Today, we see a tension between factions within the Democratic Party. During the 2016 presidential election, much of this tension centered on the divide between the Democratic Socialist positions espoused by presidential candidate and U.S. Senator Bernie Sanders (I-Vt.) and the moderately liberal views held by former U.S. Senator and Secretary of State Hillary Clinton. Some of these differences were borne out by a generational divide, where we saw Millennial voters supporting the more liberal stance, while older Democrats were more likely to support Clinton. Much of the party establishment, including Democratic members of Congress, also supported Clinton, with many elected Democrats concerned that the liberal Sanders would hurt their own electoral chances in more moderate congressional districts. When Clinton won the nomination, Sanders strongly supported her candidacy, but many of his supporters were dissatisfied by his decision to back the standard-bearer. Today, tensions between the various wings of the Democratic Party continue to be pronounced. But the Democrats have solidified in their opposition to President Trump's legislative agenda, uniformly criticizing policies of his administration, including his stance on immigration; the elimination of state and local tax credits over a certain threshold; and his foreign policy, particularly regarding North Korea and China. They also have been unified in their support of an investigation into the extent of influence Russians may have had in the 2016 presidential election and have been critical of President Trump's personality and social media presence.

As the 2020 presidential election approaches, Democrats will be weighing candidate attributes, attempting to determine which potential nominee has the skills and background to withstand the enormous scrutiny that accompanies a presidential election, as well as the ability to attract the support of demographic groups that were lost to President Trump in the 2016 election.

Changing Both Parties: New Technologies

The ways in which party members and voters give and get information, as well as the methods by which parties campaign, have changed drastically in recent years.

These changes are discussed in greater detail in Chapter 11, but today a key technological development is the use of "big data" by political parties to target potential supporters. Companies such as NGP VAN, which works with Democrats, and Aristotle, which works with Republicans, have databases containing information not only on every voter in the United States, but even on individuals they hope they can convince to become voters and support one party or the other.

Some data come from information sources openly available to the public, such as a registered voter's age, address, and years in which the voter cast a ballot. But that public information is supplemented with private information purchased by the data companies, For example, are you a member of the National Rifle Association? If so, the Republicans would know that, because the NRA sells their lists to data companies, thus enabling the Republican Party to target you (no pun intended) with information about pro–Second Amendment Republican candidates. Many companies, including CVS, grocery stores, "big box" stores, and newspaper and magazine subscription services, sell their data to companies like NGP VAN and Aristotle. The parties then supplement these databases themselves. For example, a Republican pollster might telephone and ask you what the most important issue in the campaign is, or how likely you are to support a particular candidate. This information is then analyzed and can be used to target you if you are a likely supporter of a particular candidate the party supports.

In addition to this (perhaps alarming) use, technology is changing how political parties connect with potential supporters, as more and more people in the electorate are finding information about issues on the Internet and via their cell phones. Both of the political parties communicate with their supporters and potential supporters using social media. Relying on a medium unheard of only a decade ago, both the Democrats and Republicans use YouTube (their respective channels are The Democrats and GOP) not just to disseminate information but also to create a dialogue with Americans.

During the 2018 congressional races, both the national Democrats and Republicans used their websites to drive supporters to U.S. Senate and competitive House races, encouraging them to contribute and volunteer for these efforts. Both offered downloadable apps that allowed supporters to link their social networking pages and to raise funds by linking the campaigns' sites to their own websites, and this availability has democratized the party process. Partisan activism is no longer limited to individuals who can attend meetings. Whole new forms of Internet activism have emerged. People with access to the Internet can chat, organize, plan, lobby, raise funds, contribute, and mobilize without leaving their desks.

Conclusion
Thinking Critically About What's Next in American Political Parties

Despite the cynicism with which people often view them, political parties are a vital institution for the civic engagement of Americans and are essential to democracy. For many citizens, political parties are the gateway to political participation. For others, they provide cues that guide decisions at the ballot box. The role of parties in teaching individuals essential skills that may lead to elective office, in recruiting candidates, in contesting elections, and in governing—all these valuable functions often do not get the recognition they deserve.

Despite the comparative low esteem in which the two major U.S. political parties are currently held and the significant challenges they face in satisfying their divergent groups of constituents, they both have demonstrated enormous adaptability over time. But the cultural and structural forces that perpetuate the two-party system show little sign of relenting. And although the prospect of a third party provides rich fodder for political pundits who speculate about their importance, in electoral terms third parties have demonstrated very little ability to win elections. Instead, third parties commonly advocate issues that eventually are co-opted by one or both of the major parties, and they sometimes play the role of spoiler in elections.

In the future, the parties will be challenged to adapt. In particular, they will need to adjust continually to new circumstances, as technology changes how the party organizations identify, organize, mobilize, and communicate with the party in the electorate, as well as how the party in government governs. The contemporary faces of the two major parties demonstrate their continuing evolution and responsiveness to their identifiers and constituents.

Learning Summary

1. Explain the argument that political parties today are in crisis.
   a. Explain the challenges the Republicans face in the Trump era.
   b. Explain the factionalization that characterizes the Democratic Party today.

2. Describe the functions of political parties today.
   a. Explain the four defining characteristics of political parties.
   b. Describe how political parties engage individuals.
   c. Explain how political parties promote civic engagement.
   d. Summarize the responsible party model.

3. Summarize the three faces of parties—the party in the electorate, the party organization, and the party in government.
   a. Explain how the party in the electorate is measured, what the demographic characteristics of each party are, and what the differences are between Democrats and Republicans.
   b. Describe the party organization, including the national, state, county, and local parties.
   c. Describe the party in government and the special challenges that accompany divided government.

4. Describe the five party systems identified by political scientists.
   a. Describe the development of parties.
   b. Describe the Democrats' rise to power (1828–1860).
   c. Describe the Republicans' rise to power (1860–1896).
   d. Describe the era of Republican dominance (1896–1932).
   e. Describe the era of Democratic dominance (1932–1968).
   f. Evaluate the idea that we are in a new party system.

5. Summarize the arguments that parties are in decline, are resurging, and are in a post-party era.
   a. Summarize the arguments that the era of party dominance in the United States is over.
   b. Summarize the arguments that political parties are resurging in the United States.
   c. Explain the argument that we are in a "post-party era."

6. Explain why two parties have dominated U.S. politics.
   a. Summarize the four causes of two-party dominance.
   b. Evaluate whether two-party dominance is likely to continue.

7. Outline the nature, electoral record, and influence of third parties in the United States throughout history.
   a. Describe the types of third parties.
   b. Explain the impact of third parties.

8. Describe the effects of new ideologies and new technologies on parties in the contemporary era.
   a. Explain how new ideologies are affecting the Republican Party.
   b. Describe the identity challenges the Democratic Party faces.
   c. Explain how technology is changing the operation of both political parties.

Key Terms

big tent principle 262

candidate-centered campaign 279

candidate committees 280

Citizens United v. Federal Election Commission 279

dealignment 280

divided government 272

grassroots organizing 264

independent 266

loyal opposition 269

New Deal 276

New Deal coalition 276

party identifiers 266

party in government 270

party in the electorate 265

party organization 268

party system 272

patronage 275

platform 263

political machine 275

political party 259

populism 273

primary election 278

proportional representation system 282

realignment 272

responsible party model 265

soft money loophole 270

spoils system 273

Tea Party movement 262

third party 281

ticket splitting 280

truncated government 272

winner-take-all system 282

For Review

1. Why do some political scientists assert that political parties are in crisis today?

2. What functions do political parties perform? How do these functions encourage the civic engagement of Americans?

3. What are the three faces of political parties?

4. Explain the development of the five party systems in U.S. history. Why, historically, does the majority change from one party to another?

5. Why do two parties dominate in politics and government in the United States?

6. Which arguments state that political parties are in decline? What do opponents of these arguments contend?

7. How have third parties influenced recent elections?

8. Describe the struggle today's political parties are grappling with.

For Critical Thinking and Discussion

1. How were you socialized to the two-party system? Do your views reflect your parents' views? Were third parties even mentioned in your house when you were growing up?

2. What factors explain the demographic bases of the two major parties? How could each party expand its base of support?

3. What evidence is there that a new party system is emerging? Do the 2018 election results support the claim that a new party system is taking shape?

4. In your view, how should the Republican Party balance the staunchly conservative agenda of the Tea Party faction with the desire to win national elections? How should the Democrats respond to demands from the left that the party should be more progressive?

5. In what ways beyond those discussed in the chapter might the Internet and other new technologies be used as means of communication between voters and parties? In your view, what are the most important uses for new technologies in partisan politics?

Resources for Research AND Action

Internet Resources

The American Presidency Project
www.presidency.ucsb.edu/platforms.php The American
Presidency Project website at the University of California–
Santa Barbara provides the party platforms of every party
whose presidential candidate received electoral votes.

Democratic National Committee
www.democrats.org The Democrats' website contains hotlinks
for state and local party websites and opportunities for volunteering, internships, and employment, as well as party position
papers and platforms and candidate information.

Republican National Committee
www.gop.com The Republicans' site has links for state
and local party sites and opportunities for volunteering,
internships, and employment, as well as party position papers
and platforms and candidate information.

Voter Study Group
www.voterstudygroup.org The Democracy Fund Voter Study
Group brings together analysts and scholars from across the
political spectrum to examine and glean insights from the
evolving views of the electorate.

Recommended Readings

Berlatsky, Noah. *Does the U.S. Two-Party System Still Work?*
Belmont, CA: Greenhaven Press, 2010. Part of the At Issue
series, this work examines the effectiveness of the U.S. party
system.

Flammang, Janet. *Women's Political Voice*. Philadelphia: Temple
University Press, 1997. A well-researched account of women's
political participation in general and women's participation in
political parties in particular.

Hershey, Marjorie Random. *Party Politics in America*, 17th ed.
New York: Longman, 2017. A classic work on American political
parties, analyzing the changing roles of parties in the 20th century
and the impact of the campaign finance system on political
parties.

Hetherington, Marc J., and Thomas J. Rudolph. *Why Washington
Won't Work: Polarization, Political Trust, and the Governing Crisis.*
Chicago: University of Chicago Press, 2014. The authors assert
that the increasing polarization of the American electorate
has resulted in decreasing trust, creating a dysfunctional
governmental dynamic.

Lijphart, Arend. *Electoral Systems and Party Systems: A Study
of Twenty-Seven Democracies, 1945-1990.* New York: Oxford
University Press, 1994. An exploration of the nature of party
systems in many industrialized democracies, both historically
and in modern times.

Pimlott, Jamie Pamelia. *Women and the Democratic Party: The
Evolution of EMILY's List.* Amherst, NY: Cambria Press, 2010.
Consists of both descriptive and quantitative analysis of the
growth and impact of EMILY's List, the leading fund-raising
organization that supports Democratic women candidates.

Schattschneider, E. E. *Party Government.* New York: Rinehart,
1942. A classic work that explains the nature of political parties
and their influence on party government.

Movies of Interest

Game Change (2012)
This film is based on John Heilemann and Mark Halperin's
account of Sarah Palin's entry into the 2008 presidential
race as Sen. John McCain's vice-presidential running mate.

The Ides of March (2011)
George Clooney and Ryan Gosling star in this story of the final
days of a competitive primary for the Democratic nomination
for president.

Primary Colors (1998)
Starring John Travolta, and based on the anonymously written
book of the same name, this popular movie—a fictionalized
account of Bill Clinton's 1992 campaign—provides insight into
the primary election season of a presidential nominee.

Chicago 1968 (1996)
This is an episode of *The American Experience,* an award-winning
PBS documentary, which examines the chaotic events of the
1968 Democratic National Convention in Chicago using interviews with historians, convention participants, and protesters
along with actual news footage of the events.

The War Room (1993)
This movie is a behind-the-scenes look at Bill Clinton's 1992
presidential campaign from the first primaries and caucuses,
through to the national convention and his ultimate election win.

City Hall (1996)
This film, starring Al Pacino and John Cusack, shows the
workings of a corrupt political machine—and the consequences
of that corruption.

The Best Man (1964)
This classic film shows the drama of an old-style convention
where backroom deals help determine a party's nominee.

References

1. E. E. Schattschneider, *Party Government* (New York: Farrar & Rinehart, 1942), 1.
2. Robert Griffin, "Party Hoppers: Understanding Voters Who Switched Party Affiliation," Democracy Fund Voter Study Group, 2018.
3. Stephen Ansolabehere and Brian F. Schaffner, "CCES Common Content, 2016," 2017.
4. www.pbs.org/wgbh/frontline/article/whats-driving-republican-retirements-from-congress/.
5. Marc J. Hetherington and Thomas J. Rudolph, *Why Washington Won't Work: Polarization, Political Trust, and the Governing Crisis* (Chicago: University of Chicago Press, 2014).
6. L. Sandy Maisel and Kara Z. Buckley, *Parties and Elections in America,* 4th ed. (Lanham, MD: Rowman & Littlefield, 2004).
7. Jo Freeman, *A Room at a Time: How Women Entered Party Politics* (New York: Rowman & Littlefield, 2000).
8. Ibid.
9. Melanie Gustafson, Kristie Miller, and Elisabeth Israels Perry, *We Have Come to Stay: American Women and Political Parties, 1880-1960* (Albuquerque: University of New Mexico Press, 1999).
10. V. O. Key, *Politics, Parties, and Pressure Groups* (New York: Thomas Y. Crowell, 1964).
11. Seymour Martin Lipset and Stein Rokkan, *Party Systems and Voter Alignments* (New York: Free Press, 1967).
12. Geoffrey Layman, *The Great Divide: Religious and Cultural Conflict in American Party Politics* (New York: Columbia University Press, 2002).
13. Jeffrey M. Jones, "Economy Is Paramount Issue to U.S. Voters," February 29, 2012.
14. Walter Dean Burnham, *Critical Elections and the Mainsprings of American Politics* (New York: W. W. Norton, 1997).
15. John Aldrich, *Why Parties? The Origin and Transformation of Party Politics in America* (Chicago: University of Chicago Press, 1995).
16. *Buckley v. Valeo,* 424 U.S. 1 (1976).
17. Regina Dougherty, "Divided Government Defines the Era," in *America at the Polls: 1996,* ed. Regina Dougherty, Everett C. Ladd, David Wilber, and Lynn Zayachkiwsky (Storrs, CT: Roper Center for Public Opinion Research, 1997).
18. Richard Hofstadter, "A Constitution against Parties: Madisonian Pluralism and the Anti-Party Tradition," *Government and Opposition* 4 (1969): 345-366.
19. Jefferson and Washington, quoted in Richard Hofstadter, *The Idea of a Party System: The Rise of Legitimate Opposition in the United States, 1780-1840* (Berkeley and Los Angeles: University of California Press, 1969), 2, 123.
20. Richard Hofstadter, *The Idea of a Party System: The Rise of Legitimate Opposition in the United States 1780-1840* (Berkeley: University of California Press, 1970).
21. James L. Sundquist, *Dynamics of the Party System: Alignment and Realignment of Political Parties in the United States* (Washington, DC: Brookings, 1983).
22. Everett C. Ladd, *American Political Parties* (New York: W. W. Norton, 1970).
23. David R. Mayhew, *Electoral Realignments: A Critique of an American Genre* (New Haven, CT: Yale University Press, 2002).
24. William Nisbet Chambers, *Political Parties in a New Nation: The American Experience, 1776-1809* (New York: Oxford University Press, 1963).
25. Lance Banning, *The Jeffersonian Persuasion: Evolution of a Party Ideology* (Ithaca, NY: Cornell University Press, 1978).
26. Richard L. McCormick, *The Party Period and Public Policy: American Politics from the Age of Jackson to the Progressive Era* (New York: Oxford University Press, 1986).
27. Jules Witcover, *Party of the People: A History of the Democrats* (New York: Random House, 2003).
28. Lee Benson, *The Concept of Jacksonian Democracy* (Princeton, NJ: Princeton University Press, 1961).
29. Aileen Kraditor, *The Ideas of the Woman Suffrage Movement, 1890-1920* (New York: W. W. Norton, 1981).
30. Eric Foner, *Free Soil, Free Labor, Free Men: The Ideology of the Republican Party Before the Civil War* (New York: Oxford University Press, 1995).
31. William E. Gienapp, *The Origins of the Republican Party, 1852-1856* (New York: Oxford University Press, 1987).
32. Witcover, *Party of the People.*
33. McCormick, *The Party Period and Public Policy.*
34. Joel H. Silbey, *The Partisan Imperative: The Dynamics of American Politics Before the Civil War* (New York: Oxford University Press, 1985).
35. Lewis L. Gould, *Grand Old Party: A History of the Republicans* (New York: Random House, 2003).
36. Paul Kleppner, *The Third Electoral System, 1853-1892: Parties, Voters, and Political Cultures* (Chapel Hill: University of North Carolina Press, 1979).
37. Quoted in A. James Reichley, "Party Politics in a Federal Polity," in *Challenges to Party Government,* ed. John Kenneth White and Jerome M. Mileur (Carbondale: Southern Illinois University Press, 1992), 48.
38. Kristi Anderson, *After Suffrage* (Chicago: University of Chicago Press, 1996), 30.
39. John Petrocik, *Party Coalitions: Realignment and the Decline of the New Deal Party System* (Chicago: University of Chicago Press, 1981).
40. David G. Lawrence, *The Collapse of the Democratic Majority: Realignment, Dealignment, and Electoral Change from Franklin Roosevelt to Bill Clinton* (New York: Westview, 1997).
41. Gary Orren, "The Changing Styles of American Party Politics," in *The Future of American Political Parties: The Challenge of Governance,* ed. Joel L. Fleishman (Englewood Cliffs, NJ: Prentice Hall, 1982), 31.
42. *Citizens United v. Federal Election Commission,* 558 U.S. _____ (2010).
43. The basis for this argument can be found in Larry J. Sabato and Bruce Larson, *The Party's Just Begun: Shaping Political Parties for America's Future,* 2nd ed. (New York: Longman, 2001).
44. Edward G. Carmines, John P. McIver, and James A. Stimson, "Unrealized Partisanship: A Theory of Dealignment," *Journal of Politics* 49 (1987): 376-400.

45. Party Images," www.gallup.com/poll/ 24655/Party-Images.aspx.
46. David Karol, Hans Noel, John Zaller, and Marty Cohen, "Polls or Pols? The Real Driving Force behind Presidential Nominations," *Brookings Review* 21, 3 (2003): 36–39.
47. Arend Lijphart, *Electoral Systems and Party Systems: A Study of Twenty-Seven Democracies, 1945–1990* (New York: Oxford University Press, 1994).
48. Lipset and Rokkan, *Party Systems and Voter Alignments.*
49. Maurice Duverger, *Political Parties* (New York: Wiley, 1951).
50. Steven J. Rosenstone, Roy L. Behr, and Edward H. Lazarus, *Third Parties in America,* 2nd ed. (Princeton, NJ: Princeton University Press, 1996).
51. www.npr.org/programs/all-things-considered/2018/01/30/581798328.

Campaigns, Elections, and Voting

©Jerry Holt/ZUMA Press/Newscom

THEN

Political party–dominated campaigns and grassroots activism were deciding factors in how people voted.

NOW

Candidate-centered campaigns rely on a mix of free social media to communicate with voters, paid professionals, and costly media buys to refine their messages to voters.

NEXT

How will new technologies drive how people vote and how campaigns are run?

How will changes in the campaign finance system, including the advent of super PACs, affect how campaigns are waged?

How can government, candidates, and voters protect the electoral system from fraud and corruption?

When Americans think about

politics, most think first about campaigns, elections, and voting. In the eyes of many of us, these activities are the essence of political participation, because it is through the electoral process that we feel we participate most directly and meaningfully in our democracy. Often viewed as the pinnacle of the democratic experience, the act of voting is the culmination of a wide range of forms of political engagement. In the discussion that follows, we see the interconnectedness of many aspects of political campaigns and elections, including fund-raising, the tasks that involve direct contact with potential voters called **grassroots organizing,** candidate selection, and voter mobilization. These opportunities for civic participation in the democratic process are present in such a broad variety of forms that they are accessible to everyone who wants to be engaged.

The Importance of Fair, Independent Elections

In January 2017, a jointly issued report issued by the Central Intelligence Agency, the Federal Bureau of Investigation, and the National Security Agency stated with "high confidence" that the Russian government had conducted a sophisticated campaign to influence the 2016 presidential election. According to a declassified version of the report, Russian President Vladimir Putin ordered the effort both to damage Hillary Clinton's presidential campaign and to undermine the U.S. democratic process. "Putin and the Russian government developed a clear preference for President-elect Trump," stated the report.[1] Russia denied the allegations, but in the ensuing months, executives from Facebook testified before Congress, stating that at least 120 fake Russian-backed Facebook pages created 80,000 posts that 29 million Americans received directly, as did countless others who saw the posts through user shares, likes, and follows.[2] Facebook was not alone: by January 2018, Twitter had removed 50,258 accounts that had posted automated tweets about the 2016 election and were linked to Russia. Twitter turned over details to congressional investigators who are looking into Moscow's interference with the U.S. election, but the posts reached more than 677,775 Americans before the election.[3]

Why Election Meddling Matters

Throughout U.S. history, individuals, organizations, and campaigns have attempted to influence how the American people think. From *The Federalist Papers*, which sought to convince Americans that the U.S. Constitution should be ratified, to YouTube videos advocating for Ted Cruz's election to the U.S. Senate in 2018, the art of influencing voters has been part of political life. But in 2016, the evidence that Russia meddled in the U.S. election—and is still attempting to influence public opinion and foment political strife in the United States[4]—is cause for serious concern. Of utmost importance is the issue of national sovereignty—that nations have the right of self-rule without any interference from outside. Fundamental to democracies is that the will of the people is supreme, and the concept of popular

Learning Objectives

After reading this chapter, students should be able to:

- Explain the importance of fair, independent elections.
- Categorize types of elections in the United States.
- Analyze how various methods of balloting, including vote-by-mail, may influence electoral outcomes and turnout.
- Explain the requirements and decisions related to running for office.
- Describe how increasing reliance on professional consultants and social media and technology has altered political campaigns.
- Explain efforts to regulate campaign finance, including the effect of the *Citizens United* decision on the campaign finance environment.
- Outline the process of presidential campaigns.
- Explain the factors that influence voter participation.
- Analyze how voters decide for whom they will vote.
- Explain why some people do not vote.

grassroots organizing
Tasks that involve direct contact with potential voters

RUSHIAN TROLLS BEHIND A PROTEST IN U.S. CNN

> Before the 2016 election, demonstrators, including some white suprema-
cists who learned of a protest opposing the "Islamization" of Texas from the
"Heart of Texas" Facebook page, rallied at the Islamic Da'Wah Center in
Houston. A much larger group of counter-demonstrators, who learned of the
event from the "Save Islamic Knowledge" Facebook page, gathered as well.
Both Facebook pages were the work of Russian trolls fomenting division and
dissent in the United States from a troll farm in Saint Petersburg, Russia.

Source: Cable News Network

sovereignty—that the people rule themselves by creating governments—means that governments are created with consent of the governed. But meddling by a foreign government, particularly one whose interests are often at odds with those of the United States, poses a challenge to popular sovereignty and the supremacy of the will of the people being governed. As Ben Franklin noted, "In free governments, the rulers are the servants and the people their superiors and sovereigns."[5]

Intentional Efforts at Voter Suppression

In 2018, complaints emerged that in some states, efforts were being made to suppress voter turnout, particularly voter participation by African American, Latino, and Asian American voters who would, on the whole, be more likely to support Democratic candidates. Some voters bemoaned antiquated voting machines, while others decried the reduced number of polling locations. Indeed, and analysis by the Pew Charitable Trust indicated that, nearly a thousand polling places have been closed across the United States since the 2016 election, many of them in southern black communities.[6]

In some places, allegations of intentional voter suppression tainted the electoral process. For example, a report by The Associated Press detailed how Georgia Secretary of State Brian Kemp, who was also running as a Republican for governor, had suspended more than 50,000 voter registrations.[7] A disproportionate number were the registrations of African-Americans, who constitute 32 percent of the state's population, but were almost 70 percent of the suspended applications. A coalition of civil rights group filed a lawsuit to prevent both enforcement of the suspensions in 2018[8] and similar actions leading into the 2020 elections.

Political Participation as an Expression of the Will of the People

The act of voting embodies the expression of the will of the people, a nearly sacred concept that has evolved significantly from its origins in ancient Greece. Campaigns, elections, and voting are fundamental aspects of the civic engagement of Americans and are important both for the polity as a whole and for the individuals who participate.[9] They ensure that the government is representative of the people and responsive to their needs. Representative governments, which are the product of individuals' political engagement, tend to be more stable and to make decisions that best reflect the needs and the will of the people who elect them.

Direct forms of political participation such as voting, volunteering on a campaign, and running for office are of keen interest to political scientists and scholars of civic engagement. Many scholarly analysts have noticed an overall decrease in levels of political participation. As discussed in Chapter 7, political scientist Robert Putnam argues that the United States is seeing a decline in its social capital, the social networks and reciprocal relationships characteristic of a community or a society. Some scholars have challenged Putnam's assertion that social capital has declined. They point out that new forms of social capital have arisen in the form of online social networks, instant messaging, and Internet activism to replace the traditional social networks that Putnam studied. Others point to the cyclical nature of political involvement, and argue that in modern times, candidate-centered campaigns—particularly ones that evoke high levels of voter passion and participation, including Barack Obama's 2008 race and Donald Trump's 2016 campaign—mark the ebb and flow of political participation and social capital. Despite these differing views, there is consensus that civic participation is essential and that among its most important forms is electoral political participation.

Elections in the United States

Every state holds at least two types of elections. A *primary election* comes first and determines the party's nominees—those who will run for office. In presidential elections, in most states, nominees are chosen when voters go to the polls and select a candidate's slate of delegates to the national party convention, but some states hold **caucuses**—meetings of party members where the delegates are chosen. For most political offices, there is little or no competition in the primary election. But in presidential and gubernatorial primary elections, vigorous contention is often the rule, particularly within the out-of-power party. House and Senate primary elections that lack an incumbent candidate (that is, one who has been elected to that office before) are also often highly competitive as many candidates attempt to win their party's nomination.

In a **general election,** the parties' nominees run against each other, and, in all but presidential elections, voters decide directly who should hold office, since the person with the most votes wins. (Presidential elections are determined by the Electoral College, discussed later in this chapter.) The degree of competition in general elections depends on a number of factors, including the presence of and the strength of incumbency, the degree of party competition, and the level of the office. In recent times, presidential elections have been brutally competitive, as have been certain gubernatorial races and many congressional contests in which no incumbent is seeking reelection. Some communities, particularly big cities, may also experience intense competition for office in general elections.

Nominations and Primary Elections

In a primary election, voters decide which nominees the political parties should run in the general election. But *which* voters decide varies greatly from state to state. In some states, only registered party members are eligible to vote in primary elections, whereas in other states, any registered voter can vote in any party's primary, and in North Dakota, voters are not even required to register.

In U.S. presidential primaries, voters do not vote directly for the candidate whom they would like their party to nominate. Instead, the popular vote determines which candidate's delegates will attend the party's nominating convention and vote for that party's nominee. This system of selecting delegates through primary voting is different from the earlier system, when party leaders selected the presidential nominee with little or no input from the rank-and-file party members.

The two major U.S. parties made reforms to the earlier delegate-selection process after the 1968 Democratic National Convention in Chicago. In attempting to address the concerns of anti–Vietnam War activists who had protested the nomination of pro-war candidate Vice President Hubert Humphrey, the Democratic National Committee appointed the McGovern-Fraser Commission (named

caucus
A meeting of party members held to select delegates to the national convention.

general election
An election that determines which candidates win the offices being sought.

after its co-chairs), which recommended a series of reforms to the delegate-selection process. The reforms, many of which both the Democratic Party and the Republican Party adopted, significantly increased the influence of party primary voters and caucus attendees. Voters could now select delegates to the national conventions, a power previously restricted to the party elite. The reforms also included provisions that would ensure the selection of a more representative body of delegates, with certain delegate slots set aside for women, minorities, union members, and young party voters. These slots roughly correspond with the proportion of support the party receives from those groups.

open primary
A type of primary in which both parties' ballots are available in the voting booth, and the voters simply select one on which to register their preferences.

closed primary
A type of primary in which voting in a party's primary is limited to members of that party.

TYPES OF PRIMARY ELECTIONS   In an **open primary** election, any registered voter can vote in any party's primary, as can independent voters not registered with a party. In the 20 states[10] with an open presidential primary, parties' ballots are available in the voting booth, and the voter simply selects privately or publicly one on which to register his or her preferences.

In a **closed primary** election, voting in a party's primary is limited to members of that party. In some states, voters must declare their party affiliation well in advance of the primary election—sometimes as many as 60 days before. In other states, voters can declare their party preference at the polling place on the day of the election. Such restrictions on who can vote in a party's primary originated in the parties' maneuvering to have the strongest candidate nominated. For example, if a popular incumbent president were running unopposed in a primary election, members of the president's party might choose to vote in the other party's primary as a way of scheming to get a weak candidate nominated. A closed primary aims to thwart that strategy.

Super Tuesday
The Tuesday in early March on which the most primary elections are held, many of them in southern states.

PRESIDENTIAL PRIMARIES   The states determine the timing of primary elections. Historically, states that held their presidential primaries earlier in the year had a greater say in determining the nominee than did states with later primaries. The reason is that candidates tended to drop out if they did not win primaries, did not meet media expectations, or ran out of funds. (See "Thinking Critically.") In general, past presidential primaries gave great sway to the agricultural states, because many of the more urban states' primaries fell later in the season. **Super Tuesday** is the day in early March on which the most presidential primary elections take place, many of them in southern states. Super Tuesday had been the fruit of a successful effort in 1988 by several southern and rural states to hold their primaries on the same day so as to increase their political importance and allow expression of southern voters' political will.[11]

General Elections

In a general election, voters decide who should hold office from among the candidates determined in the primary election. Most general elections, including presidential elections, are held on the first Tuesday after the first Monday in November. But because the states schedule and oversee elections, you might find that your gubernatorial election, state legislative election, or town council election occurs at a different time of the year.

General elections for Congress and most state legislatures feature a winner-take-all system. That is, the candidate who receives the most votes wins that office (even if that total is not a majority, or even if an opponent receives only one vote fewer than the victor). Thus, a member of the U.S. House of Representatives or Senate can be elected with less than a majority of the votes in his or her district, particularly when three or more candidates are seeking that seat.

Should the United States Have a National Primary?

The Issue: The party primary process that selects each party's nominee for president was a hot-button issue in the 2016 presidential race. Historically, the primary system focused enormous attention on the states of Iowa, where the first caucus is held, and New Hampshire, where the first party primary takes place. In these states, voters have had the opportunity to gain a deep familiarity with all the candidates seeking the parties' nominations. But critics of the system have charged that these two states' political cultures do not reflect that of the vast majority of Americans. Indeed, given that the party's nominees were effectively chosen by May 4, 2016, before several of the most populous states (including California and New Jersey) had even held their primaries, many questioned the democratic nature of a primary structure that effectively disenfranchised a segment of the population. Many citizens have asked, "Is this any way to begin electing a president?"

Should states matter when it comes to selecting the parties' nominees? One potential solution to the skewed emphasis on various states is to hold a national primary so that party members throughout the country can choose their nominees on the same day. People have voiced arguments for and against the idea of a national primary.

Yes: Having a national primary will help the parties, because it will ensure that the nominee chosen in each case is the best candidate for the party. With the shift to a national primary, states that currently have late primaries will no longer be forced to accept a nominee chosen by party members who might be very different from themselves. Furthermore, if more people have a say in choosing their party's nominee, voter turnout might rise in both the primary and the general election. Holding a national primary also will shorten the election season, so that voters will be less fatigued by the length of the campaign.

No: The primary system ensures that small, agricultural states have a voice in national politics. In the general election, smaller states are overshadowed because the Electoral College, which is based on state population, determines the winner. The current primary and caucus system enables voters in those states to analyze the candidates thoroughly, without the noise and distraction that would come with a large-scale, media-saturated national primary. And because the voters in states such as Iowa and New Hampshire are, after all, party members, they naturally understand that a large part of their responsibility is to select the nominee best equipped to win the general election.

Other Approaches: Some have suggested the idea of holding regional primaries instead of one national primary, with a different region holding its primary election first in each presidential election year so that no region would have the influence that Iowa and New Hampshire now enjoy. Each region would include a mix of large and small states and urban and rural areas. Candidates would need to campaign throughout each region in turn rather than the entire country, thus allowing them to focus their efforts more than they would be able to with one national primary, and with three or four regional primaries, the campaign season would still be shortened significantly, thus eliminating voter fatigue.

What do you think?

1. Do you believe that we should have a national primary? Explain.

2. What impact would a national primary have on your home state's say in the nomination process? How will small states fare compared with large states? Rural compared with urban?

3. What influence do you think a national primary or regional primaries would have on voter turnout? What effect might either type of primary have on how presidential campaigns are waged? Would money be more or less important? Why?

Because electoral law varies from state to state, and counties and municipalities within those states have their own structures of governance, less common kinds of elections are possible and are used in some locales. For example, some states require a runoff election when no candidate receives the majority of the votes cast. In a **runoff election,** if no candidate receives more than 50 percent of the vote, several of the top vote-getters (usually the top two) run in another, subsequent election. Typically, the field of candidates is winnowed down until one candidate receives the requisite 50 percent plus one vote. Runoff elections often occur in *nonpartisan* municipal elections, in which candidates do not run on a party label.

runoff election
A follow-up election that is held when no candidate receives the majority of votes cast in the original election.

Owing to advances in technology, runoff elections can occur immediately in some states when needed. In an **instant runoff election,** a computerized voting machine simulates the elimination of last-place vote-getters. How does this system work? In an instant runoff, voters rank candidates in order of preference (first choice, second choice, and so on). If any candidate garners more than 50 percent of all the first-choice votes, that candidate wins. But if no candidate gets a majority of first-choice votes, the candidate in last place is eliminated electronically. The voting machine computer then recalculates the ballots, using the second-choice vote for those voters who voted for the eliminated last-place finisher; in effect, every voter gets to choose among the candidates remaining on the ballot. This process is repeated until a candidate who receives more than 50 percent of the votes emerges. Today's voting machines allow this process to take place instantly.

instant runoff election
A special runoff election in which the computerized voting machine simulates the elimination of last-place vote-getters.

Referendum, Initiative, and Recall

Whereas primary elections and general elections select an individual to run for and serve in office, other kinds of elections are held for the purpose of deciding public policy questions. Although no national mechanism allows all Americans to vote for or against a given policy proposal, citizens can directly decide policy questions in their states by referendum or initiative.[12]

A **referendum** is an election in which voters in a state can vote for or against a measure proposed by the state legislature. Frequently, referenda concern matters such as state bond issues, state constitutional amendments, and controversial pieces of legislation. An **initiative,** sometimes called an initiative petition, is a citizen-sponsored proposal allowed in 24 states that can result in new or amended legislation or a state constitutional amendment. Initiatives differ from referenda in that they are typically propelled to public vote through the efforts of citizens and interest groups.[13] The initiative process usually requires that 10 percent of the number of the voters in the previous election in that state sign a petition agreeing that the **proposition,** or proposed measure, should be placed on the ballot. One example of an initiative is a 2018 ballot measure in Nevada that asked voters to change the state's voter registration system from an opt-in system (requiring individuals to register to vote) to an opt-out system (automatically registering individuals unless they choose to not be registered).

referendum
An election in which voters in a state can vote for or against a measure proposed by the state legislature.

initiative
A citizen-sponsored proposal that can result in new or amended legislation or a state constitutional amendment.

proposition
A proposed measure placed on the ballot in an initiative election.

A third type of special election, the recall, differs from referenda and initiatives in that it is not concerned with policy-related issues. Rather, the **recall** election allows voters to cut an officeholder's term of office short. Recall elections are typically citizen-sponsored efforts that demonstrate serious dissatisfaction with a particular officeholder. Concerned citizens circulate a petition, and, after they gather the required number of signatures, an election is held to determine whether the official should be thrown out of office.

recall
A special election in which voters can remove an officeholder before his or her term is over.

The Act of Voting

The process of voting begins when a voter registers to vote. Voting registration requirements vary greatly from state to state. Some states require registration months in advance of an election; others allow voters to register on the day of voting. In the United States, the voters use an **Australian ballot,** a secret ballot prepared by the government, distributed to all eligible voters, and, when balloting is completed, counted by government officials in an unbiased fashion, without corruption or regard to individual preferences. Because the U.S. Constitution guarantees the states the right to conduct elections, the mechanics and methods of voting vary widely

Australian ballot
A secret ballot prepared by the government, distributed to all eligible voters, and, when balloting is completed, counted by government officials in an unbiased fashion, without corruption or regard to individual preferences.

from state to state. Some states use touch-screen technology; others employ computer-based ballots or punch cards that are counted by computers. Still other states use traditional lever ballots, in which voters pull a lever to register their vote for a particular candidate. Despite those differences, all ballots are secret ballots.

Although secret ballots are the norm today, that was not always the case. From the days of the early republic through the 19th century, many citizens exercised their right to vote using oral votes cast in public or written votes witnessed by others; some made their electoral choices on color-coded ballots prepared by the political parties, which indicated which party the voter was supporting.

The 2000 Election and Its Impact

In the 2000 presidential election between Democrat Al Gore and Republican George W. Bush, an enormous controversy erupted over the voting in Florida. Because of the closeness of the electoral vote, the outcome of the Florida election turned out to be pivotal. But the tallies in that state's election were in question, not only because of the narrow difference in the number of votes won by each candidate, but also because of the voting process itself, which was marred by voting irregularities caused by poorly designed ballots that forced election officials to begin a tedious process of hand-counting ballots. In the end, the U.S. Supreme Court had the final say. On December 12, 2000, the Court halted the hand counting of ballots in Florida, with the Court's majority ruling that the differing standards of hand counting ballots from one county to the next and the absence of a single judicial officer charged with overseeing the hand counts violated the equal protection clause of the Fourteenth Amendment to the U.S. Constitution. The ruling meant that George W. Bush, who was leading in the count, was certified the winner of the Florida race, thus securing that state's 25 Electoral College votes and the presidency of the United States.

Indignation surrounding the 2000 election resulted in federal policy changes to the conduct of elections by the states. The key policy revision came through the passage of the Help America Vote Act of 2002 (HAVA). HAVA allocated $650 million to assist states in changing from punch card ballots to electronic voting systems and set a deadline of 2005 for states to comply. Most states implemented the election reforms required by HAVA, but many experienced difficulties with electronic-only voting systems, compelling many to adopt systems that create a traceable paper backup system of balloting, as shown in Figure 9.1. From that figure, we see that just five states—Louisiana, Georgia, South Carolina, Delaware, and New Jersey—now have electronic voting without any form of backup paper balloting.

Types of Ballots

Two types of ballots are most commonly used in general elections in the states today. The first, the **party-column ballot,** organizes the candidates by party so that all of a given party's candidates for every office are arranged in one column. The opposing party's candidates appear in a different column.

party-column ballot
A ballot that organizes the candidates by political party.

The impact of a party-column ballot is twofold: First, party-column ballots increase voters' tendency to vote the "party line," that is, to vote for every candidate of a given party for every office. Second, because they increase the tendency to vote the party line, party-column ballots also increase the **coattail effect,** the phenomenon whereby *down-ballot candidates* (candidates who are running for lower-level offices, such as city council) benefit from the popularity of a top-of-ticket nominee. Often, the composition of city councils, county legislatures, and even state legislatures changes because of a coattail effect from a popular presidential or gubernatorial candidate.

coattail effect
The phenomenon by which candidates running for lower-level offices such as city council benefit in an election from the popularity of a top-of-ticket nominee.

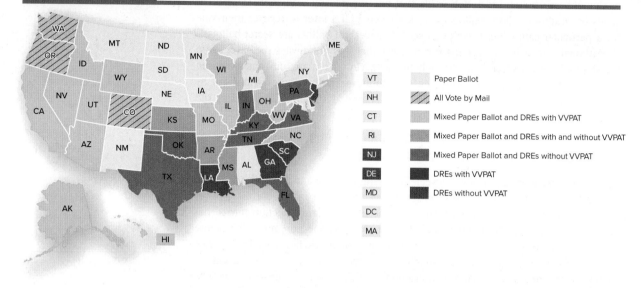

VT	▢ Paper Ballot
NH	▨ All Vote by Mail
CT	▨ Mixed Paper Ballot and DREs with VVPAT
RI	▨ Mixed Paper Ballot and DREs with and without VVPAT
NJ	▨ Mixed Paper Ballot and DREs without VVPAT
DE	▨ DREs with VVPAT
MD	▨ DREs without VVPAT
DC	
MA	

FIGURE 9.1 ■ **How Americans Vote Varies Greatly from State to State** Which states are using a vote-by-mail system exclusively? Why do you think these states would rely on this mechanism? Which states do not have backup paper ballot-ing (no VVPAT)? Why is that a risk? Does it matter that balloting occurs differently across the country?

NOTE: DRE = Direct Recording Electronic Voting Machines; VVPAT = Voter Verified Paper Audit Trail Printers.

SOURCE: Verified Voting Foundation, Inc.

office-block ballot

A type of ballot that arranges all the candidates for a particular office under the name of that office.

Because party-column ballots strengthen political parties, parties tend to favor this type of ballot, which is the most commonly used ballot in the United States.

Another type of general election ballot is the **office-block ballot,** which arranges all candidates for a particular office under the name of that office. Office-block ballots are more likely to encourage ticket splitting, where-by voters "split their ticket"—that is, divide their votes—between candidates from different parties.[14] Because office-block ballots deemphasize political parties by break-ing up the party line, the parties do not tend to favor them.

Voting by Mail

A relatively recent development is the advent of statewide voting by mail, a practice that states have adopted in an attempt to increase voter participation by making voting more convenient. Traditionally, **absentee voting,** in which voters cast their ballots in advance by mail, was allowed only when disability, illness, school, work, service in the armed forces, or travel prevented voters from casting a ballot in their voting precincts. Every state has a provi-sion that allows some voters—the elderly, the infirm, or those traveling—to vote via absentee ballot. To cast a traditional absentee ballot, an individual must typically apply (before a specific state-designated deadline) to vote by absentee in the county where he or she usually votes and is then mailed a ballot. The voter then votes and mails back the ballot. The absentee ballots are counted and added to the votes cast in the voting precincts. Requirements for absentee ballots vary from state to state.

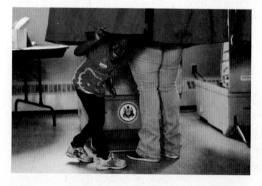

>The process of voting varies from state to state, with many states accepting mail-in ballot applications simply because absentee voting is more convenient for the voter. In every state, however, a ballot is prepared by the government, distributed to all eligible voters, and counted by government officials in an unbiased fashion. In your view, would voters be more likely to vote in person or by mail-in ballot?

©Eduardo Munoz Alvarez/AFP/Getty Images

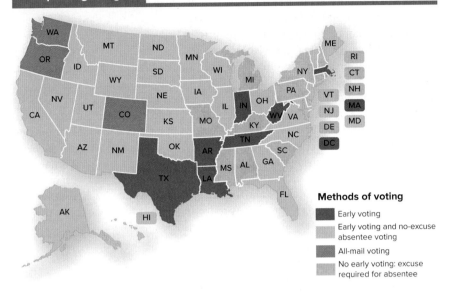

Methods of voting

- Early voting
- Early voting and no-excuse absentee voting
- All-mail voting
- No early voting: excuse required for absentee

FIGURE 9.2 ■ **Methods of Voting in the States** What is the most prevalent available form of voting in the states? Where do we find the strictest voting laws? What effect would the available method of voting have on voter turnout?

SOURCE: National Conference of State Legislatures, "Absentee and Early Voting," 2017.

Increasingly, many states accept mail-in ballot applications simply because absentee voting is more convenient for the voter. The first experiment with state-wide vote by mail occurred in Oregon in 1996. In a special election there, where officials had predicted a turnout of less than 50 percent, more than 66 percent of voters cast their ballots. This experiment brought another benefit: It saved taxpayers more than $1 million. Oregon decided to continue the practice in the presidential elections and has regularly seen voter turnout rates that exceed the national average. Oregon has now taken the drastic step of abandoning voting in polling places on Election Day.

Since that time, the practice of enabling citizens to cast their ballots by mail—often before Election Day—has become much more widespread, as indicated in Figure 9.2. In Oregon, Washington State, Colorado, and parts of Utah and California, all voters are sent mail ballots automatically. In 34 states plus the District of Columbia, any registered voter can cast a ballot in person during a designated period before Election Day. States vary in how long they allow early voting, with some states holding balloting for 4 days, others up to 45 days. Most states with early voting require that polling places—usually government offices—be open at least one weekend day, enabling those who work long hours to cast their ballots.

There are obvious advantages to voting by mail. When voting becomes easier, more people participate. Further, increased participation may bring to office candidates who are more representative of the will of the people because more people had a say in their election.

Some scholars, however, have criticized both the vote-by-mail and early voting trends. One important criticism is that early voting means that people vote before the final days of the campaign, thus casting their ballots before some additional last-minute information might be revealed about a candidate. Voting by mail also increases the chances of vote fraud. Even though states take measures to ensure the principle of "one person, one vote," voting by mail presents opportunities for

absentee voting

The casting of a ballot in advance by mail in situations where illness, travel, or other circumstances prevent voters from voting in their precincts.

corruption. Voting at the polls requires a face-to-face encounter, but voting by mail does not, so ballots could be stolen from individuals' mailboxes or intercepted after having been mailed by a voter.

Voting by mail also may eliminate the privacy associated with voting in recent times. With mail balloting, the vote occurs in a less controlled setting, and the voter might feel pressured by others to select a particular candidate. In contrast, booth voting affords privacy and secrecy that go far toward ensuring that the votes cast behind the curtain reflect the individual voter's will.

Finally, voting by mail may undermine feelings of civic engagement by eliminating a source of psychological rewards for voters. Going to a polling place, signing the voting registry, entering the voting booth, and casting your vote can elicit feelings of patriotism, civic pride, and fulfillment of civic responsibility—the sense that you are doing your duty to help ensure the election of the best-qualified candidates. Although the results may be the same with voting by mail, some evidence suggests that voting by mail does not bring with it the same sense of civic satisfaction that voting at a polling place confers.

Running for Office: The Choice to Run

The reasons that individuals become political candidates vary almost as much as the individuals do. Yet four types of motivation are generally in play when a person decides to declare a candidacy:

- Sense of civic responsibility—the feeling on the candidate's part that he or she bears an obligation to govern.
- Sense of party loyalty—of filling the need for parties to run viable candidates.
- Interest in increasing the candidate's name recognition and stature in the community, often for business reasons.
- Personal goals and, in particular, interest in electoral politics and office holding as a career.

Some people believe they have an obligation to put their experience, knowledge, and skills to work for the greater good of the community or country. Often these civically motivated people become politically involved out of concerns about specific issues. For example, 2018 saw a record number of scientists seeking congressional seats, many as part of a "pro-science resistance" spawned in response to what they perceive as an attack on scientific information and reasoning by the federal government.[15]

Sometimes an individual may choose to run for office out of a sense of party duty. The candidate may run as a "sacrificial lamb" for a seat he or she has little chance of winning, mainly with the intent to ensure that the party offers an alternative to the favored candidate. Some people run for office because of the heightened stature that a candidacy brings to their "regular" careers, through either name recognition or networking opportunities.

Other people are motivated to run for a particular office as their career. Holding office is what they do—and because of the advantages of incumbency, once elected, many remain in office for years. Other candidates run for office because of political ambitions. For example, a town council member who aspires to serve in the state legislature might run for county commissioner even if she thinks she will not win because she realizes that running a viable campaign might help her in a later bid for the statehouse.

Many candidates, of course, run for office for a combination of reasons. They might believe, for example, that they have a responsibility to serve their country *and* that they have something valuable to contribute.

Formal Eligibility Requirements

Article I of the U.S. Constitution specifies some minimum criteria for those seeking election to federal office:

- **President.** A candidate for the presidency must be a natural-born citizen. Naturalized citizens, who are born citizens of another country and then choose to become American citizens such as Ileana Ros-Lehtinen (R-Fla.), a member of the House of Representatives and a native of Cuba, cannot run for president. Presidential candidates also must be at least 35 years old. The youngest person elected president was the 43-year-old John F. Kennedy, but Theodore Roosevelt, who assumed the presidency after William McKinley's assassination, was the youngest to hold the office, at age 42. A presidential candidate also must have been a resident of the United States for 14 years by the time of inauguration.
- **Vice president.** A vice presidential candidate, like a contender for the presidency, must be a natural-born citizen and must be at least 35 years old; he or she must not be a resident of the same state as the candidate for president with whom he or she will serve. John Breckinridge, elected vice president in 1856 at age 35, was the youngest person to win the office.
- **U.S. senator.** A candidate for the Senate must have citizen status of at least 9 years, must be at least 30 years old when taking office, and must be a resident of the state from which he or she is elected. Currently the youngest person serving in the Senate is Tom Cotton (R-Ark.), born in 1977 and sworn into the Senate at age 38 in 2015.
- **U.S. representative.** A candidate for the House of Representatives must be a citizen for at least 7 years, must be at least 25 years old when taking office, and must be a resident of the state from which he or she is elected. Representative Elise Stefanik (R-N.Y.), born in 1984, was elected to the House in 2014 and sworn into office at age 30.

Typically, a state's constitution determines the minimal qualifications for the governorship and the state legislature, and these vary from state to state. In general, state requirements address the same issues as federal guidelines—citizenship, age, and residency.

Informal Eligibility Requirements

In addition to the legal eligibility requirements prescribed by the federal and state constitutions, informal eligibility criteria—that is, the characteristics that voters expect officeholders to have—help to determine who is qualified to run for a particular office. By and large, the eligibility pool for elected office depends on the office—and so although your car mechanic might be considered a good candidate for your town council, he would not likely meet the informal eligibility criteria to be elected president of the United States.

Generally speaking, the higher and more prestigious the political office, the greater the informal eligibility requirements are. On the local level, particularly in smaller communities, an individual would be considered eligible to run for town council if he or she was liked and respected in the community, had lived in the community long enough to know the voters, and was gainfully employed, a homemaker, or retired.

>Informal qualifications for Congress vary according to the political culture in the district. Openly gay members of Congress are a rarity. Mark Takano (D-Ca.), first elected in 2012, is the first openly gay person of color to be elected to the U.S. House of Representatives.

©Bill Clark/Getty Images

Farther up the political office ladder, state legislative candidates in most states are expected to have some kind of professional career. Still, there is a great deal of variation from state to state, and certainly nonprofessionals occupy many state legislative seats. State legislatures tend to be dominated by lawyers and business professionals, occupations that offer the prestige to be considered part of the informal eligibility pool and that allow enough flexibility to facilitate campaigning and legislative work.

The informal eligibility requirements for federal office are even more stringent. Voters expect candidates for the House of Representatives, the U.S. Senate, and the presidency to have higher qualifications than candidates for state and local offices. Among most congressional constituencies, candidates for federal office would be viewed as "qualified" to hold office if they had been elected to office, had a college degree, considerable professional and leadership experience, and strong communication skills. But informal qualifications vary according to the political culture in a district, with some districts favoring a particular religious affiliation, ethnicity, or other characteristic. Traditionally, in races for the U.S. Senate and the presidency, the popular press examines the minutest details of candidates' professional and educational backgrounds. For example, sometimes it is not enough that candidates are college graduates; where they went to college, whose university is more prestigious, and who had the higher grade point average are all fodder for the media and political pundits. But 2016 marked a watershed year in defining the appropriate informal eligibility requirements for a presidential candidate. When Donald Trump announced his candidacy for the Republican presidential nomination, many party insiders dismissed the celebrity candidate as not having what it takes to be president. Trump had never been elected to office, had suffered serious ups and downs in his business ventures, and was known to most of the United States as star of the reality television show *The Apprentice*. But Trump's celebrity, and his brash personality, attracted a cohort of voters perhaps weary of the predictable professional politicians who could check off all the boxes of "informal eligibility requirements," and Trump went on to win not only the GOP nomination but also the presidency itself.

The Nature of Political Campaigns Today

Campaigns today are different from the campaigns of the 1980s or even the early 1990s. The main reasons for the changes are the professionalization of campaign staffs; the dramatically expanded role of the media, the Internet, and social media and digital technologies; and the changing nature of campaign finance driven by candidates' ever-rising need for funding to keep pace with the unprecedented demands of contemporary campaigning.[16]

The Professionalization of Political Campaigns

One of the most significant changes in the conduct of campaigns is the rise in prominence of **campaign consultants,** paid professionals who specialize in the overall management of political campaigns or an aspect of campaigns, such as fund-raising or advertising. Previously, volunteers who believed in the party's ideals and in the candidate ran most campaigns. In contrast, professional consultants dominate modern campaigns for federal offices, many state offices, and some municipal offices. Typically, these advisers receive generous compensation for their services. Although professional consultants may not be as dedicated to a single candidate as earlier grassroots volunteers were, these strategists are typically committed to seeing their candidate elected and often are quite partisan, usually working only for candidates of one party throughout their careers.

One of the top jobs in a political campaign is that of **campaign manager,** a professional whose duties include a variety of strategic and managerial tasks. Among these responsibilities may be the development of the overall **campaign strategy,** the blueprint for the campaign, which includes a budget and fund-raising plan, an advertising strategy, and staffing objectives. Once the campaign strategy

campaign consultant
A paid professional who specializes in the overall management of political campaigns or an aspect of campaigns.

campaign manager
A professional whose duties comprise a variety of strategic and managerial tasks, from fund-raising to staffing a campaign.

campaign strategy
The blueprint for the campaign, including a budget and fund-raising plan, an advertising strategy, and a staffing plan.

THEN

NOW

```
                                    Scudder's Lane
                                    W. Barnstable, Mass.
                                    August 4, 1960

Senator John F. Kennedy
Hyannisport, Mass.

                                    AUG 8 1960

Dear Senator Kennedy:

      I would like to volunteer my services on behalf of
your campaign.

      I am a freelance writer living year-round on the
Cape.  I was a public relations man for General Electric
for several years, a reporter in Chicago before that.

      I am thirty-eight, have been a freelance for ten years.
I've published two novels, and am a regular contributor of
fiction to The Saturday Evening Post, Ladies' Home Journal,
McCall's, and so on.  On occasion, I write pretty well.

      I would be honored if you could use me as a volunteer
in any capacity whatsoever.



                            Yours truly,


                            Kurt Vonnegut, Jr.
```

> In 1960, campaigns, even those for the presidency, relied primarily on political party organizations and cadres of volunteers, including celebrities like famed author Kurt Vonnegut, who told then-senator Kennedy, "On occasion, I write pretty well." Now, campaigns are highly professional, with the labors of a campaign divided among many hired consultants, and technology driving participation among voters. Here, Senator Cory Booker's (D.-N.J.) website directs individuals on how to donate, keep informed, or volunteer on the campaign.

Letter: Courtesy of The Kurt Vonnegut Jr. Copyright Trust; *website:* Source: corybooker.com

GOTV
Get out the vote.

fund-raising consultant
A professional who works with candidates in identifying likely contributors to the campaign and arranges events and meetings with donors.

media consultant
A professional who brings the campaign message to voters by creating handouts and all forms of media ads.

is set, the campaign manager often hires and manages the office staff; selects the campaign's theme, colors, and slogan; shapes the candidate's image; and creates a **GOTV**–get out the vote–strategy. Another crucial campaign professional is the pollster, who conducts focus groups and polls that help develop the campaign strategy by identifying the candidate's strengths and weaknesses and by revealing what voters care about.

Other professionals round out the candidate's team. A **fund-raising consultant** works with the candidate to identify likely contributors and arranges fund-raising events and meetings with donors. Policy directors and public relations consultants help to develop the candidate's stance on crucial issues and to get the candidate's positions out to the voters, and a **media consultant** brings the campaign message to voters by creating handouts and brochures, as well as newspaper, radio, and television promotions. And now campaigns increasingly rely on social media consultants to bring the campaign to voters through YouTube, Facebook, Twitter, Snapchat, e-mail campaigns, web-based advertising, and blogs (see Chapter 11).[17]

The Media: Transforming Political Campaigns

Today, with the presence everywhere of the media in all its forms–television, Internet news sites, blogs, Twitter, radio, podcasts, newspapers, magazines–citizens' access to information is unprecedented. Whereas our ancestors had far fewer sources of news–word of mouth and the printed newspaper dominated for most of American history–people today can choose from a wide range of information sources and a bounty of information. Today, 24-hour news channels such as Fox News, CNN, and MSNBC compete with Internet news outlets, satellite radio programming, and news text messages to grab audience attention, while candidates attempt to spin coverage through the creation of videos available on their YouTube channels. But not all of the information in this bombardment is accurate.

Given the abundance of information disseminated today, engaged citizens have a greater responsibility to be discerning consumers of the news, including coverage of campaigns, voting, and elections particularly when it seems that Americans are intentionally being exposed to false information originating from foreign-sponsored trolls. They cannot be passive listeners and spoon-fed watchers of news as it is dished out on blogs or Facebook, or by daily newspapers, nightly newscasts, and the occasional weekly or monthly periodical. Vivé Griffith, at the University of Texas at Austin's Think Democracy Project, writes: "The challenge for the contemporary citizen is to be more than an audience member. Voters have unprecedented opportunities to access information and, at the same time, myriad ways to see issues obscured. An informed polity is essential to a democracy, and it can be difficult to sort through whether our media-saturated world ultimately serves to make us more or less informed."[18] We consider media coverage of elections, campaigns, and voting in detail in Chapter 10.

Revolutionizing the Campaign: New Technologies

New technologies have dramatically changed the conduct of political campaigns in recent years, and further developments promise to force campaigns to continue to evolve and adapt as technology generates new and faster ways to communicate and interact. Through texting, tweeting, Instagram, YouTube, and webchatting, candidates can use technologies to communicate with voters, mobilize supporters, and interact with the media. The Internet is among the most valuable and powerful new tools used by candidates. It serves as an efficient means by which office seekers can communicate with potential supporters, contributors, and the media. Candidates' websites and profiles provide a readily available forum where the electorate can find out about candidates' experiences, policy positions, and priorities. Voters can use this information to make more informed decisions in the voting booth. In addition, the Internet is a powerful fund-raising tool. In discussing the growth of campaign fund-raising on the Internet, Eli Pariser, founder of MoveOn.org's Peace Campaign, noted that "candidates are wasting their time with rubber-chicken donors,"[19] an allusion to donors who contribute to candidates by paying to attend campaign dinners.

Using e-mail and instant messaging, campaigns can communicate quickly with the media, both informing them of positive campaign developments and spinning negative developments in the best possible light for the candidate. Through campaign blogs, candidates can also supplement the information available in more traditional news media outlets. Internet communities and social networking sites also provide powerful tools for campaigns and important mechanisms for individuals' political engagement.

Money and Politics

Money—lots of it—is essential in electoral races today. Money and the modern campaign are inextricably linked because of the importance of costly media advertising in modern campaigns.[20] Federal regulations require any group that contributes to candidates' campaigns to register as a political action committee (PAC), and these organizations are subject to constraints in the amount of money that they can contribute to candidate campaigns. But today, as discussed in Chapter 8, in the wake of the Supreme Court ruling *Citizens United v. Federal Election Commission* in 2010, these regulations are being circumvented through the increasing use of a new class of **super PACs,** political organizations that use contributions from individuals, corporations, and labor unions to spend unlimited sums independent of the campaigns, yet influencing the outcomes of elections. Although super PACs are a relatively recent phenomenon, the influence of money

THEN NOW NEXT

How Political Campaigns Have Changed in the Past 30 Years

THEN (1980s)	NOW
Many campaigns were managed and staffed by volunteers.	Campaigns are increasingly managed professionally by "guns for hire" and often have an extensive staff dedicated to setting strategy, fund-raising, and managing social media campaigns and traditional media relations.
Grassroots activism was the norm in all but the largest campaigns.	Netroots activism—political activism driven by tweets, blogs, Snapchat, Instagram and Facebook posts, and candidates' websites—is overshadowing traditional grassroots campaign efforts.
Money was a crucial consideration in campaigns, but grassroots activism demanded fewer financial resources.	Money rules the day in most campaigns, but technology is increasingly leveling the campaign playing field.

WHAT'S NEXT?

> How can the Internet change the need for money in political campaigns?

> Given the extent of technologically driven activism during the 2018 campaigns, is there still a role for traditional grassroots activism in future campaigns? Explain.

> Will campaigns continue to be dominated by professional staffers? Why or why not?

super PACs
Political organizations that use contributions from individuals, corporations, and labor unions to spend unlimited sums independent from the campaigns, yet influencing the outcomes of elections.

in electoral politics goes back a long time, as do the efforts to regulate it.[21] Reformers have attempted to limit the influence of money on political campaigns for almost as long as campaigns have existed.

Early Efforts to Regulate Campaign Finance

Efforts to limit the influence of money started after a scandal that erupted during the administration of President Warren Harding (1921–1923). In 1921, the president transferred oil reserves at Teapot Dome, Wyoming, from the Department of the Navy to the Department of the Interior. The following year, Harding's secretary of the interior leased the oil fields without competitive bidding. A Senate investigation into the deal revealed that the lessee of the fields had "loaned" the interior secretary more than $100,000 in order to win political influence. The interior secretary was convicted and sentenced to a year in prison and a $100,000 fine. Dubbed the Teapot Dome scandal, this sordid affair led Congress to try to limit the influence of money on politics through legislation.

The Federal Corrupt Practices Act of 1925 sought to prevent future wrongdoing. This act aimed to regulate campaign finance by limiting campaign contributions and requiring public disclosure of campaign expenditures, and it was one of the first attempts at campaign finance regulation. But because the act did not include an enforcement mechanism, it was a weak attempt to fight corruption, and candidates found numerous loopholes in the law.

The Political Activities Act of 1939, also known as the Hatch Act, marked another congressional attempt to eliminate political corruption. With the growth of the federal bureaucracy as a result of the New Deal programs of President Franklin D. Roosevelt, several scandals had emerged, demonstrating the problems that could arise when government employees took an active role in politics. The Hatch Act banned partisan political activities by all federal government employees except the president, the vice president, and Senate-confirmed political appointees. The act also sought to regulate the campaign finance system by limiting the amount of money a group could spend on an election and placing a $5,000 cap on contributions from an individual to a campaign committee. Although the Hatch Act was more effective than the Federal Corrupt Practices Act of 1925, it also contained a significant loophole: Groups that wanted to spend more than the legislated limit of $3 million simply formed additional groups.

In 1971, Congress passed the Federal Election Campaign Act (FECA), the most significant attempt at overhauling the nation's campaign finance system. The law was sponsored by Democrats in Congress who were concerned about the enormous fund-raising advantage the Republicans had had during the 1968 presidential election. This law placed considerable limitations on both campaign expenditures and campaign contributions, and it provided for a voluntary tax-return check-off for qualified presidential candidates. This provision enables you, when filling out your federal income tax return, to contribute three dollars, which will go toward the matching funds that qualified presidential candidates receive.

In 1974, FECA was amended to place more stringent limitations on individual contributions and to limit expenditures by PACs, and it revamped the presidential election process by restricting spending and providing public financing for qualified candidates who abided by the limits. The act also required public disclosure of contributions and expenditures by all candidates for federal office. Most important, the act created an enforcement mechanism in the Federal Election Commission (FEC), the agency charged with enforcing federal campaign finance laws.

The Court Weighs In: Money = Speech

In the subsequent, highly significant Supreme Court case *Buckley v. Valeo* (1976), however, the plaintiffs contended that placing limitations on the amount an individual candidate could spend on his or her own campaign violated First Amendment protections of free speech. The Court agreed, ruling that "the candidate . . . has a First Amendment right to engage in the discussion of public issues and vigorously and tirelessly to advocate his own election."[22] This ruling paved the way for the subsequent explosion in the formation of PACs by recognizing political expenditures as a protected form of speech and removing limits on overall campaign spending, on personal expenditures by an individual candidate, and on expenditures not coordinated with a candidate's campaign and made by independent interest groups.

In its *Buckley* ruling, the Court boldly overturned the limitations on expenditures that to that point had been written into law. After the ruling, the number of political action committees shot up dramatically. Today, over 5,800 organizations raise and spend money to influence federal elections. Many of those PACs were formed by corporations that do business with the federal government and by associations whose members' livelihoods are significantly affected by federal regulations, including defense contractors, agricultural producers, and government employee unions. The ballooning of the number of PACs over time is indicative of the increased power that PACs have wielded in campaigns for federal office since 1980.

© N. Y. "Tribune."

>A *New York Tribune* cartoon titled "The First Good Laugh They've Had in Years" depicts the Democrats' jubilation over the Teapot Dome scandal of 1921, which saddled Republicans with a reputation for corruption. The scandal led Congress to try to limit the influence of money on politics.
©Bettmann/Getty Images

Independent Expenditures

Because expenditures are protected from limitations, many PACs now use independent expenditures to spend unlimited sums for or against political candidates.[23] **Independent expenditures** are outlays, typically for advertising supporting or opposing a candidate, that are uncoordinated with a candidate's campaign. Although PAC contributions to a candidate are limited, a PAC can spend as much as it wants on advertisements and mailings, supporting (or working against) candidates for federal office. This tactic is legal if these expenditures are not coordinated with the candidates' campaigns. Until the Court's ruling in the 2010 *Citizens United* decision, these ads could not "expressly advocate" a candidate by using terms such as "Vote for . . ." or "Elect . . . ,"[24] but the Court's decision eliminated those restrictions.

independent expenditures
Outlays by PACs and others, typically for advertising for or against a candidate, but not coordinated with a candidate's campaign.

The Bipartisan Campaign Finance Reform Act of 2002

Throughout the 1980s and 1990s, campaign finance reform was a perennial topic in presidential campaigns, and candidates roundly criticized the role of "special interests" in politics. But members of Congress had little to gain from reforming the system that had brought them to office.

Then in 2002, the world's largest energy-trading company and one of the nation's biggest corporations, Enron, collapsed after an internal accounting scandal, leaving in its wake furious stockholders, employees, and retirees whose financial health depended on the company. Investigations revealed extensive corporate fraud, including accounting improprieties that had enabled corporate leaders to lie about profits and debt. Investigations also revealed that Enron had contributed nearly $4 million to state and federal political parties in soft money contributions for "party-building activities," such as voter registration drives and later generic campaign advertising. Public indignation at the scandal flared, leading to the passage of the McCain-Feingold Act.

The McCain-Feingold Act, formally known as the Bipartisan Campaign Finance Reform Act (BCRA) of 2002, banned nearly all soft money contributions, although PACs can contribute up to a total of $10,000 to state, county, or local parties for voter registration and GOTV drives. The law also increased individual contribution limitations (shown in Table 9.1) and regulated some independent expenditure advertising.

TABLE 9.1 Contribution Limitations by Donor and Campaign Recipients Under the Bipartisan Campaign Finance Reform Act, 2018 Cycle

| | | | RECIPIENTS | | |
AMOUNT DONORS MAY GIVE	CANDIDATE OR CANDIDATE COMMITTEE PER ELECTION	NATIONAL PARTY COMMITTEE PER CALENDAR YEAR	STATE, DISTRICT, AND LOCAL PARTY COMMITTEE PER CALENDAR YEAR	ANY OTHER POLITICAL ACTION COMMITTEE PER CALENDAR YEAR	ADDITIONAL NATIONAL PARTY COMMITTEE ACCOUNTS
INDIVIDUAL	$2,700	$33,400	$10,000 (combined limit)	$5,000	$100,700 per account
NATIONAL PARTY COMMITTEE	$5,000	No limit	No limit	$5,000	No limit
STATE, DISTRICT, AND LOCAL PARTY COMMITTEE	$5,000 (combined limit)	No limit	No limit	$5,000 (combined limit)	No limit
PAC (MULTI CANDIDATE)	$5,000	$15,000	$5,000 (combined limit)	$5,000	$45,000 per account
PAC (NOT MULTI CANDIDATE)	$2,700	$33,900	$10,000 (combined limit)	$5,000	$100,700 per account
CANDIDATE COMMITTEE	$2,000	No limit	No limit	$5,000	No limit

SOURCE: Federal Election Commission, "Contribution Limits for 2015-2016."

One aspect of the McCain-Feingold Act that became the subject of a series of legal challenges was a ban on independent issue ads that aired close to elections. In many campaigns, groups would target candidates with advertisements critical of their issue positions. In 2003, Senator Mitch McConnell (R-Ky.), an opponent of the act, and a variety of groups affected by the new law (including the National Rifle Association and the California State Democratic Party) filed *McConnell v. the Federal Election Commission.*[25] The suit alleged that McCain-Feingold was a violation of the plaintiffs' First Amendment rights because the act prohibited airing these ads 30 days before a primary election and 60 days before a general election. The Supreme Court at first upheld the ban, but then reversed itself in another 5–4 decision. In 2007's *Federal Election Commission v. Wisconsin Right to Life, Inc.,*[26] the justices held that advertising within the 30- and 60-day windows could not be prohibited, thus paving the way for its extensive use in the 2008 presidential race.

Circumventing the Rules: 527s and 501(c)4s

Loopholes in the campaign finance law became apparent with the emergence of new forms of political groups, so-called 527s and 501(c)4s. **501(c)4s** are nonprofit organizations operated exclusively for the promotion of social welfare, including lobbying or engaging in political campaigning. 501(c)4s go largely unregulated by the FEC, and their activities are not subject to the transparency requirements that interest groups and campaign organizations are. Named after the section of the IRS tax code that regulates such organizations, a **527** is a tax-exempt group that raises money for political activities. If a 527 engages only in activities such as voter registration, voter mobilization, and issue advocacy, it has to report its activities only to the government of the state in which it is located or to the IRS. Disclosure to the FEC is required only if a 527 engages in activities expressly advocating for the election or defeat of a federal candidate, or if it participates in electioneering communications.

In 2016, 527s spent about $200 million to influence the outcome of federal elections through voter registration and mobilization efforts and through ads that, though purportedly issue-based, typically criticized a candidate's record. Like 527s, 501(c)4s are sometimes used by their often-wealthy organizers as a means of channeling money to influence political campaigns, but increasingly the 527 arena is becoming dominated by labor unions and offshoots of political party committees (including, for example, Bernie 2016, the Young Democrats of America, and the Young Republican National Federation).

501(c)4s
Nonprofit organizations operated exclusively for the promotion of social welfare, including lobbying or engaging in political campaigning.

527
A tax-exempt group that raises money for political activities, much like those allowed under the soft money loophole.

The Court Weighs In (Again): The Birth of Super PACs

The 1976 Supreme Court ruling in *Buckley v. Valeo* eventually would be the basis of the ruling in *Citizens United* that paved the way for super PACs. The year 2010 saw one of the most dramatic episodes in U.S. campaign finance history, with the Supreme Court's decision in the *Citizens United* case. According to this ruling, corporations and labor unions are entitled to the same First Amendment protections to freedom of speech that individuals enjoy. The impact of the *Citizens United* decision has enormously increased the importance of money in politics, as corporations and labor unions now recognize the uncontestable influence that they may have in federal elections. The controversial 5–4 decision was hailed by conservatives as a victory for free speech rights and was decried by liberals as an avenue by which corporations could increase their stranglehold on politics and the policy process.

The impact of the *Citizens United* decision could be seen in the 2016 presidential campaign: during the primary season alone, nearly 2,400 super PACs had organized and raised and spent more than $1 billion.

Presidential Campaigns

To many Americans, presidential campaigns epitomize the democratic process. In presidential election years, nonstop campaigning affords ample opportunities for the public to learn about the candidates and their positions. Campaigns also provide avenues for participation by the people—for example, by debating candidates' views on Twitter, by volunteering in or contributing to candidates' campaigns, or by voting. Although these opportunities for citizen engagement are especially abundant during a presidential election, they arise well before that time, because potential candidates typically position themselves years in advance of a presidential election to secure their party's nomination and to win the general election.

Party Conventions and the General Election Campaign

Political parties hold conventions in presidential election years to select their party's nominee for president of the United States. As discussed in Chapter 8 and as reviewed earlier in this chapter, the delegates to the national conventions are chosen by citizens in each state who vote in their parties' primary elections or who participate in party caucuses. Eligible incumbent presidents (who have served only one term) are nearly always nominated again, and the nominee of the opposing party is often determined by the primary results. After the conventions are over and the nominees have been decided (typically by late August or early September of the election year), the nominees and their vice presidential running mates begin their general election campaigns. Usually, the parties' choice of nominee is a foregone conclusion by the time of the convention.

The Electoral College

The votes tallied on Election Day determine which presidential candidate's slate of electors will cast their ballots in each state, in accordance with state law. There are 538 electors in the Electoral College because the number of electors is based on the number of members of Congress—435 in the House of Representatives, 100 in the Senate—plus 3 electors who represent the District of Columbia. A presidential candidate needs a simple majority of votes (270) to win. Note that a candidate need not win the popular vote in order to win the Electoral College and thus the presidency, as was the case in 2016 when Hillary Clinton received 65,845,063 votes to Donald Trump's 62,980,160, but Trump won the Electoral College, as shown in Figure 9.3. In most elections, the Electoral College exaggerates the winner's margin of victory (rather than reverses the popular outcome).

On the Monday following the second Wednesday of December, the slates of electors chosen in each state meet in the state capitals and cast their electoral votes. The results are then announced in a joint session of Congress in early January. In most presidential elections, however, the winner is known on election night, because analysts tabulate the outcome in each state and predict the electoral vote. The winner takes the oath of office as president in inaugural ceremonies on January 20.

Who Votes? Factors in Voter Participation

Not all people are equally likely to participate in the process of voting for the president or other government officials. Yet of all the forms of political participation, the act of voting has been analyzed perhaps more than any other.[27] Scholars such as Angus Campbell, Philip E. Converse, Warren Miller, and Donald Stokes have examined what factors influence who votes and how voters decide.[28] They and others have analyzed how characteristics such as education level, income, age, race, and the degree of party competitiveness in a given election influence whether a person will vote.[29] Of course, in considering demographic characteristics such as voter age and income level, we must remember that these are merely generalizations.

Clinton	**227**
Trump	**304**

FIGURE 9.3 ■ The 2016 Electoral College Vote In what areas of the country did President Trump get much of his support? Where did Hillary Clinton win? Which candidate won the most populous states?

Education Level—The Number-One Predictor of Voting

Historically, an individual's level of education is the best predictor of whether that person will vote, but in 2016, voters without college degrees defied long-established trends of low levels of participation and turned out to support Donald Trump. Typically, as education increases, so, too, does the likelihood of voting, with measurable differences even among those who have attended but not graduated from college and those who have graduated from college.

The Age Factor

During any presidential campaign, you will hear much about age as a factor in the likelihood of voting. Despite campus-focused initiatives by presidential campaigns, young adults are less likely to vote than are Americans who are middle aged and older, though that figure has increased in recent years.[30] In the 2016 election, the turnout rate among young Americans—those aged 18 to 29—was lower than the 2008 rates, which had seen the highest turnout rate for voters of that age group since 18-year-olds were first granted the right to vote in 1972. In both 2008 and 2012, the youth vote was a key deciding factor, with young Americans overwhelmingly supporting Barack Obama and propelling him to victory. But 2016 was a different race, with both Hillary Clinton and Donald

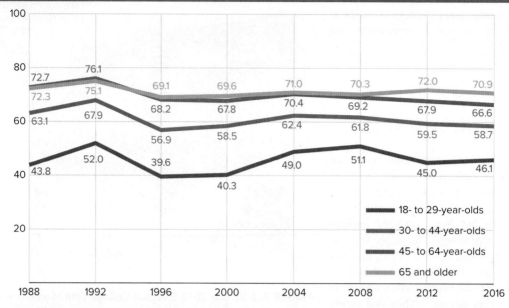

FIGURE 9.4 ■ Age and Voting in Presidential Elections For which age group is the percentage of people voting traditionally the highest? For which age group is the voting percentage lowest? In which years did all age groups' turnout increase? When did young people's increase? Do you think the youth vote will be important in 2020?

SOURCE: United States Census Bureau.

Trump struggling to attract young voters. But Figure 9.4, which plots the percentage of people in various age groups who voted in recent presidential elections, illustrates a historic trend: As Americans age, they are more likely to vote. There are numerous reasons why young people do not vote. Among 18- to 24-year-olds, the reason most often cited is that they were too busy or had a schedule conflict, but members of this age group are also more likely to report that they forgot to vote or were out of town. Age also is related to mobility—young people might move when they leave for college or to start a new job, and mobility depresses voter turnout.

Race, Ethnicity, and Voter Participation

In 2016, race and ethnicity became pivotal in the presidential contest between Democratic nominee Hillary Clinton and Republican nominee Donald Trump. During the early stages of his campaign, Trump increased the probability that race would become a wedge issue in the campaign when he initially refused to disavow white supremacists who were supporting his campaign.[31] Trump also managed to offend many Latino voters with his pejorative characterization of Mexican immigrants: "What can be simpler or more accurately stated? The Mexican Government is forcing their most unwanted people into the United States. They are, in many cases, criminals, drug dealers, rapists, etc."[32] His rhetoric alienated other voters, particularly first-generation Americans, for instance: "The United States has become a dumping ground for Mexico and, in fact, for many other parts of the world."[33]

EXPLORING RACE AND VOTING

Voter turnout rates in presidential elections, 1988–2016

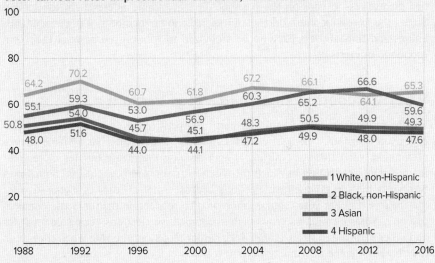

1 White, non-Hispanic
2 Black, non-Hispanic
3 Asian
4 Hispanic

NOTE: Hispanics are of any race. For the years 1988 through 2008, whites, blacks, and Asians include only non-Hispanics. For 2012 and 2016, blacks and Asians include Hispanics. Data for non-Hispanic Asians were not available in 1988.

SOURCE: United States Census Bureau.

Practice Analytical Thinking

1. In general, what has been the trend with regard to voter turnout among blacks and whites over time?

2. What has been the trend among Hispanics and Asian Americans? In your view, why has participation by members of these groups differed from that of blacks and whites?

3. From these data, we see a significant occurrence in 2012. Can you identify this event? Why might this have occurred?

Clinton sought to capitalize on Trump's divisiveness and attract the support of racial and ethnic minorities. For decades after the Voting Rights Act of 1965 ensured that African Americans could freely exercise the right to vote, turnout rates among African Americans lagged substantially behind those of non-Hispanic white Americans. But Clinton, aware that the candidacy of Barack Obama had bolstered the participation of African Americans, recognized that voter participation among African Americans had surpassed that of whites (see "Analyzing the Sources"), a trend that was years in the making. But while turnout by African American voters remained high, it was not at the record-setting pace Obama was able to generate. Participation by Latinos, who many thought would be mobilized in 2016, also dropped. Nonetheless, Latinos are viewed as an important constituency because they are an expanding proportion of the population that is becoming increasingly likely to vote.

Income—A Reliable Predictor of Voting

Besides education, income is one of the best predictors of whether an American will vote.[34] Typically in recent presidential election years, U.S. citizens with the lowest income level have had voter turnout levels of 50–60 percent, whereas those with the highest income level have had turnout levels above 85 percent.[35] As income increases, so does the likelihood of voting.

The reasons for the close correlation between income and likelihood of voting are complex.[36] One possibility is that people with lower incomes are less likely than higher-income earners to believe that the government listens to people like them. Another factor may be that individuals with lower incomes have less leisure time in which to learn about candidates and issues and even to vote. State voting registration laws also may impede participation, as individuals with unstable housing may face obstacles in determining where their polling places are, or even in finding transportation to the polls. Further, in contrast to American voters, European voters are often mobilized—by class-based trade unions and by the parties themselves—to vote on the basis of their economic interests. In the United States, the lowest-income workers are less likely to be members of organized labor unions and thus are less likely to be mobilized to vote on the basis of their own economic interests.

Party Competitiveness and Voter Turnout

Finally, researchers have found that party competitiveness in elections also influences voter turnout.[37] In tight contests, in which either party has a viable chance of winning, voter turnout typically is high because the race generates more voter interest than an election in which the winner is a foregone conclusion. Sometimes turnout is high in competitive elections because voter efficacy is higher—a voter may believe that her vote "counts" more in a close election than in a less competitive race. Voter turnout also runs high in competitive elections because the parties and other campaign organizations work harder to get out the vote when they think they have a chance at winning but know that victory is not guaranteed.

Competitive races also draw increased media attention. A tightly competitive local mayoral race might get greater than usual regional news attention, and a close race for the White House brings nearly nonstop media reports and candidate advertisements. The barrage of media coverage increases public awareness and may also boost voter efficacy by conveying the message that every vote counts.

The impact of this competitiveness can be seen in recent presidential elections. In 2016, about 139 million Americans voted, surpassing the 132 million who had voted in 2008. In 2016's elections, the **turnout rate,** the proportion of eligible voters who actually voted, was 61 percent.[38] The 2016 election saw higher turnout rates among those in competitive battleground states, where intense party competition generated turnout.

turnout rate
The proportion of eligible voters who actually voted.

How Voters Decide

When deciding for whom they will vote, some voters evaluate candidates on the basis of their positions on issues and then cast their ballots for those who best represent their views. Called **prospective voting,** this method of candidate evaluation focuses on what the candidates will do in the future. A more common form of candidate evaluation is **retrospective voting,** in which a voter evaluates an incumbent candidate on the basis of whether the incumbent's past decisions and actions are satisfactory to the voter.[39] If they are satisfactory, the voter will likely support the incumbent. If not, the voter will be disposed to support the incumbent's opponent. The prevalence of an incumbency advantage in election outcomes indicates that many voters have a favorable view of the decisions and actions of incumbent candidates for most offices.[40]

prospective voting
A method of evaluating candidates in which voters focus on candidates' positions on issues important to them and vote for the candidates who best represent their views.

retrospective voting
A method of evaluating candidates in which voters evaluate incumbent candidates and decide whether to support them based on their past performance.

TABLE 9.2 Party Loyalty in the 2016 Presidential Election

	VOTED FOR TRUMP (%)	VOTED FOR CLINTON (%)
Democrats	9	89
Independents	48	42
Republicans	90	7

SOURCE: American National Election Studies.

The most important factor that plays into how a voter decides on a candidate and perceives specific candidates, however, is the voter's party identification. Other influential determinants include those specific to a given election, such as candidates' attributes and the effectiveness of the candidates' campaigns. But as Table 9.2 indicates, even in the most controversial elections, party members tend to stay loyal to their party's candidates.

Major Factors in Voter Decision Making

Often a significant determinant of why people vote the way they do, policy priorities are to a certain extent aligned with party identification (or, even more generally, with ideology), because the political parties usually embrace differing viewpoints on issues. National issues that top the list of concerns among voters have remained consistent over many years and include several domestic policy matters, such as immigration reform, the health of the economy, education, crime, health care, and Social Security.

But how do voters decide which party and which candidate to support at the polls, based on the issues? First and foremost, an issue must be **salient** to voters—that is, it must resonate with them and reflect something that they care deeply about, an issue they are willing to base their vote on.[41] The ability of voters to cast an issue-based vote increases when candidates differ in their positions on an issue.

Incumbency, the situation of already holding an office or an official position, as we have seen, is also a key factor influencing how people vote. Because an incumbent is a "known commodity" with demonstrated experience to serve in office, voters are much more likely to vote for incumbents than for their challengers. Thus, for most offices, incumbents are much more likely to be reelected than their challengers are to be elected. Indeed, in the 2016 congressional elections, 93 percent of incumbent U.S. senators and 97 percent of incumbent members of the House of Representatives won reelection, figures that are consistent with past elections. But incumbency is also an influence in presidential elections, gubernatorial and state legislative elections, and probably even your local city council elections. Incumbents have notable advantages over challengers, namely, greater name recognition, a track record that voters can evaluate, and access to campaign contributions that help them to get their message out.

Campaign Influences on Voter Choice

As we have seen, parties and candidates conduct campaigns to influence voters' choices at the polls. Campaigns today vary a great deal in how they are waged.

salient
In relation to a voting issue—having resonance, being significant, causing intense interest.

incumbency
The situation of already holding the office that is up for reelection.

Whereas a candidate for a small town's board of selectmen might knock on the door of every voter in the community, a U.S. Senate or gubernatorial candidate might spend most of his or her time raising money to pay for expensive television and radio advertisements, while a presidential candidate might take to Twitter to get his or her views directly to voters. But generally, the lower the level of office, the greater the likelihood that the candidate will rely on grassroots activism.

Trends in modern campaigns, including a far deeper reliance on paid professional staffers, and the prevalence of the savvy use of social media and traditional media as tools for communicating with voters, are catapulting the costs of campaigns sky-high. Voter choices are also affected by increasingly negative campaigns, one outcome of the modern political campaigns' reliance on paid professionals. Outside consultants typically have far fewer qualms about "going negative" than do activists in the all-community volunteer-run campaigns that were more typical of earlier times.

Consultants use negative campaign tactics for a simple reason: research shows that the approach sways voter opinion.[42] Although the candidates themselves often prefer to accentuate a positive message that highlights their background, experience, and qualifications, paid campaign consultants generally do not hesitate to sling the mud. Once a candidate establishes name recognition and credibility with voters, many consultants believe highlighting the opponent's negative qualities and actions is an effective campaign strategy.

But the effect of negative campaigning is not limited merely to swaying voters from one candidate to another. Research by political scientists shows that negative campaigning can suppress voter turnout in several ways. For example, Shanto Iyengar and Jennifer A. McGrady note that negative advertising may suppress voter turnout among the attacked candidate's supporters.[43] Other political scientists' research shows that negative campaigning undermines the democratic process by decreasing civic engagement among all voters. According to these findings, the electorate becomes disenchanted with the candidates (about whom voters get a barrage of negative information), with the campaigns (because campaigns serve as the primary messengers for delivering negative information about opponents), or with the entire electoral process that facilitates this negativity. Some voters view negative campaigning as being completely at odds with their idealized conception of the democratic process, and this belief may discourage them from voting.

Why Some People Do Not Vote

Negative campaigning is one reason why some people do not vote, but political scientists have proposed several others. Lack of civic engagement on the part of voters underlies many of these ideas. Other reasons have to do with the nature of campaigns and the structure of elections.

Lack of Efficacy

Some voters do not vote because they do not participate in civic affairs, either locally or at the national level. Many of these nonvoters lack efficacy.[44] They do not believe that the government listens to people like them or that their vote actually matters in determining the outcome of elections and the business of government.[45]

Scholars have determined that individuals who lack efficacy exist across the social and economic spectrums but that poorer people are more likely than better-off individuals to feel that the government does not listen to people like them. While it is a common notion that people are alienated from politics or think that the government does not listen to their concerns, a study estimated that only about 9 percent of the U.S. population feels that way.[46] This same survey indicated that people lacking efficacy—a group that the study called the "disaffecteds"— typically had a low level of educational attainment and were less likely to follow current events than more engaged citizens.

Voter Fatigue and Negative Campaigns

Another explanation for why some Americans do not vote stems from the nature of political campaigns. In the United States, campaigns tend to be long-drawn-out affairs. For example, presidential campaigns typically last for more than a year, with some candidates positioning themselves three or four years in advance of an election. Contrast that with many parliamentary systems, including Germany's, in which an election must be held within 60 days of the dissolution of parliament because of a "no confidence" vote of the chancellor (similar to a prime minister). Some scholars say that the lengthiness of the campaigns leads to **voter fatigue,** the condition in which voters simply grow tired of all candidates by the time Election Day arrives, and may thus be less likely to vote.

voter fatigue
The condition in which voters grow tired of all candidates by the time Election Day arrives, and may thus be less likely to vote.

American journalist and humorist Franklin Adams commented that "elections are won by men and women chiefly because most people vote against somebody rather than for somebody."[47] The prevalence of negative campaigning compounds the phenomenon of voter fatigue. Even the most enthusiastic supporters of a candidate may feel their advocacy withering under the unceasing mudslinging that occurs in many high-level campaigns. And so, although evidence shows that negative advertising is effective in swaying voters' opinions, sometimes such advertising also succeeds in suppressing voter turnout by making voters less enthusiastic about voting.

The Structure of Elections

Political scientists also cite the structure of U.S. elections as a reason why more Americans do not vote. For years, voting rights activists claimed that the registration requirements in many states were too complicated and discouraged people from voting by making it too difficult to register, but that theory was negated when turnout failed to increase significantly after Congress passed the National Voter Registration Act in 1993, which allows people to register when interacting with many government agencies, including when they apply for a driver's license.

Critics of the structure of elections also point to their frequency.[48] In the United States, the number of elections varies from municipality to municipality, and local government charters may call for more than four elections for municipal offices alone. Although most federal offices require only two elections (a primary and a general), these elections are not always held in conjunction with state, county, and municipal elections.

The timing of elections also affects voter participation. Most general elections are held on a weekday, and research shows that holding elections on weekends or over a two-day period instead, or establishing a national voting holiday, would increase voter turnout by ensuring that voters had ample opportunity to cast their ballots.[49]

Rational Choice Theory

rational choice theory
The idea that when deciding whether to vote, individuals will consider both how much they care about the outcome of an election and the likelihood that their vote will be important in influencing its outcome.

A final explanation as to why some people do not vote is rooted in **rational choice theory**—the idea that individuals will consider both how much they care about the outcome of an election and the likelihood that their vote will be important in influencing its outcome.[50] This theory states that some individuals decide that the "costs" of voting—in terms of the time, energy, and inconvenience required to register to vote, to become informed about candidates and elections, and actually to vote—are not worth the effort when compared with the expected "benefits," or what the voters could derive from voting.

In light of these cumulative "costs," it is perhaps surprising that so many people choose to vote.[51] One explanation for why they do is that most voters report that they derive psychological rewards from exercising this citizen's right—feelings of being civically engaged, satisfied, and patriotic. But when the costs associated with voting increase too much, turnout drops; more people choose not to vote when voting becomes too inconvenient. This drop-off occurs, for example, when municipalities shorten voting hours and during inclement weather.

The Consequences of Nonvoting

From a civic engagement perspective, nonvoting is both a symptom and a result of a lack of civic involvement on the part of individuals.[52] Your room-mate might not vote because she is not civically engaged—because she feels that she has little to contribute and that the government does not listen to "people like her" anyway. But by not voting, she perpetuates this lack of efficacy by remaining outside the process rather than staking a claim to what is rightfully hers: the idea that every individual has the right to a voice in the composition and priorities of the government. Only by becoming civically engaged—learning about the candidates, discussing issues, and voting—can she break the cycle of inefficacy. Voting will make her pay more attention to campaigns, candidates, and issues.

Beyond the effects of nonvoting on individuals, low voter turnout affects the polity (see Chapter 1). When relatively few people vote in a given election, the outcome is likely to represent the will of only that subset of the electorate who voted. The process becomes cyclical: These nonvoters who disagree with the outcome conclude that the government does not represent them, they feel less efficacious, and they are less inclined to vote in the future.

Moreover, some scholars assert that democracies with low voter turnout are more likely to generate threats to their own well-being.[53] In democracies with low turnout, these scholars say, charismatic, popular political figures may rise to power and become authoritarian leaders. Corruption, too, can be a problem in low-turnout democracies where government officials might feel relatively unconcerned about the disapproval of disgruntled constituents.

Other researchers, however, contend that nonvoting is not a big problem, especially in cases where large numbers in the electorate are relatively uninformed about candidates and issues.[54] A number of scholars in this camp argue that participation by the uninformed is undesirable, because it may lead to drastic changes in government. Opponents of this view counter that because of political parties' role in selecting candidates, the menu for voter choice is actually quite limited in most elections. Those who argue that nonvoting does not matter also ignore the fact that voting tends to produce more engaged citizens who, because they vote, feel a duty to be informed and involved.

Other scholars who claim that low voter turnout is not a problem argue that low voting rates are simply a function of people's satisfaction with the status quo: Their nonvoting simply means that they do not seek change in government. This argument, however, does not explain why lower turnout is most likely to occur in populations that are least likely to be satisfied with their situation. For example, people with lower incomes are much less likely to vote than those with higher incomes. Whatever the reason—a lack of efficacy as argued by some, satisfaction as argued by others—nonvoters' best chance of having their views reflected in the policy process is to articulate them through voting.

Conclusion
Thinking Critically About What's Next in Campaigns, Elections, and Voting

The nature of political campaigns in the United States has continuously evolved, but the changes in recent decades have been especially dramatic. An era in which political parties and grassroots activism dominated campaigns has given way to the present-day realities where money, media, and mavens of strategy are key forces in shaping campaigns, which have grown increasingly candidate and technology centered. Prominently driving the changes are the simultaneous *decrease* in political party clout and *increase* in the need for money—money to pay for the small army of professional staffers that run the campaigns; and money to cover the expensive media buys that candidates, especially those running for national and state office, heavily depend on for communicating with the electorate. Increasingly, this money is being raised outside the regulated campaign finance system, with wealthy donors circumventing federal election reporting requirements by contributing to 527s, 501(c)4s, or super PACs, whose influence in federal campaigns is growing.

In 2016, we saw the possibility of meddling in U.S. elections by outside, foreign interests intent on undermining U.S. democracy, using technology to misinform and foment division within the United States. But technology offers the potential to bring the politics of electoral campaigns back to the grassroots—now perhaps more appropriately called the netroots. The options that campaigns and candidates have to communicate with voters through media such as Twitter, Facebook, YouTube, Snapchat, e-mail, and instant messaging present an exciting alternative to high-priced "campaigning-as-usual."

The election of 2016 also demonstrated that through the new media of communication, both the enormous potential and the danger that exists for the inclusion of a variety of new voices in the political campaigning process. Groups that want to influence campaigns and voters have at their disposal a vast arsenal of new technology that makes such influence possible.

Learning Summary

1. Explain the importance of fair and independent elections.
   a. Explain the implications for national and popular sovereignty.
   b. Explain why political participation is an expression of the will of the people.

2. Explain the types of elections in the United States.
   a. Compare and contrast the types of primaries.
   b. Explain the purpose of a general election.
   c. Describe the various processes of run-off elections.
   d. Compare and contrast initiative, referendum, and recall elections.

3. Describe how the act of voting varies from state to state.
   a. Describe how the 2000 elections changed the voting process in the states.
   b. Compare and contrast office-block and party-column ballots.
   c. Explain the effect of voting by mail.

4. Describe the four types of motivations typical among candidates.
   a. Explain the formal eligibility requirements for the president, vice president, U.S. senator, and U.S. House member.
   b. Explain the informal eligibility requirements for these offices.

5. Explain how modern campaigns differ from earlier campaigns.
   a. Describe the importance of paid professionals in campaigns and their roles.
   b. List ways in which the media are transforming campaigns.
   c. Explain how new technologies are revolutionizing campaigns.

6. Understand why money plays such an important role in politics.
   a. Describe early efforts to regulate campaign finance.
   b. Explain the effect of *Buckley v. Valeo*, including the growth of PACs and independent expenditures.
   c. Outline the features of the Bipartisan Campaign Finance Reform Act of 2002.
   d. Explain the purpose of new campaign-related organizations, including 527s and 501(c)4s.
   e. Explain how the *Citizens United* decision paved the way for the birth of super PACs.

7. Describe the process of presidential elections.
   a. Describe party conventions and the general election campaign.
   b. Explain the Electoral College.

8. Explain the factors in voter participation, including education, age, race and ethnicity, income, and party competitiveness.

9. Describe how voters decide for whom to vote.
   a. Compare and contrast prospective and retrospective voting.
   a. Explain the influence of issues, incumbency, and campaigns on swaying voters.

10. Explain why people do not vote.
    a. Understand what lack of efficacy is and how it influences nonvoting.
    b. Describe other explanations for why people don't vote, including voter fatigue, negative campaigns, the structure of elections, and rational choice theory.
    c. Describe the consequences of nonvoting.

Key Terms

absentee voting 307

Australian ballot 304

campaign consultant 311

campaign manager 311

campaign strategy 311

caucus 301

closed primary 302

coattail effect 305

501(c)4s 317

527 317

fund-raising consultant 312

general election 301

GOTV 312

grassroots organizing 299

incumbency 323

independent
    expenditures 315

initiative 304

instant runoff election 304

media consultant 312

office-block ballot 306

open primary 302

party-column ballot 305

proposition 304

prospective voting 322

rational choice
    theory 326

recall 304

referendum 304

retrospective voting 322

runoff election 302

salient 323

super PACs 313

Super Tuesday 302

turnout rate 322

voter fatigue 325

For Review

1. Why are fair, independent elections important?

2. What are some opportunities for civic engagement related to elections, campaigns, and voting?

3. What are the different kinds of elections in the United States? What is the difference between a primary election and a general election?

4. How do states vary in how elections are conducted?

5. What is the difference between formal and informal eligibility requirements for political office?

6. Why is regulating campaign finance so difficult? Explain the various efforts to limit the impact of money on campaigns.

7. What factors influence whether a person will vote or not?

8. What factors influence how or for whom an individual will vote?

9. What is the rational choice theory? Is it rational? What factors might not be calculated into the costs and benefits of voting?

For Critical Thinking and Discussion

1. Why do formal and informal eligibility requirements for office differ? What are the informal eligibility requirements to run for the state legislature where you live? What are the requirements for the city or town council in your hometown or the community where your school is located? How do these differences reflect the nature of the constituency for the office being sought?

2. How has the increasing cost of political campaigns changed the nature of American politics? Why have costs escalated? What effect is technology having on this trend?

3. What have been the effects of the increasing negativity in American political campaigns?

4. Using the text discussion of factors influencing whether a person votes, assess a classmate's likelihood of voting based solely on those factors. Then ask the person if he or she votes. Was your assessment accurate?

5. In your view, what are the consequences of nonvoting?

Resources for Research AND Action

Internet Resources

The Living Room Candidate
www.livingroomcandidate.org This site, maintained by the Museum of the Moving Image, provides videos of television commercials run by presidential campaigns from 1952 to 2016.

Project Vote Smart
www.votesmart.org This nonpartisan website provides independent, factual information on election procedures in each state.

Ready To Run
www.cawp.rutgers.edu/education_training/ReadytoRun/ This nonpartisan campaign training program encourages and trains women to run for elective office, position themselves for appointive office, or work on a campaign.

Vote, Run, Lead
www.voterunlead.org This is the website for an organization that encourages the civic engagement of young women as voters, activists, and candidates for political office.

Recommended Readings

Abramson, Paul R., John H. Aldrich, and David W. Rohde. *Change and Continuity in the 2016 Elections.* Washington, DC: CQ Press, 2019. The latest in this classic series of election analyses examines the tactics employed in the 2016 presidential election.

Burns, Nancy, Kay Lehman Schlozman, and Sidney Verba. *The Private Roots of Public Action: Gender, Equality, and Political Participation.* Cambridge, MA: Harvard University Press, 2003. Explores the differences in political participation between men and women.

Clinton, Hillary. *What Happened.* New York: Simon and Schuster, 2017. In this post-mortem of the 2016 election, Clinton chronicles what it was like to run for president as the first woman major-party candidate.

Gainous, Jason, and Kevin M. Wagner. *Tweeting to Power: The Social Media Revolution in American Politics.* New York: Oxford University Press, 2014. Describes the rise of social media in campaigns and elections.

Herrnson, Paul S., Richard G. Niemi, Michael J. Hanmer, Benjamin B. Bederson, and Frederick C. Conrad. *Voting Technology: The Not-So-Simple Act of Casting a Ballot.* Washington, DC: Brookings Institution Press, 2008. Explains the intricacies of voting technology, including the electoral implications of how votes are cast.

Lessig, Lawrence. *Republic, Lost 2.0.* New York: Hachette Book Group, 2015. Lessig describes how the U.S. democracy has been co-opted by outside interests, corporate money, and lobbying. He presents solutions, including a call for a constitutional convention.

Plouffe, David. *The Audacity to Win: The Inside Story and Lessons of Barack Obama's Historic Victory.* New York: Viking Press, 2009. A captivating political memoir of the 2008 campaign, written by Barack Obama's campaign manager.

Tur, Katy. *Unbelievable: My Front Row Seat to the Craziest Campaign in American History.* New York: Dey Street Books, 2017. NBC's Trump campaign correspondent describes her 2016 experience.

Zukin, Cliff, Scott Keeter, Molly Andolina, Krista Jenkins, and Michael X. Delli Carpini. *A New Engagement? Political Participation, Civic Life, and the Changing American Citizen.* New York: Oxford University Press, 2006. Describes the changing ways in which Americans are participating in the political life of their country and communities.

Movies of Interest

Game Change **(2012)**
Based on the 2010 book by journalists Mark Halperin and John Heilemann, the film stars Julianne Moore, Woody Harrelson, and Ed Harris and focuses on the selection of Alaska Governor Sarah Palin as running mate to Senator John McCain and her performance in the Republican presidential campaign.

Ides of March (2011)
George Clooney and Ryan Gosling star in this film about the drama of the primary election trail. An adaptation of the play Farragut North, the story is loosely based on the failed 2004 Democratic primary run of Howard Dean.

Recount **(2008)**
This dramatization of the 2000 presidential election shows the 36-day stalemate that comes in the wake of of the irregularities in the Florida vote count.

The Candidate **(1972)**
Robert Redford's character is convinced to run for the Senate on the premise that, with no chance at success, he can say whatever he wants. But success changes him, and his values shift as the prospect of winning becomes apparent.

References

1. www.dni.gov/files/documents/ICA_2017_01.pdf.

2. www.c-span.org/video/?436362-1/facebook-google-twitter-executives-testify-russias-influence-2016-election.

3. www.theguardian.com/technology/2018/jan/19/twitter-admits-far-more-russian-bots-posted-on-election-than-it-had-disclosed.

4. http://thehill.com/policy/technology/358025-thousands-attended-protest-organized-by-russians-on-facebook.

5. http://teachingamericanhistory.org/convention/debates/0726-2/.

6. Matt Vasilogambros, "Polling Places Remain a Target Ahead of November Elections."

7. http://www.wabe.org/voting-rights-become-a-flashpoint-in-georgia-governors-race.

8. Gregory Krieg, CNN, "Civil rights groups sue Georgia Republican Brian Kemp over 53,000 'pending' voter registrations."

9. V. O. Key, *The Responsible Electorate* (Cambridge, MA: Harvard University Press, 1966).

10. Alabama, Arkansas, Georgia, Illinois, Indiana, Michigan, Mississippi, Missouri, New Hampshire, North Dakota, Ohio, South Carolina, Tennessee, Texas, Vermont, Virginia, and Wisconsin have open primaries; Massachusetts, North Carolina, and Oklahoma allow unaffiliated or independent voters to vote in either party's primary.

11. Barbara Norrander, *Super Tuesday: Regional Politics and Presidential Primaries* (Lexington: University of Kentucky Press, 1992).

12. Thomas E. Cronin, *Direct Democracy: The Politics of Initiative, Referendum, and Recall* (Cambridge, MA: Harvard University Press, 1999).

13. David Broder, *Democracy Derailed: Initiative Campaigns and the Power of Money* (New York: Harvest Books, 2001).

14. John F. Bibby, *Politics, Parties, and Elections in America* (Belmont, CA: Wadsworth, 2000), 253.

15. www.washingtonpost.com/news/speaking-of-science/wp/2018/03/04/2018-is-the-year-of-scientists-running-for-congress/?utm_term=.368bc9a42563.

16. Pippa Norris, ed., *Politics and the Press: The News Media and Their Influences* (Boulder, CO: Lynne Rienner Publishers, 1997).

17. See, for example, Matthew Dowd, "Campaign Organization and Strategy," in *Electing the President 2004: An Insider's View*, ed. Kathleen Hall Jamieson (Philadelphia: University of Pennsylvania Press, 2006).

18. Vivé Griffith, "The Influence of Media in Presidential Politics," Think Democracy Project, University of Texas at Austin.

19. Dan Morain, "Small Democratic Donors Have an Online Pal," *Los Angeles Times*.

20. Gary Jacobson, *Money and Congressional Elections* (New Haven, CT: Yale University Press, 1980).

21. David Adamany, "Money, Politics and Democracy," *American Political Science Review* 71 (1977): 289–304.

22. *Buckley v. Valeo*, 424 U.S. (1976).

23. See Anthony Corrado, Thomas E. Mann, Dan Ortiz, Trevor Potter, and Frank Sorauf, *Campaign Finance Reform: A Sourcebook* (Washington, DC: Brookings Institute, 1997).

24. *Federal Election Commission v. National Conservative PAC*, 470 U.S. 480 (1985).

25. *McConnell v. Federal Election Commission*, 540 U.S. 93 (2003).

26. *Federal Election Commission v. Wisconsin Right to Life, Inc.*, 551 U.S. (2007).

27. Norman H. Nie, Sidney Verba, and John R. Petrocik, *The Changing American Voter* (Cambridge, MA: Harvard University Press, 1976).

28. Angus Campbell, Philip Converse, Warren Miller, and Donald Stokes, *The American Voter* (New York: Wiley, 1960).

29. Jan Leighley and Jonathan Nagler, "Who Votes Now? And Does It Matter?" (paper presented at the 2007 annual meeting of the Midwest Political Science Association, Chicago).

30. Norman H. Nie, Jane Junn, and Kenneth Stehlik-Barry, *Education and Democratic Citizenship in America* (Chicago: University of Chicago Press, 1996).

31. www.cnn.com/videos/politics/2016/02/28/sotu-tapper-donald-trump-full-interview.cnn.

32. www.washingtonpost.com/news/fact-checker/wp/2015/07/08/donald-trumps-false-comments-connecting-mexican-immigrants-and-crime/.

33. www.businessinsider.com/donald-trumps-epic-statement-on-mexico-2015-7#ixzz3fF897ElH.

34. Jan E. Leighley and Jonathan Nagler, "Socioeconomic Class Bias in Turnout, 1964–1988: The Voters Remain the Same," *American Political Science Review* 86 (1992): 725–736.

35. The Annenberg National Election Study (ANES), "Voter Turnout 1948–2004".

36. Kim Nguyen and James Garand, "The Effects of Income Inequality on Political Attitudes and Behavior" (paper presented at the 2007 annual meeting of the Midwest Political Science Association, Chicago).

37. Richard A. Brody, "The Puzzle of Political Participation in America," in *The New American Political System*, ed. Anthony King (Washington, DC: American Enterprise Institute for Public Policy Research, 1978), 287–324.

38. www.census.gov/content/dam/Census/newsroom/press-kits/2017/voting-and-registration/figure02.png.

39. Pippa Norris, "Retrospective Voting in the 1984 Presidential Election: Peace, Prosperity, and Patriotism," *Political Studies* 35 (1987): 289–300.

40. Daniel M. Shea, *Campaign Craft: The Strategies, Tactics, and Art of Political Campaign Management* (Westport, CT: Praeger, 1996).

41. Nie, Verba, and Petrocik, *The Changing American Voter*.

42. Samuel Kernell, "Presidential Popularity and Negative Voting," *American Political Science Review* 71 (1977): 44–66.

43. Shanto Iyengar and Jennifer A. McGrady, *Media Politics: A Citizen's Guide* (New York: W. W. Norton, 2006).

44. Warren E. Miller, "Disinterest, Disaffection, and Participation," *Political Behavior* 2 (1980): 7–32.

45. E. E. Schattschneider, *The Semi-Sovereign People* (New York: Holt, Rinehart, and Winston, 1960).

46. Pew Research Center for People and the Press, "Beyond Red versus Blue: Profiles of the Typology Groups," 2005.

47. Franklin Pierce Adams, *Nods and Becks* (New York: McGraw-Hill Publishers, 1944), p. 56.

48. Sebastian Garmann, "Election Frequency, Choice Fatigue, and Voter Turnout," *European Journal of Political Economy* 47 (2017): 19–35.

49. Caitlyn Bradfield and Paul Johnson, "The Effect of Making Election Day a Holiday: An Original Survey and a Case Study of French Presidential Elections Applied to the US Voting System," *Journal of Political and International Studies* 34 (2017): 19.

50. Anthony Downs, *An Economic Theory of Democracy* (New York: Harper, 1957).

51. Barbara Norrander and Bernard N. Grofman, "A Rational Choice Model of Citizen Participation in High and Low Commitment Electoral Activities," *Public Choice* 57 (1988): 187–192.

52. Sidney Verba and Norman H. Nie, *Participation in America: Political Democracy and Social Equality* (New York: Harper & Row, 1972).

53. Arend Lijphart, "Compulsory Voting Is the Best Way to Keep Democracy Strong," *The Chronicle of Higher Education,* October 18, 1996, B3–4.

54. Ruy A. Teixeira, "Just How Much Difference Does Turnout Really Make?" *The American Enterprise,* July/August 1992, 52–59.

CHAPTER 10

The Media

©Jabin Botsford/The Washington Post via Getty Images

THEN

The relationship between the media and consumers was one-way.

NOW

Technology has created a two-way relationship between the media and consumers, involving the exchange of a seemingly limitless amount of information of varying quality.

NEXT

Will the abundance and the reach of the media overload people with information?

Will people select media sources that serve only to confirm their views?

Will new technologies continue to change the nature of the news business?

If you are like most

Americans and indeed like multitudes of people across the globe—the media are a fixture in your daily life. You may wake and check Instagram before you even get out of bed. You may watch cable news over breakfast and listen to a podcast each morning when driving to school or work. In the evening, you may watch YouTube videos of televised news stories concerning the latest international crisis. You may receive real-time news updates on your cell phone, or visit Internet news sites and blogs regularly. As a citizen of the 21st century, you are bathed in a sea of news and information. Some of what the media offer you is meant to entertain, some is meant to inform, but increasingly the lines between the two have blurred.

No one can dispute that the sheer amount of information and entertainment available courtesy of the media has increased immeasurably over the past few decades. Within a generation, the modern media have transformed American life. Where once people had to seek out news and information, today they are inundated with it, and they must develop the skills needed to distinguish the reliable from the unreliable.

Although this abundance of information at times may rise to the level of a blitz, information is empowering. It serves as the basis on which people shape well-founded opinions. Those opinions are the building blocks for informed, meaningful civic engagement and political participation. In the discussion that follows, we see how the media continuously shape the ways we receive information and the ways we exercise the rights and privileges of our American democracy.

The Modern Media

At one time, it was easy to recognize the media: newspapers, television news, and cable news networks, to name a few. But defining the media today is trickier: Do tweets from your mayor, Instagrams from your roommate, or Facebook posts from your mom count as media? Although many observers regard the **media** simply as tools used to store and deliver information or data (in which case, all the preceding communications would be considered media), we must differentiate between media outlets that distribute unverifiable or opinion-based information and those that disseminate verifiable information.

The media exist in various forms today, including print media such as newspapers and magazines; electronic media, which traditionally means radio and television; and **new media,** sources of information including Internet websites, blogs, social networking sites such as Facebook and Twitter, photo- and video-sharing platforms such as Instagram and YouTube, and apps—and the cellular and satellite technologies that facilitate their use. In previous eras, media consumers often accepted what was broadcast or printed as fact, but today one must be a critical

media
Tools used to store and deliver information or data.

new media
Sources of information—including Internet websites, blogs, social networking sites such as Facebook and Twitter, photo- and video-sharing platforms such as Instagram and YouTube, and apps—and the cellular and satellite technologies that facilitate their use.

consumer of information. Just because information appears on social media, a blog, or even hundreds of blogs or reputable websites, does not necessarily mean that information is accurate. Take, for example, a story that circulated widely on social media and Internet websites in the wake of the 2018 special election in Pennsylvania's 18th congressional district, in which Democrat Conor Lamb narrowly defeated Republican Rick Saccone in a district President Trump had won handily in 2016. Entirely false reports stated that "multiple trucks full of illegals" were spotted at "six polling locations across Pennsylvania," but the reports originated with a fake news site.[1] How can today's media consumers be certain the information they are receiving is accurate? One good method is to rely on media outlets with a track record of providing solid information and adhering to journalistic standards. Another is to check sources independently: Today, the Internet has made it possible to verify some information simply by clicking on a hotlink to the original sources. More and more, news organizations will come to rely on citizen "journalists," increasing the probability that unscrupulous individuals will distribute false information widely. Thus today's media consumers must exercise a high level of caution when reading, listening, and viewing.

The Political Functions of the Media

In the United States today, the media in all forms—including print, television, radio, and new media—fulfill several key functions. Much of what the media do revolves around entertaining us, whether that means playing *Grand Theft Auto,* watching *Game of Thrones,* or reading the Sunday comics. But the media perform important political functions as well and are a vital element of our democracy. Specifically, the media perform these political functions:

- Provide political information
- Help us to interpret events and policies and influence agenda setting in the national political arena
- Provide a forum for political conversations
- Socialize children to the political culture

Providing Information

One long-standing function of the mass media is to serve up a steady diet of news and information to readers, viewers, and listeners. Indeed, the media, particularly the electronic media, are the primary source of information for most individuals. And today the quantity of information available—on blogs, websites, and cable television stations—surpasses the volume available at any other time in history. Coverage includes everything from weather watches, to sports scores, to the latest legislative developments on Capitol Hill, to serious analysis of top domestic policy issues and international problems. From this steady diet arises the problem of information overload—the constant availability of news information to the point of excess, which may cause media consumers to ignore, dismiss, or fail to see the significance of particular events. Media critics especially fault the television networks for injecting entertainment into news shows. They dub this combination **infotainment** (a hybrid of the words *information* and *entertainment*). More recent is the trend of uniting comedy with political content, as in *Saturday Night Live*'s "Weekend Update" and *Full Frontal* with Samantha Bee, both of which interpret news events with a comedic slant. But the merging of our informational and entertainment worlds could best be seen through the 2016 presidential candidacy

infotainment

A hybrid of the words *information* and *entertainment;* news shows that combine entertainment and news.

CONFIDENCE IN THE MEDIA

The Gallup Organization has asked the following question in surveys since 1972: "In general, how much trust and confidence do you have in the mass media—such as newspapers, TV, and radio—when it comes to reporting the news fully, accurately, and fairly: a great deal, a fair amount, not very much, or none at all?"

This graph illustrates survey respondents' views on that question, showing survey data at various times between May 1972 and September 2018. You can see that considerable changes have occurred in people's assessment of news organizations in this period.

Practice Analytical Thinking

1. Describe the trend during the 1970s concerning people's confidence in the media, citing specific data from the figure.

2. What has been the trend since 2001 regarding Americans' confidence in the media?

3. What do the latest data indicate concerning the issue of confidence in the media? Why do you think this is the case?

4. What do the data say about the overall trends with regard to people's confidence in the media?

5. What factors could have contributed to the changes in people's assessment of the media over time? Explain.

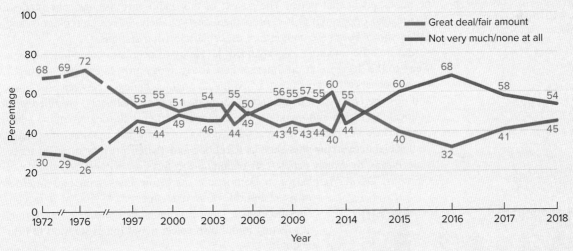

SOURCE: Gallup Poll, "Media Use and Evaluation."

of Donald Trump: Known to the American public primarily for his role on the reality television show *The Apprentice,* Trump was catapulted to the national stage when his celebrity brand attracted enough attention through his expert use of the media to win over sizeable contingents of supporters—eventually, enough to win him the Republican nomination for president and then the presidency.

Interpreting Matters of Public Interest and Setting the Public Agenda

Besides reporting information, the media help people to comprehend and interpret matters of public interest and to make informed decisions about public policies (see "Analyzing the Sources"). Political scientist Shanto Iyengar asserts that this process often begins with the media **framing**—setting a context that helps people understand important events and matters of shared interest. The media also help shape the **public agenda**—public issues that most demand the attention of government officials. Such was the case with the issue of gun violence in the United States, which generated significant media coverage in recent years, both nationally and within states. In doing so, the media engaged in **priming**—using their coverage to bring particular policies on issues to the public agenda, a common tactic used in shaping the public agenda.

Providing a Forum for Conversations About Politics

Although the media have provided an often lively forum for conversations about politics, the prominence of this role has reached new heights in the Internet era. Historically, information flowed from the media—which through the years have included everything from the political broadsides and leaflets of colonial times to modern newspapers, radio news, and television programming—to the people. The people then formed opinions based on what they read, heard, and saw. This historical one-way tradition typically featured little give-and-take between media sources and their consumers. A notable exception has been the **letter to the editor,** in which a reader responds to a newspaper story, knowing that the letter might be published in that paper. The advent of talk radio gave listeners one of their first regular opportunities to express their views publicly. Television took note, and call-in shows became common fare on cable television stations.

But no other medium has expanded the ability of people to communicate their views to the degree that the Internet has. Today, blogs provide an ideal forum for online conversations about issues, inviting an ongoing dialogue between blog hosts and posters. Discussion boards (even those that are "nonpolitical") are filled with political discussion and opinions. The comment section following an online newspaper article has become the new water cooler around which opinions are voiced. And social networking sites such as Facebook and Twitter provide an easily accessible means by which people can communicate facts, eyewitness accounts, and opinions. David Weinberger, a Democratic marketing consultant and Internet adviser, describes this phenomenon: "Think of it as conversation space. Conversation is the opposite of marketing. It's talking in our own voices about things we want to hear about."[2]

>Unlike many YouTubers with millions of subscribers, Casey Neistat has not shied away from sharing his political opinions online. What is the risk for YouTubers who discuss politics? Would you prefer to watch videos that contain political content, or avoid them?

©Kevork Djansezian/Getty Images

Socializing Children to Political Culture

The media also socialize new generations to the political culture. For young children, television remains a dominant medium for both entertainment and socialization, though iPad apps are increasingly playing these roles in the lives of today's small children. TV-viewing toddlers receive regular messages about important cultural values. Shows such as *Sesame Street* and *Sanjay and Craig* send powerful messages about the value of diversity in society. Young children's shows also subtly instruct watchers on the value of patriotism and of specific civic behaviors. TV programming for older children similarly takes on political issues. A series of episodes of *SpongeBob SquarePants* depicts

Bikini Bottom's first presidential election, in which SpongeBob's best friend, Patrick Starfish, runs against Crustacean Party candidate Larry the Lobster.

Even television and radio programs not specifically aimed at youth often reinforce democratic principles and practices. What is *The Voice* if not a televised election? And when the tribe speaks on *Survivor*, they do so through the process of voting. Talk radio and television call-in programs rest on the assumption that individuals' opinions matter and that they have the right to voice them. These kinds of programming may not directly spur a particular political behavior on the part of viewers. Nonetheless, television and other forms of media that we often think of as pure entertainment frequently reinforce and legitimize dominant American political values, including the value of participating in civic society in a democracy.

The Press and Politics: A Historical View

The sheer volume of information available through the media today makes the media's influence in our times beyond dispute. Historically, too, the media have played an essential role in setting the political agenda and shaping public policy. The power of the media was evident even in pre-Revolutionary times, when, for example, newspaper owners and readers rallied against the Stamp Act's (1765) imposition of taxes on newspapers and other kinds of legal documents. Newspaper publishers sympathetic to the colonists' cause of ejecting Great Britain from American shores used their "power of the pen" to arouse public opinion, and they strongly supported the patriot cause throughout the Revolution. Taking sides in an internal conflict was a new role for the press, one that would sow the seeds of future media influence on the country's domestic and foreign policy. The early history of media development also raised issues that continue to create conflict about the media's role in society.

The Early Role of the Press

Great leaders learned early how intimately their careers were linked to favorable press coverage and influence. From the 1790s to the 1830s, the press served primarily as a vehicle for the leaders of political parties, who expressed their opinions through newspapers known to reflect their particular viewpoints in reporting the news. The circulation of these newspapers was small, but so was their audience; most people could not read and write and did not vote.

By the 1830s, the environment had changed. For openers, the average American was now able to read. New technology made possible the **penny press**—newspapers that sold for a penny. The field of **journalism,** the practice of gathering and reporting events, flourished. Circulation increased, and the working class became interested in what the newspapers had to offer. Another reason newspapers reduced their price was the advent of advertising; newspaper owners figured out that if they sold advertising, they could increase both their profits and their papers' circulation. The 1830s was the first time advertising became part and parcel of the newspaper business, and although pressures from advertisers sometimes affected coverage and editorial opinion, few readers noticed that practice, and even fewer challenged it.

Over time, the influence of advertising grew exponentially. Although today's major newspapers do not openly change their editorial opinions to please their advertisers, occasionally advertisers flex their muscles, as General Motors did when it withdrew its advertising from the *Los Angeles Times* after the newspaper recommended the firing of the company's CEO.[3]

penny press
Newspapers that sold for a penny in the 1830s.

journalism
The practice of gathering and reporting events.

Yellow Journalism and Muckraking

Throughout the last part of the 19th century, newspapers competed vigorously with one another for ever-greater shares of readership. Publishers found that stories about sex, gore, violence, and government corruption sold papers faster than reports about garbage collection and school budgets. Well-known publishers William Randolph Hearst and Joseph Pulitzer established their reputations and their fortunes at that time, Hearst with the *New York Journal American* and Pulitzer with the *New York World*. Along with Hearst and Pulitzer at the beginning of the 20th century came the practice of yellow journalism, so named after the yellow ink used in the "Yellow Kid" cartoons in the *New York World*. The term **yellow journalism** has come to signify an irresponsible, sensationalist approach to news reporting and is used to this day to criticize certain elements of the press.

The most famous example of the impact of yellow journalism came with both Hearst's and Pulitzer's support of the United States' entry into the Spanish-American War (1898). This conflict is sometimes referred to as "the newspaper war" because of the major role of the press in President William McKinley's decision to invade Cuba and later the Philippines. Influenced by reports of Spanish cruelty toward the Cubans during and after the Cuban independence movement, public sentiment in the United States strongly favored Cuba. Hearst and Pulitzer, followed by other newspapers across the country, fanned the flames of war with sensational and lurid anti-Spanish stories, dwelling on the brutality of the Spanish toward Cuban rebels. The precipitating event, the explosion of the U.S. battleship *Maine* in Havana harbor in February 1898, may or may not have been due to a Spanish torpedo, according to recent evidence. But press reports, accompanied by the cry "Remember the *Maine*," galvanized the public and Congress. The president responded to the intensifying pressures, and Congress declared war on Spain in April. The press and the public had guided public policy.

yellow journalism
An irresponsible, sensationalist approach to news reporting, so named after the yellow ink used in the "Yellow Kid" cartoons in the *New York World*.

> Yellow journalism can influence the national policy agenda. When the battleship *Maine* exploded in Havana harbor in February 1898, newspaper coverage significantly molded public opinion, and in turn Congress declared war on Spain. Can you think of examples of recent media coverage of events that have influenced public opinion?
©Bettmann/Getty Images

Hard on the heels of the Spanish-American "newspaper war" came the era of **muckraking,** an about-face that placed journalists in the heroic role of exposing the dark underbelly of government and industry. The most famous of the muckrakers included Ida Tarbell, who exposed the oil industry in a series of articles running from 1902 to 1904 in *McClure's* magazine; Lincoln Steffens, who published *The Shame of the Cities* in 1904; and Upton Sinclair, whose novel *The Jungle* (1906) revealed the horrors of the meat-processing industry, leading to passage of the Pure Food and Drug Act and later to the establishment of the Food and Drug Administration.[4]

muckraking
Criticism and exposés of corruption in government and industry by journalists at the turn of the 20th century.

A Widening War for Readership

Yellow journalism died down after World War I, and newspapers entered a period that at least on the surface valued objectivity. Newspapers increasingly found themselves competing with the new media that were just coming into being: radio stations from 1920 to 1950; television from the 1940s to 1980; and from then on, the explosion of the new media. This increased competition has had several effects on the newspaper industry. First, for over a decade, print newspaper readership had steadily declined, particularly the audience for printed local newspapers, though in the aftermath of the 2016 election, the largest American newspapers, including *The New York Times* and *The Wall Street Journal*, saw an uptick in subscriptions. However, the additional subscriptions were not enough to counteract the overall decline seen by newspapers across the country, as shown in Figure 10.1. In response, newspaper publishers have adapted to the changes in how individuals get their news, and many newspapers have consolidated and increased their digital offerings. Indeed, some media analysts suggest that in the next several years, some newspapers will resort to digital-only formats, or publish printed editions only on Sundays. Newspapers continue in their effort to solve the challenge they face due to declining print-ad revenue. Increasingly, that solution has meant that online advertising is generating a greater portion of newspapers' revenue. And some newspapers are profiting by providing information to readers via the Internet using a **digital paywall**–the practice of limiting access to a website unless users pay a fee or purchase a subscription.

digital paywall
The practice of limiting access to a website unless users pay a fee or purchase a subscription.

Beyond changing platforms, sources of revenue, and readership, the newspaper industry has changed as society has changed. Gone are the grand urban headquarters that housed newspapers—and anchored entire downtown areas—of days gone by. Today, many city newspapers have relocated to the cheaper real estate of the suburbs, with smaller newsrooms that rely on telecommuting reporters. Large cities are now likely to have smaller weekly publications targeted to specific demographic audiences—gays, women, African Americans, for example—and to publish foreign-language newspapers appealing to diverse newcomers to the United States, such as Mexican, Brazilian, Vietnamese, Iranian, Nigerian, and Russian immigrants.

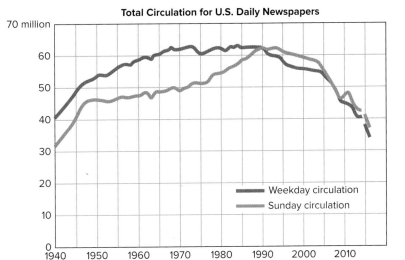

Total Circulation for U.S. Daily Newspapers

FIGURE 10.1 ■ **Newspaper Circulation Over Time**
SOURCE: Pew Research Center.

Increasing Diversity in Newsrooms

As the industry has changed, so too has the human face of the newsroom. First, there are fewer faces in the newsroom, as the long-term trend of declining revenue led many newspapers to reduce their reporting staff. Second, Figure 10.2 shows that, in 2015, more than one-third of all newsroom supervisors were women, as were more than 40 percent of all layout and copy editors and reporters. Those figures reflect societal changes from the times when "newsmen" were in fact news*men*. Among all positions measured in the annual newsroom census, women were least likely to hold jobs in the visual arts, such as photographer and artist.

Another measure of how modern newsrooms have changed along with American society is the proportion of minority journalists working at newspapers. Data indicate that minority journalists are much more likely to be employed at larger-circulation newspapers, with minorities constituting over one-fifth of the journalists at papers having a circulation of 250,000 to 500,000. That proportion is nearly as high at the largest-circulation newspapers and steadily tapers off among newspapers with a circulation of less than 250,000.

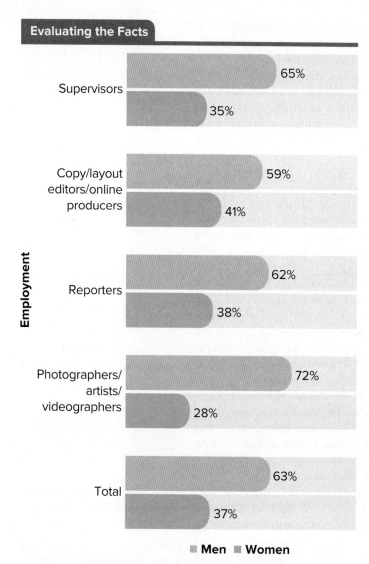

FIGURE 10.2 ■ **Newsroom Employment by Gender** In the past, "newsmen" were in fact news*men*. What does the graph indicate about women's employment in today's newsrooms?

The Media Go Electronic: The Radio and Television Revolutions

It is impossible to overemphasize the transformative impact of the early electronic media. From the time of the first U.S. radio broadcasts in the early 1920s, radio allowed listeners to hear news in real time. That immediacy marked a drastic change from the standard, delayed method of receiving news, which was by reading the morning and evening editions of newspapers, plus the occasional "extra edition" published when important breaking news warranted it. Radio also altered the relationship between politicians—particularly presidents—and their constituents, because it enabled listeners to hear the voices of their elected leaders. Television further revolutionized that relationship by making it possible for people to see their leaders (though initially only in black and white).

How Radio Opened Up Political Communication

Radio was the first electronic medium that brought people into direct contact with their leaders. Beginning in the 1920s, radios became a fixture in American living rooms, and families who could not afford a radio of their own would often spend evenings at the homes of friends or neighbors who could.

FDR'S FIRESIDE CHATS Franklin D. Roosevelt was the first politician to realize the value of radio as a device for political communication—and to exploit that value. As governor of New York (1928–1932), Roosevelt faced a Republican state legislature hostile to many of his liberal social welfare programs. To overcome the opposition, Roosevelt used radio addresses to appeal directly to his constituents, who would then lobby the legislators for his policies. Indeed, after some of Roosevelt's radio addresses, legislative offices were flooded with letters from constituents asking lawmakers to support a particular policy.

By the time Roosevelt became president in 1933, he had grasped the importance of radio as a tool for communicating directly with the people. FDR often began his radio addresses to the country—his **fireside chats**—with the greeting, "Good evening, friends," highlighting the personal relationship he wished to cultivate between himself and his listeners. (You can listen to many of Roosevelt's fireside chats in MP3 format from the Vincent Voice Library

>President Franklin D. Roosevelt was recognized as a master political communicator. Using the newest technology available of his time, Roosevelt relied on a folksy, conversational tone and the medium of radio to bring his message to the people. How does a politician's ability to communicate successfully with the people influence his or her governing?
©Bettmann/Getty Images

at Michigan State University.) Through the folksy fireside chats, Americans learned about presidential initiatives on the banking crisis, New Deal social welfare programs, the declaration of war on Japan after that nation's attack on Pearl Harbor, and the progress of U.S. forces during World War II. In all, Roosevelt had 30 fireside chats with Americans over his 12 years as president.

fireside chats
President Franklin D. Roosevelt's radio addresses to the country.

TALK RADIO: TALKING THE POLITICAL TALK Radio began to emerge from the shadows of television in the 1970s and 1980s. Those decades brought a renaissance of sorts for radio, as the medium saw tremendous growth in **talk radio**—a format featuring conversations and interviews about topics of interest, along with call-ins from listeners. As many AM station owners switched to an all-talk format in those years, music programming migrated to the FM band.

In 1987, the Federal Communications Commission (FCC), the U.S. government agency that regulates interstate and international communications by radio, television, wire, satellite and cable, repealed the **fairness doctrine,** which had required stations holding broadcast licenses to present controversial issues of public importance and to do so in a manner that was honest, fair, and balanced. Since the law's repeal, partisan radio programming has grown dramatically. Today, listeners tend to tune in to radio hosts who share—many say, reinforce—their opinions and they interact with them through call-in opportunities.

talk radio
A format featuring conversations and interviews about topics of interest, along with call-ins from listeners.

fairness doctrine
The requirement that stations holding broadcast licenses present controversial issues of public importance and do so in a manner that was honest, fair, and balanced.

Television and the Transformation of Campaigns and Elections

Although radio predates television, TV nonetheless has been the centerpiece of U.S. home entertainment for a long time. Television began to make a mark on the American scene in the 1940s, when small TV sets—their screens flecked with static snowflakes—hit the market. Its effect on the world of politics cannot be overstated. Suddenly, being **telegenic,** or looking good on TV, became almost

telegenic
The quality of looking good on TV.

THEN

NOW

> In the first-ever televised presidential debate in 1960, the importance of being telegenic emerged as an important quality for candidates. John Kennedy came across as handsome, relaxed, and articulate, while Richard Nixon, despite having a strong command of the substance, was viewed as appearing nervous and sinister. By 2016, being television savvy is a necessary trait for presidential candidates, as both Donald Trump and Hillary Clinton effectively demonstrated.

Kennedy/Nixon: ©Bettmann/Getty Images; *Clinton/Trump:* ©Pool/Getty Images

mandatory for serious political candidates. It is unlikely that President William Howard Taft (1909–1913), who weighed over 300 pounds, would ever have been elected if he had been forced to appear on television. Nor would Abraham Lincoln, whose handlers would have marched him straight to a cosmetic surgeon to have the giant mole on his cheek removed. Richard Nixon might have won the presidency in 1960 had it not been for his nervous demeanor and the "five o'clock shadow" on his face that made him look sinister in the first-ever televised presidential candidate debates that year. In appearance and demeanor, his opponent, the handsome, relaxed, and articulate John F. Kennedy, won the debate hands down, even though in hindsight most analysts agree that Nixon "won" the debate on its verbal merits. Since that election, the effective use of television has been a necessity for high-ranking elected office.

Today, people are as likely to watch cable television as they are to watch ABC, CBS, or NBC, the original three networks that dominated the United States' national political life for more than a half-century, and they are less likely to watch television at all than Americans two or three decades ago. Figure 10.3 shows one measure of the nature of these changes, as viewership of nightly network news broadcasts on ABC, CBS, and NBC plummeted between 1992 and today. Significantly, nightly news network viewership strongly correlates with age, with the youngest Americans being least likely to watch the news. But even among the oldest Americans, viewership has steeply declined as the result of the skyrocketing number of cable channels that provide tough competition for the networks.

How Americans Use the Media to Get Political Information

As cable news channels such as CNN, MSNBC, and FOX News have increased their viewing audience, it is no wonder the word *broadcasting* has spawned the term **narrowcasting:** the practice of aiming political media content at specific segments

narrowcasting
The practice of aiming media content at specific segments of the public.

media segmentation
The breaking down of the media according to the specific audiences they target.

of the public, divided according to political ideology, party affiliation, or economic interests. This winnowing of audiences has led to **media segmentation,** the breaking down of the media in general according to the specific audiences they target. Examples of segmented media include Black Entertainment Television (BET); the U.S.-based Spanish-language television network Telemundo; and the Lifestyle Network, which includes the Food Network and HGTV. Through media segmentation, advertisers can hone their advertising to the tastes of their targeted markets.

But media segmentation is only partially responsible for the decline of television networks. Since 2010, the proportion of Americans relying on digital news sources has increased, while those relying on traditional sources has declined. The trend can be seen in Figure 10.4: today, increasing numbers of Americans are getting their news online. Indeed, between 2016 and 2017 alone, the gap between those who often got news on television and those who got news online shrunk from 19 percent to 7 percent. Televisions and radios still dominate, but Figure 10.5 demonstrates that while younger Americans are more

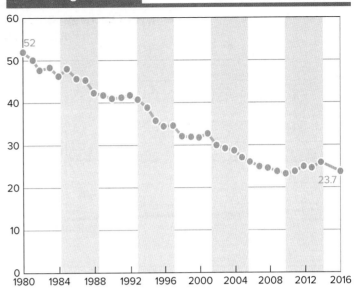

FIGURE 10.3 ■ **Evening Network News Viewership** (in Millions of Viewers) Why, in your view, are fewer people watching the nightly news? What is the likely effect of this trend? Do you think that the percentage of people watching the news will continue to dwindle?

SOURCE: Pew Research Center, "Network News Fact Sheet."

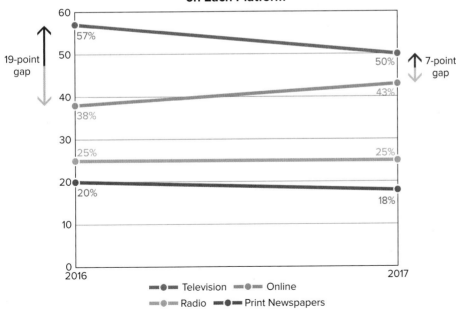

FIGURE 10.4 ■ **Where Americans Get Their News**

SOURCE: Pew Research Center.

Percentage of Each Age Group Who *Often* Get News on Each Platform

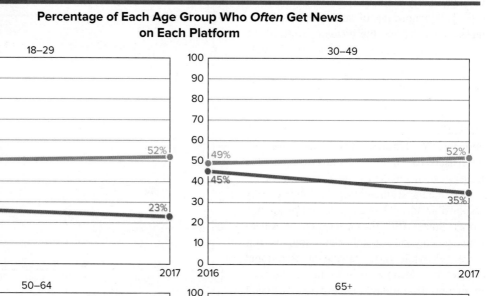

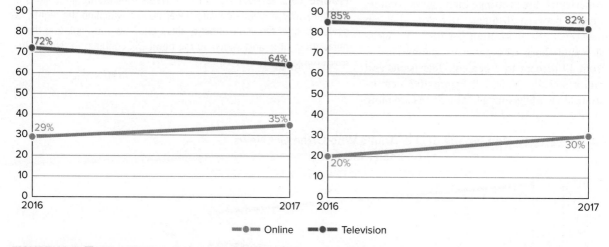

FIGURE 10.5 ■ **Who Watches Online News?** Millennials are the most likely group to watch online videos of all kinds, but older Americans are increasingly likely to get their news online. What is the relationship in changes between online news consumption and television watching? Does that trend apply to all age groups? Which group is most likely to get their news online? Which group remains most likely to rely on television? How do you predict these groups will get their news in the next five years? Why is the online audience for news likely to grow in the future?

SOURCE: Pew Research Center.

likely to get their news online, older Americans are now driving the change in how Americans get their news, with the proportion of older Americans who get their news online increasing by 10 percent in just one year.

Media Consolidation

Technology has changed the business of news. Today, our expectations of news outlets have increased. No longer will the afternoon paper delivered to your doorstep by a bicycle-riding paperboy suffice. Today's "newspapers" are media outlets: We expect

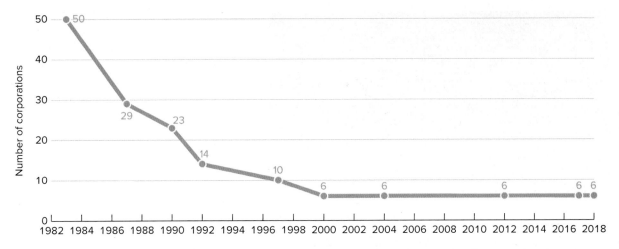

FIGURE 10.6 ■ **Media Consolidation** The number of corporations that bring the majority of news to Americans has shrunk significantly in the past 35 years. How might the fact that so few corporations control the news we receive affect public opinion?

them to tweet us updates, and we "like" them on Facebook. We are increasingly likely to read them on a tablet rather than in print form. And as our expectations of the role of the media have changed, so too have the businesses that are the media.

Today, corporations are increasingly likely to be universal providers of all our digital needs. Thus **consolidation** occurs—the phenomenon of large corporations buying smaller ones so that there are fewer and fewer companies' products available. Apple is notoriously committed to controlling the user experience from start to finish and so has created partnerships with various media outlets that distribute their content via Apple's product. In doing so, it has gobbled up several smaller companies, including the voice-recognition platform Siri. Facebook, too, has entered into agreements with technology corporations, such as the messaging service WhatsApp and the photo-sharing platform Instagram, and with media outlets, including News Corporation's *The Wall Street Journal* and also *The Washington Post* and *The Guardian.*

Consolidation has also occurred among entertainment and news media outlets. Consolidation centralizes the control of the media into the hands of a few large corporations. Some critics fear this will stifle the number of alternative viewpoints that are presented to the American public. The number of corporations responsible for supplying the majority of news to Americans has shrunk from 50 in 1983 to 6 today, as shown in Figure 10.6. The six media giants are Comcast, Walt Disney, 21st Century Fox, Time Warner, Viacom, and CBS Corporation. Some observers believe these six giants could disproportionately affect public opinion and public policy by allowing corporate interests to influence how the news is reported. Media consolidation, however, is countered by the proliferation of media sources.

consolidation
The phenomenon of large corporations buying smaller ones so that there are fewer and fewer companies' products available.

The Proliferation of News Sources and Greater Scrutiny

In the mid-20th century, rural communities could not receive broadcast signals from the big cities. As a result, hundreds of cable television systems sprang up around the country. In the early 1970s, commercial satellites enabled the advent

> During the 2018 State of the Union address, journalists caught Congresswoman Brenda Lawrence (D-Mich.) (right) playing Candy Crush. The image went viral, leading to social media outcry that Democrats were disrespectful during President Trump's address.

©Chip Somodevilla/Getty Images

of satellite networks. Media entrepreneurs established many new, nonbroadcast networks—Home Box Office (HBO) in 1975, followed by others in the 1980s, such as CNN, ESPN, and MTV. Then in the 1990s, another technological revolution created profoundly more diverse sources of news and information—the Internet.

The Cell-Phone Watchdogs

The rise of cable stations and the Internet has fundamentally changed politics by increasing the number of sources from which Americans can get their news. This trend results not only in narrowcasting but also in greater scrutiny of government officials and public policy. Things happen now in the time it takes to swipe a phone, and politicians guard against ever-present cell phone video cameras chronicling their every move for YouTube posterity. Such was the case in 2018, when Rep. Brenda Lawrence (D-Mich.) was caught playing Candy Crush Saga on her phone during President Trump's State of the Union address. Photos of the congresswoman went viral amid allegations that Democrats in Congress behaved disrespectfully during the president's speech.

The portability of cellular technology has also contributed to Americans' consumption of news. Using our smartphones, we always have access to news outlets, and this access has increased our consumption of news, including "long form" news—not just the 140-character tweet or a brief Facebook posting but real news coverage, analysis, debate, and discussion. In fact, one study found that smartphones and tablets increased traffic on major newspaper websites by 9 percent.[5] Simultaneously, the timeframe of "news" also has changed. The adage that a "week is an eternity in politics" has become an understatement in the age of the Internet and the 24-hour news cycle.

Blogs: The New Penny Papers?

Technology also has changed the format and content of written news as well. Today blogs have become an important component of how individuals communicate and convey information, and how media outlets keep us informed. Because blogs are typically written from a subjective point of view, their authors less frequently adhere to professional journalism standards. So, like the penny papers of early American times, blogs offer the opportunity for political viewpoints to infiltrate a medium whose holy grail was once neutrality. Blogging has increased enormously in the past five years, a trend that is likely to continue. Blogs are playing an increasingly important role not just in providing a platform for citizen journalists but also in shaping the agenda of the traditional media establishment. It is not uncommon for bloggers to "break" a story that then becomes a traditional media firestorm. Chapter 11 offers further discussion of the increasingly important role that blogs are playing in the American political arena.

Biased Media?

Media critics today are everywhere. All of them claim that both print and electronic media exhibit bias in their reporting, in their selection of what issues to cover, and in favoring one side of an issue (or one politician) over another. One of the most common complaints is that the media have an ideological bias.

The Question of Ideological Bias

A long-standing complaint is that the media evidence a liberal bias. For example, President Trump regularly rails against the "liberal media," calling it "so dishonest, so disgusting,"[6] and claiming the media's bias makes his job harder.

The Republicans' criticism of the "liberal media" is not a new charge. In 1964, former president Dwight D. Eisenhower, in his address to the Republican National Convention, condemned a liberal media bias: "My friends, we are Republicans. If there is any finer word in the field of partisan politics, I have not heard it. So let us particularly [scorn] the divisive efforts of those outside our family, including sensation-seeking columnists and commentators, who couldn't care less about the good of our party."[7] Many conservatives point to studies indicating that a majority of newsroom reporters identify themselves as liberal or Democrat. Conservatives charge that the ideological bent of journalists carries through to the topics covered and to the perspectives of the stories.

But in recent years, greater attention has been paid to the role that the "conservative media" plays in shaping U.S. politics. Conservative talk-show hosts, including many aired on FOX News, have been important in shaping Republican party politics. Indeed, writing for CNN, Brian Rosenwald and Michael Smerconish argue that Donald Trump's and Ted Cruz's ability to outlast their Republican rivals for the 2016 GOP presidential nomination can be attributed to the influence of the "conservative media" in politics. "Over the course of the last three decades, these media personalities have surpassed party officials and even elected representatives in their influence, ascending to exalted status atop Republican leadership.

THEN NOW NEXT

How Technology Has Changed How We Get Information

THEN (1960s)	NOW
Three television networks—ABC, NBC, and CBS—provided all the nightly news.	Americans are increasingly likely to get their news from digital sources, including websites, podcasts, and social networking sites.
Network television programming matured and revolutionized how the media entertained and provided information.	Digital cable technology and new delivery methods—including Internet television sites such as Hulu and Netflix, and Internet music-streaming sites like Spotify—are revolutionizing entertainment and information-getting.
Television accentuated a new set of candidate qualities—including being telegenic—that had not mattered much in earlier political campaigns.	Omnipresent cell phone cameras mean that candidates must consistently display the qualities that make them appealing to voters, lest their mistakes be caught in a YouTube moment.

WHAT'S NEXT?

> How will the content of television change in the next several years? What factors might influence how television content is changing?

> Is there a downside to the new pervasiveness of television and other electronic media for candidates? For voters? If so, what?

> What new media technologies will shape the evolution of television in the future?

Yet, they prioritize goals seemingly at odds with good governance, and often, even the party's sole purpose for existence," Rosenwald and Smerconish write.[8]

Numerous studies conducted by various political scientists, including C. Richard Hofstetter, Michael J. Robinson, and Margaret A. Sheehan, refute the idea that print journalists' personal viewpoints tinge the content of the news in a liberal way.[9] Indeed, studies suggest that most news stories take the form of a debate, with the journalist presenting the various sides of an issue and leaving the conclusion to the reader's interpretation. But increasingly, changes in the nature of the mass media have led to increasingly vocal charges that cable news stations and newer media outlets, particularly talk radio and the blogosphere, are ideologically biased, with some favoring a liberal bias, and others taking a conservative slant.

The Issue of Corporate Bias

Media critics also argue that another form of bias has emerged as a result of the corporate structures that dominate the news industry, altering what is considered news and how that news is covered.[10] Corporate bias—and the desire to attract, keep, and please an audience—produces skewed programming. Will corporate conglomerates be willing to report on situations that may put themselves and their advertisers in a negative light? How does the drive for profits influence what is in the news? Are viewers being fed "news" that is not particularly newsworthy? There is no doubt that profits influence the media to cover the kinds of stories that viewers and readers want. In particular, violence dominates most local news programming, so much so that the principle of "if it bleeds, it leads" now extends into the first 15 minutes of many local news broadcasts. Fires; political, sports, and sex scandals; and celebrity-heavy news are also powerful audience attractors.

Regulation of the Media: Is It Necessary?

The government regulates and controls the ownership of radio and television stations through the independent regulatory agency known as the Federal Communications Commission (FCC), founded in 1934 by Congress to regulate interstate and international communications by radio, television, wire, satellite, and cable throughout the United States.

Most of the FCC's rules have concerned ownership, such as the number of outlets a network may own. Some regulations, however, govern the content of radio and television programming, attempting to ensure that "decent" content—an ambiguous term, according to many broadcasters—is on the airwaves (see "Thinking Critically").

Other FCC regulations, however, concern how media providers operate. For example, in 2016, the FCC sought a rule change that would require video providers, including Comcast and DISH network, to open their video feeds by enabling other companies to manufacture cable or satellite ("set-top") boxes used by their subscribers. Gale Ann Hurd, a producer of television's *The Walking Dead,* argued in a *USA Today* opinion piece that reducing the security options would encourage piracy of licensed video: "let me explain why the FCC's proposal would spell disaster for those of us who are trying to figure out how to keep making the movies and TV shows audiences love. And I'm not talking about just the actors and the producers. Hundreds of thousands of crewmembers across the country will be out of jobs, too. Studios and networks can't keep making content if they stop receiving revenue from legitimate sources," Hurd argued.[11]

Should Television Be Subject to Stricter Regulations Than Other Media Are?

The Issue: In 1978, the U.S. Supreme Court ruled that the Federal Communications Commission should have the power to regulate the content that broadcasters provide. In *Federal Communications Commission v. Pacifica Foundation,** the Supreme Court asserted that regulating content served to protect children from indecent material, since broadcasted content in television and radio had become permanent fixtures in most homes in the United States. The Court also justified regulation, because the networks relied on public airwaves to broadcast their content, and that giving the FCC broad authority would protect individuals from unwanted speech in their private homes.

The case initially stemmed from a lawsuit filed by a father whose son had heard comedian George Carlin's routine called "Filthy Words" (also known as the "seven words you can never say on television"). He complained to the FCC, which fined Pacifica Foundation, the entity that owned the radio station that broadcast the comedy bit. After the ruling, content deemed indecent by the FCC (including Carlin's filthy words) was bleeped out or edited from broadcasts. In 2012, the Supreme Court ruled in *Federal Communications Commission v. Television Stations, Inc.* concerning fines issued by the FCC for the "single use of vulgar words" on the FOX television network. During the 2002 and 2003 Billboard Music Awards, Cher and Nicole Richie used obscene words and the network was fined by the FCC. FOX challenged the fines in court. The Court invalidated the fines and ruled that while the regulations at the time did not cover "fleeting expletives," the FCC's regulations do not violate the First Amendment because the FCC is regulating on behalf of the public interest. The FCC has since amended broadcasting rules to encompass fleeting expletives.

Yes: The FCC should continue to have broad authority over the regulation of television content, since the same circumstances that held true in 1978 remain a reality for many Americans today. Television networks provide a "safe haven" for children and other individuals who do not wish to be bombarded with indecency that is prevalent in cable television. Removing regulations or failing to penalize violators will mean a degeneration of the quality of the content available on network television. In addition, the public nature of the airwaves means that the content provided by broadcasters should meet common standards of decency that would be acceptable to most Americans.

No: Current FCC regulations impinge on the First Amendment free speech rights guaranteed by the Constitution and create a tiered structure in which cable television programming, the Internet, and newspapers are not held to the same standards as radio and television. This differential creates an unfair playing field and stymies free speech by individuals communicating through regulated media. In addition, the standards enforced by the FCC reflect the values of a bygone era. Moreover, technological changes in American homes allow for parental control. Nearly all televisions have V-chips, which allow for parents to control content, and most cable subscribers have parental control capability.

Other Approaches: The FCC's current policy is ambiguous, because it does not provide broadcasters with concrete guidelines as to what is indecent and what is permissible. The creation of such guidelines would enable broadcasters to create compliant programming and work within a predictable framework. In addition, broadcasters operate without a reliable guide as to what the commission would find offensive.

*438 U.S. 726 (1978).

What do you think?

1.   Do you believe that the Federal Communications Commission should regulate decency on broadcast television? Why or why not?

2.   Do such regulations stifle free speech? Do the same criteria the Court cited in 1978 apply today? Why or why not?

3.   Do you think that the Supreme Court has an obligation to voice an opinion on the matter of indecency rules? Why or why not?

Media also are regulated by the Telecommunications Act of 1996, which opened the communications markets to telephone companies. This sweeping law allowed competition in the communications industry. It presented new (often confusing) options for consumers, as individual companies began to offer a suite of services, from local and long-distance telephone service, to Internet access, to cable and satellite television.

With the combination of all of these services provided by single companies, large corporate conglomerates have increasingly gained control of the media. These firms exert a powerful influence over what news the average American sees and reads on a given day. The advent of these media titans has given rise to concerns about whether this type of control will deter balanced reporting of the news and unbiased presentations of issues. In addition, public conversations about our democracy are questioning whether the relative lack of competition (because there are so few competitors) means that a valuable check on what the media do and how they do it has been lost.

Conclusion

Thinking Critically About What's Next for the Media

The surge in the number and the variety of media outlets—along with the changes in the nature of the media and in people's interactions with them—have affected politics and government in many ways. Once defined as a one-way relationship, the relationship between the media and consumers has evolved in unforeseen ways. Even the nature of the "old media" has changed, although many people would ask whether the change has been for the better. On the one hand, narrowcasting and the resulting segmentation of media markets, a central feature of media growth, might raise the comfort level of many people who no longer have to throw soft objects at their television sets in protest but can instead pick and choose what they watch. On the other hand, media segmentation also limits the exposure of many people to new ideas. Like gated communities, segmented media are also segregated media, detached environments that expose people only to viewpoints with which they agree, thus cordoning them off from society and from many of its problems. Segmented media also confuse genuine political participation with mere ranting. After all, sounding off on a radio talk show is much easier and more entertaining than attending a zoning board meeting to fight urban congestion or becoming civically engaged in other ways.

While the number of media sources and platforms available to consumers continues to proliferate, we know that consolidation is now characteristic of the business of media. So, although we may rely on an ever-increasing number of different news outlets, these outlets are owned and operated by a shrinking number of global media conglomerates, giving those corporations nearly unprecedented power in controlling the information available to consumers. This consolidation of the business of media is offset by the proliferation of other new technologies, including the advent of citizen journalism and blogging, that have diversified the sources of information available to media consumers. Nonetheless, we can anticipate even greater levels of consolidation and convergence in the future.

Can we predict the future of the media by examining the past and the present? Certainly we can foretell increasing transparency because of the pervasive nature of today's media and the steady trend in that direction, but we cannot predict the forms media will take. What we can guarantee is continued change in the forms and usage of media and steadily increasing access to information. Will this expanding access overload people with information? It appears that many of us are developing new skills to cope with the abundance of information, much in the way that our grandparents may have developed the skill of skimming a newspaper, selecting only those stories that mattered to them. The question remains as to whether we will select only information that confirms what we already think. One trend is clear: The ever-increasing volume of information and the speed of its delivery will yield an abundance of both poor-quality and high-quality information that media consumers will need to evaluate in their efforts to get accurate information.

Learning Summary

1. Explain the concept of media, including what the new media is.

2. Describe the four political functions of the media.
   a. Explain how the media disseminate information.
   b. Describe how the media help interpret matters of public interest and set the national policy agenda.
   c. Explain how the media provide a forum for political conversations.
   d. Explain the media's role in socializing children to the political culture.

3. Describe the history of the press's involvement in U.S. politics.
   a. Explain the early role of the press.
   b. Describe how yellow journalism and muckraking altered the political agenda.
   c. Describe the expansion of new forms of media, including radio and television, and the competition that ensued.
   d. Explain how modern newsrooms have become increasingly diverse.

4. Describe the electronic revolution.
   a. Describe how television altered the nature of politics and campaigning, affecting everything from how campaigns for office are conducted to how candidates look and dress.
   b. Explain the effect that talk radio had on politics and government by providing a forum for political discourse that is open to participation by virtually everyone.
   c. Describe how digital technologies are transforming people's access to information, as well as the quantity and quality of that content.

5. Explain media consolidation and the effect that having fewer media owners has had on the nature of news.

6. Describe the proliferation of news sources, including how cell phones have increased scrutiny of government officials and how blogs have come to provide a platform for citizen journalists.

7. Analyze the claims that the media have an ideological bias, both liberal and conservative, and that corporate bias exists in the media.

8. Describe how the media are regulated by the Federal Communications Commission.
   a. Explain the effect of the Telecommunications Act of 1996.
   b. Explain how large corporate conglomerates have increasingly gained control of the media.

Key Terms

consolidation 347

digital paywall 341

fairness doctrine 343

fireside chats 343

framing 338

infotainment 336

journalism 339

letter to the editor 338

media 335

media segmentation 344

muckraking 341

narrowcasting 344

new media 335

penny press 339

priming 338

public agenda 338

talk radio 343

telegenic 343

yellow journalism 340

For Review

1. How have changing technologies affected the type of information available to media consumers?

2. What political functions do the media perform? How have these functions changed over time?

3. Describe the evolution of the press in the United States. How do newspapers today differ from newspapers in earlier centuries?

4. How did television affect how people get information? How did television change how political campaigns are waged?

5. How have changes in technology changed the media? How has our consumption of media changed? What changes do you expect to see in years to come?

6. What evidence is there to support claims of media bias? Is all bias ideological?

7. In what specific ways does the government regulate media? What aspects of the media and their coverage does the government not regulate?

For Critical Thinking and Discussion

1. Has the Internet changed how you personally participate in politics? Does virtual activism make real-world activism less likely or more likely? Explain.

2. What do you think are the most important functions the media perform? Why? Does the diversity of media outlets hinder the media's ability to serve some of their more traditional functions? Explain.

3. Compare and contrast the penny papers of the 19th century with today's blogs. What are the similarities and differences between the two? How will blogs evolve given the evolution of other media forms?

4. Discuss the dangers of the unchecked Internet in the political world. Can these dangers be combated? If so, how?

5. What difficulties are associated with government regulation of the media in an era of cable television, the Internet, and satellite radio?

Resources for

Research AND Action

Internet Resources

State of the Media
www.stateofthemedia.org Run by the Project for Excellence in Journalism, this site features an annual report on the media and tracks trends in media usage and confidence in the media.

The Pew Research Center for People and the Press
http://people-press.org This site provides independent research, surveys, data sets, and commentary on the media and issues of media interest.

Media Watch
www.mediawatch.com Visit this site to learn about the initiatives of an activist group that monitors media content and seeks to combat stereotypes and violence in the media.

Recommended Readings

Bennett, W. Lance. *News: The Politics of Illusion,* 9th ed. New York: Longman, 2015. Offers a behind-the-scenes tour of the media in politics while grappling with this question: How well does the news, as the core of the national political information system, serve the needs of democracy?

Berry, Jeffrey M., and Sarah Sobieraj. *The Outrage Industry: Political Opinion Media and the New Incivility.* New York: Oxford University Press, 2014. The book examines "outrage rhetoric," the incendiary talk common on many talk radio and cable news programs, and evaluates its impact.

Crouse, Timothy. *The Boys on the Bus.* New York: Random House, 1973. A classic tale of the presidential campaign press corps.

Graber, Doris. *Media Power and Politics.* Washington, DC: CQ Press, 2010. Analyzes the influence of the media on opinions, elections, and policies, as well as efforts to shape the content and impact of media coverage.

Iyengar, Shanto. *Media Politics: A Citizen's Guide,* 3rd ed. New York: Norton, 2015. Surveys how politicians use the media to get elected, wield power in office, and achieve policy goals.

Jamieson, Kathleen Hall, and Paul Waldman. *The Press Effect: Politicians, Journalists, and the Stories That Shape the Political World.* Oxford: Oxford University Press, 2003. Demonstrates how the national press molds the news through its reporting, using the examples of the 2000 presidential election, the Supreme Court's decision on the Florida vote that year, and the press's response to national politics after September 11.

Plissner, Martin. *The Control Room: How Television Calls the Shots in Presidential Elections.* New York: Free Press, 1999. Describes the effect of television news and advertising on presidential elections.

Wolfsfeld, Gadi. *Making Sense of Media and Politics: Five Principles in Political Communication.* New York: Taylor and Francis, 2014. Describes the relationship between the impact of politics on the news media and how the media influence politics.

Movies of Interest

The Post (2018)
The story of Katharine Graham, the first female publisher of a major American newspaper, *The Washington Post,* who, with editor Ben Bradlee, competes with *The New York Times* to expose a massive cover-up of government secrets that would come to be known as the Pentagon Papers.

Spotlight (2015)
Starring Rachel McAdams and Michael Keaton, this film is based on the true story of the *Boston Globe* reporter team who broke the sex abuse scandal involving the Boston Catholic Church.

Good Night and Good Luck (2005)
Directed by George Clooney, this film tells the story of famed CBS newsman Edward R. Murrow, who takes on Senator Joseph McCarthy and the House Un-American Activities Committee's communist witch hunt during the 1950s, despite pressure from corporate sponsors and from McCarthy himself.

Shattered Glass (2003)
Stephen Glass was a staff writer for the *New Republic* and was also freelancing for other prominent publications when it was discovered that he had fabricated stories. This film depicts his career and his downfall.

Live from Baghdad (2002)
This movie demonstrates the differences in tactics between 24-hour news channels and network news shows, telling the story of CNN's coverage of the U.S. invasion of Iraq in 1990.

All the President's Men (1976)
Starring Dustin Hoffman and Robert Redford, this film, based on Bob Woodward and Carl Bernstein's best-selling book of the same title, tells the saga of the two *Washington Post* reporters' investigation of the Watergate scandal that rocked the Nixon White House.

Network (1976)
Faye Dunaway, Peter Finch, William Holden, and Robert Duvall star in this classic satirizing the nature of newscasting in the 1970s.

Citizen Kane (1941)
This classic, directed by and starring Orson Welles, is Welles's fictionalized version of newspaper scion William Randolph Hearst, who purportedly attempted to halt release of the film.

References

1. www.snopes.com/fact-check/trucked-voters-in-pa/.
2. David Weinberger, www.hillwatch.com/PPRC/Quotes/Internet_and_Politics.aspx.
3. On April 7, 2005, General Motors pulled its advertising from the *Los Angeles Times* after columnist Dan McNeil, who covers the automotive trade for the newspaper, published several columns critical of GM, including one that chastised the company for pushing gas-guzzling SUVs rather than pursuing hybrid technology and another that called for the "impeachment" of two of the company's top executives.
4. New editions of all of these works are available: Tarbell (New York: Norton, 1969); Steffens (New York: Sangamore Press, 1957); and Sinclair (Cambridge, MA: B. Bentley, 1971).
5. Pew Research Center, *2012 State of the News Media.*
6. https://twitter.com/realDonaldTrump/status/764867963845484545.
7. Dwight D. Eisenhower, Republican National Convention Speech, July 14, 1964.
8. Brian Rosenwald and Michael Smerconish, *CNN,* "Ted Cruz and Donald Trump: Signs of Conservative Media's Grip on GOP," February 3, 2016.
9. C. Richard Hofstetter, *Bias in the News: Network Television Coverage of the 1972 Election Campaign* (Columbus: Ohio State University Press, 1976); Michael J. Robinson and Margaret A. Sheehan, *Over the Wire and on TV: CBS and UPI in Campaign '80* (New York: Russell Sage Foundation, 1983).
10. Michael Parenti, *Inventing Reality: The Politics of the Mass Media* (New York: St. Martin's Press, 1986).
11. Gale Ann Hurd, "Stop Piracy Apocalypse: 'Walking Dead' Producer," *USA Today,* April 12, 2016.

CHAPTER 11

Politics and Technology

©The Asahi Shimbun via Getty Images

Mr. Mark Zuckerberg

THEN

Technology had little influence on politics.

NOW

Technology is the most important tool for participation in democracies—shaping how voters get information, how campaigns are run, how candidates behave, and how governments provide services.

NEXT

Will people use technology as the great equalizer to facilitate participation in our democratic system?

Will campaigns use increasingly sophisticated microtargeting mechanisms and "big data" to deliver better information to voters?

Will democracies succeed in preventing foreign powers from using technology to interfere with elections?

"For most of our existence,

we focused on all the good that connecting people can bring. As Facebook has grown, people everywhere have gotten a powerful new tool to stay connected to the people they love, make their voices heard, and build communities and businesses. . . . But it's clear now that we didn't do enough to prevent these tools from being used for harm as well. That goes for fake news, foreign interference in elections, and hate speech, as well as developers and data privacy. We didn't take a broad enough view of our responsibility, and that was a big mistake. It was my mistake, and I'm sorry."[1] So began Facebook CEO Mark Zuckerberg's 2018 testimony before the House Committee on Energy and Commerce. He appeared at the committee hearing after it was revealed that Cambridge Analytica, which worked with Donald Trump's 2016 campaign, had acquired the Facebook profiles of 87 million U.S. citizens and used the data to build a software program to predict and influence voters. At the heart of the scandal—and of Zuckerberg's testimony—are both a necessity and an onerous responsibility: While tech companies strive to meet the growing demand to connect individuals in new ways, they must also protect users' privacy and ensure content that is not intentionally harmful.

The value that technology has in political and civic life can't be underestimated: It enables candidates to communicate directly with constituents, governments to connect directly with citizens, parties and other organizations to inform and mobilize voters, and citizens themselves to debate and discuss issues online. A half century ago, the advent of television changed the nature of political life in the United States in many ways—it changed the characteristics essential for candidates to be successful. It changed how campaigns were run and how voters were kept informed of issues. From the start, some Internet innovators hoped new technologies might usher in an age of better democratic governance. The founder of the World Wide Web, Tim Berners-Lee (who created the first successful communication between a hypertext transfer protocol [http] client and a server using the Internet) stated that "greater openness, accountability, and transparency in government will give people greater choice and make it easier for individuals to get more directly involved in issues that matter to them."[2] Berners-Lee's vision for the Internet has occurred, but has been accompanied by unanticipated outcomes that pose serious threats to democracies, and these threats must be addressed.

Learning Objectives

After reading this chapter, students should be able to:

- Explain the modern technological revolution and who uses new technology.
- Analyze how technology has changed and continues to change the political arena.
- Assess how technology is transforming the way governments govern.
- Understand the positive impact of new technology on politics and how it will transform political life in the future.
- List the potential negative consequences of new technologies on politics.
- Describe the arguments as to whether regulation of the Internet is necessary.

The Modern Technological Revolution: The Internet and Cellular Technology

The modern media revolution began with the birth of the Internet. As a medium of communication, a source of news and information, and a tool for political engagement and grassroots organizing, the Internet has had an incalculable—and a global—impact on the way people interact. Today, 89 percent of American adults use the Internet. In addition, the hardware of modern technology—the Internet, smartphones, and other cellular devices—is revolutionizing how politics is done in the United States. This transformation is being facilitated not only by the devices we use, but also by the platforms, software, and apps that these devices use. Of particular importance in politics are **social networking sites,** which enable users to construct a profile, specify other users with whom they share a connection, and view others' connections.[3]

social networking sites
Platforms that enable users to construct a profile, specify other users with whom they share a connection, and view others' connections.

The modern media revolution continues today as cellular technology makes the Internet portable and constantly available. Thus, we spend so much time on the Internet because we can—using cellular technology, we can Snapchat while waiting for the bus, check Instagram in line at the grocery store, blog while eating lunch in the cafeteria (but of course we would *never* text in class . . .). The convenience and power of the combination of these technologies have enormous implications for how politics takes place now and how politics will happen in the future as access to cell phones continues to increase. Today, over three-quarters (77 percent) of all American adults own a smartphone, nearly double the rate of ownership five years ago.[4] Since 95 percent of Americans own some kind of mobile phone, the number of smartphone owners is likely to increase as contracts on standard phones expire and prices of smartphones drop.[5]

Who Uses the Internet?

Even in an age when Internet usage is nearly universal, groups still differ in the extent to which they do and do not use technology. The term for this unequal access to computer technology is the **digital divide.** Historically, one of the largest sources of the digital divide has been income: Poorer people were less likely to have access to new technologies. Today, however, the chief condition fueling the digital divide is age. Still, other demographic factors, including region, income, education, and race, also play a role in predicting whether an individual will use technology, as shown in Table 11.1. Indeed, among certain populations—members of the Millennial generation, those with a household income over $75,000, and those with a college degree—Internet usage today is essentially universal (with 98 percent, 98 percent, and 97 percent of those populations, respectively, using the Internet).[6]

digital divide
Unequal access to computer technology.

The digital divide is also based on geography: 92 percent of urban and 90 percent of suburban residents use the Internet compared with 78 percent of rural residents.[7] Disabilities can also contribute to a digital divide. Today, 89 percent of Americans use the Internet, but Internet use shrinks to 77 percent among adults living with a disability that interferes with daily life, a group that constitutes about 19 percent of the U.S. population.[8]

Although the digital divide is less about income than ever before, even today, affluent individuals are more likely to have smartphones, unlimited data plans, computers, and high-speed Internet connections than are other people. Access to high-speed Internet service even in the world's most affluent democracies can be expensive,[9] and in the developing world, access to technology is nearly always limited. Where information technology is relatively broadly available, as in the United States, several political scientists, including Matthew Hindman[10] and Laura McKenna, argue that access to the Internet produces unequal benefits politically. McKenna notes that "those with lower levels of political capital are lost in a sea of facts, distracted by online poker and joke e-mails, and may be simply not interested in reading political content . . . [while] those who avail themselves of superior political resources on the Internet accelerate their political skills."[11] But evidence indicates that as the use of cellular technology increases (and becomes cheaper) and free Wi-Fi service becomes more widely available, the income-based digital divide will shrink even further. The geographic digital divide, by which residents of rural areas lack access to wired broadband technology, also is changing because of greater availability of Internet access through cellular technology, even in many remote regions.

Internet usage today is skewed toward highly educated, high-income earners. But because of the propensity for young people to use the Internet, and because of the increasing use of smartphones, Internet usage is likely to be nearly universal in the future.

Yet, despite the fact that some Americans do not own computers or have online access, the Internet has broadly transformed life in the United States in general and political life specifically. Technology has changed the structure of how information is communicated, how political participation occurs, and how governments govern. As political scientist Michael Cornfield noted: "I can't think of anything except kissing babies that you can't do online."[12] (Today, candidates probably do that by Facetiming.) In any case, the influence of the Internet has been both positive and negative, and it continues to evolve.

New Forms of Community

Internet technology also facilitates the formation of virtual communities. These networks of interested participants, although different from their IRL (in-real-life) counterparts, share features with those real-world groups.[13] Many blogs, for example, have community leaders, regular contributors, expert commentators, and participants with established roles. Blogs promote civic engagement and participation by disseminating information, exposing readers to the viewpoints of others, providing a forum allowing bloggers to share their own views, serving as a venue for the formation of online communities that can foster feelings of efficacy among participants, and channeling activism, both virtual and real.

Facebook, Instagram, and other social networking sites also create **virtual communities,** online networks—of friends, of fans, and groups—where individuals perform as leaders, information and opinions can be shared, and strategies can be

TABLE 11.1 Who Uses the Internet?

In general, what demographic groups are most likely to be Internet users? What factors might prevent less likely populations from using the Internet?

ALL ADULTS	89%
SEX	
Men	89
Women	88
RACE/ETHNICITY	
White (Non-Hispanic)	89
Black	87
Hispanic	88
Asian American*	97
AGE GROUP	
18–29	98
30–49	97
50–64	87
65 +	66
EDUCATION LEVEL	
Less than high school	65
High school grad	84
Some college	93
College +	97
HOUSEHOLD INCOME	
Less than $30,000	81
$30,000–$49,999	93
$50,000–$74,999	97
$75,000+	98
COMMUNITY TYPE	
Urban	92
Suburban	90
Rural	78

*Data for Asian Americans is from 2014 and includes only "English speaking Asians," according to the Pew Research Center.

SOURCE: Pew Research Center.

virtual communities
Online networks where individuals perform as leaders, information and opinions can be shared, and strategies can be planned, priorities organized, and roles assigned.

>Demographic factors, including income, education, race, and age, play a role in predicting whether an individual will use technology. But because of the propensity for young people to use the Internet, and because of the increasing use of smartphones, Internet usage is likely to be nearly universal in the future.

© Mario Tama/Getty Images

planned, priorities organized, and roles assigned. Clay Skirky's *Here Comes Everybody* chronicles why some online entities—including flashmobs and Wikipedia—effectively create organizational structure and channel participation, while others flounder.[14] And the success that individuals enjoy in virtual roles may spill over into real-life behaviors in political organizations. For example, much research indicates that the use of social media sources increases civic engagement and participation in the real world,[15] although some social network users are no more likely to participate in politics than are users of other media.[16] Furthermore, online groups perform many of the same positive civic functions as offline groups, specifically in terms of mobilizing political participation (although not in terms of increasing political knowledge).[17] In many ways, social networking sites undertaking political work closely resemble the in-real-life groups that preceded them and also spur activism that may not have been possible through offline groups.

The Internet has also facilitated the formation of communities by enabling people in disparate places to communicate and work toward shared goals or share information. For example, the Gay Rights cause on Facebook has over 1.3 million members from all over the world. The group is an arm of the advocacy group Change.org, which provides a community-building tool for the lesbian, bisexual, gay, and transgender (LBGT) communities to start campaigns to fight for gay rights. According to the Gay Rights' Cause Facebook page, they "empower millions of people to start, join, and win campaigns for equality in their community, city, and country." The platform enables communities to form around a wide array of issues affecting the LGBT community, including supporting anti-bullying policies in states and communities and pressuring corporations to condemn anti-gay government policies abroad. The group facilitates the replication of effective strategies by enabling local communities to rely on the tried-and-true methods that have worked in other locales.

Virtual communities have been particularly important for people with disabilities, as new technologies enable them to circumvent the physical obstacles they may face in networking with people with similar disabilities, or those without psychical challenges. For example, text messaging has greatly increased the ability of hearing-impaired individuals to communicate with others. And using the RAY app for Android phones, which allows for eye-free control with tactile keys, a non-seeing person can communicate in real time to anyone, including members of the Visually Impaired Support Group on Facebook, which connects people with vision impairment in numerous countries.

Technology Now: Changing How Candidates Campaign and Citizens Participate

The prevalent use of technology in campaigns today makes it appear that technology has been the *modus operandi* for decades. The reality, however, is that it has been just a little more than a decade—Barack Obama's first campaign for president in 2008—that was a watershed election in terms of technology use. Dubbed the Web 2.0 election, then-Senator Obama consistently had the advantage, creating a user-friendly website where supporters could access up-to-the-minute campaign news (including links to stories about the candidate and the campaign in the popular media), review talking points, download campaign posters and flyers, make computer-assisted phone calls to undecided voters in swing states, and map out door-to-door canvassing operations in their area.[18] Obama's campaign relied on social media to reach to young voters, boasting more Facebook friends than his opponent, Sen. John McCain by a 5-to-1 margin. The Obama campaign and its supporters posted twice as many videos to his official YouTube channel,[19] which bested McCain's in the number of subscribers by an 11-to-1 margin.[20] As the campaign heated up, this vast social network helped to spin news and deflate opposition messages. Finally, new cellular technologies and software platforms provided for a sophisticated get-out-the-vote effort on Election Day, with many "armchair activists" relying on their computers and telephones to encourage turnout. Obama's success made campaign organizers, political candidates, and the media realize how crucial it is to leverage emerging technology to create strategic advantages.

Since that game-changing campaign, technology has continued to transform how American politics happen. Technology has changed not only how campaigns are run, but also how we receive information and how governments provide services. Perhaps lost in all this, and yet of great importance, is technology's promise: Cellular technology and the Internet hold the potential of serving as a means by which people can exercise control over their democracy. And because of the differences in how generations use technology, it holds the greatest promise for younger people. Communications scholar Howard Rheingold argues that the digital media in particular serve as a key avenue through which young people can use their "public voice" to consume and share information.[21] This information is available immediately at any time of the day or night. Since the information superhighway is no longer a one-way street, it provides greater opportunities for political conversations, debates, and reactions. It is also increasingly serving as a platform through which communities that influence political life come together and exert influence.

>Shrinking the digital divide for the visually impaired: The RAY app enables users who are visually impaired to navigate all phone features with eyes-free operation, thus enabling the user to communicate with friends, family, and colleagues. Technology is increasingly making it easier for all people to participate in the civic life of their communities.
© Project Ray

Politics on Demand

Nightly newscasts—once the main method by which Americans got their news—now seem quaint, as information is transmitted instantaneously to our cell phones via the Internet. News websites—including those of all the network and cable news stations, plus sites maintained by Internet service providers—give Internet users access to news stories when they want them instead of at pre-determined times. And **news aggregators,** services such as *Google News*, the *Huffington Post*, and the *Drudge Report* compile all the news we want from various outlets, including news headlines, blogs, and podcasts, in one location so that we can consume information quickly. Immediate, on-demand access to political information is a recent phenomenon. Most Americans report that they follow the news using, on average, four different devices or technologies[22] and a variety of ways to connect to the Internet. These users can selectively search for specific information or sign up for alerts to keep informed about public issues that matter to them, building their knowledge base at a finger's click. Moreover, many contemporary news outlets, such as magazines and radio programs, make available downloadable podcasts that give individuals even greater access to reports on social issues, policy initiatives, and politics.

news aggregators
Services that compile in one location news we want from various outlets.

vlog
A video weblog.

YouTube provides a compelling example of how the evolving Internet has worked to provide on-demand and real-time information. This website, which debuted in February 2005 and is now owned by Google, allows individuals to post and watch original videos and provides a platform for the posting of series of video weblogs, or **vlogs.** The success of the YouTube experiment would have been inconceivable in a world of dial-up Internet connections that was the norm just a few years ago. Today, 300 hours of video are uploaded to YouTube every minute by its 1.57 billion unique users. More video is uploaded to YouTube in one month than has been broadcast by the three television networks in the past 60 years, and people watch 5 billion videos each day.[23]

One way the behemoth of YouTube is affecting political life in the United States is by furnishing an unprecedented amount and variety of on-demand data concerning candidates and elections. Today it is standard practice for candidates to have their own YouTube channels that provide original content (including biographic videos and longer advertisements than would appear on television). But the political impact of the Internet is not limited to the United States, or even to democracies. Indeed, 80 percent of YouTube views come from outside the United States. The interactivity embodied in viewing, commenting, posting, and vlogging has revolutionized civic discourse globally. Indeed, the Internet has made the world smaller, enabling the global spread of news and information and exerting an influence on national politics that was unheard of before.

Technological Tools: Paving the Two-Way Communication Street

bandwidth
The amount of data that can travel through a network in a given time period.

In its early years, the Internet functioned in much the same way that traditional media formats, such as newspapers and periodicals, functioned: It provided a convenient but "one-way" means for people to get information at times determined by the publishers. As **bandwidth**—the amount of data that can travel through a transmission medium in a given time period—has increased, so, too, has the sophistication of web content, as well as the venues and formats that serve as information sources. In the early 1990s, when Tim Berners-Lee invented hypertext and researchers at the University of Illinois introduced the first graphic web browser, Mosaic, Internet users could e-mail, post, and access text files and even communicate via rudimentary bulletin boards. Yet accessing a single page with graphics or photos could take well over a minute. By the mid-1990s, however, businesses and venture capitalists recognized the commercial potential of the World Wide Web. Cable supplanted dial-up modem-driven access and thus expanded bandwidth. Start-up companies and IT giants raced to develop hardware and software products that allowed for the exchange of text, voice, images, and videos in new ways. Cell phone towers sprang up around the world as these devices evolved to provide laptop functionalities. Within just a few years, instant messaging, voicemailing, and posting images, audio, videos, and text had become built in to the pattern of 21st-century communication.

As a result, communication is a two-way street, no longer mediated by media outlets. Governments, candidates, their organizations, grassroots organizations, interest groups, and political parties use technology to communicate directly with individuals, and vice versa. And as we saw in the 2016 presidential election, the openness of the medium of communication has exposed a key vulnerability: as authentic organizations use social media to reach individuals, so too can those who seek to undermine and disrupt democracy, as we discuss later in this chapter.

Nonetheless, civic participation has been facilitated by the rise of these forms of communication, which enable conversations about information, rather than just information reception. The Internet has also created a hybrid between producers and consumers of news, as many individuals simultaneously consume and produce information in the forms of videos, postings, and websites.

Another tool that establishes a new "two-way street" of political communication is the **blogosphere**—the community, or social network, of bloggers. Increasing numbers of people are as likely to subscribe to popular blogs such as *Daily Kos, ThinkProgress,* and *RedState* as they are to local or national newspapers. Using the blog platforms WordPress, Tumblr, Reddit, or many others, anyone can blog, and the number of blogs increases enormously each year, with some observers estimating that one million blogposts are posted each day.[24] As the number has multiplied, their variety and credibility have increased. Research indicates that there is enormous crossover between the blogosphere and traditional media outlets, with many traditional media outlets increasingly providing blogs written by professional journalists. For example, the *Washington Post*'s blog, *The Fix,* is a must-read for many D.C.-based political insiders.

THEN NOW NEXT

The Future of Facebook

Then (2004)	Now
It was called "The Facebook."	It's just Facebook.
It had 1 million users.	It has over 1.45 billion active daily users around the world.
Users posted on a Facebook wall.	Users post on a Timeline.
Fewer than 800 college networks were part of the Facebook.	Seventy-nine percent of all Americans use Facebook.

SOURCE: Facebook Investor Relations

WHAT'S NEXT?

> How can Facebook ensure that platform users do not intend harm to democracies?

> How might Facebook be used as a political tool by activists and campaigns in the future?

> What does Facebook's potential expansion internationally mean for its political utility?

Grassroots is a term that describes political efforts that start at the local level and eventually grow to reach higher levels, including the state and national levels. The blog's rise as a tool of grassroots organizing has given birth to the term **netroots** to describe Net-centered political efforts on behalf of candidates and causes. The blog provides immediate distribution of information to large numbers of users, spreading news and energizing supporters more rapidly than any other medium. Blogs, like the partisan penny papers that were a specialized medium of information in early American times, also enable people to select sources of information that mimic and confirm their own views.[25] And those who participate online tend to be among the most active citizens in offline forms of engagement as well.

blogosphere
The community of bloggers.

netroots
The Internet-centered political efforts on behalf of candidates and causes.

New Campaign Strategies and Modes of Political Participation

Technology has changed the nature of political participation and of political campaigns through the introduction of new strategies that give candidates advantages and enable new modes of political participation.

E-CAMPAIGNING   Today, it is common to open up Facebook and see a sponsored page available from your member of Congress or a candidate for other political office. Due to increasingly sophisticated software that recognizes our location, preferences, priorities, opinions, and Internet habits, we are often targeted for political ads. And as we saw in the 2016 presidential campaign, not all political ads were sponsored by legitimate organizations, as users of some social media platforms, including Facebook and Twitter, were exposed to ads created by Russian operatives. But social media platforms are not the only places where candidates advertise. Increasingly, Google is **remarketing**—that is, targeting Google political ads based on the cookies a user dropped on other websites. So, for example, say during the 2018 congressional election, you visited U.S. Senator Ted Cruz's (R-Tex.) campaign website and then read the *Houston Chronicle* online. You may have then seen a Google ad soliciting support for Ted Cruz on your screen, because when selling ads to campaigns and other organizations, Google recognizes that based on your Internet behavior, you're more likely to contribute to or support causes you have demonstrated an interest in through your online behavior.

Among the first to understand the value that information technology held for political campaigns was Jesse Ventura, a professional wrestler who served as the governor of Minnesota from 1999 to 2003. He represented the Reform Party, founded in 1995 and supported by people who were disillusioned with what they saw as the corruption and ineffectiveness of the two major parties. Ventura credited the Internet with opening up the political process by enabling grassroots mobilization through **e-campaigning,** the practice of mobilizing voters using the Internet, which allowed an outsider like him to be elected governor. Winning half of the under-30 vote, Ventura conducted the first stage of his campaign without any physical headquarters. Armed with a large e-mail list, he collected pledges of support that short-circuited the traditional doorbell ringing and telephone calls that go with the territory when running for office. His tactics gave him the final surge of voters that he needed to win. Ventura's victory foreshadowed the power of the Internet as a political campaign tool.

The potential of the Internet as a force in political campaigns came into sharp focus again in 2004, when liberal Democrat Governor Howard Dean of Vermont used the Internet extensively for recruiting volunteers and raising money. Dean's efforts proved so successful that other candidates quickly followed his strategy. By the 2008 campaign, every major presidential candidate had a staff of website designers, Internet campaign managers, and blog managers. Today, the tech side of campaigns sometimes overshadows the boots-on-the-ground campaigns taking place in each of the states.

But the rapid expansion of Internet technology also has made it more difficult for presidential campaigns (and administrations) to manage the news.[26] In a pattern established during the campaign, White House staffers are often flummoxed with President Trump's seeming unwillingness to stay "on message" and his ability to ignite firestorms by personally tweeting out incendiary comments. And the omnipresent nature of technology means that campaigns and elected officials must be aware of the always-handy cell phone, with camera and audio recording device constantly at the ready. Regarding the phenomenon of "going viral," Patrick Healy of *The New York Times* wrote that a "clip may have been trivial, but the brief episode surrounding it illustrated how visual and audio technologies like video streaming have the potential to drive political news in unexpected directions, and how White House candidates are aggressively monitoring and trying to master them."[27] The omnipresent nature of technology also must give candidates pause about behaviors they engaged in even before running for office: In 2005, when

remarketing
Targeting political Google ads based on the cookies that a user drops on other websites.

e-campaigning
The practice of mobilizing voters using the Internet.

Donald Trump bragged to Billy Bush, then of *Access Hollywood*, using vulgar terms about kissing and groping women, that "when you're a star, they let you do it," he certainly could not have imagined that the conversation would be recorded on a hot mic and obtained by the media nearly a decade later as he was pursuing a bid for the presidency.

One of the most effective means for providing immediate distribution of information to large numbers of people is through **micro-blogs,** including Twitter and other platforms that enable short communication, often targeted specifically to on-the-move audiences. And the same technology used to target potential consumers of products is now being used to target voters. Twitter currently boasts 330 million monthly active users who tweet over 500 million messages of 280 or fewer characters each day. Although Twitter has comparatively fewer users than Facebook, it is enormously important among political operatives and many activists, a fact borne out by the important role Donald Trump's use of Twitter had in propelling him to the presidency. While many candidates might view Twitter as a component of their campaign, for Trump it was the center-

>During his 2016 run for president, Donald Trump's use of Twitter—sometimes effective, sometimes damaging to his campaign—demonstrated the rapidly evolving role of technology in political campaigns.
Source: Twitter

piece, a mechanism by which he generated fast, widespread, and unfettered attention. In describing the medium, Trump explained, "I can let people know that they were a fraud. I can let people know that they have no talent, that they didn't know what they're doing. You have a voice."[28] Trump's use of Twitter—the outrageous statement, defended immediately by an army of supporters who generated enormous social media attention that was then covered by the mainstream media—proved a game changer in the practice of presidential campaigns.

Research indicates that in addition to the important role Twitter plays among political consultants and activists, it plays a significant role in shaping public opinion. Researchers Fei Xiong and Yun Liu ran 6 million tweets through a computer algorithm and discovered that the diffusiveness that characterizes initial public opinion on an issue evolves and consolidates quickly, often through endorsements of large groups, which are most effective at swaying opinions. Despite the evolved consensus, small segments of Twitter users who hold minority views may not change, but for candidates and elected officials, it is crucial to act early in order to forge the consensus view, as once public opinion solidifies around an issue on Twitter, it is difficult to change. Thus, **promoted tweets**—that is, targeted advertising—found on a Twitter page that target Twitter users based on whom they follow and who follows them may be an effective tool for candidates and elected officials to shape opinion.

BIG DATA AND MICROTARGETING   One of the hallmarks of today's technology is that it allows candidates and other organizations to rely on information derived from **big data,** or large data sets collected from numerous sources (including online searches, purchases tracked through rewards programs, location tracking, and social media use) that through computational analysis can indicate individual

micro-blog
Sites, including Twitter, that enable short communication, often targeted specifically at on-the-move audiences.

promoted tweets
Targeted advertising found on a Twitter page that targets Twitterers based on whom they follow and who follows them.

big data
Large data sets collected from numerous sources that through computational analysis can indicate individual patterns, associations, preferences, and opinions.

microtarget
Datamining techniques that facilitate the tracking of individual voter preferences so that tailored messages in various forms can be used to generate support, contributions, and votes.

patterns, associations, preferences, and opinions. Candidates can then **microtarget**—that is, use data-mining techniques to track individual voter preferences so they can tailor messages in various forms to generate support, contributions, and votes. For example, NationBuilder is a platform that mines Internet data and enables a candidate, political party, interest group, or other organization to use that mined data to create lists of potential supporters based on their online profiles. Using social networking platforms, organizations can then target these individuals and try to garner their support.

Other programs use surveys to determine voter priorities and preferences and then, based on the potential supporters' responses, campaign canvassers can access already-prescribed talking points to convince potential supporters to vote for their candidate or join their cause. They can even access compelling videos targeted at the respondents on a smartphone or an iPad. Using a smartphone, a canvasser can immediately sign up residents for text or e-mail subscriptions. Once back at headquarters, the canvasser will sync the phone with databases that will track the voter for years, and update his or her preferences and concerns.

cyber cascade
What occurs when an electronic document becomes very widely distributed digitally through e-mail, social networking, or video sharing.

E-MAIL CAMPAIGNS AND E-PETITION DRIVES Campaigns can also benefit or suffer from e-mail campaigns. With one click, you can influence how someone you know thinks about a political leader, sometimes creating a **cyber cascade**—which occurs when an electronic document "goes viral" or becomes widely distributed digitally through e-mail, social networking, or video sharing.[29] Today, people who are unsure about the accuracy of claims made in e-mails (or on the Internet) can be assisted by such fact-checking websites as Snopes.com and Politi-Fact.com, but many people pass on hoax e-mails without checking. E-mail campaigns are not always damaging, or inaccurate, though.[30] Sometimes e-mail provides a quick means by which those with a common interest, from the environment to school funding, can keep informed about issues and be advised when action is necessary. Groups will often e-mail "action alert" messages asking members to contact government officials to pass a particular piece of legislation or to join a protest against a government official or another organization.

e-petition
An online petition used as a tool to garner support for a position or cause.

From the early days of the Internet, individuals used chain e-mails to garner support and communicate with policymakers. Today, using the Internet site Change.org, any individual can create an **e-petition,** an online petition used as a tool to garner support for a position or cause.

MACRO-PROTESTING The #MeToo movement, discussed in Chapter 5, provides an example of the power of social media to foster macro-protests. The hashtag became a rallying cry as women throughout the United States shared their experiences of being sexually harassed in the workplace and lobbied for changes in workplace policies, the enforcement of harassment laws, and the dismissal of serial predators. But what started as a viral hashtag became a much larger social movement, with women advocating for changes to policy in real life. This macro-protesting generated enormous media coverage in traditional news outlets and in online news sites and blogs and created a groundswell of Internet information-sharing and activism through Facebook and Twitter.

E-MOBILIZATION Some organizations have been particularly effective at advocating for candidates and policy changes, or compelling individual actions, by using the Internet to mobilize like-minded individuals. One of the earliest, most influential groups was MoveOn.org, a liberal organization spawned by two Silicon Valley tech entrepreneurs who were frustrated with the partisan bickering surrounding President Bill Clinton's impeachment hearings. On September 18, 1998, the two started an e-petition to "Censure President Clinton and Move On to Pressing Issues Facing the Nation." The petition netted hundreds of thousands of signatures.[31] Today, MoveOn.org has 5 million members, and nearly 800,000 people "like" it on Facebook. The organization circulates electronic petitions, endorses candidates, and uses traditional advertising to sway public opinion and generate support for candidates.

HACKTIVISM   In an era in which everything from our photos of Grandma's last visit to our bank accounts is stored electronically, hackers hold considerable power. **Hacktivism** is the authorized or unauthorized use of or destruction of electronic files in pursuit of a political or social goal. One of the best-known hacktivist groups is a loosely organized collection of individuals called Anonymous. These unidentified individuals collaborate, often in denial-of-service attacks, which prevent targeted servers from functioning by overloading them. For example, in 2015, French members of Anonymous announced a hacking operation against the terror group ISIS following the coordinated attacks in Paris in November of that year. A translation of the video states, "Anonymous from all over the world will hunt you down. You should know that we will find you and we will not let you go."[32] In other acts of hacktivism, the group crippled the mail servers and websites of Monsanto, a biotech giant that supplied Agent Orange to the U.S. government during the Vietnam War and currently produces genetically modified seeds. They also took down over 40 child pornography sites and published the names of hundreds of individuals associated with these sites. Anonymous supported WikiLeaks, a website that released millions of secret government documents. During the 2016 presidential campaign, Hillary Clinton was the subject of a WikiLeaks attack when the organization published emails that indicated the Clinton campaign and the Democratic National Committee had worked in tandem against primary challenger U.S. Sen. Bernie Sanders (I-Vt.). In the wake of the scandal, the chair of the DNC, Debbie Wasserman Schultz, was forced to resign, and considerable speculation mounted that WikiLeaks would release an "October surprise," a tactical release of information that many speculated would be damaging to Hillary Clinton's presidential bid in the weeks leading in to the November general election. As hackers join forces, they resemble social movements undertaking protests in the real world, yet they have a much wider reach as they wreak havoc or work for the betterment of society.

hacktivism
The authorized or unauthorized use of or destruction of electronic files in pursuit of a political or social goal.

Technology Now: Revolutionizing How Governments Work

Governments use technology more broadly than any other entity. Indeed, the roots of most technological innovation stem from government needs, particularly in the defense and national security arenas. For example, the Internet was developed by the Defense Advanced Research Projects Agency in late 1969 so that researchers from the U.S. Department of Defense could share information with one another and with defense researchers and scientists in other government agencies and in academia. But today, this technology has grown from its cloak-and-dagger past to represent the most important mechanism by which governments are communicating

THEN

NOW

iPhone X

>In 1976, Apple Computer was founded by Steve Jobs (left), Steve Wozniak (right), and Ronald Wayne (not pictured) in the garage of Jobs's parents. Today, Apple has revolutionized how we communicate, work, and play.

Computer: ©Sal Veder/AP Images; *iPhone X:* ©Josh Edelson/AFP/Getty Images

e-Government
Employment of the Internet for delivering government information and services to the citizens.

transparency
Ability of citizens to have more and better information about governmental processes as well as services.

legacy systems
The old way of doing things, either in paper form or using outdated computer systems.

Foursquare
Geolocation app that uses an iPhone's built-in GPS to display attractions in your area.

CIA ✓
@CIA

· Follow

We can neither confirm nor deny that this is our first tweet.

↩ Reply ↨ Retweet ★ Favorite ••• More

RETWEETS	FAVORITES
302,266	188,572

10:49 AM - 6 Jun 2014

Source: Twitter/CIA

with and serving their citizens. This phenomenon, known as **e-Government,** is defined as "the employment of the Internet . . . for delivering government information and services to the citizens."[33] By using e-Government, practitioners hope that technology will enable governments to offer their services to citizens efficiently and cost-effectively. E-Government also should increase **transparency,** meaning that citizens will have more and better information about governmental processes as well as services. For example, the Federal Election Commission and state election law agencies have portals that allow citizens to learn about the sources of campaign contributions that elected officials and candidates for office accept.

Governments at all levels are using cutting-edge technology to transform the way they operate. Such practices may sometimes help governments rein in spending. For example, the Alabama Department of Conservation and Natural Resources implemented a program that enabled hunters and fishermen to obtain their licenses through an online licensing process, at an estimated cost savings of $200,000 annually.[34] But there also is evidence that technological innovation can be costly, as governments attempt to integrate **legacy systems**—that is, the old way of doing things, either in paper form or using outdated computer systems—using new, more efficient technologies.[35]

Increasingly, local governments also are using technology to improve the quality of services to residents through smartphone apps. For instance, the geolocation app **Foursquare** uses the iPhone's built-in GPS, or global positioning system (which determines your location using satellite-based radio navigation), to display civic attractions in your area as well as to broadcast your location to your friends. You can even use Foursquare to report a pothole in New York City. Soon governments will also use such programs to provide direct services to residents and visitors. For example, you may be able to search nearby restaurants by health-department grade, enabling you to pass up the sushi restaurant with a C grade in favor of walking the four blocks to its A-rated competitor. In the future, many cities will rely on this and other geolocation services to provide services, especially in times of emergency.

Governments also rely on technology to increase direct communication among government officials and between officials and constituents. For example, the town of Virginia Beach relies on **wiki,** an Internet-based editing tool that allows documents to be created and edited online by multiple individuals, to eliminate the need for cumbersome streams of e-mails containing revised versions of documents. Nicole McGee, the town's librarian, believes that wikis enable governments to be more efficient: "When comparing wikis to the traditional e-mail chain of editing/collaboration, wikis can greatly reduce inbox clutter and allow the participants in the wiki to always be working from the most up-to-date version of the document/project, since there is no need to exchange documents back and forth."[36]

Government leaders, too, rely on technology to help them better communicate with their residents. For example, local and state police departments routinely use text messages, Tweets, and Facebook posts to inform citizens about potential natural disasters, including hurricane, flood, or tornado warnings, and Amber Alerts are broadcast to cell phone subscribers. Governments also use the Internet for the more routine business of governing: Open Public Meetings Act notifications; bid alerts for public contracts; minutes of public meetings; video streams of state legislative meetings or city council meetings; texts of adopted laws, policies, or regulations; campaign finance disclosure reports; and even job openings are readily available online.

wiki
Internet-based editing tool that allows documents to be created and edited online by multiple individuals.

What Is the Impact of Technology on Political Life?

We know that technology is changing how we participate in the political life of our communities, states, nation, and world. On the whole, these changes signify greater access to information and influence by everyday people. Nonetheless, technology affects political life negatively as well.

Technology Is a Powerful Tool for Protesters and Activists

Technology has put the power to communicate into the hands of the masses and, in many circumstances, outside the reach of government control or manipulation. In 2016, that reality was reflected in the fact that the Russian government, through the activities of hackers, interfered with the process of the 2016 elections. That governments can no longer control the use of technology was reflected during the Jasmine Revolution throughout the Middle East in 2011, when anti-government protesters took to the streets, relying on social networking sites as a key medium of communication. And in 2014, as ISIS insurgents in Iraq battled their way toward Baghdad, the government attempted to thwart the rebels' use of social media sites by denying access to Twitter and Facebook, which the rebels were using to communicate. But one characteristic of modern technology is that it is becoming increasingly difficult for governments to control access. In Iraq, insurgents relied on fiber-optic lines and satellite links from Turkish, Jordanian, and Iranian telecommunications companies. Whether anti-government protesters or Islamic insurgents, technology provides an enormous tool for the masses, and increasingly this tool is outside the reach of government. The implication for this is twofold: Technology in the hands of some may foster the development of democracies; in the hands of others, it can be used by terrorists and those seeking to manipulate or overturn democratic governments.

In democratic societies, technology can also be an equalizer for candidates and for political and community groups. Before information technology, the cost of running a campaign or organizing a group could be prohibitive. Campaign mailers, lawn signs, or informational brochures might be out of reach for some candidates or groups. But for many candidates and organizations, new technology means that mobilizing can become much more affordable. For some candidates seeking local or state office, technology has revolutionized campaign costs, in some places eliminating the need for prohibitively expensive network television advertising. Though some forms of technology can be pricey for campaigns, civic organizations, interest groups, and other groups, networking through social media can provide a cost-effective and efficient means of reaching out to like-minded citizens.

Technology Increases the Amount of Political Information Available

Earlier in this chapter, we discussed the phenomenon of the on-demand news cycle. Technology has shrunk the news cycle, and candidates and organizations need to be constantly at the ready to spin events to their favor. So although officials may still attempt to manipulate the cycle (by timing announcements to garner more or less news coverage, depending on whether it is good or bad news), the reality is that today elected officials and government agencies are less capable of controlling the news cycle than in decades past. That said, the changing nature of the news makes it more susceptible to manipulation by those who seek to disrupt civic life. In addition, the advent of citizen journalism in the form of blogs, YouTube, and social networking means that relatively obscure events—gaffes or poignant moments—may go viral at any turn and create a whirlwind of unanticipated media coverage (positive or negative) for an official or a candidate.

Finally, as a result of new technology, individuals, and particularly young people, are more interested in political news, even though they may generally lack a depth of knowledge about current events, given the nature of the information they receive. This is particularly true of our shrinking global environment: Not so long ago, it would take time for news reports to emerge from hotspots around the world. Today, we are able to watch governments being overthrown live on our iPhones. Individuals may be glued to minute-by-minute coverage of an international crisis, yet these reports often do not explain the context of those events or provide in-depth analysis as to why these situations are unfolding.

What's Next: How Technology Will Continue to Transform the Political Landscape

The effect that today's technology has had on political life was unimaginable a generation ago. We know that nearly all aspects of the political landscape are being transformed, including how we register to vote, how we contribute to candidates, how we are mobilized by campaigns, and how grassroots organizing and fund-raising take place. So, although we can barely speculate about some of the ways that technology will transform political life in the generation to come, there are some very clear trends that we can say with certainty will prove to be political game-changers.

One of the most important transformative tools for politics is in the palm of your hand. Smartphone apps will continue to facilitate increasingly sophisticated targeting operations and to help candidates and other organizations create voter profiles that track voter concerns and opinions of candidates, thus facilitating enormously strategic get-out-the-vote efforts. Moreover, candidates, political parties, and interest groups are likely to invest great sums to manipulate the social media environment in favor of their candidate or their cause, using bots and other means similar to those Russian operatives used to influence the 2016 presidential election. In the future, it is likely that smaller, wearable (even implantable) devices will transform our political, social, and economic lives by altering our real-life perceptions. Imagine, for example, the experience of going on a blind date 25 years from now: Will our glasses perform facial recognition, and immediately scour the Internet for the date's social networking profile, work history, past purchases, and so on?

Decades ago, campaigns were transformed by television advertising. Suddenly a new set of candidate characteristics became mandatory, including the ability to present well on television, and campaigns had to develop expertise in media strategy. Campaign television advertising also increased negativity in campaigns, and negative charges could be spread to wider audiences than through older means of reaching voters. In the future, new strategies will emerge as paramount, as video advertisements on such outlets as YouTube and Hulu increasingly replace television ads. With fewer people watching television, and fewer still watching television in real time (a necessity for ad viewing), greater numbers of political advertisements will be seen on new IT venues. Because the length of a YouTube user session is just 15 minutes,[37] in all likelihood campaign ads will shrink to become mini sound bites that appear before videos. Decades ago, many television ads were 60 seconds long. Then 30-second ads became more common. Now, 15-second video ads appear before feature videos that have been targeted by campaigns as having viewers who will likely be sympathetic to the candidate's or group's message.

But also changing the nature of political advertising will be data-driven Internet advertising that capitalizes on technology to build better databases for campaigns. By collecting cookies from sites that constituents use, companies such as CampaignGrid can strategically target their candidate- and issue-based advertising, as shown in the example in Figure 11.1. Increasingly, these will be nonstatic

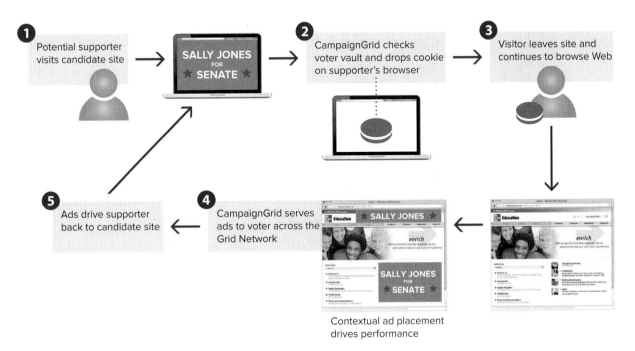

FIGURE 11.1 ■ How Grid Retargeting Works

ads: By asking viewers to click through to the campaign's website, campaigns can drop cookies to examine viewership and offer opportunities to sign up for e-mail lists, follow on Twitter, friend on Facebook, or otherwise collect identifying information about viewers. Or as CampaignGrid offers, "we help our clients target voters across all four screens—at home while watching television, at work on their computer, traveling with their tablet, or out and about on their mobile device."[38]

Another area of politics that will be affected by technological change is in absentee balloting. Although election policy expert Roy Saltman asserts that American history is replete with examples of our perception of technology as a natural way to expand the participating franchise in the United States,[39] evidence shows that, in the future, new technologies will transform how military service members and citizens living abroad will be enfranchised. This will prove increasingly important for countries with high numbers of educated citizens living abroad, including India and Turkey and other diaspora.

The Downside of Technology in Politics

The positive effects of information technology are undeniable, but technology also presents a series of challenges both to users and to society. As technology grows more sophisticated, privacy issues are becoming critical.[40] And with such an abundance of information readily available, one key challenge for those who rely on the Internet is the problem of evaluating the accuracy of information. Another is the threat of cyber attacks that can potentially upend communication, commerce, and governmental operations, including those related to security. Finally, balancing free speech rights while protecting the rights of individuals who face physical threats or threats to their reputations is another issue with which modern societies are struggling.

>This building in St. Petersburg, Russia, houses the "troll factory" where, according to U.S. government allegations, a St. Petersburg businessman, Yevgeny Prigozhin, who has connections to Russian President Vladimir Putin, sought to influence the outcome of the 2016 U.S. presidential election.
©Dmitry Lovetsky/AP Images

Election Infiltration

In the wake of the 2016 election, the U.S. intelligence community—including the Central Intelligence Agency, the Federal Bureau of Investigation, and the Director of National Intelligence—concluded that top Russian officials concocted and implemented a covert plan to influence the outcome of the U.S. elections. The Russians used various strategies: First, they hacked internal communications from Hillary Clinton's campaign and the Democratic National Committee and released them to the public. Also, using bots, they created an elaborate social media structure designed to foment dissention and division within the American electorate and to undermine Clinton's campaign (see "Analyzing the Sources"). Take one day in 2016: On May 21, Russian trolls operating out of a "troll farm" in St. Petersburg, Russia, used Facebook pages to organize both

Analyzing the Sources

TROLLING FOR VOTES

In the 18 months leading up to the 2016 presidential election, about 126 million Americans saw Facebook content that included ads and posts generated by Russian operatives. Using bots, the Russians sought to influence the outcome of the election and foment divisions and dissent among the American people. Using Facebook's advertiser tools, the Russians targeted Americans based on their self-professed "likes"—algorithms that indicate users' political preferences—and demographic characteristics including age, sex, and geography.

Source: BM (Facebook event)

Source: Being Patriotic (Facebook event)

Practice Analytical Thinking

1. Why would Russian operatives seek to create divisions within the American electorate?

2. What are the obstacles to preventing such covert disinformation attacks?

3. How can social media users protect themselves from being the target of disinformation campaigns?

an anti-Islam protest and a pro-Islam counterprotest at the same location in Houston. All told, almost 15,000 targeted Facebook users viewed the fake Russian Facebook pages, "Stop Islamization of Texas," and "Save Islamic Knowledge."

The allegations against the Russians were being investigated by U.S. special counsel Robert Mueller, who was also investigating whether anyone associated with Donald Trump's presidential campaign unwittingly or intentionally colluded with the Russians. Mueller filed charges against 13 Russian nationals and three Russian entities for perpetrating an illegal "information warfare" scheme to disrupt the 2016 presidential election and assist the candidacy of President Donald Trump.

But just as the U.S. intelligence community agreed that Russia interfered with the 2016 U.S. presidential election, they also agreed that what happened in 2016 was not an isolated incident and that the tactical mission of undermining the democratic process in which citizens elect government leaders in a fair and free method was an intentional, consistent strategy. Evidence suggested that Russia attempted to interfere with various European elections as well and had also set its sights on 2018 U.S. congressional races: "There should be no doubt that Russia perceives its past efforts as successful and views the 2018 U.S. midterm elections as a potential target for Russian influence operations," Dan Coats, the Director of National Intelligence, told the Senate Intelligence Committee's annual worldwide-threats hearing.[41]

Cyber Threats

Increasingly, cyber threats, that is, the possibility that a nation or group might intentionally do damage to the technological or financial infrastructure, are a reality. For example, using the international bank messaging system Swift (the Society for Worldwide Interbank Financial Telecommunication), a super-secure network that banks use to authorize payments from one account to another, hackers have succeeded in pulling off digital heists that eventually could threaten a nation's economy. In one such heist, hackers stole $81 million from Bangladesh's central bank in a planned and well-organized attack; when banking officials attempted to contact the Bangladesh bank to alert it about the breach, it was a weekend in Bangladesh. By the time the Bangladeshi bankers discovered the missing funds, it was a weekend in the United States. The attack eventually was linked to a hacking group called "Lazarus," based in North Korea, which has attacked, or has attempted to attack, banks in Costa Rica, Ethiopia, Gabon, India, Indonesia, Iraq, Kenya, Malaysia, Nigeria, Poland, Taiwan, Thailand, and Uruguay. In addition, the federal Justice Department indicted seven hackers it claimed attacked U.S. banks' public websites numerous times and also broke into the computer facility at a dam in Rye, New York, allegedly to disrupt the dam's operation. The individuals indicted are associated with the government of Iran. This is the first case in which state-sponsored individuals have been charged with hacking with an intent to disrupt the U.S. economy.

State-sponsored cyber threats typically involve efforts to learn about financial and infrastructure systems, in case that information could be used to further the state's goals (militarily, economically, or politically). Sometimes cyber threats are retaliatory. But whether launched for information-gathering purposes or seeking to do damage, such threats to the U.S. technological structure will likely continue to be a great risk as rogue states and disgruntled groups continue to grow more technologically sophisticated.

Domestic Surveillance, Data Breaches, and Other Privacy Issues

Today, we see that the roots of technological innovation continue to shape how governments use technology. In June 2013, a series of newspaper articles around the world described a domestic surveillance operation being conducted by the U.S. National Security Agency (NSA). A former CIA employee, Edward Snowden, leaked information that revealed that the NSA had been monitoring the actions of Americans on U.S. soil, including collecting metadata of phone communications, e-mail traffic, and other Internet communications. The NSA's domestic surveillance program began under the George W. Bush administration, and Snowden held off on whistleblowing in the hopes that President Obama would end the program after being elected. Snowden was disappointed when Obama continued and then expanded the program, so Snowden leaked documents revealing the extent of the United States' domestic surveillance program. Among the revelations was the fact that the NSA and 16 other spying agencies, working with a $56 billion "black budget,"[42] conducted a multitude of operations, including:

- Compelling U.S. telecommunications corporations, including Verizon, to provide information on a daily basis concerning telephone calls both within the United States and between the United States and other nations.[43]
- Monitoring the location of cell phones and tracking 5 billion records each day.[44]
- Using cookies acquired by Google to identify and locate targets for government hacking.[45]
- Monitoring foreign communications traffic occurring over Microsoft, Google, Yahoo!, Facebook, PalTalk, YouTube, Skype, AOL, and Apple through a secret NSA program named PRISM,[46] while copying metadata flowing from Yahoo! and Google across fiber-optic cables[47] through a program called MUSCULAR.
- Searching e-mails, online chats, and "nearly everything a typical user does on the Internet" using XKeyscore,[48] a top-secret data-mining analytical tool.
- Infiltrating multiplayer video games, including Xbox Live, World of Warcraft, and Second Life, in collaboration with its British counterpart, Government Communications Headquarters (GCHQ), in an effort to catch real-life terrorists.[49]

> Edward Snowden, a computer specialist who worked for the Central Intelligence Agency and the National Security Agency (NSA), released classified documents in 2013 that revealed that the NSA had engaged in a vast array of domestic surveillance tactics.

Snowden, who was both hailed as a hero whistleblower and reviled as a traitor to his country, feared for his own life as well as the lives of the journalists with whom he entrusted his information. He currently lives in Russia, where he has temporary asylum, though he has stated that he would like to repatriate back to the United States, hoping the felony espionage charges that await him will eventually be resolved, or that he will someday be granted a presidential pardon.

Today, government surveillance of our use of technology means that not just our communications can be monitored but also our whereabouts, our physical appearance, our habits, our associations with others, and even—to the extent that our Google search history indicates our interests—our thoughts. We live in an era in which society is attempting to balance the value that technology brings with the protection of individuals' rights. Today, privacy concerns center on the tools that law enforcement and other government officials have at their disposal to monitor individuals and their locations. But corporations also can access an enormous volume of material—from our grocery shopping habits to the kinds of apps we buy for our phones—and the challenges that our society faces will escalate with new technological innovations. Most people concerned with the issue of government surveillance agree that increased technological developments—through encryption and other surveillance-blocking mechanisms—hold the greatest promise in the potential to protect our privacy. But there is increased concern that these mechanisms will also be used by terrorists and others who would use the privacy protections offered by these new technologies to do harm.

The NSA was granted broad powers by the Foreign Intelligence Surveillance Act (FISA) Amendments passed in 2008, which forced U.S. telecommunications companies to provide information to the NSA as part of its domestic surveillance program. But

Edward Snowden @Snowden   Follow

Can you hear me now?

RETWEETS 120,601   LIKES 122,793

9:00 AM - 29 Sep 2015

> Edward Snowden, who has nearly 4 million Twitter followers, follows only the National Security Agency, the agency Snowden's whistleblowing documents revealed as conducting domestic surveillance. Above is his tweet to the NSA.

>Edward Snowden revealed that the National Security Agency, headquartered in Fort Meade, Maryland, has engaged in extensive efforts to monitor the activities, communications, and whereabouts of Americans living in the United States.

©NSA via Getty Images

unlike traditional law enforcement agencies, which have been overseen by the courts (which, for example, might produce a warrant if there is probable cause), NSA's domestic surveillance program lacked oversight. The NSA asserts that such oversight—whether by Congress or the courts—would render the program less effective. This argument has resonated when discussing foreign targets abroad, but after Edward Snowden's revelation that the NSA was spying on U.S. citizens in the United States, there was significant public outcry about these practices, which many Americans perceive as a violation of their Fourth Amendment rights. In 2015, Congress approved and President Obama signed the USA Freedom Act, a significant rollback of NSA powers, banning the agency from collecting and storing Americans' telephone dialing records unless expressly granted that legal authority by a court order.

The increasing prevalence of cloud computing, whereby files are stored on remote servers rather than on users' personal hard drives, means that our information may be more vulnerable to misuse by corporations, government officials, and hackers than if we stored our data privately. For example, web-based e-mail services (Gmail, Outlook, Yahoo!, and so on), certain word processing and spreadsheet programs (such as those stored on a Google Drive), and photo storage applications (Picasa, Snapfish) hold our information "in the cloud." Although these sites strive to protect users' privacy, the sheer volume of information available may lead to vulnerabilities as a result of both intentional damage through hacking and unintentional potential damage through technological glitches.

Fake News and the Issue of Accuracy

The explosion of the Internet into politics has also opened up a Pandora's box of misinformation. Unlike newspapers, magazines, and television networks, where editors and fact-checkers are responsible for ensuring accuracy, the Internet is almost entirely unmonitored. The problem of misinformation is compounded when the president himself communicates directly to the people using social media and spreads inaccurate information, whether unwittingly or intentionally. Consider, for example, just one week in December 2017/January 2018.

President Trump made the following statements:

- There is "substantial evidence of voter fraud."
- Dianne Feinstein said "there is no collusion" between the Trump campaign and Russia.
- "We have signed more legislation than anybody. We broke the record of Harry Truman."

The problem is that none of these statements are true.* And unlike in presidencies past, when a president might have misspoke, engaged in hyperbole, or just gotten

*First, scholarly studies have repeatedly pointed to little-to-no evidence of voter fraud, and the study cited by White House officials was grossly mischaracterized, as it concerned the number of legal voters who remained on voting rolls (not voting) after having moved or died. Also, in discussing Russia and the Trump campaign, Feinstein said that collusion was an "open question." Last, according to calculations by GovTrack.us—a nonpartisan website that collects congressional and other governmental data—Trump ranked last in legislation signed among post–World War II presidents in their first calendar year of office. www.politifact.com/truth-o-meter/statements/2018/jan/04/donald-trump/donald-trump-says-theres-substantial-evidence-vote/; www.politifact.com/california/statements/2018/jan/02/donald-trump/trumps-false-claim-dianne-feinstein-said-there-no-/; www.politifact.com/truth-o-meter/statements/2017/dec/29/donald-trump/has-donald-trump-signed-more-bills-anyone-no/.

his facts wrong, today, the presence of live news feeds, social media, and a traditional media often lacks the capacity to fact-check every statement, which means that "alternate facts" are fed to the American people, who may accept them as fact because of the source of the information, the prestige of the office, and the medium by which it has been conveyed.

In political campaigns, misinformation can be devastating, and once a damaging charge is sounded, it is often almost impossible to unring that bell, even if the allegations are false. For example, a long-standing issue that dogged President Obama throughout his first term in office was that several Internet sites, including the Drudge Report,[50] questioned his U.S. citizenship. The allegations followed the president from the early days of his 2008 presidential campaign until he released the long-form copy of his birth certificate in April 2011. Indeed, some "hybrid news sites," including Newslo, pepper fact-based news stories with outlandish fictions and enable readers to "Show Facts" or "Hide Facts." One Newslo story that was published (and was subsequently shared over the Internet as true) was the claim that Donald Trump had suggested dropping nuclear bombs on Mexico if it refused to build his proposed wall separating the nation from the United States. While Trump did propose the wall, he never proposed using nuclear weapons to compel Mexico to comply with his plan.

The sheer volume of information available online can in itself create a problem. To become and remain accurately informed, voters and other individuals must develop the critical thinking skills needed to discern what information is valuable (and sometimes rely on online fact-checking sites like Snopes.com to validate claims that seem outlandish). Consumers of information also need to consider the sources of information and determine the sources' biases or perspectives. In short, devoid of a trusted source of information, we should treat many claims made on the Internet with a healthy dose of skepticism.[51]

A Tool for Terrorists: Recruiting, Communicating, Operationalizing

In December 2015, Tashfeen Malik and Syed Farook, a married couple who were the parents of a six-month-old baby and who had been radicalized by the terror group ISIS, killed 14 people and seriously injured 22 others when they fired on a gathering of Farook's colleagues in San Bernardino, California. Malik and Farook were later killed in a gun battle with police. In the aftermath, law enforcement authorities sought access to Farook's iPhone, believing that information on it could lead investigators to other potential targets the couple may have identified, to contacts with the terror group ISIS, and to other United States–based terror cells. Apple, which had manufactured the phone, argued that it did not have the capability to override the four-digit password protection the phone had. The federal government sued Apple, and U.S. Magistrate Judge Sheri Pym ruled in favor of the Federal Bureau of Investigation's request for Apple to disable a security feature that would wipe out data on Farook's iPhone if investigators trying to access it made more than 10 incorrect password attempts. Apple challenged the ruling, and while the case was wending its way through legal channels, the FBI recovered the phone's information. It did so by hiring so-called grey hat hackers, those who exploit small glitches in companies' operating systems and sell them sometimes to the government, sometimes to the companies themselves. While the solution provided to the FBI would work on only a small number of iPhones, the issue of whether tech companies should assist governments in their attempts to get information that might thwart criminal activities, including terrorist attacks, remains a controversial one. Law enforcement officials argue that hardware-related security measures prevent them from accessing information about a wide variety of illegal activity, including issues related to illegal drug distribution, human trafficking, and potential terror plots.

But hardware is not the only obstacle for law enforcement officials: In light of revelations about the reliance of terror cells on encrypted messaging systems like WhatsApp, Telegram, Signal, and Surespot, government officials in both the United States and Europe have increased calls for regulation, with Britain and France at various points entertaining the idea of banning encryption technologies. But the tech industries, especially Apple CEO Tim Cook, have fought back, arguing, for instance, that Apple's encryption technology in its iMessaging system protects consumers from cyber criminals. Other supporters of encryption note that the technology also has the ability to protect pro-democracy activists from authoritarian governments that would persecute those advocating for democracy without the protection that encryption provides.

Technology platforms, particularly social media sites, have proved to be an important recruiting and organizational tool for terrorists. By their very nature, social media sites encourage discourse across a wide spectrum of populations, and because they are open to everyone, they have been used to radicalize individuals sympathetic to their cause. In recognition of that reality, in 2016 Twitter announced the suspension of 125,000 accounts associated with promoting terrorist acts, primarily related to ISIS, as well as the intent to step up efforts to review accounts connected to extremism so that they could be deactivated more quickly: "Like most people around the world, we are horrified by the atrocities perpetrated by extremist groups. We condemn the use of Twitter to promote terrorism and the Twitter Rules make it clear that this type of behavior, or any violent threat, is not permitted on our service."[52]

Despite the efforts by Twitter and other social media platforms, widespread evidence exists that ISIS continues to recruit and reach out to potential members—sometimes young people living in Western democracies—by relying on social media.[53]

Twitter and other tech companies including Facebook and YouTube are facing increasing criticism that the sites facilitate terrorism by providing a platform extremists can use to attract sympathizers and communicate and organize attacks. But because these sites are primarily platforms for the constant flow of user-generated content, regulation is difficult and relies on users themselves to flag inappropriate content so that site reviewers can determine whether the postings are appropriate.

Fomenting Polarized Partisanship and Extremism

Information technology can foment increased extremism domestically. The Internet makes selective exposure—the phenomenon of individuals choosing to read or view information that enforces their already-held beliefs while rejecting sources that provide contradictory views—quite easy. This lack of exposure to contradictory sources of information means that people's views—even the most extreme—will only be confirmed and reinforced. The lack of contradictory information may steer people to more-polarized ideological viewpoints, as the moderate, compromising views are eschewed by those relying on partisan information. This phenomenon is particularly problematic when foreign nations or other organizations intentionally spawn hatred, dissent, and extremism, as occurred during the 2016 presidential campaign. Some research indicates that this scenario has increased political polarization in the United States and has fostered the adoption of more extremist political viewpoints.[54]

The Internet has also contributed to the decline in civility in political discourse in the United States. In describing the political climate regarding threats to presidential candidates, Secret Service director Mark Sullivan noted that "historically, it's the same issues we've always had and the same things people are upset about. There are just a lot more venues for people to put it out there, including the Internet."[55] Some bloggers and anonymous message-board posters seek to destroy their opponents' reputations. The nature of the Internet means that lies and slanderous accusations can often be leveled with no consequence to the poster. As noted earlier, sometimes the claims—made via e-mail messages, Facebook postings, and/or tweets—are quite sophisticated and seem believable.

The Dominance of "Big Tech"

Another concern is the disproportionate influence "big tech" plays in our everyday lives, and the potentially corrupting influence technology companies *could* have. Arguing that "big tech has become way too powerful," former Secretary of Labor Robert B. Reich notes that the "most valuable intellectual properties are platforms so widely used that everyone *else* has to use them, too. Think of standard operating systems like Microsoft's Windows or Google's Android; Google's search engine; Amazon's shopping system; and Facebook's communication network. Google runs two-thirds of all searches in the United States. Amazon sells more than 40 percent of new books. Facebook has nearly 1.5 billion active monthly users worldwide. This is where the money is. . . . Sure, big platforms let creators showcase and introduce new apps, songs, books, videos and other content. But almost all of the profits go to the platforms' owners, who have all of the bargaining power."[56] Reich argues that tech monopolies have become economic and political powerhouses that have effectively controlled how markets are regulated (or not), thus ratcheting up their power even more by controlling the competitive environment.

The Internet and Free Speech

Part of the political conundrum faced by Americans is the desire to balance free speech rights with the ability of government to protect those whose person or reputation may be threatened by someone's speech. The rise of the Internet has overwhelmed our guarantees of free speech, with the volume and content of speech growing faster than society's ability to digest their impact. In parts of Europe, for example, hate speech on the Internet is forbidden and carefully regulated; in the United States, it is not. As a result, a large number of hate sites register their domains in the United States, where they can operate freely and spew their venom throughout the world without fear of government interference.

The United States is deeply wedded to the principle, refusing to regulate the Internet or any other vehicle of free speech. Throughout the nation's history, speech of all kinds has been protected, with periodic exceptions for sedition in wartime, as well as for child pornography and hate speech in peacetime. Americans have great tolerance for language and believe that fringe groups can flourish freely in a democracy without risking tears in the fabric of society. But as the threat of terrorism grows, many citizens expect lawmakers to do whatever is necessary—including setting limits on free speech—to curb violence spawned by the prevalence of hate on the Internet.[57]

Regulation of the Internet: Is It Necessary?

When Noah Kravitz left his job as an editor and videoblogger at PhoneDog, a company that reviews cell phones and other electronics, he took his Twitter account and his 17,000 followers with him. The U.S. District Court in Northern California was asked to decide whether the account and the followers are Kravitz's or whether they are legally comparable to a customer list and thus the possession of PhoneDog. The case offers another example of how technology has presented an abundance of disputes with which the law has yet to keep up. The Internet raises issues that could not have been foreseen by the framers of the U.S. Constitution. Some issues concern contract law; others, privacy rights; yet others, freedom of speech, the press, and assembly. Take, for example, freedom of the press: The framers had to be concerned only with print media when they guaranteed this freedom, one of the fundamental liberties they ensured in the Bill of Rights. As media evolved into formats such as radio and television, government created a regulatory structure to govern them as well. But technology has outpaced the government's ability to regulate certain forms of electronic media, including the Internet and cellular technology.

Net neutrality
The idea that Internet traffic should flow through the Internet pipeline without interference or discrimination by those who own or are running the pipeline.

Take, for example, the question of control over the business of the media (see "Thinking Critically"). The issue, a controversial one, centers on **Net neutrality:** the idea that Internet traffic—e-mail, websites, videos, and phone calls—should flow through the Internet pipeline without interference or discrimination by those who own or are running the pipeline. *Should* these broadband behemoths be able to use their market power to control information or to favor certain clients online? Critics charge that congressional passage of legislation supporting the service providers would destroy the neutrality and openness of the Internet. Tim Berners-Lee, the inventor of the World Wide Web, says: "The neutral communications medium is essential to our society. . . . It is the basis of democracy, by which a community should decide what to do."[58] President Obama agreed, and after a period of public comment during which over 4 million Americans voiced their views on net neutrality, in 2015 the Federal Communications Commission voted to preserve the open Internet, by adopting regulations in three key areas. First, the FCC prohibited broadband providers from blocking lawful content, services, applications, or devices. The regulations also banned providers from slowing down specific services or applications (a practice called *throttling* in the broadband industry). The third area of regulation prevented providers from isolating Internet traffic based on who is sending or receiving data, what the data is, or whether the content is viewed as competitive to the providers' own content. So, for example, under these regulations, Comcast (a broadband provider) would have been prohibited from blocking or throttling Netflix (so that Comcast subscribers would be forced to rely on Comcast's on-demand video service) or isolating content that Netflix provides. In 2017, President Trump's appointee as FCC chairman, Ajit Pai, announced a rollback of the net neutrality order, though changes have been slow, stymied somewhat by the fact that the rule changes are the subject of numerous lawsuits that promise protracted court battles.

Should We Regulate the Internet Infrastructure?

The Issue: The technological revolution has brought ongoing, exponential growth in Internet traffic. As rising numbers of people turn to the Internet for more and more uses—from viewing videos online to sending pictures to Grandma, and from buying gifts and personal items to calling friends and relatives—the volume of information that the Internet's broadband infrastructure must transmit is becoming overwhelming. The owners of that infrastructure—corporate giants such as AT&T, Verizon, and Comcast—are seeking legislation and pursuing lawsuits that would allow them to charge companies that produce high volumes of traffic. In effect, this legislation would set up a two-tiered system of broadband access, in which one tier is an "express lane" with tolls and the other is an older, slower lane with free access. One problem is that many of today's services (video streaming, for example) require the faster access to make them effective. Several Republican members of Congress have sponsored measures that would create a two-tiered system, but in 2015, the Federal Communications Commission voted by a 3-to-2 margin for regulations that would preserve the open Internet, a decision that FCC chairman Ajit Pai reversed. Industry leaders and some members of Congress supported Pai's rollback of net neutrality.

Yes: We need a two-tiered system of broadband access. The telecommunications titans in command of the Internet infrastructure argue that in order to keep up with the increasing demand for broadband space, they will continually have to expand and improve the system. These improvements cost money, and companies should be able to pass the costs and benefits on to their customers. Corporate advocates of a two-tiered system of broadband access also are interested in providing premium-quality broadband service to their own clientele. Thus, for example, Verizon wants to ensure that its Internet subscribers (rather than the subscribers of its competitors) have high-quality access to the broadband infrastructure technology that Verizon owns, so that its subscribers do not get caught in an Internet traffic jam.

No: "Fast Lane" services would hurt both businesses and consumers. In 2015, the FCC adopted regulations for Preserving a Free and Open Internet, stating that providers must have transparency of network management practices, not block lawful content, and not unreasonably discriminate in transmitting lawful network traffic. A broad coalition of businesses and interest groups, including savetheinternet.com, oppose measures that would enable broadband providers to charge for their services. These entities also include such firms as Microsoft, Google, eBay, and Yahoo! and powerful citizen organizations such as the American Association of Retired Persons (AARP).

It is the very accessibility of the Internet that has fostered strong business growth. Start-ups such as YouTube and Vonage Internet phone service are examples of ventures that might not have been able to compete and survive in a tiered broadband system. A paying system could prevent future Internet business development.

Other Approaches: Tax dollars should be used to expand the Internet infrastructure. Without essential maintenance and expansion, the Internet infrastructure will be incapable of keeping up with soaring demand. In addition, the security of the infrastructure is crucial to continued business activity and corporate financial growth, as well as to national economic health. Broadband availability is a national security issue, because if law enforcers, airports, hospitals, nuclear power plants, and first responders do not have adequate or immediate access to the information they need to perform their jobs, human lives are at risk. Because of these critical financial and security implications, a tax or user fee could be instituted that would pay for Internet infrastructure improvements.

What do you think?

1. Should the FCC or Congress accept or reject proposals to create a for-fee fast lane for Internet traffic? Why? Or do you think that the marketplace should determine which services get faster access to broadband lines? If so, why would the latter be preferable?

2. What effect could the creation of a two-tiered Internet structure have on Internet business development? On national security?

3. Should the federal government help to defray the costs of improvements to the Internet infrastructure? Why or why not?

Thinking Critically About What's Next in Politics and Technology

Technology has revolutionized how politics happens in the United States, and it is revolutionizing political life throughout the world. One of the most remarkable characteristics of the technological revolution has been the swiftness of the transformation it has propelled. Though the Internet is only 25 years old, it has spawned earth-shattering changes in our political lives and indeed throughout society. And although there remains a digital divide both within and outside the United States, that divide is shrinking domestically. Because of cellular technology and increasing access to the Internet, information technology represents one of the most powerful tools in helping people communicate with government officials, secure political information, and participate in the political life of their communities, states, and country.

Whether through traditional websites, blogging, social media, or politically specific technological platforms, technology has transformed political life by making information more easily available. But the sheer volume of information means that consumers must be wary of the information they receive and aware of concerted efforts to misinform and to foster divisions.

In particular, social media has opened up a host of opportunities for political communication and participation, but also has exposed a vulnerability enabling those who would do democracy harm to infiltrate. In addition to providing avenues of communication between constituents and elected officials, among candidate or issue supporters, and between governments and the people they serve, technology is providing more efficient and cost-effective means by which governments can provide services. In the future, technology will become a more integrated and essential part of our lives, having sweeping implications for how campaigns, governments, and citizens use technology in political life.

Learning Summary

1. Describe how the Internet and cellular technology have created a modern technological revolution.

    a. Explain how as a medium of communication, a source of news and information, and a tool for political engagement and organizing at the grassroots, the Internet and cellular technology influence the way people interact and politics is conducted.

    b. Describe the disparities that exist in who uses new technologies as political tools—in terms of age, education, and income—and the potential for equality these technologies provide as important means of participation.

    c. Explain how technologies have spawned virtual communities that break down national and physical boundaries and facilitate the formation of cohesive communities of interest.

2. Explain how technology is changing the way candidates campaign and citizens participate in political life.

    a. Understand how technology has created a two-way street for political communication between candidates and officials and their constituents.

    b. Explain how campaigns have been transformed by new forms of participation and new means of tracking supporters.

    c. Detail how campaigns are refining voter-targeting operations and data-driven Internet advertising.

3. Assess how technology is changing the way governments govern.

    a. Explain the key roles of cellular technology and the Internet in transforming governments.

    b. Describe how technology has changed how we get services and receive information from governments.

    c. Explain how the Internet has opened new avenues for citizens to voice their concerns.

4. Explain the impact of technology on political life.

    a. Describe how technology has affected political participation for average citizens, protesters, and citizen activists.

    b. Describe how technology has drastically altered the amount of information available to citizens.

5. Explain the downside of technology in politics.

    a. Describe the process of election infiltration.

    b. Explain various cyber threats and the danger they present to democracies.

    c. Describe the domestic surveillance programs undertaken by the U.S. government and related concerns over data breaches and privacy issues.

    d. Explain "fake news" and the issue of accuracy.

    e. Describe how terrorists use technology to recruit, communicate, and operationalize their plans.

    f. Explain how the Internet can foment polarized partisanship and extremism.

    g. Describe the dominance of "big tech."

    h. Explain the challenges surrounding free speech on the Internet.

Key Terms

bandwidth 364

big data 367

blogosphere 365

cyber cascade 368

digital divide 360

e-campaigning 366

e-Government 370

e-petition 368

Foursquare 370

hacktivism 369

legacy systems 370

micro-blog 367

microtarget 368

Net neutrality 382

netroots 365

news aggregators 363

promoted tweets 367

remarketing 366

social networking sites 360

transparency 370

virtual communities 361

vlog 364

wiki 371

For Review

1. How is cellular technology likely to affect politics in the decade to come?
2. What are differences among various demographic groups regarding the use of technology?
3. How are governments using technology to serve their constituents?
4. What are some of the drawbacks of technological evolution?
5. What are the arguments for regulation of the Internet?

For Critical Thinking and Discussion

1. What are the effects of very few "big tech" companies having a monopoly on how people get information, shop, and communicate? Is there any danger in this?
2. Do you believe that hacktivism is an effective political tool? Why or why not?
3. Do you believe that information technology has the potential to be the "great equalizer" in U.S. politics? Why or why not?
4. Do you support the idea of Net neutrality? Why or why not?
5. What action should the U.S. government take to protect individuals' privacy online?

Resources for Research AND Action

Internet Resource

The Guardian's NSA Files

www.theguardian.com/world/the-nsa-files This site provides a trove of documents and analyses of the NSA documents that Edward Snowden leaked, which reveal the extent of the United States' and Britain's Internet surveillance operations.

Recommended Readings

Crawford, Michael B. 2015. *The World Beyond Your Head: On Becoming an Individual in an Age of Distraction.* New York: Farrar, Straus and Giroux. Crawford presents an intriguing description of the modern "distracted" individual, exploring how technology is but one manifestation of the incongruous aspects of modern Western culture that conflict with human nature, and what the implications are for the modern individual, and for creativity, democracy, and society as a whole.

Deibert, Ronald, John Palfrey, Rafal Rohozinski, and Jonathan Zittrain, eds. 2010. *Access Controlled: The Shaping of Power, Rights, and Rule in Cyberspace.* Cambridge, MA: MIT Press. An analysis of new technologies and what they mean for relationships between citizens and states, and evaluation of how new technologies will shape civic interaction in the future.

Greenwald, Glenn. 2014. *No Place to Hide: Edward Snowden, the NSA, and the U.S. Surveillance State.* New York: Macmillan. Greenwald was one of the reporters to whom Edward Snowden leaked some of the most explosive and consequential news concerning the actions of the National Security Agency in monitoring the activities of citizens. This book tells that story and considers various reforms to how governments monitor their citizens.

Hindman, Matthew. 2009. *The Myth of Digital Democracy.* Princeton, NJ: Princeton University Press. This volume asserts that the Internet empowers a small set of elites, rather than broadening political discourse among the masses.

Howard, Philip N. 2010. *The Digital Origins of Dictatorship and Democracy: Information Technology and Political Islam.* New York: Oxford University Press. Drawing from data from 74 Muslim nations, this book examines how digital technologies, instrumental for a nation's development, are being used by young people—in particular, in creating civil society, communicating, and circumventing state and religious organizations' controls.

Rheingold, Howard. 2000. *The Virtual Community: Homesteading on the Electronic Frontier.* Cambridge, MA: MIT Press. This classic work written by the "first citizen of the Internet" examines the nexus between virtual and real-life communities and argues that a distinction between the two is not totally valid.

Stephens-Davidowitz, Seth. 2017. *Everybody Lies: Big Data, New Data, and What the Internet Can Tell Us About Who We Really Are.* New York: Harper Collins. Using big data, primarily from Google Trends, Stephens-Davidowitz sheds light on what our Google searches reveal we are thinking, including in our political life.

Sunstein, Cass R. 2006. *Infotopia: How Many Minds Produce Knowledge.* New York: Oxford University Press. This work grapples with the question of how leaders and ordinary people can challenge insular decision making and gain access to the sum of human knowledge.

Tewksbury, David, and Jason Rittenberg. 2012. *News on the Internet: Information and Citizenship in the 21st Century.* New York: Oxford University Press. This work considers the Internet both as a source of authoritative news and as a vehicle for citizens in contemporary democracies to create and share political information; it also examines the tension between these two functions in terms of increased citizen participation in a polarized climate of fragmented knowledge.

Movies of Interest

Snowden (2016)
Oliver Stone directed this film that depicts the true story of Edward Snowden, an employee of the National Security Administration, who leaked thousands of classified documents to the press in order to reveal the surveillance techniques being used by the U.S. government.

CitizenFour (2014)
The winner of the 2015 Academy Award for Best Documentary Feature, *CitizenFour* depicts Edward Snowden's revelations about the NSA's domestic surveillance program to reporter Glenn Greenwald and producer Laura Poitras.

Terms and Conditions May Apply (2013)
This eye-opening documentary sheds light on how easy it is for corporations to gather and share our information, for governments to access that information, and for the public to unknowingly agree to constant surveillance by a simple click of a button.

The Social Network (2010)
This Oscar-winning film traces the creation of Facebook by Harvard student Mark Zuckerberg and demonstrates the speed with which communication was revolutionized.

Minority Report (2002)
Tom Cruise stars in this futuristic saga in which criminals are caught before they commit crimes. It raises questions about how technology should be used by government officials.

References

1. https://docs.house.gov/meetings/IF/IF00/20180411/108090/HHRG-115-IF00-Wstate-ZuckerbergM-20180411.pdf.
2. "Ordnance Survey Offers Free Data Access," BBC News, April 1, 2010.
3. D. M. Boyd and N. B. Ellison, "Social Network Sites: Definition, History, and Scholarship," *Journal of Computer-Mediated Communication* 13 (2007), article 11.
4. Monica Anderson, "Technology Device Ownership: 2015," Pew Research Center, October 29, 2015, www.pewinternet.org/2015/10/29/technology-device-ownership-2015/.
5. www.pewinternet.org/fact-sheet/mobile/.
6. Pew Research Center, "Internet/Broadband Fact Sheet."
7. Ibid.
8. Susannah Fox, "Americans Living with Disability and Their Technology Profile," Pew Internet and American Life Project, January 21, 2011, and Monica Anderson and Andrew Perrin, "Disabled Americans Are Less Likely to Use Technology," Pew Research, April 4, 2017.
9. Mark Wheeler, *Politics and the Mass Media* (Oxford: Blackwell, 1997), 228.
10. Matthew Hindman, *The Myth of Digital Democracy* (Princeton, NJ: Princeton University Press, 2009).
11. Laura McKenna, "The Internet and American Politics: Where the Politically Rich Get Richer and the Politically Poor Get Perez Hilton," presented at the annual meeting of the American Political Science Association, Toronto, Canada, 2009.
12. Michael Cornfield, *Politics Moves Online: Campaigning and the Internet* (New York: The Century Foundation, 2004).
13. Howard Rheingold, *The Virtual Community: Homesteading on the Electronic Frontier* (Cambridge, MA: MIT Press, 2000).
14. Clay Skirky, *Here Comes Everybody* (New York: Penguin, 2008).
15. See Josh Pasek, Eian More, and Daniel Romer, "Realizing the Social Internet: Online Social Networking Meets Offline Civic Engagement," *Journal of Information Technology and Politics* 6 (2009): 197–215.
16. See Jody C. Baumgartner and Jonathan S. Morris, "MyFaceTube Politics: Social Networking Websites and Political Engagement of Young Adults," *Social Science Computer Review* 28 (2009): 24–44; and Weiwu Zhang, Thomas J. Johnson, Trent Sletzer, and Shannon Bichard, "The Revolution Will Be Networked: The Influence of Social Networking Sites on Political Attitudes and Behaviors," *Social Science Computer Review* 28 (2010): 75–92.
17. Jessica T. Feezell, Meredith Conroy, and Mario Guerrero, "Facebook Is . . . Fostering Political Engagement: A Study of Online Social Networking Groups and Offline Participation," presented at the annual meeting of the American Political Science Association, Toronto, Canada, 2009.
18. Terri L. Towner and David A. Dulio, "The Web 2.0 Election: Voter Learning in the 2008 Presidential Campaign," in *Techno Politics in Presidential Campaigning: New Voices, New Technologies, and New Voters,* ed. John Hendricks and Lynda Lee Kaid (New York: Routledge, 2008).
19. Pew Research Center Journalism Project's Staff, "McCain vs. Obama on the Web," September 15, 2008.
20. Ibid.
21. Howard Rheingold, "Using Participatory Media and Public Voice to Encourage Civic Engagement," in *Civic Life Online: Learning How Digital Media Can Engage Youth,* ed. Lance W. Bennett, The John D. and Catherine T. MacArthur Foundation Series on Digital Media and Learning (Cambridge, MA: MIT Press, 2008).
22. American Press Institute, "How Americans Get Their News," March 17, 2014.
23. https://www.omnicoreagency.com/youtube-statistics/.
24. Aaron Barlow, *The Rise of the Blogosphere* (New York: Praeger, 2007).
25. Christine Gibbs Springer, "Mastering Strategic Conversations," *PA Times* (September 2006).
26. See Howard Kurtz, *Spin Cycle–How the White House and the Media Manipulate the News* (New York: Simon & Schuster, 1998).
27. Patrick Healy, "To '08 Hopefuls, Media Technology Can Be Friend or Foe," *The New York Times,* January 31, 2007, A15.
28. Michael Barbaro, "Pithy, Mean, and Powerful: How Donald Trump Mastered Twitter for 2016," *The New York Times,* October 15, 2015.
29. Cass Sunstein, *Republic.com* (Princeton, NJ: Princeton University Press, 2001), 83.
30. Andrew Paul Williams and Evan Serge, "Evaluating Candidate E-Mail Messages in the 2008 U.S. Presidential Campaign," in *Techno Politics in Presidential Campaigning: New Voices, New Technologies, and New Voters,* ed. John Hendricks and Lynda Lee Kaid (New York: Routledge, 2001).
31. David Karpf, *The MoveOn Effect: The Unexpected Transformation of American Political Advocacy* (New York: Oxford University Press, 2012).
32. https://www.youtube.com/watch?v=BAUZnDIWu2I.
33. United Nations Department of Economic and Social Affairs, "United Nations E-Government Survey 2010."
34. NIC Core Services, "Outdoor Licensing," www.egov.com/Solutions/CoreServices/Pages/Outdoor.aspx.
35. Dana Gardner, "Staying on Legacy Systems Ends Up Costing IT More," www.zdnet.com/blog/gardner/staying-on-legacy-systems-ends-up-costing-it-more/3231.
36. Jason Rollins, "Local Government Use of the Latest Technology," April 5, 2011, International City/County Management Association Alliance for Innovation.
37. Lev Grossman, "The Beast with a Billion Eyes," *Time* (January 30, 2012).
38. www.campaigngrid.com/our-capabilities#target-all-devices.
39. Roy Saltman, *The History and Politics of Voting Technology* (New York: Palgrave Macmillan, 2008).
40. Daniel Solove, *The Digital Person: Technology and Privacy in the Information Age* (New York: New York University Press, 2004).
41. Matthew Rosenberg, Charlie Savage, and Michael Wines, "Russia Sees Midterm Elections as Chance to Sow Fresh Discord, Intelligence Chiefs Warn," *The New York Times,* February 13, 2018.
42. Barton Gellman and Greg Miller, "'Black Budget' Summary Details U.S. Spy Network's Successes, Failures and Objectives," *The Washington Post,* August 29, 2013.

43. Glenn Greenwald, "NSA Collecting Phone Records of Millions of Verizon Customers Daily," *The Guardian,* June 5, 2013.

44. Barton Gellman and Ashkan Soltani, "NSA Tracking Cellphone Locations Worldwide, Snowden Documents Show," *The Washington Post,* December 4, 2013.

45. "NSA Signal Surveillance Success Stories," *The Washington Post.*

46. Barton Gellman and Laura Poitras, "U.S., British Intelligence Mining Data from Nine U.S. Internet Companies in Broad Secret Program," *The Washington Post,* June 6, 2013.

47. Barton Gellman and Ashkan Soltani, "NSA Infiltrates Links to Yahoo, Google Data Centers Worldwide, Snowden Documents Say," *The Washington Post,* October 30, 2013.

48. Glenn Greenwald, "XKeyscore: NSA Tool Collects 'Nearly Everything a User Does on the Internet,'" *The Guardian,* July 31, 2013.

49. James Ball, "Xbox Live Among Game Services Targeted by US and UK Spy Agencies," *The Guardian,* December 9, 2013.

50. "Book to Reveal Obama's 'True' Identity?" *Drudge Report,* April 20, 2011, http://drudgereport.com/flash7.htm.

51. Sunstein, *Republic.com 2.0.*

52. Twitter, "Combating Violent Extremism," February 5, 2018.

53. See Rukmini Callimachi, Chapter 2, "The Recruit," in the podcast *The Caliphate,* www.nytimes.com/interactive/2018/podcasts/caliphate-isis-rukmini-callimachi.html.

54. Thomas E. Mann and Norman J. Ornstein, *It's Even Worse Than It Looks: How the American Constitutional System Collided with the New Politics of Extremism* (New York: Basic Books, 2012).

55. Donna Leinwand Leger, "Internet Creates Wider Venue for Political Incivility, Threats," *USA Today,* February 2, 2012, p. 6A.

56. Robert B. Reich, "Big Tech Has Become Way Too Powerful," *The New York Times,* September 15, 2015.

57. Sunstein, *Republic.com 2.0.*

58. Ibid.

CHAPTER 12
Congress

©Cliff Owen/AP Images

THEN

The framers granted to Congress both explicit powers and implied powers, by which the national government strengthened and broadened its authority.

NOW

A much more demographically diverse but ideologically polarized Congress exercises wide powers, its decision making influenced by shifting constituencies in a changing nation.

NEXT

Will increased polarization of Republicans and Democrats in Congress continue to define the congressional agenda?

Will the composition and policy making of Congress more broadly reflect the changing face of the United States?

Will technology significantly affect the ability of "average" citizens to influence Congress?

Congress is an institution

shaped by the people elected to serve there, men and women acting as the trusted representatives of the constituents who voted them into office. Congress and the policies it creates are influenced by many other factors, including the legislative body's institutional history, the lawmaking process, and the internal and external actors—congressional leaders, political parties, interest groups, the president, staff members, ordinary citizens, and the media—who seek to influence congressional actions.

The Constitution's framers structured the government so that Congress—more so than the two other institutions of the federal government—would be responsive to the needs and the will of the people. In representing their constituents, members of Congress provide an easily accessed point of contact for people to connect with their government and to have their voices heard.

Citizens today have countless opportunities to shape Congress's agenda and influence how the members of Congress vote. Among the most important of these opportunities is the ability to vote members of Congress into office. But individuals and groups of constituents can also communicate with Congress members through Twitter, Instagram, Facebook, e-mail, and telephone, and they meet face-to-face with members of Congress on issues that concern them. Constituents meet with congressional staff members for help in understanding how to deal with government bureaucracy. Through congressional campaigns and elections, citizens learn about issues of national importance and can participate in a variety of ways, such as volunteering in support of a candidate's run for office, contributing to the individual's campaign, and becoming informed about the candidates and the issues.

Throughout this chapter, we view Congress through the lens of civic engagement, seeing that Congress—the people's branch of the federal government—though imperfect, is structured to empower citizens to play a role in determining public policy priorities. And ultimately it is the people, through their choices at the ballot box, who decide who the creators of those policies will be.

The Origins of Congress

For the United States' founders, creating the Congress was a crucially important task. Fearful of a powerful executive, but having endured the problems stemming from the weak confederal government under the Articles of Confederation, the framers of the Constitution believed that the legislature should be the key branch of the newly formed government. In their vision, the Congress would be the institution responsible for making laws that would create effective public policy. In structuring the Congress, the framers strove to create a legislative branch that was at once powerful enough to govern and to check the power of the president and yet not so powerful that the legislature itself would exercise tyrannical rule.

As they debated the shape of the Congress, the Constitution's framers had to balance the desires of representation of two opposing groups. The Constitution created a bicameral, or two-house, legislature in which one house, the House of Representatives, would be based on population, and the other chamber, the Senate, would be based on state representation.[1] The constitutionally specified duties of each house of Congress reflect the framers' views of the essential nature of the two chambers and the people who would serve in them.

The House of Representatives, with the smallest constituencies of any federal office (currently about 711,000 people reside in each congressional district), is the chamber closer to the people. As such, the framers intended the House to closely represent the people's views. The Constitution thus requires, for example, that all revenue bills (bills that would impose taxes) must originate in the House of Representatives. In the framers' eyes, unwarranted taxation was an egregious offense. By placing the power to tax in the hands of the members of the House of Representatives—the officials who face more frequent federal elections—the framers sought to avoid the types of unpopular, unfair taxes that had sparked the American Revolution. A short electoral cycle, they reasoned, would allow disfavored politicians to be voted out of office. Like all other bills, revenue bills must be passed in identical form by both the House and the Senate to become law, but requiring revenue bills to originate in the House reflected a victory by the large states at the Constitutional Convention. (Smaller states wanted taxation power to reside with the Senate.)

The framers viewed the House of Representatives as the "people's chamber," and they conceived the Senate to be a more elite, more deliberative institution, one not subject to the whims of mass politics like its lower-house counterpart. Today, because of its smaller size and because its members face elections less frequently than do House members, the Senate remains a more deliberative body than the House. In addition, because of the specific constitutional duties mandated to the upper house, particularly the requirement that treaties must be ratified in the Senate, many U.S. senators have specialized in U.S. foreign policy issues. (See "The House and the Senate Compared" later in this chapter for further discussion of differences between the two chambers.)

The framers' vision was to structure the Congress to embody republican principles, ensuring that in its central policy-making responsibilities the national legislature would be responsive to the needs and the will of the people. Both historically and continuing in the present day, civically engaged citizens have exerted a strong influence on the outcome of the policy-making process. One important avenue by which individuals influence Congress and its acts is through congressional elections, a topic we now consider.

Congressional Elections

The timetable for congressional elections reflects the framers' views of the differing nature of the House of Representatives and the Senate. House members, as public servants in the legislative body that the framers conceived as closer to the people, are elected every two years, in even-numbered years (2020, 2022, and so on). But the framers also sought to check the power of the people, who they believed could be irrational and unruly, and so members of the Senate originally were chosen by state legislators. Ratification of the Seventeenth Amendment to the Constitution in 1913 shifted the election of senators to popular election within the states. Senators serve six-year terms, which are staggered so that one-third of the Senate is elected every two years. Thus, in any given congressional election year, 33 or 34 members of the Senate are up for election. Usually, the two senators from a given state will not be elected in the same cycle, unless the death or resignation of a sitting senator requires a special election. As we saw in Chapter 2, the Constitution requires that the number of seats in the House of Representatives awarded to each state be based on that state's population and that each state have two U.S. senators. On average, a successful campaign for a seat in the House of Representatives cost over $1.5 million in 2016. That is a veritable bargain compared with the price tag for a successful bid for the U.S. Senate, which averaged over $10 million that year. Compare this with the annual salary of $174,000 that rank-and-file members of the House and the Senate collect.

Incumbency

The status of already holding office—known as *incumbency*—strongly influences a candidate's ability to raise money and is probably the most important factor in determining success in a congressional campaign. Indeed, 97 percent of incumbent members of the House of Representatives running for reelection win, as do 93 percent of their Senate counterparts. These outcomes may indicate what *individual* members of Congress are doing right: representing their own constituencies effectively, engaging with their constituents, and listening to and addressing their needs. But voters typically think about Congress in terms of *a whole,* rather than individuals, viewing it as a body that is overwhelmingly composed of "other people's" representatives, who do not reflect their views.[2] Thus the voting public frequently attacks Congress as a collective entity, and typically has a negative perception of Congress as a whole. Indeed, in recent years, Congress's approval rating typically has hovered at about 14 percent.

Why do incumbents so often win reelection? Several factors make it more likely that someone already in office will be returned to that office in a reelection bid:

- **Stronger name recognition.** Having run for election before and served in government, incumbents tend to be better known than challengers are.
- **Easier access to media coverage.** Media outlets routinely publicize the activities of elected congressional officials, rationalizing that they are covering the institution of Congress rather than the individuals. Non-incumbent challengers face an uphill battle in trying to get coverage of their campaigns.
- **Redistricting that favors the incumbent party.** Often, after reapportionment, district lines are drawn to benefit the incumbent officeholder's political party, thus making it likely that the incumbent will retain the seat.
- **Franking.** The privilege of sending mail free of charge is known as **franking.** Federal law allows members of Congress free mailings to every household in their state or congressional district. These mailings make it easy for members of Congress to stay in touch with their constituencies throughout their tenure in office.
- **Campaign contributions.** Political action committees and individuals are interested in supporting candidates who will be in a position to help them once the election is over. Because donors are aware of the high reelection

franking
The privilege of sending mail free of charge by members of Congress.

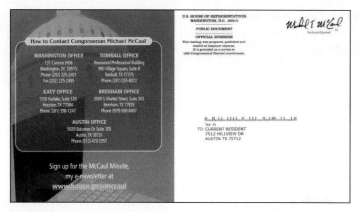

> A piece of franked mail from a congressional office. Note the signature of the sending member of Congress, which serves as a postage stamp.
©Studio 101/Alamy

rates of incumbent candidates, incumbents garner an enormous proportion of contributions, sometimes as much as 80 percent in any given congressional election year.

- **Casework.** When an incumbent personally helps constituents solve problems with the federal bureaucracy, the resulting loyalty and good word-of-mouth reputation help to attract support for that candidate during a run for reelection.

Thus incumbency is a powerful obstacle for outsiders who seek to unseat an elected member of Congress. Despite the incumbency advantage, in each congressional election, many individuals challenge incumbent members of Congress, often doing so knowing that the odds are stacked against them but believing in giving voters a ballot choice. Others run because they seek to bring attention to a particular issue or to shape the policy agenda—or sometimes because they simply underestimate the power of incumbency.

Reapportionment and Redistricting

reapportionment

Reallocation of seats in the House of Representatives to each state based on changes in state populations since the last census.

Sometimes the advantages of incumbency can be diminished, as in election years after reapportionment and redistricting. **Reapportionment** is the reallocation of seats in the House of Representatives on the basis of changes in a state's population since the last census. Every 10 years, in years ending in zero (2010, 2020, and so on), the federal government counts the number of people in the country as a whole. If the census indicates that a state's population has changed significantly, that state may gain or lose seats in the House of Representatives. **Redistricting,** the redrawing of congressional district boundaries within a state, is based on the reapportionment from the census (see "Thinking Critically").

redistricting

The redrawing of congressional district boundaries within each state, based on the reapportionment from the census.

Because the composition of a given congressional district can change as a result of reapportionment and redistricting, this process can mitigate the influence of incumbency. Frequently, the greatest shifts in the composition of the House of Representatives occur in election years ending in 2 (2002, 2012, and so on), when the first elections take place that incorporate the changes from reapportionment and redistricting. When a state loses a seat, the result is that an incumbent member of Congress is likely to lose a seat. When a state gains a seat, a new member of Congress can be elected to the open seat. In the last reapportionment and redistricting process, which occurred after the 2010 census, New York and Ohio lost the largest number of House seats (two each), while Texas gained the most (four seats), followed by Florida (two seats).

Gerrymandering

gerrymandering

The drawing of legislative district boundaries to benefit an incumbent, a political party, or another group.

In many states, the goal of congressional redistricting is to protect House incumbents. The redrawing of congressional boundaries for the purpose of political advantage is a form of **gerrymandering,** the practice of drawing legislative district boundaries to benefit an incumbent, a political party, or some other group. The

Thinking Critically

Are Congressional Elections "Rigged" Through Gerrymandering?

The Issue: In earlier times, redistricting occurred when the lines of a congressional district were redrawn to accommodate population changes. This process typically created a greater number of competitive congressional districts, and House members typically had to temper partisan impulses to placate the sizeable proportion of his or her constituency that identified with the opposing party.

Today, with the widespread use of computer-driven mapmaking technology, congressional seats can be configured to ensure a "safe seat"—one in which the party identification of the majority of a district's voters makes it likely that a candidate from that party will win an election. Thus, representatives from many of these safe seats can act in a partisan manner with impunity. Many times, a strong majority (but not all) of the member's constituency agrees with the representative's partisan stance, and the representative has little incentive to represent a moderate stance or act in a bipartisan fashion. The effect of this lopsided distribution of party identifiers within congressional districts is that the majority party is unlikely to lose an election, and the party in the minority has little hope of winning the seat, leading some to ask if the system of congressional elections is rigged through the process of gerrymandering.

Yes: Democrats, including former President Barack Obama and former Attorney General Eric Holder, contend that Republicans have rigged the redistricting system, creating congressional districts that are neither fair nor compact, but ensure that Republicans are elected to a majority of seats. They charge that Republicans (who control the majority of state legislatures, which determine the redistricting process) have hijacked the congressional redistricting system: Democrats say, "We're . . . feeling that our political system is unfair, and our votes don't count the way they should. The gerrymandering of congressional and legislative districts locks in a Republican majority and locks out the voters."[*]

No: Republicans assert that the fact that their success demonstrates a calculated strategy to win state legislative seats in states where the legislature has control over the redistricting process. "As the 2010 Census approached, the RSLC began . . . formulating a strategy to keep or win Republican control of state legislatures with the largest impact on congressional redistricting. . . . That effort, the REDistricting Majority Project (REDMAP), focused critical resources on legislative chambers in states projected to gain or lose congressional seats in 2011 based on Census data. . . . Controlling the redistricting process in these states would have the greatest impact on determining how both state legislative and congressional district boundaries would be drawn. Drawing new district lines in states with the most redistricting activity presented the opportunity to solidify conservative policymaking at the state level and maintain a Republican stronghold in the U.S. House of Representatives for the next decade."[**]

Other Approaches: Some analysts argue that the redistricting system is skewed in favor of Republicans, but that they won that advantage fair and square by developing a strategy to target state legislative seats that would determine congressional redistricting. Thus, this argument says that nothing is inherently unfair about congressional redistricting but that Democrats should adopt that strategy in 2021, when state legislative control (and redistricting) will again be up for grabs.

What do you think?

1. Why does the congressional redistricting process matter?

2. Was it fair for Republicans to target state legislative elections (spending millions of dollars) with the goal of controlling redistricting but not advising voters as to this goal? Why or why not?

3. What factors could put Democrats at a disadvantage in attempting to reconfigure the system in the 2021 elections?

*Source: National Democratic Redistricting Committee

**Source: Redistricting Majority Projedct

---

term was coined in reference to Massachusetts governor Elbridge Gerry after a district shaped like a salamander was created to favor his party in 1811. The Then/Now feature illustration shows the first gerrymander.

Most forms of gerrymandering are legal. The U.S. Supreme Court ruled in 1986 that a gerrymandering plan is unconstitutional only when it eliminates the

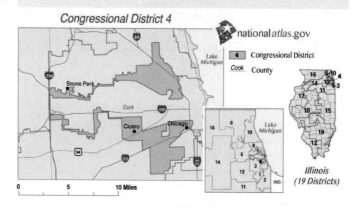

THEN

NOW

Congressional District 4

nationalatlas.gov

Illinois
(19 Districts)

>The term *gerrymander* originated from this Gilbert Stuart cartoon of a Massachusetts electoral district. To Stuart, the district looked like a salamander. A friend christened it a "Gerry-mander," after Massachusetts governor Elbridge Gerry, a signer of the Declaration of Independence and the politician who approved redrawing district lines for political advantage. What point does this famous historical cartoon of 1812, representing Massachusetts legislative districts, make about the nature of a gerrymander? Gerrymandering remains a practice today, as seen in Illinois's fourth congressional district. What are your own views on the practice?

Historical cartoon: ©Bettmann/Getty Images; *Congressional district:* U.S. Department of the Interior

minority party's influence statewide.[3] Because of the strict standards, only one partisan gerrymandering plan filed after the 1990 census was successfully challenged. Scholars believe that this ruling, along with changes in how congressional district maps are drawn, explains increased partisan voting in the House of Representatives.

Increased Partisanship and Congressional Redistricting

In earlier times, redistricting occurred through a simple redrawing of the lines of a congressional district to accommodate population changes. But today, with the widespread use of computer-driven mapmaking technology, congressional seats can be configured to ensure a "safe seat"—one in which the party identification of the majority of a district's voters makes it likely that a candidate from a given party will win election. Sometimes, for example, more than 60 percent of a district's population identifies with one political party.

The effect of this lopsided distribution of party identifiers within congressional districts is that there is little risk that the majority party will lose an election, and little hope that the party in the minority will win the seat. Thus, representatives from many of these safe seats can act in a partisan manner with impunity. Many times, a strong majority (but not all) of the member's constituency agrees with the representative's partisan stance, and the representative has little incentive to represent a moderate stance or act in a bipartisan fashion. In contrast, when congressional districts were more competitive, a House member typically would have to temper partisan impulses to placate the sizeable proportion of his or her constituency that identified with the opposing party. Otherwise, the member would risk alienating constituents and encouraging potential opponents to run. Today, that is no longer the case, and it appears that Republicans in the House of Representatives have become more conservative and their Democratic counterparts have become increasingly liberal. Consequently, House members are less likely to compromise or to be moderate in their positions in negotiating issues with the opposition. This increasing polarization is likely one additional reason why the public views Congress as an institution negatively, but individual incumbents, who represent the majority view within a district, are viewed favorably and nearly always reelected.

Majority-Minority Districts

While partisan gerrymandering tends to protect the status quo, another form of gerrymandering is sometimes relied upon to help ensure that a diversity of voices are elected to the House of Representatives. State legislatures have attempted to address the issue of racial imbalance in the House of Representatives by constructing a kind of gerrymander called a majority-minority district. A **majority-minority district** is composed of a majority of a given minority community—say, African Americans—and the creators' intent is to make it likely that a member of that minority will be elected to Congress (see "Analyzing the Sources"). The Supreme Court has ruled that such racial gerrymandering is legal unless the state legislature redrawing the district lines creates majority-minority districts at the expense of other redistricting concerns. Typically, those concerns include preserving the geographic contiguity of districts, keeping communities within one legislative district, and reelecting incumbents.

majority-minority district
A legislative district composed of a majority of a given minority community, the intent of which is to make it likely that a member of that minority will be elected to Congress.

Powers of Congress

The primary source of congressional authority is the U.S. Constitution. As shown in Table 12.1, the Constitution enumerates to Congress a number of powers. The nature of these responsibilities reveals that the Constitution is both very specific in describing congressional powers (as in punishing illegal acts on the high seas) and at the same time quite vague (as in its language establishing the federal court system). Many of the specific duties of Congress reflect Americans' bitter experience in the colonial era, in that the framers granted powers to Congress that they did not want to place in the hands of a strong executive. For example, the economic powers granted

TABLE 12.1 Enumerated Powers of the Congress

JUDICIAL POWERS
Establish the federal court system
Punish counterfeiters
Punish illegal acts on the high seas

ECONOMIC POWERS
Impose taxes
Establish import tariffs
Borrow money
Regulate interstate commerce
Coin and print money, determine the value of currency

NATIONAL SECURITY POWERS
Declare war
Raise and regulate national armed forces
Call up and regulate state national guard
Suppress insurrections
Repel invasions

REGULATORY POWERS
Establish standards of weights and measures
Regulate copyrights and patents

ADMINISTRATIVE POWERS
Establish procedures for naturalizing citizens
Establish post offices
Govern the District of Columbia

MAPPING MAJORITY-MINORITY DISTRICTS

The number of majority-minority districts in the United States has grown significantly in recent years. This figure shows that today there are 113 districts in 26 states in which an ethnic or a racial minority is in the majority.

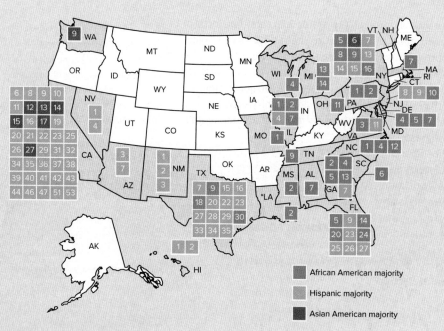

Majority-Minority Districts in Congress Today*

* In some congressional districts, combinations of racial and ethnic minorities create a majority-minority district. In those districts, the largest minority population is identified.

SOURCE: P. Bell and D. Wasserman, "Since 1982, Minority Congressional Districts Have Tripled," *National Journal,* April 13, 2012.

Practice Analytical Thinking

1. Which states have the most majority-minority districts?

2. Which racial or ethnic group has the most majority-minority districts?

3. Compare the location of majority African American districts to Hispanic districts. Which group is more dispersed? Which is more concentrated? Why do you think this is the case?

---

to Congress, including the ability to tax and spend, to establish tariffs, and to borrow money, all limit the power of the president.

Powers specifically granted to Congress still have a distinct impact on our everyday lives. For example, Congress regulates currency, establishes weights and measures, and administers post offices. As we have seen, the connection between Congress, particularly the House, and the people was crucial to the framers, and so the Constitution requires that all taxation and spending measures originate in the House, because the framers believed this chamber would be nearer to the people—and that House members would therefore ensure that the people's will was done.

The Constitution moreover imbues the Congress with an additional source of power, one that has proved important in the expansion of legislative authority over time. As discussed in Chapter 2, the necessary and proper—or elastic—clause states that the Congress shall have the power to "make all Laws which shall be necessary and proper for carrying into Execution the foregoing powers, and all other Powers vested by this Constitution in the Government of the United States, or in a Department or Officer thereof." This clause has been responsible for Congress's ability to legislate in many matters not described in the enumerated powers. Reforming our nation's health care system, determining the powers of law enforcement in investigating terrorism, and overhauling our system of immigration are all examples of powers not enumerated in the Constitution but that Congress exercises because of the broad scope of authority provided by the necessary and proper clause.

In addition to the Constitution, Congress derives power from Supreme Court decisions, the media, and the people. Supreme Court decisions often uphold the constitutionality of a law, in a sense verifying Congress's ability to create policy on a given subject. The media grant Congress power by providing members with a forum in which to communicate with constituents, sway public opinion, and create a favorable climate for the passage of legislation. The people are a key source of congressional power through civic participation in the electoral and legislative processes. Citizens communicate their views and priorities to their representatives, who then can claim public support in their endeavors to enact policy.

Functions of Congress

The Constitution is far more explicit in defining the responsibilities of the national legislature than it is in describing the function of the other branches of the government.[4] In its shaping of congressional functions, the Constitution's concerns with limited government, checks and balances, the separation of powers, and the creation of a federal system are all readily apparent. Today, Congress has a number of functions beyond lawmaking, including representation, oversight, agenda setting, and managing social conflict.

Representation Comes in Many Forms

In delineating the composition of the federal legislature and the procedures for electing its members, the Constitution shapes the congressional function of representation in several ways. Representation traditionally involves a House or Senate member's articulating and voting for the position that best represents the views of his or her constituents.[5] But sometimes a member of Congress may speak for other constituencies as well. For example, a feminist legislator might "represent" feminists nationwide,[6] just as a gay legislator might "represent" the collective interests of gays across the United States.

Often, Congress's policy-making function is at odds with its representation function. A legislator may be pressured—by his or her political party or own conscience—to vote for a policy that clashes with constituents' interests or views. In representing constituents, legislators frequently follow one of two models of representative behavior.

trustee model
A model of representation in which a member of the House or the Senate follows his or her own conscience when deciding issue positions.

MODELS OF REPRESENTATION According to the **trustee model** of representation, a member of the House or the Senate follows his or her own conscience when deciding issue positions and determining how to vote. Sometimes a legislator relying on the trustee model will act contrary to the views of his or her constituents. This model was espoused by British political theorist Edmund Burke (1729–1797), who served in Parliament as a representative of Bristol, England. Explaining his conception of representation, Burke emphasized to his constituents, however, that a member of Parliament "is not a member of Bristol, he is a member of Parliament."[7] Burke accordingly argued that a member of Parliament should follow his conscience when making decisions in the legislature: "Your representative owes you, not his industry only, but his judgment; and he betrays, instead of serving you, if he sacrifices it to your opinion."[8] In this trustee view, a legislator may act in opposition to the clear wishes of his or her constituents, such as in cases where an action is "for their own good" or the good of society.

Another model of representation is the **instructed delegate model,** the idea that a legislator, as a representative of his or her constituents, should vote in keeping with the constituents' views, *even if those views contradict the legislator's personal views.* This model of representation conceives of legislators as the agents of their constituents. A legislator hewing to the instructed delegate model faces a dilemma when his or her constituency is evenly divided on an issue.

Given these two different models of representation, which one do legislators typically follow? Most analyses of representation indicate that legislators are likely to merge the two models into a hybrid model, called **politico,** in which legislators act as instructed delegates when deciding important or high-profile issues, but for more mundane matters about which their constituents are less likely to be aware or to hold a strong position, they rely on the trustee model.

PORK BARREL AND EARMARKS Members of Congress also represent their constituencies through pork barrel politics. **Pork barrel** (also called simply *pork*) refers to legislators' appropriations of funds for special projects located within their congressional districts. Because pork brings money and jobs to a particular district, legislators who are seeking reelection work aggressively to secure monies for their states or districts—to "bring home the bacon."[9] Traditionally, members have used transportation bills as a means of creating pork barrel projects for their districts.[10] Members of Congress also use **earmarks**—designations within spending bills that provide for specific expenditures—as a means of representing constituent interests. In 2010, Republicans in Congress sought to eliminate earmarks as part of a larger effort to reign in government spending, and Republicans in both chambers endorsed a two-year moratorium on earmarks. But over time, that moratorium has fallen by the wayside, and members of Congress have resumed the practice, securing 163 earmarks in the 2017 fiscal budget, costing taxpayers $6.8 billion.[11]

CASEWORK A special form of representation called **casework** refers to providing representation in the form of personal aid to a constituent or a group of constituents, typically by getting the government to do something the constituent wants done. Members of Congress and their staffs commonly assist constituents in dealing with bureaucratic agencies. In doing so, they serve in the capacity of an **ombudsperson,** an elected or appointed representative who acts as a citizens' advocate by listening to their needs and investigating their complaints with respect to a particular government agency. For example, a member of Congress might intervene with U.S. Citizenship and Immigration Services to request that a constituent's relative in a foreign country be granted a visa to travel to the United States.

According to political scientist Morris Fiorina, casework is a valuable tool for legislators. Fiorina points out that serving constituents is relatively easy for

instructed delegate model
A model of representation in which legislators, as representatives of their constituents, should vote in keeping with the constituents' views, even if those views contradict the legislator's personal views.

politico
A hybrid model of representation in which legislators vote in keeping with constituents' views on important or high-profile matters but rely on the trustee model for more mundane matters.

pork barrel
Legislators' appropriations of funds for special projects located within their congressional districts.

earmark
A designation within a spending bill that provides for a specific expenditure.

casework
Personal work by a member of Congress on behalf of a constituent or group of constituents, typically aimed at getting the government to do something the constituent wants done.

ombudsperson
A role in which an elected or appointed leader acts as an advocate for citizens by listening to and investigating complaints against a government agency.

members of Congress, because bureaucrats—who depend on Congress for their funding—typically respond quickly to the requests of legislators.[12] The loyalty derived from assisting constituents is one aspect of the incumbency advantage that makes current members of Congress more likely to be elected than their challengers, who do not enjoy that source of constituent loyalty.

Casework benefits constituents when, for example, a member of Congress's staff works with a local branch of a Veterans' Administration clinic to secure services for a retired veteran, whose family members derive a sense of efficacy—a feeling that they can get things done and that the government works for people like them. They perceive that their individual member of Congress genuinely represents them and protects their interests, with the result that these constituents not only feel engaged but also are likely to advocate for their member's reelection bid.

Policy Making: A Central Responsibility

Each year, Congress considers laws determining everything from whether background checks should be required for gun purchases, to what law enforcers can do when they suspect someone of being a terrorist, to whether the nation's immigration policy should be overhauled. Many of these laws are passed by Congress and signed into law by the president, thus becoming the nation's policy. While all areas of congressional policy making are not explicitly listed in the Constitution (see discussion of the elastic clause in Chapter 2), it does invest Congress with some specific policy-making powers, including the authority to tax and spend, declare war, establish courts, and regulate the armed forces. This policy-making function is the central responsibility that the Congress carries out, and nearly all its other functions are related to its policy-making role. Congressional policy-making power also extends to the operations and priorities of governmental departments and agencies.

oversight
The process by which the legislative branch "checks" the executive branch to ensure that the laws Congress has passed are being administered in keeping with legislators' intent.

Oversight: A Check on the Executive Branch

In creating a system of checks and balances in the Constitution, the framers established the key congressional function of oversight.[13] **Oversight** is the process by which Congress "checks" the executive branch to ensure that the laws Congress passes are being administered in keeping with legislators' intentions. Congressional oversight is a check on the executive branch because the federal bureaucracy that implements laws is part of the executive branch. For example, oversight was important in the 2018 midterm elections, when many Democrats ran for seats in the House of Representative arguing that they would exercise more vigorous congressional oversight of the Trump administration than the Republican-led Congress had up to that point. In particular, Democrats said that with a congressional

>The oversight function of Congress was seen in the 2018 confirmation hearing of Brett Kavanaugh for a seat on the U.S. Supreme Court. During the bitterly partisan hearing, Dr. Christine Blasey Ford testified that she was "100 percent" certain that Kavanaugh had sexually assaulted her when they were both teenagers. Here, U.S. Senator Cory Booker (D-NJ), a member of the Senate Judiciary Committee who heard her testimony, provides Blasey Ford with a cup of coffee.
©Andrew Harnik-Pool/Getty Images

majority, they would ensure that special counsel Robert Mueller's probe into Russian interference in the 2016 election would continue unimpeded and that Mueller himself would be protected from unilateral removal by President Trump.

In carrying out their oversight function, members of Congress use a variety of tools, some of which are listed here:

- Congressional hearings, in which government officials, bureaucrats, and interest groups testify as to how a law or a policy is being implemented and examine the impact of its implementation.
- Confirmation hearings on presidential appointees to oversee executive departments or government agencies.
- Investigations to determine whether a law or a policy is being implemented the way Congress intended it to be, and inquiries into allegations of wrongdoing by government officials or bureaucrats.
- Budgetary appropriations that determine funding of an executive department or a government agency.

These tools ensure that Congress has some say in how the executive branch administers the laws Congress creates. Members of Congress increasingly have viewed their role of checking the executive branch as crucially important.

Agenda Setting and Civic Engagement

agenda setting
The determination by Congress of which public issues the government should consider for legislation.

Congress engages continuously in **agenda setting:** determining which public policy issues the federal legislature should consider.[14] Indeed, political scientists such as Gary Cox and Mathew McCubbins assert that agenda setting relieves the pressure that parties face in getting their members to vote with the party.[15] At the beginning of a congressional term, House and Senate leaders announce their goals for the coming session. In setting the national agenda, Congress serves as a key agent in molding the scope of civic engagement and discourse, as people learn about, discuss, and form positions about issues. Frequently, agenda setting is itself influenced by public discourse, as when constituents complain to a member of Congress about a problem that needs to be solved or when an interest group contacts a legislator about a policy its membership would like to see implemented. For example, such was the case in 2018, when students and family members of victims passionately advocated Congress for gun-safety laws in the wake of a mass shooting at Marjory Stoneman Douglas High School in Parkland, Florida. The students succeeded in setting the agenda for many of the mid-term congressional elections in 2018, particularly in some districts where incumbent legislators had accepted large campaign contributions from the National Rifle Association, which opposed the students' efforts.

Managing Societal Conflict

Congress also has a significant influence in managing the societal conflict inherent in a divided society such as the United States. Americans are divided in many ways, and in the past several years, ideological divisions have become greatly apparent as congressional district maps facilitate the election of staunchly ideological candidates, as discussed earlier.

Issues also divide Americans: Some citizens want higher wages, others advocate for more "pro-business" policies. Some want policies that benefit rural areas, and others give higher priority to urban areas. Some want more money for programs for senior citizens; others seek funding for children's programs. With respect to abortion policy, some people are pro-life, and others are pro-choice. In addition, there are divisions related to social class, race, geography, gender, sexual orientation, religion, and so on. Congress manages these conflicts by representing a wide range of views and interests, by taking stands on these positions, and then finally by compromising and negotiating on these issues.

The House and the Senate Compared

Although the House of Representatives and the Senate share numerous functions, the two chambers of Congress differ in significant ways. As President Woodrow Wilson remarked, the "House and Senate are naturally unalike."[16] Constitutionally, the two houses are conceived as unique organizations, and the framers designated their duties to match the strengths and expertise of the people who would come to hold office in each chamber. Table 12.2 highlights these major differences. As discussed earlier in this chapter, the Constitution empowers the House of Representatives, as the legislative body closer to the people, with initiating any bills that result in taxes; whereas it empowers the Senate, as the more deliberative house, to give the president advice and consent on appointments and the ratification of treaties. The differences between the House and the Senate are not limited merely to their functions, however. The electoral and legislative structures are also sources of differences between the two houses.

Each of the 435 current members of the House of Representatives represents a legislative district determined by the reapportionment and redistricting process that occurs every 10 years, as described earlier in this chapter. In more populated areas, these congressional districts are often homogeneous, cohesive units in which a House member's constituency is likely to have fairly unified positions on many issues.[17] Senators, however, are elected by the population of an entire state, and although the political culture in some states is somewhat cohesive (for example, Vermont voters are more liberal on most issues than are Kansas voters), in many states there are notable differences in constituents' views, ideologies, and policy priorities. One of

TABLE 12.2 Differences Between the House and the Senate

House	Senate
Larger (435 members)	Smaller (100 members)
Shorter electoral cycle (2-year term)	Longer electoral cycle (6-year term)
Narrow constituency (congressional districts)	Broad constituency (states)
Less prestigious	More prestigious
Originates all revenue bills	Ratifies treaties; confirms presidential nominees
Less reliant on staff	More reliant on staff
Power vested in leaders and committee chairs	Power distributed more evenly

the best examples of this vast diversity of views is California. Although it is typically viewed as having a very liberal political culture, California senators must advocate for the interests of liberal voters in the western coastal areas of the state as well as for those of more conservative voters inland to the east. Sometimes, moreover, constituents' interests divide in complex ways over a given issue: In California, for example, environmental activists and fishers have argued against programs that divert water from lakes and streams so that it can be used for irrigation on commercial farms, whereas affluent agribusinesses advocate water diversion. A U.S. senator must balance such conflicting positions when making policy decisions.

The differing lengths of representatives' and senators' terms of service affect how members of each chamber of Congress relate to their constituents. Given their short two-year terms, members of the House of Representatives naturally are reluctant to defy the will of the electorate on a given issue because of the likelihood that their opposition will be used against them during their reelection campaign. As the framers structured it, the House remains "the people's house," the chamber in which civically engaged individuals can effectively have their interests represented. And although U.S. senators naturally also want to please their constituents, they recognize that voting against their constituents' will on a particular issue might be less significant than such an action would be for a House member, especially if the issue arises early in their term and is not important enough for people to hold against them six years down the road. Take, for example, U.S. Senator Cory Booker's (D-N.J.) decision to support a nuclear agreement with Iran, despite the significant opposition of many Jewish-American and pro-Israeli groups. While an important issue to these groups and many of his constituents, because the deal came early in Booker's term, he was a bit insulated from the political fallout that would otherwise accompany such a decision, and he could vote his preference hoping that constituent passions surrounding the issue might dissipate before he faces reelection in 2020.

The size of the chambers and the length of terms also affect the relative prestige of each chamber. In general, the smaller Senate is considered more prestigious than the House of Representatives, although some individual House members may enjoy more prestige than some senators.

Although the House and the Senate differ in their constitutionally determined duties, both must pass any piece of legislation before it can become law. But the way in which legislation is considered and voted on differs in each house of Congress.

The larger size of the House of Representatives, with its 435 members, necessitates a more formal legislative structure to prevent unruliness. The House, for example, generally has more, and more formal, rules guiding debate than the Senate. Despite the differences between the two chambers, the legislative process is remarkably similar in both.

The Legislative Process

bill
A proposed piece of legislation.

Article I, Section 1, of the Constitution states, "All Legislative Powers herein granted shall be vested in a Congress of the United States, which shall consist of a Senate and House of Representatives." A **bill** is a proposed piece of legislation. As shown in Figure 12.1, every bill must be approved by *both houses* (the House and the Senate) *in identical form.* In general, bills must pass through five steps to become law:

1. **Introduction.** A member of the House of Representatives or the Senate formally proposes the bill.

The Legislative Process

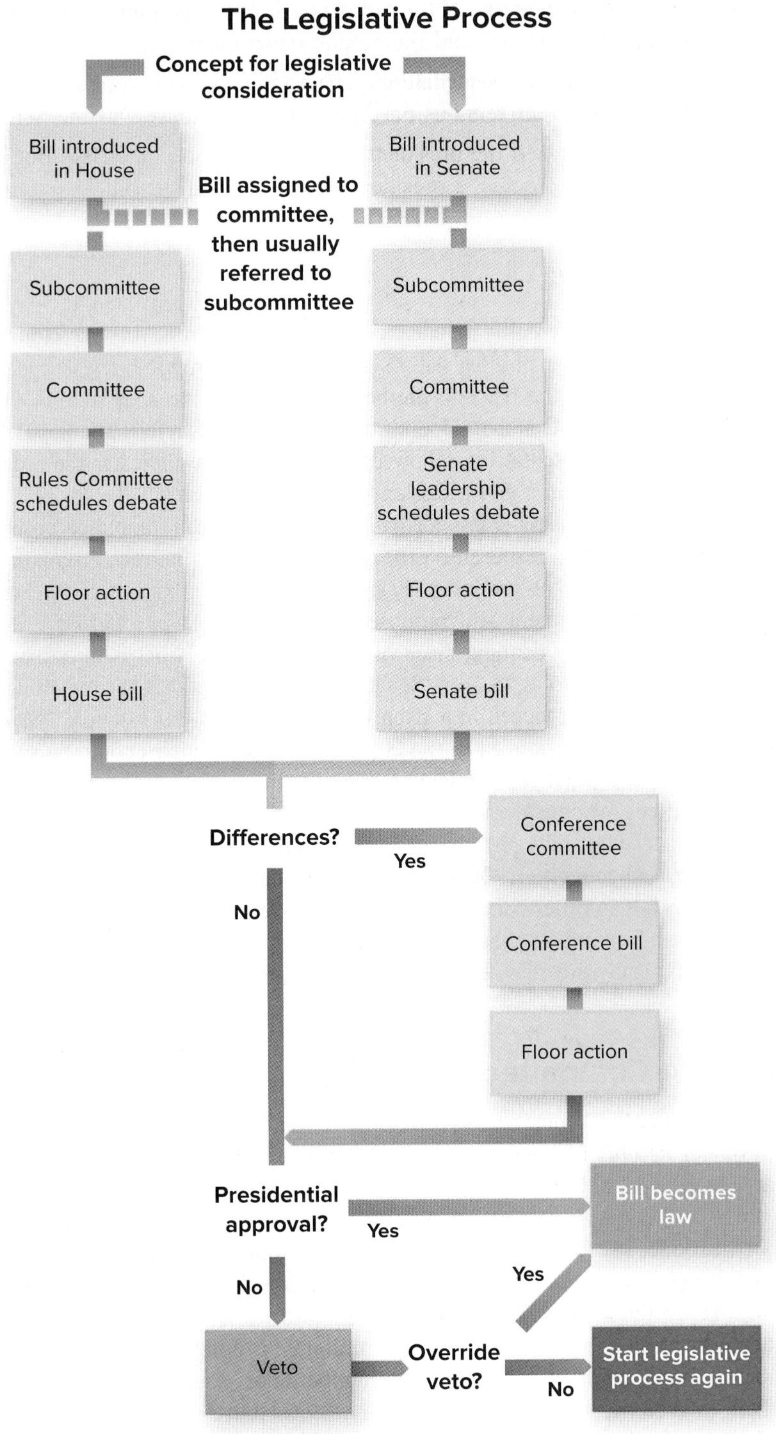

FIGURE 12.1 ■ **The Legislative Process** Where are there similarities between the House and the Senate in the legislative process? How do the Senate and the House resolve differences in versions of a bill passed in each chamber? What outcomes are possible once a bill goes to the president for approval?

2. **Committee review.** Subgroups within the House and the Senate, composed of legislators who have expertise in the bill's subject matter, review the bill.

3. **House and Senate approval.** If the bill makes it out of committee, a majority of members in the House and the Senate must approve it.

4. **Conference committee reconciliation.** The conference committee reconciles the bill when different versions have passed in the House and the Senate.

5. **Presidential approval.** If the president signs the bill, it becomes law. But even after this arduous process, a presidential veto can kill the bill.

Introducing a Bill

hopper
A wooden box that sits on a desk at the front of the House of Representatives, into which House members place bills they want to introduce.

Bills are introduced differently in each chamber of Congress. In the House of Representatives, a member of a legislator's staff drafts the proposed legislation, and the House member puts the bill into the **hopper,** a wooden box that sits on a desk at the front of the House chamber. Upon introduction, a bill is referred to as "H. R.," meaning House of Representatives, followed by a number that indicates the order in which it was introduced in a given legislative session, for example, "H. R. 207."

In the Senate, the process is less formal. Here, senators can announce proposed legislation to colleagues in a speech on the Senate floor. Alternatively, a senator can submit a written draft of the proposed legislation to an official known as the Senate clerk, or sometimes a senator will propose legislation simply by offering it as an amendment to an already pending piece of legislation. Once a bill is introduced in the Senate, it is referred to as "S.," or "Senate," followed by its number reflecting the order in which it was introduced in a given legislative session—for example, "S. 711."

joint referral
The practice, abolished in the 104th Congress, by which a bill could be referred to two different committees for consideration.

Before 1995, a bill introduced in the House of Representatives could be subject to **joint referral,** the practice of referring the bill simultaneously to two different House committees for consideration. But the 104th Congress abolished joint committee referrals. Today, bills introduced in the House are referred to one committee, called the **lead committee.** Occasionally, when the substance of a bill warrants additional referrals to other committees that also have jurisdiction over the subject of the bill, the bill might be subsequently referred to a second committee.[18] In the Senate, bills typically are referred to only one committee.

lead committee
The primary committee considering a bill.

The Bill in Committee

After introduction by a member of the House or the Senate, a bill is read into the *Congressional Record,* a formal record of all actions taken by Congress. Because of the large number of bills introduced, both chambers rely on an extensive committee structure that facilitates the consideration of so high a volume of bills.[19] Most bills that are introduced "die" in committee. That is, a committee does not consider the bill (sometimes because the committee does not have the time in a legislative session to take up the measure) or declines to forward the bill to the full chamber.

Each congressional committee and subcommittee is composed of a majority of members of the majority party in that chamber. For example, if 218 or more members (a majority in the House) elected to the House of Representatives are Republicans, then every committee and subcommittee in the House has a majority of Republicans. The parties in each chamber decide members' committee and subcommittee assignments.

seniority system
The system in which the member with the longest continuous tenure on a standing committee is given preference when the committee chooses its chair.

Though the selection of committee chairs varies between chambers and parties, committee chairs are often chosen using the **seniority system,** by which the member with the longest continuous tenure on a standing committee receives preference when the committee chooses its chair. The committee chairs run committee meetings and control the flow of work in each committee. Although the seniority system is an institution in Congress, it is an informal system, and seniority does not always determine who will be the committee chair.[20] Chairs are chosen by a secret ballot, and in recent years junior members sometimes have won out over senior committee members.

Standing committees are permanent committees with a defined legislative jurisdiction. The House has 20 standing committees, and the Senate has 21. The House Appropriations Committee and the Senate Armed Services Committee are examples of standing committees.

Select committees are specially created to consider a specific policy issue or to address a particular concern, including the controversial Select Committee on the Events Surrounding the 2012 Terrorist Attack in Benghazi, Libya. The committee was formed in 2014 and charged with investigating the attacks on the U.S. diplomatic mission in Libya, which was viewed as a partisan lob at Hillary Clinton, who had served as secretary of state during the attacks. Although the committee on the Benghazi attacks was among the most notable of all select committees formed, others have also grappled with controversial issues of the times, including climate change, the response to Hurricane Katrina, and homeland security and terrorism. There is currently one permanent Select Committee on Intelligence, which is concerned with the nation's intelligence apparatus.

Joint committees are bicameral committees composed of members of both chambers of Congress. Currently there are four joint committees; one is concerned with issues of taxation, another with economic issues, yet another deals with printing. Sometimes these committees offer administrative or managerial guidance of various kinds. For example, one joint committee supervises the administration of the Library of Congress.

In addition to the congressional committees, the House has 101 subcommittees, and the Senate has 68. **Subcommittees** typically handle specific areas of the committees' jurisdiction. For example, the House Energy and Commerce Committee is a standing committee. Within the committee there are six subcommittees: Communications and Technology, Digital Commerce and Consumer Protection, Energy, Environment, Health, and Oversight and Investigations. Each subcommittee handles bills relevant to its specified jurisdiction.

When a committee or a subcommittee favors a measure, it usually takes four actions:

1. **Agency review.** During **agency review,** the committee or subcommittee asks the executiv e agencies that would administer the law for written comments on the measure.

2. **Hearings.** Next the committee or subcommittee holds **hearings** to gather information and views from experts, including interest groups, concerned citizens, and policy experts involved with the issue.

3. **Markup.** During **markup,** the committee "marks up" the bill with suggested language changes and amendments. The committee does not actually alter the bill; rather, members recommend changes to the full chamber. In a typical bill markup, the committee may eliminate a component of the proposal or amend the proposal in some way.

4. **Report.** After agreeing to the wording of the bill, the committee issues a **report** to the full chamber, explaining the bill and its intent. The bill may then be considered by the full chamber.

standing committee
A permanent committee in Congress, with a defined legislative jurisdiction.

select committee
A congressional committee created to consider specific policy issues or address a specific concern.

joint committee
A bicameral committee composed of members of both chambers of Congress.

subcommittee
A subordinate committee in Congress that typically handles specific areas of a standing committee's jurisdiction.

agency review
Part of the committee or subcommittee process of considering a bill, wherein committee members ask executive agencies that would administer the law for written comments on the measure.

hearings
Sessions held by committees or subcommittees to gather information and views from experts.

markup
The process by which the members of legislative committees "mark up" a bill with suggested language for changes and amendments.

report
A legislative committee's explanation to the full chamber of a bill and its intent.

In the House of Representatives, a special measure known as a **discharge petition** is used to extract a bill from a committee to have it considered by the entire House. A discharge petition requires the signature of a majority (218) of the members of the House.

Debate on the House and Senate Floor

Table 12.3 compares the legislative process in the House and the Senate. For example, if a House bill is "discharged," or makes it out of committee, it then goes to the **Rules Committee,** one of the most important committees in the House, which decides on the length of debate and the scope of amendments that will be allowed on a bill. The Rules Committee sets the structure for the debate that ensues in the full House. For important bills, the Rules Committee tends to set strict limits on the types of amendments that can be attached to a bill. In general, the Rules Committee also establishes limits to floor debate in the House.

The Senate does not have a committee to do the work of the Rules Committee, but the Senate's small size allows members to agree to the terms of debate through **unanimous consent** agreements. Unanimous consent must be just that: Every senator needs to agree to the terms of debate (including time limits on debate), and if even one senator objects, unanimous consent does not take effect. Senators do not look favorably on objections to unanimous consent, and so such objections are rare. Objecting to unanimous consent agreements can potentially undermine a senator's ability to get legislation passed by provoking the ire of other senators.

If the Senate does not reach unanimous consent, the possibility of a **filibuster** arises—a procedural move that attempts to halt passage of the bill.[21] Sometimes the mere threat of a filibuster is enough to compel a bill's supporters to alter a bill's content. During a filibuster, a senator can speak for an unlimited time on the Senate floor. A filibuster can end by a vote of **cloture,** in which a supermajority of

Evaluating the Facts

TABLE 12.3 Differences Between the Legislative Process in the House and Senate

What are the root causes of the differences between the House and Senate? Which chamber has a greater number of rules and procedures? Why do you think this is the case?

HOUSE	SENATE
Bill introduced by member placing bill in hopper	Bill introduced by member
Relies on Rules Committee to schedule debate on House floor and to establish rules for amendments	Relies on unanimous consent agreements to determine rules for debate and amendments
Has a rule barring nongermane amendments	No rule banning nongermane amendments
Does not allow filibusters	Allows filibusters
Discharge petition can be used to extract a bill from a committee	Does not allow discharge petitions

60 senators agrees to end debate. Cloture is initiated if 16 senators sign a cloture petition. Filibustering senators do not need to restrict themselves to speaking only on the subject of the bill—they just need to keep talking. Some senators have read the Bible, cookbooks, and in 2013, Sen. Ted Cruz even read Dr. Seuss's *Green Eggs and Ham* into the *Congressional Record.* Former senator Strom Thurmond (R-S.C.) holds the Senate record for the longest filibuster. In an attempt to block passage of the Civil Rights Act of 1957, Thurmond filibustered for 24 hours and 18 minutes.

In recent years, President Trump has repeatedly expressed his frustration with the procedural maneuver, which has sometimes stymied his ability to win legislative votes, tweeting in 2018: "With the ridiculous Filibuster Rule in the Senate, Republicans need 60 votes to pass legislation, rather than 51. Can't get votes, END NOW!"[22] Despite the president's criticism, senators in both political parties have expressed reluctance to end the filibuster rule.[23]

In 2018, a unique filibuster occurred on the Senate floor when a bipartisan coalition of three Democrats and two Republicans committed to filibustering the FISA Amendments Reauthorization Act of 2017, a bill that effectively expands the warrantless surveillance of American citizens. Led by Republican Sen. Rand Paul (Ky.) and Democratic Sen. Ron Wyden (Ore.), the filibuster ended after only 2½ hours because the Senate obtained a cloture vote of 60–38, which limited debate on the bill to 30 hours. The full Senate approved the six-year extension by a 65–34 vote, and the measure, which had already passed in the House, was signed into law by President Trump.

In 2017, facing significant Democratic opposition, Republicans exercised the so-called **nuclear option,** a maneuver eliminating the possibility of filibusters on federal judicial nominations to confirm Neil Gorsuch as President Donald Trump's nominee to the Supreme Court. Doing so marked a break with precedent because the nuclear option had never been used as a mechanism in a Supreme Court nominee's confirmation; however, in 2013, Senate Democrats had used the option to pave the way for confirming appointments to the executive branch. The nuclear option is based on a 1957 opinion drafted by then–Vice President Richard M. Nixon, who asserted that the Constitution grants the presiding officer of the Senate the power to override Senate rules. In 2013, Democrats in charge of the Senate declared that filibusters on appointments and nominations could be subjected to a simple majority vote, requiring 51 votes rather than the 60 votes that would otherwise be necessary to end a filibuster. This 60-vote minimum had prevented President Obama—and Presidents Bill Clinton and George W. Bush before him— from getting many of their executive and judicial appointments confirmed in the Senate. Then–Senate majority leader Harry Reid (D-Nev.) argued that a backlog of appointments to the Obama administration and the federal courts was a result of Republican opposition to President Obama's administration overall rather than a reflection of the qualifications of individuals nominated to various positions, an argument that resurfaced during Gorsuch's confirmation.

After a bill is debated by the full chamber, the members vote on it. Before a bill can become law, identical versions of the bill must pass in both the House and the Senate. If only one chamber passes a bill during a congressional term, the bill dies. If both the House and the Senate pass bills on the same topic but with differences between the bills, the bills are then sent to a **conference committee,** a bicameral, bipartisan committee composed of legislators whose job is to reconcile the two versions of the bill. After the committee develops a compromise version of the bill, the bill then goes back to both chambers for another vote. If the bill does not pass in both chambers during a congressional term, the bill is dead, although it can be reintroduced in the next session. If both chambers approve the bill, it then goes to the president for signature or veto.

nuclear option
A maneuver exercised by the presiding officer in the Senate that eliminates the possibility of filibusters by subjecting votes on certain matters to a simple majority vote.

conference committee
A bicameral, bipartisan committee composed of legislators whose job is to reconcile two versions of a bill.

Presidential Action

When both the House and the Senate manage to pass a bill in identical form, it proceeds to the president, who may take one of three actions. First, the president may sign it, in which case the bill becomes a law. Second, the president may choose to do nothing. If the president does nothing and Congress is in session, the bill becomes law after 10 days without the president's signature. A president may take this route if he or she does not support the bill but knows that Congress would override a veto. If, however, Congress has adjourned (that is, the bill was passed at the end of a legislative session), then the president may exercise a pocket veto. A **pocket veto** occurs when Congress has adjourned and the president waits 10 days without signing the bill; the president effectively "puts the bill in his pockct," and the bill dies. Finally, a president may exercise the executive power of a *veto:* rejecting the bill and returning it to Congress with a message explaining why the bill should not become law. Congress can vote to override the veto by a two-thirds vote in both houses, in which case the bill becomes law. But overriding a presidential veto is a difficult and rare achievement.

pocket veto
A special presidential veto of a bill passed at the conclusion of a legislative session, whereby the president waits 10 days without signing the bill, and the bill dies.

Congressional Leadership

In earlier eras, forceful politicians rose to the position of majority leader in both houses and strongly influenced congressional priorities and legislation.[24] But allegiance to party leaders in these institutions has dwindled, a function of the decreasing role that political parties play in individual members' election to Congress.[25] Today's congressional power brokers face members whose loyalty to the party and the leadership is tempered by the increase in the number of highly ideological members hailing from safe congressional districts and the increasing need to please constituencies that themselves are less loyal to the parties than in bygone times.[26] The era has long passed in which individuals could essentially control what members of Congress do through their assertive personalities.[27] Nonetheless, despite the evolution in the role of congressional leader, partisanship remains a strong aspect of congressional politics.

Leadership in the House of Representatives

Although Article I, Section 2, of the Constitution states, "The House of Representatives shall choose their Speaker and other Officers," and all members of the House vote for the Speaker, it is really the members of the majority party who select their **Speaker of the House.** Second in the line of presidential succession (after the vice president), the Speaker serves as the presiding officer and manager of the House. In this capacity, the Speaker chairs floor debates, makes majority party committee assignments, assigns members to the powerful Rules Committee, negotiates with members of the minority party and the White House, and guides legislation through the House.[28] But the Speaker is also the leader of his or her party in the House, and a key duty associated with this role is helping party members to get reelected. Finally, the Speaker is himself or herself an elected member of the House.

In September 2015, John Boehner (pronounced BAY-ner) (R-Ohio), then the Speaker of the House of Representatives, shocked many by announcing his resignation. Boehner, a moderate Republican who served at the helm since 2010, was a victim of the factionalism that has plagued the Republican Party since that time.

Speaker of the House
The leader of the House of Representatives, chosen by the majority party.

Specifically, Boehner's inability to rein in conservative Freedom Caucus members within his party became apparent in 2013 when he could not corral them to compromise with Democrats on the budget, resulting in a 16-day shutdown of the federal government. In 2015, Freedom Caucus members, their numbers bolstered by the 2014 mid-term elections, threatened to shut down the government again by withholding votes on a budget measure, prompting Boehner's resignation.

When Rep. Boehner stepped down as Speaker, Republicans in the House of Representatives floundered for a short time in deciding his successor. They sought a Speaker who could unify but also was conservative enough to placate the Tea Party caucus, whose intraparty rumblings had caused Boehner's downfall. Paul D. Ryan (R-Wis.) emerged as that consensus candidate, winning all but nine of the Republican House votes. When he was elected, he acknowledged the challenge he

>Sen. Mitch McConnell (R-Ky.) was elected Senate Majority Leader when the Republicans took control of the Senate in 2014. When they maintained their majority in the chamber in 2016 and 2018, McConnell was re-elected to that role. He is viewed as a skilled political tactician by members of his party, and as an obstructionist by his opponents.

©Chip Somodevilla/Getty Images

faced: reforming an institution that he characterized as "broken,"[29] with deep divisions between Republicans and Democrats, and within the Republican party itself. After President Trump's inauguration in 2017, Ryan enjoyed the advantage of having a president of his party in the White House, but that presented many challenges, and President Trump's priorities and positions often varied greatly with members of his caucus. The reluctant Speaker, who often seemed disturbed by President Trump's behavior, often faced factionalism within his caucus. When it became evident that there was a possibility that Democrats might gain enough seats in the 2018 mid-term elections to take control of the House, Ryan announced that he was retiring from Congress.

The House leadership—which, in addition to the Speaker, includes the majority leader, the minority leader, and the party whips—is chosen at the beginning of each session of Congress through a conference also known as a *caucus*. During a caucus, all the members of the political party meet and elect their chamber leaders, approve committee assignments, and elect committee chairpersons. Party leaders also may call a party caucus during a legislative session to shore up support on an issue being voted upon or to formulate the party's position on an issue on the agenda.[30]

The Speaker relies on the **House majority leader** to help develop and implement the majority party's legislative strategy, to work with the minority party leadership, and to encourage unity among majority party legislators. In this last task, the Speaker and the House majority leader are assisted by the **majority whip,** who acts as a go-between with the leadership and the party members in the House. The term *whip* comes from the English hunting term *whipper-in,* a hunter whose job is to keep the foxhounds in the pack and to prevent them from straying during a fox hunt. Similarly, the job of the party whip is to keep party members together, encouraging them to vote with the party on issues and preventing them from straying off into their own positions. The minority party in the House also elects leaders, the **House minority leader** and the **minority whip,** whose jobs mirror those of their majority-party colleagues but without the power that comes from holding a majority in the House.

House majority leader
The leader of the majority party, who helps the Speaker to develop and implement strategy and who works with other members of the House of Representatives.

majority whip
The go-between with the majority leadership and party members in the House of Representatives.

House minority leader
The leader of the minority party, whose job mirrors that of the majority leader but without the power that comes from holding a majority in the House of Representatives.

minority whip
The go-between with the minority leadership, whose job mirrors that of the majority whip but without the power that comes from holding a majority in the House of Representatives.

Leadership in the Senate

In the Senate, the vice president of the United States serves as the president of that body, according to the Constitution. But in actual practice, vice presidents preside over the Senate only rarely. Vice presidents, however, have one power in the Senate that, although rarely exercised, is enormously important. If a vote in the upper house of Congress is tied, the vice president breaks the tie. Vice President Mike Pence has cast a record number of tie-breaking votes in the Senate, including the deciding vote on a plan that allows states to block funding for Planned Parenthood and the deciding vote on the nomination of Betsy DeVos to be secretary of education.

The majority party in the Senate elects a Senate leader called the **president pro tempore.** Meaning "president for the time," this position is often referred to as "president pro tem." The job of the president pro tem is to chair the Senate in the vice president's absence. Historically, this position has been honorary, with the majority-party senator who has the longest record of continuous Senate service being elected to the office. Although the position is honorary, the Senate's president pro tem is third in the line of presidential succession (following the vice president and the Speaker of the House). Senator Orrin Hatch (D-Utah), who was first elected to the Senate in 1976, has served as the president pro tem since 2015.

The real power in the U.S. Senate is held and wielded by the **Senate majority leader,** whose job is to manage the legislative process so that favored bills are passed; to schedule debate on legislation in consultation with his or her counterpart in the minority party, the **Senate minority leader;** and to act as the spokesperson for the majority party in the Senate. The majority and the minority leaders both play crucial roles in ushering bills through the Senate, and the majority leader facilitates the numerous negotiations that arise when senators bargain over the content of a given piece of proposed legislation.[31]

Senate majority leader Mitch McConnell (R-Ky.) was elected after the Republicans won a majority of seats in the 2014 Senate elections and was reelected in 2016, when the Republicans retained control of the Senate. McConnell was elected after serving as minority leader and has a reputation as a skillful and tough-minded politician. As majority leader, McConnell faces pressure both from more conservative members of his party and from the Trump administration on an array of issues. Notably, McConnell forcefully went toe to toe with President Trump after the president criticized Robert Mueller, defending and supporting the special counsel who was investigating Russian interference in the 2016 presidential election.[32]

Decision Making in Congress: The Legislative Context

When deciding whether to "toe the party line" on a legislative vote, members of Congress do not operate independently and in isolation. Throughout the legislative process, they face a variety of external pressures that influence their views. Some of these pressures are subtle; others are more pronounced. Moreover, the effectiveness of the pressure varies according to the timing and type of legislation being considered. For example, political scientist Barry C. Burden has noted that the personal experiences of legislators sometimes have a bearing on their policy stances on issues.[33] Among the most important influences on members of Congress with respect to the legislative process are political parties, members' colleagues and staff, interest groups, the president, and of course their constituents—the people who elected them to serve as their representatives in our system of republican government.

Party Breakdowns in the House and Senate, 1991–2021*

FIGURE 12.2 ■ **Party Representation Trends** What trends does this graph show with respect to party representation in the House of Representatives since 1991? What trends does it indicate for the Senate? Generally speaking, do the patterns for the House resemble those for the Senate?

* At time of publication, eight House races and two Senate races had not yet been officially decided.

Political Parties and Partisanship in Decision Making

Figure 12.2 shows the party breakdown in Congress since 1991. The data show that 1994 was a pivotal year, ending Democratic control in the House and the Senate. For nearly all of the next 12 years, Republicans retained control over both the House and the Senate. (Republicans lost their narrow majority in the Senate in 2001 when one Republican senator switched parties, but they regained control in the 2002 elections.) But in 2006 the balance of power shifted back to the Democrats, who won majorities in both houses, squeaking out a majority in the Senate with a one-member lead. That year, Democratic candidates benefited from Republican President George W. Bush's unpopularity and the public's weariness with the war in Iraq. In 2008 the Democrats continued to increase their majorities in both houses, as a result of voters' continuing dislike of Bush's policies, and–for some Democratic congressional candidates–from Barack Obama's coattails. But this trend was reversed in 2010, when Republicans won a majority of seats in the House of Representatives and increased their numbers in the U.S. Senate (see "Thinking Critically"). In the 2012 elections, in which President Obama topped the Democratic ticket, Democrats increased their margins slightly in both the House and the Senate, but again, this trend reversed itself in 2014, with Republicans increasing their majority in the House and winning a majority in the U.S. Senate. In 2016, Republicans lost several seats but maintained control of the House of Representatives. The 2018 elections were largely seen as a referendum on the Trump presidency, and Democrats succeeded in recapturing the House by flipping over 30 seats, many in affluent, suburban areas (Figure 12.3).

The partisan breakdown of Congress is important because most major legislative votes cast are "party votes," meaning that most members of one political party vote one way, and most members of the other party vote the other way. In some cases,

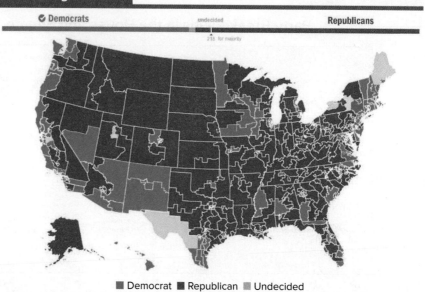

☑ Democrats   undecided   **Republicans**

218 for majority

■ Democrat ■ Republican ■ Undecided

FIGURE 12.3 ■ Party Representation in the House of Representatives, 2019–2021
How many seats in the House do the Republicans have as a result of the 2018 election?
How many seats do the Democrats have? Which party has the majority? Given the party
of the president, how do you think the new House composition might affect lawmaking?

* At time of publication, House races in the following districts had not yet been officially decided: California's 39th and 45th,
Georgia's 7th, Maine's 2nd, New Jersey's 3rd, New York's 27th, Texas' 23rd, and Utah's 4th.

this divide is due to the differing ideologies. In other instances, party voting is simply
pure partisanship: Democrats vote against something because Republicans vote for
it and vice versa. Partisan voting increased after the Watergate scandal in the 1970s,
rose again after the 1994 congressional elections, in which Republicans took control
of Congress, and again when the conservative Tea Party members of Congress began
flexing their political muscle after the 2010 elections. Partisan voting tends to be
particularly acrimonious immediately before congressional and presidential elections.
It occurs more often when members are voting on domestic policy issues, including
environmental policies, economic regulatory policies, or policies concerning entitlement programs. Policy decisions such as these tend to crystallize ideological differences between the parties, as the Affordable Care Act did.

As previously discussed, the increasingly sophisticated ability of mapmakers to draw
congressional districts that offer partisan advantage to one party means that partisanship has increased in the House of Representatives. But many scholars assert that a
similar bifurcation of political ideology has not occurred in the Senate. They claim that,
because state populations as a whole tend to be more ideologically diverse and less
homogeneous than House districts, U.S. senators often must temper their views to
reflect the wider range of their constituents' perspectives. Thus senators tend to
be more willing than their House counterparts are to compromise and to take a more
moderate stance in negotiating with the opposing party. Nonetheless, on some issues,
other scholars note that the Senate is increasingly divided along strongly partisan lines.[34]

Colleagues and Staff: Trading Votes and Information

Congressional colleagues provide cues for members of the House and the Senate in
their decision making over whether to vote for a pending piece of legislation. Members
may seek the opinions of like-minded colleagues in determining how to vote on a
proposed bill. In addition, legislators may consult with peers who are policy experts.

Members of Congress also engage in **logrolling,** the practice of trading votes between members. Logrolling is a reciprocal tactic by which a member agrees to vote on one piece of legislation in exchange for a colleague's vote on another. For example, a representative from an urban area might agree to vote for a farm aid bill that has little effect on her constituents in exchange for a colleague's vote for increased funds for community policing in cities.

In addition, House and Senate members rely on their staffs to inform their decision making on legislation.[35] Staff members frequently have policy expertise that can guide a legislator's decision on an upcoming vote. They also figure in the legislative voting process by communicating with legislators about the desires of constituents and interest groups with respect to a pending piece of legislation.

logrolling
The practice of members of Congress agreeing to vote for a bill in exchange for their colleague's vote on another bill.

Interest Groups: Influence Through Organization

In various ways, interest groups also influence congressional elections. They can affect electoral outcomes, for example, through an endorsement process by which a group notifies its members that it backs a certain candidate in the hope that members get on the bandwagon and express their support at the polls. In addition, through their political action committees, interest groups make financial contributions to congressional campaigns. And interest groups whose memberships are mobilized to support or oppose a candidate often provide grassroots activists to political campaigns.[36] In 2018, one interest group, the National Rifle Association, became a focal point, as momentum gathered throughout the United States for more gun-safety laws following several mass shootings. When these efforts to pressure Congress were thwarted by legislators who had been backed by the NRA, the interest group became the target of intense criticism and scrutiny.

As we considered in Chapter 7, interest groups also shape the legislative process. They make their mark by influencing congressional campaigns, by providing information to members of Congress as they try to decide whether to vote for a particular piece of legislation, and by lobbying members of Congress to support or oppose legislation.[37]

The President's Effect on Decision Making

As we have seen, the president determines whether to sign or to veto legislation that reaches his or her desk. But often, before a bill reaches the signing stage, the president's position on it carries enough influence to sway members of Congress, particularly members of the president's political party, to vote for or against the proposed legislation.

President Trump succeeded in shepherding his federal tax plan through Congress and in pressuring lawmakers to break with tradition and use the "nuclear option" (described earlier in this chapter) to confirm his nominee for the U.S. Supreme Court, Neil Gorsuch, and later Brett Kavanaugh. He has also succeeded in convincing Congress to repeal a wide variety of regulations concerning gun ownership, environmental protection, and business. But he has had less success with other measures, including repealing the Affordable Care Act, securing funding to build a wall between the United States and Mexico, and reforming immigration policy. Where he has had less success it is, in part, because members of Congress have been pressured by other entities, including their constituents.[38]

Constituents: The Last Word

Of all the players with a voice in the legislative process, congressional constituents—the people whom the members of Congress represent—wield perhaps the strongest,

THEN NOW NEXT

Partisanship in Congress

Then (1980s)	Now
Congress was divided; Democrats controlled the House of Representatives, and Republicans controlled the Senate.	Congress is divided; Democrats control the House of Representatives, and Republicans control the Senate.
Although incumbents enjoyed a considerable advantage, many congressional districts were a mix of constituents of both major parties.	Fewer congressional districts are competitive. Many districts are more homogeneous because district boundaries can be drawn with sophisticated computer programs.
Partisan voting was evident, but legislators were often forced to base their positions on constituent preferences in addition to their own party loyalty.	With the advent of less competitive districts, legislators are more partisan than their predecessors.

WHAT'S NEXT?

> Has the outcome of the 2018 elections increased or decreased party tensions, in your view? Why?

> In recent years, partisanship has increased when there has been a president of one party and a Congress of another. Does such a scenario exist today? What implications does that have for the future of partisanship in Congress for the next several years?

> Increases in technological sophistication could make redistricting an even more exact science. What effect would this change have on partisanship in Congress?

attentive public
The segment of voters who pay careful attention to political issues.

if indirect, influence with respect to congressional decision making. Most members of Congress want to be reelected, and representing constituents' views (and being able to convince voters that their views are represented well) is a major avenue to reelection to Congress. Thus constituents influence the legislative process by ensuring that their representatives in Congress work hard to represent their perspectives and policy interests, whether those concerns are over environmental pollution, crime, or the soaring cost of higher education.

In fact, some research shows that the public's "potential preferences" can motivate legislators to espouse a policy position likely to be embraced by constituents.[39] But other research shows that most voters are not especially vigilant when it comes to monitoring their elected officials in Congress. In fact, only a very small percentage of voters, sometimes called the **attentive public,** pay careful attention to the public policies being debated by Congress and to the votes cast by their representatives and senators. But the fact that the attentive public is a relatively small minority does not mean that votes taken in Congress are insignificant as far as constituents' opinions go. Indeed, if a member of Congress should disregard constituents' views in voting on a major issue, it is quite likely that an opposing candidate or political party will bring this misstep to the public's attention during the individual's next congressional campaign.

The People and Their Elected Representatives

Although members of Congress may make it a priority to represent the viewpoints and interests of their constituents, demographically speaking, they do not represent the American public at large. As Table 12.4 shows, Congress, especially the Senate, is older, whiter, more educated, and more likely to be male than the population as a whole. That said, Congress is not designed to be a perfect sampling of American demographics.[40] Yet Congress is more diverse today than at any other point in history, with 2018 ushering in a slew of historic "firsts" among elected House members, including Reps. Sharice Davids (D-KS) and Deb Haaland (D-NM), the first Native American women elected to the House of Representatives.

TABLE 12.4 Demographic Characteristics of the 114th Congress Compared to the U.S. Population

	House (%)	Senate (%)	Population (%)
PARTY			
Democrat	44	44	27
Republican	56	54	28
Independent/Unaffiliated	0	2	42
AVERAGE AGE	57 years	61 years	38 years
SEX			
Male	80	80	49
Female	20	20	51
RACE			
White	78	93	60
Black	10	2	12
Hispanic (any race)	8	4	19
Asian/Pacific Islands	3	1	8
Native American	.45	0	.72
EDUCATION			
Bachelor's degree	94	100	30
Master's degree	19	16	9
Law degree	36	54	>1
Ph.D.	5	1	>1
M.D.	5	3	>1

SOURCES: Jennifer E. Manning, *Membership of the 114th Congress: A Profile* (Washington, DC: Congressional Research Service), and U.S. Census Bureau, *Population Estimates*, and The Gallup Organization.

2018: The Year of the Woman Redux

The year 2018 saw a record number of women's candidacies for Congress, and a particularly large number of Democratic women running against Republican House members. In many of these cases, the women candidates said that they were motivated to run because of their objection to President Trump's rhetoric and behavior toward women and because of the policy stances of their Republican representatives, many of whom had supported the president's legislative initiatives, including the repeal of the Affordable Care Act and a budget that was perceived as punitive to states that had voted Democratic in the 2016 presidential election. The candidacies also were part of a larger women-centered social movement born in the aftermath of President Trump's election, spawned through marches after his inauguration, kindled by the #MeToo social media protests surrounding sexual harassment, and nurtured through anti-gun violence demonstrations that occurred in the wake of school shootings.

Because of the strong advantage associated with incumbency, many women candidates were not successful, but in some cases, the threat of their candidacies alone caused an unprecedented occurrence: faced with sometimes well-financed and formidable challengers (and several in the wake of allegations of sexual harassment), large numbers of incumbent members of Congress decided to retire. These changes were particularly evident in Republican districts: in 2018, nine House Democrats outright retired (i.e., they did not retire in order to pursue a U.S. Senate seat) compared to 25 House Republicans. These retirements presented opportunities for many women candidates in those districts.

Figure 12.4 shows that most states have women as part of their congressional delegations. While Congress as a whole is becoming increasingly diverse and a record number of women won seats in 2018, the proportion of women in Congress is not nearly equal to their proportion in the national population. In 2018, 101 women were elected to the House of Representatives, constituting 23 percent of the 435 members. In addition, 23 women (or 23 percent of the 100 members) serve in the Senate. Despite an upward trend, the United States lags behind many industrialized democracies with respect to the proportion of women serving in the national legislature.

Interpreting Images

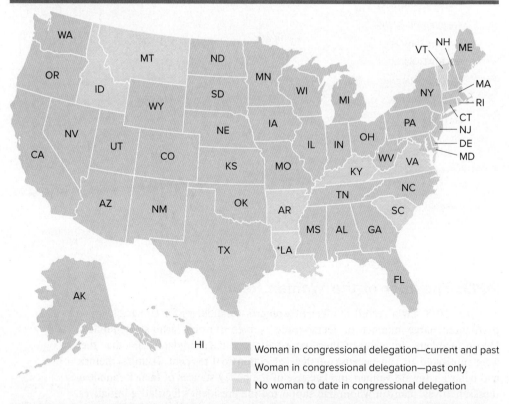

Woman in congressional delegation—current and past

Woman in congressional delegation—past only

No woman to date in congressional delegation

FIGURE 12.4 ■ States Represented by Women in the U.S. Congress What commonalities exist among the states that have never had a woman in their congressional delegations? Where are the states that no longer have women in their delegations primarily located? Why do you think this is the case?

* At time of publication, Rep. Mia Love (R-UT) had sought a judicial order to halt counting ballots in a tightly-contested race until ballot challenges are resolved.

SOURCE: Center for American Women and Politics, Eagleton Institute of Politics, Rutgers, The State University of New Jersey, and authors' calculations.

Racial and Ethnic Diversity in Congress

Similarly, African Americans have historically been underrepresented in Congress. To date, only nine African Americans have served in the Senate, including two, Hiram Revels and Blanche Bruce, who served during the Reconstruction era that followed the Civil War. After Bruce left the Senate in 1881, no other African American would be elected to that chamber until 1967, when Senator Edward Brooke (R-Mass.) was elected for one term. More recently, Senator Carol Moseley Braun (D-Ill.) was elected in 1992 and served for one term, and Barack Obama was elected from the state of Illinois in 2004. From 2011 through 2013, no African Americans served in the U.S. Senate, but in 2013, Cory Booker (D-N.J.) was elected to fill the remainder of the term vacated when Senator Frank Lautenberg passed away. Booker was reelected to a full six-year term in 2014, and was joined in the Senate by Tim Scott (R-S.C.), the first African American to be elected to the Senate from the South since the Reconstruction era that year. In 2016, Sen. Kamala Harris (D-Calif.), became the first mixed-race senator (Harris is black and Asian American).

Figure 12.5 traces the increasing success of African Americans in getting elected to the House of Representatives. The figure shows that, as in the Senate, African Americans' initial service in the House came about in the Reconstruction period. But the successes of that era were short lived, and the numbers of African Americans in Congress would not match those of the immediate post-Reconstruction period until after the civil rights movement of the 1960s. Today, as is the case for women, more African Americans serve in Congress than at any other point in U.S. history, and with each election history continues to be made. In 2014, for example, Mia Love (R-Utah) made history by becoming the first Republican African American woman elected to the House of Representatives.

Evaluating the Facts

African Americans in the House of Representatives

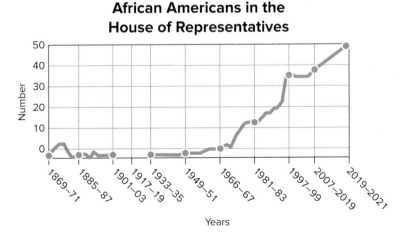

FIGURE 12.5 ■ **African Americans Elected to the House** What explains the rise in African American representation in the House from 1871 through 1887? Why did African Americans' representation fall after 1887? What pattern do you see since the late 1960s, and what political and social changes explain it?

In 2018, Latinos saw marked success in gaining representation in Congress. Ten new Latinos were elected to the House, joining 30 incumbents, bringing the total number of representatives of Hispanic heritage to 40. In addition, four current members of the U.S. Senate are Latino, including Senators Catherine Cortez Masto (D-Nev.), Robert Menendez (D-N.J.), Marco Rubio (R-Fla.), and Ted Cruz (R-Tex). Many states, including New Mexico, California, Texas, and Arizona, are seeing rising numbers of Latinos elected to state legislatures, providing a pool of candidates who could move on to run for Congress. As women, African Americans, and ethnic minorities make up an increasing proportion of the eligibility pool—the group of people deemed qualified for office—diversity in Congress is sure to grow.

Conclusion
Thinking Critically About What's Next in Congress

Congress is an ever-evolving institution. The national legislature is shaped by the framers' vision that created it; by the groups and individuals that seek to, and do, influence it; and by the broader electorate who vote for the representatives who serve in it. The Constitution's framers ingeniously created a strong legislative system designed to dominate the national government. In doing so, they simultaneously— and significantly—checked the power of the executive.

The framers ensured that the legislative branch of the federal government would be responsive to changing times. Today, Congress is more demographically diverse than ever before in history. In recent years, it has also responded to modern challenges, including internal struggles and low approval ratings. Congressional decision making today is influenced by shifting constituencies in a country that is rapidly growing more diverse. How will continued increasing diversity affect congressional decision making in the future?

With Congress well-structured to respond to constituents' needs, ongoing technological advances and the spread of inexpensive technology to more and more citizens mean that members of Congress and their staffs should be increasingly accessible to the people. And representatives' district offices will continue to provide constituents another easily accessed channel through which to convey their needs and interests to their representatives—and through which their representatives, in turn, can monitor the opinions of their constituents so that they may better represent them. But technology also has driven the process of congressional redistricting, rendering more highly partisan districts and creating a more polemic legislature that often prioritizes party issues, sometimes at the expense of the national interest.

Congress has proved itself to be a remarkably flexible institution, responding to changes in society, shifting constituencies, and increasingly diverse members, particularly in recent times. That Congress will become even more diverse is certain.

Learning Summary

1. Explain the origins of Congress, including the compromise that led to a bicameral legislature.

2. Describe the process of congressional elections.
   a. Explain incumbency advantage.
   b. Describe the processes of reapportionment and redistricting.
   c. Define gerrymandering and explain its effect on elections.

3. Describe the powers of Congress.

4. Discuss the functions of Congress.
   a. Explain representation.
   b. Describe the policy-making process as a function.
   c. Explain congressional oversight.
   d. Explain how Congress can set the national agenda.
   e. Discuss how Congress manages societal conflict.

5. Compare and contrast the House of Representatives and the Senate.

6. Explain the process of how a bill becomes a law, including the differing procedures in each chamber.

7. List the leadership positions in Congress and explain how congressional leadership affects the legislature's ability to perform its functions.

8. Explain congressional decision making in the legislative context.
   a. Describe the role of political parties.
   b. Explain how staff assist in decision making.
   c. Analyze the role of interest groups in influencing Congress members' decisions.
   d. Explain how the president might affect congressional decisions.
   e. Describe why constituents have a strong role in influencing Congress members.

9. Analyze the demographic similarities and differences between the people and their elected representatives.

Key Terms

agency review 407
agenda setting 402
attentive public 416
bill 404
casework 400
cloture 408
conference committee 409
discharge petition 408
earmark 400

filibuster 408
franking 393
gerrymandering 394
hearings 407
hopper 406
House majority leader 411
House minority leader 411
instructed delegate
   model 400

joint committee 407
joint referral 406
lead committee 406
logrolling 415
majority whip 411
majority-minority
   district 397
markup 407
minority whip 411

For Review

1. Why was Congress created in the way it was?

2. How does incumbency affect congressional elections?

3. What is the difference between reapportionment and redistricting?

4. How has technology changed the process of congressional redistricting?

5. Historically, what has been the impact of the necessary and proper (elastic) clause?

6. Describe the two types of congressional powers.

7. What influence do the constitutionally enumerated duties of the House and the Senate have on the expertise of each chamber?

8. Outline the basic steps of the legislative process.

9. How do the qualities of congressional leaders differ today from those needed in earlier eras?

10. Why has party-line voting increased in Congress in recent years?

For Critical Thinking and Discussion

1. If you were serving in Congress, would you tend to follow the instructed delegate model of representation, the trustee model, or the politico model? Why? What might be the likely outcome of your choice?

2. How does the legislative process differ in the House and the Senate? In which chamber is the process more streamlined? More deliberative? Why?

3. What do you and the people you know think about the work and contributions of Congress? Would you give Congress high or low approval ratings as an institution, or something in between? Who is your own congressional representative, and what rating would you give her or him? Why?

4. Log on to the Library of Congress website (www.loc.gov) and read about issues currently on the floor of the House of Representatives. Can you identify any of the external influences mentioned in this chapter on the legislative process? Describe these influences, and discuss how they are shaping the process.

5. Why do you think so few women and racial and ethnic minorities have been elected to Congress? Why is this situation changing? What do you imagine that Congress will look like, demographically, in the year 2050?

Resources for Research AND Action

Internet Resources

C-Span
www.c-span.org The cable television network C-Span provides a large amount of information on Congress, including Internet video, audio, and podcast programs of congressional hearings, committee meetings, C-Span video series, and a variety of public affairs information.

Library of Congress
www.loc.gov The website for the Library of Congress, the most important clearinghouse for information about Congress, legislation, hearings, votes, and other federal matters.

Roll Call
www.rollcall.com This website for *Roll Call,* the "source for news on Capitol Hill since 1955," offers an insider's look at the world of Capitol Hill, including issue analysis, politics, and opinions.

U.S. Senate and U.S. House of Representatives
www.senate.gov and **www.house.gov** These websites for the Senate and the House provide information about members of Congress, votes, pending legislation, committees, and session schedules, plus information about the Capitol and information for visitors.

Recommended Readings

Ahuja, Sunil. *Congress Behaving Badly: The Rise of Partisanship and Incivility and the Death of Public Trust.* Santa Barbara, CA: Praeger, 2008. This analysis examines the causes and the results of increased party cleavages in Congress.

Bordewich, Fergus M. *The First Congress.* New York: Simon & Schuster, 2016. The story of the first federal Congress of 1789–1791 and how, in just two years, the founding fathers created the Constitution of the United States and laid the framework for our modern Congress.

Corning, Trevor, Reema Dodin, and Kyle W. Nevins. *Inside Congress: A Guide for Navigating the Politics of the House and Senate Floors.* Washington, DC: Brookings, 2017. Written by congressional insiders, this volume sheds light on the structures, procedures, and politics that rule each chamber.

Dodd, Lawrence C., and Bruce J. Oppenheimer. *Congress Reconsidered,* 11th ed. Washington, DC: CQ Press, 2016. The most recent edition of a classic series providing comprehensive coverage of the evolution of the American Congress.

Fenno, Richard F., Jr. *Home Style: House Members in Their Districts.* New York: Longman, 2009. Fenno traveled the United States observing members of Congress at home in their districts and explains how constituent interaction affects congressional decision making.

Forman, Sean D., and Marcia Godwin. *The Roads to Congress 2016.* New York: Palgrave Macmillan. 2018. This work examines the processes and issues associated with key congressional races in 2016.

Kaiser, Robert G. *Act of Congress: How America's Essential Institution Works, and How It Doesn't.* New York: Vintage Books, 2014. A look at the inner workings of Congress and the financial reform bill in a post-crash America.

Loomis, Burdett, and Wendy J. Schiller. *The Contemporary Congress,* 7th ed. Lanham, MD.: Rowman and Littlefield, 2018. A concise yet comprehensive analysis of Congress, particularly the legislative context that influences the legislative process.

O'Neill, Thomas P. *Man of the House: The Life and Political Memoirs of Speaker Tip O'Neill.* New York: Random House, 1987. The political memoir of a long-term Speaker of the House of Representatives provides a fascinating glimpse into the "real world" of Capitol Hill politics from the 1960s through the 1980s.

Thomas, Sue. *How Women Legislate.* New York: Oxford University Press, 1994. Groundbreaking analysis of the differences and similarities between how men and women approach the task of legislating.

Movies of Interest

The Congress (1988)
This Ken Burns documentary provides a fine introduction to the U.S. Congress (both the institution and the Capitol building). Burns traces the history of the institution and the people who have served in it, including 19th-century statesmen Henry Clay and Daniel Webster and continuing to Congress's modern leaders.

The Ugly American (1963)
This drama stars Marlon Brando as Harrison Carter MacWhite, who, after surviving an acrimonious Senate confirmation hearing, becomes ambassador to a Southeast Asian nation on the brink of civil war.

Mr. Smith Goes to Washington (1939)
This classic Frank Capra movie features Jimmy Stewart as Jefferson Smith, who, after the death of a senator, is appointed to serve in the U.S. Senate despite his political naiveté. Stewart's depiction of a filibuster informs most Americans' perception of this political maneuver.

References

1. See, for example, David E. Price, *The Congressional Experience: A View from the Hill* (Boulder, CO: Westview, 1992).

2. Richard F. Fenno Jr., *Home Style: House Members in Their Districts* (New York: Longman, 2002).

3. *Davis v. Bandemer,* 478 U.S. 109 (1986).

4. Samuel Kernell, ed., *James Madison: The Theory and Practice of Republican Government* (Stanford, CA: Stanford University Press, 2003), 5.

5. Richard F. Fenno Jr., *Congressional Travels* (New York: Pearson Longman, 2007).

6. Sue Thomas, *How Women Legislate* (New York: Oxford University Press, 1994).

7. Edmund Burke, *Speeches at His Arrival at Bristol,* November, 3, 1774, http://books.google.com.

8. Ibid.

9. Diana Evans, *Greasing the Wheels: Using Pork Barrel Projects to Build Majority Coalitions in Congress* (New York: Cambridge University Press, 2004).

10. Bret Schulte, "A Bridge (Way) Too Far," *U.S. News and World Report,* 139:5, August 8, 2005, p. 26.

11. www.cagw.org/reporting/pig-book.

12. See, for example, Bruce Cain, John Ferejohn, and Morris Fiorina, *The Personal Vote: Constituency Service and Electoral Independence* (Cambridge, MA: Harvard University Press, 1987).

13. Walter J. Oleszek, *Congressional Procedures and the Policy Process,* 7th ed. (Washington, DC: CQ Press, 2007).

14. See Janet M. Martin, *Lessons from the Hill: The Legislative Journey of an Education Program* (New York: St. Martin's, 1994).

15. Gary Cox and Mathew D. McCubbins, *Setting the Agenda* (Cambridge: Cambridge University Press, 2004).

16. Woodrow Wilson, *Constitutional Government in the United States* (New York: Columbia University Press, 1911), 87.

17. David Butler and Bruce Cain, *Congressional Redistricting: Comparative and Theoretical Perspectives* (New York: Macmillan, 1992).

18. Christopher J. Deering and Steven S. Smith, *Committees in Congress,* 3rd ed. (Washington, DC: Congressional Quarterly, 1997).

19. Garrison Nelson, *Committees in the U.S. Congress, 1947–1992,* 2 vols. (Washington, DC: CQ Press, 1993).

20. Steven S. Smith, Jason M. Roberts, and Ryan J. VanderWielen, *The American Congress,* 5th ed. (New York: Cambridge University Press, 2007).

21. Lawrence C. Dodd and Bruce I. Oppenheimer, *Congress Reconsidered,* 8th ed. (Washington, DC: CQ Press, 2004).

22. https://twitter.com/realDonaldTrump/status/908640949605163010?.

23. www.youtube.com/watch?time_continue=4&v=6NjDrnCWW84.

24. Sarah H. Binder, *Minority Rights, Majority Rule: Partisanship and the Development of Congress* (New York: Cambridge University Press, 1997).

25. David W. Brady and Mathew D. McCubbins, *Party, Process, and Political Change in Congress: New Perspectives on the History of Congress* (Stanford, CA: Stanford University Press, 2002).

26. Gary W. Cox, *Legislative Leviathan: Party Government in the House* (Berkeley: University of California Press, 1993).

27. Joseph Martin Hernon, *Profiles in Character: Hubris and Heroism in the U.S. Senate, 1789–1990* (Armonk, NY: M. E. Sharpe, 1997).

28. Ronald M. Peters Jr., *The American Speakership: The Office in Historical Perspective,* 2nd ed. (Baltimore: Johns Hopkins University Press, 1997).

29. Mike DeBonis, "Paul Ryan Elected House Speaker," *The Washington Post,* October 29, 2015.

30. Susan Webb Hammond, *Congressional Caucuses in National Policy Making* (Baltimore: Johns Hopkins University Press, 2001).

31. Barbara Sinclair, *Majority Leadership in the US House and the Transformation of the US Senate* (Baltimore: Johns Hopkins University Press, 1990).

32. www.cnn.com/2018/03/20/politics/mitch-mcconnell-mueller-defense-schumer/index.html.

33. Barry C. Burden, *Personal Roots of Representation* (Princeton, NJ: Princeton University Press, 2007).

34. Sean Theriault, "Party Polarization in Congress" (paper presented at the annual meeting of the American Political Science Association, Washington, DC, September 1, 2005).

35. Michael J. Malbin, *Unelected Representatives: Congressional Staff and the Future of Representative Government* (New York: Basic Books, 1980).

36. Burdett A. Loomis, *The Contemporary Congress,* 3rd ed. (Boston: Bedford/St. Martin's, 2000).

37. John R. Wright, *Interest Groups and Congress* (New York: Allyn and Bacon, 1996).

38. www.dispatch.com/news/20170202/for-legislators-now-pressures-on-to-meet-constituents.

39. R. Douglas Arnold, *The Logic of Congressional Action* (New Haven, CT: Yale University Press, 1990).

40. For a discussion of the potential goals of demographic representation, see, for example, David T. Canon, "Representing Racial and Ethnic Minorities," in *The Legislative Branch,* eds. Paul J. Quirk and Sarah A. Binder (New York: Oxford University Press, 2005).

CHAPTER 13
The Presidency

©Jeff J Mitchell/Getty Images

THEN

Presidential power grew over the centuries to "imperial" proportions and then ebbed in the late 20th century in the wake of scandals.

NOW

A controversial president exercises presidential power in new and unprecedented ways.

NEXT

Will President Trump unify a divided American electorate?

Will future presidents take a page from the Trump presidency and use technology in an unfettered and unfiltered manner?

Has President Trump forever changed the presidency, or will it revert to the traditional institution it once was?

President Donald Trump's

most ardent supporters and his most vocal critics agree on very little, but both groups agree that he has transformed the office of the presidency in an unprecedented fashion. During his tenure, President Trump has learned that each presidency is shaped not only by the person who holds the office but also by the support of constituencies within the public, congressional approval of presidential policy priorities, and the societal context of the day. Each presidential term can be molded and manipulated in many ways, with the result that one president may appear strong, and the next, weak—or a president may be both effective and ineffectual during the course of just one term. In looking at the roles presidents play in conducting their office, as well as the sources of their power, we consider in this chapter why some presidents are more effective than others.

The presidency is constantly evolving. The institution of the presidency that Donald Trump has is not the one that George Washington left behind. In the discussion that follows, we examine the development of the presidency to gain historical perspective on how the individuals who have served as president have changed the nature of the institution over time and what the impacts of those changes are for presidents today.

The presidency has changed in part because of the way this institution—which for many Americans embodies their government—has evolved.[1] We consider that even within this most "imperial" of the American institutions of government, the people play a vital part in determining not only who serves as president but also how effective and successful the president is in exercising the executive power.[2]

Presidential Elections

The relationship between Americans and their president begins well before a president takes the oath of office. In presidential election years, nonstop campaigning provides ample opportunities for the public to learn about candidates and their positions on issues, as we could see during the 2016 campaign, which offered nearly thirty debates between candidates in the primaries alone, plus nearly nonstop coverage of the Trump and Clinton campaigns. Campaigns are opportunities for voters to familiarize themselves with the policy stances and personal traits of candidates. Campaigns also present many avenues for participation by the people—for example, by volunteering in or contributing to candidates' campaigns or even just by debating candidates' views around the water cooler or on Facebook. Although these opportunities for citizen engagement are especially abundant during a presidential election year, similar chances to get involved arise well before, because potential candidates typically position themselves years in advance of Election Day to secure their party's nomination and to win the general election.

Should We Abolish the Electoral College?

The Issue: In the world's oldest democracy, the idea that the president of the United States might not be the choice of the majority of the voting population is a distinct reality. Such was the case in the 2016 presidential election: The candidate with the most popular votes, Democrat Hillary Clinton, lost the presidential election to her opponent, Republican Donald J. Trump. According to the Federal Election Commission's official election results, Clinton won the popular vote 65,853,516 to Trump's 62,984,825.* In every other election for federal office, the candidate with the most popular votes wins that seat. But instead of the direct election of the president, the Constitution requires that the president be elected by the Electoral College. Essentially, the winner is determined by the cumulative results of 51 separate elections, one conducted in each state plus the District of Columbia, with the number of electoral votes determined in proportion to the size of the state's congressional delegation. Is the Electoral College system unfair? Should we abolish it?

Yes: The Electoral College is exclusive and undemocratic. The Electoral College system demands that candidates focus nearly exclusively on key swing states that will be pivotal to their election and on populous states that carry the most electoral votes. The system is undemocratic because of its reliance on plurality elections within the states. In a plurality, the candidate with the most votes wins, even if that candidate does not receive a majority of the votes. The ultimate victory in both the 2000 and 2016 presidential elections by the candidates whom the most people did not prefer (George W. Bush and Donald Trump) highlights the undemocratic nature of the Electoral College. The Electoral College should be abolished.

No: The constitutionally mandated Electoral College system provides a crucial check on what would otherwise be the unchecked will of the people. In structuring the Electoral College as they did, the Constitution's framers devised a way of representing the views of both the *people* who elect the electors and the *states* because of the state-based nature of the elections. Other checks on the will of the people include staggered senatorial elections (in which one-third of that body is elected every two years) and appointed Supreme Court justices, and these are evidence of the framers' view that the will of the people needed to be tempered. If the Electoral College were abolished, the most populous geographical regions would dominate in presidential elections. Urban areas would have tremendous clout in presidential elections, and less densely populated rural areas would be virtually ignored. The current structure strengthens the power of the states and in this way ensures that our federal system remains strong.

Other Approaches: Because of the difficulty of abolishing the Electoral College, various schemes have been proposed that would make it almost impossible for the loser of the popular vote to win the presidency, including awarding a state's electoral votes proportionally instead of on a winner-take-all basis, dividing electoral votes by congressional district (currently done in Maine and Nebraska), and awarding extra electoral votes to the winner of the popular vote. Legislation recently passed in Maryland, Hawaii, Illinois, and New Jersey would commit those states' electors to vote for the winner of the popular vote if states representing a 270-vote majority in the Electoral College enact similar legislation.

What do you think?

1. Do you think that the Electoral College should be abolished, should remain the same, or should be reformed? Why? If your answer is "should be reformed," what changes would you implement?

2. If the Electoral College were abolished, what impact would the change likely have on voters in your home state? Does that scenario influence your view?

3. Americans revere the Constitution as a near-sacred document. Typically, citizens are reluctant to advocate amending the "supreme law of the land." What is your view concerning amending the Constitution?

*https://transition.fec.gov/pubrec/fe2016/2016presgeresults.pdf.

As discussed in Chapter 8, citizens in each state who vote in their party's primary election choose the delegates to the national conventions, where the parties' nominees are officially chosen (see "Thinking Critically"). After the nominees have been decided, typically by late August, they and their vice presidential running mates begin their general election campaign. Usually, the parties' choice of nominee is a foregone conclusion by the time of the convention. The votes tallied on Election Day determine which presidential candidate's slate of electors will cast their ballots, in accordance with state law. There are 538 electors in the Electoral College because the number of electors is based on the number of members of Congress—435 in the House of Representatives, 100 in the Senate— plus 3 electors who represent the people of the District of Columbia, though these elected officials are not the actual electors (see "Thinking Critically"). A presidential candidate today needs a simple majority of electoral votes (270) to win the presidency. On the Monday following the second Wednesday of December, the slate of electors chosen in each state meets in their respective state capitals and casts their electoral votes. The results are then announced in a joint session of Congress in early January. In most presidential elections, however, the winner is known on election night because analysts tabulate the outcome in each state and predict the electoral vote. The winner takes the oath of office as president in inaugural ceremonies on January 20.

Presidential Roles and Responsibilities

Newly elected presidents quickly discover that they need to perform a variety of functions each day. Many of these are closely related to the president's constitutionally ascribed duties,[3] including the role of commander in chief of the U.S. armed forces, and others relate to the president's role as chief diplomat. Other roles reflect the growth of the presidency in modern times,[4] whether it was Donald Trump's desire to bring industrial jobs back to the United States, Barack Obama's desire to overhaul health care, George W. Bush's priority of reforming schools, or all presidents' need to keep the economy sound and growing. Presidents also must conduct the "politics" of the job: they must interact with Congress and serve as the leader of their party.[5]

Chief of State

The president's role as chief of state reflects the chief executive's embodiment of the values and ideals of the nation, both within the United States and abroad. The function of chief of state is similar to the ceremonial role played by the constitutional monarch in parliamentary systems such as Great Britain's. In the United States, the role of symbolic leader of the nation enhances the president's image and authority and promotes national unity. We may experience this sense that we are one indivisible nation when, for example, the president, as chief of state, makes a formal state visit to another nation, or hosts Olympic medalists at the White House.

The President's Role in Congressional Agenda Setting

Although the separation of powers precludes the president from actually creating laws, presidents nonetheless have significant legislative power.[6] Presidents can influence Congress by lobbying its members to support or oppose pending legislation and by defining the congressional agenda in the annual presidential State of the Union message, a constitutionally required address to Congress. Presidents also "legislate" when they submit the budget for the entire federal government to Congress annually, although Congress ultimately passes the spending plan.

Today, one of the most important legislative tools at a president's disposal is the authority either to sign legislation into law or to veto it,[7] as described in Chapter 2. Although a veto allows the president to check the power of Congress, it also provides Congress with the opportunity to check presidential power by overriding the veto with a two-thirds majority vote.[8] In giving the president the right to veto laws, the Constitution essentially integrates the executive into the legislative process.[9]

There are several variations on the veto. During a regular legislative session, if the president does not sign or veto a bill within 10 days after receiving it from Congress, the bill becomes law even without the president's consent. But if the president receives a congressional bill to sign and Congress is scheduled to adjourn within 10 days, the president can exercise a pocket veto, in which the bill is vetoed if the president takes no action at all.

Figure 13.1 shows that the use of the veto varies widely from president to president. Modern presidents are generally much more likely to veto legislation than their predecessors were. A primary determinant of whether a president will regularly exercise veto power is whether the president's party has a majority in Congress. For example, President Trump has not vetoed any measures passed by the Republican-controlled Congress. When Democrats had control of Congress during President Obama's administration, he issued only two vetoes, neither of which was controversial. But after Republicans took control of Congress in 2014, Obama went on to veto 10 additional measures, including a controversial one, the Keystone XL pipeline bill, that would have allowed construction of an oil pipeline running from Alberta, Canada, to Steele City, Nebraska, where it would join an existing pipe. Obama vetoed another measure that would have repealed his own health care act.

An exception to this trend was the presidency of Franklin D. Roosevelt. As Figure 13.1 shows, during his 12-year term in the White House, Roosevelt issued 372 vetoes, or 12 percent of all presidential vetoes. Roosevelt chalked up this exceptional record despite having strong Democratic majorities in Congress throughout his tenure. But Roosevelt used the veto much differently than most presidents do. Because he was such a strong president, he exercised his veto power to prevent the passage of even small pieces of legislation with which he disagreed. Most presidents save the veto for important legislative matters, because they are unwilling to offend members of Congress over smaller laws that they do not favor.

But presidents today use a different tactic—the signing statement—to influence how policies are to be administered during their tenure in office. A presidential **signing statement** is a written message that the president issues upon signing a bill into law. A presidential signing statement may, for example, direct executive departments in how they should implement a law, taking into account constitutional or political considerations. Controversy arose during the administration of George W. Bush over the perception that, by using the tool widely, he was modifying the intent of the laws by asserting unconstitutional legislative authority.[10] Nonetheless, the use of signing statements was continued by President Obama, who actually increased his use of signing statements in the wake of the 2012 presidential election. Indeed, during almost every year of Obama's presidency, Congress included a provision in the nation's Defense Authorization Act that sought to ban the transfer of detainees in Guantánamo Bay, Cuba—which at one time held more than 800 individuals the United States identified as potential terrorists—to the United States. President Obama had vowed to close the facility early in his administration, but faced significant resistance in Congress and among

signing statement
A written message that the president issues upon signing a bill into law.

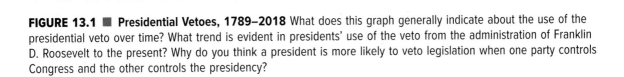

FIGURE 13.1 ■ Presidential Vetoes, 1789–2018 What does this graph generally indicate about the use of the presidential veto over time? What trend is evident in presidents' use of the veto from the administration of Franklin D. Roosevelt to the present? Why do you think a president is more likely to veto legislation when one party controls Congress and the other controls the presidency?

the public, which led to the inclusion of the bans in the bills. Each year, Obama signed the defense measure, but issued a signing statement objecting to Congress's attempts to constrict his efforts to close the facility, saying, "Any attempt to deprive the executive branch of that tool undermines our Nation's counterterrorism efforts and has the potential to harm our national security."[11]

Manager of the Economy

Although the Constitution makes no mention of presidential responsibilities with respect to the economy, we can see the enormous power presidents have in this regard by examining priorities of the Trump administration. Consider, for example, the far-reaching implications of President Trump's decision to impose tariffs, or import taxes, on several raw and manufactured goods, including solar panels, washing machines, aluminum, and steel coming from China, in an effort to recover American jobs that had been lost because lower-priced imports were available. Reaction to the tariffs was mixed, with many Republicans and most economists criticizing the move and charging that it would lead to higher prices and a potential trade war. Some Democrats were supportive of the tariffs, hoping they would restore some jobs. But whatever the outcome, the strong influence of the president on the nation's economy is apparent.

This influence could also be seen in the 2018–2019 federal budget process, during which President Trump and his administration lobbied for and won key changes to the U.S. tax code. Supporters note that most Americans will pay less in taxes for the five years following the budget cycle, but critics point out the serious increase in the national debt and the negative consequences that could have on the national economy (see Chapter 16 for further discussion of economic policy). By submitting a budget to Congress President Trump, like all presidents before him, affects where federal tax dollars are spent and thereby sets the economic priorities of the legislative agenda. Presidents also help to establish the regulatory and economic environment in which businesses must operate, and in that way they can influence economic growth and employment levels.

Central in presidents' oversight of economic performance is the appointment of the Federal Reserve Board ("the Fed") and its chair, who play a crucial role in managing the economy. The position of Fed chair tends to be less partisan than many other appointments, and a given chair often serves under presidents of both political parties. In 2018, President Trump surprised many by choosing not to renominate Janet Yellin, who President Obama had appointed as Fed chair, as presidents often renominate chairs from previous administrations if the economy is growing. But Trump chose Jerome Powell, a member of the Fed since Obama nominated him in 2012, to be the new chair. Powell enjoys a reputation as a bipartisan consensus builder, as he convinced some Republicans in Congress not to follow through on promises to default on the federal debt if GOP policies were not adopted, pointing out the deleterious impact such a move would have on the economy.

The appointment of a Fed chair has a lot to do with consumer confidence, as well as with support from economically influential individuals on Wall Street, including investment bankers, stockbrokers, and mortgage lenders. The fact that a Fed action (such as increasing the interest rate that banks charge one another for loans, which affects other interest rates charged to private individuals and businesses) can send the stock market plummeting sheds light on why presidential appointments to the Fed are watched so closely.

>One way presidents try to affect the nation's economy is through the appointment of the Fed chair, who oversees the Federal Reserve Board,—a body that plays a crucial role in managing the economy. In 2017, President Trump replaced Obama appointee Janet Yellin and appointed Jerome Powell as chair of the Federal Reserve. The move surprised some because Yellin had overseen a period of economic growth and job creation. During his confirmation, Powell pledged to continue many of the same monetary policies, including incremental interest-rate increases as the economy continues to improve.

©Chip Somodevilla/Getty Images

Chief Diplomat

Serving in the capacity of chief diplomat, the president (along with advisers) shapes and administers the nation's foreign policy. Supported by a wide array of foreign policy resources, including the State Department, the National Security Council, the Central Intelligence Agency, and the various branches of the U.S. military, the president creates and administers foreign policy. In setting foreign policy, the president can act more unilaterally than with most domestic policies. Members of Congress, who, in reflection of their constituents' main interests, tend to be concerned primarily with domestic policy issues, are much less likely to challenge presidents in the foreign policy arena.

As chief diplomat, the president, in conjunction with his or her staff, negotiates treaties and other international agreements with foreign nations and represents the United States at international summits. The president also has the authority to enter into an **executive agreement,** a kind of international agreement. Executive agreements are based on the constitutional authority vested in the president, and, unlike treaties, they may not be binding on future presidents nor do they require Senate approval.

The Constitution also empowers the president to appoint ambassadors to other nations. As high-ranking diplomats, ambassadors are the official representatives of the United States in their host nation. Ambassadors' duties vary widely, depending on the locale of their appointment. Some ambassadors play an influential, highly visible role in carrying out U.S. foreign policy, but others remain in the background.

The president, acting in the role of chief diplomat, is the leader of the diplomatic corps. In the capacity of chief diplomat, the president also hosts state dinners at the White House and formally receives the ambassadors of other nations.

As commander in chief, the president is the supreme military commander of the U.S. Army, Navy, Air Force, Marines, and Coast Guard. Counseled by advisers, the president decides when to send troops into battle (although only Congress can formally declare war) and sets military strategy in times of both peace and war.[12]

Today, serving as commander in chief of the military is, perhaps, among the most onerous responsibilities of the president. In earlier eras, the president's actions as commander in chief often would be accompanied by a congressional declaration of war, so that both branches bore the responsibility of sending troops into harm's way. Today, however, the rapid-fire nature of many conflicts means that presidents often make unilateral decisions to send "boots on the ground." And so, for example, when faced with evidence in 2018 that Syrian President Bashar al-Assad had used chemical weapons in that country's civil war against civilians in the rebel-held town of Douma, it was President Trump who unilaterally ordered retaliatory air strikes targeting three suspected chemical weapons development or storage sites being used by the al-Assad government.

executive agreement
An international agreement between the United States and other nations, not subject to Senate approval and in effect only during the administration of the president who negotiates the agreement.

>Serving as commander in chief is one of the most onerous responsibilities, as modern presidents are forced to act unilaterally when quick military action is needed. Both President Trump and President Obama used airstrikes against Syrian targets as a flexible tactic in response to foreign policy challenges there.
©Halil el-Abdullah/Anadolu Agency/Getty Images

Party Leader

One of the most important domestic roles for the president is political: the function of party leader. Such a role is sometimes difficult, particularly given the fractured nature of both political parties. But President Trump assumed the role of party leader and he has succeeded in attracting candidates who embrace his agenda and message. While President Trump is popular in some areas of the country, in other areas Republican members of the House and Senate face constituencies who have low opinions of the president, and so sometimes attempt to distance themselves from him. Many in the Republican party establishment were at odds with Donald Trump during his campaign, leading to concern about his ability to lead the party that he had vocally criticized, and whose members had often criticized him. But Trump has seized control of the GOP, effectively silencing—at least temporarily—many of his critics within the Republican party. As chief of one of the two main parties, the president is a symbolic leader for the party members and asserts influence in the party's operations by selecting the national party chair and serving as the party's premier fund-raiser. The presidential function of party leader has become even more significant in recent White House administrations, with presidents working ever more aggressively to promote the reelection of candidates from their party by ensuring that enough money is available for their campaigns.

The president also acts as party head in the day-to-day operations of the executive branch, because many of the staff appointments to the White House Office, cabinet, subcabinet, ambassadorships, and judiciary typically come from party ranks. Finally, at the end of a president's term, the president likely campaigns on behalf of the party's new presidential nominee.

Chief Executive

As the nation's leader in domestic and foreign policy initiatives, the president serves as chief executive. In this capacity, the president appoints the *secretaries* (top administrators) of the cabinet—the 15 departments of the federal government—as well as the heads of other federal government agencies charged with developing and implementing the administration's policy. As chief executive, the president also appoints other staff members and numerous advisers, including staff in the Executive Office of the President. In the capacity of chief executive, the president determines how the bureaucracy will implement the laws Congress has passed and which policies—those concerning education, crime, social welfare, and so on—will be emphasized.[13]

The President and the Executive Branch

As chief executive, the president is constitutionally charged with ensuring that the "laws be faithfully executed." Today, this responsibility means that the president oversees a bureaucracy of more than four million government employees, including the members of the military, while presiding over an astonishing annual federal budget of nearly *$4 trillion*. In addition, as we now consider, the president is the leader of the executive branch of government, which includes the vice president, the cabinet, the offices within the White House, and the entire federal bureaucracy.

The Vice President's Role

John Nance Garner, Franklin D. Roosevelt's vice president from 1933 to 1941, vulgarly commented that "the vice presidency isn't worth a pitcher of warm piss."[14] This insider's observation on the vice presidential office matches the perceptions of many Americans fairly well. But although the media and the public tend to ignore the vice presidency and to marginalize the responsibilities of the second-in-command, vice presidents have an enormously important function. They are first in the line of succession to the presidency if the president should die or become incapacitated. Only eight presidents have died while in office, and although presidential succession may not be the foremost consideration in selecting a running mate for many presidential candidates, it can be an issue. Bill Clinton, in describing his selection of Tennessee Senator Al Gore as his running mate, explained that his choice of Gore in part reflected Clinton's belief that Gore would make a good president "if something happened to me."[15]

THE VICE PRESIDENT'S JOB   Many vice presidents serve a largely ceremonial function, performing such activities as attending state dinners, visiting foreign nations, and attending the funerals of foreign dignitaries. But vice presidents may have more substantive responsibilities, depending on their skills and the needs of the administration. Sometimes, for example, a vice president acts as legislative liaison with Congress, particularly if the vice president has more experience in dealing with the legislative branch than the president. For example, before being elected governor of Indiana, Vice President Mike Pence served a dozen years in Congress, including a stint as chair of the House Republican Conference, where he forged deep relationships with fellow Republicans, and these relationships have benefited the Trump administration. In other instances, vice presidents' policy expertise is a crucial resource for the administration. In the case of Vice President Dick Cheney, experience in foreign policy and national security determined the pivotal role he played in developing the foreign policy of George W. Bush's administration.

Although vice presidents are only "a heartbeat away" from the presidency, their own election to the presidency (should they decide to run) is not ensured when their term as second-in-command has ended. It is true that several vice presidents—among them, George H. W. Bush and Lyndon B. Johnson—have won election to the presidency in their own right; but many other former vice presidents have failed.[16] Notably, Al Gore, Walter Mondale, and Gerald Ford (the vice presidents of Bill Clinton, Jimmy Carter, and Richard Nixon, respectively) all went down to defeat at the polls in their bids for the White House.

balanced ticket
The selection of a running mate who brings diversity of ideology, geographic region, age, gender, race, or ethnicity to the slate.

CHOOSING A VICE PRESIDENT   In selecting a vice presidential running mate, traditionally, presidential candidates weigh several considerations. Would-be presidents strive for a **balanced ticket;** that is, to broaden their appeal to the electorate and increase their chances of getting elected, they select a running mate who brings diversity of ideology, geographic region, age, gender, race, or ethnicity to the slate. Such was the case in 2016, when Republican presidential nominee Donald Trump chose Indiana Governor Mike Pence as his running mate; many party supporters were heartened with Trump's choice of an experienced, conservative politician who could balance Trump's lack of political experience. Similarly, as a candidate vying for the presidency against Senator John McCain of Arizona, an older and respected member of the U.S. Senate, Barack Obama chose Senator Joe Biden of Delaware, who was thought to complement Obama in terms of age (Biden was 65 years old, compared with Obama's 47); experience (Biden had served in the Senate since 1972, Obama

>When presidential nominees select a running mate, they often strive to increase their own chances of being elected to the presidency and of being able to govern effectively after taking office. In 2016, Donald Trump chose Indiana Governor Mike Pence, an experienced, conservative politician as his potential vice president.
©Chip Somodevilla/Getty Images

FIGURE 13.2 ■ **The Departments of the President's Cabinet** The presidential cabinet consists of the heads of the 15 departments shown in the figure. Which department is concerned with finding alternatives to the use of fossil fuels? Which one addresses the problems of the dedicated service men and women who served in Afghanistan and Iraq? Which department arose as a result of the September 11, 2001, terrorist strikes?

Source (Line 1): United States Department of Justice; United States Department of Agriculture; United States Department of Commerce; United States Department of Defense; United States Department of Education, Line 2: United States Department of Energy; United States Department of Health and Human Services; ©Win McNamee/Getty Images; ©Nicholas Kamm/AFP/Getty Images, Line 3: United States Department of the Interior; United States Department of Labor; United States Department of Transportation; United States Department of Treasury; United States Trade Representative.

since 2000); and expertise (Biden was chair of the Senate Foreign Relations Committee, Obama had faced media criticism about his lack of foreign policy experience).

The Cabinet

cabinet

The group of experts chosen by the president to serve as advisers on running the country.

Since George Washington's presidency, every president has depended on the advice of a **cabinet,** the group of experts chosen by the president to serve as advisers on running the country. These advisers serve as the heads of each of the executive departments. Figure 13.2 shows the 15 departments of the cabinet and their respective websites. Each cabinet member except the head of the Department of Justice is called the *secretary* of that department. The head of the Department of Justice is called the attorney general.

President George W. Bush created the newest department, the Department of Homeland Security, in 2002. This department is charged with increasing the nation's preparedness, particularly with respect to catastrophic events such as terrorist attacks and natural disasters. George Washington's cabinet consisted of the heads of only four departments—justice, state, treasury, and war. (The last is now called the Department of Defense.) Subsequent presidents added other departments.

Each president may also designate cabinet rank to other advisers whose agencies are not permanent cabinet departments. Typically, presidents have specified that their national security adviser, director of the Office of Management and Budget, and administrator of the Environmental Protection Agency be included in their administration's cabinet. In addition to these advisers, President Trump has included the Small Business Administrator in his cabinet.

Today, presidents and the public typically scrutinize presidential cabinet appointments to determine whether, in the words of Bill Clinton, they "look like America." As the data in Table 13.1 confirm, this is a relatively new gauge, since only three women and two members of ethnic minority groups had served in presidential cabinets until the Carter administration. Although President Trump's cabinet is less diverse than those of recent presidents, before his tenure, presidential

TABLE 13.1 Women and Minoritles Appointed to Presidential Cabinets

PRESIDENT	NUMBER OF WOMEN* CABINET MEMBERS	NUMBER OF MINORITY** CABINET MEMBERS	TENURE
Trump	6	4	2017–
Obama	14	15	2009–2017
G. W. Bush	7	10	2001–2009
Clinton	13	11	1993–2001
G. H. W. Bush	4	3	1989–1993
Reagan	4	2	1981–1989
Carter	4	1	1977–1981
Ford	1	1	1974–1977
Nixon	0	0	1969–1974
Johnson	0	1	1963–1969
Kennedy	0	0	1961–1963
Eisenhower	1	0	1953–1961
Truman	0	0	1945–1953
F. Roosevelt	1	0	1933–1945

*Includes cabinet and cabinet-level appointments.

**Includes African Americans, Latinos/as, and Asian Americans.

SOURCES: Brigid C. Harrison, *Women in American Politics: An Introduction* (Belmont, CA: Wadsworth Publishing, 2003); the Center for the American Woman and Politics, National Information Bank on Women in Public Office, Eagleton Institute of Politics, Rutgers University.

>The tenure of President Trump's second White House Chief of Staff Gen. John Kelly has been a controversial one. Many outsiders speculated that Kelly would bring stability and moderation to the West Wing and were surprised at some of his hard-line stances on policy issues. But over the course of his tenure, it seems that Kelly's influence has dwindled.

©Michael Candelori/Shutterstock

cabinets were becoming increasingly diverse, with significant strides made during President Bill Clinton's administration.[17] Clinton became the first president to appoint a woman to any of the "big four" posts when he named Janet Reno attorney general and Madeleine Albright secretary of state. George W. Bush named Colin Powell the first black secretary of state, and when Powell resigned, Bush replaced him with Condoleezza Rice, an African American woman who had served previously as national security adviser.

The Obama administration continued the trend of increasing diversity. During his two terms, President Obama appointed 14 female cabinet members, including several to "big four" posts: Hillary Clinton served as secretary of state during his first term, and Loretta Lynch served as attorney general during his second. Obama also appointed a record number of racial and ethnic minorities to cabinet posts. President Trump's cabinet has been less diverse than his immediate predecessors': Secretary of Housing and Urban Development Benjamin S. Carson Sr. is the only African American, and Secretary of Labor Alexander Acosta is the only Hispanic; Secretary of Transportation Elaine L. Chao is Asian American, and former Representative of the United States to the United Nations Nikki R. Haley is Indian American. Chao and Haley are joined by three other women in the Trump cabinet: Secretary of Education Betsy DeVos, Secretary of Homeland Security Kirstjen Nielsen, and Central Intelligence Agency Director Gina Haspel.

The Executive Office of the President

Whereas the cabinet usually functions as an advisory board for the president, the **Executive Office of the President (EOP)** typically is the launchpad for the implementation of policy. The offices, councils, and boards that compose the EOP help the president to carry out the day-to-day responsibilities of the presidency and similarly assist the first lady and the vice president in their official activities. The EOP also coordinates policies among different agencies and departments.

Among the EOP offices, several are particularly important, including the White House Office, the National Security Council, the Office of Management and Budget, and the Council of Economic Advisers. These offices are crucial not only because of the prominent issues with which they deal but also because of their strong role in developing and implementing policy in these issue areas.[18]

THE WHITE HOUSE OFFICE Playing a pivotal role in most presidential administrations, **White House Office (WHO)** staff members develop policies favored by the presidential administration and protect the president's legal and political interests. They research policy and keep the president informed about policy issues on the horizon. WHO staffers also regularly interact with members of Congress, their primary goal being to get presidential policy priorities enacted into law. They strive to ensure that those policies, once passed into law, are administered in keeping with the president's expectations.

Executive Office of the President (EOP)
The offices, counsels, and boards that help the president to carry out his day-to-day responsibilities.

White House Office (WHO)
The office that develops policies and protects the president's legal and political interests.

Because of the enormous influence of staff members in the White House Office, presidents take pains to ensure their loyalty and trustworthiness, a task that has proven difficult in President Trump's White House Office, which has faced criticism because of an unusually high level of turnover in key positions. Among the top staff members of the White House Office is the **chief of staff,** who serves as both an adviser to the president and the manager of the WHO. Other staff members with clout include the **press secretary,** the president's spokesperson to the media, and the **White House counsel,** the president's lawyer. The president's secretary and appointments secretary are also influential WHO employees; they act as gatekeepers by controlling access to the president by other staffers and by members of Congress and the cabinet.

NATIONAL SECURITY COUNCIL   The president consults members of the **National Security Council (NSC)** on domestic and foreign matters related to national security. Since its creation in 1947 during the Truman administration,[19] the NSC has advised presidents on key national security and foreign policy decisions and assisted in the implementation of those decisions by coordinating policy administration among different agencies. For example, once the president has decided on a specific policy, the NSC might coordinate its implementation among the Department of State, the Central Intelligence Agency, various branches of the military, and diplomatic officials.

The president officially chairs the National Security Council. Its other regular members include the vice president, the secretary of defense, the secretary of state, the secretary of the treasury, and the assistant to the president for national security affairs, often called the **National Security Advisor,** who is responsible for administering the day-to-day operations of the NSC and its staff. Other administration officials serve the NSC in advisory capacities or are invited to meetings when matters concerning their area of expertise are being decided.

Within the Trump administration, the position of National Security Advisor has been both a powerful position and one fraught with controversy. President Trump's first National Security Advisor, Michael T. Flynn, resigned after revelations that he had misled administration officials, including Vice President Mike Pence, about conversations he had with the Russian ambassador to the United States. Flynn was replaced with Lt. Gen. H. R. McMaster, who had led troops in Afghanistan and Iraq. It was hoped that McMaster would bring stability to the administration's foreign policy, but McMaster resigned after a year, never having developed a strong bond with President Trump. In March 2018, McMaster was replaced by John Bolton, a former U.S. Ambassador to the United Nations, known for taking hard-line stances in international disputes.

OFFICE OF MANAGEMENT AND BUDGET   Once part of the Department of the Treasury, the **Office of Management and Budget (OMB**—originally called the Bureau of the Budget) has been a separate office within the EOP since 1939. Its chief responsibility is to create the president's annual budget, which the president submits to Congress each January. The budget outlines all of the anticipated revenue that the government will receive in the next year, usually from taxes and fees paid by businesses and individuals. The budget also lists the anticipated expenditures for the coming year, detailing how much money the various departments and agencies in the federal government will have available to spend on salaries, administrative costs, and programs. The OMB is among the president's most important agencies for policy making and policy implementation.

chief of staff
Among the most important staff members of the White House Office (WHO); serves as both an adviser to the president and the manager of the WHO.

press secretary
The president's spokesperson to the media.

White House counsel
The president's lawyer.

National Security Council (NSC)
Consisting of top foreign policy advisers and relevant cabinet officials, this is an arm of the Executive Office of the President that the president consults on matters of foreign policy and national security.

National Security Advisor
The assistant to the president for national security affairs, adviser to the president on national security policy, and administrator over the day-to-day operations of the National Security Council.

Office of Management and Budget (OMB)
The office that creates the president's annual budget.

The director of the Office of Management and Budget (OMB), a presidential appointee confirmed by the Senate, has a staff of about six hundred career civil servants. In recent decades, the OMB director has figured prominently in presidential administrations and typically has been designated a member of the cabinet. The director's job is complex. He or she interacts intensively with Congress, trying to ensure that the budget that passes resembles the president's proposed budget as closely as possible. The director also lobbies members of Congress with the goal of ensuring that the key provisions of the budget that are important to the president remain intact in the congressionally approved version.

Once Congress approves the budget, the director of the OMB turns attention to its implementation, since it is the job of the OMB staff to manage the budget's execution by federal departments and agencies—to ensure that monies are spent on their designated purposes and that fraud and financial abuse do not occur. This managerial responsibility of the OMB was the reasoning behind the change in the office's name (from the Bureau of the Budget) in 1970.

Presidential Succession

No examination of the executive branch would be complete without considering the question, What happens if the president dies? Presidential succession is determined by the Presidential Succession Law of 1947. But sometimes incapacitation other than death prevents presidents from fulfilling their duties. In such cases, the Twenty-Fifth Amendment, ratified in 1967, determines the course of action.

When the President Dies in Office

When the president dies, the course of action is clear in most cases: The vice president assumes the presidency. Such was the situation when Harry S. Truman became president upon Franklin D. Roosevelt's death from natural causes in 1945 and when Lyndon B. Johnson was sworn in as president after the assassination of John F. Kennedy in 1963. Vice presidents sometimes fill the unexpired term of their president for reasons other than the president's death, as when Gerald Ford acceded to the presidency upon the resignation of Richard Nixon after the Watergate scandal.

The Presidential Succession Law of 1947 determines presidential succession if the vice president also dies or is unable to govern. Table 13.2 shows that after the vice president, the next in line for the presidency is the Speaker of the House of Representatives, then the president pro tem of the Senate, followed by a specified order of the members of the cabinet. Notice that as new cabinet departments have been established, their secretaries have been added to the bottom of the line of succession. As a precaution, at the State of the Union address each year, one cabinet member is chosen not to attend the president's speech

>When a president dies in office, the line of presidential succession is clear. Crowds watched the funeral procession for President Franklin D. Roosevelt, who died in office in 1945 and was succeeded by his vice president, Harry S. Truman (1945–1953).

©George Skadding/Time Life Pictures/Getty Images

before Congress but, rather, to stay behind at the White House. This measure ensures that if a catastrophe should occur in Congress during the address, someone in the line of succession will be able to assume the duties of the president.

When the President Cannot Serve: The Twenty-Fifth Amendment

What happens when a president is alive but unable to carry out the responsibilities of the office? Until the ratification of the Twenty-Fifth Amendment in 1967, the course of action was not clear. Such was the case in 1881, when an assassin shot President James Garfield, and Garfield lived two and a half months before succumbing to his injuries. In another such instance, President Woodrow Wilson was so ill during his last months in office that he was incapacitated. First Lady Edith Wilson assumed some of his responsibilities and decision making. Questions about presidential health also arose toward the end of Franklin D. Roosevelt's tenure; and during Dwight D. Eisenhower's administration, the president authorized Vice President Richard Nixon to determine whether Eisenhower, who was battling a series of illnesses, was competent to govern. President John F. Kennedy, who suffered from a host of physical ailments, including severe, chronic back pain and Addison's disease, similarly empowered Vice President Lyndon B. Johnson: in an informal agreement, the men arranged that if Kennedy was physically unable to communicate with Johnson, Johnson was authorized to assume the presidency.

After Kennedy's assassination, the ratification of the Twenty-Fifth Amendment (1967) finally put codified procedures in place for dealing with an incapacitated president. According to the Twenty-Fifth Amendment, if a president believes he or she is unable to carry out the duties of the office, the president must notify Congress, and the vice president becomes the acting president until the president can resume authority. The amendment would apply in the case when a president is anesthetized for surgery, for example, or perhaps recuperating from a debilitating illness.

In other situations, a president might be incapable of carrying out the duties of office and incapable of notifying Congress. In such a case, the Twenty-Fifth Amendment requires that the vice president and a majority of the cabinet notify Congress, and the vice president becomes the acting president. If a question arises as to whether the president is fit to reassume the duties of office, a two-thirds vote of Congress is required for the acting president to remain.

TABLE 13.2 The Line of Presidential Succession

1. Vice president
2. Speaker of the House of Representatives
3. President pro tem of the Senate
4. Secretary of state
5. Secretary of the treasury
6. Secretary of defense
7. Attorney general
8. Secretary of the interior
9. Secretary of agriculture
10. Secretary of commerce
11. Secretary of labor
12. Secretary of health and human services
13. Secretary of housing and urban development
14. Secretary of transportation
15. Secretary of energy
16. Secretary of education
17. Secretary of veterans affairs
18. Secretary of homeland security

Sources of Presidential Power

The presidency that Donald Trump assumed on January 20, 2017, scarcely resembled George Washington's presidency in the 1790s. From the late 18th century to today, the powers of the president have evolved, reflecting the expansion of the federal government, changes in public attitudes about the proper role of government, and the personalities and will of those who have served as president.

In describing the powers that would guide presidents for centuries to come, the framers of the Constitution created a unique office. These visionary authors had lived through a repressive era in which an authoritarian monarch had exercised absolute power. They subsequently had witnessed the new American nation's struggles under the ineffectual Articles of Confederation, in which the federal government had too little power and the states too much. Thus the framers sought to establish an office that would balance the exercise of authority with the preservation of the rights and the will of the people.

Given their colonial experience, it was no surprise that the framers granted the presidents both *expressed powers* and *inherent powers* in the Constitution. Congress grants presidents additional powers, called *statutory powers,* through congressional action. We consider these various powers in this section.

Additional presidential powers have emerged over time. These newer authorities reflect both changes in the institution of the presidency and shifts in popular views on the appropriate role of government and the president. These powers include emergency powers granted in Supreme Court decisions and powers that, though not formalized, are given to presidents by the public through election mandates, presidential popularity, or unified public opinion on a particular issue or course of action.

The Constitution: Expressed Powers

expressed powers
Presidential powers enumerated in the Constitution.

The primary source of presidential power comes from the Constitution in the form of the **expressed powers,** which are those enumerated in the Constitution. Article II, Sections 2 and 3, list the following powers of the president:

- Serve as commander in chief of the armed forces.
- Appoint heads of the executive departments, ambassadors, Supreme Court justices, people to fill vacancies that occur during the recess of the Senate, and other positions.
- Pardon crimes, except in cases of impeachment.
- Enter into treaties, with two-thirds consent of the Senate.
- Give the State of the Union address to Congress.
- Convene the Congress.
- Receive ambassadors of other nations.
- Commission all officers of the United States.

The expressed powers outlined in the Constitution provide a framework for presidential responsibilities and an outline of presidential power. They also shape how presidents themselves develop their authority.

The Constitution: Inherent Powers

take care clause
The constitutional basis for inherent powers, which states that the president "shall take Care that the Laws be faithfully executed."

inherent powers
Presidential powers that are implied in the Constitution.

One of the principal ways by which the Constitution provides for presidents themselves to assert additional powers, beyond those expressed in the Constitution, is the **take care clause,** which states that "the executive Power shall be vested in a President of the United States of America" and that the president "shall take Care that the Laws be faithfully executed." On the basis of that clause, presidents throughout U.S. history have asserted various **inherent powers,** which are powers that are not expressly granted by the Constitution but are inferred.

President Thomas Jefferson exercised inherent powers in his far-reaching Louisiana Purchase in 1803. Jefferson authorized this $15 million purchase of

800,000 square miles of land, even though the Constitution did not authorize any such action on the part of a president. Interestingly, in the civic discourse over the Constitution, Jefferson, an Anti-Federalist, had argued for states' rights and against a strong central government and a powerful presidency. Jefferson had believed that the powers enumerated in the Constitution defined the powers of the government. But Jefferson thought that the purchase of the Louisiana Territory was of crucial strategic and economic importance. He believed that the deal was key to the United States averting war with France and to securing the port of New Orleans, which was essential for the new American republic's fortunes in trade. Jefferson could not wait for a constitutional amendment to authorize the transaction, and so he forged ahead with the purchase. Congress and many Americans of the day agreed with his actions, and so there were no negative consequences to them.

President Franklin D. Roosevelt also drew on the inherent powers when he expanded the size of the federal government in the 1930s to administer his New Deal programs, designed to relieve the economic and human distress of the Great Depression. Beginning in 2002, President George W. Bush used the inherent powers when he suspended the civil liberties of foreign nationals being held in a military prison at the U.S. naval base at Guantánamo Bay, Cuba, as part of the administration's war on terror. The individuals at Guantánamo Bay have been detained indefinitely for questioning about their possible terrorist activities. These instances of presidents' exercise of inherent powers generated varying degrees of controversy among Americans of the times.

More recently, President Obama exercised his inherent powers by again expanding the scope of the federal government through passage of the Patient Protection and Affordable Care Act of 2010, also known as Obamacare. This health care reform act, which was approved by the Democrat-controlled Congress at President Obama's behest, expands Medicaid, subsidizes health insurance premiums for middle-income families, offers incentives for employers to provide health care to their employees, and mandates that uninsured individuals purchase government-approved health insurance. The measure, which has been vehemently opposed by many Republicans in Congress since its passage, marked the entrance of the federal government into previously uncharted territory.

Statutory Powers

The Constitution's expressed and inherent powers provided a foundation for presidential power that has evolved over time. Those powers have been supplemented by additional powers, including **statutory powers,** which are explicitly granted to presidents by congressional action.

statutory powers
Powers explicitly granted to presidents by congressional action.

An example of such a grant of statutory powers is the 1996 Line Item Veto Act, which gave the president the power to strike down specific line items on an appropriations bill while allowing the rest of the bill to become law. In 1997 the Supreme Court declared the line-item veto unconstitutional on the grounds that the congressional action violated the separation of powers.

Special Presidential Powers

Presidents also have special powers that have evolved from various sources, including the Constitution and Supreme Court decisions. These powers, which numerous presidents have exercised, have come to be regarded as accepted powers and privileges of the presidency. They include *executive orders, emergency powers,* and *executive privilege.*

THEN NOW NEXT

Evolution of the Modern Presidency

Then (1970s)	Now
The presidency had become an increasingly powerful institution, shaped by the predecessors of Richard Nixon, who assumed office in 1969.	President Trump relies on unprecedentedly bold tactics to act as a unilateral actor.
The presidency supplanted Congress as the epicenter of power in the federal government.	Presidential exercise of authority in the foreign policy realm serves to limit Congress's ability to rein in presidential power.
Backlash against abuses of executive power in the Nixon administration paved the way for the election of Jimmy Carter, a comparatively weak president.	While Democrats decry President Trump's uses of executive power, even members of his own party sometimes object to his actions.

WHAT'S NEXT?

> Will a parallel backlash against President Trump's exercise of authority occur, like the one seen in the post-Nixon era?

> What public policy issues will likely dominate in the months and years to come? How will these issues influence the ways presidential power is exercised?

> What conditions facilitate the creation of "imperial" presidencies? Do these conditions exist now?

executive order
The power of the president to issue orders that carry the force of law.

emergency powers
Broad powers exercised by the president during times of national crisis.

EXECUTIVE ORDERS The president has the power to issue **executive orders** that have the force of law. Executive orders carry the same weight as congressional statutes and have been used in a variety of circumstances to guide the executive branch's administrative functions.[20] Executive orders have very few limitations and stipulations, though one limitation is that presidents cannot use them to create new taxes or appropriate funds, because the Constitution reserves those powers for Congress. In general, executive orders:

- Direct the enforcement of congressional statutes or Supreme Court rulings.
- Enforce specific provisions of the Constitution.
- Guide the administration of treaties with foreign governments.
- Create or change the regulatory guidelines or practices of an executive department or agency.

Executive orders can be an important strategic tool, because they convey the president's priorities to the bureaucracy that implements the laws. For example, in 1948 President Harry Truman signed Executive Order 9981, which states, "It is hereby declared to be the policy of the President that there shall be equality of treatment and opportunity for all persons in the armed services without regard to race, color, religion, or national origin."[21] This executive order effectively banned segregation in the U.S. military. Why would Truman issue an executive order instead of working for congressional passage of a statute that would desegregate the military? Many analysts think that Truman, who ardently believed that the military should be desegregated, not only doubted that Congress would pass such a measure but also faced pressure from early civil rights activists who had pledged an African American boycott of military service if the military was not desegregated.

EMERGENCY POWERS Broad powers that a president exercises during times of national crisis have been invoked by presidents since Abraham Lincoln's claim to **emergency powers** during the Civil War. Lincoln used emergency powers during the war to suspend the civil liberties of alleged agitators, to draft state militia units into national service, and to federalize the governance of southern states after the war.

In 1936, the U.S. Supreme Court acknowledged the existence of presidential emergency powers in *United States v. Curtiss-Wright Export Corp.*[22] In this case, the U.S. government charged the Curtiss-Wright Corporation with conspiring to sell 15 machine guns to Bolivia, in violation of a joint resolution of Congress and a presidential proclamation. Without congressional approval, President Franklin D. Roosevelt had ordered an embargo on the machine-gun shipment. The Court supported Roosevelt's order, ruling that the president's powers, particularly in foreign affairs, are not limited to those powers expressly stated in the Constitution. The justices also stated that the federal government is the primary actor in foreign affairs and that the president in particular has inherent powers related to the constitutionally derived duties in foreign relations.

EXECUTIVE PRIVILEGE Presidents also can exercise **executive privilege,** the authority of the president and other executive officials to refuse to disclose information concerning confidential conversations or national security to Congress or the courts. In invoking executive privilege, presidents draw on the idea that the Constitution's framework of separation of powers justifies the withholding of certain information from Congress or the judiciary,[23] a claim initially asserted when George Washington refused to grant Congress access to all documents pertaining to treaty negotiations. Typically, presidents claim executive privilege so that they can get advice from aides without fear that such conversations might be made public or scrutinized by members of Congress or the judiciary. Presidents also have invoked executive privilege when negotiating foreign policies with other heads of state, to shield these leaders from having sensitive negotiations examined by the other branches of the federal government.

On occasion, the judicial branch of the federal government has successfully challenged executive privilege. For example, when President Richard Nixon refused to turn over tapes of Oval Office conversations to a special prosecutor investigating the Watergate scandal in 1974, the Supreme Court intervened. In *United States v. Richard M. Nixon,* the Court asserted that although executive privilege does exist, it was not applicable regarding the tapes because President Nixon's claim of executive privilege concerning the tapes was too broad.[24]

In general, the courts have allowed executive privilege in cases where a clear issue of separation of powers exists—as with respect to international negotiations and conversations regarding matters of policy or national security. The courts have tended to limit the use of executive privilege when presidents have exercised it in an effort to prevent the revelation of misdeeds by members of the executive branch. During the Monica Lewinsky scandal, when Bill Clinton evoked executive privilege to prevent White House aides from testifying before special prosecutor Kenneth Starr, the courts ruled that executive privilege did not apply, and his aides were compelled to testify. (Clinton was accused of having extramarital relations with Lewinsky, a White House intern.) President Trump also has threatened to evoke executive privilege to keep current and former aides from answering questions as part of an inquiry being conducted by special council Robert Mueller concerning meddling by Russia in the 2016 presidential election.

executive privilege
The right of the chief executive and members of the administration to withhold information from Congress or the courts, or the right to refuse to appear before legislative or judicial bodies.

The People as a Source of Presidential Power

One of the most important sources of presidential power today comes from the people. Although one president generally will have the same formal powers as the next, presidents' ability to wield their power, to control the political agenda, and to get things done typically is a function of political skill, charisma, and what political scientist Richard Neustadt has called "the power to persuade."[25]

The President and the Bully Pulpit

Modern presidents work to persuade the public on a virtually continuous basis. They know that if they win popular support for their views and political agenda, they will have an easier time getting their policy priorities through Congress. In their efforts to persuade the people, they exploit the power of their office, using the presidency as a forum from which to speak out on any matter—and to have their views listened to. This ready access to the public ear and broad power of the president to communicate led President Theodore Roosevelt to exclaim, "I have got such a bully pulpit!"[26]

In using their bully pulpit, presidents seek to communicate that their stances on important issues are the right choices and that their actions, particularly controversial decisions, should be supported. Presidents also strive to persuade the public that they are doing a good job on key policy fronts such as economic and foreign policy. Sometimes presidents seek to mobilize the public to take specific actions or to adopt certain beliefs. For example, although President Trump has faced stern criticism (from both his supporters and detractors), his mastery of Twitter, the modern bully pulpit, illustrates his ability not only to inform the public, but also to single-handedly determine the national agenda, often steering media coverage toward one issue or another simply through a 140-character message (which often ends in exclamation points)!!!

The reason why presidents work so tirelessly to win public support for their agenda is that they understand that getting Congress to act on policy priorities, to approve budgets, and to pass favored legislation depends heavily on the perception that the public supports presidential initiatives. Indeed, political scientist Richard Neustadt argues that the modern institution of the presidency is weak and that presidents in fact must rely on public and congressional support in order to enact their agendas.[27] Getting Congress to do what the president wants is more difficult when a president faces divided government, the situation in which the president belongs to one political party and Congress is controlled by a majority of members of the other party, or when the president must deal with a truncated government, in which the president and one house of Congress are controlled by one party, but the other house of Congress is controlled by the other.

But beyond partisan differences, presidents' ability to get things done in Congress also is a function of their popularity with the people. A popular president can use that clout to persuade members of Congress that favored positions are the right ones; an unpopular president, or one distracted by issues not related to policy, will face greater obstacles in getting Congress's cooperation to enact the preferred legislative agenda.

The President and Public Approval

When presidents are sworn in to office, they are typically met with a time of hope and optimism on the part of the public who elected them. The advantage of this **honeymoon period,** a time early in a new president's administration characterized by optimistic approval by the public, varies in strength from president to president (see "Analyzing the Sources"). But during this time a president's **approval rating,**

honeymoon period
A time early in a new president's administration characterized by optimistic approval by the public.

approval ratings
The percentage of survey respondents who say that they "approve" or "strongly approve" of the way the president is doing his job.

PRESIDENTIAL JOB APPROVAL

Measuring presidential job approval is relatively simple: pollsters ask survey respondents whether they approve or disapprove of the job the president is doing. But these ratings are a powerful indicator of how the public views the president and how much they support the president's agenda. Presidential approval ratings are also an indicator of power in and of themselves—that is, Congress will be reluctant to defy an extremely popular president, while they may perceive little harm in resisting an unpopular president's priorities or agenda.

Practice Analytical Thinking

1. Which presidents enjoyed the highest approval ratings? When did these high ratings occur? What prompted the American people to be so supportive of these presidents in those times?

2. In general, in looking at the approval trend of modern presidents, how do two-term presidents differ in their overall approval trend from one-term presidents?

3. How does President Trump's approval rating compare with President Obama's? With President George W. Bush's?

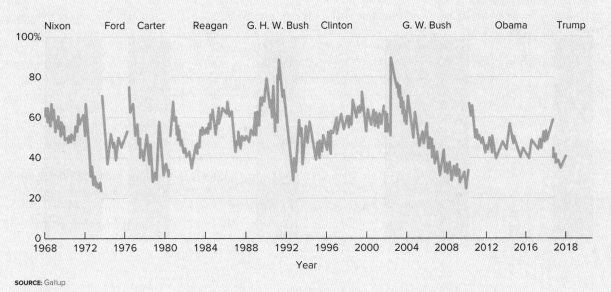

SOURCE: Gallup

the percentage of survey respondents who say they "approve" or "strongly approve" of the way the president is doing the job, is above 55 percent.

While some presidents, on average, are more popular than others, the approval ratings for many presidents varies a great deal during their terms in office. Take, for example, President George W. Bush: after the September 11, 2001, terrorist attacks and President Bush's rapid and dignified response to them, Bush enjoyed record high approval ratings. Immediately after September 11, President Bush's approval ratings hovered in the high 80s, occasionally reaching 90 percent, meaning that 90 percent of those surveyed indicated that they approved of the way the president was handling his job. (In contrast, the average presidential approval rating since the Franklin D. Roosevelt administration was 56 percent.) During this time, Bush had enormous legislative successes. These included the passage of the USA PATRIOT Act of 2001, which gave law enforcement officers greater authority in handling suspected terrorist acts, and the congressional declaration of a "war on terror." When Bush's popularity subsequently waned because of the people's dissatisfaction with the rate of progress in the war in Iraq, the high number of casualties in the war, and continued weakness in the American economy, so, too, did support decrease for the continuation of the war, the president's economic policies, and a proposed extension of the USA PATRIOT Act.

While President Obama's approval ratings did not show the same enormous variations, we can see that he enjoyed a strong and sustained honeymoon period, followed by a gradual decline in approval, with an uptick during his reelection campaign in 2012.

In general, presidential approval ratings reveal that some presidents are simply more popular than others. For example, Presidents Ronald Reagan and Bill Clinton tended to enjoy high approval ratings, with President Clinton's second-term ratings running particularly high, especially in light of the Monica Lewinsky scandal and the subsequent impeachment proceedings against him. When the United States engages in a short-term military action or is the subject of an attack by terrorists, we see similar peaks in approval ratings, sometimes referred to as the **rally 'round the flag effect.** A president rarely sustains high public approval continuously. Once achieved, however, high ratings help the chief executive succeed by demonstrating the people's support of the presidential agenda.[28]

Scratching beneath the surface, however, it is apparent that while high approval ratings can bolster presidential power, lower approval ratings can sometimes signal something other than universally low regard. Take, for example, President Trump's approval rating. During the first year of his presidency, Trump earned a national approval rating of 38 percent. But as shown in Figure 13.3, that rating varied greatly from state to state. For example, only 26 percent of Vermonters approved of the president's job performance, but 61 percent of West Virginians did. All in all, President Trump received approval ratings above 50 percent in 12 states, while he received ratings below 40 percent in 18 states. These figures demonstrate the polarized nature of opinion of President Trump but also are demonstrative of his efforts to build and maintain support in certain areas of the country, particularly areas where he received strong support for his 2016 presidential bid.

Technology and the Media as Tools of Presidential Influence

Just as President Trump has transformed the presidency by using social media to convey his priorities and views to the American people, so too have his predecessors embraced technological innovation as a means of wielding influence. In the 1930s, Franklin D. Roosevelt changed the relationship between the president and his constituents by using radio to communicate directly with the American people. President Kennedy would replicate this transformation using the medium of television in the 1960s (see Chapter 11 for further discussion of the president's use of technology).

For every president, technology and the media can be used as a tool of influence as the expertise of the White House communications office can "spin" news in a favorable light for the administration. In particular, the White House can manage direct communication using new technologies by releasing videos on the president's Facebook page or YouTube channel, or by holding "office hours" on

rally 'round the flag effect
The peaks in presidential approval ratings during short-term military action.

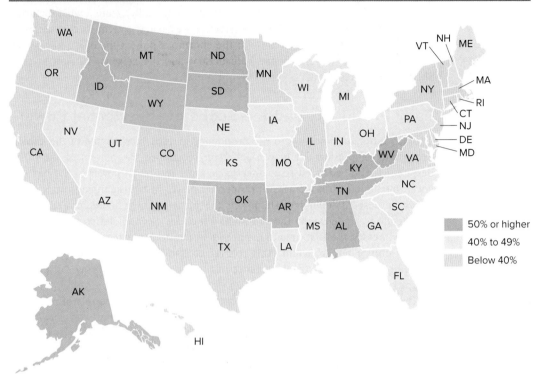

FIGURE 13.3 ■ **Approval of President Donald Trump Varies from State to State** Geographically, where is President Trump the most popular? The least popular? Assess President Trump's popularity in the states with the largest populations.

SOURCE: Gallup

Twitter. Relying on traditional media, the communication director forges relationships with the most prominent media outlets by providing access, exclusive interviews, and scoops on breaking stories to reporters considered friendly to the administration.

Although the nature of presidential press conferences and other media forums has evolved over time, the mass media have served as a key avenue by which modern presidents have communicated directly to the population at large. Because the nature of the president's relationship with his constituency is constantly evolving, so, too, is presidential power.

The Evolution of Presidential Power

Although the constitutional powers of the presidency have changed little over time, the power of the presidency has evolved a great deal.[29] This development stems in part from some presidents' skillful use of powers not granted by the Constitution, such as the powers to persuade and to assert more authority. But the political environment within which presidents have governed has also contributed to the evolution of presidential power.[30]

The history of the early republic saw an incremental expansion of the power of the presidency, whereas the Great Depression of the 1930s and the election of

Franklin D. Roosevelt in 1932 spawned an enormous growth in presidential authority.[31] As successor presidents inherited the large bureaucracy that Roosevelt built, presidential powers have expanded further—gradually creating what historian Arthur Schlesinger Jr. has called the **imperial presidency,** a term used to describe some modern presidencies because of the enormous powers the office has gained through assertion, the size of the bureaucracy, and the presence of staff loyal to an individual president.

imperial presidency
A term coined by Arthur Schlesinger Jr. to describe the modern executive branch and the enormous powers the office has gained through assertion, the size of the bureaucracy, and the presence of staff loyal to an individual president.

Early Presidents and the Scope of Presidential Power

Thomas Jefferson's election to the presidency in 1801 marked one of the earliest expansions of presidential power. Jefferson broadened the powers of the office despite his Anti-Federalist reluctance to delegate too much power to the national government. Jefferson increased presidential power in two significant ways. First, as we have seen, Jefferson established the principle of inherent powers of the presidency by undertaking the Louisiana Purchase. Second, Jefferson's tenure in office witnessed the first time that a president had to act as party leader. Jefferson had no choice but to assume this role: If he had not, he would not have been elected president, given the dominance of the Federalist Party during this era (see Chapter 8).

Twenty-five years later, Andrew Jackson would also adopt the role of president-as-party-leader, but he would add a new twist. Jackson's emphasis on *populism,* a political philosophy that emphasizes the needs of the common person, spawned a new source of presidential power, because Jackson was the first president to derive real and significant power from the people. Whereas earlier politics had mostly emphasized the needs of the elite, Jackson's populism mobilized the masses of common people who traditionally had not been civically engaged. This populism augmented the power of the presidency by increasing the popularity of the president and investing the president with power that came from the people's goodwill.

In the 20th century, the nature and scope of presidential power changed as a consequence of the prevailing political environment. One of the most extraordinary shifts in the nature of the presidency occurred during Franklin D. Roosevelt's administration, which lasted from 1932 until his death in 1945. (Roosevelt was elected to an unprecedented four terms; the Twenty-Second Amendment to the Constitution, which allows only two elected presidential terms, was ratified six years after his death.)

Having come to power during the Great Depression, Roosevelt engineered a significant change in the function of the federal government. He called for a New Deal for the American people, a series of social welfare programs that would provide employment for many of the nation's unemployed workers. Roosevelt's New Deal was based on the ideas of economist John Maynard Keynes, who argued for temporary deficit spending by the government (that is, going into debt) to spur the economy during economic downturns.

Roosevelt's primary weapon in his New Deal arsenal was the **Works Progress Administration (WPA),** a federal government program that employed 8.5 million people at a cost of more than $11 million between 1935 and 1943. The idea was that government-funded employment would create economic growth in the private sector because those employed by the government would have the money to buy goods and services, thus creating spiraling demand. The rising demand for goods and services would mean that the private sector could then employ more people, and the cycle of recovery and growth would continue. For example, if during the

Works Progress Administration (WPA)
A New Deal program that employed 8.5 million people at a cost of more than $11 million between 1935 and 1943.

1930s the government employed your great-great-grandfather to work on a road-building project in his town, he might have put his paycheck toward buying more bread and other baked goods than he previously could have afforded. If enough people in town could have similarly patronized the bakery, then the baker might have had to hire an assistant to keep up with demand, and consequently the assistant would have had money to spend on, say, new shoes for his children. In that way, the increased demand for products and services would continue, creating additional economic growth.

Roosevelt's New Deal was important to the presidency for two reasons. First, it dramatically changed people's views of the role of the federal government. Many people now tend to think of the federal government as the provider of a "safety net" that protects the most vulnerable citizens—a safeguard that did not exist before the New Deal, when those needing assistance had to rely on the help of family, friends, churches, and private charities. Second, this popular perception and the programs that emerged—the WPA, unemployment insurance, Social Security—meant that the federal government would have to grow larger in order to administer these programs. As a result, the president's role as chief executive of a large federal bureaucracy would become much more important to modern presidents than it had been to those who served before Roosevelt.[32]

> William Frazee, the chief of the presses for the *Washington Post*, makes the victory sign after learning of the Supreme Court's decision allowing newspapers to publish the *Pentagon Papers*. Applause broke out in the press room as the first print run began rolling.
©Bettmann/Getty Images

The Watershed 1970s: The *Pentagon Papers*, Watergate, and the "Imperial Presidency"

Americans' penchant for strong presidents modeled after Roosevelt diminished drastically in the 1970s. In 1971, Daniel Ellsberg, a Defense Department employee, leaked a classified, top-secret 7,000-page history of the nation's involvement in and thinking on Vietnam dating from the Truman administration in 1945 to the Nixon administration then in the White House. Called the *Pentagon Papers,* the work first appeared as a series of articles in *The New York Times.* When the Nixon administration in 1971 successfully petitioned the Department of Justice to prevent the publication of the remainder of the articles, the *Washington Post* assumed publication of them. When the Department of Justice sued the *Post,* the *Boston Globe* resumed their publication. Two weeks later, in an expedited appeals process, the U.S. Supreme Court ruled in *The New York Times Co. v. The United States* that the government "carries a heavy burden of showing justification for the imposition of such a restraint" and that the government had failed to meet that burden, thus allowing the continued publication of the papers.[33]

The *Pentagon Papers* tainted the public's view of the presidency. The published work revealed miscalculations by policymakers in presidential administrations from Truman's to Nixon's, as well as arrogance and deception on the part of policymakers, cabinet members, and presidents. Specifically, the *Pentagon Papers* revealed that the federal government had repeatedly lied about or misrepresented the fact of increasing U.S. military involvement in Southeast Asia. In particular, the analysis in the *Pentagon Papers* indicated not only that U.S. marines had conducted offensive military maneuvers well before the public was informed but also that the U.S. military had engaged in other actions, including air strikes over Laos and military raids throughout the North Vietnamese coastal regions. The Nixon administration's legal wrangling to prevent release of the *Pentagon Papers* cast a dark cloud over the public's perception of the presidency.

Cynicism about the presidency continued to grow in light of the **Watergate** scandal that took place a year later. In 1972, men affiliated with President Nixon's reelection campaign broke into the headquarters of the Democratic National Committee (located in the Watergate Hotel in Washington, D.C.) to retrieve wiretaps that they had previously installed to monitor their opponents. *Washington Post* reporters Bob Woodward and Carl Bernstein, in a groundbreaking series of stories, traced the burglaries and the subsequent cover-up to high-level officials in the Nixon administration. This crime and the Nixon administration's attempts at cover-ups became known as the Watergate scandal. A Senate investigation revealed that President Nixon had secretly taped conversations in the Oval Office that would shed light on "what the president knew [about the break-in] and when he knew it."[34] Nixon claimed executive privilege and refused to turn over the tapes to a special prosecutor who had been appointed to investigate the scandal. When the U.S. Supreme Court ruled in *United States v. Richard Nixon* that Nixon must provide the tapes to the special prosecutor, one key tape was found to have a gap of almost 20 minutes where someone, reportedly his secretary, Rosemary Woods, had erased part of the recording.

Meanwhile, all the Watergate burglars had pleaded guilty and been sentenced, and only one refused to name the superiors who had orchestrated the break-in. But the testimony of burglar James W. McCord Jr. linked the crime to the Committee to Re-Elect the President (CREEP), Nixon's campaign organization, and to high-ranking Nixon White House officials. The disclosure prompted John Dean, Nixon's White House counsel, to remark: "We have a cancer within, close to the presidency, that is growing."[35] With indictments handed down for many of Nixon's top aides, and with a Senate investigation and a special prosecutor's investigation in progress, the House Judiciary Committee took up the matter of impeachment. The committee handed down three articles of impeachment against Nixon—one for obstruction of justice, a second for abuse of power, and a third for contempt of Congress. When a newly released tape documented that Nixon had planned to block the investigations by having the Federal Bureau of Investigation and the Central Intelligence Agency falsely claim that matters of national security were involved, the tape was referred to as a "smoking gun."[36] Nixon lost the support of his few loyalists in Congress and, on August 8, 1974, announced that he would resign from office the following day.

Watergate might seem like a relatively insignificant event in the history of the American presidency, but the impact of the Watergate scandal on the presidency has been enormous. Watergate badly wounded the trust that many Americans held for their president and for their government. Combined with the unpopularity of the Vietnam War and the release of the *Pentagon Papers,* it created a deep cynicism that pervades many Americans' perception of their government even today— a pessimistic attitude that has passed from generation to generation.

Watergate also dramatically demonstrated how enormously the presidency had changed. Modern presidents had supplanted Congress as the center of federal power and in so doing had become too powerful. Historian Arthur Schlesinger Jr. and other presidential scholars have decried the problem of the growth of the executive branch and, in particular, the imperial "courts"—the rising number of Executive Office of the President staff members, many of whom are not subject to Senate confirmation and share a deep loyalty to the person who is president rather than to the institution of the presidency. In juxtaposition with an attitude like that expressed by Richard Nixon in his comment that "when the president does it, that means it is not illegal,"[37] the imperial presidency left much room for abuse.

The Post-Watergate Presidency

With the election of Jimmy Carter to the White House in 1976, many observers believed that the era of the imperial presidency had passed. Carter, the mild-mannered governor of Georgia and thus a Washington outsider, seemed to be the antidote the nation needed after the display of power-run-amok during Nixon's tenure. But given the significant challenges Carter faced during his term, many people believed that he did not exercise *enough* authority—that he acted weakly when faced with various crises. Ronald Reagan's election in 1980 in some ways represented a return to a more powerful, "imperial" presidency. Reagan, a former actor, was Hollywood swagger personified, speaking tough talk that many Americans found appealing. His administration was not unlike an imperial court, featuring a group of advisers with deep loyalties to Reagan. Although the era of unchecked presidential power was gone for good, many would argue that the George W. Bush administration was best at re-creating a form of an imperial presidency.

> On the basis of an investigation by special prosecutor Kenneth Starr, the House impeached President Bill Clinton in 1998 for committing perjury by lying to a grand jury about his relationship with White House intern Monica Lewinsky and for obstructing justice. The Senate voted to acquit Clinton on those perjury charges.
©APTN/AP Images

Bush was able to exercise strong authority because of the fear created both among the citizenry and in Congress after the September 11, 2001, terror attacks. And given President Bush's activist foreign policy, he exercised great authority in that realm, with Congress having little ability to check him. Ironically, many critics of the Bush administration would assert that he was assisted in creating a modern imperial presidency by many of the same staff members who were part of the Nixon administration. But administration supporters would note that a strong presidency was necessary at this critical juncture in the nation's history.

Many Democrats were frustrated by President Obama's comparative lack of assertiveness when exercising presidential power in the early years of his first term. Many analysts faulted his conciliatory, consensus-building nature as an impediment to exercising strong authority. These abilities, however, enabled the president to get the hallmark achievement of his administration passed: the Affordable Care Act of 2010. After the congressional elections later that year, which saw a Republican majority elected in the House, many viewed Obama's powers as dissipating. In particular, the Republican majority in the Senate served as a heavy check on the latter portion of his first term. After the government shutdown in 2013, President Obama seemed more willing to exert strong authority in exercising presidential duties, oftentimes while circumventing Congress. But in 2014, Republicans also won control of the U.S. Senate, and Obama faced even more roadblocks to his policy proposals and initiatives. The check provided by Republicans in the Congress thwarted any prospect of the Obama administration becoming an imperial one.

Impeachment: A Check on Abuses of Presidential Power

Although presidential powers are flexible and can be shaped by the individuals holding the office, these powers do not go unchecked. One crucial check on presidential power is **impeachment,** the power of the House of Representatives to

impeachment
The power of the House of Representatives to formally accuse the president (and other high-ranking officials, including the vice president and federal judges) of crimes.

articles of impeachment
Charges against the president during an impeachment.

formally accuse the president (and other high-ranking officials, including the vice president and federal judges) of crimes. The Constitution specifically refers to charges of "Treason, Bribery, or other high Crimes and Misdemeanors," an appropriately vague description of the potential offenses a president could commit. An impeachment can be thought of as an indictment: If a majority of the members of the House of Representatives vote to impeach the president, they forward the charges against the president, called the **articles of impeachment,** to the Senate. The Senate then tries the president and, in the event of conviction for the offenses, determines the penalty. In convicting a president, the Senate has the authority to punish the president by removing him from office.

Although the Senate can force a president to step down, it has never done so in practice, and only two presidents have been impeached by the House of Representatives. The first was Andrew Johnson, who succeeded Abraham Lincoln as president in 1865 upon the latter's assassination. When he assumed the presidency, Johnson faced not only a divided nation but also a government in turmoil. The 11 articles of impeachment against him had to do primarily with his removal of the secretary of war, Edwin Stanton, who was working with Johnson's congressional opponents to undermine Johnson's reconstruction policies in the South. The so-called Radical Republicans in the House believed that Johnson's policies were too moderate, and they sought to treat the Confederate states as conquered territories and to confiscate the land of slaveholders. Those same House members wanted to protect their ally Stanton and prevent him from being removed from office. The Senate ultimately recognized the politically motivated nature of the articles of impeachment against Johnson and acquitted him on all counts.

The most recent occurrence of the impeachment of a president was in 1998, when the House of Representatives approved two articles of impeachment against President Bill Clinton. On the basis of an investigation by a special prosecutor, the House impeached Clinton for lying to a grand jury about his relationship with White House intern Monica Lewinsky and for obstructing justice. The Senate acquitted Clinton on both counts.

During the Watergate scandal that rocked Richard Nixon's presidency, the House Judiciary Committee approved articles of impeachment against the president and sent them to the full House for a vote. Republican members of Congress convinced Nixon that the House would vote to impeach him and that the Senate would convict him and remove him from office. Faced with the inevitable, Nixon became the first president to resign from office before the House could vote to impeach him.

Women and the Presidency

Many believed that the 2016 election would result in a historic first: the election of Hillary Clinton as the first woman president of the United States. Clinton's candidacy was historic, but her failure to win represents a stark political reality concerning the difficulty of any woman to win the most powerful position in the world. Of the three branches of government, the executive branch has been the most challenging for women to enter as formal participants. Historically, part of that struggle has come because sizeble portions of Americans were unwilling to vote for a qualified woman for president, as shown in Figure 13.4. For example, in 1937, only 33 percent of Americans said they would cast their presidential ballot for a qualified woman, but that figure has risen steadily. By 1999, 92 percent of respondents said they would vote for a female presidential candidate. In 2005,

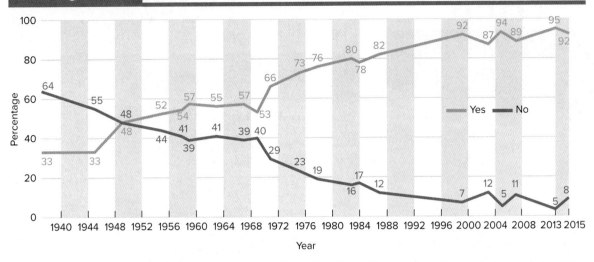

FIGURE 13.4 ■ **America's Willingness to Vote for a Woman President** What has been the trend since the late 1930s in the American electorate's willingness to vote for a woman president? What factors do you think explain this shift?

SOURCES: Roper Center for Public Opinion Research and Gallup

that number declined to 89 percent. One explanation for this drop could be that at the time of the poll, then-Senator Hillary Clinton was frequently mentioned as a likely 2008 presidential candidate and respondents unwilling to support her candidacy said they were unwilling to vote for a woman for president. By 2013, though, the number had risen again, and 95 percent of Americans said they were willing to vote for a woman for president. Again, in 2015, with the prospect of a Hillary Clinton candidacy emerging, there was a slight down-tick in the percentage, again presumably because some respondents viewed Clinton as that likely woman candidate. Nonetheless, while the trend is a positive one, it remains disconcerting that a statistically significant proportion of the American electorate would be unwilling to vote for a qualified woman for president.

The First Lady

Much like the presidency itself, the role of the president's spouse has been defined by the individuals who have occupied it. And today, Melania Trump, a modern mother who once worked as a model, is shaping the office to suit her own personality and her marriage. Historically, some first ladies have preferred to take a very hands-on approach when it comes to politics and policy while others stay out of the spotlight. That the American people typically accept both types of first spouses is evidence of the open-mindedness with which the American people view the role.

Some first ladies have used their proximity to the chief executive to influence policy concerns broadly and forcefully. Several have acted "behind the scenes," as was the case with Edith Wilson, the wife of Woodrow Wilson. Others have taken a more public role. Eleanor Roosevelt, the wife of Franklin D. Roosevelt, fought for many causes during her husband's administration, including human rights and civil rights for African Americans. Hillary Clinton transformed the office of first lady by serving, at her husband's appointment, as the chair of a presidential task

THEN

NOW

> Virginia "Bess" Truman, Edith Wilson, and Eleanor Roosevelt were modern first ladies of their era. Wilson assumed some presidential responsibilities and decision making while her husband, Woodrow, was ill. Truman was recognized as a strong campaign asset, and Roosevelt is widely regarded as being the first modern feminist first lady. Today, Melania Trump is a thoroughly modern First Lady. The role of First Lady is shaped enormously by the women who serve in that capacity.

Truman, Wilson, Roosevelt: ©Bettmann/Getty Images; Trump: ©Andrze J Hulimka/AFP/Getty Images

force on health care reform. Her role in the task force, and indeed throughout the Clinton administration, proved to be a lightning rod for critics who thought that a first lady should not be so prominent.

Laura Bush, Hillary Clinton's successor, by contrast was a more reserved and less public first lady, a persona that Michelle Obama seemed to emulate. Both shunned the policy-oriented role that Hillary Clinton had forged, though each had causes to which they drew attention. For Bush, that issue was reading and libraries (Bush was a schoolteacher and a librarian before serving as First Lady), while Obama prioritized the issue of childhood obesity, using her status to bring attention to the problem and to shape policy affecting it. By and large, though, Obama preferred to focus on raising the Obamas' daughters, Malia and Sasha, and on the more ceremonial aspect of serving as first lady.

Similar to Michelle Obama, Melania Trump has embraced a traditional interpretation of the role, shying away from the policy and politics some former First Ladies have pursued. Instead, she has participated in the ceremonial duties associated with the position, and has also focused on raising the Trumps' young son, Barron, who was just 10 years old when his father was elected president. Melania Trump has also prioritized the issue of cyber-bullying, advocating for more civility on the Internet, particularly directed at children.

Conclusion

Thinking Critically About What's Next in the Presidency

The American presidency is a dynamic institution, one that is molded by the individuals who serve and by the American people—by their changing interests, viewpoints, struggles, and needs. The presidency has a symbiotic relationship with the larger culture in which it exists; it is at once shaped by, and shapes, the culture.

The executive branch of the federal government is also flexible, incorporating the needs of diverse constituencies and participants, particularly in recent times. The continued evolution of the presidency as a more diverse institution is relatively ensured. How will this evolution take place in the next several decades?

The presidency is a product of both the design of the framers and the desires of the citizenry. As the country's need for stronger presidents has increased, the resources and authorities of presidents have grown to accommodate new powers. Since the activist administration of Franklin D. Roosevelt, the characterization of the presidency as an "imperial" institution has dogged numerous presidents, most recently former president George W. Bush. But divided government has meant that modern presidents are increasingly "checked" in their efforts to expand presidential authority by Congress.

Looking ahead, how will the citizens of the future view the scope of presidential power? The answer will depend in large part on the people themselves, particularly those who vote. It will depend on whom citizens elect to the highest office in the land; on how the people's opinions shape (or, in some cases, fail to shape) presidential actions; and on how the people's relationship with their presidents develops. Although the Constitution created a system in which presidential powers can be checked institutionally, the framers did not foresee the most significant checks on modern presidents: the will of the people and a ruthlessly investigatory media, both of which ensure that presidential power is not unrestrained.[38]

Learning Summary

1. Explain the process of presidential election.

2. Describe presidential roles and responsibilities.
    a. Explain the responsibilities associated with the position of chief of state.
    b. Describe the president's role in congressional agenda setting.
    c. Explain the tools available to the president as manager of the economy.
    d. Explain how the president acts as chief diplomat.
    e. Describe the political role of the president as party leader.
    f. Describe the role of the president as chief executive.

3. Describe the executive branch and how it helps the president create and implement policy.
    a. Describe the role of the vice president.
    b. Discuss the various cabinet departments and the roles they play in a president's administration.

c. Describe key offices in the Executive Office of the President.
  i. The White House Office.
  ii. The National Security Council.
  iii. The Office of Management and Budget.

4. Describe the process of presidential succession.
  a. Explain what happens when a president dies in office.
  b. Explain what happens when a president cannot serve.

5. Explain the sources of presidential power.
  a. Describe the expressed presidential powers coming from the Constitution.
  b. Explain inherent powers derived from the Constitution.
  c. Explain what a statutory power is.
  d. Describe special presidential powers.
    i. Explain executive orders.
    ii. Describe the president's emergency powers.
    iii. Explain executive privilege and how presidents have used it.

6. Describe the people as a source of presidential power.
  a. Define the bully pulpit, and explain how presidents use it.
  b. Describe presidential approval ratings as a source of presidential power.
  c. Explain how presidents use technology to increase their power.

7. Describe the evolution of presidential power.
  a. Explain the power of early presidents.
  b. Describe the imperial presidency.
  c. Evaluate the post-Watergate presidency.
  d. Explain how impeachment provides a check on abuses of presidential power.

8. Analyze the role of women in the White House, particularly the role of the First Lady.

Key Terms

approval ratings 446

articles of impeachment 454

balanced ticket 435

cabinet 436

chief of staff 439

emergency powers 444

executive agreement 433

Executive Office of the President (EOP) 438

executive order 444

executive privilege 445

expressed powers 442

honeymoon period 446

impeachment 454

imperial presidency 450

inherent powers 442

National Security Adviser 439

National Security Council (NSC) 439

Office of Management and Budget (OMB) 439

press secretary 439

rally 'round the flag effect 448

signing statement 430

statutory powers 443

take care clause 442

Watergate 452

White House counsel 439

White House Office (WHO) 438

Works Progress Administration (WPA) 450

For Review

1. Explain the process of presidential elections. What role do states play in the process?
2. List the various roles of the president, and provide an example of each.
3. What are the sources of presidential power?
4. How has presidential power evolved over time?
5. Explain the organization and the functions of the Executive Office of the President.
6. Discuss the role that women have played to date in the American presidency.

For Critical Thinking and Discussion

1. What do you think are the most important roles for presidents today? Why do these roles matter more than others?
2. Who do you think has been the greatest president in U.S. history? What characteristics do you admire about the president you chose?
3. What factors affect how frequently a president vetoes legislation? Does vetoing legislation signify presidential strength or weakness? Explain.
4. How did Watergate affect people's perception of the presidency and of government? Have there been lasting effects from this scandal? Explain.
5. What is your perception of the role of first spouse? Should that person take on a role in influencing policy decisions? Should the first spouse instead be relegated to more-ceremonial functions? If so, why?

Resources for Research AND Action

Internet Resources

270 to Win

www.270towin.com This interactive website demonstrates how the Electoral College outcome is determined; users can experiment with altering the results of elections. It also contains past voting information for all states.

Cabinet Websites

The websites of the cabinet departments listed in this chapter (Figure 13.2) each contain information about the cabinet members, their staffs, and the services each department provides.

Center for the Study of the Presidency

www.thepresidency.org This research center analyzes presidential leadership and offers seminars and symposia for presidential researchers, including the Center Fellows program for undergraduate students.

Presidential Libraries

You can find the websites of the libraries of recent presidents, which typically include a wealth of information about individual presidencies and archival resources, by searching "[President's name] Presidential Library."

The White House

www.whitehouse.gov You can visit the White House website for information about current issues and news, the text of presidential speeches, links to cabinet departments, the EOP, and information about the first lady and the vice president.

Recommended Readings

Borrelli, MaryAnne. *The President's Cabinet: Gender, Power, and Representation.* Boulder, CO: Lynne Rienner, 2002. Analysis of the evolution of presidential cabinets in terms of gender representation.

Clinton, Hillary Rodham. *What Happened.* New York: Simon and Schuster, 2017. In *Time* magazine's best book of the year, Clinton describes the unique experience of becoming the first woman nominated to the presidency by a major party in one of the most controversial and unpredictable presidential elections in history.

Comey, James. *A Higher Loyalty: Truth, Lies, and Leadership.* New York: Flatiron Books, 2018. Former FBI director Comey, who learned that he was fired by President Trump by television, shares his thoughts on leadership and an insider's view on Washington's inner-workings.

Ehrenhalt, Alan. *The United States of Ambition: Politicians, Power and the Pursuit of Office.* New York: Times Books, 1991. Interesting account of the importance of personal drive and ambition in catapulting would-be presidents to the White House.

Halberstam, David. *The Best and the Brightest.* New York: Fawcett Books, 1993. Riveting analysis of how the Kennedy and Johnson administrations entrenched the United States in the war in Vietnam.

Meacham, Jon. *The Soul of America: The Battle for Our Better Angels.* New York: Random House, 2018. This uplifting work by the Pulitzer Prize–winning Meacham looks back at troubled times in our nation's history and reminds us that hope has the power to overcome division and fear.

Milkis, Sidney M. *The American Presidency: Origins and Development, 1776–2011.* Washington, DC: CQ Press, 2011. This volume describes the constitutional foundations as well as the social, economic, political, and international factors that have shaped the Constitution's expansion through its origins to the Obama presidency.

Neustadt, Richard E. *Presidential Power and the Modern President.* New York: The Free Press, 1990. Update of the author's classic 1960 volumes, explaining the evolution of power in the modern presidency and probing, in particular, presidents' ability to persuade.

Schlesinger, Arthur M., Jr. *The Imperial Presidency.* Boston: Houghton Mifflin, 1973. Classic volume describing how the presidency has become a rarely checked, "imperial" institution (introduction updated in the 2004 edition).

Wolff, Michael. *Fire and Fury: Inside the Trump White House.* New York: Henry Holt and Company, 2018. A behind-the-scenes description of the tumult in the first nine months of one of the most controversial presidencies of our time.

Woodward, Bob, and Carl Bernstein. *All the President's Men,* 2nd ed. New York: Simon & Schuster, 1994. Classic work that launched investigative journalism, particularly concerning the presidency, in which the authors describe their investigation of the Watergate scandal that led to President Richard Nixon's resignation.

Movies of Interest

Mark Felt: The Man Who Brought Down the White House (2017) Liam Neeson stars as Mark Felt (also known as "Deep Throat"), the anonymous source who helped journalists Bob Woodward and Carl Bernstein uncover the Watergate scandal in 1972.

Southside with You (2016) This film tells the story of an afternoon in summer 1989 when the future president of the United States, Barack Obama, wooed his future First Lady, Michelle Obama, on a first date across Chicago's South Side.

Lincoln (2012)

Daniel Day-Lewis stars in the title role in a film depicting the later days of Lincoln's presidency as he seeks to end the Civil War and secure ratification of the Thirteenth Amendment, which abolished slavery.

John Adams (2008)

This television mini-series stars Paul Giamatti and Stephen Dillane in a chronicle of the first 50 years of the U.S. presidency.

Recount (2008)

This movie chronicles the 2000 presidential election, focusing on the controversy surrounding ballot counting in Florida that culminated in the U.S. Supreme Court case *Bush v. Gore*.

Air Force One (1997)

In this suspense thriller, the president of the United States, played by Harrison Ford, is forced to do battle with terrorist hijackers aboard Air Force One.

The American President (1995)

Rob Reiner directed this comedic drama about an unmarried male president (portrayed by Michael Douglas) and a lobbyist (Annette Bening), who fall in love.

All the President's Men (1976)

In this 1976 film adaptation of the book by the same name, Robert Redford and Dustin Hoffman star as *Washington Post* reporters Bob Woodward and Carl Bernstein (respectively), who uncover the details of the Watergate scandal that led to President Nixon's resignation.

In addition, there are numerous biographical movies of American presidents, including many that air on the A&E network's *Biography* series. You can find these programs at www.biography.com.

References

1. George C. Edwards III, John H. Kessel, and Bert A. Rockman, eds., *Researching the Presidency: Vital Questions, New Approaches* (Pittsburgh, PA: University of Pittsburgh Press, 1993).

2. Theodore J. Lowi, *The Personal President* (Ithaca, NY: Cornell University Press, 1985).

3. George C. Edwards III and Steven J. Wayne, *Studying the Presidency* (Knoxville: University of Tennessee Press, 1983).

4. Jean Reith Schroedel, *Congress, the President, and Policymaking: A Historical Analysis* (Armonk, NY: M. E. Sharpe, 1994).

5. William W. Lammers, *The Presidency and Domestic Policy: Comparing Leadership Styles, FDR to Clinton* (Washington, DC: CQ Press, 2000).

6. Andrew Rudalevige, *Managing the President's Program: Presidential Leadership and Legislative Policy Formulation* (Princeton, NJ: Princeton University Press, 2002).

7. Richard A. Watson, *Presidential Vetoes and Public Policy* (Lawrence: University of Kansas Press, 1993).

8. Robert J. Spitzer, *The Presidential Veto: Touchstone of the American Presidency* (Albany: SUNY Press, 1988).

9. Sidney M. Milkis and Michael Nelson, *The American Presidency: Origins and Development, 1776–1998,* 4th ed. (Washington, DC: CQ Press, 2003).

10. American Bar Association Recommendation, adopted by the House of Delegates August 7–8, 2006.

11. Statement by the President on H.R. 1540, December 31, 2011.

12. Louis Fisher, *Presidential War Power* (Lawrence: University of Kansas Press, 1995).

13. Cornell G. Hooton, *Executive Governance: Presidential Administrations and Policy Change in the Federal Bureaucracy* (Armonk, NY: M. E. Sharpe, 1997).

14. O. C. Fisher, *Cactus Jack: A Biography of John Nance Garner* (Waco, TX: Texian Press), chap. 11.

15. Bill Clinton, *My Life* (New York: Knopf, 2004), 414.

16. Stephen Skowronek, *The Politics Presidents Make: Leadership from John Adams to George Bush* (Cambridge, MA: Belknap Press, 1997).

17. MaryAnne Borrelli, *The President's Cabinet: Gender, Power, and Representation* (Boulder, CO: Lynne Rienner, 2002).

18. Joel D. Aberbach and Mark A. Peterson, eds., *The Executive Branch* (New York: Oxford University Press, 2005).

19. William E. Leuchtenburg, *In the Shadow of FDR: From Harry Truman to Ronald Reagan* (Ithaca, NY: Cornell University Press, 1989).

20. Kenneth R. Mayer, *With the Stroke of a Pen: Executive Orders and Presidential Power* (Princeton, NJ: Princeton University Press, 2002).

21. Executive Order 9981, www.trumanlibrary.org/9981.htm.

22. *United States v. Curtiss-Wright Export Corp.,* 229 U.S. 304 (1936).

23. Mark J. Rozell, *Executive Privilege: Presidential Power, Secrecy, and Accountability,* 2nd ed. rev. (Lawrence: University of Kansas Press, 2002).

24. *United States v. Richard M. Nixon,* 418 U.S. 683 (1974).

25. Richard Neustadt, *The Power to Persuade* (New York: Wiley, 1960).

26. *Outlook,* February 27, 1909.

27. Richard E. Neustadt, *Presidential Power and the Modern President* (New York: The Free Press, 1990).

28. George C. Edwards III with Alec M. Gallup, *Presidential Approval: A Sourcebook* [Eisenhower to Reagan] (Baltimore: Johns Hopkins University Press, 1990).

29. Harry A. Bailey Jr. and Jay M. Shafritz, *The American Presidency: Historical and Contemporary Perspectives* (Pacific Grove, CA: Brooks/Cole, 1988).

30. Marc Landy and Sidney M. Milkis, *Presidential Greatness* (Lawrence: University of Kansas Press, 2000).

31. Harold J. Laski, *The American Presidency* (New York: Harper & Row, 1940).

32. William M. Goldsmith, *The Growth of Presidential Power: A Documented History,* 3 vols. (New York: Chelsea House, 1974).

33. *New York Times Co. v. United States,* 403 U.S. 713 (1971).

34. Statement of Senator Howard Baker (R-Tenn.) during the Senate Committee investigation.

35. John Dean, the Nixon presidential transcripts, March 21, 1973.

36. Watergate Special Prosecution Force (WSPF) conversations, Nixon Presidential Library and Museum.

37. David Frost, *I Gave Them a Sword* (New York: William Morrow, 1978).

38. Charles C. Thach Jr., *The Creation of the Presidency, 1775–1789: A Study in Constitutional History* (Baltimore, MD: Johns Hopkins University Press, 1969).

CHAPTER 14

The Bureaucracy

©Ann Hermes/The Christian Science Monitor via Getty Images

THEN

The federal bureaucracy under President George Washington had three departments and two offices staffed with public servants engaged in mostly clerical work, serving a national population of 4 million.

NOW

Approximately 4 million national bureaucrats—plus at least 13 million state and local bureaucrats, and private for-profit and nonprofit shadow bureaucrats—implement national public policies that serve the country's population of over 323 million.

NEXT

Will the best and the brightest respond to the call to serve while elected officials denigrate the work and independence of federal bureaucrats?

Will the use of e-government boost citizen knowledge of public policies and their satisfaction with the bureaucracy?

Will the federal government address the transparency and accountability concerns raised by its expanding use of contracts and therefore shadow bureaucrats to implement public policies?

Drain the Swamp. This is

what Trump pledged to do if elected president. There are different understandings of what he meant by "drain the swamp." Candidate Trump first used the phrase when announcing his plans for ethics reforms to "make government honest once again." A White House statement provided four examples of President Trump attacking the swamp in his first few months in office: his executive order on ethics, his call for regulatory reform, a hiring freeze for federal civil servants, and a directive to examine waste in federal agencies. In a video about government efficiency, Director of the Office of Management and Budget Mike Mulvaney said that what draining the swamp really means is "making the government more accountable to you [the citizens], more effective and more efficient."[1]

Citizens turn to their governments to solve individual and community problems and to provide public services and benefits. After Congress and the president approve policies and the funding to pay for their implementation, millions of public servants (at all levels of government) and private-sector employees take on the work of putting public policies into action. It is the daily implementation of public policies that citizens focus on when they evaluate government performance. They don't base their level of satisfaction on the number of laws Congress enacts or the amount of money it spends to implement the laws. Citizens' satisfaction is based on the quality of public services and benefits they receive from bureaucrats.

For their trillions of tax dollars, Americans expect the millions of public servants and private employees involved in implementing public policies to provide services and benefits efficiently (without wasting resources including tax dollars) and effectively (successfully addressing the need or problem). Americans also expect accountability—as Mike Mulvaney suggested. When public services and programs are not effective, efficient, or provided fairly, we want to know who to blame. Typically, we—along with our elected officials—blame bureaucrats. However, the reality of public policy implementation suggests that accountability goes beyond bureaucrats; often, blame for poor outcomes can be found in the actions or inactions of elected officials.

If the promise to drain the swamp means making all public officials accountable to us, then we need to understand the roles and responsibilities of all our elected officials and government bureaucrats. We also need to understand the tools at our disposal to hold them accountable. Citizens must recognize that if there is a swamp in the national government (inefficiencies and ineffective policies), then we all have a role to play in draining it.

Learning Objectives

After reading this chapter, students should be able to:

- Describe who bureaucrats are and the characteristics of bureaucracies.
- Distinguish among the three categories of federal bureaucrats.
- Explain the federal government's use of local, state, and shadow bureaucrats.
- Summarize the evolution of the federal bureaucracy, from small and simple to large and complex.
- Explain the roles and responsibilities of bureaucrats throughout the public policy process.
- Identify the means by which a variety of actors hold bureaucracies accountable.
- Explain barriers and opportunities for improving government performance.

Bureaucrats and Bureaucracy

The national government is the largest single employer of Americans; it even employs more Americans than WalMart! A government employee hired by an executive branch unit (an agency, bureau, commission, department, or office) is a **bureaucrat.** Currently, the national **bureaucracy,** the collection of all national executive branch units, employs approximately 4.1 million public servants: 2.8 million civilian bureaucrats including postal workers, and 1.3 million uniformed military personnel.[2]

What do these millions of public employees do? Ultimately, they work to meet the goals presented in the Preamble of the Constitution: establish justice, ensure domestic tranquility, provide for the common defense, promote the general welfare, and secure the blessings of liberty to all people and to future generations. To accomplish these ambitious and broad (some would say vague) goals, congresses and presidents since 1789 have enacted policies and created thousands of executive branch units to implement the policies. Elected officials determine the size, structures, and activities of the bureaucracy and then must fund it. In addition, elected officials delegate to the bureaucrats the authority to interpret laws and the discretion to determine the best ways to implement them.

Unlike private, for-profit organizations, whose bottom-line goal is making the most profit possible, the bottom-line goal for government is citizen satisfaction. To achieve that goal, the government must do a million things right, most important of which, perhaps, is to hire the best and the brightest.

Who Are the Bureaucrats?

Very few children say they want to be bureaucrats when they grow up. Bureaucrats themselves prefer the label public servant, because that phrase captures how they see themselves and their essential job goal. Yet millions aspire to careers through which they can serve the public good, including as teachers, police officers, health

>From A (astronaut) to Z (zookeeper), and every occupation in between, whatever your dream job, you can do it as a bureaucrat. As a matter of fact, some occupations are available only as government jobs. Can you think of one or two occupations for which only governments hire? Can you think of a (legal) occupation for which the government does not hire?

Space photo: NASA/JSC; *Zoo photo:* ©McGraw-Hill Education care professionals, and lawyers. In 2016, public-sector jobs (national, state, and local government jobs) accounted for 15 percent of total employment in the United States,[3] which includes approximately 3 million national bureaucrats, 5 million state bureaucrats, and 14 million local bureaucrats.

According to the Congressional Research Service,[4] 47 percent of federal civilian employees have at least a bachelor's degree, compared to 35 percent of private-sector employees. More federal bureaucrats work in managerial, professional, and related occupations than private employees (49 percent to 38 percent, respectively) and in sales, office, and administrative support than private employees (28 percent to 13 percent, respectively).

Due to slow-moving federal hiring practices and a large proportion of Baby Boomers who have not retired at the predicted rates, today "just 17 percent of federal workers are under 35 years old" compared to 40 percent of private-sector workers. In addition, only about 1 percent of federal employees are under age 24, compared with 13 percent in the private sector. Nearly a quarter of federal bureaucrats are over 55 years old and 13 percent are over 60 years old.[5]

According to Charles Goodsell, a respected scholar of public administration and public policy, studies show government employees to be very hard workers who are motivated by the recognition of the importance of public service.[6] Compared with private-sector employees, government bureaucrats must comply with more stringent codes of behavior and they express a greater concern for serving the public.[7] According to a 2015 Gallup poll,[8] public servants are more satisfied with their traditional benefits than are private-sector employees. These traditional benefits include retirement plans, health insurance, and vacation time. Public servants are also slightly more satisfied than private employees with their job security, chances for promotion, relations with coworkers, and money earned.

By the beginning of 2018, federal public servants were showing signs of dissatisfaction. About one year earlier, shortly after his inauguration, Trump imposed

THEN NOW NEXT

Federal Civil Servant Hiring Process

THEN (2000)	NOW (2017)
Majority of job applications require lengthy essays and extensive job application forms and questionnaires.	Almost all job applications require the uploading of a résumé and cover letter; no lengthy essays, application forms, or questionnaires.
Many applicants experience a "black hole," never receiving a response to their applications.	www.usajobs.gov allows applicants to follow the flow of their applications through the hiring process.
Majority of applicants apply directly to the Office of Personnel Management (OPM).	Majority of applicants apply directly to the agency with the open position.
usajobs.gov lists open positions for which OPM accepts applications.	All federal agencies must post their job openings on usajobs. gov; many also post them on their own websites.

WHAT'S NEXT?

> Will perpetually changing technology, which leads to increased efficiency in the usajobs.gov application process, make it easier for the federal government to recruit and hire the best and the brightest?

> Will an important tool for evaluating applicants be lost by dropping the essay requirement? Why or why not?

> Will partisan politics and the fear of future government shutdowns affect federal hiring?

> Will proposals to freeze federal pay and cut back on benefits such as paid time off spark retirements?

> Will proposals to freeze federal pay and cut back on benefits affect federal hiring?

a federal hiring freeze. This was part of his long-term plan to "drain the swamp" by reducing the size of the federal bureaucracy through *attrition;* that is, when public servants leave the government, they are not to be replaced. Although the hiring freeze was lifted quickly, by September 2017, the federal government had 16,000 fewer permanent workers than it had in January 2017. Then, the Trump administration budget for 2019 proposed a federal pay freeze, reducing paid time off, having employees pay a higher proportion of their health insurance premiums, and increasing employee contributions to the federal employee retirement system, which is a major benefit of working for the federal government. Democrats and Republicans on the Homeland Security and Governmental Affairs Committee's federal management panel criticized the pay freeze. Senator Heidi Heitkamp (D-N.D.), the top Democrat on the panel, claimed that these proposals would have a "grave impact" on federal employees and on the recruitment of new federal employees if they were implemented.[9]

The Bureaucratic Structure

Max Weber (1864–1920), the "father of sociology," is famous for creating an ideal model of a bureaucracy. Weber's **bureaucratic structure** had the following features: a division of labor, specialization of job tasks, hiring systems based on worker competency, hierarchy with a vertical chain of command, and standard operating procedures. Today, government agencies as well as large, nongovernmental organizations typically conform to this bureaucratic structure. Review Figure 14.1 to identify bureaucratic structures in the national government.

Colleges and universities (public and private) are good examples of organizations with bureaucratic structures. They have a division of labor with specialization of tasks. (Consider the various academic departments, each specializing in a different discipline.) They hire employees (such as professors, computer technicians, and student affairs staff) with the knowledge, skills, and abilities essential to doing their jobs well. Colleges and universities also have a hierarchy with a vertical chain of command (faculty members report to chairpersons, who report to a dean, who reports to the vice president for academic affairs, who reports to the president, who makes final decisions). University employees implement standardized procedures to register students for classes, determine financial aid eligibility, and punish violations of the conduct code.

For most people, the word *bureaucracy* conjures up the image of a large government organization with rules and procedures that are inefficient and dehumanizing, and that require tedious paperwork: **red tape.** They visualize long lines at the Department of Motor Vehicles as uncaring workers, who they believe the government cannot fire, slowly process mounds of forms. Taxpayers are not the only people who think and speak negatively of the bureaucracy. Even our presidents and congressional members—who rely on bureaucrats to implement their policy promises—do not hesitate to criticize bureaucrats. Are the negative images and criticisms fair? The reality is that much of the red tape is a product of the bureaucratic structure, and the expectations we have for equal treatment and government accountability.

Although most people think of government when they hear the word *bureaucracy,* a bureaucracy is *any* organization with Weber's bureaucratic structure. Yet in this chapter, as is appropriate to our study of American national government, we focus on the departments and agencies that compose the national government bureaucracy. And even though most people think of government employees when they hear the term *bureaucrat,* nongovernment employees, as we will see, may also

bureaucratic structure
A large organization with the following features: a division of labor, specialization of job tasks, hiring systems based on worker competency, hierarchy with a vertical chain of command, and standard operating procedures.

red tape
Bureaucratic rules and procedures that are viewed as inefficient, dehumanizing, and requiring tedious paperwork.

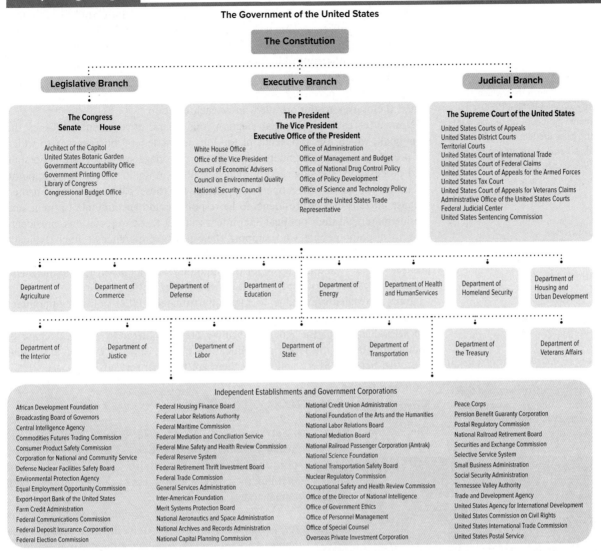

The Government of the United States

The Constitution

Legislative Branch | **Executive Branch** | **Judicial Branch**

The Congress
Senate   House

Architect of the Capitol
United States Botanic Garden
Government Accountability Office
Government Printing Office
Library of Congress
Congressional Budget Office

The President
The Vice President
Executive Office of the President

White House Office
Office of the Vice President
Council of Economic Advisers
Council on Environmental Quality
National Security Council

Office of Administration
Office of Management and Budget
Office of National Drug Control Policy
Office of Policy Development
Office of Science and Technology Policy
Office of the United States Trade Representative

The Supreme Court of the United States

United States Courts of Appeals
United States District Courts
Territorial Courts
United States Court of International Trade
United States Court of Federal Claims
United States Court of Appeals for the Armed Forces
United States Tax Court
United States Court of Appeals for Veterans Claims
Administrative Office of the United States Courts
Federal Judicial Center
United States Sentencing Commission

Department of Agriculture | Department of Commerce | Department of Defense | Department of Education | Department of Energy | Department of Health and HumanServices | Department of Homeland Security | Department of Housing and Urban Development

Department of the Interior | Department of Justice | Department of Labor | Department of State | Department of Transportation | Department of the Treasury | Department of Veterans Affairs

Independent Establishments and Government Corporations

African Development Foundation
Broadcasting Board of Governors
Central Intelligence Agency
Commodities Futures Trading Commission
Consumer Product Safety Commission
Corporation for National and Community Service
Defense Nuclear Facilities Safety Board
Environmental Protection Agency
Equal Employment Opportunity Commission
Export-Import Bank of the United States
Farm Credit Administration
Federal Communications Commission
Federal Deposit Insurance Corporation
Federal Election Commission

Federal Housing Finance Board
Federal Labor Relations Authority
Federal Maritime Commission
Federal Mediation and Conciliation Service
Federal Mine Safety and Health Review Commission
Federal Reserve System
Federal Retirement Thrift Investment Board
Federal Trade Commission
General Services Administration
Inter-American Foundation
Merit Systems Protection Board
National Aeronautics and Space Administration
National Archives and Records Administration
National Capital Planning Commission

National Credit Union Administration
National Foundation of the Arts and the Humanities
National Labor Relations Board
National Mediation Board
National Railroad Passenger Corporation (Amtrak)
National Science Foundation
National Transportation Safety Board
Nuclear Regulatory Commission
Occupational Safety and Health Review Commission
Office of the Director of National Intelligence
Office of Government Ethics
Office of Personnel Management
Office of Special Counsel
Overseas Private Investment Corporation

Peace Corps
Pension Benefit Guaranty Corporation
Postal Regulatory Commission
National Railroad Retirement Board
Securities and Exchange Commission
Selective Service System
Small Business Administration
Social Security Administration
Tennessee Valley Authority
Trade and Development Agency
United States Agency for International Development
United States Commission on Civil Rights
United States International Trade Commission
United States Postal Service

FIGURE 14.1 ■ **U.S. Government Organizational Chart** How is the federal bureaucracy's division of labor evident in the national government organizational chart? How is the vertical chain of command evident in the chart? What other characteristics of Weber's ideal bureaucracy can you identify in this organizational chart?

be paid with taxpayer money to serve the public, and so it is appropriate that we consider these shadow bureaucrats, too.

Federal Bureaucrats

Political scientists distinguish among federal bureaucrats according to several factors, including the processes by which they are hired, the procedures by which they can be fired, and the grounds for which they can be fired. On the basis of these factors, we examine three categories of national civilian bureaucrats: political appointees, Senior Executive Service appointees, and civil servants.

Political Appointees

In 1863, President Abraham Lincoln, suffering from smallpox, told his secretary to "send all the office seekers in here. I finally have something I can give to them all." Indeed, before the creation of the federal civil service system in 1883, presidents had the authority to hire bureaucrats, selecting whomever they wanted and establishing whatever qualifications they desired, through the **patronage system** of hiring. Under the patronage system, hordes of men seeking government jobs presented themselves to the president after each election.

Now, after each presidential election, the federal government publishes the **plum book,** which lists thousands of top jobs in the federal bureaucracy to which the president will appoint people through the patronage system. There is no standard process for assessing the knowledge, skills, and abilities needed for appointive positions, nor is there open competition for these patronage jobs. Further, because citizens expect presidents to be responsive and accountable to them, and presidents rely on their political appointees to meet those expectations, presidents tend to appoint people who support their policy preferences, which typically means they are affiliated with the same political party as the president. Patronage positions come with a downside for the appointees: no job security. The president not only hires but also can fire political appointees at his pleasure.

Today, presidents are able to hire approximately 3,000 political appointees through the patronage system. These appointees serve under the president, in the top several layers in the federal executive branch's hierarchy (vertical chain of command). Below the layers of political appointees are members of the Senior Executive Service (SES), and below them are the civil servants.

Senior Executives

The keystone of the Civil Service Reform Act of 1978 was the creation of the **Senior Executive Service (SES).**[10] The SES is composed of the top managerial, supervisory, and policy positions that link the political appointees to the rest of the federal bureaucracy.

The SES bureaucrat is a hybrid of the political appointee and the civil servant. At least 90 percent of SES bureaucrats are career appointees hired based on merit through an open, competitive process. These employees can be moved from job to job and from agency to agency, as can political appointees. However, unlike political appointees, they cannot be fired at the discretion of the president. To fire a SES career appointee, the government must prove that the employee is not performing the job, is performing it poorly, or is performing it in a manner that violates agency rules or the law.

The remaining 10 percent of SES bureaucrats are noncareer and temporary appointees hired without open, competitive procedures, similar to political appointees. Their appointments are approved by the Office of Personnel Management (the federal government's central personnel office) and the White House Office of Presidential Personnel, and they can be removed at the pleasure of the president.[11]

patronage system
A personnel system in which the chief executive officer (CEO) can appoint whomever he or she wants to top bureaucratic positions, without the need for open competition for applicants; those hired through patronage typically serve at the pleasure of the CEO who hired them.

plum book
A publication that lists the top jobs in the bureaucracy to which the president will appoint people through the patronage system.

Senior Executive Service (SES)
A unique personnel system for top managerial, supervisory, and policy positions offering less job security but higher pay than the merit-based civil service system.

> President Donald Trump stands with Vice President Michael Pence as Pence swears in senior staff members in a January 22, 2017, ceremony in the East Room of the White House. By March of 2018, 56 percent of Trump's 621 nominees needing Senate confirmation had been confirmed. This confirmation rate is lower than that of President Obama (67%), President G. W. Bush (71%), and President Clinton (81%) during the same period of their presidencies, according to the nonprofit organization Partnership for Public Service. What might explain this lower rate of confirmations?
©Andrew Harrer/Getty Images

Civil Servants

During the first century of U.S. history, all federal bureaucrats were hired through the patronage system. Then in 1883, after the assassination of President James Garfield by a man who did not get the patronage position he sought, Congress and President Chester Arthur (1881–1885) approved the Pendleton Civil Service Act. The goal of the act was to eliminate the expectation that government jobs were the spoils of an electoral victory, distributed by the winning candidate. The act established a **merit-based civil service** in the national government. The hiring principles of this system included open competition, competence, and political neutrality, which would ensure the independence and integrity of civil servants. **Civil servants** are bureaucrats hired through the merit-based personnel system established by the Pendleton Act and reinforced by the 1978 Civil Service Reform Act.

By the 1970s, there was widespread criticism of federal government performance. As President Jimmy Carter (1977–1981) said in 1978, "The public suspects that there are too many government workers, that they are underworked, overpaid, and insulated from the consequences of incompetence."[12] To address the criticisms, Carter proposed the Civil Service Reform Act (CSRA). The CSRA reaffirmed and expanded the merit principles established by the Pendleton Act, established the SES, and reorganized the management of the national civil service.

OPEN COMPETITION, COMPETENCE, AND EQUAL OPPORTUNITY Today, merit-based civil service jobs, which compose the majority of the federal bureaucracy, are open and accessible to all who wish to compete for a position. The competition requires that candidates prove their competence to do the job (their merit). This may be done by evaluation of the applicants' education and work experiences, written exams, or some other examination of their knowledge, skills, and abilities that are relevant to job performance.

The Office of Personnel Management (OPM), the central personnel office for the federal government, determines which positions it will evaluate candidates for and for which positions individual agencies can conduct their own evaluations. Regarding the positions for which it conducts evaluations, the OPM analyzes and ranks them on the basis of the knowledge, skills, and abilities needed to do the job competently. A job's rank determines its salary. The pay scales are expected to offer equal pay for jobs of equal worth. (Table 14.1 presents the pay scales and education requirements for white-collar federal government jobs evaluated by the OPM.)

As the proportion of jobs that require the hiring of professionals has increased, the OPM has delegated to a growing number of agencies more control over hiring processes and establishing salaries.

Several national laws that mandate equal opportunities have helped to make today's civil servants, as a group, look more like the U.S. population at large than they did in the past. Title VII of the 1964 Civil Rights Act, as amended, prohibits employers, including governments, from making personnel decisions based on factors irrelevant to job competence, such as sex, race, color, ethnicity, age, and disabilities that can be reasonably accommodated. The merit principles of the CSRA reiterate this prohibition against discrimination in personnel practices. The Title VII and CSRA bans against discrimination do not apply to the positions of elected officials or political appointees.

Title VI of the 1964 Civil Rights Act prohibits discrimination based on race, color, religion, and ethnicity in educational opportunities offered by institutions receiving federal funding. Title IX, which was added to the act in 1972, extended

merit-based civil service
A personnel system in which bureaucrats are hired on the basis of the principles of competence, equal opportunity (open competition), and political neutrality; once hired, these public servants have job protection.

civil servants
Bureaucrats hired through a merit-based personnel system and who have job protection.

TABLE 14.1 Education Requirements and Salary Ranges for White-Collar Federal Civil Servants (2018)

LEVEL	SALARY RANGE	QUALIFYING EDUCATION
GS-1	$18,785–$23,502	No high school diploma required
GS-2	$21,121–$26,585	High school graduation or equivalent
GS-3	$23,045–$29,957	One academic year above high school
GS-4	$25,871–$33,629	Two academic years above high school, or associate's degree
GS-5	$28,945–$37,630	Four academic years above high school leading to a bachelor's degree, or a bachelor's degree
GS-6	$32,264–$41,939	Experience required in addition to the stated level of education
GS-7	$35,854–$46,609	Bachelor's degree with superior academic achievement or one academic year of graduate education or law school
GS-8	$39,707–$51,623	Experience required in addition to the stated level of education
GS-9	$43,857–$57,015	Master's (or equivalent graduate degree) or two academic years of progressively higher level graduate education
GS-10	$48,297–$62,787	Experience required in addition to the stated level of education
GS-11	$53,062–$68,983	PhD or equivalent degree or three academic years of progressively higher level graduate education
GS-12	$63,600–$82,680	Completion of all requirements for a doctoral or equivalent degree (for research positions only)
GS-13	$75,628–$98,317	Appropriate specialized experience
GS-14	$89,370–$116,181	Appropriate specialized experience
GS-15	$105,123–$136,659	Appropriate specialized experience

SOURCE: U.S. Office of Personnel Management, "Salary Table, 2018 GS," "What Determines Where You Stand on the GS Scale?"

this prohibition to sex-based discrimination. Enforcement of these laws has increased the diversity of people who are able to gain the education and experience needed to do government jobs competently. Titles VI, VII, and IX, combined with the merit principles of the Pendleton Act and the CSRA, have fostered movement toward a **representative bureaucracy,** which means that bureaucrats, as a group, resemble the larger population whom they serve in demographic characteristics such as race, age, ethnicity, sex, religion, and economic status.

representative bureaucracy
A bureaucracy in which the people serving resemble the larger population whom they serve in demographic characteristics such as race, age, ethnicity, sex, religion, and economic status.

POLITICAL NEUTRALITY Civil servants cannot be fired merely because someone with different political beliefs is elected or appointed to supervise them. They can be fired for poor quality of work (misfeasance), or for nonperformance of their work (nonfeasance), or for violating the law or the rules and regulations that guide their work (malfeasance). The merit-based civil service system thus gives competent civil servants job protection and does not require them to adhere to the president's policy preferences (unlike political appointees). Hence, the civil service system supports political neutrality in hiring. To bolster political neutrality, the federal government limits through the Hatch Act the rights of bureaucrats to run for partisan office and participate in campaigning during work hours. The expectation is that civil servants hired through the merit system will be competent and will make work decisions that are nonpartisan and that serve the public good.

THEN

NOW

> In the summer of 1981, 12,000 of the 17,000 air traffic controllers complied with their union's request to strike. The striking Professional Air Traffic Controllers Organization (PATCO) members broke the law because it is illegal for federal civil servants to strike. President Reagan took a hard line, stating that if the controllers did not return to work within 48 hours, they would be fired. Indeed, the striking public servants were fired and the federal government decertified PATCO (it was no longer a legally recognized union). It took 10 years for the Federal Aviation Administration (FAA) to fill the 12,000 open positions created by the mass firing. Today, the National Air Traffic Controllers Association, the union representing the 14,000 controllers, supports efforts to privatize its operations because the government has not resolved the chronic controller understaffing and has not made progress on modernizing operations.

PATCO strike: © Bourdier/AP Images; *control tower:* © Monty Rakusen/Cultura/Getty Images

MANAGING THE FEDERAL CIVIL SERVICE The CSRA of 1978 established three new independent administrative agencies—the Office of Personnel Management (OPM), the Merit System Protection Board (MSPB), and the Federal Labor Relations Authority (FLRA)—to replace the old Civil Service Commission created by the Pendleton Act. Today, the OPM, as the central personnel office, is responsible for developing and implementing merit-based civil service personnel policies and procedures. The MSPB ensures proper implementation of the merit system by investigating allegations of improper implementation. The CSRA, which legislated for the collective bargaining rights (unionization rights) of national civil servants, created the FLRA to monitor relations between unionized bureaucrats and the federal government.

UNIONIZED CIVIL SERVANTS Twenty-eight percent of U.S. federal civil servants belong to labor unions. By comparison, the percentage of unionized workers among private-sector employees is 7 percent.[13] Whereas about 68 percent of U.S. Postal Service employees are union members,[14] the level of union membership among bureaucrats in the State Department is close to zero.

Unionized civil servants have leverage to negotiate certain conditions of work. For example, they may bargain for improved training opportunities and enhanced due process protections in disciplinary matters. Federal civil service employee unions cannot negotiate salaries or work hours, however. And unlike private-sector unions, federal civil servant unions do not have the legal right to strike. The prohibition of strikes by federal civil servants is typically justified by the fact that these workers provide essential services that are vital to public safety. A strike by these workers would therefore threaten public safety and health.

State, Local, and Shadow Bureaucrats

shadow bureaucrats

People hired and paid by private for-profit and nonprofit organizations that implement public policy through a government contract.

contracting-out

Also called *outsourcing;* a process by which the government contracts with a private for-profit or nonprofit organization to provide public services, such as disaster relief, or resources needed by the government, such as fighter planes.

When it comes to implementing federal policies, joining the national bureaucrats are state and local bureaucrats and **shadow bureaucrats**—employees on the payroll of private for-profit businesses and private nonprofit organizations that have received government contracts and grants. Through a process of **contracting-out** (also called *outsourcing*), the government signs work contracts with these private organizations to assist in implementing national policy as well as producing certain resources needed to serve the public. In other words, shadow bureaucrats do some of the work of government, but they do not receive government paychecks.

Examples of outsourcing include the federal government's contracting with Lockheed Martin and Boeing for the production of defense resources such as helmets, fighter planes, and laser-guided missiles. As part of the Affordable Care Act of 2010 (also known as Obamacare), the government contracted out the bulk of the work to develop the website through which citizens can purchase health insurance. Traditionally, the government also undertakes large capital projects such as the construction of roads and government buildings through contracts with private businesses. Furthermore, the federal government outsources medical as well as social research to cure diseases and address the ills of society. And through government contracts, the Red Cross has dispensed disaster relief for decades. The federal government's contracts totaled approximately $438 billion in 2015.[15]

The federal government expects that contracting-out will reduce the expense of government by eliminating the overhead costs (including employee benefits and basic operating costs) of producing public goods and services. Outsourcing also provides a means by which the government can hire experts and specialists only when they are needed. Proponents of outsourcing argue that private- and nonprofit-sector employees and organizations are more efficient and effective than government bureaucracies. However, as we discuss later in this chapter, the benefits of contracting-out are debatable.

Political scientist John DiIulio estimates that at least 10 million shadow bureaucrats and 3 million state and local bureaucrats receive paychecks that are at least partially funded by federal tax dollars due to contracts and grants-in-aid.[16] As you may recall from Chapter 3, the federal government has devolved greater responsibility for financing and administering national public policies to state and local governments, putting the implementation of national policy in the hands of state and local bureaucrats. Either through grants-in-aid conditions or unfunded mandates in federal laws, state and local bureaucrats implement national policies. In cases where federal law preempts (takes precedence over) state and local law, state and local bureaucrats may have to implement federal policy instead of state or local policies if their policies are weaker than the federal policy, or if they have no policy on the matter.

Even with the increased use of state, local, and shadow bureaucrats, the federal bureaucracy is neither small nor streamlined. It is composed of thousands of executive units with a variety of names and organizational structures. The federal bureaucracy continues to grow in complexity even as it contracts out and devolves more of its work.

The Evolution of the Federal Bureaucracy

Four million people resided in the United States in 1789, the year George Washington was sworn in as the first president. Most of them lived off the land and were self-sufficient; they expected few services from the federal government.

The federal bureaucracy consisted of the Department of War, Department of Foreign Affairs, Treasury Department, Attorney General's Office, and Postal Services Office. Those three departments and two offices handled the core functions demanded of the national government at that time: respectively, providing defense, managing foreign affairs, collecting revenues and paying bills, resolving lawsuits and legal questions, and delivering mail. With the exception of defense, the work of public servants was mostly clerical in nature.

Since the nation's founding, congresses and presidents have enacted laws creating thousands of executive branch bureaucracies. The size, scope, and complexity of today's federal bureaucracy are products of elected officials' efforts to respond to the ever-changing needs and growing demands of U.S. citizens. Elected policymakers rely on the federal bureaucracy to faithfully execute the laws they enact, providing a range of services and benefits that would shock George Washington.

Today, with the U.S. population of 326 million, approximately 2,000 federal executive branch units, employing close to 3 million civilian employees and 1.3 million active duty military personnel, implement volumes of national policies. The number of bureaucrats is comparable to the nation's total population in 1789. Figure 14.2 presents the growth in the size of federal, state, and local workforces since 1940. Figure 14.3 shows the growth in cost of the national bureaucracy since 1940. The "Thinking Critically" feature debates whether the federal government is too big.

Political scientists distinguish among five categories of executive branch organizations based on their structure and the type of work they perform: (1) departments, (2) independent administrative agencies, (3) independent regulatory commissions, (4) government corporations, and (5) agencies in the Executive Office of the President. Within each category there is much variation in size, structure, and function. When Congress and the president authorize a new policy, they must decide whether they will assign its implementation to an existing agency or create a new agency. If they choose the latter option, they must determine which type of agency to create.

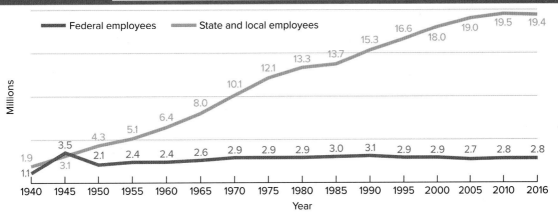

FIGURE 14.2 ■ **Growth in Civilian Workforce** What has been the trend regarding federal employees since 1965? What has been the pattern for the growth regarding state and local bureaucrats over the same period? What helps to explain these patterns?

SOURCES: U.S. Census Bureau. *Statistical Abstracts of the United States.* 1955, Table 476; 1968, Table 567; 1978, Table 504; 1990, Table 487; 2012, Table 461.
2016 data source: U.S. Bureau of Labor Statistics, Employment Projections program, Table 2.1 Employment by major industry sector, 2006, 2016, and projected 2026.

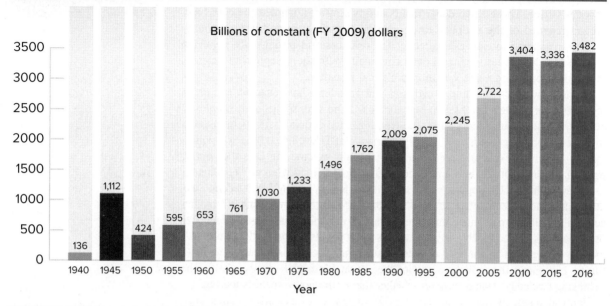

FIGURE 14.3 ■ **Trends in Federal Expenditures** What has been the overall trend in federal government spending since 1940? What has the pattern been since 2000? What factors might explain the trend in federal spending since 2000?

SOURCE: Office of Management and Budget. *Historical Tables*, "Table 1.3—Summary of Receipts, Outlays, and Surpluses or Deficits in Current Dollars, Constant (FY 2009) Dollars, and as Percentages of GDP: 1940–2023."

Departments

department
One of 15 executive branch units responsible for a broadly defined policy area and whose top administrator (secretary) is appointed by the president, is confirmed by the Senate, and serves at the discretion of the president.

The Department of Homeland Security, established in 2002, is the newest of 15 federal **departments,** each responsible for one broadly defined policy area. The president holds the 15 departments accountable through the appointment of a head official. *Secretary* is the title of this top political appointee in all departments except the Department of Justice, where the head is the attorney general. Although the Senate must confirm them, these top appointees report to the president and serve at the president's pleasure. In addition to appointing the department secretaries, the president names bureaucrats to positions in several levels of the hierarchy below the secretaries. These political appointees have titles such as *deputy secretary, assistant deputy secretary, agency director,* and *deputy director.* Table 14.2 lists the 15 departments, from oldest to newest.

Independent Administrative Agencies

independent administrative agency
An executive branch unit created by Congress and the president that is responsible for a narrowly defined function and whose structure is intended to be protected from partisan politics.

Whereas each executive branch department has authority for a broadly defined policy area, a host of **independent administrative agencies** are each responsible for a more narrowly defined function of the national government. Congress and the president create these agencies to fulfill one of several purposes. Some of them, such as the Smithsonian Institution, were established to handle new governmental functions that did not easily fall within the scope of responsibilities of existing departments. Other independent administrative agencies support the work of existing departments and agencies, including recruiting and training employees (Office

Is the Federal Government Too Big?

The Issue: Many taxpayers complain that the federal government is too big. For some this means the government spends too much money. For others it means it is doing things that individuals or businesses should do. For still others, too big means too involved in their daily lives. Is the federal government too big?

Yes: The federal government spends close to $4 trillion per year, which is almost one-quarter of the value of all goods and services produced in the country each year. In contrast, total spending by the 50 states is less than $2 trillion per year. The national government has many more employees and contractors than any state government. To pay its bills, the national government must borrow money because it cannot cover its annual costs with the revenue it collects each year. The federal government has taken on too many responsibilities. It should devolve many of its domestic policies to the states and their local governments; this is how the framers expected our federal system to function.

No: The amount of money the federal government spends does not tell you how big the government is. The largest single expense in the federal budget is Social Security, which is a transfer of money to individuals that does not require the employment of large numbers of people. Elimination of Social Security would decrease the cost of government, but it would not have a significant impact on the number of federal bureaucrats. Almost half of all full-time federal civilian bureaucrats work to implement defense and homeland security policies. These policies are the responsibility of the federal government, per the Constitution. They cannot be devolved to the state and local governments, which already engage in implementing numerous national policies.

Other Approaches: According to the PEW Research Center, 29 percent of Democrats think the government is doing too many things that are better left to businesses and individuals. At the same time, 71 percent of Republicans hold this view. This partisan gap in perception of scope of government (which relates to size of budget and number of employees) suggests that there is no consensus opinion on what is the "right" size for the federal government. Even those who say the federal government is too big don't necessarily agree on what programs or costs can be cut to shrink it, a sentiment that can be summarized as "Cut government spending, but don't cut *my* services or benefits."

What do you think?

1. How should the size of the federal government be measured: cost, number of employees, number of citizens served? Is there some other measure you can justify?

2. If the federal government devolved domestic policies to the state governments, would people begin to complain about the size of state governments? If so, what would stop state governments from devolving more responsibilities to their local governments? Would devolution actually decrease costs for taxpayers or merely lead to increases in state and local taxes?

3. Are there public programs, services, or goods the federal government provides that the majority of people will agree to shrink or eliminate? How likely are people to willingly give up a benefit they currently receive?

of Personnel Management) and managing government properties and records (General Services Administration). Still others, such as the National Science Foundation and the National Aeronautics and Space Administration, focus on research and preservation of national resources.

These agencies are "independent" because congresses and presidents place them outside the cabinet departments, which means they do not report to a cabinet secretary. In addition, some independent administrative agency heads serve fixed terms, making their agencies independent from the president. In other agencies, the heads serve at the pleasure of the president, but the president must have a cause (such as misconduct) to remove them. In yet other agencies, the president can remove the head without specifying a cause. Although the structures of

TABLE 14.2 Establishment of Cabinet Departments

What do the names of the departments indicate about the concerns and interests that have won federal policymakers' attention over the country's history? What mobilized the government to establish the Department of Homeland Security? Do you have an area of national concern for which you would advocate Congress create a department? Is there a department you think we no longer need? If so, explain why it is no longer needed.

DEPARTMENT	YEAR ESTABLISHED
State	1789
Treasury	1789
War	1789
Army	1798
Navy	1798
Interior	1859
Justice (Attorney General's Office, 1789)	1870
Agriculture	1889
Commerce and Labor	1903
Commerce (separated from Commerce and Labor)	1913
Labor (separated from Commerce and Labor)	1913
Defense (pulled War, Army, and Navy into one department)	1947
Health, Education, and Welfare	1953
Housing and Urban Development	1965
Transportation	1966
Energy	1977
Health & Human Services (separated from Health, Education, and Welfare)	1979
Education (separated from Health, Education, and Welfare)	1979
Veterans Affairs	1988
Homeland Security	2002

>James Smithson, a French citizen who never visited the United States, willed his estate as a donation to establish an educational institution in Washington, D.C. His donation was used to establish the Smithsonian Institute in 1846, the first independent administrative agency created by the federal government. Today, the Smithsonian includes 19 museums and galleries. The newest addition to the Smithsonian is the Museum of African American Culture, which opened in 2016.

©Jahi Chikwendiu/The Washington Post via Getty Images

independent administrative agencies are expected to make them "independent" of partisan politics, ultimately such agencies still need to earn the support of those who authorize the spending of money and who have authority to restructure the agency or its mission—Congress and the president.

Independent Regulatory Commissions

Over time, congresses and presidents have recognized the need for expertise in regulating the country's diverse economic activities and in evaluating their impact on the overall economy, workers, consumers, and the environment. Acknowledging their own lack of such expertise, they have created numerous **independent regulatory commissions,** bureaucracies outside of the cabinet departments with the authority to develop standards of behavior for specific industries and businesses, to monitor compliance with these standards, and to impose sanctions on those it finds guilty of violating the standards.

Initially, government regulation centered on *economic regulation*—matters such as setting the prices of goods and services and ensuring competition in the marketplace. The first independent regulatory commission, the Interstate Commerce Commission, was set up in 1887 to oversee the prices and services of the railroad industry. By the 1970s, Congress had turned more in the direction of *social regulation,* establishing regulatory commissions that focused on how business practices affected the environment, and the health and safety of consumers and workers. For example, legislation created the Consumer Product Safety Commission in 1972.

Independent regulatory agencies are under the direction of bipartisan boards whose members do not need to be loyal to the president's preferences. Typically, the president nominates and the Senate confirms an odd number of board members. Board members serve staggered fixed terms. This structure allows the agency to make decisions based on the expertise of its board members, not on the preferences of the president or Congress. Still, the agencies need both presidential and congressional support to survive.

independent regulatory commission
An executive branch unit outside of cabinet departments, responsible for developing standards of behavior within specific industries and businesses, monitoring compliance with these standards, and imposing sanctions on violators.

Government Corporations

Like private businesses, **government corporations** sell a service or a product and compete for customers; but unlike private businesses, they are government owned. Congress and the president create government corporations when they believe it is in the public interest for the federal government to engage in a commercial activity, such as selling stamps to pay for the cost of delivering mail. Unlike the other categories of bureaucracies, government corporations, such as the U.S. Postal Service, are expected to make enough money to cover their costs, instead of being funded by tax dollars.

A bipartisan board typically directs each government corporation. The president appoints the board members to serve for staggered fixed terms. Typically, the Senate is not required to confirm the board members. Like regulatory commissions and administrative agencies, government corporations are independent of cabinet departments.

government corporation
An executive branch unit that sells a service and is expected to be financially self-sufficient.

Executive Office of the President

By 1939, the federal bureaucracy had grown tremendously in size and diversity. Acknowledging that the president, who serves as the chief executive of the bureaucracy, needed help to manage this constellation of departments, independent administrative agencies, independent regulatory commissions, and government corporations, President Franklin Roosevelt and Congress created the Executive Office of the President (EOP).

The EOP is composed of dozens of offices and councils that assist the president in managing the complex and sprawling executive branch of the bureaucracy. The president appoints the top-level bureaucrats in EOP units, and the majority of these appointments are not subject to Senate confirmation. The president has the authority to fire these appointees at his pleasure. Therefore, the EOP serves the president; it is in fact the presidential bureaucracy. (See Chapter 13 for a detailed discussion of the EOP.)

As the U.S. government organizational chart (Figure 14.1) indicates, the legislative branch has several offices supporting its work (including the Government Accountability Office, the Government Printing Office, and the Library of Congress). In addition, there are offices in the judicial branch supporting the work of the courts (the Administrative Office of the United States Courts, the Federal Judicial Center, and the United States Sentencing Commission). Federal bureaucrats employed in these legislative and judicial bodies support the formulation, implementation, and evaluation of public policies.

The Work of Bureaucrats

Although the primary work of bureaucrats is policy implementation—putting public policy into action—bureaucrats play an active, vital role in all six stages of the public policy cycle. These stages are (1) agenda setting, (2) policy formulation, (3) policy approval, (4) appropriation approval, (5) policy implementation, and (6) policy evaluation. (Figure 14.4 presents an example of how the Affordable Care Act of 2010 is working through the six-stage policy cycle.)

politics-administration dichotomy
The concept that elected government officials, who are accountable to the voters, create and approve public policy, and then competent, politically neutral bureaucrats implement the public policy.

According to the **politics-administration dichotomy,** there is a clear line between *politics* (deciding what government should accomplish, enacting those goals into laws, and allocating money to pay to execute laws) and the *administration* of public policy (the real work of putting the laws into action). The dichotomy says that elected officials (whom citizens hold accountable through the ballot box) have authority for politics and that competent bureaucrats (hired through merit-based civil service) have authority for policy administration. Theoretically, this arrangement fosters not only government by and for the people (responsive government) but also efficient and effective public services.

The politics-administration dichotomy may sound good, but the reality of public policy processes does not allow for such a clean separation between those who "do politics" and those who administer policy. Although bureaucrats are hired to implement policy made by elected officials, elected officials tap the expertise of bureaucrats throughout the other five stages of the policy process, allowing bureaucrats to influence and even make policies themselves, as we now shall see.

Agenda Setting

In the first stage of the public policy cycle, elected officials decide what issues they want to discuss and possibly address by placing them on their lists of items to work on, their policy agendas. Bureaucrats play an instrumental role in helping to set the policy agenda. Because their focus is to implement public policy at the

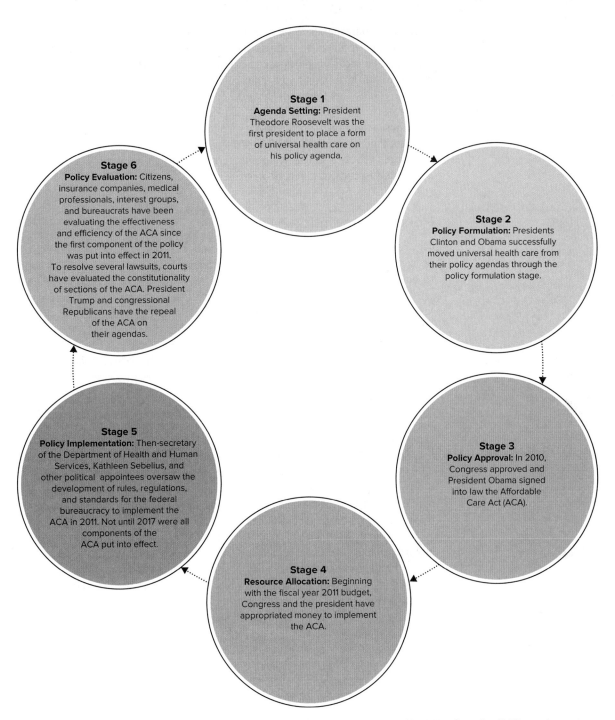

FIGURE 14.4 ■ **Stages of the Policy Process** This flowchart shows how the Affordable Care Act (ACA) continues to work through the policy cycle. In reality, the stages of the policy cycle often overlap. Today, additional rules and regulations are being established as the ACA is implemented. At the same time, critics and supporters are evaluating the ACA, as are government agencies and courts (as they resolve lawsuits). Calls for reforms to the act may force it back to the agenda-setting stage, which could lead to the formulation of new legislation revising the ACA or even to repealing it.

The circles in the figure contain the following text:

Stage 1
Agenda Setting: President Theodore Roosevelt was the first president to place a form of universal health care on his policy agenda.

Stage 2
Policy Formulation: Presidents Clinton and Obama successfully moved universal health care from their policy agendas through the policy formulation stage.

Stage 3
Policy Approval: In 2010, Congress approved and President Obama signed into law the Affordable Care Act (ACA).

Stage 4
Resource Allocation: Beginning with the fiscal year 2011 budget, Congress and the president have appropriated money to implement the ACA.

Stage 5
Policy Implementation: Then-secretary of the Department of Health and Human Services, Kathleen Sebelius, and other political appointees oversaw the development of rules, regulations, and standards for the federal bureaucracy to implement the ACA in 2011. Not until 2017 were all components of the ACA put into effect.

Stage 6
Policy Evaluation: Citizens, insurance companies, medical professionals, interest groups, and bureaucrats have been evaluating the effectiveness and efficiency of the ACA since the first component of the policy was put into effect in 2011. To resolve several lawsuits, courts have evaluated the constitutionality of sections of the ACA. President Trump and congressional Republicans have the repeal of the ACA on their agendas.

street level, bureaucrats have a clear view of the societal problems that citizens expect the government to address and strong views on how best to address those problems. Political scientists use the term *iron triangle* to describe long-term collaborative efforts among bureaucrats in a government agency, the members of an interest group, and the members of a legislative committee to get their mutual concerns on the agenda and then addressed through approved public policies. *Issue networks,* which are temporary collaborations among bureaucrats, elected officials, and the members of numerous interest groups, also work to set the agenda as well as to influence policy formulation and approval. For more about iron triangles and issue networks, see Chapter 7.

Policy Formulation

The second stage of the policy process, policy formulation, involves defining a problem that has made it to an agenda and developing a plan of action (a policy) to address the problem. Many issues that reach an elected official's agenda—or even the agendas of numerous elected officials—do not make it to the policy formulation stage. Although anyone can formulate a public policy, only elected officials can officially introduce policy proposals into the lawmaking process. Thus individuals and groups outside government, as well as bureaucrats, must identify members of Congress to introduce policy proposals for federal legislative action. The president can also make policy by issuing an executive order, a lawmaking authority that lies outside the legislative process (see Chapter 13).

Because bureaucrats are the people who actually provide public service daily, they often have specialized knowledge of societal problems. Recognizing their expertise, elected officials rely on bureaucrats when formulating policies. House and Senate committees frequently call on bureaucrats to review and comment on bills that, if approved, the bureaucrats will implement. Bureaucrats often testify at the hearings congressional members hold to investigate and study problems. Thus bureaucrats regularly take part in policy formulation, whether at their own impetus or at the request of elected officials.

In recognition of bureaucrats' expertise, Congress often includes vague or ambiguous language in legislation, relying on bureaucrats to fill in the program details as they implement the policy. Vague legislative language may also reflect the congressional sponsors' need to win majority votes in both the House and the Senate and to secure presidential approval of the policy.

Policy Approval

Policy approval, the third stage of the policy cycle, occurs when Congress and the president vote to approve or reject a bill that presents a formulated public policy. When Congress and the president, or Congress alone over a president's veto, approve bills, the laws thus created authorize government action. These **authorization laws** provide the plan of action to address a given societal concern and identify the executive branch unit that will put the plan into effect. The law may authorize an existing executive unit to carry out the policy, or it may establish a new unit to do the job. Although some authorization laws mandate the spending of money every year to achieve the law's goals, such as the law that created Social Security, most authorization laws do not authorize the spending of money. Instead, the majority of public policies rely on congressional and presidential approval of annual spending bills for their funding.

authorization law
A law that provides the plan of action to address a given societal concern and identifies the executive branch unit that will put the plan into effect.

Appropriation Approval

In the next phase of the policy process, appropriation, Congress and the president specify how much money each bureaucracy is authorized to spend during the budget year. Through the budget process (see Chapter 16), Congress and the president formulate appropriation bills, which are plans for the distribution of government revenue to government entities, including bureaucracies, legislative bodies, and judicial bodies. Approved appropriation bills—**appropriation laws**—give bureaucracies the legal authority to spend money during a specific fiscal year.

Bureaucrats play three key roles in the budget process. First, at the request of the president, bureaucrats develop an annual budget request for their agencies. Second, Congress calls on bureaucrats to justify their budget requests. In turn, bureaucrats lobby members of Congress to allocate to their agencies the funds they requested. With limited money available, bureaucracies typically do not receive all the funding they request. Therefore, bureaucracies compete with one another for their piece of the limited budget pie. Once Congress and the president approve the appropriation bills, bureaucrats take on their primary public policy role; they put public policy into action.

appropriation law
A law that gives bureaucracies and other government entities the legal authority to spend money.

Policy Implementation

Policy implementation, the second-to-last stage of the policy cycle, is the main work of bureaucrats. To put policy into action, bureaucrats must first interpret the authorization law and then carry it out. Congress and the president delegate to bureaucrats the authority to determine the best way to implement the policy; this authority is called **administrative discretion.** Applying administrative discretion, bureaucrats use their expertise and best judgment to interpret vague laws, establish programs and procedures aimed at achieving the policy goals, and make the day-to-day decisions necessary to execute public policy. Elected officials risk the loss of control over the content of public policy when they delegate administrative discretion to bureaucrats. However, they have numerous tools to hold bureaucrats accountable, which we discuss later in this chapter.

Bureaucrats use administrative discretion to establish programs, rules, regulations, and standards necessary for the effective and efficient implementation of policy. **Administrative rule making** is the process by which upper-level bureaucrats use their administrative discretion to create rules, regulations, and standards that the bureaucracy will then enforce. For example, recognizing its lack of expertise in the specifics of how to prevent air and water pollution, Congress delegated to the Environmental Protection Agency (EPA) the authority to establish policy. The EPA sets specific pollution emissions standards to implement the Clean Water and Clean Air Acts. Although Congress does not approve these EPA administrative standards, the standards have the force of law.

Agencies involved in administrative rule making also engage in **administrative adjudication;** they have the authority to determine if their rules are violated and to impose penalties on the violators. Citizens who disagree with an agency's application of its administrative rules or those whom an agency finds guilty of violating its rules may challenge the agency's decisions through a lawsuit. For example, if the Social Security Administration denies an individual benefits, that person can appeal the decision through Social Security Administration procedures. Once she has exhausted those administrative procedures, if the denial is upheld, she can file a lawsuit challenging it.

administrative discretion
The authority delegated to bureaucrats to use their expertise and judgment when determining how to implement public policy.

administrative rule making
The process by which an independent commission or agency fills in the details of a vague law by formulating, proposing, and approving rules, regulations, and standards that will be enforced to implement the policy.

administrative adjudication
The process by which agencies resolve disputes over the implementation of their administrative rules.

Policy Evaluation

The last stage of the policy process is policy evaluation—the assessment of the intended and unintended effects of policy implementation. As mentioned earlier, people assess government by determining the effectiveness and efficiency of public services and benefits delivered. Therefore, the implementation of policy by bureaucrats, that is, bureaucratic performance, is the key to citizens' satisfaction with government, and the key to government success.

In 1973, political scientists Jeffrey L. Pressman and Aaron B. Wildavsky published their study of a federally funded economic development program, which concluded that it is "amazing that federal programs work at all" given the hurdles bureaucrats encounter.[17] Their landmark research fueled outcries for increased transparency and evaluations of public policies. As a result, policy evaluation has become a larger component of the workload of legislators and bureaucrats.

Because elected officials and citizens want proof of the efficiency and the effectiveness of implemented policies, agencies must document what they do and the impact of their work. Because citizens do not elect bureaucrats, they do not have the opportunity to fire public servants whose performance is unsatisfactory. Therefore, citizens defer the responsibility for bureaucratic accountability to members of Congress, the president, and the judges who preside over the courts because these elected and appointed government officials have legal means to monitor bureaucrats' work and to hold them accountable.

Bureaucratic Accountability

When it comes to public service, everyone is watching. The courts, through the mechanism of lawsuits, review the actions of the executive and legislative branches to ensure that they are constitutional and legal. Congress and the president, as the creators and funders of bureaucracies, can threaten to revamp or eliminate any bureaucratic organization, or to decrease its funding, if its performance falls short of expectations. Congress and the president not only structure bureaucracies to foster efficient, effective, and accountable public service but also pass laws to increase self-policing by bureaucrats.

sunshine laws
Legislation that opens up government functions and documents to the public.

People outside government, including many ordinary citizens, also keep a close eye on bureaucracies. **Sunshine laws** open up government activities and documents to the public, fostering transparency and supporting the public's right to know about government actions and decision making. However, laws, including sunshine laws, are effective only if citizens know about them and take advantage of them.

Accountability to the People

One of the first national sunshine laws was the Administrative Procedure Act (APA) of 1946. The APA responded to citizens' and interest groups' concerns about the fast growth in the number of agencies involved in administrative rule making and the lack of transparency and accountability of the bureaucratic rule makers. The APA standardized rule-making procedures, and all federal agencies except those specifically excluded by their authorization legislation must comply with them. These procedures include requiring bureaucracies to publicize their proposed rules in the *Federal Register*, a daily national government publication. Agencies also must publish an invitation for people to offer comments on their proposals.

To facilitate this open process, www.regulations.gov, the national government website, posts proposed administrative rules and accepts electronically submitted comments on the rules. In this way, people can have a voice in administrative rule making. Such citizen input is essential to democracy, because bureaucrats propose and approve more administrative rules each year than Congress proposes and approves pieces of legislation. Once the agency collects and reviews the comments that people have submitted, it must publish its approved rules in the *Federal Register*.

The Freedom of Information Act (FOIA), a 1966 amendment to the APA, requires national agencies to give citizens access to government documents on request and at a reasonable cost. Today, the act also requires all federal executive units to proactively post on their websites information of interest to the public, without the need for a FOIA request.

The Government in the Sunshine Act of 1976 requires all multi-headed national agencies, except those in the Executive Office of the President, to conduct open, public meetings where citizens can testify and present their concerns about these agencies' procedures as well as their past, current, and potential actions.

As discussed in Chapter 11, all levels of government are using the Internet to offer services to citizens more efficiently and cost effectively, and to foster accountability. In September 2000, the General Services Administration (GSA) launched the national government's one-stop portal to national, state, local, and tribal government agency websites. The site, www.usa.gov, puts government information and services at your fingertips.

In a democracy, bureaucrats, like elected officials, operate in a fishbowl. Working face to face, or computer screen to computer screen, with the people whom they serve, they are in full view of anyone interested in monitoring them. Sunshine laws and e-government provide citizens with the means to find out what is going on in the bureaucracy. When citizens or watchdog groups identify a problem with bureaucratic operations, they frequently turn to the media to bring public attention to the issue, because the media are always ready to report on bureaucratic inefficiency and impropriety. A more expensive option for citizen and interest group action against bureaucratic waste and misconduct is the filing of a lawsuit.

Accountability to the Courts

Through the litigation process, the U.S. judicial system seeks to ensure that bureaucrats and bureaucracies comply with the law, including the authorization laws that create them, the appropriation laws that fund them, the constitutional protections for due process and equal treatment, the Administrative Procedures Act, the sunshine laws, and any other laws Congress applies to them. If an individual or group believes that a bureaucrat or bureaucracy has violated the law, they can file a lawsuit. For example, people or organizations can file lawsuits against the National Security Administration if they believe NSA employees violated the Fourth Amendment's protection against unreasonable search and seizure.

In July 2017, a federal court ruled that the Environmental Protection Agency did not have the authority to impose a two-year moratorium on enforcing parts of new methane regulations. Environmental interest groups, including the Environmental Defense Fund, had sued the EPA, claiming that the moratorium was illegal because the new methane regulations had successfully navigated the Administrative Procedure Act's rule-making process during the Obama administration. The court indicated that if the Trump administration did not want to enforce the new regulations, then it must follow the APA procedures to repeal the regulations; in the meantime, the regulations must be enforced.[18]

Accountability to Congress

Bureaucrats must always keep in mind the preferences of Congress if they want to survive, for Congress approves the legislation that creates (and eliminates), regulates, and funds bureaucracies. The Senate has an additional mechanism for promoting bureaucratic accountability, in that more than one-quarter of the president's appointees are subject to Senate confirmation. The confirmation process for political appointees gives senators a degree of influence over the leadership and direction of executive departments and agencies.

Another means by which Congress encourages bureaucratic accountability is through the monitoring of bureaucracies' policy implementation, a form of legislative oversight. When the media, citizens, or interest groups bring concerns about a bureaucracy's policy implementation to the attention of legislators, Congress might launch an investigation. If, consequently, Congress and the president are dissatisfied with that bureaucracy's performance or behavior, they can cut its budget, modify its legal authority, or even eliminate the agency.

Congress can force itself to evaluate a bureaucracy's performance by including a **sunset clause** in the authorization law that establishes an agency or a program. A sunset clause creates an expiration date for a program or policy, meaning the program or policy will end unless Congress and the president reauthorize it through new legislation.

sunset clause
A clause in legislation that sets an expiration date for an authorized program or policy unless Congress reauthorizes it.

Accountability to the President

The president also has several tools for holding bureaucracies accountable. Like Congress, the president can use the legislative process to ensure accountability by approving or vetoing authorization and appropriation bills. In addition, because

>On June 8, 2017, former FBI director James Comey testified in front of the Senate Select Committee on Intelligence as part of its investigation into possible ties between the Trump presidential campaign and Russia. Comey was also asked questions about his interactions with the president up to the time when the president fired Comey from his position of FBI director. What were the findings and results of the Senate Select Committee on Intelligence's investigation?

©Mandel Ngan/AFP/Getty Images

most top political appointees serve at the president's pleasure, they are responsive to the president's policy preferences—and in this way, they and their agencies are accountable to the president.

Today, the Office of Management and Budget (OMB), an EOP agency, is the key lever in the president's efforts to hold the bureaucracy accountable. The OMB evaluates bureaucratic performance for the president. The OMB also spearheads the development of the president's budget, controls the implementation of appropriation laws, and regulates administrative rule making. Through its Office of Information and Regulatory Affairs, the OMB ensures that regulations created by executive branch agencies through the administrative rule-making processes are not "unnecessarily costly"[19] and that they support the president's policy preferences.

Internal Accountability

The president, Congress, the courts, and ordinary citizens have multiple means by which to hold bureaucrats accountable. But bureaucrats, who themselves are taxpayers, also worry about inefficiency and waste in public service. Legislated codes of behavior, whistleblower protections, and inspectors general help foster accountability from within bureaucracies.

ETHICS IN GOVERNMENT ACT   The Ethics in Government Act of 1978 established the Office of Government Ethics (OGE), which is charged with preventing conflicts of interest by bureaucrats (political appointees, SES bureaucrats, and civil servants). A **conflict of interest** arises when a public servant is in a position to make a work decision or take a work action from which he or she can personally benefit. In such a situation, the public servant's private interest is in conflict with his or her responsibility to serve the public interest.

In 1992, the OGE published a comprehensive set of ethical standards for federal bureaucrats, which provides guidelines for ethical, efficient, and effective behavior. Some agencies also have their own codes of behavior. Moreover, many of the professions in which bureaucrats are members (lawyers, doctors, nurses, accountants, engineers, and so on) also have established codes of behavior. Importantly, however, codes of behavior are just guidelines. They do not stipulate what a bureaucrat should do in a given situation. Thus bureaucrats must use discretion when applying such codes to their daily work of providing public service.

WHISTLEBLOWER PROTECTIONS AND INSPECTORS GENERAL   **Whistleblowers** are people who disclose government misconduct, waste, mismanagement, abuse of authority, or a threat to public health or safety. They can be bureaucrats or private parties. To enhance bureaucratic accountability, the 1978 Civil Service Reform Act provided some protections to civil servants who are whistleblowers, including the establishment of the Office of Special Counsel to protect the jobs of public servants who blow the whistle.

In another attempt to improve internal accountability, Congress approved the Inspector General Act in 1978. This law aims to ensure the integrity of public service by creating government watchdogs, called **inspectors general,** appointed by the president and embedded in government agencies to monitor policy implementation and investigate alleged misconduct. The law requires the appointment of the inspectors general without regard to their political affiliation and strictly based on their abilities in accounting, auditing, or investigation. Today 72 federal agencies have inspectors general.

conflict of interest
In the case of public servants, the situation in which they can personally benefit from a decision they make or an action they take in the process of doing their jobs.

whistleblower
A bureaucrat or private party who discloses to the government mismanagement, fraud, waste, corruption, or threats to public health and safety.

inspectors general
Political appointees who work within a government agency to ensure the integrity of public service by investigating allegations of misconduct by bureaucrats.

"We're supposed to check our politics at the door and call things as we see them. If we uncover things that reflect badly on the government, we're legally and morally obliged to report it. We're obliged to do that for the good of the country." So explained Clark Ervin, who held the position of inspector general at the Departments of State and Homeland Security.[20]

In summary, codes of ethics, whistleblower protection laws, and inspectors general enhance the ability of the bureaucrats themselves to police the agencies in which they work, and sunshine laws give government outsiders various instruments for monitoring the bureaucracy. But many citizens and government officials believe that more needs to be done to improve bureaucrats' record of performance.

Can Bureaucratic Performance Be Improved?

In the United States, bureaucrats perform every job imaginable. They generally do their jobs so well that we rarely think about how their work positively affects us around the clock. We and our elected officials are nevertheless quick to bash the bureaucracy at the slightest hint of inefficiency. Similarly, the media seize upon any opportunity to report on problems with bureaucrats and bureaucracies. When was the last time you heard a news report or were involved in a friendly conversation that praised a public servant?

Yet the U.S. Postal Service delivers hundreds of millions of pieces of mail 6 days a week, and rarely is a letter or a package lost. Thousands of planes safely take off from and land at U.S. airports every hour, guided by federal bureaucrats in the person of air traffic controllers. Millions of senior citizens receive a Social Security benefit on time every month.

Policy scholar Charles Goodsell has found that two-thirds to three-fourths of Americans report their encounters with government bureaucrats and bureaucracy as "satisfactory."[21] However, Pew Research Center surveys show that Americans' views on government performance are mixed and can change quickly.[22] Table 14.3 shows that in 2015 the majority of survey respondents believed the government was doing a very or somewhat good job in nine policy areas. Two years later, the majority of respondents believed the same in only six of those nine areas. In addition, while in 2015 the majority of respondents indicated that the government was doing a bad job in three policy areas, by 2017 the majority indicated that the government was doing a bad job in six policy areas. The "Analyzing the Sources" feature shows how partisanship may explain the changing viewpoints on government performance.

The Best-Performing Bureaucracies

Research consistently shows that some federal agencies perform better than do others. Political scientists William T. Gormley and Steven Balla reviewed national performance data and summarized the characteristics of federal agencies that perform well.[23] They found several characteristics common among better-performing bureaucracies. They include language in the agency's authorization legislation that clearly states what the agency is expected to accomplish and that delegates high levels of administrative discretion, which allows bureaucrats to determine the best way to achieve the agency's goal. Better-performing bureaucracies tend to be those with easily measured goals, especially goals that include providing resources to citizens (such as Social Security benefits) as opposed to taking

TABLE 14.3 Public Ratings of Government Performance on Select Issues

Majority of respondents said the "government is doing a very/somewhat good job . . ."

2015	2017
Responding to natural disasters (79%)	Responding to natural disasters (64%)
Setting workplace standards (76%)	Setting workplace standards (65%)
Ensuring safe food and medicine (72%)	Ensuring safe food and medicine (61%)
Keeping country safe from terrorism (72%)	Keeping country safe from terrorism (66%)
Maintaining infrastructure (52%)	Maintaining infrastructure (51%)
Strengthening the economy (51%)	Strengthening the economy (53%)
Protecting the environment (59%)	
Ensuring access to health care (56%)	
Ensuring access to quality education (52%)	

Majority of respondents said the government is doing a bad job . . .

2015	2017
Managing U.S. immigration system (72%)	Managing U.S. immigration system (68%)
Helping people get out of poverty (54%)	Helping people get out of poverty (74%)
Ensuring basic income for 65+ (52%)	Ensuring basic income for 65+ (59%)
	Ensuring access to health care (64%)
	Ensuring access to quality education (56%)
	Protecting the environment (56%)

SOURCE: Pew Research Center, "Government Gets Lower Ratings for Handling Health Care, Environment, Disaster Response," December 14, 2017.

resources (tax collection). Another factor correlated with good performance is high levels of support for the agency's mission from elected officials, the media, and diverse groups of citizens. High levels of support typically result in an agency's receiving the funding it needs to accomplish its goals. Effective agency leaders who develop and maintain high levels of support from government officials and interested citizens and groups also are important to well-performing bureaucracies.

Does Contracting-Out Improve Performance?

Contracting-out to private businesses certainly decreases the number of bureaucrats on the federal payroll. But does outsourcing foster more effective public service? Does it save taxpayer dollars? For-profit organizations must make a profit to survive, so how can they accomplish public service at a lower cost?

Paul Light, a renowned political scientist, notes that although the salaries of shadow bureaucrats are about the same as government bureaucrats doing similar

IS IT GOVERNMENT PERFORMANCE OR PARTISANSHIP?

When surveys ask citizens their views on government performance, the expectation is that respondents are assessing the quality of services provided. The data below and that are presented in Table 14.3 are from two Pew Research Center surveys conducted just two years apart. The data below report the percentage of Democratic and Democratic-leaning respondents (one category) and Republican and Republican-leaning respondents (a second category) who say "the federal government is doing a very/somewhat good job. . . ." Use the data below and the data presented in Table 14.3 in your analysis.

Practice Analytical Thinking

1. Summarize the shifts in the opinions in each table. What events between November 2016 and November 2017 might have contributed to the shifts in opinion?

2. If you were a bureaucrat in an agency with the mission of strengthening the economy, responding to natural disasters, or managing the U.S. immigration system, what would you take away from these survey results?

3. What do these data suggest about citizens' satisfaction survey results such as these?

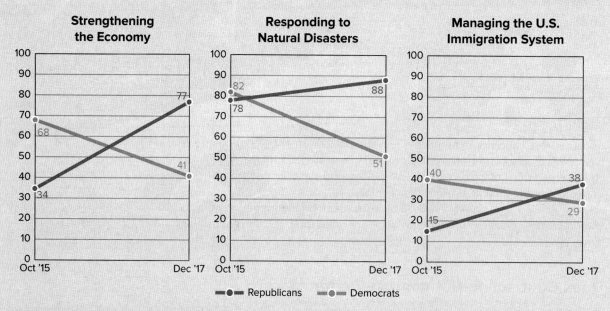

SOURCE: Pew Research Center.

work, the full cost to the government for contracted work includes administrative costs and profit. Therefore, in many cases, the government pays more for work contracted out to shadow bureaucrats. In addition, Light notes that the federal bureaucracy does not have enough bureaucrats to monitor government contractors,[24] which means that holding contractors accountable for delays, cost overruns, and quality of results is difficult.

The problems the Internal Revenue Service (IRS) encountered with contracting-out collection of late payments in 1996 and 2006 provide a good study. The contracted debt collectors were paid up to 25 percent of what they collected. However, due to cost overruns and concerns about abuses of taxpayer rights, the IRS abandoned the use of contractors. According to the IRS, the outsourcing cost the government millions more than it actually collected from taxpayers. Yet, in 2017, following a provision in a 2015 law and a congressional order, the IRS began contracting with debt collectors again.[25]

In his review of the status of federal contracting-out, Peter Schuck, professor of law emeritus at Yale University, found that "the vast amount of contracting reduces accountability and transparency, and raises serious questions about agencies' ability to manage these contracts effectively and measure contractors' performance."[26] The lack of accountability for the results of contractors' work is a growing concern for the Government Accountability Office (GAO), the independent agency that functions as Congress's watchdog for bureaucratic performance and use of taxpayer money. The GAO has determined contract management to be a high-risk function for numerous federal agencies.[27]

>On September 7, 2017, Hurricane Irma skirted Puerto Rico, leaving one million people without electricity and much damage to buildings and infrastructure. FEMA Disaster Survivor Assistance team members and members of the Small Business Administration arrived in Puerto Rico within days to register survivors for assistance and to assess damage. Then on September 20, 2017, Hurricane Maria slammed Puerto Rico, crippling the island and leaving its 3.4 million residents in a humanitarian crisis. FEMA's response to the devastation of Irma and Maria in Puerto Rico has been severely criticized by Puerto Ricans, politicians, nonprofit organizations, and media outlets.

Source: Kenneth Wilsey/FEMA

In 2018, the Senate Homeland Security and Government Affairs Committee and the House Oversight and Government Reform Committee both initiated investigations of the Federal Emergency Management Agency's (FEMA) handling of a failed contract. The $156 million contract to provide 300 million emergency meals to hurricane victims in Puerto Rico was canceled after the contractor was unable to fulfill the contract. Senators stated that the contract was "further evidence of systemic weaknesses in FEMA's contracting practices."[28]

Unlike government bodies, private businesses, including those with government contracts, can legally function behind closed doors—unless and until concerned citizens, watchdog groups, the media, and government officials force the doors open through congressional investigations or lawsuits. In 1986, the federal government enacted the False Claims Act. This law allows a private party with information about fraud against a government program committed by a person or a company (typically a federal contractor) to file a lawsuit on behalf of the government. If the government wins such a lawsuit and recovers money, the whistleblower is eligible to receive 15–30 percent of the recovered money.

Three Americans working for a Dubai-owned shipping services company blew the whistle in 2010, filing a suit claiming that the company overcharged the U.S. Navy by close to $50 million. Two of the three whistleblowers are former federal bureaucrats. In November 2015, the Justice Department announced that it was moving forward with the lawsuit after two years of unsuccessful settlement talks with the company.[29] Between 1986 and 2015, the federal government recovered approximately $48 billion under the False Claims Act.[30]

Citizens' Role in Bureaucratic Performance

Citizens turn to the government to provide services and solve problems. Unfortunately, the solutions to many societal problems are not known. How can government prevent crime? How can government solve homelessness and poverty? Can government find a cure for cancer? Often several potential solutions are offered, but elected officials might not agree on what potential solution to try. This is why political scientists describe a policy cycle: a circular, ongoing process that typically yields incremental changes while attempting to improve current policies based on policy evaluations.

As we have discussed, the national government's success in serving the people well depends on many factors. The president and Congress play key roles in providing the resources bureaucrats and bureaucracies need to perform well so citizens are satisfied. They must appoint good leaders who hire competent civil servants, legislate clear policy goals, delegate ample administrative discretion, and fund agencies and programs at sufficient levels. Ultimately, even if all other factors correlated with a well-performing bureaucracy are in place, the bureaucracy will fail without the participation and compliance of the people it serves.

The effectiveness of public policies depends on people's knowledge of and compliance with the law. It depends on their applying for the government programs for which they qualify. It depends on their conformity to the rules, regulations, standards, and directions of bureaucrats. This symbiotic relationship is essential to the success of government. Governments are tapping into new media technologies to enhance citizens' knowledge of and ability to apply for government services and benefits. Governments are also using new media technologies to increase transparency and, hence, accountability and hopefully citizens' satisfaction.

Thinking Critically About What's Next in the Bureaucracy

Ultimately, for citizens to be satisfied with their governments, elected officials must "do politics" well by formulating and agreeing to enact sound solutions to societal problems, and by appropriating the funds necessary to properly and fully implement public policies. To be successful in "doing politics," elected officials must rely on the expertise, competence, and neutrality of bureaucrats who participate in every stage of the policy cycle, with their primary responsibility being the provision of public goods and services (administering policy) daily.

Although bureaucrat bashing pervades the media and is a common practice among candidates and elected officials—such as calls to "drain the swamp"—surveys consistently find that the majority of citizens are satisfied with their interactions with bureaucrats and with how the national bureaucracy is addressing their top areas of concern. However, there are always challenges to the efficiency, effectiveness, and accountability of the bureaucracy, as well as opportunities to make improvements.

E-government and one-stop web portals are proliferating as governments attempt to provide education about and easy access to public goods and services. The objective is to improve efficiency, accountability, and ultimately, citizen satisfaction. The national government is also attempting to improve transparency and accountability by increasing reporting requirements for federal contractors and grant recipients, and posting much of this information on government websites, such as www.usaspending.gov.

Citizens' satisfaction with their governments depends on governments' abilities to address the challenges and take advantage of the opportunities that present themselves to bureaucrats and bureaucracies.

Learning Summary

1. Define *bureaucrat* and *bureaucracy*.
   a. Compare bureaucrats and private-sector employees in terms of their education, occupations, age, and job satisfaction.
   b. Describe the characteristics of Max Weber's ideal bureaucratic structure.

2. Explain what differentiates the three categories of federal bureaucrats.
   a. Explain the hiring processes and criteria as well as the job security of political appointees.
   b. Explain the hiring processes and job security of those in the Senior Executive Service.
   c. Explain the hiring processes and criteria as well as the job security of civil servants.
   d. Explain the concept of a representative bureaucracy.
   e. Identify the three independent administrative agencies established by the Civil Service Reform Act of 1978 and the main function of each.
   f. Identify at least two legal limits imposed on national employees who are unionized that private employees who are unionized do not experience.

3. Summarize the role of state, local, and shadow bureaucrats in national public policy implementation.
   a. Describe some of the work the federal government outsources/contracts out.
   b. Explain the relationship between the growth in the federal budget, the growth in number of state and local bureaucrats, and the stability in the number of federal bureaucrats.

4. Compare the size and scope of the national bureaucracy in 1789 with the size, scope, and complexity of the national bureaucracy today.
   a. Describe federal departments by summarizing the types of responsibility, leadership structure, and accountability to the president they have.
   b. Describe independent administrative agencies by summarizing the type of responsibilities they have and how they are structured to be independent of partisan politics.
   c. Describe regulatory commissions by summarizing the type of responsibilities they have and how they are structured to be independent of partisan politics.
   d. Describe the functions of government corporations.
   e. Explain the function of the Executive Office of the President.

5. Summarize the breadth of the work of bureaucrats.
   a. Explain the politics-administration dichotomy and why it is an ideal, not a reality.
   b. Identify the roles of bureaucrats in each of the six stages of the policy process: agenda setting, policy formulation, policy approval, appropriation approval, policy implementation, and policy evaluation.
   c. Identify the stage at which the main work of bureaucrats is done, and describe why and how they use their administrative discretion at this stage of the policy process.

6. Explain who holds the bureaucracies accountable and how they hold them accountable
   a. Identify several ways the people can hold bureaucracies accountable.
   b. Identify what the courts hold bureaucracies accountable for.
   c. Identify several ways Congress holds bureaucracies accountable.
   d. Identify several ways the president holds bureaucrats and bureaucracies accountable.
   e. Explain the internal mechanisms created by Congress to hold bureaucrats accountable.

7. Explain some of the barriers and opportunities to improving bureaucratic performance.
   a. Describe the nature of citizen satisfaction with government performance.
   b. Identify some of the characteristics of the best-performing bureaucracies.
   c. Describe some of the expected benefits, as well as some of the problems, of contracting-out.
   d. Identify what Congress, the president, and citizens can do to improve the performance of the bureaucracy.

Key Terms

administrative adjudication 483

administrative discretion 483

administrative rule making 483

appropriation law 483

authorization law 482

bureaucracy 466

bureaucratic structure 468

bureaucrats 466

civil servants 471

conflict of interest 487

contracting-out (privatizing, outsourcing) 474

department 476

government corporation 479

independent administrative agency 476

independent regulatory commission 479

inspectors general 487

merit-based civil service 471

patronage system 470

plum book 470

politics-administration dichotomy 480

red tape 468

representative bureaucracy 472

Senior Executive Service (SES) 470

shadow bureaucrats 474

sunset clause 486

sunshine laws 484

whistleblower 487

For Review

1. List and describe the structures of a bureaucracy as identified by Max Weber.
2. Compare and contrast the following categories of bureaucrats: political appointees, civil servants, Senior Executive Service bureaucrats, and shadow bureaucrats.
3. What accounts for the fact that the national budget and the scope of its responsibilities have continued to grow in recent decades, yet the number of its civilian employees has remained stable?
4. Differentiate the five categories of national bureaucracies by discussing differences in their structures and the type of services they provide.
5. Describe the role that bureaucrats play at each of the six stages of the policy process.
6. List the many people, groups, and government officials outside a bureaucracy to whom bureaucrats are accountable, and give examples of how they hold bureaucrats accountable. Describe some mechanisms of internal accountability for federal bureaucrats and bureaucracies.
7. Describe some of the benefits government officials expect from contracting-out. Describe some of the disadvantages of contracting-out.
8. According to Gormley and Balla, what are three or four characteristics of bureaucracies that perform well?

For Critical Thinking and Discussion

1. Do citizens expect too much from government and hence from bureaucrats and bureaucracies? Explain your answer.
2. Identify at least one public service that you believe the national government should not contract-out to private-sector organizations, and defend your choice(s).
3. How often do you interact with national bureaucrats? What about state bureaucrats? Local bureaucrats? Give some recent examples of each interaction and your satisfaction with those interactions. Can you identify some shadow bureaucrats that have provided you with public goods or services? If so, were you satisfied with their performance?
4. Compose a list of public services provided to you since you woke up this morning. Were you satisfied with the services? Which of those services do people generally take for granted?

Resources for Research AND Action

Internet Resources

Office of Management and Budget
www.whitehouse.gov.omb This website provides access to the current and previous federal budget documents and historical budget tables.

Office of Personnel Management
www.usajobs.gov To find out about government job opportunities as well as apprenticeships, fellowships, and internships, visit this Office of Personnel Management website.

Partnership for Public Service
www.ourpublicservice.org/OPS/ This nonprofit, nonpartisan organization is working to revitalize the federal government by inspiring a new generation of public servants.

Regulations.gov
www.regulations.gov You can review proposed and approved rules, regulations, and standards of federal executive agencies and submit your comments about them.

U.S. Government Printing Office
www.gpoaccess.gov/gmanual/browse This website allows you to view the most current *United States Government Manual* as well as several older editions of the manual.

USA.gov
www.usa.gov Use this site as a one-stop portal to national, state, and local government officials, agencies, and documents.

Recommended Readings

DiIulio, John. *Bring Back the Bureaucrats: Why More Federal Workers Will Lead to Better (and Smaller!) Government.* West Conshohocken, PA: Templeton Press, 2014. DiIulio makes the argument, supported by statistics and facts, that the national government has too few of its own bureaucrats to function well. Instead, the national government relies on state, local, and shadow bureaucrats because elected officials know that citizens claim to prefer smaller government.

Goodsell, Charles T. *The Case for Bureaucracy: A Public Administration Polemic,* 4th ed. Washington, DC: CQ Press, 2004. A review of the common myths and criticisms of bureaucracy, with evidence to show that they are indeed unsupported.

Gormley, William T., Jr., and Steven J. Balla. *Bureaucracy and Democracy: Accountability and Performance.* Washington, DC: CQ Press, 2004. Uses case studies and examples to illustrate what the national bureaucracy does and why it is important, and draws on social science theories to describe how bureaucracy works and the complex and conflicting demands put on it.

Light, Paul. *A Government Ill Executed: The Decline of the Federal Service and How to Reverse It.* Boston: Harvard University Press, 2008. Claiming that the federal government is no longer able to "faithfully execute the laws," Light offers an agenda for reform to reverse the decline in federal service, which includes decreasing the size of the bureaucracy and reducing federal outsourcing.

Schuck, Peter H. *Why Government Fails So Often: And How It Can Do Better.* Princeton and Oxford: Princeton University Press, 2014. By studying domestic policy failures and a few successes, Schuck identifies bureaucratic, political, and cultural factors that assist in explaining why public policies perform poorly and reforms that would improve the likelihood of policy successes.

Movies of Interest

Argo (2012)
Based on real events, this movie tells the story of a collaboration between the U.S. State Department, the CIA, Hollywood moviemakers, and the Canadian government to smuggle American officials out of Iran after the 1979 invasion of the U.S. embassy there. The plan to save 6 U.S. officials hiding in the Canadian Embassy in Iran, while Iranians hold 56 other U.S. officials hostage, revolves around the claim that the U.S. officials are part of a Canadian movie crew searching for a location for their movie.

Pentagon Papers (2003)
In this made-for-TV movie, a Department of Defense bureaucrat, Daniel Ellsberg, has access to classified documents that he decides should be brought to the public's attention. The documents detail the secret history of U.S. involvement in Vietnam, which includes bureaucrats misinforming decision makers and the public. Ellsberg risks his career and his freedom to try to get the truth to the public. Based on a true story.

Mississippi Burning (1989)
Two committed FBI agents, with very different personal styles, investigate the disappearance of three civil rights workers during the 1960s. Based on a true story.

Serpico (1973)
The story of a New York City police officer who is living his dream of being a cop. His dream job turns life threatening when he blows the whistle on corruption in the police force, the existence of which shows that not all of Serpico's coworkers are as committed to public service as he is. Based on a true story.

References

1. Peter Overby, "Trump's Efforts to 'Drain The Swamp' Lagging Behind His Campaign Rhetoric," *NPR Politics,* April 26, 2017, www.npr.org.
2. Governing Data, January 19, 2018, www.governing.com/gov-data/federal-employees-workforce-numbers-by-state.html.
3. Bureau of Labor Statistics, "Employment Projections," Table 2.1, Employment by Major Industry Sector, 2006, 2016, and projected 2026.
4. Gerald Mayer, "Selected Characteristics of Private and Public Sector Workers," Congressional Research Service. March 2014.
5. Danny Vinik, "America's Government Is Getting Old," *Politico,* September 27, 2017.
6. Charles T. Goodsell, *The Case for Bureaucracy: A Public Administration Polemic,* 4th ed. (Washington, DC: CQ Press, 2004), 104–106.
7. Norman J. Baldwin, "Public Versus Private Employees: Debunking Stereotypes," *Review of Public Personnel Administration* 12 (Winter 1991): 1–27.
8. Gallup, http://gallup.com/poll/185396/gov-workers-happier-retirement-plans-benefits.aspx.
9. Eric Katz, "Key GOP Senator Calls Trump's Pay Freeze Plan Ill-Advised," *Government Executive,* March 1, 2018, www.govexec.com.
10. Office of Personnel Management, "Senior Executive Service Overview and History."
11. Ibid.
12. Jimmy Carter, "Federal Civil Service Reform Remarks Announcing the Administration's Proposals to the Congress: March 2, 1978."
13. Bureau of Labor Statistics, "News Release: Union members–2015," Table 3: Union affiliation of employed wage and salary workers by occupation and industry, 2014–2015 annual averages.
14. Gerald Mayer, "Selected Characteristics of Private and Public Sector Workers," Congressional Research Services, March 2014.
15. https://www.usaspending.gov/Pages/TestView.aspx?data=OverviewOfAwardsByFiscalYearTextView.
16. George Will, "'Big Government' Is Ever Growing, on the Sly," *National Review,* February 25, 2017.
17. Jeffrey L. Pressman and Aaron Wildavsky, *Implementation: How Great Expectations in Washington Are Dashed in Oakland: Or, Why It's Amazing That Federal Programs Work at All* (Berkeley and Los Angeles: University of California Press, 1973).
18. Lisa Friedman, "Court Blocks E.P.A. Effort to Suspend Obama-Era Methane Rule," *The New York Times,* July 3, 2017.
19. William T. Gormley Jr. and Steven J. Balla, *Bureaucracy and Democracy: Accountability and Performance* (Washington, DC: CQ Press, 2004), 67.
20. Matt Kelley, "Probes at NASA Plummet Under Its Current IG," *USA Today,* January 11, 2008.
21. Charles T. Goodsell, *The Case for Bureaucracy,* 54.
22. Pew Research Center, "Government Gets Lower Ratings for Handling Health Care, Environment, Disaster Response," December 14, 2017.
23. Gormley and Balla, *Bureaucracy and Democracy,* 164–178.
24. Paul Light, "Contractors in Federal Workforce," November 12, 2013.
25. Stacy Cowley and Jessica Silver-Greenberg, "Outside Collectors for I.R.S. Are Accused of Illegal Practices," *The New York Times,* June 23, 2017, https://nyti.ms/2tXfXdC.
26. Peter H. Schuck, *Why Government Fails So Often: And How It Can Do Better,* (Princeton and Oxford: Princeton University Press, 2014), 325.
27. Ibid.
28. Charles S. Clark, "FEMA Meals Contractor's Proposal Was Rife with False Claims, Senators Allege," *Government Executive,* February 23, 2018.
29. Christopher Drew and Danielle Ivory, "U.S. to Sue Contractor It Says Bilked the Navy," *The New York Times,* November 18, 2015.
30. Whistleblower Legal Center, "The False Claims Act," http://www.whistleblowerlegalcenter.com/false-claims-act.php?keyword=false%20claims%20act.

CHAPTER 15

The Judiciary

Source: ©Fred Schilling/Supreme Court of the United States/Getty Images

THEN

The federal judiciary did not affect the daily lives of citizens due to its limited jurisdiction as established by the Judiciary Act of 1789.

NOW

All major policy issues—social, economic, and political—eventually end up in the courts, where judges interpret laws; therefore, courts make policies that affect the daily lives of citizens.

NEXT

Will calls to reform the term of office of federal judges and justices succeed?

Will the partisan battles over judicial appointments and over the Senate's advice and consent powers continue?

Will the judicial branch retain its status as the most trusted branch of government?

"The interpretation of the

laws is the proper and peculiar province of the courts. A constitution is in fact, and must be, regarded by the judges as a fundamental law. It therefore belongs to them to ascertain its meaning as well as the meaning of any particular act proceeding from the legislative body," declared Alexander Hamilton in *Federalist No. 78.*

Courts resolve legal disputes, which are conflicts over law, and in the process, judges and jurors must determine the facts of the case. At the same time, judges must interpret relevant laws and then apply them to the facts of the case while protecting the constitutional rights of all parties involved in a lawsuit.

Why do judges have to interpret laws before applying them? As discussed throughout this textbook and acknowledged by Hamilton in *Federalist No. 78,* laws are often vague, ambiguous, and even contradictory. Therefore judges, through their interpretation and application of laws in the context of a lawsuit, play an important role in ascertaining the meaning of laws and ensuring their constitutionality. In so doing, the courts make policy.

The inevitability that the courts will make policy has politicized the process by which federal judges are nominated and confirmed. The battles over replacing deceased Justice Antonin Scalia and then retired Justice Anthony Kennedy on the Supreme Court bench highlight how partisan politics affect the most trusted branch of government: the courts.

Learning Objectives

After reading this chapter, students should be able to:

- Explain how courts resolve legal disputes.
- Describe the various federal courts, their jurisdictions, and the methods for selecting judges to staff them.
- Outline the process by which the U.S. Supreme Court selects and resolves legal disputes.
- Describe judicial policy making and the constraints on it.
- Present a brief history and status report of the Roberts Court.

What Do Courts Do?

In our federal system of government, with dual sovereignty, both the national government and the state governments are sovereign, each having its own authority to make laws, execute laws, and resolve conflicts over its laws (as explained in Chapters 2 and 3). One characteristic of this dual sovereignty is that the national government establishes national law, and each state government establishes its own state laws. A second characteristic of dual sovereignty is the **dual court system,** in which each state has a judicial system that is responsible for resolving legal disputes over the state's laws, while the federal judicial system is responsible for resolving legal disputes over national laws (Figure 15.1).

Unlike the legislative and executive branches, which proactively respond to citizens' needs and demands by formulating, approving, funding, and implementing laws, judges (and the courts in which they work) are reactive. Judges must wait for someone to file a lawsuit (a legal dispute) before they can do their work. In addition, while elected legislators and executives represent their constituents, judges do not have constituents to represent. Judges are responsible for resolving disputes over whether accused persons have harmed society or another person by their actions or inactions, as well as determining the constitutionality of laws and their applications. Therefore, in our democracy we expect elected legislators and executives to be partial to the majority of their constituents—the principle of

dual court system
The existence of 50 independently functioning state judicial systems, each responsible for resolving legal disputes over its state laws, and one national judicial system, responsible for resolving legal disputes over national laws.

majority rule. At the same time, we expect judges to be independent—that is, impartial to individuals or groups—and uphold the Constitution and laws that comply with it.

To clarify what judges and courts do, we first explore the sources of law in the United States. Then we consider how the courts resolve disputes over laws.

Sources of Law in the United States

law
A body of rules established by government officials that bind governments, individuals, and nongovernment organizations.

Law is a body of rules established by government officials that bind governments, individuals, and nongovernment organizations. A goal of law is to create a peaceful, stable society by establishing rules of behavior that government enforces, with punishments imposed on those whom the government finds guilty of violating the law. Another goal of law is to create processes by which conflicts about the rules and expected behaviors can be resolved. There is a variety of sources of law in the United States, including constitutions, pieces of legislation, executive orders, rules and regulations made by administrative bodies, and judicial decisions. From these sources come different types of law, all of which must comply with the U.S. Constitution.

common law
Judge-made law grounded in tradition and previous judicial decisions, instead of in written law.

doctrine of *stare decisis*
From the Latin for "let the decision stand," a common-law doctrine that directs judges to identify previously decided cases with similar facts and then apply to the current case the rule of law used by the courts in the earlier cases.

precedent cases
Previous cases with similar facts that judges identify for use in a new case they are deciding; judges apply the legal principles used in the precedent cases to decide the legal dispute they are currently resolving.

JUDICIAL DECISIONS: COMMON LAW **Common law** is judge-made law grounded in tradition and previous judicial decisions. When there is no written law for judges to apply when resolving disputes, the judges use their understanding of the societal norms of justice and fairness to resolve conflicts. The legal principle established by the court (common law) is binding on other judges when resolving later cases with similar facts. The common-law **doctrine of *stare decisis*** (Latin for "let the decision stand") directs judges to identify previously decided cases with similar facts and then apply to the current case the rule of law used by the courts in the earlier cases. The previous cases with similar facts identified by judges are **precedent cases.**

The United States inherited, and then built on, a system of common law from England. When a newly established court in the United States had no written law to guide its decision, it used British common law, and then eventually U.S. common law. Common law was the predominant form of law in the United States in the 19th century, before the volume of state and national legislation, rules, and regulations expanded. Eventually, many of the legal rules and principles developed by judges to resolve disputes over property, contracts, and harm caused by another person's negligent behavior were enacted in written laws.

Although the doctrine of *stare decisis* directs judges to ground their decisions in precedents, judges do have the discretion to step away from precedent if there are contradictory precedents, or if they believe the earlier decision was wrong (that is, if it misinterpreted or misapplied the law). Ultimately, common law gives judges the responsibility for interpreting law, especially if there are few precedents to guide them.[1]

In her book *The Majesty of the Law: Reflections of a Supreme Court Justice,* Sandra Day O'Connor notes, "the genius of the common law in the United States has been its capacity to evolve over time—case by case and issue by issue—as the courts apply basic legal principles developed over the past to resolve the challenges posed by new situations."[2]

constitutional law
The body of law that comes out of the courts in cases involving the interpretation of the Constitution.

CONSTITUTIONS: CONSTITUTIONAL LAW Constitutions regulate the behavior of governments and the interactions of governments with their citizens. The body of law established in constitutions is **constitutional law.**

In the United States, the U.S. Constitution is the supreme law of the land. All other laws must comply with the U.S. Constitution. National laws and treaties cannot violate the U.S. Constitution. State constitutions and laws cannot violate the U.S. Constitution. Throughout U.S history, courts have had to resolve disputes over the meaning of the language in the U.S. Constitution. For example, in 1974 the Supreme Court had to resolve a conflict arising from President Nixon's claim of constitutionally established executive privilege—the right to withhold information from other branches of the government. As the Court stated in *United States v. Nixon,* "In the performance of assigned constitutional duties, each branch of the Government must initially interpret the Constitution, and the interpretation of its powers by any branch is due great respect from the others. [President Nixon's] counsel, as we have noted, reads the Constitution as providing an absolute privilege of confidentiality for all Presidential communications. Many decisions of this Court, however, have unequivocally reaffirmed the holding of *Marbury v. Madison* (1803), that '[i]t is emphatically the province and duty of the judicial department to say what the law is.'"[3] In this case, the Court acknowledged executive privilege of presidents to keep some communications confidential. At the same time, the Court determined that Nixon had refused to provide subpoenaed material for use in a criminal case in order to protect the general concept of executive privilege and that this refusal could not prevail over constitutional due process rights in the criminal case.

>President Nixon, with his daughter at his side, says farewell to members of the cabinet and White House staff after resigning from the presidency in August 1974. Nixon's resignation came after the U.S. Supreme Court ruled that presidential executive privilege did not extend to his refusal to provide material subpoenaed in a criminal case. The Court found that constitutional due process rights of the accused prevailed over Nixon's use of executive privilege to withhold tapes of phone conversations he had in his possession.
Source: National Archives and Records Administration (NLNP-WHPO-MPF-E3384C(12).)

LEGISLATION: STATUTES   By the early 20th century, rapid changes in society and the economy forced legislators in Congress and the states to create laws to regulate the behavior of individuals and organizations to further the public good and protect individual liberties and rights. Laws written by legislatures are called legislation, acts, and statutes. Governments often compile legislative law in one document. All legislation may be in one consolidated document, such as is found in the **U.S. Code,** which is a compilation of all the laws ever passed by the U.S. Congress. The U.S. Code has 50 sections spanning a range of issues including agriculture, bankruptcy, highways, the postal service, and war and defense. At the state level, each state has a **penal code,** which is the compilation of all its criminal law.

U.S. Code
A compilation of all the laws passed by the U.S. Congress.

penal code
The compilation of a state's criminal law—legislation that defines crime—into one document.

EXECUTIVE ORDERS   Article II, Section 1, of the U.S. Constitution states that "the executive power shall be vested in [the] president of the United States." This power has been interpreted to allow the president to issue orders that create and guide the bureaucracy in implementing policy as well as orders that establish commissions. A president can enact an executive order without input from the other branches of government, though executive orders are subject to judicial review and depend on the legislature for funding. Because executive orders have the force and

> Reacting to President Trump's executive order imposing a temporary ban on admitting all refugees and citizens from seven mostly Muslim nations, hundreds of people protested at airports around the country, including Miami International Airport, on January 29, 2017. Did the U.S. Supreme Court ultimately find Trump's executive order banning admission of citizens from several mostly Muslim nations constitutional or unconstitutional?

©C.M. Guerrero/Miami Herald/TNS via Getty Images

effect of law, they represent a crucial tool in the president's lawmaking toolbox.

Within his first two weeks in office in January 2017, President Trump signed an executive order that temporarily banned admission to the United States for all refugees and citizens from seven mostly Muslim nations. Several successful lawsuits filed in federal courts blocked the implementation of this travel ban. Trump issued a second travel-ban executive order in March 2017. Lawsuits again followed the executive order. Ultimately, the Supreme Court allowed part of the ban to go into effect. That travel ban expired in October 2017 before the Court heard several appeals, so the Court dismissed the appeals. In September 2017, Trump put forth a third ban, which has no expiration date. The third ban restricts travel from eight nations, six of which are predominantly Muslim, and two that are not: North Korea and Venezuela. Again, lawsuits were filed. In January 2018, the Supreme Court agreed to hear an appeal of a lower federal court's finding that the third travel ban was not legal. The brief urging the Supreme Court to hear the appeal argued that the lower federal courts "have overridden the president's judgments on sensitive matters of national security and foreign relations, and severely restricted the ability of this and future presidents to protect the nation."[4] In June 2018, the Supreme Court sent the case back to the 9th Circuit Court to reconsider.

ADMINISTRATIVE RULES AND REGULATIONS: ADMINISTRATIVE LAW As we saw in Chapter 14, legislation that creates policies and programs also delegates discretion to the bureaucrats in the executive branch whose job it is to implement them. Applying their administrative discretion, bureaucrats determine the best means to achieve the goals of the policies they execute. In the lawmaking process known as administrative rule making, bureaucrats use their administrative discretion to establish specific rules, regulations, and standards necessary for the effective and efficient implementation of policy. The rules, regulations, and standards made by bureaucrats through administrative rule making have the force of law.

An example of administrative law is the standards established by the Social Security Administration to determine eligibility for Social Security disability benefits. Once established, bureaucrats in the Social Security Administration offices apply the standards case-by-case in their review of medical documentation to determine which applicants are qualified to receive disability benefits. Conflicts over the application of the standards can end up in a courtroom for resolution.

Resolving Legal Disputes

adversarial judicial system
A judicial system in which two parties in a legal dispute each present its case and the court must determine which side wins the dispute and which loses.

To resolve legal disputes raised in lawsuits, courts in the United States have an **adversarial judicial system,** in which the two sides (parties) in a legal dispute each presents its set of facts. At the end of a lawsuit, one party will win and the other party will lose. Two kinds of legal disputes are brought to courts: questions of facts are resolved in trial courts, and questions of interpretation and application of law are resolved in appellate courts.

TRIAL COURTS   **Trial courts** have **original jurisdiction,** which means they are the first courts to hear a case. Trial courts resolve lawsuits by determining the truth of what occurred—the facts of the case. The dispute in a trial court may involve the claim that a defendant harmed society by violating criminal law, or it may involve the claim that a defendant caused harm to an individual, a group, or an organization by violating civil law.

Trials include the questioning of witnesses by lawyers for both parties and the presentation of evidence. The accused usually has the choice between a bench trial and a jury trial. In a **jury trial,** a group of citizens selected to hear the evidence determines guilt or liability. Each juror (member of the jury) is expected to be impartial and neutral and base her or his decision on the facts presented in the courtroom. In a **bench trial,** the judge who presides over the court proceedings decides guilt or liability; there is no jury. In federal trial courts, the jurors must unanimously agree on the verdict.

CRIMINAL TRIALS   **Criminal law** is the body of law dealing with conduct considered harmful to the peace and safety of society as a whole, even when directed against an individual. Each state establishes its own criminal law, compiled in its penal code. In addition, Congress has established national criminal law; however, the vast majority of crimes are defined by state legislation, not national legislation. Therefore, state courts resolve the overwhelming majority of criminal lawsuits. The government whose criminal statute was violated—either the national or state government—files the lawsuit, as the prosecutor against the defendant. For example, when a government arrests and accuses a person of setting a house on fire (arson), it is the state in whose territory the crime occurred that has the authority to bring a lawsuit, charging the person with violating its criminal law. At times, an act may violate both state and federal criminal law. In that situation, the state government and the national government can each prosecute based on its own law.

In a criminal case, the government as prosecutor has the burden to prove its case against the defendant **beyond a reasonable doubt,** which means there is no doubt in the mind of the judge (bench trial) or the jury that the defendant is guilty of violating the criminal law as charged. When a court finds a criminal defendant guilty, typically the judge (even where there is a jury) determines the punishment. However, because the overwhelming majority of defendants charged with criminal offenses plead guilty before trial, most criminal cases never go through a trial. In criminal cases, punishments can range from community service to capital punishment, depending on the severity of the crime.

As discussed in Chapter 4, criminal defendants who go to trial have a variety of constitutional rights to guarantee due process before the government infringes on their life, liberty, or pursuit of happiness through punishment. Some of these rights include the right to a speedy trial; to exclusion of evidence that law enforcement gained through an unreasonable search or seizure; to assistance of counsel, including counsel paid for by the government for indigent defendants accused of serious crimes; and to protection from cruel and unusual punishment. Defendants found guilty have the legal right to an appeal, although the overwhelming majority do not appeal guilty verdicts. Because the Constitution protects people from double jeopardy, which is the trying of a person again for the same crime he or she has been cleared of in court, the government does not have the right to appeal not-guilty verdicts.

State and federal courts resolve criminal cases. However, both levels of government spend much more time resolving the larger volume of civil cases brought to them.

trial court
Court with original jurisdiction in a legal dispute that decides guilt or liability based on its understanding of the facts presented by the two disputing parties.

original jurisdiction
Judicial authority to hear cases for the first time and to determine guilt or liability by applying the law to the facts presented.

jury trial
A trial in which a group of people selected to hear the evidence presented decides on guilt or liability.

bench trial
A trial in which the judge who presides over the trial decides on guilt or liability.

criminal law
The body of law dealing with conduct so harmful to society as a whole that it is prohibited by statute, and is prosecuted and punished by the government.

beyond a reasonable doubt
The standard of proof the government must meet in criminal cases; the government must convince the judge or the jury that there is no reasonable doubt that the defendant committed the crime.

CIVIL TRIALS **Civil law** is the body of law dealing with private rights and obligations that are established by voluntary agreements (written and oral contracts) or laws.[5] Civil lawsuits involve disputes between individuals, between an individual and a corporation, between corporations, and between individuals or corporations and a government. In civil law disputes, one party (the complainant) alleges that some action or inaction by the other party (the respondent) has caused harm to his or her body, property, psychological well-being, reputation, or civil rights or liberties.

When the harm is to a person's body or property and is caused by another person's negligence or other wrongful act it is known as a **tort.** Well-publicized tort lawsuits include medical malpractice suits (disputes over claims that negligence of medical professionals caused harm) and product liability lawsuits (disputes over claims that a product, from toys to makeup to medicine, caused harm). The most common civil lawsuits stem from traffic accidents. Divorce and other family conflicts are also resolved in civil lawsuits because these disputes deal with obligations and rights created by a marriage contract.

Courts have a range of procedures that the variety of civil lawsuits must follow. However, some common practices are seen across civil suits. For example, the complainant who files the lawsuit has the burden to prove that the respondent caused the harm. The burden of proof used in civil lawsuits is lower than that used in criminal trials. In civil trials, the complainant must prove that the **preponderance of evidence** is on his or her side—that is, the evidence indicates that the respondent is more likely than not to have caused the harm and is therefore liable.

Unlike criminal defendants, the respondents in civil suits do not have a constitutional right to the assistance of counsel. Nor do the complainants. This may explain why so many people who are harmed by the action or inaction of another, and have grounds to file a civil lawsuit, decline to do so; they often cannot afford a lawyer. In addition, the overwhelming majority of civil lawsuits are settled (resolved) before trial. Respondents found liable for causing harm are not punished like those found guilty in criminal cases, but instead are required to remedy the harm, which often means paying monetary damages to the complainant. (See Table 15.1 for a summary comparison of criminal and civil trials.)

Verdicts in both criminal and civil trials may be appealed to correct errors in the interpretation or application of law made by the judge presiding over the trial. We now turn to differentiating appellate procedures from trial procedures.

TABLE 15.1 Comparison of Criminal and Civil Trials

Characteristic	Criminal trial	Civil trial
The accusation	Defendant harmed the peace and safety of society by violating the criminal law	Respondent's action or inaction caused harm to an individual or group
Accuser	State or federal government whose criminal law was alleged violated (prosecutor)	Individual or group that alleges harm (complainant)
Standard of proof	Beyond a reasonable doubt	Preponderance of evidence
Verdict	Guilty or acquitted (not guilty)	Liable or not liable
Outcome	Punishment	Remedy

APPELLATE COURTS   **Courts of appeal** have **appellate jurisdiction,** which means they are responsible for identifying and correcting errors made by judges in previous lawsuits when they interpreted and applied law. Often, courts of appeal must clarify laws to determine if the judge(s) in the previous trial/hearing properly interpreted and applied the relevant laws to the case. At other times, courts of appeal must choose between laws that conflict. In the process of clarifying laws and choosing between conflicting laws, courts of appeal determine what the law is, and in so doing, they make law.

Appellate court cases do not include the questioning of witnesses, nor do they use juries. Instead, each party to the legal dispute submits a legal brief that presents the facts as it sees them and legal material, including what they see as relevant law and favorable legal findings in precedent cases. The goal of each party's legal brief is to persuade the court to rule in its favor. A panel of judges reviews the legal briefs as well as transcripts from the trial court and any previous appellate court hearings from the case. The judges may allow each party to make a brief oral argument, typically about 20 minutes per side. The panel of judges decides the case (with a simple majority vote) based on the review of this paperwork, oral arguments when they are allowed, and conversations among themselves and their law clerks. Appellate courts often write, announce, and publish opinions that provide the legal rationale for the court's decision. Table 15.2 summarizes the differences between trial and appellate courts.

JUDICIAL REVIEW   In resolving disputes, courts are responsible for ensuring that the U.S. Constitution is not violated. In the landmark case *Marbury v. Madison* (1803), the Supreme Court, led by Chief Justice John Marshall, grabbed for itself the power of judicial review.[6] **Judicial review** is the Court's authority to determine that an action taken by any government official or governing body violates or does not violate the Constitution (see Chapter 2). In the *Marbury* case, the Supreme Court ruled that a section of the Judiciary Act of 1789 was unconstitutional. In its ruling, the U.S. Supreme Court argued something it had never argued before: that it had the power not only to review acts of Congress and the president, but also to decide whether those acts (including laws enacted) were consistent with the Constitution and to strike down laws that conflicted with constitutional principles.

Legal scholar Joel B. Grossman observes that in *Marbury*, "[Chief Justice John] Marshall made it abundantly clear that the meaning of the Constitution was rarely self-contained and obvious and that those who interpreted it—a role he staked out

courts of appeal
Courts with authority to review cases heard by other courts to correct errors in the interpretation or application of law.

appellate jurisdiction
Judicial authority to review the interpretation and application of the law in previous decisions reached by another court in a case.

Marbury v. Madison
The 1803 Supreme Court case that established the power of judicial review, which allows the Court to strike down laws passed by the other branches that it views to be in conflict with the Constitution.

judicial review
Court authority to determine that an action taken by any government official or governing body violates or does not violate the Constitution; established by the Supreme Court in the 1803 *Marbury v. Madison* case.

TABLE 15.2 Comparison of Trial and Appellate Courts

Characteristic	Trial Courts	Appellate Courts
Type of Jurisdiction	Original	Appellate
Conflict to be resolved	Is the accused guilty or not guilty?	Did an error of interpretation or application of law occur?
Evidence	Witnesses testify to facts.	Legal briefs and court transcripts are reviewed.
Who decides?	Judge in bench trial; jury in jury trial	Panel of judges

for the federal courts but one that did not reach its full flowering until the mid-twentieth century—made a difference."[7] Judicial review is the most significant power the Supreme Court exercises. Over time, the Court has extended this power to apply not only to acts of Congress, the president, and federal bureaucrats, but also to laws passed by state legislatures and executives, as well as to state court rulings and acts of state and local bureaucrats. Today, all courts in the United States, federal and state, have judicial review authority. We now turn to an examination of the federal judicial system.

The Federal Court System

Under the Articles of Confederation, there was no national judiciary. State courts handled all lawsuits, unless the suit was between states. Congress had jurisdiction over those suits. During the Constitutional Convention, delegates agreed on the need for a national judiciary, but they sparred over the appropriate structure and powers of a national judiciary. The debate was not resolved at the Constitutional Convention. Instead, Article III of the Constitution established that "Judicial power of the United States shall be vested in one supreme Court and in such inferior Courts as the Congress may from time to time ordain and establish."

Article III also stated that the power of the national judiciary extended to all disputes over the U.S. Constitution, national laws, and treaties. While the Constitution provided for the basic structure of the U.S. Supreme Court and power of the federal judiciary, it is through legislation that Congress established inferior courts and special courts with distinctive jurisdiction. In addition, through legislation and judicial decision making, the authority of the federal courts has evolved.

Jurisdiction of Federal Courts

federal question
A question of law based on interpretation of the U.S. Constitution, federal laws, or treaties.

diversity of citizenship
The circumstance in which the parties in a legal case are from different states or the case involves a U.S. citizen and a foreign government.

court of last resort
The highest court in a court system.

The ability of a court to hear a case depends on whether that court has jurisdiction—the authority of a court to hear and decide a case. Article III, Section 2, of the Constitution strictly defines federal court jurisdiction. In this passage, federal courts are empowered to hear only cases involving a federal question or diversity of citizenship. A **federal question** is a question of law based on interpretation of the U.S. Constitution, federal laws (including common law, statutory law, administrative law, and executive orders), or treaties. **Diversity of citizenship** means that the parties in the case are individuals from different states or that the case involves a U.S. citizen and a foreign government. It may also mean that the suit centers on the complaint of one or more states against another state or states.

One twist to the independent functioning of state and federal courts in the U.S. dual court system, as presented in Figure 15.1, is that a lawsuit that began in a state court can end up in the federal court system. Specifically, if a state court case raises questions about federal laws (typically about U.S. constitutional rights during an appeal), then the case may be brought to a federal appeals court after the state **court of last resort**, the highest court in the state's court system, has an opportunity to hear the case.

The Structure of the Federal Courts

The federal court system is a three-tier hierarchical system. At the bottom, in the first tier, are the U.S. district courts, which are the federal trial courts with original jurisdiction over a case. In the middle tier of the federal system are the U.S. courts of appeals,

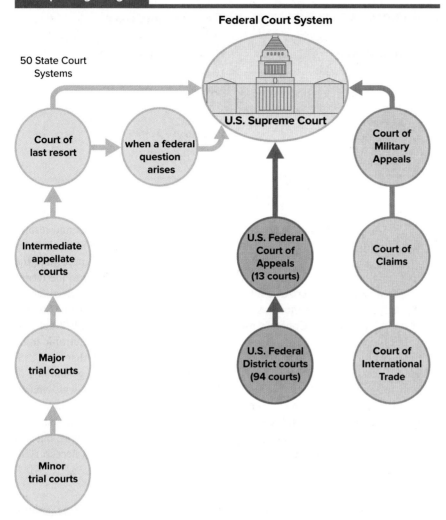

Federal Court System

U.S. Supreme Court

50 State Court Systems

Court of last resort

when a federal question arises

Intermediate appellate courts

Major trial courts

Minor trial courts

U.S. Federal Court of Appeals (13 courts)

U.S. Federal District courts (94 courts)

Court of Military Appeals

Court of Claims

Court of International Trade

FIGURE 15.1 ■ **Jurisdiction in the Dual Court System** In the dual court system, the cases that state courts have authority to hear differ from those that the federal courts have authority to hear. What cases are within the jurisdiction of a state's court system? What cases are within the jurisdiction of the federal court system? When can a case that began in a state court system move into the federal court system?

which have appellate jurisdiction. At the top of the federal court hierarchy, in the top tier, is the U.S. Supreme Court. The U.S. Supreme Court has appellate jurisdiction and rarely used, very limited original jurisdiction. The U.S. Supreme Court is the federal court of last resort. Table 15.3 summarizes the types of jurisdiction each Article III court has.

Congress has complemented the three-tier system of Article III courts (district courts, courts of appeals, and the U.S. Supreme Court) with specialized courts. Congress established the specialized courts through legislation grounded in its authority under Article I of the Constitution to "constitute tribunals inferior to the Supreme Court," and so the specialized courts are known as Article I courts.

Article I courts

Courts created by Congress under constitutional authority provided in Article I that help administer and resolve conflicts over specific federal legislation.

ARTICLE I COURTS Congress establishes **Article I courts** to administer and resolve conflicts regarding specific federal laws.[8] Article I courts include U.S. Bankruptcy Courts, the U.S. Court of Military Appeals, and the U.S. Tax Court. Unlike the judges sitting on the benches in Article III courts, who are appointed to life terms, the judges who preside over Article I courts are appointed to serve for fixed terms.

Probably the most well-known Article I court is the Foreign Intelligence Surveillance Act (FISA) court. Congress established the FISA court in a 1978 act that spells out the procedures for government collection of human and electronic intelligence.[9] In June 2013, Britain's *Guardian* newspaper reported that the U.S. National Security Agency (NSA) was collecting telephone records of millions of Verizon customers. Then, *The Washington Post* reported that the NSA was wiretapping servers of nine companies, including Google and Facebook. The FISA court approved the national government's applications for this electronic surveillance. This government infringement on their privacy startled American citizens, but was quickly defended by President Obama and members of Congress as necessary to national security.

district courts

The federal trial courts with mandatory jurisdiction.

mandatory jurisdiction

The requirement that a court hear all cases filed with it.

U.S. DISTRICT COURTS There are 94 federal district courts with 677 judgeships. Each state has between one and four district courts, and Washington, D.C., and Puerto Rico each have a district court. These **district courts** do the bulk of the work of the federal judiciary because these trial courts have original, **mandatory jurisdiction,** which means they must hear every case filed with them. A judge presides over the trial court. The judge, or a jury if the defendant chooses a jury trial, decides what happened in the case, based on the application of the law to the facts presented in the courtroom. It is in the trial court that two parties to the lawsuit present evidence and witnesses testify. Congress, through legislation, can modify the jurisdiction of district courts as well as change the number of district court judgeships.

Defendants who lose in the district courts have the right to appeal their cases to a federal court of appeals if they believe the presiding judge misinterpreted or misapplied the law. However, the majority of cases decided by the district courts are not appealed. Therefore, the overwhelming majority of federal lawsuits that go to trial are resolved in the district courts.

federal courts of appeals (circuit courts)

Federal courts with mandatory, appellate jurisdiction.

U.S. COURTS OF APPEALS At the middle level of the federal judicial hierarchy are 13 **federal courts of appeals,** also called **circuit courts,** with a total of 179 congressionally created judgeships. The First through Twelfth Circuit Courts each has a geographic area over which it has appellate jurisdiction. Each of these circuit courts hears appeals from the district courts in its geographic area (circuit). The Twelfth Circuit is better known as the D.C. Circuit because that is the area its jurisdiction covers, which includes appeals stemming from federal administrative agencies located in Washington, D.C.

The Thirteenth Circuit is better known as the Federal Circuit. The jurisdiction of the Federal Circuit Court is not geographically based; it is issue based. The Federal Circuit Court handles appeals of cases that cover specific federal matters such as international trade, government contracts, and patents. Judges on the courts of appeals work in panels of three to review cases. Similar to the U.S. district courts, the U.S. courts of appeals have mandatory jurisdiction; therefore, they hear all cases that are filed with them. Losing parties can appeal to the U.S. Supreme Court; however, only a very small percentage do. Therefore, the courts of appeals are in fact the last court to hear most cases appealed from the district courts.

THE U.S. SUPREME COURT   At the top of the federal judicial hierarchy sits the **U.S. Supreme Court.** Although the Court has a very limited original jurisdiction, it hears appeals from both the federal courts and the state courts of last resort when cases decided there concern a conflict over federal law (known as a federal question). The framers limited the Supreme Court's original jurisdiction to those cases that concern ambassadors, public ministers, and consuls, and those involving two or more states. But over time, Congress, in cooperation with the Court, has decided that the Court should retain original jurisdiction only in cases involving suits between two or more states.

The U.S. Supreme Court's appellate jurisdiction is **discretionary jurisdiction,** which means the justices choose the cases they will hear from among all the cases appealed to the Court. Ultimately, the justices select to hear only a fraction of the cases appealed to the Supreme Court each term.

Since legislation enacted in 1869, nine judges, called justices, sit on the Supreme Court. One of these justices has been specially selected by a president to serve as the **chief justice,** the judge who provides both organizational and intellectual leadership on the Court. Each of the remaining eight justices is an **associate justice.** Political scientists distinguish periods of court activity by changes in the chief justices; therefore, Supreme Courts are named for the chief justice. Today, we have the Roberts Court, named for the current chief justice, John Roberts, whom President George W. Bush nominated and the Senate confirmed in 2005.

Appointing Federal Judges

The framers wanted to ensure **judicial independence** so that federal judges could make impartial decisions based on the law, protected from the need to win the votes of citizens or support from elected officials to keep their job. See the "Analyzing the Sources" feature to consider the argument for judicial independence made by Alexander Hamilton in *Federalist No. 78.* To foster judicial independence, the

U.S. Supreme Court
Serves as the court of last resort for conflicts over the U.S. Constitution and national laws; in addition to its appellate jurisdiction, the Court has limited original jurisdiction.

discretionary jurisdiction
The authority of a court to select the cases it will hear from among all the cases appealed to it.

chief justice
The leading justice on the Supreme Court, who provides both organizational and intellectual leadership.

associate justice
Title of the eight Supreme Court justices who are not the chief justice.

judicial independence
Insulating judges from the need to be accountable to voters or elected officials so that they can make impartial decisions based on the law.

> When the first woman Supreme Court justice, Sandra Day O'Connor, announced her retirement in the summer of 2005, President G. W. Bush nominated John Roberts to replace her. Before the Senate had an opportunity to vote on the Roberts nomination, Chief Justice William Rehnquist died. Bush withdrew his nomination of Roberts for associate justice, instead nominating him for chief justice. Roberts has served as chief justice since 2005. To keep the bench full (with nine justices) O'Connor agreed to remain on the Court until the Senate confirmed her replacement—Samuel Alito, in January 2006.
©Universal History Archive/UIG/Getty Images

JUDICIAL INDEPENDENCE: IS IT NEEDED? HAS IT BEEN ACHIEVED?

The Constitution guarantees rights on paper. However, the framers understood that a mechanism was needed to ensure that government officials did not abridge those fundamental rights. The mechanism the framers adopted was an independent judiciary, as discussed in the quotes from *Federalist No. 78* presented below.

Federalist No. 78 (Alexander Hamilton, May 28, 1788)

The complete independence of the courts of justice is peculiarly essential in a limited constitution. By a limited constitution I understand one which contains certain specified exceptions to the legislative authority. . . . Limitations [on legislative authority] can be preserved in practice no other way than through the medium of the courts of justice; whose duty it must be to declare all acts contrary to the manifest tenor of the constitution void.

The standard of good behaviour for the continuance in office of the judicial magistracy is certainly one of the most valuable of the modern improvements in the practice of government . . . : In a republic it is a no less excellent barrier to the encroachments and oppressions of the representative body. And it is the best expedient which can be devised in any government, to secure a steady, upright and impartial administration of the laws . . . Periodical appointment, however regulated, or by whomsoever made, would in some way or other be fatal to their necessary independence. If the power of making them was committed either to the executive or legislature, there would be danger of an improper complaisance to the branch which possessed it; if to both, there would be an unwillingness to hazard the displeasures of either; if to the people, or to persons chosen by them for the special purpose, there would be too great a disposition to consult popularity, to justify a reliance that nothing would be consulted but the constitution and the laws.

Practice Analytical Thinking

1. What argument does Hamilton put forward to support the Constitution's creation of an independent judiciary?

2. What mechanism does Hamilton propose to protect judicial independence?

3. Reflect on the following portions of the Constitution and then explain the mechanisms it established to create an independent judiciary: Article II, Section 2, Clause 2; Article II, Section 4; and, Article III, Section 1, Clause 1.

4. Do you think "bad behavior" of a justice is an impeachable offense according to Article II, Section 4? If so, provide some examples of impeachable bad behavior for a justice.

5. Do you believe the constitutional mechanisms established to create an independent judiciary are sufficient? Explain.

framers stated that Article III judges "shall hold their offices during good behavior," which has been interpreted to mean their term extends until they resign, retire, or pass away, or until Congress removes them through the impeachment process. In addition, Article III states that judges "shall at stated times, receive for their services, a compensation, which shall not be diminished during their continuance in office." Their salary cannot be cut by a president or Congress unhappy with their decisions.

Article II of the Constitution establishes the president's authority to appoint, with the advice and consent of the Senate, Supreme Court justices and other federal officers, including federal judges. Therefore, the power to appoint federal judges is a power shared by the president and the Senate. Presidents and senators are aware of the long-term effect a judge, particularly a Supreme Court justice, can have on constitutional interpretation and public policies. However, the Constitution does not establish qualifications for judgeships. Therefore, presidents are left to use their own discretion when nominating judges, and senators also use their discretion when providing advice and consent. What criteria do presidents and senators use in the judicial appointment process?

Selection Criteria

Presidents seek competent nominees who will win Senate consent. In addition, presidents since at least Jimmy Carter have also considered demographic characteristics in efforts to make federal courts more representative of the nation's growing diversity. Unfortunately, as judicial scholars Christoper P. Banks and David M. O'Brien claim, "because the meaning of senatorial 'advice and consent' has never been settled, the political self-interest of presidents and senators makes the federal judicial appointment process politically contentious."[10] The lack of constitutionally enumerated judicial qualifications opens the door even wider to a politically contentious process.

JUDICIAL COMPETENCE What knowledge, skills, and capacities make a judge competent? Constitutionally, federal judges are not required to have a law degree, nor do Supreme Court justices need to have prior judicial experience. Today, a law degree is expected, and judicial experience has also become a means to assess competence of judicial nominees. Prior to President Dwight Eisenhower's presidency (1953–1961), about one-third of Supreme Court nominees were sitting judges. Since 1953, more than two-thirds of the nominees have been sitting judges.[11] Of the justices currently on the Court, only one, Justice Elena Kagan, was not a sitting judge when appointed.

THEN NOW NEXT

Supreme Court Diversity

Characteristic	Then (1981)	Now (2018)
Sex	First woman appointed	Second, third, and fourth woman serving
Race	First African American man serving	Second African American man and first Latina serving
Religion	3 Episcopalian 3 Presbyterian 1 Lutheran 1 Methodist 1 Roman Catholic	6 Catholic 3 Jewish
Average age	67 years	66 years
Age range	51 to 75 years	51 to 85 years
Party affiliation	5 Republicans 4 Democrats	5 Republicans 4 Democrats
Law schools	4 Harvard 1 Howard 1 Northwestern 1 Stanford 1 William Mitchell 1 Yale	4 Harvard 4 Yale 1 Columbia
Prior judicial experience	3 justices had no prior judicial experience	1 justice has no prior judicial experience
Chief justice	15th chief 15th white man	17th chief 17th white man

WHAT'S NEXT?

> Assume that during the next few years, at least one of the two justices in their 80s will retire. What impact do you expect her/his replacement will have on the balance of liberals and conservatives on the bench? Explain your answer.

> Consider the data in this table and the data in Table 15.4. Do you think the Court will become more diverse any time soon? Explain your answer.

> Will a woman chief justice be appointed during your lifetime? What supports your answer?

In addition to legal education and experience, presidents and senators look for candidates who evidence professional and personal integrity, and solid oral and written communication skills. President Obama calculated that Elena Kagan's reputation as a skilled peacemaker who could bring divergent ideological sides together outweighed her lack of experience on the bench when he nominated her to the Supreme Court in 2010. In addition to adding a peacemaker to the ideologically divided bench, Kagan's confirmation by the Senate increased the number of women sitting on the Court to three, an all-time high.

REPRESENTATION OF DEMOGRAPHIC GROUPS The impulse to diversify the Court's membership serves the goal of **descriptive representation,** which is representation on governing bodies of the country's leading demographic groups in proportion to their representation in the population at large. There is an implicit assumption that a justice will better understand and serve the concerns of the racial, ethnic, gender, or other groups to which he or she belongs, thereby offering **substantive representation.** That is, the Latina justice will take the perspective of Latinas, the male justice will consider the policy preferences of men, and so on. However, the representation may be more symbolic than real because not all men have the same views, nor do all women, even if they are of the same race or ethnicity. Therefore, one female or Latino judge cannot represent the diversity of views of the people they look like. Nevertheless, many public figures and citizens say that the Court should mirror as closely as possible the main contours of the national demographic profile, because such descriptive representation offers **symbolic representation,** which indicates that our democracy is functioning appropriately by offering equal opportunity to all to influence government as a government official.

Some presidents appear more concerned than others with enhancing diversity on the federal bench. Table 15.4 suggests that, compared to Republican presidents, Democratic presidents have been more concerned about descriptive representation.

descriptive representation
The attempt to ensure that governing bodies include representatives of major demographic groups—such as women, African Americans, Latinas, Jews, and Catholics—in proportions similar to their representation in the population at large.

substantive representation
Assumption that a government official will best serve the concerns of the racial, ethnic, gender, or other group to which he or she belongs.

symbolic representation
Diversity among government officials is a symbol, an indication, that our democracy, our government by and for the people, is functioning appropriately by offering equal opportunity to influence government by becoming a government official.

TABLE 15.4 Demographics of Federal Judges as a Percentage of Those Confirmed

Characteristic	J. Carter	R. Reagan	G. W. H. Bush	B. Clinton	G. W. Bush	B. Obama	D. Trump
Total number of appointees	261	364	188	372	324	324	29*
Hispanic	6%	4%	4%	6%	9%	9%	0%
Black	14%	2%	7%	17%	7%	19%	0%
White	78%	94%	89%	76%	82%	64%	90%
Female	16%	8%	19%	29%	22%	42%	21%
Male	84%	92%	81%	71%	78%	58%	79%

*Trump's appointees through March 20, 2018.

SOURCE: Pew Research Center, "Trump's Appointed Judges Are a Less Diverse Group than Obama's," March 20, 2018.

Justice Antonin Scalia, in his 2015 dissent in the case establishing a constitutional right to same-sex marriage, wrote that "To allow the policy question of same-sex marriage to be considered and resolved by a select, patrician, highly unrepresentative panel of nine is to violate a principle even more fundamental than no taxation without representation: no social transformation without representation." Scalia went on to say that "The striking unrepresentative character of the body voting on today's social upheaval would be irrelevant if they were functioning as judges, answering [a] legal question." However, because he believed some of his colleagues were making decisions based on their policy preferences, he believed that the lack of diversity on the bench mattered.[12]

POLITICAL IDEOLOGY Mindful that federal judges typically serve far beyond the tenure of the presidents who appoint them, presidents often regard these nominations as a way of cementing their own legacies. Using party affiliation and previous decisions on the bench to assess a nominee's political ideology, presidents nominate judges, including Supreme Court justices, with whom they are ideologically compatible. Liberal presidents nominate liberal judges, and conservative presidents nominate conservative judges.

In February 2016, just ten days before Associate Justice Antonin Scalia died, Chief Justice John Roberts criticized the Supreme Court confirmation process, noting it "is not functioning very well." More specifically, Roberts stated, "Look at my more recent colleagues, all extremely well qualified for the court, and the votes were, I think, strictly on party lines for the last three of them, or close to it, and that doesn't make any sense. That suggests to me that the process is being used for something other than ensuring the qualifications of the nominees."[13]

The battle over Justice Scalia's replacement highlights the partisan battles that have become common in the selection of Supreme Court justices. When Scalia died in February 2016, a partisan battle exploded. Within 24 hours of Scalia's death, Senate Majority Leader Mitch McConnell (R) said that Scalia's seat should remain vacant until the newly elected president would take office in 2017. Republicans argued that President Obama should refrain from nominating a candidate. Democrats fervently disagreed and argued that the Senate should fulfill its constitutional obligation once President Obama nominated a candidate to fill Scalia's vacant seat.

President Obama (D) nominated Merrick Garland for Scalia's seat on March 16, 2016. Garland had won confirmation to the D.C. Circuit Court in 1997 with bipartisan support. However, in 2016, the Senate Judiciary Committee refused to hold hearings on Garland's nomination, which expired on January 3, 2017, when the newly elected 115th Congress convened. Newly elected President Trump (R) nominated Neil Gorsuch on January 31, 2017. On April 3, 2017, the Judiciary Committee voted 11–9, along party lines, to support his confirmation. On April 6, 2017, Senate Democrats filibustered the Senate's vote on Gorsuch. In turn, Senate Republicans invoked the nuclear option for the first time in the selection process for a Supreme Court justice, ending the filibuster with a simple majority vote. Gorsuch was confirmed with a 54–45 vote, with three Democrats joining the Republicans. Vice President Mike Pence (R) presided over the Senate during the vote, just in case his vote was needed to break a tie.[14]

Should There Be a Retirement Age for Supreme Court Justices?

The Issue: If no sitting Supreme Court justices leave the bench, by 2021 at least six justices will qualify for Social Security; their ages will range from 66 to 88. Calls for justices to retire are not unusual, although the call is typically sparked by ideological disagreements. However, as the average age of retirement for justices has risen from 68 before 1971 to 79 today, calls for a mandatory retirement age have grown louder.

Yes: The 9 justices that sit on the Supreme Court are responsible for solving some of the most controversial legal disputes that are dividing our nation today. We cannot afford to leave these vital decisions to justices who may be experiencing even normal, age-related cognitive decline. Although mandatory retirement was made illegal in 1986, there are some exceptions to the law. Most state governments have taken advantage of this and established mandatory retirement ages for their judges; most set the retirement age between 70 and 75. The legitimacy of the Court is at stake.

No: Americans are living longer and healthier lives with each generation. Life expectancy at birth for people born in 1900 was 49 years; for people born in 1950 it was 68 years. For people born in 2012, life expectancy is 79 years. People should not be forced to retire simply because of the number of years they have lived. Retirement should be voluntary unless an employer can prove the employee is no longer competent to do the job. If there is evidence that a justice is declining cognitively and is no longer competent, the justice can be encouraged to retire. If the justice chooses not to retire, then impeachment might be an option; lack of good behavior could be the accusation. This approach serves fairness and due process.

Other Approaches: The federal government should establish successful programs already piloted. For example, the Ninth Circuit Court of Appeals offers a series of mental health assessments, hosts educational programs with neurological experts, and has a hotline for staff and judges to report signs of cognitive decline of judges. Another approach would be to offer an incentive for justices to accept "senior status," which is a form of semi-retirement available to judges at a certain combination of years served and age. Constitutional scholars have suggested another approach: Establish an 18-year term for federal judges.

What do you think?

1. A constitutional amendment is needed to establish an age of retirement or a fixed term for justices. Do you think that Congress and three-quarters of state legislatures would support either amendment? Why or why not?

2. Do you think the statement that justices "shall hold their offices during good behavior" means that they serve a life term until they retire, die, or get impeached? Could it mean "shall keep their job as long as they are competent"? Justify your answer.

3. If a change is made to the term of Supreme Court justices (either by establishing a retirement age or a fixed term), should it apply to all federal judges? Explain why or why not.

The Senate's Role: Advice and Consent

Article II of the Constitution gives the president the authority, with the advice and consent of the Senate, to appoint federal judges. This sharing of power, with the president nominating judges and the Senate confirming them, operates in accordance with our system of checks and balances.

In practice, the Senate's power of advice and consent for presidential nominations to federal offices and judgeships involves the tradition of **senatorial courtesy;** the Senate will not confirm a nominee if a senator from the nominee's home state opposes the nominee. In the case of federal judicial appointments, the Senate Judiciary Committee sends to the nominee's home-state senators a form

senatorial courtesy
A custom whereby the Senate will not confirm a presidential nominee if the nominee is opposed by one (or both) senators from the nominee's home state.

THEN

NOW

> In 1991, the Senate confirmed Supreme Court nominee Clarence Thomas with a 52–48 vote. The reason most often cited for the narrow vote is the testimony of Anita Hill during contentious, nationally televised hearings. Hill claimed that Thomas sexually harassed her ten years earlier when he was her boss at the Equal Employment Opportunity Commission. In 2018, during the Senate confirmation hearings for Supreme Court nominee Brett Kavanaugh, Christine Blasey Ford testified that Kavanaugh sexually assaulted her when they were both teenagers in the 1980s. Kavanaugh was confirmed with a 50–48 Senate vote, which was the narrowest vote since 1881, when Stanley Matthews was confirmed as a Supreme Court justice with a 24–23 vote.

Hill: ©Bettmann/Getty Images; *Ford:* ©Melina Mara/Getty Images

called a "blue slip," so called because it is printed on blue paper, on which the senator can indicate support or opposition to a judicial nominee. At the discretion of the Senate Judiciary Committee chairperson, if one of the home-state senators does not support the nominee, or does not return the blue slip, then the nomination will not move forward in the confirmation process. Today, senatorial courtesy is used in the selection of district court and courts of appeals judges.

The Senate Judiciary Committee gathers information on and interviews judicial nominees. Then, the Committee votes on whether to recommend the nominees to the full Senate. The full Senate uses this vote to signal whether a nominee is acceptable. Sometimes the judiciary committee does not make a recommendation about a nominee, as when members split their vote 7-7 on the nomination of Clarence Thomas to the U.S. Supreme Court in 1991. The full Senate followed this split recommendation with a 52-48 vote to confirm Thomas.

President Obama, like Presidents Bill Clinton and George W. Bush before him, ran into problems with many of his judicial nominees, particularly those nominated to the courts of appeals. Sparked by partisanship, senators from both political parties have used the filibuster to block votes on judicial nominees to promote partisan bias on specific courts. In November 2013, after repeated filibustering of President Obama's nominees, the Democratic majority in the U.S. Senate argued that the Republican minority had gone too far in its efforts to thwart the president. Without one vote from the Republican minority, the Democratic majority approved a filibuster rule change, called the nuclear option, prohibiting the use of the filibuster to block votes on presidential nominees to executive branch positions and all judicial positions except those for the U.S. Supreme Court. In the 2017 confirmation of Justice Gorsuch, the Senate Republicans voted to prohibit the use of the filibuster to block his confirmation to the Supreme Court.

Once Supreme Court justices and other Article III judges are confirmed by the Senate, they serve for as long as they want, or until death, or conviction by the Senate of an impeachable offense. Although lifetime tenure is controversial, as debated in the "Thinking Critically" feature, it also means that such appointees often are the longest-lasting legacies of the presidents who appoint them.

How the U.S. Supreme Court Functions

collegial court

A court made up of a group of judges who must evaluate a case together and decide on the outcome; compromise and negotiation take place as members try to build a majority coalition.

As a **collegial court,** the Supreme Court is made up of a panel of justices who must work closely together to evaluate a case and decide, with a simple majority vote, the outcome. Collegially, they decide what cases to hear, resolve each case heard, and develop the legal reasoning that, as presented in the Court's written opinion, will persuade the public that the Court's decision is correct. The *correct decision* means the justices upheld the legal principles found in the Constitution. Today's reality is that it is common for Supreme Court cases to be decided by a 5–4 vote, which indicates that the justices do not all agree on the same interpretation of constitutional language and its legal principles.

The overwhelming majority of cases decided by the U.S. Supreme Court are appeals. Therefore, we focus on how the Court processes the appeals that are filed with it.

Choosing Cases for Review

certiorari petition

A petition submitted to the Supreme Court requesting review of a case already decided.

Between 7,000 and 8,000 *certiorari* **petitions** are filed with the Court each year, each asking for the review of a case already decided.[15] Ultimately, the justices agree to review about 80 cases in each annual term that begins in October and typically runs through the following June or July.[16] For the thousands of cases the Court decides not to hear, the decision made by the last court to hear the case stands. How do the justices decide which cases to hear? Like the other stages of the decision-making process, "deciding to decide," as Supreme Court scholar H. W. Perry puts it, is a joint activity.[17]

cert memo

Description of the facts of a case filed with the Court, the pertinent legal arguments, and a recommendation as to whether the case should be taken, written by one of the justices' law clerks and reviewed by all justices participating in the pool process.

The decision to place a case on the Supreme Court's docket (schedule of cases it will review) is a collaborative one, with the nine justices and their law clerks (four clerks per associate justice, and five for the chief justice) working together. The Supreme Court justices pool their law clerks so that only one clerk reviews a *certiorari* petition and writes a **cert memo,** which includes a description of the facts of the case, the pertinent legal arguments, and a recommendation as to whether the Court should hear the case. The clerk's cert memo is shared with all the justices. After reviewing the cert memos, the chief justice distributes a list of possible cases, the discuss list. The associate justices may add cases to the discuss list based on their own reviews of cert memos.

writ of *certiorari*

Latin for "a request to make certain"; issued by a higher court, this is an order for a lower court to make available the records of a past case it decided so that the higher court can review the case.

On Fridays throughout the Court's term, the justices meet in conference to discuss the cases on the discuss list.[18] At this point, they vote on whether to issue a writ of *certiorari*–a Latin term roughly translated as "a request to make certain"–for specific cases. The **writ of *certiorari*** is a higher court's order to a lower court to make available the records of a past case so that the higher court can review the case.[19] A writ of *certiorari* is sent when the justices, using their discretionary jurisdiction, agree to hear a case. The justices determine which cases to hear according to a practice known as the **Rule of Four,** under which the justices will hear a case if four or more of the nine justices decide they want to hear it. They do not need to give reasons for wanting or not wanting to hear a case–they simply must vote.

Rule of Four

Practice by which the Supreme Court justices determine if they will hear a case if four or more justices want to hear it.

Considering Legal Briefs and Oral Arguments

When the justices agree to put a case on the docket, the parties in the litigation shift into high gear (see Figure 15.2). The petitioner (the party that sought the Court's review) files with the Court a brief—a document detailing the legal argument for the desired outcome. After the filing of this brief, the opposing party files its own brief with the Court.

Today, *amicus curiae* briefs are a common part of Supreme Court litigation. Filed by a person or group that is not a party to the lawsuit, an **amicus curiae brief,** or **"friend of the court" brief,** is written to influence the Court's decision in a specific case. Controversial cases with the potential to affect public policy trigger the filing of many *amicus* briefs. In 2013, the 136 amicus briefs submitted in the lawsuit challenging parts of the Affordable Care Act was the highest number filed in one case up to that date. Then, in 2015, 148 amicus briefs were filed in the same-sex marriage case *Obergefell v. Hodges.* One of those 148 briefs was filed on behalf of 370 businesses.[20]

In comparison with the legal briefs filed by the two parties involved in the legal dispute, *amicus curiae* briefs typically put forth new legal arguments, and discuss broader societal effects of potential Court decisions (not just the effect on the litigants). Justices do not legally have to consider the information provided in *amicus curiae* briefs. However, research indicates that justices often use the information or the legal arguments contained in *amicus curiae* briefs to help them decide cases.[21] Judicial scholar Paul Collins found that no type of interest group dominated *amicus* activity, but instead "*amicus* participation in the Court is pluralistic."[22] Associate Supreme Court justice Stephen Breyer argues that the participation of organized interests in the judicial decision-making process provides an avenue for citizen engagement and civic discourse, which support a healthy democracy.[23]

In addition to reviewing legal briefs, justices listen to oral arguments—attorneys' formal spoken arguments that lay out why the Court should rule in their client's favor. Heard in the Supreme Court's public gallery, oral arguments give the justices the opportunity to ask the parties and their lawyers specific questions about the arguments in their briefs. To assist in their preparation for oral argument, justices typically have their law clerks prepare **bench memos,** which summarize the case and outline relevant facts and issues presented in the case documents and the legal briefs. The bench memos may also suggest questions for the justices to ask during oral arguments.[24]

In typical cases, each side's lawyers have 30 minutes to make a statement to the Court and to answer the justices' questions. However, the justices can provide more time for oral argument, as they did in 2012 when they scheduled six hours of oral argument, over the course of three days, for the case challenging the constitutionality of the Patient Protection and Affordable Care Act (2010). The justices frequently interrupt the attorneys during their oral arguments by asking questions and sometimes seem to ignore the lawyers entirely, instead talking with one another. Chief Justice Roberts points out that the justices do not discuss the cases before oral argument. "When we get out on the bench, it's really the first time we start to get some clues about what our colleagues think. So we are often using questions to bring out points that we think our colleagues ought to know about."[25] Associate Justice Kagan notes that "part of what oral argument is about is a little bit of the justices talking to each other with some helpless person standing at

amicus curiae brief ("friend of the court" brief)
A legal brief, filed by an individual or a group that is not a party in the case; it is written to influence the Court's decision.

bench memo
Written by a justice's law clerk, a summary of the case, outlining relevant facts and issues presented in the case documents and briefs, that may also suggest questions for the justices to ask during oral arguments.

FIGURE 15.2 ■ Decision Making on the Supreme Court

the podium who you're talking through."[26] This discourse takes place entirely in public view, and transcripts and even audiotapes are readily available to the public.

After the oral arguments, the justices meet in a private, justice-only conference to deliberate; no law clerks are present, and no information is shared with the public. The justices take a nonbinding vote on the case. If the chief justice votes with the majority, he chooses whether he wants to write the opinion that will provide the legal reasoning for the Court's decision or if he will assign the task to one of the other justices in the likely majority. If the chief justice is not with the majority, the senior member of the majority decides whether to write the opinion or assign the opinion to another justice. The assignment of the majority opinion is crucial to the resolution of the case because, in writing the opinion, the justice may persuade some justices to change their votes, making for a larger majority or possibly turning the majority into the minority, turning the losing party (based on the nonbinding conference vote) into the winning party. So let's consider how judges decide cases.

Resolving the Legal Dispute: Deciding How to Vote

How does each justice decide how to vote in a particular case? Judicial scholars offer several judicial decision-making models. The **legal model** focuses on legal norms and principles as the guiding force in judicial decision making. Specifically, according to the legal model, judges consider existing precedents, relevant constitutional and statutory law, and the intent of those who wrote the relevant laws, when deciding cases. Law schools train lawyers, and therefore judges, to follow the legal model. The **attitudinal model** indicates that judges allow their policy and ideological preferences to influence their decisions. In fact, evidence suggests that Supreme Court justices are for the most part ideologically consistent in their own decision making.[27] Constitutional law professor Dale Carpenter notes, "There's evidence that the justices do vote against their policy preferences from time to time, enough to disrupt the general narrative that they just vote their ideological preferences. But that doesn't stop the general story from being true."[28]

According to the **strategic model,** "while justices' decisions are primarily motivated by policy concerns (thus accepting the attitudinal model), institutional constraints exist that limit the ability of the justices to vote in a manner that is compatible with their attitudes and values in every case."[29] The institutional constraints identified by proponents of the strategic model include the preferences of congress, the president, and other justices sitting on the collegial court, as well as concern for maintaining the legitimacy of the court system. If the Court makes decisions that are too far afield from societal norms, the public might begin to question the legitimacy of the Court in our democracy.

Research on the decision making of the Supreme Court justices suggests that none of these models explains every aspect of judicial decision making. Indeed, the three models must be combined to better understand these decision makers. Judicial scholars Bryan W. Marshall, Richard L. Pacelle Jr., and Christine Ludowise argue that "the behavior of the Supreme Court is governed by the personal preferences of the justices, but that is tempered by the need to attend to precedent as well as the institution's sense of duty and obligation to the law and the Constitution."[30]

legal model
Judicial decision-making model that focuses on legal norms and principles as the guiding force in judicial decision making, including existing precedents, relevant constitutional and statutory law, and the lawmakers' intent.

attitudinal model
Judicial decision-making model that claims judicial decision making is guided by policy and ideological preferences of individual judges.

strategic model
Judicial decision-making model that states that the primary guide for judges is their individual policy preferences; however, their preferences are tempered by their consideration of institutional factors, as well as concern over the legitimacy of the court system.

Legal Reasoning: Writing the Opinions

After the conference at which the nonbinding vote to decide a case occurs, justices and their law clerks begin writing opinions. The justices' law clerks often write the first draft of their opinions and frequently take the lead in communicating with the other justices through their law clerks. In fact, judicial scholar Artemus Ward states: "Modern justices now see themselves and their clerks as comprising an opinion writing team."[31]

The justice assigned the majority opinion will circulate a draft and revise it based on input from the other justices. Revisions are made to strengthen the legal reasoning, to win new votes from justices who were in the minority, or to keep the votes of justices in the majority. Other justices, with their clerks, will draft and circulate opinions with their legal reasoning. Some of these drafts may become concurring opinions; others may become dissenting opinions. **Concurring opinions** agree with the majority decision in the case but disagree with at least some of the legal reasoning or conclusions reached in the majority opinion. **Dissenting opinions** not only disagree with the legal reasoning but also reject the underlying decision in the case.

After the opinions are written and signed off on, the Court announces the decision by publishing it. On rare occasions, the justices read their opinions from the bench. In 2007, Justice Ginsburg read her dissenting opinion in the *Ledbetter v. Goodyear Tire & Rubber*[32] case to bring immediate attention to a decision that she believed would have great, negative consequences, especially on women. Ginsburg's reading was a catalyst for Congress to formulate and enact the Lilly Ledbetter Fair Pay Act in 2009, which overruled the Court's interpretation of a piece of the 1964 Civil Rights Act.

In the *Ledbetter* case, the Court decided that when Ledbetter finally found out about her discriminatory pay, 19 years after her first discriminatory paycheck, it was too late for her to sue. The majority of justices interpreted the 1964 Civil Rights Act as limiting the time to file a lawsuit to no more than 180 days after the first discriminatory paycheck was issued. However, the Fair Pay Act of 2009 states that the 180-day statute of limitation to file an equal pay lawsuit established in the 1964 law resets after each new discriminatory paycheck. The Fair Pay Act is now the law the Supreme Court must apply in discrimination cases.

Although the U.S. Supreme Court is the court of last resort, it does not always have the final word. As in the *Ledbetter* case, Congress can write new legislation to overrule the Court's interpretation of law. In this way, the U.S. Supreme Court is part of an ongoing dialogue, with officials in the other branches and levels of government, on laws and policies.

>The Supreme Court began audio recording oral arguments in 1955, but to date does not allow video recording of, or even photographs to be taken during, oral arguments. Therefore, the only images we have of Supreme Court cases are artists' sketches. The public can download the audio files or listen to the recordings on the Court's website. The National Archives serves as the repository for the Court's recordings.

©Dana Verkouteren/AP Images

concurring opinion
A judicial opinion agreeing with the majority decision in the case but disagreeing with at least some of the legal interpretations or conclusions reached in the majority opinion.

dissenting opinion
A judicial opinion disagreeing both with the majority's disposition of a case and with their legal interpretations and conclusions.

Judges as Policymakers

Courts make law—common law—by deciding cases and establishing legal principles that guide future litigants and judges. The lawmaking function of courts ensures that judges have a powerful role as public policymakers, because the decisions they make profoundly affect not only the parties in the case but also society, the economy, and politics.

Law professor Tom Ginsburg, who compares constitutions from across the globe adopted since 1787, notes that the U.S. Constitution is briefer and covers fewer topics than do more recently approved constitutions. It also does not cover contemporary issues and topics because it was ratified over 225 years ago and has been amended only 27 times. This means that the U.S. Constitution leaves more room for courts to fill in gaps. According to Ginsburg, "all of these factors perversely empower the Supreme Court and make the court much more likely to engage in public policy."[33]

From Judicial Review to Judicial Policy Making

The Court's decision in *Marbury v. Madison* (1803) claimed the power of judicial review for the courts, making the courts a major policymaker. The courts determine what government actions are constitutional. In 1896, the Supreme Court decided in *Plessy v. Ferguson*[34] that the Fourteenth Amendment did not prohibit segregation of people based on race and color in public accommodations, specifically train cars. The Court in *Plessy* established the common-law legal principle of separate but equal. That decision allowed state and local governments to enact laws that permitted, and in some cases even required, segregation by race in a variety of venues, from movie theaters to housing developments to public schools. Then the Court struck a blow to segregation policies with its decision in *Brown v. Board of Education of Topeka, Kansas* (1954).[35] In *Brown,* using the common-law principle of judicial review, the Court reinterpreted the Fourteenth Amendment's equal protection clause, ruling the legal principle of separate but equal unconstitutional, and found segregation laws unconstitutional. The Court took its decision further, calling for integration of public schools with all deliberate speed. Clearly, the Court was engaged in policy making, and the policy has had a tremendous effect on society, the economy, and politics.

Supreme Court Justice Sandra Day O'Connor argues that the *Brown* case was a catalyst for lawsuits in which litigants claim violations of their constitutional rights to equal protection of the law and due process. O'Connor notes that prior to the *Brown* case, conflicts over the separation of powers within the national government and the distribution of powers between the national and state governments dominated the Supreme Court's docket. However, since the *Brown* case, "the Supreme Court's decisions on individual rights have recognized for the first time many of the freedoms that most Americans today assume as our birthrights. Among them are the right to speak freely and advocate for change, the right to worship as we please, and the privilege of political participation."[36] Therefore, judicial policy making includes defending and creating individual rights through the courts' interpretations of laws.

Judicial Activism, Living Constitution, Judicial Restraint, and Originalism

judicial activism
An approach to judicial decision making whereby judges are willing to strike down laws made by elected officials as well as step away from precedents.

When considering the courts' role as policymakers, legal analysts often categorize judges and justices as exercising either judicial activism or judicial restraint. **Judicial activism** refers to the courts' willingness to strike down laws made by

elected officials as well as to step away from precedents, thereby creating new laws and policies. It reflects the notion that the role of the courts is to check the power of the federal and state executive and legislative branches when those governmental entities exceed their authority or violate the Constitution. In contrast, some judges reject the idea that the courts' role is to actively check legislative and executive authority. Noting that people elect officials to those branches to carry out the people's will, these judges observe **judicial restraint**–the limiting of their own power as judges. Practitioners of judicial restraint believe that the judiciary, as the least democratic branch of government, should not check the power of the democratically elected executive and legislative branches unless their actions clearly violate the Constitution.[37]

During the Warren Court (the tenure of Chief Justice Earl Warren, 1953–1969), using the common-law doctrine of judicial review, the Supreme Court took an activist stance, most notably in rejecting the constitutionality of racial segregation. By barring southern states from segregation in a variety of contexts–including schools and other public facilities–the Warren Court powerfully bolstered the efforts of civil rights activists. The activism of the Warren Court also shaped the modern rights of the accused and the modern definitions of the privacy rights of individuals, which later formed the framework for the Court's thinking about abortion rights. Supported by presidents who enforced its rulings, the Warren Court took on a leadership role in changing the nature of U.S. society. Therefore, the majority on the Warren Court, in racial segregation cases and with regard to due process in the criminal justice system, treated the Constitution as a **living Constitution;** that is, their legal interpretations took into consideration changes in social customs and norms.

Although many people connect judicial activism with liberal-leaning court decisions, such as those made by the Warren Court, the reality is that judicial activism is also used to further conservative causes. In fact, judicial scholar Thomas Keck labeled the Rehnquist Court (1986–2005) "the most activist Supreme Court in history."[38] The Rehnquist Court's conservative-leaning activism is evident in cases in which the Court overturned laws enacted by Congress such as the Gun-Free School Zones Act[39] and a section of the Violence Against Women Act that created a right for victims of sexual misconduct to sue in federal courts.[40] For some, the ultimate judicial activism occurred during the 2000 presidential election, when

judicial restraint
An approach to judicial decision making whereby judges defer to the democratically elected branches of government unless their actions clearly violate the Constitution.

living Constitution
View that legal interpretation of the Constitution can and should adapt to changing social customs and norms.

the U.S. Supreme Court overturned the Florida Supreme Court's interpretation of Florida election law on counting votes.[41]

Originalism (textualism), the judicial principle that the Constitution means no more or less than what it meant to those who wrote it, is often coupled with judicial restraint when characterizing a justice's judicial decision making. Presented as the opposite of those who acknowledge the Constitution as a living document, originalists try to interpret constitutional language based on the time, culture, norms, and customs at the time of its writing. However, even the most well-known originalist and advocate for judicial restraint, former Supreme Court justice Antonin Scalia, was not always faithful to the "original" meaning of the Constitution. For example, in the majority opinion he wrote in *District of Columbia v. Heller,*[42] Scalia used legislative history (not custom and culture from 1789) to justify, for the first time in U.S. history, that the Second Amendment protects an individual right to keep and bear arms for self-defense.[43]

Today, political scientists argue that "judicial activism simply means that the courts make public policy when the elected branches cannot or will not, often by declaring the actions of other political actors to be unconstitutional."[44] But, as noted, the term *judicial activism* is also applied to judges who view the Constitution as a living, evolving document. However, the term is also often used by people to criticize judges when they do not agree with a court's decision.

Although the policy making of judges, particularly U.S. Supreme Court justices, is an acknowledged reality today, justices do not have the last word. Associate Justice Sandra Day O'Connor notes, "The Constitution is interpreted first and last by people other than judges. The judicial branch is only an intermediate step in the continuing process of making our Constitution work."[45]

Constraints on Judicial Policy Making

The U.S. judiciary is a powerful institution. Nonetheless, judges and justices face checks and constraints that limit how they decide cases, make law, and act as policymakers. Among the most important checks on the judiciary's power are the other branches of government. But lawyers, interest groups, and individual citizens also check the courts and constrain their activism. Moreover, judges and justices are trained to, and actively attempt to, make good law by correctly interpreting the Constitution.

CHECKS AND BALANCES   Article II of the Constitution explicitly gives the legislative and executive branches crucial checks on the structure of the courts. It grants Congress the power to create all federal courts other than the Supreme Court. It also gives the president and the U.S. Senate important powers in determining who sits on all federal courts, providing the president and the Senate with significant control over the judiciary.

Beyond giving the president a check on the judiciary through the power to nominate judges, the Constitution also empowers the president and the executive branch because the courts must rely on the executive branch to enforce their decisions. Specifically, if presidents fail to direct the bureaucracy to carry out judicial decisions, those decisions carry little weight. Frequently, it is executive implementation that gives teeth to the judiciary's decisions.

The Constitution also creates a legislative check on the judiciary because the framers established only the Supreme Court and left it up to Congress to create the lower federal courts. In addition, the Constitution allows Congress to control the Supreme Court's jurisdiction. Congress also can control, through legislation, the number of judges or justices who serve in the federal judiciary. Historically,

originalism (textualism)
View that the Constitution means no more or less than it meant to those who wrote it.

Congress has been willing to increase the number of judges only when its majority is of the same party affiliation as the incumbent president, who will have the authority to nominate judges to the newly created judgeships. In 2013, Republicans in the Senate used the filibuster to prevent President Obama from filling three vacancies on the D.C. Circuit Court, claiming the Court did not have a sufficient workload for its eleven judgeships and therefore there was no need to fill the three vacancies. However, they did not propose legislation to reduce the number of judgeships on the D.C. Circuit Court. This conflict resulted in the nuclear option, which prevents the use of a filibuster to block Senate voting on presidential nominees.

The two houses of Congress moreover have a central role in deciding whether to impeach federal judges. The House issues the articles of impeachment, and the Senate conducts the impeachment trial. Finally, Congress initiates the process of constitutional amendment and can attempt to change the Constitution to overrule a court decision with which it disagrees. In fact, in several cases Congress has embarked on constitutional amendment procedures in direct response to a Court decision with which members of Congress or their constituencies have disagreed. For example, the Twenty-Sixth Amendment (1971), which standardized the voting age to 18 years, came about after the Supreme Court ruled that states could set their own age limits for state elections.[46]

Although the courts can check the lawmaking (and hence policy-making) power of the legislative and executive branches by exercising judicial review, the legislature and the executive can check the courts' power of judicial review through the creation of new laws. For example, as discussed earlier in this chapter, in response to the Supreme Court's interpretation of a piece of the Civil Rights Act of 1964 in *Ledbetter v. Goodyear Tire & Rubber* in 2007, Congress approved and President Obama signed the Lilly Ledbetter Fair Pay Act in 2009, which overruled the Court's interpretation of law.

PUBLIC ACCOUNTABILITY   Public opinion seems to have a distinct influence on what the courts do, especially appellate courts such as the U.S. Supreme Court. The Court rarely issues a decision that is completely out of step with the thinking of the majority of the population. In fact, most cases seem to follow public opinion. When the Court does break with public opinion, it opens itself up to harsh criticism by the president, Congress, interest groups, and/or the general public.

But sometimes in the case of a landmark decision that is out of touch with public sentiment, the Court's ruling and people's opinions align over time. This shift can occur either because later courts adjust the original, controversial decision or, less commonly, because the Supreme Court's decision changes public opinion. One example of the interplay between public opinion and judicial decisions can be seen in the *Brown v. Board of Education* Court ruling. Initially, many southern state legislatures and even judges in federal district and appellate courts in the South did not comply with the Court's call to integrate schools. Not only did some school districts continue to segregate, but more than 100 southern legislators signed the "Southern Manifesto," a document that claimed the U.S. Supreme Court had overstepped its authority. By the 1970s, progress in integrating schools had been made. However, there are still legal conflicts over segregation and integration today.

Citizens can also constrain the courts by threatening to ignore their rulings. When members of the public disagree with judicial decisions, or with any law for that matter, they can engage in civil disobedience. In acts of civil disobedience, individuals or groups flout the law to make a larger point about its underlying unfairness. Keep in mind that the courts have little ability to enforce their decisions, and if people refuse to recognize those decisions and the other branches of the government fail to enforce them, the courts risk losing their authority and power. Fear of losing authority may explain in part why judicial decisions rarely fall out of step with the larger public stance on an issue. Like legislators, executives, and their colleagues sitting on the bench, citizens can impose significant constraints on courts and probably limit how judges handle cases and interpret laws. These constraints may not be written into the U.S. Constitution as the checks by the other branches are, but they are nonetheless very powerful and have a significant impact on how judges decide cases.

INTERNAL CONSTRAINTS Judges and justices also face powerful internal constraints on their judicial actions. Law schools train lawyers, and hence judges, to focus on the facts of the case and the relevant legal principles (found in law and precedent cases) when deciding cases. For lower-court judges, precedents from higher courts, as well as earlier decisions made by the court itself, impose limitations through the common-law doctrine of *stare decisis*. In addition, federal district court and appeals court judges do not diverge far from Supreme Court precedent because if they did so, they would risk having their decisions overturned by the Supreme Court. According to judicial scholar Paul Collins, "Judges are concerned with making good law: attempting to determine the *most* legally appropriate answer to the controversy."[47]

The Supreme Court Today: The Roberts Court

John G. Roberts became chief justice of the Supreme Court in September 2005. President George W. Bush nominated him to fill the vacant position left by the death of Chief Justice William Rehnquist. With the appointment of Roberts, the bench was composed of four justices nominated by Democratic presidents and five nominated by Republican presidents. Justice Sandra Day O'Connor was the most moderate of Republicans serving on the Court, and was considered a swing voter because she often voted with the more liberal justices.

Justice O'Connor announced her retirement from the bench in the summer of 2005, but stayed until January 2006, when the Senate confirmed Samuel Alito to replace her. The appointment of Alito (a conservative) to replace the moderate O'Connor was viewed as the most significant ideological shift on the bench since 1991. In that year, Clarence Thomas (viewed by many as the most conservative justice on the bench today) replaced Thurgood Marshall (viewed by many as the most liberal justice in modern history). After Alito joined the bench, the Court's decisions on matters of race, abortion, campaign finance, religion, and rights of corporations shifted in a more conservative direction. At the same time, Justice Anthony Kennedy became the swing voter on the Court—a Republican justice most apt to vote with the liberal justices, particular on social and civil rights issues.

The death of Associate Justice Antonin Scalia in February 2016 sparked headlines about the probability that his replacement would "reshape American life."[48] Scalia's death left four Republican appointees and four Democratic appointees on the bench. The headlines highlighted the ideological split on the Court and the reality that a President Obama replacement for Scalia could swing the balance in a liberal direction, which would change the direction of Court decisions on matters where the ideological split has been evident. However, the Senate did not consider Merrick Garland, President Obama's nominee for the vacant seat, because the Republican Senate leadership refused to process the nomination.

Only eight justices sat on the bench for the majority of the Supreme Court's 2016 term—October 3, 2016, through April 10, 2017, when President Trump's nominee, Neil Gorsuch, was sworn in as the ninth justice. According to Adam Liptak, lawyer and

Supreme Court correspondent for the *New York Times*, during the 2016 term, the justices "dodged the most provocative or consequential cases" and had "a level of agreement unseen at the court in more than 70 years." Liptak and Stanford law professor Jeffrey Fisher agree that the Court's consensus could be attributed to the lack of cases dealing with divisive social and civil rights issues and the justices' efforts to decide cases on narrow grounds so as not to get tangled up in philosophic, legal arguments.[49] William Baude, a law professor at the University of Chicago, summarized the 2016 term this way: "It has been a quiet term, and that is a good thing for the country. . . . We will look back on [the 2016] term as the calm before the storm.[50]

A storm indeed erupted in response to President's Trump nomination of Brett Kavanaugh to replace Justice Anthony Kennedy, who announced his retirement from the bench in June of 2018 (Table 15.5). Both Democrats and Republicans viewed Kavanaugh as considerably more conservative than the swing-voter Kennedy he would replace. Not since Justice Alito replaced the more moderate Justice O'Connor, which led to Kennedy becoming the swing voter, did a Supreme Court nominee threaten the ideological balance of the Court. According to Irv Gornstein, executive director of the Supreme Court Institute at Georgetown University, "Justice Kennedy's departure is likely to lead to far more dramatic change in the court than the departure of Justice O'Connor did."[51]

Will the Roberts Court swing in a more consistent and staunch conservative direction, or will one of the more moderate Republican appointees move into the swing-voter position? Chief Justice Roberts is now viewed as the Court's ideological center. He has confronted criticism from conservatives for his 2012 vote that rejected challenges to the Affordable Care Act (ACA), a key legislative initiative

>Within minutes of President Obama's nomination of Merrick Garland to replace deceased Associate Justice Antonin Scalia, the Republican majority in the Senate made it clear it would not provide advice or consent on the nominee. Indeed, they stated that Scalia's replacement should not be considered until after the 2016 presidential election, which was eight months away. Protests calling for the Senate to do its job of advice and consent did not influence the Republicans in the Senate. Who was confirmed to replace Scalia 14 months later? Who nominated Scalia's replacement?

©Al Drago/CQ Roll Call/Getty Images

Evaluating the Facts

TABLE 15.5 The Roberts Court

Considering the age of the Supreme Court justices nominated by President Barack Obama, what do you think will be President Obama's long-term effect on the decision making of the Court? What might explain the pattern of change in confirmation votes from 1988 through 2018? How many justices do you predict President Trump will be able to appoint?

Justice	Year Appointed	Nominating President	Confirmation Vote	Year of Birth
Clarence Thomas	1991	George H. W. Bush (R)	52–48	1948
Ruth Bader Ginsburg	1993	Bill Clinton (D)	96–3	1933
Stephen G. Breyer	1994	Bill Clinton (D)	87–9	1938
John G. Roberts	2005	George W. Bush (R)	78–22	1955
Samuel Anthony Alito	2006	George W. Bush (R)	58–42	1950
Sonia Sotomayor	2009	Barack Obama (D)	68–31	1954
Elena Kagan	2010	Barack Obama (D)	63–37	1960
Neil Gorsuch	2017	Donald Trump (R)	54–45	1967
Brett Kavanaugh	2018	Donald Trump (R)	50–48	1963

SOURCE: U.S. Supreme Court

of the Democrats. In 2015, Roberts again voted to reject an effort to find pieces of the ACA unconstitutional, and again conservatives questioned his conservatism. However, Justin Driver, a law professor at the University of Chicago, argues that "John Roberts would be the least swinging swing justice in the post-World War II era."[52]

Thinking Critically About What's Next for the Judiciary

Rooted in a common-law tradition and framed by the Constitution, the American judiciary in its early form strongly reflected its English heritage, with its emphasis on law made by judges. Over the past two-plus centuries, the judiciary has evolved powerfully to accommodate a broad spectrum of societal changes in a continuously developing country. Today the policy-making role of the courts is acknowledged, if not appreciated, by political scientists, government officials, and most citizens.

The judicial activism practiced by liberal and conservative justices, as they apply the common-law doctrine of judicial review, feeds concerns that the courts are engaged in partisan policy making, just like the other two branches of government. Although judges strive to make decisions that are legally correct, grounded in the fundamental rights found in the U.S. Constitution, the reality of 5–4 Supreme Court decisions indicates that not everyone agrees on what the Constitution means. The Senate's adoption of the nuclear option to limit the power of the partisan minority in the judicial appointment process and the Republican senators' reaction to Associate Justice Scalia's death with 342 days left in Obama's presidency speak volumes about the partisan battles to control the direction of court decisions on the meaning of laws—constitutional law, legislation, executive orders, administrative law, and common law.

Although many people criticize appellate courts for judicial activism when they disagree with a court decision, as noted in Chapter 6, citizens trust the nonelected policymakers (judges and justices) of the federal judicial branch more than they trust their elected federal representatives in the executive and legislative branches. A Gallup September 2017 poll showed that 68 percent of Americans had a "great deal" or a "fair amount" of trust in the judicial branch. This was more trust in the courts than in September 2016, when 61 percent of Americans had that level of trust in the courts. The 2017 poll also found that 45 percent of Americans had a "great deal" or "fair amount" of trust in the executive branch, and 35 percent had that level of trust in the legislative branch.[53] The high level of trust in the judicial branch challenges those who believe that in a representative democracy, only elected government officials should make policy. Because of the vague and ambiguous language in the laws that courts must apply to resolve conflicts, judicial policy making is inevitable.

Learning Summary

1. Explain how courts resolve legal disputes.
   a. Identify and explain the sources of U.S. law.
   b. Compare trial courts with appellate courts.
   c. Compare criminal trials with civil trials.

2. Describe the federal court system.
   a. Explain the differences between Article III and Article I courts.
   b. Compare the jurisdictions of the three categories of Article III courts.
   c. Outline the judicial selection process and the criteria used in the process.
   d. Describe how and why the selection process was delayed after the death of Justice Scalia.

3. Outline the processes of the U.S. Supreme Court.
   a. Explain how the Court implements its discretionary jurisdiction.
   b. Outline the flow of a case from filing of briefs to the Court's published opinion.

4. Discuss judicial policy making.
   a. Explain why the courts make policy.
   b. Explain judicial review.
   c. Compare judicial activism and judicial restraint.
   d. Compare originalism and the Constitution as a living document.
   e. Discuss the constraints on judicial policy making.

5. Present a brief history and status report of the Roberts Court.
   a. Describe who the current justices are in terms of their demographics and partisan leanings.
   b. Discuss the level of trust Americans have in the three branches of national government.

Key Terms

adversarial judicial system 502

amicus curiae brief ("friend of the court" brief) 517

Article I courts 508

appellate jurisdiction 505

associate justice 509

attitudinal model 518

bench memo 517

bench trial 503

beyond a reasonable doubt 503

cert memo 516

certiorari petition 516

chief justice 509

civil law 504

collegial court 516

common law 500

concurring opinion 519

constitutional law 500

courts of appeal 505

court of last resort 506

criminal law 503

descriptive representation 512

discretionary jurisdiction 509

dissenting opinion 519

district courts 508

diversity of citizenship 506

doctrine of *stare decisis* 500

dual court system 499

federal courts of appeal (circuit courts) 508

federal question 506

judicial activism 520

judicial independence 509

judicial restraint 521

judicial review 505

jury trial 503

law 500

legal model 518

living Constitution 521

mandatory jurisdiction 508

Marbury v. Madison 505

original jurisdiction 503

originalism (textualism) 522

penal code 501

precedent cases 500

preponderance of evidence 504

Rule of Four 516

senatorial courtesy 514

strategic model 518

substantive representation 512

symbolic representation 512

tort 504

trial court 503

U.S. Code 501

U.S. Supreme Court 509

writ of *certiorari* 516

For Review

1. What are the five sources of law in the U.S. legal system, and for each source, who has the authority to create law?

2. What legal disputes do trial courts resolve? What disputes do appellate courts resolve? What does the power of judicial review allow the courts to decide?

3. What differentiates criminal law from civil law and a criminal lawsuit from a civil lawsuit?

4. What is the structure of the federal court system? Which courts have original jurisdiction and which have appellate jurisdiction? How can a state lawsuit end up in a federal appellate court?

5. What criteria do presidents use when selecting judicial nominees? What role does the Senate play in the judicial selection process?

6. Outline the stages by which the Supreme Court handles appeals. Explain the three judicial decision-making models.

7. In what ways do federal judges participate in civic discourse as policymakers? How is judicial policy making constrained?

8. What are the characteristics (mix of sex, political ideology, and level of activism) of the Roberts Court?

For Critical Thinking and Discussion

1. Explain the principles of judicial activism, judicial restraint, originalism, and the Constitution as a living document. Which judicial principles do you believe best serve the country? Why?

2. The Supreme Court has the power of judicial review, that is, the power to strike down federal and state laws that it views to be in conflict with the U.S. Constitution. In a representative democracy, what argument can be made against allowing the Court to overturn laws passed by the democratically elected branches? In a government founded on the principle of protecting rights of all people, even those in the minority, what argument can be made in support of allowing the Court to overturn laws passed by democratically elected branches?

3. When a president nominates a prospective federal judge, a number of factors are at play, and the nominee's qualifications are only one of these. What are the other factors? Should they be in play? Why or why not? In what ways do these factors reinforce or undermine democratic principles?

4. Which do you think impose greater limitations on policy making by federal courts: legal norms, the constitutional system of checks and balances, or public opinion? Explain your answer.

5. Unlike in the federal court system, in many states, judges are elected by the voters. Which system of judicial selection do you think best protects civil rights and liberties for all citizens, popular election or appointment (nomination by the chief executive and confirmation by a senate)? Explain.

6. Did the framers believe that judges should be accountable to the people or independent of the people and public opinion? Do you think Americans expect judicial accountability or judicial independence? What is your preference? Explain.

Resources for Research AND Action

Internet Resources

FindLaw

www.findlaw.com This website provides a wealth of information about lawmaking in the federal and state judiciaries, as well as ongoing cases in the news. It allows users easy access to federal and state code law, case law, and regulatory law. It also helps prelaw and law students stay connected to helpful information about legal education and practice.

Legal Information Institute (LII)

www.law.cornell.edu This is a valuable resource for information not only on the U.S. Supreme Court but also on the other courts in the federal and state judiciaries. The site provides an excellent catalog of statutory, regulatory, and administrative laws, as well as executive orders. It also allows you to search for all sources of law in a particular area of the law, including federal and state court decisions as well as laws coming out of the other branches.

Oyez

www.oyez.org/oyez/frontpage This interactive website allows you to access recordings of the oral arguments in a select group of cases. You can also visit the site to take a virtual tour of the Supreme Court building and to learn interesting trivia about the Court, including a list of the most active lawyers before the Court.

U.S. Supreme Court

www.supremecourtus.gov The official website of the U.S. Supreme Court is an excellent resource for information on the Court. You can access the briefs and oral argument transcripts for cases currently before the Court, as well as for cases decided recently. The site also allows easy access to nearly all cases that the Court has decided, including historical decisions.

Recommended Readings

Breyer, Stephen. *The Court and the World: American Law and the New Global Realities.* New York: Alfred A. Knopf, 2015. Associate Justice Breyer explores what he calls the "foreign aspect" of the Supreme Court's docket in today's interdependent, global world. Breyer presents his belief that American courts must develop an understanding of and ability to appropriately apply international and foreign law.

Collins, Paul M., Jr. *Friends of the Supreme Court: Interest Groups and Judicial Decision Making.* New York: Oxford University Press, 2008. A study of the influence *amicus curiae* briefs have on judicial decision making, including an explanation for the increased occurrence of split decisions, concurring opinions, and dissenting opinions.

Miller, Mark C. *Exploring Judicial Politics.* New York: Oxford University Press, 2009. An edited volume offering studies by political scientists on the role of the courts as both legal institutions and political institutions.

O'Connor, Sandra Day. *The Majesty of the Law: Reflections of a Supreme Court Justice.* New York: Random House, 2003. In her reflections, O'Connor offers a history of the Supreme Court and discusses the important influence of several justices on the shape of the Court, the effect the Court has had on public policy, and the role of the Court in the 21st century.

Savage, David G. *Guide to the U.S. Supreme Court.* Washington, DC: Congressional Quarterly, 2010. Contains a thorough description of the U.S. Supreme Court, including its origins, its functions, and its influence.

Tribe, Laurence, and Joshua Matz. *Uncertain Justice: The Roberts Court and the Constitution.* New York: Picador, 2014. The authors analyze momentous decisions of the first 10 years of the Roberts Court and show how it "has wrought remarkable and directed changes in many areas of the law, forever transforming how the Constitution is understood."

Movies of Interest

12 Citizens (2015)

Chinese director Xu Ang has redone the 1957 classic movie *12 Angry Men* for a Chinese audience. Following protocol in China, Xu had to get approval from the government to make the film, which was tricky given the closed court systems in China that are often corrupted by local governments. Xu wanted to bring the movie's examination of social biases in an era of social media to his countrymen.

The Runaway Jury (2003)

This film provides critical examination of the role of the jury in the American judicial system.

Gideon's Trumpet (1980)

This classic film starring Henry Fonda traces the true story of Clarence Gideon's fight to have a counsel appointed to his case at the expense of the state. *Gideon v. Wainright* was the 1963 Supreme Court decision that extended state-appointed attorneys to all criminal defendants.

12 Angry Men (1957)

Henry Fonda starred in and produced this classic drama depicting the acrimonious deliberations of a jury in a death penalty case where a juror forces his fellow jurors to come to grips with the concept of reasonable doubt and their own prejudices.

References

1. Brian L. Porto, *May It Please the Court: Judicial Processes and Politics in America* (New York: Longman, 2001), 4.
2. Sandra Day O'Connor, *The Majesty of the Law: Reflections of a Supreme Court Justice* (New York: Random House, 2003), 271–272.
3. *United States v. Nixon,* 418 U.S. 683 (1974).
4. Adam Liptak, "Supreme Court to Consider Challenge to Trump's Latest Travel Ban," *New York Times,* January 19, 2018.
5. G. Alan Tarr, *Judicial Process and Judicial Policymaking,* 5th ed. (Boston: Wadsworth/Cengage Learning, 2010), 209.
6. Charles D. Shipan, *Designing Judicial Review* (Ann Arbor: University of Michigan Press, 1997).
7. Joel B. Grossman, "Paths to the Bench: Selecting Supreme Court Justices in a 'Juristocratic' World," in *The Judicial Branch,* ed. Kermit L. Hall and Kevin T. McGuire (Oxford: Oxford University Press, 2005), 143.
8. Porto, *May It Please the Court,* 32.
9. 50 U.S.C. §§1801–1811, 1821–29, 1841–46, and 1861–62.
10. Christopher P. Banks and David M. O'Brien, *Courts and Judicial Policymaking* (Upper Saddle River, NJ: Pearson Prentice Hall, 2008), 130.
11. Adam Liptak, "Suggestions on a Successor: Scalia Urged a More Varied Membership," *New York Times,* February 16, 2016: A1, A13.
12. Ibid.
13. Adam Liptak, "Roberts Had Criticized Supreme Court Confirmation Process," *The Times-Tribune,* March 22, 2016: A7.
14. Ariane de Vogue and Dan Berman, "Neil Gorsuch Confirmed to the Supreme Court," *CNN,* April 7, 2017.
15. About the Supreme Court, "The Justices' Caseload," www.supremecourt.gov/about/justicecaseload.aspx.
16. Robert M. Yablon, "Justice Sotomayor and the Supreme Court's Certiorari Process," 123 *Yale L.J. F.* 551 (2014).
17. H. W. Perry Jr., *Deciding to Decide: Agenda Setting in the United States Supreme Court* (Cambridge, MA: Harvard University Press, 1994).
18. Bob Woodward, *The Brethren: Inside the Supreme Court* (New York: Simon & Schuster, 2005).
19. Henry J. Abraham, *The Judicial Process* (New York: Oxford University Press, 1998).
20. Nina Totenberg, "Record Number of Amicus Briefs Filed in Same-Sex-Marriage Cases," *NPR,* April 28, 2015.
21. Benjamin N. Cardozo, *The Nature of the Judicial Process* (Mineola, NY: Dover, 2005); Paul Collins Jr., *Friends of the Supreme Court: Interest Groups and Judicial Decision Making* (New York: Oxford University Press, 2008); Allison Orr Larsen, "The Trouble with Amicus Facts," *Virginia Law Review* 100, no. 8 (December 2014).
22. Paul Collins Jr., *Friends of the Supreme Court: Interest Groups and Judicial Decision Making* (New York: Oxford University Press, 2008), 71–72.
23. Stephen Breyer, *Active Liberty: Interpreting Our Democratic Constitution* (New York: Vintage Books, 2006).
24. Artemus Ward, "Sorcerers' Apprentices: U.S. Supreme Court Law Clerks," in *Exploring Judicial Politics,* ed. Mark C. Miller (New York: Oxford University Press, 2009), 159.
25. Adam Liptak, "A Most Inquisitive Court? No Argument There," *New York Times,* October 8, 2013.
26. Ibid.
27. Bryan W. Marshall, Richard L. Pacelle Jr., and Christine Ludowise, "A Court of Laws or a Superlegislature? An Integrated Model of Supreme Court Decision Making," in *Exploring Judicial Politics,* ed. Mark C. Miller (New York: Oxford University Press, 2009), 194.
28. Black, "Something Changed."
29. Collins, *Friends of the Supreme Court,* 12.
30. Marshall, Pacelle, and Ludowise, "A Court of Laws or a Superlegislature?"
31. Ward, "Sorcerers' Apprentices," 168.
32. *Ledbetter v. Goodyear Tire & Rubber,* 550 U.S. 618 (2007).
33. Quoted in Eric Black, "How the Supreme Court Has Come to Play a Policymaking Role," November 20, 2012.
34. *Plessy v. Ferguson,* 163 U.S. 537 (1896).
35. *Brown v. Board of Education of Topeka, Kansas,* 347 U.S. 483 (1954).
36. O'Connor, *The Majesty of the Law,* 266.
37. Antonin Scalia, *A Matter of Interpretation: Federal Courts and the Law* (Princeton, NJ: Princeton University Press, 1998).
38. Thomas M. Keck, *The Most Activist Supreme Court in History: The Road to Modern Judicial Conservatism* (Chicago: University of Chicago Press, 2004).
39. *U.S. v. Lopez,* 514 U.S. 549 (1995).
40. *U.S. v. Morrison,* 529 U.S. 598 (2000).
41. *Bush v. Gore,* 531 U.S. 98 (2000).
42. *District of Columbia v. Heller,* 554 U.S. 570 (2008).
43. Sheldon Whitehouse, "Conservative Judicial Activism: The Politicization of the Supreme Court Under Chief Justice Roberts," *Harvard Law & Policy Review,* March 18, 2015.
44. Mark C. Miller, "The Interactions between the Federal Courts and the Other Branches," in *Exploring Judicial Politics,* ed. Mark C. Miller (New York: Oxford University Press, 2009), 278–279.
45. O'Connor, *The Majesty of the Law,* 41.
46. *Oregon v. Mitchell,* 400 U.S. 112 (1970).
47. Collins, *Friends of the Supreme Court,* 175.

48. Adam Liptak, "Supreme Court Appointment Could Reshape American Life," *New York Times,* February 19, 2016: A1.

49. Adam Liptak, "A Cautious Supreme Court Sets a Modern Record for Consensus," *New York Times,* June 27, 2017.

50. Liptak, "A Cautious Supreme Court Sets a Modern Record for Consensus."

51. Adam Liptak, "How Brett Kavanaugh Would Transform the Supreme Court," *New York Times,* Sept. 2, 2018.

52. Adam Liptak, "How Brett Kavanaugh Would Transform the Supreme Court," *New York Times,* Sept. 2, 2018.

53. Jeffrey Jones, "Trust in Judicial Branch Up, Executive Branch Down," *News Gallup,* September 20, 2017.

CHAPTER 16

Economic Policy

©Eduardo Munoz Alvarez/Getty Images

THEN

The federal government played a limited role in the economy, and there was consensus about the need for a balanced federal budget.

NOW

The federal government makes taxing, spending, regulatory, and monetary policies that affect the health of the economy, and it persistently borrows money to balance the federal budget.

NEXT

Will the 2017 Tax Cuts and Jobs Act bolster the country's economic health?

Will rolling back federal regulations have a positive or negative effect on the national economy?

Will your generation and future generations achieve the American dream?

Is the American dream still

a realistic goal in the United States? A 2015 *American Values Survey* conducted by The Atlantic/Aspen Institute found that three in four Americans said the American dream was "suffering."[1] However, a 2017 Pew Research Center survey found that while 17 percent of respondents believed the American dream was out of reach for their family, 46 percent believed their family was on the way to achieving the American dream, and 36 percent believed their family had already achieved it.[2] What do you think about your ability to achieve the American dream?

Although individuals have different definitions of the American dream (see Table 16.1), financial security is a foundational building block. Therefore, the health of a country's economy is a key to its people achieving the American dream. Congress and the president battle over enacting a variety of laws that will affect the U.S. economic system with the goal of ensuring economic prosperity and the American dream. These laws include tax laws, laws that regulate economic activity in the domestic and international marketplaces, laws that protect the health and safety of workers and consumers, and spending policies that encourage economic growth as well as provide for the public good. In addition, the Federal Reserve—the United States' central banking system—makes policy decisions that affect the amount of money in circulation, which in turn affects consumer prices and employment rates, and hence, the economy.

Debates among elected and appointed officials at the national and state levels and among economists, business leaders, and taxpayers about the proper role for the national government in creating and maintaining a healthy economy have been ongoing since the birth of the American republic. This chapter explores how national policies affect the U.S. economic system and the possibility of achieving the American dream. In the exploration, we consider various measures of economic health, economic theories, fiscal policy, monetary policy, regulatory policy, and trade policy.

Learning Objectives

After reading this chapter, students should be able to:

- Explain how a healthy economy supports pursuit of the American dream.
- Describe how the health of a country's economy is measured.
- Summarize the goals and tools of laissez-faire economics, Keynesian economics, supply-side economics, and monetarism.
- Explain the process of creating fiscal policy, where the money comes from, and what it is spent on.
- Describe monetary policy.
- Explain the effect regulatory policy has on the economy.
- Summarize the key differences between protectionist trade policy and free-market trade policy.
- Explain recent shifts in economic policy.

The American Dream and the American Economy

The American national government seeks a healthy economy so that it can raise the revenue it needs to serve the people in compliance with the mission laid out in the Preamble to the Constitution: to establish justice, ensure domestic tranquility, provide for the common defense, promote the general welfare, and secure the blessings of liberty today and in the future. On a more personal level, many U.S. citizens desire a healthy economy so that they can achieve the American dream.

The American Dream

The desire for enough money to buy not only what we require to meet our basic needs (food, shelter, and clothing) but also what many people would consider luxuries seems natural to most Americans. In developed countries such as the United States, "luxuries" typically include owning a home instead of renting, owning a car or two, dining at a nice restaurant now and then, taking vacations, and sending children to good schools. U.S. citizens and many immigrants to the United States seek a financially secure, happy, and healthy life, with upward mobility, attained through an individual's hard work and persistence, and an even better life for their children, which collectively are known as the **American dream.** Table 16.1 presents information on what Americans think is essential or important to achieving the American dream.

Clearly, it takes money to live the American dream. For some, being born into a wealthy family or just dumb luck (winning the lottery!) may provide the means to live the American dream. For most individuals, however, the ability to earn enough money to attain the American dream is the product of several factors, including their education level, their work ethic, and the availability of well-paying jobs.

Why are you attending college? Are you taking classes to develop your intellectual capacities? To better understand yourself and the world around you? To get a better-paying job so you can live the American dream? If you read your college's mission statement, you will find that your institution hopes to facilitate all those accomplishments.

American dream

The belief that in the United States hard work and persistence will reap a financially secure, happy, and healthy life, with upward mobility.

Evaluating the Facts

TABLE 16.1 What Is Needed to Achieve the American Dream?

The data in this table summarize the responses to the question: *Do you think each is essential, important but not essential, or not important to your own view of the American dream?*

Identify anything in the survey responses that surprises you, and explain why it surprises you. Identify other factors that you believe should be added to the list in future surveys, and explain why you think each additional factor should be included.

Factors	Essential	Important, But Not Essential	Not Important
Have freedom of choice in how to live	77%	22%	1%
Have a good family life	70%	28%	2%
Retire comfortably	60%	36%	3%
Make valuable contributions to community	46%	46%	5%
Own a home	43%	48%	9%
Have a successful career	43%	60%	6%
Become wealthy	11%	49%	40%

SOURCE: Pew Research Center, "Most Think the 'American Dream' Is within Reach for Them," October 31, 2017.

Although you may be able to increase your level of education, and you have control over your work ethic, the availability of well-paying jobs commensurate with your level of education is not within your control. The health of the national economy determines the availability of jobs and affects their compensation (pay and benefits). So, although achieving the American dream depends on individual attributes and opportunities to develop those attributes, the health of the national economy also plays a major role.

A healthy national economy supports a nation's ability to raise sufficient revenue to serve its people. The better the economy's performance, the greater the **tax base**: the overall *wealth* (income and assets, such as property) of citizens and corporations that governments tax to raise revenue to pay the costs of providing public goods and services.

tax base
The overall *wealth* (income and assets of citizens and corporations) that the government can tax to raise revenue.

The American Economy

In the United States and other countries, national government policies influence the **economy**—the system for producing, selling, buying, and using goods and services. **Economic policy** is a collection of public policies that affect the health of the economy, which includes taxing and spending policies (fiscal policy), monetary policy, regulatory policy, and trade policy. Economists view a healthy economy as one in which unemployment is low, the prices of consumer goods are relatively stable, and the productivity of individual workers and the economy as a whole is increasing.

Although labeled as a capitalist system, the U.S. economy is not an example of pure capitalism. In a **pure capitalist economy**, private individuals and companies own the modes of producing goods and services, and the government does *not* enact laws aimed at influencing the marketplace transactions that distribute those goods and services. In other words, a pure capitalist economy has a government-free marketplace. Although private ownership of the modes of production dominates the U.S. marketplace, it is not a government-free marketplace. National government policies in some cases encourage, and in other cases mandate, certain business practices that the government deems essential to sustain a healthy economy as well as a clean environment and a safe and productive citizenry. Because of the many national policies enacted to influence the economy, the U.S. economy is an example of a **regulated capitalist economy (mixed economy),** not a pure capitalist economy.

People around the world want their governments to engage in actions that ensure a healthy economy. Yet the actions a government takes to ensure a healthy economy depend on the economic theories its lawmakers follow. In the United States, Democrats and Republicans traditionally disagree on economic policies, each justifying their preferences with different economic theories. Next, we survey several economic theories that have influenced U.S. national economic policy in various historical periods.

economy
A system for producing, selling, buying, and using goods and services.

economic policy
A collection of public policies that affect the health of the economy, which includes taxing and spending policies (fiscal policy), monetary policy, regulatory policy, and trade policy.

pure capitalist economy
An economy in which private individuals and companies own the modes of producing goods and services, and the government does not enact laws aimed at influencing the marketplace transactions that distribute those goods and services.

regulated capitalist economy (mixed economy)
An economy in which private ownership of the modes of production dominate and the government enacts policies to influence the health of the economy.

Measuring Economic Health

Economists and government officials describe a **healthy economy** as one that has these characteristics: increasing domestic product (GDP), low unemployment rate, and low inflation rate. These traditional measures of economic health together provide a useful snapshot of how the national economy is doing. Other measures

healthy economy
According to economists, an economy experiencing an increase in its gross domestic product (GDP), low unemployment rate, and low inflation rate.

of economic health focus on the general well-being of the people by accounting for factors such as rates of poverty and literacy and the financial situation of households. These less traditional measures include the United Nations Human Development Index, real median household income, income inequality, and the poverty rate.

Traditional Measures of Economic Health

Most economists assume that growth in the gross domestic product translates into a prosperous nation with improving living standards—hence progress toward living the American dream. **Gross domestic product (GDP)** is the total market value of all goods and services produced within a country's borders. Rising GDP is a sign of an expanding economy, which means the production of more goods and services—and thus the availability of more goods and services for consumers.

Economists also expect a healthy economy to correlate with a low level of **inflation,** which is a decreased value of money as evidenced by increased prices. When inflation occurs, consumers' purchasing power falls and they cannot buy as much this year with the same amount of money they spent last year. The government agency known as the Bureau of Labor Statistics publishes the **consumer price index (CPI),** which measures the average change in prices over time of a "market basket" of goods and services, including food, clothing, shelter, fuel, transportation costs, and selected medical costs. The CPI is the most commonly used measure of the impact of inflation on people. According to economists, when the economy is healthy, the inflation rate (measured by the change in CPI) ranges between 1 and 3 percent.

A low unemployment rate, 5 percent or less, is also characteristic of a healthy economy, according to economists. When more people are working, the financial situation of families overall should improve. In addition, in a growing economy with falling unemployment, government revenues should increase because there is more corporate and personal income to tax, and government spending for social welfare programs should decrease because fewer people should need public assistance. These trends create a healthier financial situation for government.

In sum, a high or rising GDP, low inflation rate, and low unemployment rate suggest a healthy national economy. (The "Analyzing the Sources" feature presents recent changes in these traditional measures of economic health.) Yet as the U.S. Department of Commerce's Bureau of Economic Analysis points out, "While the GDP is used as an indicator of economic progress, it is not a measure of well-being."[3] Therefore, we next describe other measures that attempt to assess the well-being of individuals and households, which most people expect is a product of a healthy economy and is correlated with achieving the American dream.

Other Measures of Economic Health

The United Nations (UN) created the **Human Development Index (HDI)** to measure the standard of living of the people of various nations. The HDI assesses three components of human development that people in prosperous nations should be able to enjoy: a long and healthy life, educational opportunities, and a decent standard of daily living. These measures of economic health shed light on the ability of individuals and households to earn enough to *enjoy a decent quality of life.* Thus, they are probing into something quite different from the traditional measures of national economic health that we have just discussed.

gross domestic product (GDP)
The total market value of all goods and services produced by labor and properties within a country's borders.

inflation
The decreased value of money as evidenced by increased prices.

consumer price index (CPI)
The most common measure of inflation, it gauges the average change in prices over time of a "market basket" of goods and services including food, clothing, shelter, fuel, transportation costs, and selected medical costs.

Human Development Index (HDI)
A UN-created measure to determine how well a country's economy is providing for a long and healthy life, educational opportunity, and a decent standard of daily living.

TABLE 16.2 Human Development Index Rankings

On which continent(s) are the top five countries located? On which continent(s) are the bottom five countries located? What is the pattern of change in the HDI for the top five countries from 2013 to 2016? What is the pattern of change in the HDI for the bottom five countries from 2013 to 2016?

TOP FIVE COUNTRIES 2013	TOP FIVE COUNTRIES 2016
1. Norway (.955)	1. Norway (.945)
2. Australia (.938)	2. Australia (.936)
3. United States (.937)	3. Switzerland (.936)
4. Netherlands (.921)	4. Denmark (.926)
5. Germany (.920)	5. Netherlands (.923)

BOTTOM FIVE COUNTRIES 2013	BOTTOM FIVE COUNTRIES 2016
183. Burkina Faso (.343)	184. Burundi (.404)
184. Chad (.340)	185. Burkina Faso (.402)
185. Mozambique (.327)	186. Chad (.396)
186. Democratic Republic of Congo (.304)	187. Niger (.353)
186. Niger (.304)	188. Central African Republic (.352)

SOURCES: United Nations Development Programme, *Human Development Report 2013*, "Table 1: Human Development Index and Its Components."; United Nations Development Programme, *Human Development Report 2016*, "Table 1: Human Development Index and the Components."

With an HDI score of .920 (1.0 is the highest score possible), the United States ranked tenth out of 188 countries in the Human Development Report of 2016.[4] Table 16.2 presents the countries with the five highest HDI scores and those with the five lowest HDI scores in the Human Development Reports of 2013 and 2016. How do we know what this rank means to American households and their ability to live the American dream? Additional measures—looking at household income, income inequality, and the level of poverty within the population—can help us answer this question.

The ideal healthy economy would ensure that all workers earn enough to stay out of **poverty**—the condition of lacking sufficient income to purchase the necessities for an adequate living standard. The **poverty rate** is the percentage of the population with income below the nationally designated poverty level. In 2016, the poverty rate was 12.7 percent, or 40.6 million people living in poverty in the United States.[5] The U.S. Census Bureau calculates the poverty rate by using its **poverty thresholds**—an annually updated set of income measures (adjusted for family size) that define who is living in poverty. According to the poverty thresholds for 2017,[6] a family of four, with two children under the age of 18 years, earning less than $24,858 was living in poverty. In 2017, one person under 65 years of age earning less than $12,752 was living in poverty, according to the Census Bureau. What quality of life would you have earning $12,753, just $1 over the poverty threshold?

poverty
The condition of lacking the income sufficient to purchase the necessities for an adequate living standard.

poverty rate
The proportion of the population living below the poverty line as established by the national government.

poverty thresholds
The U.S. Census Bureau's annually updated set of income measures (adjusted for family size) that defines who is living in poverty.

Sources

HOW IS THE U.S. ECONOMY DOING?

	2008	2010	2012	2014	2016
Annual change in U.S. GDP	1.7%	3.8%	4.1%	4.1%	3.0%
Average annual inflation rate	3.8	1.6	2.1	1.6	1.3
Average annual unemployment rate	5.8	9.6	8.1	6.2	4.9
Poverty rate	13.2	15.1	15.0	14.8	12.7
Median household income in 2016 inflation-adjusted dollars	$56,076	$54,245	$53,331	$54,398	$59,039

SOURCES: U.S. Bureau of Economic Analysis, "Gross Domestic Product; Percent Change From Preceding Period," U.S. Inflation Calculator, "Historical Inflation Rates: 1914–2016," U.S. Census Bureau, "Historical Poverty Tables—People," Table 23.

Practice Analytical Thinking

1. Referencing the data presented above and the discussion on how economists define a healthy economy, how do you think the U.S. economy is doing? Explain.

2. Does the fact that the unemployment rate does not account for people who have given up hope and stopped looking for a job call into question the rate's accuracy? Justify your answer.

3. The GDP takes into account the total amount of consumer spending, government spending, business investment in new capital resources (such as equipment, computers, and facilities), and the total net exports (the difference between the value of all the nation's exports and the value of all its imports). The GDP does not include the value of unpaid work done in the home, such as home-cooked meals, child care, adult care, house cleaning, and laundry. Should it include the costs of those services? Why or why not?

4. What measure, or combination of measures, would you argue provides citizens with the most accurate picture of the health of the nation's economy? Explain.

real income
Earned income adjusted for inflation.

household income
The total pretax earnings of all residents over the age of 15 living in a home.

median household income
The middle of all household incomes—50 percent of households have incomes less than the median and 50 percent have incomes greater than the median.

In addition to presenting poverty rates, the "Analyzing the Sources" feature presents real median household income data, which is another important measure of the financial well-being of American households. **Real income** is earned income adjusted for inflation so that it can be compared across years. **Household income** is the total pretax earnings of all residents over the age of 15 living in a home. **Median household income** is the income level in the middle of all household incomes; 50 percent of the households have incomes less than the median and 50 percent have incomes greater than the median. An increase in real median household income should characterize a healthy, expanding economy if we assume that increases in workers' productivity will translate into increases in workers' incomes. In 2016, the real median household income was $59,039.[7]

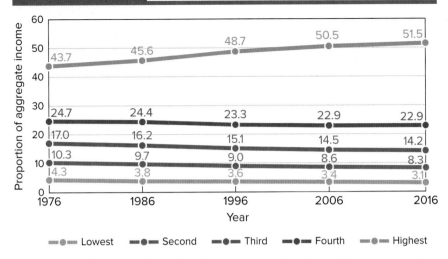

FIGURE 16.1 ■ **Income Inequality** What is the overall pattern of income inequality over the past few decades?

SOURCE: U.S. Census Bureau, Data, "Historical Income Tables: Income Inequality," Table H-2: Share of Aggregate Income Received by Each Fifth and Top 5 Percent of Households.

To determine whether people at all income levels are benefiting from a healthy economy, the government measures changes in **income inequality,** which is the gap in the proportion of national income held by the richest compared to that held by the poorest. Governments and economists use several measures to assess income inequality. One measure calculates the percentage of the total national income possessed by households in five income groups, five *quintiles,* each comprised of 20 percent of the households in the nation, based on total household income. The bottom quintile comprises the 20 percent of households with the lowest incomes, and the top quintile comprises the 20 percent of households with the highest incomes. In 2016, the lowest quintile held 3 percent of the money income while the highest quintile held 52 percent of the total money income.[8] Changes in the percentage of the total income held by each quintile over time indicate whether income inequality is growing or shrinking (see Figure 16.1). The ideal is to see a shrinking of income inequality as the national economy expands.

We have seen that not only traditional economic measures such as GDP, inflation, and unemployment rates serve as indicators of national economic health, but also other measures shed light on the quality of life of people in the United States. With this context in mind, we next explore some economic theories that influence the policies elected officials support to maintain a healthy economy.

income inequality

The gap in the proportion of national income held by the richest compared to that held by the poorest.

Economic Theories That Shape Economic Policy

Today's debates about the proper role of the national government in the economy are nothing new. It was the lack of an economic role for the national government and the poor health of the economy under the Articles of Confederation that sparked rebellions and the call for a constitutional convention in 1787. The framers of the new system of government established by the Constitution envisioned a national government more involved in the economy. Citizens initially supported a limited role for the government in the economy—a *laissez-faire* economic policy. However, as the national economy evolved and experienced ups and downs, citizens and corporations sought greater government involvement in creating and maintaining a healthy economy. In addition, economists developed new theories about the proper role for governments in the economy: Keynesian economics, supply-side economics, and monetarism.

Laissez-Faire Economics: An Unrealized Policy

laissez-faire

The hands-off stance of a government in regard to the marketplace.

Until the late 1800s, a majority of the American people believed that the national government should take a relatively **laissez-faire,** or "hands-off," stance with regard to the marketplace. That is, they thought that the government should neither encourage nor discourage (through its laws) business practices that affected economic health. In his *Wealth of Nations* (1776), economist Adam Smith described the principles underlying the theory of laissez-faire economics. Smith's classical capitalist argument emphasized that the most effective means of supporting a strong and stable economy in the long term is to allow unregulated competition in the marketplace. According to Smith, people's pursuit of their self-interest in an unregulated marketplace would yield a healthy economy. Although it supported a hands-off approach in general, the national government became involved in economic activity as early as 1789, when Congress approved and President George Washington signed the first import tariff (tax on imported goods).

As a manufacturing economy replaced the farming-dominated economy during the 19th century, the general laissez-faire stance of the national government disappeared. Technological advances fueled industrialization and the movement of workers from farms to manufacturing jobs in the cities. As immigrants flocked to the United States in search of the American dream, the supply of cheap labor ballooned. Giant corporations formed, and individuals with money to invest accumulated great wealth. Monopolies and trusts also developed, limiting competition in a variety of industries. Although the economy grew (with increased productivity) and unemployment was low, "a huge gap between rich and poor defined the Gilded Age" (1870–1900) when 80 percent of workers "who toiled twelve to sixteen hours a day, stayed poor."[9] The quality of life for most working-class citizens deteriorated as additional family members, including children, needed to work to pay for life's basic necessities. As fewer and fewer people achieved the American dream, even with all family members working, many Americans began to look to the federal government to improve working and living conditions.

In the late 19th century, the federal government began to respond to workers' demands for better wages and working conditions and

> In the late 19th and early 20th centuries, very low wages forced many American families to rely on the income brought home by their children who worked in mines, glass and textile factories, agriculture, canneries, and home industries such as cigar making. Today, child labor is illegal in the United States and most countries in the world.
Source: Library of Congress [LC-DIG-nclc-02949]

to business owners' calls for uniform (national) rules for business practices. Moreover, by the early 20th century, the national government took steps to protect public health by passing laws regulating the processing of foods and drugs, and the cleanliness and safety of manufacturing plants. Though not directed at the health of the economy, such regulations increased the costs of doing business and, hence, affected the economy.

Clearly, the national government never fully implemented a laissez-faire economic policy. Moreover, as the national economy grew with industrialization, Americans accepted and even called for a mixed economy featuring regulated capitalism. Today, consensus exists on the need for some level of government involvement in the marketplace to ensure a healthy and sustainable economy, environment, and standard of living. But debate continues over how much government involvement is appropriate and what specific policies the government should enact.

Keynesian Economics

Before the Great Depression of the 1930s, government officials and economists believed that a **balanced budget** was important for a healthy economy. When the budget is balanced, the government's expenditures (costs of providing goods and services) are equal to or less than its revenues (money raised from taxes and other sources excluding borrowing). Yet officials and economists recognized that during wartime the government might need to engage in **deficit spending,** spending more than is raised during the budget year, to pay for the military effort.

During the Great Depression, when unemployment rates soared to 25 percent, President Franklin D. Roosevelt and Congress supported deficit spending to address the severe economic depression that engulfed the nation. The Roosevelt administration implemented numerous economic regulations and a number of innovative work and public assistance programs. Those policies drove up government spending at a time of shrinking government revenues. A key objective of the government's increased spending was to trigger economic growth by lowering unemployment rates, thereby increasing demand for goods because more employed people means more people with money to spend. Deficit spending, Roosevelt said, would provide the solution to the American people's economic woes by boosting the national economy.

The new economic theory of John Maynard Keynes supported Roosevelt's unprecedented peacetime deficit spending. **Keynesian economics** recommends that during a **recession**—an economic downturn during which unemployment is high and the production of goods and services is low—the national government should increase its spending to create jobs and decrease taxes so that people have more money to spend to stimulate the economy. Based on this theory, deficit spending is also justified during a **depression,** which is a long-term and severe recession. During times of rapid economic growth—an **economic boom,** when unemployment is low and productivity is increasing rapidly—Keynesian theory recommends cutting government spending and possibly increasing taxes. In the long term, deficit spending during recessions and depressions and collecting a surplus when the economy is booming should lead to a balanced budget. Hence Keynesian economic theory advocates using **fiscal policy,** the combination of tax policy and spending policy, to ensure a healthy economy. Fiscal policy is one type of economic policy.

In response to the Great Recession (2007–2009), President George W. Bush used fiscal policy to stimulate the economy. In February 2008, Congress and

balanced budget
A budget in which the government's expenditures are equal to or less than its revenues.

deficit spending
Government expenditures costing more than is raised in taxes, during the budget year, leading to borrowing and debt.

Keynesian economics
The theory that recommends that during a recession the national government increase its spending and decrease taxes, and during a boom, cut spending and increase taxes.

recession
An economic downturn during which unemployment is high and the production of goods and services is low.

depression
A long-term and severe recession.

economic boom
Rapid economic growth.

fiscal policy
Government spending and taxing and their effect on the economy.

THEN NOW NEXT

Tax Law Before and After the 2017 Tax Cuts and Jobs Act

	2017	2018
Top individual tax rate	39.6%	37% (tax cut expires in 2025)
Personal exemptions	$4,150 per taxpayer and dependent	No personal exemptions
Child tax credit	$1,000	$2,000
Credit for non-child dependents	none	$500
Student loan interest deduction	Up to $2,500	Up to $2,500
State & local tax deduction	Income or sales and property taxes are deductible	All state and local tax deductions limited to $10,000
Top corporate tax rate	35%	21% (tax cut does not expire)

WHAT'S NEXT?

> Will the national government cut spending to address the predicted increased deficit created by the 2017 Tax Cuts and Jobs Act?

> Will the expiration of the lowered top tax rate for individual income in 2025 occur, increasing the income tax for some Americans? What could prevent the expiration of this tax cut?

> Some states in which the state and local tax deductions average more than $10,000 have suggested they will change their laws to work around the new limit on tax deductions for their residents. Will state governments find a way to ameliorate the new limit on state and local tax deductions?

supply-side economics
The theory that advocates cutting taxes and deregulating business to stimulate the economy.

President Bush approved tax refunds for citizens totaling $168 billion along with tax cuts for select businesses. Later the same year, Congress and the president pledged to spend $300 billion to rescue three giant mortgage, insurance, and financial services companies from financial disaster and $700 billion to bail out faltering Wall Street financial institutions.

President Barack Obama and Congress continued to stimulate the sagging economy by enacting the American Recovery and Reinvestment Act (ARRA) in February 2009, which authorized $787 billion in combined tax cuts and federal spending. The goals of the ARRA, better known as the "stimulus package," were to create and save jobs, jump-start the nation's economy, and build the foundation for long-term economic growth. Although the success of the stimulus package was debated due to the slow pace of recovery from the Great Recession, most economists agree that the recession would have been even worse without the ARRA.[10]

Supply-Side Economics

Not all administrations have embraced Keynesian economics. President Ronald Reagan (1981–1989) stepped away from Keynesian theory and introduced the nation to **supply-side economics,** which advocates tax cuts and a decrease in government regulation to stimulate the economy in times of recession. Supply-siders argue that the government collects so much money in income taxes from workers that they are discouraged from working more than they absolutely need to (because any extra effort will just mean they pay more in taxes). In addition, supply-siders argue that high taxes drain the economy because they diminish people's ability to save and corporations' ability to invest to increase productivity. Therefore, the theory goes, if the government cuts taxes, workers will be more productive and corporations will have more money to invest, thus stimulating economic growth. Supply-siders also argue that, because government regulation increases the cost of producing goods, **deregulation**—reduction or elimination of government rules that businesses must follow—will reduce production costs.

President Donald Trump is also applying supply-side economic theory to his policies. The 2017 Tax Cuts and Jobs Act that he signed into law included several reforms to decrease the taxes paid by corporations; the most talked about was the cut in the top corporate tax rate from 35 percent to 21 percent. At the same time, Trump's administration was rolling back regulation, as discussed later in this chapter.

Monetarism

Economist Milton Friedman, a one-time supporter of Keynesian economics, is today best known for yet another economic theory, **monetarism,** which advocates that the government's proper role in promoting a healthy economy is through its regulation of the amount of money circulating in the economy (including coin, currency, and bank deposits). By controlling the amount of money in the economy, the government tries to ensure that the rate of inflation remains low.

Monetarists believe that *too much* money in circulation leads to a high inflation rate, which slows economic growth as people buy less because of higher prices. In addition, as the rate of inflation increases, investors begin to worry about the health of the economy, and investments may decline as a result, ultimately limiting economic growth. On the flip side, the monetarists say, *too little* money in circulation means there is not enough for new investments and that consequently new jobs are not created; this situation, too, retards economic growth. Today, monetarists target an inflation rate of 1–3 percent per year to ensure an adequate money supply for a healthy economy. They believe that the national government must use its **monetary policy,** which is the body of Federal Reserve actions (discussed later in this chapter) aimed at adjusting the amount of money in the economy to maintain a stable, low level of inflation.

Should One Economic Theory Predominate?

Although economists, government officials, and citizens broadly agree that the government should act to ensure a healthy economy, there is perpetual debate over the proper level of government involvement in the economy and what specific policy actions it should take. Where people stand in this debate depends on which economic theory they advocate. Each theory supports the use of different government policies to promote a healthy economy.

Democrats and Republicans traditionally disagree on economic policies, each justifying their preferences with different economic theories. Since Reagan, Republicans have advocated policies based on supply-side economics, and Democrats have advocated policies more in line with Keynesian economics. The Federal Reserve, which is expected to be nonpartisan, continues to adjust monetary policy in attempts to maintain a healthy economy.

Fiscal Policy

As noted earlier, fiscal policy comprises a government's spending and tax policies. The national government, through its budget process, annually approves a 12-month plan for raising revenue and spending revenue. The 12-month accounting period

deregulation
The reduction or elimination of government rules and regulations (laws) that businesses and industries must follow.

monetarism
The theory that says the government's proper economic role is to control the rate of inflation by controlling the amount of money in circulation.

monetary policy
The body of Federal Reserve actions aimed at adjusting the amount of money (coin, currency, and bank deposits) in the economy to maintain a stable, low level of inflation.

fiscal year (FY)
The 12-month accounting period for revenue raising and spending, which for the national government begins on October 1 and ends on September 30 of the following year.

for revenue raising and spending is a **fiscal year (FY).** The national government's fiscal year runs from October 1 through September 30 of the following calendar year, and is named for the calendar year in which it ends. Therefore, the federal FY 2020 runs from October 1, 2019, through September 30, 2020.

Although government spending certainly can create jobs, its primary goal is to provide the goods and services necessary to fulfill the Constitution's mission. The other side of the coin, tax policy, raises revenue needed by the national government to serve the people. Although the main goal of tax policy is to collect revenue, taxation also decreases the amount of money taxpayers have to spend in the marketplace and corporations have to invest. Hence, taxation may reduce consumer demand for goods and services, with possible effects on the unemployment rate as well as company profits. It may also affect investment, which contributes to economic growth. Thus tax policy, like spending policy, powerfully affects the economy.

Tax Policy

The Constitution delegates the power of the purse to Congress. By the authority of the Constitution, Congress formulates and approves (and then sends to the president for approval or rejection) *tax laws* to raise money along with *appropriations laws*—legislation that authorizes the spending of government money for a fiscal year. The Constitution specifies that the House must introduce revenue-raising bills before the Senate can consider them. The House Ways and Means Committee and the Senate Finance Committee are the congressional standing committees from which tax bills emerge.

Figure 16.2 presents the tax mix for the FY 1967 and FY 2017 budgets. Today, the national tax on individual income is the largest revenue source for the national government. The federal individual income tax is imposed on each individual's *earned income* (salaries and wages) and *unearned income* (profits made from investments).

The second-largest revenue category, social insurance receipts, includes taxes collected for Social Security and Medicare. Because employers deduct from workers' paychecks the amount they owe for social insurance taxes, these taxes are referred to as **payroll taxes.** The federal government's third-largest revenue source is corporate income taxes. The national government also collects *excise taxes,* which are taxes levied against a specific item such as gasoline or liquor, *estate and gift taxes,* and *customs duties* (import taxes).

Taxes levied by the federal government do not affect the income of all taxpayers in the same way. The national income tax is a **progressive tax** because it takes a larger percentage of the income of wealthier taxpayers and a smaller percentage of the income of less-well-off taxpayers. Most taxpayers view a progressive tax as fair. However, some people believe that a **proportional tax (flat tax),** which takes the same percentage of each taxpayer's income, is fairer than a progressive tax. A flat tax of 10 percent would equal $3,500 for a person earning $35,000 and $13,500 for a person earning $135,000. Although these two taxpayers pay a different amount of money in taxes, the *proportion* of their income collected is the same—hence the name proportional tax. Taxes can also be regressive. A **regressive tax** takes a greater percentage of the income of lower-income earners than of higher-income earners. States' sales taxes are the prime example of a regressive tax because lower-income households spend a larger proportion of their income to pay for sales taxes than do wealthier households, when the two are purchasing the same items.

payroll taxes
Taxes employers deduct from workers' paychecks that pay for social insurance programs including Social Security and Medicare.

progressive tax
A tax that takes a larger percentage of the income of wealthier taxpayers and a smaller percentage of the income of lower-income taxpayers.

proportional (flat) tax
A tax that takes the same percentage of each taxpayer's income.

regressive tax
A tax that takes a greater percentage of the income of lower-income earners than of higher-income earners.

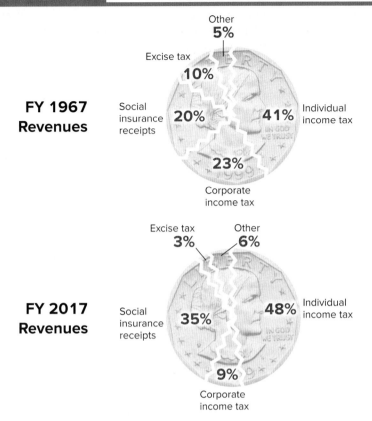

FY 1967 Revenues

Other
5%

Excise tax
10%

Social insurance receipts
20%

Individual income tax
41%

23%
Corporate income tax

FY 2017 Revenues

Excise tax
3%

Other
6%

Social insurance receipts
35%

Individual income tax
48%

9%
Corporate income tax

FIGURE 16.2 ■ **Revenues** Compare the revenue sources of 1967 and 2017 and summarize the differences. Reflect on the differences. What stands out to you? Given the 2017 Tax Cuts and Jobs Act, what pattern of changes do you predict for the future?

PHOTO: U.S. Mint

SOURCE: Office of Management and Budget, Historical Tables, Table 2.2: Percentage Composition of Receipts by Source: 1934–2023.

Taxes may also affect various taxpayers differently because the government grants **tax expenditures** (better known as *tax breaks* or *tax loopholes*). These are government financial incentives, in other words, a decreased tax burden, that encourage individuals and corporations to behave in a way that promotes the public good. For example, to encourage home ownership, the government gives tax breaks to individuals paying interest on a home mortgage. The government also offers tax breaks to businesses for job creation and worker retraining.

State and local governments, as well as nonprofit organizations that provide a public service, pay no federal taxes. Thus we say that they are exempt from federal taxes. Included in this group of tax-exempt organizations are the overwhelming majority of colleges and universities, which are public or nonprofit institutions. They are tax exempt because they provide the public good of higher education without making a profit; they must invest any surplus money back into the institution.

Tax expenditures and tax cuts, such as the cuts established in the Tax Cuts and Jobs Act of 2017, would not be a concern if the government raised enough money to balance its budget. Unfortunately, the national government spends more than it raises in annual revenues. How is the government spending all this money?

tax expenditures

(also, *tax breaks* or *loopholes*) Government financial incentives that allow individuals and corporations to pay reduced taxes, to encourage behaviors that promote the public good.

Spending Policy

Decisions the federal government makes about spending significantly affect both the national economy and the ability of individuals to achieve the American dream. Although setting the budget is an annual process, with Congress and the president approving a spending plan one fiscal year at a time, not all national government spending is approved annually.

For the government to spend money, Congress and the president must enact laws that establish **budget authority,** which is the legal authority for agencies to spend federal money. Programs granted budget authority each year are **discretionary spending** programs. There are two categories of discretionary spending programs: defense programs and nondefense programs. As Figure 16.3 indicates, in FY 2017, discretionary defense spending was the same proportion of the budget pie as discretionary nondefense spending. Nondefense spending covers the majority of domestic programs, including the administration of justice, agriculture, education, energy, environment, health, housing, income security for those who are poor and disabled, and transportation.

Annual appropriations acts are pieces of legislation that define how much money can be spent in the fiscal year. Congress and the president deliberate each year over how much budget authority to include in these acts for discretionary spending programs. Typically, Democrats and Republicans differ on their priorities for such programs.

The share of the budget spent on discretionary spending has been shrinking due to the growth in **mandatory spending,** spending required by the authorization legislation that created a government program (see Figure 16.3). Social Security (income security for retired Americans and people with certain disabilities), Medicare (health insurance for elderly individuals), and Medicaid (health insurance for low-income individuals) are prime examples of mandatory spending programs. The government is obligated to pay for the program every year, whatever the cost may be, as long as the program exists. Because the government is legally obligated to pay back money it borrows, payments for the national debt also fall within the category of mandatory spending.

In the annual budget process, Congress and the president do not make annual decisions about most of the money spent by the national government because most expenditures are mandatory. Other than interest payments on the debt, mandatory spending could be controlled by Congress and the president by rewriting the legislation that established these open-ended budget obligations. For example, eligibility for receiving Social Security could be changed so that very wealthy, retired individuals would not receive Social Security. However, recent attempts to rewrite the legislation that created the Social Security retirement program have shown that mandatory programs are difficult to change. This is partly because elected officials fear the impact such changes would have on their reelection prospects, and partly because of partisanship. Therefore, most mandatory spending is considered **politically uncontrollable spending.** Not only do Democrats and Republicans disagree on the proper reforms, but also members of each party disagree among themselves on specific reforms. Without major reforms to programs like Social Security and Medicare, mandatory spending will continue to grow as a percentage of the federal budget.

National Budget Process: Creating Fiscal Policy

The federal government creates its policies and programs through authorization legislation that specifies policy goals and establishes whether the policy will be

---

budget authority
The authority provided by law for agencies to spend government funds.

discretionary spending
Payment on programs for which Congress and the president must approve budget authority each year in appropriation legislation.

mandatory spending
Government spending for debt and programs whose budget authority is provided in legislation other than annual appropriation acts; this budget authority is open ended, obligating the government to pay for the program whatever the cost, every year.

politically uncontrollable spending
Spending on programs that are so popular that elected officials are not willing to change the laws that authorize the programs for fear of the effect on their reelection prospects.

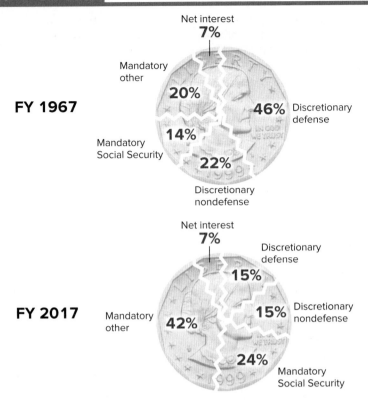

Net interest
7%

Mandatory
other

FY 1967

20%

46% Discretionary
defense

14%

Mandatory
Social Security

22%

Discretionary
nondefense

Net interest
7%

Discretionary
defense

15%

FY 2017

Mandatory
other

Discretionary
nondefense

42%

15%

24%

Mandatory
Social Security

FIGURE 16.3 ■ **Federal Expenditures by Budget Categories (as a Percentage of Total)** The figures present the proportion of actual budget outlays by budget category for 1967 and 2017. What category of spending has increased the most as a proportion of total spending since 1967? What category has decreased the most since 1967? What percentage of the spending was mandatory in 1967? In 2017? What is the impact of the change in mandatory spending on the difficulty of budget decisions?

PHOTO: U.S. Mint

SOURCE: Office of Management and Budget, Historical Tables, Table 8.3: Table 8.2—Outlays by Budget Enforcement Act Category in Constant (FY 2009) Dollars: 1962–2023.

funded through budget authority obligated for the life of the program (open-ended, mandatory spending) or budget authority that must be set annually (discretionary spending). In an annual appropriations process, Congress and the president establish yearly funding for discretionary spending programs and possibly change tax policy to increase revenue raised—to pay the bills—or to cut taxes in an effort to stimulate the economy. This process begins in the executive branch.

THE PRESIDENT'S EXECUTIVE BUDGET   The budget process officially starts about a year and a half before the beginning of the fiscal year for which budget authority will be obligated. For example, work on the budget for FY 2020 (which covers the spending period of October 1, 2019, through September 30, 2020) began during the spring of 2018. The process begins when the Office of Management and Budget (OMB) sends the president's budget priorities (policy and financing preferences) to the executive branch agencies. Executive branch agencies use the president's guidelines to formulate their funding requests. Typically, these requests are incremental changes (small increases) to their current fiscal year's budget authority.

The budget requests work their way back up the executive branch hierarchy to the OMB. The OMB reviews the budget requests, conducts hearings in which the agencies justify their requests, and analyzes the requests in light of economic forecasts. The OMB then submits its budget recommendations to the president, who works with the OMB to create a proposed fiscal plan for the entire national government for the upcoming fiscal year. The OMB drafts a budget document and a budget message, collectively labeled the **executive budget,** which explains the president's fiscal plan. The president is to submit the executive budget to Congress by the first Monday in February, eight months before the fiscal year begins.

executive budget
The budget document and budget message that explains the president's fiscal plan.

CONGRESSIONAL ACTION Once Congress receives the president's executive budget, the Congressional Budget Office (CBO), the legislative branch's counterpart to the OMB, swings into action. The CBO analyzes the executive budget in light of economic forecasts and predicted government revenues. The House Budget Committee and the Senate Budget Committee use the CBO's analysis, along with reports from other congressional committees, to develop the concurrent budget resolution. The **concurrent budget resolution** establishes a binding expenditure ceiling (the maximum amount that can be spent) and a binding revenue floor (the minimum amount that must be raised) as well as proposed expenditure levels for major policy categories. The House and the Senate must both agree to the concurrent budget resolution. This agreement is to occur by April 15, less than six months before the fiscal year begins.

concurrent budget resolution
A document approved by the House and the Senate at the beginning of their budget processes that establishes binding expenditure ceilings and a binding revenue floor as well as proposed expenditure levels for major policy categories.

After approval of the concurrent budget resolution, the House Appropriations Committee and the Senate Appropriations Committees each draft 12 appropriations bills to provide budget authority for all the discretionary spending for the upcoming fiscal year. To comply with the concurrent budget resolution, Congress may also need to revise the legislation that authorized selected government programs to stay below the expenditure ceiling, or it may have to agree to changes in tax legislation to meet the revenue floor. **Budget reconciliation** is the process of rewriting authorization legislation to comply with the concurrent budget resolution. The deadline for completion of the reconciliation process is June 15, less than four months before the fiscal year begins.

budget reconciliation
The annual process of rewriting authorization legislation to comply with the expenditure ceiling and revenue floor of the concurrent budget resolution for the upcoming fiscal year.

Congress has until the end of June to approve the 12 appropriations bills that fund discretionary spending for the upcoming fiscal year. This timetable leaves two months for the president to approve all 12 bills so that by October 1 the national government can begin the new fiscal year with budget authority.

The nature of the annual budget process is such that, at any given time, some government body in the executive or legislative branch is preparing a future budget, even as the executive branch is implementing the current budget. At the same time, the Government Accountability Office (GAO), a congressional office, is evaluating the implementation of the previous fiscal year's budget. Thus budgeting is a perpetual government activity, one that takes up a great deal of national officials' time.

>Copies of President Trump's FY2019 Executive Budget are unpacked for review by the House Budget Committee and the Senate Budget Committee. The president's FY2019 budget was presented to Congress in February of what year?
©Bill Clark/CQ Roll Call/Getty Images

Today's Federal Budget Realities

Although the budget process just outlined was established through legislation beginning with the 1974 Congressional Budget and Impoundment Control Act, the process is not often followed. By the 21st century, the federal budget process included these realities:

1. Appropriations bills that were not approved by October 1.
2. Continuing resolutions that were approved to fund some, if not all, of the fiscal year.
3. Efforts to shrink annual deficit spending by establishing spending caps on annual discretionary spending.
4. Regular increases to the debt ceiling to pay for debt already incurred.

CONTINUING RESOLUTIONS   If Congress and the president fail to approve one or more of the appropriations bills before the new fiscal year begins on October 1, Congress needs to approve a **continuing resolution** to authorize spending for agencies and programs not covered by the approved appropriations bills. Typically, the level of spending authority approved in a continuing resolution is the same level as in the previous fiscal year, with adjustments for inflation. If a program or agency is not extended budget authority through either an appropriation law or a continuing resolution, then it cannot operate and must shut down until Congress and the president approve its budget authority.

For FY 2018, Congress approved five continuing resolutions (CRs) between October 1, 2017, and February 8, 2018, to fund the national government. During that period, the government shut down for 2.5 days between the approval of CR 3 and CR 4. It also shut down for a few hours between the approval of CR 4 and CR 5. Then on March 23, 2018, just hours before another shutdown, Congress passed and the president signed $1.3 billion of appropriations for the remainder of FY 2018, which would end on September 30, 2018.

continuing resolution
An agreement of the House and Senate that authorizes agencies not covered by approved appropriation laws to continue to spend money within their previous budget year's levels.

DEFICIT SPENDING, SPENDING CAPS, AND SEQUESTRATION   Most Americans highly value the ideal of a balanced budget, in which the government spends no more than the revenues that it raises. Although the nation had a **budget surplus** (money left over when all expenses are paid) for several years at the end of the 1990s, **budget deficits** (more money spent than collected through revenues) recurred as the first decade of the 21st century unfolded. Indeed, deficit spending has been the norm, not the exception (see Figure 16.4).

The Budget Control Act of 2011 set caps on annual federal discretionary funding for 2012–2021 in an attempt to decrease (and eventually eliminate) budget deficits. The caps limited how much discretionary spending could be increased in each fiscal year. However, for most fiscal years since 2011, Congress has agreed to increase the established caps, and so deficit spending continues.

The Budget Control Act also established a congressional committee to find savings in the federal budget. In FY 2013, when savings were not identified and the spending caps were kept in place, automatic spending cuts went into effect through the process called **sequestration**. Sequestration also occurred in FY 2014 and FY 2015. The spending cuts were across-the-board, meaning that all agencies had to cut their spending by a set percentage during the fiscal year. Still, deficit spending continues.

budget surplus
Money left over after all expenses are paid.

budget deficit
More money spent than collected through revenues.

sequestration
Automatic spending cuts during the fiscal year.

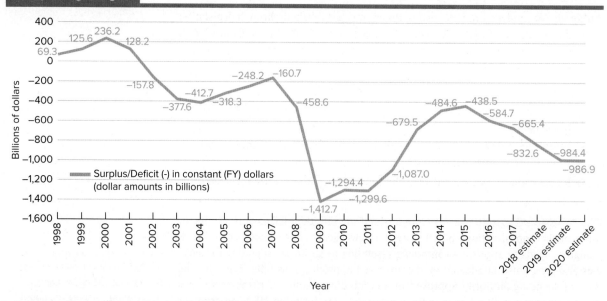

FIGURE 16.4 ■ **Deficit Spending Since Last Surplus Years** How did the 2009 American Recovery and Reinvestment Act (ARRA)—the stimulus package enacted to address the Great Recession—affect the deficit? What actions can the national government take to decrease annual deficits?

SOURCE: Office of Management and Budget, Historical Tables, Table 1.3—Summary of Receipts, Outlays, and Surpluses or Deficits (−) in Current Dollars, Constant (FY2000) Dollars, and as Percentages of GDP: 1940–2023.

national debt

The total amount of money the government owes to all the individuals and groups that loaned it money.

debt ceiling

The legal borrowing limit for the national government.

NATIONAL DEBT A government that engages in deficit spending borrows money and hence goes into debt. The **national debt** is the total amount of money the national government owes to all the creditors (individuals and groups) that loaned it money. Figure 16.5 indicates who these creditors are and the percentage of the debt owed to each creditor group. The long-term impact of debt is the legal obligation to pay back not only the money initially borrowed (the *principal*) but also *interest,* an additional amount of money equal to a percentage of the amount initially borrowed. In the case of government borrowing, future generations must pay back the debt of their parents and grandparents. In March 2018, to pay off the $21 trillion national debt, each citizen (man, woman, and child) would have had to chip in $64,275.[11] Even as politicians, some economists, and many concerned citizens call for a balanced budget, deficit spending continues, and so the national debt grows.

Democrats and Republicans battle annually over what taxing and/or spending policies they should change to decrease annual deficits, moving the government toward a balanced budget. These battles grow more intense and bitter as the proportion of the budget that goes to mandatory spending grows.

To pay its annual financial obligations, including debt already incurred, Congress and the president have to regularly increase the **debt ceiling,** the legal borrowing limit for the national government. Congresses and presidents have raised the debt ceiling almost 100 times since it was first established in 1917.[12] Democrats and Republicans battle regularly about raising the debt ceiling, even though a decision not to raise the debt ceiling would leave the national government unable to pay all its financial obligations—a *default.* Countries around the globe worry

FIGURE 16.5 ■ **Who Owns the $21 Trillion National Debt by Proportion of Debt Owed** Which creditor group do you think Americans are most worried about owing money to? Why?

SOURCE: The Balance

[a] Among foreign governments, China holds the largest proportion, Japan the second largest, and Ireland the third largest.
[b] Intragovernmental holdings are the portion of the debt owed to 230 federal agencies.
[c] Other U.S. government entities include the Federal Reserve System, state governments, and local governments.
[d] Private funds include mutual funds and private pension funds.
[e] Businesses include banks and insurance companies.

that a U.S. government default on its debt would spark a global financial and economic disaster.

Elected officials fear that citizens harmed by spending cuts and tax increases will not vote for them on Election Day; therefore, attempts to shrink annual deficits often fail. While elected officials struggle with budget decisions and their impact on reelection hopes, appointed officials, whom citizens cannot hold accountable through the ballot box, make monetary policy that, like fiscal policy, affects the national economy.

Monetary Policy: The Federal Reserve System

The federal government seeks to influence the value of money by controlling its availability. When more money is in circulation, it is lower in value; consequently, consumers need to spend more money to keep buying the same goods and services. Inflation is at work. The costs of running a business also increase with inflation. As a result of increased costs and decreased sales (because fewer people can maintain their levels of spending), businesses may choose to lay off workers. To avert these potential problems, the Federal Reserve, the nation's central banking system, works to maximize employment, ensure stable prices (keep inflation low), and moderate long-term interest rates.

Congress and President Woodrow Wilson established the Federal Reserve System (the Fed) in 1913. The Fed is composed of the Board of Governors (a government agency whose seven members the president nominates and the Senate must confirm), 12 Federal Reserve banks, and the Federal Open Market Committee (FOMC). The Board of Governors, the president of the Federal Reserve Bank of New York, and the presidents of four of the other Federal Reserve banks, who serve on a rotating basis, make up the FOMC. Today, the Fed's responsibilities include (1) setting *monetary*

policy—the body of government policies aimed at maintaining price stability; (2) supervising and regulating banking institutions; (3) maintaining the stability of financial markets; and (4) providing financial services to depository institutions, the national government, and foreign official institutions—central banks of other nations, and international organizations such as the International Monetary Fund.

The Fed has three primary tools for setting monetary policy. It can raise or lower the *reserve requirement*—the amount of money that financial institutions must keep out of circulation. In times of high inflation, the Fed may raise the reserve requirement to decrease the amount of money available through credit, hence, decreasing the money supply. The Fed can also raise or lower the *discount rate*—the interest charged to financial institutions that borrow money from the Federal Reserve banks—and thereby make it more or less costly to borrow money. The Fed action that most influences the money supply, however, is its decision to buy or sell Treasury Securities (bills, notes, and bonds, which represent loans of money to the government). The Fed sells Treasury Securities when it wants to decrease the money supply and buys them to increase the supply.

>The Federal Reserve sells and buys Treasury Securities, including Savings Bonds, which represent loans of money to the government, to affect the amount of money in circulation. Although savings bonds are viewed as an old-fashioned gift given to new babies and grandchildren, they are one of the safest investments because the U.S. government fully backs them. Has someone invested in the government by giving you a Treasury Savings Bond?

©John Parrot/Stocktrek Images/Getty Images

Regulatory Policy

Marketplace competition among private entities, each trying to make a profit, may threaten economic health as well as public safety, people's health, and the environment. Consider, for example, the unsafe products, including dangerous food and drugs, which may be manufactured and sold to make a profit. Think about production and manufacturing processes that may pollute the air, water, and land, creating conditions that are injurious to public health. Competition may also lead firms to cut salaries and benefits to ensure their profits, or their very survival. Such cuts decrease workers' ability to earn wages and benefits that keep them in the middle class, or even out of poverty. Unsafe and unhealthful working conditions may be another "cost" that workers "pay" so that firms can hold down or reduce production expenses. Moreover, if marketplace competition results in a few firms driving out their competition, they then have the power to raise prices or produce goods of lower quality, harming consumers.

In the U.S. economy today, the government regulates marketplace practices to protect the public and the economy. This regulation occurs in two broad categories: business regulation and social regulation. **Business regulation** includes government policies that aim to preserve competition in the marketplace. **Social regulation** refers to government policies directed at protecting workers, consumers, and the environment from the harm caused by marketplace competition. In Chapter 14, we surveyed the administrative rule-making process by which executive branch agencies establish business and social regulations. In this discussion, we trace the evolution of these two types of regulatory policy.

business regulation
Government rules, regulations, and standards directed at preserving competition in the marketplace.

social regulation
Government rules, regulations, and standards aimed at protecting workers, consumers, and the environment from market failure.

Business Regulation

The federal government created the first agency for the purpose of regulating business, the Interstate Commerce Commission (ICC), in 1887. The ICC initially regulated the prices of and services provided by the railroad industry to ensure that farmers could transport their goods to distant markets. Next, in 1914, the federal government established regulations to prevent large corporations from engaging in business practices that harmed marketplace competition and established the Federal Trade Commission (FTC) to oversee these regulations.[13] In 1934, during the Great Depression, the government created the Securities and Exchange Commission (SEC) to regulate and make transparent the nation's stock markets and financial markets.

More recently, the United States experienced a failure in the financial market because of risky decisions by numerous financial and banking institutions. Loans and credit lines were extended to people without the means to repay the borrowed money. Ultimately, this sparked an increase in the number of people who could not pay their mortgages and therefore lost their homes. Hundreds of billions of dollars' worth of mortgages could not be repaid by the fall of 2008, and several large, prominent financial and banking companies collapsed. President Bush and Congress began discussions about the need for new regulations for the banking and financial industries to prevent similar market failures in the future.

Congress and President Obama's administration continued those discussions, focusing on protecting consumers of the banking and financial industries. In the summer of 2010, President Obama signed legislation establishing the Consumer Financial Protection Bureau (CFPB), an independent unit within the Fed. The CFPB has the authority to regulate a wide range of financial products, including mortgages and credit cards, and to collect and monitor consumer complaints about the financial and banking industries. The CFPB also has a responsibility to educate consumers about financial products and services.

Social Regulation

The national government also uses social regulatory policy—which aims to protect the public's health and safety—to safeguard workers, consumers, and the environment from the potential harm created by the competitive quest for profits in the marketplace. Like business regulation, social regulation has an economic impact because it increases the costs of doing business.

The federal government first established social regulation when it passed two 1906 laws that protected *public* health—the Pure Food and Drug Act and the Meat Inspection Act. Upton Sinclair's descriptions of the dangerous and unsanitary conditions in the Chicago meatpacking industry in his novel *The Jungle* motivated President Theodore Roosevelt (1901–1909) to sign those two laws. The Pure Food and Drug Act created the Food and Drug Administration (FDA) and charged it with testing all foods and drugs produced for human consumption. It also requires individuals to present prescriptions from licensed physicians to purchase certain drugs and mandates the use of warning labels on habit-forming drugs. The Meat Inspection Act requires government inspection of animals that are slaughtered and processed for human consumption and establishes standards of cleanliness for slaughterhouses and meat processing plants.

The federal government first addressed working conditions that jeopardized *workers'* health and general welfare when it enacted the Fair Labor Standards Act (FLSA) in 1938. The FLSA established standards for a legal workweek, overtime pay for those working more than the standard workweek, a minimum wage, record keeping of workers' hours, and limits on child labor. President Franklin D. Roosevelt characterized the law as the "most far-reaching, far-sighted program to the benefit of workers ever adopted."[14]

THEN

NOW

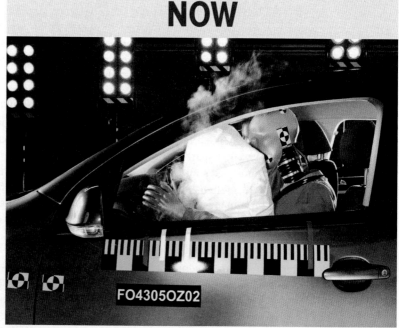

FO4305OZ02

> By the early 1900s, speeding and car accidents with fatalities were a growing problem in the United States. In the 1950s, crash testing helped identify causes and effects of bodily impacts during car accidents. Seat belts and padded dashboards became options when buying a car. State governments began to regulate the auto industry's safety standards in the early 1960s by requiring seat belts in new cars. Learning from the state experiments, in 1966 Congress authorized the federal government to establish safety standards for new cars. By 1968, seat belts and padded dashboards were mandatory in new cars. By 1999, airbags were mandatory in new cars. These government regulations have saved hundreds of thousands of lives. However, beginning in 2014, cars were being recalled due to faulty, malfunctioning airbags that caused numerous deaths.

In the 1960s, the government focused anew on growing concerns about product quality and safety. In his 1965 book *Unsafe at Any Speed,* attorney and consumer advocate Ralph Nader warned that "a great problem of contemporary life is how to control the power of economic interests which ignore the harmful effects of their applied science and technology."[15] Although Nader's book targeted the unsafe cars rolling off the assembly lines of the U.S. auto industry, his warning was equally relevant to the countless American industries that were discharging chemicals and toxins into the environment. Nader's book helped ignite an environmental movement and a consumer safety movement.

Lobbying by concerned citizens and interest groups led to passage of the Consumer Product Safety Act (CPSA) of 1973. The federal Consumer Product Safety Commission (CPSC), created through the CPSA, is charged with protecting the public from unreasonable risk of injury associated with more than 15,000 consumer products, including toys, products for children, products for inside and outside the home, and products made for sports and recreation. The CPSC can recall such products if it deems them unsafe, just as the FDA can recall food and prescription medicines it judges to be unsafe. To better serve the public today, there is a website, www.recall.gov, that provides the latest information on recalls.

The Benefits and Costs of Regulation

Business and social regulation has unquestionably lowered the risk of harm to citizens and the environment caused by marketplace competition. It also has cushioned economic downfalls. But the burden of government regulations has driven up the cost of doing business and of government expenditures, and in the end, consumers pay for this cost. In many industries, this increased cost poses greater problems for smaller firms than for larger ones. The higher costs caused by compliance with government regulations may also put U.S. industries and firms at a competitive disadvantage in the global marketplace, because many other countries do not have business or social regulations. Therefore, the production costs of firms in other countries are often lower than those in the United States.

>President Trump highlights his administration's deregulation efforts by cutting a red tape tied between a stack of papers representing government regulations in the 1960s (left) and a stack representing government regulation at the end of 2017 (right). How successful has the Trump administration been in cutting government red tape through deregulation?
©Saul Loeb/AFP/Getty Images

President Obama "was among the most prolific authors of major regulations in presidential history."[16] His successor, President Trump, "declared that rolling back regulations will be a defining theme of his presidency." He put this declaration into action by signing an executive order that called for the elimination of two regulations for each new regulation approved.[17] He also ordered federal agencies to form teams to deregulate.[18] By July 2017, the Environmental Protection Agency was already working on undoing more than 30 environmental rules.[19] The Trump administration claimed that between January 2017 and January 2018, they had "delayed, withdrawn or made inactive nearly 1,600 planned regulatory actions."[20] Trump's deregulation efforts combined with the tax cuts he signed into law indicate that he supports supply-side economics.

Trade Policy in the Global Economy

The next time you are shopping, try to purchase only American-made products. Is it possible? Stores in the United States offer products that are domestic (that is, American made) as well as imported (made overseas by American or foreign companies). Moreover, many American-made products have imported components and ingredients. For example, U.S. International Trade Commission data show that ingredients for food products are imported from more than 100 countries.[21] Today, marketplaces in every country offer products grown and produced in countries from throughout the world. Hence, national economies are integrated and interdependent—holistically forming the **global economy.**

To navigate in this global economy, each nation creates its own **trade policy**—a collection of tax laws and regulations that support the country's international commerce. In addition, international organizations whose mission is to establish trade rules for all nations to follow have created a global trade policy. The goal of trade policy, like the other economic policies we have discussed, is ostensibly to promote prosperous economies.

global economy
The worldwide economy created by the integration and interdependence of national economies.

trade policy
A collection of tax laws and regulations that support the country's international commerce.

protectionist trade policy
The establishment of trade barriers to shelter domestic goods from foreign competition.

tariff
A special tax on imported goods paid by the importer.

nontariff trade barriers
Business and social regulations as well as subsidies aimed at creating a competitive advantage in trade.

government subsidy
A tax break or another kind of financial support that encourages behaviors the government deems beneficial to the public good.

free trade policy
The elimination of tariffs and nontariff trade barriers so that international trade is expanded.

A government's trade policy may take one of two basic forms—free trade or protectionism—or it may be a combination of the two. **Protectionist trade policy** aims at sheltering domestic producers and businesses from foreign competition through tariffs and nontariff trade barriers. A **tariff** is a special tax on imported goods paid by the importer. **Nontariff trade barriers** include government business regulations (such as limits on the number of imports allowed into a country or bans on the sale of imports that a government deems unsafe). **Government subsidies**—tax breaks or another kind of financial support that encourages behaviors the government deems beneficial to the public good—are another form of nontariff barriers. Most subsidies are given to producers or distributors of goods to promote economic growth. Proponents of national government subsidies to U.S. farmers argue that to decrease these subsidies would place the farmers at a competitive disadvantage because European farmers receive even larger subsidies from their governments.

Opponents of protectionist policy argue that prices of domestic goods increase as a result of limited competition. In addition, the price of imported goods increases due to tariffs. Proponents of protectionist policy argue that businesses benefit from the limited competition, and workers' salaries benefit as business profits increase. Therefore, wealth remains in the country.

From the 1790s until the 1930s, protectionism was the aim of U.S. trade policy. The first secretary of the Treasury, Alexander Hamilton, argued successfully that taxes on imported goods could be set high enough to protect American-made products in the domestic marketplace. In 1930, even as the American economy was failing, Congress hiked tariffs 20 percent—so high that it set off an international tariff war. This tariff hike fueled the Great Depression, whose economic toll was global.

After World War II, the United States and its international partners gradually shifted toward **free trade policy,** which aims at lowering or eliminating tariffs and nontariff barriers to trade. Free trade policies decrease the costs of bringing products to markets throughout the world and, in this way, open markets to a greater diversity of products and brisker competition. When other nations eliminate tariffs, American companies can participate in the global marketplace at a lower cost. These opportunities encourage an increase in the supply of U.S. goods and thus lead to an expansion of the U.S. economy. By the same token, when the United States eliminates its tariffs, more foreign products make their way into the American marketplace, increasing the diversity of consumer goods and producer competition and decreasing consumer prices in the United States. Opponents of free trade claim that the increased competition decreases profits of domestic businesses, and therefore, unemployment increases. Proponents counter that in the long term, poorer countries will develop healthier economies due to increased competition and increased employment opportunities and will become new consumers for the products of wealthier countries. Therefore, proponents argue, in the long term, all countries benefit from free trade policy.

In 1947, the United States and 23 other nations signed the General Agreement on Tariffs and Trade (GATT), which advocated for free trade and punishment of protectionism. This multilateral agreement on guidelines for conducting international trade had three basic objectives. First, the signatory countries would not discriminate against one another in trade matters. Second, the signatory countries would work toward eliminating all tariff and regulatory barriers to trade among their countries. Third, the signatory countries would consult and negotiate with one another to resolve any trade conflicts or damages caused by trading activities of another signatory country. Through multilateral negotiations, the GATT established the guidelines for international trade and resolved trade disputes from 1947 to 1995. Then, in 1995, the World Trade Organization (WTO) came into being. The WTO continues the GATT's advocacy of free trade and punishment of protectionism. Specifically, the WTO monitors adherence to international trade rules and resolves charges of rule violations raised by any of its over 150 member countries, of which the United States is one.

The American Dream in Today's Economy

It was during the Great Depression that historian James Truslow Adams coined the term "American dream." In his book *The Epic of America* (1931), Adams argued that what made America a unique nation was its inhabitants' "dream of a better, richer, and happier life" for all citizens based on equal "opportunity for each according to his [or her] ability or achievement."[22]

In the fall of 2017, the Pew Research Center[23] found that the majority of people (82 percent) believe they have already achieved the American dream (36 percent) or they are on their way to achieving it (46 percent). The people who are most apt to see the American dream as out of their reach are those with a high school degree or less than a high school degree (24 percent). (Read the "Thinking Critically" feature for a discussion of whether college tuition should be free.) The survey asked about the American dream as each respondent defined it; the survey did not provide a definition of the American dream.

When asked to select factors that are needed to achieve the American dream, the majority of respondents to the survey identified the following as essential or important: have a good family life (98 percent), retire comfortably (96 percent), own a home (91 percent), and become wealthy (60 percent) (see Table 16.1 at the beginning of this chapter). A healthy economy with low unemployment and low rates of inflation are foundational to those factors, and therefore to the American dream.

According to the results of a Pew Research Center survey, conducted January 10–15, 2018,[24] as presented in Table 16.3, a majority of Americans say the

TABLE 16.3 The Majority of Americans' Top Priorities for Trump and Congress in 2018

Defending against terrorism	73%
Improving education	72%
Strengthening the economy	71%
Reducing health care costs	68%
Securing Social Security	67%
Securing Medicare	66%
Protecting the environment	62%
Improving job situation	62%
Problems of poor and needy	58%
Reducing crime	56%
Addressing race relations	52%

SOURCE: Pew Research Center, "Economic Issues Decline among Public's Policy Priorities," January 25, 2018.

Should College Tuition Be Free?

The Issue: Although a college degree is viewed as a path to the American dream, many are having a tough time paying for it. College costs keep increasing, and at a rate that is more than the rate of inflation. This is especially problematic for middle-class families, who are typically ineligible for most government scholarship and grant programs that are available for lower-income families and that wealthier families do not need. Graduates are delaying marriage and home purchases while they pay down their college debt from student loans. Many are asking whether college should be free.

Yes: Today, a college degree has replaced a high school degree as the path to the American Dream and a middle-class lifestyle. Moreover, it is not only a private good for individuals, allowing them to become financially self-sufficient; it is also a public good. When more people earn college degrees, our workforce is more highly skilled and better educated, and therefore, our economy is more productive and more competitive. Free college tuition is good for the individual and for the economy.

No: Free tuition is not really free. Taxpayers will need to pay more (national and state taxes) to cover the cost of tuition for everyone, including the wealthy, who can afford to pay for their own tuition. The increased cost to taxpayers might lead to decreased access to college, as the actual cost of a college education will keep increasing (due to increasing salaries and benefits for employees and keeping up with technology) while the ability and willingness of taxpayers to pay ever more in taxes is limited. If taxpayers cannot keep up with the increasing cost, then the quality of the education will be harmed. The current system, in which financial assistance is available based on financial need, is the best way to finance higher education.

Other Approaches: Deferring a proportion of tuition payments until after graduation would increase access and affordability for low- and middle-income families. Repayment plans could be based on the graduate's earnings. Payments could be a percentage of money earned; that is, as salary increases so do the payments.

What do you think?

1. Is a college degree essential or important to achieving the American dream? Explain your answer.

2. Currently, a majority of students at community colleges (where tuition is on average the lowest among colleges) have to take remedial courses to succeed. Should we improve the quality and access to elementary and secondary education before (or at the same time) that we consider increasing access to college by making it more affordable?

economy, jobs, and the problems of the poor and needy should be among the top priorities for President Trump and Congress. Therefore, Americans are looking for national government policies that attempt to ensure a healthy economy with low unemployment. As we have explored in this chapter, the national government can utilize fiscal policy, regulatory policy, trade policy, and monetary policy to affect those top priorities. President Trump and Congress have enacted tax legislation—the 2017 Tax Cuts and Jobs Act—to boost the economy. Because the tax cuts are predicted to reduce the revenue raised beginning in FY 2018, with a deficit of about $800 billion in FY 2018, spending is a concern.[25]

To address the predicted ongoing deficits, many in Congress are proposing cuts in spending. Unfortunately, Americans identify some of the most expensive mandatory spending programs—Social Security and Medicare—as top priorities for Trump and Congress. Those two programs compose a large percentage of federal expenditures, 43 percent in FY 2017,[26] and therefore are worthy of exploration for cuts. Traditionally, however, they are politically uncontrollable, with both Democrats and Republicans hesitant to cut benefits and, therefore, spending in either program.

On the regulatory front, by the beginning of 2018, President Trump's deregulation efforts seemed to have "created a wave of optimism" among American business leaders. Their "newfound confidence" was "beginning to translate into the sort of investment in new plants, equipment and factory upgrades that bolsters economic growth, spurs job creation—and may finally raise wages significantly."[27]

Clearly, the national government has many tools it can use in its efforts to create and maintain a healthy economy and support each individual's pursuit of the American dream. Typically, there is not consensus on spending policies, tax policies, regulatory policies, trade policies, or monetary policies. Often, the disagreements are clearly partisan. Yet overall, traditional measures of economic health (unemployment rate, rate of inflation) indicate that the U.S. economy is healthy, and surveys suggest that the majority of Americans are confident that they have been or will be successful in their pursuit of the American dream.

Conclusion
Thinking Critically About What's Next in Economic Policy

Governments throughout the world seek to maintain healthy economies using economic policy. U.S. economic policy comprises taxing and spending policies (fiscal policy), monetary policy, regulatory policy, and trade policy. Today, the economic decisions made by the president, Congress, and the Fed are influenced by the realities of the global economy. Partisan battles over fiscal policy and shrinking the deficit have shut down the national government and brought it to the brink of debt defaults. Will the partisan battles over fiscal and regulatory policies continue, resulting in ongoing deficit spending and growth in the national debt?

The viability of the American dream depends on a healthy national economy. The gap between those who have the largest share of the nation's wealth and everyone else has expanded in the past few decades, and wages have stagnated. Will the 2017 tax reform and deregulation stimulate wage growth? Will the shift from Keynesian-based economic policies to supply-side-based policies support continued improvement in the health of the U.S. economy, or even speed economic growth?

Learning Summary

1. Explain what "American dream" means.
   a. Describe the relationship between a healthy national economy and achievement of the American dream.
   b. Define *regulated capitalism*.

2. Identify traditional and other ways that economists, politicians, and others measure the health of a country's economy.
   a. Identify the unemployment rate, inflation rate, and growth in GDP that economists view as indications of a healthy economy.
   b. Summarize what the measures of economic health indicate about the health of the U.S. economy.

3. Compare the goals of and policies advocated by each of the following economic theories: laissez-faire; Keynesian; supply-side; monetarism.
   a. Describe partisan preferences for particular economic theories that elected officials use to support their economic policy choices.

4. Explain what fiscal policy is.
   a. Identify the revenue sources of the national government from the largest source of revenue to the smallest.
   b. Discuss the effects taxes and tax expenditures can have on a person's income.
   c. Compare mandatory spending, discretionary spending, and politically uncontrollable spending.
   d. Outline the national budget process and who has authority for it.
   e. Describe the reality of the national budget process as it works today.

5. Explain monetary policy.
   a. Identify who controls monetary policy.
   b. Describe the tools of monetary policy.

6. Explain how regulatory policy affects the economy.
   a. Compare business regulation and social regulation.
   b. Identify some costs and benefits of rolling back regulations.

7. Summarize the goals and means of protectionist trade policy and free-trade policy.

8. Describe the recent shifts in economic policy since the election of President Trump.
   a. Discuss the viability of the American dream for you and your peers.

Key Terms

American dream 534
balanced budget 541
budget authority 546
budget deficit 549
budget reconciliation 548
budget surplus 549
business regulation 552
concurrent budget resolution 548
consumer price index (CPI) 536
continuing resolution 549
debt ceiling 550
deficit spending 541
depression 541
deregulation 543
discretionary spending 546

economic boom 541
economic policy 535
economy 535
executive budget 548
fiscal policy 541
fiscal year (FY) 544
free trade policy 556
global economy 555
government subsidy 556
gross domestic product (GDP) 536
healthy economy 535
household income 538
Human Development Index (HDI) 536
income inequality 539
inflation 536

Keynesian economics 541
laissez-faire 540
mandatory spending 546
median household income 538
monetarism 543
monetary policy 543
national debt 550
nontariff trade barriers 556
payroll taxes 544
politically uncontrollable spending 546
poverty 537
poverty rate 537
poverty thresholds 537
progressive tax 544

For Review

1. What is the American dream? Describe one effect that each of the following national policies can have on the American dream: tax policy, spending policy, business regulation, social regulation, monetary policy, trade policy.

2. What distinguishes a pure capitalist economy from a regulated capitalist economy?

3. Differentiate among Keynesian economics, supply-side economics, and monetarism.

4. Explain at least four measures of economic health.

5. What is fiscal policy and who makes it?

6. What is monetary policy and who makes it?

7. Distinguish between business regulation and social regulation. Indicate how each type of regulation affects the economy.

8. Differentiate between the goals as well as the techniques of free trade policy and protectionist trade policy.

9. What is the health of the U.S. economy as well as the American dream at the beginning of the 21st century?

For Critical Thinking and Discussion

1. If you were president of the United States and wanted to balance the annual budget, what programs' cost cuts do you think you could get partisans in the other political party to support? What tax increases or new taxes do you think you could get partisans in the other political party to support? Explain your choices.

2. Consider your family's financial situation. What economic policy would you propose the national government implement to improve your family's financial situation? Explain.

3. Which type of tax do you think is the most fair: progressive, proportional, or regressive? Explain your choice.

4. If the national government deregulates with regard to environmental protection, product safety, and/or working conditions, would there be negative consequences? Give some examples, or explain why there would not be negative consequences.

5. Some politicians have suggested that a flat income tax of about 17 percent could raise about the same amount of revenue for the national government as the current progressive income tax and should replace it. Politically speaking, who would support such a proposal, and who would oppose it?

6. Do you think Democrats and Republicans can agree on a plan to stop deficit spending through reform of tax policies and spending policies?

Resources for Research AND Action

Internet Resources

American Enterprise Institute (AEI)
www.aei.org The AEI sponsors research on government policy and economic policy and advocates limited government involvement in the marketplace.

American Institute for Economic Research
www.aier.org This nonprofit research and educational organization provides studies and information on economic and financial issues.

Bureau of Economic Analysis (BEA)
www.bea.gov The BEA, an agency in the Department of Commerce, produces and disseminates data on regional, national, and international economies.

Economic Policy Institute
www.epi.org This nonprofit organization aims to broaden public debate on strategies to achieve a prosperous and fair economy.

Office of Management and Budget (OMB)
www.whitehouse.gov/omb The OMB's site has links to the most recent executive budget and historical budget documents.

U.S. Census Bureau
www.census.gov The Census Bureau, a bureau in the Department of Commerce, collects and disseminates data about the people and economy of the nation.

Recommended Readings

Bittle, Scott, and Jean Johnson. *Where Does the Money Go? Your Guided Tour to the Federal Budget Crisis.* Revised Edition. New York: Harper, 2011. This easy-to-understand book guides the reader through the jargon and essentials of the nation's fiscal problems with a nonpartisan perspective. It is informative and entertaining.

Derber, Charles. *People Before Profit.* New York: Picador, 2003. A disturbing analysis of globalization to date with a blueprint for a new form of globalization that will lead to a more stable and just global community.

Schick, Allen. *The Federal Budget.* Washington, DC: Brookings Institute, 2000. A comprehensive, in-depth consideration of the national budget process.

Sinclair, Upton. *The Jungle.* New York: Doubleday, Jabber & Company, 1906; and New York: Signet Classics, 2001. Sinclair's gruesome descriptions of work life and family life in Chicago at the beginning of the 20th century brought attention to income inequality, poverty, and deplorable and dangerous living and working conditions. The novel sparked enactment of national policies to protect public health and safety through regulation of the meat processing and packaging industries. The effect of this novel on government regulatory policy is immeasurable.

Woodward, Bob. *Maestro: Greenspan's Fed and the American Boom.* New York: Simon & Schuster, 2000. A probing look into how the Fed operated under the leadership of Alan Greenspan from 1987 to 2000. The effect of the evolving global economy on the economic health of the United States is an intriguing part of Woodward's account.

Movies of Interest

The Big Short (2015)
Based on the book by Michael Lewis, the film tells the stories of three groups of men who predict the home mortgage crisis of 2007–2008 and bet against the financial industry to profit from the upcoming collapse.

Too Big to Fail (2011)
A docudrama, this film shows federal government officials from the Treasury Department, the Federal Reserve, and the Securities and Exchange Commission working between late March and mid-October 2008 to prevent a national financial meltdown as banks and financial institutions move toward the brink of bankruptcy.

Inside Job (2010)
Narrated by Matt Damon, this is the first film to explore the global financial crisis that began in 2008. This sober, comprehensive analysis, based on extensive research, including interviews with politicians, financial professionals, journalists, and academics, indicates that the meltdown was predictable and preventable.

Enron: The Smartest Guys in the Room (2005)
Based on the best-selling book of the same title, this documentary spotlights the human drama of Enron's fall—the biggest corporate scandal in American history—including the company's collapse, the elimination of thousands of jobs, and the loss of $60 billion in market value and $2 billion in pension plans.

Commanding Heights: The Battle for the World Economy (2002)
This documentary exploration of the political side of today's global economy looks at the people, ideas, and events that fostered the liberalization of trade policies around the globe.

References

1. Catey Hill, "White People Have Least Confidence in the American Dream," January 31, 2016.
2. Samantha Smith, "Most Think the 'American Dream' Is within Reach for Them," October 31, 2017.
3. U.S. Bureau of Economic Analysis, "Measuring the Economy: A Primer on GDP and the National Income and Product Accounts," September 2007.
4. United Nations Development Programme, *Human Development Report 2016,* "Table 1: Human Development Index and Its Components".
5. U.S. Census Bureau, *Newsroom,* "Income, Poverty & Health Insurance Coverage in the United States: 2016," September 12, 2017.
6. U.S. Census Bureau, *Data,* "Poverty Thresholds by Size of Family and Number of Children: 2017".
7. Ibid.
8. U.S. Census Bureau, *Data,* "Historical Income Tables: Income Inequality," Table H-2: Share of Aggregate Income Received by Each Fifth and Top 5 Percent of Households, www.census.gov/data/tables/time-series/demo/income-poverty/historical-income-inequality.html.
9. Charles Derber, *People Before Profit* (New York: Picador, 2002), 48.
10. David Leonhardt, "Judging Stimulus by Job Data Reveals Success," *The New York Times,* February 17, 2010.
11. "U.S. National Debt Clock," www.usdebtclock.org.
12. Ariana Eunjung Cha, "What's in the Debt Ceiling, and Why Is Everyone in Washington Talking About It?" *The Washington Post,* April 18, 2011.
13. Sherman Antitrust Act (1890); Clayton Antitrust Act (1914).
14. "United States History: Fair Labor Standards Act," www.u-s-history.com/pages/h1701.html.
15. Ralph Nader, *Unsafe at Any Speed: The Designed-in Dangers of American Automobiles* (New York: Grossman Publishing, 1965), ix.
16. Steve Eder, "Neomi Rao, the Scholar Who Will Help Lead Trump's Regulatory Overhaul," *New York Times,* July 9, 2017.
17. Binyamin Appelbaum and Jim Tankersley, "The Trump Effect: Business, Anticipating Less Regulation Loosens Purse Strings," *New York Times,* January 1, 2018.
18. Danielle Ivory and Robert Faturchi, "Secrecy and Suspicion Surround Trump's Deregulation Teams," *New York Times,* August 7, 2017.
19. Eder, "Neomi Rao, the Scholar Who Will Help Lead Trump's Regulatory Overhaul."
20. Appelbaum and Tankersley, "The Trump Effect: Business, Anticipating Less Regulation, Loosens Purse Strings."
21. Alexei Barrionuevo, "Globalization in Every Loaf," *The New York Times,* June 16, 2007.
22. Quoted in David Kamp, "Rethinking the American Dream," *Vanity Fair,* April 2009.
23. Smith, "Most Think the 'American Dream' Is within Reach for Them."
24. Pew Research Center, "Economic Issues Decline Among Public's Policy Priorities," January 25, 2018.
25. Herb Jackson, "Deficit Could Hit $1 Trillion in 2018, and That's before the Full Impact of Tax Cuts," *USA Today,* December 20, 2017.
26. Office of Management and Budget, *Historical Tables,* Table 8.3—Percentage Distribution of Outlays by Budget Enforcement Act Category 1962–2021.
27. Appelbaum and Tankersley, "The Trump Effect: Business, Anticipating Less Regulation, Loosens Purse Strings."

CHAPTER 17

Domestic Policy

©Roel Slootweg/Shutterstock

THEN

Before the Great Depression, state and local governments dominated domestic policy matters; the federal government had limited engagement in citizens' daily lives.

NOW

The federal government is responsible for a host of domestic policy issues, from the high cost of maintaining the safety net to managing environmental degradation, promoting energy independence, and reforming immigration policies.

NEXT

Will the national government continue to push energy dominance to the detriment of environmental protection?

Will federal safety-net programs continue to expand, or will Congress rein them in to ensure they are available for our posterity?

Will immigration policy continue to be a source of tension between the national and state governments?

The U.S. Constitution says

that American governments must ensure a just and safe society in which citizens can live their lives freely, in pursuit of their happiness. Today, our multiple governments—at the national, state, and local levels—often work together to implement domestic policies that are essential to meeting those goals.

Often (but certainly not always) citizens and elected officials agree on policy goals, but they do not agree on the means to achieve the goals. For example, it is hard to argue against the goal of a clean environment; however, there are debates over what causes environmental degradation and therefore what policies are needed to address it. Since the Great Depression, the national government has taken on the responsibility of providing a safety net for the disadvantaged living among us; however, we still debate how best to provide security of income, housing, food, and health care for low-income people of all ages and persons with disabilities.

Since September 11, 2001, homeland security has become a concern for Americans. Calls for immigration reform have grown louder and more frequent as the incidence of terrorism throughout the world expands. Yet, there is no agreement on the best means to address these concerns.

In this chapter we explore several domestic policies and a variety of tools used by governments—laws and regulations, cash transfers, loans and insurance, grants, contracts, and direct provision of services by government employees—to ensure a just and safe society where citizens can live healthy lives as they pursue their happiness.

Citizen Engagement and Domestic Policy

The Constitution established a government that is by and for the people. Previous chapters have explored the many ways in which individuals and groups engage with government officials and political processes to influence what government does and does not do. Yet a widespread national affliction is the **NIMBY,** or **"not-in-my-backyard," syndrome.** People with the NIMBY syndrome are not inspired to participate in politics until a government action or inaction threatens them directly. Lobbying government officials is a common first step in citizen engagement, and it may be as basic as making a phone call, sending an e-mail, or writing a letter. Additional modes of participation include joining public protests and demonstrations, attending open government meetings, and testifying at government hearings. Citizens may also use lawsuits to press government officials to focus on issues of concern and to eventually address them through policy making.

NIMBY ("not in my-backyard") syndrome
A pattern of citizens' behavior in which people are not inspired to participate in politics until a government action or inaction threatens them directly.

Complicating the work of U.S. policymakers is the diversity of citizens' needs and expectations for government action. Almost every call for action sparks a call for either a different action or no action. The diversity of citizens' needs and priorities, the constantly changing priorities of citizens, and the range of political ideologies among citizens make for ongoing public conversations and legislative debates over which policies warrant government spending and who will pay the taxes to cover the bills. To explore the plurality of citizens' priorities, the "Analyzing the Sources" feature presents the differing policy priorities of two groups of citizens: those who are Democrats or independents who lean Democratic and those who are Republicans or independents who lean Republican.

In general, Democrats are liberal in inclination and tend to support **safety net programs**—public policies aimed at ensuring that citizens' basic physiological needs (food, water, shelter, health care, and a clean environment) are met. Republicans more commonly have a conservative ideology and focus more on public safety and national security issues. A growing plurality of citizens do not affiliate with either major party, and their collective views sometimes mirror Democratic tendencies, sometimes mirror Republican tendencies, and at still other times are distinct from both major parties. Ultimately, elected officials—who typically want to get reelected—find it much easier to add new policies and programs than to eliminate programs or to decrease program costs. Hence, the federal government's breadth of domestic responsibilities has grown, as has its costs.

As we have seen in preceding chapters, the government makes policy in several ways. For one, Congress and the president set policy by approving *authorization bills,* which establish a policy and identify who will implement it, and *appropriations bills,* which authorize the spending of national revenue to pay for policies (see Chapters 12, 13, and 16). As discussed in Chapter 14, federal, state, local, and shadow bureaucrats also make policy, through both the administrative rule-making process and their daily use of administrative discretion as they implement policies. In addition, the presidential power of the executive order amounts to making policy, because it gives the president the authority to tell bureaucrats how to carry out a national policy (see Chapter 13). Finally, as explored in Chapter 15, the federal courts resolve conflicts over the meaning and proper implementation of laws and, in doing so, make policy. In summary, each of the three branches of the national government has policy-making authority that it uses to fulfill the government's constitutionally established mission to serve present generations and their posterity.

Since 1789, the national government's scope of responsibility for addressing domestic matters has gradually expanded as individuals and groups have lobbied for their interests. Federal authority now covers a diverse collection of public policies. The national budget lists 17 functions of the federal government. The data in Table 17.1 show that today, most federal government functions are directed at (and most government spending goes toward) **domestic policies,** which are policies addressing the problems, needs, and relations of people residing within the country's borders, as opposed to matters involving relations with other countries and nations. In 2017, 77 percent of federal expenditures paid for domestic policies and 16 percent paid for international affairs and defense policies. The remaining 7 percent of expenditures paid for interest on the national debt incurred by past borrowing to cover deficit spending.[1]

Because it would be impossible for us to examine every domestic policy program, we limit our focus in this chapter to a subset of national domestic policies. Specifically, we concentrate on national policies that address the most basic of human needs and are essential to sustaining life, liberty, and opportunities to

safety net programs
A collection of public policies aimed at ensuring that citizens' basic physiological needs are met.

domestic policies
Policies addressing the problems, needs, and relations of people residing within the country's borders.

PARTISAN DIFFERENCES ON TOP PRIORITIES FOR PRESIDENT TRUMP AND CONGRESS

Citizens in representative democracies expect their elected officials to listen to their concerns and then enact policies that address them. However, citizens do not speak with one voice. Moreover, their opinions and priorities change because the world around them is dynamic and life situations change. The policy priorities of citizens differ due to their differing life experiences, which are in turn a product of multiple demographic factors including sex, ethnicity, age, and religion as well as environmental and socialization factors such as urban or rural residence and political ideology of parents.

The table below presents the views of Democrats and independents who lean Democratic and Republicans and independents who lean Republican on the top priorities for President Trump and Congress for 2018.

Top Policy Priorities by Party/Partisan Leaning

Values are the percentage of respondents who indicated the policy as a top priority for President Trump and Congress for 2018.

POLICY	DEMOCRAT/ DEMOCRATIC LEANING	REPUBLICAN/ REPUBLICAN LEANING
Improving education	78%	61%
Strengthening economy	64%	78%
Reducing health care costs	72%	64%
Securing Social Security	68%	68%
Securing Medicare	72%	62%
Protecting the environment	81%	37%
Improving job situation	58%	66%
Problems of poor and needy	68%	48%
Reducing crime	52%	63%
Addressing race relations	61%	40%
Improving transportation	48%	50%
Drug addiction	51%	47%
Immigration	39%	62%
Strengthening military	30%	69%
Global climate change	35%	44%

SOURCE: Pew Research Center, "Economic Issues Decline Among Public's Policy Priorities," January 25, 2018.

Practice Analytical Thinking

1. Compare the highest-rated four priorities for Democrats/ Democratic-leaners and the highest-rated four priorities for Republicans/ Republican-leaners. Are there any overlapping top priorities? Where do the priorities differ between the two groups? Does it fit the pattern of Democrats tending to support safety net policies and Republicans supporting public safety and national security?

2. On what priority is the gap between Democrats/ Democratic-leaners and Republican/Republican-leaners the largest? Identify any event or situation that might shrink this partisan gap.

3. Is there a policy area that may now be of greater concern to Democrats and/or Republicans because of a recent event or situation? Explain your answer.

4. Review the discussion on measuring public opinion in Chapter 6. What do you need to know about the Pew Research Center methodology to have confidence in the survey results presented in the table?

TABLE 17.1　Percentage of FY 2017 Expenditures by Functions

Social Security	24%
Medicare	15%
National defense	15%
Health	13%
Income security	13%
Net interest	7%
Education, training, employment, and social services	4%
Veterans benefits and services	4%
Administration of justice	2%
Transportation	2%
International affairs	1%
Natural resources and environment	1%
Community and regional development	1%
General science, space, and technology	1%
Agriculture	1%
General government	1%
Energy	<1%
Commerce and housing credit	−1%
Undistributed offsetting receipts	−2%

SOURCE: Office of Management and Budget, Historical Tables, "Table 3.1—Outlays by Superfunction and Function: 1940–2023".

pursue happiness: environmental, energy, and income security policies. We also look at the controversial policy area of immigration, defined by some as a national security concern, by others as an economic issue, and by still others as a humanitarian cause reflecting the United States' roots and highest ideals.

Tools of Domestic Policy

The national government attempts to address citizens' problems and to provide benefits and services to the people by using various policy tools. Domestic policy tools include laws and regulations, direct provision of public goods, cash transfer payments, loans, loan guarantees, insurance, grants-in-aid to state and local governments, and contracting-out the provision of public goods to nongovernmental entities (shadow bureaucracies and bureaucrats, as discussed in Chapter 14).

Laws and Regulations

At the federal, state, and local levels alike, governments strive to accomplish their domestic policy goals by creating rules of behavior through laws with which individuals and organizations must comply. These include tax laws, environmental laws, and laws to ensure public health and safety. Many laws assign administrative agencies the authority to establish the specific rules, regulations, and standards that are essential to their effective implementation. As discussed in Chapter 16, business regulations are aimed at preserving competition in the marketplace, and social regulations are directed at protecting workers, consumers, and the environment from the harms caused by marketplace competition. For example, the Food and Drug Administration (FDA) establishes rules and regulations to ensure the safety of foods and drugs produced and sold in the country.

The overwhelming majority of people and organizations comply with most laws and regulations. But because some individuals and organizations fail to do so, the government must monitor compliance. For example, the FDA hires inspectors to ensure that meat, poultry, and eggs are processed safely, are wholesome, and are labeled correctly. The government counts on citizens, interest groups, and the media to assist in overseeing compliance by identifying violators.

Direct Provision of Public Goods

In addition to creating rules of behavior through laws and regulations, governments provide services and benefits directly to people. Using the domestic policy tool of **direct provision,** governments hire public servants—bureaucrats who receive a government paycheck—to dispense the services. For example, veterans hospitals hire doctors, nurses, and physical therapists to administer health care to veterans; the U.S. Postal Service hires mail carriers, postal clerks, and postal processing machine operators to deliver billions of pieces of mail each week. The workers hired by the national government to provide these services directly are on the payroll of the national government.

>A Food and Drug Administration (FDA) inspector checks imported seafood for signs of contamination or spoilage, and prepares samples for laboratory testing for contaminants. The FDA receives notice of every entry of seafood from a foreign country, and FDA labs analyze samples for contaminants. It also conducts in-plant inspections that focus on seafood safety. Working in collaboration with state and foreign regulators and the Centers for Disease Control (CDC), the FDA works to ensure food safety so you do not have to worry every time you eat a meal.

Source: US Food and Drug Administration. Photo by Michael J. Ermath.

Cash Transfers

Another instrument of government policy is the **cash transfer**—the direct provision of cash (in various forms) to eligible individuals or to the providers of goods or services to eligible individuals. **In-kind assistance** is a form of a cash transfer in which the government pays cash to those who provide goods or services to eligible individuals. Approximately 70 percent of the money spent by the national government goes toward cash transfers to citizens.[2] Nearly half of the American population lives in a household that receives a cash transfer.[3]

Examples of cash transfers include unemployment and Social Security checks, and Pell grants to college students. The Supplemental Nutrition Assistance Program (SNAP; better known to most by its old name, the food stamp program) was created in 1964 and is an example of in-kind assistance. The government provides cash to the stores that accept SNAP debit cards for food purchases.

The main cash transfer programs are of two kinds, depending upon their sources of revenue. For **noncontributory programs,** the general revenues collected by the government pay for the program. This means that a proportion of the money collected from all taxpayers funds the cash transfer. Temporary Assistance for Needy Families, the income security program for families who have children and no or very low income, is an example of a noncontributory cash-transfer

direct provision
A policy tool whereby the government that creates a policy hires public servants to provide the service.

cash transfer
The direct provision of cash (in forms including checks, debit cards, and tax breaks) to eligible individuals or to providers of goods or services to eligible individuals.

in-kind assistance
A cash transfer in which the government pays cash to those who provide goods or services to eligible individuals.

noncontributory program
A benefit provided to a targeted population, paid for by a proportion of the money collected from all taxpayers.

contributory program (social insurance program)
A benefit provided only to those who paid the specific tax created to fund the benefit.

entitlement program
A government benefit guaranteed to all who meet the eligibility requirements.

direct subsidy
A cash transfer from general revenues to particular persons or private companies engaged in activities that the national government believes support the public good.

program. In contrast, **contributory programs,** or **social insurance programs,** are funded by revenue collected specifically for these programs, which benefit only those who have paid into the programs. Social insurance programs are **entitlement programs,** meaning the government guarantees the programs' benefits to all who meet the eligibility criteria. Thus workers who pay the payroll tax for Social Security will receive Social Security checks when they retire.

With a **direct subsidy,** another type of cash transfer, the government provides financial support, often through tax breaks, to specific persons or organizations that engage in activities that the government believes benefit the public good. Individual farmers and agricultural corporations, for example, receive money from the government to grow specified crops or to limit how much they grow.

Loans, Loan Guarantees, and Insurance

In addition to using tax breaks and grants to encourage behaviors that accomplish its goals, the national government lends money to individuals and organizations, and it guarantees loans made by private businesses. Some examples are government loan programs to assist individuals in purchasing homes, reflecting the widespread belief that home ownership promotes the general welfare and domestic tranquility, and Stafford loans for college students and their parents. The Small Business Administration provides government-backed loan guarantees on loans made through private banks, credit unions, and other lenders. These loan guarantees make it easier for entrepreneurs who are beginning or expanding small businesses to acquire credit because lenders' risks are limited by the government's promise to pay back some of the borrowed money if the entrepreneur is unable to pay it back.

The national government is also in the insurance business. The Federal Deposit Insurance Corporation (FDIC) is one example of a national insurance program. The FDIC insures bank deposits up to $250,000 in member banks to encourage people to save money not only for their own sake but also for the good of the national economy. A controversial national insurance program is its flood insurance program, which is discussed in this chapter's "Thinking Critically" feature.

Grants-in-Aid and Contracting-Out

State and local governments and private-sector organizations implement a growing proportion of national government policies. Through funded and unfunded mandates as well as grants-in-aid (explored in Chapter 3), the federal government requires and encourages state and local governments to carry out national policies. We see these forms of intergovernmental relations in policies as diverse as homeland security, primary and secondary education, and environmental protection.

The government also contracts with private and nonprofit organizations to produce essential resources or to deliver services. One example of contracting-out, or outsourcing (see Chapter 14), is the government's contracts with corporations such as Lockheed Martin and Boeing to build the planes and missiles it needs to defend the country. Another example is medical research funded by the government and conducted by private companies and institutions of higher education.

By means of contracting-out and the other various tools we have surveyed, the government delivers goods and services to its citizens. In the rest of this chapter, we examine how government uses these tools to implement overall policy in several domestic policy areas, including environmental protection, energy, income security, health care, and immigration.

Should the Federal Government Mandate Flood Insurance?

The Issue: 2017 was the most expensive year on record for natural disasters in the United States. According to the National Oceanic and Atmospheric Administration, extreme weather occurrences caused more than $300 billion in damage. Flooding, caused by that extreme weather, accounted for much of that damage. Hurricane Harvey caused $125 billion in damage; Maria caused $90 billion; Irma, $50 billion. Missouri, Arkansas, and California each experienced flooding in 2017 that cost a total of more than $3 billion.[*]

One big storm can flood whole neighborhoods, and yet, most people—including those who live in hurricane-prone areas—do not have federal flood insurance, which is the back-up when private insurance companies won't insure a property. In Florida, hit by Maria and Irma, fewer than half its residents had federal flood insurance. Maria and Irma also hit Puerto Rico, where just 1 percent of residents had flood insurance. In Houston, hit by Harvey, only about 15 percent of residents had federal flood insurance. This means that after a catastrophic flood, everyone turns to the federal government for help.[**] Should the federal government mandate flood insurance for those with buildings and property in hurricane-prone areas?

Yes: Our governments were created to protect life, liberty, and pursuit of happiness as well as to serve the general welfare and ensure domestic tranquility. With the creation of the Department of Homeland Security, the federal government took on responsibilities to prevent as well as respond to natural and man-made disasters. To prevent the harms to body, buildings, and the economy caused by flooding, the federal government should mandate flood insurance for those with property in government-identified flood-prone areas. The government requires car insurance to drive, and under the Affordable Care Act, it also required people to buy health insurance. Mandated flood insurance makes sense.

No: If people choose to build in flood-prone areas, then the cost for damages due to extreme weather is their responsibility. If they decide not to purchase flood insurance or are denied it through the private market, then that is on them. If the government mandates insurance, and private insurance companies will not sell it to people living in flood-prone zones, or if the insurance is too expensive for some, then the government will have to offer flood insurance or subsidize the cost of private insurance as it does with health insurance. Why should my tax dollars go to protect other people from a risky choice they made?

Other Approaches: The federal government could work with local governments to identify flood-prone areas and create zoning laws that restrict new construction in those areas. The government could also insure owners of existing buildings in those zones and mandate that they relocate after devastating flooding. Or the federal and local governments could work together to purchase all buildings in flood zones and force people to relocate, just as it did in Love Canal, New York, where buried toxic chemicals were causing health problems.

What do you think?

1. Economists view the private insurance option as the most efficient answer to flood insurance—that is, define the risks, allow people to build where they want, encourage them to buy insurance, and leave the rest to nature, not the federal government. Do you think that is a politically feasible option for elected officials with constituents living and doing business in flood-prone zones?

2. How do you think people would respond to a government that restricted people from building homes in flood-prone areas? Explain.

3. Traditionally, zoning and land-use are the responsibility of local governments. Do you think the federal government should get more involved in zoning and land-use decisions, or should such decisions remain at the local level of government? Explain.

[*] Kendra Pierre-Louis, "These Billion-Dollar Natural Disasters Set a U.S. Record in 2017," *New York Times*, January 8, 2018, www.nytimes.com/2018/01/08/climate/2017-weather-disasters.html?emc=edit_th_20180109&nl=todaysheadlines&nlid=54430813.

[**]Donald Kettl, "Whose Disaster Is It?" *Governing*, December 2017, pp. 16–17.

Environmental Policy

At the most basic level, providing for the general welfare means ensuring that people have the basic necessities for sustaining life. These needs include clean and drinkable water, breathable air, and unpolluted land on which to grow food that is safe for consumption. No one argues against a clean environment. Yet there is no consensus on how to achieve and maintain one. In addition, appeals for environmental protection often conflict with demands for ample supplies of energy and for economic development, specifically job creation.

The national government first acknowledged environmental degradation as a problem in the 1960s. In the 1970s, national environmental protection laws were enacted to address air, land, and water pollution. Beginning in the 1990s, concern for environmental protection became a global focus, with attempts to negotiate international agreements that would address newly recognized environmental concerns.

Environmental Degradation

Since the 1940s, farmers have used chemicals to destroy insects, weeds, fungi, and other living organisms that harm their crops. The threats such pesticides pose to air, water, and land became the focus of public concern and political debate after the publication of Rachel Carson's eye-opening best seller *Silent Spring* in 1962. Carson's book documented how pesticides were contaminating the environment and getting into human food. The use of chemicals, she warned, threatened the existence not only of birds—whose extinction would mean a silent spring—but of humankind itself.

Then, in 1969, those growing environmental apprehensions became a spectacular reality when the heavily polluted Cuyahoga River in Ohio caught fire. Around the same time, arsenic was found in the Kansas River, and millions of fish went belly-up in major waterways such as Lake Superior, killed by the chemicals and untreated waste emitted by industrial plants and local sewage systems. In response, state and local governments banned fishing in many waterways because of their excessive pollution.

The mounting environmental crises and additional governmental studies brought amplified calls to action from both citizens' groups and elected officials during the 1960s and 1970s. In 1965, 17 percent of citizens listed this as one of their top three political priorities; by 1970, 53 percent of citizens listed it as one of their top three priorities.[4]

U.S. senator Gaylord Nelson (D-Wisc.) responded to citizens' growing environmental concerns by proposing a national teach-in, organized at the grassroots level. He hoped the teach-ins would mobilize the national government to establish an environmental protection agenda. Nelson's vision became a reality on April 22, 1970. More than 200,000 people gathered on the National Mall in Washington, D.C., and 20 million more congregated across the country.[5] Earth Day, as that day in 1970 was called, is celebrated every year and involves millions of people around the globe. Earth Day keeps concerns about environmental degradation on public policy agendas throughout the world.

Since the 1990s, scientists and governments throughout the world have been raising concerns about air pollution, particularly emissions of carbon dioxide. Mounting evidence indicates that air pollution caused by burning fossil fuels (to create energy) produces a **greenhouse effect,** which is the heating of the earth's atmosphere as carbon dioxide and other gases build up and trap solar heat in the earth's atmosphere. The greenhouse effect causes **global warming,** the rising

greenhouse effect
The heating of the earth's atmosphere as a result of humans' burning of fossil fuels and the resultant buildup of carbon dioxide and other gases.

global warming
The rising temperature of the earth as a result of pollution that traps solar heat, keeping the air warmer than it would otherwise be.

temperature of the earth. Today, people who discuss global warming often refer to the phenomenon of climate change.

A 2014 report by the Intergovernmental Panel on Climate Change, a United Nations group, concluded that "climate change is already having sweeping effects on every continent." As examples, it noted that climate change is causing extremes in weather leading to floods, droughts, and other natural disasters. Moreover, coastal communities are being affected by melting ice caps, water supplies are under stress, and the world's food supply is at "considerable risk."[6]

Environmental Protection

In 1969, Congress passed the Environmental Protection Act, which established the Environmental Protection Agency (EPA) to oversee implementation of laws protecting the quality of air, water, and land. Then a cascade of national environmental protection legislation followed the first Earth Day.

CLEAN AIR The landmark Clean Air Act of 1970 delegates authority to the EPA to establish standards for regulating emissions of hazardous air pollutants. The act also mandated each state to develop and implement plans to meet EPA standards. Today, states typically delegate some of their enforcement responsibilities to local governments. If states and their local governments do not enforce compliance with the national standards or their own stricter standards, then the EPA can take over, enforcing national law through preemption (discussed in Chapter 3).

To bolster compliance with the Clean Air Act, the law gives citizens the right to sue those who are violating the standards. Citizens also have the right to sue the EPA if it does not enforce the Clean Air Act. Citizens and environmental interest groups have availed themselves of their right to sue, pushing the government and industries to comply with the law. For example, in 2007, Massachusetts and 11 other states, three cities, and several

THEN NOW NEXT

Federal Websites and Climate Change

Then (2016)	Now (2018)
Term *climate change* pervasive on multitude of department and agency websites	Term *climate change* deleted or replaced with the term *sustainability* on multitude of department and agency websites
Term *carbon* pervasive on multitude of agency websites	Term *carbon* replaced with term *emissions* on multitude of agency websites
Hundreds of websites connected to state and local climate change programs	Removal of hundreds of websites connected to state and local climate change programs
Raw government data on climate change, such as historical records of temperature and emission levels, easily accessible	Raw government data on climate change, such as historical records of temperature and emission levels, available but hard to find
Clean Power Plan website	No website for Clean Power Plan

SOURCE: Scott Waldman, "Climate Web Pages Erased and Obscured under Trump," *Scientific American,* January 10, 2018.

WHAT'S NEXT?

> What do the website changes indicate about the policy direction of President Trump compared with his predecessor?

> Will removal of the terms *climate change* and *carbon* affect the public understanding and debate on global warming? Explain.

> If people have to rely on information from advocacy groups or private citizens instead of the national government, how will that affect the public understanding and debate?

> How might the removal of the Clean Power Plan website affect the review process of the Trump administration's proposal to repeal the Clean Power Plan—a review process that includes a public comment period? Explain.

environmental groups successfully challenged the EPA and President George W. Bush's interpretation of the law. Although the Clean Air Act of 1970 did not specifically discuss greenhouse gases such as carbon dioxide as pollutants to be regulated, the U.S. Supreme Court determined that carbon dioxide is a pollutant that the EPA has the authority to regulate.[7]

Since 1992, United Nations negotiators have held annual meetings aimed at developing a global climate change treaty. In 1997, world leaders signed the Kyoto Protocol, which established binding targets for cutting greenhouse gases in the world's largest economies in developed countries. By 2012, 191 countries had ratified the treaty; the United States did not. Although the national government did not sign on to the Kyoto Protocol, state and local governments acted to meet the protocol's provisions. For example, in 2007, 10 northeastern and mid-Atlantic states signed the Regional Greenhouse Gas Initiative (RGGI), committing to capping emissions from power plants in their states. Today, additional states are discussing joining RGGI.[8]

In 2015, the EPA enacted the Clean Power Plan, the first U.S. climate change policy. The plan established new regulations designed to reduce greenhouse gases emitted by power plants. Under the plan, the EPA set emission targets for each state, and each state could develop its own strategies to meet its target. If a state did not develop a plan, then the EPA could impose one on it.

Internationally, the Obama administration's Clean Power Plan was viewed as a sign that the United States was ready to join the international efforts to reduce carbon dioxide emissions. In December 2015, 195 nations reached a landmark international agreement, the Paris Accord, which commits each nation to decreasing its emission of greenhouse gases. The accord was touted as a turning point for climate change.

In 2017, however, President Trump pulled the United States out of the Paris Accord. The Trump administration also focused on eliminating numerous EPA regulations. In response, an alliance among a group of U.S. states, cities, businesses, and universities, called the "American Pledge," stated its commitment to working toward meeting the Paris Accord. At a global climate meeting in Bonn, Germany, in 2017, California governor Jerry Brown spoke on behalf of the alliance: "In the United States, we have a federal system, and states have real power, as do cities. And when cities and states combine together, and then join with powerful corporations, that's how we get stuff done."[9]

CLEAN WATER The 1972 Federal Water Pollution Control Act (Clean Air Act), with the goal of making waterways clean enough to swim in and to eat fish from, authorizes the EPA to set water quality standards and to require permits for anyone discharging contaminants into any waterway. Under the act, state and local governments must monitor water quality, issue permits to those discharging waste into waterways, and enforce the national standards. If states and localities fail to carry out these mandated responsibilities, the EPA can step in and do the job. The law also provides for federal loans to local governments, funneled through state governments, for building wastewater treatment plants.

The Safe Drinking Water Act of 1974 authorizes the EPA to establish purity standards for drinking water. Because states or localities typically operate water systems, this act effectively requires the EPA to regulate state and local governments. The act provides for national grants to state and local governments for research and for improving their water systems. It also requires frequent testing of water samples from public water systems.

>Women in Flint, Michigan, show bottles filled with water from their home faucets to government officials and offer them a drink. Would you want to drink the water in those bottles?
©Mark Wilson/Getty Images

In 2015, a water crisis in Flint, Michigan, sparked lawsuits, government investigations, and calls for the state's governor to resign. The crisis was created when the city government switched the public water source from Lake Huron to the Flint River during the construction of a new water pipeline from Flint to Lake Huron. The Flint River has had contamination problems for decades, and within a year of the switch, the city's water had unhealthy levels of lead because the water had not been properly treated to meet state and federal purity standards. The Flint water crisis highlights the fact that the country's water supply is threatened by a deteriorating public water structure full of lead pipes that Congress banned in 1986, but that have not yet been replaced.[10]

CLEAN LAND The Resource Conservation and Recovery Act of 1976, administered by the EPA, regulates the disposal of household, industrial, and manufacturing solid and hazardous wastes, and encourages recycling. Although this act authorized the cleanup of toxic waste sites, thousands of which the government identified in the 1970s, no national funding was made available for the cleanup. Then in 1980, just as Congress was focused on the crisis at Love Canal, New York, where 833 families had to be relocated because of health problems tied to the toxic waste buried below their homes and school, an abandoned site for the storage, treatment, and disposal of hazardous waste in Elizabeth, New Jersey, exploded. Shortly thereafter, Congress approved the Comprehensive Environmental Response, Compensation and Liability Act of 1980 (known as the Superfund law) to pay for cleanup of the nation's most toxic waste dumps.

The Superfund has protected human health and the environment by improving the identification and cleanup of hazardous waste sites. It has also increased the accountability of the parties responsible for creating hazardous waste problems. However, close to two thousand identified sites must still be cleaned, and new sites continue to be added to the list.[11]

Citizens with resources, including money and the time to organize, can fight to prevent the location of undesirable land uses (such as landfills, industrial plants, and toxic waste sites) in their communities. Lower-income communities are more likely than more affluent communities to bear the burden of land uses with negative environmental impacts. **Environmental racism** is the term used to describe the higher incidence of environmental threats and subsequent health problems in lower-income communities, which frequently are also communities populated by people of color.[12]

ENVIRONMENTAL PROTECTION, ENERGY PRODUCTION, AND JOBS Although no one argues against a clean environment, tensions persist between the need for environmental protection and other policy areas. Energy production, both extraction of resources from the earth and the burning of fossil fuels, damages the environment and human health; it sometimes also takes lives. The tragic explosion of a BP oil rig in 2010 killed 11 people and injured at least 17, caused oil to be pumped into the Gulf of Mexico for 87 days, led to tens of millions of dollars in lost income for people who made their living from the Gulf, and killed and harmed wildlife along the 16,000 miles of coastline affected by the spill.[13]

Efforts to reduce greenhouse emissions affect energy production businesses, particularly plants that burn fossil fuels such as coal and natural gas. Hence, environmental protection bumps up against economic health in terms of jobs. This tension was evident in the seven-year battle over the proposed 1,700-mile Keystone XL pipeline. A Canadian firm applied to build the pipeline to transport crude oil from Alberta, Canada, through the United States to Texas. Proponents of the pipeline argued it would create jobs. Opponents argued it would harm the environment. Because the proposed pipeline crossed an international border, the State Department had to issue a federal permit allowing the pipeline's construction. In November 2015, President Obama concurred with the State Department's recommendation and rejected the pipeline's construction. Then, in 2017, President Trump reversed that decision and approved the pipeline's construction.

Today, as the nation and the world act to address environmental degradation, particularly global warming, new energy sources are being explored and developed. This exploration and development is good for the environment and also creates jobs.

Energy Policy

Energy creation—the production of electricity and heat, as well as fuels to power automobiles, trucks, planes, trains, and other transport vehicles—is essential to the prosperity of the U.S. economy and to the American way of life. The high energy demands of the U.S. economy and the lifestyle of U.S. residents are problematic for several reasons, as we shall see.

In 1973 the Organization of Petroleum Exporting Countries (OPEC) refused to sell oil to the United States and Western European nations. The OPEC oil embargo caused oil and gas prices in United States to skyrocket, and people quickly found themselves stuck in hours-long waits at gas stations. OPEC's actions focused national government attention on U.S. dependence on foreign oil as an economic, quality of life, and national security concern. In response, the national government began to develop energy policy aimed at reducing the nation's dependence on foreign oil.

THEN

NOW

> By 1905, when the THEN photo of coal miners at the bottom of a mine shaft in Scranton, Pennsylvania, was taken, coal had become the dominant source of energy in the United States. Coal continued to be the primary energy source through the middle of the 20th century, when petroleum overtook it as the primary source. Today in the United States, Wyoming produces the most coal. Texas produces the most energy from crude oil, natural gas, and wind turbines.

Coal miners: ©Universal History Archive/UIG via Getty Images; *wind turbines:* ©Michael Mcmurray/Getty Images

In 1975, the national government established the Strategic Petroleum Reserve, a store of crude oil to mitigate the security consequences of any future interruption in the supply of imported oil. The government also enacted legislation encouraging energy conservation and providing funding for research and development of alternative energy sources (such as solar, wind, and geothermal). Legislation created fuel efficiency standards for passenger cars and light trucks, the Corporate Average Fuel Economy (CAFE) standards. Then in 1976, the federal government created the Department of Energy to develop and oversee a comprehensive national energy plan.

In 1977, President Jimmy Carter declared an "energy crisis" and called for energy conservation and for research and development into alternative energy. Toward that end, the United States established a national speed limit of 55 miles per hour, Daylight Saving Time, weatherization assistance programs, tax incentives to insulate homes, and building codes related to energy efficiency.

Since the 1970s, with energy independence as its goal, U.S. energy policy has swung back and forth between (1) a focus on conservation, research on alternative renewable energy sources, and tax breaks supporting that research and (2) calls for increased use of coal and other domestic fossil fuel resources. In the most recent swing, in his first year in office, President Trump signed an executive order aimed at repealing President Obama's 2015 Clean Power Plan, which focused on limiting emissions from burning fossil fuels and supporting renewable energy industries. Trump argued that the plan killed jobs and created barriers to energy independence.[14]

Trump's overall goal is to put in place his "America First Energy Plan," which declares U.S. energy dominance to be a strategic economic and foreign policy goal and promises to create a huge number of new jobs by lifting regulations on American energy.[15] In support of his energy plan, Trump approved the Keystone XL and Dakota Access Pipelines, opened much of the Atlantic and Pacific coasts to offshore drilling, lifted restrictions on coal mining on federal lands, and is attempting to repeal the Clean Power Plan. In December 2017, Trump announced his administration's National Security Strategy (NSS) document, which makes this statement: "Access to domestic sources of clean, affordable, and reliable energy underpins a prosperous, secure, and powerful America for decades to come. . . . Unleashing these abundant energy resources—coal, natural gas, petroleum, renewables, and nuclear—stimulates the economy and builds a foundation for future growth."[16]

Energy independence coupled with clean air, clean water, and clean land are foundational to the pursuit of happiness and quality of life of all Americans. Other conditions important to those goals include income security, food security, housing security, and health care, which we explore next.

Income Security Programs

Before the Great Depression of the 1930s, Americans who could not provide for their basic needs relied on relief from family, friends, charities, and, in some cases, local or state government. During the Depression, however, the excessively weak economy left one-quarter of the U.S. labor force unemployed. Families lost jobs, savings, and homes. Charities were overwhelmed. State and local governments lacked the resources needed to assist the millions of people without incomes. Citizens, as well as state and local governments, looked to the federal government for assistance.

Within his first hundred days in office, President Franklin D. Roosevelt proposed a sequence of revolutionary bills to stimulate and regulate sectors of the depressed economy and to provide income to those in need. His administration's radical proposals placed the national government at the center of issues it had historically left to local and state governments. Those and the subsequent New Deal policies approved in Roosevelt's first few years in office provided income security for retired citizens and a safety net for people in financial need. Many of the New Deal programs are still in place today, though in modified form.

Social Security

The Social Security Act of 1935, a centerpiece of the New Deal, established a range of landmark income security programs. To this day, these programs provide financial assistance to individuals who are elderly, disabled, dependent, and unemployed.

OLD-AGE AND SURVIVORS INSURANCE (OASI)   The Social Security Act established the Old-Age and Survivors Insurance (OASI) program, which initially provided income to individuals or families when a worker covered by the program retired. This contributory cash-transfer program is the traditional retirement insurance component of Social Security; most people are aware of it and anticipate benefiting from it in retirement. OASI is a social insurance entitlement program, funded by contributions that employees as well as employers make. Each year, the federal government establishes the amount of earnings subject to the 12.4 percent Social Security tax (6.2 percent paid by employee and 6.2 percent paid by employer). In 2018, an individual's earned income up to $128,400 was subject to the tax.[17]

A formula that accounts for how much individuals paid into Social Security over their years of employment determines the amount of each beneficiary's monthly Social Security check. Because OASI is an **indexed benefit,** the government makes regularly scheduled, automatic cost-of-living adjustments (COLAs), increasing the benefit based on the rate of inflation. The 1937 Federal Insurance Contribution Act (FICA) established the pay-as-you-go funding mechanism for OASI. Through FICA contributions, current workers and employers deposit money in the Social Security Trust Fund, and the government uses the money contributed today to pay today's beneficiaries. The money left over after today's payments are made is invested so that the trust fund will grow; income from investments will be combined with future FICA revenues to pay for future Social Security checks.

Most people collect more from Social Security than they pay into the fund, and the number of retirees is growing. With the increasing number of retirees and with those retirees living longer, the pay-as-you-go system will eventually reach the point at which it will not cover the full costs of OASI. If Congress does not legislate changes to the program that increase revenues, decrease costs, or do both, then the trust fund reserves will be gone by 2034. At that time, the income for OASI will only be enough to cover about 75 percent of the cost of scheduled benefits.[18]

>On January 31, 1940, Ida Mae Fuller was the first person to receive an OASI check. Ms. Fuller paid a total of $22 into the Social Security insurance program from 1937 to her retirement in 1940. Her first check was for $22.54 and over the next 35 years, she collected a total of $22,000 (1,000 times what she paid into the system). Today, people paying into Social Security can visit the Social Security Administration website and create an account that allows them to review their earnings record and the government's estimate of their retirement, disability, and survivor's benefits. When you are ready to retire, you can apply for your OASI benefits online. To create your own account, go to www.ssa.gov/myaccount/.
©AP Photo/AP Images

AMENDMENTS TO THE SOCIAL SECURITY ACT Congress amended the Social Security Act in 1939 to provide benefits to the dependents and surviving spouse of a deceased worker. In 1956, the act was further amended to assist workers who, because of physical or mental disabilities, had to stop working after age 50 but before the OASI-designated retirement age. The new benefit program thus created, called Social Security Disability Insurance (SSDI), provides income to those covered by the Social Security program and to their families if they meet the guidelines for disability. Similar to OASI, SSDI is a contributory (social insurance) program.

In 1972, Congress again amended the Social Security Act by establishing the Supplemental Security Income (SSI) program, a noncontributory program. Recipients of SSI include low-income elderly people whose Social Security benefits are so low they cannot provide for themselves, individuals with disabilities, and blind people. Unlike other Social Security programs, SSI is a **means-tested benefit,** meaning that the eligibility criteria to receive the benefit include a government-specified income level, which is very low.

indexed benefit
A government benefit with an automatic cost-of-living increase based on the rate of inflation.

means-tested benefit
A benefit for which eligibility is based on having an income below a government-specified amount, typically based on a percentage of the poverty guideline.

Unemployment Compensation

The Federal-State Unemployment Insurance Program, created by the Social Security Act of 1935, requires each state government to administer its own unemployment insurance program within guidelines established by federal law. Through this program, employees who lose their jobs through no fault of their own, and meet other eligibility requirements established by their state, can collect unemployment compensation from the state for up to 26 weeks. Employees fired for cause (based on their own behavior) cannot receive unemployment compensation.

In general, the benefit received is based on a percentage of an individual's most recent earnings.

During economic recessions, the national government has sometimes extended the 26-week benefit period if the unemployment rate remains high for a long time. When the federal government extends the benefit period in times of high, long-term unemployment, it (not the states) pays for the additional benefits.

Minimum Wage

We can thank Frances Perkins for the federal minimum wage. When President Franklin D. Roosevelt asked her to serve as his secretary of labor, Perkins told him she would join his cabinet only if he agreed to establish a minimum wage.[19] He agreed, she became the first woman to serve as a department secretary, and the minimum wage became law through the 1938 Fair Labor Standards Act.

The aim of the minimum wage was to guarantee most employed workers a **living wage**—a wage high enough to keep them out of poverty. Yet, there have always been some workers not guaranteed the federal minimum wage. Today these include full-time students, youths under 20 years of age for the first 90 days of their employment, workers who earn tips, commissioned sales employees, farm laborers, and seasonal and recreational workers. For workers guaranteed the minimum wage, employers must pay overtime (equal to one and a half times an employee's regular hourly rate) for all hours over 40 worked during a workweek.

In 2015, the Obama administration introduced changes to the rules regulating minimum wage. The changes made millions more Americans eligible for overtime pay by clarifying that some workers, who employers claimed were contracted workers and therefore not eligible for overtime pay, are indeed permanent workers who are eligible for overtime pay. At the same time, federal courts upheld an earlier Obama administration regulation change that extended minimum wage and overtime pay coverage to approximately two million home care workers who had been exempt from minimum wage coverage.[20]

living wage
A wage high enough to keep workers and their families out of poverty and to allow them to enjoy a basic living standard.

>Frances Perkins became the first woman to serve in the cabinet. She was secretary of labor from 1933 to 1945. As chair of the President's Committee on Economic Security, she led the development of the Social Security Act (1935), which created the programs for Old-Age and Survivors Insurance (OASI, or Social Security retirement income) and Aid to Dependent Children. In addition, she was instrumental in establishing the minimum wage and the other worker benefits provided by the 1938 Fair Labor Standards Act. Here we see her standing behind President Roosevelt as he signs the Social Security Act.
©FPG/Archive Photos/Getty Images

In 1938, the government set the federal minimum wage at 25 cents per hour. Because the minimum wage is not an indexed benefit, increases in the wage must be enacted through legislation, and so congressional battles to increase the minimum wage occur regularly. In 2009, Congress increased the minimum wage to $7.25. Since then, there have been numerous unsuccessful efforts to have Congress increase the minimum wage. Unable to get Congress to legislate a new federal minimum wage, in 2015, Obama issued an executive order that raised the minimum wage for federal contractors to $10.10.[21]

State and local governments can establish a minimum wage higher than the federal minimum for covered workers, and they can extend a minimum wage to workers not covered by the federal minimum wage. At the beginning of 2018, 31 states and the District of Columbia had minimum wages higher than the federal level. In addition, 17 states have enacted laws to index their minimum wage, which means they have a system of automatic annual adjustments tied to a measure of inflation.[22] But even with these more generous benefits, many minimum wage workers still live in poverty. Hence, today's minimum wage is not necessarily a living wage. To reduce the financial hardship on minimum and low-wage workers, the national government established the Earned Income Tax Credit program.

Earned Income Tax Credit and Child Tax Credit

In addition to providing cash transfers and regulating wages, the government supports income security through programs offering tax breaks such as the Earned Income Tax Credit (EITC) and the Child Tax Credit (CTC) programs. The EITC offers a tax credit to working citizens with low to moderate earned income who file an income tax return. Working parents are eligible for larger EITC credits than are workers without children. The amount of the tax credit decreases (eventually reaching zero) as earned income increases. The CTC is worth up to $1,000 per child for working families. Because the EITC and CTC reward work by supplementing the earnings of workers, there is broad bipartisan support for both programs. According to the Center on Budget and Policy Priorities, a research organization concerned with the status of poor people, in 2015 the EITC and CTC lifted an estimated 14 million people out of poverty, including 5 million children. Unfortunately, the Center on Budget and Policy Priorities estimates that 20 percent of eligible people do not claim their EITC benefits.[23]

Temporary Assistance for Needy Families

The Social Security Act established Aid to Dependent Children (ADC), which evolved into Aid to Families with Dependent Children (AFDC) and was then replaced by Temporary Assistance for Needy Families (TANF). These income security programs target families with children and no or very low income (a means test).

ADC supported stay-at-home single widows with children. AFDC evolved into a program that supported one- and two-parent families with children. Federal grants and state funds paid for the ADC and AFDC noncontributory cash transfer, entitlement programs, and a formula in the national law determined what percentage of each state's annual program costs the federal government would cover. The federal law also gave each state discretion to determine the level of benefits as well as the eligibility criteria for program recipients in that state.

Beginning in the late 1950s, the number of households headed by women with children living in poverty began to increase, a development referred to as the **feminization of poverty.** Although the overwhelming majority of AFDC beneficiaries

feminization of poverty
The phenomenon of increasing numbers of unmarried, divorced, and separated women with children living in poverty.

were children, myths about a poor work ethic and irresponsible sexual practices on the part of their typically single mothers fueled many calls for reform. Although AFDC was modified several times over the next few decades, a major reform did not occur until the 1990s.

In 1996, President Bill Clinton signed the Personal Responsibility and Work Opportunity Reconciliation Act (PRWORA), which radically changed both the nature and the provision of income security for low-income families with children. PRWORA replaced the AFDC entitlement program and several other grant assistance programs for low-income families with one block grant: Temporary Assistance for Needy Families (TANF). Unlike AFDC, TANF is not an entitlement program. The focus moreover has changed from one of encouraging women to stay home with their children to one of requiring recipients to work (those in both single- and dual-parent households) and requiring fathers (particularly those not living with their children) to take on greater financial responsibilities for their children.

TANF is designed to foster self-sufficiency among families with children by providing financial assistance for basic needs (like food, housing, and clothing), job training, child care, and transportation, among other needs. States receive block grants from the federal government that give them discretion to design programs that meet the purposes of the TANF program.

Although PRWORA gives state governments a great deal of flexibility in determining TANF eligibility, benefits, and programs, it comes with several very specific regulations. For example, a family can receive benefits only for two consecutive years and a lifetime maximum of five years. Moreover, program beneficiaries must work or be enrolled in an educational or training program that prepares them for work. Ultimately, the success of this radical approach to welfare reform depends on the availability of jobs that pay well and offer benefits; hence, its success depends on the overall health of the U.S. economy.

Other Safety Net Programs

Despite the various income security programs we have considered, tens of millions of Americans, including millions who work full time, live in *poverty*—the condition of lacking sufficient income to purchase the necessities for an adequate living standard. Millions of others are one problem away from poverty, meaning that a health emergency, significant car repair, family relations issue, or job layoff could land them in poverty. The government defines poverty using two measures: *poverty thresholds* and *poverty guidelines.*

Since the 1960s, the U.S. Census Bureau has used the gauge of *poverty thresholds*—an annually updated set of income measures adjusted for family size that define who is living in poverty (see Chapter 16). The government uses these thresholds to collect data on how many families and individuals are living in poverty.

Using 100 percent of the poverty threshold as the definition of poverty, according to the Census Bureau, in 2016, 41 million individuals (13 percent of the U.S. population) were living in poverty. There were 13 million children below the age of 18 years (18 percent) living in poverty, and almost 5 million people over the age of 64 (9 percent) in the same situation. The poverty rate among blacks was 22 percent; Hispanics, 19 percent; Asians, 12 percent; and non-Hispanic whites, 9 percent.[24]

poverty guidelines
A simplified version of the U.S. Census Bureau's poverty thresholds developed each year by the Department of Health and Human Services; used to set financial eligibility criteria for benefits.

Government agencies that offer additional safety-net programs beyond those we have considered so far do not use the Census Bureau's poverty thresholds to determine eligibility. Instead, many use **poverty guidelines** established by the Department of Health and Human Services (HHS). These guidelines are a version of the poverty thresholds simplified for administrative use (see Table 17.2).

TABLE 17.2 **Department of Health and Human Services Poverty Guidelines for the 48 Contiguous States and Washington, D.C., 2018 ($ per year)**

What quality of life could you, as a single person, achieve at the income of 100 percent of the poverty guidelines? What quality of life could you, as a single person, achieve at the income of 185 percent of the poverty guidelines?

PERSONS IN HOUSEHOLD	100 PERCENT OF POVERTY	185 PERCENT OF POVERTY*
1	12,140	22,270
2	16,460	30,451
3	20,780	38,443
4	25,100	46,435
5	29,420	54,427
6	33,740	62,419
7	38,060	70,411
8	42,380	78,403

*Calculated from the HSS poverty guidelines.

SOURCE: U.S. Department of Health and Human Services, "2018 Poverty Guidelines."

Most in-kind assistance safety-net programs allow families with incomes of a certain percentage above the HHS poverty guidelines (say, 185 percent) to receive benefits. Administrators recognize that families with even those income levels experience difficulties in meeting their basic needs. Programs that use the HHS poverty guidelines as the basis for determining eligibility include SNAP and the National School Lunch Program. These programs target the problem of **food insecurity,** the situation in which people have limited or uncertain ability to obtain, in socially acceptable ways, enough nutritious food to sustain a healthy and active life.

Housing insecurity—the condition in which people have limited or uncertain ability to obtain, in socially acceptable ways, housing that is affordable, safe, of decent quality, and permanent—is another problem for a proportion of the U.S. population. The U.S. Department of Housing and Urban Development reported that in one night in January 2017, there were 553,742 people homeless; 65 percent were staying in emergency shelters or transitional housing, and 35 percent were living in unsheltered locations. This is a little less than a 1 percent decrease in homelessness from 2016.[25] Advocates for the homeless question the one-night-in-January count and argue that many homeless persons were not counted.[26]

Even with the billions spent on homelessness programs, the most federal revenue spent on housing assistance is in the form of tax breaks to homeowners, developers, and property owners who rent to low-income householders. However, the programs that are most in the public eye are means-tested public housing and housing-choice-voucher (Section 8 rent subsidy) programs for which low-income households can apply. Affordable housing is a growing problem as incomes are stagnant and home prices and rents increase.[27]

food insecurity
The situation in which people have a limited or an uncertain ability to obtain, in socially acceptable ways, enough nutritious food to live a healthy and active life.

housing insecurity
The situation in which people have limited or uncertain ability to obtain, in socially acceptable ways, affordable, safe, and decent-quality permanent housing.

Health Care Policy

Lack of health insurance is an additional problem for low-income households, although the 2010 Patient Protection and Affordable Care Act attempted to ensure that everyone has health insurance. According to the U.S. Census Bureau, in 2016 about 9 percent of the U.S. population was without health insurance. Of those with insurance, 68 percent had private insurance; and 56 percent were covered by employer-provided insurance. Some 37 percent of the insured were covered by government health programs: 17 percent Medicare, 19 percent Medicaid.[28] These two programs were established in 1965 as part of President Lyndon B. Johnson's (1963–1969) Great Society plan, which included government programs to address the effects of poverty during a time of national economic prosperity. Medicare and Medicaid are part of today's safety net.

Medicaid

Title XIX, added to the Social Security Act in 1965, created Medicaid—a joint federal-state entitlement program providing health care to people meeting a means test. Because the national legislation delegates substantial discretion to state governments regarding eligibility and benefits, there are really 50 different Medicaid programs.

In this cash transfer program, state governments pay health care providers, and then the national government reimburses the states for a percentage of those bills. The national government's share of each state's cost is based on a formula that takes into account the state's wealth. The national government pays as little as 50 percent of the Medicaid bill in the wealthiest states and as much as 74 percent in the poorest state, Mississippi.[29]

The State Children's Health Insurance Program (SCHIP), established in 1997, covers medical costs for low-income uninsured children under the age of 19 who are not eligible for Medicaid. In this joint federal-state cash transfer program, eligibility is based on a family income that is generally less than 200 percent of the HHS poverty guidelines. States participating in SCHIP can expand their current Medicaid program to cover these children, or they can create a new program that provides the standard coverage mandated by the national government.

The Affordable Care Act allows states to expand Medicaid and SCHIP eligibility for children, pregnant women, parents, and other adults who were excluded previously from the programs by decreasing the income requirements. Specifically, it allows states to extend Medicaid to low-income individuals and adults in families with incomes up to 133 percent of the federal poverty level.[30]

Traditionally, although most of those who benefit from Medicaid are women and children, the bulk of Medicaid spending pays for nursing home and long-term care services, which Medicare does not cover.

Medicare

In 1965, President Lyndon Johnson signed legislation enacting Medicare, a program that provides health insurance to persons over age 65 and those under 65 who have been receiving SSDI for at least two years. Today, Medicare has four components.

Part A, Medicare's Hospital Insurance Program, is a social insurance program funded by a 1.45 percent tax paid by employees and employers that helps to pay for hospital stays. (This tax and the Social Security tax make up the "FICA" deduction from your paychecks.) All who pay into Medicare are eligible for Part A benefits when they reach the age of 65. Also eligible for Part A are persons under age 65 who have been receiving SSDI for at least two years. *Part B,* Medicare's Supplemental Medical Insurance, covers a percentage of physician costs and other outpatient health care expenses, such as laboratory fees and ambulance services. *Part C,* Medicare + Choice, allows Medicare beneficiaries to choose private health plans that provide them with the same coverage found in Medicare Parts A and B. *Part D* is a prescription drug plan that took effect in 2006.

The Affordable Care Act extended several preventive services to Medicare recipients at no cost, including cholesterol screening, mammograms, diabetes screening, and screening for colorectal, prostate, and cervical cancers. The act also filled in a prescription coverage gap in the Medicare Part D program.[31]

The Patient Protection and Affordable Care Act (ACA)

On March 23, 2010, President Obama signed into law the Patient Protection and Affordable Care Act (ACA), which had been approved by Congress without a single vote from a Republican congressional member. The ACA has several goals, including expanding consumers' protections in their dealings with health insurance companies, improving the quality and lowering the costs of health care, and increasing access to affordable health care. The ACA included numerous important regulations:

- Prohibiting insurance companies from denying coverage based on preexisting health conditions.
- Prohibiting insurance companies from discontinuing coverage when a customer gets sick.
- Eliminating lifetime dollar limits on insurance coverage.
- Providing preventive care services.
- Requiring insurance coverage to allow young adults to stay on their parents' health plan until they turn 26 years old.
- Requiring that at least 80 to 85 percent of all premium dollars paid to health insurance companies be spent on benefits for the insured and quality improvements (thereby limiting the money that can be spent on administrative costs and that can go into the company's profits).
- Prohibiting insurance companies from charging higher rates due to a person's sex or health status.

The federal government makes subsidies available to individuals with incomes between 133 percent and 400 percent of the federal poverty level to help them pay for insurance. Moreover, employers with more than 50 employees must provide health insurance or pay annual fines for each of their employees who receive federal subsidies to purchase insurance.

On June 28, 2012, the Supreme Court upheld the health insurance mandate and a tax penalty for those who did not have insurance. The 2017 Tax Cuts and Jobs Act eliminated the tax penalty. In 2012, the Court limited the law's expansion of Medicaid by finding that each state government had the option to expand or not to expand Medicaid to all families earning less than 133 percent of the federal poverty level. Figure 17.1 shows the Medicaid expansion decision made by each state. Some of the states received waivers from ACA rules so that they can try innovations with their Medicaid expansion plans.[32]

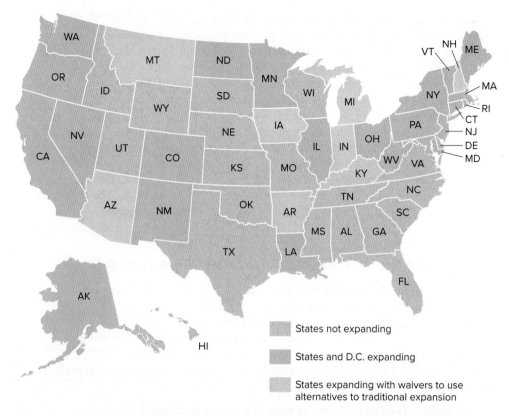

States not expanding

States and D.C. expanding

States expanding with waivers to use alternatives to traditional expansion

FIGURE 17.1 ■ States' ACA-Medicaid Expansion Decisions Through 2018

SOURCE: National Academy for State Health Policy, "Where States Stand on Medicaid Expansion Decisions."

Implementation of the ACA has seen its ups and downs. In addition to lawsuits, by January 2016 Congress had taken a vote to repeal the ACA 62 times. On the 62nd try, the bill to repeal was approved in Congress and sent to President Obama, who vetoed it. In 2017, President Trump and Republicans in Congress continued efforts to repeal and replace the ACA.

Immigration Policy

The majority of immigrants to the United States are young people seeking two goals: reunification with family members residing here and work that will provide a better quality of life than they are able to achieve in their home countries. U.S. immigration policy, the collection of laws that specify which people the government will authorize to emigrate to the United States, allows approximately 1 million people to do so legally each year. Figure 17.2 shows that legal immigrants come from around the globe. In addition to the legal newcomers, since 2009, an average of about 350,000 unauthorized immigrants come into the United States annually.[33]

Authorized and Unauthorized Immigration

Federal immigration policy determines who may emigrate to the United States as permanent residents ("green card" recipients) and as temporary visitors (officially labeled nonimmigrant admissions, including tourists, students, diplomats, businessmen and businesswomen, and guest workers). Since the Immigration and Nationality Act of 1965, the largest category of immigrants authorized to come to the United States permanently is those seeking to reunify with immediate family members who are either U.S. citizens or authorized permanent residents. Currently, U.S. citizens can sponsor immediate family members—spouses, minor children, and parents—for visas, and there is no limit on the number of these the government can issue. In addition, U.S. citizens may sponsor their siblings and adult children, who receive preferences under a program that offers a limited number of visas each year to citizens' relatives. Immigrants with green cards can also apply for visas for their spouses and children.[34]

The second-largest category—less than one-fifth of those admitted—is made up of individuals welcomed for their employment skills; this group includes highly skilled professionals and wealthy entrepreneurs expected to invest in job creation. Persons to whom the United States offers humanitarian protection from persecution (or likely persecution) because of race, religion, nationality, membership in a particular social group, or political views compose the third-largest category of authorized immigrants. An additional 5 percent of immigrants are admitted through the State Department's diversity lottery. The diversity lottery awards permanent residency to people from countries with low rates of immigration to the United States.[35] Figure 17.3 presents the breakdown of the 1 million people obtaining lawful permanent resident status in 2016.

Who is not eligible for permanent authorized immigration to the United States? In addition to foreigners who do not fall within one of the categories described previously, foreign nationals perceived to be anarchists or political extremists have been excluded since 1901, when a Polish anarchist assassinated President William McKinley (1897–1901). More recently, in 2002, the USA PATRIOT Act established new criteria for denying entry to the United States. Today, the national government can deny authorized immigration to foreigners who it perceives as security or terrorist threats, who have a criminal history, who have previously been removed from the United States, or who present a health risk.[36]

Interpreting Images

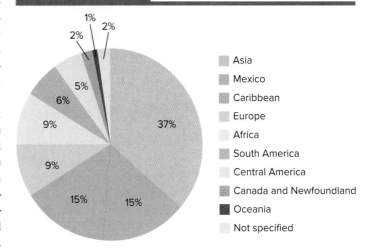

Legend:
- Asia
- Mexico
- Caribbean
- Europe
- Africa
- South America
- Central America
- Canada and Newfoundland
- Oceania
- Not specified

FIGURE 17.2 ■ **Where U.S. Lawful Permanent Residents Come From, 2016** What world region is the source of most U.S. immigrants today? With respect to the Americas, what country or larger geographical unit is the source of most immigrants to the United States? From what area of the world do you think most Americans believe the largest proportion of immigrants come to the United States? Do you think these statistics would surprise most Americans?

SOURCE: Homeland Security, 2016 *Yearbook of Immigration Statistics,* "Table 2—Persons Obtaining Lawful Permanent Resident Status by Region and Selected Country of Last Residence: FY 2014–2016."

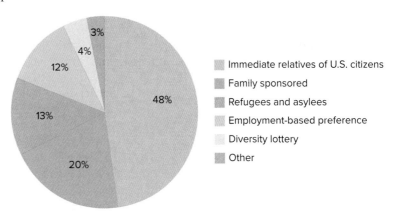

Legend:
- Immediate relatives of U.S. citizens
- Family sponsored
- Refugees and asylees
- Employment-based preference
- Diversity lottery
- Other

FIGURE 17.3 ■ **Classification of Immigrants Granted Lawful Permanent Resident Status, 2016**

SOURCE: Homeland Security, 2016 *Yearbook of Immigration Statistics,* "Table 6: Persons Obtaining Lawful Permanent Resident Status by Type and Major Class of Admission: FY 2014–2016."

Why do immigrants enter the United States without authorization each year? There are several answers to that question. One is that the United States may offer more economic opportunities than does the home country. Yet, unless an individual fits into one of the categories for authorized immigration, he or she has no basis on which to apply for permanent, legal entry into the United States. In addition, each admission category has annual quotas. The result is a backlog of more than 4 million applications, which may mean up to a 20-year wait for authorized immigration.[37] Those are just some explanations for why so many undocumented immigrants enter the United States each year.

What most people do not realize is that the main source of undocumented immigrants is travelers who overstay their visas. According to the Department of Homeland Security, in 2015, more than 527,000 people did so.[38]

Although undocumented immigrants are not eligible for safety-net benefits such as programs for income security and food security, all children born on U.S. soil—even those born to undocumented immigrants—are citizens and hence are eligible for these benefits. Moreover, the government guarantees a public education to all children—citizens and undocumented immigrants alike. State and local governments cover approximately 92 percent of the cost of public education, and the national government funds the remaining 8 percent. With respect to legal rights, the Fourteenth Amendment to the Constitution guarantees all people—not just citizens—due process before the government can infringe on their life, liberty, or pursuit of happiness, as well as equal protection of the law. Typically, the costs of these constitutional guarantees fall to state and local governments. Most undocumented immigrants do pay taxes and so are contributing to government revenues collected to pay these bills.

Proposed Immigration Policy Reforms

Discussions about immigration reform typically include four general questions. What can the government do about the more than 11 million immigrants living in the United States without legal permission? How can the government tighten border security to decrease the number of undocumented immigrants? How can the government prevent employers from hiring undocumented immigrants, thereby eliminating the jobs that lure so many people to the United States without legal permission? Finally, what must the government do to fix the current immigration system so that those following the rules to immigrate legally do not have to wait two decades to gain legal permanent resident status?

Immigration policy reform has been a topic of debate for more than two decades. However, disagreement among congressional members (typically along party lines) has resulted in no legislated national immigration policy reforms. Thus, the long history of presidents using their discretionary powers to execute legislation has continued. President Obama put forth executive orders to direct the implementation of immigration policies. In addition, state and local governments have stepped into the gap left by Congress, enacting their own policies to address concerns about undocumented immigrants. In turn, courts have had to resolve conflicts over the constitutionality of state and local policies, as well as presidential executive orders.

By early 2012, federal judges had struck down or prevented the implementation of portions of state immigration laws in Alabama, Arkansas, Georgia, Indiana, Pennsylvania, South Carolina, and Utah. The courts ruled that state and local governments cannot craft their own immigration policies because it infringes on the federal government's constitutional authority over such matters.

An Obama 2012 executive order established the Deferred Action for Childhood Arrivals (DACA) program. Affecting approximately 1.5 million people, this program allows children and young adults who were brought to the United States illegally as children to apply for temporary deportation relief. A 2014 Obama executive order called for the expansion of the DACA program and the creation of a new program, Deferred Action for Parents of Americans and Lawful Permanent Residents (DAPA). DAPA would allow undocumented immigrants who are the parents of U.S. citizens or of lawful permanent residents to be shielded from deportation and allowed to apply for work permits. DAPA could affect close to 4 million people.[39]

Immediately, 26 state governments filed lawsuits claiming that although the president has enforcement power over immigration policies, DAPA was too broad a policy to be enacted through executive order; legislation is required. They also argued that DAPA harms states that have laws providing benefits to lawful immigrants because of the additional costs they will incur providing the benefits to DAPA program recipients. In 2015, a federal district court placed a temporary injunction on the government's implementation of the DAPA program. The Supreme Court heard the case in June 2016. The 4–4 split vote left the injunction in place. Then in June 2017, the Department of Homeland Security (DHS) secretary ended the DAPA program. In September 2017, following President Trump's directive, the DHS secretary initiated the phase-out of the DACA program. In early 2018, a federal court ordered the U.S. Customs and Immigration Service to resume accepting requests to renew DACA protections from deportation.[40]

In his 2018 State of the Union address, Trump outlined four pillars of his plan for immigration reform: protection for DACA recipients; an end to family reunification immigration; an end to the diversity lottery; and full funding for the border wall he has been calling for since his presidential campaign, which is estimated to cost $25 billion over 10 years.[41]

Then in March 2018, the Justice Department filed suit against the state of California. Modeled on the Obama administration's 2010 mostly successful lawsuit against Arizona's immigration law that cracked down on undocumented immigrants, the 2018 lawsuit attempted to prevent three California laws from being implemented, claiming they violate the Constitution's supremacy clause. In this case, the California laws created barriers to state and local officials cooperating with federal immigration-enforcement efforts. California officials argued that the Supreme Court had determined in previous cases that the Constitution does not allow the national government to "commandeer local officials into federal service."[42]

> In his 2018 State of the Union, President Trump requested full funding for a wall to be built at the United States border with Mexico as one of the four pillars of his immigration reform plan. Here we see President Trump in March 2018, viewing several prototypes for the wall. What is the current status of the border wall?

©Doug Mills/The New York Times/Redux

Thinking Critically About What's Next in U.S. Domestic Policy

A healthy environment is essential to human health, happiness, and survival. Reliance on nonrenewable energy sources, specifically fossil fuels, combined with the production of volumes of waste by the world's growing population harm the global environment. Today, people across the globe agree that countries must decrease their reliance on fossil fuels to limit climate change and its harmful effects. However, debates in the United States continue on how to accomplish this while not harming economic development and while increasing economic independence.

Ensuring a healthy and safe society in which citizens can live their lives freely, in pursuit of their happiness, means more than protecting air, water, and land quality. Today, the ever-increasing cost of ensuring a just and safe society is forcing U.S. policymakers to take a hard look at income security, food security, housing security, and health care policies. There is bipartisan concern about the growing costs of several safety net policies, particularly OASI, Medicare, and Medicaid. However, there is not bipartisan agreement on how to address the financial problems so that the benefits program recipients currently enjoy will also be available to their posterity.

The national government regularly works with state and local governments to provide the phenomenal range of domestic policies from which citizens benefit. Only through a unity of effort, which requires clear communication and cooperation, can intergovernmental relations succeed, whether the goal is protecting the environment, establishing energy independence, or maintaining a safety net. Today, healthy intergovernmental relations are key elements of effective and efficient national domestic policies. However, in several policy areas, including environmental protection and immigration, intergovernmental tension is growing as many state and local governments move in directions at odds with that of the national government. Intergovernmental cooperation and intergovernmental tension are both realities in U.S. domestic policy today.

Learning Summary

1. Explain several ways citizens can engage in domestic policy making.
  a. Explain the NIMBY syndrome.
  b. Differentiate between domestic policy and international policy.

2. Describe several policy tools the national government uses to accomplish policy goals.
  a. Provide an example of each of the following policy tools: laws; regulations; direct provision of services; cash transfer; in-kind service; grants; loans; insurance; contracting-out.
  b. Differentiate a contributory program (social insurance program) from a noncontributory program.

3. Outline the history of national environmental protection policy through the current presidential administration.
   a. Identify the policy tools the national government has used in environmental policy.
   b. Discuss the roles of state and local governments in environmental policy.
   c. Explain the tensions among environmental protection policy, energy policy, and economic development policy.

4. Outline the history of national energy policy through the current presidential administration.

5. Explain the goals of and policy tools used in national safety net programs, including income security programs, food security programs, and housing security programs.
   a. Outline the history of income security programs.
   b. Explain how the government defines poverty.

6. Explain the goals and policy tools of national health care policy, including Medicaid, Medicare, and the Affordable Care Act.
   a. Compare the beneficiaries of Medicaid and Medicare.
   b. Present some legal challenges to components of the Affordable Care Act.

7. Describe current immigration policy and policy debates.
   a. Explain the categories of legal admissions to the United States.
   b. Summarize the data on where legal immigrants to the United States come from.
   c. Describe the efforts of state and local governments to create immigration policy.
   d. Summarize the four pillars of President Trump's immigration reform plan.

Key Terms

cash transfer 569

contributory program (social insurance program) 570

direct provision 569

direct subsidy 570

domestic policies 566

entitlement program 570

environmental racism 576

feminization of poverty 581

food insecurity 583

global warming 572

greenhouse effect 572

housing insecurity 583

indexed benefit 579

in-kind assistance 569

living wage 580

means-tested benefit 579

NIMBY ("not in my backyard") syndrome 565

noncontributory program 569

poverty guidelines 582

safety net programs 566

For Review

1. Explain the NIMBY syndrome.

2. Describe four or five of the domestic policy tools used by the federal government.

3. Discuss how the federal policy tools used for environmental protection make intergovernmental relations a key component of environmental policy.

4. Explain how the goals of environmental protection, economic development, and energy independence are in tension with each other.

5. Use the following terms to distinguish between OASI and TANF: contributory program, noncontributory program, means-tested program, and entitlement program.

6. Differentiate among Medicaid, Medicare, and the Affordable Care Act in terms of who benefits from each program.

7. What are the major questions raised in conversations about reforming immigration policy?

For Critical Thinking and Discussion

1. Although the majority of scientists argue that human behavior is a main cause of climate change, not everyone agrees. Some argue that global warming is not even occurring. What do you think, and what data can you gather to support your view?

2. Which cash transfer programs (including tax expenditures) will the majority of Americans benefit from at some point in their lives? Explain.

3. A government concerned with sustainability makes policy decisions today that serve today's citizens without threatening the quality of life of future generations. Explain how at least two of the programs discussed in this chapter are important to a sustainable community that is safe and free.

4. What might explain why Social Security and Medicare are entitlements but TANF is not an entitlement? Keep in mind the nature of the programs (contributory or noncontributory) and the populations each program targets.

5. Frequently, a crisis or a disaster is the catalyst for revolutionary, new public policies. Discuss one or two crises or disasters that have occurred in your lifetime that led to major changes in public policy.

Resources for Research AND Action

Internet Resources

Center for Budget and Policy Priorities
www.cbpp.org The center focuses on the impact of public policies on low-income households. On the website, you will find links to numerous reports elaborating on the effects of public policies on such households.

Environmental Protection Agency
www2.epa.gov/enforcement This section of the EPA's website provides information on its enforcement actions, efforts to clean up contaminated sites, and investigations of environmental law violations.

USA Government Information
www.usa.gov This easy-to-use first stop for government information offers links to government agencies and their programs.

Recommended Readings

Carson, Rachel. *Silent Spring.* New York: Houghton Mifflin, 1962. Thorough and alarming description of how the pesticide DDT harmed the food chain, caused cancer and genetic damage, and threatened the world as we know it.

Ehrenreich, Barbara. *Nickel and Dimed: On (Not) Getting By in America.* New York: Henry Holt, 2001. Documentation of the author's experiences when she joined the millions of Americans working full time, year round, for wages higher than the minimum wage at the time ($6 to $7 per hour) in jobs with no benefits.

Gore, Al. *Earth in the Balance: Ecology and the Human Spirit.* Boston: Houghton Mifflin, 1992. Comprehensive assessment of the major post–Cold War threat to the United States and the world: planetary destruction due to overpopulation, deforestation, soil erosion, air pollution, and water pollution. Written before his more popularly known *An Inconvenient Truth,* Gore recommends far-reaching and specific governmental and corporate actions.

Movies of Interest

An Inconvenient Sequel: Truth to Power (2017)
Former Vice President Al Gore continues his environmental advocacy, pursuing the idea that human ingenuity and passion can address the perils of climate change.

Gasland (2010)
In 2008, Josh Fox was offered $100,000 to lease his family's land in northeast Pennsylvania to a natural gas company that wanted to frack for gas. Fracking, a process developed by Halliburton to get natural gas out of the ground, was a relatively new drilling process, and Josh traveled across the country to learn about how it affected communities: the air, water, land, and people's health. This documentary was not well received by the natural gas drilling industry.

An Inconvenient Truth (2006)
A rallying cry for citizens and government to address the problem of global warming, this documentary presents the science of global warming as it follows Al Gore's environmental advocacy from his college years to today.

United 93 (2006)
An account of the fate of United Flight 93—the fourth plane hijacked on September 11, 2001, this fact-based film documents the plight of the passengers (who had become aware of the other hijackings) and their struggle to prevent another catastrophe. It also reveals the national government's lack of preparedness for the emergency.

Erin Brockovich (2000)
This movie tells the real-life story of a single mom who, while working in a law firm, uncovers the fact that the Pacific Gas & Electric Company is covering up its improper and illegal dumping of toxic waste in a small Northern California town. The toxic waste is making residents sick. Brockovich's findings lead to one of the largest successful class-action lawsuits against a multibillion-dollar corporation in U.S. history.

The Grapes of Wrath (1940)
The winner of two Academy Awards, this movie, set during the Great Depression, tells the story of the Joad family (and their acquaintances) as they struggle to meet their basic needs, first in the Oklahoma Dust Bowl and later in California.

References

1. Office of Management and Budget, *Historical Tables,* "Table 3.1—Outlays by Superfunction and Function: 1940–2023," www.whitehouse.gov/omb/historicals.

2. Office of Management and Budget, "Table 11.1: Summary of Outlays for Payments for Individuals," *Historical Tables.*

3. U.S. Census Bureau, "Measuring America," December 12, 2013.

4. "Gaylord Nelson and Earth Day—Introduction: The Earth Day Story and Gaylord Nelson," nelsonearthday.net/earth-day/index.htm.

5. Ibid.

6. Justin Gillis, "Panel's Warning on Climate Risk: Worst Is Yet to Come," *The New York Times,* March 31, 2014.

7. *Massachusetts v. EPA,* 549 U.S. 497 (2007).

8. J. B. Wogan, "The Cap-and-Trade Comeback," *Governing,* February 2018, pp. 40–45.

9. Frank Jordans and Dorothee Thiesing, "Cities, States Defy Trump, Back Paris Climate Deal," *Scranton Times-Tribune,* November 2, 2017.

10. Hroko Tabuchi, "What's at Stake in the Cuts Proposed for the EPA," *New York Times,* April 11, 2017.

11. https://www.epa.gov/superfund/search-superfund-sites-where-you-live

12. David Hosansky, *The Environment A to Z* (Washington, DC: CQ Press, 2001), 80–81.

13. https://www.dosomething.org/facts/11-facts-about-bp-oil-spill

14. Coral Davenport and Adam Nagourney, "Fighting Trump on Climate, California Becomes a Global Force," *New York Times,* May 23, 2017.

15. Dan Byers, "Energy Policy in Trump Era Bodes Well for Americans and Business," *The Hill,* January 26, 2018.

16. Michael T. Klare, "Donald Trump's Extract-Everything Energy Policy Dooms Us All," *The Nation,* February 12, 2018.

17. Social Security Administration, Research, Statistics, & Policy Analysis, "OASDI and SSI Program Rates & Limits, 2018," www.ssa.gov/policy/docs/quickfacts/prog_highlights/index.html.

18. Social Security and Medicare Board of Trustees, *A Summary of the 2017 Annual Reports,* www.ssa.gov/oact/trsum/.

19. Jim Dwyer, "Exhausted Workers Recall Minimal Efforts to Enforce a Minimum Wage Law," *The New York Times,* November 7, 2013.

20. Noam Scheiber, "As His Term Wanes, Obama Champions Workers' Rights," *New York Times,* August 31, 2015.

21. Ibid.

22. National Conference of State Legislatures, "State Minimum Wages: 2018 Minimum Wage by State," www.ncsl.org/research/labor-and-employment/state-minimum-wage-chart.aspx.

23. Center on Budget and Policy Priorities, "Chart Book: The Earned Income Tax Credit and Child Tax Credit," November 2, 2015.

24. U.S. Census Bureau, Newsroom, "Income, Poverty and Health Insurance Coverage in United States: 2016, www.census.gov/newsroom/press-releases/2017/income-poverty.html.

25. U.S. Department of Housing and Urban Development, "*The Annual Homeless Assessment Report to Congress: December 2017,* www.hudexchange.info/resources/documents/2017-AHAR-Part-1.pdf.

26. Maria Foscarinis, "Homeless Problem Bigger Than Our Leaders Think: Report Misleads on Those Without Shelter," *USA Today,* January 16, 2014.

27. Patrick Clark, "The Affordable Housing Crisis Moves Inland," *Bloomberg,* April 15, 2016.

28. Jessica C. Smith and Carla Medalia, U.S. Census Bureau, Current Population Reports, P60-253, *Health Insurance Coverage in the United States: 2014,* p. 3, https://www.census.gov/content/dam/Census/library/publications/2015/demo/p60-253.pdf.

29. U.S. Census Bureau, "Income, Poverty and Health Insurance Coverage in United States: 2016."

30. Centers for Medicare and Medicaid, "Timeline: The Affordable Care Act Becomes Law," www.medicaid.gov/AffordableCareAct/Timeline/Timeline.html.

31. U.S. Department of Health and Human Services, "Key Features of the Affordable Care Act by Year," www.hhs.gov/healthcare/facts/timeline/timeline-text.html#Page_4.

32. National Academy for State Health Policy, "Where States Stand on Medicaid Expansion Decisions," https://nashp.org/states-stand-medicaid-expansion-decisions/.

33. Jeffrey S. Passel, "Unauthorized Immigrant Population Stable for Half a Decade," July 22, 2015, http://www.pewresearch.org/fact-tank/2015/07/22/unauthorized-immigrant-population-stable-for-half-a-decade/.

34. Julie Hirschfeld Davis, "'Merit-Based' Rules Could Reshape Immigration," *New York Times,* March 3, 2017.

35. Ibid.

36. "Inadmissibility: When the U.S. Can Keep You Out," *NOLO Law for All,* www.nolo.com/legal-encyclopedia/us-deny-entry-inadmissibility-reasons-29715.html.

37. Julia Preston, "Legal Immigrants Seek Reward for Years of Following the Rules," *The New York Times,* July 15, 2013.

38. Adriana Gomez Licon, "Border Plan Overlooks Expired-Visa Holders," *Scranton Times-Tribune,* April 14, 2017.

39. Drew Desilver, "Executive Actions on Immigration Have Long History," Pew Research Center, November 21.

40. U.S. Immigration and Customs Enforcement, "Deferred Action for Childhood Arrivals (DACA) and Deferred Action for Parents of Americans and Lawful Permanent Residents (DAPA)," www.ice.gov/daca.

41. Sheryl Gay Stolberg, "Senate Begins 'Wild' Week of Debate on Immigration, Outcome Unknown," *New York Times,* February 12, 2018.

42. Josh Gerstein, "Trump Administration Goes on Offense, Sues California over Sanctuary Laws," *Politico.com,* March 6, 2018.

CHAPTER 18

Foreign Policy and National Security

©Saul Loeb/AFP/Getty Images

THEN

The emergence of
the United States as a
superpower and the
Cold War dominated
U.S. foreign policy in
the aftermath of
World War II.

NOW

Unpredictability
and uncertainty
characterize U.S.
foreign and national
security policy in a
rapidly changing
global context.

NEXT

What will be the long-term repercussions of President Trump's
foreign policy on the United States?

How will the continuing threat of terrorism against the United
States and other Western democracies influence foreign and
national security policy in the future?

Will U.S. foreign policy in the coming years increasingly reflect
a clash of civilizations between Western democracies and
fundamentalist Islamic actors?

In a 2018 tweet, President

Trump wrote, "North Korean Leader Kim Jong Un just stated that the 'Nuclear Button is on his desk at all times.' Will someone from his depleted and food starved regime please inform him that I too have a Nuclear Button, but it is a much bigger & more powerful one than his, and my Button works!" The insult and threat sent shock waves through the U.S. diplomatic and foreign service communities, who typically operate on a premise that it is unwise to evoke the ire of foreign dictators who possess nuclear weapons. Months later, Kim joined his South Korean counterpart at a summit and announced a new era of peace and a denuclearization of the Korean peninsula, which paved the way for for a summit between Trump and Kim, who forged a close relationship during their meetings in June 2018. While it is unclear whether President Trump's braggadocio had any bearing on Kim's willingness to negotiate with South Korea and the United States, since assuming the presidency in 2017, he has conducted an unpredictable brand of near-unilaterally created foreign policy. Often, Trump's actions seem intended to offend long-standing allies while cozying up to historic rivals. Other times, President Trump embraces policies only to overturn them months later.

President Trump's seeming willingness to turn conventional foreign policy wisdom on its head comes at a time when the foreign policy arena is the most volatile. During the past 65 years, the goals of U.S. foreign policy have shifted significantly, from preventing the spread of communism in the post–World War II era, to redefining the nation as the world's only superpower in the 1990s, to responding to the terrorist attacks of September 11, 2001, to waging multi-front wars in Iraq and Afghanistan, to responding to the instability that remains in those and adjacent areas, including Syria, and the increasing threats of terrorism from insurgent groups seizing control in the power vacuum left behind. As the objectives and the worldviews of policymakers have changed in concert with unprecedented world developments, so too have their priorities and the instruments available to them in implementing U.S. foreign policy.

The Tools of U.S. Foreign Policy

Government officials use a variety of instruments to shape foreign policy. That is, in creating foreign policy, policymakers rely on a variety of tactics to get foreign nations to bend to the will of the United States. Among these tools are diplomacy, trade and economic policies, and military options. Often, policymakers rely on more than one tool in their dealings with foreign nations.

Learning Objectives

After reading this chapter, students should be able to:

- Describe the tools of U.S. foreign policy.
- Understand who creates U.S. foreign policy.
- Describe U.S. foreign policy's historical context, and trace its development from the ratification of the Constitution until World War II.
- Analyze the postwar era and the status of the United States as superpower.
- Describe 21st-century U.S. foreign policy.
- Explain the future challenges in U.S. foreign policy.

Diplomacy

Covering a gamut of situations, diplomacy is often foreign policymakers' tool of choice. **Diplomacy** can generally be defined as the conduct of international relations, particularly involving the negotiation of treaties and other agreements between nations. It can include an occurrence as attention-grabbing as a Twitter war between two heads of state, or as mundane as the communication between two embassies when a citizen of one country commits a crime in another. Or it can involve an event as significant as a major summit attended by world leaders. When diplomacy works, we typically do not hear about it.

Among the central figures in the diplomatic arena are **foreign service officers,** the diplomatic and consular staff at American embassies abroad. Foreign service officers, who are employees of the Department of State, conduct formal communications among nations. They are frequently responsible for negotiating many types of international agreements, including economic and trade policies.

Trade and Economic Policies

Almost a century ago, President Woodrow Wilson made this observation: "A nation that is boycotted is a nation that is in sight of surrender. Apply this economic, peaceful, silent, deadly remedy and there will be no need for force. It does not cost a life outside the nation boycotted, but it brings a pressure upon the nation which, in my judgment, no modern nation could resist."[1] It is within this context that U.S. foreign policymakers rely on trade policies, economic aid (foreign aid), and economic penalties to compel foreign governments to conform to the United States' will. Consider President Trump's 2018 decision to impose steep tariffs on steel and aluminum imports: in an effort to save American jobs in those industries, Trump sought to drive up the price of imported steel and aluminum, hoping to increase demand for domestically produced steel and aluminum. Opposition to the president's plan was swift and fierce, with members of his own party being his harshest critics, as Republicans traditionally have favored pro-business free-trade policies. Both Republicans in Congress and a clear consensus of economists argued that imposing tariffs would compel other nations to retaliate by imposing tariffs on goods produced in the United States but sold abroad. In response to those concerns, President Trump tweeted that "trade wars are good, and easy to win." But critics argue that in the past trade wars have contributed to global recessions. Indeed, the Smoot-Hawley Tariffs of 1930, which imposed large tariffs on imported goods in the early days of the Great Depression, led to retaliatory trade wars that were viewed as exacerbating global economic decline. With that knowledge, the goal of most presidential administrations has been to broadly confer **normal trade relations (NTR) status,** meaning that a country grants a particular trading partner the same, least restrictive trade conditions (that is, the lowest tariff rates) that the country offers to its other favored trading partners—its "most favored nations." U.S. foreign policymakers can bestow most favored nation status on a country to influence it to enact policies the United States prefers. Conversely, they can withhold this status to punish a nation that does not institute policies supportive of the United States' goals.

The controversial nature of President Trump's trade policies also was the subject of acrimony between the United States and some of its key economic allies at a G7 summit in 2018. The G7 is made up of seven nations: Canada, France, the United States, the United Kingdom, Germany, Japan, and Italy. The summit was characterized by tense negotiations between Trump administration officials and representatives of the other G7 governments, resulting in a compromise communique that was issued by the G7, only to be repudiated by Trump as he departed the summit in tweets lashing out at Canadian Prime Minister Justin Trudeau. The ill will between the United States and its traditional allies could be seen with promises of retaliatory tariffs targeting the United States by G7 nations.

Governments also use trade agreements as a tool of foreign policy. Among the most important of these agreements in the United States was the North American Free Trade Agreement (NAFTA), whose members included the United States, Mexico, and Canada. NAFTA eliminated barriers to trade and financial investments across the economies of the three nations, but after being a focal point of criticism by President Trump, was replaced with a renegotiated agreement, the United States-Mexico-Canada Agreement (USMCA). One key component of that agreement was to bolster the automotive parts industry, so starting in 2020, a car or truck must have 75 percent of its components manufactured in Canada, Mexico or the United States to qualify for zero tariffs, an increase over the 62.5 percent required under NAFTA. Trump administration officials also were able to increase the amount of U.S. dairy products that will be imported to Canada.

Beyond trade policy, American diplomats frequently use economic enticements in the form of foreign aid to pressure other countries into enacting and enforcing policies that the United States supports. Such was the case in the aftermath of the terrorist attacks of September 11, 2001, when the George W. Bush administration sought the cooperation of the Pakistani government in Operation Enduring Freedom, the U.S. military offensive in neighboring Afghanistan. The United States sought to overthrow the Islamic fundamentalist Taliban regime, which had harbored and provided training grounds for terrorists, and to capture 9/11 mastermind Osama bin Laden, who was believed to have been hiding in Afghanistan. Before the 9/11 terrorist strikes on domestic U.S. targets, Pakistan had received comparatively little aid from the United States—only about $3.4 million in 2001. But in 2002, Pakistan received more than $1 billion in U.S. aid. This amount tapered off in subsequent years, hovering at just under $800 million in 2008. President Obama continued the policy of relying on economic enticements to compel Pakistani cooperation, but those efforts soured in 2011 when it was discovered that bin Laden had been hiding in the Pakistani city of Abbottabad. U.S. forces launched a surprise attack in May 2011, killing bin Laden. Throughout the remainder of President Obama's tenure, aid to Pakistan was reduced and was sometimes withheld if the United States perceived that Pakistan was not supporting U.S. interests. President Trump has continued to use foreign aid to further U.S. interests in Pakistan. In 2018, he announced that the United States was temporarily suspending aid to that country amid allegations that Pakistan was aiding and harboring anti-American terrorist organizations.[2] In 2019, the budget contained $256 million in civilian assistance and $80 million in military aid to Pakistan,[3] but was contingent on Pakistan taking action "to address areas of national divergence," including ceasing to provide safe haven to terrorists.

Increasingly, world leaders have recognized that economic policy must be coupled with other types of policies to effectively compel or deter desired actions. For example, after Iranian state media reported that the nation had begun the uranium-enrichment process, President Obama announced that the United States and its allies were developing a host of **sanctions**—penalties that halt economic exchanges (and that may include boycotts and a suspension of cultural exchanges)—on Iran. However, as former senator Christopher Dodd (D-Conn.), who chaired the Banking, Housing, and Urban Affairs Committee, noted: "Economic sanctions

sanctions
Penalties that halt economic exchanges.

are a critical element of U.S. policy toward Iran. But sanctions alone are not sufficient. They must be used as effective leverage, undertaken as part of a coherent, coordinated, comprehensive diplomatic and political strategy which firmly seeks to deter Iran's nuclear ambitions and other actions which pose a threat to regional stability."[4] Under economic pressure from the United States, Great Britain, China, Russia, Germany, and the member states of the European Union, Iran agreed to halt its uranium-enrichment activities in a deal implemented in January 2014. In return, the United States and other nations agreed to lift some sanctions on Iran. The sanctions had effectively crippled Iran's economy, pressuring its leaders to negotiate with the United States and the other nations. After the International Atomic Energy Agency (IAEA) certified that it had succeeded in restricting Iran's sensitive nuclear activities, some sanctions were lifted. Specifically, the deal allows Iran to export petrochemicals and to import goods and services for its automotive manufacturing and civilian aviation sectors, and to trade in gold and other precious metals. But in 2018, President Trump announced that the United States would withdraw from the deal, opening the possibility that sanctions and bans on imported goods could be unilaterally reinstated by the United States.

The Military Option

In 2018, President Trump announced that the United States and its allies, France and Great Britain, would conduct a series of strategic air strikes in Syria, targeting chemical weapons factories in response to an alleged chemical weapon attack by the Syrian government in the rebel-held town of Douma. The move was one in a series of actions by the U.S. government over the course of the presidencies of Donald Trump and his predecessor, Barack Obama, in which the United States and its allies flexed some muscle in the Syrian civil war, but also demonstrated an unwillingness to become involved in a full-on ground war. For example, in 2016, President Obama sent 300 U.S. military personnel to Syria to combat the insurgent group **ISIS,** the Islamic State in Iraq and Syria, a radical international fundamentalist terror organization. ISIS had gained a foothold in Syria in the wake of an anti-government uprising, and while U.S. efforts succeeded in thwarting ISIS's efforts, the conflict has escalated into a full-scale civil war, which has seen the displacement of over 11 million people.

ISIS

The Islamic State in Iraq and Syria, a radical international fundamentalist terror organization.

THE USE OF THE MILITARY OPTION AFTER THE 9/11 TERROR ATTACKS The military action in the Middle East today is a consequence of foreign policy in the aftermath of the September 11, 2001, terrorist strikes, and the subsequent U.S. government reactions, demonstrating how the creators of foreign policy use the military option as an instrument of foreign policy. Hungry for an enemy after the 2001 deadly attacks on American soil, the United States targeted Afghanistan's Taliban regime. The Taliban had supported and harbored members of al-Qaeda ("The Base"), the radical Islamic fundamentalist terrorist organization that took credit for the 9/11 bloodshed. Foreign intelligence had pointed to Osama bin Laden, a Saudi millionaire living in Afghanistan, as the engineer of the attacks. U.S. military presence in Afghanistan has continued through 2019, with insurgent violence escalating and the United States responding with increased numbers of U.S. troops, in an attempt to quell concern that the Taliban regime will continue to allow anti-U.S. terrorist organizations to operate training camps in unsecured areas of the nation, camps that could train terrorists for missions outside Afghanistan.

A NEW BRAND OF ENEMY: NON-STATE ACTORS   That fear is grounded in the reality that world terrorist activity today transcends national borders. Like ISIS militants today, the September 11 terrorists themselves were not citizen-soldiers of any one country but were nationals from countries across the globe. They had trained in various nations, including Afghanistan, and had been supported by citizens of still other countries. Thus no single, clear nation-state was the enemy. Without a concrete enemy (over which a victory could be defined and declared), the Bush administration requested, and Congress passed, a formal declaration of a "war on terror."

One part of that war on terror included an invasion of Iraq, though that nation had not played a part in the September 11 attacks. But the George W. Bush administration, particularly then-secretary of state Colin Powell, made a case to the United Nations and to the American people alleging that U.S. intelligence indicated that the Saddam Hussein regime in Iraq was harboring **weapons of mass destruction (WMDs)**–nuclear, chemical, and biological weapons.[5] In response to what at the time appeared to be a credible threat, American troops invaded Iraq on March 20, 2003. The military strike toppled the Hussein regime, which the United States had supported for years through foreign aid.[6] Following the invasion, weapons inspectors conducted a thorough search of suspected weapons sites, but no WMDs were ever found, leaving many critics of the Bush administration to question the administration's motives and to ask whether the intelligence community had been pressured by administration officials to find intelligence rationalizing the war in Iraq.[7] From 2003 to 2016, over 4,500 U.S. troops died in Iraq, along with hundreds of other coalition forces and 500,000 Iraqi civilians, a figure that is increasing as insurgent violence continues. In the power vacuum that existed after American troops left Iraq, ISIS was able to seize control in many areas of the nation.

weapons of mass destruction (WMDs)
Nuclear, chemical, and biological weapons.

THE GOAL OF THE MILITARY OPTION   When military conflict occurs on a grand scale–for the United States, that would include the wars in Afghanistan and Iraq, as well as the Gulf War (1990–1991), the Vietnam War (1965–1975), the Korean War (1950–1953), and the two world wars (1914–1918 and 1939–1945), the goal often is **regime change,** the replacement of a country's government with another government by facilitating the deposing of its leader or leading political party. That is, rather than attempting to change another nation's policies, historically wars were typically fought to end the reign of the enemy nations' leaders. On the other hand, most military action by the United States in the past century has occurred on a smaller scale, as policymakers have sought to change the policy in another country, as has been the case with the U.S. air strikes on Syrian targets.

regime change
The replacement of a country's government with another government by facilitating the deposing of its leader or leading political party.

Who Decides? The Creators and Shapers of Foreign Policy

In the United States, the executive and legislative branches are the primary foreign policymakers, with the president and the executive branch playing the dominant role. However, a variety of interests–from the media, to interest groups, to other nations, and even private individuals–provide the context of the foreign policy process and contribute to shaping the policy outcomes of that process.

The President and the Executive Branch

The president of the United States is the foremost foreign policy actor in the world. This vast power derives in part from the president's constitutionally pre-scribed duties, particularly the role of commander in chief of the U.S. armed forces. Presidents' foreign policy powers also have roots in the way the institution of the presidency has evolved and continues to evolve. Other government institutions, especially the U.S. Congress, have some ability to rein in the president's foreign policy authority. But U.S. presidents in the 21st century remain the central figures in the foreign policy arena, owing to presidential resources such as cabinet departments and the national intelligence community, as well as the executive prestige that supplements presidents' legal and administrative powers.

THE DEPARTMENTS OF STATE AND DEFENSE In the executive branch, the Departments of State and Defense take the lead in advising the president about foreign and military policy issues. Specifically, the Department of State, headed by the secretary of state, has more than 30,000 employees located both within the United States and abroad. (State Department employees work at more than 300 U.S. consular offices around the world.) These staff members are organized according to topical specialty (trade policy, environmental policy, and so on) and geographic area specialty (the Middle East or Southeast Asia, for example). Polit-ical appointees hold many of the top ambassadorial posts. These ambassadors and the career members of the foreign service who staff each **country desk**—the official operation of the U.S. government in each country with diplomatic ties to the United States—help to shape and administer U.S. foreign policy in those countries.

> **country desk**
> The official operation of the U.S. government in each country that has diplomatic ties to the United States.

The Department of Defense, often referred to as the Pentagon for its five-sided headquarters, is headed by the secretary of defense. The modern Department of Defense traces its history to the end of World War II, although it is the successor of the Department of War established at the nation's founding. The Defense Department is the cabinet department that oversees all branches of the U.S. mil-itary. Thus, although the Army, Navy, Marines, Air Force, and Coast Guard oper-ate independently, administratively they are part of the Department of Defense. The commanding officers of each branch of the military, plus a chairperson and a vice chairperson, make up the Joint Chiefs of Staff, important military advisers to the president. Increasingly, both the State and the Defense Departments rely on private contractors to perform some functions typically associated with these respective departments, particularly overseas.

THE NATIONAL SECURITY COUNCIL AND THE INTELLIGENCE COMMUNITY As discussed in Chapter 13, the National Security Council, consisting of the vice president, the secretary of state, the secretary of the treasury, the secretary of defense, and the national security adviser, advises and assists the president on national security and foreign policy.

Through the input of the National Security Council, the president's administration considers the country's top security matters. The National Security Council also coordinates foreign policy approaches among the various government agencies that will implement them. A recent addition to the foreign policy apparatus, the national security adviser has traditionally competed with the secretary of state for influence over foreign policy—and for influence over the president as well. The tension between the two advisers also stems from the differing approaches each agency takes in shap-ing foreign policy. Frequently, the State Department has a long-term view of world affairs and advocates for foreign policies in keeping with long-term goals. In contrast, the National Security Council focuses more on short-term crises and objectives.

A key resource in presidential foreign policy making is the intelligence community. Chief among the agencies in this community is the Central Intelligence Agency (CIA). This independent agency of the federal government is responsible for collecting, analyzing, evaluating, and disseminating foreign intelligence to the president and senior national policymakers. Like the National Security Council, the modern CIA was created by the National Security Act of 1947 at the dawn of the Cold War to monitor the actions of the expansionist Soviet Union. During the Cold War, the CIA expanded its mission, using agents to penetrate the governments of foreign countries, influence their politics, and foment insurrections when the president deemed such tactics necessary to promote American interests. At times, particularly after September 11, critics have argued that the agency, along with the Federal Bureau of Investigation (FBI), had failed in their duty to avert the terrorist strikes. Congress scrutinized both agencies for lapses in intelligence and apprehension. Because the CIA and the FBI had been seriously understaffed in Arabic translators, neither agency had the means to interpret intercepted messages that might have enabled them to prevent the tragedy.

Spurred by the 9/11 Commission's findings, President Bush announced in 2005 the appointment of a national intelligence czar, called the **director of national intelligence (DNI).** This individual is responsible for coordinating and overseeing all the intelligence agencies within the executive branch.

> **director of national intelligence (DNI)**
> The person responsible for coordinating and overseeing all the intelligence agencies within the executive branch.

Congress

Along with the president, Congress enjoys significant constitutional authority in foreign policy making. The constitutional provisions that outline congressional authority with respect to foreign relations include, prominently, Congress's power to declare war. In modern times, however, presidential administrations have circumvented this congressional power by using U.S. troops without a formal congressional declaration of war. Such was the case in the Vietnam War, for example.

In response to this presidential tactic, Congress in 1973 passed the **War Powers Act.** This law limits presidential use of military forces to 60 days, with an automatic extension of 30 days if the president requests such an extension. But the nature of modern warfare has quickly made the War Powers Act less effective than in the days of traditional warfare, since most modern warfare is measured in weeks rather than months (the wars in Iraq and Afghanistan being exceptions). Thus it has been possible for modern presidents to wage full-scale wars without congressional involvement.

> **War Powers Act**
> A law that limits presidential use of military forces to 60 days, with an automatic extension of 30 additional days if the president requests such an extension.

But Congress's ability to shape foreign policy does not rest merely with its authority to declare war. Congressional powers with respect to foreign relations also include the authority of the U.S. Senate to ratify treaties, as well as to confirm presidential appointees to ambassadorial posts and to cabinet positions (including those of the secretaries of defense and state). Furthermore, one of Congress's greatest powers is its control of the purse strings. This control means that although the president can order troops into action, the members of Congress must authorize spending for such an operation.

The Military-Industrial Complex

In his farewell address, President Dwight D. Eisenhower (1953–1961), Supreme Allied Commander of Europe during World War II, warned the nation of the influence of the expanding military-industrial complex. Eisenhower stressed that the American people and their representatives in government must "guard against the acquisition of unwarranted influence" and noted that "only an alert and knowledgeable citizenry can compel the proper meshing of the industrial and military machinery of defense with our peaceful methods and goals so that security and liberty may prosper together."[8]

Eisenhower was describing the mutually advantageous—and potentially corrupting—collusion among the U.S. armed forces, the defense industry, and Congress. These three entities have the potential to develop "unwarranted influence" over foreign policy in general and defense spending in particular, for several reasons. First, the goals of the military and the goals of the defense industry often intersect. Consider, for example, the military's need to supply soldiers with the appropriate equipment to fight wars. Both the military complex and the defense industry benefit from doing so: The military wants to protect its troops and help ensure their success on the battleground, and the defense industry seeks to sell such goods to the military—and reap a healthy profit.

A second reason that the military-industrial complex has the potential to be so highly influential is the close personal and professional relationships that flourish between the individuals in the military and their counterparts in the defense industry. These relationships are similar to the associations that develop in the case of iron triangles (see Chapter 15). Indeed, many retired military personnel often put their military expertise to work in "retirement jobs" with defense contractors or as congressional lobbyists.

For many congressional districts throughout the United States, spending by the federal government for military bases, personnel, and defense contracts represents an important infusion of money into the local economy. When this economic influence is combined with the clout members of the military, veterans, their interest groups, and their families can wield, we can see why many members of Congress support the military-industrial complex.

The Media and New Technologies

Because of the pervasiveness and reach of the media, foreign policy decisions provide prime fodder for news reporting. But the media and new technologies go well beyond monitoring and reporting on foreign policy; they also frequently play a role in shaping the country's foreign policy, and in influencing the conduct of that policy.

Since the beginning of the 20th century, the U.S. government has used the news media in an organized way to promote its foreign policy priorities. During World War I, newspapers ran ads calling on Americans to take all kinds of actions to help the war effort, from cleaning their plates and planting "victory gardens" (to conserve food supplies for soldiers) to buying war bonds to help finance the war. By World War II, filmmakers spurred Americans to action, from enlisting in the armed services to conserving food fats and saving scrap metal for the war effort. In those various wartime initiatives, the media worked hand in hand with the government and generally took a highly patriotic and supportive stance. By the era of the Vietnam War, however, journalists, particularly television reporters stationed among U.S. troops in the faraway Asian country, painted a grimmer, more realistic canvas, focusing on the ravages of war that most Americans had never before seen. Today, new technologies can provide a check both on the government and on the media, as private citizens now have the ability to communicate directly with news and Internet platforms, enabling the whole world to watch events across the globe unfold. In this way, citizen activists rely on social media outlets to organize and mobilize across geographic borders.

The news media and technology influence the conduct and substance of foreign policy by increasing public awareness and thus by shaping the foreign policy agenda. This has often been the case throughout Donald Trump's presidency, as he frequently takes to Twitter and heightens awareness of his foreign policy positions, whether concerning North Korea, China, Iran, or even concerning relations with U.S. allies. By focusing public attention on a certain area of the world or on a particular aspect of foreign policy, the media shape the priorities of, and the policies made by, the foreign policy apparatus.

New technologies have also been used as a tool for foreign policymakers, specifically as a means of surveillance against foreign governments, including U.S. allies, but other forms of new technologies, specifically unmanned drones, also have been used in conducting attacks against targets in Afghanistan, Pakistan, Somalia, and Yemen. According to investigative journalist sources, nearly 5,000 U.S. drone attacks have killed as many as 7,500 individuals, nearly 1,000 of them civilians, and as many as 300 children.[9] The media also play a powerful role by serving as a watchdog to ensure that the actions of men and women who implement foreign policy "in the trenches" are consistent with the intentions of policymakers who craft the policies.

Public Opinion

In general, public opinion tends to play a less influential role in shaping specific foreign policies than it does in domestic issues. The public might voice strong opinions and call for politicians to fight terrorism in the wake of the saturated media reporting after a terrorist attack. But in general, people tend to be less concerned, less informed, and less interested in foreign policy matters than in domestic issues. Thus the public at large is likely to accept the views and actions of the individuals who make their country's foreign policy.

Public opinion plays a comparatively small role in shaping foreign policy for several reasons. First, foreign policy is made incrementally, over years and decades, and keeping up with international developments in different parts of the world is not something that many individuals or even news organizations do. Often, international issues must reach crisis proportions before media coverage becomes significant and exerts an impact on public opinion.

Many Americans also feel less connected to foreign policy decisions than they do to domestic policy issues. While individuals may feel empathy for the victims of the refugee crisis, foreign policy crises typically have less bearing on their own lives than, say, whether their mortgage payments will increase because of Federal Reserve policy or whether more student loans will be available to pay their tuition. Despite this disconnect between most people's everyday lives and pressing issues in foreign policy, individuals nonetheless can and do influence foreign policy decisions, as we now consider.

Private Citizens

Individuals can have an impact on the foreign policy process. Consider the various educational exchange programs that arrange for students from one country to visit another. In effect, such visitors act as **public diplomats**–individuals who promote

public diplomat
An individual outside government who promotes his or her country's interests and thus helps to shape international perceptions of the nation.

their country's interests by shaping the host country's perception of their homeland, not only through educational but also through business or entertainment initiatives that advance mutual understanding.

World events can become an influence in American foreign policy, too, when individuals take personal causes that are related to their ethnic origins to the White House and Congress. The influence of domestic interests on foreign policy, called **intermestics,** plays a distinct part in foreign policy making.

A powerful example of intermestics involves the large number of Cuban immigrants in Florida, many of them refugees or descendants of refugees from the regime of Fidel Castro. This influential group effectively swayed U.S. policy toward imposing the embargo against the Castro government and keeping it in effect since 1962, as well as encouraged tightened travel and currency restrictions between the United States and Cuba. But as the revolution generation of immigrants has aged, many younger Cuban Americans hold less pronounced hostility toward Cuba's Castro regime, and they believe that normalizing relations with Cuba will both improve the lot of the Cuban people and bring proximity to openness and democracy, which might in turn plant seeds for reforms that isolationism has failed to bring about.

U.S. Foreign Policy in Historical Context

As those who make and shape U.S. foreign policy continue to confront contemporary challenges, they can look back on two broad historical traditions with respect to American foreign relations: isolationism and intervention. Historically, an initial policy of **isolationism,** a foreign policy characterized by a country's unwillingness to participate in international affairs, gave way to **interventionism,** the willingness of a country to take part and intervene in international situations, including another country's affairs.

The Constitutional Framework and Early Foreign Policy Making

In drafting the Constitution, the founders sought to remove the United States from international affairs. They reasoned that it was best for the new American republic to stay out of the deadly wars that had plagued Europe for centuries and because of which many Americans had left their native lands. Because of that isolationist outlook, the founders structured the Constitution so that responsibility for conducting foreign affairs rests exclusively with the national government rather than with the states.

THE CONSTITUTION AND FOREIGN POLICY POWERS The Constitution provides for shared responsibility for foreign policy making in the national government between the executive and the legislative branches. The Constitution grants the president very specific powers. These include powers related to the role of commander in chief, to making treaties, and to appointing and receiving ambassadors. In comparison, Congress's powers in foreign policy making are broader. Moreover, the Constitution structures executive and legislative powers as complementary. Note that the Constitution provides for checks and balances: although the president is commander in chief, Congress declares war and raises and supports an army and navy. Political scientist Roger Davidson has termed the give-and-take between presidential and congressional power "an invitation to struggle," reflecting the founders' attempt to ensure that neither entity dominates the process.[10]

EARLY ISOLATIONISM   In keeping with the founders' emphasis on isolationism, President George Washington's Farewell Address in 1796 warned the young government against involving the United States in entangling alliances. Washington feared that membership in such international associations would draw a war-weary people and a war-weakened nation into further conflicts. He refused to accept the advice of either his secretary of state, Thomas Jefferson, who favored an alliance with France, or his treasury secretary, Alexander Hamilton, who wanted stronger ties to Great Britain. As a general who knew firsthand about the ravages of war and who also was the first American leader to connect foreign and defense policy, Washington set the tone for the United States' role in the world for the next 200 years.

FOREIGN TRADE AND THE EROSION OF U.S. ISOLATIONISM   During Washington's tenure as president and in the next several successive administrations, the United States' primary activity in the international arena was trade. Rich in natural resources and blessed with an industrious labor force, the United States sought to increase its wealth by selling raw materials and supplies to all sides in the Napoleonic Wars (1792–1815), the latest in the never-ending series of European conflicts. The French Empire took exception to the United States' provision of supplies to its enemies, and when France captured ships that it alleged were bound for enemy ports, the United States was forced into an undeclared naval war with France in the 1790s.

Neutral international trade was a difficult feat to accomplish in the American republic's early years. American ships had to cross sea lanes where neutrality was not the governing principle; instead, pirates, warring nations, and the allies of warring nations controlled the seas, and nationality counted for little. When pirates off the Barbary Coast of Africa seized ships and their crews, which they held for ransom, the United States fought the Barbary Wars (1801–1805 and 1815) against the North African Barbary states (what are now Morocco, Algeria, Tunisia, and Libya).

Throughout the early part of the 19th century, the seas proved a difficult place for American sailors. During that time, the British Navy began the practice of **impressment,** or forcing merchant sailors off U.S. ships—in effect, kidnapping them—on the spurious grounds that American sailors were "deserters" from the British Navy. In protest of this policy, Congress passed the Embargo Act of 1807, which forced U.S. ships to obtain approval from the American government before departing for foreign ports. But the British continued impressments, and the Embargo Act seriously curtailed the amount of U.S. goods being exported. Overall, the Embargo Act harmed the U.S. economy, as the decline in trade spurred more economic woes.

The tensions between the United States and Great Britain escalated as the practice of impressment continued. When the United States sought to increase its territory northward into Canada (then still part of the British Empire), the United States and Great Britain fought the War of 1812 over the United States' desire to

> *Burning of the Frigate Philadelphia in the Harbor of Tripoli, February 16, 1804,* a painting by Edward Moran (1829–1901), shows the USS *Philadelphia* aflame in Tripoli Harbor during the Barbary Wars.
©Universal History Archive/UIG via Getty images

impressment
The forcible removal of merchant sailors from U.S. ships on the spurious grounds that the sailors were deserters from the British Navy.

annex portions of Canada and to put a halt to the practice of impressments. The war was relatively short-lived, ending with the signing of the Treaty of Ghent in 1814, when the British decided that their military resources could be better used against France in the Napoleonic Wars.

Hegemony and National Expansion: From the Monroe Doctrine to the Roosevelt Corollary

After the conclusion of the War of 1812 in 1814 and of the Napoleonic Wars in 1815, peace settled over the United States and Europe. Still, some American politicians feared that European nations—especially France, Spain, and Russia—would attempt to assert or reassert their influence in the Western Hemisphere. Thus, the view arose in American foreign policy-making circles that the United States should establish **hegemony**—a form of imperial geographic dominance—over its own hemisphere. In 1823, President James Monroe declared that "the American continents by the free and independent condition which they have assumed and maintain, are henceforth not to be considered as subjects for future colonization by any European power." Known as the **Monroe Doctrine,** this policy attempted to prevent European nations from colonizing any nations in North or South America. Monroe's declaration, however, sounded more like bravado than policy, because the United States was still too weak militarily to chase a European power away from South America, Central America, or the Caribbean. But the United States' interest in preventing the colonization of the Americas was consistent with the interest of the British, who did not want to see European rivals dominating in the Americas. Thus Monroe's doctrine had the backing of the still-formidable British fleet.

With the Americas out of play, European countries were expanding their colonial empires in Africa and the Middle East during the first half of the 19th century. Meanwhile, the United States also extended its territories westward and solidified its borders. Supporters of the theory of **manifest destiny**—the idea that it was the United States' destiny to expand throughout the North American continent—used this concept to rationalize the spread of U.S. territory. As the philosophy of manifest destiny took hold on the popular imagination, the United States expanded west to the Pacific Ocean, as well as south and southwest.

During this era, too, the United States became increasingly active in profitable international trade, particularly with China and Japan. To facilitate this Pacific trade—which was a primary goal of American policymakers—the United States acquired the islands of Hawaii, Wake, and Midway and part of Samoa in the 1890s. In 1898, on the pretext of ending Spanish abuses in Cuba and instigated by a jingoistic (extremely nationalistic and aggressive) President William McKinley and press, the United States decided to fight Spain, which by then was the weakest of the colonial powers. The United States won the Spanish-American War handily, and the victory increased the country's international prestige.

Theodore Roosevelt, who later became president, achieved enormous national popularity during the Spanish-American War for his leadership of the Rough Riders, a cavalry regiment. Their charge up San Juan Hill in Cuba in 1898 was the war's bloodiest and most famous battle. As spoils, the United States obtained the Philippines, Guam, Puerto Rico, and—temporarily—Cuba from Spain. Roosevelt supported the United States' entry into the war and later, as president (1901–1909), added his own famous dictum to the Monroe Doctrine: the **Roosevelt Corollary.** He announced that to ensure stability in the region, the United States had the right

hegemony
A form of imperial geographic dominance.

Monroe Doctrine
President James Monroe's 1823 declaration that the Americas should not be considered subjects for future colonization by any European power.

manifest destiny
The idea that it was the United States' destiny to spread throughout the North American continent; used to rationalize the expansion of U.S. territory.

Roosevelt Corollary
The idea, advanced by President Theodore Roosevelt, that the United States had the right to act as an "international police power" in the Western Hemisphere to ensure stability in the region.

>The Panama Canal improved the flow of international trade by reducing the length of time ships took to travel between the Atlantic and Pacific Oceans. This is an aerial view of the Gatun Locks.
©Viagens E. Caminhos/Shutterstock

to act as an "international police power" and intervene in Latin America—and indeed, the entire Western Hemisphere—if the situation in any country warranted the intervention of a "civilized society."

After Roosevelt became president, the United States intervened in Panama, where U.S.-backed revolutionaries won independence from Colombia in 1903. The United States then immediately began construction on the Panama Canal in 1904. The canal improved the flow of trade by reducing the length of time ships took to travel between the Atlantic and Pacific Oceans.

World War I and the End of U.S. Isolationism

Encouraged by its successful efforts at colonization and strong enough by this time to ignore George Washington's admonition about avoiding foreign entanglements, the nation became embroiled in two major European wars in the 20th century: World War I and World War II. The United States' isolation from the world ended with these two wars, even though strong isolationist forces in Congress and the White House continued to play a role during the first half of the 20th century.

World War I came about primarily because of the balance of power system that dominated the world's foreign policy decisions from the end of the Napoleonic Wars in 1815 until the conclusion of World War I in 1918. The **balance of power system** was a system of international alliances that, in theory, would balance the power of one group of nations against the power of another group and thus discourage war. So, for example, when it was perceived that England was becoming too powerful in this European balance of power in the 1770s, France, Spain, and Holland assisted the colonial forces in the American Revolution in an effort to bring the British down a notch. For nearly a century, that attempt to bring order to international relations worked, and Europe enjoyed a long period of peace. But a flaw of the balance of power system was that a relatively small skirmish could escalate into a major international incident because of agreements

balance of power system
A system of international alliances that, in theory, would balance the power of one group of nations against the power of another group and thus discourage war.

for **collective defense**—the idea that allied nations agree to defend one another in the face of invasion—that were inherent in the system. Such was the case in 1914 in Sarajevo when a young Bosnian Serb student assassinated Archduke Ferdinand, heir to the Austro-Hungarian throne. The assassin was a member of a group seeking Bosnia's independence from the Austro-Hungarian Empire. The empire demanded that Serbia respond to the assassination, and when it determined that Serbia had not responded, it declared war. Austria-Hungary's declaration of war led to a sweeping domino effect that had the European continent in full-scale war within weeks of that initial declaration because of those alliances and collective defense obligations between nations.

The United States entered World War I in 1917, three years after the conflict began and largely at the behest of Britain. U.S. participation led President Woodrow Wilson to formulate the first conceptual framework for world governance that had ever been articulated. The most effective way to maintain peace, Wilson believed, was through **collective security**—the idea that peace could be achieved if nations agreed to collectively oppose any nation that attacked another country. By using this approach, nations at peace could prevent war by working together to restrain the lawlessness inherent in more unstable parts of the world.

Internationalism and the League of Nations

In negotiating the end of World War I at the Paris Peace Conference, Wilson sought to organize a **League of Nations,** a representative body that would ensure the collective security of nations. Wilson was successful in convincing representatives at the Paris meetings of the need for such an organization. But he was less successful in convincing Congress of the merits of the League of Nations. In 1918, the Republican-controlled Senate (Wilson was a Democrat) refused to ratify the Treaty of Versailles, which included among the terms for ending World War I the formation of the League of Nations. Without the United States, the League died a natural death before being replaced near the end of World War II by the United Nations.

In the dawning days of World War I, the United States was still heeding George Washington's call to avoid entangling alliances. At the war's conclusion, isolationism remained a key tenet of U.S. foreign policy. In the years immediately following the war, trade reasserted itself as the key component of U.S. foreign policy. The Industrial Revolution was in full swing, and the United States depended on the import of raw materials and the export of manufactured goods to grease the wheels of its prosperous economy in the 1920s. During this time, however, Europe was healing from the ravages of World War I, and growth in its manufacturing sector meant serious competition for American industry.

The U.S. economy suffered another blow in 1929 when the stock market crashed, marking the beginning of the Great Depression. And the trade war that resulted from the Smoot-Hawley Tariff exacerbated the Depression, causing industrialists, as well as citizens who saw the economic impact of an isolated United States, to question the isolationism that had characterized U.S. foreign policy to date—from the era of Washington to the era of Smoot-Hawley.

World War II: U.S. Foreign Policy at a Crossroads

World War I was supposed to be the "war to end all wars." In hindsight, however, many observers believed that the victors only sowed the seeds of World War II (1939-1945). By impoverishing the defeated Germany through the imposition of huge reparations (compensation paid by a defeated nation to the victors for war damages) and the loss of 13 percent of its territory, the Treaty of Versailles (1919) created the environment that gave Adolf Hitler, the fascist leader of Germany, the opportunity to succeed politically. With his aggressive foreign policy, Hitler aimed to expand the German homeland at the expense of non-Germanic populations.

Influenced by a strong isolationist group in Congress, the United States waited until two years after the official start of the war in 1939 to declare war. Following a deadly Japanese attack on the U.S. naval base at Pearl Harbor, Hawaii, in December 1941, the United States declared war first on Japan and then on the other Axis powers (Germany and Italy) after those countries declared war on the United States. Following years of fighting on multiple fronts, in August 1945 the United States dropped two atomic bombs on the Japanese cities of Hiroshima and Nagasaki. Those devastating attacks ended the war.

The question remains whether the United States would have joined the efforts of the Allies (the United States, England, France, China, and the Soviet Union) sooner had policymakers known about the **Holocaust**—the murder by Hitler and his subordinates of six million Jews, along with political dissidents, Catholics, homosexuals, individuals with disabilities, and gypsies. Newspapers did not report the genocide until 1943, well after the war was under way. The experience of fighting World War II and dealing with its aftermath forced U.S. policymakers to reassess the country's role in the world, as well as the policies that governed its entire approach to foreign affairs.

Holocaust
The genocide perpetrated by Adolf Hitler and the Nazis of six million Jews, along with political dissidents, Catholics, homosexuals, individuals with disabilities, and gypsies.

The Postwar Era: The United States as Superpower

The post–World War II era saw the emergence of two of the Allied victors, the United States and the Soviet Union, as **superpowers**—leader nations with dominating influence in international affairs. The United States' role as superpower in a new international system, and the relationship between these superpowers, would shape America's foreign policy for the remainder of the 20th century. Increasingly important in this new era was the role that **multilateral** (many-sided, or supported by numerous nations) organizations and agreements would play.

superpowers
Leader nations with dominating influence in international affairs.

multilateral
Many-sided; having the support of numerous nations

International Agreements and Organizations

In the aftermath of World War II, the United States was intent on avoiding the mistakes of the Treaty of Versailles, which many policymakers felt had led directly to the conditions that produced the war. They proceeded to address those mistakes one by one, often forming international organizations equipped to respond to the public policy challenges confronting the postwar world.

A key component of the postwar recovery effort was the **Marshall Plan.** Named for Secretary of State George Marshall, the program provided the funds necessary for Western European countries—even the United States' enemies during World War II—to rebuild. War-ravaged nations, including defeated (West) Germany, soon became economic powerhouses, thanks to initial help from the Marshall Plan. Ironically, by forcing the Germans to demilitarize as a condition of their surrender, the Allies freed Germany from spending large amounts of its own tax money on defense, thus enabling the German people to devote more of their resources to

Marshall Plan
The U.S. government program that provided funds necessary for Western European countries to rebuild after World War II.

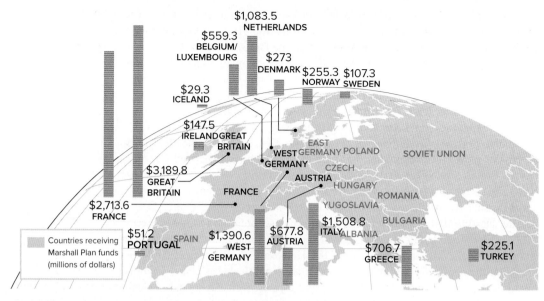

FIGURE 18.1 ■ Recipients of Marshall Plan Aid, 1948–1951

SOURCE: CNN, Cold War 3/24, Marshall Plan

economic development. Other countries impoverished by war also benefited from the Marshall Plan (Figure 18.1), creating new markets for U.S. products. Eastern European nations, now securely under Soviet influence, were prevented from participating. Because of the plan's success in Western Europe, the United States recognized that economic development and peace were intertwined, that economic stability was critical if future wars were to be prevented, and that an international approach was preferable to isolationism in foreign policy.

THE UNITED NATIONS   The Allied victors of World War II recognized the need for a structure to ensure collective security. In that spirit, U.S. officials organized a meeting in San Francisco in 1945 with 50 U.S. allies, all of whom agreed to create the **United Nations (UN).** Participants hoped that this international body, through collective security, would develop the capacity to prevent future wars. The charter of the United Nations created these components:

United Nations (UN)

An international body established in 1945 in order to prevent future wars by achieving collective security and peace.

- *United Nations (UN):* established in 1945, an international body intended to prevent future wars by achieving collective security and peace.
- *Security Council:* 11 members, 5 of which—including the United States, the Soviet Union (now Russia), China, Great Britain, and France—are permanent members with the power to veto any action taken by the council. Today, the Security Council consists of 15 members, with the permanent members and their veto power remaining unchanged.
- *General Assembly:* consisting of all the member nations, each with a single vote (in 1945, there were 51 member nations; today there are 193).
- *Secretariat:* headed by a secretary-general with a staff at UN headquarters in New York City. The secretary-general in 2019 is Antonio Guterres of Portugal.
- Several specialized organizations to handle specific public policy challenges, including the Economic and Social Council, the Trusteeship Council, and the International Court at The Hague.

The United Nations' mission includes the promotion of economic and social development. Since its founding, it has added peacekeeping to its functions and has had some limited success in that endeavor in areas of the former Yugoslavia, the Middle East, and Africa. But in the immediate post–World War II era, the ability of the United Nations in general, and of the Security Council in particular, to provide for collective security was seriously undermined by the Soviet Union's presence on the Security Council. Because the Soviet Union was a permanent member with veto power, any attempt by the Security Council to thwart Soviet aggression was blocked by the Soviets' veto.

NATO It did not take long for the United States and the Western democracies to be disappointed by the inability of the United Nations to provide for collective security. The UN's failure to halt the militaristic expansion of the Soviet sphere of influence particularly troubled them. Their frustrations led the United States and its Western allies to attempt to bring order to international relations through the creation of regional security alliances. **Regional security alliances** typically involve a superpower and nations that are ideologically similar in a particular area of the world.

>At the United Nations, heads of state, including Russian Prime Minister Vladimir Putin and UN delegates, discuss policies, including global policy and economic strategy. Here Putin addresses the UN Security Council.
©Drew Angerer/Getty Images

The first regional security alliance was the **North Atlantic Treaty Organization (NATO).** Established in 1949, NATO created a structure for regional security for its 15 member nations through a declaration that "an armed attack against one or more NATO nations . . . shall be considered an attack against them all."[11] Through the formation of NATO, the United States made a specific commitment to defend Western Europe in the event of a Soviet attack. In response to the creation of NATO, the Soviet Union and its seven satellite states in Eastern Europe formed a similar regional security alliance, the **Warsaw Pact,** in 1955.

Both NATO and the Warsaw Pact reflected the tensions and the rivalry that existed between the United States and the Soviet Union. They also reflected the failure of the United Nations to provide for collective security, that is, the security of *all* nations. Instead, the regional security alliances more closely resembled the balance of power alliances established after the Napoleonic Wars.

NATO's role as a structure for regional security was highlighted in 2014, when Russia annexed Crimea, which had been part of the Ukraine. Stationing 40,000 troops along the border with Ukraine, Russia evoked fears that it intended to annex more of the Ukraine, or even parts of Eastern European and Baltic nations. In response to Russia's actions in Crimea, NATO ceased practical cooperation with Russia and drew up plans to reinforce NATO's defenses in NATO member states in the area.

regional security alliance
An alliance typically between a superpower and nations that are ideologically similar in a particular region.

North Atlantic Treaty Organization (NATO)
An international mutual defense alliance formed in 1949 that created a structure for regional security for its 15 member nations.

Warsaw Pact
A regional security structure formed in 1955 by the Soviet Union and its seven satellite states in Eastern Europe in response to the creation of the North Atlantic Treaty Organization (NATO).

INTERNATIONAL FINANCIAL ORGANIZATIONS In addition to establishing the United Nations and NATO for the purposes of conflict management and security, the United States recognized the need to relinquish a great deal of its own economic power in exchange for the economic stability that would come from international financial institutions. Doing so would benefit the global economy in general but also the U.S. economy in particular.

To that end, in 1944, an international agreement made in Bretton Woods, New Hampshire—the Bretton Woods Agreement—established the **International Monetary Fund (IMF).** The meeting delegates charged the newly created international financial institution with regulating monetary relationships among nations. One of the IMF's key purposes was to establish exchange rates for currencies, determining, for example, how many dollars a British pound or a Japanese yen was worth. To the present day, IMF member states provide the resources the IMF needs to operate through a formula by which nations pay amounts roughly proportional to the size of their economies. Based on these IMF contribution quotas, nations are allocated votes proportional to their contributions. Thus the IMF perpetuates the dominance of the high-contributing economic powerhouses. Today, the United States has more than 17 percent of the IMF votes. The Bretton Woods agreement also established the institution that would become the **World Bank,** which initially focused on lending money to countries devastated in World War II. Today, the World Bank lends money to developing nations to help them become self-sufficient.

Still reeling from the effects of high tariffs on international trade during the Depression, the United States also encouraged an international agreement that would heal the economies of nations by lowering tariffs and promoting international trade. In 1948, 23 nations signed the General Agreement on Tariffs and Trade (GATT). The GATT is based on the most favored nation principle.

In 1995, the **World Trade Organization (WTO)** replaced the GATT. Whereas the GATT was a series of agreements among nations, the WTO is an actual organization that negotiates, implements, and enforces international trade agreements. Today, the WTO consists of 159 member nations. Although it has a one-nation, one-vote policy, this policy is moot because the largest economies have the greatest say. The organization's goal—to remove all types of trade barriers, including obstacles to investment—is more ambitious than that of the GATT.

The Cold War: Superpowers in Collision

During World War II, the United States, Great Britain, and the Soviet Union were allies against the Nazis. But events at the wartime Yalta Conference in 1945 sowed the seeds of what would become known as the Cold War. The **Cold War** refers to the political, ideological, and military conflict that lasted from 1945 until 1990 between the Soviet Union and its allies, and the United States and its allies. The causes of the Cold War included the competing desires to have dominant influence in Europe, as well as the fundamental dispute between communist versus capitalist economic systems.

Each leader came to the Yalta Conference with an agenda. The United States' Franklin D. Roosevelt needed Soviet help in battling Japan in the naval wars of the Pacific. England's Winston Churchill sought democratic elections in Eastern Europe. And Soviet premier Joseph Stalin wanted Eastern Europe as a Soviet sphere of influence, arguing that the Soviet Union's national security depended on its hegemony in the region.

International Monetary Fund (IMF)
The institution charged with regulating monetary relationships among nations, including establishment of exchange rates for major world currencies; established in 1944 by the Bretton Woods Agreement.

World Bank
The international financial institution created by the Bretton Woods Agreement of 1944 and charged with lending money to nations in need.

World Trade Organization (WTO)
The organization created in 1995 to negotiate, implement, and enforce international trade agreements.

Cold War
The political, ideological, and military conflict that lasted from 1945 until 1990 between communist nations led by the Soviet Union and Western democracies led by the United States.

>In 1945, British prime minister Winston Churchill, U.S. president Franklin Roosevelt, and Soviet premier Joseph Stalin each attended the Yalta Conference with an agenda. Roosevelt was seeking Soviet help in battling Japan; Churchill wanted democracy in Eastern Europe; Stalin wanted Eastern Europe as a Soviet sphere of influence. The results of the Yalta Conference shaped the global relations for decades to come.

©Public Record Office/HIP/The Image Works

At the conference, Stalin agreed to allow free elections in the region, but he later broke that promise. In response, former British prime minister Churchill warned Americans in a 1946 speech that the Soviets were dividing Europe with an "Iron Curtain." Churchill's characterization was accurate, because Stalin's brutal dictatorship, combined with the force of the Soviet Red Army, would install a communist government in every Eastern European nation. When Stalin also refused to cooperate in the planned cooperative allied occupation of Germany, the result was the division of Germany into separate zones, one administered by the Soviet Union and the other three by the United States, Great Britain, and France. In 1947, when the Soviets backed communist guerrillas who were attempting to take over Greece and Turkey, U.S. president Harry Truman (1945–1953) committed the United States to "support free people who are resisting attempted subjugation by armed minorities or by outside pressures."[12] This policy—the United States' foreign policy commitment to assist efforts to resist communism—was called the **Truman Doctrine.**

U.S. Efforts to Contain Communism: Korea, Cuba, and Vietnam

The Truman Doctrine reflected the ideas of George F. Kennan, the State Department's Soviet expert at the time. Specifically, Kennan advocated the principle of **containment,** the policy of preventing the spread of communism, mainly by providing military and economic aid as well as political advice to

Truman Doctrine
Articulated by President Harry Truman, a foreign policy commitment by the United States to assist countries' efforts to resist communism in the Cold War era.

containment
The Cold War–era policy of preventing the spread of communism, mainly by providing military and economic aid as well as political advice to countries vulnerable to a communist takeover.

beleaguered countries that were vulnerable to communist takeover. Kennan argued: "It is clear that the main element of any United States policy toward the Soviet Union must be that of a long-term vigilant containment of Russian expansive tendencies."[13] The idea of containment would spur the United States to fight in two protracted wars, the Korean War and the Vietnam War, to contain communism.

THE KOREAN WAR, 1950–1953 The first military effort the United States engaged in to check the spread of communism occurred in 1950. In June of that year, North Korea, with the backing of Stalin and the Soviet Union, invaded South Korea in an attempt to reunify the Korean peninsula under communism. During that summer, the United States sent in forces as part of a UN force to help the South Koreans repel the attack. The defensive strategy quickly succeeded, but by October the United States changed military strategy. Instead of merely containing the spread of communism, the United States sought to reunify North and South Korea—and, in doing so, to depose the communists from North Korea. But as U.S. and South Korean forces edged north, they also came closer and closer to the North Korea–China border.

That October, China, wary of a potential invasion, came to the aid of fellow communists in North Korea. The two countries' combined forces repelled the UN forces back to the 38th parallel, the original border between North and South Korea. Over the next two years, U.S. forces (as part of the UN contingent), North and South Koreans, and Chinese soldiers would continue to do battle, with very little territory changing hands. When an armistice was reached in July 1953, the border established was the 38th parallel—exactly what it had been before the war—although a demilitarized zone (DMZ) was created.

The Korean War marked an escalation and expansion of the Cold War. Not only was the war the first occasion in which the two superpowers clashed militarily, but it also brought the Cold War outside the boundaries of Europe. Significantly, the outbreak of the Korean War also gave rise to the concept of **limited war**—a combatant country's self-imposed limitation on the tactics and strategy it uses, particularly its avoidance of the deployment of nuclear weapons. The idea of limited war would set the stage for subsequent conflicts.

limited war
A combatant country's self-imposed limitation on the tactics and strategy it uses, particularly its avoidance of the use of nuclear weapons.

THE CUBAN MISSILE CRISIS, 1962 Another tactic of U.S. foreign policy during the Cold War was brinkmanship, a term coined by John Foster Dulles, the secretary of state under President Dwight D. Eisenhower (1953–1961). In essence, **brinkmanship** meant fooling the enemy by going to the edge (the brink), even if the party employing brinkmanship had no intention of following through to its logical conclusion.

The Cuban Missile Crisis in October 1962 turned out to be a perfect example of brinkmanship, even though that was not the intention of President John F. Kennedy (1961–1963). Reacting to Soviet premier Nikita Khrushchev's decision to put ballistic missiles in Cuba, Kennedy imposed a naval blockade around that island nation 94 miles off the coast of Florida, and warned the Soviet Union to withdraw its missiles, or else—never specifying what he meant by "or else." Although this confrontation seemed like brinkmanship, it was no bluff; rather, it was an act of bravado that could easily have led to nuclear war. Luckily for the United States and the rest of the world, the Soviets backed down, withdrew their missiles, and entered a period of improved relations with the United States.[14]

brinkmanship
The Cold War–era practice of fooling the enemy by going to the edge (the brink), even if the party using the brinkmanship strategy had no intention of following through.

THEN

NOW

> Since 1953, soldiers from South Korea and the United States on one side and North Korean soldiers on the other have patrolled the military demarcation line separating North and South Korea. Since the historic summit between South Korean President Moon Jae In (R) and North Korean leader Kim Jong Un, there is hope that relations between North and South Korea can be normalized. Paramount to that process would be denuclearization on the part of North Korea.

Soldiers: ©Ute Grabowsky/Photothek via Getty Images; *Leaders:* ©Kyodo News via Getty Images

THE VIETNAM CONFLICT, 1965–1975   The United States' involvement in the war in Vietnam was motivated in large part by policymakers' acceptance of the **domino theory,** the principle that if one nation fell to communism, other nations in its geographic vicinity would also succumb. As described by President Eisenhower, "You have broader considerations that might follow what you would call the 'falling domino' principle. You have a row of dominoes set up, you knock over the first one, and what will happen to the last one is the certainty that it will go over very quickly. So you could have a beginning of a disintegration that would have the most profound influences."[15]

And so the United States again sought to contain the spread of communism in Southeast Asia. Although Vietnam was not of particular strategic importance to the United States, it represented the second "domino" in the faraway region. U.S. involvement in Vietnam started in the late 1950s, and by 1963, the United States became enmeshed in an all-out ground, naval, and air war there. The United States supported the South Vietnamese against the North Vietnamese in the decade-long civil war that would take the lives of almost 60,000 U.S. soldiers and at least 3 million Vietnamese soldiers and civilians. On April 29, 1975, when the South Vietnamese capital, Saigon, fell to the North Vietnamese Vietcong forces, the event marked the first military failure by the United States in its efforts to contain communism.

domino theory
The principle that if one nation fell to communism, other nations in its geographic vicinity also would succumb.

Détente: A Thaw in the Cold War Chill

Richard M. Nixon (1969–1974) was elected to the presidency in 1968, largely on his promise to end the war in Vietnam. Although several years would pass before the war actually ended, Nixon's approach to the top foreign policy issues of the day marked a departure from that of his predecessors. Specifically, the **Nixon Doctrine** emphasized the responsibility of U.S. allies to provide for their own national defense and security and sought to improve relations with the two communist world powers, the Soviet Union and China. As early as 1970, his administration sought

Nixon Doctrine
Policy emphasizing the responsibility of U.S. allies to provide for their own national defense and security, aimed at improving relations with the communist nations, including the Soviet Union and China.

>The United States supported the South Vietnamese against the North Vietnamese in the decade-long civil war that took the lives of almost 60,000 U.S. soldiers, who are memorialized on the Vietnam War Memorial in Washington, D.C. Three million Vietnamese soldiers and civilians also died in the conflict. Here, family members of a soldier killed in action find his name on the monument.
©Joe Raedle/Getty Images

détente
The easing of tensions between the United States and its communist rivals.

mutual assured destruction (MAD)
The doctrine that if one nation attacked another with nuclear weapons, the other would be capable of retaliating and would retaliate with such force as to ensure mutual annihilation.

deterrence
The idea that nations would be less likely to engage in nuclear war if adversaries each had first-strike capability.

strategic arms limitation talks (SALT talks)
Discussions between the United States and the Soviet Union in the 1970s that focused on cooling down the nuclear arms race between the two superpowers.

détente, or the easing of tensions between the United States and its communist rivals. In keeping with this idea, the Nixon administration normalized diplomatic relations with China and began a series of nuclear arms control talks that would occur throughout the 1970s. Critics of the Nixon Doctrine argued that President Nixon's approach to foreign policy was accommodationist—that it sought the easy solution and ignored the moral and philosophical implications of improving relations between the Western democracies and their communist rivals.

Part of the motivation for détente was the recognition that any escalation of tensions between the superpowers would increase the probability of nuclear war. Since the early 1960s, the United States and the Soviet Union had engaged in a nuclear arms race in which each country attempted to surpass the other's nuclear capability. According to the doctrine of **mutual assured destruction (MAD),** if one nation attacked another with nuclear weapons, the other would be capable of retaliating, and *would* retaliate, with such force as to ensure mutual annihilation. The goal of the arms race (which would continue through the 1980s) was first-strike capability, meaning that each nation sought the ability to use nuclear weapons against the other nation and to eliminate the possibility of that nation's retaliating in a second-strike attack.

Many foreign policymakers in both the United States and the Soviet Union believed in the power of **deterrence,** the idea that nations would be less likely to engage in nuclear war if the adversaries each had first-strike capability. But Nixon and his primary foreign policy adviser, Henry Kissinger (who served first as Nixon's national security adviser and then as his secretary of state), sought negotiations with the Soviets that would dampen the arms race.

SALT I AND SALT II In 1972, the United States and the Soviet Union concluded two and a half years of **strategic arms limitation talks (SALT talks)** that focused on cooling the superheated nuclear arms race between the two superpowers. The resulting treaty, SALT I, limited the two countries' antiballistic missiles and froze the number of offensive missiles that each nation could have. The SALT II treaty set an overall limit on all strategic nuclear launchers and limited the number of missiles that could carry multiple independently targeted reentry vehicles (MIRVs) with nuclear warheads.

Later in 1979, however, the Soviet Union invaded Afghanistan, sparking a new round of U.S-Soviet tensions. In response, President Jimmy Carter withdrew the SALT II treaty from consideration for ratification by the Senate. Nevertheless, Carter announced (as did his successor, Ronald Reagan) that the United States would abide by all the terms of SALT II as long as the Soviet Union complied as well. During his one term in office, Carter also sought to engage the world in a campaign for human rights, while attempting to convert the vast U.S. military apparatus to peacetime functions—a policy known as **defense conversion.**

defense conversion
President Jimmy Carter's attempt to convert the nation's vast military apparatus to peacetime functions.

The Reagan Years and Soviet Collapse

Ronald Reagan's presidency (1981–1989) marked a pivotal time in U.S.-Soviet relations. On the one hand, the Reagan administration pushed for a *reduction* in missiles and nuclear warheads, not merely a limitation on increases. Because of this new direction, Reagan named these arms reduction talks the **strategic arms reduction talks (START talks).** Despite this overture, the Reagan administration was passionate in the pursuit of a ballistic missile defense system, called the **strategic defense initiative (SDI, or "Star Wars").** In protest of the development of this system, the Soviet Union walked out of the START meeting in 1983. The two superpowers would return to the table in 1985, after Reagan won reelection with a resounding victory.

strategic arms reduction talks (START talks)
Talks between the United States and the Soviet Union in which reductions in missiles and nuclear warheads, not merely a limitation on increases, were negotiated.

strategic defense initiative (SDI, or "Star Wars")
A ballistic missile defense system advocated by President Ronald Reagan.

In 1987, the United States and the Soviet Union signed the Intermediate-Range Nuclear Forces Treaty (INF), the first agreement that resulted in the destruction of nuclear weapons. It eliminated an entire class of weapons—those with an intermediate range of between 300 and 3,800 miles. A pathbreaking treaty, the INF shaped future arms control talks. It provided for reductions in the number of nuclear weapons, established the principle of equality because both nations ended up with the same number of weapons (in this case, zero), and, through the establishment of on-site inspections, provided a means of verifying compliance.

In retrospect, many analysts credit the Soviet Union's eventual collapse to President Reagan. During his tenure, Reagan ratcheted up the rhetoric with his many speeches referring to the Soviet Union as "the Evil Empire." Under his administration, the U.S. defense budget also doubled, with much of the expenditure going toward the SDI. The Soviets reacted with fear and a surge in spending. These developments all came at a time when the Soviet Union was dealing with unrest in 15 republics that eventually would secede. The last straw, however, was the country's troubled economy, because to compete with the U.S. ballistic missile system, the Soviet Union had to increase its military budget to the point where its economy collapsed—and with it, the government.

Post-Soviet Times: The United States as Solo Superpower in an Era of Wars

The START talks, which had resumed in 1985, resulted in a long-awaited agreement that reduced the number of long-range strategic nuclear weapons to 3,000 for each side. In 1991, the agreement was signed by U.S. president George H. W.

THEN NOW NEXT

Defining U.S. Foreign Policy

Then (1984)	Now
The Cold War was the defining feature of U.S. foreign policy.	U.S. foreign policy is being reshaped with ongoing crises in the Middle East and Asia, and a resurgence in the aggressiveness of Russia.
The United States and the Soviet Union competed as the two world superpowers.	A rapidly changing global context means that the United States competes for its world power status, along with China, Russia, and the European Union.
The arms race resulted in unprecedented military spending.	Military spending has increased as President Trump has prioritized new ships for the U.S. Navy, funding for a fighter-jet program, and increased missile-defense spending.

WHAT'S NEXT?

> What new realities will shape U.S. foreign and national defense policy?

> Will the United States continue as the world's only superpower? How will a superpower be defined in the future? Will the term refer to military or economic might or a combination of these (and/or other) factors?

> What impact will continued military spending have on the U.S. and global economy?

Bush and Soviet president Mikhail Gorbachev, whose tenure had ushered in the ideas of *glasnost* (openness) and *perestroika* (economic restructuring) in the Soviet Union. That same year, the Soviet Union broke apart, and Russia democratically elected its president, Boris Yeltsin. Upon Yeltsin's election, in another series of talks called START II, Yeltsin agreed to even deeper cuts in nuclear weapons. The START II agreement of 1992 between the superpowers was fully implemented in 2003 and significantly decreased the likelihood of a massive nuclear attack.

As a result of the breakup of the Soviet Union, a whole new order emerged in Eastern Europe, with the Balkan nations of Latvia, Lithuania, and Estonia reasserting their independence, and an additional 15 former Soviet republics establishing independent states. These sweeping changes meant a changed role for NATO, which in 1999 expanded to include Poland, Hungary, and the Czech Republic in the organization, over the objections of Russia. In 2004, another seven countries in central and Eastern Europe—Estonia, Latvia, Lithuania, Slovenia, Slovakia, Bulgaria, and Romania—joined NATO. Five years later, in 2009, Albania and Croatia also became members of the collective security alliance, in which each member nation pledges protection should any member of NATO be attacked.

The 1990s proved to be a watershed era in global relations in both Asia and Europe. In Asia, China emerged as a world power and has continued to increase its influence on the world stage. In Europe, the Maastricht Treaty, signed in 1992, paved the way for the formation of the European Union. The European Union is a political and economic alliance that prioritizes peace in Europe based on economic cooperation and stability. What started out as an economic union between six nations has grown into an enormous single market in which citizens of the 28 member states can move freely between states, and all members use a single currency, the euro. While Great Britain voted in 2016 to exit the EU (the so-called Brexit vote), there has relatively little fallout from that decision, with other European nations not following suit.

The 1990s also proved to be a novel time in U.S. foreign relations. For the first time in over half a century, the United States was without an enemy, and it found itself the world's lone superpower. The tumult following the collapse of communism ushered in an era of wars—many of them fueled by long-standing ethnic rivalries or disputes—and the creation of new borders and new nations. By the start of the new century, 14 wars were going on around the globe. Some, such as the decades-long conflict in Northern Ireland, now seem to be resolved. Others seemed intractable, such as the conflict in the Middle East over the Palestinian question. Still others, such as the tribal wars in Africa, were all too often manipulated by foreign interests and by corrupt indigenous leaders who were reluctant to give up their power. And other events—such as fighting that erupted between UN and U.S. forces against Somali militia fighters loyal to warlord Mohamed Farrah Aidid in 1993; the 1998 attacks on U.S. embassies in Nairobi, Kenya, and Dar es Salaam, Tanzania; and the 2000 suicide bombing of the U.S. Navy guided missile destroyer USS *Cole* in the port of Aden, Yemen—were harbingers of clashes to come. It was as if a giant hand had lifted a rock at the end of the Cold War, freeing long-submerged problems to crawl out and presenting new challenges for U.S. foreign policymakers as the United States assumed its role as the world's leader.

U.S. Foreign Policy in the 21st Century

U.S. foreign policymakers' challenges in the 1990s pale in comparison with those they have faced since the terrorist attacks of September 11, 2001. The incidents on that day have profoundly defined and determined recent American foreign policy.

The Bush Doctrine: A Clash of Civilizations

One prism for viewing the September 11 attacks is that posited by political scientist Samuel P. Huntington. He asserts that "the clash of civilizations will be the battle lines of the future."[16] Huntington's **clash of civilizations thesis** asserts that bitter cultural conflict will continue and escalate between modern Western democracies, whose culture emphasizes values rooted in democracy and capitalism, and fundamentalist Islamic states, where traditional values grounded in religious beliefs dominate. Huntington, whose thesis remains controversial, argues that the ideological divisions that characterized the 20th century—the clash between communism and democratic capitalism, for example—will be replaced by an older source of conflict: cultural and religious identity. Huntington initially posited his ideas in 1993, and his theories seemed particularly relevant during the 1990s when ethnic and religious warfare broke out in Bosnia and in parts of Africa. After September 11, 2001, Huntington's neoconservative theory appears to have significantly shaped the foreign policy of both George W. Bush and Donald Trump.

Huntington's clash of civilizations thesis provides one explanation of *why* contemporary U.S. foreign policy has focused on the areas that it has. President George W. Bush himself articulated his views on the *how* of that policy's implementation. According to the **Bush Doctrine,** the United States has a responsibility to further the spread of democracy and create a global order that ensures the security of the United States and its allies, even if it means that the United States acts alone. This unilateral action, according to the Bush Doctrine, is both justifiable and feasible. The Bush Doctrine also asserted that the United States should use its role as the world's only remaining superpower to spread democracy and to create conditions of security that will benefit itself and its allies.

clash of civilizations thesis
Samuel Huntington's idea that bitter cultural conflict will continue and escalate between modern Western democracies and fundamentalist Islamic states.

Bush Doctrine
The argument, articulated by President George W. Bush, that unilateral action directly targeted at an enemy is both justifiable and feasible.

MAJOR U.S. TROOP DEPLOYMENTS OVERSEAS

Deployment numbers as of Sept. 2017

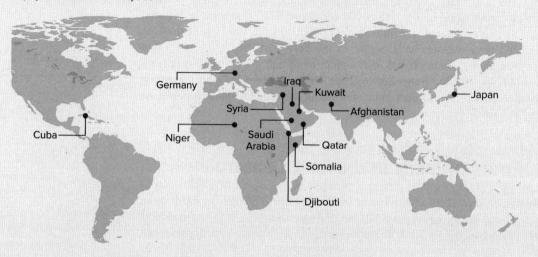

Country	Troops in September 2017	Change in Troops from December 2016	How the U.S. Is Involved Here
Japan	44,925	5,299 ↑	Largest number of U.S. forces based in any foreign country
Germany	36,145	−269 ↓	Largest number of U.S. forces in a European country
Kuwait	16,197	3,332 ↑	The Largest concentration of U.S. forces in the Middle East and the Gulf
Afghanistan	15,298	4,162 ↑	Battling the Taliban
Iraq	8,892	2,080 ↑	Bombing campaign against ISIS
Qatar	6,567	1,567 ↑	Home to a U.S. air base that carries out strikes throughout the region
Djibouti	4,694	1,085 ↑	Home to the one permanent U.S. base in Africa
Syria	1,720	1,442 ↑	Bombing campaign against ISIS
Cuba	900	−33 ↓	U.S. forces at Guantánamo Bay
Saudi Arabia	634	207 ↑	U.S. Air Base houses security forces that work with Saudi host forces
Niger	546	539 ↑	U.S. special ops forces advise local troops battling Boko Haram and al Oaeda
Somalia	289	151 ↑	Taking part in fight against al-Shabab militia

Notes
Troop numbers include active-duty, National Guard, and reserve troops, but not Department of Defense civilian personnel or civilian contractors.

SOURCE: "Under Trump, U.S. Troops In War Zones Are on the Rise," NPR.

Since President Trump was sworn into office in January 2017, the number of U.S. troops deployed around the world has increased. Most of the troops stationed abroad are engaged in peacetime missions, and those engaged in tactical missions are primarily involved in air campaigns or training of local allied forces. While the number of troops stationed abroad is much lower than the 200,000 who were stationed abroad when the United States was involved in boots-on-the-ground conflicts in Iraq and Afghanistan, the president's policy shift can be seen in the figure.

Practice Analytical Thinking

1. Where are the majority of U.S. troops stationed abroad? In general, what has been the trend regarding the number of troops stationed in these places since President Trump took office?

2. In which countries are U.S. troops involved in war time actions? What has been the trend regarding the number of troops stationed in these places since President Trump took office?

3. Which countries have seen the largest proportional increase in troops? Are these forces involved in peace time or war time actions?

WAR IN AFGHANISTAN The United States' first response to the 9/11 attacks was based on the connection of Osama bin Laden and the al-Qaeda terror network to the masterminding and execution of those attacks. For several years before the September 11 attacks, the fundamentalist Taliban regime in Afghanistan had allowed al-Qaeda training camps to operate in that country. In retaliation for the terror strikes, in late 2001 the United States, a coalition of allies, and anti-Taliban rebels from within Afghanistan attacked the training camps and the Taliban government itself. Within weeks the Taliban government fell.

The multilateral forces worked to create first an interim government in Afghanistan and then, in 2004, a democratically elected government. Attacks from Taliban insurgents continue, and about 15,000 American troops were stationed in Afghanistan in late 2018, nearly double the number present in 2017 (see "Analyzing the Sources"). Toppling the Taliban regime proved easier than creating peace in Afghanistan, where government officials and everyday citizens who participate in civic life are routinely targeted by terrorist organizations, including the Taliban, Haqqani Network, and ISIS.

WAR IN IRAQ After the Taliban's fall, President Bush set his sights on changing another regime: that of Iraq's Saddam Hussein. During the presidency of Bush's father, George H. W. Bush (1989–1993), the United States had gone to war with Iraq when that country invaded Kuwait, an ally of the United States. During the younger Bush's 2003 State of the Union address, the president claimed that Iraq possessed weapons of mass destruction and said that the Iraqis were attempting to purchase the components of nuclear weapons. In the ensuing weeks, the Bush administration made a case for going to war with Hussein's regime to both the UN Security Council and the American people. In doing so, Bush introduced the concept of **preventive war,** the strategy of waging war on countries regarded as threatening to the United States in order to avoid future conflicts.

preventive war
The strategy of waging war on countries that are regarded as threatening in order to avoid future conflicts.

The concept of preventive war represents a shift in policy from responding to attacks to anticipating attacks. The idea of preventive war is in part an outgrowth of the drastically altered nature of warfare. The biological, chemical, and nuclear weapons of today can cross borders with far deadlier efficiency than troops, ships, or aircraft. In addition, U.S. enemies no longer declare themselves as openly as they did before. The national defense policymakers who advocate preventive war thus argue that the only way to defend the country against these various new threats is to invade *before* the fact, in hopes of deterring another attack.

The invasion of Iraq in March 2003 was initially successful in toppling Saddam Hussein's regime. Despite insurgency violence that prevented peace from taking root, elections were finally held in 2004 and 2005, and power officially passed to an elected government. In the face of continued violence, the Bush administration enacted a military surge policy, resulting in the addition of more than 20,000 troops in Baghdad and Al Anbar Province. The surge strategy was credited with temporarily quelling much of the insurgent violence in these areas. Unfortunately, violence has greatly increased in recent years, so that today Iraq is in the midst of a full-blown civil war.

Nation building in Iraq proved troublesome—far more so than the rebuilding of Japan after World War II, for example. There, U.S. general Douglas MacArthur undertook the task of reconstructing the nation and creating a system of democratic self-governance. It took four years, but when MacArthur left for duty in Korea, Japan was as close to democracy as any Far Eastern country. Japan's feudal aristocracy was abolished, the country had a new constitution that empowered the legislature to make laws, civil liberties and collective bargaining were guaranteed, the legal equality of the sexes was established, and citizens had been given the right of *habeas corpus* (a petition that allows a prisoner to go to a court where a judge will determine whether he or she is being held illegally). MacArthur also suspended banks that had financed the war, destroyed (at least temporarily) the giant monopolies, and refused to allow "war profiteers" to invade Japan at the expense of local businesses.

> In the United States' crosshairs for over a decade, Osama bin Laden, mastermind of the September 11, 2001, terror attacks, was caught and killed in Abbottabad, Pakistan, in 2011. The terror attacks, and the U.S. response to them, have been the defining feature of U.S. foreign policy since they occurred.

©Aqeel Ahmed/AP Images

Fifty years later, as the United States sought to rebuild Iraq's war-torn infrastructure and feed its people after toppling Hussein's regime, a powerful insurgency thwarted American efforts. Unlike MacArthur, the U.S. military had allowed widespread looting in the early days of the occupation, including the looting of munitions warehouses. These munitions later helped to arm the insurgents, including ISIS, who continue to do battle in Iraq today. Also unlike MacArthur, who had some familiarity with Japanese culture, few commanders knew either the Arabic language or Iraqi culture and rituals. Even fewer knew how to stem the war profiteering of the multinational corporations that had also "invaded" the country, making millions off the reconstruction of Iraq's infrastructure.

The Obama Doctrine: A More Conciliatory Approach to Foreign Policy

Throughout his tenure both as a candidate and as president, Barack Obama used language that seemed to reject Huntington's clash of civilizations thesis, which was instrumental in shaping Bush administration policy. For example, in what was billed as an "address to the Muslim world," given in Egypt in 2009, Obama referred to the differences between his worldview and those of his predecessors:

> Violent extremists have exploited these tensions in a small but potent minority of Muslims. The attacks of September 11th, 2001, and the continued efforts of these extremists to engage in violence against civilians has led some in my country to view Islam as inevitably hostile not only to America and Western countries, but also to human rights. This has bred more fear and mistrust. . . .
>
> I have come here to seek a new beginning between the United States and Muslims around the world; one based upon mutual interest and mutual respect; and one based upon the truth that America and Islam are not exclusive, and need not be in competition. Instead, they overlap, and share common principles—principles of justice and progress; tolerance and the dignity of all human beings.

From his rhetoric, it appeared that President Obama had rejected the idea that the United States and Islamic nations were destined to clash, and he instead sought to build bridges between the United States and the Muslim nations. Nowhere is this in greater evidence than in Iran, where the Obama administration negotiated a halting of that country's nuclear program. Nonetheless, many observers were surprised at the similarities between the Obama and Bush administration policies, despite the change in rhetoric. For example, some analysts say that the success of President Bush's "surge strategy" in Iraq was the guiding principle behind President Obama's troop surge in Afghanistan, with Obama hoping that such a strategy would pave the way for a withdrawal of U.S. forces from Afghanistan, which, though a key tenet of his campaign promise in 2008, did not occur during his eight years in office. Others remark on President Obama's failure to close military prisons at Guantánamo Bay (see "Thinking Critically"), and still others point to his continuation of drone attack programs, in which unmanned combat air vehicles carried out attacks abroad on people and other targets deemed a threat to the United States.

The Trump Doctrine: America First

From the earliest stages of his presidency—indeed, even during the course of his presidential campaign—it was apparent that President Trump fundamentally disagreed with Obama's foreign policy doctrine. In some instances, Trump has seemed to embrace Huntington's clash of civilizations thesis, most demonstrably by demonizing Muslims through his rhetoric.[17] Take, for example, an exchange between Trump and CNN host Anderson Cooper, who asked whether there is "a war between the west and radical Islam or between the west and Islam itself." Trump replied, "Well, it's radical, but it's very hard to define. It's very hard to separate because you don't know who is who."[18] The president's repeated efforts through executive orders to ban all citizens of predominantly Muslim countries from entering the United States also suggest an adherence to Huntington's thesis. The federal courts rejected two such efforts as discriminatory, while the third ban, which also barred citizens from North Korea and leaders and their families from

Thinking Critically

Do the Geneva Conventions Apply When Terrorists Have So Drastically Altered the Rules of War?

The Issue: The Geneva Conventions are a set of four treaties signed in Geneva, Switzerland, in 1949, in the aftermath of World War II. The conventions established standards for the protection of humanitarian concerns under international law. They apply to injured or ill members of the armed forces, prisoners of war, and civilians. Article 13 of the Third Geneva Convention, which specifically guides the treatment of prisoners of war, states that "prisoners of war must at all times be humanely treated. Any unlawful act or omission by the Detaining Power causing death or seriously endangering the health of a prisoner of war in its custody is prohibited, and will be regarded as a serious breach of the present Convention. In particular, no prisoner of war may be subjected to physical mutilation or to medical or scientific experiments of any kind which are not justified by the medical, dental or hospital treatment of the prisoner concerned and carried out in his interest. Likewise, prisoners of war must at all times be protected, particularly against acts of violence or intimidation and against insults and public curiosity. Measures of reprisal against prisoners of war are prohibited."*

Beginning in 2002, military authorities at the U.S. naval base at Guantánamo Bay in Cuba have detained about 775 "enemy combatants." Captured primarily in Afghanistan, these individuals were transported to Guantánamo for questioning. Although authorities in the Bush and Obama administrations have released 90 percent of the prisoners, about 41 remain, with President Trump signing an executive order in 2018 to keep the facility open, saying "In the past, we have foolishly released hundreds and hundreds of dangerous terrorists only to meet them again on the battlefield."** As designated enemy combatants, the prisoners have not enjoyed the legal rights granted to individuals charged with a crime in the United States. The detainees have no legal rights to a lawyer, a trial, or *habeas corpus*.

Yes: The Geneva Conventions clearly apply in this situation. As many human rights organizations, including Amnesty International, argue, the detention of prisoners at Guantánamo amounts to a violation of the Geneva Conventions. Specifically, as these critics cite, there have been emphatic allegations of torture by individuals who have been released. Furthermore, the indefinite nature of the detentions—combined with the captors' acknowledged practices of sleep deprivation and constant light exposure, plus the disrespect of the Muslim religion on the part of some—constitutes the abuse of their human rights in violation of the Geneva Conventions. The moral high ground usually occupied by the United States is at stake, and if the United States does not grant these prisoners rights that are consistent with the Geneva Conventions, our own soldiers will be at risk of having their rights denied when they are captured by enemy forces.

No: The Geneva Conventions do not apply when the rules of engagement of war have changed so drastically. The Bush administration convincingly argued that the Geneva Conventions apply only to "prisoners of war" (POWs) and not to "unlawful combatants." Because the nature of the war on terror and of the tactics used by terrorists is in stark contrast to accepted international conventions of war, the treatment of combatants in that war should also vary. The Supreme Court has thus far agreed with the Bush administration's assessment that holding enemy combatants is legal.***

Other Approaches: The Geneva Conventions do not apply to detainees at Guantánamo because they are not conventional enemy combatants, but the detainees should be afforded their human rights. In times like these, when international terrorist organizations do not follow centuries-old rules of engagement in warfare, the United States cannot follow antiquated rules and expect to keep its citizens safe. Therefore, detention can prevent further terrorist attacks if potential terrorists are prevented from carrying them out. Nevertheless, the detainees are entitled to humane treatment and to a hearing before an impartial judge to determine if they are truly a threat.

What do you think?

1. Are the prisoners held at Guantánamo different from the prisoners of war held in other wars? If so, how?

2. Are the Geneva Conventions, drafted soon after the conclusion of World War II, still applicable in the post-9/11 world, in which terrorism is such an urgent problem in international affairs?

3. How does the context of actions including the brutal murder of civilians, journalists, and aid workers by terror groups such as ISIS shape your views of adhering to the Geneva Convention?

*You can read the rules and explore other topics at this International Committee of the Red Cross site: www.icrc.org/ihl.nsf/7c4d08d9b287a42141256739003e636b/6fef854a3517b75ac125641e004a9e68.

**www.npr.org/sections/thetwo-way/2018/01/31/582033937/trump-signs-order-to-keep-prison-at-guantanamo-bay-open.

***Hamdi v. Rumsfeld, 542 U.S. 507 (2004).

Venezuela, was challenged in the U.S. Supreme Court, which ruled the ban constitutional in a 5-4 decision.

But President Trump's foreign policy worldview often seems disjointed: at times, he seems bent on antagonizing long-standing allies while flattering heads of state whose interests may be contrary to those of the United States, including North Korea's Jong Un, Russian President Vladimir Putin, and Chinese President Xi Jinping. Trump also has demonstrated a willingness to defy both political wisdom and his own political and business allies in order to implement unpopular policies he believes will help save American jobs. Such was the case in enacting a series of tariffs on imported goods, a policy that promises to present challenges for U.S. foreign policymakers in the future.

Future Challenges in American Foreign Policy

The volatility and complexity of events in the global arena show no sign of abating. In the foreseeable future and beyond, U.S. foreign policymakers will undoubtedly continue to face a number of pressing issues, including foreign trade policy. And among the most urgent are the ongoing, acute threat of further terrorism directed at domestic and foreign targets and the continued concern over Russia's attempt to expand its influence. Other issues that promise to remain a fixture on the U.S. foreign policy agenda in the years to come include problems related to the environment, human rights, and technology.

Trade Policy

Calling it a "horrible deal," as a candidate, Donald Trump railed against the Trans-Pacific Partnership. The TPP, negotiated during the Obama administration, was a trade agreement among 12 countries that border the Pacific Ocean, including the United States, Australia, Brunei, Canada, Chile, Japan, Malaysia, Mexico, New Zealand, Peru, Singapore, and Vietnam. The nations—which represent about 40 percent of global economic production—sought to encourage trade among the countries by cutting tariffs. The long-term goal was to eventually create closer economic ties among the partners and perhaps even create a unified market that could negotiate more favorable trading terms with countries outside the TPP (including the European Union). A shorter-term purpose was to strengthen the United States' trading position in the Asian-Pacific region, in the hopes that stronger economic ties with the TPP member states would curtail some of China's growing influence in that region. The agreement would have eliminated about 18,000 separate tariffs imposed by the various members. Under the agreement, tariffs on U.S.-manufactured goods and nearly all American agricultural products would have been ended immediately. The deadline for ratification by all its member states was February 2018, but President Trump rejected the partnership and thus killed the deal.

In an effort to protect American jobs, President Trump imposed tariffs on imported steel, aluminum, washing machines, and solar panels. The tariffs were targeted at the Chinese, but the Trump administration faced blowback from European and North American allies, who both argued for exemptions based on previously negotiated trade deals, and threatened retaliatory tariffs if the exemptions were not granted. In response to the new tariffs, China also imposed tariffs on 128 U.S. products, making items like American-made wine, strawberries, and oranges more expensive in the vast Chinese market.[19]

The Trump administration responded in kind, imposing new taxes on Chinese televisions, batteries, and other manufactured goods, making those products more expensive to the American consumer. This tit-for-tat trade retaliatory policy evoked fears that a global trade war would ensue. It also forced President Trump to reconsider his position on the Trans-Pacific Partnership, in that increasing U.S. influence through favorable trading conditions in the Asian-Pacific market could provide needed stability in the demand for U.S.-produced goods given the uncertainty surrounding trade relations with China.

The Ongoing Threat of Terrorism

As the terrorist attacks of 9/11 demonstrated tragically, foreign affairs can be unpredictable. Nonetheless, U.S. foreign policymakers are certain to confront some clear challenges in the years to come. First among these is the continued threat of terrorism. As a tactic, terrorism has proven enormously effective in accomplishing the goals of the attackers. Specifically, it breeds terror—disrupting economies, creating instability, and acting as a polarizing force.

The increasing availability of chemical and biological weapons to nations as well as terror groups also promises to create a tough challenge for U.S. and other foreign policymakers. The potential, enormous damage of these weapons of mass destruction cannot be underestimated.

Russian Expansion and Influence

For decades, Russian expansionism seemed like a threat from the past. But in March 2014, Russian troops moved onto the Crimean Peninsula and annexed the area that had been under control of Ukraine. In the aftermath, large numbers of Russian troops moved onto the border with Ukraine, stirring fears that the nation, under the rule of Vladimir Putin, would continue its push. Fears were also raised in Eastern European nations, especially in the Balkan states of Latvia, Lithuania, and Estonia, which had been overtaken by the Soviets in the 1940s. The specter of Russian aggression is troublesome to foreign policymakers in the United States who recognize that the United States' role in NATO, the regional security organization, would necessitate the use of U.S. troops (likely as part of NATO forces) should a member of the NATO alliance be attacked. In 2016, the United States began repurposing old Warsaw Pact military facilities in Poland as missile defense bases to demonstrate that NATO would defend Eastern European allies in the event of an attack, while reassuring Russia that the facility was for defense purposes only. Although they do not involve Russian troops, allegations that individuals connected to Putin interfered in the 2016 U.S. presidential election and continue to use technology to foment divisions within the United States present the possibility of perhaps a more insidious form of aggression.

Nuclear Proliferation

Not all challenges to come are new, however. The continued proliferation of nuclear weapons presents a serious problem to foreign policymakers throughout the world. Figure 18.2 shows that eight nations have a declared nuclear weapons capability, including India and Pakistan, and another, Israel, has the undeclared

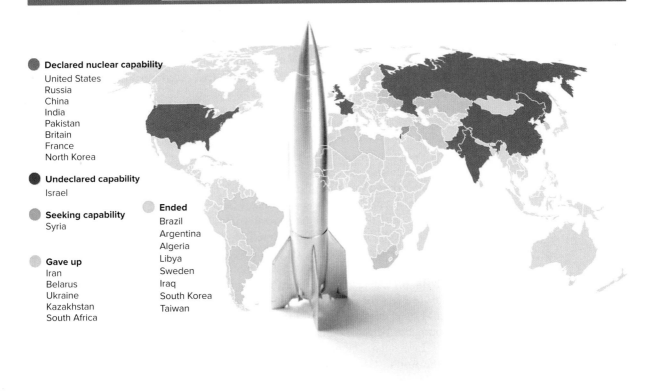

- **Declared nuclear capability**
  - United States
  - Russia
  - China
  - India
  - Pakistan
  - Britain
  - France
  - North Korea

- **Undeclared capability**
  - Israel

- **Seeking capability**
  - Syria

- **Gave up**
  - Iran
  - Belarus
  - Ukraine
  - Kazakhstan
  - South Africa

- **Ended**
  - Brazil
  - Argentina
  - Algeria
  - Libya
  - Sweden
  - Iraq
  - South Korea
  - Taiwan

FIGURE 18.2 ■ **The Nuclear Club** What, if anything, do most or all of the countries that gave up or ended their nuclear programs have in common, either among themselves or with the countries that have nuclear capability? What do most or all of the countries that have nuclear capability—either declared or undeclared—have in common? What conclusions can you draw about these commonalities?

Photo: ©F_/Getty Images

potential. The fact that dangerous weapons of mass destruction are in such wide distribution increases the likelihood of their use—either accidentally or intentionally.

Environmental and Health Issues

Environmental concerns that by their very nature are worldwide challenges promise to remain on the United States' foreign policy agenda deep into the future, though concerns about these issues are less of a focal point in the Trump administration than they were with his predecessor, President Obama. Environmental concerns that are sure to have a secure place in foreign policymakers' agendas for the future include climate change, greenhouse gas emissions, enormous world consumption of fossil fuels, deterioration of the oceans, worldwide deforestation, and ongoing air and water contamination. In recent years, global influenza pandemics plus the outbreak and spread of other viruses, including Zika and Ebola, demonstrate a vulnerability that increased globalism has created, and forced policymakers to grapple with difficult questions concerning global health issues.

Technology's Potential in Foreign Affairs

Although there are many uncertainties about what's next in the foreign policy arena, one certainty is that the impact of technology—as a tool in foreign policy and in citizens' efforts to influence the policies and institutions of government—will continue to increase. Nowhere can that be better seen than in the conclusion reached by the U.S. Intelligence Community that determined that, using technology, Russia succeeded in interfering with the 2016 U.S. presidential election. In addition, technology has transformed not only how nations communicate with each other but also how non-state actors, including terrorists, can harness the power of social media to communicate directly with policymakers and private citizens. Video technologies increasingly enable nongovernmental organizations, cyberjournalists, and others to make compelling cases directly to individuals. It allows terror cells to radicalize individuals, turning private citizens into lone wolf terrorists. Technology also is increasingly being relied on as a tool by private citizens, lobbying their governments for favored foreign policies, while governments are using technology in unprecedented ways to monitor the actions of their citizens as well as their adversaries and allies.

Technology also is being used as a tool for those seeking to foster democracy. In 2018, protesters, many of them students, took to the streets of Nicaragua in an effort to press for democratic reforms. The protests were spurred in part by President Daniel Ortega's reforms to the nation's social security system, but grew when a journalist, Angel Gahona, was killed while reporting on the protests on a Facebook Live video. The protesters relied on technology to disseminate their message to the world. Also, as discussed in Chapter 11, the impact of new technologies could be seen in Jasmine Spring protest movements throughout the Middle East. In the spring of 2011, cellular and social networking technology provided the organizing tools that facilitated populist uprisings against oppressive regimes, toppling governments in Tunisia and Egypt. The likelihood is great that technology will play an increasingly prevalent role in shaping new democracies, checking the authority and policies of governments, and providing a means for cross-national movements.

Conclusion

Thinking Critically About What's Next in Foreign Policy and National Security

In retrospect, the development of the United States' foreign policy over time seems to have followed a natural progression as the nation itself grew and changed. The nation's initial isolationism, spawned by a healthy suspicion of foreign powers and their motives, gave way to international relations in the limited sphere of trade. Then, in both World War I and World War II, the importance of global alliances in helping to shape U.S. foreign policy became evident. With the end of World War II, the United States emerged as a superpower whose foreign policy came to be defined largely by its relations with its chief rival in the global arena, the Soviet Union. After the collapse of the Soviet empire in the 1990s, the foreign policy arena was murky as U.S. and world policymakers searched for a new prism through which to view the nations of the world. Could policymakers have anticipated the threat of terrorism that was to come?

On September 11, 2001, U.S. foreign policy instantly acquired a new focus. Their morning hardly going according to their daily planners, a shaken president and his aides scrambled to respond appropriately to the unforeseen and unprecedented terrorist attacks on U.S. soil. They asked the same question that the millions of Americans who watched the unbelievable events unfold on television asked: Why? Ultimately, the administration's responses to the terrorist strikes showed that significant cultural and political differences separate the United States and the other Western democracies on the one hand, and fundamentalist non-Western states that harbor terrorists on the other hand. The attacks crystallized perceptions both among U.S. policymakers and in the general public that no longer could the terrorist states be viewed simply as potential threats or as insignificant to the United States' interests. Do those perceptions remain widely held by the public and policymakers today?

Challenges facing U.S. foreign policymakers in the next several years are particularly acute, given their unpredictable nature. Uncertainty surrounding foreign trade policy will likely be a factor in the U.S. economy and in international relations. And the randomness of terrorism confounds policymakers and other experts and prevents them from making accurate predictions and determining adequate modes of defense. Nonetheless, given the high stakes of another potential attack, the threat of terrorism—and the imperative to prevent it—clearly will remain a defining characteristic of U.S. foreign policy in the decades to come.

Learning Summary

1. Explain the tools of foreign policy.
   a. Understand diplomacy, by which nations conduct political negotiations with one another and settle disagreements.
   b. Describe how the United States uses economic policy to cajole other nations into enacting policies the United States supports.
   c. Explain the circumstances in which the United States relies on the military to force other countries to align with U.S. interests.

2. List the creators and shapers of foreign policy.
   a. Explain how the Constitution grants important foreign policy-making powers to the president and the executive branch.
   b. Describe how Congress plays an important role in creating foreign policy, particularly through its decision making with respect to declaring war and appropriating funds.
   c. Explain the role interest groups play in the foreign policy process.
   d. Understand the media's role in shaping foreign policy.
   e. Describe how private individuals influence the foreign policy process.

3. Explain U.S. foreign policy in its historical context.
   a. Explain early influences on the conduct of foreign policy.
   b. Describe the role of international trade as the U.S. economy developed.
   c. Explain the balance of power system that drew the United States into global conflict in World War I.
   d. Describe the role of isolationism during the Great Depression.
   e. Explain the international alliances that helped to precipitate U.S. entry into World War II.

4. Describe the postwar era with the United States as a superpower.
   a. Explain the emergence of the United States and the Soviet Union as competing superpowers with clashing ideologies after World War II.
   b. Describe the Cold War rivalry that defined U.S. foreign policy and the international organizations charged with ensuring security and facilitating economic relations among nations.
   c. Describe the impetus for conducting proxy wars on the Korean peninsula and in Vietnam.
   d. Describe President Richard Nixon's policy of détente.
   e. Explain President Ronald Reagan's policy to outspend the Soviets, which forced the collapse of the Soviet Union.

5. Describe U.S. foreign policy in the 21st century.
   a. Explain Huntington's clash of civilizations thesis.
   b. Explain the Bush Doctrine of preventive war and regime change.
   c. Describe President Obama's foreign policy practices.
   d. Explain the Trump Doctrine of America first.

6. Describe the likely future challenges in American foreign policy.
   a. Explain the controversy over President Trump's foreign trade policy.
   b. Explain how the continued threat of terrorism affects the United States in the foreign policy arena.
   c. Explain the trend regarding nuclear proliferation.
   d. Describe the environmental challenges and global health crises that continue to challenge foreign policymakers.
   e. Explain the impact of technology on international relations and foreign policy in the future.

Key Terms

For Review

1. What are the primary tools that policymakers use in the foreign policy process?

2. Why is the president the primary foreign policymaker in the United States? What tools do presidents have to assist them in creating foreign policy? Who are the other actors in foreign policy decision making?

3. How did the United States evolve from a nation that emphasized isolationism in its early years to internationalism in the post–World War II era? What factors spurred this transformation?

4. How did the Cold War between the United States and the Soviet Union affect U.S. foreign policy? How did it influence relations between the United States and other nations?

5. September 11, 2001, led to a significant shift in how the United States viewed itself and the world. What theories best explain how the United States now sees itself in today's global context?

6. What specific, major challenges will U.S. foreign policymakers face in the years to come?

For Critical Thinking and Discussion

1. How have the 9/11 terrorist attacks changed the structure of the foreign policy-making apparatus in the executive branch?

2. How did World War II change the way the United States was perceived by other nations around the world? How did the war alter U.S. policymakers' perceptions of what the international order should look like?

3. In retrospect, was the theory of containment an accurate description of how the United States should have attempted to stem the tide of communism during the Cold War? Why or why not?

4. Does Samuel Huntington's clash of civilizations theory accurately reflect the current state of world affairs? Explain. What present-day realities are in keeping with Huntington's theory? What other realities defy it?

5. What additional challenges, beyond those we examined in the text, are likely to face the makers of U.S. foreign policy in the next decade?

Resources for

Research AND Action

Internet Resources

Central Intelligence Agency
www.cia.gov This is the official website of the CIA. Its *World Factbook,* available online at this site, is an excellent resource for research on various nations. The site also hosts news and information, history, and career opportunities.

North Atlantic Treaty Organization
www.nato.int This site hosts an informative eLibrary as well as an impressive multimedia collection of documentation about NATO-related events and history.

State Department and Defense Department
www.state.gov and www.defense.gov These government sites offer a plethora of information from these two cabinet departments. Included are news and information, policy statements, career opportunities, virtual tours, and reports.

World Bank
www.worldbank.org This site explains the World Bank's policy priorities and offers data, research reports, and a wide variety of related international news.

Recommended Readings

Allison, Graham. *Nuclear Terrorism: The Ultimate Preventable Catastrophe.* New York: Times Books, 2004; and *The Essence of Decision: Explaining the Cuban Missile Crisis.* Boston: Little, Brown, 1971. This key scholar of U.S. foreign policy making uses the Cuban Missile Crisis as a model to explain foreign policy making. In his more recent work, he analyzes the foreign policy dilemma of nuclear terrorism.

Cameron, Fraser. *U.S. Foreign Policy after the Cold War.* New York: Routledge, 2002. This introduction to U.S. foreign policy looks at some aspects of U.S. foreign policy from the perspective of their domestic origins. Critical of the United States' unilateralism, Cameron also details relations between the United States and the European Union.

Coleman, Isobel, and Terra Lawson-Remer. *Pathways to Freedom.* New York: Council on Foreign Relations Press, 2013. This book offers a prescription on how the United States and other nations can foster the development of prosperous and stable democracies.

Huntington, Samuel P. *The Clash of Civilizations and the Remaking of World Order.* New York: Simon & Schuster, 1998. Huntington asserts that Western democracies are engaged in a clash of civilizations, particularly with Islamic societies.

Jervis, Robert. *American Foreign Policy in a New Era.* New York: Routledge, 2005. A noted foreign policy scholar explains the issues of and influences on American foreign policy in today's international circumstances.

Keohane, Robert. *Neo-Realism and Its Critics.* New York: Columbia University Press, 1986. This classic work explains neorealism, a theory that emphasizes the power of state actors in international affairs.

Movies of Interest

Zero Dark Thirty (2012)
A thriller that depicts the 10-year hunt for Osama bin Laden and what eventually led the Navy SEALs Team 6 to his Pakistan hideout in 2011.

Argo (2012)
This film is based on the true story of the 1980 U.S. Hostage Crisis in Iran, directed by and starring Ben Affleck as Tony Mendez, a CIA agent who launches a mission with the help of Hollywood and the Canadian Embassy to rescue six Americans amidst extreme political tension in Tehran.

Tinker Tailor Soldier Spy (2011)
Gary Oldman stars in this story of a Cold War veteran spy who is forced from semi-retirement to uncover a Soviet agent within MI6.

The Hurt Locker (2008)
This 2009 Oscar-winning film follows the story of a U.S. Army Explosive Ordnance Disposal (EOD) team during the war in Iraq.

The Good Shepherd (2006)
Directed by Robert De Niro and starring Matt Damon, Alec Baldwin, and Angelina Jolie, this film traces the creation of the CIA and its evolution through the Cold War.

The Killing Fields (1984)
Based on a true story, this film tells the story of an American journalist and his Cambodian guide during the vicious genocide by Cambodia's Khmer Rouge regime during the Vietnam War.

Dr. Strangelove or: How I Learned to Stop Worrying and Love the Bomb (1964)
This Stanley Kubrick film probes the dangers of the Cold War when an insane army general tries to start a nuclear war over the objections of political leaders and other generals.

The Mouse That Roared (1959)
This Peter Sellers comedy takes a satirical look at how the United States used foreign aid to ensure the support of allies. It features a fictional impoverished European nation that invades the United States with the goal of losing so that it can receive foreign aid.

References

1. Saul K. Padover, ed., *Wilson's Ideals* (Washington, DC: American Council on Public Affairs, 1942), 108.
2. www.vox.com/world/2018/1/8/16850116/trump-pakistan-suspend-aid.
3. www.whitehouse.gov/wp-content/uploads/2018/02/budget-fy2019.pdf.
4. "Dodd Assesses Efforts by U.S. to Increase Economic, Diplomatic, Political Pressure on Iran," March 21, 2007.
5. Secretary of State Colin L. Powell, remarks to the United Nations Security Council, February 5, 2003.
6. Alex Chadwick and Mike Shuster, "U.S. Links to Sadaam During Iran-Iraq War," September 22, 2005.
7. See, for example, James Risen, *State of War: The Secret History of the CIA and the Bush Administration* (New York: Free Press, 2006).
8. "President Dwight D. Eisenhower's Farewell Address (1961)," www.ourdocuments.gov/doc.php?flash=true&doc=90.
9. www.thebureauinvestigates.com/projects/drone-war.
10. Roger H. Davidson, "Invitation to Struggle: An Overview of Legislative-Executive Relations," *Annals of the American Academy of Political and Social Science* 499 (1988): 1, 9–21.
11. Article 5 of the North Atlantic Treaty, Washington, D.C., April 4, 1949.
12. President Harry S. Truman's address before a joint session of Congress on March 12, 1947.
13. George F. Kennan, writing under the pseudonym "X," "Sources of Soviet Conduct," *Foreign Affairs,* July 1947: 25.
14. Graham T. Allison and Philip Zelikow, *Essence of Decision: Explaining the Cuban Missile Crisis,* 2nd ed. (New York: Longman, 1999).
15. President Eisenhower's News Conference, April 7, 1954, *Public Papers of the Presidents*, 1954, p. 382.
16. Samuel P. Huntington, "The Clash of Civilizations?" *Foreign Affairs* 72, no. 3 (Summer 1993): 22–49.
17. www.vox.com/policy-and-politics/2017/11/29/16714788/trump-retweet-britain-first-islamophobia.
18. www.brookings.edu/blog/markaz/2017/01/04/what-does-it-mean-to-be-at-war-with-radical-islam-on-the-attractions-and-dangers-of-a-vague-term/.
19. http://fortune.com/2018/04/02/china-tariffs-128-us-products/.

GLOSSARY

501(c)4s Nonprofit organizations operated exclusively for the promotion of social welfare, including lobbying or engaging in political campaigning.

527 A tax-exempt group that raises money for political activities, much like those allowed under the soft money loophole.

A

absentee voting The casting of a ballot in advance by mail in situations where illness, travel, or other circumstances prevent voters from voting in their precincts.

administrative adjudication The process by which agencies resolve disputes over the implementation of their administrative rules.

administrative discretion The authority delegated to bureaucrats to use their expertise and judgment when determining how to implement public policy.

administrative rule making The process by which an independent commission or agency fills in the details of a vague law by formulating, proposing, and approving rules, regulations, and standards that will be enforced to implement the policy.

adversarial judicial system A judicial system in which two parties in a legal dispute each present its case and the court must determine which side wins the dispute and which loses.

advice and consent The Senate's authority to approve or reject the president's top appointments and negotiated treaties.

affirmative action In the employment arena, intentional efforts to recruit, hire, train, and promote underutilized categories of workers (women and minority men); in higher education, intentional efforts to diversify the student body.

agency review Part of the committee or subcommittee process of considering a bill, wherein committee members ask executive agencies that would administer the law for written comments on the measure.

agenda setting The determination by Congress of which public issues the government should consider for legislation.

agents of socialization The individuals, organizations, and institutions that facilitate the acquisition of political views.

American dream The belief that in the United States hard work and persistence will reap a financially secure, happy, and healthy life, with upward mobility.

amicus curiae **brief ("friend of the court" brief)** A legal brief, filed by an individual or a group that is not a party in the case; it is written to influence the Supreme Court's decision.

Anti-Federalists Individuals who opposed ratification of the Constitution because they were deeply suspicious of the powers it gave to the national government and of the impact those powers would have on states' authority and individual freedoms.

appellate jurisdiction Judicial authority to review the interpretation and application of the law in previous decisions reached by another court in a case.

appropriation law A law that gives bureaucracies and other government entities the legal authority to spend money.

approval ratings The percentage of survey respondents who say that they "approve" or "strongly approve" of the way the president is doing his job.

Article I courts Courts created by Congress under constitutional authority provided in Article I that help administer and resolve conflicts over specific federal legislation.

articles of impeachment Charges against the president during an impeachment.

associate justice Title of the eight Supreme Court justices who are not the chief justice.

attentive public The segment of voters who pay careful attention to political issues.

attitudinal model Judicial decision-making model that claims judicial decision making is guided by policy and ideological preferences of individual judges.

Australian ballot A secret ballot prepared by the government, distributed to all eligible voters, and, when balloting is completed, counted by government officials in an unbiased fashion, without corruption or regard to individual preferences.

authoritarianism System of government in which the government holds strong powers but is checked by some forces.

authorization law A law that provides the plan of action to address a given societal concern and identifies the executive branch unit that will put the plan into effect.

B

bad tendency test A standard extended in the 1925 case *Gitlow v. New York* whereby any speech that has the likelihood of inciting crime or disturbing the public peace can be silenced.

balance of power system A system of international alliances that, in theory, would balance the power of one group of nations against the power of another group and thus discourage war.

balanced budget A budget in which the government's expenditures are equal to or less than its revenues.

balanced ticket The selection of a running mate who brings diversity of ideology, geographic region, age, gender, race, or ethnicity to the slate.

ballot measure A proposed piece of legislation, a constitutional amendment, or some other policy proposal placed on the Election Day ballot for voters to approve or reject.

bandwidth The amount of data that can travel through a network in a given time period.

bench memo Written by a justice's law clerk, a summary of the case, outlining relevant facts and issues presented in the case documents and briefs, that may also suggest questions to be asked during oral arguments.

bench trial A trial in which the judge who presides over the trial decides on guilt or liability.

beyond a reasonable doubt The standard of proof the government must meet in criminal cases; the government must convince the judge or the jury that there is no reasonable doubt that the defendant committed the crime.

bicameral legislature Legislature comprising two parts, called *chambers.*

big data Large data sets collected from numerous sources that through computational analysis can indicate individual patterns, associations, preferences, and opinions.

big tent principle A strategy in which a political party seeks to build a broad coalition among individuals with wide-ranging beliefs, backgrounds, and priorities.

bill A proposed piece of legislation.

Bill of Rights The first 10 amendments to the Constitution, which were ratified in 1791, constituting an enumeration of the individual liberties with which the government is forbidden to interfere.

Black Codes Laws passed immediately after the Civil War by the confederate states that limited the rights of "freemen" (people formerly enslaved).

block grant A grant-in-aid for a broadly defined policy area, whose funding amount is typically based on a formula.

blogosphere The community of bloggers.

brinkmanship The Cold War–era practice of fooling the enemy by going to the edge (the brink), even if the party using the brinkmanship strategy had no intention of following through.

Brown v. Board of Education of Topeka This 1954 Supreme Court decision ruled that segregated schools violated the equal protection clause of the Fourteenth Amendment.

budget authority The authority provided by law for agencies to spend government funds.

budget deficit More money spent than collected through revenues.

budget reconciliation The annual process of rewriting authorization legislation to comply with the expenditure ceiling and revenue floor of the concurrent budget resolution for the upcoming fiscal year.

budget surplus Money left over after all expenses are paid.

bureaucracy The collection of all national executive branch organizations.

bureaucratic structure A large organization with the following features: a division of labor, specialization of job tasks, hiring systems based on worker competency, hierarchy with a vertical chain of command, and standard operating procedures.

bureaucrats People employed in a government executive branch unit to implement public policy; public administrators; public servants.

Bush Doctrine The argument, articulated by President George W. Bush, that unilateral action directly targeted at an enemy is both justifiable and feasible.

business regulation Government rules, regulations, and standards directed at preserving competition in the marketplace.

C

cabinet The group of experts chosen by the president to serve as advisers on running the country.

campaign consultant A paid professional who specializes in the overall management of political campaigns or an aspect of campaigns.

campaign manager A professional whose duties comprise a variety of strategic and managerial tasks, from fund-raising to staffing a campaign.

campaign strategy The blueprint for the campaign, including a budget and fund-raising plan, an advertising strategy, and a staffing plan.

candidate committees Organizations that candidates form to support their individual election.

candidate-centered campaign A campaign in which the individual seeking election, rather than an entire party slate, is the focus.

capital budget A budget that accounts for the costs and revenues for expensive building and purchasing projects from which citizens will benefit for many years and for which governments can borrow money.

capitalism An economic system in which the means of producing wealth are privately owned and operated to produce profits.

casework Personal work by a member of Congress on behalf of a constituent or group of constituents, typically aimed at getting the government to do something the constituent wants done.

cash transfer The direct provision of cash (in forms including checks, debit cards, and tax breaks) to eligible individuals or to providers of goods or services to eligible individuals.

categorical formula grant A grant-in-aid for a narrowly defined purpose, whose dollar value is based on a formula.

categorical project grant A grant-in-aid for a narrowly defined purpose for which governments compete with each other by proposing specific projects.

caucus A meeting of party members held to select delegates to the national convention.

centralized federalism Intergovernmental relations in which the national government imposes its policy preferences on state and local governments.

cert memo Description of the facts of a case filed with the Supreme Court, the pertinent legal arguments, and a recommendation as to whether the case should be taken, written by one of the justices' law clerks and reviewed by all justices participating in the pool process.

***certiorari* petition** A petition submitted to the Supreme Court requesting review of a case already decided.

charter The constitution of a local government.

checks and balances A system in which each branch of government can monitor and limit the functions of the other branches.

chief justice The leading justice on the Supreme Court, who provides both organizational and intellectual leadership.

chief of staff Among the most important staff members of the White House Office (WHO); serves as both an adviser to the president and the manager of the WHO.

citizens Members of the polity who, through birth or naturalization, enjoy the rights, privileges, and responsibilities attached to membership in a given nation.

Citizens United v. Federal Election Commission Supreme Court ruling stating that corporations and labor unions are entitled to the same First Amendment protections that individuals enjoy, resulting in drastically increased spending through super PACs by corporations and labor organizations.

civic engagement Individual and collective actions designed to identify and address issues of public concern.

civil disobedience Active, but nonviolent, refusal to comply with laws or governmental policies that are morally objectionable, while accepting the consequences of violating these laws.

civil law The body of law dealing with disputes between individuals, between an individual and corporations, between corporations, and between individuals and their governments over harms caused by a party's actions or inactions.

civil liberties Constitutionally established guarantees that protect citizens, opinions, and property against arbitrary government interference.

civil rights The rights and privileges guaranteed to all citizens under the equal protection and due process clauses of the Fifth and Fourteenth Amendments; the idea that individuals are protected from discrimination based on characteristics such as race, national origin, religion, and sex.

civil servants Bureaucrats hired through a merit-based personnel system and who have job protection.

clash of civilizations thesis Samuel Huntington's idea that bitter cultural conflict will continue and escalate between modern Western democracies and fundamentalist Islamic states.

clear and present danger test A standard established in the 1919 Supreme Court case *Schenck v. U.S.* whereby the government may silence speech or expression when there is a clear and present danger that this speech will bring about some harm that the government has the power to prevent.

clear and probable danger test A standard established in the 1951 case *Dennis v. U.S.* whereby the government could suppress speech to avoid grave danger, even if the probability of the dangerous result was relatively remote; replaced by the imminent lawless action (incitement) test in 1969.

climate control The practice of using public outreach to build favorable public opinion of an organization.

closed primary A type of primary in which voting in a party's primary is limited to members of that party.

cloture A procedural move in which a supermajority of 60 senators agrees to end a filibuster.

coattail effect The phenomenon by which candidates running for lower-level offices such as city council benefit in an election from the popularity of a top-of-ticket nominee.

Cold War The political, ideological, and military conflict that lasted from 1945 until 1990 between communist nations led by the Soviet Union and Western democracies led by the United States.

collective defense The concept that allied nations agree to defend one another in the face of an invasion.

collective goods Outcomes shared by the general public; also called *public goods*.

collective security The idea that peace could be achieved if nations agreed to collectively oppose any nation that attacked another country.

collegial court A court made up of a group of judges who must evaluate a case together and decide on the outcome; compromise and negotiation take place as members try to build a majority coalition.

commercial speech Advertising statements that describe products.

commission A form of local government that is more common in county and

township governments than in other general-purpose governments and for which voters elect a body of officials who collectively hold legislative and executive powers.

common law Judge-made law grounded in tradition and previous judicial decisions, instead of in written law.

concurrent budget resolution A document approved by the House and the Senate at the beginning of their budget processes that establishes binding expenditure ceilings and a binding revenue floor as well as proposed expenditure levels for major policy categories.

concurrent powers Basic governing functions that are exercised by the national and state governments independently, and at the same time, including the power to make policy, raise revenue, implement policies, and establish courts.

concurring opinion A judicial opinion agreeing with the majority decision in the case but disagreeing with at least some of the legal interpretations or conclusions reached in the majority opinion.

confederal system A government structure in which several independent sovereign states agree to cooperate on specified policy matters by creating a central governing body; each sovereign state retains ultimate authority over other governmental matters within its borders, so the central governing body is not a sovereign government.

confederation A union of independent states in which each state retains its sovereignty, that is, its ultimate power to govern, and agrees to work collaboratively on matters the states expressly agree to delegate to a central governing body.

conference committee A bicameral, bipartisan committee composed of legislators whose job is to reconcile two versions of a bill.

conflict of interest In the case of public servants, the situation in which they can personally benefit from a decision they make or an action they take in the process of doing their jobs.

conflicted federalism Intergovernmental relations in which elements of dual federalism, cooperative federalism, and centralized federalism are evident in the domestic policies implemented by state and local governments.

Connecticut Compromise The compromise between the Virginia Plan and the New Jersey Plan that created a bicameral legislature with one chamber's representation based on population and the other chamber having two members for each state (also known as the *Great Compromise*).

consent of the governed The idea that, in a democracy, the government's power derives from the consent of the people.

conservatism An ideology that emphasizes preserving tradition and relying on community and family as mechanisms of continuity in society.

consolidation The phenomenon of large corporations buying smaller ones so that there are fewer and fewer companies' products available.

constitution The fundamental principles of a government and the basic structures and procedures by which the government operates to fulfill those principles; may be written or unwritten.

constitutional law The body of law that comes out of the courts in cases involving the interpretation of the Constitution.

constitutionalism Government that is structured by law, and in which the power of government is limited.

consumer price index (CPI) The most common measure of inflation, it gauges the average change in prices over time of a "market basket" of goods and services including food, clothing, shelter, fuel, transportation costs, and selected medical costs.

containment The Cold War–era policy of preventing the spread of communism, mainly by providing military and economic aid as well as political advice to countries vulnerable to a communist takeover.

continuing resolution An agreement of the House and Senate that authorizes agencies not covered by approved appropriation laws to continue to spend money within their previous budget year's levels.

contracting-out Also called *outsourcing;* a process by which the government contracts with a private for-profit or non-profit organization to provide public services, such as disaster relief, or resources needed by the government, such as fighter planes.

contributory program (social insurance program) A benefit provided only to those who paid the specific tax created to fund the benefit.

cooperative federalism Intergovernmental relations in which the national government supports state governments' efforts to address the domestic matters reserved to them.

Council of Governments (COG) A regional agency composed of representatives from several local governments who share resources to address one or more mutual problems.

council-manager (commission-administrator) A form of general-purpose local government found in many counties and the majority of cities; it is composed of an elected body with legislative and executive powers whose members hire a professional manager to oversee the government's day-to-day operations.

council-mayor (council-executive) A form of general-purpose local government comprising (1) a legislative body elected by voters and (2) an independently elected chief executive.

country desk The official operation of the U.S. government in each country that has diplomatic ties to the United States.

county government A general-purpose local government created by states to assist them in implementing policy in geographic subdivisions of the state.

court of last resort The highest court in a court system.

courts of appeal Courts with authority to review cases heard by other courts to correct errors in the interpretation or application of law.

criminal due process rights Safeguards for those accused of crime; these rights constrain government conduct in investigating crimes, trying cases, and punishing offenders.

criminal law The body of law dealing with conduct so harmful to society as a whole that it is prohibited by statute, and is prosecuted and punished by the government.

cyber cascade What occurs when an electronic document becomes very widely distributed digitally through e-mail, social networking, or video sharing.

D

de facto segregation Segregation maintained by practice.

de jure segregation Segregation mandated by law.

dealignment The situation in which fewer voters support the two major political parties, instead identifying themselves as independent, or splitting their ticket between candidates from more than one party.

debt ceiling The legal borrowing limit for the national government.

defense conversion President Jimmy Carter's attempt to convert the nation's vast military apparatus to peacetime functions.

deficit spending Government expenditures costing more than is raised in taxes, during the budget year, leading to borrowing and debt.

democracy Government in which supreme power of governance lies in the hands of its citizens.

department One of 15 executive branch units responsible for a broadly defined policy area and whose top administrator (secretary) is appointed by the president, is confirmed by the Senate, and serves at the discretion of the president.

depression A long-term and severe recession.

deregulation The reduction or elimination of government rules and regulations (laws) that businesses and industries must follow.

descriptive representation The attempt to ensure that governing bodies include representatives of major demographic groups—such as women, African Americans, Latinas, Jews, and Catholics—in proportions similar to their representation in the population at large.

détente The easing of tensions between the United States and its communist rivals.

deterrence The idea that nations would be less likely to engage in nuclear war if adversaries each had first-strike capability.

devolution The process whereby the national government returns policy responsibilities to state or local governments.

digital divide Unequal access to computer technology.

digital paywall The practice of limiting access to a website unless users pay a fee or purchase a subscription.

Dillon's Rule The ruling articulated by Judge John Forrest Dillon in 1868 that local governments are creatures of the state that created them, and they have only the powers expressly mentioned in the charters written and approved by the state and those necessarily implied by the formally expressed powers.

diplomacy The conduct of international relations, particularly involving the negotiation of treaties and other agreements between nations.

direct democracy A structure of government in which citizens discuss and decide policy through majority rule.

direct provision A policy tool whereby the government that creates a policy hires public servants to provide the service.

direct subsidy A cash transfer from general revenues to particular persons or private companies engaged in activities that the national government believes support the public good.

director of national intelligence (DNI) The person responsible for coordinating and overseeing all the intelligence agencies within the executive branch.

discharge petition A special tactic used to extract a bill from a committee to have it considered by the entire House.

discretionary jurisdiction The authority of a court to select the cases it will hear from among all the cases appealed to it.

discretionary spending Payment on programs for which Congress and the president must approve budget authority each year in appropriation legislation.

dissenting opinion A judicial opinion disagreeing both with the majority's disposition of a case and with their legal interpretations and conclusions.

district courts The federal trial courts with mandatory jurisdiction.

diversity of citizenship The circumstance in which the parties in a legal case are from different states or the case involves a U.S. citizen and a foreign government.

divided government The situation that exists when Congress is controlled by one party and the presidency by the other.

divine right of kings The assertion that monarchies, as a manifestation of God's will, could rule absolutely without regard to the will or well-being of their subjects.

doctrine of *stare decisis* From the Latin for "let the decision stand," a common-law doctrine that directs judges to identify previously decided cases with similar facts and then apply to the current case the rule of law used by the courts in the earlier cases.

domestic policies Policies addressing the problems, needs, and relations of people residing within the country's borders.

domino theory The principle that if one nation fell to communism, other nations in its geographic vicinity also would succumb.

double jeopardy The trying of a person again for the same crime that he or she has been cleared of in court; barred by the Fifth Amendment.

dual court system The existence of 50 independently functioning state judicial systems, each responsible for resolving legal disputes over its state laws, and one national judicial system, responsible for resolving legal disputes over national laws.

dual federalism The initial model of national and state relations in which the national government takes care of its enumerated powers while the state governments independently take care of their reserved powers.

dual sovereignty A system of government in which ultimate governing authority is divided between two levels of government, a central government and regional governments, with each level having ultimate authority over different policy matters.

due process The legal safeguards that prevent the government from arbitrarily depriving citizens of life, liberty, or property; guaranteed by the Fifth and Fourteenth Amendments.

E

e-campaigning The practice of mobilizing voters using the Internet.

e-Government Employment of the Internet for delivering government information and services to the citizens.

e-petition An online petition used as a tool to garner support for a position or cause.

earmark A designation within a spending bill that provides for a specific expenditure.

economic boom Rapid economic growth.

economic incentive Motivation to join an interest group because the group works for policies that will provide members with material benefits.

economic policy A collection of public policies that affect the health of the economy, which includes taxing and spending policies (fiscal policy), monetary policy, regulatory policy, and trade policy.

economy A system for producing, selling, buying, and using goods and services.

efficacy Citizens' belief that they have the ability to achieve something desirable and that the government listens to people like them.

electioneering Working to influence the election of candidates who support the organization's issues.

Electoral College The name given to the body of representatives elected by voters in each state to elect the president and the vice president.

elite theory A theory that holds that a group of wealthy, educated individuals wields most political power.

emergency powers Broad powers exercised by the president during times of national crisis.

entitlement program A government benefit guaranteed to all who meet the eligibility requirements.

enumerated powers The powers of the national government that are listed in the Constitution.

environmental racism The term used to describe the higher incidence of environmental threats and subsequent health problems in lower-income communities, which frequently are also communities dominated by people of color.

equal protection clause The Fourteenth Amendment clause stating that no state shall "deny to any person within its jurisdiction the equal protection of the laws."

essential services Public services provided by state and local governments on a daily basis to prevent chaos and hazardous condtions in society.

establishment clause The First Amendment clause that bars the government from passing any law "respecting an establishment of religion"; often interpreted as a separation of church and state but this is increasingly challenged.

exclusionary rule The criminal procedural rule stating that evidence obtained illegally cannot be used in a trial.

executive agreement An international agreement between the United States and other nations, not subject to Senate approval and in effect only during the administration of the president who negotiates the agreement.

executive budget The budget document and budget message that explains the president's fiscal plan.

Executive Office of the President (EOP) The offices, counsels, and boards that help the president to carry out his day-to-day responsibilities.

executive order The power of the president to issue orders that carry the force of law.

executive privilege The right of the chief executive and members of the administration to withhold information from Congress or the courts, or the right to refuse to appear before legislative or judicial bodies.

exit polls Polls conducted at polling places on Election Day to project the winner of an election before the polls close.

expressed powers Presidential powers enumerated in the Constitution.

extradition The return of individuals accused of a crime to the state in which the crime was committed upon the request of that state's governor.

F

fairness doctrine The requirement that stations holding broadcast licenses present controversial issues of public importance and do so in a manner that was honest, fair, and balanced.

federal courts of appeals (circuit courts) Federal courts with mandatory, appellate jurisdiction.

federal question A question of law based on interpretation of the U.S. Constitution, federal laws, or treaties.

federal system A governmental structure with two levels of government in which each level has sovereignty over different policy matters and geographic areas; a system of government with dual sovereignty.

Federalists Individuals who supported the new Constitution as presented by the Constitutional Convention in 1787.

feminization of poverty The phenomenon of increasing numbers of unmarried, divorced, and separated women with children living in poverty.

fighting words Speech that is likely to bring about public disorder or chaos; the Supreme Court has held that this speech may be banned in public places to ensure the preservation of public order.

filibuster A procedural move by a member of the Senate to attempt to halt passage of a bill, during which the senator can speak for an unlimited time on the Senate floor.

fireside chats President Franklin D. Roosevelt's radio addresses to the country.

fiscal federalism The relationship between the national government and state and local governments whereby the national government provides grant money to state and local governments.

fiscal policy Government spending and taxing and their effect on the economy.

fiscal year (FY) The 12-month accounting period for revenue raising and spending, which for the national government begins on October 1 and ends on September 30 of the following year.

food insecurity The situation in which people have a limited or an uncertain ability to obtain, in socially acceptable ways, enough nutritious food to live a healthy and active life.

foreign service officers The diplomatic and consular staff at U.S. embassies abroad.

Foursquare Geolocation app that uses an iPhone's built-in GPS to display attractions in your area.

framing The process by which the media set a context that helps people understand important events and matters of shared interest.

franking The privilege of sending mail free of charge by members of Congress.

free exercise clause The First Amendment clause prohibiting the government from enacting laws prohibiting an individual's practice of his or her religion; often in contention with the establishment clause.

free rider problem The phenomenon of someone deriving benefit from others' actions.

free trade policy The elimination of tariffs and nontariff trade barriers so that international trade is expanded.

full faith and credit clause The constitutional clause that requires states to comply with and uphold the public acts, records, and judicial decisions of other states.

fund-raising consultant A professional who works with candidates in identifying likely contributors to the campaign and arranges events and meetings with donors.

G

gender gap The measurable difference in the way women and men vote for candidates and in the way they view political issues.

general election An election that determines which candidates win the offices being sought.

general-purpose government A government providing services in numerous and diverse policy and functional areas to the residents living within its borders.

generational effect The impact of an important external event in shaping the views of a generation.

gerrymandering The drawing of legislative district boundaries to benefit an incumbent, a political party, or another group.

global economy The worldwide economy created by the integration and interdependence of national economies.

global warming The rising temperature of the earth as a result of pollution that traps solar heat, keeping the air warmer than it would otherwise be.

GOTV Get out the vote.

government The institution that creates and implements policy and laws that guide the conduct of the nation and its citizens.

government corporation An executive branch unit that sells a service and is expected to be financially self-sufficient.

government subsidy A tax break or another kind of financial support that encourages behaviors the government deems beneficial to the public good.

grandfather clause A clause exempting individuals from voting conditions such as poll taxes or literacy tests if they or their ancestors had voted before 1870, thus sparing most white voters.

grant-in-aid (intergovernmental transfer) The transfer of money from one government to another government that does not need to be paid back.

grassroots organizing Tasks that involve direct contact with voters or potential voters.

greenhouse effect The heating of the earth's atmosphere as a result of humans' burning of fossil fuels and the resultant buildup of carbon dioxide and other gases.

gross domestic product (GDP) The total market value of all goods and services produced by labor and properties within a country's borders.

H

habeas corpus An ancient right that protects an individual in custody from being held without the right to be heard in a court of law.

hacktivism The authorized or unauthorized use of or destruction of electronic files in pursuit of a political or social goal.

hate crime A crime committed against a person, property, or society, in which the offender is motivated, in part or in whole, by his or her bias against the victim because of the victim's race, religion, disability, sexual orientation, or ethnicity.

healthy economy According to economists, an economy experiencing an increase in its gross domestic product (GDP), low unemployment rate, and low inflation rate.

hearings Sessions held by committees or subcommittees to gather information and views from experts.

hegemony A form of imperial geographic dominance.

heightened scrutiny test (intermediate scrutiny test) The guidelines used most frequently by the courts to determine the legality of sex-based discrimination; on the basis of this test, sex-based discrimination is legal if the government can prove that it is substantially related to the achievement of an important public interest.

Holocaust The genocide perpetrated by Adolf Hitler and the Nazis of 6 million Jews, along with political dissidents, Catholics, homosexuals, individuals with disabilities, and gypsies.

home rule Power delegated by a state government to its citizens to formulate and adopt their municipal and county government charters and to determine the extent of those governments' powers and responsibilities as long as they comply with state and national law.

home rule charter A local government constitution written and approved by citizens following state-mandated procedures, including a referendum.

honeymoon period A time early in a new president's administration characterized by optimistic approval by the public.

hopper A wooden box that sits on a desk at the front of the House of Representatives, into which House members place bills they want to introduce.

horizontal federalism The state-to-state relationships created by the U.S. Constitution.

House majority leader The leader of the majority party, who helps the Speaker to develop and implement strategy and who works with other members of the House of Representatives.

House minority leader The leader of the minority party, whose job mirrors that of the majority leader but without the power that comes from holding a majority in the House of Representatives.

household income The total pretax earnings of all residents over the age of 15 living in a home.

housing insecurity The situation in which people have limited or uncertain ability to obtain, in socially acceptable ways, affordable, safe, and decent-quality permanent housing.

Human Development Index (HDI) A UN-created measure to determine how well a country's economy is providing for a long and healthy life, educational opportunity, and a decent standard of daily living.

I

imminent lawless action test (incitement test) A standard established in the 1969 *Brandenburg v. Ohio* case, whereby speech is restricted only if it goes beyond mere advocacy, or words, to create a high likelihood of immediate disorder or lawlessness.

impeachment The power of the House of Representatives to formally accuse the president (and other high-ranking officials, including the vice president and federal judges) of crimes.

imperial presidency A term coined by Arthur Schlesinger to describe the modern executive branch and the enormous powers the office has gained through assertion, the size of the bureaucracy, and the presence of staff loyal to an individual president.

implied powers The powers of the national government that are not enumerated in the Constitution but that Congress claims are necessary and proper for the national government to fulfill its enumerated powers in accordance with the necessary and proper clause of the Constitution.

impressment The forcible removal of merchant sailors from U.S. ships on the spurious grounds that the sailors were deserters from the British Navy.

in-kind assistance A cash transfer in which the government pays cash to those who provide goods or services to eligible individuals.

income inequality The gap in the proportion of national income held by the richest compared to that held by the poorest.

incumbency The situation of already holding the office that is up for reelection.

independent A voter who does not belong to any organized political party; often used as a synonym for an unaffiliated voter.

independent administrative agency An executive branch unit created by Congress and the president that is responsible for a narrowly defined function and whose structure is intended to be protected from partisan politics.

independent expenditures Outlays by PACs and others, typically for advertising for or against a candidate, but not coordinated with a candidate's campaign.

independent regulatory commission An executive branch unit outside of cabinet departments, responsible for developing standards of behavior within specific industries and businesses, monitoring compliance with these standards, and imposing sanctions on violators.

indexed benefit A government benefit with an automatic cost-of-living increase based on the rate of inflation.

indirect democracy Sometimes called a *representative democracy,* a system in which citizens elect representatives who decide policies on behalf of their constituents.

individualistic political culture The view that the decision to take part in government is an individual choice and those who choose to participate determine the purpose of government and personally benefit from their participation.

inflation The decreased value of money as evidenced by increased prices.

infotainment A hybrid of the words *information* and *entertainment;* news shows that combine entertainment and news.

inherent characteristics Individual attributes such as race, national origin, religion, and sex.

inherent powers Presidential powers that are implied in the Constitution.

initiative A citizen-sponsored proposal allowed in 24 states that can result in new or amended legislation or a state constitutional amendment.

inspectors general Political appointees who work within a government agency to ensure the integrity of public service by investigating allegations of misconduct by bureaucrats.

instant runoff election A special runoff election in which the computerized voting machine simulates the elimination of last-place vote-getters.

instructed delegate model A model of representation in which legislators, as representatives of their constituents, should vote in keeping with the constituents' views, even if those views contradict the legislator's personal views.

interest group An organization that seeks to achieve goals by influencing government decision making.

intergovernmental relations (IGR) The interactions of two or more governments (national, state, and local) in their collective efforts to provide goods and services to the people they each serve.

intermestics The influence of domestic interests on foreign policy.

International Monetary Fund (IMF) The institution charged with regulating monetary relationships among nations, including establishment of exchange rates for major world currencies; established in 1944 by the Bretton Woods Agreement.

intersectionality The experience of multiple forms of oppression (based on race, gender, class, sexual orientation, or sexual identity) simultaneously.

interstate compacts Agreements between states that Congress has the authority to review and reject.

interventionism A foreign policy characterized by a nation's willingness to participate and intervene in international situations, including another country's affairs.

iron triangle The interaction of mutual interests among members of Congress, executive agencies, and organized interests during policy making.

ISIS The Islamic State in Iraq and Syria, a radical international fundamentalist terror organization.

isolationism A foreign policy characterized by a nation's unwillingness to participate in international affairs.

issue network The fluid web of connections among those concerned about a policy and those who create and administer the policy.

J

Jim Crow laws Laws requiring the strict separation of racial groups, with whites and "nonwhites" required to attend separate schools, work in different jobs, and use segregated public accommodations, such as transportation and restaurants.

joint committee A bicameral committee composed of members of both chambers of Congress.

joint referral The practice, abolished in the 104th Congress, by which a bill could be referred to two different committees for consideration.

journalism The practice of gathering and reporting events.

judicial activism An approach to judicial decision making whereby judges are willing to strike down laws made by elected officials as well as step away from precedents.

judicial federalism State courts' use of their state constitutions to determine citizens' rights, particularly when state constitutions guarantee greater protections than does the U.S. Constitution.

judicial independence Insulating judges from the need to be accountable to voters or elected officials so that they can make impartial decisions based on the law.

judicial restraint An approach to judicial decision making whereby judges defer to the democratically elected legislative and executive branches of government.

judicial review Court authority to determine that an action taken by any government official or governing body violates or does not violate the Constitution; established by the Supreme Court in the 1803 *Marbury v. Madison* case.

jury trial A trial in which a group of people selected to hear the evidence presented decides on guilt or liability.

K

Keynesian economics The theory that recommends that during a recession the national government increase its spending and decrease taxes, and during a boom, cut spending and increase taxes.

L

laissez-faire The hands-off stance of a government in regard to the marketplace.

law A body of rules established by government officials that bind governments, individuals, and nongovernment organizations.

lead committee The primary committee considering a bill.

League of Nations A representative body founded in the aftermath of World War I to establish the collective security of nations.

legacy systems The old way of doing things, either in paper form or using outdated computer systems.

legal model Judicial decision-making model that focuses on legal norms and principles as the guiding force in judicial decision making, including existing precedents, relevant constitutional and statutory law, and the lawmakers' intent.

legitimacy A quality conferred on government by citizens who believe that its exercise of power is right and proper.

Lemon test A three-part test established by the Supreme Court in the 1971 case *Lemon v. Kurtzman* to determine whether government aid to parochial schools is constitutional; the test is also applied to other cases involving the establishment clause.

letter to the editor A letter in which a reader responds to a story in a newspaper, knowing that the letter might be published in that paper.

libel False written statements about others that harm their reputation.

liberalism An ideology that advocates change in the social, political, and economic realms to better protect the well-being of individuals and to produce equality within society.

libertarianism An ideology whose advocates believe that government should take a "hands off" approach in most matters.

liberty The most essential quality of American democracy; it is both the freedom from governmental interference in citizens' lives and the freedom to pursue happiness.

limited government Government that is restricted in what it can do so that the rights of the people are protected.

limited war A combatant country's self-imposed limitation on the tactics and strategy it uses, particularly its avoidance of the use of nuclear weapons.

literacy test A test to determine eligibility to vote; designed so that few African Americans would pass.

living Constitution View that legal interpretation of the Constitution can and should adapt to changing social customs and norms.

living wage A wage high enough to keep workers and their families out of poverty and to allow them to enjoy a basic living standard.

lobby To communicate directly with policymakers on an interest group's behalf.

logrolling The practice of members of Congress agreeing to vote for a bill in exchange for their colleague's vote on another bill.

loyal opposition A role that the party out of power plays, highlighting its objections to policies and priorities of the government in power.

M

majority rule The idea that in a democracy, only policies with 50 percent plus one vote are enacted, and only candidates that win 50 percent plus one vote are elected.

majority whip The go-between with the majority leadership and party members in the House of Representatives.

majority-minority district A legislative district composed of a majority of a given minority community—say, African Americans—the intent of which is to make it likely that a member of that minority will be elected to Congress.

mandates Clauses in legislation that direct state and local governments to comply with national legislation and national standards.

mandatory jurisdiction The requirement that a court hear all cases filed with it.

mandatory spending Government spending for debt and programs whose budget authority is provided in legislation other than annual appropriation acts; this budget authority is open ended, obligating the government to pay for the program whatever the cost, every year.

manifest destiny The idea that it was the United States' destiny to spread throughout the North American continent; used to rationalize the expansion of U.S. territory.

Marbury v. Madison The 1803 Supreme Court case that established the power of judicial review, which allows the Court to strike down laws passed by the other branches that it views to be in conflict with the Constitution.

marketplace of ideas A concept at the core of the freedoms of expression and press, based on the belief that true and free political discourse depends on a free and unrestrained discussion of ideas.

markup The process by which the members of legislative committees "mark up" a bill with suggested language for changes and amendments.

Marshall Plan The U.S. government program that provided funds necessary for Western European countries to rebuild after World War II.

matching funds requirement A grant requirement that obligates the government receiving the grant to spend some of its own money to match a specified percentage of the grant money provided.

McCulloch v. Maryland The 1819 case that established that the necessary and proper clause justifies broad understandings of enumerated powers.

means-tested benefit A benefit for which eligibility is based on having an income below a government-specified amount, typically based on a percentage of the poverty guideline.

media Tools used to store and deliver information or data.

media consultant A professional who brings the campaign message to voters by creating handouts and all forms of media ads.

media segmentation The breaking down of the media according to the specific audiences they target.

median household income The middle of all household incomes—50 percent of households have incomes less than the median and 50 percent have incomes greater than the median.

merit selection process A process for selecting judges in which a nonpartisan committee nominates candidates, the governor or legislature appoints judges from among those candidates to a short term of service, and then the appointed judges face a retention election at the end of the short term.

merit-based civil service A personnel system in which bureaucrats are hired on the basis of the principles of competence, equal opportunity (open competition), and political neutrality; once hired, these public servants have job protection.

micro-blog Sites, including Twitter, that enable short communication, often targeted specifically at on-the-move audiences.

microtarget Data-mining techniques that facilitate the tracking of individual voter preferences so that tailored messages in various forms can be used to generate support, contributions, and votes.

minority whip The go-between with the minority leadership, whose job mirrors that of the majority whip but without the power that comes from holding a majority in the House of Representatives.

Miranda rights A criminal procedural rule, established in the 1966 case *Miranda v. Arizona,* requiring police to inform criminal suspects, on their arrest, of their legal rights, such as the right to remain silent and the right to counsel; these warnings must be read to suspects before interrogation.

monarchy Government in which a member of a royal family, usually a king or queen, has absolute authority over a territory and its government.

monetarism The theory that says the government's proper economic role is to control the rate of inflation by controlling the amount of money in circulation.

monetary policy The body of Federal Reserve actions aimed at adjusting the amount of money (coin, currency, and bank deposits) in the economy to maintain a stable, low level of inflation.

Monroe Doctrine President James Monroe's 1823 declaration that the Americas should not be considered subjects for future colonization by any European power.

moralistic political culture The view that the purpose of government is to serve the public good, including providing for those who are disadvantaged, and that all citizens should participate in government.

muckraking Criticism and exposés of corruption in government and industry by journalists at the turn of the 20th century.

multilateral Many-sided; having the support of numerous nations.

municipal government Self-governing general-purpose government—including city, borough, and town governments—created by states to provide goods and services within a densely populated area.

mutual assured destruction (MAD) The doctrine that if one nation attacked another with nuclear weapons, the other would be capable of retaliating and would retaliate with such force as to ensure mutual annihilation.

N

narrowcasting The practice of aiming media content at specific segments of the public.

national debt The total amount of money the government owes to all the individuals and groups that loaned it money.

National Security Advisor The assistant to the president for national security affairs, advisor to the president on national security policy, and administrator over the day-to-day operations of the National Security Council.

National Security Council (NSC) Consisting of top foreign policy advisers and relevant cabinet officials, this is an arm of the Executive Office of the President that the president consults on matters of foreign policy and national security.

natural law The assertion that standards that govern human behavior are derived from the nature of humans themselves and can be applied universally.

natural rights The rights possessed by all humans as a gift from nature, or God, including the rights to life, liberty, and the pursuit of happiness (also called *unalienable rights*).

naturalization The process of becoming a citizen by means other than birth, as in the case of immigrants.

necessary and proper clause (elastic clause) A clause in Article I, Section 8, of the Constitution that gives Congress the power to do whatever it deems necessary and constitutional to meet its enumerated obligations; the basis for the implied powers.

Net neutrality The idea that Internet traffic should flow through the Internet pipeline without interference or discrimination by those who own or are running the pipeline.

netroots The Internet-centered political efforts on behalf of candidates and causes.

New Deal Franklin D. Roosevelt's broad social welfare program in which the government would bear the responsibility of providing a safety net to protect the most disadvantaged members of society.

New Deal coalition The group composed of southern Democrats, northern city dwellers, immigrants, the poor, Catholics, labor union members, blue-collar workers, African Americans, and women who elected Franklin D. Roosevelt to the presidency four times.

New Jersey Plan The proposal presented in response to the Virginia Plan by the less populous states at the Constitutional Convention, which called for a unicameral national legislature in which all states would have an equal voice (equal representation), an executive office composed of several people elected by Congress, and a Supreme Court whose members would be appointed by the executive office.

new media Sources of information—including Internet websites, blogs, social networking sites such as Facebook and Twitter, photo- and video-sharing platforms such as Instagram and YouTube, and apps—and the cellular and satellite technologies that facilitate their use.

news aggregators Services that compile in one location news we want from various outlets.

NIMBY ("not in my backyard") syndrome A pattern of citizens' behavior in which people are not inspired to participate in politics until a government action or inaction threatens them directly.

Nixon Doctrine Policy emphasizing the responsibility of U.S. allies to provide for their own national defense and security, aimed at improving relations with the communist nations, including the Soviet Union and China.

noncontributory program A benefit provided to a targeted population, paid for by a proportion of the money collected from all taxpayers.

nonpartisan election An election in which the candidates are not nominated by political parties and the ballot does not include party affiliations.

nontariff trade barriers Business and social regulations as well as government subsidies aimed at creating a competitive advantage in trade.

normal trade relations (NTR) status The international trade principle holding that the least restrictive trade conditions (best tariff rates) offered to any one national trading partner will be offered to every other nation in a trading network (also known as *most favored nations*).

North Atlantic Treaty Organization (NATO) An international mutual defense alliance formed in 1949 that created a structure for regional security for its 15 member nations.

nuclear option A maneuver exercised by the presiding officer in the Senate that eliminates the possibility of filibusters by subjecting votes on certain matters to a simple majority vote.

nullification A legal theory that state governments have the authority to invalidate national actions they deem unconstitutional.

O

obscenity Indecent or offensive speech or expression.

Office of Management and Budget (OMB) The office that creates the president's annual budget.

office-block ballot A type of ballot that arranges all the candidates for a particular office under the name of that office.

oligarchy Government in which an elite few hold power.

ombudsperson A role in which an elected or appointed leader acts as an advocate for citizens by listening to and investigating complaints against a government agency.

open primary A type of primary in which both parties' ballots are available in the voting booth, and the voters simply select one on which to register their preferences.

operating budget A budget that accounts for all the costs of day-to-day government operations and covers such items as salaries and benefits, utilities, office supplies, and rent.

ordinary scrutiny test (rational basis test) On the basis of this test, sex-based discrimination is legal if it is a reasonable means by which the government can achieve a legitimate public interest.

originalism (textualism) View that the Constitution means no more or less than it meant to those who wrote it.

original jurisdiction Judicial authority to hear cases for the first time and to determine guilt or liability by applying the law to the facts presented.

oversight The process by which the legislative branch "checks" the executive branch to ensure that the laws Congress has passed are being administered in keeping with legislators' intent.

P

partisan election An election in which candidates are nominated by political parties and the ballot lists each candidate's political party affiliation.

partisan federalism The phenomenon of preference for state or national government action (hence, preference for dual federalism, cooperative federalism, or centralized federalism) depending on policy substance and partisan makeup of government at the other levels.

party identifiers Individuals who identify themselves as a member of one party or the other.

party in government The partisan identifications of elected leaders in local, county, state, and federal government.

party in the electorate Individuals who identify with or tend to support a party.

party organization The formal party apparatus, including committees, party leaders, conventions, and workers.

party system The categorization of the number and competitiveness of political parties in a polity.

party-column ballot A ballot that organizes the candidates by political party.

patronage The system in which a party leader rewarded political supporters with jobs or government contracts in exchange for their support of the party.

patronage system A personnel system in which the chief executive officer (CEO) can appoint whomever he or she wants to top bureaucratic positions, without the need for open competition for applicants; those hired through patronage typically serve at the pleasure of the CEO who hired them.

payroll taxes Taxes employers deduct from workers' paychecks that pay for social insurance programs including Social Security and Medicare.

penal code The compilation of a state's criminal law—legislation that defines crime—into one document.

penny press Newspapers that sold for a penny in the 1830s.

platform The formal statement of a party's principles and policy objectives.

Plessy v. Ferguson 1896 Supreme Court ruling creating the separate but equal doctrine.

plum book A publication that lists the top jobs in the bureaucracy to which the president will appoint people through the patronage system.

plural executive system A state and local government structure in which the citizens elect more than two people to top positions in the executive branch of government.

pluralist theory A theory that holds that policy making is a competition among diverse interest groups that ensure the representation of individual interests.

pocket veto A special presidential veto of a bill passed at the conclusion of a legislative session, whereby the president waits 10 days without signing the bill, and the bill dies.

police powers The states' reserved powers to protect the health, safety, lives, and properties of residents in a state.

political action committee (PAC) An entity whose specific goal is to raise and spend money to influence the outcome of elections.

political culture The people's collective beliefs and attitudes about government and political processes.

political engagement Citizen actions that are intended to solve public problems through political means.

political ideology An integrated system of ideas or beliefs about political values in general and the role of government in particular.

political machines Big-city organizations that exerted control over many aspects of life and lavishly rewarded supporters.

political party An organization that recruits, nominates, and elects party members to office in order to control the government.

political socialization The process by which we develop our political values and opinions.

politically uncontrollable spending Spending on programs that are so popular that elected officials are not willing to change the laws that authorize the programs for fear of the effect on their reelection prospects.

politico A hybrid model of representation in which legislators vote in keeping with constituents' views on important or high-profile matters but rely on the trustee model for more mundane matters.

politics The process of deciding who gets benefits in society and who does not.

politics-administration dichotomy The concept that elected government officials, who are accountable to the voters, create and approve public policy, and then competent, politically neutral bureaucrats implement the public policy.

poll tax A fee for voting; levied to prevent poor African Americans in the South from voting.

popular sovereignty The theory that government is created by the people and depends on the people for the authority to rule.

population In a poll, the group of people whose opinions are of interest and/or about whom information is desired.

populism A philosophy supporting the rights and empowerment of the masses as opposed to elites.

pork barrel Legislators' appropriations of funds for special projects located within their congressional districts.

poverty The condition of lacking the income sufficient to purchase the necessities for an adequate living standard.

poverty guidelines A simplified version of the U.S. Census Bureau's poverty thresholds developed each year by the Department of Health and Human Services; used to set financial eligibility criteria for benefits.

poverty rate The proportion of the population living below the poverty line as established by the national government.

poverty thresholds The U.S. Census Bureau's annually updated set of income measures (adjusted for family size) that define who is living in poverty.

precedent cases Previous cases with similar facts that judges identify for use in a new case they are deciding; judges apply the legal principles used in the precedent cases to decide the legal dispute they are currently resolving.

preemption The constitutionally based principle that allows a national law to supersede state or local laws.

preponderance of evidence The standard of proof used in civil cases; the evidence must show that it is more likely than not that the accused caused the harm claimed by the complainant.

president pro tempore Also called *president pro tem;* theoretically, the chair of the Senate in the vice president's absence; in reality, an honorary title, with the senator of the majority party having the longest record of continuous service being elected to the position.

press secretary The president's spokesperson to the media.

preventive war The strategy of waging war on countries that are regarded as threatening in order to avoid future conflicts.

primary election An election in which voters choose the party's candidates who will run in the later general election.

priming Bringing certain policies on issues to the public agenda through media coverage.

prior restraint A form of censorship by the government whereby it blocks the publication of news stories viewed as libelous or harmful.

privileges and immunities clause The Constitution's requirement that a state extend to other states' citizens the privileges and immunities it provides for its citizens.

progressive tax A tax that takes a larger percentage of the income of wealthier taxpayers and a smaller percentage of the income of lower-income taxpayers.

promoted tweets Targeted advertising found on a Twitter page that targets Twitterers based on whom they follow and who follows them.

property Anything that can be owned.

proportional (flat) tax A tax that takes the same percentage of each taxpayer's income.

proportional representation system An electoral structure in which political parties win the number of parliamentary seats equal to the percentage of the vote the party receives.

proposition A proposed measure placed on the ballot in an initiative election.

prospective voting A method of evaluating candidates in which voters focus on candidates' positions on issues important to them and vote for the candidates who best represent their views.

protectionist trade policy The establishment of trade barriers to shelter domestic goods from foreign competition.

public agenda The public issues that most demand the attention of government officials.

public diplomat An individual outside government who promotes his or her country's interests and thus helps to shape international perceptions of the nation.

public employee unions Labor organizations comprising federal, state, and municipal workers, including police officers and teachers.

public goods Goods whose benefits cannot be limited and that are available to all.

public opinion The public's expressed views about an issue at a specific point in time.

public opinion poll A survey of a given population's opinion on an issue or a candidate at a particular point in time.

pure capitalist economy An economy in which private individuals and companies own the modes of producing goods and services, and the government does not enact laws aimed at influencing the marketplace transactions that distribute those goods and services.

purposive incentive Motivation to join an interest group based on the belief in the group's cause from an ideological or a moral standpoint.

push polls A special type of poll that both attempts to skew public opinion about a candidate and provides information to campaigns about candidate strengths and weaknesses.

Q

quota sample A method by which pollsters structure a sample so that it is representative of the characteristics of the target population.

R

rally 'round the flag effect The peaks in presidential approval ratings during short-term military action.

random sampling A scientific method of selection in which each member of the population has an equal chance of being included in the sample.

rational choice theory The idea that from an economic perspective it is not rational for people to participate in collective action when they can secure the collective good without participating.

real income Earned income adjusted for inflation.

realignment A shift in party allegiances or electoral support that propels a political party to majority status.

reapportionment Reallocation of seats in the House of Representatives to each state based on changes in state populations since the last census.

recall A special election in which voters can remove an officeholder before his or her term is over.

recession An economic downturn during which unemployment is high and the production of goods and services is low.

Reconstruction era The time after the Civil War between 1866 and 1877 when the institutions and infrastructure of the South were rebuilt.

red tape Bureaucratic rules and procedures that are viewed as inefficient, dehumanizing, and requiring tedious paperwork.

redistricting The redrawing of congressional district boundaries within each state, based on the reapportionment from the census.

referendum An election in which voters in a state can vote for or against a measure proposed by the state legislature.

regime change The replacement of a country's government with another government by facilitating the deposing of its leader or leading political party.

regional security alliance An alliance typically between a superpower and nations that are ideologically similar in a particular region.

regressive tax A tax that takes a greater percentage of the income of lower-income earners than of higher-income earners.

regulated capitalist economy (mixed economy) An economy in which private ownership of the modes of production dominate and the government enacts policies to influence the health of the economy.

remarketing Targeting political Google ads based on the cookies that a user drops on other websites.

report A legislative committee's explanation to the full chamber of a bill and its intent.

representative bureaucracy A bureaucracy in which the people serving resemble the larger population whom they serve in demographic characteristics such as race, age, ethnicity, sex, religion, and economic status.

republic A government that derives its authority from the people and in which citizens elect government officials to represent them in the processes by which laws are made; a representative democracy.

reserved powers The matters referred to in the Tenth Amendment over which states retain sovereignty.

responsible party model Political scientists' view that a function of a party is to offer a clear choice to voters by establishing priorities or policy stances different from those of rival parties.

retention election A noncompetitive election in which an incumbent judge's name is on the ballot and voters decide whether the judge should be retained.

retrospective voting A method of evaluating candidates in which voters evaluate incumbent candidates and decide whether to support them based on their past performance.

right to privacy The right of an individual to be left alone and to make decisions freely, without the interference of others.

Roosevelt Corollary The idea, advanced by President Theodore Roosevelt, that the United States had the right to act as an "international police power" in the Western Hemisphere to ensure stability in the region.

Rule of Four Practice by which the Supreme Court justices determine if they will hear a case if four or more justices want to hear it.

Rules Committee One of the most important committees in the House, which decides the length of debate and the scope of amendments that will be allowed on a bill.

runoff election A follow-up election that is held when no candidate receives the majority of votes cast in the original election.

S

safety net programs A collection of public policies aimed at ensuring that citizens' basic physiological needs are met.

salient In relation to a voting issue—having resonance, being significant, causing intense interest.

sampling error Also called *margin of error;* a statistical calculation of the difference in results between a poll of a randomly drawn sample and a poll of the entire population.

sanctions Penalties that halt economic exchanges.

select committee A congressional committee created to consider specific policy issues or address a specific concern.

selective incorporation The process by which, over time, the Supreme Court applied those freedoms that served *some* fundamental principle of liberty or justice to the states, thus rejecting total incorporation.

Senate majority leader The most powerful position in the Senate; the majority leader manages the legislative process and schedules debate on legislation.

Senate minority leader The leader of the minority party in the Senate, who works with the majority leader in negotiating legislation.

senatorial courtesy A custom whereby the Senate will not confirm a presidential nominee if the nominee is opposed by one (or both) senators from the nominee's home state.

Senior Executive Service (SES) A unique personnel system for top managerial, supervisory, and policy positions offering less job security but higher pay than the merit-based civil service system.

seniority system The system in which the member with the longest continuous tenure on a standing committee is given preference when the committee chooses its chair.

separate but equal doctrine Established by the Supreme Court in *Plessy v. Ferguson,* it said that separate but equal facilities for whites and nonwhites do not violate the Fourteenth Amendment's equal protection clause.

separation of powers The Constitution's delegation of authority for the primary governing functions among three branches of government so that no one group of government officials controls all the governing functions.

sequestration Automatic spending cuts during the fiscal year.

shadow bureaucrats People hired and paid by private for-profit and nonprofit organizations that implement public policy through a government contract.

signing statement A written message that the president issues upon signing a bill into law.

slander False verbal statements about others that harm their reputation.

social capital The many ways in which our lives are improved in many ways by social connections.

social contract An agreement between people and their leaders in which the people agree to give up some liberties so that their other liberties are protected.

social contract theory The idea that individuals possess free will, and every individual is equally endowed with the God-given right of self-determination and the ability to consent to be governed.

social movement Large, often informal groups of individuals or organizations striving for a broad, common goal, frequently centered on significant change to the social or political order.

social networking sites Platforms that enable users to construct a profile, specify other users with whom they share a connection, and view others' connections.

social regulation Government rules, regulations, and standards aimed at protecting workers, consumers, and the environment from market failure.

socialism An ideology that advocates economic equality, theoretically achieved by having the government or workers own the means of production (businesses and industry).

soft money loophole The Supreme Court's interpretation of campaign finance law that enabled political parties to raise unlimited funds for party-building activities such as voter registration drives and get-out-the-vote (GOTV) efforts.

solidary incentive The motivation to join an interest group based on the companionship and the satisfaction derived from socializing with others that it offers.

Speaker of the House The leader of the House of Representatives, chosen by the majority party.

special-purpose government A government providing one service or function for residents living within its borders.

spoils system The practice of rewarding political supporters with jobs.

standing committee A permanent committee in Congress, with a defined legislative jurisdiction.

standing to sue The legal right to bring lawsuits in court.

statutory powers Powers explicitly granted to presidents by congressional action.

strategic arms limitation talks (SALT talks) Discussions between the United States and the Soviet Union in the 1970s that focused on cooling down the nuclear arms race between the two superpowers.

strategic arms reduction talks (START talks) Talks between the United States and the Soviet Union in which reductions in missiles and nuclear warheads, not merely a limitation on increases, were negotiated.

strategic defense initiative (SDI, or "Star Wars") A ballistic missile defense system advocated by President Ronald Reagan.

strategic model Judicial decision-making model that states that the primary guide for judges is their individual policy preferences; however, their preferences are tempered by their consideration of institutional factors, as well as concern over the legitimacy of the court system.

stratified sampling A process of random sampling in which the national population is divided into fourths and certain areas within these regions are selected as representative of the national population.

strict scrutiny test Guidelines the courts use to determine the legality of suspect classification based discrimination; on the basis of this test, discrimination is legal if it is a necessary means by which the government can achieve a compelling public interest.

strong mayor An elected municipal government executive who holds the powers traditionally delegated to elected chief executives (veto power, power to formulate the budget, and power to appoint many executive branch officials).

subcommittee A subordinate committee in Congress that typically handles specific areas of a standing committee's jurisdiction.

substantive representation Assumption that a government official will best serve the concerns of the racial, ethnic, gender, or other group to which he or she belongs.

sunset clause A clause in legislation that sets an expiration date for an authorized program or policy unless Congress reauthorizes it.

sunshine laws Legislation that opens up government functions and documents to the public.

super PACs Political organizations that use contributions from individuals, corporations, and labor unions to spend unlimited sums independent from the campaigns, yet influencing the outcomes of elections.

Super Tuesday The Tuesday in early March on which the most primary elections are held, many of them in southern states.

superpowers Leader nations with dominating influence in international affairs.

supply-side economics The theory that advocates cutting taxes and deregulating business to stimulate the economy.

supremacy clause A clause in Article VI of the Constitution that states that the Constitution and the treaties and laws created by the national government in compliance with the Constitution are the supreme law of the land.

supreme law of the land The U.S. Constitution's description of its own authority, meaning that all laws made by governments within the United States must be in compliance with the Constitution.

suspect classifications Distinctions based on race, religion, and national origin, which are assumed to be illegitimate.

symbolic representation Diversity among government officials is a symbol, an indication, that our democracy, our government by and for the people, is functioning appropriately by offering equal opportunity to influence government by becoming a government official.

symbolic speech Nonverbal "speech" in the form of an action such as picketing, flag burning, or wearing an armband to signify a protest.

T

take care clause The constitutional basis for inherent powers, which states that the president "shall take Care that the Laws be faithfully executed."

talk radio A format featuring conversations and interviews about topics of interest, along with call-ins from listeners.

tariff A special tax on imported goods paid by the importer.

tax base The overall *wealth* (income and assets of citizens and corporations) that the government can tax to raise revenue.

tax expenditures (also, *tax breaks* or *loopholes*) Government financial incentives that allow individuals and corporations to pay reduced taxes, to encourage behaviors that promote the public good.

Tea Party movement A grassroots, conservative protest movement that opposed recent government actions, including economic stimulus spending and health care reform.

telegenic The quality of looking good on TV.

The Federalist Papers A series of essays, written by James Madison, Alexander Hamilton, and John Jay, that argued for the ratification of the Constitution.

third party A party organized in opposition or as an alternative to the existing parties in a two-party system.

Three-Fifths Compromise The negotiated agreement by the delegates to the Constitutional Convention to count each slave as three-fifths of a free man for the purpose of representation and taxes.

ticket splitting The situation in which voters vote for candidates from more than one party.

time, place, and manner restrictions Regulations regarding when, where, or how expression may occur; must be content neutral.

tort Situation when a person's body or property is harmed by another person's negligence or other wrongful act, other than the violation of a contract.

total incorporation The theory that the Fourteenth Amendment's due process clause requires the states to uphold *all* freedoms in the Bill of Rights; rejected by the Supreme Court in favor of selective incorporation.

totalitarianism System of government in which the government essentially controls every aspect of people's lives.

township A unit of government that serves people living outside municipalities, in rural areas where the population is more dispersed than in areas served by municipal governments.

tracking polls Polls that measure changes in public opinion over the course of days, weeks, or months by repeatedly asking respondents the same questions and measuring changes in their responses.

trade policy A collection of tax laws and regulations that support the country's international commerce.

traditionalistic political culture The view that the purpose of government is to maintain the status quo and that participants in government should come from the society's elite.

transgender Individuals whose gender identity does not match the sex they were assigned at birth.

transparency Ability of citizens to have more and better information about governmental processes as well as services.

trial court Court with original jurisdiction in a legal dispute that decides guilt or liability based on its understanding of the facts presented by the two disputing parties.

Truman Doctrine Articulated by President Harry Truman, a foreign policy commitment by the United States to assist countries' efforts to resist communism in the Cold War era.

truncated government The situation that exists when one chamber of Congress is controlled by the same party that controls the White House, while the other chamber is controlled by the other party.

trustee model A model of representation in which a member of the House or the Senate follows his or her own conscience when deciding issue positions.

turnout rate The proportion of eligible voters who actually voted.

U

U.S. Code A compilation of all the laws passed by the U.S. Congress.

U.S. Supreme Court The court of last resort for conflicts over the U.S. Constitution and national laws; in addition to its appellate jurisdiction, the Court has limited original jurisdiction.

umbrella organizations Interest groups that represent collective groups of industries or corporations.

unanimous consent An agreement by every senator to the terms of debate on a given piece of legislation.

unicameral legislature A legislative body with a single chamber.

unitary system A governmental system in which one central government is *the* sovereign government and it creates other, regional governments to which it delegates some governing powers and responsibilities; however, the central government retains ultimate authority (sovereignty).

United Nations (UN) An international body established in 1945 in order to prevent future wars by achieving collective security and peace.

V

veto The president's rejection of a bill, which is sent back to Congress with the president's objections noted.

Virginia Plan The new governmental structure proposed by the Virginia delegation to the Constitutional Convention, which consisted of a bicameral legislature (Congress), an executive elected by the legislature, and a separate national judiciary; state representation in Congress would be proportional, based on state population; the people would elect members to the lower house, and members of the lower house would elect the members of the upper house.

virtual communities Online networks where individuals perform as leaders, information and opinions can be shared, and strategies can be planned, priorities organized, and roles assigned.

vlog A video weblog.

voter fatigue The condition in which voters grow tired of all candidates by the time Election Day arrives, and may thus be less likely to vote.

W

waivers Exemptions from particular conditions normally attached to grants.

War Powers Act A law that limits presidential use of military forces to 60 days, with an automatic extension of 30 additional days if the president requests such an extension.

Warsaw Pact A regional security structure formed in 1955 by the Soviet Union and its seven satellite states in Eastern Europe in response to the creation of the North Atlantic Treaty Organization (NATO).

Watergate During the Nixon administration, a scandal involving burglaries and the subsequent cover-up by high-level administration officials.

weak mayor An elected municipal government executive who holds few, if any, of the powers traditionally delegated to elected chief executives.

weapons of mass destruction (WMDs) Nuclear, chemical, and biological weapons.

whistleblower A bureaucrat or private party who discloses to the government mismanagement, fraud, waste, corruption, or threats to public health and safety.

White House counsel The president's lawyer.

White House Office (WHO) The office that develops policies and protects the president's legal and political interests.

white primary A primary election in which a party's nominees for general election were chosen but in which only white people were allowed to vote.

wiki Internet-based editing tool that allows documents to be created and edited online by multiple individuals.

winner-take-all system An electoral system in which the candidate who receives the most votes wins that office, even if that total is not a majority.

Works Progress Administration (WPA) A New Deal program that employed 8.5 million people at a cost of more than $11 million between 1935 and 1943.

World Bank The international financial institution created by the Bretton Woods Agreement of 1944 and charged with lending money to nations in need.

World Trade Organization (WTO) The organization created in 1995 to negotiate, implement, and enforce international trade agreements.

writ of *certiorari* Latin for "a request to make certain"; issued by a higher court, this is an order for a lower court to make available the records of a past case it decided so that the higher court can review the case.

Y

yellow journalism An irresponsible, sensationalist approach to news reporting, so named after the yellow ink used in the "Yellow Kid" cartoons in the *New York World.*

evaluation, of policy, 484
evidence, 504
ex post facto laws, 69
exclusionary rule, 142–143, *143*
executive branch, 436*f*, 437*t. See also* presidents
  chief executive, 434
  departments for, 476
  Electoral College, 45–46
  executive budgets, 547–548, *548*
  Executive Office of the President, 438–440, 479–480
  executive orders, 80, 444, 501–502, *502*
  executive privilege, 445
  foreign policy for, 602–603
  history of, 449–454, *451, 453*
  Office of Management and Budget, 437, 439–440, 487
  oversight of, 401–402
  policy for, 43–44, 44*f*
  powers for, 70–72
  press secretary, 439
  propaganda for, 449
  special presidential powers, 443–445
  structure of, 51
  vetoes for, 51
exit polls, 216
expenditures, 545, 547*f*, 568*t*
expert testimony, 246
exports, 70
expressed powers, 442
expression, 126–127
extradition, 96
extremism, 380–381

F

FAA (Federal Aviation Administration), 108, *473*
Facebook, 8, *300*, 335–336
  activism on, 362
  in elections, 374–375
  politics on, 359
  trends for, 365
faces, of politics, 265–272, 265*f, 267, 268t, 269f, 271, 271f,* 292
facts
  for age, 22*f*, 511
  in critical thinking, 7
  Factcheck, 29
  for race, 23*f*
  for Supreme Court, 517
Fair Labor Standards Act, 553, 580
fair trials, 143–144, 144*t*
fairness doctrine, 343
faith, 201–202
fake news, 7, 378–379
False Claims Act, 492
family
  Aid to Dependent Children, 581
  for Americans, 25–26
  child tax credits, 581
  community and, 16
  Deferred Action for Childhood Arrivals, 589
  Deferred Action for Parents of Americans and Lawful Permanent Residents, 589
  family values, 244
  politics and, 282–283
  public assistance for, 104*t*, 106
  in public opinion, *198–199*, 198–200, 254
  State Children's Health Insurance Program, 584

Supplemental Nutrition Assistance Program, 569
Temporary Assistance to Needy Families, 106, 581–582
farming, 241–242
Farook, Syed, 379–380
FBI (Federal Bureau of Investigation), 286, 299
FCC (Federal Communications Commission), 343, 350–352, 382–383
FDA (Food and Drug Administration), 553, 569, *569*
FDIC (Federal Deposit Insurance Corporation), 570
FDR. *See* Roosevelt, Franklin D.
Feagin, Clairece Booher, 183
Feagin, Joe R., 183
FEC (Federal Election Commission), 315, 317, 370, 428
Federal Aviation Administration (FAA), 108, *473*
Federal Bureau of Investigation (FBI), 286, 299
Federal Communications Commission (FCC), 343, 350–352, 382–383
Federal Communications Commission v. Television Stations, Inc., 351
Federal Corrupt Practices Act, 314
federal courts
  federal court of appeals, 508–509
  ideology of, 72–73, 527
  systems for, 506–509, 507*f*, 508*t, 509*
Federal Deposit Insurance Corporation (FDIC), 570
Federal Election Campaign Act, 314
Federal Election Commission (FEC), 315, 317, 370, 428
Federal Election Commission v. Wisconsin Right to Life, Inc., 317
Federal Emergency Management Agency (FEMA), 232, 492
federal grants, 104–105, 105*f*
Federal Insurance Contribution Act, 579
Federal Open Market Committee (FOMC), 551–552
federal questions, 506
Federal Reserve Board, 432, *432*, 533, 551–552, *552*
federal system, 43, 48. *See also* bureaucracy
  authority in, 91–100
  centralized federalism, 101–102
  concurrent powers in, 82
  conflicted federalism, 102
  cooperative federalism, 101
  critical thinking about, 112–113
  debates on, 53
  dual federalism, 101
  FAA in, 108
  federal grants, 104–105, 105*f*
  fiscal federalism, 104–105, 104*t*
  government and, *103*
  history of, 100–104
  IGR in, 104–112
  learning objectives for, 87, 113
  "Observations on the New Constitution" (Warren, M.), 53
  partisan federalism, 102–104
  readings for, 116
  states in, 87
  theory of, 88–91
  trends in, 86, 111–112
Federal Trade Commission (FTC), 553
Federal Water Pollution Control Act, 574

The Federalist Papers, 53–56, 100, 299–300, 510
Federalist Party, 273
federalists
  Anti-Federalists and, 53–56
  in bureaucracy, 469–473, *470*, 472*t, 473*
  ratification process for, 59
Federal-State Unemployment Insurance Program, 579–580
Feinstein, Dianne, 378
FEMA (Federal Emergency Management Agency), 232, 492
feminism. *See also* #MeToo
  activism for, 238–239, *239*
  Bradwell v. Illinois, 174–175, 177
  in Constitution (U.S.), 175–176
  history of, 173–174, 192
  legislation for, 176–177, *177*
  NOW, 204–206, 204*f*–205*f, 206*
  in politics, 417–418, 418*f*
  presidents and, 454–456, 455*f*
  in states, 174–175, *175*
  suffrage, 173–176, *175*
  trends in, 178–179
Ferdinand (Archduke), 610
fifth party system, 276–277
fighting words, 132
filibusters, 408–409, 408*t*, 522
FindLaw, 61
fines, 78
Fiorina, Morris, 400–401
Fire and Fury (Wolf), *130*
fireside chats, 343, *343*
first lady, 441, 455–456, *456*
first party system, 272–273
fiscal policy
  data for, 545*f*, 547*f*, 550*f*, 551*f*
  fiscal federalism, 104–105, 104*t*
  fiscal year, 544
  ideology of, 533, 543–551, *548*
  theory of, 541
Fisher, Jeffrey, 525
527, 317, 327
501(c)4s, 317, 327
The Fix (blog), 365
Fleming, Jonathan, *143*
floor action, 405*f*
Florida, 25, 248–249, 305
Flynn, Michael T., 439
FOMC (Federal Open Market Committee), 551–552
Food and Drug Administration (FDA), 553, 569, *569*
food insecurity, 583
Ford, Gerald, 85, 277, 435
foreign policy, 244–245, 340–341, 551*f*, 566
  chief diplomat, 433
  Congress, 603
  critical thinking about, 626, 630–631, 633
  diplomacy in, 597
  economic policy in, 598–600
  economics and, 392
  environment in, 629
  for executive branch, 602–603
  Foreign Intelligence Surveillance Act (1978), 146, 377–378, 508
  globalization and, 611–621, 612*f, 613, 615, 617–618,* 628
  learning objectives for, 596, 631–633
  media and, 604–605
  military for, 600–601, 603–604
  military-industrial complex in, 603–604
  movies about, 634

North American Free Trade Agreement, 599
  nuclear option in, 628–629, 629*f*
  for presidents, 602–603
  for private citizens, 605–606
  public opinion and, 605
  technology in, 604–605, 630
  for terrorism, 621–627, *624*
  for trade, 598–600, 627–628
  trends in, 596
  for U.S., 340–341, 392, 433, 435, 601, 606–611, *607, 609*
  for vice presidents, 435
foreign service officers, 598
formal eligibility, 309
formulation, of policy, 482
Foursquare (app), 370
fourth party system, 275–276, *276*
framing, 337–338
France, 443–444, 607–608
Francis (Pope), 7
franking, *393*, 394
Franklin, Ben, 300
fraud, 492
Frazee, William, *451*
free exercise clause, 136–138
free rider problem, 242
free speech. *See also* censorship
  for artists, 131, *131*
  assembly and, 146
  commercial speech, 131
  in education, 148–150
  fighting words, 132
  history of, 127–129
  Internet and, 381–382
  libel, 131
  lobbying and, 251
  obscenity, 131
  politics of, 353
  pure speech, 129–131
  redress of grievances, 132–133
  for religion, 134–138
  slander, 131
  for Supreme Court, 129–131
  symbolic speech, 129–131
  unprotected speech, 131–132
freedom of assembly, 132–133
Freedom of Information Act (1966), 485
freedoms, 120, 124–126
Friedman, Milton, 543
friend of the court briefs, 516
FTC (Federal Trade Commission), 553
fuel, 577
Fugitive Slave Act, 161
full faith and credit clause, 96
Full Frontal with Samantha Bee (TV show), 200, 336–337
Fuller, Ida Mae, *579*
functions, 3, 27
fundamental principles, 39–40
funded mandates, 107
funding, 9
fund-raising consultants, 312
Furman v. Georgia, 145

G

Gahona, Angel, 630
Gallup polls, 5–6, 218–220, 218*f*–219*f*
gambling, *182*, 182–183
Game of Thrones (TV show), 336
Garfield, James, 441, 471
Garland, Merrick, 513
Garner, John Nance, 434–435
gay people, 179–181, *310*

symbolic speech, 129–131
Syria, 597
  history of, 433
  ISIS, 5
systems. *See also* federal system; legal
    system
  adversarial judicial system, 502
  balance of power system, 609–610
  confederal system, 88–89
  dual court system, 499, 507*f*
  federal court system, 506–509,
    507*f*, 508*t*, *509*
  fifth party system, 276–277
  first party system, 272–273
  fourth party system, 275–276, *276*
  for government, 89*f*
  horizontal system, 95–96
  legacy systems, 370
  legal model, 517–518
  Merit System Protection Board, 473
  party system, 272
  patronage system, 470
  proportional representation
    system, 282
  second party system, 273–274, *274*
  seniority system, 406
  spoils system, 273
  Swift messaging, 376
  third party system, 274–275, *275*
  two-party system, 281–288,
    284*f*, 294
  unitary system, 88
  winner-take-all system, 282, 293

T

Taft, William Howard, 276, 344
Takano, Mark, *310*
take care clause, 442–443
Taliban. *See* Afghanistan
talk radio, 343, *343*
Tarbell, Ida, 341
tariffs, 598
  for China, 627–628
  General Agreement on Tariffs and
    Trade, 556–557
  history of, 540
  nontariff trade barriers, 556
  policy for, 432
Tax Cuts and Job Act, 543, 558
taxes
  Article I courts, 508
  banking and, 97–98
  child tax credits, 581
  Congress and, 67, 81
  debates on, *86*, 477
  duties and, 70
  Earned Income Tax Credit
    program, 581
  in elections, 84, 285
  government subsidies and, 556
  for health care, 4–5, 9
  Internal Revenue Service, 491
  law and, 432
  in legal system, 64
  in local politics, 545
  payroll taxes, 544
  policy for, 36, 41, 541–542,
    544–545, 545*f*
  poll tax, 164
  progressive taxes, 544
  proportional (flat) tax, 544
  psychology of, 91, 432, 488–489
  regressive taxes, 544
  for revenues, 545*f*
  for Social Security, 578–579, 585

Social Security Act (1935), 98–99
  states and, 69
  tax base, 535
  tax cuts, 532, 543, 558–559
  tax expenditures, 545
  trends in, 542
Tea Act (1773), 37
Tea Party, 260, 262, 287–288,
    290, 294
Teapot Dome scandal, 314, *315*
technology
  for activism, 252, 371–374
  bandwidth, 364–365
  big tech, 381, 386
  cell-phone watchdogs, 348
  for citizens, 362–369
  computers, 369–371, *370*
  for corporations, 347
  in courts, 141
  critical thinking about,
    383–384, 386
  data as, 384
  digital paywalls, 341
  for diplomacy, 604–605
  in education, 558
  e-government, 369–370, 464, 493
  in foreign policy, 604–605, 630
  for global warming, 573
  globalization of, 288, 290–291
  for government, 28, 369–371
  Internet as, 360–362
  learning objectives for, 359,
    384–385
  media and, 217, 342–347, 449
  movies on, 387
  national security and, 630
  for participation, 2, 5
  politics and, 4, 27, 374–382, 391
  propaganda and, 278, 354
  psychology and, 335
  public opinion and, 196, 220–221
  regulation of, 14, 382–383
  strategic arms limitation talks,
    618–619
  strategic arms reduction talks,
    619–621
  *Torrey Dale Grady v. North
    Carolina*, 143
  trends in, 348, 353, 358
  vlogs, 364
  for voting, 303–304, 312–313
  weapons of mass destruction, 601
  wiki, 370
Telecommunications Act (1996), 352
telegenic, 343–345, *345*
telephone polls, 217
television, 343–346, 344*f*–346*f*, *345*,
    351, 373, 373*f*. *See also specific
    TV shows*
Temporary Assistance to Needy
    Families, 106, 581–582
Tennessee, 167–170, *170*, 435
tensions
  in expression, 126–127
  psychology of, 109–110, 121
term limits
  in debates, 83
  for presidents, 70, 82
  for vice presidents, 82
terminology, 23
territory, 74
terrorism, 436*f*, 628
  blogs for, 381
  for Bush, G. W., 447–448
  in California, 379–380
  clash of civilizations thesis, 621
  counterterrorism, 430, 432

economics of, 599
  in elections, 630
  foreign policy for, 621–627, *624*
  globalization of, 147–148
  for government, 407
  Guantánamo Bay, 626
  history of, 597
  Internet for, 369, 379–380
  in Iraq, 5
  in media, 219–220
  military for, 600–601
  non-state actors in, 601
  operationalizing of, 379–380
  policy for, 77, 565
  security and, 146
  testimony, 246
Texas, 25
  Lawrence v. Texas, 140–141
  New Mexico and, *96*
  Texas v. Johnson, 130–131
text messaging, 379–380
textualism, 521–522
theory
  attentive public, 416
  balanced budget, 541
  balanced tickets, 435
  big tent principle, 262, 293
  brinkmanship, 616
  bully pulpit, 446
  casework, 394
  of centralization, 47
  chief diplomat, 433
  chief of state, 429
  coattail effect, 305–306
  collective defense, 609–610
  collective force, 229
  collective security, 610
  of conflict, 281–282
  of consensus, 432
  consent of the governed, 15
  contracting-out, 474
  of criminal due process, 141–142
  dealignment, 280
  debates in, 543
  deficit spending, 541, 549,
    550*f*, 566
  deregulation, 542–543, *555*
  deterrence, 618
  devolution, 101–102
  digital divide, 360–361, *362*
  domino theory, 617
  dualism, 281–282
  economic policy and, 539–543, *540*
  of economics, 450–451
  elitism, 230
  environmental racism, 576
  family values, 244
  of federal system, 88–91
  first lady, 455–456, *456*
  of fiscal policy, 541
  generational effect, 207–208
  global warming, 572–573
  for government, 278
  greenhouse effect, 572–573
  healthy economy, 535–536
  hegemony, 608–609, *609*
  of hierarchies, 268–269, 269*f*
  honeymoon period, 446–447
  of IGR, 100–101
  imperial presidency, 450, 453
  of independent sovereigns, 87
  inflation, 536, 543, 558
  information warfare, 375
  in-kind assistance, 569
  intermestics, 606
  intersectionality, 179–180
  interstate compacts, 96–97

interventionism, 606
  limited war, 616
  of lobbying, 245–246
  of loyal opposition, 269
  manifest destiny, 608
  of minimum wage, *580*, 580–581
  monetarism, 543
  multilateralism, 611
  mutually assured destruction, 618
  nation building, 624
  national debt, 550
  net neutrality, 382–383
  of neutrality, 135
  nuclear option, 409
  of party in the electorate,
    265–268, 268*t*
  pluralism, 230
  pluralist theory, 253
  of political socialization, 197–199
  politics-administration
    dichotomy, 480
  populism, 273
  preventive war, 623–624
  principal, 550
  proportional (flat) tax, 544
  protectionism, 556
  pure capitalist economy, 535
  rational choice theory, 326
  realignment, 272
  regime changes, 601
  regulated capitalist economy, 535
  salience, 323
  of social contract, 12–13
  of sovereignty, 88
  standing to sue, 162
  of success, 236–240
  supply-side economics, 542–543
  supreme law of the land, 92–93
  transparency, 369–370
Think Democracy Project, 312
ThinkProgress (blog), 365
third party system, 274–275, *275*
  democracy and, 285
  in partisanship, 281–288, 284*f*
Thomas, Clarence, 524
Three-Fifths Compromise, 47–48, 59
Thurmond, Strom, 408
ticket splitting, 280
Till, Emmett, 167–168, *168*
time, place, and manner restrictions,
    132–133
Tinker v. Des Moines, 130
tobacco, 91
*Torrey Dale Grady v. North
    Carolina*, 143
tort, 504
total incorporation, 122–123
totalitarianism, 10
town meetings, 13, 310–311
Townshend Act (1766), 36
tracking polls, 214, 216
trade
  authority for, 40
  foreign policy for, 598–600,
    627–628
  free trade policy, 556
  General Agreement on Tariffs and
    Trade, 556–557
  in national security, *607*, 607–608
  nontariff trade barriers, 556
  normal trade relations status, 598
  North American Free Trade
    Agreement, 599
  Organization of Petroleum
    Exporting Countries, 576
  professionalism and, 242
  tariffs, 432, 540, 556–567, 598

Students—study more efficiently, retain more and achieve better outcomes. Instructors—focus on what you love—teaching.

SUCCESSFUL SEMESTERS INCLUDE CONNECT

FOR INSTRUCTORS

You're in the driver's seat.

Want to build your own course? No problem. Prefer to use our turnkey, prebuilt course? Easy. Want to make changes throughout the semester? Sure. And you'll save time with Connect's auto-grading too.

65%

Less Time Grading

They'll thank you for it.

Adaptive study resources like SmartBook® help your students be better prepared in less time. You can transform your class time from dull definitions to dynamic debates. Hear from your peers about the benefits of Connect at **www.mheducation.com/highered/connect**

Make it simple, make it affordable.

Connect makes it easy with seamless integration using any of the major Learning Management Systems—Blackboard®, Canvas, and D2L, among others—to let you organize your course in one convenient location. Give your students access to digital materials at a discount with our inclusive access program. Ask your McGraw-Hill representative for more information.

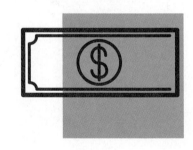

©Hill Street Studios/Tobin Rogers/Blend Images LLC

Solutions for your challenges.

A product isn't a solution. Real solutions are affordable, reliable, and come with training and ongoing support when you need it and how you want it. Our Customer Experience Group can also help you troubleshoot tech problems—although Connect's 99% uptime means you might not need to call them. See for yourself at **status.mheducation.com**

Effective, efficient studying.

Connect helps you be more productive with your study time and get better grades using tools like SmartBook, which highlights key concepts and creates a personalized study plan. Connect sets you up for success, so you walk into class with confidence and walk out with better grades.

©Shutterstock/wavebreakmedia

"" I really liked this app—it made it easy to study when you don't have your textbook in front of you. ""

- Jordan Cunningham,
Eastern Washington University

Study anytime, anywhere.

Download the free ReadAnywhere app and access your online eBook when it's convenient, even if you're offline. And since the app automatically syncs with your eBook in Connect, all of your notes are available every time you open it. Find out more at **www.mheducation.com/readanywhere**

No surprises.

The Connect Calendar and Reports tools keep you on track with the work you need to get done and your assignment scores. Life gets busy; Connect tools help you keep learning through it all.

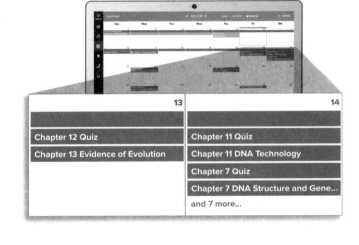

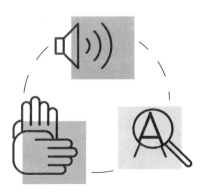

Learning for everyone.

McGraw-Hill works directly with Accessibility Services Departments and faculty to meet the learning needs of all students. Please contact your Accessibility Services office and ask them to email accessibility@mheducation.com, or visit **www.mheducation.com/about/accessibility.html** for more information.